Scandinavia

THIS EDITION WRITTEN AND RESEARCHED BY

Andy Symington,
Carolyn Bain, Cristian Bonetto, Peter Dragicevich,
Anthony Ham, Anna Kaminski

PLAN YOUR TRIP

ON THE ROAD

BANANA PANCAKE/GETTY IMAGES ©
NUSFJORD, LOFOTEN ISLANDS P343

ANNHFHUNG/GETTY IMAGES ©
TALLINN P208

ALEX ROBINSON/AWL IMAGES LTD/GETTY IMAGES ©

Contents

KUUSAMO P185

Contents

ON THE ROAD

JOHNER ROYALTY-FREE/GETTY IMAGES ©

DOG-SLEDDING, KIRUNA P463

G.L. CHENG/GETTY IMAGES ©

Contents

SURVIVAL GUIDE

GULLFOSS WATERFALL, THE GOLDEN CIRCLE P238

Welcome to Scandinavia

Effortlessly chic cities meet remote forests, drawing style gurus and wilderness hikers alike. Endless day, perpetual night. Rocking festivals, majestic aurora borealis. Scandinavia's menu is anything but bland.

Epic Outdoors

The great outdoors is rarely greater than in Europe's big north. Epic expanses of wilderness – forests, lakes, volcanoes – and intoxicatingly pure air mean engaging with nature is utter pleasure. National parks cover the region, offering some of Europe's best hiking as well as anything from kayaking to glacier-walking to bear-watching. Spectacular coasts – rugged fjords, cliffs teeming with seabirds, archipelagos so speckled with islands it looks like an artist flicked a paintbrush at a canvas – invite exploration from the sea.

City Style

Stolid Nordic stereotypes dissolve in the region's vibrant capitals. Crest-of-the-wave design can be seen in them all, backed by outstanding modern architecture, excellent museums, imaginative solutions for 21st-century urban living, internationally acclaimed restaurants and a nightlife that fizzes along despite hefty beer prices. Live music is a given: you're bound to come across some inspiring local act whether your taste is Viking metal or chamber music. Style here manages to be conservative and innovative at the same time, or perhaps it's just that the new and the old blend with less effort than elsewhere.

Seasons

They have proper seasons up here. There are long, cold winters with thick snow carpeting the ground and the sun making only cameo appearances – if at all. Despite the scary subzero temperatures, there's a wealth of things to do: skiing, sledding behind huskies or reindeer, snowmobile safaris to the Arctic Sea, ice fishing, romantic nights in snow hotels, visiting Santa Claus and gazing at the soul-piercing northern lights. Spring sees nature's tentative awakening before the explosive summer's long, long days, filled with festivals, beer terraces and wonderful boating, hiking and cycling. Autumn in Scandinavia's forested lands can be the most beautiful of all, as the birches and other deciduous trees display a glorious array of colours, offering marvellous woodland walking before the first snows.

Green Choices

You'll rarely come across the word *ecotourism* in Scandinavia, but those values have long been an important part of life here. Generally, green and sustainable solutions are a way of living rather than a gimmick to attract visitors. Scandinavia will likely be significantly affected by climate change, and big efforts to reduce emissions are being made across the region.

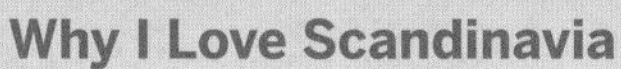

Why I Love Scandinavia

By Andy Symington, Author

I've been visiting regularly for a couple of decades; right from the moment I arrive, those first breaths of Nordic air always seem fresh and pure. I'm entranced by Scandinavia's smart modern cities and cosy cottage culture. My first love, though, is the wilderness. Spotting the first roadside reindeer tells me I've reached the far north, whether for endless Arctic summer days or the eerily sunless polar night. Then, depending on season and place, it's time for brilliant hikes, the northern lights, baying huskies, smoking volcanoes, indigenous culture or intriguing wildlife. It fascinates me that there's such untamed nature in these modern nations.

For more about our authors, see p512

Above: Aurora borealis, Tromsø (p350), Norway

Scandinavia

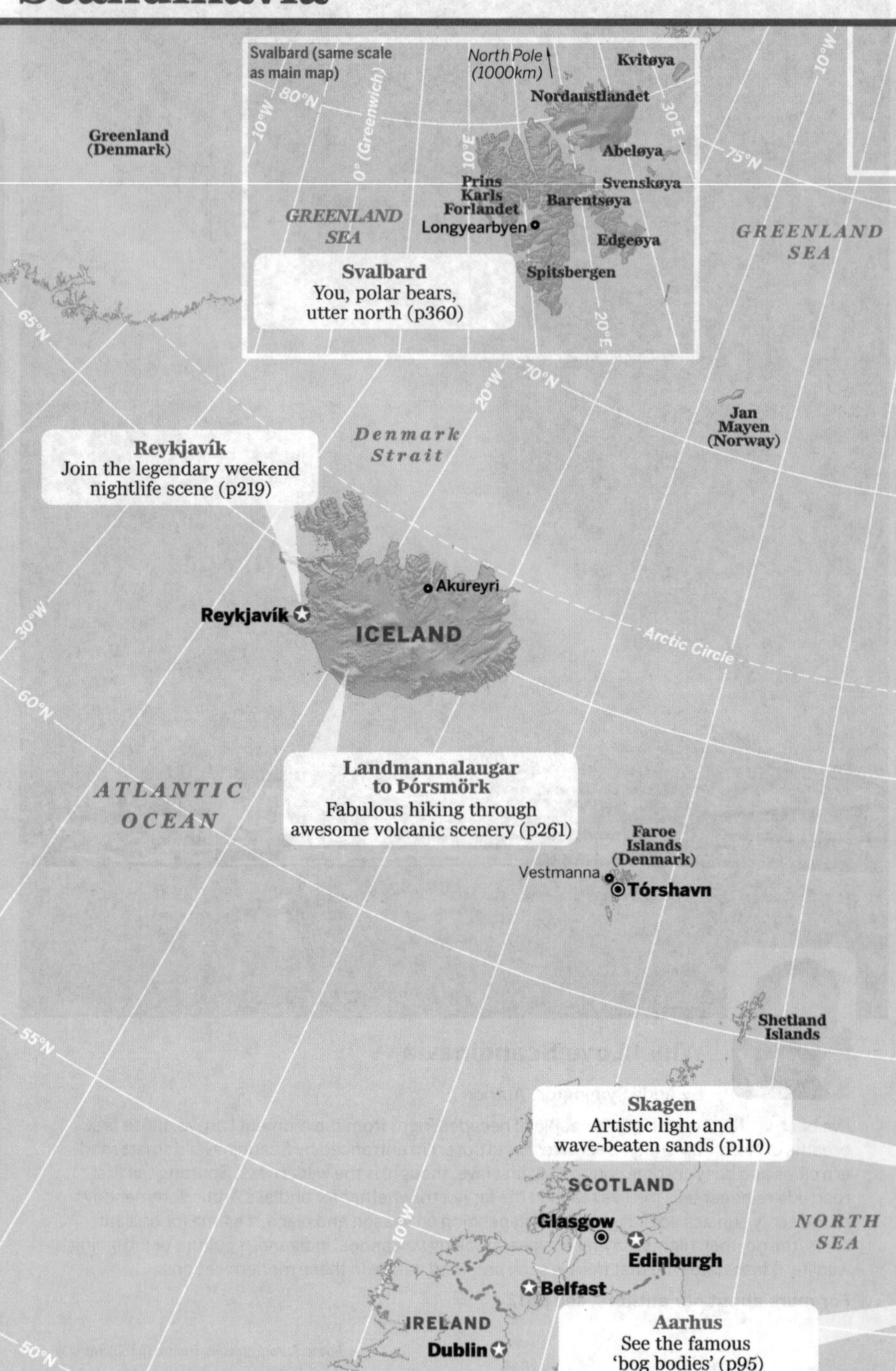

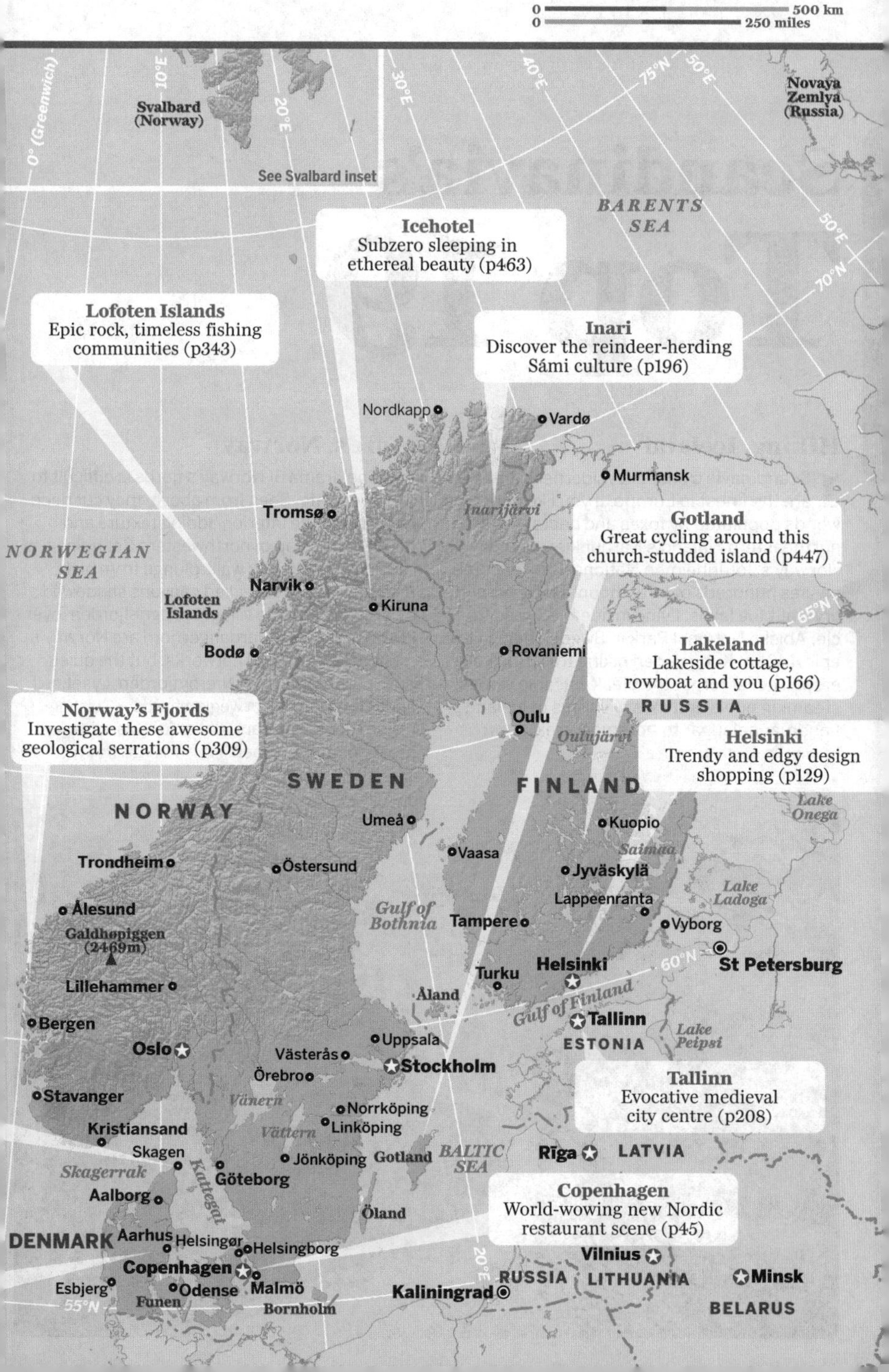

0 — 500 km
0 — 250 miles

Icehotel
Subzero sleeping in ethereal beauty (p463)

Lofoten Islands
Epic rock, timeless fishing communities (p343)

Inari
Discover the reindeer-herding Sámi culture (p196)

Gotland
Great cycling around this church-studded island (p447)

Lakeland
Lakeside cottage, rowboat and you (p166)

Norway's Fjords
Investigate these awesome geological serrations (p309)

Helsinki
Trendy and edgy design shopping (p129)

Tallinn
Evocative medieval city centre (p208)

Copenhagen
World-wowing new Nordic restaurant scene (p45)

Svalbard (Norway)
See Svalbard inset
Novaya Zemlya (Russia)
BARENTS SEA
NORWEGIAN SEA
Nordkapp
Vardø
Murmansk
Inarijärvi
Tromsø
Narvik
Lofoten Islands
Kiruna
Bodø
Rovaniemi
RUSSIA
Oulu
Oulujärvi
SWEDEN
FINLAND
NORWAY
Umeå
Kuopio
Lake Onega
Saimaa
Vaasa
Trondheim
Östersund
Jyväskylä
Ålesund
Gulf of Bothnia
Lappeenranta
Lake Ladoga
Galdhøpiggen (2469m)
Tampere
Vyborg
St Petersburg
Helsinki
Turku
Lillehammer
Åland
Gulf of Finland
Tallinn
Bergen
Uppsala
Lake Peipsi
ESTONIA
Oslo
Västerås
Stockholm
Örebro
Stavanger
Vänern
Norrköping
Kristiansand
Vättern
Linköping
Skagen
Jönköping
Gotland
BALTIC SEA
Rīga
LATVIA
Skagerrak
Kattegat
Göteborg
Aalborg
Öland
DENMARK
Aarhus
Helsingør
Helsingborg
Vilnius
Copenhagen
Esbjerg
Odense
Malmö
Kaliningrad
RUSSIA
LITHUANIA
Minsk
Funen
Bornholm
BELARUS
0° (Greenwich)
10°E
20°E
30°E
40°E
50°E
75°N
70°N
65°N
60°N
55°N

Scandinavia's Top 19

Hiking, Iceland

1 Scandinavia's unspoilt wilderness areas are the finest in Europe. If you like dark pine woods populated by foxes and bears, head for northeastern Finland's Karhunkierros trail. Norway's Jotunheimen National Park encompasses hundreds of lofty mountain peaks and crystal-blue lakes. Lying inside the Arctic Circle, Abisko National Park in Sweden begins the epic 440km Kungsleden hiking trail. But walkers will never forget the bleak volcanic slopes, steaming pools and mossy valleys of Iceland's Landmannalaugar to Þórsmörk trek. Below: Landmannalaugar region (p260)

Fjords, Norway

2 The drama of Norway's fjords is difficult to overstate. Seen from above, they cut deep gashes into the interior, adding texture and depth to the map of northwestern Scandinavia. Up close, sheer rock walls plunge from high meadows into water-filled canyons shadowed by pretty fjord-side villages. Sognefjorden, over 200km long, and Hardangerfjord are Norway's most extensive fjord networks, but the quiet, precipitous beauty of Nærøyfjorden, Lysefjord and – the king of Norwegian fjords – Geirangerfjord are prime candidates for Scandinavia's most beautiful corner. Right: Geirangerfjord (p330)

1

TYLER STABLEFORD/GETTY IMAGES ©

Aurora Borealis, Lapland

3 Whether caused by the collision of charged particles in the upper atmosphere, or sparked, as Sámi tradition tells, by a giant snow fox swishing its tail as it runs across the Arctic tundra, the haunting splendour of the aurora borealis, or northern lights, is never to be forgotten. Though it is theoretically visible year-round, it's much easier to see and more spectacular in the darker winter months. The further north you go, such as the Lapland region of Finland, Norway or Sweden, the better your chances of gazing on nature's light show.

Lofoten Islands, Norway

4 Few visitors forget their first sighting of the Lofoten Islands, laid out in summer greens and yellows or drowned in the snows of winter, their razor-sharp peaks poking dark against a cobalt-clear sky. In the pure, exhilarating air, there's a constant tang of salt and, in the villages, more than a whiff of cod, that giant of the seas whose annual migration brings wealth. A hiker's dream and nowadays linked by bridges, the islands are simple to hop along, whether by bus, car or bicycle.

Right: Svolvær (p343)

DOUG PEARSON/GETTY IMAGES ©

LOVE STRANDELL/GETTY IMAGES ©

BEN CRANKE/GETTY IMAGES ©

Cycling Gotland

5 A lazy bike ride around the perimeters of Gotland, the holiday-friendly Baltic Sea island, is one of the most rewarding ways to spend your time in Sweden: the mostly flat, paved Gotlandsleden cycle path circles the island, passing fields of poppies, shady woodlands, historic churches and ancient rune stones at regular intervals. Also a short ferry ride from Stockholm, the autonomous Åland islands have a network of bridges and ferries that makes them a pleasure to pedal around. Or try the 105km-long ride around Bornholm, one of Denmark's National Routes.

Svalbard, Norway

6 The subpolar archipelago of Svalbard is a true place of the heart. Deliciously remote and yet surprisingly accessible, Svalbard is Europe's most evocative slice of the polar north and one of the continent's last great wilderness areas. Shapely peaks, massive ice fields (60% of Svalbard is covered by glaciers) and heartbreakingly beautiful fjords provide the backdrop for a rich array of Arctic wildlife (including one-fifth of the world's polar bears, which outnumber people up here) and for summer and winter activities that get you out amid the ringing silence of the snows.

Icehotel, Sweden

7 Somewhere between a chandelier and an igloo, the famed Icehotel (p463) at Jukkasjärvi is a justifiably popular destination – it may be a gimmick, but it's also really cool (and not just literally). Sleep among reindeer skins in a hotel sculpted anew from ice each winter, and hang out in the attached Icebar, sipping chilled vodka out of ice glasses. Beyond its own appeal, the hotel makes a good base for admiring the aurora borealis and learning about Sámi culture in this part of Lapland. Similar hotels exist in Norway and Finland.

Sámi Culture, Inari

8 The indigenous Sámi have a near-mystical closeness to the natural environment: in this case the awesome wildernesses of Lapland. Reindeer-herding is still a primary occupation, but these days it's done with all-terrain vehicles and snowmobiles, leaving more time for other endeavours. The Sámi are a modern people, but still in touch with their roots. Check out the museums, parliament buildings and craft workshops in Inari and Karasjok, and try to catch a festival or cultural event, whether reindeer-racing or *yoiking* (singing).

7

PER RANUNG/GETTY IMAGES ©

DOUG PEARSON/GETTY IMAGES ©

CESCASSAWIN/GETTY IMAGES ©

TOTORORO/GETTY IMAGES ©

Thermal Springs, Iceland

9 Geothermal pools are Iceland's pride. The most famous of the bathing places is the Blue Lagoon (p238) spa, where the waters are packed with skin-softening minerals. Visitors can also sink back into warm milky-blue waters at Mývatn Nature Baths, or even inside a volcanic crater at Víti lake at the Askja caldera. The soothing springs plus the mind-bending scenery make for utter relaxation. Top right: Blue Lagoon (p238)

Old Town, Tallinn

10 The jewel in Tallinn's crown is its Unesco-protected Old Town, a 14th- and 15th-century two-tiered jumble of turrets, spires and winding streets. Most travellers' experiences of Estonia's capital begin and end with the cobblestoned, chocolate-box landscape of intertwining alleys and picturesque courtyards. Enjoy it from up high (climb one of the observation towers) or down below (refuel in one of the vaulted cellars turned into cosy bars and cafes), or simply stroll and soak up the medieval magic.

INGOLF POMPE/LOOK-FOTO/GETTY IMAGES ©

MARK HANNAFORD/GETTY IMAGES ©

AYNIA BRENNAN/SHUTTERSTOCK ©

Cottage Retreat, Finland's Lakeland

11 Vast numbers of Scandinavians head for summer cottages at the first hint of midyear sunshine. The typical one is simple, by a lake or on an island, with few modern comforts but probably a rowing boat or canoe, a barbecue, a bit of old fishing line and maybe a sauna. The holidays are spent enjoying nature and getting away from city life. Across the region there are numerous rental cottages that can become venues for you to experience a slice of authentic Nordic peace. Above: Summer cottage near Porvoo (p143)

Sledding, Lapland

12 Once there's healthy snow cover in the north, a classic experience is to hitch up a team of reindeer or husky dogs to a sled and swish away under the pale winter sun. Short jaunts are good for getting the hang of steering, stopping and letting the animals know who's boss; once your confidence is high, take off on an overnight trip, sleeping in a hut in the wilderness and thawing those deserving bones with a steaming sauna. Pure magic.

New Nordic Cuisine, Copenhagen

13 Copenhagen's culinary prowess is a byword these days. Once known for *smørrebrød* (open sandwiches) and *frikadeller* (meatballs), Denmark's capital has re-invented itself as a hotbed of gastronomic innovation, with the revamped Nordic cuisine and its forage ethos turning heads around the globe. Other countries have followed Denmark's lead, and exciting new restaurants now stock all the region's capitals, with more popping up like chanterelle mushrooms.

Viking History, Oslo

14 Mead-swilling pillaging hooligans or civilising craftspeople, poets and merchants? Your Viking preconceptions will likely be challenged. A series of memorable burial sites, rune stones, settlements and museums – Oslo's (p290) are perhaps the finest – across the region brings this fascinating age to life. Gods and beliefs, their stupendous feats of navigation, customs, longships, intricate jewellery, carvings and sagas – it's all here. Just forget about the horned helmets; they didn't wear them. Below: Vikingskipshuset (p290)

Bog Bodies, Denmark

15 If you've read Seamus Heaney's 'bog people' poems, you'll know all about the eerily preserved, millennia-old bodies exhumed from Denmark's peat bogs. Skin still intact and frown lines clear, these ancients seem caught in perpetual slumber. The Grauballe Man near Aarhus is a compelling Bronze Age whodunit: was he a noble sacrifice or the victim of foul play? More serene is Tollund Man (p103), his face so well preserved that people mistook him for a modern-day crime victim upon discovery in 1950. Bottom: Tollund Man (p103)

14

15

Design Shopping, Helsinki

16 If design is defined as making the practical beautiful, then Scandinavia rules the roost. Elegant, innovative yet functional takes on everyday items mean that you won't have to look far before you get an 'I need that!' moment. There's great design and handicrafts to be found right across the region, but Copenhagen and Helsinki, closely followed by Stockholm, are where modern flagships can be found alongside the best of the edgier new ideas. Below: Marimekko store, Design District Helsinki (p141)

Bar Life, Reykjavík

17 In Scandinavia's capital cities summer is short and winter is long and bitter. Driving away the darkness is a necessity – so it's no wonder a near-legendary nightlife has evolved in these cities. After all, what could be better than gathering your friends into a snug, sleek bar to talk, drink, joke, sing, laugh, flirt and dance the night away? Natural Nordic reserve melts away with local firewaters as *brennivín*, *salmiakkikossu*, *snaps* or aquavit, or plain old beer. Join the party and make fast friends. Right: Laundromat Café (p233)

16

BLOOMBERG/GETTY IMAGES ©

17

ARCTIC-IMAGES/CORBIS ©

18

TOVE, JAN/GETTY IMAGES ©

19

FARLEY BARICUATRO/GETTY IMAGES ©

Skagen, Denmark

18 Sweeping skies, moving sands and duelling seas: the appeal of Skagen (p110) is both ephemeral and constant. The lure of the light has drawn many – packing paintbrushes – from far beyond its coastline, and its blending colour of sky, sea and sand can inspire awe in the most hardened of souls. This is both Jutland's northern tip and Denmark's 'end of the line', where gentle fields give way to ghostly dunes, a buried church and the shape-shifting headland of Grenen, where the Baltic meets its murky North Sea rival.

Wooden Town, Bergen

19 Wooden buildings, once comprising whole towns, are a feature of Scandinavia. But 'great fires' – whether through somebody smoking in bed or burning the toast – were understandably common, and comparatively few of these historic districts remain. They are worth seeking out for their quaint, unusual beauty; among others, Bergen, Rauma, Stavanger and Göteborg preserve excellent 'timbertowns', perfect neighbourhoods for strolling around. Above: Bergen (p309)

Need to Know

For more information, see Survival Guide (p479)

Currency

Denmark: Danish krone (Dkr; DKK)
Finland & Tallinn: euro (€; EUR)
Iceland: Icelandic króna (Ikr; ISK)
Norway: Norwegian krone (Nkr; NOK)
Sweden: Swedish krona (Skr; SEK)

Language

Danish, Estonian, Finnish, Icelandic, Norwegian and Swedish. English is widely spoken.

Visas

Generally not required for stays of up to 90 days; some nationalities will need a Schengen visa.

Money

ATMs are widespread. Credit/debit cards are accepted for any transaction.

Mobile Phones

Local SIM cards cheap, widely available. Need an unlocked phone. Data packages cheap and easy. Normal tariff for EU SIM cards in EU countries, otherwise roaming rates. No public phones.

When to Go

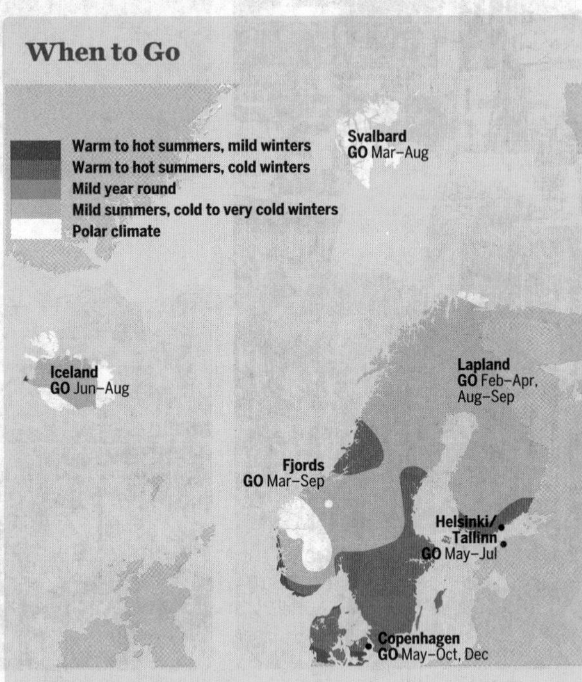

High Season (Jun–Aug)

- Attractions and lodgings are open.
- Hotels in many parts are often substantially cheaper.
- Summer budget accommodation is open.
- Boat cruises running.
- Numerous festivals.

Shoulder (Apr & May, Sep & Oct)

- Expect chilly nights and even snow.
- Not the cheapest time to travel as summer hostels and camping grounds have closed.
- Many attractions close or shorten their opening hours.

Low Season (Nov–Mar)

- Outside cities, many attractions are closed.
- Hotels charge top rates except at weekends.
- December to April is busy for winter sports.
- Short, cool or cold days.

Websites

Lonely Planet (www.lonelyplanet.com) Destination information, accommodation bookings, traveller forum and more.

Go Scandinavia (www.goscandinavia.com) Combined tourist-board website for the four mainland Nordic countries.

IceNews (www.icenews.is) Presents the latest English news snippets from the Nordic nations.

Direct Ferries (www.directferries.co.uk) Useful booking site for Baltic and Atlantic ferries.

Important Numbers

Eliminate the initial zero from area/mobile codes if dialling from abroad.

International access code ☎00

General emergency ☎112

Country codes

Denmark	☎45
Finland	☎358
Iceland	☎354
Norway	☎47
Sweden	☎46
Tallinn	☎372

Daily Costs

Budget: less than €140

- Dorm beds: €15–40 (HI membership gets you discounts)
- Bike hire: €10-20 per day
- Lunch specials: €10-16
- National parks: free

Midrange: €140–250

- Standard hotel double room: €80-150
- Week-long car hire: €40-60 per day
- Two-course meal for two with wine: €100-150
- Museum entry: €5-15

Top end: more than €250

- Room in boutique hotel: €150-300
- Upmarket degustation menu for two with wine: €200-300
- Taxi across town: €20-40

What to Take

- For winter visits: decent thermal underwear, waterproof boots and top layer, woolly hat, gloves and a neck warmer.
- A credit or debit card: plastic's an easy option throughout, and saves working out which country that 50-krone banknote is from.
- A HI membership card, towel and sleep sheet if you plan to use hostels.
- A tent and sleeping bag if you're going hiking.
- Insect repellent in summer, especially in Finland and Iceland.
- An eye mask for sleeping under the summer sun.
- Swimsuit – there are lots of hot springs, spa hotels and lakes to jump in.
- Mobile phone – buying a local SIM card is the easiest way to get connected.

Arriving in Scandinavia

Copenhagen Kastrup Airport (p63) Trains run every 10 minutes into the centre; taxis cost around Dkr300 for the 20-minute ride.

Stockholm Arlanda Airport (p405) Express trains run all day from Stockholm; airport buses are cheaper but slower. Taxis cost around Skr600 for the 45-minute drive.

Oslo Gardermoen Airport (p297) Regular shuttle buses make the 40-minute journey to the centre. A train from the airport takes 20 minutes.

Helsinki Vantaa Airport (p205) Local buses and faster Finnair buses do the 30- to 45-minute run into town. By taxi, plan on €45 to €55 for the half-hour trip. An airport-to-city rail link (30 minutes) is opening in 2015.

Getting Around

Bus Comprehensive network throughout region; only choice in many areas.

Train Efficient services in the continental nations, none in Iceland.

Car Drive on the right. Hire is easy but not cheap. Few motorways, so travel times can be long. Compulsory winter tyres.

Ferry Great-value network around the Baltic; spectacular Norwegian coastal ferry, and a service to Iceland via the Faroe Islands.

Bike Very bike-friendly cities and lots of options for longer cycling routes. Most transport carries bikes for little or no charge. Hire is widely available.

Air Decent network of budget flights connecting major centres. Full-fare flights are comparatively expensive.

For much more on **getting around**, see p486

If You Like...

Coastal Scenery

Scoured by glaciers, speckled with islands and buffeted by wind and rain, the Nordic coastlines are spectacular. The Atlantic coasts are the most jagged, while the more sedate Baltic archipelagos offer a gentler beauty.

Dueodde On Bornholm, Nordic forest and snow white dunes back one of Europe's most spectacular beaches. (p78)

Møns Klint Gleaming white cliffs against the Baltic blue. (p73)

Kvarken A constantly changing pattern of land and water as the Earth's crust bounces back from the weight of the glaciers in the last Ice Age. (p164)

The High Coast See northern Sweden's dramatic Höga Kusten. (p453)

Lofoten Marvel at nature's sheer improbability in these northern Norwegian islands. (p343)

Svalbard Be spellbound where vast glaciers meet the Arctic Ocean at this remote outpost. (p360)

Jökulsárlón Watch glaciers float to sea from this glittering lagoon. (p259)

Ingólfshöfði An isolated Iceland headland and nature reserve, accessible only by tractor-towed hay cart. (p259)

Kystriksveien Norway's lightly-travelled but utterly extraordinary route into the Arctic. (p340)

Hiking

Wide open spaces, majestic landscapes and bracing air offer brilliant hiking. Multiday treks are easily accomplished with a great network of national parks, camping grounds and huts. Norway and Iceland offer magnificent scenery, while Finland and Sweden have spectacular autumn forestscapes.

Kungsleden Trek along the King's Trail in Swedish Lappland. (p465)

Norwegian peaks Traverse the roof of Norway in the Jotunheimen National Park. (p307)

Rjukan Hike in search of wild reindeer atop Norway's Hardangervidda plateau. (p319)

Hornstrandir Accessible only by boat in high summer, this isolated Icelandic peninsula is the ultimate escape. (p244)

Laugavegurinn Trek Iceland's most famous hike, from Landmannalaugar to Þórsmörk, over rainbow-coloured mountains and through deserts of pumice. (p261)

Finnish Lapland Hit Lapland's Urho Kekkonen National Park for some top trekking in one of Europe's last great wildernesses. (p196)

Cycling

Bikes are part of life here: the cities are full of cycle lanes, grab-a-bike stands and marked routes. There are great options for multiday cycling holidays, particularly in the Baltic islands. Bikes are easily transported throughout the region.

Bornholm Pedal your way across this perfect Danish island. (p76)

Tallinn Get out of the Old Town and take a bike tour to the far-flung corners of the capital. (p208)

Gotland Make the easy loop around this Swedish island. (p447)

Rjukan Ride across Norway's Hardangervidda, Europe's highest mountain plateau. (p319)

CHRIS MELLOR/GETTY IMAGES ©

TIM E WHITE/GETTY IMAGES ©

Top: Oslo Opera House (p286; architect Tarald Lundevall for Snøhetta), Norway

Bottom: Svalbard (p360), Norway

Mývatn The best way to explore the charms of Iceland's Lake Mývatn is on a day-long bicycle circuit. (p251)

Åland This archipelago between Finland and Sweden is ideal for two-wheeled touring, with numerous flat islands to explore. (p151)

Vikings

Whether you're interested in the structured society, extensive trade networks, dextrous handicrafts and well-honed navigational skills of this advanced civilisation, or you glorify in tales of plunder, pillage, dragonships and the twilight of the gods, there's something for you here.

Roskilde Set sail on a faithful Viking replica in Denmark. (p70)

Ribe Vikingecenter Schmooze with modern-day Danish Vikings. (p117)

Gotland Visit this Swedish island's numerous rune stones and ship settings. (p448)

Oslo Admire a Viking longboat at Oslo's marvellous Vikingskipshuset. (p290)

Lofotr Vikingmuseum Norway's largest Viking-era building. (p347)

Reykjavík 871 +/-2 Fascinating hi-tech exhibition, based around an original Viking longhouse. (p222)

Saga Museum A kind of Viking Madame Tussauds, this Reykjavík museum is heaps of fun. (p224)

Northern seas Follow the mighty wake of the Viking colonists by taking the boat from Denmark to Iceland via the Faroes. (p113)

Winter Wonders

Sled safaris Head out pulled by huskies or reindeer, or aboard a snowmobile to explore the frozen wildernesses; there are excellent places to do this right across northern Norway, Sweden and Finland, whether it's a short hour-long swoosh or a multiday adventure.

Skiing/snowboarding There are excellent resorts in Norway and flatter, family-friendly slopes in northern Sweden and Finland; these places usually offer a host of other wintry activities like snowshoe treks and ice fishing.

Breaking the ice Crunch through the frozen Gulf of Bothnia aboard an icebreaker at Kemi in Finland. (p192)

Snow hotels It's tough to beat the romance of snow hotels, ethereally beautiful creations sculpted from snow and ice; the most famous is at Jukkasjärvi (near Kiruna; p463) in Sweden but others we like are at Alta (p354) and Kirkenes (p357) in Norway, and Kemi (p192) in Finland.

Santa Claus Visit the world's most famous beardie in his eerie Finnish grotto. (p190)

Tivoli Put the magic back into Christmas with wonderful lights and warming mulled wine. (p45)

Aurora borealis (northern lights) Get as far north as you can; find a place without much light, then you'll need patience and a slice of luck; one of the best viewing spots is Abisko in Sweden. (p187)

Canoeing & Kayaking

It's hard to beat this region for kayaking and canoeing, whether you're planning a multiday sea-kayaking or afternoon lake-canoeing adventure.

Danish Lake District Glide on silent lakes in bucolic Jutland. (p94)

Stockholm Rent a canoe for the day from Djurgårdsbrons Sjöcafe. (p396)

Norway Kayak some of Norway's prettiest corners, such as Svalbard (p330) or the World Heritage–listed Geirangerfjorden and Sognefjorden (p323).

Ísafjörður This Icelandic destination is perfect for beginners. (p242)

Seyðisfjörður Guided kayaking tours with affable Hlynur in Iceland. (p256)

Åland Paddle around the low, rocky islands of this quietly picturesque Finnish archipelago. (p154)

Seal Lakes Explore these watery Finnish national parks by boat and try to spot a rare inland seal. (p170)

Modern Art & Architecture

Louisiana Art meets vistas at this Copenhagen modern-art must-see. (p65)

ARoS Walk among giants at this Danish cultural showpiece. (p95)

Stockholm Visit one of Scandinavia's best modern-art museums, Moderna Museet. (p395)

Malmö Marvel at the Turning Torso. (p419)

Oslo Enjoy a modern architectural icon: the Oslo Opera House or the young-at-20 Astrup Fearnley modern art museum. (p286)

Helsinki Iconic Kiasma (p132) still turns heads with its exuberant exterior and excellent exhibitions; the adjacent Musiikkitalo (p140) is a stunning concert venue.

Alvar Aalto Make an architectural pilgrimage to Jyväskylä, the city where one of the giants made his name. (p172)

Northern Lights Cathedral Alta's astonishing swirl of rippling titanium, best appreciated with an aurora backdrop. (p353)

Historic Buildings & Churches

Kronborg Slot Channel Shakespeare at Hamlet's old haunt in Helsingør. (p65)

Tallinn Stroll back to the 14th century around the Old Town's narrow, cobbled streets. (p208)

Gotland Historic churches dot this Swedish island. (p447)

Norwegian stave churches Admire World Heritage–listed Urnes Stave Church on the banks of a fjord. (p327)

Gamle Stavanger One of Europe's most spectacular districts of wooden buildings sits at the heart of this Norwegian city. (p320)

Olavinlinna This spectacular Finnish island castle presides over the centre of its prettiest town. (p168)

Reindeer, Svalbard (p360), Norway

Roskilde Domkirke Eight centuries of Danish architecture under one roof. (p70)

Nidaros Domkirke Scandinavia's largest medieval building and tapestry in stone dedicated to St Olav. (p335)

Wildlife-Watching

Seabirds clamour in the Atlantic air while whales roll beneath. Elk are widespread, Finnish forests harbour serious carnivores and mighty polar bears still lord it – for now – over Svalbard.

Fanø Witness mass feathery migration in Denmark. (p115)

Iceland Nesting colonies of the comical puffin are found all across the island. (p266)

Reindeer These roam at will across the north of Sweden, Norway and Finland. (p382)

Central Norway Track down the prehistoric musk ox. (p367)

Svalbard Watch out for Europe's last polar bears in Svalbard, with Arctic foxes, and walrus also present. (p360)

Whale watching Head to Norway's Andenes or Húsavík in Iceland. (p349)

Látrabjarg These dramatic cliffs are the world's biggest bird breeding grounds. (p244)

Bear-watching Head out to the Finnish forests to observe bears, elk or wolverines. (p181)

Month by Month

TOP EVENTS

Sled safaris & skiing, March

Midsummer, June

Roskilde Festival, June & July

Aurora watching, November

Christmas, December

January

It's cold. Very cold and very dark. But this is the beginning of the active winter; there's enough snow for ice hotels, and winter sports are reliable.

Skábmagovat, Finland

In the third week of January, this film festival with an indigenous theme is held in the Finnish Sámi village of Inari. Associated cultural events also happen here throughout the winter. (p197)

Kiruna Snöfestivalen, Sweden

This Lapland snow festival, based around a snow-sculpting competition that draws artists from all over, is held on the last weekend in January. There's also a husky dog competition and a handicrafts fair.

February

There's enough light now for it to be prime skiing season in northern Scandinavia. Local holidays mean it gets very busy (and pricey) on the slopes mid-February.

Jokkmokk Winter Market, Sweden

The biggest Sámi market of the year with all manner of crafts for sale, preceded by celebrations of all things Sámi and featuring reindeer races on the frozen lake. (p461)

Þorrablót, Iceland

Held all across the country, nominally in honour of the god Thor, this midwinter festival's centrepiece is a feast for the fearless that includes delicacies such as fermented shark.

Rørosmartnan, Norway

An old-fashioned and traditional winter fair livens the streets of the historic Norwegian town of Røros. (p306)

March

As the hours of light dramatically increase and temperatures begin to rise again, this is an excellent time to take advantage of the hefty snow cover and indulge in some winter fun.

Vasaloppet, Sweden

Held on the first Sunday in March, this ski race salutes Gustav Vasa's history-making flight on skis in 1521; it has grown into a week-long ski fest and celebration with different races – short, gruelling or just for fun. (p417)

Sled Safaris & Skiing, Northern Norway, Sweden & Finland

Whizzing across the snow pulled by a team of huskies or reindeer is a pretty spectacular way to see the northern wildernesses. Add snowmobiling or skiing to the mix and it's a top time to be at high latitude.

Reindeer Racing, Finland

Held over the last weekend of March or first of April, the King's Cup is the grand finale of Finnish Lapland's reindeer-racing season and a great spectacle. (p197)

April

Easter is celebrated in a traditional fashion across the region. Spring is underway in Denmark and the southern parts, but there's still solid snow cover in the northern reaches.

Sámi Easter Festival, Norway

Thousands of Sámi participate in reindeer racing, theatre and cultural events in the Finnmark towns of Karasjok and Kautokeino. The highlight is the Sámi Grand Prix, a singing and *yoiking* (traditional Sámi form of song) contest attended by artists from across Lapland (www.samieasterfestival.com).

Valborgsmässoafton, Sweden

This public holiday (Walpurgis Night) on 30 April is a pagan holdover that's partly to welcome the arrival of spring. Celebrated across the country, it involves lighting huge bonfires, singing songs and forming parades.

Jazzkaar, Tallinn

Late April sees jazz greats from all around the world converge on Estonia's picturesque capital for a series of performances (www.jazzkaar.ee).

May

A transitional month in the north, with snow beginning to disappear and signs of life emerging after the long winter. In the south, spring is in full flow. This is a rewarding time to visit the southern capitals.

Copenhagen Marathon, Denmark

Scandinavia's largest marathon (www.copenhagenmarathon.dk) is on a Sunday in mid-May and draws around 5000 participants and tens of thousands of spectators. A series of shorter, lead-up races in the preceding months are a fun way to see the city.

Reykjavík Arts Festival, Iceland

Running for two weeks from late May to June, this wide-ranging festival sees Iceland's capital taken over by theatre performances, films, lectures and music. (p229)

Bergen International Festival, Norway

One of the biggest events on Norway's cultural calendar, this two-week festival, beginning in late May, showcases dance, music and folklore presentations, some international, some focusing on traditional local culture. (p311)

June

Midsummer weekend in late June is celebrated with great gusto, but it's typically a family event; unless you've got local friends it's not necessarily the best moment to visit. Lapland's muddy, but the rest of the region is warm and welcoming.

Old Town Days, Tallinn

This week-long Estonian festival (www.vanalinnapaevad.ee) in early June features dancing, concerts, costumed performers and plenty of medieval merrymaking in the heart of Tallinn's stunning historic centre.

Skagen Festival, Denmark

Held over four days in late June or early July, this festival at Denmark's picturesque northern tip features folk and world music performed by Danish and international artists.

Independence Day, Iceland

Held on 17 June, this is the largest nationwide festival in the country. It commemorates the founding of the Republic of Iceland in 1944 with big parades and general celebration.

Roskilde Festival, Denmark

Northern Europe's largest music festival rocks Roskilde for four consecutive days each summer. It takes place from late June to early July, but advance ticket sales are on offer in December and the festival usually sells out. (p70)

Midsummer, Denmark, Norway, Sweden & Finland

The year's biggest event in continental Nordic Europe sees fun family feasts, joyous celebrations of the summer, heady bonfires and copious drinking, often at peaceful lakeside summer cottages. It takes place on the weekend that falls between 19 and 26 June.

Extreme Sports Festival, Norway

Adventure junkies from across the world converge on Voss in late June for a week of skydiving, paragliding, parasailing and base jumping; music acts keep the energy flowing. (p319)

July

Peak season sees long, long days and sunshine. This is when the region really comes to life, with many festivals, boat trips, activities, cheaper hotels and a celebratory feel. Insects in Lapland are a nuisance.

Frederikssund Vikingespil, Denmark

Held in Frederikssund over a two-week period from late June to early July, this Viking festival (www.vikingespil.dk) includes a costumed open-air drama followed by a banquet with Viking food and entertainment.

Wife-Carrying World Championships, Finland

The world's premier wife-carrying event is held in the village of Sonkajärvi in early July. Winning couples (marriage not required) win the woman's weight in beer as well as significant kudos. (p174)

Ruisrock, Finland

Finland's oldest and possibly best rock festival takes place in early July on an island just outside the southwestern city of Turku. Top Finnish and international acts take part. (p147)

Copenhagen Jazz Festival, Denmark

This is the biggest entertainment event of the year in the capital, with 10 days of music at the beginning of July. The festival features a range of Danish and international jazz, blues and fusion music, with more than 500 indoor and outdoor concerts. (p54)

Moldejazz, Norway

Norway has a fine portfolio of jazz festivals, but Molde's version in mid-July is the most prestigious. With 100,000 spectators, world-class performers and a reputation for consistently high-quality music, it's easily one of Norway's most popular festivals. (p334)

Ólavsøka, Faroe Islands

The largest and most exciting traditional festival in the Faroes celebrates the 10th-century Norwegian king Olav the Holy, who spread the Christian faith on the isles. The big days are 28 and 29 July.

Savonlinna Opera Festival, Finland

A month of excellent performances in the romantic location of one of Europe's most picturesquely situated castles makes this Finland's biggest summer drawcard for casual and devoted lovers of opera. (p169)

August

Most Scandinavians are back at work, so it's quieter than in July but there's still decent weather across most of the region. It's a great time for hiking in Lapland, biking the islands or cruising the archipelagos.

Medeltidsveckan Visby, Sweden

Find yourself an actual knight in shining armour at Medieval Week, an immensely popular annual Swedish fest in Visby, Gotland's medieval jewel. It takes place over a week in early August.

Aarhus Festival, Denmark

The 10-day Aarhus Festival starts in late August and features scores of musical performances, theatre, ballet, modern dance, opera, films and sports events at indoor and outdoor venues across Denmark's second-largest city. (p97)

Air Guitar World Championships, Finland

Tune your imaginary instrument and get involved in this crazy rockstravaganza held in Oulu in late August. This surfeit of cheesy guitar classics and seemingly endless beer is all in the name of world peace. (p182)

Copenhagen Cooking, Denmark

Scandinavia's largest food festival focuses on the gourmet. It's a busy event that will let you catch up on the latest trends in fashionable New Nordic cuisine. (p54)

Menningarnótt, Iceland

On a Saturday in late August, this 'cultural night' (www.menningarnott.is) rocks Reykjavík, when the whole city seems to be out on the streets for quality Icelandic bands on a variety of stages in the city. (p229)

Þjódhátíð, Iceland

Held over the first weekend in August, this festival on the Vestmannaeyjar islands is Iceland's biggest piss-up, with three days of music, fireworks and frivolity. It's a big thing for young Icelanders: an enormous bonfire is a focal point.

September

The winter is fast approaching: pack something warm for those chilly nights. Autumn colours are spectacular in northern forests, making it another great month for hiking. Many attractions and activities close down or go onto winter time.

Reykjavík International Film Festival, Iceland

This annual event right at the end of September sees blockbusters make way for international art films in cinemas across the city, as well as talks from film directors from home and abroad. (p229)

Ruska Hiking, Finland & Sweden

Ruska is the Finnish word for the autumn colours, and there's a mini high season in Finnish and Swedish Lapland as hikers take to the trails to enjoy nature's brief artistic flourish.

October

Snow is already beginning to carpet the region's north. It's generally a quiet time, as locals face the realities of yet another long winter approaching.

Stockholm Jazz Festival, Sweden

Held on the island of Skeppsholmen, this well-known jazz fest brings artists from all over, including big international names. (p397)

November

Once the clocks change in late October, there's no denying the winter. November's bad for winter sports as there's little light and not enough snow. It can be a good month to see the aurora borealis, though.

Aurora Watching, Iceland, Norway, Sweden & Finland

Whether you are blessed with seeing the aurora borealis is largely a matter of luck, but the further north you are, the better the chances. Dark, cloudless nights, patience and a viewing spot away from city lights are other key factors.

Iceland Airwaves, Iceland

This five-day event in Reykjavík is one of the world's most cutting-edge music festivals: don't expect to sleep. It focuses on new musical trends rather than mainstream acts. (p229)

Stockholm International Film Festival, Sweden

Screenings of new international and independent films, director talks and discussion panels draw cinephiles to this important annual festival. Tickets go fast; book early. (p397)

December

The Christmas period is celebrated enthusiastically across the region, with cinnamon, mulled drinks, romantic lights and festive traditions putting the meaning back into the event.

Christmas, Regionwide

Whether visiting Santa and his reindeer in Finnish Lapland, admiring the magic of Copenhagen's Tivoli at night or sampling home-baked delicacies, Christmas – especially if you know a friendly local family to spend it with – is a heart-warming time to be here.

Plan Your Trip
Itineraries

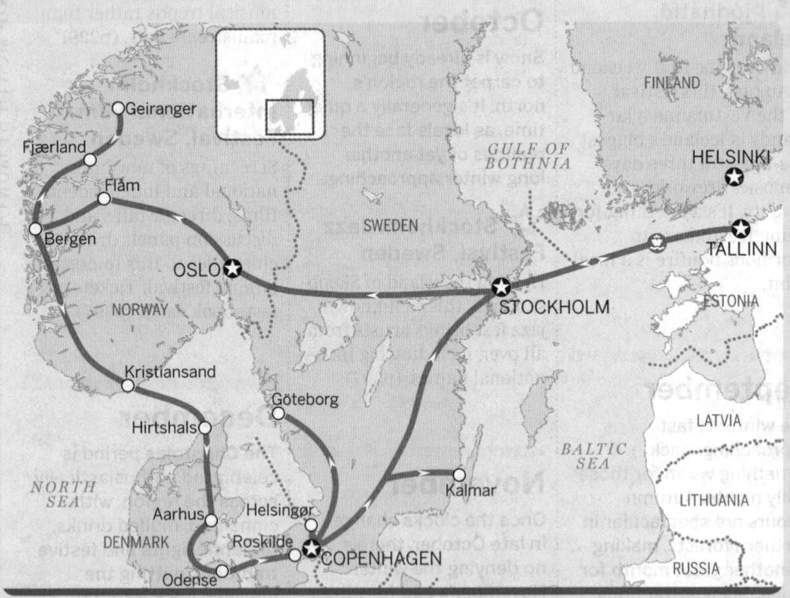

Scandinavia in a Nutshell

This quick hop jaunts around southern Scandinavia's classic sights. With just a week, it's essentially one city in each of Denmark, Sweden and Norway; extra time allows more detailed exploration and side trips.

Start in **Copenhagen**, admiring the waterfront, museums and lights of Tivoli at night. Day-trip to the cathedral and Viking Ship Museum at **Roskilde** or Hamlet's castle at **Helsingør**.

Next, train it to **Stockholm** and get into the design scene and the stately, watery town centre. An overnight train takes you to **Oslo**, to check out Munch's work and the city's extraordinary portfolio of museums. From Oslo, a long but very scenic day includes the rail trip to **Flåm** and a

Fjærlandsfjorden (p329), Norway

combination boat/bus journey along the Sognefjord to **Bergen**, Norway's prettiest city. Out of time? Fly out from Bergen.

Otherwise, head to **Kristiansand**, where there's a ferry to **Hirtshals**. Nose on down to **Aarhus** – don't miss the ARoS art museum. From here, it's an easy train to Copenhagen.

Extra days? A side trip from Stockholm on a Baltic ferry could take you to **Helsinki** or picturesque **Tallinn**. Other stops could include **Göteborg** or **Kalmar**; more fjord-y Norwegian experiences at **Fjærland** and **Geiranger**; or extra Danish time at **Odense**.

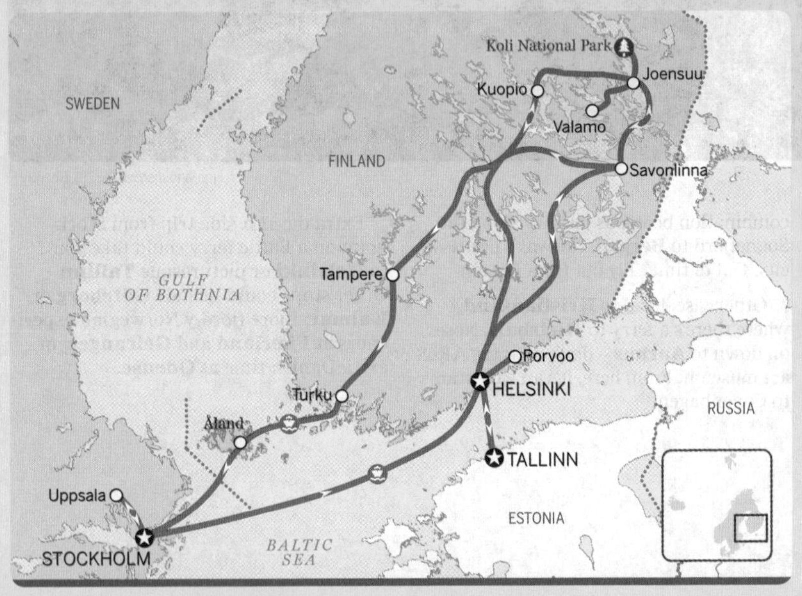
Koli National Park
Joensuu
Kuopio
SWEDEN
Valamo
FINLAND
Savonlinna
Tampere
GULF OF BOTHNIA
Porvoo
HELSINKI
Turku
Åland
RUSSIA
TALLINN
Uppsala
ESTONIA
STOCKHOLM
BALTIC SEA

Finland & the Baltic

Starting in Stockholm, this itinerary follows the old trading routes around the Baltic and covers plenty of Finland, including the capital, Helsinki, and beautiful Lakeland, as well as taking in the sumptuous Baltic city of Tallinn.

Kick things off in **Stockholm**, for centuries a Baltic trading powerhouse. Admire its picturesque Old Town and ponder that famously neutral Sweden once ruled most of the Baltic from here. Take a day trip to ancient **Uppsala** before taking advantage of Stockholm's cheap, luxurious overnight ferries to Finland. Don't overdo it on the duty-free booze, because you'll want a good view of the spectacular arrival in **Helsinki**, where you should investigate the cathedrals, market halls, modern architecture and design scene. Catch a classical concert at Musiikkitalo or a rock gig at legendary Tavastia.

From here, a good excursion heads east to the town of **Porvoo**, with its picturesque wooden warehouses and cathedral. Back in Helsinki, it's an easy boat ride across the Baltic to medieval **Tallinn**, a historic treasure trove that's worth a couple of days' exploration. If time's short, take a day trip.

In summer, take the train to the shimmering lakes of **Savonlinna**, with its awesome medieval castle and opera festival, and/or **Kuopio**, to steam up in its large smoke sauna. If you have the time, historic lake boats travel between these and other inland Finnish towns, a fabulously leisurely way to travel on a sunny day. A side trip from either of these towns can take you to **Joensuu**, from where you can visit the Orthodox monastery of **Valamo** or what is deservingly claimed to be Finland's best view at **Koli**.

Turning west again, head to the dynamic cultural city of **Tampere**, visiting its quirky museums and re-imagined fabric mills, and patronising its interesting cafes and restaurants. Then it's on to the third member of the trinity of Finnish cities, intriguing **Turku**, with excellent museums of its own, a towering castle and cathedral, and some very quirky drinking dens. From here you can get a ferry back to Sweden via the **Åland islands**. Stop off here for as long as you wish and tour the archipelago by bike.

MATTI NIEMI/GETTY IMAGES ©

JAMES MARGOLIS/GETTY IMAGES ©

Top: Stockholm (p386), Sweden
Bottom: Strawberries in a Helsinki market, Finland

4 WEEKS Beyond the Arctic Circle

This visit to the north takes in Santa, Sámi culture, spectacular coastal scenery viewed from the sea and opportunities for excellent activities. It'll be a completely different experience in summer or in winter.

Take the overnight train from **Helsinki** to **Rovaniemi**. Visit the fabulous Arktikum, chat with Santa Claus and stock up on anything you might need for your wilderness adventure; it will be a while before you see another town this big. Head north, crossing the Arctic Circle to **Saariselkä**, a base for great activities, whether summer hiking in the adjacent Urho Kekkonen National Park or husky-sledding trips in winter. There's a huge range of other things on offer year-round, too.

From here it's a short hop to the Sámi village of **Inari**, where Siida is a wonderful exhibition on Lapland's nature and indigenous cultures. Check out the craft shops too, and the impressive parliament building. To continue the theme, head onwards to **Karasjok**, Inari's Norwegian counterpart and an important meeting place for representatives of different Sámi groups.

From Karasjok (and Inari) summer buses run to **Nordkapp**, where you can stand at the top of Europe and gaze out towards the utter north. From nearby **Honningsvåg**, catch the *Hurtigruten* coastal steamer to the stunning **Lofoten Islands**, possibly stopping in lively **Tromsø**. Did we say Nordkapp was the top of Europe? We lied; from Tromsø there are flights way north to **Svalbard**, demesne of polar bears and an epic Arctic experience to really impress the folks back home.

Take some time to enjoy the Lofoten Islands, doing some cycling and visiting the Lofotr Vikingmuseum. When you're done, the *Hurtigruten* heads right down to Bergen, but jump off in **Narvik** and take the train to **Kiruna**, a remote Swedish mining town, and, in winter, home to the famous Icehotel. On the way, stop off for some hiking or aurora-watching at stunning **Abisko National Park**. Also be sure to check out the Sámi village and typical reindeer-herding region of **Jokkmokk**.

From here, you could fly, train or bus all the way south to **Stockholm**, cut back into Norway to continue your trip down the coast, or head to the Finnish border at **Haparanda/Tornio** to head back to Helsinki from there.

DOUG PEARSON/GETTY IMAGES ©

GAVIN HELLIER/GETTY IMAGES ©

Top: Nordkapp (p355), Norway
Bottom: Icehotel (p463), Jukkasjärvi, Sweden

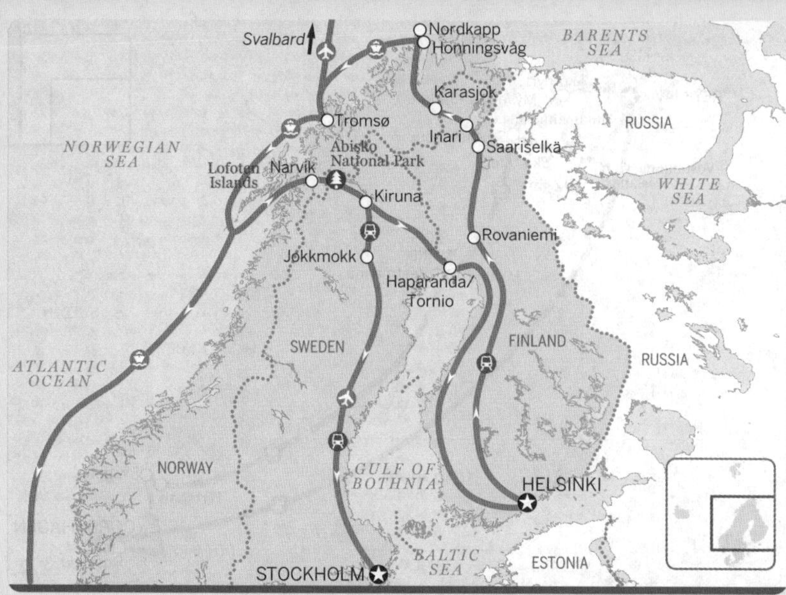
Svalbard
Nordkapp
Honningsvåg
BARENTS SEA
Karasjok
Tromsø
Inari
Saariselkä
RUSSIA
NORWEGIAN SEA
Abisko National Park
Lofoten Islands
Narvik
WHITE SEA
Kiruna
Rovaniemi
Jokkmokk
Haparanda/Tornio
SWEDEN
FINLAND
ATLANTIC OCEAN
RUSSIA
NORWAY
GULF OF BOTHNIA
HELSINKI
BALTIC SEA
ESTONIA
STOCKHOLM

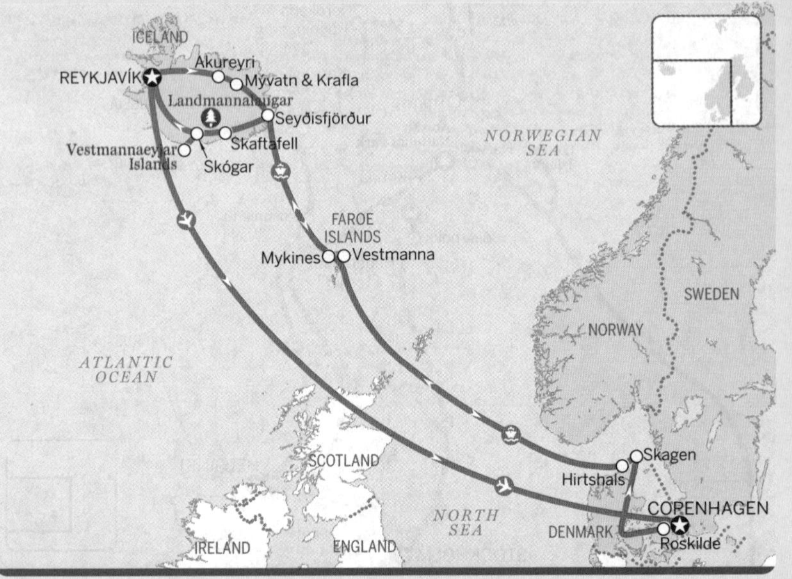

ICELAND
REYKJAVÍK
Akureyri
Mývatn & Krafla
Landmannalaugar
Seyðisfjörður
Skaftafell
Vestmannaeyjar Islands
Skógar
NORWEGIAN SEA
FAROE ISLANDS
Mykines
Vestmanna
SWEDEN
NORWAY
ATLANTIC OCEAN
SCOTLAND
Skagen
Hirtshals
COPENHAGEN
NORTH SEA
DENMARK
Roskilde
IRELAND
ENGLAND

MINT IMAGES/FRANS LANTING/GETTY IMAGES ©

Northern Islands

Fly into Copenhagen, taking some time to absorb its addictive atmosphere. Get in the mood for your sea crossing by visiting the Viking Boat Museum at nearby Roskilde. Then hit north Jutland and the beautiful dunes at Skagen, where at the sandy headland of Grenen, two seas meet at Denmark's northernmost tip.

Jump aboard the Smyril Line ferry leaving from nearby **Hirtshals**. In summer there are two ferries running per week, so you can make a three-day stop in the remote **Faroe Islands**, but in the off season it's either nine hours there or a whole week. If you manage some time on the islands, giggle at the comical puffins on the awesome cliffs of **Mykines** and take a boat trip to visit the immense seabird colonies at **Vestmanna**.

The ferry (April to late October only, with some limited departures in winter) continues to Iceland, arriving at **Seyðisfjörður**. From here journey along the south coast past **Skaftafell**, a national park area that is one of Iceland's most spectacularly scenic regions, offering great hiking and unforgettable glacier walks. If you've got time to explore, head to the interior for the amazing geoscapes of **Landmannalaugar**. Take the spectacular three-day hike to Þórsmörk, one of Europe's most spectacular walks. The tough day's extension to **Skógar** takes you across some of the country's newest lava fields. Next, you could head out to see the birdlife and traditional communities of the **Vestmannaeyjar** islands.

Hit the capital **Reykjavík**, enjoy the nightlife, visit the Saga Museum and take trips to the Blue Lagoon, then travel around the Ring Rd to the north of the island, where an R&R stop at peaceful fjord-side **Akureyri** can include a side trip to the **Mývatn** natural thermal baths and the steaming volcanic landscape of **Krafla**.

From here, you can return to the ferry terminal to head back to Denmark by sea if you're still game, otherwise you can fly back from Reykjavík.

ANDREA RICORDI, ITALY/GETTY IMAGES ©

Top: Landmannalaugar (p260), Iceland
Bottom: Puffin, Faroe Islands (p113), Denmark

Countries at a Glance

The seductive call of the north is one of wild landscapes, crisp air and cutting-edge city style coloured by the epic changes of the Scandinavian seasons.

Scenically, it's hard to beat. Norway's noble, breathtaking coastline, serrated with fjords, competes with Iceland's harsh, volcanic majesty. Soothing Swedish and Finnish lake- and forestscapes offer a gentler beauty.

Though the towns and cities all have a definite allure – Copenhagen is the one worth the most time – the big attraction is the outdoors. There are so many ways to get active on land, water and snow. Hiking, kayaking and wildlife-watching are among Europe's best, while the bike-friendly culture makes it great for cyclists too, particularly in Denmark, southern Sweden and various Baltic islands.

Denmark

Cycling
History
Gastronomy

Two-Wheeled Pleasure

With a highest point as lofty as your average big-city office building, it's no surprise to find that Denmark is a paradise for cycling. With thousands of kilometres of dedicated cycle routes and islands designed for two-wheeled exploration, it's the best way to get around.

Past Echoes

Denmark's historical sites are excellent. Hauntingly preserved bog bodies take us back to prehistoric times, while Roskilde's Viking boats and majestic cathedral are important remnants of other periods. Hamlet may have been a fictional character, but his home, Kronborg Slot (Elsinore Castle), is a major attraction.

New Nordic Cuisine

Nordic food has taken the world by storm in recent years, and Denmark is at the forefront of modern trends in Scandinavian cuisine. Copenhagen has a great eating scene, with Noma one of the world's most highly regarded restaurants.

p42

Finland

Hiking
Winter Activities
Design

Wild Nature

Finland's vast forested wildernesses are some of Europe's least populated areas. Large national parks with excellent networks of trails, huts and camping grounds make this prime hiking country. Kayaking and canoeing are also great options.

Active Winters

Northern Finland's numerous ski resorts aren't very elevated but are great for beginners and families. Skiing's just the start, though: snowy wildernesses crossed in sleds pulled by reindeer or huskies, snowmobile safaris, ice-breaker cruises, nights in snow hotels and a personal audience with Santa Claus are other wintry delights.

Design & Architecture

Finnish design is world-famous; browsing Helsinki's shops, from flagship emporia to edgy bohemian studios, is one of the city's great pleasures. Some of the world's finest modern architecture can also be found scattered around Finland's towns.

p126

Tallinn

Medieval Streets
Culture
Bars & Cafes

Historic Jewel

A short trip across the water from Helsinki, Estonia's capital, Tallinn, is the jewel of the nation. The medieval Old Town is its highlight, and weaving your way along its narrow, cobbled streets is like strolling back to the 14th century.

Traditional Culture

Despite (or perhaps because of) centuries of occupation, Estonians have tenaciously held onto their national identity and are deeply, emotionally connected to their history, folklore and national song traditions.

Bar Life

Tallinn has numerous cosy cafes decorated in plush style, ideal spots to while away a few hours if the weather's not being kind. Nightlife, with alcohol not such a wallet drain as in other Nordic countries, is pretty vibrant.

p208

Iceland

Scenery
Activities
Wildlife

Volcanic Landscapes

Iceland, forged in fire, has a scenic splendour matched by few other nations. It's a bleak, epic grandeur that seems designed to remind visitors of their utter insignificance in the greater scheme of things. Get among the steaming pools, spouting geysers and majestic glaciers to really appreciate the unique nature of this country.

Outdoors

There are so many ways to get active. Truly spectacular hikes give awesome perspectives of Iceland's natural wonder; kayaks let you see it all from the sea. Horse riding is a must; and what better way to soothe those aching muscles than luxuriating in a thermal spring?

Whales & Birds

The land may seem inhospitable, but the seas and skies teem with life. Iceland is one of the world's premier spots for whale watching, and the quantity of seabirds – some 10 million puffins! – has to be seen to be believed.

p217

Norway

Fjords
Activities
Wildlife

Coastal Majesty

The famous serrations of the coast are justly renowned; from base to tip, Norway's jagged geography is deeply momentous, inspiring profound awe.

Outdoor Appeal

The rough and rugged contours make this a prime outdoors destination. Mountains and plateaux attract hikers and cyclists, while the coastline invites getting out on the water in anything from a kayak to a cruise ship. Winter switches over to husky-sledding and snowmobile safaris, as well as the region's best skiing.

Unusual Creatures

For a modern European country, Norway has an impressive range of beasts, from whales sporting offshore to roaming elk and reindeer. There's even a reintroduced population of the weird-looking musk ox, as well as plentiful seabird life. Right up north, Svalbard is bossed by polar bears and walruses.

p282

Sweden

Winter Activities
Museums
Boating

Snowy Seduction

Northern Sweden has several top-drawer winter attractions, one of which is the aurora borealis (northern lights). Dark places like Abisko, in the country's top-left corner, make great observatories; other attractions up here include dog-sledding, skiing and Kiruna's famous Icehotel.

Proud Heritage

Sweden, which once controlled much of northern Europe, has a rich history and proud artistic heritage, which is displayed at great galleries and museums around the country. But it's not all about the rich and famous. Excellent open-air displays dotted across the country document the humbler traditions of everyday life.

Water World

The abundance of water once the snow melts means it's a country that's beautifully set up for boating, whether you're canoeing inland waterways, boating in the many archipelagos, or exploring the coastline in a yacht or kayak.

p383

On the Road

Iceland
p217
Finland
p126
Sweden
p383
Norway
p282
Tallinn
p208
Denmark
p42

Denmark

Includes ➡

Best Places to Eat

- ➡ Noma (p58)
- ➡ Schønnemann (p57)
- ➡ Kadeau (p78)
- ➡ Kähler Villa Dining (p99)
- ➡ Mortens Kro (p108)

Best Places to Stay

- ➡ Hotel Nimb (p56)
- ➡ Helenekilde Badehotel (p69)
- ➡ Dragsholm Slot (p72)
- ➡ Pension Vestergade 44 (p93)

Why Go?

Denmark is the bridge between Scandinavia and northern Europe. To the rest of Scandinavia, the Danes are chilled, frivolous party animals, with relatively liberal, progressive attitudes. Their culture, food, architecture and appetite for conspicuous consumption owe as much, if not more, to their German neighbours to the south than to their former colonies – Sweden, Norway and Iceland – to the north.

Packed with intriguing museums, shops, bars, nightlife and award-winning restaurants, Denmark's capital, Copenhagen, is one of the hippest, most accessible cities in Europe. And while Danish cities such as Odense and Aarhus harbour their own urbane drawcards, Denmark's other chief appeal lies in its photogenic countryside, sweeping coastline and historic sights, from neolithic burial chambers and frozen-in-time peat-bog bodies, to castles.

When to Go

Copenhagen

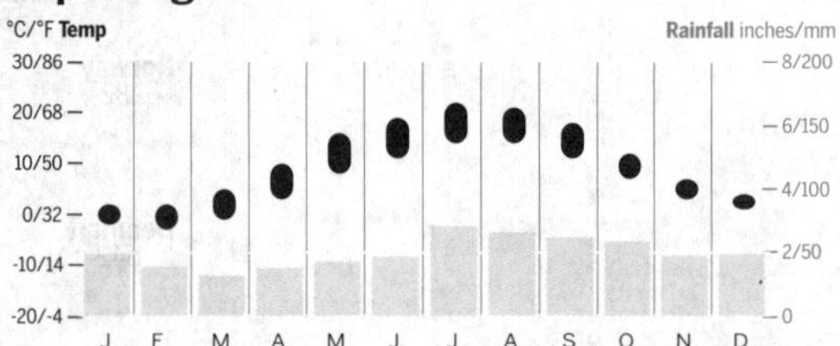

Jun & Jul Long days, buzzing beachside towns, Copenhagen Jazz and A-list rock fest Roskilde.

Sep & Oct Fewer crowds, golden landscapes and snug nights by crackling open fires.

Dec Twinkling Christmas lights, ice-skating rinks and gallons of warming *gløgg* (mulled wine).

Connections

Denmark's modern, efficient transport network is well connected to the region and the rest of the world. Located in Copenhagen, its main airport, Kastrup, offers excellent and numerous long- and short-haul connections, while Billund and Aarhus in Jutland (regional airports) offer numerous European short-haul options. Good road and rail connections link Sweden and Germany to Denmark. Plentiful ferries link Denmark with all major Baltic destinations and with Atlantic-coast destinations in Norway, the Faroe Islands and Iceland.

ITINERARIES

One Week

You could comfortably spend four days in **Copenhagen** exploring the museums, hunting down Danish design and taste-testing its lauded restaurants and bars. A trip north along the coast to the magnificent modern-art museum, **Louisiana**, and then further north still to Kronborg Slot, before returning south via **Frederiksborg Slot** and **Roskilde**, would be a great way to spend the other three days. If the weather is on your side, head for the north coast of **Zealand** for historic fishing villages and gorgeous sandy beaches.

Two Weeks

After time in **Copenhagen**, a quick catamaran ride will take you to the Baltic island of **Bornholm**, reputedly the sunniest slice of Denmark, and famed for cycling, beaches and its cheap, tasty smokehouses. Alternatively, head west, stopping off on the island of Funen to see Hans Christian Andersen's birthplace in **Odense**. Continue further west to the Jutland peninsula for the understated hipster cool of **Aarhus** and further north to magnificent **Skagen**, where the Baltic and North Seas clash.

Essential Food & Drink

Smørrebrød Rye bread topped with anything from beef tartar to egg and shrimp, the open sandwich is Denmark's most famous culinary export.

Sild Smoked, cured, pickled or fried, herring is a local staple and best washed down with generous serves of akvavit (schnapps).

Kanelsnegle A calorific delight, 'cinnamon snails' are sweet, buttery scrolls, sometimes laced with chocolate.

Akvavit Denmark's best-loved spirit is caraway-spiced akvavit from Aalborg, drunk straight down as a shot, followed by a chaser of *øl* (beer).

Lashings of beer Carlsberg may dominate, but Denmark's expanding battalion of microbreweries includes Rise Bryggeri, Brøckhouse and Grauballe.

AT A GLANCE

Capital Copenhagen

Area 42,915 sq km

Population 5.6 million

Country code ☎45

Language Danish

Currency Danish krone (Dkr)

Exchange Rates

Australia	A$1	Dkr5.14
Canada	C$1	Dkr5.18
Euro Zone	€1	Dkr7.44
Japan	¥100	Dkr5.46
New Zealand	NZ$1	Dkr4.66
UK	UK£1	Dkr9.42
USA	US$1	Dkr5.83

Set Your Budget

Double room in a budget hotel Dkr500–Dkr650

Museum entrance free–Dkr140

Bike hire per day free–Dkr100

Train ticket Copenhagen–Aarhus Dkr382

Main course in a top-end restaurant Dkr250 and up

Resources

Visit Denmark (www.visitdenmark.com)

AOK (www.aok.dk)

Rejseplanen (www.rejseplanen.dk)

Lonely Planet (www.lonelyplanet.com/denmark)

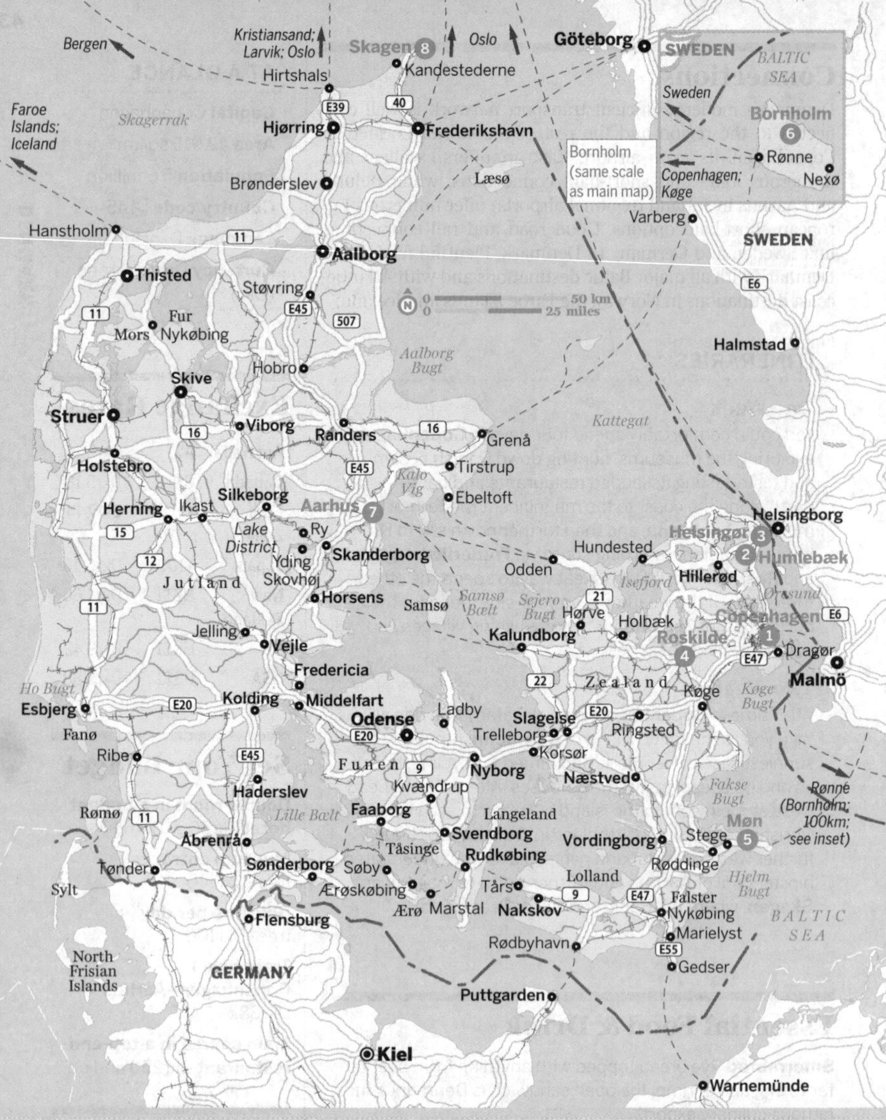

Denmark Highlights

1 Shop, nosh and chill in Scandinavia's capital of cool, **Copenhagen** (p45)

2 Be inspired by the art and the views at the **Louisiana** (p65) in Humlebæk

3 Snoop around **Kronborg Slot** (p65), Hamlet's epic home in Helsingør

4 Get your groove on at Denmark's top annual music event, **Roskilde Festival** (p70)

5 Tackle the toothpaste-white cliffs of **Møns Klint** (p73) on picture-perfect Møn

6 Lose yourself in nature and smoked fish on the Baltic island of **Bornholm** (p76)

7 See Aarhus through technicolor glass at impressive art museum **ARoS** (p95)

8 Watch angry seas duel above luminous, northern **Skagen** (p110)

COPENHAGEN

POP 1.9 MILLION

Copenhagen is the coolest kid on the Nordic block. Edgier than Stockholm and worldlier than Oslo, the Danish capital gives Scandinavia the X-factor.

While this thousand-year-old harbour town has managed to retain much of its historic good looks (think copper spires and cobbled squares), the focus here is on the innovative and cutting edge. Denmark's overachieving capital is home to a thriving design scene, its streets awash with effortlessly hip shops, cafes and bars; world-class museums and art collections; intelligent new architecture; and no fewer than 15 Michelin-starred restaurants. This is also a royal city, home to the multitalented Queen Margrethe II and her photogenic family.

And as if this wasn't impressive enough, a bounty of beautiful beaches, wooded parks and elegant lakes await just minutes away.

History

For more millennia than anyone can be sure of, Copenhagen was a fishing settlement on the shores of what we now call the Øresund Strait, the narrow belt of water between Denmark and Sweden.

Wendish pirates, who marauded the coast in the 12th century, prompted the locals, led by Bishop Absalon, to build a fort on a small island in the harbour – where the modern-day Danish parliament stands on Slotsholmen; you can still see the foundations of the original fort in the cellar museum.

The city of København (*'købe'* means 'to buy', *'havn'* is 'harbour') gradually grew to the north of Slotsholmen (where the restaurants of Gammel Strand now stand), founded on the wealth that came from the herring caught by the local fishermen. But it wasn't until the 15th century that Copenhagen stole Roskilde's thunder as the new capital of Denmark.

Denmark's great Renaissance king, Christian IV (1588–1648), transformed Copenhagen into an impressive capital. From there he controlled much of Scandinavia – with numerous ambitious buildings including Rosenborg Slot and the Rundetårn. Eventually Christian IV brought the country to its knees with overspending and reckless foreign forays.

By the early 19th century, the once-mighty Danish empire was greatly diminished. Twice in the early 19th century the British navy bombarded the city but its people bounced back with a cultural Golden Age, led by the likes of Hans Christian Andersen and Søren Kierkegaard.

Sights

Two of the great things about Copenhagen are its accessibility and size. You can walk across the city centre in an hour, and travel further with great ease thanks to the cycle paths, metro, trains and buses, all of which mean you can pack many of the sights into two days.

Around Tivoli

★**Tivoli Gardens** AMUSEMENT PARK

(www.tivoli.dk; adult/child under 8yr Dkr99/free; ⏲11am-10pm Sun-Thu, to 12.30am Fri, to midnight Sat early Apr-late Sep, reduced hours rest of year; 🚻; 🚌2A, 5A, 9A, 12, 26, 250S, 350S, 🚆S-train København H) Dating from 1843, tasteful Tivoli wins fans with its dreamy whirl of amusement rides, twinkling pavilions, carnival games and open-air stage shows. Visitors can ride the renovated, century-old **roller coaster**, take in the famous Saturday-evening **fireworks display** or just soak up the story-book atmosphere. A good tip is to go on Fridays during the summer season, when the open-air Plænen stage hosts free rock concerts from Danish bands (and the occasional international superstar) from 10pm – go early if it's a big-name act.

Each of Tivoli's numerous entertainment venues has a different character. Perhaps

> **COPENHAGEN CARD**
>
> The **Copenhagen Card** (www.copenhagencard.com; 24hr adult/child 10-15yr Dkr339/179, 48hr Dkr469/239, 72hr Dkr559/289) secures unlimited travel on buses and trains around Copenhagen and North Zealand. This covers the city's metro system, as well as suburban trains. It also gives free or discounted admission to around 70 of the region's museums and attractions. Cards can be purchased directly online and are also sold at the Copenhagen tourist office, Central Station, major Danske Statsbaner (DSB) stations and at many hotels, camping grounds and hostels. Be aware, though, that several of the city's attractions are either free or at least free one day of the week.

best known is the open-air pantomime theatre, built in 1874 by Vilhelm Dahlerup, the Copenhagen architect who also designed the royal theatre. Tivoli's large concert hall features performances by international symphony orchestras and ballet troupes, as well as popular musicians. While the numerous open-air performances are free of charge, there's usually an admission fee for the indoor performances; check the website for venue details, line-ups and prices.

Amusement-ride tickets cost Dkr25 (some rides require up to three tickets), making the multiride ticket (Dkr199) better value in most cases.

Outside the main summer season, Tivoli also opens for around three weeks around Halloween and from mid-November to early January for Christmas. For up-to-date opening times, see the Tivoli website.

★ **Nationalmuseet** MUSEUM
(National Museum; www.natmus.dk; Ny Vestergade 10; ⏲10am-5pm Tue-Sun; 👪; 🚌1A, 2A, 11A, 33, 40, 66, 🚆S-train København H) FREE For a crash course in Danish history and culture, spend an afternoon at Denmark's National Museum. It has first claims on virtually every antiquity uncovered on Danish soil, including Stone Age tools, Viking weaponry, rune stones and medieval jewellery. Among the many highlights is a finely crafted 3500-year-old Sun Chariot, as well as bronze *lurs* (horns), some of which date back 3000 years and are still capable of blowing a tune.

You'll find sections related to the Norsemen and Inuit of Greenland, and an evocative exhibition called 'Stories of Denmark', covering Danish history from 1660 to 2000. Among the highlights here are re-created living quarters (among them an 18th-century Copenhagen apartment) and a whimsical collection of toys, including a veritable village of doll's houses. The museum also has an excellent **Children's Museum**, as well as a classical-antiquities section complete with Egyptian mummies. For a little cerebral relief, find refuge in the decent museum cafe and well-stocked gift shop.

★ **Ny Carlsberg Glyptotek** MUSEUM
(www.glyptoteket.dk; Dantes Plads 7, HC Andersens Blvd; adult/child Dkr75/free, Sun free; ⏲11am-5pm Tue-Sun; 🚌1A, 2A, 11A, 33, 40, 66, 🚆S-train København H) Fin de siècle architecture dallies with an eclectic mix of art at Ny Carlsberg Glyptotek. The collection is divided into two parts: northern Europe's largest booty of antiquities, and an elegant collection of 19th-century Danish and French art. The latter includes the largest collection of Rodin sculptures outside of France, and no less than 47 Gauguin paintings. These are displayed along with works by greats like Cézanne, Van Gogh, Pissarro, Monet and Renoir.

COPENHAGEN IN...

Two Days

Orient yourself with a **canal tour** (p53) before strolling **Nyhavn** (p47) and design shopping at **Hay House** (p62) and **Illums Bolighus** (p61). Gourmet graze at **Torvehallerne KBH** (p57) and dive into Danish history at the **Nationalmuseet** (p46). If dining at **Kadeau** (p58), cap the night at **Ruby** (p60). If eating at **Kødbyens Fiskebar** (p57), kick on at **Mesteren & Lærlingen** (p60). The following day, visit **Statens Museum for Kunst** (p51), sample smørrebrød (Danish open sandwiches) at **Schønnemann** (p57) and take in the panorama atop **Rundetårn** (p51). Amble through free-spirited **Christiania** (p52) before New Nordic noshing at **Noma** (p58; assuming you booked months ahead!), **Kadeau** (p58) or **Pony** (p56). If it's summer, Halloween or Christmas, indulge your inner child at **Tivoli** (p45). If it's not, opt for craft suds at **Mikkeller** (p60).

Four Days

Spend day three gazing at art and Sweden at the **Louisiana** (p65) or head further north to Hamlet's 'home' in Helsingør, **Kronborg Slot** (p65). Head back into town for an early dinner at **Cock's & Cows** (p57), followed by jazz at **Jazzhouse** (p61) or weekend clubbing at **Culture Box** (p60). Spend day four exploring **Ny Carlsberg Glyptotek** (p46), lunching at romantic **Orangeriet** (p58) and eyeing the crown jewels at **Rosenborg Slot** (p52). After dark, catch an aria at Copenhagen's head-turning opera house, **Operaen** (p61).

Slotsholmen

An island separated from the city centre by a moatlike canal on three sides and the harbour on the other side, Slotsholmen is the site of Christiansborg Palace, home to Denmark's parliament.

Christiansborg Palace PALACE
(☎33 92 64 92; www.christiansborg.dk; Slotsholmen; 🚌1A, 2A, 9A, 26, 40, 66, 🚢Det Kongelige Bibliotek, Ⓜ Christianshavn) Of Christiansborg Palace's numerous museums (which include a theatre museum and an arsenal museum), the cake-taker is **De Kongelige Repræsentationslokaler** (Royal Reception Rooms; www.ses.dk; adult/child Dkr80/40; ⏰10am-5pm daily May-Sep, closed Mon rest of yr, guided tours in Danish 11am, in English 3pm), an ornate Renaissance hall where the queen entertains heads of state.

Beneath the building lurk the **Ruins of Bishop Absalon's Fortress** (Ruins under Christiansborg; www.ses.dk; adult/child Dkr40/20; ⏰10am-5pm daily, closed Mon Oct-Apr, guided tours in English noon Sat, in Danish noon Sun), the excavated foundations of Bishop Absalon's original castle of 1167 and of its successor, Copenhagen Slot.

★**Thorvaldsens Museum** MUSEUM
(www.thorvaldsensmuseum.dk; Bertel Thorvaldsens Plads; adult/child Dkr40/free, Wed free; ⏰10am-5pm Tue-Sun; 🚌1A, 2A, 11A, 26, 40, 66) What looks like a colourful Graeco-Roman mausoleum is in fact a museum dedicated to the works of illustrious Danish sculptor Bertel Thorvaldsen (1770–1844). Heavily influenced by mythology after four decades in Rome, Thorvaldsen returned to Copenhagen and donated his private collection to the Danish public. In return the royal family provided this site for the construction of what is a remarkable complex housing Thorvaldsen's drawings, plaster moulds and statues. The museum also contains Thorvaldsens' own collection of Mediterranean antiquities.

Det Kongelige Bibliotek LIBRARY
(Royal Library; ☎33 47 47 47; www.kb.dk; Søren Kierkegaards Plads; ⏰8am-7pm Mon-Sat Jul & Aug, to 10pm rest of year; 🚌1A, 2A, 9A, 11A, 26, 40, 66, 🚢Det Kongelige Bibliotek) FREE Scandinavia's largest library consists of two very distinct parts: the original, 19th-century red-brick building and the head-turning 'Black Diamond' extension, the latter a leaning parallelogram of sleek black granite and smoke-coloured glass. From the soaring, harbour-fronting atrium, an escalator leads up to a 210-sq-metre ceiling mural by celebrated Danish artist Per Kirkeby. Beyond it, at the end of the corridor, is the 'old library' and its Hogwarts-like northern Reading Room, resplendent with vintage desk lamps and classical columns.

Around Nyhavn & Harbourfront

Just east of Kongens Nytorv, the bustling waterfront and the surrounding area are home to a number of iconic landmarks and cultural riches.

Nyhavn CANAL
There are few nicer places to be on a sunny day than sitting at the outdoor tables of a cafe on the quayside of the Nyhavn canal. The canal was built to connect Kongens Nytorv to the harbour, and was long a haunt for sailors and writers, including Hans Christian Andersen, who lived there for most of his life at, variously, numbers 20, 18 and 67. These days Nyhavn is a tourist magnet of brightly coloured gabled town houses, herring buffets and foaming beers.

Amalienborg Slot PALACE
(☎33 12 21 86; http://dkks.dk/amalienborgmuseet/amalienborg; Amalienborg Plads; adult/child Dkr90/free; ⏰10am-4pm daily May-Oct, reduced hours rest of year; 🚌1A, 26) Home of the current queen, Margrethe II, Amalienborg Slot consists of four austere, 18th-century palaces around a large cobbled square. The changing of the guard takes place here daily at noon, the new guard having marched through the city centre from the barracks on Gothersgade at 11.30am. One of the palaces features exhibits of the royal apartments used by three generations of the monarchy from 1863 to 1947, its reconstructed rooms decorated with gilt-leather tapestries, trompe l'œil paintings, family photographs and antiques.

Marmorkirken CHURCH
(Marble Church; ☎33 15 01 44; www.marmorkirken.dk; Frederiksgade 4; dome adult/child Dkr35/20, church admission free; ⏰church 10am-5pm Mon, Tue, Thu & Sat, 10am-6.30pm Wed, noon-5pm Fri & Sun, dome 1pm & 3pm daily mid-Jun–Aug, 1pm & 3pm Sat & Sun rest of year; 🚌1A) Consecrated in 1894, the neobaroque Marble

Central Copenhagen (København)

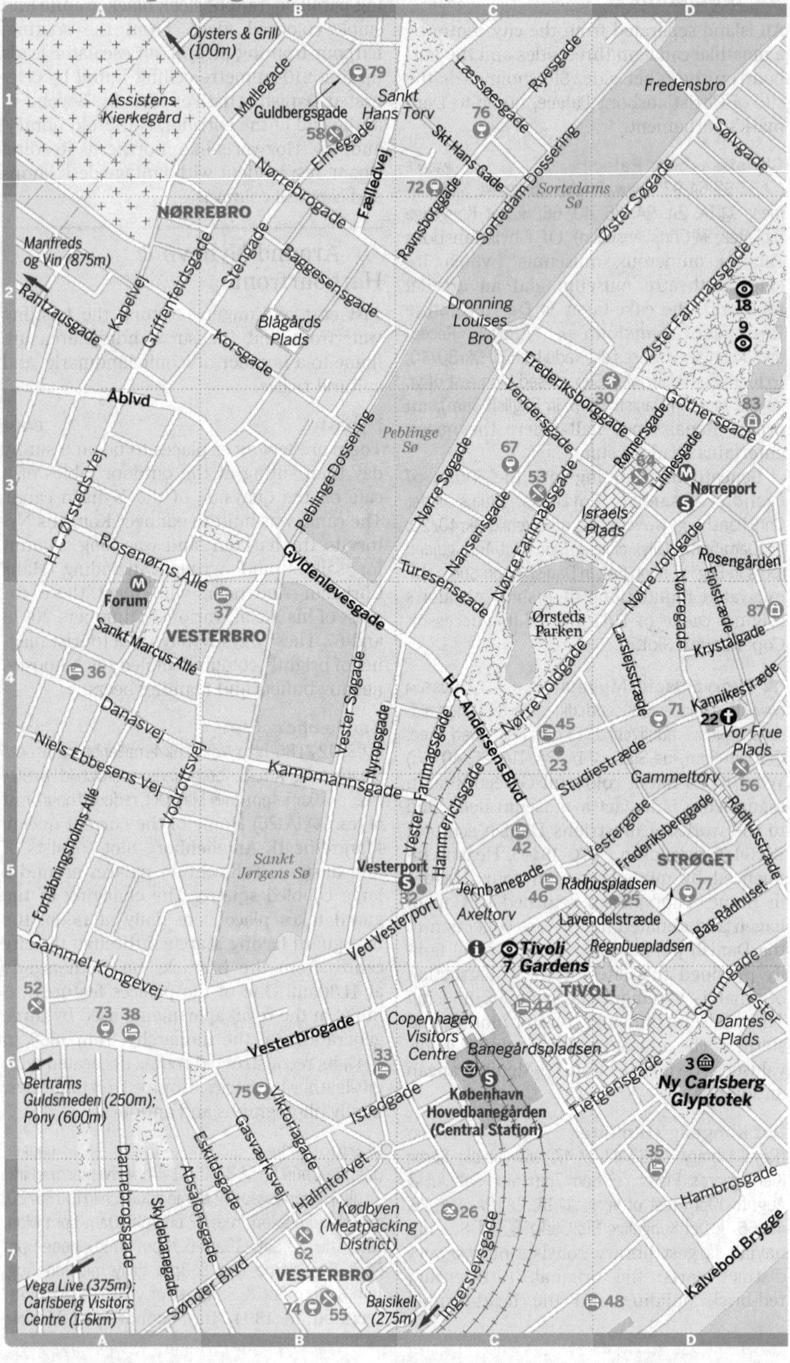

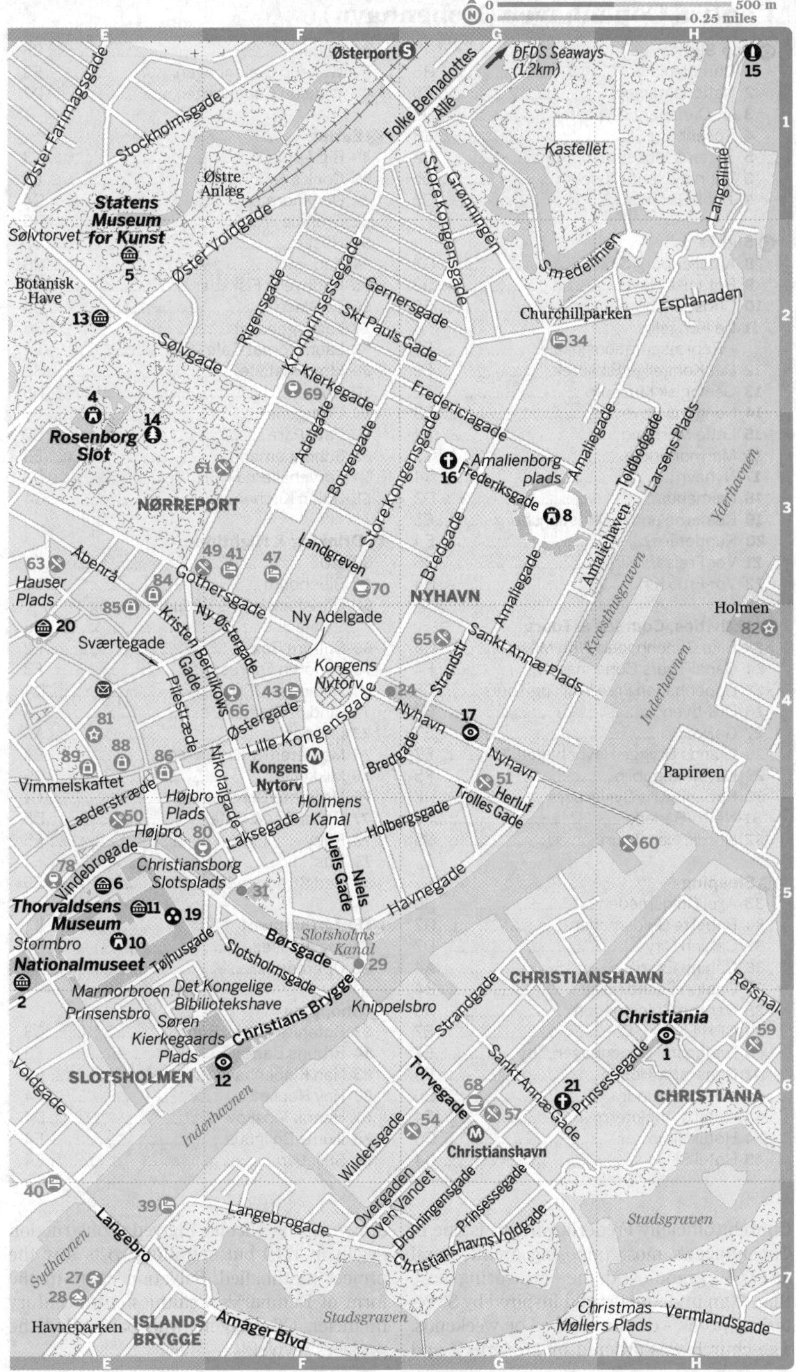
0 500 m
0 0.25 miles
Østerport
DFDS Seaways (1.2km)
Folke Bernadottes Allé
Kastellet
Langelinie
Øster Farimagsgade
Stockholmsgade
Østre Anlæg
Statens Museum for Kunst
Sølvtorvet
Øster Voldgade
Botanisk Have
Store Kongensgade
Grønningen
Smedelinien
Gernersgade
Skt Pauls Gade
Rigensgade
Kronprinsessegade
Esplanaden
Churchillparken
Sølvgade
Klerkegade
Fredericiagade
Rosenborg Slot
Adelgade
Borgergade
Amalienborg plads
Frederiksgade
Amaliegade
Toldbodgade
Larsens Plads
Yderhavnen
NØRREPORT
Landgreven
Bredgade
Amaliehaven
Åbenrå
Hauser Plads
Gothersgade
NYHAVN
Holmen
Kristen Bernikows Gade
Ny Østergade
Ny Adelgade
Sankt Annæ Plads
Kvæsthusgraven
Sværtegade
Kongens Nytorv
Strandstr
Inderhavnen
Pilestræde
Østergade
Nyhavn
Lille Kongensgade
Nikolajgade
Kongens Nytorv
Bredgade
Papirøen
Vimmelskaftet
Læderstræde
Højbro Plads
Holmens Kanal
Herluf Trolles Gade
Højbro
Laksegade
Holbergsgade
Juels Gade
Niels
Vindebrogade
Christiansborg Slotsplads
Havnegade
Thorvaldsens Museum
Stormbro
Tøjhusgade
Slotsholms Kanal
Børsgade
Nationalmuseet
Slotsholmsgade
CHRISTIANSHAWN
Refshale
Marmorbroen
Det Kongelige Bibiliotekshave
Christians Brygge
Knippelsbro
Strandgade
Prinsensbro
Søren Kierkegaards Plads
Christiania
Sankt Annæ Gade
Prinsessegade
SLOTSHOLMEN
Torvegade
CHRISTIANIA
Voldgade
Inderhavnen
Wildersgade
Christianshavn
Overgaden Oven Vandet
Dronningensgade
Prinsessegade
Christianshavns Voldgade
Langebrogade
Stadsgraven
Langebro
Sydhavnen
Stadsgraven
Christmas Møllers Plads
Vermlandsgade
Havneparken
ISLANDS BRYGGE
Amager Blvd
E
F
G
H
1
2
3
4
5
6
7
1
2
4
5
6
8
10
11
12
13
14
15
16
17
19
20
21
24
27
28
29
31
34
39
40
41
43
47
49
50
51
54
57
59
60
61
63
65
66
68
69
70
78
80
81
82
84
85
86
88
89

Central Copenhagen (København)

Top Sights
1 Christiania H6
2 Nationalmuseet E5
3 Ny Carlsberg Glyptotek D6
4 Rosenborg Slot E3
5 Statens Museum for Kunst E2
6 Thorvaldsens Museum E5
7 Tivoli Gardens C5

Sights
8 Amalienborg Slot G3
9 Botanisk Have D2
10 Christiansborg Palace E5
11 De Kongelige Repræsentationslokaler E5
12 Det Kongelige Bibliotek F6
13 Geologisk Museum E2
14 Kongens Have E3
15 Little Mermaid H1
16 Marmorkirken G3
17 Nyhavn G4
18 Palmehus D2
19 Ruinerne under Christiansborg E5
20 Rundetårn E4
21 Vor Frelsers Kirke G6
22 Vor Frue Kirke D4

Activities, Courses & Tours
23 Bike Copenhagen With Mike C4
24 Canal Tours Copenhagen F4
25 Copenhagen Free Walking Tours D5
26 DGI-byen C7
27 GoBoat E7
28 Islands Brygge Havnebadet E7
29 Kayak Republic F5
30 Københavns Cyklerbørs D2
31 Netto-Bådene F5
32 Nordic Noir Tours C5

Sleeping
33 Axel Guldsmeden B6
34 Babette Guldsmeden G2
35 Cabinn City D7
36 Cabinn Express A4
37 Cabinn Scandinavia B4
38 Carlton Guldsmeden A6
39 CPH Living E7
40 Danhostel Copenhagen City E7
41 Generator Hostel F3
42 Hotel Alexandra C5
43 Hotel d'Angleterre F4
44 Hotel Nimb C6
45 Hotel SP34 C4
46 Square C5
47 Wakeup Copenhagen F3
48 Wakeup Copenhagen D7

Eating
49 Big Apple F3
50 Cock's & Cows E5
51 Damindra G4
52 Granola A6
53 Höst C3
54 Kadeau G6
55 Kødbyens Fiskebar B7
56 La Glace D4
57 Lagkagehuset G6
58 Laundromat Cafe B1
59 Morgenstedet H6
60 Noma H5
61 Orangeriet F3
62 Paté Paté B7
63 Schønnemann E3
64 Torvehallerne KBH D3
65 Union Kitchen G4

Drinking & Nightlife
66 1105 F4
67 Bibendum C3
68 Christianshavns Bådudlejning og Café G6
69 Culture Box F2
70 Forloren Espresso F3
71 Jailhouse CPH D4
72 Kind of Blue C1
73 Lidkoeb A6
74 Mesteren & Lærlingen B7
75 Mikkeller B6
76 Nørrebro Bryghus C1
77 Oscar Bar & Cafe D5
78 Ruby E5
79 Rust B1
80 Ved Stranden 10 E5

Entertainment
81 Jazzhouse E4
82 Operaen H4

Shopping
83 Botanisk Haves Butik D3
84 Bruuns Bazaar E3
85 Han Kjøbenhavn E4
86 Hay House E4
87 Henrik Vibskov D4
88 Illums Bolighus E4
89 Stilleben E4

Church (officially Frederikskirken) is one of Copenhagen's most imposing architectural assets. Its grandiose dome – measuring more than 30m in diameter and inspired by St Peter's in Rome – can be climbed on weekends. The church was ordered by Frederik V and drawn up by Nicolai Eigtved. Construction began in 1749 but spiralling costs saw the project mothballed. Salvation came in the form of Denmark's wealthiest 19th-century financier, CF Tietgen, who bankrolled the project's revival.

★ **Designmuseum Danmark** MUSEUM
(www.designmuseum.dk; Bredgade 68; adult/child Dkr75/free; ⏲11am-5pm Tue & Thu-Sun, to 9pm Wed; 🚌1A) The 18th-century Frederiks Hospital is now the outstanding Denmark Design Museum. A must for fans of the applied arts and industrial design, its fairly extensive collection includes Danish silver and porcelain, textiles, as well as the iconic design pieces of modern innovators like Kaare Klint, Poul Henningsen and Arne Jacobsen. Also on display are ancient Chinese and Japanese ceramics, and 18th- and 19th-century European decorative arts.

Around Strøget

Rundetårn HISTORIC BUILDING
(www.rundetaarn.dk; Købmagergade 52; adult/child Dkr25/5; ⏲10am-8pm late May-late Sep, reduced hrs rest of year, observatory usually 7-9pm Tue & Wed Oct & Mar, 6-9pm Tue & Wed Nov-Feb; 🚌5A, 14, 11A, Ⓜ Nørreport) Haul yourself to the top of the 34.8m-high, red-brick 'Round Tower' and you will be following in the footsteps of such luminaries as King Christian IV, who built it in 1642 as an observatory for the famous astronomer Tycho Brahe. You'll also be following in the hoofsteps of Tsar Peter the Great's horse and, according to legend, the track marks of a car that made its way up the tower's spiral ramp in 1902.

The tower still functions as an excellent stargazing platform, making it the oldest functioning observatory in Europe. Visitors wanting to view the night sky from the 3m-long telescope mounted within the rooftop dome should call ahead to confirm opening times and days, as they can vary.

Vor Frue Kirke CHURCH
(www.koebenhavnsdomkirke.dk; Nørregade 8; ⏲8am-5pm, closed during services & concerts; 🚌11A) Founded in 1191 and rebuilt three times after devastating fires, Copenhagen's current cathedral dates from 1829, its neoclassical looks the work of CF Hansen. Sporting high-vaulted ceilings and columns, it's home to sculptor Bertel Thorvaldsen's statues of Christ and the apostles, completed in 1839 and considered his most acclaimed works. The sculptor's depiction of Christ, with comforting open arms, remains the most popular worldwide model for statues of Jesus. In May 2004 the cathedral hosted the wedding of Crown Prince Frederik to Australian Mary Donaldson.

Around Kongens Have

★ **Statens Museum for Kunst** MUSEUM
(www.smk.dk; Sølvgade 48-50; special exhibitions adult/child Dkr110/free; ⏲10am-5pm Tue & Thu-Sun, to 8pm Wed; 🚌6A, 26, 42, 173E, 184, 185) FREE Denmark's National Gallery straddles two contrasting, interconnected buildings: a late-19th-century 'palazzo' and a sharply minimalist extension. The museum houses medieval and Renaissance works, and impressive collections of Dutch and Flemish artists including Rubens, Breughel and Rembrandt. It claims the world's finest collection of 19th-century Danish 'Golden Age' artists, among them Eckersberg, Krøyer and Hammershøi, foreign greats like Matisse and Picasso, and modern Danish heavyweights including Per Kirkeby, Richard Mortensen and Asger Jørn. Among the contemporary stars are Danish/Norwegian duo Elmgreen

THE LITTLE MERMAID

New York has its Lady Liberty, Sydney its (Danish-designed) Opera House. When the world thinks of Copenhagen, chances are they're thinking of the **Little Mermaid** (Den Lille Havfrue; 🚌1A, ⛴ Nordre Toldbod). Love her or loathe her (watch Copenhagers cringe at the very mention of her), this small, underwhelming statue is arguably the most photographed sight in the country, as well as the cause of countless 'is that it?' shrugs from tourists who have trudged the kilometre or so along an often-windswept harbourfront to see her.

In 1909 the Danish beer baron Carl Jacobsen was so moved after attending a ballet performance based on the Hans Christian Andersen fairy tale 'The Little Mermaid' that he commissioned sculptor Edvard Eriksen to create a statue of the eponymous lady-fish to grace Copenhagen's harbourfront. The face of the famous statue was modelled after the ballerina Ellen Price, while Eline Eriksen, the sculptor's wife, modelled for the body.

In 2006, Carlsberg commissioned Danish artist Bjørn Nørgaard to create a new *Little Mermaid*. The result is a 'genetically altered' mermaid, sitting only a few hundred metres from the original.

and Dragset, and Vietnamese-born Danish artist Danh Vo.

The museum also has an extensive collection of drawings, engravings and lithographs representing the works of such prominent artists as Degas and Toulouse-Lautrec, as well as a strikingly colourful geometric cafe created by designer Peter Lassen and artist Bjørn Nørgaard. Check the website for upcoming temporary exhibitions.

★ Rosenborg Slot CASTLE
(http://dkks.dk; Øster Voldgade 4A; adult/child Dkr90/free, incl Amalienborg Palace Dkr125/free; 10am-5pm daily Jun-Aug, 10am-4pm daily May, Sep & Oct, reduced hours rest of year; 6A, 11A, 42, 150S, 173E, 184, 185, 350S, M Nørreport) A 'once-upon-a-time' combo of turrets, gables and moat, the early-17th-century Rosenborg Slot was built between 1606 and 1633 by King Christian IV in Dutch Renaissance style to serve as his summer home. Today, the castle's 24 upper rooms are chronologically arranged, housing the furnishings and portraits of each monarch from Christian IV to Frederik VII. The pièce de résistance, however, is the basement Treasury, home to the dazzling crown jewels, among them Christian IV's glorious crown and the jewel-studded sword of Christian III.

Kongens Have PARK
(King's Gardens; 6A, 11A, 42, 150S, 173E, 184, 185, 350S, M Nørreport) FREE The oldest park in Copenhagen was laid out in the early 17th century by Christian IV, who used it as his vegetable patch. These days it has a little more to offer, including immaculate flower beds, romantic garden paths, and a marionette theatre with free performances during the summer season (2pm and 3pm Tuesday to Sunday). Located on the northeastern side of the park, the theatre occupies one of the neoclassical pavilions designed by Danish architect Peter Meyn.

Botanisk Have GARDENS
(Botanical Gardens; botanik.snm.ku.dk; main entrance Gothersgade 140; 8.30am-6pm daily May-Sep, 8.30am-4pm Tue-Sun Oct-Apr; ; 6A, 11A, 14, 40, 42, 150S, 173E, 184, 185, M Nørreport, S-train Nørreport) Restorative and romantic, Copenhagen's Botanic Garden lays claim to the largest collection of living plants in Denmark. You can amble along tranquil trails punctuated with quotes from Danish poets and writers (in Danish), escape to warmer climes in the 19th-century **Palmehus** (10am-3pm May-Sep, closed Mon Oct-Apr) glasshouse, and even pick up honey made using the garden's own bees at the gorgeous little **gift shop** (10am-5pm Apr-Sep, to 3.30pm Tue-Sun rest of yr). At the garden's northwest corner lies the old-fashioned **Geologisk Museum** (Geology Museum; Øster Voldgade 5-7; adult/child Dkr40/free; 10am-1pm Tue-Fri, 1-4pm Sat & Sun), worth a trip for its exhibition of botanical drawings, dazzling mineral displays and riotously colourful staircase mural by revered Danish artist Per Kirkeby.

Christianshavn

★ Christiania NEIGHBOURHOOD
(www.christiania.org; Prinsessegade; 9A, 2A, 40, 350S, M Christianshavn) Escape the capitalist crunch at Freetown Christiania, a dreadlocks-heavy commune straddling the eastern side of Christianshavn. Since its establishment by squatters in 1971, the area has drawn nonconformists from across the globe, attracted by the concept of collective business, workshops and communal living. Explore beyond the settlement's infamous 'Pusher St' – lined with shady hash and marijuana dealers – and you'll stumble upon a semibucolic wonderland of whimsical DIY homes, cosy gardens, and a handful of craft shops, eateries, beer gardens and music venues.

The main entrance into Christiania is on Prinsessegade, 200m northeast of its intersection with Bådsmandsstræde. From late June to the end of August, 60- to 90-minute guided tours (Dkr40) of Christiania run daily at 3pm (weekends only September to late June). Tours commence just inside Christiania's main entrance on Prinsessegade.

Vor Frelsers Kirke CHURCH
(www.vorfrelserskirke.dk; Sankt Annæ Gade 29; church free, tower adult/child Dkr40/10; 11am-3.30pm, closed during services, tower 10am-7.15pm Mon-Sat, 10.30am-7.15pm Sun Jun-Sep, reduced hours rest of year; 9A, 2A, 40, 350S, M Christianshavn) It's hard to miss this 17th-century church and its 95m-high spiral tower. For a soul-stirring panoramic city view, make the head-spinning 400-step ascent to the top – the last 150 steps run along the outside rim of the tower, narrowing to the point where they literally disappear at the top. Inspired by Borromini's tower of St Ivo in Rome, the colourful spire was added in 1752 by Lauritz de Thurah. Inside, the church wows with its elaborately carved pipe organ from 1698 and an ornate baroque altar.

Outer Copenhagen

Den Blå Planet AQUARIUM

(www.denblaaplanet.dk; Jacob Fortlingsvej 1, Kastrup; adult/child 3-11yr Dkr160/95; 10am-9pm Mon, to 6pm Tue-Sun; 5A, Kastrup) Designed to look like a whirlpool from above, Copenhagen's new, aluminum-clad aquarium is the largest in northern Europe. The space is divided into climatic and geographic sections, the most spectacular of which is 'Ocean/Coral Reef'. Home to swarms of technicolor tropical fish, the exhibition is also home to the centre's largest tank, a massive 4,000,000-litre showcase brimming with sharks, stingrays and other majestic creatures. If possible, visit the aquarium on a Monday evening, when it's at its quietest and most evocative.

Carlsberg Visitors Centre BREWERY

(33 27 12 82; www.visitcarlsberg.dk; Gamle Carlsberg Vej 11, Vesterbro; adult/child Dkr80/60; 10am-5pm Tue-Sun; 18, 26) Adjacent to the architectually whimsical Carlsberg brewery, the Carlsberg Visitors Center explores the history of Danish beer from 1370 BC (yes, they carbondated a bog girl who was found in a peat bog caressing a jug of well-aged brew). Dioramas give the low-down on the brewing process, and en route to your final destination you'll pass antique copper vats and the stables with a dozen Jutland dray horses. The self-guided tour ends at the bar, where you can knock back two free beers.

Activities

GoBoat BOATING

(40 26 10 25; www.goboat.dk; Islands Brygge 10; boat hire 1/3hr Dkr395/999; 10am-sunset;) What could be more 'Copenhagen' than sailing around the harbour and canals in your own solar-powered boat? You don't need prior sailing experience and each comes with a built-in picnic table (you can buy supplies at GoBoat or bring your own). Boats seat up to eight and rates are per boat, so the more in your group, the cheaper per person.

DGI-byen SWIMMING, GYM

(www.dgi-byen.dk; Tietgensgade 65, Vesterbro; day pass adult/child Dkr65/45, day pass before 9am Mon-Fri Dkr45/30; 6.30am-10pm Mon-Thu, 6.30am-7.30pm Fri, 9am-7pm Sat, 9am-6pm Sun; ; 1A, 820, København H) An extravagant indoor swim centre with several pools, including a grand ellipse-shaped affair with 100m lanes, a deep 'mountain pool' with a climbing wall, a hot-water pool and a children's pool. If you've forgotten your togs or towels, they can be hired for Dkr25 each (bring photo ID as a deposit). There's also a small gym on the premises.

Islands Brygge Havnebadet SWIMMING

(Islands Brygge; 7am-7pm Mon-Fri, 11am-7pm Sat & Sun Jun-Aug; ; 5A, 12, Islands Brygge) FREE Copenhagen's coolest outdoor pool complex sits right in the central city's main canal. Water quality is rigorously monitored, and the lawns, BBQ facilities and eateries make it a top spot to see and be seen on a warm summer day, whether you get wet or not. In 2014 plans were underway for winter-friendly saunas and thermal baths, as well as a sixth pool.

Tours

Canal Tours

The best way to see Copenhagen is from the water. There are several ways to take a boat tour around the city's canals and harbour, with multilingual guides giving a commentary in English.

Canal Tours Copenhagen BOAT TOUR

(32 66 00 00; www.stromma.dk; adult/child/family Dkr75/35/190; 9.30am-9pm late Jun-late Aug, reduced hours rest of year;) Canal Tours Copenhagen runs one-hour cruises of the city's canals and harbour, taking in numerous major sights, including Christiansborg Slot, Christianshavn, the Royal Library, the Opera House, Amalienborg Palace and the *Little Mermaid*. Embark at Nyhavn or Ved Stranden. Boats depart up to six times per hour from late June to late August, with reduced frequency the rest of the year.

Netto-Bådene BOAT TOUR

(32 54 41 02; www.havnerundfart.dk; adult/child Dkr40/15; tours 2-5 per hr, 10am-7pm Jul & Aug, to 5pm Apr-Jun & Sep–mid-Oct;) Netto-Bådene operates good-value one-hour cruises of Copenhagen's canals and harbour. Embarkation points are at Holmens Kirke and Nyhavn. From mid-July to August, boats also depart from the *Little Mermaid*. Check the website for timetable updates.

Walking Tours

Copenhagen Free Walking Tours WALKING TOUR

(www.copenhagenfreewalkingtours.dk) FREE Departing daily at 11am and 2pm from outside the rådhus (city hall), these free, three-hour walking tours take in famous landmarks and interesting anecdotes. Tours are in English and require a minimum of five people. Free

90-minute tours of Christianshavn depart at 4pm Friday to Monday from the base of the Bishop Absalon statue on Højbro Plads.

Nordic Noir Tours WALKING TOUR
(http://nordicnoirtours.com; per person Dkr150, if booked online Dkr100; ⌚Borgen tour 2pm Sat, The Killing/The Bridge tour 4pm Sat) Fans of Danish TV dramas *Borgen, The Bridge* and *The Killing* can visit the shooting locations on these themed 90-minute walks. Tours commence at Vesterport S-train station. Bookings are not required, though tickets purchased online at least 48 hours in advance are Dkr50 cheaper.

Cycling & Kayaking

Bike Copenhagen With Mike BICYCLE TOUR
(☎26 39 56 88; www.bikecopenhagenwithmike.dk; Skt Peders Stræde 47; per person Dkr299) If you don't fancy walking, Bike Mike runs three-hour cycling tours of the city, departing from Skt Peders Stræde 47 in the city centre, just east of Ørstedsparken (which is southwest of Nørreport station). The tour cost includes bike and helmet rental. Seasonal options are also offered, including a Saturday-evening 'Ride & Dine' tour from June to September. Cash only.

Kayak Republic KAYAK TOUR
(☎30 49 86 20; www.kayakrepublic.dk; Børskaj 12; per person 150-575kr; ⌚10am-8pm) Kayak Republic runs two-hour and full-day kayak tours along the city's canals. It also rents out kayaks for self-exploration (single kayak per one/two hours Dkr150/250).

Festivals & Events

Distortion MUSIC
(www.cphdistortion.dk) Taking place over five heady days in early June, Copenhagen Distortion celebrates the city's street life and club culture. Expect raucous block parties and top-name DJs spinning dance tracks in bars and clubs across town.

Copenhagen Jazz Festival MUSIC
(http://jazz.dk) Copenhagen's single largest event, and the largest jazz festival in northern Europe, hits the city over 10 days in early July. The program covers jazz in all its forms, with an impressive line-up of local and international talent.

Copenhagen Cooking FOOD
(www.copenhagencooking.dk) Scandinavia's largest food festival serves up a gut-rumbling program spanning cooking demonstrations from A-list chefs to tastings and foodie tours of the city. Events are held in venues and restaurants across town, usually in August. A monthlong winter edition takes place in February.

Strøm MUSIC
(www.stromcph.dk) Copenhagen's electronic-music festival runs for a week in August. Considered the top festival of its kind in Scandinavia, its 60-plus events include workshops and masterclasses, concerts, raves and parties across the city.

Art Copenhagen ART
(www.artcopenhagen.dk) This major, three-day art fair in September involves around 60 art galleries from Scandinavia and beyond. Showcasing a good number of contemporary artists from Denmark, Sweden, Norway, Finland, Iceland and the Faroe Islands, the event usually takes place at Forum Copenhagen.

Sleeping

Copenhagen's slumber spots cover all bases.

It's a good idea to book in advance – rooms in many of the most popular mid-range hotels fill quickly, particularly during the convention season, typically from August to October, when prices increase significantly too. That said, prices for rooms do fluctuate greatly, depending on the time of year or even the time of week, with most hotels tempting guests with special offers throughout the year.

The tourist office (p62) can book rooms in private homes (Dkr350/500 for singles/doubles); there is a Dkr100 booking fee if you do it via the tourist office when you arrive, otherwise it's free online.

★ **Generator Hostel** HOSTEL €
(www.generatorhostel.com; Adelgade 5-7; dm Dkr230-325, r Dkr800-1070; @; 🚌11A, 350S, Ⓜ Kongens Nytorv) A solid choice for 'cheap chic', upbeat, design-literate Generator sits on the very edge of the city's medieval core. It's kitted out with designer furniture, slick communal areas (including a bar and outdoor terrace) and friendly, young staff. While the rooms can be a little small, all are bright and modern, with bathrooms in both private rooms and dorms.

Danhostel Copenhagen City HOSTEL €
(☎33 11 85 85; www.danhostel.dk/copenhagencity; HC Andersens Blvd 50; dm/d Dkr225/610; @; 🚌12, 33, 1A, 2A, 11A, 40, 66) With interiors by design company Gubi and a cafe-bar in the

lobby, this friendly, ever-popular hostel is set in a tower block overlooking the harbour just south of Tivoli Gardens (did we mention the views?). Both the dorms and private rooms are bright, light and modern, each with bathroom. Book ahead.

Cabinn HOTEL €
(www.cabinn.com; s/d/tr Dkr545/675/805; @) Well managed, functional and cheap, the Cabinn chain has four hotels in Copenhagen, the most central being **Cabinn City** (☎33 46 16 16; Mitchellsgade 14; @; 🚌5A, 9A, 11A, 30, 🚆S-train København H), just south of Tivoli. Although small and anonymous, rooms are comfortable, with cable TV, phone, free wi-fi, and private bathroom. Both **Cabinn Scandinavia** (☎35 36 11 11; Vodroffsvej 57, Frederiksberg; 🚌2A, 68, 250S, Ⓜ Forum) and **Cabinn Express** (☎33 21 04 00; Danasvej 32, Frederiksberg; @; 🚌3A, 30, Ⓜ Forum) are less than 2km west of Tivoli, while the newer **Cabinn Metro** (☎32 46 57 00; Arne Jakobsens Allé 2; Ⓜ Ørestad) is a short walk from Ørestad metro station, and close to the airport.

★ **Hotel Guldsmeden** BOUTIQUE HOTEL €€
(www.hotelguldsmeden.dk) The gorgeous Guldsmeden hotels include **Bertrams** (☎70 20 81 07; Vesterbrogade 107; s/d from Dkr895/995; 🚌6A, 3A), **Carlton** (☎33 22 15 00; Vesterbrogade 66; s/d from Dkr695/795; 🚌6A), **Axel** (☎33 31 32 66; Helgolandsgade 7-11; s/d Dkr765/895; 🚌6A, 26, 🚆S-train København H) and newcomer **Babette** (☎33 14 15 00; Bredgade 78; s/d from Dkr795/945; 🚌1A). Only the latter is not in Vesterbro, instead located between Amalienborg and Kastellet on the northern side of the city centre. All four deliver subtle, Balinese-inspired chic, with raw stone, bare wood, four-poster beds and crisp white linen.

★ **Hotel Alexandra** HOTEL €€
(☎33 74 44 44; www.hotelalexandra.dk; HC Andersens Blvd 8; s/d from Dkr750/950; @; 🚌10, 11A, 2A, 12, 26, 250S, 🚆S-train Vesterport) The furniture of Danish design deities such as Arne Jacobsen, Ole Wanscher and Kaare Klint grace the interiors of the refined yet homely Alexandra. Recently renovated, rooms are effortlessly cool, each decked out in mid-century Danish style. Contemporary concessions include flat-screen TVs. Staff are attentive, and the hotel's refined retro air makes a refreshing change from all that white-on-white Nordic minimalism.

Wakeup Copenhagen HOTEL €€
(☎44 80 00 10; www.wakeupcopenhagen.com; Carsten Niebuhrs Gade 11; r Dkr450-1500; @; 🚌11A, 🚆S-train København H) An easy walk from Central Station and Tivoli, this is one of two Wakeup Copenhagen branches in town, well known for offering style on a budget (assuming you've booked online and in advance). The foyer is an impressive combo of concrete, glass and Arne Jacobsen chairs, while the 500-plus rooms are sharp and compact, with flat-screen TV and capsulelike showers.

Wakeup's second **branch** (☎44 80 00 00; Borgergade 9) enjoys an even more central location close to Nyhavn.

Hotel SP34 BOUTIQUE HOTEL €€
(☎33 13 30 00; www.brochner-hotels.dk; Skt Peders Stræde 34; rm from Dkr1255; 🚌5A, 6A, 14, 10, 11A, 🚆S-train Vesterport) Urbane SP34 is one of Copenhagen's newest boutique options. Tans and subtle pastels underline the communal areas, among them a plush, light-drenched lounge, modernist-inspired reading room, and svelte lobby bar. The 118 rooms keep things smart and simple, with slate-coloured walls, muted accents and REN bathroom amenities. Nibble on organic produce at breakfast, and sip complimentary vino between 5pm and 6pm.

CPH Living FLOATING HOTEL €€
(☎61 60 85 46; www.cphliving.com; Langebrogade 1C; r incl breakfast from Dkr1000; 🚌5A, 12) Located on a converted freight boat, Copenhagen's only floating hotel consists of 12 stylish, contemporary rooms, each with harbour and city views. Perks include modern bathrooms with rainforest shower, and a communal sundeck for summertime lounging. Breakfast is a simple continental affair, while the central location makes it an easy walk to the city centre, Christianshavn and the harbour beach at Islands Brygge.

LAST-MINUTE CHEAP SLEEPS

If you arrive in Copenhagen without a hotel booking, luck may yet be on your side. The Copenhagen Visitors Centre (p62) books unfilled hotel rooms at discounted rates of up to 50% (sometimes even more). These discounts, however, are based on supply and demand, and are not always available during busy periods.

★**Hotel Nimb** BOUTIQUE HOTEL €€€

(☎88 70 00 00; www.nimb.dk; Bernstorffsgade 5; r from Dkr2600; @; 2A, 5A, 9A, 12, 26, 250S, 350S, S-train København H.) Located at Tivoli, this boutique belle offers 17 individually styled rooms and suites fusing clean lines, beautiful art and antiques, luxury fabrics and high-tech perks such as Bang & Olufsen TVs and sound systems. All rooms except three also feature a fireplace while all bar one come with views over the amusement park. In-house perks include a smart cocktail lounge with crackling fire.

Hotel d'Angleterre HOTEL €€€

(☎33 12 00 95; www.dangleterre.com; Kongens Nytorv 34; r from Dkr2750; ; M Kongens Nytorv) Hitting the scene in 1755, the neo-classical d'Angleterre is Copenhagen's most glamourous slumber palace. Fresh from an ambitious facelift, it's once again fit for royalty and mere-mortal sybarites. Regal portraits, fireplaces and art nouveau flourishes keep things suitably posh in the public areas, while the hotel's rooms and suites deliver contemporary twists on classic luxury, with powdery accents, luxurious fabrics and marble bathrooms.

Square HOTEL €€

(☎33 38 12 00; www.thesquarecopenhagen.com; Rådhuspladsen 14; s/d from Dkr925/1030; @; 2A, 12, 26, 250S, S-train Vesterport) Pimped with Jacobsen chairs and red leather, the Square is an excellent three-star hotel with designer flair and amenities generally associated with greater expense and more stiffness. Standard rooms are a little small but well equipped, and some have sterling views of the main square – plus all the city's main sights are within walking distance.

Eating

Copenhagen's dining scene is hot, with more Michelin-starred restaurants than any other city in Scandinavia. Among these is New Nordic pioneer Noma, topping the World's Best 50 Restaurants list three years running. Beyond the fine-dining meccas are a growing number of smart-yet-casual hot spots – among them Pony, Kødbyens Fiskebar and Höst – putting new-school Nordic gastronomy in the reach of kroner-conscious gourmands.

New Nordic scene aside, you can expect a multifaceted culinary landscape, spanning everything from superlative sushi restaurants to hipster pizza bars, cheap-eat cafes and old-school institutions like Schønnemann, where *smørrebrød* (open sandwiches), herring and akvavit come with a side of nostalgia.

You'll find many of Copenhagen's coolest nosh spots in the Vesterbrø neighbourhood, while bohemian Nørrebro has its fair share of cheaper, student-friendly eateries.

Before you tuck in, consider the following: Copenhagen is not Barcelona, meaning that if you like to eat late, you'll have trouble finding a kitchen open after 10pm. Secondly, hot-spot 'New Nordic Scandinavian' restaurants should always be booked ahead; tables are highly coveted and often booked out days ahead (three months ahead in Noma's case!). Conveniently, many restaurants allow you to book tables on their websites.

Around Tivoli & Vesterbro

Pony MODERN DANISH €€

(☎33 22 10 00; www.ponykbh.dk; Vesterbrogade 135; dishes Dkr110-185, 4-course menus Dkr450; 5.30-10pm Tue-Sun; 6A) If your accountant forbids dinner at Kadeau, opt for its bistro spin-off, Pony. While the New Nordic grub here is simpler, it's no less stunning, with palate-punching marvels like tartar with black trumpet mushrooms, blackberries and mushroom broth, or lemon sole with cauliflower, pickled apples, kale, almonds and capers. The vibe is convivial and intimate. Book ahead, especially on Friday and Saturday.

Paté Paté INTERNATIONAL €€

(☎39 69 55 57; www.patepate.dk; Slagterboderne 1; dishes Dkr80-130; 9am-10pm Mon-Thu, 9am-11pm Fri, 11am-11pm Sat; 10, 14) A Kødbyen favourite, this pâté factory turned restaurant/wine bar gives Euro classics modern twists. While the menu changes daily, signature dishes include refreshing *burrata* (a type of cheese) with roasted peach, pesto, chilli and browned butter, and earthy grilled piglet with *mojo rojo* (chilli sauce), *sobrasada* (raw cured sausage), borlotti beans and grilled carrots. Hip and bustling, yet utterly convivial, bonus extras include clued-in staff, a well-versed wine list, and solo-diner-friendly bar seating.

Granola CAFE €€

(☎40 82 41 20; Værndemsvej 5, Vesterbro; lunch Dkr75-145, dinner mains Dkr135-195; 7am-10pm Mon-Fri, 9am-10pm Sat, 9am-4pm Sun; 9A, 6A,

26) A top spot for breakfast or brunch (head in early on weekends), Granola packs a cool Vesterbro crowd with its retro mix of industrial lamps, terrazzo flooring and 'General Store' cabinets. Start the day with uncomplicated standards like fruit-laced oatmeal, *croque monsieur* or pancakes, or head in later for well-rounded classics like *moules marinière,* braised pork cheek, and Niçoise salad.

★Kødbyens Fiskebar SEAFOOD €€€
(☎32 15 56 56; http://fiskebaren.dk; Flæsketorvet 100; mains Dkr215-255; ⏲5.30-11pm; 🚌10, 14) Concrete floors, industrial tiling and a 1000L aquarium meets impeccable seafood at this Michelin-listed must, slap bang in Vesterbro's trendy Kødbyen ('Meat City' district). Ditch the mains for three or four starters; the oysters are phenomenal, while the silky razor clams, served on a crisp, rice-paper 'shell', are sublime. While you can book a table, dining at the Manhattan-style bar is much more fun.

Around Nyhavn & Harbourfront

Union Kitchen CAFE €€
(Store Strandstræde 21; ⏲7.30am-5pm Mon & Tue, to 11pm Wed & Thu, to midnight Fri, 8am-midnight Sat, 8am-5pm Sun; 🚌11A, 66, Ⓜ Kongens Nytorv) Just around the corner from Nyhavn is new-school Union Kitchen, where inked staffers look like punk-pop rockers, the colour scheme is grey-on-grey, and the clipboard menu is packed with contemporary cafe grub like homemade granola and toasted sourdough with cottage cheese, tomato, thyme and olive oil. Best of all is the 'Balls of the Day', a daily-changing combo of succulent homemade meatballs served with interesting sides.

Damindra JAPANESE €€€
(☎33 12 33 75; www.damindra.dk; Holbergsgade 26; lunch dishes Dkr175-398, 7-course dinner tasting menus with 2-person min Dkr750; ⏲11am-3pm & 5-10pm Tue-Sat; 🚌11A, 66, Ⓜ Kongens Nytorv) We wouldn't be surprised if Japanese Damindra lands a Michelin star in the next few years. From the buttery sashimi to an unforgettable prawn tempura, dishes are obscenely fresh and mesmerising. The evening 'Chef's Choice' set sushi menu (Dkr398) provides the perfect culinary tour, while desserts such as green tea ice cream with plum compote and fresh wasabi cream make for a wicked epilogue.

Around Strøget

Torvehallerne KBH MARKET €
(www.torvehallernekbh.dk; Israels Plads; ⏲10am-7pm Mon-Thu, to 8pm Fri, to 6pm Sat, 11am-5pm Sun) Since debuting in 2011, food market Torvehallerne KBH has become an essential stop on the Copenhagen foodie trail. A gut-rumbling ode to the fresh, the tasty and the artisanal, its beautiful stalls peddle everything from seasonal herbs and berries to smoked meats, seafood, cheeses, smørrebrød, fresh pasta, and hand-brewed coffee. You could easily spend an hour or more exploring its twin halls, chatting to the vendors and taste-testing their products. Best of all, you can enjoy some of the city's best sit-down meals here...with change to spare.

Cock's & Cows BURGERS €
(☎69 69 60 00; http://cocksandcows.dk; Gammel Strand 34; burgers Dkr89-129; ⏲noon-9.30pm Sun-Thu, to 10.30pm Fri & Sat; 🚌1A, 2A, 26, 40, 66) When burger lust hits, satiate your urges at Cock's. In a setting best described as American diner meets Danish modernist (picture red leather booths against Poul Henningsen lamps), energetic staff deliver fresh, made-from-scratch burgers that are generous and insanely good. The meat is Danish and charcoal grilled, and there's a vegie burger for herbivores. Make sure to order a side of the onion rings.

La Glace BAKERY €
(www.laglace.dk; Skoubougade 3; cake slices Dkr57, pastries from Dkr36; ⏲8.30am-6pm Mon-Fri, 9am-6pm Sat, 10am-6pm Sun, closed Sun Easter-Sep; 🚌11A) Copenhagen's oldest *konditori* (pastry shop) has been compromising waistlines since 1870. Succumb to a slice of the classic *valnøddekage* (walnut cake), a sinful concoction of crushed and caramelised walnuts, whipped cream and Mocca glacé. Alternatively, betray your personal trainer with the *sportskage* (crushed nougat, cream and caramelised profiteroles). Your secret is safe.

★Schønnemann DANISH €€
(☎33 12 07 85; www.restaurantschonnemann.dk; Hauser Plads 16; smørrebrød Dkr72-178; ⏲11.30am-5pm Mon-Sat; 🚌6A, 11A, Ⓜ Nørreport) A verified institution, Schønnemann has been lining bellies with smørrebrød (open sandwiches) and snaps since 1877. Originally a hit with farmers in town peddling their produce, the restaurant's current fan base includes revered chefs like Noma's René

Redzepi. Two smørrebrød per person should suffice, with standouts including the King's Garden (potatoes with smoked mayonnaise, fried onions, chives and tomato). Make sure to order both a beer and a glass of snaps to wash down the goodness, and always book ahead (or head in early) to avoid long lunchtime waits.

★Höst MODERN DANISH €€

(☎89 93 84 09; http://cofoco.dk/da/restauranter/hoest; Nørre Farimagsgade 41; mains Dkr195-215, 3-course set menus Dkr295; ⏰5.30-9.30pm; 🚌40, Ⓜ Nørrebro) Höst's phenomenal popularity is a no-brainer: warm, award-winning interiors, mere-mortal prices, and New Nordic food that's equally fabulous and filling. The set menu is great value, with three smaller 'surprise dishes' thrown in, and evocative creations like salted Faroe Island scallops with corn, raw plums, pickled black trumpet mushrooms and wild garlic. The 'deluxe' wine menu is significantly better than the standard option.

Around Kongens Have

Big Apple SANDWICHES €

(Kronprinsessegade 2; sandwiches Dkr50, salads Dkr55; ⏰8am-6pm Mon-Fri, 9am-6pm Sat & Sun; 🚌11A, Ⓜ Kongens Nytorv) Concrete floors, rustic communal tables, and splashes of vibrant green keep things Nordic and natural at this popular sandwich peddler. The bread is vegan, toasted and stuffed with combos like goat's cheese, avocado, cucumber and homemade pesto. Liquids include freshly squeezed juices and fantastic coffee from top local roastery The Coffee Collective. *And* it has soy milk!

Orangeriet MODERN DANISH €€

(☎33 11 13 07; www.restaurant-orangeriet.dk; Kronprinsessegade 13; smørrebrod Dkr75, 3-/5-course dinners Dkr375/495; ⏰11.30am-3pm & 6-10pm Mon-Sat, noon-4pm Sun; 🚌11A, 350S, 26) Take a vintage conservatory, add elegant, seasonal menus, and you have Orangeriet. Skirting the eastern edge of Kongens Have, its main man is award-winning chef Jasper Kure, whose contemporary creations focus on simplicity and premium produce. Savour the brilliance in clean, intriguing dishes like rimmed cod with celeriac, cabbage, cress and clam sauce with smoked cod roe. Lunch is a simple affair of smørrebrød. Book ahead.

Christianshavn

Lagkagehuset BAKERY €

(☎32 57 36 07; www.lagkagehuset.dk; Torvegade 45; pastries from Dkr18, sandwiches Dkr50; ⏰6am-7pm Sat-Thu, to 7.30pm Fri; 🚌2A, 9A, 40, 350S, Ⓜ Christianshavn) Right opposite Christianshavn metro station, this is the original (and some would say the best) of the Lagkagehuset bakeries. Handy for a quick bite on the go, its counters heave with luscious pastries, salubrious sandwiches, mini pizzas and heavyweight loaves of rye bread. You'll find a handful of counter seats as well as free wi-fi if you insist on Instagramming your *kanelsnegle*.

Morgenstedet VEGETARIAN €

(www.morgenstedet.dk; Langgaden; mains Dkr80-100; ⏰noon-9pm Tue-Sun; 📝; 🚌9A, 2A, 40, 350S, Ⓜ Christianshavn) 🌿 A homely, hippy bolthole in the heart of Christiania, Morgenstedet offers but two dishes of the day, one of which is usually a soup. Choices are always vegetarian and organic, and best devoured in the bucolic bliss of the cafe garden.

★Noma MODERN DANISH €€€

(☎32 96 32 97; www.noma.dk; Strandgade 93; degustation menus Dkr1600; ⏰noon-4pm & 7pm-12.30am Tue-Sat; 🚌2A, 9A, 11A, 40, 66, 350S, Ⓜ Christianshavn) Noma is a Holy Grail for gastronomes across the globe. Using only Scandinavian-sourced produce such as musk ox and *skyr* (Icelandic yoghurt) curd, head chef René Redzepi and his team create extraordinary symphonies of flavour and texture. Tables are booked months ahead, so expect to join the waiting list. Tip: parties of four or more have a better chance of landing a table with shorter notice.

★Kadeau MODERN SCANDINAVIAN €€€

(☎33 25 22 23; www.kadeau.dk; Wildersgade 10a; 4-/8-course menus Dkr550/850; ⏰noon-3.30pm Wed-Fri & 6pm-late Tue-Sun) This is the Michelin-starred sibling of Bornholm's critically acclaimed Kadeau, its outstanding New Nordic cuisine now firmly on the radar of both local and visiting gastronomes. Whether it's salted and burnt scallops drizzled in clam bouillon, or an unexpected combination of toffee, crème fraiche, potatoes, radish and elderflower, dishes are evocative, revelatory and soul-lifting. An equally exciting wine list and sharp, warm service make this place a must. Book ahead.

Nørrebro

★Manfreds og Vin MODERN DANISH €€

(☎36 96 65 93; http://manfreds.dk; Jægersborggade 40; small plates Dkr75-95, 7-course tasting menus Dkr250; ⊙noon-3.30pm & 5.30-10pm; ✎; 🚌18, 5A, 350S) On hip strip Jægersborggade, convivial Manfreds is the fantasy local bistro, with passionate staffers, boutique wines, and a menu that favours local, organic produce cooked simply and sensationally. Swoon over nuanced, gorgeously textured dishes like sauteed spinach with lard-roasted croutons and warm poached egg, or slightly charred broccoli served with cheese cream, pickled onion and toasted bulgur.

Oysters & Grill SEAFOOD €€

(☎70 20 61 71; http://cofoco.dk/en/restaurants/oysters-and-grill; Sjællandsgade 1B; mains Dkr155-195; ⊙5.30-9.30pm Mon-Thu, to 10pm Fri & Sat, to 9.15pm Sun; 🚌5A) Finger-licking surf and turf is what you get at this rocking, unpretentious classic, complete with kitsch vinyl tablecloths and a fun, casual vibe. If you're a seafood fan, make sure your order includes both the ridiculously fresh oysters and the common cockles drizzled with parsley oil. Meat lovers won't to be disappointed either, with cuts that are lust-inducingly tender and succulent. Book ahead.

Laundromat Cafe INTERNATIONAL €€

(www.thelaundromatcafe.com; Elmegade 15; dishes Dkr45-155; ⊙8am-midnight Mon-Fri, from 10am Sat & Sun; 🚌3A, 5A, 350S) Cafe, bookshop, and laundrette in one, this retrolicious Nørrebro institution is never short of a crowd. It's an especially popular brunch spot, with both 'clean' (vegetarian) and 'dirty' (carnivorous) brunch platters, strong coffee and fresh juices. Breakfast options include porridge and *croque madame,* while all-day comforters span hamburgers (vegie option included), chilli con carne, and a pear and goat's cheese salad.

Drinking & Nightlife

Copenhagen heaves with an eclectic booty of drinking and party spots, from old-school cellar bars or bodegas to slinky cocktail dens and cult-status clubs dropping experimental beats. On the drinking scene, the line between cafe, bar and restaurant is often blurred, with many places changing role as the day progresses. And while you can hit the dance floor most nights of the week, the club scene really revs into gear from Thursday to Saturday. Club admission is usually around Dkr70 to Dkr100, though you can often get in for free before a certain time in the evening. Keep in mind that Danes tend to be late-nighters and, unlike the restaurants, many nightspots don't start heaving until 11pm or midnight. Popular drinking and clubbing hot spots include Nørrebro and Vesterbro (especially along Istedgade, west of the red-light district, and Kødbyen, closer to the station).

★Ved Stranden 10 WINE BAR

(www.vedstranden10.dk; Ved Stranden 10; ⊙noon-10pm Mon-Sat; 🚌1A, 2A, 26, 40, 66) Politicians and well-versed oenophiles make a beeline for this canalside wine bar, its enviable cellar stocked with classic European vintages, biodynamic wines and more obscure drops. Adorned with modernist Danish design and friendly, clued-in staff, its string of rooms lend the place an intimate, civilised air that's perfect for grown-up conversation. Chat terroir and tannins over vino-friendly nibbles like olives, cheeses and smoked meats.

Christianshavns Bådudlejning og Café CAFE, BAR

(☎32 96 53 53; www.baadudlejningen.dk; Overgaden Neden Vandet 29; ⊙9am-midnight daily Jun–mid-Aug, reduced hours rest of year, closed Oct-Mar; 🚌2A, 9A, 40, 350S, Ⓜ Christianshavn) Right on Christianshavn's main canal, this festive, wood-decked cafe-bar is a wonderful spot for drinks by the water. It's a cosy, affable hang-out, with jovial crowds, strung lights and little rowboats (available for hire) docked like bath-time toys. There's grub for the peckish, and gas heaters and tarpaulins to ward off any northern chill.

★Forloren Espresso CAFE

(www.forlorenespresso.dk; Store Kongensgade 32; ⊙8am-4pm Tue-Fri, from 9am Sat; 🚌1A, 26, 11A, Ⓜ Kongens Nytorv) Coffee snobs weep joyfully into their nuanced espressos and third-wave brews at this cute, light-filled cafe, decorated with photography tomes. Bespectacled owner Niels tends to his brewing paraphernalia like an obsessed scientist, turning UK- and Swedish-roasted beans into smooth, lingering cups of Joe. Whatever your poison, pair it with a Danablu Horn, a ridiculously delicious horn-shaped bread stuffed with blue cheese, honey and walnuts.

Ruby COCKTAIL BAR

(www.rby.dk; Nybrogade 10; 4pm-2am Mon-Sat, 7pm-1am Sun; 1A, 2A, 11A, 26, 40, 66) Cocktail connoisseurs raise their glasses to high-achieving Ruby. Here, hipster-geek mixologists whip-up near-flawless libations such as the Green & White (vodka, dill, white chocolate and liquorice root) and a lively crowd spills into a labyrinth of cosy, decadent rooms. For a gentlemen's-club vibe, head downstairs into a world of Chesterfields, oil paintings, and wooden cabinets lined with spirits.

Mikkeller BAR

(http://mikkeller.dk; Viktoriagade 8B-C, Vesterbro; 1pm-1am Sun-Wed, to 2am Thu & Fri, noon-2am Sat; 6A, 26, 10, 14, S-train København H) Low-slung lights, moss-green floors and 20 brews on tap: cult-status Mikeller flies the flag for craft beer, its rotating cast of suds including Mikkeller's own acclaimed creations and guest drops from microbreweries from around the globe. The bottled offerings are equally inspired, with cheese and snacks to soak up the foamy goodness.

Mesteren & Lærlingen BAR

(Flæsketorvet 86, Vesterbro; 8pm-3am Wed-Sat) In a previous life, Mesteren & Lærlingen was a slaughterhouse bodega. These days it's one of Copenhagen's in-the-know drinking holes, its tiled walls packing in a friendly, hipster crowd of trucker caps and skinny jeans. Squeeze in and knock back a rum and ginger (the house speciality) to DJ-spun retro, soul, reggae and country.

Lidkoeb COCKTAIL BAR

(33 11 20 10; www.lidkoeb.dk; Vesterbrogade 72B, Vesterbro; 4pm-2am Mon-Sat, 8pm-1am Sun; 6A, 26) Lidkoeb loves a game of hide and seek: follow the 'Lidkoeb' signs into the second, light-strung courtyard. Once found, this top-tier cocktail lounge rewards with passionate barkeeps and clever, seasonal libations. Slip into a Børge Mogensen chair and toast to Danish ingenuity with Nordic bar bites and drinks like the Koldskål; a vodka-based twist on Denmark's iconic buttermilk dessert. Extras include a dedicated upstairs whisky bar with over 100 drops.

★1105 COCKTAIL BAR

(www.1105.dk; Kristen Bernikows Gade 4; 8pm-2am Wed, Thu & Sat, 4pm-2am Fri; 11A, Kongens Nytorv) Head in before 11pm for a bar seat at this dark, luxe cocktail lounge. It's the domain of world-renowned barman Hardeep Rehal, who made the top 10 at the 2014 Diageo World Class, the unofficial Olympics of mixology. While Rehal's martini is the stuff of legend, 1105's seductive libations include both classics and classics with a twist. Whisky connoisseurs will be equally enthralled.

Bibendum WINE BAR

(Nansensgade 45; 4pm-midnight Mon-Sat; 40, 5A, 350S, Nørreport) Cosily set in a rustic cellar on trendy Nansensgade, Bibendum is an oenophile's best friend. Dive in and drool over a savvy list that offers over 30 wines – including drops from Australia, New Zealand, Spain, France and Italy – by the glass. The vibe is intimate but relaxed, and the menu of small plates (Dkr89 to Dkr95) is simply gorgeous.

Nørrebro Bryghus BREWERY

(38 60 38 60; www.noerrebrobryghus.dk; Ryesgade 3, Nørrebro; 11am-midnight Mon-Thu, to 2am Fri & Sat; 3A, 5A, 350S) This now-classic brewery kick-started the microbrewing craze a few years back. Thankfully, the concept remains as alluring as ever, and the place remains a great place to wash down local suds. Rumbling bellies are also accounted for, with the brewery's in-house restaurant serving up tasty, reasonably priced grub like pan-roasted scallops, fish and chips, and risotto.

Kind of Blue BAR

(26 35 10 56; http://kindofblue.dk; Ravnsborggade 17, Nørrebro; 4pm-midnight Mon-Wed, to 2am Thu-Sat; 5A) Chandeliers, heady perfume and walls painted a hypnotic 1950s blue: the spirit of the Deep South runs deep at intimate Kind of Blue. Named after the Miles Davis album, it's never short of a late-night, hipster crowd, kicking back porters and drinking in owner Claus' personal collection of soul-stirring jazz, blues and folk. You'll find it on Nørrebro's bar-packed Ravnsborggade.

Culture Box CLUB

(www.culture-box.com; Kronprinsessegade 54A; White Box 9pm-late Fri & Sat, Red Box 10pm-late Fri & Sat, Black Box midnight-late Fri & Sat; 26) Electronica connoisseurs swarm to Culture Box, known for its impressive local and international DJ line-ups and sharp sessions of electro, techno, house and drum and bass. The club is divided into three spaces: preclubbing bar White Box, intimate club space Red Box, and heavyweight Black Box, where big-name DJs play the massive sound system.

Rust CLUB, LIVE MUSIC

(☎35 24 52 00; www.rust.dk; Guldbergsgade 8, Nørrebro; ⏲hrs vary, club usually 11pm-5am Fri & Sat; 🚌3A, 5A, 350S) A smashing place attracting one of the coolest crowds in Copenhagen. Live acts focus on alternative or upcoming indie rock, hip hop or electronica, while the club churns out hip hop, dancehall and electro on Wednesdays, and house, electro and rock on Fridays and Saturdays. From 11pm, entrance is only to over 18s (Wednesday and Thursday) and over 20s (Friday and Saturday).

Gay & Lesbian Venues

Denmark was the first country to permit same-sex marriage and has had a swinging gay scene for more than 30 years. Beyond the city's string of LGBT cafes, bars and clubs, queer drawcards include **Copenhagen Pride** (www.copenhagenpride.dk) in August, and queer film fest **Mix Copenhagen** (mixcopenhagen.dk) in October. For listings and events, see www.out-and-about.dk.

Oscar Bar & Cafe GAY

(www.oscarbarcafe.dk; Regnbuepladsen 77; ⏲11am-11pm Sun-Thu, to 2am Fri & Sat; 🚌12, 26, 33, 11A, 🚆S-train København H) In the shadow of the rådhus, this corner cafe-bar remains the most popular gay venue in the village. There's food for the peckish and a healthy quota of eye-candy locals and out-of-towners. In the warmer months, its alfresco tables are packed with revellers, one eye on friends, the other on Grindr.

Jailhouse CPH GAY

(http://jailhousecph.dk; Studiestræde 12; ⏲3pm-2am Sun-Thu, to 5am Fri & Sat; 🚌5A, 6A, 11A) Trendy, attitude-free and particularly popular with an older male crowd, this themed bar promises plenty of penal action, with uniformed 'guards' and willing guests.

☆ Entertainment

Copenhagen's 'X factor' fuels its entertainment options. Its live-music scene is healthy and kicking, with choices spanning intimate jazz and blues boltholes to mega rock venues.

Further up the entertainment ladder, a string of arresting, 21st-century cultural venues, including Operaen (Copenhagen Opera House), have injected the city's cultural scene with new verve.

Most events can be booked through **Billetnet** (☎70 15 65 65; www.billetnet.dk). You can also try **Billetlugen** (☎70 26 32 67; www.billetlugen.dk). For listings, scan www.aok.dk and www.visitcopenhagen.com.

Live Music & Clubs

★ **Jazzhouse** JAZZ

(☎33 15 47 00; www.jazzhouse.dk; Niels Hemmingsensgade 10; 🚌11A) Copenhagen's leading jazz joint serves up top Danish and visiting talent, with music styles running the gamut from bebop to fusion jazz. Doors usually open at 7pm, with concerts starting at 8pm. On Friday and Saturday, late-night concerts (from 11pm) are also offered. Check the website for details and consider booking big-name acts in advance.

Vega Live LIVE MUSIC

(☎33 25 70 11; www.vega.dk; Enghavevej 40, Vesterbro; 🚌10, 14, 3A) The daddy of Copenhagen's live-music and club venues, Vega hosts everyone from big-name rock, pop, blues and jazz acts to underground indie, hip hop and electro up-and-comers. Gigs take place on either the main stage (Store Vega), small stage (Lille Vega) or the revamped ground-floor Ideal Bar. The venue itself is a 1950s former trade-union HQ by leading Danish architect Vilhelm Lauritzen. Performance times vary; check the website.

Operaen OPERA

(Copenhagen Opera House; ☎box office 33 69 69 69; www.kglteater.dk; Ekvipagemestervej 10; 🚌9A, ⛴Opera) Designed by the late Henning Larsen, Copenhagen's state-of-the-art opera house has two stages: the Main Stage and the smaller, more experimental Takkeløftet. The repertoire runs the gamut from classic to contemporary opera. Productions usually sell out in advance, so book ahead or you might miss the fat lady singing.

🛍 Shopping

Copenhagen is a superb, if expensive, shopping destination. The city shines with small, independent boutiques selling must-have Danish homewares, fashion and jewellery. Be aware that aside from major retail chains, department stores and supermarkets, most shops are closed on Sunday.

Illums Bolighus DESIGN

(www.illumsbolighus.dk; Amagertorv 8-10, Strøget; ⏲10am-7pm Mon-Fri, to 6pm Sat, 11am-6pm Sun; 🚌11A) Revamp everything from your wardrobe to your living room at this multilevel department store, dedicated to big names in Danish and international design. Coveted goods include fashion, jewellery, silverware and glassware, and no shortage of Danish furniture, textiles and fetching office accessories.

THE SHOPPING-STREET LOW-DOWN

Strøget (City Centre) Local and global fashion chains, Danish design stores, department stores; downmarket at its western end, upmarket at its eastern end.

Kronprinsensgade, Store Regnegade, Pilestræde, Købmagergade (City Centre) High-end independent fashion labels, local jewellery and homewares.

Istedgade (Vesterbro) Street fashion, vintage threads, shoes and food.

Elmegade, Jægersborggade and Ravnsborggade (Nørrebro) Antiques, hipster fashion labels, homewares.

Bredgade (Nyhavn) Upmarket art and antiques.

Hay House DESIGN
(www.hay.dk; Østergade 61, Strøget; ⌚10am-6pm Mon-Fri, to 5pm Sat; 🚌11A) Rolf Hay's fabulous interior-design store sells its own coveted line of furniture, textiles and design objects, as well as those of other fresh, innovative Danish designers. Easy-to-pack gifts include anything from notebooks and ceramic cups to building blocks for style-savvy kids. There's a second branch at Pilestræde 29-31.

Han Kjøbenhavn FASHION, ACCESSORIES
(www.hankjobenhavn.com; Vognmagergade 7; ⌚11am-6pm Mon-Thu, to 7pm Fri, 10am-5pm Sat; 🚌11A, Ⓜ Kongens Nytorv) While we love the modernist fitout, it's what's on the racks that will hook you: original, beautifully crafted men's threads that merge Scandinavian sophistication with hints of old-school Danish working-class culture. Accessories include painfully cool eyewear, as well as sublime leather goods from America's Kenton Sorensen.

Bruuns Bazaar FASHION
(www.bruunsbazaar.com; Vognmagergade 2; ⌚10am-6pm Mon-Thu, to 7pm Fri, to 5pm Sat; 🚌11A, 350S) You'll find both men's and women's threads at the flagship store for Bruuns Bazaar, one of Denmark's most coveted and internationally respected brands. The style is contemporary, archetypal Scandinavian, with a focus on modern daywear that's crisp, well cut and classically chic with a twist.

Stilleben DESIGN
(☎33 91 11 31; www.stilleben.dk; Niels Hemmingsensgade 3; ⌚10am-6pm Mon-Fri, to 5pm Sat; 🚌11A) Owned by Danish Design School graduates Ditte Reckweg and Jelena Schou Nordentoft, Stilleben stocks a bewitching range of contemporary ceramics, glassware, jewellery and textiles from mostly emerging Danish and foreign designers. A must for design fans and savvy shoppers seeking 'Where did you get that?' gifts.

Henrik Vibskov FASHION
(www.henrikvibskov.com; Krystalgade 6; ⌚11am-6pm Mon-Thu, to 7pm Fri, to 5pm Sat; 🚌11A, Ⓜ Nørreport, 🚆S-train Nørreport) Not just a drummer and prolific artist, Danish enfant terrible Henrik Vibskov pushes the fashion envelope too. Break free with his bold, bright, creatively silhouetted threads for progressive guys and girls, as well as other fashion-forward labels such as Issey Miyake, Walter Van Beirendonck and Denmark's own Stine Goya.

ℹ Information

Dial ☎112 to contact police, ambulance or fire services.

Copenhagen Visitors Centre (☎70 22 24 42; www.visitcopenhagen.com; Vesterbrogade 4A; ⌚9am-6pm Mon-Sat, to 2pm Sun May, Jun & Sep, 9am-7pm Jul & Aug, 9am-4pm Mon-Fri, to 2pm Sat rest of yr) Copenhagen's excellent information centre has multilingual staff, as well as a bakery and lounge with free wi-fi and power sockets. It's the best source of information in town: free maps, masses of brochures and guides to take away, and booking services and hotel reservations available for a fee. It also sells the Copenhagen Card.

Frederiksberg Hospital (☎38 16 38 16; www.frederiksberghospital.dk; Nordre Fasanvej 57) Private doctor and dentist visits vary in price. To contact a doctor, call ☎60 75 40 70.

Hovedbiblioteket (15 Krystalgade; ⌚8am-7pm Mon-Fri, 9am-4pm Sat) The main public library provides computer terminals with internet access, as well as free wi-fi.

København H Post Office (Central Station; ⌚9am-7pm Mon-Fri, noon-4pm Sat) Post office in Central Station.

Politigården (☎33 14 88 88; Polititorvet 14) Police headquarters; south of Tivoli.

Post office (Købmagergade 33; ⌚10am-6pm Mon-Fri, to 2pm Sat) A handy post office near Strøget and the Latin Quarter.

Steno Apotek (Vesterbrogade 6C) A 24-hour pharmacy opposite Central Station.

Getting There & Away

AIR

Copenhagen Airport (www.cph.dk) is Scandinavia's busiest hub, with direct connections to other destinations in Denmark, as well as in Europe, North America and Asia. It is located in Kastrup, 9km southeast of the city centre.

BOAT

DFDS Seaways (☎33 42 30 10; www.dfdsseaways.com; Dampfærgevej 30) operates daily ferries to Oslo. See p485 for details.

BUS

Long-distance buses leave from opposite the DGI-byen sports complex on Ingerslevsgade, a quick walk southwest of Central Station. Advance reservations on most international routes can be made at Eurolines (p124).

CAR & MOTORCYCLE

The main highways into Copenhagen are the E20, which goes west to Funen and east to Malmö, Sweden; and the E47, which connects to Helsingør. If you're coming into Copenhagen from the north on the E47, exit onto Lyngbyvej (Rte 19) and continue south to get into the heart of the city.

As well as airport booths, the following rental agencies have city branches:

Avis (☎70 24 77 07; www.avis.com; Kampmannsgade 1)

Europcar (☎33 55 99 00; www.europcar.com; Gammel Kongevej 13A)

Hertz (☎33 17 90 20; www.hertzdk.dk; Ved Vesterport 3)

TRAIN

Long-distance trains arrive and depart from **Central Station** (⏲5.30am-1am Mon-Sat, 6am-1am Sun), known officially as København Hovedbanegård (København H). *Billetautomats* (coin-operated ticket machines) are the quickest way to purchase a ticket. **DSB Billetsalg** (www.dsb.dk; ⏲7am-8pm Mon-Fri, 8am-6pm Sat & Sun) is best for reservations and for purchasing international train tickets. Alternatively, you can make reservations on its website.

Central Station also offers **left-luggage services** (☎24 68 31 77; per 24hr per piece Dkr55-65, max 10 days; ⏲5.30am-1am Mon-Sat, 6am-1am Sun) and **lockers** (per 24hr small/large Dkr50/60, max 72hr), both on the lower level near the Reventlowsgade exit.

Getting Around

TO/FROM THE AIRPORT

Train

DSB trains (www.dsb.dk) link the airport with Copenhagen's Central Station (Dkr36, 14 minutes, every 12 minutes).

Metro

The 24-hour **metro** (www.m.dk) runs every four to 20 minutes between the airport arrival terminal (the station is called Lufthavnen) and the eastern side of the city centre. It does not stop at København H (Central Station) but is handy for Christianshavn and Nyhavn (get off at Kongens Nytorv for Nyhavn). Journey time to Kongens Nytorv is 14 minutes (Dkr36).

Taxi

A taxi between the city centre and airport will cost between Dkr250 and Dkr300, with a journey time of around 20 minutes, subject to traffic.

BICYCLE

Bikes can be carried free on S-Train services, but are banned at Nørreport station during weekday peak hours. Bikes can also be carried on the metro (except from 7am to 9am and 3.30pm to 5.30pm on weekdays from September to May). Metro bike tickets cost Dkr13.

Københavns Cyklerbørs (www.cykelboersen.dk; Gothersgade 157; bicycles per day/week Dkr75/350; ⏲8.30am-5.30pm Mon-Fri, 10am-2pm Sat, plus 6-9pm Sat & Sun May-Aug) Close to the Botanisk Have (Botanical Gardens) on the northwest edge of the city centre.

Baisikeli (☎26 70 02 29; http://baisikeli.dk; Ingerslevsgade 80, Vesterbro; bicycles per 6hr/week from Dkr50/270; ⏲10am-6pm) Baisikeli is Swahili for bicycle, and the profits from this rental outlet are used to ship 1200 much-needed bikes to African communities annually. It's located beside Dybøllsbro S-train station and just south of the Kødbyen restaurant and bar precinct in Vesterbro.

PUBLIC TRANSPORT

Copenhagen's bus and train network has an integrated ticket system based on seven geographical zones. Most of your travel within the city will be within two zones. Travel between the city and airport covers three zones.

- The cheapest ticket (*billet*) covers two zones, offers unlimited transfers, and is valid for one hour (adult/12 to 15 years Dkr24/12). Children under 12 travel free if accompanied by an adult.
- Buses, metro and trains use a common fare system based on zones. The basic fare of Dkr24 for up to two zones covers most city runs and allows transfers between buses and trains on a single ticket within one hour.
- If you plan on exploring sights outside the city, including Helsingør, the north coast of Zealand and Roskilde, you're better off buying a 24-hour ticket (all zones adult/12 to 15 years Dkr130/65) or a seven-day FlexCard (all zones Dkr590).
- Alternatively, you can purchase a Rejsekort, a touch-on, touch-off smart card that covers all zones and all public transport across the

country. Available from the Rejsekort machines at metro stations, Central Station or the airport, the card costs Dkr180 (Dkr80 for the card and Dkr100 in credit). When your credit is low, simply top up at the machines.

➡ All tickets are valid for travel on the metro, buses and S-tog (S-train or local train) even though they look slightly different, depending on where you buy them.

➡ The free Copenhagen city maps that are distributed by the tourist office show bus routes (with numbers) and are very useful for finding your way around the city.

➡ The website www.rejseplanen.dk offers a handy journey planner, with transport routes, times and prices.

Metro (www.m.dk) Consists of two lines (M1 and M2), with a city circle (Cityringen) line due for completion in late 2018 or early 2019. Trains run a minimum of every two minutes and connect Nørreport and Kongens Nytorv (near Nyhavn) to Christianshavn and the airport. Purchase tickets from *billetautomats* at the station. Trains run around the clock, with reduced frequency at night.

S-Tog (S-train; www.dsb.dk) Copenhagen's suburban train network runs seven lines through Central Station (København H). Popular tourist towns covered by the network include Helsingør and Køge. Services run every four to 20 minutes from approximately 5am to 12.30am. All-night services run hourly on Friday and Saturday (half-hourly on line F).

Bus (www.moviatrafik.dk) Copenhagen's vast bus system has seven primary routes, each with the letter 'A' in the route number. These routes run every three to seven minutes in peak hour, and about every 10 minutes at other times. Night buses (denoted by an 'N' in the route number) run on a few major routes between 1am and 5am nightly.

Harbour Bus Movia also operates the city's commuter ferries, known as Harbour Buses. There are three routes, servicing 10 stops along the harbourfront, including the Royal Library, Nyhavn and the Opera House.

CAR & MOTORCYCLE

➡ Weekday morning and evening rush hour aside, traffic is usually manageable, though parking can be hard to find. It's far better to explore sights within the city centre on foot or by using public transport.

➡ For street parking, buy a ticket from a kerbside *billetautomat* (automated ticket machine) and place it inside the windscreen. Ticket machines accept credit cards.

➡ Copenhagen parking is zoned. Those in the central commercial area (red zone) are the most costly (Dkr30 per hour). Blue-zone parking, located on the fringe of the city centre, is the cheapest, costing Dkr11 per hour. Closer to the centre, green zone parking costs Dkr18 per hour. These rates are valid between 8am and 6pm, with reduced rates at other times. Parking is free from 5pm Saturday to 8am Monday and on public holidays.

TAXI

➡ Taxis can be flagged on the street and there are ranks at various points around the city centre. If the yellow *taxa* (taxi) sign is lit, the taxi is available for hire.

➡ The fare will start at Dkr37 (Dkr50 from 11pm to 7am Friday and Saturday) and costs Dkr14.20 per kilometre from 7am to 4pm Monday to Friday, and Dkr18.75 from 11pm to 7am Friday and Saturday. The rate at all other times is Dkr15 per kilometre. Most taxis accept major credit cards.

➡ The main companies are **DanTaxi** (☎70 25 25 25; www.dantaxi.dk in Danish), **Taxa** (☎35 35 35 35; www.taxa.dk) and **Amager-Øbro Taxi** (☎27 27 27 27; www.amagerobrotaxi.dk in Danish).

ZEALAND

Though Copenhagen is the centre of gravity for most visitors to Denmark's eastern island, there is no shortage of drawcards beyond the city limits. Zealand is an island with a rich history, beautiful coastline and plenty of rolling countryside. Then there are the region's pedigree castles, most notably Kronborg Slot (famously known as Hamlet's castle, Elsinore) and the Renaissance showstopper Frederiksborg Slot. Older still are the remarkable Viking ships of Roskilde, excavated from Roskilde fjord in the 1950s and housed in a purpose-built museum.

North Zealand

One of the most popular day trips from Copenhagen is a loop tour taking in Frederiksborg Slot in Hillerød and Kronborg Slot in Helsingør. With an early start you might even have time to reach one of the north-shore beaches before making your way back to the city, although it is more rewarding to allow an extra day for wandering between shoreline towns along this gorgeous coastline.

If you're driving between Helsingør and Copenhagen, ditch the motorway for the coastal road, Strandvej (Rte 152), which is far more scenic (though admittedly quite crowded on summer weekends).

DON'T MISS

LOUISIANA: A MODERN-ART MUST

Even if you don't have a burning passion for art, Denmark's outstanding **Louisiana** (www.louisiana.dk; Gammel Strandvej 13, Humlebæk; adult/child Dkr110/free; ⏲11am-10pm Tue-Fri, to 6pm Sat & Sun) should be high on your 'To-Do' list. It's a striking modernist-art mecca, sprawling across a sculpture-laced park, burrowing down into the hillside and nosing out again to wink at the sea (and Sweden).

The museum's permanent collection, mainly postwar paintings and graphic art, covers everything from constructivism, CoBrA movement artists and minimalist art to abstract expressionism and pop art. Pablo Picasso, Francis Bacon, Andy Warhol and Robert Rauschenberg are some of the international luminaries you'll encounter, while Henry Moore's monumental bronzes and Max Ernst's owl-eyed creatures lurk behind the hillocks of the garden. Then there are the home-grown stars, among them Asger Jorn, Carl-Henning Pedersen, Robert Jacobsen and Richard Mortensen.

Adding extra X-factor is the museum's program of fantastic temporary exhibitions, its dedicated (and diverting) children's wing, fantastic gift shop, not to mention its airy cafe (complete with sunny terrace and international vista).

Louisiana is in the leafy commuter town of Humlebæk, 30km north of central Copenhagen and roughly 35 minutes from there on the S-train's C line. From Humlebæk station, the museum is a 900m signposted walk north along Strandvej. If day-tripping it from Copenhagen, the 24-hour ticket (adult/child Dkr130/65) is better value.

Frederiksborg Slot

Hillerød, 30km northwest of Copenhagen, is the site of **Frederiksborg Slot** (www.frederiksborgmuseet.dk; adult/child Dkr75/20; ⏲10am-5pm Apr-Oct, 11am-3pm rest of yr), an impressive Dutch Renaissance castle spread across three islands. The oldest part of the castle dates from Frederik II's time, though most of the present structure was built by his son Christian IV in the early 17th century. After parts of the castle were ravaged by fire in 1859, Carlsberg beer baron JC Jacobsen spearheaded a drive to restore the castle and make it a national museum.

The sprawling castle has a magnificent interior, with gilded ceilings, full wall-sized tapestries, royal paintings and antiques. The richly embellished **Riddershalen** (Knights' Hall) and the **coronation chapel**, where Danish monarchs were crowned between 1671 and 1840, are well worth the admission fee.

The S-train (Line B) runs every 10 to 20 minutes between Copenhagen and Hillerød (24-hour travel card adult/child Dkr130/65), a 40-minute ride. From Hillerød station follow the signs to Torvet, then continue along Slotsgade to the castle, a 1.5km walk in all. Alternatively, take bus 301 or 302, which will drop you in front of the castle grounds.

Helsingør (Elsinore)

POP 46,400

Generally, visitors come to the harbour town of Helsingør, at the northeastern tip of Zealand, for one of two reasons. If they are Swedish, they come to stock up on cheap(er) booze (this is the closest point to Sweden, and ferries shuttle back and forth across the Øresund frequently). Or, more often, they come to soak up the atmosphere of Denmark's most famous and awe-inspiring castle, Kronborg, home of Shakespeare's indecisive antihero, Hamlet. The **tourist office** (☎49 21 13 33; www.visitnordsjaelland.com; Havnepladsen 3; ⏲10am-5pm Mon-Fri, to 2pm Sat & Sun Jul-early Aug, reduced hours rest of year) is opposite the train station.

Sights

★**Kronborg Slot** CASTLE

(www.kronborg.dk; Kronborgvej; interior incl guided tour adult/child Dkr80/35; ⏲10am-5.30pm Jun-Aug, 11am-4pm Apr-May & Sep-Oct, shorter hours rest of year; guided tours 11.30am & 1.30pm daily) The Unesco World Heritage–listed Kronborg Slot began life as Krogen, a formidable tollhouse built by Danish king Erik of Pomerania in the 1420s. Expanded by Frederik II in 1585, the castle was ravaged by fire in 1629, leaving nothing but the outer walls. The tireless builder-king Christian IV rebuilt Kronborg, preserving the castle's earlier Renaissance

North Zealand

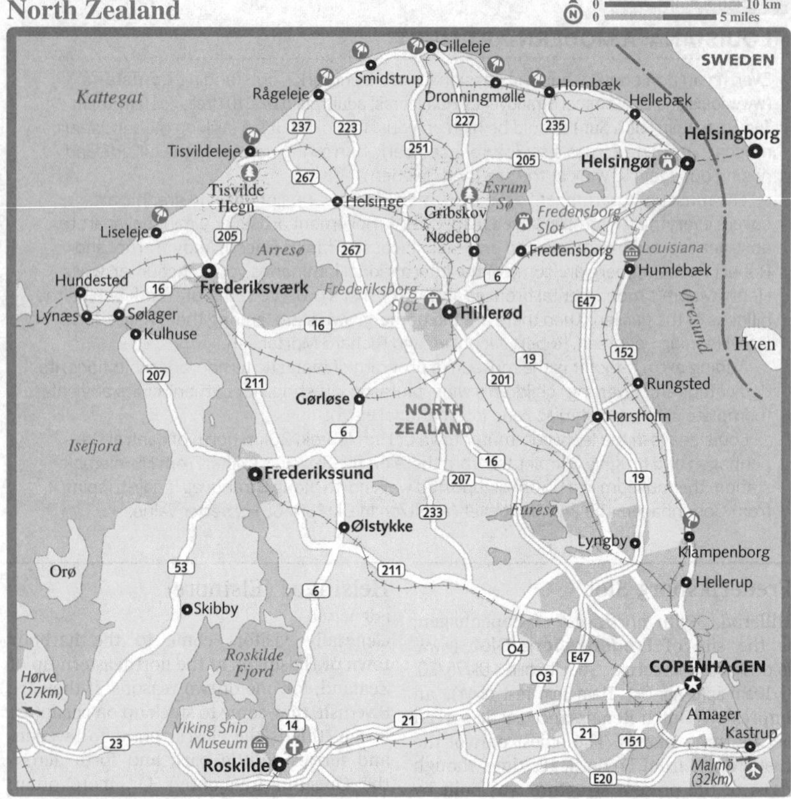

style and adding his own baroque touches. The galleried chapel was the only part of Kronborg that escaped the flames in 1629 and gives a good impression of the castle's original appearance.

★M/S Museet for Søfart MUSEUM

(Maritime Museum of Denmark; www.mfs.dk; Ny Kronborgvej 1; adult/child Dkr110/free; ⊙10am-5pm daily Jul & Aug, 11am-5pm Tue-Sun rest of yr) Ingeniously built in and around a dry dock beside Kronborg Slot, Denmark's subterranean Maritime Museum merits a visit as much for its design as for its enlightened, multimedia galleries. The latter explore Denmark's maritime history and culture in dynamic, contemporary ways. Alongside the usual booty of nautical instruments, sea charts and wartime objects, exhibitions explore themes as varied as the representation of sailors in popular culture; trade and exploitation in Denmark's overseas colonies; and the globe-crossing journeys of modern shipping containers.

Sankt Olai Domkirke CATHEDRAL

(⊙10am-4pm May-Aug, to 2pm Sep-Apr) Surrounded by lime trees, handsome, red-brick Sankt Olai Domkirke is a Gothic cathedral built in 1559. Eclectic features include an over-the-top white-and-gold altarpiece (one of Denmark's largest at 12m high), an ominous black stone slab where the names of wrongdoers were written, and, wedged in an archway, an English cannonball fired en route to the Battle of Copenhagen (1801).

Sankt Mariæ Kirke & Karmeliterklostret CHURCH, CLOISTER

(www.sctmariae.dk; Sankt Anna Gade 38; ⊙10am-3pm Tue-Sun) Slip into this medieval church for some rather eclectic 15th-century frescoes, in which frogs, foxes, bulls and rams spring from bizarre-looking faces, and where pipers and lute players burst from giant flowers. Other highlights include an ornate rococo gallery and a 17th-century organ, the latter played by Dieterich Buxtehude (1637–1707), a baroque composer who greatly influenced Bach; the frequent organ concerts are attended by aficionados. Sankt Mariæ Kirke is attached to one of Scandinavia's best-preserved medieval monasteries, Karmeliterklostret.

Sleeping

Danhostel Helsingør HOSTEL €
(☎49 28 49 49; http://danhostelhelsingor.dk; Nordre Strandvej 24; dm/s/d/tr Dkr225/495/550/595; P) This 180-bed hostel is based in a coastal manor house 2km northwest of town, on a little beach looking directly across to Sweden. The run-of-the-mill dorms are in one of the smaller attached buildings. Facilities include a self-catering kitchen, small playground and outdoor ping-pong tables to keep kids amused. From Helsingør, bus 842 (Dkr24) will get you there.

Helsingør Camping CAMPGROUND €
(☎49 28 49 50; www.helsingorcamping.dk; Strandalleen 2; campsites adult/child Dkr70/35, cabins with bathroom Dkr850; ⊙year-round) A well-spaced, low-key beachside camping ground east of Danhostel Helsingør and approximately 1.5km northwest of the town centre. Facilities include a shop and laundry, and it's close to one of the area's best beaches. To get here, take bus 842 from Helsingør train station.

Marienlyst Hotel & Casino HOTEL €€
(☎49 21 40 00; www.marienlyst.dk; Nordre Strandvej 2; s Dkr800-1425, d Dkr 1000-1625; P@) Stretching along the seafront, Helsingør's four-star hotel features a swimming pool, casino, and views across the sea to Sweden. Rooms are neutrally hued and classically styled, and while they won't win any design awards, all are comfortable and utterly satisfactory.

Eating

There's a cluster of restaurants and beer gardens around the main square, Axeltorv. For coffee and cake, head for pedestrianised Stengade.

You'll find a **Kvickly** (Stjernegade 25; ⊙8am-8pm Mon-Fri, to 6pm Sat & Sun) supermarket and bakery west of Axeltorv.

Rådmand Davids Hus DANISH €
(☎49 26 10 43; Strandgade 70; dishes Dkr38-98; ⊙10am-5pm Mon-Sat) What better place to gobble down Danish classics than a snug, lop-sided 17th-century house, complete with cobbled courtyard? Refuel with honest, solid staples like smørrebrød, herring, and the special 'shopping lunch', typically a generous plate of salad, salmon pâté, and slices of pork, cheese and homemade ryebread. Leave room for the Grand Marnier pancakes.

Spisehuset Kulturværftet INTERNATIONAL €
(www.kulturvaerftet.dk; Allegade 2; meals Dkr45-95; ⊙10am-7pm Mon-Fri, to 5pm Sat & Sun) Part of The Culture Yard (a striking waterfront cultural centre housing theatres, exhibition spaces and the Helsingør library), this casual, light-filled eatery peddles fresh, modern cafe grub. Gaze out over Hamlet's pad while chowing down open sandwiches, creative soups and salads, or the more substantial daily special. If the view inspires the scribe within, there's free wi-fi, good coffee and nibble-friendly pastries and cookies.

Rustica ITALIAN €€
(☎20 68 56 44; www.rustica.dk; Stengade 26E; mains Dkr179-229; ⊙11am-late Tue-Sat) At the far end of a courtyard, up a flight of stairs, Rustica serves beautiful, seasonal dishes in a contemporary rustic setting of whitewashed wooden beams, filament bulbs and long

WORTH A TRIP

FREDENSBORG SLOT

A 20-minute train ride southwest of Helsingør takes you to a very different kind of royal castle from Kronborg Slot. **Fredensborg Slot** (www.ses.dk; Slotsgade 1; tours adult/child Dkr75/30; ⊙tours in English 1.45-3.30pm daily Jul-early Aug) evolved during the early 18th century as a royal hunting lodge. Its present-day role is as the royal family's summer residence and number-one party palace. It's a peaceful spot for a stroll or a picnic, with lush rolling lawns, forest and formal gardens beside Esrum Sø (Lake Esrum). By the lake, seasonal restaurant **Skipperhuset** (☎48 48 10 12; www.skipperhuset.dk; Skipperallé 6; lunch Dkr89-145, dinner mains Dkr195-285; ⊙noon-5pm Tue-Sun mid-Apr–Sep, plus 6-9pm Fri & Sat May-Aug) serves beautiful dishes made with ingredients from the palace garden. Fredensborg is midway between Hillerød (Dkr24, 10 minutes) and Helsingør (Dkr60, 25 minutes). Trains run about twice hourly. The palace is about 1km from the train station, and well signposted.

communal tables made by the chef himself. The Italian-inspired menu is reassuringly short, with only a handful of antipasti, mains, pizzas and desserts, driven by quality produce and an emphasis on clean, natural flavours.

Getting There & Away

BOAT

Scandlines (www.scandlines.com) sails between Helsingør and Helsingborg in Sweden (person/car plus nine passengers Dkr59/745 return, 20 minutes). Car tickets are cheaper booked online.

TRAIN

Trains between Copenhagen and Helsingør run about three times hourly (Dkr108, 45 minutes) from early morning to midnight. If you're day-tripping it from Copenhagen, buy a 24-hour pass (Dkr130).

Trains between Helsingør and Hillerød (Dkr72, 30 minutes) run at least once hourly until around midnight.

The Lokalbanen train from Helsingør to Gilleleje (Dkr72, 45 minutes) runs once to twice hourly until around midnight.

Zealand's North Coast

The entire stretch of coast from Helsingør west to Liseleje is in effect Zealand's holiday zone, with literally thousands of traditional Danish summer houses packing the woodlands and beachfronts. Long, sandy beaches and the festive summer vibe that grips its half-timbered fishing villages make the region worth a visit.

Hornbæk, the next main town west of Helsingør, has the best and most easily accessible beach on the north coast. The beach is a vast expanse of white sand and grassy dunes that run the entire length of the town, and it has a **Blue Flag** (www.blueflag.org) eco-friendly label. From the train station, it's just a five-minute walk directly down Havnevej to the harbour, where you'll find a great seafood kiosk and the yacht marina. Simply climb the dunes to the left and you're on the beach. The library doubles as the **tourist office** (☎49 70 47 47; www.hornbaek.dk; Vestre Stejlebakke 2A; ⏲1-5pm Mon & Thu, 10am-3pm Tue, Wed & Fri, 10am-2pm Sat).

Zealand's northernmost town, **Gilleleje**, has the island's largest fishing port. Visitors usually head straight for the harbour and adjacent sandy beach. The harbour has several wonderful seafood kiosks, selling freshly caught crayfish platters, fish and chips and even sushi. The **tourist office** (www.visitnordsjaelland.dk; Gilleleje Stationsvej 10; ⏲10am-5pm Mon-Fri, to 2pm Sat Jul-early Aug, 10am-4pm Mon-Fri May-Jun & mid-Aug–late Sep) is in the centre. There are excellent beaches either side of the town and others along the coast to the west, especially at **Rågeleje**, **Dronningmølle** and at **Smidstrup Strand**, where conditions are often good for windsurfing. All have Blue Flags.

Tisvildeleje is a pleasant seaside village known for its bohemian and artistic communities, with a long, straggling main street that leads to an even longer beach. It really transforms in July when the holidaymakers arrive. Behind the beach is **Tisvilde Hegn**, a windswept forest of twisted trees and heather-covered hills laced with good walking paths. You can pick up brochures and tourist information at the train station. Out of season the town feels desolate.

Sleeping

Danhostel Tisvildeleje HOSTEL €

(☎48 70 98 50; www.helene.dk; Bygmarken 30; dm/s/d Dkr200/680/700; ⏲year-round; P @) One kilometre east of Tisvildeleje, this modern hostel shares the excellent facilities of the Sankt Helene holiday complex. The grounds cover 12 hectares, with walking trails, sports fields, playgrounds, kids' activities and a decent restaurant, as well as easy access to a sandy beach. By train, get off at Godhavn station, one stop before Tisvildeleje: the hostel is a short walk north.

Gilleleje Badehotel HOTEL €€

(☎48 30 13 47; www.gillelejebadehotel.dk; Hulsøvej 15, Gilleleje; r incl breakfast from Dkr1090; P) Kierkegaard was a frequent guest at this luxurious beach hotel. The atmosphere is so richly nostalgic you half expect the hotel to be sepia-tinted, but instead a soothing egg-white colour scheme prevails. All the rooms are bright and sunlit and most have balconies with views of Sweden. The hotel also offers a sauna, steam room and massage treatments. You'll find it 1km west of town.

Hotel Villa Strand HOTEL €€

(☎49 70 00 88; www.villastrand.dk; Kystvej 12, Hornbæk; s/d incl breakfast Dkr895/995, without bathroom Dkr725/825; ⏲Jun-Aug; P) If this hotel was any closer to the sea, it would be floating towards Sweden. Rooms in the main building are large, with cool white decor, floorboards and a lofty air.

Ewaldsgården Guest House GUESTHOUSE €€
(☎49 70 00 82; www.ewaldsgaarden.dk; Johannes Ewalds Vej 5, Hornbæk; s/d incl breakfast Dkr565/875; ⊙mid-Jun–mid-Aug; P@) This 17th-century farmhouse pension is a delight, with a picture-perfect garden and a cosy mix of antiques and cottage-style furnishings. All 12 rooms have washbasins; showers and toilets are off the hall. There's also a simple guest kitchen. Ewaldsgården is a five-minute walk southeast of the train station.

★**Helenekilde Badehotel** BOUTIQUE HOTEL €€€
(☎48 70 70 01; www.helenekilde.com; Strandvejen 25, Tisvildeleje; r with sea view incl breakfast from Dkr1695, r without seaview incl breakfast from Dkr1395; P) Like Tisvildeleje Strand, the interior of this enchanting beachfront hotel was designed by the ballet dancer Alexander Kolpin. The cosy communal areas feature beautiful furnishings, art and the odd vintage suitcase turned coffee table, while the rooms themselves are simple yet elegant, with 16 of them looking out over the waves.

Eating

For eating out along Zealand's northern coast you can't beat the seafood restaurants – usually little more than a few kiosks, really – that you find in the harbours.

Fiskehuset Hornbæk SEAFOOD €
(Havenevej 32, Hornbæk; dishes Dkr45-75; ⊙11am-8pm summer, shorter hours rest of year) Hornbæk's harbourside gem is the Fiskehuset, a humble fishmonger-cum-kiosk where punters happily devour the likes of smoked-cod's roe, cured herring, smoked mackerel, fresh prawns, *fiskefrikadeller* (fish cakes), mussel soup and all manner of wonderful, fresh, local seafood. Best of all, you'll have change to spare.

Adamsen's Fisk SEAFOOD €
(Gilleleje Havn; meals Dkr50-79; ⊙11am-9pm, sushi bar 11am-8pm) This popular harbourside takeaway dishes up fish, seafood, sides of chips and more salubrious salads. The fish and seafood are heavily battered, so delicate stomachs and waist-watchers may prefer the grilled options. After selecting your combo, you're given a token which flashes when your order is ready. For those who prefer their fish raw, Adamsen's has a sushi bar next door (10-piece sushi set Dkr130).

Hansens Café DANISH €€
(☎49 70 04 79; Havnevej 19, Hornbæk; lunch Dkr72-149, dinner mains Dkr178-238; ⊙4pm-midnight Mon-Fri, 1pm-midnight Sat & Sun) Hansens is in the town's oldest house, an earthen-roofed half-timbered building with a pleasant pub-like atmosphere. The menu changes daily but you can expect to find solid grub such as *fiskefrikadeller* (fishballs) with homemade remoulade or *moules marinière*.

Tisvildeleje Cafeen INTERNATIONAL €€
(Hovedgaden 55; mains Dkr129-162; ⊙11am-11pm daily summer, shorter hours rest of year) A popular spot, complete with alfresco summertime seating, Tisvildeleje Cafeen delivers a worldly menu spanning salads and burgers to curry and fish soup. Happy hour runs from 5pm to 7pm Friday to Sunday, with cheaper beer and cocktails. The cafe features live music and DJs on Friday and Saturday nights in summer.

Getting There & Away

Train connections to/from Helsingør include the following:

Gilleleje Dkr72, 45 minutes, once or twice hourly.

Hornbæk Dkr36, 25 minutes, once or twice hourly.

Tisvildeleje via Hillerød Dkr84, 30 minutes, once or twice hourly.

There is no direct rail link between Gilleleje and Tisvildeleje. Bus 360R runs between Gilleleje and Helsinge, from where trains run to Tisvildeleje. A one-way ticket costs Dkr36, with an overall travel time of 50 minutes (80 minutes on Sunday). Services run once or twice hourly.

Roskilde

POP 47,800

Most foreigners who have heard of Roskilde know it either as the home of one of northern Europe's best outdoor music festivals, or the sight of several remarkable Viking ship finds, now housed in an excellent, purpose-built museum. To the Danes, however, it is a city of great royal and religious significance, as it was the capital city long before Copenhagen and is still the burial place of 39 monarchs stretching back several hundred years. Located on the southern tip of Roskilde Fjord, the city was a thriving trading port throughout the Middle Ages. It was also the site of Zealand's first Christian church, built by Viking king Harald Bluetooth in AD 980.

Sights

★Roskilde Domkirke CATHEDRAL

(www.roskildedomkirke.dk; Domkirkepladsen; adult/child Dkr60/free; ⏲9am-5pm Mon-Sat, 12.30-5pm Sun Apr-Sep, shorter hours rest of year) Not merely the crème de la crème of Danish cathedrals, this twin-towered giant is a designated Unesco World Heritage Site. Started by Bishop Absalon in 1170, the building has been rebuilt and tweaked so many times that it's now a superb showcase of 800 years' worth of Danish architecture. As the royal mausoleum, it contains the crypts of 37 Danish kings and queens – contemplating the remains of so many powerful historical figures is a moving memento mori.

★Viking Ship Museum MUSEUM

(☎46 30 02 00; www.vikingeskibsmuseet.dk; Vindeboder 12; adult/child May–mid-Oct Dkr115/free, mid-Oct–Apr Dkr80/free, boat trip excl museum Dkr90; ⏲10am-5pm late Jun–mid-Aug, to 4pm rest of yr, boat trips daily mid-May–Sep) Viking fans will be wowed by the superb Viking Ship Museum, which displays five Viking ships discovered at the bottom of Roskilde Fjord. The museum is made up of two main sections: the Viking Ship Hall, where the boats themselves are kept; and Museumsø, where archaeological work takes place. There are free 45-minute guided tours in English daily at noon and 3pm from late June to the end of August, and at noon on weekends from May to late June and in September.

If you've always had an urge to leap aboard a longboat for a spot of light pillaging, join one of the museum's hour-long boat trips. Traditional Nordic boats are propelled across the water by you and the rest of your shipmates.

From mid-May to the end of September, 50-minute trips run one to three times daily, with an additional two to three trips daily from late June to mid-August, weather dependent. Call ahead to confirm sailing times. Tickets (Dkr90) are additional to the main museum entry ticket.

Museum for Samtidskunst MUSEUM

(http://samtidskunst.dk; Stændertorvet 3d; adult/child Dkr40/free; ⏲noon-4pm Tue-Sun, to 8pm 1st Wed of month) Housed in the elegant 18th-century Roskilde Palace (built to be used by Christian VI whenever he was in town) is this surprisingly cutting-edge contemporary-art space. Exhibitions lean towards new media, with often perplexing sound, video or performance installations by both Danish and international artists.

Danmarks Rockmuseum MUSEUM

(www.danmarksrockmuseum.dk; Rabalderstræde 1) Scheduled to open in mid-2015, the Denmark Museum of Rock Music will deliver a multisensory journey through the wild, often transgressive history of rock and roll. Interactive exhibitions will have visitors laying and remixing hits, practising various dance steps, and rocking to a virtual Roskilde Festival crowd. Check the website for opening times and pricing. From Roskilde train station, buses 202A and 212 stop 350m from the museum.

Festivals & Events

Roskilde Festival MUSIC FESTIVAL

(www.roskilde-festival.dk) Denmark's answer to Glastonbury, Roskilde Festival is northern Europe's largest music festival. This four-day-long binge of bands and booze rocks Roskilde every summer on the last weekend in June.

Sleeping & Eating

Roskilde has limited accommodation for its size; being so close to Copenhagen, it's a popular day-trip destination.

Danhostel Roskilde HOSTEL €

(☎46 35 21 84; www.danhostel.dk/roskilde; Vindeboder 7; dm/s/d/tr Dkr250/575/700/750; P) Roskilde's modern hostel sits right next door to the Viking Ship Museum, on the waterfront. Pimped with funky black and white murals, each of the 40 large rooms has its own shower and toilet. Staff are friendly, although the mattress we slept on was frustratingly lopsided. Cheekily, wi-fi is an extra Dkr20 per hour (Dkr100 per 24 hours).

Hotel Prindsen HOTEL €€€

(☎46 30 91 00; www.prindsen.dk; Algade 13; s/d incl breakfast Dkr1395/1495; P @) First opened in 1695, the centrally located Prindsen is Denmark's oldest hotel, with former guests including King Frederik VII and Hans Christian Andersen. Rooms are comfortable and classically styled, with many featuring blue carpet and fleur-de-lis-patterned drapes. The carpet-free Nordisk rooms (s/d Dkr1505/1605) are larger than the standard rooms, but not really worth the extra cost. Rates often drop on weekends and public holidays.

Café Vivaldi INTERNATIONAL €€

(Stændertorvet 8; sandwiches & salads Dkr99-109, mains Dkr169-199; ⏲10am-10pm Sun-Thu, to 11pm

Fri & Sat) Slap bang on the main square (cathedral views included), this faux bistro is a good place to sit back and people-watch over abundant servings of tasty cafe grub. Edibles include soup, sandwiches, wraps, burgers and salads, as well as more substantial pasta and meat dishes. It's particularly handy on Sundays, when most of the town shuts down.

Raadhuskælderen DANISH, INTERNATIONAL €€
(www.raadhuskaelderen.dk; Stændertorvet; smørrebrød Dkr68-118, dinner mains Dkr188-348; ⌚11am-9pm Mon-Sat) Another reliable nosh spot is this atmospheric restaurant in the cellar of the old town hall (c 1430). Herring platters, shrimps, salads, a burger and open sandwiches feature on the lunch menu. Come dinner, you might see racks of lamb paired with tzatziki and rosemary sauce, or smoked-salmon carpaccio prepared with breadcrumbs, radishes and cress mayo. Vegetarians may struggle.

Restaurant Mumm DANISH, INTERNATIONAL €€€
(☎46 37 22 01; www.mummroskilde.com; Karen Olsdatters Stræde 9; dishes Dkr120; ⌚5.30-11pm Mon-Sat) One of Roskilde's more exclusive dining destinations, intimate Mumm melds Danish and global influences to create contemporary tasting dishes like glazed veal sweetbread with pickled onions and malt soil. Four to six dishes should fill most bellies. Book ahead.

Information

Post Office (Algade 51; ⌚10am-5.30pm Mon-Fri, to 1pm Sat) Inside the Kvickly supermarket building.

Tourist Office (☎46 31 65 65; www.visit-roskilde.com; Stændertorvet 1; ⌚10am-5pm Mon-Fri, to 1pm Sat) The tourist office provides information, as well as accommodation options.

Getting There & Around

Trains from Copenhagen to Roskilde are frequent (Dkr96, 25 minutes). From Copenhagen by car, Rte 21 leads to Roskilde; upon approaching the city, exit onto Rte 156, which leads into the centre.

Parking discs are required in Roskilde and can be purchased at the tourist office. There are free car parks at Gustav Weds Plads and near the Viking Ship Museum.

Jupiter Cykler (☎46 35 04 20; www.jupiter-cykler.dk; Gullandsstræde 3; per day Dkr100; ⌚9am-5.30pm Mon-Thu, to 6pm Fri, to 2pm Sat), just off Skomagergade, rents out bikes.

WORTH A TRIP

SAGNLANDET LEJRE

If Roskilde's Viking Ship Museum has given you a taste for the history of the region, 7km southwest of town is the fascinating **Sagnlandet Lejre** (www.sagnlandet.dk; Slangealleen 2, Lejre; adult/child Dkr130/85; ⌚10am-5pm daily late Jun–mid-Aug, reduced hours rest of year). An experimental-archaeology centre, its enthusiastic reenactors use ancient technology to test out various theories: How many people does it take to build a dolmen? What plants might have been used to dye clothing? And how do you stop the goats eating your reed roof? Kids can let loose in the hands-on Fire Valley, paddling dug-out canoes, attempting to work a fire drill and chopping up logs using primitive axes. To reach it, catch a train from Roskilde to Lejre, then local bus 207 (weekdays only) to Gl Lejre (Dkr24, 37 minutes). From here, Sagnlandet Lejre is a 2.2km walk.

Køge

POP 35,770

Køge is a pretty town that, if not worth a special visit, offers a pleasant diversion if you're passing through on your way to Bornholm (by ferry) or the south islands. The one-time medieval trading centre, 42km south of Copenhagen, retains a photogenic core of narrow cobbled streets flanked by Denmark's best-preserved 17th- and 18th-century buildings. At its heart is broad and bustling **Torvet**, the nation's largest square.

A short stroll through the central part of Køge takes you to Denmark's oldest **half-timbered building** (c 1527) at Kirkestræde 20, a marvellous survivor with a fine raked roof. Set to reopen in 2015 after major renovations, the high-tech **Køge Museum** (☎56 63 42 42; www.koegemuseum.dk; Nørregade 4) occupies a splendid building that dates from 1619. Another gem is **Brogade 23**, decorated with cherubs carved by the famed 17th-century artist Abel Schrøder. Elsewhere, best efforts have been made to improve a not-very-attractive industrial harbour with open-air cafes and restaurants. Køge also has Denmark's only museum dedicated to the artistic process, **KØS** (www.koes.dk; Vestergade 1; adult/18-24yr/child

WORTH A TRIP

DRAGSHOLM SLOT

Fancy a night in a culinary castle? Then pack your bag and your appetite and check in at **Dragsholm Slot** (☎59 65 33 00; www.dragsholm-slot.dk; Dragsholm Allé, Hørve; s/d from Dkr1895/1995; P). Located at the edge of Zealand's fertile Lammefjorden (Denmark's most famous 'vegetable garden'), its medieval walls are home to **Slotskøkkenet** (Castle Kitchen; 5/7 courses Dkr700/900; 6-10pm Wed-Sat Jun, 6-10pm Tue-Sat Jul-early Sep, reduced hours rest of year), a New Nordic hot spot headed by ex-Noma chef Claus Henriksen. From the area's prized carrots to herbs from the castle's own garden, 'locally sourced' is the catch-cry here. The end results are deceptively simple, sublime creations such as candied herbs with *skyr* (Icelandic yoghurt) and celeriac. Upstairs, the more casual **Lammefjordens Spisehus** (2-course lunches Dkr245, 3-course dinners Dkr345; noon-3pm & 6-10pm) offers cheaper, pared-back Nordic dishes using the same top-notch ingredients (think herb-marinated herring or hay-smoked salmon). Bookings are a must for Slotskøkkenet and recommended for Spisehus.

Nosh aside, whitewashed Dragsholm is famed for its 800-year history, which includes the imprisonment of Roskilde's last Catholic bishop and the secret burial of a love-struck girl in the castle walls (eerily visible behind a plexiglass panel). While some rooms – spread across the castle and the nearby porter's lodge – feature contemporary styling, most ooze a distinguished baronial air, with anything from canopy beds to fleur-de-lis wallpaper and (in some cases) jacuzzis. Add to this a string of Late Romantic salons and ballrooms and rambling fairy-tale gardens, and you'll soon be feeling like a well-fed noble.

Check the website for dinner and accommodation packages (often cheaper than the official room rates), and request a room with field or garden views. Dragsholm Slot is located 91km west of Copenhagen via motorway 21.

Dkr50/20/free; 10am-5pm Tue-Sun), which includes the sketches for the statue of the *Little Mermaid* and for Queen Margrethe II's birthday tapestries.

Sleeping & Eating

The tourist office can book rooms in private homes for around Dkr500 per double; there's a Dkr25 booking fee.

Danhostel Køge HOSTEL €
(☎56 67 66 50; www.danhostel-koege.dk; Vamdrupvej 1; dm Dkr200, r from Dkr380; P) In a quiet area 2km northwest of town, this friendly 116-bed hostel offers pleasant, cosy rooms; those upstairs have Velux windows with relaxing sky views. The more expensive rooms come with bathrooms. There's a laundry, small playground and breakfast buffet (Dkr60). To get here from Køge, catch bus 101A and get off at Norsvej, from where the hostel is an 850m walk.

Hotel Niels Juel HOTEL €€
(☎56 63 18 00; www.hotelnielsjuel.dk; Toldbodvej 20; s/d incl breakfast Dkr1225/1395; P) Overlooking the harbour a couple of blocks south of the train station, this pleasant hotel/restaurant combo offers 51 well-furnished rooms in two colour schemes: maritime blue or warm and earthy. All include phone, minibar and satellite TV. Check the hotel website for discounts and special offers.

★ **Restaurant Arkens** SEAFOOD €€
(☎56 66 05 05; www.restaurant-arken.dk; Bådehavnen 21; lunch Dkr68-168, dinner mains Dkr158-288; 11.30am-9pm Mon-Thu & Sun, to 9.30pm Fri & Sat) This Skagen import has quite a reputation for sterling seafood, and its Køge outpost is no less drool-inducing. It's a case of top ingredients cooked well; superlative choices include the garlic gratin Norwegian lobster tails. There's a savvy choice of wines by the glass, as well as house-made snaps and beer from Skagen. You'll find Arkens right on Køge marina, 2.5km north of Torvet.

Café Vivaldi INTERNATIONAL €€
(☎56 63 53 66; www.cafevivaldi.dk; Torvet 30; lunch Dkr95-149, dinner mains Dkr169-199; 10am-10pm Sun-Thu, to 11pm Fri, to midnight Sat) This chain 'bistro' is a safe bet for tasty, straightforward cafe nosh like salads, sandwiches, burgers, burritos as well as more substantial meat and fish dishes. Order at the counter. There's seating right on the square and, at weekends, a buzzing bar vibe.

Information

Tourist Office (☎56 67 60 01; www.visitkoege.com; Vestergade 1; ⊙9.30am-6pm Mon-Fri, 10am-3pm Sat Jul & Aug, 9.30am-5pm Mon-Fri, 10am-1pm Sat rest of yr) Just off the town's main square, the tourist office offers information and free wi-fi, and can also book accommodation.

Getting There & Away

Car drivers can park in Torvet, but only for an hour; turn down Brogade, then follow Fændediget round for less-restricted free parking off Bag Haverne and north of the harbour.

BOAT

Bornholmer Færgen (☎70 23 15 15; www.faergen.dk; adult/child 12-15/under 11 Dkr290/145/free, car incl 5 passengers Dkr1625) operates an overnight service from Køge to Bornholm, departing daily at 12.30am and arriving at 6am. It is quicker and almost as cheap to take a train via Copenhagen to Ystad in Sweden, and then a catamaran to Rønne from there (total journey time is around 3½ hours), although it can make sense to sleep while you sail if your itinerary is tight.

TRAIN

Køge's train and bus stations are at Jernbanegade 12 on the east side of town. The train station is the last stop on the A line on Copenhagen's S-Tog network. Trains to Copenhagen run at least three times an hour (Dkr108, 45 minutes).

Vordingborg

POP 11,750

Vordingborg's modern-day quaintness is deceptive. Now best known as Zealand's gateway to the south islands, the town played a starring role in early Danish history. It was the royal residence and Baltic power base of Valdemar I (Valdemar the Great), famed for reuniting the Danish kingdom in 1157 after a period of civil war. And it was here that Valdemar II (Valdemar the Victorious) signed the Law of Jutland in 1241, a civil code which declared that legitimate laws must be based on objective and sovereign justice. The code would become a forerunner to Danish national law.

Starting as a small wooden fortification in the 1160s, the town's historic fortress expanded over the following two centuries, becoming one of Denmark's most important castles. The remnants of that 14th-century giant, the 26m **Gåsetårnet** (Goose Tower), is Vordingborg's most prominent landmark, and part of the multimillion-dollar **Danmarks Borgcenter** (Danish Castle Centre; www.danmarksborgcenter.dk; Slotsruinen 1; adult/child Dkr115/free; ⊙10am-5pm daily). Known in English as the Danish Castle Centre, this intriguing, new, high-tech museum explores the castle's history, as well as that of medieval Danish power, politics and castle life.

When the Vordingborg **tourist office** (☎55 34 11 11; www.visitmoen.dk; Algade 97; ⊙10am-3pm Mon-Fri) is closed, you can find information on the region at the museum.

MØN

POP 9580

The three islands of Møn, Falster and Lolland mark the southernmost part of Denmark. Of these, Møn is the most bewitching. Its most famous drawcards are its spectacular white cliffs, Møns Klint. Soft, sweeping and crowned by deep green forest, they're the stuff paintings are made of...which possibly explains the island's healthy quota of artists. Yet the inspiration doesn't end there, with beautiful beaches spanning sandy expanses to small secret coves, haunting Neolithic graves and medieval churches lined with some of Denmark's most vivid medieval frescoes. The island's main stettlement is Stege, an everyday place enlivened by its role as the island's gateway town and main commercial centre.

Sights

Møns Klint — OUTDOORS

The chalk cliffs at Møns Klint were created 5000 years ago when the calcareous deposits from aeons' worth of seashells were lifted from the ocean floor. The gleaming white cliffs rise sharply 128m (420ft) above an azure sea, making one of the most striking landscapes in Denmark.

GeoCenter Møns Klint — MUSEUM

(www.moensklint.dk; Stengårdsvej 8, Borre; adult/child Dkr120/80; ⊙10am-6pm late Jun-early Aug, shorter hours rest of year) Located at Store Klint, the high-tech GeoCenter Møns Klint manages to make geology utterly engrossing. Imaginative displays (in Danish, German and English) explain how the cliffs were formed, show off an orderly fossil collection and bring other-worldly Cretaceous sea creatures to life. Kids absolutely love the inventive hands-on nature centre, and there are roaming experts to answer any questions. Ponder nature's craftiness at the smart upstairs cafe, which serves coffee, cakes and open sandwiches.

Passage Graves HISTORIC SITE

FREE There are a 119 megalithic tombs on Møn, dating from 4000 to 1800 BC. Two of the best-known passage graves (*jættestuer*, or 'giants' rooms') are Kong Asgers Høj and Klekkende Høj, each about 2km from the village of Røddinge. Northwest of Røddinge, **Kong Asgers Høj** (Kong Asgersvej) is Denmark's largest passage grave, with a burial chamber 10m long and more than 2m wide. Southeast of Røddinge, **Klekkende Høj** is the only double passage grave on Møn: the side-by-side entrances each lead to a 7m-long chamber.

Stege Kirke CHURCH

(Provstesstræde, Stege; ⏲9am-5pm) It looks as though a demented nine-year-old has been let loose inside Stege Kirke, built in the 13th century by one of the powerful Hvide family. The interior is covered in endearingly naive 14th- and 15th-century frescoes in red and black paint: monkeylike faces sprout from branches, a hunter chases unidentifiable animals, and a sorrowful man is covered in big blobs...measles? The church has a splendidly carved pulpit dating from 1630.

Thorsvang MUSEUM

(http://thorsvangdanmarkssamlermuseum.dk; Thorsvangs Allé 7, Stege; adult/child Dkr50/25; ⏲10am-5pm mid-Apr–mid-Oct, shorter hours rest of year) Fastidiously detailed and highly atmospheric, this collectors' museum recreates 30 old shops and workshops, from a barber, butcher and bakery to a cinema lobby adorned with vintage film magazines, candy and a 1967 Italian projector. The museum is also home to a small yet fascinating collection of historic motor vehicles, including Ford's final T-Model car (1927) and its first A-Model vehicle (1928).

You'll find Thorsvang 800m southwest of the tourist office in Stege, just off Route 59.

A FEAST OF FRESCOES

Given Møn's artistic sensibility, it seems apt that the island should claim some of the best-preserved primitive frescoes in Denmark. You'll find them in many of Møn's churches, most of which are of medieval origin. The frescoes depict biblical scenes, often interpreted through light-hearted rustic imagery. Fearful of what they saw as too much Roman exuberance, post-Reformation Lutherans whitewashed them, ironically preserving the artworks. The style of Møn fresco painting owes much to the Emelunde-mestteren (the Elmelunde Master), an accomplished stylist whose name is unknown. Some of his finest work can be seen at **Elmelunde Kirke** (Kirkebakken 41; ⏲8am-4.45pm Apr-Sep, to 3.45pm rest of yr) on the road to Møns Klint.

Activities

Although testing at times, cycling on Møn is rewarding given the island's uncharacteristic hilliness. The tourist office has maps of cycling routes on the island. In Stege, bike rental is available at **Point S** (Storegade 91; per day Dkr65; ⏲7.30am-5pm Mon-Fri, 9am-1pm Sat). The **Min Købmand** (Thyravej 6; ⏲7am-8pm) supermarket in Klintholm Havn also hires out bikes.

Sleeping & Eating

The tourist office has a brochure with a list of B&Bs on the island. You're welcome to use the tourist-office phone free of charge to book accommodation. Singles/doubles in a private home average Dkr300/400.

In Stege, there's a good bakery, **Din Bager** (Storegade 36; pastries from Dkr11; ⏲5am-5pm Mon-Fri, 6am-2pm Sat, 6am-1pm Sun), and several large supermarkets, including **SuperBrugsen** (Vasen 3; ⏲9am-7pm Mon-Fri, 8am-6pm Sat, 10am-6pm Sun). The most central supermarket is **Kiwi Mini Pris** (Storegade 44; ⏲8am-10pm).

Camping Møns Klint CAMPGROUND €

(☎55 81 20 25; www.campingmoensklint.dk; Klintevej 544, Børre Møn; campsites per adult/child/tent Dkr90/66/30; ⏲mid-Apr–Oct; @ 🏊) This massive, family-friendly, three-star site is about 3km northwest of Møns Klint. The camping ground has impressive facilities: a 25m outdoor swimming pool, guest kitchen, coin laundry, tennis court, mini-golf, bike hire (Dkr100 per day), boat hire (Dkr50 per hour), internet cafe and a shop. In high summer there are guided kayak tours (Dkr350) and nature workshops in English, German and Danish.

Danhostel Møns Klint HOSTEL €

(☎55 81 24 34; www.danhostel.dk/hostel/danhostel-moens-klint; Klintholm Havnevej 17A,

Borre; dm/s/d/tr from Dkr180/340/380/470; P) With lots of shady trees and scurrying hares, this hostel has a pleasant lakeside location 3km northwest of Møns Klint. There are 29 rooms, cosy seating areas and plenty of kids' toys. The hostel also offers bike rental (per day Dkr70). From Stege, take bus 667.

★Tohøjgaard Gæstgivern GUESTHOUSE €€
(☎55 81 60 67; www.tohoejgaard.com; Rytsebækvej 17, Hjelm; r Dkr480-700; ⊙mid-Mar–mid-Oct; P) Book ahead to slumber at one of Denmark's most coveted guesthouses: an 1875 farmhouse surrounded by fields, a 4000-year-old burial mound and calming sea views. Six eclectic, individually themed guest rooms are a cosy combo of flea-market finds, books and fluffy bathrobes, while the welcome tray of organic local chocolates, seasonal fruit and juice is a sweet extra touch. Breakfast is an extra Dkr70.

On Fridays and Saturdays, host Christine serves fabulous Scandinavian dinners (two courses Dkr195) at a communal table in the converted milking room. On all other nights, she offers a simpler 'biker's supper' (from Dkr130). The guesthouse lies 9.5km southwest of Stege; if catching public transport, you'll need to walk about 4km to get here.

★Liselund Ny Slot HOTEL €€
(☎55 81 20 81; www.liselundslot.dk; Langebjergvej 6; s/d incl breakfast Dkr800/1200, 2nd night d Dkr900; P) If the idea of slumbering in a romantic, 19th-century manor house appeals, Liselund Ny Slot has your name all over its art-clad walls. The 17 rooms are simply yet elegantly furnished, with old wooden floorboards and views of the calming gardens. Each room is named after a Hans Christian Andersen fairy tale, and the in-house **cafe** (cakes Dkr25, lunch Dkr85-135; ⊙10am-6pm daily late Jun-early Aug, shorter hours rest of year) comes with enchanting lawn seating.

Motel Stege MOTEL €€
(☎55 81 35 35; www.motel-stege.dk; Provstestræde 4; s Dkr550-650, d Dkr575-750; P) Your best bet in central Stege, Motel Stege offers 12 rooms that are simple yet smart. Those in the main building have a mezzanine level (accessible by ladder), and sleep up to four. Rooms in the annexe have their own kitchenette, while all guests have access to a homely communal kitchen and dining area. Added comforts include a washer and dryer.

Bryghuset Møn DANISH, INTERNATIONAL €€
(Storegade 18, Stege; lunch Dkr65-115, dinner mains Dkr119-180; ⊙11am-9pm daily Apr–mid-Oct, shorter hours rest of year) Tucked away inside Luffes Gård courtyard, Møn's well-known microbrewery serves good-quality lunch grub, including smørrebrød (open sandwiches), butter-fried fish fillet with homemade pickles, and hearty meatballs with red cabbage and cucumber salad. The dinner menu is a more limited affair, usually with one meat and one fish option. Wash it all down with one of the microbrewery's silky beers.

David's INTERNATIONAL €€
(www.davids.nu; Storegade 11a, Stege; dishes Dkr89-150; ⊙10am-5pm Mon-Fri, to 4pm Sat & Sun) David's open kitchen prepares fabulous, contemporary cafe fare. Tuck into the celebrated 'tapas' platter or opt for gems like the roll of smoked salmon and apples with trout mousse and green salad. House-made cakes keep gluttons happy. Sunny days mean alfresco noshing in the leafy courtyard. No credit cards.

Klintholm Røgeri SEAFOOD €€
(Thyravej 25, Klintholm Havn; lunch/dinner buffet Dkr125/165; ⊙noon-4pm & 6-9pm) Head to Klintholm's harbourside smokehouse to tackle a lip-smacking buffet of grilled, smoked and marinated ocean treats. Kids under 12 are charged half-price.

ℹ Information

Møn tourist office (☎55 86 04 00; www.visitmoen.dk; Storegade 2, Stege; ⊙9.30am-4pm Mon-Fri, 9.30am-12.30pm & 2.30-4pm Sat Jun & Aug, 9.30am-5pm Mon-Fri, 9.30am-12.30pm & 2.30-5pm Sat Jul, shorter hours rest of year) is at the entrance to Stege. As well as offering information on the island, the website allows you to book accommodation online out of hours.

ℹ Getting There & Around

From Copenhagen take the train to Vordingborg (Dkr138, 1½ hours, at least once hourly). From Vordingborg, bus 660R (and occasionally bus 664) run to Stege (Dkr48, 45 minutes), half-hourly on weekdays and hourly on weekends.

On Møn, the most frequent service is bus 667, which goes from Stege to Klintholm Havn (Dkr24, 30 minutes) via Keldby, Elmelunde and Magleby. Bus 678 runs hourly between Stege and Møns Klint (Dkr24, 35 minutes). The last bus to Møns Klint departs Stege at 5.40pm. The last bus back from Møns Klint is at 6.06pm (6.36pm on weekends).

BORNHOLM

POP 39,920

Bornholm is a little Baltic pearl: a Danish island, yet lying some 200km east of the mainland, north of Poland. It boasts more hours of sunshine than any other part of the country, as well as gorgeous sandy beaches, idyllic fishing villages, numerous historic sights, endless cycling paths and a burgeoning reputation for culinary curiosities and ceramic artists and glassmakers.

Unique among Bornholm's attractions are its four 12th-century round churches, splendid buildings with whitewashed walls, 2m thick, that are framed by solid buttresses and crowned with black, conical roofs. Each was designed as both a place of worship and a fortress against enemy attacks, with a gun-slot-pierced upper storey. All four churches are still used for Sunday services, but are otherwise open to visitors. The island's tourist website, with information on accommodation, activities, events and transport, is at www.bornholm.info.

History

Bornholm's history reflects its position at the heart of the Baltic and, in its time, Sweden, Germany and Soviet Russia have occupied it. A Danish possession since the Middle Ages, the island fell into Swedish hands in the 17th century, but was won back for Denmark by a fierce local rebellion.

The island suffered cruelly in the chaos at the end of WWII. It was occupied by the Nazis, but when Germany surrendered in May 1945 the commander on Bornholm resisted and Rønne and Nexø suffered heavy damage from Soviet air raids. On 9 May, the island was handed over to the Soviets, who remained in situ until the following year, when Bornholm was returned to Denmark.

Getting There & Away

AIR

Danish Airport Transport (p125) operates several flights a day between Copenhagen and Rønne. Book ahead for cheaper flights.

BOAT & TRAIN

Bornholmer Færgen (70 23 15 15; www.faergen.dk; adult/child 12-15/under 11 Dkr290/145/free, car incl 5 passengers Dkr1625) operates an overnight ferry service from Køge, 39km south of Copenhagen, to Bornholm. The ferry departs daily at 12.30am and arrives at 6am. On the upside, the overnight journey makes good use of your travel time. On the downside, the trip to Køge (around 30 minutes by train) adds additional cost and time if travelling from Copenhagen.

Bornholm

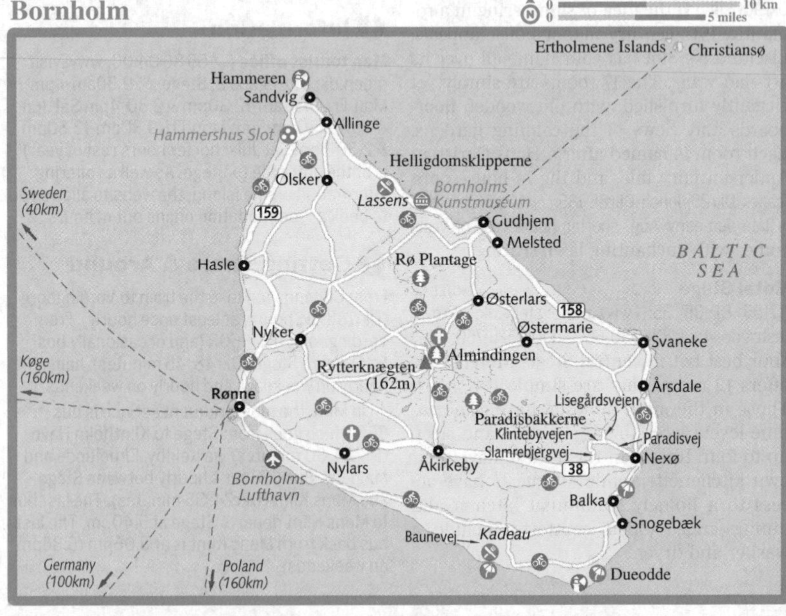

From Copenhagen, **DSB** (www.dsb.dk) offers a combined train/catamaran ticket (one way adult/child Dkr328/149) that includes train travel to Ystad (Sweden) and high-speed catamaran from Ystad to Rønne on Bornholm. This is the most cost- and time-effective option from Copenhagen, usually taking no more than 3½ hours. It's also possible to drive to Ystad and cross with your car from there.

Getting Around

TO/FROM THE AIRPORT

Bornholms Lufthavn is located 5km southeast of Rønne, on the road to Dueodde. Buses 6 and 7 connect the airport to Rønne.

BICYCLE

Bornholm is criss-crossed by more than 230km of bike trails. The tourist office in Rønne sells the 82-page English-language *Bicycle Routes on Bornholm* (Dkr129), which maps out routes and describes sights along the way. It also provides a free, simple map of cycling routes on the island.

Next to the tourist office in Rønne, **Bornholms Cykeludlejning** (bike rental per 1/2/7 days Dkr70/140/390; 9.30am-5.30pm Mon-Fri, 9am-noon & 2-5.30pm Sat) has bikes for hire. Rental bikes are commonly available at hostels and camping grounds.

BUS

Bornholms Amts Trafikselskab (BAT; www.bat.dk) operates bus services on the island. Fares cost Dkr13 per zone; the maximum fare is for five zones. Ask the bus driver about the 'RaBATkort' (10 rides; Dkr80), which can be used by more than one person and saves about 20%. Day/week passes cost Dkr150/500. Children travel for half-price. Buses operate all year, but services are less frequent from October to April. Buses 7 and 8 circumnavigate the island, stopping at all major towns and settlements. Other buses make direct runs from Rønne to Nexø, Svaneke, Gudhjem and Sandvig.

CAR & SCOOTER

Europcar (56 95 43 00; www.europcar.com; Nordre Kystvej 1, Rønne) is at the Q8 petrol station and rents cars from around Dkr600 per day as well as scooters. It has another branch at the airport.

Rønne

POP 13,570

Though Rønne is not the most charming of the island's harbour towns, virtually everyone who visits Bornholm will end up spending time here. The town offers some engaging museums, an old quarter of cobbled streets and cottages, and a reasonably sized shopping area.

Sights

With its handsome period buildings and cobblestone streets, the old neighbourhood west of Store Torv is especially charming. Two standout streets here are **Laksegade** and **Storegade**.

Bornholms Museum MUSEUM
(www.bornholmsmuseum.dk; Sankt Mortensgade 29; adult/child incl entry to Hjorths Fabrik Dkr70/free; 10am-5pm Jul–mid-Aug, closed Sun mid-May–Jun & mid-Aug–mid-Oct, shorter hours rest of year) Prehistoric finds including weapons, tools and jewellery are on show at Bornholm's main museum, which has a surprisingly large and varied collection of local history exhibits, including some interesting Viking finds. A good maritime section is decked out like the interior of a ship and there's a hotchpotch of nature displays, antique toys, Roman coins, pottery and paintings.

Hjorths Fabrik MUSEUM
(www.bornholmsmuseum.dk/hjorths; Krystalgade 5; adult/child incl entry to Bornholms Museum Dkr70/free; museum 10am-5pm Jul–mid-Aug, closed Sun mid-May–Jun & mid-Aug–mid-Oct, shorter hours rest of year, studio 10am-4pm Mon-Fri mid-May–mid-Oct) This ceramics museum features a working studio, and watching the master artisans turn clay into beautifully moulded works of art is the real highlight. You'll find some fetching, locally made wares for sale in the shop in front (which is free to enter).

★**Nylars Rundkirke** CHURCH
(Kirkevej 10K, Nylars; 7am-6pm Apr-Sep, 8am-3.30pm Oct-Mar) Built in 1150, Nylars Rundkirke is the most well-preserved and easily accessible round church in the Rønne area. Its central pillar is adorned with wonderful 13th-century frescoes, the oldest in Bornholm. The works depict scenes from the Creation myth, including Adam and Eve's expulsion from the Garden of Eden. The cylindrical nave has three storeys, the top one a watchman's gallery that served as a defence lookout in medieval times.

Sleeping

The tourist office can book rooms (singles/doubles Dkr225/400) in private homes in Rønne; there's no booking fee.

Danhostel Rønne HOSTEL €
(☎56 95 13 40; www.danhostel-roenne.dk; Arsenalvej 12; dm/s/d/tr Dkr200/350/450/530; ⊙Apr-late Oct; P) The immaculately kept 140-bed hostel near Galløkken Camping is a secluded, whitewashed building with a neatly tended garden. Expect small, tidy, if somewhat-soulless dorms.

Radisson Blu Fredensborg Hotel HOTEL €€
(☎56 90 44 44; www.bornholmhotels.dk; Strandvejen 116; r incl breakfast from Dkr1125; P@) Perched on a pleasant knoll overlooking wave-pounded rocks at the southern end of Rønne, the Fredensborg has 72 comfortable rooms with classic 20th-century Scandi style (admittedly, some rooms are due for a revamp), all with sea views, some with rather pokey '70s-style bathrooms and a few with access for people in wheelchairs. There's also a sauna, tennis court and restaurant.

Eating & Drinking

There's a reasonable variety of restaurants and cafes in and around the main square of Store Torv, though no standout venues.

Jensen's Bageri BAKERY €
(Snellemark 41; focaccias Dkr16, pastries Dkr10; ⊙6am-5.30pm Mon-Fri, to 3pm Sat & Sun) Nibble on freshly baked focaccias, sausage rolls and Danish pastries at this petite bakery, located between the tourist office and the main town square, Store Torv.

Oste-Hjørnet DELI €
(Ostergade 40B; cheese boards from Dkr70; ⊙9am-5.30pm Mon-Thu, to 6pm Fri, to 1pm Sat) This gut-rumbling little deli stocks both local and foreign slabs of gourmet cheeses, as well as locally made charcuterie, stuffed savoury pancakes and fresh bread – the perfect ingredients for a picnic.

Information

There's free internet access at the **library** (Pingels Allé; ⊙9.30am-6pm Mon-Fri, to 2pm Sat).

Tourist Office (Bornholms Velkomstcenter; ☎56 95 95 00; www.bornholm.info; Nordre Kystvej 3; ⊙9am-6.30pm late Jun-early Aug, shorter hours rest of year) A few minutes' walk from the harbour, this large, friendly office has masses of information on all of Bornholm and Christiansø.

Dueodde

Backed by deep green woodlands and dramatic dunes, Dueodde has a vast stretch of white-sand beach that most of Europe can only dream about. There's no village, just a bus stop with a single hotel, a steakhouse restaurant, a cluster of kiosks selling ice cream and hot dogs, and the necessary public toilets to cope with the rush from tour coaches in summer. It can be a crowded trek for a couple of hundred metres along boardwalks to reach the superb beach. Once there, head left or right for wide-open spaces.

Sleeping & Eating

Dueodde Vandrerhjem & Camping Ground HOSTEL, CAMPGROUND €
(☎56 48 81 19; www.dueodde.dk; Skorkkegårdsvejen 17; s/d/tr/q Dkr225/375/450/530, campsites per adult/child Dkr72/37, tents Dkr30-40; ⊙May-Sep; P) This upbeat beachside hostel-and-campground combo is a 10-minute walk east of the bus stop. The place also offers pleasant, pine-clad cabins/apartments for rent at Dkr4500 per week for two persons. Perks include an indoor swimming pool.

★**Kadeau** MODERN SCANDINAVIAN €€€
(☎56 97 82 50; www.kadeau.dk; Baunevej 18; lunch dishes Dkr125-150, 4-/6-/8-course dinner from Dkr600/750/950; ⊙noon-4pm & 5.30pm-midnight Jul–mid-Aug, shorter hours rest of year) Book ahead to experience one of Denmark's most exciting and innovative destination restaurants. The menu is a confident, creative celebration of Nordic produce and foraged ingredients, including wild herbs from the adjacent beach and woods. Lunch options are limited but inspired, though the true tour de force is dinner, where dishes such as sugar-cured scallops in chamomile-infused milk, served with pickled celeriac, will have you swooning.

Take note that although Kadeau's address is in Åkirkeby, the restaurant is actually 8km southeast of the town, right on the beach.

Bornholm's East Coast

Bornholm's east coast tends to be fairly built-up and is punctuated by several settlements, all with some interest as stopping-off places.

Snogebæk is a small shoreside fishing village that hangs on to its authenticity because of its small fleet of working boats and its scat-

LOCAL KNOWLEDGE

RASMUS KOFOED: SOMMELIER

Bornholm native Rasmus Kofoed is the founder of Dueodde restaurant Kadeau.

Must-Eats

Don't miss smoked herring and a beer at a *rogeri* (smokehouse). Smokehouses are part of Bornholm's history, and one of the island's simple pleasures. One of the best and most consistent is Rogeriet i Svaneke (p80). Ditch the chips (they're for the tourists) and ask the staff for a platter of whatever is best that day.

Must-Dos

Walk around **Svaneke**. The locals have been very active in protecting its built heritage and I think it's the most beautiful town on Bornholm. Then there's **Paradisbakkerne**, with its changing landscapes and sublime views. It's called 'Paradise Hills' with good reason.

Did You Know?

We can grow figs on Bornholm. The island is one of the mildest areas of Denmark. It takes a while to warm up in June but then it stays warm for longer, which allows some exotic things to grow. Bornholm is also home to Denmark's biggest chef competition, **Sol Over Gudhjem** (Sun Over Gudhjem; www.solovergudhjemkonkurrence.dk). It takes place in June and sees some of the country's best chefs battle it out using local produce.

tering of fishing huts and cabins. Just north of Snogebæk is the fine beach of **Balka Strand**.

Nexø is Bornholm's second-largest town. It took a hammering from Soviet bombers in WWII and today much of what you see from the harbour outwards is a fairly functional reconstruction. **Nexø Museum** (Havnen 2; adult/child Dkr30/10; ⏲10am-4pm Mon-Fri, to 1pm Sat Jul & Aug, shorter hours rest of year) is at the harbour and is packed with maritime flotsam and jetsam, including an old-fashioned diving suit, cannons, WWII mines and the inner workings of a lighthouse. The town's **tourist office** (☎56 49 70 79; www.bornholm.info; Sdr Hammer 2G; ⏲10am-5pm Mon-Fri, to 2pm Sat & Sun Jul & Aug, closed Sun May, Jun, Sep & Oct, shorter hours rest of year) is down by the harbour.

Three kilometres northwest of Nexø lies **Paradisbakkerne**, a natural wonderland of forest, high-heath bogs and rift valleys. To get here from Nexø, take Paradisvej (which becomes Klintebyvejen) inland and turn right at Lisegårdsvejen, which leads to a car park, toilets and a map of the area's colour-coded walking tracks.

The harbour town of **Svaneke** has award-winning historic buildings, especially those near the village church, a few minutes' walk south of the centre. The seasonal **tourist office** (☎56 49 70 79; Peter F Heerings Gade 7; ⏲10am-4pm Mon-Fri mid-Jun–mid-Sep) is down by the harbour.

Sleeping

Danhostel Svaneke HOSTEL €
(☎56 49 62 42; www.danhostel-svaneke.dk; Reberbanevej 9, Svaneke; dm/s/d Dkr160/450/510; ⏲Apr-late Oct; P) A basic but modern low-roofed hostel, 1km south of the centre of Svaneke. Facilities include a communal kitchen and laundry facilities.

Hotel Balka Strand HOTEL €€
(☎56 49 49 49; www.hotelbalkastrand.dk; Boulevarden 9; s/d incl breakfast Dkr875/1075; P ≋) Only 200m from Balka's sandy beach, this smart, friendly hotel has double rooms and cheery apartments, all with modern decor. On-site pluses include a pool, massage treatments, bar and restaurant.

Hotel Siemsens Gaard HOTEL €€
(☎56 49 61 49; www.siemsens.dk; Havnebryggen 9, Svaneke; s incl breakfast Dkr850, d incl breakfast from Dkr1275; ⏲closed Jan & Feb; P @) Although the straightforward rooms at this harbourside hotel are a little dowdy, they are comfortable and equipped with fridge and bath (some doubles even have kitchenettes). Request a room in the old wing, a beautiful half-timbered building that dates from the mid-17th century. Service is friendly and guests can rent bikes for Dkr75 per day.

Eating & Drinking

★ **Rogeriet i Svaneke** SEAFOOD €

(Fiskergade 12; counter items Dkr35-115; ⏲9am-8.30pm Jul & Aug, shorter hours rest of year) You'll find a fine selection of excellent, smoked fare at the long counter here, including wonderful smørrebrød (open sandwiches), great trout, salmon, herring, shrimp, fried fish cakes and tasty *frikadeller* (Danish meatballs). Chow inside with a view of the massive, blackened doors of the smoking ovens or at the outdoor picnic tables overlooking the old cannons.

Bryghuset MICROBREWERY

(Torv 5; lunch Dkr69-129, dinner mains Dkr149-298; ⏲10am-midnight, kitchen closes 9.30pm) This is one of the most popular dining and drinking options on the island, known throughout Denmark for its excellent beers brewed on the premises. If you haven't already eaten, it also serves decent, hearty pub grub. Danish lunch classics include smørrebrød (open sandwiches) and *fiskefrikadeller* (fish cakes) with rye bread remouldade. Dinner mains are mostly juicy, fleshy affairs.

Gudhjem

POP 710

Gudhjem is the best-looking of Bornholm's harbour towns. Its rambling high street is crowned by a squat windmill standing over half-timbered houses and sloping streets that roll down to the picture-perfect harbour. The town is a good base for exploring the rest of Bornholm, with cycle and walking trails, convenient bus connections, plenty of places to eat and stay and a boat service to Christiansø. Interestingly, the harbour was one of the settings for the Oscar-winning film *Pelle the Conqueror*, based on the novel by Bornholm writer Martin Andersen Nexø.

Sights

A bike path leads inland 4km south from Gudhjem to the thick-walled, buttressed **Østerlars Rundkirke**, the most impressive of the island's round churches – buses 1 and 9 go by the church.

★ **Oluf Høst Museet** MUSEUM

(www.ohmus.dk; Løkkegade 35; adult/child Dkr75/35; ⏲11am-5pm mid-Jun–Aug, shorter hours rest of year; 👪) This wonderful museum contains the workshops and paintings of Oluf Høst (1884–1966), one of Bornholm's best-known artists. The museum occupies the home where Oluf lived from 1929 until his death. The beautiful back garden is home to a little hut with paper, paints and pencils for kids with a creative itch.

★ **Bornholms Kunstmuseum** MUSEUM

(www.bornholms-kunstmuseum.dk; Otto Bruuns Plads 1; adult/child Dkr70/free; ⏲10am-5pm Jun-Aug, closed Mon Apr, May, Sep & Oct, shorter hours rest of year) Occupying a svelte, modern building and overlooking sea, fields and (weather permitting) the distant isle of Christiansø, Bornholms Kunstmuseum echoes Copenhagen's Louisiana. The museum exhibits paintings by artists from the Bornholm School, including Olaf Rude, Oluf Høst and Edvard Weie, who painted during the first half of the 20th century. The art museum also has works by other Danish artists, most notably paintings of Bornholm by Skagen artist Michael Ancher.

There's a cafe on-site. Buses stop in front of the museum (bus 2 from Rønne; bus 4 or 8 between Gudhjem and Sandvig).

Sleeping & Eating

Danhostel Gudhjem HOSTEL €

(☎56 48 50 35; www.danhostel-gudhjem.dk; Løkkegade 7; dm/s/d Dkr220/385/490) Right by the harbour, this hostel has cosy, bright six-bed dorms. The reception is at a small grocery shop on Løkkegade, about 75m northwest of the hostel. Bikes can be hired for Dkr90 per day.

★ **Stammershalle Badehotel** BOUTIQUE HOTEL €€

(☎56 48 42 10; www.stammershalle-badehotel.dk; Sdr Strandvej 128, Rø; s/d incl breakfast from Dkr700/900; Ⓟ) Bornholm's most fabulous slumber spot occupies an imposing, early-20th-century bathing hotel overlooking a rocky part of the coast a few kilometres north of Gudhjem. It's a calming blend of whitewashed timber and understated Cape Cod–esque chic, not to mention the home of one of Denmark's up-and-coming New Nordic restaurants, Lassens. Book well ahead, especially in the summer high season.

Jantzens Hotel HOTEL €€

(☎56 48 50 17; www.jantzenshotel.dk; Brøddegade 33; s Dkr850, d Dkr1200-1300) One of the island's true charmers, Jantzens offers smallish but supremely cosy, stylish rooms in a handsome period building. Some rooms have sea views and the breakfast is one of Bornholm's best.

Gudhjem Rogeri SEAFOOD €
(Gudhjem Harbour; lunch/dinner buffet Dkr120/180; ⏲10am-9pm Jul-Aug, shorter hours rest of year) Gudhjem's popular smokehouse serves deli-style fish and salads, including the classic Sol over Gudhjem (Sun over Gudhjem; smoked herring with a raw egg yolk). There's both indoor and outdoor seating, some of it very challenging to get to (the upper floor is reached by a rope ladder!). There's live folk, country or rock most nights in the summer.

★ **Lassens** MODERN SCANDINAVIAN €€€
(☎56 48 42 10; www.stammershalle-badehotel.dk; Sdr Strandvej 128, Rø; small/large tasting menu Dkr450/550; ⏲6-11pm Jul & Aug, closed Mon May, Jun & Sep, shorter hours rest of year) There are two restaurants foodies cannot afford to miss on Bornholm: Kadeau and Lassens, located at Stammershalle Badehotel. The latter is home to award-winning chef Daniel Kruse, whose pure, showstopping compositions might include smoked scallops with Icelandic *skyr* (strained yoghurt), dehydrated olives, truffle mayonnaise, parsley sauce and malt chips. Service is knowledgable and personable, and the sea-and-sunset panorama as inspired as the kitchen's creations. Bookings are essential.

ℹ Information

Tourist Office (☎56 48 64 48; Ejnar Mikkelsensvej 17, Gudhjem Harbour; ⏲10am-4pm Mon-Sun Jun-Aug) Gudhjem Turistbureau is at the library, just a block inland from the harbour.

Sandvig & Allinge

Sandvig and Allinge have grown together over the years and are generally referred to as Sandvig-Allinge. They are tucked away to the east of Bornholm's rocky northwestern

WORTH A TRIP

CHRISTIANSØ

If you think Bornholm is as remote as Denmark gets, you're wrong. Even further east, way out in the merciless Baltic, is tiny Christiansø, an intensely atmospheric 17th-century fortress-island about 500m long and an hour's sail northeast of Bornholm. It's well worth making time for a day trip; its rugged, moss-covered rocks, historic stone buildings and even hardier people are reminiscent of the Faroe Islands. A seasonal fishing hamlet since the Middle Ages, the island fell briefly into Swedish hands in 1658, after which Christian V decided to turn the island into an invincible naval fortress. Bastions and barracks were built; a church, school and prison followed.

By the 1850s the island was no longer needed as a forward base against Sweden and the navy withdrew. Soldiers who wanted to stay on as fishermen were allowed to live as free tenants in the old cottages. Their offspring, and a few latter-day fisherfolk and artists, currently comprise Christiansø's 100 residents. The entire island is an unspoiled reserve – there are no cats or dogs, no cars and no modern buildings – allowing the rich birdlife, including puffins, to prosper.

There's a small **local history museum** (Little Tower; museum adult/child 20/5kr; ⏲museum 11.30am-4pm Jul-Aug, 11.30am-4pm Mon-Fri, 11.30am-2pm Sat & Sun May-Jun & Sep) in Lille Tårn (LittleTower) and a great 360-degree view from the top of **Store Tårn** (Great Tower; ⏲noon-4pm Jun-Aug) FREE. Otherwise, the main activity is walking the footpaths along the fortified walls and batteries that skirt the island. There are skerries with nesting seabirds and a secluded **swimming cove** on Christiansø's eastern side.

In summer camping is allowed at **Christiansø Teltplads** (☎24 42 12 22; campsites Dkr75-100; ⏲May-Aug), a small field called the Duchess Battery. **Christiansø Gæstgiveriet** (☎56 46 20 15; www.christiansoekro.dk; s/d without bathroom Dkr1050/1150; ⏲closed late Dec-Jan), the island's only inn, has six rooms with shared bathroom and a restaurant. Booking ahead for a room is advised. There's a small food store and a kiosk.

Christiansøfarten (☎56 48 51 76; www.bornholmexpress.dk; return ticket adult/child Dkr250/125) operates passenger ferries to Christiansø from Gudhjem year-round. Check the website for up-to-date timetables.

tip and boast an excellent sandy beach to add to their beguiling appeal. Sandvig is a small fishing village, while Allinge has a good a range of restaurants and hotels.

Bornholm's best-known sight, **Hammershus Slot**, is 3km south on the road to Rønne. The impressive, substantial ruins of this 13th-century castle are the largest of their kind in Scandinavia. They are perched dramatically over the sea, flanked by cliffs and a deep valley. One of the best ways of reaching the castle is by following footpaths from Sandvig through the heather-covered hills of Hammeren – a wonderful hour-long hike. The trail begins by the camping ground. If there is a must-see sight on Bornholm, this castle is it.

Sleeping

Byskrivergarden GUESTHOUSE €€
(☎56 48 08 86; www.byskrivergaarden.dk; Løsebækegade 3, Allinge; s/d incl breakfast Dkr750/1000; ⏲mid-May–mid-Sep; P) This enchanting, white-walled, black-beamed converted farmhouse right on the water is our choice of places to stay in Allinge. The rooms (try to get the sea-facing not the road-facing ones) are simply yet smartly decorated in a contemporary style. There's a pleasant garden, a large, cheerful breakfast room and kelp-filled rock pools nearby if you fancy taking a dip.

Hotel Romantik HOTEL €€
(☎20 23 15 24; www.hotelromantik.dk; Stranvejen 68, Sandvig; s/d from Dkr650/800, 2- to 4-person apt per week from Dkr3402; P @) The coast-hugging Romantik offers smart, comfortable hotel rooms, some with sea views. Even better are the 40 stylish apartments, complete with modern kitchenettes. The hotel also offers simple, satisfactory budget rooms (singles/doubles from Dkr600/700) in a nondescript annexe across the street.

Eating

Nordbornholms Røgeri SEAFOOD €
(Kæmpestranden 2, Allinge; buffet Dkr180; ⏲11am-9pm daily) Several of Bornholm's best chefs praise this smokehouse as the island's best. Not only does it serve a drool-inducing buffet of locally smoked fish, salads and soup, but its waterside setting makes it the perfect spot to savour Bornholm's Baltic flavours. Kids aged between five and 11 can tackle the buffet at half price.

FUNEN

POP 466,280

Funen is Denmark's proverbial middle child. Lacking Zealand's capital-city pull or Jutland's geographic dominance, it's often overlooked by visitors, who perhaps make a whistle-stop visit to Hans Christian Andersen's birthplace and museum in the island's capital, Odense. But there is more to Funen (Fyn in Danish): the beautiful harbour towns of Svendborg and Faaborg, and Denmark's only Viking ship grave at Ladby, not to mention the island's manor houses and castles, some dating back to the 14th century.

Odense

POP 172,500

Currently undergoing a major revamp, Funen's millennium-old capital is a cheerful, compact city, ideal for feet and bicycles, and with enough diversions to keep you hooked for a day ot two. It was here that Hans Christian Andersen entered the world, a fact hard to miss given the city's string of Andersen-related attractions, not to mention its Andersen-themed pedestrian lights. Yet there's more to the place than hatted storytellers, including contemporary-art-hub Brandts, Denmark's best zoo, and a buzzing cafe and bar scene.

Sights

★HC Andersens Hus MUSEUM
(www.museum.odense.dk; Bangs Boder 29; adult/child Dkr95/free; ⏲10am-5pm Jul & Aug, 10am-4pm Tue-Sun Sep-Jun) Lying amid the miniaturised streets of the old poor quarter (now often referred to the HCA Quarter), this museum delivers a thorough, lively telling of Andersen's extraordinary life and times. His achievements are put into an interesting historical context and leavened by some engaging audiovisual material and quirky exhibits (such as the display on his height – HCA was 25cm taller than the national average at the time).

Børnekulturhuset Fyrtøjet CULTURAL CENTRE
(www.museum.odense.dk; Hans Jensens Stræde 21; admission Dkr80-95; ⏲10am-4pm Fri-Sun Feb–mid-Dec, daily during school holidays; 👪) Next to HC Andersens Hus is the charming Fyrtøjet (The Tinderbox culture house for children), where kids are encouraged to explore the world of Hans Christian Andersen through storytelling and music (the storytelling is

in Danish, but the activities are suitable for all languages). Kids can dress up, have their face painted, act out stories and draw fairy-tale pictures in the art studio.

HC Andersens Barndomshjem MUSEUM
(www.museum.odense.dk; Munkemøllestræde 3-5; adult/child Dkr30/free; ⏲10am-5pm Jul & Aug, to 3pm or 4pm Tue-Sun Sep-Jun) The small childhood home of Hans Christian Andersen paints a picture of the writer's poverty-stricken childhood. He lived here from 1807 to 1819, aged two to 14.

Odense Zoo ZOO
(www.odensezoo.dk; Sønder Blvd 306; adult/child Dkr175/95; ⏲from 10am daily; 🚸) Denmark's showpiece zoo borders both banks of the river, 2km south of the city centre. It's an active supporter of conservation and education programs, and its residents include tigers, lions, giraffes, zebras and chimpanzees, plus an 'oceanium' with penguins and manatees.

The highlight is the zoo's Kiwara area, an open space that aims to mimic the African savannah. You can feed giraffes (Dkr70) or take in the views from the upper deck of the excellent visitor centre.

Child-friendly drawcards include a playground and lots of animal-related games. Check the website's calendar for details of feeding times and daily events. Closing time varies – generally from 4pm (winter) to 7pm (summer).

Odense Aafart boats stop at the zoo during peak season. A number of buses run here frequently (40, 42, 51, 52, 151, 152; Dkr23), or you can walk or cycle the 2km-long wooded riverside path that begins at Munke Mose.

★**Brandts** MUSEUM
(www.brandts.dk; Brandts Torv; combined ticket adult/child Dkr90/free, after 5pm Thu free; ⏲10am-5pm Tue, Wed & Fri-Sun, noon-9pm Thu) The former textile mill on Brandts Passage has been beautifully converted into a sprawling art centre, with thought-provoking, well-curated changing displays (including a riveting exhibition on tattooing when we last stopped by).

Brandts Samling (the permanent collection) traces 250 years of Danish art, from classic to modern, and includes an impressive assemblage of international photography.

Art highlights include portraits by Christoffer Wilhelm Eckersberg (the 'father of Danish painting'), plus HA Brendekilde's powerful *Udslidt* (Worn Out; 1889), depicting a collapsed farm worker, and PS Krøyer's radiant *Italienske markarbejdere* (Italian Field Laborers; 1880). Funen artists also feature – Johannes Larsen's *Svanerne letter, Fiil Sø* is a stunning depiction of swans taking flight.

On the 3rd floor, **Danmarks Mediemuseum** traces the history of the Danish media (primarily in Danish, but with a tablet provided for coverage in other languages).

The area around Brandts is worth a wander for great street art and murals.

Den Fynske Landsby MUSEUM
(www.museum.odense.dk; Sejerskovvej 20; adult/child Dkr85/free; ⏲10am-6pm daily Jul-Aug, 10am-5pm Tue-Sun Apr-Jun & Sep-Oct) Wind back the clock at this delightful open-air museum, which has relocated period houses from around Funen and created a small country village, complete with barnyard animals, a duck pond, apple trees and flower gardens. Costumed 'peasants' tend to the geese, while children in knickerbockers play with hoops and sticks.

The museum is in a green zone 4km south of the city centre; buses 110 and 111 (Dkr23) run nearby. The best way to get here is by boat: from May to August, Odense Aafart boats sail hourly from Munke Mose past the zoo to the end station at Fruens Bøge, from where it's a 15-minute woodland walk to reach the museum.

Sankt Knuds Kirke CHURCH
(www.odense-domkirke.dk; Klosterbakken; ⏲10am-5pm Apr-Oct, to 4pm Nov-Mar) Odense's imposing 14th-century Gothic cathedral reflects the city's medieval wealth and stature. Its most intriguing attraction lies in

ℹ BRIDGE CROSSINGS

Funen is connected to Zealand by the **Storebælts Forbindlesen** (Great Belt's Bridge) and to Jutland by the **Lillebælts Bro** (Little Belt's Bridge). Storebælts Forbindlesen is an impressive span, running between the industrial towns of Korsør and Nyborg. It covers 18km – even longer than the Øresunds Fixed Link to Sweden. If you're taking a train, the cost of crossing is included in your fare; however, if you're driving, there's a costly bridge toll each way (one-way toll motorcycle Dkr125, small/medium/large car Dkr125/235/360). For more information, click onto www.storebaelt.dk.

the chilly crypt, down an inconspicuous staircase to the right of the altar. Here you'll find a glass case containing the 900-year-old skeleton of Denmark's patron saint, King Canute (Knud) II, alongside the bones of his younger brother Benedikt.

Møntergården MUSEUM
(www.museum.odense.dk; Mønterstræde; adult/child Dkr50/free; ⌚10am-5pm Jun-Aug, 10am-4pm Tue-Sun Sep-May) This revamped city showcase is a model of good museum design (something the Danes excel at). In 'Funen – Centre of the Universe', you walk through a chronological display of world events and see how Funen experienced them, including the effects of the Industrial Revolution on villages, and how locals experienced WWII occupation and the Cold War. Plus there are Viking-era finds, and information on how Funen came to be known as 'Denmark's garden' (hint: apples play a key role).

Carl Nielsen Museet MUSEUM
(www.museum.odense.dk; Claus Bergs Gade 11; ⌚11am-3pm Wed-Sun May-Aug, 3-7pm Thu-Fri, 11am-3pm Sat & Sun Sep-Apr) FREE In Odense's concert hall, displays detail the career of the city's native son Carl Nielsen (1865–1931), Denmark's best-known composer, and a skilled conductor and violinist. His music includes six symphonies, several operas and numerous hymns and popular songs.

Jernbanemuseet MUSEUM
(www.jernbanemuseet.dk; Dannebrogsgade 24; adult/child Dkr90/45; ⌚10am-4pm) Clamber aboard a diverting collection of 19th-century locomotives at the Danish Railway Museum, just behind the train station. The museum has two-dozen engines and wagons, including double-decker carriages and the Royal Saloon Car belonging to Christian IX, fully kitted out with everything a king might need.

Odense

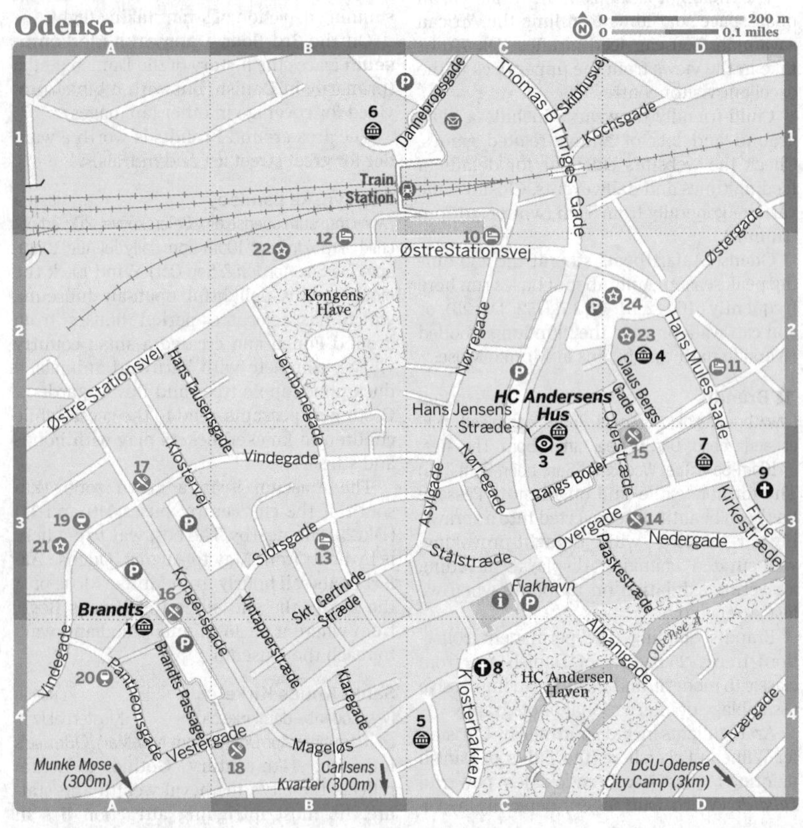

Sleeping

Danhostel Odense City HOSTEL €
(☎63 11 04 25; www.odensedanhostel.dk; Østre Stationsvej 31; dm/d from Dkr250/470; @) Perfectly placed for travellers, with the train and bus stations as neighbours and Kongens Have (a large park) directly opposite. All rooms at this large, modern hostel have bathrooms, and there's a guest kitchen, laundry and a basement TV room.

CabInn Odense Hotel HOTEL €
(☎63 14 57 00; www.cabinn.com; Østre Stationsvej 7; s/d from Dkr495/625; @) Facing off with the nearby Danhostel, fighting for the budget-conscious, train-travelling custom, is this member of the popular budget-bed chain. Sure, the beds are narrow and the no-frills rooms lack charm, but at these prices it's decent value.

DCU-Odense City Camp CAMPGROUND €
(☎66 11 47 02; www.camping-odense.dk; Odensevej 102; sites per adult/child/tent Dkr80/50/48, cabins from Dkr560; @ ≋ ♣) A neat campground in a wooded area (close to walking and cycling paths), with TV lounge, outdoor swimming pool and kids' amusements. There are also simple cabins for rent. It's about 4km south of the city centre, not far from Den Fynske Landsby museum. Take bus 21, 22 or 23.

First Hotel Grand HOTEL €€
(☎66 11 71 71; www.firsthotels.dk; Jernbanegade 18; r from Dkr750; P) Odense's grand dame dates from 1897 and her exterior is still a head-turner; she's had a skilful makeover in recent times, bringing the interior up to date, with lots of warm chocolate tones in the crisp, business-style room decor. The location is good and the breakfast excellent; the lovely lounge and brasserie areas are the best features. Online deals are good.

City Hotel HOTEL €€
(☎66 12 12 58; www.city-hotel-odense.dk; Hans Mules Gade 5; s/d incl breakfast from Dkr735/1035; P @) Handy for the gems of the HCA Quarter (museums, concert hall, farmers market), this hotel has friendly service and free parking, plus unremarkable but comfortable rooms. Its best features: the rooftop terrace, bike hire, and discounts at Den Gamle Kro (p86; under the same ownership). Discounted weekend and summer rates are good value.

Eating

The pedestrianised main street Vestergade houses several good restaurants and cafes, and there's a cluster of buzzing bars/bistros around Kongensgade and in Brandts Passage. Kitchens usually stop taking food orders at 9pm or 10pm.

Bazar Fyn INTERNATIONAL €
(www.bazarfyn.dk; Thriges Plads 3; ⌚10am-9pm Tue-Sun) More than just a great place to buy groceries, Bazar Fyn offers an insight into the multicultural side of Odense. The roofed market is about five minutes' walk from the train station. There's fresh fruit and veg and deli items (stores close 6pm), plus a food court where you can eat cheaply: Lebanese shwarma, Greek souvlaki, Indian curries, Vietnamese pho.

Odense

Top Sights
1 Brandts ... A4
2 HC Andersens Hus ... C3

Sights
3 Børnekulturhuset Fyrtøjet ... C3
4 Carl Nielsen Museet ... D2
5 HC Andersens Barndomshjem ... C4
6 Jernbanemuseet ... B1
7 Møntergården ... D3
8 Sankt Knuds Kirke ... C4
9 Vor Frue Kirke ... D3

Sleeping
10 CabInn Odense Hotel ... C2
11 City Hotel ... D2
12 Danhostel Odense City ... B2
13 First Hotel Grand ... B3

Eating
14 Den Gamle Kro ... D3
15 Fresh-Produce Market ... D3
16 LEI:K ... A3
17 Restaurant no.61 ... A3
18 Simoncini ... B4

Drinking & Nightlife
19 Den Smagløse Café ... A3
20 Nelle's Coffee & Wine ... A4

Entertainment
21 Dexter ... A3
22 Musikhuset Posten ... B2
23 Odense Koncerthus ... D2
24 Odeon (under construction) ... D2

DON'T MISS

STORY-BOOK SIDE STREETS

The east side of Odense's city centre has some of the city's oldest buildings. You can follow a rewarding walking route from the centre by crossing the busy Torvegade and strolling down Nedergade, a cobblestoned street lined with leaning, half-timbered houses and antique shops, and then returning via Overgade. En route you'll pass the 13th-century **Vor Frue Kirke** (Frue Kirkestræde 12B; ⏲10am-3pm Mon-Fri, to noon Sat).

From Overgade turn right into Overstræde, which spills into Sortebrødre Torv. This square (and adjoining Claus Bergs Gade) is the setting for Odense's belly-rumble-inducing outdoor **produce market** (Sortebrødre Torv; ⏲8am-1pm Wed & Sat), where vendors peddle a sprawling feast of fruits, vegetables, meats and seafood, bread, pastries, cheeses and flowers.

From the square, turn left into Bangs Boder, and then immediately right into what is a continuation of Bangs Boder. Awaiting is a charming cobblestoned street lined with pastel-coloured cottages. At the end of Bangs Boder, turn left into Hans Jensens Stræde, which leads back to busy Thomas B Thriges Gade and the centre of town beyond (note the Hans Christian Andersen–themed pedestrian lights).

★**Restaurant no.61** EUROPEAN €€
(☎61 69 10 35; www.no61.dk; Kongensgade 61; 2/3 courses Dkr255/295; ⏲from 5pm Tue-Sat) Winning plaudits for its embrace of classic European cooking, this cosy, farmhouse-chic bistro has a menu that changes monthly and is short, simple and seasonal. Each course presents two options: dishes plucked straight from the Funen fields might include white asparagus with truffle-infused hollandaise sauce, or a confection of strawberry, rhubarb, white chocolate and crème anglais. Reservations recommended.

Simoncini ITALIAN €€
(☎66 17 92 95; www.simoncini.dk; Vestergade 70; pasta Dkr110-140, mains Dkr195-250; ⏲from 5.30pm Mon-Sat) Seasonal, local produce with an authentic Italian spin is on offer in this rustically elegant dining space off the main drag. Guinea-fowl-filled ravioli, asparagus risotto and grilled octopus bring on an appetite; the monthly set menu offers excellent value (two/three/four courses Dkr199/249/299).

LEI:K INTERNATIONAL €€
(☎66 11 66 12; www.leik.dk; Brandts Passage 33-35; lunch Dkr99-119, dinner mains Dkr185-395; ⏲noon-11pm Mon-Wed, to 1am Thu-Sat) Odense looks all grown up at this scene-y hot spot, with a NYC-inspired, industrial-chic interior and a menu of burgers and fine cuts of beef (pimp your steak with foie gras or langoustine). Long hours are kept: lunch is served until 4pm, and a late-night kitchen opens until midnight Thursday to Sunday (to feed the cocktail-supping crowd).

Den Gamle Kro DANISH, FRENCH €€
(☎66 12 14 33; www.dengamlekro.eu; Overgade 23; smørrebrød Dkr71-135, dinner mains Dkr218-348; ⏲11am-10pm Mon-Sat, to 9pm Sun) The romantic Gamle Kro spreads through several half-timbered 17th-century houses, with a glass-roofed courtyard and medieval cellar. Lunch options include classic smørrebrød, while dinner is a decadent French affair: terrine of foie gras, duck breast with truffle sauce, plaice *meunière,* tournedos rossini. Seasonal set menus represent the best value (two/three courses Dkr298/385).

Drinking

★**Den Smagløse Café** BAR
(http://densmagloesecafe.dk; Vindegade 57; ⏲noon-midnight or later) This friendly, offbeat place describes itself as 'bringing to mind your grandmother's living room or your German uncle Udo's campervan'. It's *hyggelig* (cosy) in a slightly mad, wonderful way: old sofas and lamps, books and bric-a-brac. It serves all manner of drinks (coffee, cocktails, beer) and you can bring food if you like (there are pizzerias nearby).

Nelle's Coffee & Wine BAR
(www.nelles.dk; Pantheonsgade; ⏲9am-10pm Mon-Thu, to midnight Fri & Sat, 9am-5.30pm Sun) Get your morning caffeine fix here (Nelle's brews the city's best coffee), then return at wine time, to select from some 20 wines by the glass (from Dkr45). Nelle's doesn't serve meals but you won't go hungry: there are morning pastries, afternoon cakes and wine-time nuts or cheeseboards.

Carlsens Kvarter PUB
(www.carlsens.dk; Hunderupvej 19; ⌚noon-1am Mon-Sat, 1-7pm Sun) If soulful sipping appeals more than party crowds, this cosy neighbourhood pub has you covered. Friendly staff recommendations help ease you into the huge selection of microbrewed beer and whiskies – 138 on the beer menu alone, including Trappist ales and plenty of local stuff. If bad weather strikes, this could well be a place to hole up.

☆ Entertainment

Nightlife is centred on Brandts Passage, a pedestrian corridor lined with boutiques, restaurants, bars and cafes, many with outdoor seating in summer, leading to Brandts Klædefabrik.

Dexter LIVE MUSIC
(www.dexter.dk; Vindegade 65) An intimate live-music venue, where the music is primarily (but not exclusively) jazz, blues, folk and world, from Danish and international artists. There are jam sessions every Monday (free entry). Check the concert calendar online.

Musikhuset Posten LIVE MUSIC
(www.postenlive.dk; Østre Stationsvej 35) In an old postal warehouse close to the station, Posten presents live music (rock, pop, hip hop etc) from established and upcoming artists. There's often something interesting going on in one of its two halls; check listings online.

Odense Koncerthus CONCERT VENUE
(www.odensesymfoni.dk; Claus Bergs Gade 9) Home of the Odense Symphony Orchestra. The classical-music program commonly includes works by native son Carl Nielsen. Ticket prices vary according to the concert (generally starting around Dkr140). Check the program online, and note the new concert hall/theatre, Odeon, being built in the vicinity.

ℹ Information

Main Post Office (Dannebrogsgade 2; ⌚10am-6pm Mon-Fri, to 1pm Sat) North of the train station.

Odense Centralbibliotek (www.odensebib.dk; Østre Stationsvej; ⌚10am-7pm Mon-Thu, to 4pm Fri, to 2pm Sat, also to 2pm Sun Oct-Mar) Library inside the train station, with free internet use and foreign-language newspapers.

Tourist Office (☎63 75 75 20; www.visitodense.com; Vestergade 2; ⌚9.30am-6pm Mon-Fri, 10am-3pm Sat, 11am-2pm Sun Jul & Aug, 10am-4.30pm Mon-Fri, to 1pm Sat Sep-Jun) Helpful, well-stocked office, in the town hall about 700m from the train station.

ℹ Getting There & Away

Odense is on the main railway line between Copenhagen (Dkr276, 1½ hours, at least twice hourly), Aarhus (Dkr240, 1¾ hours, twice hourly) and Esbjerg (Dkr218, 1½ hours, one to two times hourly).

Regional buses leave from Dannebrogsgade, at the rear of the train station. **Fynbus** (www.fynbus.dk) runs bus services from Odense to all major towns on Funen.

Odense is just north of the E20; access from the highway is clearly marked. Rte 43 connects Odense with Faaborg; Rte 9 connects Odense with Svendborg.

ℹ Getting Around

Odense is a delight to explore by bike, especially along the many riverside bike paths. The tourist office has free cycling maps.

The city council runs an extensive bike-share scheme; if you don't have a Danish mobile phone, you need to register online with your credit-card details, then use your mobile phone to access bikes. Full instructions are on www.cibi.dk – scroll down to find 'Bycykel turist' under Odense.

It's a long-winded process if all you want is a bike for a couple of hours – a simpler alternative is to rent bikes at **Odense Cykeludlejning** (☎29 29 25 89; www.odensecykler.dk; Nedergade 36; ⌚9am-1pm Mon-Fri May-Aug) for Dkr100 per day. Outside of opening hours, you can book via the website, or rent bikes through City Hotel.

If you're driving, you'll find large undercover car parks around Brandts (access from Vindegade) and by the train station. Parking costs around Dkr12 per hour.

Ladbyskibet & Vikingemuseet Ladby

Denmark's only Viking Age **ship grave** is a captivating site. Around the year 925, a Viking chieftan was laid to rest in a splendid 21.5m-long warship, surrounded by weapons, jewellery, clothing, riding equipment, pots and pans, coins and a gaming board. All the wooden planks from the Ladby ship decayed long ago, leaving the imprint of the hull moulded into the earth, along with iron nails, an anchor and the grinning skulls of sacrificed dogs and horses.

The site's **museum** (www.vikingemuseet-ladby.dk; Vikingevej 123; adult/child Dkr60/free; ⌚10am-5pm Jun-Aug, 10am-4pm Tue-Sun Sep-May) does a great job of recounting what is known of the story, displaying finds from the grave and a reconstructed mock-up of the boat before it was interred. The result is a vivid sense of the scale and trouble taken over the chieftan's burial.

By car or bike, follow Rte 315 out of Kerteminde, then the signs to Ladby. In Ladby village, 4km southwest, turn north onto Vikingevej, a one-lane road through fields that ends after 1.2km at the museum car park. The ship mound is a few minutes' walk along a field path.

From Banegården Plads C in Odense, catch bus 151 to Kerteminde (Dkr41, 40 minutes, once or twice hourly). From here, local bus 482 makes the six-minute trip from Kerteminde to Ladby (you'll have to walk the Vikingevej section) but it operates only on schooldays, so hiring a bike is a better summertime option. See www.rejseplanen.dk for bus times.

Egeskov Slot

This magnificent **castle** (www.egeskov.dk; Egeskov Gade 18, Kværndrup; adult/child castle & grounds Dkr210/130, grounds only Dkr180/110; ⏲10am-7pm Jul–mid-Aug, to 5pm mid-Apr–Jun & mid-Aug–mid-Oct), complete with moat and drawbridge, is an outstanding example of the lavish efforts that sprang up during Denmark's Golden Age, the Renaissance. There are enough sights and activities here to keep anyone happily occupied for a day. The castle exteriors are the best features. The interior is heavily Victorian in its furnishings and hunting trophies of now-rare beasts.

The castle's expansive 15-hectare park contains century-old privet hedges, a herd of deer, space-age sculptures and manicured English-style gardens. Visitor attractions include a handful of first-class museums displaying outstanding collections of vintage cars and aircraft, antique motorcycles and bikes, emergency vehicles and horse-drawn vehicles, plus a wartime grocery shop.

The grounds usually stay open an hour longer than the castle. Check the website for 'Open By Night' events (usually Wednesdays in peak summer), when the grounds stay open until 11pm, with a program of evening concerts and fireworks. There's also pre-Christmas activity.

Egeskov Slot is 2km west of Kværndrup on Rte 8, and is well signposted. If you're in Faaborg, bus 920 (roughly hourly) runs 500m from the castle – ask the driver where to alight. Otherwise take a train to Kværndrup station and catch the 920 bus, walk or take a taxi.

Faaborg

POP 7200

In its 17th-century heyday, Faaborg claimed one of the country's largest commercial fishing fleets. It might be a lot sleepier these days, but vestiges of those golden years live on in cobblestone streets like Holkegade, Adelgade and Tårngade. Add to this a fine art museum and you have a deeply pleasant pit stop on your way to or from the unmissable, time-warped island of Ærø.

Sights & Activities

Faaborg Museum MUSEUM

(www.faaborgmuseum.dk; Grønnegade 75; adult/child Dkr60/free; ⏲10am-4pm daily Jun-Aug, closed Mon Sep-May) You'll find a notable collection of Funen art, including works by Johannes Larsen, Peter Hansen, Jens Birkholm and Anna Syberg, and a flower-filled garden and cafe inside this handsome, imposing building. Kai Nielsen's original granite sculpture of the *Ymerbrønd* is also here.

Den Gamle Gaard HISTORIC BUILDING

(www.ohavemuseet.dk; Holkegade 1; ⏲11am-3pm Mon-Wed Aug–mid-Sep) FREE Den Gamle Gaard is a beautiful timber-framed house that dates back to about 1720. Inside are 22 rooms, arranged to show how a wealthy merchant lived in the early 19th century – full of antique furniture, porcelain, toys and maritime objects. When we visited it was open only limited hours; check the website.

Torvet SQUARE

The star of Faaborg's main square is sculptor Kai Nielsen's striking bronze fountain **Ymerbrønd**, which caused a minor uproar on its unveiling. It depicts a Norse creation myth: the naked frost giant Ymir (from whose body the sky and earth were made) suckling at the udder of a cow.

Sleeping & Eating

Danhostel Faaborg HOSTEL €

(☎62 61 12 03; www.danhostelfaaborg.dk; Grønnegade 71-72; dm/d Dkr175/375; ⏲Apr-Sep) This is a simple, oh-so-cosy hostel, based in two historic buildings – an old cinema and a half-timbered poorhouse, both full of sunshine and creaking woodwork. There are few frills (bathrooms are shared). Dorm beds are available in high summer.

Hotel Faaborg HOTEL €€
(☎62 61 02 45; www.magasingaarden.dk; Torvet; s/d incl breakfast Dkr750/950) Plumb in the centre square, this pretty-as-a-picture boutique-style hotel has fresh rooms and a lovely downstairs courtyard and cafe.

Faaborg Røgeri SEAFOOD €
(www.faaborgroegericafe.com; Vestkaj 3; fish dishes Dkr32-76; ⏰10am-9pm daily mid-Jun–mid-Aug, reduced hours rest of year) Nothing says 'Danish holiday' better than eating *fiskefrikadeller* (fishballs) and remoulade from a paper plate in the salty-smelling harbourside sunshine.

Det Hvide Pakhus DANISH €€
(☎62 61 09 00; www.dethvidepakhus.dk; Christian IXs Vej 2; lunch Dkr88-135, dinner mains Dkr155-265; ⏰11.30am-10pm daily mid-Jun–Aug, reduced hours rest of year) Set in a light, airy harbourside warehouse, Det Hvide Pakhus is as much a hit with locals as it is with out-of-towners. Lunch is a lesson in old-school Danish cuisine (heavy on the fish, direct from local fishers), while dinner gets a bit fancier and skews towards fine cuts of beef. Kitchen closes 8pm.

Information

Tourist Office (☎63 75 94 44; www.visitfaaborgmidtfyn.com; Torvet 19; ⏰9am-5pm Mon-Fri, 9am-2pm Sat Jun-Aug, 10am-4pm Mon-Fri Sep-May) With bike hire, cycling and hiking maps, fishing licences etc. Can book accommodation and ferry tickets for a small fee.

Getting There & Away

BOAT

Ærøfærgerne (☎62 52 40 00; www.aeroeferry.dk) runs car ferries between Faaborg and Søby on the island of Ærø (p94).

BUS

Faaborg's bus station is on Banegårdspladsen, at the defunct train station on the southern side of town.

From Odense, buses 111 and 141 (Dkr71) run regularly (bus 141 is the most direct, and takes an hour). From Svendborg, take frequent bus 931 (Dkr51, 55 minutes).

CAR

From the north, simply follow Rte 43. From Svendborg, Rte 44 leads directly west into Faaborg.

Lyø, Avernakø & Bjørnø

This trio of islands off the coast of Faaborg make pleasant day trips – fans of feathered creatures will especially love the rich birdlife. Of the three, Lyø has the most to see: an old village with an unusual **circular churchyard**; the **Klokkesten**, a 1000-year-old dolmen that rings like a bell when struck; and several bathing **beaches**.

From Faaborg, **Ø-Færgen** (☎72 53 18 00; www.oefaergen.com; return adult/child Dkr120/85, bicycle Dkr30) sails around five times daily to Avernakø and Lyø, taking between 30 and 70 minutes. For Bjørnø, the passenger-only **M/S Lillebjørn** (☎20 29 80 50; www.bjoernoe-faergen.dk; return adult/child Dkr59/30, bicycle Dkr18) runs about to nine times daily Monday to Friday, and up to five times daily on weekends. Journey time is approximately 20 minutes.

The Visit Faaborg site (www.visitfaaborg.dk) has information on all three islands.

Svendborg

POP 26,700

Darling of the Danish yachting fraternity, who pack the town's cafe-dotted streets each summer, hilly Svendborg is a major sailing and kayaking centre. There are more Danish boats registered here than anywhere else beyond Copenhagen, and the place is the main gateway to Funen's beautiful southern islands. Although predominantly a modern industrial settlement, the town has no shortage of elegant old buildings, not to mention a harbour packed with beautiful old wooden boats from across the Baltic.

Sights & Activites

Maritimt Center Danmark HISTORIC BUILDING
(☎63 75 94 92; www.maritimt-center.dk; Havnepladsen 2; cruises adult/child Dkr270/170) At the Ærø ferry dock is the Maritime Centre, with its HQ inside a candy-striped timber warehouse (Pakhuset) from the late 19th century. The centre arranges cruises on historic sailing ships in high summer (late June to mid-August), with the possibility of sailing from various ports in the area (Svendborg, Faaborg, Marstal and Ærøskøbing on Ærø, Rudkøbing on Langeland). The website outlines the schedule.

★**Sejlskibsbroen** WATERFRONT
Don't miss Sejlskibsbroen, a jetty lined with splendidly preserved wooden sailing ships, and with an adjoining marina catering for the great number of yachts that sail local waters.

Naturama MUSEUM
(www.naturama.dk; Dronningemaen 30; adult/child Dkr140/free; ⏰Feb-Nov; 👪) Make a date with

nature at Svendborg's impressive natural-history museum. Its three levels focus on water, land and air: whale skeletons dominate the basement, Scandinavian mammals congregate on the middle floor, and birds soar above it all. There's state-of-the-art sound and lighting, plus regular film shows and a good hands-on section for kids.

Note: confirm opening days online, as the museum is closed Mondays outside Danish school holidays.

Sleeping & Eating

Svendborg and its surrounds have good, inexpensive B&Bs, many of which are listed in the Funen and the Islands B&B brochure (found in tourist offices across Funen and online at www.bed-breakfast-fyn.dk). The nearest campground is on Tåsinge, on the southern side of Svendborg Sound.

Hotel Ærø HOTEL €€
(☎62 21 07 60; www.hotel-aeroe.dk; Brogade 1; s/d incl breakfast Dkr850/1025) This handsome mustard-and-white hotel occupies an unbeatable harbourside position (right by where the Ærø ferry docks), and has bags of atmosphere. The annexe of large, modern rooms is light and airy. The 'British-colonial' style – big comfy wooden beds, mock mahogany desks and wood floors – is restrained and relaxed. Harbour views cost Dkr100 extra.

★Danhostel Svendborg HOSTEL €€
(☎62 21 66 99; www.danhostel-svendborg.dk; Vestergade 45; dm/d incl breakfast & linen Dkr275/750; P @) This is a slick, professional hostel – more like a hotel really, and prices reflect this. Simple, spotless rooms, each with bathroom and TV, are based in a renovated 19th-century iron foundry in the city centre. It's a popular conference centre in winter, and has oodles of facilities: laundry, large kitchen, garden, breakfast buffet (Dkr75) and plentiful lounge nooks.

Bendixens Fiskehandel SEAFOOD €
(www.bendixens-fiskehandel.dk/; Jessens Mole 2; meals Dkr40-95; ⊙grill 11am-8pm or 9pm Mon-Sat) What could be better than fish and chips for Dkr70, and a boat-filled harbour as your view? This fish shop has an attached bargain-priced grill where you can buy fresh fish dishes to down at alfresco picnic tables.

Jettes Diner BURGERS €
(www.jettesdiner.dk; Kullinggade 1; burgers Dkr66-85; ⊙11.30am-9pm Sun & Mon, to 9.30pm Tue-Sat) It's all about bumper burgers at Jettes, a popular and inexpensive spot favoured by everyone, from workers nipping in for a beer to yachties from the nearby harbour. There's a good selection too, from standard beef to chicken, pulled pork and even some vegetarian options (and gluten-free buns).

★Vintapperiet FRENCH €€
(☎62 22 34 48; Brogade 37; lunch Dkr70-125, 2/3/4 courses Dkr200/250/300; ⊙11am-5.30pm Mon, 11am-10pm Tue-Sat Jun-Aug, shorter hours rest of year) There's a clever blend of rustic-France-meets-Denmark at this appealing little bistro, tucked into a half-timbered house. Cheese or charcuterie for lunch, a small, sweet menu of selections for dinner (coq au vin, braised lamb nicoise), and always lots of wine options by the glass – perhaps even some live music to accompany it. *C'est bon.*

Information

Tourist Office (☎63 75 94 80; www.visitsvendborg.dk; Centrumpladsen 4; ⊙10am-4pm or 5pm Mon-Fri, to 1pm Sat) Has lots of information on south Funen; can book accommodation, ferry tickets etc.

Getting There & Around

The train and bus stations are two blocks northwest of the ferry terminal.

There are frequent bus services between Svendborg and Faaborg (bus 931, Dkr51, 55 minutes). Trains leave Odense for Svendborg twice hourly (Dkr78, 40 minutes).

Ærøfærgerne (☎62 52 40 00; www.aeroe-ferry.dk) runs car ferries to Ærøskøbing on Ærø (p94). The ticket is valid for any one of Ærø's four ferry routes.

For bike rental, hit **Svendborg Cykeludlejning** (☎30 17 69 27; www.svendborgcykeludlejning.dk; Jernbanegade 10; ⊙9am-1pm Jun-Aug, shorter hours rest of year).

SOUTH FUNEN ARCHIPELAGO

Tåsinge

Just over the bridge from Svendborg is the island of Tåsinge, with its pretty harbourside village of **Troense** and the nearby 17th-century castle **Valdemars Slot** (www.valdemarsslot.dk; Slotsalléen 100, Troense; adult/child Dkr85/45; ⊙10am-5pm daily Jun-Aug, closed Mon May & Sep). The castle was built in the early 17th century by Denmark's great Renaissance king, Christian IV, for his son, but later awarded to the naval hero Admiral Niels Juel; it remains in his family to this day. The palatial interior is crammed with antique furniture and eccentricities: lavish Venetian glass, 17th-century Gobelin tapestries, a toilet hidden in a window frame, a secret ammo store, Niels Juels' sea chest pasted with engravings, and autographed photos of visiting celebs. In the attic is the grisly **Jagt- & Trofæmuseet**, featuring ethnographical objects and animal trophies collected by hunter Børge Hinsch and others.

Another museum can be found in the pond-filled courtyard: Danmarks **Museum for Lystsejlads** (Yachting Museum; www.lystsejlads.dk; adult/child incl castle Dkr99/55; ⌚10am-5pm Jun-Aug) contains a collection of sleek, varnished sailboats.

You can get to Valdemars Slot by bus (route 250 stops 1km short), but a better way is via **M/S Helge** (www.mshelge.dk), a boat that ferries passengers from Svendborg. From mid-May to mid-September, the vintage vessel sails three or four times daily on a schedule that makes five stops in the area, at Svendborg Sund campground on the northern tip of Tåsinge, then at Christiansminde, a popular beach area east of Svendborg, before continuing to Troense and Valdemars Slot on Tåsinge. It turns around at Valdemars Slot to retrace its steps back to Svendborg harbour. You can use it as a long sightseeng tour (Dkr60 one way) or a short-hop transport option (riding two stops for Dkr30). See the ferry website (in Danish) for sailing times.

Langeland

POP 13,280

The long, narrow grain-producing island of Langeland, connected by bridge to Funen via Tåsinge, is a natural haven and popular holiday destination for Danes. It has some excellent sandy beaches, enjoyable cycling and rewarding bird-watching. A large part of the island around Dovns Klint has been protected as a wildlife reserve. It is also well known in Denmark for its annual **Langeland Festival** (langelandsfestival.dk; ⌚late Jul-early Aug), a popular family-oriented music festival often referred to as 'Denmark's largest garden party'.

Sights

Langeland's main town of **Rudkøbing** has a fairly desolate harbour area, but the town centre is attractive and there's a booty of fine old buildings around Rudekøbing Kirke, to the north of Brogade, the street leading inland from the harbour to the main square of Torvet.

For beaches, head for Ristinge about 15km south of Rudkøbin.

Tranekær Slot CASTLE

(www.tranekaergods.dk) The little village of Tranekær stretches between its church and the salmon-coloured Tranekær Slot, which has been in the hands of one family since 1659 (there's been a fortification here since the 13th century). The castle's interior is only open to the public on tours conducted over two weeks in July (see the website), but the grounds are open daily and known as Tickon.

Tickon GARDENS

(Tranekær International Centre for Art & Nature; adult/child Dkr25/free; ⌚sunrise-sunset) The wooded grounds of Tranekær Slot are home to the magical Tickon, a collection of outdoor art installations. You can wander around the lake and arboretum, inhabited by a herd of red deer. There are surprises round every corner: a unicorn's horn sprouts in a glade, a river of tree trunks floods down a hillside. There are 19 sculptures to enjoy, and the fun is finding them in the landscape.

Activities

Cycling is a good way to explore Langeland. You can hire bikes at **Lapletten** (☎62 51 10 98; www.lapletten.dk; Engdraget 1).

For bird-watching, you'll find a sighting tower at Tryggelev Nor, 5km south of Ristinge, and a sanctuary at Gulstav Bog, the island's southern tip.

Sleeping & Eating

Æblegaarden B&B €€

(☎59 64 02 44; www.aeblegaarden.dk; Fæbækvej 25; per person incl breakfast Dkr385) On a beautiful, bountiful rural property (the name means 'The Apple Farm') about 8km north of Tranekær Slot, friendly hosts offer two stylish, light-filled rooms for rent (shared kitchenette and bathroom). Breakfast is a highlight, utilising farm-fresh produce; dinners are also possible (advance notice usually required).

Tranekær Gæstgivergaard GUESTHOUSE €€
(☎62 59 12 04; www.tranekaerkro.dk; Slotsgade 74; s/d Dkr750/950; P) This village inn 200m south of the castle dates from 1802 and retains its period ambience. Most rooms have peaceful garden views (they're in a more-modern annex out the back). The highly rated restaurant (mains Dkr250 to Dkr390) is strong on local game, such as venison and pheasant.

Hotel Rudkøbing Skudehavn HOTEL, APARTMENT €€
(☎62 51 46 00; www.rudkobingskudehavn.dk; Havnegade 21; s/d incl breakfast Dkr575/795; P) Down by the modern marina, this bright holiday centre includes small, modern hotel rooms, but the nicest options are the two-bedroom apartments (sleeping six, and all with bathroom, kitchen, TV and private balcony or terrace). A two-night stay in these costs from Dkr1500, with significant discounts for extra nights (and low-season stays). There's also a restaurant and bar.

Slagterpigerne DELI €
(www.slagterpigerne.dk; Torvet 6; smørrebrød Dkr22-45; ⏲9am-5pm Mon-Thu, to 6pm Fri, to 1pm Sat) Put a picnic together with some takeaway smørrebrød and deli items from this butcher's shop on Rudkøbing's main square.

★ **Skovsgaard MadMarked** CAFE, DELI €
(www.danmarksnaturfond.dk; Kågårdsvej 12; lunch plates Dkr75; ⏲10am-5pm mid-May–Sep, to 9pm Thu) 'MadMarked' sounds worrying but in fact means 'food market', and this bright, pretty cafe-deli at the entrance to the Skovsgaard estate is brimming with fresh, organic local produce (some of it grown on the estate). You can lunch on a plate of various meats and salads; we'll understand if you go straight for coffee and dessert (eg rhubarb crumble).

Information

Pick up information about the island from Langeland's **tourist office** (☎62 51 35 05; www.langeland.dk; Torvet 5; ⏲9.30am-4.30pm Mon-Fri year-round, also 9.30am-2.30pm Sat Jul & Aug).

Getting There & Away

BOAT

A ferry operates from Spodsbjerg to Tårs on Lolland. The ferry service from Rudkøbing to Marstal on Ærø has ceased; to reach Ærø you need to return to Svendborg and take the ferry from there.

BUS

Route 9 connects Langeland to Tåsinge, via the Langeland bridge. Bus 930 makes the 20km run from Svendborg to Rudkøbing (Dkr41, 30 minutes) at least hourly. See www.fynbus.dk for schedules.

Ærø

POP 6670

Just 30km long and 8km wide, Ærø (pronounced 'with difficulty') holds a special place in the hearts of Danes. Mention it and they will sigh wistfully and perhaps recall a long-ago childhood visit to the quaint old town of Ærøskøbing, or cycling holidays amid the beautiful, gentle countryside peppered with crooked, half-timbered houses with traditional hand-blown glass windows and decorative doorways beautified by hollyhocks. Most young residents leave as soon as they can, however, as, though Ærø is one of the most enchanting of all the islands of the south Funen archipelago, there isn't a great deal going on here out of season. There are some good, small beaches, one of the best being Risemark Strand on the southern tip of the island; it's a great place to tour by bicycle, not least as this is in keeping with the spirit of an island that is run almost entirely on sustainable energy sources such as wind and solar power.

Ærø has three main towns: Ærøskøbing, Marstal and Søby. The island's tourist website is www.arre.dk.

Sights

Ærøskøbing

The words 'higgledy' and 'piggledy' could have been invented to describe Ærøskøbing (population 930). A prosperous merchants' town in the late 17th century, its winding cobblestone streets meander between crooked houses, cheerfully painted and gently skewed, with hand-blown glass windows, doorways bursting with bright hollyhocks, and half-timbered courtyards.

The town's former poorhouse is now **Flaske Peters Samling** (www.arremus.dk; Smedegade 22; adult/child Dkr40/free; ⏲10am-4pm Jul-Aug, 11am-3pm Mon-Sat mid-Apr–Jun & Sep–mid-Oct, by appointment rest of yr), a small museum displaying the amazing life's work of Peter Jacobsen ('Bottle Peter'), who crafted 1700 ships in bottles. A mere 95m to the north, **Æro Museum** (www.arremus.dk; Brogade 3-5; adult/child Dkr30/free; ⏲11am-4pm Mon-Fri, 11am-3pm Sat & Sun Jul-Aug, by appointment rest of year) offers a sweet assemblage of maritime paraphernalia, traditional clothing, furniture and household utensils.

Søby

This quiet little port has a shipyard, which happens to be the island's biggest employer, a sizeable fishing fleet and a busy yacht marina. Five kilometres beyond Søby, at Ærø's northern tip, there's a pebble beach with clear water and a stone **lighthouse** with a view.

Marstal

On the southeastern end of the island, Marstal is Ærø's most modern-looking town and has a web of busy shopping streets at its centre. Marstal has an emphatically maritime history; even its street names echo the names of ships and famous sailors. The town's **Søfartsmuseum** (www.marmus.dk; Prinsensgade 1; adult/child Dkr60/free; ⏲ 9am-5pm Jun-Aug, 10am-4pm Apr, May, Sep & Oct, 11am-3pm Mon-Sat Nov-Apr) has an absorbing collection of nautical artefacts, including ships' models and full-size boats. You'll find a reasonably good **beach** on the southern side of town.

Sleeping

The *Ærø Guide,* available in tourist offices, lists B&Bs around the island, as does www.aeroe.dk. There are also plenty of holiday cottages for rent.

Andelen Guesthouse GUESTHOUSE €
(☎ 61 26 75 11; www.andelenguesthouse.com; Søndergade 28A, Ærøskøbing; s/d/tr without bathroom Dkr600/700/900) After big renovations, a young, well-travelled Danish-English family have opened this great option: wooden floors, timber beams, stylish modern (shared) bathrooms, pretty courtyard. It's in a building with lots of history and character – it houses Bio Andelen, the sweet local 50-seat cinema (complimentary tickets for guests) that's been the venue for many jazz-fest gigs. Breakfast is Dkr75.

Danhostel Marstal HOSTEL €
(☎ 62 53 39 50; www.marstalvandrerhjem.dk; Færgestræde 29; dm Dkr220, d without/with bathroom Dkr400/550; ⏲ May–mid-Sep) Nicely positioned halfway between the harbour and the beach, this is a well-run, high-quality hostel with a pretty cobbled courtyard and stylish dining area with wood fire. A handful of rooms have bathrooms; some also have sea views. Dorms are available in high season. A fine choice.

Ærøskøbing Camping CAMPGROUND €
(☎ 62 52 18 54; www.aeroecamp.dk; Sygehusvej 40; per site adult/child Dkr78/48) Near Vesterstrand beach (about 1km north of the town centre), this green campground has hedges for shelter, plus neat facilities, playground and bike rental. The small, cute, no-frills huts are great if you'd like a roof over your head. Marstal and Søby also have campgrounds.

★ **Pension Vestergade 44** GUESTHOUSE €€
(☎ 62 52 22 98; www.vestergade44.com; Vestergade 44, Ærøskøbing; s/d without bathroom incl breakfast Dkr990/1090) The large timbered house was built in 1784 by a sea captain for his daughter. It's now owned and run as a guesthouse by lovely Susanna (originally from England), and she gets it right, down to the finest detail: the six rooms are decorated with period charm, the large garden is delightful, and the breakfast comprises freshly laid eggs and homemade jam.

Eating & Drinking

All three towns have bakeries, restaurants and food stores.

ANCIENT ÆRØ

Ærø once had more than 100 prehistoric sites and, although many have been lost, the island still has some atmospheric Neolithic remains, especially in its southeast district, to the west of Marstal. At the small village of Store Rise is the site of **Tingstedet**, the remains of a passage grave in a field behind an attractive **12th-century church**.

At **Lindsbjerg** is the superb hilltop site of a long barrow and two passage graves, one of which has a nicely poised capstone. Just over 1km south of here, follow signs to a spot right on the coast where you'll find the fascinating medieval relic of **Sankt Albert's Kirke**. It's within a Viking defensive wall from about the 8th century.

Another striking site is at **Kragnæs**, about 4km west of Marstal. Head through the village of Græsvænge and follow the signs for 'Jættestue' along narrow lanes to reach a small car park, from where it's about 600m along field tracks to the restored grave site.

Ærøskøbing Røgeri SEAFOOD €
(Havnen 15; meals Dkr36-82; ⌚10am-9pm Jul–mid-Aug, 11am-7pm mid-Apr–Jun & mid-Aug–mid-Oct) Get an authentically salty-dog feel at this fish smokehouse, adjacent to the harbour. It serves bargain-priced smoked-fish plates (the halibut with potato salad is delicious) or fish-stuffed sandwiches. Wash it down with a plastic cup full of locally brewed beer.

Kongensgade 34 INTERNATIONAL €€
(www.kongensgade34.dk; Kongensgade 34, Marstal; meals Dkr85-169; ⌚10am-midnight Sun-Thu, to 2am Fri & Sat Jul-Aug, shorter hours rest of year) A relaxed, all-day bar-bistro that moves from lunch into dinner then late-night drinks. There's a menu of Danish and global classic hits: sit in the sun and enjoy a burger, steamed mussels or a pile of *'pilselv rejer'* (unpeeled prawns) with citron-mayo.

Café Aroma INTERNATIONAL €€
(☎62 52 40 02; www.cafe-aroma.dk; Havnepladsen, Ærøskøbing; mains Dkr72-225; ⌚11am-10pm Jul & Aug, to 8pm Apr-Jun & Sep-Oct) This cafe's interior is the essence of *hyggelig* (cosy): film posters, old cinema seats, a battered sofa, even a barber's chair – but on warm summer evenings, the outdoor terrace is in hot demand. There's a good all-day menu where local produce shines – try fish (of course) or the gourmet hot dog, then follow with delicious homemade ice cream.

Above the cafe, **Hotel Aroma** offers outstanding rooms and apartments (double from Dkr695), stylish and colourful with plenty of character.

Restaurant Edith MODERN DANISH €€€
(☎62 25 25 69; www.restaurantedith.dk; Kirkestræde 8, Marstal; 3-/5-/7-course menus Dkr445/599/699; ⌚6-11pm) Pretty, mint-green Edith is a smart showcase for regional produce (locally caught fish, island-reared meat, plenty of herbs, vegetables and summer berries), put to good use in innovative creations. Outside the summer season it's only open for dinner Friday and Saturday, and only if booked ahead.

ℹ Information

Ærøskøbing tourist office (☎62 52 13 00; www.visitaeroe.dk; Havnen 4; ⌚9am-4pm Mon-Fri) is by the waterfront.

ℹ Getting There & Away

Ærøfærgerne (p90) runs year-round car ferries:

Svendborg–Ærøskøbing The main service, running up to 12 times daily. 75 minutes.

Faaborg–Søby Runs two to three times a day. One hour.

Fynshav–Søby From Fynshav on the island of Als (southern Jutland). Runs two to three times a day. 70 minutes.

Prices are the same on all three routes:

Adult one way/return Dkr130/199

Child one way/return Dkr82/115

Car one way/return Dkr280/437

Bicycle one way return Dkr27/41

If you have a car it's a good idea to reserve, particularly on weekends and in summer (you can do this online).

ℹ Getting Around

BICYCLE

Both the tourist offices in Ærøskøbing and Marstal sell a Dkr20 cycling map of the island.

Bike Erria (☎32 14 60 74; www.bike-erria.dk) is a useful company that promotes bicycle tourism on the island and can help you plan a cycle-tour itinerary.

Pilebækkens Cykler (☎62 52 11 10; Pilebækken 11, Ærøskøbing) You can rent bikes for 45kr to 50kr per day in Ærøskøbing at Pilebækkens Cykler.

Søby Cykeludlejning (☎62 58 14 60; Havnevejen 2; per day Dkr75)

BUS

Bus 790 runs the length of the island, from Søby harbour to Marstal harbour and vice versa, via Ærøskøbing (a full journey takes just under an hour). The bus is free, and operates hourly from 5am to 9pm weekdays (slightly less frequently and shorter hours on weekends). Pick up the schedule at tourist offices.

JUTLAND

Denmark doesn't have a north–south divide; culturally, spiritually and to a great extent politically, it is divided into Jutland… and all the rest. Jutlanders are different. Sturdy, down to earth, unpretentious, hard-working; you will find an old-fashioned hospitality here and an engaging frankness. Then there are those Jutland landscapes, an arresting melange of windswept islands, duelling seas and brooding lakes that have inspired centuries of great Danish art. Add to this fine art museums, Denmark's oldest town, and the understated cool of 'second-city' Aarhus, and you too might concede that there's something about Jutland.

Aarhus

POP 310,000

Always the bridesmaid, never the bride, Aarhus (*oar*-hus) stands in the shadow of its bigger, brasher sibling, Copenhagen. Yet Denmark's affable runner-up city has a few unexpected surprises up its sleeve, from hipster boutiques, bars and cafes, to world-class dining and some fantastic museums. The city is home to ARoS (one of Denmark's best art museums), a thriving student population, as well as the country's best music scene. Expect its stature to grow in the lead-up to 2017, when it is one of the European Capitals of Culture (www.aarhus2017.dk).

Sights & Activities

There are sandy beaches on the outskirts of Aarhus. The most popular one to the north is **Bellevue**, about 4km from the city centre (bus 17 or 20), while the favourite to the south is Moesgård Strand (take bus 18 or 31).

★**ARoS Aarhus Kunstmuseum** ART MUSEUM
(www.aros.dk; Aros Allé 2; adult/child Dkr110/free; ⌚10am-5pm Tue-Sun, to 10pm Wed; 👪) Inside the cubist, red-brick walls of Aarhus' showpiece art museum are nine floors of sweeping curves, soaring spaces and white walls, showcasing a wonderful selection of Golden Age works, Danish modernism, and an abundance of arresting and vivid contemporary art. The museum's cherry-on-top is the spectacular **Your Rainbow Panorama**, a 360-degree rooftop walkway offering technicolour views of the city through its glass panes in all shades of the rainbow.

Intriguingly, ARoS' main theme is Dante's *The Divine Comedy;* the entrance is on level 4, and from there you either descend into hell or climb towards heaven. Hell is **De 9 Rum** (The 9 Spaces), on the bottom floor, painted black and home to moody installation pieces; Heaven is the rooftop rainbow halo, the brainchild of Olafur Eliasson, a Danish-Icelandic artist famed for big, conceptual pieces.

Another iconic piece is Ron Mueck's **Boy** on level 1, an astoundingly lifelike, oversized (5m-high) sculpture of a crouching boy.

The museum stages varied special exhibitions – check what's on when you're in town. ARoS also houses a great gift shop and light-filled cafe on level 4 (free entry), and restaurant on level 8.

Den Gamle By MUSEUM
(The Old Town; www.dengamleby.dk; Viborgvej 2; adult/child Dkr135/free; ⌚10am-5pm; 👪) The Danes' seemingly limitless enthusiasm for dressing up and re-creating history reaches its zenith at Den Gamle By. It's an engaging, picturesque open-air museum of 75 half-timbered houses brought here from all corners of Denmark and reconstructed as a provincial market town from the era of Hans Christian Andersen. Re-created neighbourhoods from 1927 and 1974 are the latest additions.

You can take a **horse-drawn wagon ride** (adult/child Dkr40/30) around the site, and then visit each building, store and workshop to see craftspeople practising their trade. Small museums cater to different interests: the **Danish Poster Museum** has some fabulous retro pieces, the **Toy Museum** showcases antique playthings, and the **Gallery of Decorative Arts** displays silverware, porcelain and clocks. Don't miss the apartment block from 1974 for a peek into past lives, or the TV and hi-fi store stocking authentic 1970s gear.

The website details kid-friendly activities for visitors; these peak in July and August, and in the lead up to Christmas.

Den Gamle By is 1.5km west of the city centre (a 20-minute walk from the train station); buses 3A, 19 and 44 stop nearby. There's a detailed schedule of opening hours and admission prices (set according to the museum's activities) outlined on the website. Outside of opening hours you can stroll the cobbled streets for free.

Aarhus Domkirke CHURCH
(www.aarhus-domkirke.dk; Bispetorv; ⌚9.30am-4pm Mon-Sat May-Sep, 10am-3pm Mon-Sat

CITY DISCOUNTS

If you're planning to tick off city sights, the **AarhusCard** is a worthwhile investment. The bus station and most accommodation providers sell the pass (24-hour pass adult/child Dkr129/69, 48-hour pass Dkr179/79), which allows unlimited transport on local buses as well as free or discounted admission to most sights.

In a city full of students, an ISIC or ID card from your home university is an asset. If you have one, flaunt it. From pubs to restaurants to museums, students are given favourable prices.

Aarhus

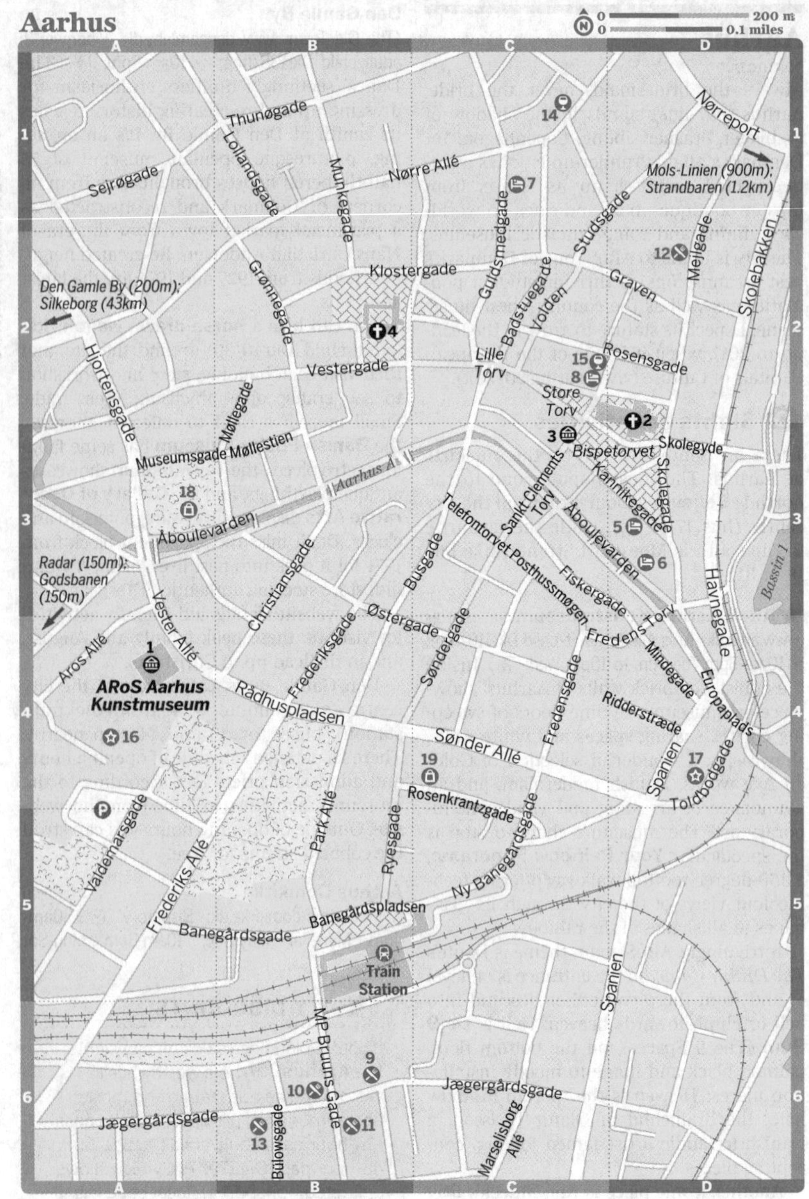

Oct-Apr) With a lofty nave spanning nearly 100m in length, Aarhus Domkirke is Denmark's longest church. The original Romanesque chapel at the eastern end dates from the 12th century, while most of the rest of the church is 15th-century Gothic.

Like other Danish churches, the cathedral was once richly decorated with frescoes that served to convey biblical parables to unschooled peasants. After the Reformation in 1536, church authorities, who felt the frescoes smacked too

Aarhus

Top Sights
1 ARoS Aarhus Kunstmuseum A4

Sights
2 Aarhus Domkirke D2
3 Vikingemuseet C3
4 Vor Frue Kirke B2

Sleeping
5 CabInn Aarhus Hotel D3
6 Hotel Ferdinand D3
7 Hotel Guldsmeden C1
8 Hotel Royal C2

Eating
9 Kvickly B6
10 Lagkagehuset B6
11 Nordisk Spisehus B6
12 Oli Nico D2
13 St Pauls Apothek B6

Drinking & Nightlife
14 Løve's Bog- & VinCafé C1
15 Under Masken C2

Entertainment
16 Musikhuset Aarhus A4
17 Train D4

Shopping
ARoS Aarhus Kunstmuseum .... (see 1)
18 Flagstang Markeder A3
19 HAY C4

much of Roman Catholicism, had them all whitewashed, but many have now been uncovered and restored. They range from fairy-tale paintings of St George slaying a dragon to scenes of hellfire.

A highlight of the cathedral is the ornate, five-panel gilt altarpiece made in Lübeck by the renowned woodcarver Bernt Notke in the 15th century.

Vor Frue Kirke CHURCH
(www.aarhusvorfrue.dk; Frue Kirkeplads; ⊙10am-4pm Mon-Fri, to 2pm Sat May-Sep; shorter hrs Oct-Apr) Set back from Vestergade, the Church of Our Lady is like a Russian *matryoshka* (nesting doll), opening to reveal multiple layers. It was here that the original Aarhus cathedral was erected shortly after 1060. That cathedral stood until about 1240, when it was replaced by the current red-brick church, the main treasure of which lies in its basement: the vaulted **crypt** of the original cathedral (enter via the stairs beneath the chancel), uncovered by chance in 1955 during a restoration.

Vikingemuseet MUSEUM
(www.moesmus.dk; Sankt Clements Torv 6; ⊙10.15am-5pm Mon-Fri) FREE There's more than the expected vaults in the basement of Nordea bank, a stone's throw from the cathedral. In the mid-1960s this site was excavated and artefacts from the Viking era were unearthed. Concise exhibits include a skeleton, a reconstructed pithouse, 1000-year-old carpentry tools and pottery.

Festivals & Events

NorthSide Festival MUSIC
(www.northside.dk) A three-day music festival in mid-June that's building a big reputation – line-ups rival the legendary Roskilde Festival.

Aarhus Festival PERFORMING ARTS
(www.aarhusfestuge.dk) The city dons its shiniest party gear at the end of August, when this festival transforms the town for 10 days, celebrating music, food, short film, theatre, visual arts and outdoor events for all ages (many of which are free).

Sculpture by the Sea CULTURAL
(www.sculpturebythesea.dk) This monthlong festival is held biennially (June in odd-numbered years) and transforms the city's southern beachfront into an outdoor gallery, with dozens of sculptures from Danish and foreign artists displayed beside (and in) the water.

Sleeping

CabInn Aarhus Hotel BUDGET HOTEL €
(☎86 75 70 00; www.cabinn.com; Kannikegade 14; s/d/tr from Dkr495/625/805; P@) 'Best location, best price' is the CabInn chain's motto, and given that this branch doubled in size in 2014, it's clearly doing something right. The functional rooms are based on ships' cabins (hence the name) – the cheapest is *tiny,* but all come with bathroom, kettle and TV. The location is indeed top-notch. Breakfast costs Dkr70.

WORTH A TRIP

MOESGÅRD

Visit Moesgård, 5km south of the Aarhus city centre, for its glorious beech woods and the trails threading through them towards sandy beaches. The spectacular, reinvented **Moesgård Museum** (www.moesmus.dk; Moesgård Allé; adult/child Dkr110/free; ⌚10am-5pm Tue-Sun, to 9pm Wed, open Mon Jul-Sep) features well-presented history exhibits from the Stone Age to the Viking Age. Its most dramatic exhibit is the 2000-year-old **Grauballe Man** (Grauballe-manden), whose astonishingly well-preserved body was found in 1952 at the village of Grauballe, 35km west of Aarhus.

Behind the museum is an enjoyable trail dubbed the 'prehistoric trackway' or Oldtidsstien, which leads across fields of wildflowers, past grazing sheep and through beech woods down to **Moesgård Strand**, Aarhus' best sandy beach. The trail, marked by red-dotted stones, passes reconstructed historic sights including a dolmen, burial cists and an Iron Age house. The museum has a brochure with details. You can walk one way and catch a bus back to the city centre, or follow the trail both ways as a 5km round trip. It's all well worth a half-day or full-day visit, with a picnic perhaps if the weather behaves itself.

From central Aarhus, bus 18 runs here frequently. With your own wheels, it's a lovely drive; take Strandvejen south and follow the signs.

Danhostel Aarhus HOSTEL €
(☎86 21 21 20; www.aarhus-danhostel.dk; Marienlundsvej 10; dm Dkr250, d without/with bathroom Dkr550/720; ⌚mid-Jan–mid-Dec; P @) The main building here is as pretty as a picture: it's a large octagonal room that was once a dancehall. Accommodation is bright and basic; some rooms have private bathrooms (linen costs extra). Breakfast costs Dkr64. The hostel is 3km north of the city centre, in pretty woods close to the beach; take bus 17, 18 or 20.

DCU-Camping Blommehaven CAMPGROUND €
(☎86 27 02 07; www.blommehaven.dk; Ørneredevej 35; adult/child Dkr80/50, sites Dkr48-70; ⌚late Mar-late Oct;) This big beachside campground 6km south of the city centre lies in the scenic Marselisborg woods en route to Moesgård. It's got loads of family-oriented facilities, plus simple four-berth huts (Dkr635). If you're driving, follow Strandvejen south; otherwise, take bus 18 or (in summer) 31.

★**Hotel Guldsmeden** BOUTIQUE HOTEL €€
(☎86 13 45 50; www.hotelguldsmeden.com; Guldsmedgade 40; d without/with bathroom from Dkr995/1395) A top pick for its excellent location, warm staff, French Colonial–style rooms with Persian rugs, pretty garden oasis and relaxed, stylish ambience. Bumper breakfasts (mainly organic) are included, as is Guldsmeden's own organic toiletries range. *Guldsmed* means both 'goldsmith' and 'dragonfly' in Danish – look for sweet use of the dragonfly motif in the decor.

Hotel Ferdinand BOUTIQUE HOTEL €€
(☎87 32 14 44; www.hotelferdinand.dk; Åboulevarden 28; s/d studio from Dkr950/1150, ste from Dkr1100/1300) Ferdinand is in the centre of the Åboulevarden action, with a swanky French brasserie downstairs. There are eight suites above the restaurant (large and luxurious); in the neighbouring building are five studio apartments with kitchen, washing machine and balconies overlooking Åboulevarden.

Hotel Royal HOTEL €€€
(☎86 12 00 11; www.hotelroyal.dk; Store Torv 4; s/d incl breakfast from Dkr1295/1495; P) If you've come to expect restrained Scandi style in your top-end Danish hotels, prepare to be surprised. From the over-the-top entrance portico to the chandelier-lit reception area and incredible murals, the Royal seems a little, well, gaudy in parts. But fun too – we love the fish-tank reception desk and the rich colour schemes. The rooms are appropriately lavish.

Eating

Away from the same-same feeling you may get along Åboulevarden, fertile hunting grounds come dinner time include the Latin Quarter (good for bistro-style cafes); Mejlgade (home to some excellent budget options); and the cool Frederiksbjerg neighbourhood, south of the train station (centred on MP Bruuns Gade and Jægergårdsgade). Adjacent to the train station, Bruun's Galleri shopping centre is home to a handy **Kvickly** (MP Bruuns Gade 25; ⌚8am-8pm Mon-Fri, to 6pm Sat & Sun) supermarket.

★Oli Nico INTERNATIONAL €

(www.olinico.dk; Mejlgade 35; dishes Dkr55-125; ⌚11.30am-2pm & 5.30-9pm Mon-Fri, noon-2pm & 5.30-9pm Sat, 5.30-9pm Sun) You may need to fight for one of the sought-after tables at Oli Nico, a small deli-restaurant with a menu of classic dishes at astoundingly good prices (*moules frites* for Dkr60, rib-eye steak for Dkr125 – both with homemade chips!). The daily-changing three-course dinner menu (for a bargain Dkr130) may be Aarhus' best-kept food secret. No reservations; takeaway available.

Lagkagehuset BAKERY €

(MP Bruunsgade 34; sandwiches & salads around Dkr60; ⌚6.30am-7pm Mon-Fri, to 6pm Sat & Sun) There's a whole lot of baked-good deliciousness going on here – take a number and wait for your chance to order from the display of breads, cakes and pastries. Lunchtime sandwiches and salads are decent value, and the coffee is good.

★St Pauls Apothek MODERN SCANDINAVIAN €€

(☎86 12 08 33; www.stpaulsapothek.dk; Jægergårdsgade 76; 2-/3-course menu Dkr245/295; ⌚5.30pm-midnight Tue-Thu, to 2am Fri & Sat) What was once a pharmacy is now one of Aarhus' hottest, best-value dining destinations: a Brooklyn-esque combo of hipster mixologists, vintage architectural detailing and slinky mood lighting. The menu is small on choice but big on Nordic produce and confident food pairings – and for Dkr595, you can enjoy three courses matched with inspired, delicious cocktails. Book ahead.

★Kähler Villa Dining MODERN DANISH €€€

(☎86 17 70 88; www.villadining.dk; Grenåvej 127; 4-course dinner incl wine Dkr599; ⌚6.30-9.30pm Mon-Sat) Aarhus' culinary A-lister lies about 5km north of the centre, in a gracious old villa where gustatory magic happens, at a delightfully accessible price. It's a clever concept: for a flat rate of Dkr599, and at a set starting time, diners enjoy a set menu of appetiser, starter, main, dessert and coffee, plus as much wine as they fancy.

Nordisk Spisehus MODERN DANISH €€€

(☎86 17 70 99; www.nordiskspisehus.dk; MP Bruuns Gade 31; 3-/5-course lunch Dkr199/299, 3-/5-/8-course dinner Dkr399/599/799; ⌚noon-10pm Mon-Sat) Another clever concept restaurant, where the menu is usually geographically themed ('Rome', for example, or 'New York Meets Paris') and dishes are loaned from (consenting) Michelin-starred restaurants around the globe, then given a Nordic twist. Menus change every two months – it's no doubt a huge challenge, but the kitchen handles it with aplomb. Lunch is excellent value.

Drinking & Entertainment

Aarhus is the nation's music capital, with no shortage of quality-music gigs in venues from dignified concert halls to beer-fuelled boltholes. For the low-down on what's happening around town, click onto www.visitaarhus.com or www.aoa.dk.

★Strandbaren BAR

(www.facebook.com/strandbarenaarhus; Havnebassin 7, pier 4; ⌚May-Sep) Plonk shipping containers and sand on a harbourfront spot and voila: beach bar. This chilled hang-out at Aarhus Ø (just beyond the ferry port) offers food, drink, flirting, and weather-dependent activities and events. Check hours and location on the Facebook page (harbour redevelopment may require an annual location change; opening hours are 'when the sun is shining').

Bus 33 runs out this way. While you're here, check out the new architectural developments of Aarhus Ø, including the head-turning 'Iceberg'.

★Løve's Bog- & VinCafé BAR

(www.loeves.dk; Nørregade 32; ⌚9am-midnight Mon-Fri, from 10am Sat, 10am-5pm Sun) This snug 'book and wine cafe' is full of book-lined shelves and old furniture, and reading/laptopping regulars. Occasional poetry readings and jazz bands add to the cultured air, while the short, simple tapas menu nicely fills in any writer's-block moments.

Under Masken BAR

(Bispegade 3; ⌚noon-2am Mon-Sat, 2-10pm Sun) Artist-run Under Masken keeps things kooky with its jumble of gilded mirrors, African tribal masks, sailor pictures and glowing fish tanks. Slide in a for a loud, smoky and fun night on the tiles. Note: no food served.

Train LIVE MUSIC, CLUB

(www.train.dk; Toldbodgade 6; ⌚club from midnight Fri & Sat) Aarhus' premier club, Train is first and foremost a concert venue, with shows a couple of nights a week and some big international acts on the program. Train opens as a late-night club as well, on Friday and Saturday nights, with room for up to 1700 party people and top-notch DJ talent. The complex also incorporates Kupé, a funky lounge club.

Radar LIVE MUSIC
(www.radarlive.dk; Godsbanen, Skovgaardsgade 3) Radar offers a glimpse into Aarhus' indie scene with a wide range of music (including rock, techno, punk and folk) from its home inside the very cool Godsbanen freight yard, a new cultural hub for the city. **Godsbanen** (www.godsbanen.dk; Skovgaardsgade 3) is home to stages, workshops and a quality cafe, and hosts exhibitions and events – it's worth a look.

Musikhuset Aarhus LIVE MUSIC
(www.musikhusetaarhus.dk; Thomas Jensens Allé 2) Aarhus' concert hall is a large, glass-fronted venue that hosts a range of musical events, from Rod Stewart to *Rigoletto*, and performances from Den Kongelige Ballet (the Royal Danish Ballet) or the Aarhus Symphony Orchestra.

Shopping

ARoS Aarhus Kunstmuseum BOOKS, GIFTS
(Aros Allé 2; ⏲10am-5pm Tue-Sun, to 10pm Wed) The art museum's gift shop has an extensive range of art books, homewares, accessories and nifty knick-knacks.

HAY DESIGN
(www.hay.dk; Rosenkrantzgade 24; ⏲10am-6pm Mon-Fri, to 4pm Sat) Well-chosen examples of the latest Danish furniture as well as fabulous designer homewares, textiles and rugs.

Flagstang Markeder FLEA MARKET
(www.flagstang-markeder.dk; Mølleparken; ⏲10am-4pm Sun monthly) Scour Aarhus' monthly flea market for anything from Cheap Monday jeans to Royal Copenhagen porcelain and plastic-fantastic 70s Danish kitchenware (plus a good deal of junk). Check the website calendar for dates. In winter the market moves inside, to the foyer of Musikhuset.

Information

VisitAarhus (☎87 31 50 10; www.visitaarhus.com) no longer has a central tourist office, but aims to reach travellers via its website, phone line, mobile info booths (in peak periods), and touch-screen computers at many of the town's attractions, transport hubs and accommodation providers.

If you have questions and want face-to-face help, staff at the bus station can usually help. Otherwise, do some advance prep: visit the website, download the app, check social-media pages for up-to-date info (see 'This is why I love Aarhus' on Facebook; follow @VisitAarhus on Twitter).

Aarhus Universitetshospital (☎78 45 00 00; Nørrebrogade 44) Hospital with a 24-hour emergency ward; call before arriving.

Getting There & Away

AIR

Aarhus Airport (www.aar.dk), also known as Tirstrup airport, is 45km northeast of the city. Scandinavian Airlines (SAS) has daily flights to/from Copenhagen; Sun-Air (affiliated with British Airways) operates direct connections to Stockholm, Gothenburg and Oslo. Ryanair has daily connections to/from London (Stansted).

BOAT

Mols-Linien (☎70 10 14 18; www.mols-linien.dk) operates high-speed ferries between Aarhus and Odden in north Zealand (one-way adult/child/car Dkr349/175/699kr, 70 minutes, minimum five sailings daily). Rates for car passage include passengers.

BUS

The **bus station** (Fredensgade) has a DSB cafe and a small supermarket. **Abildskou** (☎70 21 08 88; www.abildskou.dk) runs express bus line 888 up to 10 times daily between Aarhus and Copenhagen's Valby station (Dkr310, three to 3½ hours), with connections to Copenhagen airport. Good fare discounts are available; see the website.

CAR & MOTORCYCLE

The main highways to Aarhus are the E45 from the north and south, and Rte 15 from the west. The E45 doesn't make it into the city itself; take exits 46 to 50.

Cars can be rented from **Europcar** (☎89 33 11 11; www.europcar.com; Sønder Allé 35).

TRAIN

Aarhus is well connected by train. There's a ticket-queuing system at the station: red for domestic and green for international. For domestic journeys, skip the queues by using one of the ticket machines (instructions available in English; credit cards accepted). Friday trains are always busy, and it's best to reserve a seat (Dkr30) for long journeys.

Destinations include Aalborg (Dkr194, 1½ hours, twice hourly) and Copenhagen via Odense (Dkr382, three to 3½ hours, twice hourly).

Getting Around

A new light-rail line (known as the Aarhus Letbane) is expected to open in 2016. Phase 1 includes the construction of a 12km tramway from Aarhus train station via the harbour to Nørreport. The rail link to Grenaa in Djursland will carry trams. The opening of the *letbane* will impact upon bus services – the Midttrafik website (www.midttrafik.dk) will keep you informed; its phone line and the service counter at the bus station are your best bets for info.

TO/FROM THE AIRPORT

A bus service (route 925X) connects Aarhus with the airport at Tirstrup (Dkr100, 50 minutes). Buses depart outside the train station (close to the post office) and the changeable schedule is geared to meet all incoming and outgoing flights; phone 70 21 02 30 for up-to-date information or see www.midttrafik.dk.

A taxi between the airport and the city centre will set you back a hefty Dkr650.

BICYCLE

Free **Aarhusbycykel** (www.aarhusbycykel.dk) city bikes are available from locations around the city from April to October (download a map from the website, or ask at your accommodation). There are a few bikes close to the Subway store opposite the train station, and some outside the town hall. You need to put a Dkr20 coin into the slot to obtain the bike (refunded when you return it).

If you're visiting from November to March, or you want a better-quality bike for a lengthy period, **Bikes4Rent** (20 26 10 20; www.bikes-4rent.dk; per day/week Dkr95/250) can help. Staff deliver bikes to a central city location (the Radisson hotel by Musikhuset).

BUS

Aarhus has an extensive, efficient local bus network. Most in-town (yellow) buses stop close to the train station on Park Allé. Buy your ticket from the on-board machine (Dkr20, allowing up to two hours' travel). Information on tickets, routes and schedules is available from the bus station on Fredensgade, via the website www.midttraffik.dk (good info in English) or by dialling 70 21 02 30.

CAR & MOTORCYCLE

A car is convenient for getting to sights such as Moesgård on the city outskirts, though the city centre is best explored on foot.

There's paid undercover parking in municipal car parks, including one near Musikhuset Aarhus and at Bruun's Galleri shopping centre. There are also numerous *billetautomat* (parking meters) along city streets. You'll usually need to pay for street parking from 9am to 7pm Monday to Friday and 9am to 4pm Saturday (outside those hours parking is generally free). Parking costs Dkr12/17 for the first/second hour, and Dkr22 per hour after that.

TAXI

Taxis are available at the train station and at a rank by the cathedral; you can also flag one on the street or order one by phone (89 48 48 48). All taxis have a meter – expect to pay up to Dkr100 for destinations within the inner city.

Jelling

A sleepy town with a big history, Jelling is revered as the birthplace of Christianity in Denmark, the monarchy and all that is truly Danish. The town served as the royal seat of King Gorm during the Vikings' most dominant era; Gorm the Old was the first in a millennium-long chain of Danish monarchs that continues unbroken to this day. The site of Gorm's ancient castle remains a mystery, but other vestiges of his reign can still be found at Jelling Kirke.

The town is a kind of spiritual touchstone for the Danes, Virtually all of them will visit at some point, to pay homage at the church,

WORTH A TRIP

RANDERS

Located 36km north of Aarhus, the town of Randers is famous for two rather eclectic attractions. The first is **Randers Regnskov** (www.regnskoven.dk; Tørvebryggen 11; adult/child Dkr170/100; 10am-4pm or later;), a dome-enclosed tropical zoo. Trails within the sultry trio of domes – which re-create the tropical environments of South America, Africa and Asia – pass through enclosures housing crocodiles, monkeys, iguanas, a manatee, orchids, hibiscus and other tropical fauna and flora. Closing times vary, from 4pm to 6pm (check the website).

Two kilometres southeast of the town centre is **Graceland Randers** (www.elvispresley.dk; Graceland Randers Vej 3; museum adult/child Dkr99/69; 10am-9pm), Denmark's very own Elvis Presley Museum. Housed in a replica Graceland mansion (double the size of the original), it's a showcase for one obsessed fan's personal collection of memorabilia. The kitschy complex also includes a well-stocked Elvis shop, American diner and mini movie theatre.

All trains between Aarhus (Dkr58, 30 minutes) and Aalborg (Dkr111, 50 minutes) stop at Randers.

inspect the two rune stones and climb the burial mounds. The area became a Unesco World Heritage Site in 1994.

Sights

Jelling Kirke CHURCH
(www.jellingkirke.dk; Vejlevej; ⌚8am-8pm May-Aug, to 6pm Sep-Oct & Mar-Apr, to 5pm Nov-Feb) Inside this small whitewashed church, erected around 1100, are some vividly restored 12th-century **frescoes**; the main attractions, however, are the two well-preserved **rune stones** just outside the church door.

The smaller stone was erected in the early 10th century by King Gorm the Old in honour of his wife. The larger one, raised by Gorm's son, Harald Bluetooth, is adorned with the oldest representation of Christ found in Scandinavia and is commonly dubbed 'Denmark's baptismal certificate'.

The stone reads: 'King Harald ordered this monument to be made in memory of Gorm his father and Thyra his mother, the Harald who won for himself all Denmark and Norway and made the Danes Christians.' A replica of the stone (in full colour, as the original would once have appeared) is at Kongernes Jelling, opposite the church.

Harald Bluetooth did, in fact, succeed in routing the Swedes from Denmark and began the peaceful conversion of the Danish people from the pagan religion celebrated by his father to Christianity.

Two large **burial mounds** flank Jelling Kirke. The barrow to the north was long believed to contain the bones of Gorm and his queen, Thyra, but when it was excavated in 1820 no human remains were found. The southern mound was excavated in 1861 but, again, no mortal remains unearthed.

In the 1970s archaeologists dug beneath Jelling Kirke itself and hit pay dirt. They found the remains of three earlier wooden churches; the oldest is thought to have been erected by Harald Bluetooth. A burial chamber was also unearthed and human bones and gold jewellery were discovered. Archaeologists now believe that the remains are those of Gorm, who had originally been buried in the northern mound but was later reinterred by his son. Presumably Harald Bluetooth, out of respect, moved his parents' remains from pagan soil to a place of honour within the church. The bones of Queen Thyra have yet to be found.

Archaeological investigations in the area are ongoing. Read about them online (http://jelling.natmus.dk), or learn more at Kongernes Jelling.

Kongernes Jelling MUSEUM
(http://natmus.dk/en/royal-jelling; Gormsgade 23) FREE In summer 2015, a newly expanded visitors centre will open opposite the church. Expect high-quality interactive exhibitions: before its expansion, Kongernes Jelling provided enthralling insight into the town's monuments and their importance to Danish royal history. The museum is part of the National Museum organisation; check the website for opening hours.

Eating

Jelling Kro TRADITIONAL DANISH €€
(www.jellingkro.dk; Gormsgade 16; lunch Dkr75-125, dinner mains Dkr98-210; ⌚11am-9.30pm daily Jun-Aug, shorter hours rest of year) In a 1780 bright-yellow building bristling with character, this country inn serves up traditional, meat-heavy Danish fare.

Information

Jelling Kirke is in the centre of town, a three-minute walk due north from the train station along Stationsvej. Tourist information will likely be offered at Kongernes Jelling when it reopens. There is online information at www.visitvejle.com.

Getting There & Away

Jelling is 10km northwest of Vejle on Rte 442. From Vejle, trains run at least hourly on weekdays, less frequently at weekends (Dkr30, 15 minutes). Bus 211 covers the same ground for the same price.

The Lake District

This is a perhaps misleading name for what is more like a gently hilly region with a few medium-sized lakes and Denmark's highest point, Yding Skovhø. It is unlikely to induce nosebleeds, but this is a delightful area for rambling. There is also ample opportunity for canoeing, biking and longer-distance hiking here. This is also where you'll find Denmark's longest river, the Gudenå, and Mossø, Jutland's largest lake. This area is south and southwest of Silkeborg, slap bang in the centre of Jutland, half an hour's drive west of Aarhus.

Silkeborg

POP 43,200

Silkeborg overcomes its rather bland modern character with a friendly openness. It is the Lake District's biggest town and is an ideal base for exploring the surrounding forests and waterways. The town has some good restaurants and lively bars and cafes. A compelling reason to visit is to see the Tollund Man, the body of a preserved Iron Age 'bog man' who looks as if he's merely asleep.

Sights

Museum Silkeborg MUSEUM
(www.museumsilkeborg.dk; Hovedgårdsvej 7; adult/child Dkr50/free; 10am-5pm daily May–mid-Oct, noon-4pm Sat & Sun Nov-Apr) Here you can check out the amazingly well-preserved body of the 2350-year-old **Tollund Man**, the central (albeit leathery) star in an otherwise smart but predictable collection. The well-preserved face of the Tollund Man is hypnotic in its detail, right down to the stubble on his chin. Like the Grauballe Man at Aarhus' Moesgård Museum, the life (and death) of the Tollund Man remains a mystery.

Museum Jorn ART MUSEUM
(www.museumjorn.dk; Gudenåvej 7-9; adult/child Dkr80/free; 11am-5pm Tue-Fri, 10am-5pm Sat & Sun) This wonderful art space contains some striking works. It displays many of the works of native son Asger Jorn and other modern artists, including Max Ernst, Le Corbusier and Danish artists from the influential CoBrA group. It's 1km south of the town centre.

KunstCentret Silkeborg Bad ART MUSEUM
(www.silkeborgbad.dk; Gjessøvej 40; adult/child Dkr60/free; 10am-5pm Tue-Sun May-Sep, noon-4pm Mon-Fri, 11am-5pm Sat & Sun Oct-Apr) This former spa dates from 1883 and is now a beautiful, modern art space, with permanent works and changing exhibitions of art, sculpture, ceramics, glassware, design and architecture, surrounded by parkland (always open) featuring contemporary sculpture. It's about 2km southwest of town; catch local bus 10.

Activities

Outdoor activities are at the heart of the Lake District's appeal. The track of the old railway from Silkeborg to Horsens is now an excellent **walking** and **cycling** trail of about 50km or so. The tourist office has plenty of brochures on hiking and cycling routes and **Silkeborg Kayak og Cykel Udlejning** (www.skcu.dk; Åhave Allé 7; kayak/mountain bike per day Dkr350/175; 9am-8pm Jun-Aug, to 5pm May, by arrangement Sep, Oct, Apr;) has mountain bikes for hire.

Canoeing is a marvellous way to explore the Lake District and you can plan trips for several days staying at lakeside camping grounds along the way. The canoe-hire places can help plan an itinerary and will rent canoes by the hour (Dkr100) or day (Dkr400). Among them is **Silkeborg Kanocenter** (86 80 30 03; www.silkeborgkanocenter.dk; Østergade 36; 9am-8pm Jun-Aug, to 5pm Apr, May, Sep;).

The world's oldest operating **paddle steamer** (86 82 07 66; www.hjejlen.com; 1-way/return Dkr90/140; May-Sep) offers tours on the lake during summer, departing opposite Slusekiosken.

Sleeping

Budget and midrange choices in town are limited, making B&B accommodation an especially good (and good-value) option. The website www.silkeborg.com lists all the choices, and the tourist office can help. There are oodles of camping grounds in the region.

★**Villa Zeltner** B&B €
(29 82 58 58; www.villa-zeltner.dk; Zeltnersvej 4; s/d/apt from Dkr350/500/600) Supercentral and with loads of style, this great-value B&B houses a handful of rooms with shared bathroom and kitchen access, plus a couple of small apartments with private kitchen and bathroom. There's garden access and a grill too, plus a few bikes for guest use. Breakfast can be arranged at additional cost.

★**Danhostel Silkeborg** HOSTEL €
(86 82 36 42; www.danhostel-silkeborg.dk; Åhavevej 55; dm Dkr275, d without/with bathroom Dkr520/720; Mar-Nov; @) The gorgeous riverbank location, good facilities and lack of budget alternatives in town make this hostel popular, so book ahead. Once here, enjoy the outdoor tables and homely communal areas alongside cyclists, families, school groups and Euro-backpackers. Dorm beds are available July to mid-September; breakfast costs Dkr75.

Gudenåens Camping CAMPGROUND €
(86 82 22 01; www.gudenaaenscamping.dk; Vejlsøvej 7; per adult/child/site Dkr85/52/70; @) Follow the signs for Aqua to find this tree-filled riverside park, about 2km south of the town centre (just south of

Indelukket). Cabins and caravans are available for hire (only by the week in July and August), and there's a lovely natural pool for swimming. Local bus 4 runs down this way.

Radisson BLU Hotel HOTEL €€
(☎88 82 22 22; www.radissonblu.com/hotel-silkeborg; Papirfabrikken 12; d incl breakfast Dkr1125-1575; @) This polished performer lives in the redeveloped paper factory that was once the backbone of the local economy. It's right on the river, among a clutch of restaurants, and the designer rooms are petite but comfy and well equipped. Weekend rates are cheaper than midweek.

Eating

There are two areas to investigate when scouting for eating (and drinking) options: the reinvigorated Papirfabrikken (the old paper factory) and the fast-food and international cuisines on Nygade. Self-caterers can stock the hamper at the **Fotex Supermarket** (Torvet; ⏲8am-9pm), on the main square. End-of-week nightlife clusters around the corner of Nygade and Hostrupsgade.

Café Evald INTERNATIONAL €€
(www.evald.nu; Papirfabrikken 10B; lunch Dkr100-150, dinner mains Dkr150-290; ⏲11am-midnight or 1am Mon-Sat, 9.30am-9.30pm Sun) Among the family restaurants, cinema and cafe-bars of Papirfabrikken is bustling Evald, wooing patrons with a crowd-pleasing menu. Sit at a riverside table, order a beer from the local Grauballe Bryghus (brewery) and try the 'tapas' plate (a sampler plate comprising five small tastes of seasonal favourites).

★**Restaurant Gastronomisk Institut** EUROPEAN €€€
(☎86 82 40 97; www.gastronomiske.dk; Søndergade 20; lunch Dkr117-199, dinner mains Dkr199-299; ⏲11.30am-3pm & 5.30-9.30pm Tue-Sat) The ambitious name creates high expectations, and this elegant central restaurant delivers, with changing menus highlighting seasonal produce (and good-value set menus, including four evening courses for Dkr399). Leisurely lunchers might like crayfish soup; dinner ranges from suckling calf to fresh fish. Dinner bookings recommended.

Information

Tourist Office (www.silkeborg.com; Torvet 2A; ⏲10am-5pm Mon-Fri, 10am-2pm Sat Jul-Aug, shorter hrs Sep-Jun) Well-stocked office on the main square.

Getting There & Away

Silkeborg is 44km west of Aarhus on Rte 15. Half-hourly trains connect Silkeborg with Aarhus (Dkr85, 50 minutes) via Ry (Dkr39, 15 minutes).

Skanderborg & Ry

Two smaller, quieter Lake District towns east of Silkeborg are Ry and Skanderborg. **Ry**, the closer of the two to Silkeborg, is a particularly peaceful place from which to base your exploration of the Lake District. **Skanderborg** is a rather humdrum town, but with a lovely setting on Skanderborg Lake. It is best known in Denmark for the Smukfest.

Sights & Activities

Himmelbjerget OUTDOORS
The Lake District's most visited spot is the whimsically named Himmelbjerget (Sky Mountain), which, at just 147m, is one of Denmark's highest hills. It was formed by water erosion during the final Ice Age as a *kol* (false hill), the sides of which are quite steep. There are a number of interesting memorials surrounding the hilltop's crowning glory, the 25m-tower (admission Dkr10), reached via a marked 6km footpath north east of Ry, or by bus or boat.

Ry Kanofart CANOEING
(☎86 89 11 67; www.kanoferie.dk; Kyhnsvej 20; ⏲9am-6pm daily Jun-Aug, 9am-6pm Sat & Sun May & Sep) Ry Kanofart has canoes for hire, costing Dkr100/400 per hour/day. As with the operators in Silkeborg, staff here can help you plan multiday river trips on the Gudenå and lakes.

Festivals & Events

Smukfest MUSIC
(www.smukfest.dk) If music festivals are your thing, you *definitely* need to know about the annual Skanderborg Festival, held on the second weekend in August and billed as 'Denmark's most beautiful festival', due to its gorgeous location among beech forest in the Lake District. Skanderborg is about 28km southwest of Aarhus, and roughly the same distance from Silkeborg.

Sleeping & Eating

Hotel Blicher HOTEL €€
(☎86 89 19 11; www.hotelblicher.dk; Kyhnsvej 2; d standard/superior Dkr990/1250; P@) There are two room categories at Ry's only hotel:

the superior rooms are newly renovated and a fresher option than the older, unrenovated wing. It's a large, pleasant place, popular for conferences and weddings, and staff can help arrange canoeing and cycling.

La Saison DANISH €
(Kyhnsvej 2; lunch smørrebrød 1/3 pieces Dkr49/125, dinner mains Dkr175; ⌚11am-9pm) Easily Ry's fanciest dining option, this shiny outfit is attached to Hotel Blicher and has a lunchtime menu of smørrebrød classics, and a short but high-quality dinner menu.

Le Gâteau BAKERY €
(Klostervej 12; sandwiches Dkr45; ⌚7am-5.30pm Mon-Fri, to 2pm Sat, to noon Sun) Flaky pastries, good coffee and handy sandwiches await at this smart little bakery, opposite the Ry train station and tourist office.

Information

Ry's **tourist office** (☎86 69 66 00; www.visitskanderborg.com; Klostervej 3, Ry; ⌚10am-4pm Mon-Fri, 10am-noon Sat May-Aug, 10am-2pm Mon-Fri Sep-Apr) is in the train station.

Getting There & Away

Ry is on Rte 445, 22km southeast of Silkeborg and 35km west of Aarhus. Half-hourly trains connect Ry with Silkeborg (Dkr39, 15 minutes) and Aarhus (Dkr66, 30 minutes).

Viborg

POP 38,600

Rich in religious history and bordering two idyllic lakes, Viborg is a sweetly romantic getaway. During its holiest period (just prior to the Reformation), 25 churches lined the streets. Nowadays, only two can be found in the town centre.

Sights & Activities

Viborg Domkirke CHURCH
(www.viborgdomkirke.dk; Sankt Mogens Gade 4; admission Dkr10; ⌚11am-5pm Mon-Sat, noon-5pm Sun May-Aug, to 3pm Sep-Apr) The striking, twin-towered cathedral is equally impressive inside and out, with **frescoes**, painted over five years (1908–13) by artist Joakim Skovgaard, evocatively portraying the story of the Protestant bible. In 1876 the cathedral was almost entirely rebuilt, becoming the largest granite church in Scandinavia (an enduring claim to fame). The crypt is all that survives from its birth date, 1100.

Skovgaard Museet MUSEUM
(www.skovgaardmuseet.dk; Domkirkestræde 2-4; adult/child Dkr50/free; ⌚10am-5pm Tue-Sun Jun-Aug, 11am-4pm Tue-Sun Sep-May) Just outside the cathedral, this museum highlights further work of cathedral-artist Joakim Skovgaard, among other works by his contemporaries, plus changing exhibitions.

Viborg Museum MUSEUM
(www.viborgmuseum.dk; Hjultorvet 4; adult/child Dkr40/free; ⌚11am-5pm Tue-Sun Jul–mid-Aug, shorter hours rest of year) This local history museum tells the story of Viborg's rich religious past.

Margrethe I BOAT TRIPS
(adult/child Dkr50/30; ⌚2pm mid-May–Aug) Jump onboard the *Margrethe I* for a one-hour cruise of the town lakes. There are additional cruises from mid-June (at 3.15pm); the boat departs from outside Golf Salonen on Randersvej. The surrounding park is lovely; from mid-May to September you can rent canoes and rowboats from the park kiosk for lake exploration.

Sleeping & Eating

The Sankt Mathias Gade Centre has cafes, a supermarket, bakery, fruit shop and a butcher.

Danhostel Viborg HOSTEL €
(☎86 67 17 81; www.danhostelviborg.dk; Vinkelvej 36; dm/s/d Dkr210/415/515; ⌚mid-Jan–Nov; @) This well-run place feels like a country escape, 3km from town in green surrounds and backed by botanic gardens down to the lakeshore. Rooms are top-notch too (most with bathrooms). Note that the town's camping ground is next door. No bus services.

★**Niels Bugges Hotel** BOUTIQUE HOTEL €€
(☎86 63 80 11; www.nielsbuggeskro.dk; Egeskovvej 26, Hald Ege; d Dkr1250-1450, without bathroom Dkr790) This old inn, set amid forest on the outskirts of town, is a destination hotel where design and gastronomy are taken seriously and the result is something special. Rooms epitomise farmhouse chic, all florals, patchworks and antiques. Add a library, romantic grounds and wonderful New Nordic-inspired restaurant, **Skov** (meaning 'forest'), and you too will be dreading checkout.

To reach the hotel from Viborg, take Rte 13 south then follow signs for 'Hald Ege'. Bus 53 runs out this way.

Oasen GUESTHOUSE €€
(☎86 62 14 25; www.oasenviborg.dk; Nørregade 13; s/d Dkr400/550, with bathroom Dkr450/650;) Oasen is an inviting complex of central rooms and apartments, nicely bridging the gap between hostels and business hotels. Some rooms have shared bathroom, but all have cable TV and free wi-fi, plus kitchen access. Breakfast (Dkr75) is taken in a sweet little 'cafe' in the garden.

Café Morville INTERNATIONAL €€
(www.cafemorville.dk; Hjultorvet; lunch Dkr69-124, dinner dishes Dkr69-179; ⊙10am-10pm Mon & Tue, to 11pm Wed & Thu, to 1am Fri & Sat, 11am-5pm Sun) One of those chic all-day cafes that seem compulsory in Danish towns. You can park yourself on the leather banquettes for a midmorning coffee or late-night drink and everything in between.

Information

Tourist Office (☎87 87 88 88; www.visit-viborg.dk; Skottenborg 12-14; ⊙10am-5pm Mon-Fri, to 2pm Sat Jun-Aug, 10am-4pm Mon-Fri Sep-May) Clued up on the area, with good brochures and maps, plus bike hire (Dkr100 per day). This office is a little out of the centre; there's a smaller second branch inside the Viborg Museum on central Hjultorvet.

Getting There & Around

Viborg is 66km northwest of Aarhus on Rte 26 and 44km west of Randers on Rte 16. Regular trains run to/from Aarhus (Dkr138, 70 minutes). The train station is 1km southwest of the cathedral.

Aalborg

POP 130,900

Things are on the way up for Aalborg, Denmark's fourth-largest city. It sits at the narrowest point of the Limfjord (the long body of water that slices Jutland in two), and recent developments have seen the waterfront become the focal point of the town. A concerted effort is being made to rejuvenate the central industrial areas and turn neglected spaces into something far more appealing.

Traditionally Aalborg has flown under the traveller's radar, but that could easily change. There are enough low-key diversions here to occupy a few days for most visitors, from architecture fans to families, party animals to history boffins.

Sights

★Utzon Center ARCHITECTURE, MUSEUM
(www.utzoncenter.dk; Slotspladsen 4; adult/child Dkr60/free; ⊙10am-5pm Tue-Sun, open Mon in Jul) An impressive 700-sq-metre design-and-architecture space, the Utzon Center, with its distinctive silver roofscape, sits pretty on the waterfront. It bills itself as 'a dynamic and experimental centre of culture and knowledge' and is the last building designed by celebrated Danish architect, Jørn Utzon (1918–2008). Utzon famously designed the Sydney Opera House; he grew up in Aalborg and died shortly after the eponymous centre was finished.

The centre hosts a changing program of exhibitions on architecture, design and art; there's also a high-quality restaurant.

★Waterfront LANDMARK
The Aalborg waterfront promenade, extending east from Limfjordsbroen, is a good example of urban regeneration, taking what was a scruffy dockside area and opening it up to locals. Here you'll find restaurants, a park, playground, basketball courts and moored boats (including an old ice-breaker, now a restaurant-bar). One of the best features is the **Aalborg Havnebad** (Jomfru Ane Parken 6; ⊙daily mid-Jun–Aug) FREE, a summertime outdoor pool that lets you take a dip in the Limfjord.

East of the Utzon Center there's more new development, including university buildings and smart, low-cost housing for the city's growing student population. The latest addition is the shiny new **Musikkens Hus** (www.musikkenshus.dk; Musikkens Plads 1), a first-class, futuristic-looking concert hall that opened in 2014.

An anachronism among all this new development, the mid-16th-century, half-timbered **Aalborghus Slot** (Slotspladsen; ⊙dungeon 8am-3pm Mon-Fri May-Oct) FREE is more an administrative office than a castle, but there's a small dungeon you can visit.

Nordkraft CULTURAL CENTRE
(www.nordkraft.dk; Kjellerups Torv; ⊙7am-11pm) Once a power station, this cultural centre is home to a theatre, concert venue, art-house cinema, gallery, fitness centre, plus a couple of eateries. The small tourist office is also here, so it's worth popping in to see what's happening.

Budolfi Domkirke CHURCH
(www.aalborgdomkirke.dk; Algade 40; ⊙9am-4pm Mon-Fri, to 2pm Sat Jun-Aug, 9am-3pm Mon-Fri, to noon Sat Sep-May) This 12th-century cathedral

marks the centre of the old town and its elegant carillon can be heard every hour, on the hour. Its whitewashed interior creates an almost Mediterranean ambience.

As you enter the cathedral from Algade, look up at the foyer ceiling to see colourful frescoes from around 1500. The interior boasts some beautifully carved items, including a gilded baroque altar and a richly detailed pulpit.

Aalborg Historiske Museum MUSEUM
(www.nordmus.dk; Algade 48; adult/child Dkr30/free; ⌚10am-5pm Tue-Sun Apr-Dec, to 4pm Jan-Mar) Just west of Budolfi Domkirke is the town's history museum, with artefacts from prehistory to the present, and furnishings and interiors that hint at the wealth Aalborg's merchants enjoyed during the Renaissance.

Helligåndsklostret MONASTERY
(CW Obels Plads; adult/child Dkr50/free; ⌚tours 2pm Tue & Thu Jul-Aug) An alley off Algade leads to the rambling Monastery of the Holy Ghost, which dates from 1431 and is home to some fascinating frescoes. The interior can only be visited on a guided tour.

Kunsten MUSEUM
(www.kunsten.dk; Kong Christians Allé 50) Housed in a modular, marble building designed by the great Finnish architect Alvar Aalto, Kunsten is Aalborg's museum of modern and contemporary art. The building's light-filled interior complements a fine collection of predominantly Danish works.

Kunsten will reopen after major renovations in October 2015 (before then, you can see some of its collection inside the train station). Check the website for opening hours and prices.

To get to Kunsten, take the tunnel beneath the train station, which emerges into **Kildeparken**, a green space with statues and water fountains. Go directly through the park, cross Vesterbro and continue through a wooded area to the museum, a 10-minute walk in all. Alternatively, take bus 15.

Lindholm Høje VIKING SITE
(Vendilavej; ⌚dawn-dusk) FREE The Limfjord was a kind of Viking motorway providing easy, speedy access to the Atlantic for longboat raiding parties. It's not surprising, then, that the most important piece of Aalborg's historical heritage is a predominantly Viking one.

The atmospheric Lindholm Høje is a Viking burial ground where nearly 700 graves from the Iron Age and Viking Age are strewn around a hilltop pasture ringed by a wall of beech trees.

Many of the Viking graves are marked by stones placed in the oval outline of a Viking ship, with two larger end stones as stem and stern. At the end of the Viking era the whole area was buried under drifting sand and thus preserved until modern times.

Lindholm Høje Museet (www.nordmus.dk; Vendilavej 11; adult/child Dkr60/free; ⌚10am-5pm daily Apr-Oct, 10am-4pm Tue-Sun Nov-Mar) adjoins the site and explains its history, and has displays on finds made during its excavation. Murals behind the exhibits speculate on how the people of Lindholm lived.

Lindholm Høje is 15 minutes north of central Aalborg via bus 2. With your own wheels, head north from the centre over Limfjordsbroen to Nørresundby, and follow the signs.

Sleeping

If only the sleeping options matched the quality of the eating choices! With few exceptions, Aalborg's hotel scene is lacklustre. The tourist office has details of budget-priced rooms in private homes.

CabInn Aalborg HOTEL €
(☎96 20 30 00; www.cabinn.com; Fjordgade 20; s/d/tr from Dkr495/625/835; @) The cheap, reliable CabInn chain added Aalborg to its portfolio with this large, central hotel across the road from the Utzon Center and neighbouring the Friis shopping centre. All 239 rooms have TV and bathrooms, but there's little room for cat-swinging in the cheaper rooms. Breakfast costs Dkr70.

Danhostel Aalborg HOSTEL €
(☎98 11 60 44; www.bbbb.dk; Skydebanevej 50; dm/d Dkr345/590; P @) The hostel is handy for boating activities on the fjord (you can hire kayaks here in summer) but it's hardly central. The surrounds are green and the accommodation is basic (all rooms have bathrooms); dorm beds are available in summer. There's an adjoining campground with budget cabins. It's in the marina area about 3km west of the town centre; take bus 13 (which stops short of the hostel).

Villa Rosa GUESTHOUSE €€
(☎98 12 13 38; www.villarosa.dk; Grønnegangen 4; r & apt Dkr500-800; P) Book early to snare one of only six theatrically decorated rooms over three floors (no lift) at this late-19th-century villa. The standout bargains here are the

three small self-contained apartments – the English Room is especially lovely. Three rooms share a large bathroom and guest kitchen. It's the most interesting option in town, so the reasonable rates and central location are added bonuses.

First Hotel Aalborg HOTEL €€
(☎98 10 14 00; www.firsthotels.com; Rendsburggade 5; d incl breakfast from Dkr740; P @) Some of the newly renovated rooms at this smart fjordside hotel near the Utzon Center have water views, and the (limited) free parking is a bonus, as is the central location, and onsite gym and bar. Best rates are found online.

Hotel Aalborg HOTEL €€
(Sømandshjemmet; ☎98 12 19 00; www.hotelaalborg.com; Østerbro 27; s/d from Dkr715/760; P) This old seamen's hotel was once oddly placed, but encroaching harbourside redevelopment now sees it in the heart of the action, with Nordkraft and Musikkens Hus as neighbours. Comfortable, no-frills rooms are on offer, but there are exciting plans for a big extension and dramatic makeover (including the addition of high-end rooms). Free parking and friendly staff too.

Eating

★**Abbey Road** CAFE €
(http://abbeyroadcafe.dk; Kjellerupsgade 1A; meals Dkr89-135; ⊙8am-10pm Mon-Sat) Opposite Nordkraft is this near-perfect all-day cafe: quality coffee and tea, mismatched furniture, and *hygge* by the bucketload. A new little sister to the long-established Penny Lane, Abbey Road dispenses salads, sandwiches and tapas plates, plus some seriously tasty baked goods (including healthy seeded breads – but hello pear-and-chocolate tart).

Penny Lane CAFE, DELI €
(pennylanecafe.dk; Boulevarden 1; meals Dkr89-135; ⊙8am-6pm Mon-Thu, to 7pm Fri, to 4pm Sat) This ace cafe-delicatessen has an inhouse bakery, so its freshly baked bread, local cheeses and cured meats are extremely picnicworthy. There's an in-house cafe offering a cracker brunch platter (Dkr105) or lunchtime sandwiches, salads and tarts. Leave room for something sweet.

Pingvin Tapas & Vincafé INTERNATIONAL €€
(☎98 11 11 66; www.cafepingvin.dk; Adelgade 12; dinner 4/6/8 tapas Dkr198/238/268; ⊙noon-11pm Mon-Sat) This chic restaurant-bar offers a selection of up to 30 'tapas' (not so much shared dishes, but more of an individual tasting-plate approach). Enjoy small portions of lobster soup, grilled prawns with Vietnamese mango salad, or smoked duck breast. There's an excellent global wine list, plus lunchtime offers.

★**Mortens Kro** MODERN DANISH €€€
(☎98 12 48 60; www.mortenskro.dk; Møllea 4-6; 4-course menus Dkr598; ⊙5.30-10pm Mon-Sat) Hands down both the best and priciest in town, sleek Mortens Kro is owned by celebrity chef Morten Nielsen. It's a stylish, well-hidden place where top-quality local, seasonal produce is showcased: home-smoked trout and salmon, Norwegian lobster soup, cherry meringue with raspberry sorbet. Book ahead and dress to impress. Mølleå Arkaden is accessed from Peder Barkes Gade 40A or Mølleplads.

Morten Nielsen is also the chef behind the excellent restaurant at the Utzon Center – a great place to go for top-shelf smørrebrød or weekend brunch.

Drinking

If it's a flirt, a drink or loud beats you're after, trawl Jomfru Ane Gade, Aalborg's take-no-prisoners party street, jammed solid with bars. The venues themselves are pretty homogenous, so it's best to explore until you hear your kind of music or spy your type of crowd. Things are pretty tame early in the week, but get rowdy later from Thursday night.

You won't have trouble finding somewhere to whet your whistle along Jomfru Ane Gade, so we've listed a few places away from the main strip.

Irish House PUB
(www.theirishhouse.dk; Østerågade 25; ⊙1pm-1am Mon-Wed, to 2am Thu, noon-4am Fri & Sat, 2pm-midnight Sun) It's almost too beautiful a setting in which to get sloshed. Inside a 17th-century building loaded with timber carvings and stained glass, this cheerful pub offers live music Thursday to Saturday, cheap pub grub and a big range of beers.

Søgaards Bryghus MICROBREWERY
(www.soegaardsbryghus.dk; CW Obels Plads 4; ⊙11am-11pm Mon-Thu, to late Fri & Sat, 11.30am-10pm Sun) Every Danish town worth its salt has a microbrewery, and Aalborg's is a cracker. It has loads of outdoor seating and a long menu of beer accompaniments, so you could easily lose an afternoon sampling Søgaard's impressive array of brews.

Information

Post Office (Slotsgade 14; ⌚9.30am-6pm Mon-Fri, to 1pm Sat) Inside Føtex supermarket.

Tourist Office (☎99 31 75 00; www.visitaalborg.com; Nordkraft, Kjellerups Torv 5; ⌚10am-5.30pm Mon-Fri, to 2pm Sat) A small but well-stocked office inside Nordkraft. In summer, information is also dispensed from the delightful 1896 Kochs Kiosk (Gabels Torv).

Getting There & Away

BUS & TRAIN

Trains run to Aarhus (Dkr194, 1½ hours, at least hourly), Frederikshavn (Dkr100, 70 minutes, hourly), and Copenhagen (Dkr431, 4½ to five hours, at least hourly). **Abildskou** (☎70 21 08 88; www.abildskou.dk) runs express bus 888 to Copenhagen's Valby station (Dkr360, 5½ hours).

In summer the good-value NT Travel Pass covers 24/72 hours of transport in northern Jutland (train and bus) for Dkr150/250. Two children under 12 years can accompany a paying adult for free. Buy the pass online (www.nordjyllandstrafikselskab.dk) and it's delivered to your phone.

CAR & MOTORCYCLE

Aalborg is 117km north of Aarhus and 65km southwest of Frederikshavn. The E45 bypasses the city centre, tunnelling under the Limfjord, while Rte 180 (which links up with the E45 both north and south of the city) leads into the centre.

Getting Around

BUS

Almost all city buses leave from south of JF Kennedys Plads and pass the city-centre stops on Østerågade and Nytorv, near Burger King. The standard local bus fare is Dkr20.

From late June to late August, a free City Circle bus runs half-hourly from 10am to 6pm (until 2pm on weekends). The circuit takes in major sites, including Kunsten and the waterfront.

Information on tickets, routes and schedules is available at the helpful **bus station information desk** (☎98 11 11 11; ⌚7am-5pm Mon-Fri, 9.30am-4pm Sat, 10.30am-5.30pm Sun).

CAR

Despite a few one-way streets, central Aalborg is a fairly easy place to get around by car. There's free (but time-restricted) parking on many side streets, and metered parking in the city centre. There are also several large commercial car parks, including at Ved Stranden 11 (opposite the Radisson hotel), at Kennedy Arkaden (enter from Østre Allé), and under the Friis shopping centre (enter from Nyhavnsgade). These aren't cheap (up to Dkr18 per hour, maximum Dkr160 for a 24-hour period).

Frederikshavn

POP 23,300

If you plan on catching a ferry to Sweden or Norway, you may find yourself boarding in Frederikshavn. Those with time to kill can head to **Bangsbo** (www.kystmuseet.dk; Dronning Margrethesvej 6; adult/child Dkr50/free; ⌚10am-4pm Mon-Fri, 11am-4pm Sat & Sun Jun-Aug, Mon-Fri only Sep-May), an old country estate with eclectic exhibits. Among these are the reconstructed remains of a 12th-century, Viking-style merchant ship dug up from a nearby stream bed. Located 3km south of the centre, the museum can be reached by bus 3, which stops near the estate's entrance.

Sleeping

In case you have a late or early ferry, here are a couple of decent options within walking distance of the port.

★**Danhostel Frederikshavn City** HOSTEL € (☎98 42 14 75; http://danhostelfrederikshavn.dk; Læsøgade 18; dm/s/d Dkr220/530/590; P@) Frederikshavn's hostel is perfectly positioned behind the tourist office, with a supermarket and cafe-bar as neighbours. It's busy with ferry passengers enjoying the fresh new facilities (all rooms have bathrooms). Communal areas are top-notch, as is the courtyard garden with barbecue. Breakfast costs Dkr60.

Best Western Hotel Herman Bang HOTEL €€ (☎98 42 21 66; www.hermanbang.dk; Tordenskjoldsgade 3; standard s/d from Dkr795/995) The standard rooms here are bright and comfortable, and the most expensive ('business' rooms) are quite luxurious. The cheapest (called 'budget' rooms) are poor value – you're better off at the hotel's newly decorated budget annex, **Herman Bang Bed & Breakfast** (www.hbbb.dk; Skolegade 2; d with/without bathroom Dkr650/500). The hotel has an upmarket spa and American-style diner.

Eating

Numerous, mainly fast-food, places line central Danmarkgade. You'll also find a cluster of eateries at the eastern end of Lodsgade, the best of which is **Karma Sushi** (www.karmasushi.dk; Lodsgade 10; 8-piece sushi Dkr98-135; ⌚5-10pm Tue-Thu, to 11pm Fri & Sat).

Getting There & Away

BOAT

Stena Line (☎96 20 02 00; www.stenaline.com) connects Frederikshavn with Gothenburg (Sweden) and Oslo (Norway).

TRAIN

Frederikshavn is the northern terminus of Danske Statsbaner (DSB) train lines (the national rail network); however, a private train line operates hourly trains north to Skagen (Dkr60, 35 minutes). DSB trains depart about hourly south to Aalborg (Dkr100, 1¼ hour) and Aarhus (Dkr252, 2¾ hours).

Skagen

POP 8200

Skagen is a magical place, both bracing and beautiful. If you are driving from the south, to get there you pass through kilometre after kilometre of, well, pretty much nothing really, until first pine forests and then an extraordinary landscape of grassy sand dunes herald this popular vacation region. The town of Skagen (pronounced 'skain') is a busy working harbour and is Denmark's northernmost settlement, just a couple of kilometres from the dramatic sandy spit where the country finally peters out at Grenen, a slender point of wave-washed sand, where seals bask and seagulls soar.

Artists discovered Skagen's luminous light and its colourful, wind-blasted, heath-and-dune landscape in the mid-19th century and fixed eagerly on the romantic imagery of the area's fishing life that had earned the people of Skagen a hard living for centuries. Painters such as Michael and Anna Ancher and Oscar Björck followed the contemporary fashion of painting *en plein air* (out of doors), often regardless of the weather. Their work established a vivid figurative style of painting that became known internationally as the 'Skagen School'.

Today, Skagen is a highly popular tourist resort, completely packed during high summer. But the sense of a more picturesque Skagen survives and the town's older neighbourhood, Gammel Skagen, 5km west, is filled with distinctive, single-storey, yellow-walled, red-roofed houses (they're traditionally painted every Whitsuntide with lime and ochre).

The peninsula is lined with fine beaches, including a sandy stretch on the eastern end of Østre Strandvej, a 15-minute walk from the town centre.

The Skagen Festival (p27) packs the town out with official performers, buskers and appreciative visitors during the first weekend of July; book accommodation well in advance.

Sights

Grenen OUTDOORS

Appropriately enough for such a neat and ordered country, Denmark doesn't end untidily at its most northerly point, but on a neat finger of sand just a few metres wide. You can actually paddle at its tip, where the waters of the Kattegat and Skagerrak clash, and you can put one foot in each sea – but not too far. Bathing here is forbidden because of the ferocious tidal currents.

The tip is the culmination of a long, curving sweep of sand at Grenen, about 3km northeast of Skagen along Rte 40. Where the road ends there's a car park (Dkr13 per hour), excellent restaurant and small art gallery. From the car park the 30-minute walk up the long, sweeping stretch of sand passes the grave of writer Holger Drachmann (1846–1908).

The tractor-pulled bus, the **Sandormen** (adult/child return Dkr25/15; ⏲Apr-Oct), can take you out to the point; it leaves from the car park at Grenen from 10am daily and runs regularly all day, according to demand.

Skagens Museum MUSEUM

(www.skagensmuseum.dk; Brøndumsvej 4; adult/child Dkr90/free; ⏲10am-5pm daily May-Aug, Tue-Sun Sep-Apr) This wonderful gallery (which has just undergone major renovation and expansion) showcases the outstanding art that was produced in Skagen between 1870 and 1930.

Den Tilsandede Kirke RUIN

The 'sand-covered church', built during the late 14th century, was once the region's biggest church. It fell victim to a sand drift that began in the 17th century and became progressively worse – so much so that churchgoers eventually had to dig their way in. In 1795 the relentless sand drift broke the will of the congregation and the church was closed. The main part of the church was torn down in 1810 but the whitewashed **tower** (adult/child Dkr20/3; ⏲11am-5pm daily Jun-Aug, weekends only Apr, May & Sep) still stands.

Sleeping

You'll need to book ahead for summer visits, when hotel accommodation can be scarce (and at its highest rate; outside July and August most prices drop).

Danhostel Skagen HOSTEL €
(98 44 22 00; www.danhostelskagen.dk; Rolighedsvej 2; dm/s/d Dkr180/525/625; Mar-Nov; P) Always a hive of activity, this hostel is modern, functional and spick and span. It's decent value, particularly for families or groups. Low-season prices drop sharply. It's 1km towards Frederikshavn from the Skagen train station (if you're coming by train, get off at Frederikshavnsvej).

Grenen Strand Camping CAMPGROUND €
(98 44 25 46; www.campone.dk/grenen; Fyrvej 16; campsites from Dkr50, plus per adult Dkr90; Apr–mid-Sep; @) This busy, well-organised place is in a fine seaside location on the outskirts of town towards Grenen. There's plenty of tree cover and good facilities, including wee four-bed cabins.

★ **Badepension Marienlund** GUESTHOUSE €€
(28 12 13 20; www.marienlund.dk; Fabriciusvej 8; s/d incl breakfast Dkr650/1100; Apr-Oct; P) A cosy atmosphere, idyllic garden and pretty lounge and breakfast areas make Marienlund a top option. There are only 14 rooms, all light, white and simply furnished (all with bathrooms). You'll find the hotel in a peaceful residential neighbourhood west of the centre; bike hire available.

Finns B&B GUESTHOUSE €€
(98 45 01 55; www.finns.dk; Østre Strandvej 63; s/d incl breakfast from Dkr525/750; May–mid-Sep) Take a 1923-vintage 'log cabin' built for a Norwegian count, fill it with art, antiques and memorabilia, and you have this fabulously quirky slumber spot. Gay-friendly, TV-free and adults-only (no kids under 15), Finns is a stone's throw from the beach and has six individually decorated rooms (a few with shared bathroom).

Eating & Drinking

Perhaps a dozen seafood shacks line the harbour selling fresh seafood. *Rejer* (prawns/shrimp) are the favourite order, costing around Dkr100 for a generous helping.

Havnevej, the road connecting the harbour and the town centre, has a cluster of eateries and bars. At Havneplads things get a little seedier (well, as seedy as Denmark gets), with some late-opening summertime nightclubs.

Supermarket **Super Brugsen** (Sankt Laurentii Vej 28; 8am-10pm) has a bakery.

★ **Skagens Museum Cafe** CAFE €
(www.skagensmuseum.dk; Brøndumsvej 4; lunch Dkr85-100; 10am-5pm) For lunch or a cuppa in a magical setting, head to the Garden House cafe at Skagens Museum, serving lunchtime dishes plus a super spread of home-baked cakes and tarts. Note: you don't need to pay the museum's admission if you're just visiting the cafe.

Pakhuset SEAFOOD €€
(98 44 20 00; www.pakhuset-skagen.dk; Rødspættevej 6; lunch Dkr85-230, mains Dkr170-240; 11am-late) Seafood is the star at Pakhuset, from simple fish cakes with remoulade to swoon-inducing flambéed Norwegian lobster tails. It has long hours and superb ambience both outdoors (slap bang on the harbour) and indoors (think wooden beams and cheerful ship mastheads). Fine-dine in the restaurant upstairs (from 6pm), or keep it cheaper in the downstairs cafe.

Jakobs Café & Bar INTERNATIONAL €€
(www.jakobscafe.dk; Havnevej 4; lunch Dkr75-155, dinner mains Dkr190-280; 9am-1am Sun-Thu, to 3am Fri & Sat) The terrace of this relaxed cafe-bar is primed for people-watching, and the comprehensive menu has favourites such as burgers, Caesar salad, *moules-frites* and steaks (the kitchen closes at 10pm). On summer nights the place is generally heaving with young Danes enjoying warm-up drinks; there's live music on weekends.

Ruths Gourmet MODERN DANISH €€€
(98 44 11 24; www.ruths-hotel.dk; Gammel Skagen; 3/5/9 courses Dkr595/865/1395; 6pm-late Tue-Sat Jul & Aug, Thu-Sat Apr-Jun & Sep, Fri & Sat Oct-Mar) New Nordic cuisine is in the spotlight at this intimate restaurant at Ruths Hotel, under the leadership of acclaimed chef Thorsten Schmidt. The menu has a regional focus, utilising fine local produce to stunningly innovative and creative effect (choose menus from three to nine courses). You'll need to book ahead to score one of only 22 seats.

Information

Tourist Office (☎98 44 13 77; www.skagen-tourist.dk; Vestre Strandvej 10; ⊙9am-4pm Mon-Sat, 10am-2pm Sun late Jun–mid-Aug, shorter hours rest of year) In front of the harbour, with loads of info on regional sights, attractions and activities.

Getting There & Away

Trains run hourly to Frederikshavn (Dkr60, 35 minutes), where you can change for destinations further south.

From late June/early July to mid-August, bus 99 runs a few times daily between Grenen, Skagen, Gammel Skagen, Hirtshals, Tornby Strand, Hjørring, Lønstrup, Løkken and Fårup Sommerland (where it connects with bus 200 to Aalborg) and Blokhus. Pick up a timetable or call ☎98 11 11 11; the website for **Nordjyllands Trafikselskab** (NT, North Jutland Transport Association; www.nordjyllandstrafikselskab.dk) is in Danish, but timetables should be easy enough to access (just look for 'Sommerbus').

Getting Around

The best way to get around is by bike, and loads of places offer rental. **Skagen Cykeludlejning** (www.skagencykeludlejning.dk; Banegårdspladsen, Sankt Laurentii Vej 22; bike hire per day/week Dkr90/375) is adjacent to the train station and has a range of bikes. It has a second outlet close to the harbour, in the bike shop at Fiskergangen 10.

Parking is at a premium in summer;– there's paid parking (Dkr13 per hour, from 9am to 6pm) beside and in front of the tourist office, and beside the train station.

Hirtshals

POP 6000

Situated 50km southwest of Skagen, the port town of Hirtshals services year-round ferries to Norway and seasonal ferries to the Faroe Islands and Iceland. Its one notable sight is **Nordsøen Oceanarium** (www.nordsoenoceanarium.dk; Willemoesvej 2; adult/child Dkr170/90; ⊙9am-6pm daily Jul-Aug, 10am-4pm or 5pm rest of year, closed Dec–early Jan; 👪), an impressive aquarium that re-creates a slice of the North Sea in a massive four-storey tank.

Sleeping

Hotel Hirtshals HOTEL €€
(☎98 94 20 77; www.hotelhirtshals.dk; Havnegade 2; s/d/f from Dkr695/795/1295) On the main square above the fishing harbour, Hotel Hirtshals has bright, comfortable rooms with steepled ceilings – try for one with a sea view (at the time of research a new wing was under construction). It's well positioned for enjoying the town's restaurants and is heavily peopled by ferry-going Norwegians.

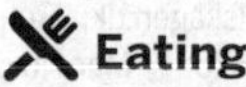

Eating

There are cafes at the northern end of Hjørringgade, and there are also a couple of pizza and kebab places on Nørregade. Your best bet for a decent feed is **Hirtshals Fiskehus** (http://hirtshalsfiskehus.dk; Sydvestkajen 7; meals Dkr59-129; ⊙11am-9pm Jun-Aug, to 8pm May & Sep), down by the fishing harbour.

Getting There & Away

BOAT

Ferries connect Frederikshavn to five Norwegian ports: Bergen, Kristiansand, Stavanger, Langesund and Larvik. Seasonal ferries run to Tórshavn (Faroe Islands) and Seyðisfjörður (Iceland).

TRAIN

Hirtshals' train station is on Havnegade, west of the ferry terminals. A private railway connects Hirtshals with Hjørring at least hourly (Dkr30, 20 minutes). At Hjørring you can connect with DSB trains to Aalborg, Frederikshavn or destinations further south.

Esbjerg

POP 71,600

Esbjerg fails to pull heartstrings on first impressions. Made big and rich from North Sea oil, its silos and smokestacks hardly compete with the crooked, story-book streets of nearby Ribe. Away from the industrial grit, however, Esbjerg redeems itself with a handsome town square, a fantastic art museum and easy access to the beautiful, time-warped island of Fanø, a quick 12-minute ferry ride away.

Sights & Activities

Esbjerg Kunstmuseum MUSEUM
(www.eskum.dk; Havnegade 20; adult/child Dkr60/free; ⊙10am-4pm) The Utzon-designed Musikhuset is home to the modern-art collection of Esbjerg Kunstmuseum. In an admirable display of openness (and a nod to restricted space), the Åbne Magasiner (Open Stores) downstairs allows you to look up

WORTH A TRIP

FAROE ISLANDS

The far-flung Faroes (Føroyar) may be under Danish sovereignty, but this self-governing slice of Scandinavia is a universe unto itself. Midway between Iceland and Scotland, it's an 18-piece jigsaw of majestic rocks jutting out of the frothing North Atlantic swells, a place where multicoloured cottages and grass-roofed wooden churches add focus to grandly stark, treeless moorlands. It's a curiously bewitching place, infused with ancient Norse legends and tight-knit rural communities alive with art and music.

Running the show is capital-city **Tórshavn** (Thor's Harbour), its transport links, solid restaurants and hotels making the place an excellent base from which to explore the rest of the country. Take a day or two to explore the turf-roofed cottages of its historic Tinganes district, as well as the islands' idiosyncratic culture at museums such as **Føroya Fornminnissavn** (www.fornminni.fo; Brekkutún 6, Hoyvík; adult/child Dkr30/free; ⏲10am-5pm Mon-Fri, 2-5pm Sat & Sun mid-May–mid-Sep) and **Listasavn Føroya** (www.art.fo; Gundadalsvegur 9; adult/child Dkr50/free; ⏲11am-5pm Mon-Fri, 2-5pm Sat & Sun May-Aug, reduced hours rest of year).

The Faroes' ethereal pull, however, lurks beyond the city limits. Sharing the island of **Streymoy** with Tórshavn is tiny **Vestmanna**, from where tour boats reach the inspirational **Vestmanna Bird Cliffs**, bobbing beneath towering cliff faces, passing spiky rock pinnacles and squeezing through tight stone arches. You'll spy the breeding areas of guillemots and razorbills as screeching fulmars and kittiwakes soar above like thousands of white dots.

Another bird-watchers' paradise is the far western island of **Mykines**. Its hiking trail to the 1909 Mykinesholmur Lighthouse leads through densely packed puffin burrows and across a 35m footbridge over a sea gorge brimming with birdlife, including the Faroes' only significant gannet colonies.

Long and thin enough to make a supermodel cry, the northeast island of **Kalsoy** delivers a surreal succession of abrupt peaks and swales. Nicknamed the 'flute' for its many tunnel holes, the scenery glimpsed all too briefly between them is nothing short of majestic.

Arresting scenery is something the island of **Eysturoy** does especially well. Wedged between Kalsoy and Streymoy, it's here that you'll find the country's grandest fjords and highest peaks. Northern Eysturoy serves up especially spectacular scenery at every turn, and travelling between its criminally cute villages makes for one of the most magical experiences in the country.

Facing Kalsoy's jagged northern tip, the petite village of **Elduvík** is a dreamily cute snaggle of tar-blackened traditional cottages divided into two photogenic clumps by the meandering mouth of the Stórá stream. Then there's **Gøta**. Caught in a fjord end between two jagged mountain arms, this sprawling three-villages-in-one wakes the neighbours in July with the Faroes' foremost rock festival, **G!** (www.gfestival.com), improbably held on a sandy little beach.

While July and August cover the main tourist season, consider visiting in June, when the days are dreamily long, most hotels and museums are open, yet tourist numbers are low. From September to May, rain abounds, and much infrastructure is shut, though the brooding skies, pounding ocean and haunting landscapes will speak to more meditative travellers.

All flights fly into the Faroe Islands' only airport, **Vágar** (www.floghavn.fo). National carrier **Atlantic Airways** (www.atlantic.fo) runs direct flights to/from numerous destinations, including Copenhagen, Billund, Bergen and Reykjavík. Seasonal destinations include Stavanger, Barcelona and Milan. **Air Iceland** (www.airiceland.is) also has flights to Reykjavík.

For details on ferry connections to/from Hirtshals (Denmark) and Seyðisfjörður (Iceland), see p485. For more information on the Faroe Islands themselves, click onto www.faroeislands.com.

undisplayed works from the collection. Another benefit: from the museum it's easy to admire the angles and details of the Utzons' architectural prowess.

Mennesket ved Havet MONUMENT
(Hjertingvej) On the waterfront opposite Fiskeri og Søfartsmuseet is Esbjerg's most interesting landmark, *Mennesket ved Havet* (Man Meets the Sea): four stark-white, 9m-high, stylised human figures, sitting rigid and staring out to sea. They were created by Danish sculptor Svend Wiig Hansen to commemorate the city's centennial in 1995 and they make a striking backdrop to holiday snaps.

Seal Safari BOAT TOUR
(www.faergen.com/sealsafari; adult/child Dkr130/70; ⌚Esbjerg departures 10.45am & 1.45pm Mon-Thu, 10.45am Fri Jul-Aug; 👪) In July and August you can enjoy a 2½-hour sightseeing cruise around the harbour and into Ho Bugt (Ho Bay), with a chance of seeing seals in their natural habitat. Tours operate once or twice a day, Monday to Friday, and depart from the ferry harbour in Esbjerg (by the Fanø ferry).

There is also the option to join the tour from Fanø (boats depart Nordby 20 minutes before the Esbjerg departure times listed here).

Sleeping

CabInn Esbjerg BUDGET HOTEL €
(☎75 18 16 00; www.cabinn.com; Skolegade 14; s/d from Dkr545/675; @🛜) Esbjerg's best value is found in this classy century-old building that's been thoroughly renovated and sits in a prime inner-city location. It's a hit with international and local visitors, who enjoy its good rates and light-filled rooms, all with bathroom, kettle and TV. Free parking, a decent breakfast buffet (Dkr70) and free wi-fi add up to a good deal.

Danhostel Esbjerg HOSTEL €
(☎75 12 42 58; www.esbjerg-danhostel.dk; Gammel Vardevej 80; dm Dkr230, d without/with bathroom Dkr560/720; @👪) An excellent choice if you don't mind being out of the city centre. It's in a spiffy location, neighbouring a sports stadium, swimming pool, park and cinema. The old building is lovely and the communal facilities top-notch; rooms in the new wing all have private bathrooms. It's 3km northwest of the city centre on bus 4.

Eating & Drinking

Most restaurants and grocery stores are east of Torvet on Kongensgade.

Sand's Restaurant DANISH €€
(www.sands.dk; Skolegade 60; lunch Dkr42-139, dinner mains Dkr109-249; ⌚11.30am-9.30pm Mon-Sat) The menu at this classy 100-year-old restaurant is an ode to old-school Danish favourites: lunchtime smørrebrød and herring platters, evening fish (try the *bakskuld,* a local fish not unlike a flounder) and plenty of classic *bøf* (beef).

Dronning Louise INTERNATIONAL €€
(www.dr-louise.dk; Torvet 19; lunch Dkr90-145, dinner mains Dkr190-300; ⌚10am-1am Mon-Wed, to 3am Thu, to 4am Fri, to 5am Sat, to midnight Sun) Jack of all trades, the Queen Louise commands a great central position on Torvet: she's a restaurant, pub and even a nightclub (Friday and Saturday), with occasional live music too. You can dine from the broad, classic-hits menu on the square, inside or in the rear courtyard. Kitchen closes 10.30pm Monday to Saturday, 9.30pm Sunday.

Paddy Go Easy PUB
(Skolegade 42) Skolegade is where to head to when you're thirsty; it's virtually wall-to-wall bars. We like Paddy Go Easy for the real Irish accents behind (and often in front of) the bar, Kilkenny and Guinness on tap, and decent *craic* all round.

Information

Tourist Office (☎75 12 55 99; www.visitesbjerg.dk; Skolegade 33; ⌚10am-4pm Mon-Fri) On the corner of Torvet. Offers self-service screens, plus racks of brochures and maps.

Getting There & Away

If you're driving into Esbjerg, the E20 (the main expressway from the east) leads directly into the heart of the city and down to the ferry harbour.

There are regular train services running south to Ribe (Dkr60, 35 minutes) and east to Aarhus (Dkr265, two hours).

Thinggaard Express (www.expressbus.dk) operates bus 980 from Esbjerg to Frederikshavn once daily (Dkr340, 5¼ hours), calling at Viborg and Aalborg en route.

Getting Around

Most city buses can be boarded at the train station; local tickets cost Dkr20. Bus 5 runs to the harbour every 20 minutes.

Fanø

POP 3200

If Esbjerg has one silver lining, it is that one of the treasures of the Danish Wadden Sea – famed for its seals, birdlife and national-park status – is just a short ferry ride away. The island of Fanø, a popular holiday island for Danes and Germans, pulls in the punters with its picture-perfect villages; broad, endless sandy beaches; and lively summertime vibe. Its two fishing villages, northerly Nordby (where the majority of the islanders live) and southerly Sønderho, are time-warped jumbles of historic, thatched cottages and cobblestone streets.

Sights & Activities

The main villages of **Nordby** and **Sønderho** lie at each end of the 16km-long island; ferries from Esbjerg arrive at Nordby. Sønderho in particular is one of Denmark's most charming villages. It dates from the 16th century and has more than a hint of Middle Earth to its jumble of thatched houses.

The tourist office can provide brochures and maps outlining on-foot exploration of Nordby and Sønderho. The villages are home to a few low-key **museums** detailing Fanø's rich maritime history. Fanø's golden age peaked in the late 19th century, when it boasted the largest fleet outside Copenhagen; over a period of 150 years it was the site for the construction of more than 1000 vessels.

With time and interest, check out Nordby's maritime or history museum. Sønderho has an art museum and an original 19th-century sea-captain's house known as Hannes Hus.

Beaches BEACHES

Families and water-sports fans (and amber-hunters, too) come to Fanø above all else for the great beaches – the best swimming is found between **Rindby Strand** and **Fanø Bad** (Denmark's first international seaside resort). Further north is the vast sand spit, Søren Jessens Sand. South of Rindby, the beach is full of activity: windsurfing, kitesurfing and blokarts.

Fanø Klitplantage NATURE RESERVE

Wildlife-watchers and nature lovers will feel at home in the centre of the island, where 1162 hectares make up this nature reserve. Hit the walking tracks and you'll find birds, deer and rabbits in abundance. Stop by the popular picnic site and forest playground near Pælebjerg.

Sleeping & Eating

There are seven campgrounds on Fanø, virtually all within a short walk of the coast. All are family-focused and most have cabins for rent. For more information, see www.visitfanoe.dk.

For information on booking summer-holiday flats and houses (which typically sleep four to six people and are rented by the week), contact the tourist office. There are booking agents (eg www.danibo.dk), but their websites are generally only in Danish and German.

As well as the inns serving food, take a stroll along Nordby's Hovedgaden and Sønderho's Sønderland and you'll be tripping over inviting little eateries and sunny courtyard gardens.

There are supermarkets and bakeries in the main villages on the island. Heather honey is a local speciality, as is lamb, and it's worth seeking out beer brewed at the local microbrewery, Fanø Bryghus.

★**Møllesti B&B** GUESTHOUSE €

(☎75 16 29 49; www.mollesti.dk; Møllesti 3, Nordby; s Dkr300, d Dkr450-500; ⊙Jun-Aug) This well-priced B&B is hidden away in the atmospheric lanes of Nordby. It's home to four simple, stylish bedrooms sharing two bathrooms and a kitchenette-lounge, in a restored sea-captain's house from 1892. It can open for guests on weekends outside of summer, but you'll need to arrange this in advance. Breakfast costs an additional Dkr50; there's a two-night minimum stay.

Fanø Krogaard INN €€

(☎76 66 01 66; www.fanoekrogaard.dk; Langelinie 11, Nordby; d from Dkr895) In operation since 1664, this charming inn on the Nordby waterfront has cosy antique-filled rooms (plus more modern ones in a newer annex) and an intimate atmosphere, plus a large, sunny terrace and an appealling menu of local specialities (lunch Dkr79 to Dkr139, dinner mains Dkr129 to Dkr239).

★**Sønderho Kro** INN €€€

(☎75 16 40 09; www.sonderhokro.dk; Kropladsen 11, Sønderho; s/d incl breakfast from Dkr1195/1495;

(P) The loveliest place to stay on the island (and renowned around the country) is this thatched-roof slice of *hyggelig* heaven. It dates from 1722, and its 14 individually decorated rooms feature local antiques. The inn has an acclaimed gourmet restaurant (lunch Dkr129 to Dkr179, dinner three/five courses Dk495/695), which showcases local and seasonal specialities in a steeped-in-time dining room.

Information

Tourist Office (☎70 26 42 00; www.visitfanoe.dk; Skolevej 5, Nordby; ⊙9am-5pm Mon-Fri, 10am-4pm Sat & Sun Jul-Aug, 10am-5pm Mon-Fri Sep-May) In Nordby, about 700m from the ferry harbour (via Hovedgaden).

Getting There & Around

If you're doing a day trip or overnight stay from Esbjerg, it's much cheaper to leave your car on the mainland and hire a bike or take the bus once on the island.

Fanø Færgen (☎70 23 15 15; www.fanoe-faergen.dk) ferries depart from Esbjerg for Nordby one to three times hourly from 5am to 2am. Sailing time is 12 minutes. A return ticket for a foot passenger/bike is Dkr45/40. It costs Dkr300/415 in low/high season to transport a car (return trip, including passengers).

Bicycles can be hired from a number of places, including **Fri BikeShop** (☎75 16 24 60; Mellemgaden 12, Nordby).

There's a local bus service (route 431) from the ferry dock that runs about once an hour, connecting Nordby with Fanø Bad (Dkr20), Rindby Strand (Dkr20) and Sønderho (Dkr30).

Ribe

POP 8200

The charming crooked, cobblestone streets of Ribe date from AD 869, making it one of Scandinavia's oldest and Denmark's most attractive towns. It is a delightful confection of half-timbered, 16th-century houses, clear-flowing streams and water meadows. Almost everything, including the hostel and train station, is within a 10-minute walk of Torvet, the town square, which is dominated by the huge Romanesque cathedral.

WORTH A TRIP

LEGOLAND

Revisit your tender years at Denmark's most visited tourist attraction (beyond Copenhagen). **Legoland** (www.legoland.dk; Nordmarksvej; adult/child Dkr309/289; ⊙10am-8pm or 9pm Jul–mid-Aug, shorter hrs Apr-Jun & Sep-Oct, closed Nov-Mar; (♿)). Located 1km north of the town of Billund, the sprawling theme park is a gob-smacking ode to those little plastic building blocks, with everything from giant Lego models of famous cities, landmarks and wild beasts, to re-created scenes from the Star Wars film series. And while the park's booty of rides and activities is mostly geared to preteens, adrenalin junkies can scream to their heart's content on the Legoland roller coasters.

Legoland closing times vary – from 6pm to 9pm. Also worth knowing (and not well publicised) is that the park opens its gates a half-hour before the rides close, and no ticket is necessary to enter. Rides normally close one or two hours before the park itself (check the website), so with a bit of luck you could end up with 2½ hours to browse and check out Miniland for free. Also, consider buying your tickets online to avoid the queues.

In 2016 the 'experience centre' **Lego House** is set to open in Billund town itself. Featuring a bold design that resembles a stack of gigantic Lego bricks, it will incorporate exhibition areas, rooftop gardens, a cafe, a Lego store and a covered public square, and is expected to attract 250,000 visitors annually.

Billund is 63km northeast of Esbjerg. If you're travelling by train, the most common route is to disembark at Vejle and catch a bus from there. Bus 43 runs between Vejle and Billund airport (Dkr60, 30 minutes); bus 143 runs a slower route from Vejle and stops at Legoland (60kr, 40 minutes), Billund town centre and the airport. Buses run up to 10 times daily between Aarhus and Billund airport (Dkr160kr, one hour). Other buses run to the airport from major Jutland towns including Esbjerg, Ribe and Kolding. To plan your travel, use www.rejseplanen.dk.

Sights

For a charmed stroll that takes in some of Ribe's handsome half-timbered buildings and winding cobbled lanes, head along any of the streets radiating out from Torvet, in particular Puggårdsgade or Grønnegade, from where narrow alleys lead down and across Fiskegarde to Skibbroen and the picturesque old harbour.

Ribe Domkirke CHURCH

(www.ribe-domkirke.dk; Torvet; tower adult/child Dkr20/10; 10am-5pm Mon-Sat, noon-5pm Sun May-Sep, shorter hours Oct-Apr) Dominating Ribe's skyline is the impressive Ribe Cathedral, which dates back to at least 948 (the earliest record of the existence of a bishop in Ribe) – making it the oldest in Denmark. The cathedral was largely rebuilt in 1150 when Ribe was at the heart of royal and government money, which in turn paved the way for some fine architectural structures.

★Ribe Kunstmuseum MUSEUM

(www.ribekunstmuseum.dk; Sankt Nicolaj Gade 10; adult/child Dkr70/free; 10am-5pm Thu-Tue, to 8pm Wed Jul & Aug, 11am-4pm Tue-Sun Sep-Jun) An undeniable benefit of being the oldest town in the land is the opportunity to amass an impressive art collection. Ribe's beautifully restored art museum has been able to acquire some of Denmark's best works, including those by 19th-century 'Golden Age' painters.

Museet Ribes Vikinger MUSEUM

(www.ribesvikinger.dk; Odins Plads 1; adult/child Dkr70/free; 10am-6pm Thu-Tue, to 9pm Wed Jul & Aug, 10am-4pm rest of yr, closed Mon Nov-Mar;) To better come to grips with Ribe's Viking and medieval history, visit the informative displays of the Museum of Ribe's Vikings. Two rooms provide snapshots of the town in 800 and during medieval times in 1500. These portrayals are complemented by rare archaeological finds and good explanations, which add real substance to the tales.

Ribe VikingeCenter MUSEUM

(www.ribevikingecenter.dk; Lustrupvej 4; adult/child Dkr100/50; 11am-5pm late Jun-late Aug, 10am-3.30pm Mon-Fri early May-late Jun & late Aug–mid-Oct;) Embrace your inner Viking (ignore any pillaging tendencies, OK?) at this hands-on, open-air museum. It attempts to re-create a slice of life in Viking-era Ribe using various reconstructions, including a 34m longhouse. The staff, dressed in period clothing, bake bread over open fires, demonstrate archery and Viking-era crafts such as pottery and leatherwork, and offer falconry shows and 'warrior training' (for kids, using a sword and shield). You'll undoubtedly learn more about Viking life than you could from a textbook.

Tours

Night-Watchman Tour WALKING TOUR

(8pm May-mid–Sep, also 10pm Jun-Aug;) FREE One of the best free activities in Denmark is Ribe's 45-minute night-watchman tour, which departs from out the front of Weis Stue, on Torvet, once or twice a night in the warmer months.

Sleeping

The tourist-office's brochure lists some 35 private homes in and around Ribe that rent great-value rooms and apartments (doubles cost Dkr350 to Dkr600, excluding breakfast). You can see pictures of the accommodation online at www.visitribe.dk.

Weis Stue GUESTHOUSE €

(75 42 07 00; www.weisstue.dk; Torvet; s/d Dkr395/495) An ancient wooden-beamed house from 1600, Weis Stue has eight small, crooked rooms (with shared bathrooms) above its restaurant. They have lashings of character: creaking boards, sloping walls and low overhead beams.

Danhostel Ribe HOSTEL €

(75 42 06 20; www.danhostel-ribe.dk; Sankt Pedersgade 16; dm Dkr220, s/d from Dkr435/470; P@) An ideal location, knowledgable staff, sparkling rooms (all with bathroom) and impressive facilities make this a top option suited to both backpackers and families. It rents bikes and is a stone's throw from Ribe's historic centre; equally impressive is its commitment to the environment, from the Good Origin coffee in its vending machines to its promotion of sustainable travel in the Wadden Sea region.

Hotel Dagmar HOTEL €€€

(75 42 00 33; www.hoteldagmar.dk; Torvet; s/d incl breakfast from Dkr1095/1295; @) Classy, central Hotel Dagmar is Denmark's oldest hotel (1581) and exudes all the charm you'd expect. There's a golden hue to the hallways and rooms, with old-world decor alongside tiling, artworks and antiques. See the website for packages involving meals and accommodation.

Eating & Drinking

Postgaarden CAFE

(www.postgaarden-ribe.dk; Nederdammen 36; meals Dkr69-119; ⊙10am-5.30pm Mon-Fri, to 4pm Sat) Postgaarden has a range of Danish and international microbrews for sale in its delicatessen, and a changing selection of boutique (and sometimes obscure) brews on tap to accompany its cafe-style menu, best enjoyed in the photogenic 1668 courtyard.

Sælhunden DANISH €€

(www.saelhunden.dk; Skibbroen 13; lunch Dkr99-159, dinner mains Dkr135-220; ⊙11am-10pm) This handsome old black-and-white restaurant is by the riverfront, with outdoor seating by the *Johanne Dan* boat. *Sælhund* means 'seal', so it's no surprise this place dedicates itself to serving quality seafood in traditional Danish guises. Try the delicious house specialty, *stjerneskud* (one fried and one steamed fillet of fish served on bread with prawns, caviar and dressing).

Weis Stue TRADITIONAL DANISH €€

(www.weisstue.dk; Torvet 2; lunch Dkr84-118, dinner mains Dkr154-208; ⊙11.30am-10pm) Don't come here looking for modern, could-be-anywhere cuisine. As befits the setting (one of Denmark's oldest inns, wonky and charming), the menu is a traditionalist's dream. The large meat-and-potatoes portions are full of northern-European flavour (pepper pork medallions, Wiener schnitzel), best washed down with locally brewed beer. There's bags of atmosphere, but little joy for vegetarians.

Information

Tourist Office (☎75 42 15 00; www.visitribe.dk; ⊙9am-6pm Mon-Fri, 10am-5pm Sat Jul-Aug, reduced hours rest of year) Has an abundance of information on the town and surrounding areas, plus internet access. Ask here about the RibePas (adult/child Dkr20/10, or free from a handful of accommodation providers) that grants the holder up to 20% discount at many local attractions. It may be superseded by a new type of pass by the time you visit.

Getting There & Away

Ribe is 31km south of Esbjerg via Rte 24 and 47km north of Tønder via Rte 11.

Trains from Ribe run hourly on weekdays and less frequently at weekends to Esbjerg (Dkr60, 35 minutes).

UNDERSTAND DENMARK

History

Humble Hunters to Mighty Vikings

First settled around 4000 BC, most probably by prehistoric hunter-gatherers from the south, Denmark has been at the centre of Scandinavian civilisation ever since, and there are plenty of reminders of that past in the shape of the ancient burial chambers that pepper the countryside and the traces of fortifications at, for example, Trelleborg.

The Danes themselves are thought to have migrated south from Sweden in around AD 500 but it was their descendants, who were initially a peaceful, farming people who are better known today. What we think of as modern Denmark was an important trading centre within the Viking empire and the physical evidence of this part of Denmark's history is to be found throughout the country today. In the late 9th century, warriors led by the Viking chieftain, Hardegon, conquered the Jutland peninsula. The Danish monarchy, Europe's oldest, dates back to Hardegon's son, Gorm the Old, who reigned in the early 10th century. Gorm's son, Harald Bluetooth, completed the conquest of Denmark and spearheaded the conversion of the Danes to Christianity; his story and his legacy is well showcased in the tiny hamlet of Jelling. Successive Danish kings sent their subjects to row their longboats to England and conquer most of the Baltic region. They were accomplished fighters, sword-smiths, shipbuilders and sailors, qualities well illustrated at the excellent Viking Ship Museum (p70) in Roskilde.

Reformation & Renaissance

In 1397, Margrethe I of Denmark established a union between Denmark, Norway and Sweden to counter the influence of the powerful Hanseatic League that had come to dominate the region's trade. Sweden withdrew from the union in 1523 and over the next few hundred years Denmark and Sweden fought numerous border skirmishes and a few fully fledged wars, largely over control of the Baltic Sea. Norway remained under Danish rule until 1814.

In the 16th century, the Reformation swept through the country, accompanied by church burnings and civil warfare. The fighting ended in 1536, the Catholic Church was ousted and the Danish Lutheran Church headed by the monarchy was established.

Denmark's Golden Age was under Christian IV (1588–1648), with Renaissance cities, castles and fortresses flourishing throughout his kingdom. A superb example is Egeskov Slot (p88) on Funen. In 1625, Christian IV, hoping to neutralise Swedish expansion, entered an extremely ill-advised and protracted struggle known as the Thirty Years' War. The Swedes triumphed and won large chunks of Danish territory. Centuries' worth of Danish kings and queens are laid to rest in sarcophagi on dramatic display at Roskilde's cathedral.

The Modern Nation

Literature, the arts, philosophy and populist ideas flourished in the 1830s, and Europe's Year of Revolution in 1848 helped inspire a democratic movement in Denmark. Overnight, and in typically orderly Danish fashion, the country adopted male suffrage and a constitution on 5 June 1849, forcing King Frederik VII to relinquish most of his power and become Denmark's first constitutional monarch. Denmark lost the Schleswig and Holstein regions to Germany in 1864.

Denmark remained neutral throughout WWI and also declared its neutrality at the outbreak of WWII. Nevertheless, on 9 April 1940, the Germans invaded, albeit allowing the Danes a degree of autonomy. For three years the Danes managed to walk a thin line, running their own internal affairs under Nazi supervision, until in August 1943 when the Germans took outright control. The Danish Resistance movement mushroomed and 7000 Jewish Danes were smuggled into neutral Sweden.

Although Soviet forces heavily bombarded the island of Bornholm, the rest of Denmark emerged from WWII relatively unscathed. Postwar Social Democrat governments introduced a comprehensive social-welfare state in the postwar period, and still today Denmark provides its citizens with extensive cradle-to-grave social security.

Political Controversies

In 2004 the country's most eligible bachelor, Crown Prince Frederik, married Australian Mary Donaldson in a hugely popular and exhaustively covered story-book wedding. They now have four children.

It has not all been fairy tales, though. The growing political sway of the nationalist, right-wing Danish People's Party (DPP) in the late 1990s and early 2000s led Denmark to impose some of the toughest immigration laws in Europe in 2002. Its influence also contributed to Denmark's joining the USA, UK and other allies in the 2003 Iraq War, as well as to its commitment to maintain its role in Afghanistan.

In 2006, the country became the focus of violent demonstrations around the Middle East following the publication of a cartoon depicting the prophet Mohammed – a deep taboo for many Muslims but an issue of freedom of speech for liberal news editors – in the *Jyllands-Posten* newspaper.

Discontent over the country's stuttering economic performance influenced the election of a new, centre-left coalition in 2011, led by Social Democrat Helle Thorning-Schmidt. During the first year in office her government rolled back anti-immigration legislation enacted by the previous government, and passed a tax reform with support from the liberal-conservative opposition.

Taxation and immigration have remained controversial issues among the parties of Thorning-Schmidt's ruling coalition. It has not been all smooth sailing: her government was weakened in early 2014 when the small Socialist People's Party left the coalition amid disagreements over plans to sell off a stake in the state utilities giant Dong Energy to investment bank Goldman Sachs, among others.

People

Denmark's 5.6 million people are a generally relaxed bunch. It takes a lot to shock a Dane, and even if you do, they probably won't show it. This was the first country in the world to legalise same-sex marriages, and it became (in)famous during the 1960s for its relaxed attitudes to pornography.

They are an outwardly serious people, yet with an ironic sense of humour. They have a strong sense of family and an admirable environmental sensitivity. Above all, they are the most egalitarian of people (they officially have the smallest gap between rich and poor in the world), proud of their social equality in which none have too much or too little.

The vast majority of Danes are members of the National Church of Denmark, an Evangelical Lutheran denomination (a proportion of each Dane's income tax goes directly to the church), though less than 5% of the population are regular churchgoers.

Arts

Literature

By far the most famous Danish author is Hans Christian Andersen. Other prominent Danish writers include religious philosopher Søren Kierkegaard, whose writings were a forerunner of existentialism, and Karen Blixen, who wrote under the name Isak Dinesen and penned *Out of Africa* and *Babette's Feast,* both made into acclaimed movies in the 1980s.

Another successful novel turned screenplay is Peter Høeg's 1992 world hit *Miss Smilla's Feeling for Snow,* a suspense mystery about a Danish Greenlandic woman living in Copenhagen. And while the hugely popular genre of Scandinavian crime fiction is dominated by authors from Sweden (Henning Mankell and Stieg Larsson) and Norway (Jo Nesbø), Denmark is not without its noteworthy contributors. Among them is Jussi Adler-Olsen, whose novel *The Message That Arrived in a Bottle* won the 2010 Glass Key award, an annual prize given to a Nordic crime novel. The prize was once again swagged by a Dane in 2012, this time by Erik Valeur for his debut work, *The Seventh Child.*

Architecture & Design

For a small country Denmark has had a massive global impact in the fields of architecture and design. Arne Jacobsen, Verner Panton, the late Jørn Utzon and Hans J Wegner are now considered among the foremost designers of the 20th century, and the tradition of great furniture and interior design remains strong in the country's design schools, museums and independent artisanal workshops.

In recent years, a new league of eco-conscious architectural firms has emerged on the world stage. Among them is Effekt, designers of Tallinn's striking new Estonian Academy of Arts building, and BIG (Bjarke Ingels Group), whose head-turning projects include the cascading VM Bjerget housing complex in Copenhagen's Ørestad district. Indeed, Copenhagen is Denmark's architectural and design powerhouse, with museums such as Desigmuseum Danmark and architectural show-stealers like the Opera House and Royal Library extension maintaining the country's enviable international reputation.

Film & TV

As with its design prowess, Denmark punches well above its weight in the realm of cinema and televison. The country has scored regular Oscar success with films such as *Babette's Feast* (1987), Gabriel Axel's adaptation of a Karen Blixen novel; Bille August's *Pelle the Conqueror* (1988); and Anders Thomas Jensen's short film *Valgaften* (1998). In 2011, Susanne Bier's family drama *In a Better World* (2010) won Best Foreign Film at both the Academy Awards and the Golden Globe Awards. In 2010, Mads Brügger's subversively comic documentary about North Korea, *The Red Chapel* (2009), swooped the World Cinema Documentary Jury Prize at the Sundance Film Festival. Among the trio of films competing to be Denmark's Best Foreign Film contender at the 2015 Academy Awards was director Niels Arden Oplev's offbeat 1970s period flick *Speed Walking* (2014).

The most prolific and controversial of Denmark's 21st-century directors remains Lars von Trier, whose best-known films to date include the award-winning *Breaking the Waves* (1996) and *Dancer in the Dark* (2000). Dubbed the enfant terrible of contemporary cinema, von Trier first scored international attention as a cofounder of the Dogme95, an artistic manifesto pledging a minimalist approach to film-making using only hand-held cameras, shooting in natural light and rejecting special effects and prerecorded music.

Over the past 15 years, Denmark has also cemented its reputation for superlative TV drama. The most successful series to date include *The Killing* – featuring a Copenhagen police detective known for her astute crime solving abilities and love of Faroese knitwear – and *The Bridge*, which begins with the discovery of severed corpses on the Øresund Bridge. Police tape gives way to spin doctors in the acclaimed political drama *Borgen*, whose idealistic female protagonist is suddenly thrown into the position of Denmark's *statsminister* (prime minister).

Visual Arts

Before the 19th century, Danish art consisted mainly of formal portraiture, exemplified by the works of Jens Juel (1745–1802). A Golden Age ushered in the 19th century with such fine painters as Wilhelm Eckersberg (1783–1853) and major sculptors like Bertel Thorvaldsen (1770–1844), although he chose to spend most of his life in Rome.

Later in the century, the Skagen School evolved from the movement towards alfresco painting of scenes from working life, especially of fishing communities on the northern coasts of Jutland and Zealand. Much of it is exhibited at the Skagens Museum (p110). Leading exponents of the Skagen School were PS Krøyer and Michael and Anna Ancher. In the mid-20th century, a vigorous modernist school of Danish painting emerged, of which Asger Jorn (1914–73) was a leading exponent. Many of his works are on display at the art museum in Silkeborg (p103).

A number of contemporary Danish artists enjoy international acclaim, including conceptual artists Jeppe Hein, duo Elmgreen & Dragset, and Danish-Icelandic Olafur Eliasson. The latter's famously large-scale projects have included four temporary 'waterfalls' along New York's East River, as well as a whimsical multicoloured walkway atop the acclaimed ARoS gallery (p95) in Aarhus.

Like Aarhus, many Danish towns and cities contain a vibrant selection of homegrown and international contemporary art; even the smallest towns can surprise. Two of the best small art museums and galleries outside the capital are Faaborg's art museum (p88) and Herning's contemporary-art museum, **HEART** (www.heartmus.dk; Birk Centerpark 8, Herning; adult/child Dkr75/free; ⌚10am-5pm Tue-Sun). Topping it all off is the magnificent Louisiana (p65), on the coast north of Copenhagen.

Environment

Wildlife

On the nature front, common critters include wild hare, deer and many species of birds, including eagles, magpies, coots, swans, and ducks. Stretching along Jutland's west coast from Ho Bugt to the German border (and including the popular island of Fanø), the Nationalpark Vadehadet (Wadden Sea National Park) provides food and rest for between 10 and 12 million migratory birds each spring and autumn. Among the feathered regulars are eiders, oystercatchers, mallards and widgeons, as well as brent geese and barnacle geese. The park, Denmark's largest and newest, is part of an ambitious plan to restore many of Denmark's wetlands and marshes, and to help endangered species such as the freshwater otter make a comeback.

Environmental Issues

While some Western governments continue to debate the veracity of climate-change science, Denmark gets on with (sustainable) business. Wind power generates around 30% of Denmark's energy supply, and the country is a market leader in wind-power technology, exporting many wind turbines.

The long-term goal for Danish energy policy is clear: the entire energy supply – electricity, heating, industry and transport – is to be covered by renewable energy by 2050. The city of Copenhagen has pledged to go carbon-neutral by 2025.

The cycling culture is another example of Denmark's green outlook. Copenhagen has around 430km of continuous, safe cycle paths, and 52% of all Copenhageners cycle to their place of work or education every day.

Food & Drink

Denmark has rebranded itself from 'dining dowager' to 'cutting-edge gastronome' in less than two decades. At the heart of the revolution is Copenhagen, home to 15 Michelin-starred restaurants and 2010, 2011, 2012 and 2014 San Pellegrino World's Best Restaurant winner, Noma (p58). Along with restaurants like Kadeau (p58), Kødbyens Fiskebar (p57) and Pony (p56), Noma has helped redefine New Nordic cuisine by showcasing native produce and herbs, prepared using traditional techniques and contemporary experimentation, and focused on clean, natural flavours.

Staples & Specialities

Proud of it though they are, even the Danes would concede that their traditional cuisine is rather heavy and unhealthy. They eat a great deal of meat, mostly pork and usually accompanied by something starchy and a gravylike sauce. However, one Danish speciality has conquered the world: *smørrebrød*, the Danish open sandwich.

Meaty staples include *frikadeller* (fried minced-pork balls) and *fiskefrikadeller* (the fish version), *flæskesteg* (roast pork with crackling), *hvid labskovs* (beef-and-potato stew), *hakkebøf* (beefburger with fried onions) and the surprisingly tasty *pariserbøf* (rare beef patty topped with capers, raw egg yolk, beets, onions and horseradish).

It's not all turf, with coast-sourced classics including *sild* (herring), fresh *rejer* (shrimp) and *hummer* (lobster). The Danes are great fish smokers too; you'll find smokehouses (called *røgeri* in Danish) preserving herring, eel, cod livers, shrimp and other seafood all around the coast. The most renowned are on Bornholm.

Where to Eat

Beyond Copenhagen, Denmark's food scene can be less inspiring. Culinary clichés continue to plague too many menus, from nachos and burgers to inauthentic pasta, pizza and Thai. Yet things are slowly changing. Seasonality and local produce are informing an ever-growing number of kitchens. In Aarhus, New Nordic hot spots such as St Pauls Apothek and Nordisk Spisehus have pushed the city onto the foodie radar. Beyond the big cities, destinations like Zealand's Dragsholm Slot, Bornholm's Kadeau, and Skagen's Ruths Gourmet fly the flag for quality and innovation. And then there are the country's traditional *kroer* (inns), many of which serve authentic Danish home cooking.

SURVIVAL GUIDE

Directory A–Z

ACCOMMODATION

Price Ranges

The following price indicators are for a double room with private bathroom and breakfast unless stated otherwise. Rates include all taxes.

€€€ more than Dkr1500

€€ Dkr700 to Dkr1500

€ less than Dkr700

Camping & Cabins

➡ Denmark is very well set up for campers, with nearly 600 campgrounds. Some are open only in the summer months, while others operate from spring to autumn. About 200 stay open year-round (and have low-season rates).

➡ The per-night charge to pitch a tent or park a caravan typically costs around Dkr75 for an adult, and about half that for each child. In summer, some places also tack on a site charge of Dkr50 per tent/caravan; some also have a small eco tax.

➡ Many camping grounds offer cabins for rent; expect to pay around Dkr3500 per week during the peak summer season.

➡ You need a camping card (Dkr110) for stays at all campgrounds. You can buy a card at the first campground you arrive at, at local tourist offices, or from the Danish Camping Board (see www.danishcampsites.dk). The cost for an annual pass for couples is Dkr110; it covers all accompanied children aged under 18.

➡ See www.danishcampsites.dk and www.dk-camp.dk for further details.

Hostels

➡ Some 88 hostels make up the **Danhostel association** (☎ 33 31 36 12; www.danhostel.dk), which is affiliated with Hostelling International (HI). Some are dedicated hostels in holiday areas, others are attached to sports centres (and hence may be busy with travelling sports teams etc).

➡ Advance reservations are advised, particularly in summer. In a few places, reception closes as early as 6pm. In most hostels the reception office is closed, and the phone not answered, between noon and 4pm.

➡ Typical costs are Dkr200 to Dkr275 for a dorm bed. For private rooms, expect to pay Dkr400 to Dkr600 per single, Dkr450 to Dkr720 per double, and up to Dkr100 for each additional person in larger rooms. All hostels offer family rooms. Many rooms come with bathroom.

➡ All hostels provide an all-you-can-eat breakfast costing around Dkr70, and some also provide dinner. Most hostels have guest kitchens with pots and pans.

➡ If you hold a valid national or international hostel card, you receive a 10% discount on rates (these can be purchased from hostels and cost Dkr70 for Danish residents, Dkr160 for foreigners). We list prices for noncardholders.

Hotels

➡ Some hotels have set rates published on their websites; others have rates that fluctuate according to season and demand. Most hotel websites offer good deals, as do booking engines.

➡ Many business hotels offer cheaper rates on Friday and Saturday nights year-round, and during the summer peak (from about Midsummer in late June until the start of the school year in early/mid-August).

➡ There is no hard-and-fast rule about the inclusion of breakfast in prices – many hotels include it in their price, but for others it is optional. It is never included in the price of budget hotels (you can purchase it for around Dkr70).

Other Accommodation

- Hundreds of places (summer cottages, inner-city apartments, family-friendly houses) can be rented direct from the owner via **AirBnB** (www.airbnb.com).
- Many tourist offices book rooms in private homes for a small fee, or provide a free list of the rooms on their website so travellers can book online or phone on their own.

ACTIVITIES

Denmark is well set up for a diversity of outdoor activities, from walking and cycling to fishing and water sports. The official **Visit Denmark** (www.visitdenmark.com) tourist website offers useful information and links.

The best way to tour Denmark by bike is by grabbing a map and planning it yourself – a fantastic resource is the **Cyclistic** (http://cyclistic.dk/en/) website.

Each county produces its own detailed 1:100,000 cycle-touring maps; many of them come with booklets detailing accommodation, sights and other local information. These maps cost around Dkr129, and are available at tourist offices or online via the Danish cycling federation, Dansk Cyklist Forbund (its shop is at http://shop.dcf.dk).

FOOD

Generally speaking, eating out in Denmark is not cheap. You can expect to pay Dkr400 for a decent three-course meal in the capital, rising easily to Dkr1000 and above in the finest restaurants.

The following price ranges refer to a standard main course:

€ less than Dkr125

€€ Dkr125–250

€€€ more than Dkr250

GAY & LESBIAN TRAVELLERS

- Denmark is a popular destination for gay and lesbian travellers. Copenhagen in particular has an active, open gay community with a healthy number of gay venues.
- For general info, contact **Landsforeningen for Bøsser, Lesbiske, Biseksuelle og Transpersoner** (www.lgbt.dk), the Danish national association for the GLBT community.
- A useful website for travellers with visitor information and listings in English is www.copenhagen-gay-life.dk. Also see www.out-and-about.dk.

INTERNET ACCESS

- With the proliferation of wi-fi, and most locals and travellers carrying iPads and/or smartphones, the old-fashioned internet cafe is a dying breed in Denmark. Public libraries are your best bet in midsized and small towns for free use of computers with internet access.

MONEY

ATMs Major bank ATMs accept Visa, MasterCard and the Cirrus and Plus bank cards.

Cash If you're exchanging cash, there's a Dkr30 fee for a transaction. Post offices exchange foreign currency at rates comparable to those at banks.

Credit cards Visa and MasterCard are widely accepted in Denmark. American Express and Diners Club are occasionally accepted. A surcharge of up to 3.75% is imposed on foreign credit-card transactions in some restaurants, shops and hotels.

Tipping Restaurant bills and taxi fares include service charges in the quoted prices. Further tipping is not expected, although rounding up the bill is not uncommon when service has been particularly good.

OPENING HOURS

Opening hours vary throughout the year. We've provided high-season opening hours; in tourist areas and establishments, hours will generally decrease in the shoulder and low seasons.

Family-friendly attractions (museums, zoos, fun parks) in holiday hot spots will generally open from June to August (possibly May to September), plus open for the spring and autumn school holidays.

Banks 10am–4pm Monday to Friday

Bars 4pm–midnight, to 2am or later Friday & Saturday (clubs on weekends may open until 5am)

Cafes 8am–5pm or later

Restaurants Noon–10pm (maybe earlier on weekends for brunch)

Shops 10am–6pm Monday to Friday (possibly until 7pm on Friday), to 4pm Saturday; some larger stores may open Sunday

Supermarkets 8am–8pm or to 9pm or 10pm (many with bakeries opening around 7am)

PUBLIC HOLIDAYS

Many Danes take their main work holiday during the first three weeks of July. Banks and most businesses close on public holidays and transport schedules are commonly reduced.

New Year's Day 1 January

Maundy Thursday Thursday before Easter

Good Friday Friday before Easter

Easter Day Sunday in March or April

Easter Monday Day after Easter Day

Great Prayer Day Fourth Friday after Easter

Ascension Day Sixth Thursday after Easter

Whitsunday Seventh Sunday after Easter

Whitmonday Seventh Monday after Easter

Constitution Day 5 June
Christmas Eve 24 December
Christmas Day 25 December
Boxing Day 26 December
New Year's Eve 31 December

TELEPHONE

- To call Denmark from abroad, dial your country's international access code, then ☎45 (Denmark's country code), then the local number. There are no regional area codes within Denmark.
- To call internationally from Denmark, dial ☎00, then the country code for the country you're calling, followed by the area code (without the initial zero if there is one) and the local number.
- Public payphones accept coins, phonecards and credit cards. Phonecards are available from kiosks and post offices.

TIME

Denmark is normally one hour ahead of GMT/UTC. Clocks are moved forward one hour for daylight-saving time from the last Sunday in March to the last Sunday in October. Denmark uses the 24-hour clock.

TOURIST INFORMATION

Visit Denmark (www.visitdenmark.com), Denmark's official tourism website, lists tourist offices throughout the country.

TRAVELLERS WITH DISABILITIES

- Denmark is improving access to buildings, transport and even forestry areas and beaches all the time, although accessibility is still not ubiquitous.
- The official www.visitdenmark.com website has a useful series of links for travellers with disabilities.
- A good resource is **God Adgang** (www.godadgang.dk), which lists service providers who have had their facilities registered and labelled for accessibility.

VISAS

Citizens of the USA, Canada, Australia and New Zealand need a valid passport to visit Denmark, but do not need a visa for stays of less than 90 days. In addition, no entry visa is required by citizens of EU and Nordic countries. Citizens of many African, South American, Asian and former Soviet-bloc countries do require a visa. See www.nyidanmark.dk.

WOMEN TRAVELLERS

Women travellers are less likely to encounter problems in Denmark than in most other countries. Naturally, use common sense when it comes to potentially dangerous situations such as hitching or walking alone at night. Dial ☎112 for emergencies.

Getting There & Away

Flights, cars and tours can be booked online at lonelyplanet.com.

AIR

The majority of international flights into Denmark land at Copenhagen Airport (p63) in Kastrup, about 9km southeast of central Copenhagen.

A number of international flights, mostly those coming from other Nordic countries or the UK, land at smaller regional airports, in Aarhus, Aalborg, Billund, Esbjerg and Sønderborg.

LAND

Germany

The E45 is the main motorway running between Germany and Denmark's Jutland peninsula.

Bus

- The most extensive European bus network is maintained by **Eurolines** (☎33 88 70 00; www.eurolines.dk), a consortium of 30 bus operators. Eurolines Scandinavia offers connections to more than 500 major European cities in 26 countries. Destinations, timetables and prices are all online; advance reservations are advised.
- **Abildskou** (☎70 21 08 88; www.abildskou.dk) links Aarhus and Berlin (one way Dkr495, nine hours, daily) with stops in Kolding and Vejle (Denmark) and Flensburg and Neumünster (Germany) en route. There is an option to connect to services to Hamburg.

Train

There are both direct and indirect train services from Copenhagen to Germany; see www.bahn.com for more information. Direct services include Berlin (from Dkr663, 7¾ to 9¾ hours, one or two daily).

Norway

Train

There are numerous daily services between Copenhagen and Oslo, although most require several interchanges. One to two daily services require only one interchange in Göteborg, Sweden (from Dkr728, 8¼ hours). See www.sj.se for more information.

Sweden

Bus

Eurolines (☎33 88 70 00; www.eurolines.dk) runs buses between Göteborg and Copenhagen (Dkr242, 4½ hours, daily). **Swebus Express** (www.swebus.se) and **Nettbuss Express** (www.nettbuss.se) both run regular buses on the same routes.

Train

Trains run many times a day between Denmark and Sweden via the Øresund bridge linking Copenhagen with Malmö (Dkr95, 35 minutes). If you're travelling by train, the bridge crossing is included in the fare, but for those travelling by car, there's a Dkr335 toll per vehicle. For train timetables, ticket offers and bookings, see www.sj.se. From Copenhagen, other direct Swedish connections include the following:

Göteborg From Dkr450, 3¾ hours, up to 15 daily

Stockholm From Dkr360, 5½ hours, up to six daily

SEA

International ferries run between Denmark and Sweden, Norway, Iceland, Germany and Poland.

Getting Around

AIR

Denmark's small size and efficient train network mean that domestic air travel is mostly the domain of business folk and people connecting from international flights through Copenhagen.

SAS (☎70 10 20 00; www.flysas.com) Links Copenhagen with Aalborg (at least five times daily) and Aarhus (at least four times daily).

Danish Airport Transport (DAT; ☎76 92 30 40; www.dat.dk)

BICYCLE

- Cyclists here are very well catered for, with excellent cycling routes throughout the country.
- Bike-rental prices average around Dkr100/400 per day/week for something basic.
- Bicycles can be taken on ferries and trains for a modest fee.
- On Intercity trains, reservations should be made at least three hours prior to departure as bikes generally travel in a separate section of the train.

BOAT

Ferries link virtually all of Denmark's populated islands. See individual towns for details.

BUS

Long-distance buses run a distant second to trains. Still, some cross-country bus routes work out to about 25% cheaper than trains. Popular routes include Copenhagen to Aarhus or Aalborg.

The main bus companies operating in Denmark:

Abildskou (☎70 21 08 88; www.abildskou.dk) Runs from Copenhagen to Aarhus, Silkeborg and Aalborg.

Thinggaard Express (☎98 11 66 00; www.expressbus.dk) Operates between Frederikshavn and Esbjerg via Aalborg.

CAR & MOTORCYCLE

Denmark is perfect for touring by car. Roads are in good condition and well signposted. Traffic is manageable, even in major cities such as Copenhagen (rush hours excepted). Denmark's extensive network of ferries carries motor vehicles for reasonable rates. It's always a good idea for drivers to call ahead and make reservations, especially in the summer.

Car Hire

The following applies when renting a car:

- You must be 21.
- You must have a valid home driving licence.
- You must have a major credit card.
- You may need to supply a passport.
- You may get the best deal by booking through an international rental agency before you arrive. Be sure to ask for promotional rates.
- Ensure you get a deal covering unlimited kilometres.
- Check car-rental websites for special online deals.
- Drivers aged 21 to 25 may need to pay an additional 'young driver fee'.

Car-hire companies in Denmark:

Avis (www.avis.com)

Europcar (www.europcar.com)

Hertz (www.hertzdk.dk)

Road Rules

- Drive on the right-hand side of the road.
- The use of seatbelts is mandatory.
- Cars and motorcyles must have dipped headlights on at all times.
- Motorcyclists (but not cyclists) must wear helmets.
- Speed limits: 50km/h in towns and built-up areas, 80km/h on major roads, 110km/h or 130km/h on motorways.
- The legal blood-alcohol limit is 0.05%.
- Using a hand-held mobile phone while driving is illegal; hands-free use is permitted.
- Use of a parking disc (P-skive) is usually required. Resembling a clock, the device is placed on the dashboard to indicate the time of arrival at a car-parking space. Discs are commonly available at petrol stations and tourist offices.

TRAIN

With the exception of a few short private lines, **Danske Statsbaner** (DSB; ☎70 13 14 15; www.dsb.dk) runs all Danish train services. Overall, train travel in Denmark is not expensive, in large part because distances are short.

Reservations During morning and evening peak times, it's advisable to make reservations (Dkr30) if travelling on the speedy InterCityLyn (ICL) and Intercity (IC) trains.

Discounts and passes People aged 65 and older are entitled to a 25% discount on Friday and Sunday and a 50% discount on other days. Children under the age of 12 usually travel free if they are with an adult travelling on a standard ticket (one adult can take two children free).

Finland

Includes ➡

Best Places to Eat

- ➡ Olo (p137)
- ➡ Gustav Wasa (p165)
- ➡ Musta Lammas (p175)
- ➡ Smor (p149)
- ➡ Hietalahden Kauppahalli (p137)

Best Places to Stay

- ➡ Lossiranta Lodge (p170)
- ➡ Dream Hostel (p159)
- ➡ Lumihotelli (p193)
- ➡ Hotel Fabian (p135)
- ➡ Hotel Kantarellis (p164)

Why Go?

There's something pure in the Finnish air; it's an invitation to get out and active year-round. A post-sauna dip in an ice hole under the majestic aurora borealis (northern lights), after whooshing across the snow behind a team of huskies, isn't a typical winter's day just anywhere. And hiking or canoeing under the midnight sun through pine forests populated by wolves and bears isn't your typical tanning-oil summer either.

Although socially and economically in the vanguard of nations, large parts of Finland remain gloriously remote; trendsetting modern Helsinki is counterbalanced by vast forested wildernesses elsewhere.

Nordic peace in lakeside cottages, summer sunshine on convivial beer terraces, avant-garde design, dark melodic music and cafes warm with aromas of homebaking are other facets of Suomi (Finnish) seduction. As are the independent, loyal, warm and welcoming Finns, who tend to do their own thing and are much the better for it.

When to Go

Helsinki

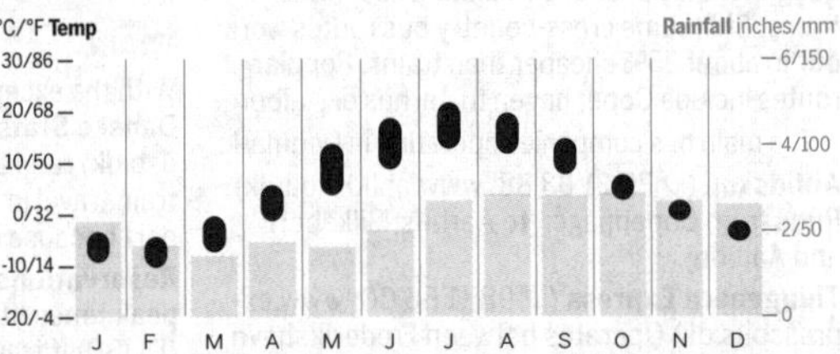

Mar & Apr There's still plenty of snow, but enough daylight to enjoy winter sports.

Jul Everlasting daylight, countless festivals and discounted accommodation.

Sep The stunning colours of the *ruska* (autumn) season make this prime hiking time up north.

Connections

Good roads and bus connections make getting around easy, while there's a comprehensive train network in the south and centre. Road connections with Norway and Sweden are way up north, but ferries are big on the Baltic; an overnight boat can take you to Stockholm or as far as Germany. Helsinki's harbour also offers quick and easy connections to Tallinn in Estonia, launch pad for the Baltic states and Eastern Europe. Finland's also a springboard for Russia, with boat, bus and train services available, some visa-free.

ITINERARIES

One Week

Helsinki demands at least a couple of days and is a good base for a day trip to Tallinn (Estonia) or **Porvoo**. In summer, head to the eastern Lakeland and explore **Lappeenranta**, **Savonlinna** and **Kuopio** (catch a lake ferry between the latter towns). In winter, take an overnight train or budget flight to **Lapland** (Rovaniemi) for a few days, visiting Santa at **Napapiiri**, exploring Sávuomi culture and mushing with huskies. A Helsinki–Savonlinna–Kuopio–Rovaniemi–Helsinki route is a good option.

Two Weeks

Spend a few days in **Helsinki** and **Porvoo**, visit the harbour town of **Turku** and lively **Tampere**. Next stops are **Savonlinna** and **Kuopio** in the beautiful eastern Lakeland. Head up to **Rovaniemi**, and perhaps as far north as the Sámi capital **Inari**. You could also fit in a summer festival, some hiking in **Lapland** or **North Karelia**, or a quick cycling trip to **Åland**.

Essential Food & Drink

Coffee To fit in, eight or nine cups a day is about right, best accompanied with a *pulla* (cardamom-flavoured pastry).

Offbeat meats Unusual meats appear on menus: reindeer is a staple up north, elk is commonly eaten, and bear is also seasonally available.

Fresh food The kauppahalli (market hall) is where to go for a stunning array of produce. In summer, stalls at the kauppatori (market square) sell delicious fresh vegetables and fruit.

Gastro Helsinki is the best venue for fabulous New Suomi cuisine, with sumptuous degustation menus presenting traditional Finnish ingredients in crest-of-the-wave ways.

Alcoholic drinks Beer is a staple, and great microbreweries are on the increase. Finns also love dissolving things in vodka; try a shot of *salmiakkikossu* (salty-liquorice flavoured) or *fisu* (Fisherman's Friend–flavoured).

Fish Salmon is ubiquitous; tasty lake fish include arctic char, lavaret, pike-perch and scrumptious fried *muikku* (vendace).

AT A GLANCE

Capital Helsinki

Area 338,145 sq km

Population 5.46 million

Country code ☎358

Languages Finnish, Swedish, Sámi languages

Currency euro (€)

FINLAND

Exchange Rates

Australia	A$1	€0.72
Canada	C$1	€0.71
Japan	¥100	€0.73
New Zealand	NZ$1	€0.64
UK	UK£1	€1.25
USA	US$1	€0.77

Set Your Budget

Budget hotel room €75

Two-course evening meal €45–€60

Museum entrance €7–€12

Beer €6–€8

City transport ticket €3–€4

Resources

Visit Finland (www.visitfinland.com)

Helsinki Times (www.helsinkitimes.fi)

Matkahuolto (www.matkahuolto.fi)

Metsähallitus (www.outdoors.fi)

This is Finland (finland.fi)

VR (www.vr.fi)

Finland Highlights

1. Immerse yourself in harbourside **Helsinki** (p129), creative melting pot for the latest in Finnish design and nightlife
2. Marvel at the shimmering lakescapes of handsome **Savonlinna** (p168), and see top-quality opera in its medieval castle
3. Cruise Lakeland waterways, gorge on tiny fish, and sweat it out in the huge smoke sauna at **Kuopio** (p173)
4. Cross the Arctic Circle, hit the awesome Arktikum museum, and visit Santa in his official grotto at **Rovaniemi** (p187)
5. Trek the Bear's Ring Trail or kayak in picturesque **Oulanka National Park** (p186)
6. Learn about Sámi culture, husky-sledding and meeting reindeer at **Inari** (p196)
7. Cycle the picturesque islands of the **Åland archipelago** (p151)
8. Check out the quirky museums of **Tampere** (p156)
9. Take an unusual pub crawl around the offbeat watering holes of **Turku** (p146)
10. Crunch out a shipping lane aboard an icebreaker and spend a night in the ethereal Snow Castle at **Kemi** (p192)

HELSINKI

☎09 / POP 1.09 MILLION (TOTAL URBAN AREA)

It's fitting that harbourside Helsinki, capital of a country with such watery geography, melds so graciously into the Baltic. Half the city seems liquid, and the writhings of the complex coastline include any number of bays, inlets and islands.

Though Helsinki can seem a younger sibling to other Scandinavian capitals, it's the one that went to art school, scorns pop music and works in a cutting-edge studio. The design scene here is legendary, whether you're browsing showroom brands or taking the backstreet hipster trail. The city's gourmet side is also flourishing, with new gastro eateries offering locally sourced tasting menus popping up at dizzying speed.

Nevertheless, much of what is lovable in Helsinki is older. Its understated yet glorious art-nouveau buildings, the spacious elegance of its centenarian cafes, dozens of museums carefully preserving Finnish heritage, restaurants that have changed neither menu nor furnishings since the 1930s: all part of the city's quirky charm.

History

Helsinki (Swedish: Helsingfors) was founded in 1550 by the Swedish king Gustav Vasa, who hoped to compete with the Hanseatic trading port of Tallinn across the water. In the 18th century the Swedes built a mammoth fortress on the nearby island of Suomenlinna, but it wasn't enough to keep the Russians out. Once the Russians were in control of Finland, they needed a capital closer to home than the Swedish-influenced west coast. Helsinki was it, and took Turku's mantle in 1812. Helsinki grew rapidly, with German architect CL Engel responsible for many noble central buildings. In the bitter postwar years, the 1952 Olympic Games symbolised the city's gradual revival.

Sights

The heart of central Helsinki is the harbourside **kauppatori**, where cruises and ferries leave for archipelago islands. It's completely touristy these days, with reindeer souvenirs having replaced most market stalls, but there are still some berries and flowers for sale, and adequate cheap food options.

★Tuomiokirkko CHURCH

(Lutheran Cathedral; www.helsinginseurakunnat.fi; Unioninkatu 29; ⌚9am-6pm, to midnight Jun-Aug) FREE One of CL Engel's finest creations, the chalk-white neoclassical Lutheran cathedral presides over Senaatintori. Created to serve as a reminder of God's supremacy, its high flight of stairs is now a meeting place for canoodling couples. The spartan, almost mausoleum-like interior has little ornamentation under the lofty dome apart from an altar painting and three stern statues of Reformation heroes Luther, Melanchthon and Mikael Agricola, looking like they've just marked your theology exam and taken a dim view of your prospects.

Uspenskin Katedraali CHURCH

(Uspenski Cathedral; http://hos.fi/uspenskin-katedraali; Kanavakatu 1; ⌚9.30am-4pm Tue-Fri, 10am-3pm Sat, noon-3pm Sun) FREE Facing the Lutheran cathedral, the eye-catching red-brick Uspenski Cathedral stands on nearby Katajanokka island. The two buildings face off high above the city like two queens on a theological chessboard. Built as a Russian Orthodox church in 1868, it features classic onion-topped domes and now serves the Finnish Orthodox congregation. The high, square interior has a lavish iconostasis with the Evangelists flanking panels depicting the Last Supper and the Ascension.

Helsingin Kaupunginmuseo MUSEUM

(Helsinki City Museum; www.helsinkicitymuseum.fi; Sofiankatu 4; ⌚9am-5pm Mon-Fri, to 7pm Thu, 11am-5pm Sat & Sun) FREE A group of small museums scattered around the city centre constitute this city museum: all have free entry and focus on an aspect of the city's past or present through permanent and temporary exhibitions. The must-see of the bunch is the main museum, just off Senaatintori.

HELSINKI CARD

The **Helsinki Card** (www.helsinkiexpert.com; adult per 24/48/72hr €36/46/56, child €15/18/21) gives you free travel, entry to more than 50 attractions in and around Helsinki, and discounts on day tours to Porvoo and Tallinn. It's cheaper online; otherwise, get it at the tourist office, hotels, R-kioskis or transport terminals. To make it worthwhile, you'd need to pack lots of sightseeing into a short time.

Helsinki

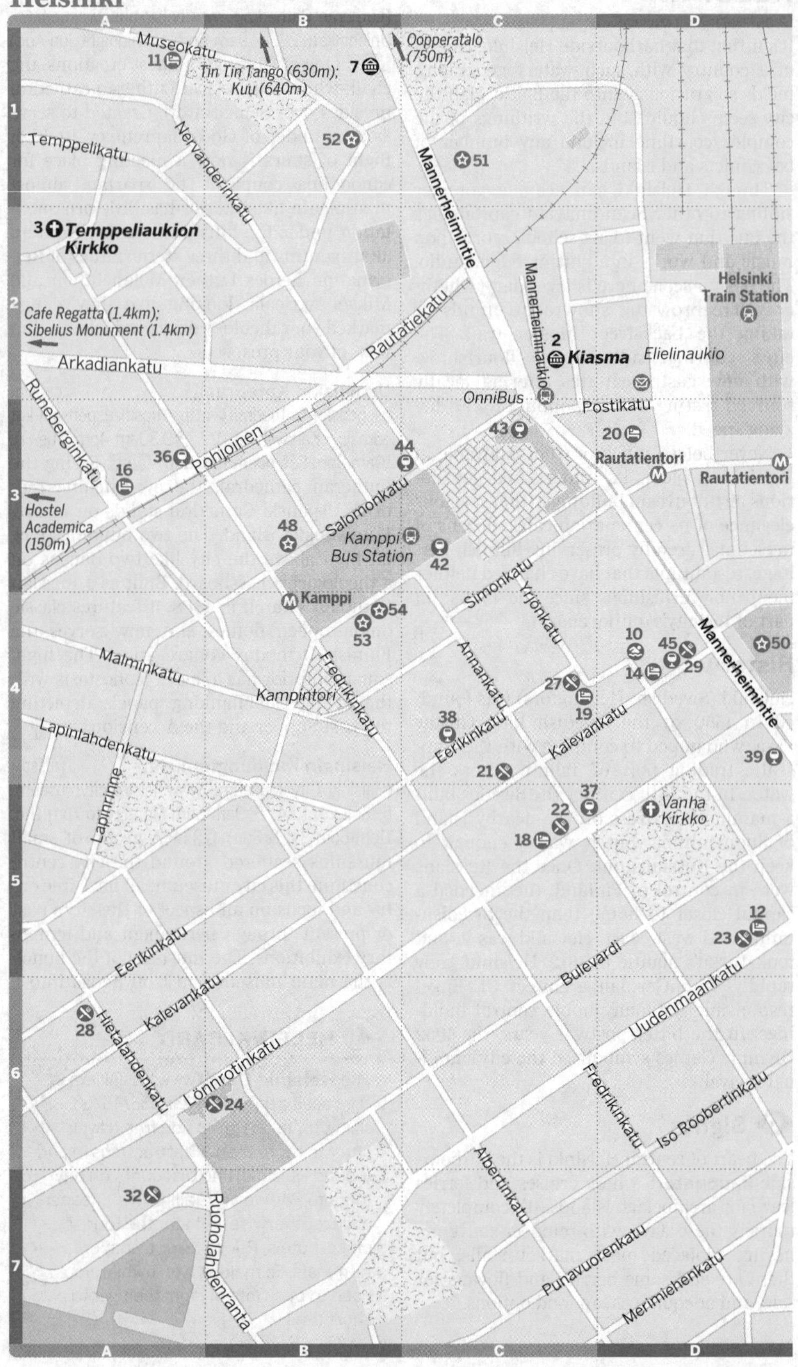

Museokatu
Tin Tin Tango (630m); Kuu (640m)
Oopperatalo (750m)
Temppelikatu
Nervanderinkatu
Mannerheimintie
Temppeliaukion Kirkko
Cafe Regatta (1.4km); Sibelius Monument (1.4km)
Arkadiankatu
Rautatiekatu
Mannerheiminaukio
Kiasma
Elielinaukio
Helsinki Train Station
OnniBus
Postikatu
Runeberginkatu
Pohjoinen
Rautatientori
Hostel Academica (150m)
Salomonkatu
Kamppi Bus Station
Kamppi
Simonkatu
Yrjönkatu
Malminkatu
Fredrikinkatu
Annankatu
Kampintori
Lapinlahdenkatu
Eerikinkatu
Kalevankatu
Lapinrinne
Vanha Kirkko
Bulevardi
Uudenmaankatu
Hietalahdenkatu
Lönnrotinkatu
Iso Roobertinkatu
Albertinkatu
Ruoholahdenranta
Punavuorenkatu
Merimiehenkatu

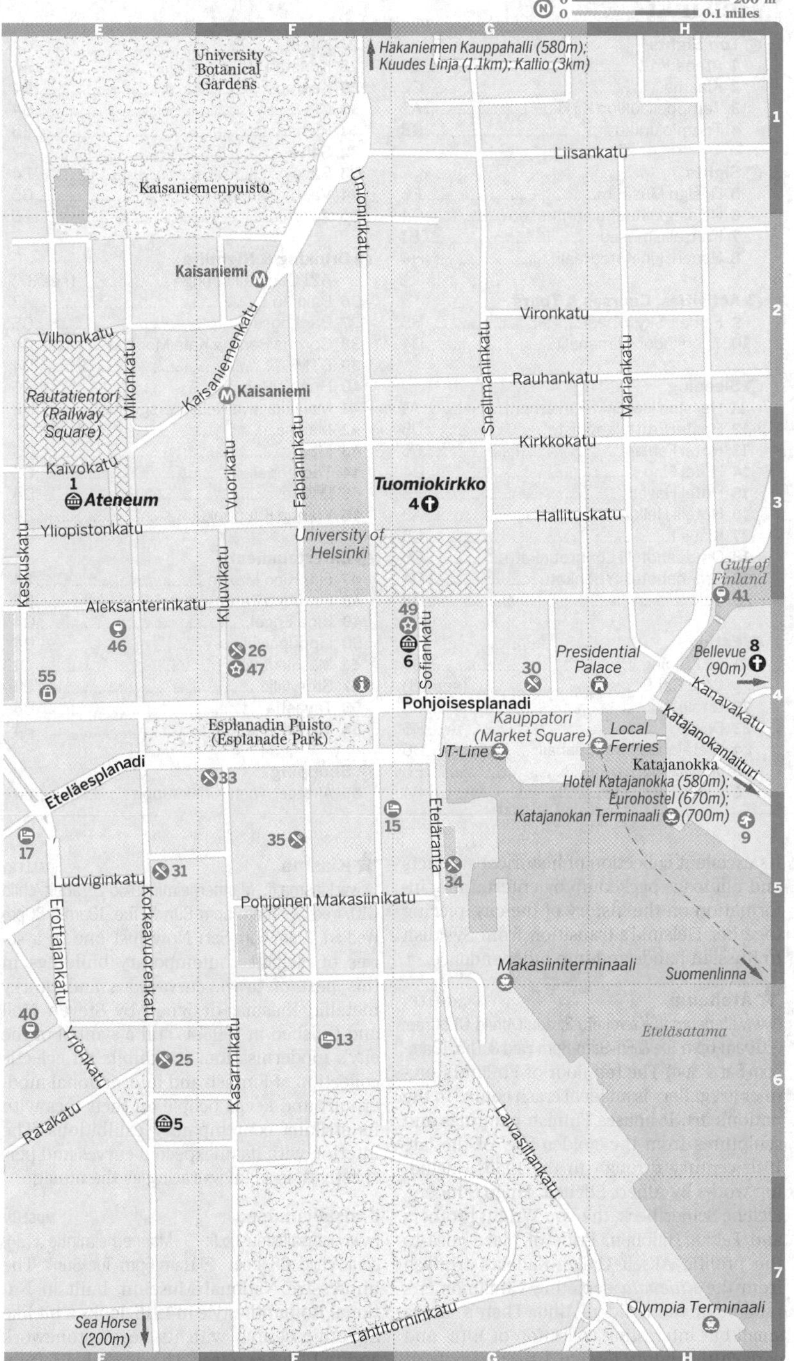

0 200 m
0 0.1 miles
University Botanical Gardens
Hakaniemen Kauppahalli (580m); Kuudes Linja (1.1km); Kallio (3km)
Liisankatu
Unioninkatu
Kaisaniemenpuisto
Kaisaniemi
Vironkatu
Vilhonkatu
Kaisaniemenkatu
Mikonkatu
Snellmaninkatu
Mariankatu
Rauhankatu
Rautatientori (Railway Square)
Kaisaniemi
Kirkkokatu
Kaivokatu
Fabianinkatu
Vuorikatu
Tuomiokirkko
Ateneum
Hallituskatu
Yliopistonkatu
University of Helsinki
Keskuskatu
Kluuvikatu
Gulf of Finland
Aleksanterinkatu
Sofiankatu
Presidential Palace
Bellevue (90m)
Kanavakatu
Pohjoisesplanadi
Kauppatori (Market Square)
Local Ferries
Katajanokanlaituri
Esplanadin Puisto (Esplanade Park)
JT-Line
Katajanokka
Eteläesplanadi
Hotel Katajanokka (580m); Eurohostel (670m); Katajanokan Terminaali (700m)
Eteläranta
Ludviginkatu
Korkeavuorenkatu
Erottajankatu
Pohjoinen Makasiinikatu
Makasiiniterminaali
Suomenlinna
Eteläsatama
Yrjönkatu
Kasarmikatu
Ratakatu
Laivasillankatu
Olympia Terminaali
Sea Horse (200m)
Tähtitorninkatu

Helsinki

Top Sights
1 Ateneum ... E3
2 Kiasma ... C2
3 Temppeliaukion Kirkko ... A2
4 Tuomiokirkko ... G3

Sights
5 Design Museum ... E6
6 Helsingin Kaupunginmuseo ... G4
7 Kansallismuseo ... B1
8 Uspenskin Katedraali ... H4

Activities, Courses & Tours
9 Finnair Sky Wheel ... H5
10 Yrjönkadun Uimahalli ... D4

Sleeping
11 Hellsten Helsinki Parliament ... A1
12 Hostel Erottajanpuisto ... D5
13 Hotel Fabian ... F6
14 Hotel Finn ... D4
15 Hotel Haven ... F5
16 Hotelli Helka ... A3
17 Klaus K ... E5
18 Omenahotelli Lönnrotinkatu ... C5
19 Omenahotelli Yrjönkatu ... C4
20 Sokos ... D3

Eating
21 A21 Dining ... C4
Café Bar 9 ... (see 23)
22 Cholo ... C5
23 Demo ... D5
24 Hietalahden Kauppahalli ... B6
25 Juuri ... E6
26 Karl Fazer Café ... F4
27 Kitch ... C4
28 Konstan Möljä ... A6
29 Kosmos ... D4
30 Olo ... G4
31 Rikhards ... E5
32 Salve ... A7
33 Savoy ... F4
34 Vanha Kauppahalli ... G5
35 Zucchini ... F5

Drinking & Nightlife
A21 Cocktail Lounge ... (see 37)
36 Bäkkäri ... A3
37 Bar Loose ... C5
38 Corona Baari & Kafe Mockba ... C4
39 DTM ... D4
40 Hugo's Room ... E6
41 Majakkalaiva Relandersgrund ... H3
42 Maxine ... C3
43 Mbar ... C3
44 Teerenpeli ... C3
45 U Kaleva ... D4
46 Wanha Kauppakuja ... E4

Entertainment
47 FinnKino Maxim ... F4
48 FinnKino Tennispalatsi ... B3
49 Kino Engel ... G4
50 Lippupalvelu ... D4
51 Musiikkitalo ... C1
52 Storyville ... B1
53 Tavastia ... B4
54 Tiketti ... B4

Shopping
55 Akateeminen Kirjakauppa ... E4

Its excellent collection of historical artefacts and photos is backed up by entertaining information on the history of the city, piecing together Helsinki's transition from Swedish to Russian hands and into independence.

★Ateneum GALLERY
(www.ateneum.fi; Kaivokatu 2; adult/child €12/free; 10am-6pm Tue & Fri, 9am-8pm Wed & Thu, 10am-5pm Sat & Sun) The top floor of Finland's premier art gallery is an ideal crash course in the nation's art. It houses Finnish paintings and sculptures from the 'golden age' of the late 19th century through to the 1950s, including works by Albert Edelfelt, Hugo Simberg, Helene Schjerfbeck, the Von Wright brothers and Pekka Halonen. Pride of place goes to the prolific Akseli Gallen-Kallela's triptych from the *Kalevala* depicting Väinämöinen's pursuit of the maiden Aino. There's also a small but interesting collection of 19th- and early-20th-century foreign art.

★Kiasma GALLERY
(www.kiasma.fi; Mannerheiminaukio 2; adult/child €10/free; 10am-5pm Sun & Tue, 10am-8.30pm Wed-Fri, 10am-6pm Sat) Now just one of a series of elegant contemporary buildings in this part of town, curvaceous and quirky metallic Kiasma, designed by Steven Holl and finished in 1998, is still a symbol of the city's modernisation. It exhibits an eclectic collection of Finnish and international modern art and keeps people on their toes with its striking contemporary exhibitions. The interior, with its unexpected curves and perspectives, is as invigorating as the outside.

Kansallismuseo MUSEUM
(www.kansallismuseo.fi; Mannerheimintie 34; adult/child €8/free; 11am-6pm Tue-Sun) The impressive National Museum, built in National Romantic style in 1916, looks a bit like a Gothic church with its heavy stonework and tall square tower. This is Finland's pre-

mier historical museum and is divided into rooms covering different periods of Finnish history, including prehistory and archaeological finds, church relics, ethnography and changing cultural exhibitions. It's a very thorough, old-style museum – you might have trouble selling this one to the kids – but provides a comprehensive overview.

Design Museum MUSEUM
(www.designmuseum.fi; Korkeavuorenkatu 23; adult/child €10/free; ⌚11am-8pm Tue, 11am-6pm Wed-Sun Sep-May, 11am-6pm daily Jun-Aug) The Design Museum has a permanent collection that looks at the roots of Finnish design in the nation's traditions and nature. Changing exhibitions focus on contemporary design – everything from clothing to household furniture.

★Temppeliaukion Kirkko CHURCH
(☎09-2340-6320; www.helsinginseurakunnat.fi; Lutherinkatu 3; ⌚10am-5.45pm Mon-Sat, 11.45am-5.45pm Sun Jun-Aug, to 5pm Sep-May) The Temppeliaukio church, designed by Timo and Tuomo Suomalainen in 1969, remains one of Helsinki's foremost attractions. Hewn into solid stone, it feels close to a Finnish ideal of spirituality in nature – you could be in a rocky glade were it not for the 24m-diameter roof covered in 22km of copper stripping. There are regular concerts, with great acoustics. Opening times vary depending on events, so phone or search for its Facebook page updates. There are less groups midweek.

★Seurasaaren Ulkomuseo MUSEUM
(Seurasaari Open-Air Museum; www.seurasaari.fi; adult/child €8/2.50; ⌚11am-5pm Jun-Aug, 9am-3pm Mon-Fri, 11am-5pm Sat & Sun late May & early Sep) West of the city centre, this excellent island museum has a collection of historic wooden buildings transferred here from around Finland. There's everything from haylofts to a mansion, parsonage and church, as well as the beautiful giant rowboats used to transport churchgoing communities. Prices and hours refer to entering the buildings themselves, where guides in traditional costume demonstrate folk dancing and crafts. Otherwise, you're free to roam the picturesque wooded island, where there are several cafes.

Sibelius Monument MONUMENT
This famous, striking sculpture was created by artist Eila Hiltunen in 1967 to honour Finland's most famous composer. Bus 24 takes you there, but it's a pleasant walk or cycle.

Activities

Finnair Sky Wheel FERRIS WHEEL
(www.finnair-skywheel.com; Katajanokanlaituri 2; adult/child €12/9; ⌚10am-10pm Mon-Thu, 10am-11pm Fri & Sat, 10am-8pm Sun) Rising over the harbour, this ferris wheel gives good perspectives over the comings and goings of central Helsinki. If you fancy forking out €195, you get the VIP gondola, with glass floors below, leather seats and a bottle of champagne.

★Kotiharjun Sauna SAUNA
(www.kotiharjunsauna.fi; Harjutorinkatu 1; adult/child €12/6; ⌚2-8pm Tue-Sun, sauna to 9.30pm) This traditional public wood-fired sauna in Kallio dates back to 1928. This type of place largely disappeared with the advent of shared saunas in apartment buildings, but it's a classic experience, where you can also

HELSINKI IN...

One Day

Finns are the world's biggest coffee drinkers, so first up it's a caffeine shot with a *pulla* (cardamon-flavoured bun) at a classic central **cafe**. Then down to the **kauppatori** (market square), and the fresh produce in the adjacent **kauppahalli** (covered market). Put a picnic together and boat out to the island fortress of **Suomenlinna**. Back in town, check out **Senaatintori** (Senate Square) and nearby **Uspenskin Katedraali**. Then take the metro to legendary **Kotiharjun Sauna** for a predinner sweat. Eat traditional Finnish at **Konstan Möljä** or **Sea Horse**.

Two Days

Investigate the art and design scene. Head to the **Ateneum** for a perspective on the golden age of Finnish painting, then see contemporary works at still-iconic **Kiasma**. Feet tired? Catch the **number 2 & 3 trams** for a circular sightseeing trip around town, before browsing design shops around **Punavuori**. In the evening, head up to **Ateljee Bar** for great views, then to **Tavastia** for a rock gig.

get a scrub down and massage. There are separate saunas for men and women; bring your own towel or rent one (€3). It's a short stroll from Sörnäinen metro station. Closes Sundays June to mid-August.

Yrjönkadun Uimahalli SWIMMING
(www.hel.fi; Yrjönkatu 21; swimming €5-5.40, swimming plus saunas €14; ⏲ open Sep-May, men 6.30am-8pm Tue & Thu, 8am-8pm Sat, women noon-8pm Sun & Mon, 6.30am-8pm Wed & Fri) For a sauna and swim, these art deco baths are a Helsinki institution – a fusion of soaring Nordic elegance and Roman tradition. There are separate hours for men and women. Nudity is compulsory in the saunas; bathing suits are optional in the pool.

Tours

There are a couple of the standard hop-on hop-off bus tours running; expect to pay around €25 to €30 for a ticket. An excellent budget alternative is to do a circuit of town on **Tram 2** then **3** or vice versa; pick up the free *Sightseeing on Tram 2/3* brochure as your guide around the city centre and out to Kallio.

When strolling through the kauppatori in summer, you won't have to look for cruises – the boat companies will find you. One-and-a-half hour cruises cost €20 to €25, while dinner cruises, bus-boat combinations and sunset cruises are also available.

Festivals & Events

There's something going on in Helsinki year-round. Some of the biggies:

Vappu STUDENT
(May Day) This student graduation festival is celebrated by gathering around the Havis Amanda statue, which receives a white graduation cap, at 6pm on 30 April. The following day, May Day, is celebrated with plenty of sparkling wine, preferably outdoors.

Helsinki Päivä CITY
(Helsinki Day; www.helsinkipaiva.fi) Celebrating the city's anniversary, Helsinki Day brings many free events to Esplanadi on 12 June.

Tuska Festival MUSIC
(www.tuska-festival.fi) A big metal festival in late June or early July.

Helsingin Juhlaviikot PERFORMING ARTS
(Helsinki Festival; www.helsinginjuhlaviikot.fi) From late August to early September, this arts festival features chamber music, jazz, theatre, opera and more.

Flow Festival MUSIC
(www.flowfestival.com) An August weekend festival that sees indie, hip-hop, electronic and experimental music rock the suburb of Suvilahti.

Sleeping

From mid-May to mid-August, bookings are strongly advisable, although July's a quieter time for midrange and top-end hotels.

The **Sokos** (www.sokoshotels.fi) and **Scandic** (www.scandichotels.com) chains have several business hotels in the centre, and other multinationals are present.

Hostel Academica HOSTEL €
(☎09-1311-4334; www.hostelacademica.fi; Hietaniemenkatu 14; dm/s/d €28.50/63/75; ⏲ Jun-Aug; P @ 🛜 🏊) Finnish students live well, so in summer take advantage of this residence, a clean busy spot packed with features (pool and sauna) and cheery staff. The modern rooms are great, and all come with bar fridges and their own bathrooms. Dorms have only two or three berths so there's no crowding. It's also environmentally sound. Breakfast available. HI discount.

Hostel Erottajanpuisto HOSTEL €
(☎09-642-169; www.erottajanpuisto.com; Uudenmaankatu 9; dm/s/d €30/60/75; @ 🛜) Helsinki's most characterful and laid-back hostel occupies the top floor of a building in a lively street of bars and restaurants. Forget curfews, lockouts, school kids and bringing your own sleeping sheet – this is more like a guesthouse with (crowded) dormitories. Shared bathrooms are new; private rooms offer more peace and there's a great lounge and friendly folk. HI members get 10% off; breakfast is extra.

Eurohostel HOSTEL €
(☎09-622-0470; www.eurohostel.eu; Linnankatu 9; dm €31, s €54-60, d €60-70; @ 🛜) On Katajanokka island close to the Viking Line ferry and easily reached on tram 4, this hostel is busy and convenient, if impersonal. Two grades of room are similar and both come with share bathrooms; the 'Eurohostel' rooms are more modern with TV and parquet floors. Dorm rates mean sharing a twin – a good deal.

Hostel Stadion HOSTEL €
(☎09-477-8480; www.stadionhostel.fi; Pohjoinen Stadiontie 3; dm/d/q €24/60/104; P @ 🛜) An easy tram ride from town, this well-equipped hostel is actually part of the Olympic Stadium. There are no views though, and it feels

old-style, with big dorms and heavy decor. Nonetheless, it's a cheap bed and there are good facilities, including laundry, kitchen, bike hire, a cafe and free parking. Linen and towels included; HI discount.

Rastila Camping CAMPGROUND, COTTAGES €
(☎09-3107-8517; www.rastilacamping.fi; Karavaanikatu 4; campsites €14, plus per adult/child €5/1, 2-to 4-person cabins €79, cottages €107-213; P@🛜👪) Only 20 minutes on the metro from the city centre (Rastila station), this year-round campground makes a good budget option. Though scarcely rural, it's green and well equipped, with a supermarket nearby. As well as grassy tent and plenty of van sites, there are wooden cabins and more-upmarket log cottages, plus a gentle beach and facilities, including good showers, fast wi-fi, saunas and bike hire.

★**Hotelli Helka** HOTEL €€
(☎09-613-580; www.helka.fi; Pohjoinen Rautatiekatu 23; s €110-132, d €142-162; P@🛜) One of the centre's best midrange hotels, the Helka has competent, friendly staff and excellent facilities, including free parking if you can bag one of the limited spots. Best are the rooms, which seem to smell of pine with their Artek furniture, ice-block bedside lights and print of a rural Suomi scene over the bed, backlit to give rooms a moody glow.

Hotel Finn HOTEL €€
(☎09-684-4360; www.hotellifinn.fi; Kalevankatu 3B; s €59-119, d €109-199; P🛜) High in a central-city building, this friendly two-floor hotel is upbeat with helpful service and corridors darkly done out in sexy chocolate and red, with art from young Finnish photographers on the walls. Rooms all differ but are bright, with modish wallpaper and tiny bathrooms. Some are furnished with recycled materials. Rates vary widely – it can be a real bargain.

Hellsten Helsinki Parliament APARTMENT €€
(☎09-251-1050; www.hellstenhotels.fi; Museokatu 18; apt €120-190; ⏱reception 7am-10pm Mon-Fri; @🛜👪) A step up in style and comfort from many hotels, the apartments here have sleek modern furnishings, kitchenette, internet connections and cable TV. Prices vary seasonally and there are discounts for longer stays. It's in a great location. You will receive a keycode if you arrive outside hours.

Omenahotelli HOTEL €€
(☎0600-18018; www.omenahotels.com; r €70-130; 🛜) This good-value staffless hotel chain has two handy Helsinki locations: **Lönnrotinkatu** (www.omena.com; Lönnrotinkatu 13); **Yrjönkatu** (www.omena.com; Yrjönkatu 30). As well as a double bed, rooms have fold-out chairs that can sleep two more, plus there's a microwave and minifridge. Book online or via a terminal in the lobby. Windows don't open, so rooms can be stuffy on hot days.

★**Hotel Fabian** HOTEL €€€
(☎09-6128-2000; www.hotelfabian.fi; Fabianinkatu 7; r €200-270; ❄@🛜) Central, but in a quiet part without the bustle of the other designer hotels, this place gets everything right. Elegant standard rooms with whimsical lighting and restrained modern design are extremely comfortable; they vary substantially in size. Higher-grade rooms add extra features and a kitchenette. Staff are super helpful and seem very happy to be here.

★**Hotel Haven** HOTEL €€€
(☎09-681-930; www.hotelhaven.fi; Unioninkatu 17; s/d from €189/220; P❄@🛜) The closest hotel to the kauppatori is elegant, welcoming and scores high on all levels. All room grades feature excellent beds and linen, soft colour combinations, classy toiletries and thoughtful extras such as sockets in the safes. 'Comfort' rooms face the street and are very spacious; higher grades give add-ons – like a Nespresso machine in 'Lux' category – and some offer a magnificent harbour view.

Klaus K HOTEL €€€
(☎020-770-4700; www.klauskhotel.com; Bulevardi 2; d €175-315; ❄@🛜) 🍃 Boasting excellent service and extremely comfortable beds, this central, independent design hotel has a theme of *Kalevala* quotes throughout, and easy-on-the-eye space-conscious architecture. A range of slick new 'Sky Loft' rooms offer a more modern feel; some come with balconies. A host of amenities ease the stay, but the best bit is the fabulous breakfasts.

Hotel Katajanokka HOTEL €€€
(☎09-686-450; www.bwkatajanokka.fi; Merikasarminkatu 1A; d €150-250; P❄@🛜) Set in a refurbished prison, this place offers character in spades on Katajanokka island. Rooms stretch over two to three ex-cells, so they're anything but pokey, and boast not slop buckets but sleek modern bathrooms. Penitentiary jokes – handcuffs for sale at reception – aside, there's plenty of luxury and a sumptuous sauna. Tram 4 stops right outside. This jailhouse rocks.

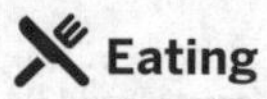

Helsinki has by far the nation's best range of restaurants, whether for Finnish classics, New Suomi cuisine or international dishes. Good budget options are in shorter supply: cafes offer lunch choices and there are plenty of self-catering opportunities.

Restaurants

Zucchini VEGETARIAN €

(Fabianinkatu 4; lunch €8-12; ⏲11am-4pm Mon-Fri; ✎) One of the city's few vegetarian cafes, this is a top-notch lunchtime spot; queues out the door are not unusual. Piping-hot soups banish winter chills, and freshly baked quiche on the sunny terrace out the back is a summer treat. For lunch, you can choose soup or salad/hot dish or both.

Café Bar 9 CAFE €

(www.bar9.net; Uudenmaankatu 9; mains €10-16; ⏲food 11am-11pm Mon-Fri, noon-11pm Sat & Sun; ☎) It's tough to find low-priced food at dinnertime in Helsinki that's not shaved off a spinning stick, so this place stands out. It would anyway, with its retro red formica tables and unpretentious artsy air. Plates vary, with some solid Finnish fare backed up by big sandwiches, Thai-inspired stir-fries and pastas. Portions are generous so don't overdo it: you can always come back.

Konstan Möljä FINNISH €

(☎09-694-7504; www.konstanmolja.fi; Hietalahdenkatu 14; buffet €18; ⏲5-10pm Tue-Fri, 4-10pm Sat) The maritime interior of this old sailors' eatery hosts an impressive husband-and-wife team who turn out a great-value Finnish buffet for dinner. Though these days it sees plenty of tourists, it serves solid traditional fare, with salmon, soup, reindeer and friendly explanations of what goes with what. There's also limited à la carte available.

> **BRUNSSI**
>
> Finns like a lie-in on the weekend, after the debauches of Friday and Saturday nights, so *brunssi*, or brunch, was sure to catch on. Usually served as a buffet with everything from fruit and pastries to canapes, salads and pasta, it's so popular that you'll often have to book or wait. Expect to pay around €15 to €25 for this meal, which is served around 10.30am to 3.30pm, weekends only. The blog brunssipartio.fi keeps tabs on the scene; there's an English section.

Cholo MEXICAN €

(www.cholo.fi; Lönnrotinkatu 9; meals €9.80; ⏲11am-8pm Tue-Fri, noon-9pm Sat) This pint-sized place packs out with a young hipster crowd who are prepared to queue for the really tasty burritos and tacos that come bursting with colour and flavour. It gets a bit cramped, so head out and eat in the park opposite on a nice day.

★Kuu FINNISH €€

(☎09-2709-0973; www.ravintolakuu.fi; Töölönkatu 27; mains €19-30; ⏲11.30am-midnight Mon-Fri, 2pm-midnight Sat, 2-10pm Sun) Tucked away on a corner behind the Crowne Plaza hotel on Mannerheimintie, this is an excellent choice for both traditional and modern Finnish fare. The short menu is divided between the two; innovation and classy presentation drive the contemporary dishes, while quality ingredients and exceptional flavour are keys to success throughout. Wines are very pricey, but at least there are some interesting choices.

Salve FINNISH €€

(☎010-766-4280; www.ravintolasalve.fi; Hietalahdenranta 11; mains €19-27; ⏲10am-midnight Mon-Sat, 10am-11pm Sun) Down by the water in the west of town, this centenarian establishment has long been a favourite of nautical types, and has appropriately high-seas decor, with paintings of noble ships on the walls. They serve great Finnish comfort food such as meatballs, fried Baltic herring and steaks in substantial quantities. The atmosphere is warm and the service kindly.

Kosmos FINNISH €€

(☎09-647-255; www.kosmos.fi; Kalevankatu 3; mains €20-34; ⏲11.30am-1am Mon-Fri, 4pm-1am Sat) Designed by Alvar Aalto, and with a bohemian history, this nonagenarian place is a Helsinki classic. It combines a staid, traditionally Finnish atmosphere with tasty not-very-modern dishes, including reindeer, sweetbreads, kidneys and succulent fish options. Service can be no-nonsense but comes straight from the days when waiting tables was a career.

Sea Horse FINNISH €€

(☎010-837-5700; www.seahorse.fi; Kapteeninkatu 11; mains €18-27; ⏲10.30am-midnight, to 1am Fri & Sat) Sea Horse dates back to the 1930s and is as traditional a Finnish restaurant as you'll find anywhere. Locals gather in the gloriously unchanged interior to meet and drink over hefty dishes of Baltic herring, Finnish meatballs, liver and cabbage rolls.

DON'T MISS

HELSINKI'S MARKET HALLS

While food stalls, fresh produce and berries can be found at the kauppatori (market square), the real centre of Finnish market produce is the kauppahalli (market hall). There are three in central Helsinki, and they are fabulous places, great for self-catering, picnics and take-away food, and all have cafes and other casual eateries where you can sit in.

Hietalahden Kauppahalli (www.hietalahdenkauppahalli.fi; Lönnrotinkatu 34; 8am-6pm Mon-Fri, to 5pm Sat, plus 10am-4pm Sun Jun-Aug;) This renovated market at Hietalahti has a fabulous range of food stalls and eateries, including enticing cafes with upstairs seating at each end. Take tram 6.

Vanha Kauppahalli (www.vanhakauppahalli.fi; Eteläranta 1; 8am-6pm Mon-Sat;) Alongside the harbour, this is Helsinki's classic market hall. Built in 1889 and recently renovated, some of it is touristy these days (reindeer kebabs?), but it's still a traditional Finnish market.

Hakaniemen Kauppahalli (www.hakaniemenkauppahalli.fi; Hämeentie; 8am-6pm Mon-Fri, to 4pm Sat;) This traditional-style Finnish food market is near the Hakaniemi metro. It's got a good range of produce and a cafe, and textile outlets upstairs. There's a summer market on the square outside.

Soppakeittiö (www.sopakeittio.fi; soups €8-10; 11am-3.30pm Mon-Fri, 11am-3pm Sat) A great place to warm the cockles in winter; its bouillabaisse is famous. There's a branch at each kauppahalli.

Rikhards GASTROPUB €€
(010-423-3256; www.rikhards.fi; Rikhardinkatu 4; mains €19-29; food 4-10pm Tue-Fri, 2-10pm Sat, 1-6pm Sun;) The latest venture of Finnish chef Hans Välimäki, this corner gastropub blends the stylish and the casual with notable success. Some intriguing creations – try the 'popcorn' – back up classic bistro dishes – sausage and mash, succulent pork chop, fish 'n' chips – all of which reach great taste levels. A classy meal at a decent price.

Bellevue RUSSIAN €€
(09-179-560; www.restaurantbellevue.com; Rahapajankatu 3; mains €20-33; 11am-midnight Tue-Fri, 5pm-midnight Sat Aug-Jun) Helsinki's best Russian restaurant, complete with pot-roasted bear (€70). More standard choices include *zakuska* (mixed starters) and a range of blini choices. The atmosphere is elegant and old-fashioned. Closes Saturday lunch in summer.

Kitch CAFE €€
(www.kitch.fi; Yrjönkatu 30; mains €15-23; 11am-2pm & 4-10pm, to 11pm Wed-Fri, noon-11pm Sat;) Handily located in a central area, this is great for watching the world go by. Simply furnished, it offers good-value lunches as well as generous tapas portions, original salads and fat burgers with slabs of goat cheese. Plenty of the produce is sustainably sourced.

★**Olo** MODERN FINNISH €€€
(010-320-6250; olo-ravintola.fi; Pohjoisesplanadi 5; lunch €53, degustations €89-137, with drinks €224-292; 11.30am-3pm Mon, 11.30am-3pm & 6pm-midnight Tue-Fri, 6pm-midnight Sat) Thought of by many as Helsinki's best restaurant, Olo occupies smart new premises in a handsome 19th-century harbourside mansion. It's at the forefront of New Suomi cuisine, and its memorable degustation menus incorporate both the 'forage' ethos and a little molecular gastronomy. The shorter 'journey' turns out to be quite a long one, with numerous small culinary jewels. Book a few weeks ahead.

★**Savoy** FINNISH €€€
(09-6128-5300; www.savoy.fi; Eteläesplanadi 14; mains €44-47; 11.30am-2.30pm & 6pm-midnight Mon-Fri, 6pm-midnight Sat) Originally designed by Alvar and Aino Aalto, this is definitely a standout dining room, with some of the city's best views. The food is a modern Nordic tour de force, with the 'forage' ethos strewing flowers and berries across plates that bear the finest Finnish game, fish and meat.

★**Demo** MODERN FINNISH €€€
(09-2289-0840; www.restaurantdemo.fi; Uudenmaankatu 9; 4-/5-/6-/7-course menu €62/75/92/102; 4-11pm Tue-Sat) Book to get a table at this chic spot, where the young chefs wow a designer-y crowd with modern Finnish cuisine. The quality is excellent, the

combinations innovative, the presentation top notch and the slick contemporary decor appropriate. A place to be seen, not for quiet contemplation.

★A21 Dining MODERN FINNISH €€€
(☎040-171-1117; www.a21.fi; Kalevankatu 17; 5-/7-course menu €65/79, cocktail flight €49-63; ⏲5pm-midnight Tue-Sat) A very out-of-the-ordinary experience is to be had here, with a blinding white interior and innovative degustation menu accompanied by a mood-setting intro to each course. The idea is to transport you into Finland's natural world, and it works, with stunning flavour combinations accompanied by unusual cocktails.

Juuri MODERN FINNISH €€€
(☎09-635-732; www.juuri.fi; Korkeavuorenkatu 27; mains €28-30; ⏲11am-2.30pm & 4-10pm Mon-Fri, 4-10pm Sat & Sun) Creative takes on classic Finnish ingredients draw the crowds to this stylish modern restaurant, but the best way to eat is to sample the 'sapas', which are tapas with a Suomi twist (€4.70 per plate). You might graze on marinated fish, smoked beef or homemade sausages. There are good lunches too, but they're not as interesting.

Cafes

Karl Fazer Café CAFE €
(www.fazer.fi; Kluuvikatu 3; light meals €6-11; ⏲7.30am-10pm Mon-Fri, 9am-10pm Sat, 10am-6pm Sun; 📶) This classic cafe can feel a lit-

DON'T MISS

SUOMENLINNA

Just a 15-minute ferry ride from the kauppatori (market square), a visit to **Suomenlinna** (Sveaborg; www.suomenlinna.fi), the 'fortress of Finland', is a Helsinki must-do. Set on a tight cluster of islands connected by bridges, the UNESCO World Heritage Site was originally built by the Swedes as Sveaborg in the mid-eighteenth century.

At the main quay, the pink Rantakasarmi (Jetty Barracks) building is one of the best-preserved of the Russian era. It holds a small exhibition and helpful multilingual **tourist office** (☎0295-338 410; www.suomenlinna.fi; ⏲10am-6pm May-Sep, 10am-4pm Oct-Apr), with downloadable content for smartphones. Near here are Suomenlinna's hostel, a supermarket and the islands' distinctive **church** (⏲noon-4pm Wed-Sun, plus Tue Jun-Aug), which doubles as a lighthouse.

A blue-signposted walking path connects the main attractions. By the bridge that connects Iso Mustasaari and the main island, Susisaari-Kustaanmiekka, is **Suomenlinna-museo** (adult/child €6.50/free; ⏲10.30am-4.30pm Oct-Apr, 10am-6pm May-Sep), a two-level museum covering the history of the fortress. It's very information-heavy, but the first part gives good background. There's also an audiovisual display. Guided walks from here (adult/child €10/4) run in English three times daily from June to August, and 1.30pm Saturdays and Sundays the rest of the year.

Suomenlinna's most atmospheric part is on Kustaanmiekka at the end of the blue trail. Exploring the old bunkers, crumbling fortress walls and cannons lets you appreciate the fortress, and there are plenty of grassy picnic spots. Monumental **King's Gate** was built in 1753–54. In summer you can get the JT-Line waterbus back to Helsinki from here, saving you the walk back to the main quay.

Several other museums dot the islands. Perhaps most interesting is **Ehrensvärd-museo** (adult/child €3/1; ⏲11am-4pm May & Sep, 11am-6pm Jun-Aug), once home to the man responsible for designing and running the fortress. Nearby, the **Vesikko** (adult/child €5/free; ⏲11am-6pm May-Sep) is the only WWII-era submarine remaining in Finland. It saw action against the Russians.

Taking a picnic is a great way to make the most of Suomenlinna's grass and views. Around 5.15pm find a spot to watch the enormous Baltic ferries pass through the narrow gap between islands.

Ferries head from Helsinki's kauppatori to Suomenlinna's main quay. Tickets (single/return €2.50/5, 15 minutes, three times hourly, less frequent in winter, 6.20am to 2.20am) are available at the pier. In addition, **JT-Line** (www.jt-line.fi; one way/return €4.50/7; ⏲May–mid-Sep) runs a waterbus at least hourly from the kauppatori, making three stops on Suomenlinna (single/return €4.50/7, 20 minutes, 8am to 7pm May to mid-September).

tle cavernous, but it's the flagship for the mighty chocolate empire of the same name. The cupola famously reflects sound, so locals say it's a bad place to gossip. It is ideal, however, for buying Fazer confectionery, fresh bread, salmon or shrimp sandwiches or enjoying the towering sundaes or slabs of cake. Good special-diets options.

Tin Tin Tango CAFE €

(www.tintintango.info; Töölöntorinkatu 7; light meals €7-10; ⌚7am-midnight Mon-Fri, 9am-midnight Sat, 10am-midnight Sun; 📶) This buzzy neighbourhood cafe decorated with prints from the quiffed Belgian's adventures has a bit of everything. There's a laundry and a sauna, as well as lunches, brunches and cosy tables where you can sip a drink or get to grips with delicious rolls absolutely stuffed full. The welcoming, low-key bohemian vibe is the real draw, though.

Cafe Regatta CAFE €

(Merikannontie 10; pastries €1.50-3; ⌚10am-11pm) Near the Sibelius monument in a marvellous waterside location, this historic cottage is scarcely bigger than a sauna, but has great outdoor seating on the bay. You can hire a canoe or paddleboards alongside, buy sausages and grill them over the open fire, or just kick back with a drink or cinnamon pastry. Expect to queue on sunny weekends.

Drinking & Nightlife

Finns don't mind a drink and Helsinki has some of Scandinavia's most diverse nightlife. In winter, locals gather in cosy bars, while in summer, early-opening beer terraces sprout all over town. Some club nights have minimum age of 20 or more, so check event details on websites before you arrive.

★Teerenpeli PUB

(www.teerenpeli.com; Olavinkatu 2; ⌚noon-2am Mon-Thu, noon-3am Fri & Sat, 3pm-midnight Sun; 📶) Get away from the Finnish lager mainstream with this excellent pub right by Kamppi bus station. It serves very tasty ales, stouts and berry ciders from its microbrewery in Lahti, in a long, split-level place with romantic low lighting, intimate tables and an indoor smokers' patio. The highish prices keep it fairly genteel for this zone.

★Bar Loose CLUB

(www.barloose.com; Annankatu 21; ⌚4pm-2am Tue, 4pm-4am Wed-Sat, 6pm-4am Sun; 📶) The opulent blood-red interior and comfortably cosy seating seem too stylish for a rock bar, but this is what this is, with portraits of guitar heroes lining one wall and an eclectic mix of people filling the upstairs, served by two bars. Downstairs is a club area, with live music more nights than not and DJs spinning everything from metal to mod/retro classics.

A21 Cocktail Lounge COCKTAIL BAR

(www.a21.fi; Annankatu 21; ⌚6pm-midnight Wed, 6pm-1am Thu, 6pm-2am Fri & Sat) You'll need to ring the doorbell to get into this chic club but it's worth the intrigue to swing with Helsinki's arty set. The interior is sumptuous in gold, but the real lushness is in the cocktails, particularly the Finnish blends that toss cloudberry liqueur and rhubarb to create the city's most innovative tipples.

U Kaleva PUB

(www.ukaleva.fi; Kalevankatu 3A; ⌚2pm-2am) Part of a knot of bars on this street just off Mannerheimintie in the heart of town, this unpretentious place stands out for its old-time Finnish atmosphere, cordial owners, eclectic local crowd and heated terrace.

Bäkkäri BAR, CLUB

(www.bakkari.fi; Pohjoinen Rautatiekatu 21; ⌚4pm-4am) Central and atmospheric, this bar is devoted to the heavier end of the spectrum, with lots of airplay for Finnish legends including Nightwish, HIM, Children of Bodom and Apocalyptica. Outdoor tables are where the socialising goes on, while upstairs is a club space. Beer's cheap until 8pm.

Corona Baari & Kafe Mockba BAR

(www.andorra.fi; Eerikinkatu 11-15; ⌚Corona 11am-2am Mon-Thu, 11am-3am Fri & Sat, noon-2am Sun, Kafe Mockba 6pm-2am Mon-Thu, 6pm-3am Fri & Sat; 📶) Those offbeat film-making Kaurismäki brothers are up to their old tricks with this pair of conjoined drinking dens. Corona plays the relative straight man with pool tables, no doorperson, an island bar and a relaxed mix of people. Mockba is back in the USSR with a bubbling samovar and Soviet vinyl. At closing they clear the place out by playing Brezhnev speeches.

Mbar BAR

(www.mbar.fi; Mannerheimintie 22; ⌚9am-midnight Mon-Tue, 9am-2am Wed-Thu, 9am-4am Fri & Sat, noon-midnight Sun; 📶) Not just a geek haunt with internet terminals, this cafe-bar in the Lasipalatsi complex has a great terrace to soak up the sun, accompanied by DJs on most summer nights. It's one of Helsinki's most enjoyable spots, with great atmosphere.

OFF THE BEATEN TRACK

THE CALL OF KALLIO

For Helsinki's cheapest beer (around €3 to €4 a pint), hit working-class Kallio (near Sörnäinen metro station), north of the centre. Here, there's a string of dive bars along Helsinginkatu, but it, the parallel Vaasankatu, and cross-street Fleminginkatu are also home to several more characterful bohemian places: go for a wander and you'll soon find one you like.

Maxine BAR, CLUB
(www.maxine.fi; 6th fl, Kamppi; admission €3.50; ⏲4pm-4am Tue-Sat, shorter hours winter; 📶) On the top of Kamppi shopping centre, this refurbished venue makes the most of the inspiring city views from this high perch. It's divided into three sections, with a bar area – a great spot for a sundowner – and two dancefloors, one of which (the name, Kirjasto, or Library, gives it away) is quieter and aimed at an older crowd.

Majakkalaiva Relandersgrund BAR
(www.majakkalaiva.fi; Pohjoisranta; ⏲noon-10pm or later May–mid-Oct) The deck of this elegant old lightship provides a fabulous and unusual venue for a coffee, beer or cider on a sunny afternoon.

Kuudes Linja CLUB
(www.kuudeslinja.com; Hämeentie 13; entry from €8; ⏲7pm-1am Sun-Thu, 10pm-4am Fri & Sat) Between Hakaniemi and Sörnäinen metros, this is the place to find Helsinki's more experimental beats from top visiting DJs playing techno, industrial, post-rock and electro. There are also live gigs.

Wanha Kauppakuja BAR
(www.center-inn.fi) This covered laneway off Aleksanterinkatu has a boisterous, meat-markety summer scene once the restaurant terraces are done with serving food for the night. There's usually a €5 admission charge.

☆ Entertainment

Live music is big in Helsinki, from metal to opera. The latest events are publicised in *Helsinki This Week*. Tickets for big events can be purchased from **Lippupalvelu** (☎0600-10800; www.lippupalvelu.fi), **Lippupiste** (☎0600-900-900; www.lippu.fi), **Tiketti** (☎0600-11616; www.tiketti.fi; Urho Kekkosenkatu 4; ⏲11am-7pm Mon-Fri) and **LiveNation** (www.livenation.fi).

Cinemas

Cinemas show original versions with Finnish and Swedish subtitles.

Kino Engel CINEMA
(☎020-155-5801; www.cinemamondo.fi; Sofiankatu 4; adult €9.50-12.50) As well as the *kesäkino* (summer cinema) in the courtyard of Café Engel, in the warmer months this independent theatre shows art-house and Finnish indie films.

FinnKino CINEMA
(☎0600-007-007; www.finnkino.fi; adult €7-16) Several Helsinki cinemas screening big-name films; prices vary by day and session time. Branches include **Tennispalatsi** (www.finnkino.fi; Salomonkatu 15) and **Maxim** (www.finnkino.fi; Kluuvikatu 1).

Gay & Lesbian

Helsinki has an active scene with several dedicated venues and a host of gay-friendly spots. There's a list of gay-friendly places at www.visithelsinki.fi, and the tourist office stocks a couple of brochures on gay Helsinki.

Hugo's Room GAY
(www.hugosroom.fi; Iso Roobertinkatu 3; ⏲2pm-2am; 📶) This popular lounge bar is elegant but doesn't take itself too seriously. It's got a great streetside terrace on this always-intriguing pedestrian thoroughfare.

DTM GAY, CLUB
(www.dtm.fi; Mannerheimintie 6; ⏲9pm-4am; 📶) Finland's most famous gay venue (Don't Tell Mama) now occupies smart premises in a very out-of-the-closet location on the city's main street. There are various club nights with variable entry fees.

Theatre & Concerts

★ **Musiikkitalo** CONCERT VENUE
(www.musiikkitalo.fi; Mannerheimintie 13) As cool and crisp as a gin and tonic on a glacier, this striking modern building is a great addition to central Helsinki. The interior doesn't disappoint either – the main auditorium, visible from the foyer, has stunning acoustics. There are regular classical concerts, and prices are kept low, normally around €20. The bar is a nice place to hang out for a drink.

Oopperatalo OPERA, BALLET
(Opera House; ☎09-4030-2211; www.opera.fi; Helsinginkatu 58; tickets from €14) Opera, ballet and classical concerts are held here, though not during summer. Performances of the Finnish National Opera are surtitled in Finnish.

Live Music

Various bars and clubs around Helsinki host live bands. Big-name rock concerts and international acts often perform at Hartwall Areena.

Tavastia LIVE MUSIC
(www.tavastiaklubi.fi; Urho Kekkosenkatu 4; ⏲8pm-1am Sun-Thu, 8pm-3am Fri, 8pm-4am Sat) One of Helsinki's legendary rock venues, this attracts both up-and-coming local acts and bigger international groups. There's a band every night of the week. Also check out what's on at Semifinal, the venue next door.

Storyville JAZZ
(www.storyville.fi; Museokatu 8; ⏲6pm-2am Tue, 6pm-3am Wed-Thu, 6pm-4am Fri & Sat) Helsinki's number-one jazz club attracts a refined older crowd swinging to boogie woogie, trad jazz, Dixieland and New Orleans most nights. As well as the club section (from 8pm Wednesday to Saturday), there's a stylish bar that has a cool outside summer terrace in the park opposite.

Juttutupa JAZZ, FUSION
(www.juttutupa.com; Säästöpankinranta 6; ⏲10.30am-midnight Mon-Tue, 10.30am-1am Wed-Thu, 10.30am-3am Fri, 11am-3am Sat, noon-11pm Sun) A block from Hakaniemi metro station in an enormous granite building, Juttutupa is one of Helsinki's better music bars, focusing on contemporary jazz and rock fusion. Great beer terrace.

Sport

Between September and April, ice hockey reigns supreme; going to a game is a good Helsinki experience. The World Championships in May are avidly watched on big screens.

Hartwall Areena SPECTATOR SPORT
(www.hartwall-areena.com; Areenakuja 1) The best place to see top-level hockey matches is at this arena, about 4km north of the city centre (take bus 23 or 69, or tram 7A or 7B). It's the home of Jokerit Helsinki, who now play in the international Kontinental Hockey League.

Shopping

Helsinki is a design epicentre, from fashion to the latest furniture and homewares. Central but touristy Esplanadi has the chic boutiques of Finnish classics. The most intriguing area to browse is nearby Punavuori, with a great retro-hipster vibe and numerous boutiques, studios and galleries to explore. A couple of hundred of these are part of **Design District Helsinki** (www.designdistrict.fi), whose invaluable map you can find at the tourist office.

Akateeminen Kirjakauppa BOOKS
(www.akateeminen.com; Pohjoisesplanadi 39; ⏲9am-9pm Mon-Fri, 9am-6pm Sat, noon-6pm Sun; 📶) Finland's biggest bookshop, with a huge travel section, maps, Finnish literature and an impressively large English section including magazines and newspapers.

Information

EMERGENCY

General Emergency (☎112)

INTERNET ACCESS

Internet access at public libraries is free. Large parts of the city centre have free wi-fi, as do many bars and cafes.

MEDICAL SERVICES

Haartman Hospital (☎09-3106-3231; www.hel.fi; Haartmaninkatu 4; ⏲24hr) For emergency medical assistance.

MONEY

There are currency-exchange counters at the airport and ferry terminals. ATMs are plentiful in the city.

Forex (www.forex.fi; Train station; ⏲8am-8pm Mon-Fri, 9am-7pm Sat, 9.30am-5pm Sun) One of several branches. Hours change through the year.

POST

Main Post Office (www.posti.fi; Elielinaukio; ⏲8am-8pm Mon-Fri, 10am-4pm Sat, noon-4pm Sun) Across from the train station; enter via the supermarket.

TOURIST INFORMATION

Helsinki City Tourist Office (☎09-3101-3300; www.visithelsinki.fi; Pohjoisesplanadi 19; ⏲9am-8pm Mon-Fri, 9am-6pm Sat & Sun mid-May–mid-Sep, 9am-6pm Mon-Fri, 10am-4pm Sat & Sun mid-Sep–mid-May) Busy multilingual office with a great quantity of information on the city. Also has an office at the airport (www.visithelsinki.fi; Terminal 2, Helsinki-Vantaa airport; ⏲10am-8pm May-Sep, 10am-6pm Oct-Apr).

LOCAL KNOWLEDGE

ALEXIS KOUROS, FILM-MAKER & FOUNDING EDITOR OF THE HELSINKI TIMES

What Finnish film would you recommend? People could watch a couple of the Kaurismäki brothers' movies. Aki has *Man Without a Past*, for example, which won a prize at the Cannes festival. His films are always a bit exaggerated, like a sort of caricature of Finnish society. But that sort of exaggerated view can give you an idea about the Finnish people's shyness.

Favourite building in Helsinki? My favourite building is the Temppeliaukion Kirkko, which is a round church built into the environment which is basically a big hill with stones. It's a fantastic building and I really am amazed that the church authorities let it happen, because the roundness is pointing back to the pagan religions before Christianity.

For Finnish food? In the summertime, there are some tents in the kauppatori (market square) which will give you an assortment of fish, potatoes, these kind of things. Those are really very typically Finnish. Then there is a newish restaurant called Juuri, with Finnish tapas: *sapas*.

For design shopping? Well, there is a design district, which goes from the centre of the city towards Punavuori. It evolves all the time, and there are always new shops. Lots of Finnish design.

Helsinki in one word? One word! I would say fresh. From the top of my head.

WEBSITES

City of Helsinki (www.hel.fi) Helsinki City website, with links to copious information.
HSL/HRT (www.hsl.fi) Public-transport information and journey planner.
Visit Helsinki (www.visithelsinki.fi) Excellent tourist board website full of information.

ℹ Getting There & Away

There are lockers at the bus and train stations and lockers or left-luggage counters at ferry terminals.

AIR

There are direct flights to Helsinki, Finland's main air terminus, from many major European cities and several intercontinental ones. The airport is at Vantaa, 19km north of Helsinki.

Between them, **Finnair** (☎ 0600-140140; www.finnair.fi) and cheaper **FlyBe** (www.flybe.com) cover 18 Finnish cities, usually at least once per day.

BOAT

Ferries (p485) travel to Sweden (via the Åland archipelago), Russia, and Germany from Helsinki. There are regular ferries and fast-boat services to Tallinn, Estonia.

There are five main terminals, three close to the kauppatori: Katajanokka is served by tram 4T, Makasiini by tram 1A and 2 and Olympia by trams 1A, 2 and 3. Länsiterminaali (West Terminal) is served by trams 6T and 9, while further-afield Hansaterminaali (Vuosaari) can be reached on bus 90A or 78 from Vuosaari metro.

Purchase tickets at the terminal, ferry company offices, online or (in some cases) the tourist office. Book well in advance during high season (late June to mid-August), and at weekends.

BUS

Regional and long-distance buses dock at underground **Kamppi Bus Station** (www.matkahuolto.fi). There are services to all major towns in Finland. OnniBus (p206) runs budget routes to several Finnish cities from a stop outside Kiasma: book online in advance for the best prices.

TRAIN

Helsinki's **train station** (Rautatieasema; www.vr.fi) is central, linked to the metro (Rautatientori stop) and a short walk from the bus station.

The train is the fastest and cheapest way to get from Helsinki to major centres: express trains run daily to Turku, Tampere, Kuopio and Lappeenranta among others, and there's a choice of day and overnight trains to Oulu, Rovaniemi and Joensuu. There are also daily trains (buy tickets from the international counter) to the Russian cities of Vyborg, St Petersburg and Moscow.

Getting Around

TO/FROM THE AIRPORT

Bus 615/620 (€5, 30 to 45 minutes, 5am to midnight) shuttles between Helsinki-Vantaa airport (platform 21) and platform 3 at Rautatientori next to the main train station. Faster **Finnair buses** depart from Elielinaukio platform 30 on the other side of the train station (€6.30, 30 minutes, every 20 minutes 5am to midnight). The last service leaves the airport at 1.10am. The 415 bus departs from the adjacent stand but it's slower than the other two.

Door-to-door **airport taxis** (☎0600-555-555; www.airporttaxi.fi; 2/4passengers €29.50/39.50) need booking the previous day before 6pm if you're leaving Helsinki. A normal cab should cost €45 to €55.

There's a new airport–city rail link due to open in late 2015. It will be a 30-minute journey from the central railway station and also means that, if you're coming by train from the north or east, you can change at Tikkurila and head to the airport (8 minutes) without going into the centre.

BICYCLE

With a flat inner city and well-marked cycling paths, Helsinki is ideal for cycling. Get hold of a copy of the Helsinki cycling map at the tourist office.

Greenbike (☎050-404-0400; www.greenbike.fi; Bulevardi 32; per day €20-35, per week €75-105; ⏲10am-6pm early May-Aug) Offers a range of good-quality road and mountain bikes to hire. The entrance is actually around the corner on Albertinkatu. Call for low-season hiring.

PUBLIC TRANSPORT

The city's public-transport system **HSL** (www.hsl.fi) operates buses, metro and local trains, trams and a ferry to Suomenlinna. A one-hour flat-fare ticket for any HSL transport costs €3 when purchased on board or €2.50 when purchased in advance. The ticket allows unlimited transfers but must be validated at the machine on board on first use. A single tram ticket is €2.20 advance purchase. Order any of these tickets for €2.40 using your Finnish SIM card: send an SMS to 16355 texting A1. Day or multiday tickets (24/48/72 hours €8/12/16, tickets up to seven days available) are worthwhile. The Helsinki Card gives you free travel anywhere within Helsinki.

Sales points at Kamppi bus station and Rautatientori and Hakaniemi metro stations sell tickets and passes, as do many R-kioski shops and the tourist office. The *Helsinki Route Map*, available at the city tourist office, maps bus, metro and tram routes. Online, www.reittiopas.fi is a useful route planner.

SOUTH COAST

The south coast of Finland meanders east and west of Helsinki, a summer playground for Finnish families, with a handful of resort towns and the pretty bays, beaches and convoluted islands and waterways of the southern archipelago. Medieval churches, old manors and castles show the strong influence of early Swedish settlers, and Swedish is still a majority language in some of the coastal towns.

Porvoo

☎019 / POP 49,500

A great day trip from Helsinki, charming medieval Porvoo is Finland's second-oldest town (founded in 1346). There are three distinct sections to the city: Vanha Porvoo (the Old Town), the New Town and the 19th-century Empire quarter, built Russian-style under the rule of Tsar Nicholas I.

Sights & Activities

★**Vanha Porvoo** HISTORIC SITE

(Old Town) One of Finland's most enticing old quarters, this tangle of cobbled alleys and wooden warehouses is still entrancing. Once a vibrant port and market, Porvoo now has craft boutiques, art galleries, souvenir stores and antique shops jostling for attention on the main roads, Välikatu and Kirkkokatu. The rows of **rust-red storehouses** along the Porvoonjoki are a local icon: cross the old bridge for the best photos. The relatively less-touristed area is east of the cathedral; Itäinen Pitkäkatu is one of the nicest streets.

Tuomiokirkko CATHEDRAL

(www.porvoonseurakunnat.fi; ⏲10am-2pm Tue-Sat, 2-4pm Sun Oct-Apr, 10am-6pm Mon-Fri, 10am-2pm Sat, 2-5pm Sun May-Sep) Porvoo's historic stone-and-timber cathedral sits atop a hill looking over the quaint Old Town. This is where the first Diet of Finland assembled in 1809, convened by Tsar Alexander I, giving Finland religious freedom. Vandalised by fire in 2006, it has been completely restored, so you can admire the ornate pulpit and tiered galleries. The magnificent exterior, with free-standing bell tower, remains the highlight.

Porvoon Museo MUSEUM

(www.porvoonmuseo.fi; Vanha Raatihuoneentori; adult/child €6/3; ⏲10am-4pm Mon-Sat & 11am-4pm Sun May-Aug, noon-4pm Wed-Sun Sep-Apr)

WORTH A TRIP

ST PETERSBURG

A short side trip from Finland, beguiling St Petersburg makes a tempting destination. Russia's most outward-looking metropolis is a fascinating hybrid where one moment you can be inhaling incense in the mosaic-heavy interior of an Orthodox church or strolling the gilded halls of a tsar's palace, the next knocking back vodka shots in a trendy bar or taking in cutting-edge contemporary art.

One of the world's premier museums and art galleries, the **Hermitage** (Государственный Эрмитаж; www.hermitagemuseum.org; Dvortsovaya pl 2; adult/student R400/free, 1st Thu of month free, camera R200; ⏲10.30am-6pm Tue & Thu-Sun, to 9pm Wed; Ⓜ Admiralteyskaya) is sumptuously located in the Winter Palace. It's a scarcely believable collection of archaeological treasures and Western art which would take days to fully appreciate. Buy tickets online to avoid the frightening queues. Nearby, Nevsky Prospekt is the city's main boulevard and well worth a stroll to observe a slice of St Petersburg life. It bridges canals that criss-cross the city and takes you close to several other principal sights. The **Russian Museum** (Русский музей; www.rusmuseum.ru; Inzhenernaya ul 4; adult/student R350/150, 4-palace ticket adult/child R600/300; ⏲10am-6pm Wed & Fri-Sun, to 5pm Mon, 1-9pm Thu; Ⓜ Nevsky Prospekt) offers a comprehensive overview of Russian art, while adjacent **Church of the Saviour on Spilled Blood** (Церковь Спаса на Крови; http://cathedral.ru; Konyushennaya pl; adult/student R250/150; ⏲10.30am-6pm Thu-Tue; Ⓜ Nevsky Prospekt) is a multidomed dazzler with impressive interior mosaics.

The tsars' lavish lifestyle is best appreciated at one of their summer palaces outside town. The best, **Petrodvorets** (www.peterhof.ru; ul Razvodnaya 2; ⏲grounds daily, individual sights vary), has a series of splendid chambers and ballrooms overlooking the sumptuously over-the-top Grand Cascade water feature.

Getting out on the water lets you appreciate St Petersburg's noble buildings along the Neva and the intricate network of canals. One of many operators, **Anglo Tourismo** (☎921-989 4722; www.anglotourismo.com; 27 nab reki Fontanki; 1hr tour adult/student R650/550; Ⓜ Gostiny Dvor) has the advantage of offering English commentary.

The historic centre offers plenty of choice from the stunning designer interiors of **W Hotel** (☎812-610 6161; www.wstpetersburg.com; Voznesensky pr 6; r from R18,630; ❄@📶🏊; Ⓜ Admiralteyskaya) to the Italianate boutique charm of **Casa Leto** (☎812-314 6622; http://casaleto.com; Bolshaya Morskaya ul 34; r incl breakfast from R7900; ❄@📶; Ⓜ Admiralteyskaya). One of several central 'mini-hotels', **Guest House Nevsky 3** (☎812-710 6776; www.nevsky3.ru; Nevsky pr 3; s/d incl breakfast R4700/5300; 📶; Ⓜ Admiralteyskaya) offers excellent value. Budget travellers have **Friends Hostel** (☎812-571 0151; www.friendsplace.ru; nab kanala Griboyedova 20; dm/d R500/2500; @📶; Ⓜ Nevsky Prospekt) at several distinct, appealing locations.

For restaurants, look around the side streets rather than along Nevsky Prospekt itself, which is tourist-trap territory. If you are up for a night of bar-hopping, **Dumskaya ulitsa** (Ⓜ Gostiny Dvor) has dozens of St Petersburg's hottest spots for drinking and dancing crammed into a crumbling, classical facade. St Petersburg's Kirov ballet company are world-famous, and seeing a performance in the **Mariinsky Theatre** (Мариинский театр; ☎812-326 4141; www.mariinsky.ru; Teatralnaya pl 1; R1000-6000; Ⓜ Sadovaya) is an unforgettable experience. Book tickets online in advance.

You can travel to St Petersburg from Helsinki by air, overnight ferry (13 hours, from €60), bus (nine hours, €35) or train (2nd/1st class around €86/250, 3½ hours). St Petersburg is an hour ahead of Finland in summer and two in winter.

Visas are required by all. Applying in your home country is easiest; if you want to do it in Finland, it's best via a travel agent. Think €60 to €100 for the normal seven working days processing time, plus a hefty fee for express processing (three to four working days). You'll require a 'visa support' document – essentially an invitation that can be obtained via a hotel booking or by paying a fee to a travel agent. You can travel visa-free to St Petersburg (maximum stay three days) by ferry from Helsinki, or cruise from Lappeenranta.

Porvoo's town museum occupies two buildings on the beautiful cobbled square at the heart of the Old Town. The town-hall building houses most of the collection, with a clutter of artefacts relating to the town's history, including work by painter Albert Edelfelt and sculptor Ville Vallgren, two of Porvoo's celebrated artists. The other building recreates an 18th-century merchant's home.

JL Runeberg CRUISE
(☎ 019-524-3331; www.msjlruneberg.fi; ⏲ Tue, Wed, Fri, Sat mid-May–early Sep, plus Sun Jun-Aug & Mon Jul) This noble old steamship cruises from Helsinki's kauppatori to Porvoo (adult one way/return €27/39, daily except Thursday) in summer and makes an excellent day trip, with various lunch options available. The trip takes 3½ hours each way, so you may prefer to return by bus.

Sleeping

Porvoon Retkeilymaja HOSTEL €
(☎ 019-523-0012; www.porvoohostel.fi; Linnankoskenkatu 1-3; dm/s/d €22/37/52; P 📶) Four blocks south and two east of the kauppatori, this historic wooden house holds a well-kept hostel in a grassy garden. It caters for groups, so you'll need to book ahead to ensure a spot, and linen is extra, so be prepared. There's a great indoor pool and sauna complex over the road. Check-in is from 4pm. HI discount.

Ida-Maria B&B €€
(☎ 045-851-2345; http://ida-maria.fi; Välikatu 10A; s/d/f €65/85/125; 📶) Right on the square in the heart of old Porvoo, this can't be beaten for location, and the hospitable owner does her utmost to make you feel welcome. Historic character is the order of the day in this wooden building – the rooms share one bathroom – but the ambience, sauna and appetizing breakfast make it a winner.

★**Hotelli Onni** BOUTIQUE HOTEL €€€
(☎ 044-534-8110; www.hotelonni.fi; Kirkkotori 3; r/ste €182/292; P ❄ 📶) Right opposite the cathedral, this gold-coloured wooden building couldn't be better placed. There's a real range here, from the four-poster bed and slick design of the Funkishuone to the rustic single Talonpoikaishuone. Top of the line is the honeymoon suite, a small self-contained apartment with bathtub and complimentary champagne. Breakfast is downstairs where there's a terraced cafe and upmarket restaurant space.

Eating & Drinking

Porvoo's most atmospheric cafes, restaurants and bars are in the Old Town and along the riverfront. Porvoo is famous for its sweets; the Runeberg pastry is ubiquitous.

Wanha Laamanni FINNISH €€
(☎ 020-752-8355; www.wanhalaamanni.fi; Vuorikatu 17; mains €20-29; ⏲ 11am-11pm Mon-Sat, noon-8pm Sun) Top of the town in both geographic and culinary terms, this old judges' chambers serves up a short menu of classy Finnish favourites and a rather tasty six-course surprise menu (€60). The building itself is a rambling late-18th-century conversion with a roaring fireplace and sprawling terrace that's ideal for people-watching.

Timbaali FINNISH €€
(☎ 019-523-1020; www.timbaali.com; Jokikatu 43; mains €20-27; ⏲ 11am-11pm Jun-Aug, 11am-10pm Mon-Sat, noon-6pm Sun) In the heart of the Old Town, this well-loved restaurant specialises in slow food: locally farmed snails (€18 for a dozen) prepared with garlic or cheese. There's also other tasty Finnish cuisine, served in quaint dining rooms or the inner courtyard. In summer a fish buffet (€26) is served at lunchtimes.

★**Porvoon Paahtimo** CAFE, PUB
(www.porvoonpaahtimo.fi; Mannerheiminkatu 2; ⏲ 10am-midnight Sun-Thu, 9am-3am Fri & Sat) On the main bridge, this atmospheric red-brick former storehouse is a cosy, romantic spot for drinks of any kind: it roasts its own coffee and has tap beer and several wines. There's a terrace and boat deck, which come with blankets on cooler evenings.

Information

Summer Tourist Kiosk (www.visitporvoo.fi; Jokikatu 35B; ⏲ 10am-6pm Mon-Fri, 10am-4pm Sat & Sun May-Aug; 📶) Under the bridge near the entrance to the Old Town. Rent bikes for €7.50/20 per one/four hours.

Tourist Office (☎ 040-489-9801; www.visitporvoo.fi; Läntinen Aleksanterinkatu 1; ⏲ 9am-6pm Mon-Fri, 11am-4pm Sat; 📶) Offers maps and local information in the Taidetehdas (Art Factory) building across the river. This former tractor factory is now an exhibition space, cinema and shopping mall.

Getting There & Away

Buses depart for Porvoo from Helsinki Kamppi every 30 minutes or so (€11.80, one hour) and there are frequent buses to/from towns further east.

Hanko

019 / POP 9270

On a long sandy peninsula, Hanko (Swedish: Hangö) recalls its heyday as a well-to-do Russian spa town in the late 19th century, and its opulent seaside villas from the era remain a star attraction. Visitors still flock here for the sun, sand and party atmosphere of the huge **Hanko Regatta** (www.hangoregattan.fi).

Sleeping & Eating

Several of Hanko's Empire-era Russian-style villas operate as B&Bs. Don't expect luxury, but do come with an open mind and a lively appreciation of history! You can book private accommodation (sometimes in villas) through the tourist office.

★Villa Maija RUSSIAN VILLA €€
(050-505-2013; www.villamaija.fi; Appelgrentie 7; s/d €135/175, without bathroom €100/130, f €200; P) Built in 1888, this is Hanko's best villa accommodation. Flawlessly restored rooms are so cosy and packed with character that it's difficult to prise yourself away. Prices vary according to the size of the room, and whether it has a private bathroom and balcony facing the sea. Breakfast is excellent.

På Kroken SEAFOOD €€€
(040-358-1815; www.pakroken.fi; Tegelbruksvägen 12; cafe buffet €8, mains €10, restaurant buffet €26, mains €24-42; cafe 9am-8pm May-Sep, restaurant 11am-10pm Jun-Aug, 11am-10pm Fri & Sat, 11am-5pm Sun Sep-May) With its own smokehouse and boat-fresh lobster and shellfish (it sells to Helsinki's Hakaniemi market), På Kroken's yacht-shaped buffet teems with choices. If the restaurant's beyond your budget, its adjoining cafe serves cheaper dishes including fabulous salmon soup with dark archipelago bread, or you can stock up on picnic fare at its fish shop.

Information

Tourist Office (019-220-3411; www.hanko.fi; Raatihuoneentori 5; 9am-4pm Mon-Fri Sep-May, 9am-6pm Mon-Fri, 10am-4pm Sat & Sun Jun-Aug) Helpful office with a large list of private accommodation.

Getting There & Away

Buses run to/from Helsinki (€25.20, 2¼ hours, 10 daily) via Ekenäs (€8.20, 35 minutes, nine daily).

Direct trains serve Helsinki (€25.60, 1¼ hours, hourly). Trains for Turku (€29, two hours, four daily) meet connecting trains or buses in Karjaa.

Turku

02 / POP 182,280

The historic castle and cathedral point to the city's rich cultural history, and contemporary Turku is a hotbed of experimental art and vibrant festivals, thanks in part to its spirited university population (the country's second-largest), who make Turku's nightlife young and fun. As the first city many visitors encounter arriving by ferry from Sweden and Åland, it's a splendid introduction to the Finnish mainland.

Once the capital under the Swedes, Turku (Swedish: Åbo) was founded in 1229, and grew into an important trading centre despite being ravaged by fire many times.

Sights & Activities

Soak up Turku's summertime vibe by walking or cycling along the riverbank between the cathedral and the castle, crossing via bridges or the pedestrian ferry.

Turun Linna CASTLE
(Turku Castle; 02-262-0300; www.turunlinna.fi; Linnankatu 80; adult/child €9/5, guided tours €2; 10am-6pm daily Jun-Aug, 10am-6pm Tue-Sun Sep-May) Founded in 1280 at the mouth of the Aurajoki, mammoth Turku Castle is easily Finland's largest. Highlights include two dungeons and sumptuous banqueting halls, as well as a fascinating **historical museum** of medieval Turku in the castle's Old Bailey. Models depict the castle's growth from a simple island fortress to a Renaissance palace. Guided tours in English run several times daily from June to August.

★Turun Tuomiokirkko CATHEDRAL
(Turku Cathedral; 02-261-7100; www.turunseurakunnat.fi; cathedral free, museum adult/child €2/1; cathedral & museum 9am-8pm mid-Apr–mid-Sep, 9am-7pm mid-Sep–mid-Apr) The 'mother church' of Finland's Lutheran faith, Turku Cathedral towers over the town. Consecrated in 1300, the colossal brick Gothic building was rebuilt many times over the centuries after damaging fires.

Upstairs, a small **museum** traces the stages of the cathedral's construction, and contains medieval sculptures and religious paraphernalia.

Free **summer organ concerts** take place at 8pm Tuesday and 2pm Wednesday. English-language services are held at 4pm every Sunday except the last of the month year-round.

★Aboa Vetus & Ars Nova MUSEUM, GALLERY
(☎020-718-1640; www.aboavetusarsnova.fi; Itäinen Rantakatu 4-6; adult/child €8/5.50; ⏰11am-7pm; 👪) Art and archaeology unite here under one roof. **Aboa Vetus** (Old Turku) draws you underground to Turku's medieval streets, showcasing some of the 37,000 artefacts unearthed from the site (digs still continue). Back in the present, **Ars Nova** presents contemporary art exhibitions. The themed Turku Biennaali (www.turkubiennaali.fi) takes place here in summer of odd-numbered years.

Opening to a grassy courtyard, the museums' cafe, Aula, hosts Sunday jazz brunches and Thursday night DJ sessions from June to August.

★Luostarinmäki Handicrafts Museum MUSEUM
(☎02-262-0350; www.turunmuseokeskus.fi; Vartiovuorenkatu 2; adult/child €6/4, guided tours €2.50; ⏰10am-6pm daily Jun-Aug, 10am-6pm Tue-Sun May & early Sep–mid-Sep, 10am-4pm Tue-Sun Dec–mid-Jan) When the savage Great Fire of 1827 swept through Turku, the lower-class quarter Luostarinmäki escaped the flames. Set along tiny lanes and around grassy yards, the 19th-century wooden workshops and houses now form the outdoor handicrafts museum, a national treasure since 1940.

All of the buildings are in their original locations and house 30 workshops (including a silversmith, watchmaker, bakery, pottery, shoemaker, printer and cigar shop), where artisans in period costume practise their trades in summer.

Forum Marinum MUSEUM, SHIPS
(www.forum-marinum.fi; Linnankatu 72; adult/child €8/5, incl museum ships €16/10, museum ships each €6/4; ⏰11am-7pm May-Sep, 11am-6pm Tue-Sun Oct-Apr, museum ships 11am-7pm Jun-Aug) Partly housed in an old granary, this excellent maritime museum offers a comprehensive look at ships and shipping, from scale models to full-sized vessels. Anchored outside is a small fleet of **museum ships**, which you can climb aboard. The mine-layer *Keihässalmi* and the corvette *Karjala* take you back to WWII, while the full-rigger *Suomen Joutsen* recalls more-carefree prewar days. The beautiful three-masted barque *Sigyn* (moored 500m upstream) was originally launched from Göteborg in 1887 and has well-preserved cabins.

S/S Ukkopekka CRUISE
(www.ukkopekka.fi; one way/return adult €24/29, child €12/14.50, Moomin package adult/child return €49/36) The historic steamship S/S *Ukkopekka* cruises to Naantali at 10am and 2pm Tuesday to Saturday mid-June to mid-August, docking next to Muumimaailma (Moomin World; p150). The trip takes 1¾ hours.

Evening dinner cruises (€43 to €49), with dancing on the pier of the island of Loistokari run from May to August.

Festivals & Events

★Ruisrock MUSIC
(www.ruisrock.fi; 1-/3-day ticket €78/128) For three days in July, Finland's oldest and largest annual rock festival – held since 1969 and attracting 100,000-strong crowds – takes over Ruissalo island.

Sleeping

Ruissalo Camping CAMPGROUND €
(☎02-262-5100; www.turkutouring.fi; tent sites €17 plus per person €5, 2-/4-/6-person cabin €68/125/165; ⏰May-Sep; 🅿👪) On idyllic Ruissalo island, 10km west of the city centre, this sprawling campground has gently sloping grassy sites and a great choice of cabins, along with saunas, a cafe and Turku's closest beaches (including a naturist beach). Book way, *way* ahead for the Ruisrock festival and Midsummer. Bus 8 runs from the kauppatori.

Laivahostel Borea HOSTEL €
(☎040-843-6611; www.msborea.fi; Linnankatu 72; s €49, d €78-105.50, tr €102, q €124; 📶) Built in Sweden in 1960, the enormous passenger ship S/S *Bore* is docked outside the Forum Marinum museum, just 500m northeast of the ferry terminal. It now contains an award-winning HI-affiliated hostel with vintage ensuite cabins. Most are squishy

SCANDINAVIA? NOT US!

Despite its proximity, Finland isn't actually geographically part of Scandinavia, and many Finns will be quick to remind you of the fact. Technically, Scandinavia refers to the Scandinavian Peninsula (Norway plus Sweden) along with Denmark. Linguistically, Scandinavia includes Iceland, the Faroe Islands and Swedish-speaking Finns, while the term Nordic countries is a more general term for all these lands.

but if you want room to spread out, the higher-priced doubles have a lounge area. Rates include a morning sauna.

★ Park Hotel BOUTIQUE HOTEL €€
(☎ 02-273-2555; www.parkhotelturku.fi; Rauhankatu 1; s €89-124, d €115-162; @ 📶) Overlooking a hilly park, this art nouveau building is a genuine character, with a resident squawking parrot, Jaakko, and classical music playing in the lift (elevator). Rooms are decorated in a lovably chintzy style and equipped with minibars. Family owners and facilities such as a lounge with pool table make it the antithesis of a chain hotel.

Hotelli Helmi HOTEL €€
(☎ 020-786-2770; www.hotellihelmi.fi; Tuureporinkatu 11; s/d/tr/f €85/110/120/170; ❄ 📶) Next door to the bus station, family-owned Helmi (literally, 'pearl') has 34 autumnal-hued soundproofed rooms with minifridges, comfy mattresses and good-sized bathrooms. If you're catching an overnight ferry or late-night flight, day rooms (€55) are available.

Centro Hotel HOTEL €€
(☎ 02-211-8100; www.centrohotel.com; Yliopistonkatu 12; s/d €111/119; @ 📶) The 62-room Centro Hotel is (as its name implies) central, but its courtyard location cuts out street noise. Service is friendly and the blonde-wood rooms are a good compromise between size and price. The breakfast buffet is worth getting out of bed for. Arrive early to nab one of the 14 parking spaces.

✕ Eating

There are plenty of cheap eateries on and around Turku's bustling central **kauppatori** (⏲ 8am-4pm Mon-Sat May-Sep).

CaféArt CAFE €
(www.cafeart.fi; Läntinen Rantakatu 5; dishes €2.20-4.80; ⏲ 10am-7pm Mon-Fri, 10am-5pm Sat, 11am-5pm Sun) With freshly ground coffee,

Turku

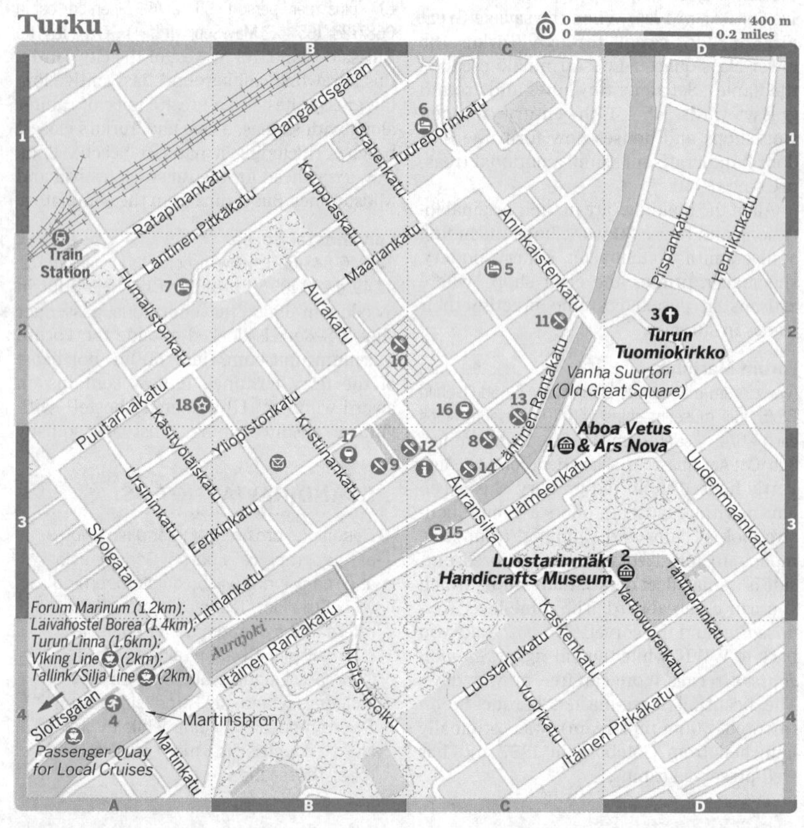

prize-winning baristas, a beautifully elegant interior and artistic sensibility, there's no better place to get your caffeine-and-cake fix. In summer, the terrace spills onto the riverbank, shaded by linden trees.

Kauppahalli MARKET €

(www.kauppahalli.fi; Eerikinkatu 16; 8am-6pm Mon-Fri, 8am-4pm Sat;) Filled with speciality products, this historic covered market also contains the converted train carriage **Sininen Juna Aschan Café** (kauppahalli; pastries & sandwiches €2.50-6; 8am-6pm Mon-Fri, 8am-4pm Sun), run by top-quality Turku bakery chain Aschan.

★Tintå GASTROPUB €€

(02-230-7023; www.tinta.fi; Läntinen Rantakatu 9; lunch €8.50-13.50, pizza €12-16, mains €25-30; 11am-midnight Mon, 11am-1am Tue-Thu, 11am-2am Fri, noon-2am Sat, noon-10pm Sun) With a cosy exposed-brick interior, this riverside wine bar also offers weekday lunches, gourmet pizzas such as asparagus and smoked feta or prosciutto and fig, and classy mains like organic beef skewers with horseradish aioli. Grab a glass of wine and watch the world walking along the shore from the summer terrace.

Turku

Top Sights
1 Aboa Vetus & Ars Nova....C3
2 Luostarinmäki Handicrafts Museum....D3
3 Turun Tuomiokirkko....D2

Activities, Courses & Tours
4 S/S Ukkopekka....A4

Sleeping
5 Centro Hotel....C2
6 Hotelli Helmi....C1
7 Park Hotel....A2

Eating
8 CaféArt....C3
9 Kauppahalli....B3
10 Kauppatori....B2
11 Mami....C2
12 Sininen Juna Aschan Café....C3
13 Smor....C2
14 Tintå....C3

Drinking & Nightlife
15 Boat Bars....C3
16 Cosmic Comic Café....C2
17 Panimoravintola Koulu....B3

Entertainment
18 Klubi....A2

Mami BISTRO €€

(02-231-1111; www.mami.fi; Linnankatu 3; lunch €9-10, mains €20-25; 11am-10pm Tue-Fri, 1-10pm Sat) Mami's riverside summer terrace is perfect for people-watching, though its abiding popularity means you'll have to fight for a table with half of Turku. Seasonal ingredients from local, small-scale suppliers – chanterelles, perch, salmon, cockerel – are prepared with care.

★Smor MODERN FINNISH €€€

(02-536-9444; www.smor.fi; Läntinen Rantakatu 3; mains €29, 3-/6-course tasting menu €47/65, incl wine €81/130; 11am-2pm & 4.30-10pm Mon-Fri, 4-10pm Sat) A vaulted cellar lit by flickering candles makes a romantic backdrop for stunning, often organic Modern Finnish cuisine: spinach waffle with quail egg and air-dried pork, roast Åland lamb with cauliflower purée and nettle sauce, or whitefish with bronze fennel. Desserts such as almond pastry with yoghurt pudding and lemon-and-thyme sorbet are equally inspired.

Drinking & Entertainment

Turku also has some of Finland's most eccentric bars that make for an offbeat pub crawl.

★Panimoravintola Koulu BREWPUB

(www.panimoravintolakoulu.fi; Eerikinkatu 18; 11am-2am) In a former school complete with inkwells, desks and a playground-turned-summer beer garden, this fantastic brewpub only serves its own brews – around five lager-style beers that change with the seasons, and a couple of interesting ciders flavoured with cranberries and blackcurrants. The exception is the whisky collection, with 75 or so to sample.

Boat Bars BAR

Summer drinking begins on the decks of the boats lining the south bank of the river. Although most serve food, they are primarily floating beer terraces with music and shipboard socialising. If the beer prices make you wince, join locals gathering on the grassy riverbank drinking takeaway alcohol.

Cosmic Comic Café BAR

(www.cosmic.fi; Kauppiaskatu 4; 3pm-2am Mon-Thu, 3pm-3am Fri & Sat, 4pm-2am Sun) This fab late-night haunt is a fanboy's dream – comics paper the walls and you can browse its huge (mostly English-language) collection. Over 70 different kinds of beer and 25 ciders rotate on the eclectic menu. Occasional live music.

OFF THE BEATEN TRACK

TURKU ARCHIPELAGO

Twenty thousand islands and skerries make up the Swedish-speaking Turku archipelago. The five largest inhabited islands – from east to west, Pargas, Nagu, Korpo, Houtskär and Iniö – are clustered in a tight crescent, and are known collectively as Väståboland (Länsi-Turunmaan). There are no big-ticket sights, just quiet settlements, abundant birdlife, and ever-changing views of sea and land. Grab a bike from Turku and plan a route of a few days.

Klubi LIVE MUSIC
(www.klubi.net; Humalistonkatu 8A; ⏲8pm-4am Wed & Thu, 10pm-4am Fri & Sat, midnight-4am Sun) Part owned by a local record label, this massive complex has several speeds, from casual drinking at Kolo to the DJ-fuelled nightclub Ilta and big-name Finnish bands at Live.

Information

Tourist Office (☎02-262-7444; www.visitturku.fi; Aurakatu 4; ⏲8.30am-6pm Mon-Fri, 9am-4pm Sat & Sun) Busy but helpful office with information on the entire region.

Getting There & Away

AIR

Finnair (www.finnair.com) flies daily to Turku's tiny airport from Helsinki; SAS has flights to Stockholm-Arlanda. Business airline **Turku Air** (www.turkuair.fi) flies to Mariehamn on weekdays.

BOAT

Turku is a major gateway to Sweden and Åland. The harbour, about 3km southwest of the centre, has terminals for **Silja Line** (www.tallinksilja.fi) and **Viking Line** (www.vikingline.fi). Both companies sail to Stockholm (11 hours) and Mariehamn (six hours).

BUS

Long-distance buses use the bus terminal at Aninkaistenkatu 20, while regional buses (including for Naantali) depart from the kauppatori.

Major intercity services:

Helsinki (€31.50, 2½ hours, hourly)

Tampere (€25.60, 2½ hours)

TRAIN

Turku's train station is 400m northwest of the centre; trains also stop at the ferry harbour.

Services:

Helsinki (€34, two hours, hourly or better)

Rovaniemi (€91.40, 12 hours, four daily, usually change in Tampere)

Tampere (€28.20, 1¾ hours, every two hours)

Getting Around

BICYCLE

Turku's tourist office rents seven-gear bikes (per half-/full day €15/20) and publishes an excellent free *pyörätiekartta* (bike-route map) of the city and surrounding towns.

BUS

Bus 1 runs between the kauppatori and the airport (€3, 25 minutes). The same bus continues from the kauppatori to the harbour.

Naantali

☎02 / POP 18,835

The lovely seaside town of Naantali is just 18km from Turku and is set around a picturesque horseshoe-shaped harbour. It's a delightfully peaceful, historic spot…or it would be, were it not for the presence of its extraordinarily popular main attraction.

Sights

The harbour, lined with cafes and restaurants, the delightful cobbled **Old Town** and the huge **Convent Church** (www.naantalinseurakunta.fi; admission free, organ concerts €5-10; ⏲10am-4pm Wed-Sun mid-May–end May, 10am-4pm Tue-Sun Jun–mid-Aug, noon-2pm Wed, 9am-noon Sun mid-Aug–mid-May) are enough incentive for a day trip here from Turku. Out of season Muumimaailma closes its gates, and the Old Town acquires the melancholic air of an abandoned film set.

Muumimaailma AMUSEMENT PARK
(Moomin World; ☎02-511-1111; www.muumimaailma.fi; 1-/2-day pass €26/36, winter magic 1-day pass €18; ⏲summer season 10am-6pm early Jun–mid-Aug, noon-6pm late Aug, winter magic 10am-4pm mid-Feb–late Feb; 👪) Crossing the bridge from the Old Town to Kailo island takes you into the delightful world of the **Moomins**. The focus is on hands-on activities and exploration, not rides; littlies love the costumed characters wandering through the Moominhouse, Snork's Workshop (where they can help with inventions) and other places from the books and cartoons.

Older adventure seekers can rock climb and track down buccaneer relics at nearby pirate island **Väski** (☎02-511-1111; www.vaski.fi; over 3yr €22, 2-day ticket incl Moominworld entry €41; ⏲11am-7pm early Jun–mid-Aug), reached by boats (included in admission) departing regularly from Naantali.

Sleeping & Eating

Although an easy day trip from Turku, Naantali has some lovely guesthouses and a famous spa hotel.

★Hotel Bridget Inn GUESTHOUSE €€
(02-533-4026; www.bridgetinn.fi; Kaivokatu 18; d €120-140, f €160, apt €220;) Steeped in history, this dove-white 1880-built wooden inn (a one-time cafe frequented by former Finnish president PE 'Ukko-Pekka' Svinhufvud) has gorgeous period-furnished rooms in champagne and chocolate hues, some with patios or balconies. Double-storey apartments include full kitchens. Parents can watch the kids romp in the playground from the umbrella-shaded terrace.

Naantalin Kylpylä SPA HOTEL €€€
(02-445-5100; www.naantalispa.fi; Matkailijantie 2; spa hotel d €168-188, ste hotel d €188-248; @) Indulge at this large, upmarket **spa** (02-445-5100; www.naantalispa.fi; Matkailijantie 2; pool entry per 3hr adult/child Sun-Fri €20/8, Sat €24/12, day spa packages from €92; nonguests 8am-8pm Mon-Sat, to 7pm Sun) complex and its first-rate restaurants Le Soleil and Thai Garden. Rooms in the Spa Hotel and Suite Hotel are spacious (the latter has Moomin-themed rooms!), and spiffing Spa Residence apartments (double from €218) come with balconies. The spa also owns the neighbouring budget family hotel Naantalin Kylpylä Perhehotelli (2-/3-bedroom apartment €120/180).

Uusi Kilta INTERNATIONAL €€
(02-435-1066; www.uusikilta.fi; Mannerheiminkatu 1; mains €18-33; kitchen 10am-10pm May-Sep) Naantali's best restaurant has a sundrenched terrace overlooking the pier and a superb, mostly seafood-oriented menu of whitefish with warm apple and fennel salad, fried perch with crayfish and potato gratin, and aromatic salmon soup with homemade bread; land-based dishes include lamb rump with garlic mash and brandy sauce.

Information

Naantalin Matkailu (02-435-9800; www.naantalinmatkailu.fi; Kaivotori 2; 9am-6pm Mon-Fri, 10am-4pm Sat & Sun Jun-Aug, 9am-4.30pm Mon-Fri Sep-May) By the harbour.

Getting There & Away

Naantali's bus station is 1km east of the harbour. Buses run to/from Turku's kauppatori (€3, 20 minutes, four per hour).

S/S Ukkopekka (p147) sails between Turku and Naantali in summer, arriving at the passenger quay on the south side of the harbour.

ÅLAND ARCHIPELAGO

018 / POP 28,700

The glorious Åland archipelago is a geopolitical anomaly: the islands belong to Finland, speak Swedish, but have their own parliament, fly their own blue-gold-and-red flag, issue their own stamps and have their own web suffix: 'dot ax'. Their 'special relationship' with the EU means they can sell duty free and make their own gambling laws.

Åland is the sunniest spot in northern Europe and its sweeping white-sand beaches and flat, scenic cycling routes attract crowds of holidaymakers during summer. Yet outside the lively capital, Mariehamn, a sleepy haze hangs over the islands' tiny villages and finding your own remote beach among the 6500 skerries and islets is surprisingly easy. A lattice of bridges and free cable ferries connect the central islands, while larger car ferries run to the archipelago's outer reaches.

Getting There & Away

AIR

Åland's airport is 4km northwest of Mariehamn, served by **NextJet** (www.nextjet.se; Turku and Stockholm-Arlanda, Sweden), **FlyBe** (www.flybe.com; Helsinki) and business airline **Turku Air** (020-721-8800; www.turkuair.fi; Turku).

BOAT

Several car ferries head to Åland. Prices vary with season and web specials are common; cars and cabins cost extra.

Alternatively, consider travelling via the archipelago ferries (p156).

Eckerö Linjen (018-28000) Branches at Mariehamn (018-28000; www.eckerolinjen.ax; Torggatan 2, Mariehamn) and Eckerö (018-28300; www.eckerolinjen.ax; Berghamn, Eckerö). Sails from Eckerö to Grisslehamn, Sweden (adult/adult and car €4/18, two hours).

Tallink/Silja Lines (018-16711; www.tallinksilja.com; Torggatan 14, Mariehamn) Runs direct services to Mariehamn from Turku (adult/adult and car €12/32, five hours), Helsinki (€33/80, 12 hours) and Stockholm (€12/32, six

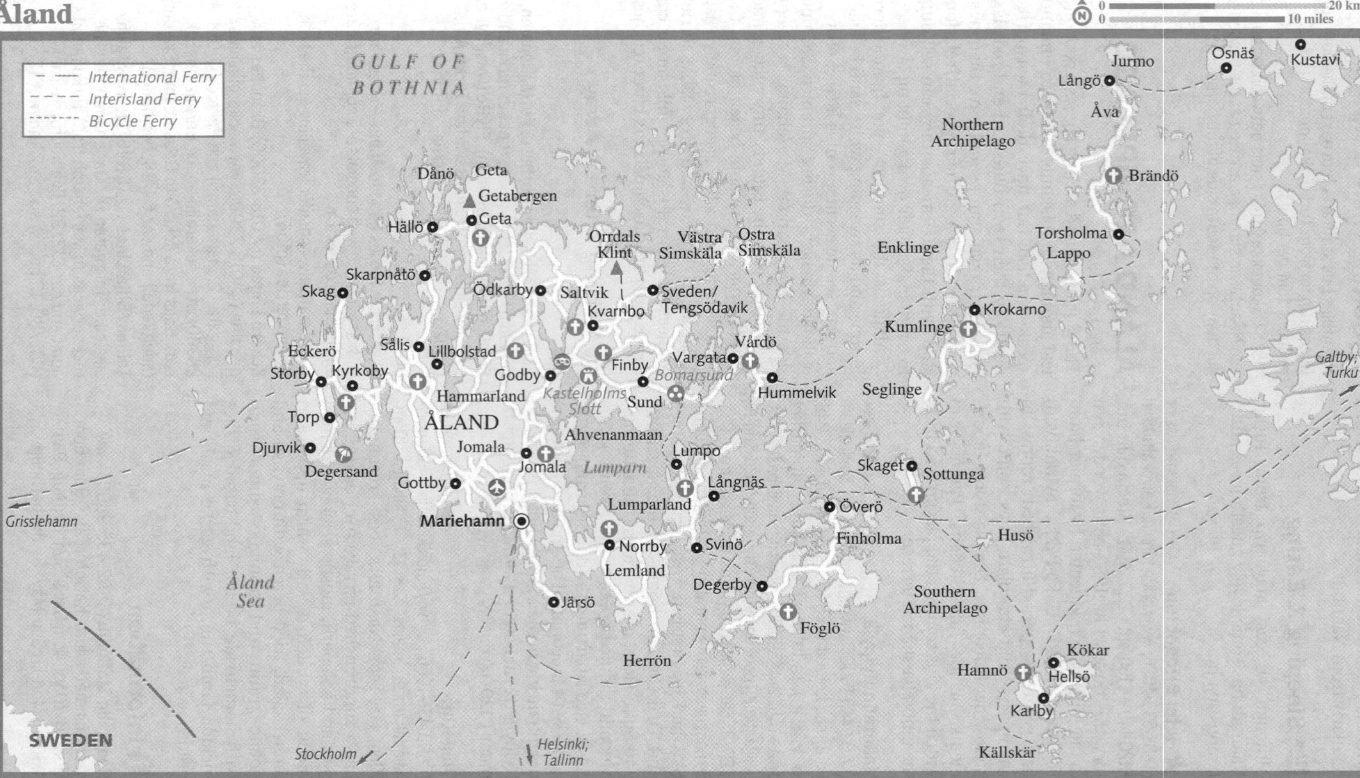
Åland
0 20 km
0 10 miles
International Ferry
Interisland Ferry
Bicycle Ferry
GULF OF BOTHNIA
Dånö
Geta
Getabergen
Geta
Hällö
Skarpnåtö
Skag
Ödkarby
Saltvik
Orrdals Klint
Västra Simskäla
Ostra Simskäla
Sveden/ Tengsödavik
Kvarnbo
Sålis
Lillbolstad
Eckerö
Storby
Kyrkoby
Godby
Finby
Vargata
Vårdö
Hummelvik
Bomarsund
Hammarland
Kastelholms Slott
Sund
Torp
ÅLAND
Djurvik
Degersand
Jomala
Jomala
Ahvenanmaan
Lumpo
Lumparn
Gottby
Grisslehamn
Mariehamn
Lumparland
Långnäs
Norrby
Svinö
Lemland
Järsö
Degerby
Föglö
Herrön
Åland Sea
SWEDEN
Stockholm
Helsinki; Tallinn
Enklinge
Kumlinge
Krokarno
Seglinge
Skaget
Sottunga
Överö
Finholma
Husö
Southern Archipelago
Northern Archipelago
Jurmo
Långö
Åva
Brändö
Torsholma
Lappo
Osnäs
Kustavi
Galtby; Turku
Kökar
Hamnö
Hellsö
Karlby
Källskär

hours). Ferries also run to Långnäs, Lumparland, from Stockholm (€18/59, 5½ hours) and Turku (€12/44, five hours).

Viking Line (☎018-26211; www.vikingline.fi; Storagatan 3, Mariehamn) Ferries to Mariehamn from Turku (adult/adult and car €14/32, five hours), Helsinki (€30/66, 11 hours) and Stockholm (€11/32, 5½ hours). Ferries also link Långnäs, Lumparland, with Stockholm (€42/66, 5½ hours).

Getting Around

BICYCLE

Cycling is a great way to tour these flat, rural islands. **Ro-No Rent** (☎018-12820; www.rono.ax; bicycles per day/week from €8/40, mopeds €80/200; ⊙Jun–mid-Aug), which also rents boats, has offices at both Mariehamn harbours as well as Eckerö. Green-and-white signs trace the excellent routes through the islands.

BOAT

Timetables for all inter-island ferries are available at the main tourist office in Mariehamn and online at www.alandstrafiken.ax. Nonstop free ferries connect adjacent islands, while there are programmed departures for longer routes.

BUS

Five main bus lines depart from Mariehamn's regional bus terminal on Styrmansgatan, in front of the police station. Rte 1 goes to Hammarland and Eckerö; rte 2 to Godby and Geta; rte 3 to Godby and Saltvik; rte 4 to Godby, Sund and Vårdö (Hummelvik); and rte 5 to Lemland and Lumparland (Långnäs). Tickets from Mariehamn to the ferry ports cost around €4.50. Bicycles can be carried (space permitting) for €8.

Mariehamn

☎018 / POP 11,390

Village-y Mariehamn is Åland's main port and capital, a pretty place lined with linden trees and timber houses set between two large harbours. Compared to the rest of the archipelago, it's a metropolis, getting quite busy in summer with tourists off the ferries, and yachts stocking the marinas. Outside peak season, you could safely fire a cannon through the town.

Sights & Activities

★Sjöfartsmuseum MUSEUM
(Maritime Museum; www.sjofartsmuseum.ax; Hamngatan 2; adult/child incl Museum Ship Pommern €10/6; ⊙10am-5pm Jun-Aug, 11am-4pm Sep-May) Centred on a re-creation of a ship with mast, saloon, galley and cabins, preserved boats make up most of the exhibitions at this state-of-the-art museum exploring Åland's marine heritage. It's a great place to discover your inner pirate with plenty of ships in bottles, sea chests and accoutrements. Anchored outside is the beautiful 1903-built four-masted merchant barque, the **Pommern** (☎018-531-423; Sjopromenaden; adult/child incl Sjöfartsmuseum €10/6; ⊙10am-5pm Jun-Aug, 11am-4pm May & Sep), which plied the trade route between Australia and England. Also here is Mariehamn's best restaurant, Nautical (p155).

Ålands Museum & Ålands Konstmuseum MUSEUM, GALLERY
(www.museum.ax; Stadhusparken; adult/child €4/3; ⊙10am-5pm Jun-Aug, 10am-8pm Tue & Thu, 10am-4pm Wed & Fri, noon-4pm Sat & Sun Sep-May) Åland's museum offers an insight into the islands' history, with exhibits including a replica of a Stone Age boat made of sealskin and a large illustration of Bomarsund in all its glory. The adjoining art gallery has changing exhibitions and paintings by local artists. Both are expected to reopen after renovations for summer 2015.

Sjökvarteret BOATYARD, MUSEUM
(☎018-16033; www.sjokvarteret.com; Österleden 110; museum adult/child €4/free; ⊙museum 11am-5pm Jun–mid-Aug, by arrangement mid-Aug–May) At the northern end of Österhamn, Sjökvarteret has long been devoted to boat-building. You can stroll along the quay, lined with

NEED TO KNOW

Currency Euro; most places accept Swedish krona.

Language Swedish.

Mobile Phones Åland uses the Finnish mobile phone network but it can be sketchy, especially in the outer islands.

Post Mail sent in Åland must have (highly collectable) Åland postage stamps.

Time Åland shares Finland's time zone, one hour ahead of Sweden.

Tourist Information The website www.visitaland.com has tourist info; www.alandsresor.fi lets you book accommodation online. There's a wealth of cottages for rent across the islands; **Destination Åland** (☎0400-108-800; www.destinationaland.com; Östra Esplanadgatan 7, Mariehamn) has a comprehensive list.

MIDSUMMER POLES

Åland's Midsummer poles are a fixture on the landscape in summer. Up to 25m tall, the whitewashed spruce poles are a cross between a mast and a totem pole. Each village usually has at least one, decorated in a public gathering the day before Midsummer with leaves, ribbons, tissue paper, miniature flags and various trinkets, the nature and symbolism of which differs from place to place. Atop the poles is the Fäktargubbe, a figure representing toil and diligence. Other motifs include sailing boats, ears of corn representing the harvest, a wreath symbolising love, a sun facing east and other icons of community togetherness. Once raised, the pole then stands until the following Midsummer.

When the Midsummer pole came to Åland remains a mystery. Although some theorists believe that the pole is a manifestation of an ancient fertility rite, its origins on Åland itself are probably more recent. Others point to the resemblance to ships' masts, with cross-spars and cords, which suggests an appeal to a higher power for safe seas.

traditional schooners, and perhaps see boats under construction. The **museum**, with exhibitions on ship-building (no English information), is located in a small timber boatshed. Also here is a **reconstructed seafarers' chapel** as well as galleries, unique **jewellery** (www.guldviva.com; Sjökvarteret; 10am-5pm Mon-Fri, to 2pm Sat late Jun–mid-Aug) and an excellent **craft shop** (www.salt.ax; Sjökvarteret; 10am-6pm Mon-Fri, to 3pm Sat, 11am-3pm Sun Jun-early Aug).

Ro-No Rent OUTDOORS
(018-12820; www.rono.ax; 9am-6pm Jun–mid-Aug, by arrangement Sep-May) Ro-No rents out a variety of bicycles (per day/week €10/50), kayaks (€80/150), small boats (that don't require a licence; per four hours/day €100/200) and mopeds (that do require a licence; per day/week €60/180) from its outlet at Österhamn. The smaller outlet at **Västerhamn** just has bicycles.

Sleeping

Rates for Mariehamn's hotels and guesthouses peak in July and August. The hotels are all much of a muchness, with no standout option.

Gröna Udden Camping CAMPGROUND €
(018-528-700; www.gronaudden.com; Östernäsvägen; tent site €10 plus per adult €10, d €80, 2-/4-/6-person cabins €95/115/160; early May-early Sep) By the seaside, 15 minutes' stroll south of the city centre, this campground is a family favourite so you'll need to book its fully equipped spruce cabins ahead in summer. Outdoor fun includes a safe swimming beach, minigolf course (admission €5) and bike hire (€15). Linen costs €8.50 per person.

Pensionat Solhem GUESTHOUSE €€
(018-16322; www.visitaland.com/solhem; Lökskärsvägen 18; s/d without bathroom €45/75; May-Oct) Situated 3km south of the city centre, this seaside spot feels like your own villa. Simple rooms share bathrooms but you can use rowing boats and the sauna and cheerful staff keep the place running like clockwork. Local buses stop nearby.

Park Alandia Hotel HOTEL €€
(018-14130; www.parkalandiahotel.com; Norra Esplanadgatan 3; s/d €98/116) Spacious, modern rooms at this sophisticated spot on the main boulevard are done out in sandy hues and hardwood floors, and guests can borrow bikes for free. On sunny days its restaurant terrace packs in the crowds.

Hotell Arkipelag HOTEL €€€
(018-24020; www.hotellarkipelag.com; Strandgatan 35; s/d €134/164, with sea view €158/188, ste €280) High-class Arkipelag is popular with business visitors, though water views from the balconies are tempting for anyone. Rooms are large, with minimalist decoration and bathrooms contain both baths and showers. Super facilities include indoor and outdoor pools, a freshly refurbished sauna, nightclub, casino, three restaurants and several bars.

Eating & Drinking

Mariehamn's many cafes serve the local speciality, *Ålandspannkaka* (Åland pancakes), a fluffy square pudding made with semolina and served with stewed prunes.

Pub Niska PIZZA €
(018-19151; www.mickesmat.ax; Sjökvarteret; pizza €11.50-12.50; 11am-7pm Mon-Sat, 3-9pm Sun May & Sep, 11am-9pm Jun-Aug) Star chef Mi-

chael 'Micke' Björklund, the mastermind behind Åland's sublime 'taste village' **Smakbyn** (www.smakbyn.ax; Slottsvägen 134, Kastelholm; lunch mains €10, dinner mains €29, 2-/3-course evening menus €39/49; kitchen 11am-7pm Mon-Fri, 1-8pm Sat & Sun;), recently shifted his smuggler-named *plåtbröd* (Åland-style pizza) restaurant from the west harbour here to Mariehamn's maritime quarter. Condiments are homemade, cheese is from Åland's dairy, and toppings include cold smoked salmon and horseradish cream. There are also meal-sized baked potatoes and salads.

Seapoint Restaurant & Bar REGIONAL CUISINE €€
(018-15501; www.taste.ax; Österhamn; lunch mains €10.50-16, dinner mains €22-28; kitchen 11am-10pm Mon-Fri, 1-10pm Sat & Sun May–mid-Aug) Local ingredients are used to intriguing effect at this smart harbour pavilion: grilled fennel with roasted root vegetables, perch with wild garlic, smoked whitefish roe, and crème brûlée with seabuckthorn and strawberries. Tapas-style platters (€15) offer a taste of three seafood, meat or vegetable dishes.

Indigo REGIONAL CUISINE €€
(018-16550; www.indigo.ax; Nygatan 1; lunch mains €12-13, dinner mains €20-32.50; kitchen 11am-3pm & 5-10pm Mon-Sat year-round plus 2-10pm Sun mid-May–early Sep) The building might be historic brick and timber but the menu is contemporary, with expertly cooked dishes such as grilled Åland beef with béarnaise sauce and homemade fries. There's a buzzing summer courtyard and beautiful upstairs loft space. It's a stylish spot for a drink; the bar stays open to midnight Monday to Thursday and 3am on Friday and Saturday.

★**Nautical** REGIONAL CUISINE €€€
(018-19931; www.nautical.ax; Hamngätan 2; lunch mains €13-24, dinner mains €30-36, 6-course tasting menu €75; 11am-10pm Jun-Aug, 5-10pm Sep-May;) Taking its cue from its maritime museum location, this spiffing marine-blue restaurant overlooking the western harbour and *Pommern* is decked out with a ship's wheel and has a splendid umbrella-shaded summer terrace. Sea-inspired dishes span salmon tartare with horseradish and fennel to pan-fried Åland perch with caraway foam; land-based options include red-wine-braised ox tail with forest mushrooms.

Information

Ålandsresor (018-28040; www.alandsresor.fi; Torggatan 2; 8.30am-5pm Mon-Fri year-round, plus 9am-2pm Sat Jun & Jul) Handles hotel, guesthouse and cottage bookings for the entire archipelago.

Tourist Office (Ålands Turistinformation; 018-24000; www.visitaland.com; Storagatan 8; 9am-6pm early Jun-early Aug, 9am-5pm Mon-Fri, to 4pm Sat & Sun early Jun & mid-Aug–late Aug, 9am-4pm Mon-Fri, 10am-3pm Sat & Sun Apr, May & Sep, 9am-4pm Mon-Fri Oct-Mar;) Helpful office with region-wide info.

Around the Islands

Sund

Crossing the bridge into the municipality of Sund brings you to Åland's most striking attraction: the medieval 14th-century **Kastelholms Slott** (018-432-150; www.kastelholm.ax; adult/child €6/4.50; 10am-5pm mid-May–Jun & Aug–mid-Sep, to 6pm Jul), a striking and beautifully situated castle. Next to the castle, **Jan Karlsgårdens Friluftsmuseum** (018-432-150; www.kastelholm.ax; 10am-5pm May–mid-Sep) FREE is a typical open-air museum consisting of about 20 wooden buildings, including three windmills, transported here from around the archipelago.

Further east, the ruins of the Russian fortress at **Bomarsund** (www.bomarsund.ax) are accessible all year. The impressive fortifications date from the 1830s and were destroyed during the Crimean War (1853–56). Near Bomarsund, **Puttes Camping** (018-44016; www.visitaland.com/puttescamping; Bryggvägen 2, Bomarsund; tent sites €12 plus per person €4, cabins from €35; May-Aug) is a large, well-equipped site with a beach sauna, a cafe and cabins. For eats, seek out Smakbyn. This 'taste village' incorporates a farm shop, cookery courses, a distillery, bar, and airy open-kitchen restaurant using seasonal organic produce.

Eckerö

Finland's westernmost municipality, Eckerö is all blonde hair and tanned bodies in summer, packed with holidaying Swedish families making the short ferry-hop across. **Storby** (Big Village), at the ferry terminal, is the main centre, with a petrol station and bank. The best beach is at **Degersand** in

OFF THE BEATEN TRACK

EASTERN ARCHIPELAGO ROUTES

If you have a bit of time on your hands it's possible to island-hop eastwards through the northeast and southeast archipelago routes. Accommodation options are limited so carry a tent or make advance bookings.

To the north you can travel through **Vårdö** then take the ferry to **Kumlinge**. Another 1½ hours by ferry via **Lappo** brings you to **Torsholma** on the scattered island group of **Brändö**. It's then possible to hop via **Jurmo** all the way to Turku. By public transport, take bus 4 from Mariehamn to Hummelvik harbour on Vårdö island. From Turku, take a bus to Kustavi, and on to Vartsala island to reach the harbour of Osnäs (Vuosnainen).

To the south, it's an easier trip to the port of **Långnäs**, from where you can hop via **Föglö** and **Sottunga** to the far-flung but picturesque island of **Kökar**, with hiking trails, a 14th-century abbey and an 18th-century church. By local transport from Mariehamn, take bus 5 to Långnäs harbour. From Kökar there are ferries to Galtby harbour on Korppoo island (two hours), then it's 75km by bus to Turku.

If you're taking a car on these ferries, it's substantially cheaper if you spend a night en route between Finland and mainland Åland. Plus, stopover tickets take priority in summer, so you might not even get on if you don't.

the south, but away from the coast, Eckerö is typical rural Åland, with winding country lanes and tiny villages.

Storby was once the western extremity of the Russian Empire, and the Bear wanted a show of power for Europe, so CL Engel was commissioned to design a massive, er, post office. The **Post och Tullhuset** (Post & Customs House; Storby; ⊙10am-5pm May-Aug, individual business hours vary) is enormous and now houses a cafe, exhibition gallery and the small **mailboat museum** (www.aland.com; admission €3; ⊙10am-3pm early Jun–mid-Aug), which tells the story of the gruelling archipelago mail route that cost many lives over two and a half centuries.

Bang on Åland's most beautiful beach, **Degersands Resort** (☎018-38004; www.degersand.nu; Degersandsvägen 311; tent sites €8 plus per person €6, 1-2 person/3-4 person cabins €140/165;) has stunning cottages in sleek Scandinavian blond wood.

Bus 1 runs to Mariehamn.

SOUTHWESTERN FINLAND

Tampere

☎03 / POP 217,400

Scenic Tampere, set between two vast lakes, has a down-to-earth vitality that makes it a favourite for many visitors. Through its centre churn the Tammerkoski rapids, whose grassy banks contrast with the red brick of the imposing fabric mills that once drove the city's economy. Regenerated industrial buildings now house quirky museums, enticing shops, pubs, cinemas and cafes.

Sights

★Tuomiokirkko CHURCH
(www.tampereenseurakunnat.fi; Tuomiokirkonkatu 3; ⊙10am-5pm May-Aug, 11am-3pm Sep-Apr) FREE An iconic example of National Romantic architecture, Tampere's cathedral dates from 1907. Hugo Simberg created the frescoes and stained glass; you'll appreciate that they were controversial. A procession of ghostly childlike apostles holds the 'garland of life', graves and plants are tended by skeletal figures, and a wounded angel is stretchered off by two children. There's a solemn, almost mournful feel; the altarpiece, by Magnus Enckell, is a dreamlike Resurrection in similar style.

Finlayson Centre CULTURAL CENTRE
(Satakunnankatu 18) Tampere's industrial era began with Scot James Finlayson, who established a cotton mill by the Tammerkoski in the 1820s. Later it grew massively and was the first building in the Nordic countries to have electric lighting, which started operating in 1882. It has now been sensitively converted into a mall of cafes and shops; you'll also find a cinema here, as well as a great brewery pub and a couple of intriguing museums.

★Amurin Työläismuseokortteli MUSEUM
(Amuri Museum of Workers' Housing; www.tampere.fi/amuri; Satakunnankatu 49; adult/child €7/3;

⏲10am-6pm Tue-Sun mid-May–mid-Sep) An entire block of 19th-century wooden houses, including 32 apartments, a bakery, a shoemaker, two general shops and a cafe, is preserved here. It's one of the most realistic house-museums in Finland and entertaining backstories (English translation available) give plenty of historical information.

Vakoilumuseo MUSEUM
(Spy Museum; www.vakoilumuseo.fi; Satakunnankatu 18, Finlayson Centre; adult/child €8/6; ⏲10am-6pm Mon-Sat, 11am-5pm Sun Jun-Aug, noon-6pm Mon-Sat, 11am-5pm Sun Sep-May; 👪) The offbeat spy museum under the Finlayson Centre offers a small but well-assembled display of devices of international espionage, mainly from the Cold War era. As well as histories of famous Finnish and foreign spies, it has numerous Bond-style gadgets and some interactive displays. English translations are slightly unsatisfying. For €5 extra, kids can take a suitability test for KGB cadet school.

Lenin-Museo MUSEUM
(www.lenin.fi; Hämeenpuisto 28; adult/child €5/free; ⏲11am-4pm Sep-May, 11am-6pm Jun-Aug) Admirers of bearded revolutionaries won't want to miss this small museum in the Workers' Hall where Lenin and Stalin first met in 1905. His life is documented with photos and papers; it's a little dry but it's fascinating to see, for example, his old school report (Vladimir was a straight-A student) or a threadbare couch that he slept on. The gift shop stocks Lenin pens, badges, T-shirts and other Soviet-era souvenirs.

Muumilaakso MUSEUM
(Moomin Valley; www.tampere.fi/muumi; Puutarhakatu 34; adult/child €7/3, incl Tampereen taidemuseo €10/4; ⏲9am-5pm Tue-Fri, 10am-6pm Sat & Sun) Explore the creation of Tove Jansson's enduringly popular Moomins in this atmospheric museum in the basement of the art gallery, Tampereen taidemuseo. It contains original drawings and beautiful dioramas depicting scenes from these quirky stories (English explanations available). It's scheduled to move to a new home in the Tampere-talo building in 2016.

Vapriikki MUSEUM
(www.vapriikki.fi; Veturiaukio 4; adult/child €10/4; ⏲10am-6pm Tue-Sun) A bright, modern glass-and-steel exhibition space in the renovated Tampella textile mill. As well as regularly changing exhibitions on anything from bicycles to Buddhism, there's a permanent display on Tampere's history, a beautiful **mineral museum**, a **natural history museum** and a small but cluttered **ice-hockey museum**, with memorabilia of star players and teams from Finland's sporting passion. There's also a **museum of shoes** – Tampere was known for its footwear industry – and a pleasant cafe.

★**Särkänniemi** AMUSEMENT PARK
(www.sarkanniemi.fi; day pass adult/child €37/31; ⏲rides roughly 10am-7pm mid-May–Aug) This promontory amusement park complex has numerous attractions, including dozens of rides, an observation tower, art gallery, aquarium, farm zoo, planetarium and dolphinarium. Buy all-inclusive entry or pay per attraction (€10/5 per adult/child). Opening times are complex; check the website, where you can also get discounted entry. Indoor attractions stay open year-round. Take bus 20 from the train station or central square.

Rides include the Tornado roller coaster, super-fast High Voltage, speedboat rides on the lake and an Angry Birds area for younger kids. The **aquarium** (www.sarkanniemi.fi; adult/child day pass up to €29/€18; ⏲noon-7pm mid-May–Aug, 11am-9pm Sep–mid-May) is mediocre, with Finnish fish more interesting than the hobby-tank favourites. The planetarium is in the same complex, above which soars 168m **Näsinneula Observation Tower** (www.sarkanniemi.fi; adult/child €10/5; ⏲11am-11.30pm), the tallest in these northern lands. It's overpriced but gives spectacular city and lake views. There's a revolving restaurant.

Sara Hildénin taidemuseo (☎03-5654-3500; www.tampere.fi/sarahilden; adult/child €8/4; ⏲10am-6pm Tue-Sun Sep–mid-May, noon-7pm daily mid-May–Aug) has a collection of international and Finnish modern art and sculpture; the space is normally devoted to excellent exhibitions showcasing particular artists.

Activities

Pyynikki PARK
Rising between Tampere's two lakes, this forested ridge has fine views plus walking and cycling trails. It soars 85m above the lakeshores – an Everest by southern Finnish standards – and claims to be the world's highest gravel ridge. A stone **observation tower** (www.munkkikahvila.net; adult/child €2/1; ⏲9am-8pm, 9am-9pm Jun-Aug) holds a cafe serving brilliant doughnuts (€1.90).

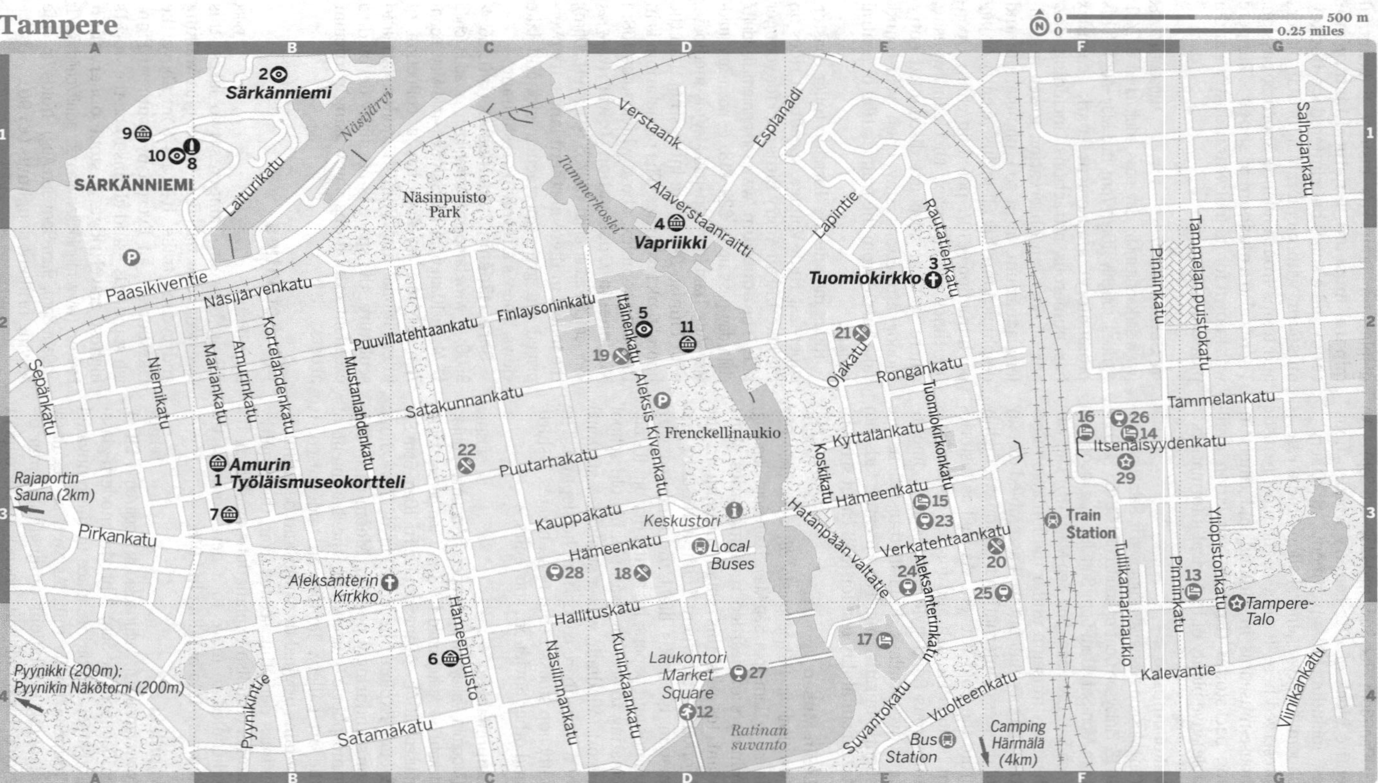
Tampere
500 m
0.25 miles
Särkänniemi
Näsijärvi
SÄRKÄNNIEMI
Laiturikatu
Näsinpuisto Park
Tammerkoski
Verstaank
Esplanadi
Alaverstaanraitti
Vapriikki
Lapintie
Rautatienkatu
Tuomiokirkko
Salhojankatu
Pinninkatu
Tammelan puistokatu
Paasikiventie
Näsijärvenkatu
Finlaysoninkatu
Puuvillatehtaankatu
Itäinenkatu
Ojakatu
Ronganakatu
Sepänkatu
Niemikatu
Mariankatu
Amurinkatu
Kortelahdenkatu
Mustanlahdenkatu
Aleksis Kivenkatu
Satakunnankatu
Tuomiokirkonkatu
Tammelankatu
Kyttälänkatu
Itsenäisyydenkatu
Frenckellinaukio
Koskikatu
Puutarhakatu
Amurin Työläismuseokortteli
Rajaportin Sauna (2km)
Hämeenkatu
Kauppakatu
Keskustori
Train Station
Pirkankatu
Hatanpään valtatie
Verkatehtaankatu
Local Buses
Tullikamarinaukio
Pinninkatu
Yliopistonkatu
Aleksanterin Kirkko
Aleksanterinkatu
Tampere-Talo
Hallituskatu
Hämeenpuisto
Näsilinnankatu
Kuninkaankatu
Laukontori Market Square
Kalevantie
Pyynikki (200m); Pyynikin Näkötorni (200m)
Pyynikintie
Satamakatu
Ratinan suvanto
Suvantokatu
Vuolteenkatu
Bus Station
Camping Härmälä (4km)
Viinikankatu

Tampere

Top Sights

1 Amurin Työläismuseokortteli B3
2 Särkänniemi B1
3 Tuomiokirkko E2
4 Vapriikki D1

Sights

5 Finlayson Centre D2
6 Lenin-Museo C4
7 Muumilaakso B3
8 Näsinneula Observation Tower A1
9 Sara Hildénin taidemuseo A1
10 Särkänniemi Aquarium A1
11 Vakoilumuseo D2

Activities, Courses & Tours

12 Suomen Hopealinja D4

Sleeping

13 Dream Hostel G3
14 Hotelli Victoria F3
15 Omenahotelli E3
16 Scandic Tampere Station F3
17 Sokos Hotel Ilves E4

Eating

18 Kauppahalli D3
Neljä Vuodenaikaa .... (see 18)
19 Panimoravintola Plevna D2
20 Ravintola C F3
21 Runo E2
22 Tuulensuu C3

Drinking & Nightlife

23 Café Europa E3
24 Nordic Gastropub E3
25 O'Connell's F3
26 Ruma F3
27 Suvi D4
28 Teerenpeli C3

Entertainment

29 Klubi F3

Rajaportin Sauna SAUNA
(www.rajaportinsauna.fi; Pispalan Valtatie 9; adult/child €8/2, midweek €5; 6-10pm Mon & Wed, 3-9pm Fri, 2-10pm Sat) This traditional place is Finland's oldest operating public sauna. It's a great chance to experience the softer steam from a traditionally heated sauna rather than the harsher electric ones. It's a couple of kilometres west of the city centre; buses 8, 11 and 13 among others head out there. There's a cafe on-site, and massages can be arranged. Take a towel or rent one there.

Tours

There are plenty of summer options on Tampere's two magnificent lakes. Trips on Näsijärvi leave from Mustalahti Quay, while Laukontori Quay serves Pyhäjärvi. All cruises can be booked at the tourist office.

Suomen Hopealinja CRUISE
(Finnish Silverline; 010-422-5600; www.hopealinja.fi) From Laukontori Quay, short cruises run on Pyhäjärvi from June to August, as well as a shuttle service (adult/child return €12/6) to nearby **Viikinsaari**, a pleasant picnic island. There are various lunch- and dinner-cruise options, and pirate cruises for kids.

★ **Poet's Way** CRUISE
(010-422-5600; www.runoilijantie.fi; early Jun–mid-Aug) From Mustalahti Quay, the glorious steamship S/S *Tarjanne* operates one of Finland's finest lake cruises, departing on Wednesdays and Fridays and returning from Virrat on Thursdays and Saturdays. One way to Ruovesi (4¾ hours) is €50; Virrat (8¼ hours) is €58.

Festivals & Events

There are events held in Tampere almost year-round.

Tampere Film Festival FILM
(www.tamperefilmfestival.fi) A respected international festival of short films, usually held in early March.

Tampere Biennale MUSIC
(www.tamperemusicfestivals.fi) This festival of new Finnish music is held in April of even-numbered years.

Tammerfest ROCK
(www.tammerfest.fi) The city's premier rock festival, held over four days in mid-July with concerts at various stages around town.

Sleeping

★ **Dream Hostel** HOSTEL €
(045-236-0517; www.dreamhostel.fi; Åkerlundinkatu 2; dm €24-29, tw/q €79/108; P @) Sparky, stylish and spacious, this is Finland's best hostel. Helpful staff, super-comfortable wide-berth dorms (unisex and female) in various sizes, a heap of facilities including bike hire, original decor and the right attitude about everything make it a real winner.

It's a short walk from the train station in a quiet area.

Camping Härmälä CAMPGROUND €
(☎020-719-9777; www.suomicamping.fi/harmala; Leirintäkatu 8; campsites €16 plus per person €5, one-person tent €16, 2-/4-person cabin €54/72; ⊙early May-late Sep; P ☎) Four-and-a-half kilometres south of the city centre (take bus 1 or 11), this is a spacious campground on the Pyhäjärvi lakeshore. There's a cafe, saunas and rowboats, as well as bike hire.

★**Scandic Tampere Station** HOTEL €€
(☎03-339-8000; www.scandichotels.com; Ratapihankatu 37; s/d €139/159; P ❄ @ ☎ ♿) As the name suggests, this is right by the train station. It's a sleek, beautifully designed place with a minimalist feel to the decor, based on soothing pink and mauve lighting breaking up the chic whites and blacks. Superior-plus rooms are particularly enticing, with darkwood sauna and balcony, and don't cost a whole lot more. Facilities are modern, service excellent and prices competitive.

Hotelli Victoria HOTEL €€
(☎03-242-5111; www.hotellivictoria.fi; Itsenäisyydenkatu 1; s/d €139/172; P ❄ @ ☎ ≈) Just on the other side of the train station from the city centre, this friendly hotel offers sound summer value with its spruce rooms, free internet and commendable breakfast spread. Rooms are light and quiet despite the busy road and there's a good sauna (included), 20m pool and free parking. It's usually cheaper than these maximum rates. Closed most of December. Bike hire available.

Omenahotelli HOTEL €€
(☎0600-18018; www.omenahotels.com; Hämeenkatu 7; r €60-96; ☎ ♿) On the main drag and very handy for the train station, this receptionless hotel offers the usual comfortable rooms with twin beds, a microwave, a kettle and a fold-out couch. Rooms are great value for a family of four, for example. Book online or via the terminal at the entrance.

Sokos Hotel Ilves HOTEL €€€
(☎020-123-4631; www.sokoshotels.fi; Hatanpään valtatie 1; s/d €165/185; P ❄ @ ☎ ≈) This tower hotel was big news when it opened in the 1980s, and still keeps standards high. Very high: the view from upper-floor rooms is memorable, so ask for as lofty a chamber as you can get. Rooms are attractively furnished with Finnish design classics; superiors are the same size but with even better views.

Eating

Tampere's speciality, *mustamakkara*, is a mild, rather tasty sausage made with cow's blood, normally eaten with lingonberry jam. Try it at the kauppahalli or Laukontori market.

★**Neljä Vuodenaikaa** BISTRO €
(4 Saisons; www.4vuodenaikaa.fi; Kauppahalli; dishes €10-25; ⊙11am-3.45pm Mon-Fri, 11am-2.30pm Sat) Tucked into a corner of the kauppahalli, this recommended spot brings Gallic flair to the Finnish lunch hour with delicious plates such as bouillabaisse and French country salad augmented by excellent daily specials and wines by the glass.

Kauppahalli MARKET €
(Hämeenkatu 19; ⊙8am-6pm Mon-Fri, 8am-3pm Sat; ✎) This intriguing indoor market is one of Finland's best, with picturesque wooden stalls serving a dazzling array of wonderful meat, fruit, baked goodies and fish. There are good places to eat here too; this is the best place to try cheap *mustamakkara* with berry jam.

Runo CAFE €
(www.kahvilaruno.fi; Ojakatu 3; sandwiches €4-6; ⊙9am-8pm Mon-Sat, 10am-8pm Sun) With an arty crowd and bohemian feel, Runo (Poem) is an elegant, almost baroque cafe with books, paintings, decent coffee and huge windows that allow you to keep tabs on the weather. It's a top hang-out for either a light lunch or a spot of quiet contemplation.

Panimoravintola Plevna BREWPUB €
(www.plevna.fi; Itäinenkatu 8; mains €11-23; ⊙food 11am-10pm; ☎) Inside the Finlayson Centre, this barn of a place offers a wide range of delicious beer, cider and perry brewed here, including an excellent strong stout. Meals are large and designed to soak it all up: massive sausage platters and enormous slabs of pork in classic beer-hall style. Vegetables here mean potatoes and onions, preferably fried, but it's all tasty, and service is fast.

★**Tuulensuu** GASTROPUB €€
(www.gastropub.net/tuulensuu; Hämeenpuisto 23; mains €17-26; ⊙11am-midnight Mon-Fri, from noon Sat, from 3pm Sun; ☎) The best of several Tampere gastropubs, this has a superb range of Belgian beers, good wines and a lengthy port menu. Food is lovingly prepared and features staples such as liver or schnitzel, as well as more elaborate plates like duck confit and other bistro fare inspired by Bel-

gium and northeastern France. Even the bar snacks are gourmet: fresh-roasted almonds. Closed Sundays in summer.

Ravintola C MODERN FINNISH €€€
(☎010-617-9760; www.ravintola-c.fi; Rautatienkatu 20; mains €25-29; ⊙5pm-midnight Tue-Sat) In a pristine, off-white dining room near the train station, this top Tampere restaurant creates innovative, beautifully presented modern dishes from a short menu with a focus on local ingredients and traditions. Meat tends to be slow-cooked and treated with respect, and there's always a non-dull vegetarian option.

Drinking & Nightlife

Panimoravintola Plevna and Tuulensuu are also fine places for a beer or two.

★Café Europa BAR
(www.ravintola.fi/europa; Aleksanterinkatu 29; ⊙noon-midnight Mon-Tue, noon-2am Wed-Thu, noon-3am Fri & Sat, 1pm-midnight Sun; 📶) Lavishly furnished with horsehair couches, armchairs, mirrors, chandeliers and paintings, this successfully fuses a re-creation of a 1930s-style old-Europe cafe, and is a popular meeting spot for students and anyone else who appreciates comfort, board games, Belgian and German beers, and generously proportioned sandwiches and salads. There's good summer seating out the front.

Teerenpeli PUB
(www.teerenpeli.com; Hämeenkatu 25; ⊙noon-2am Sun-Thu, noon-3am Fri & Sat) On the main street, this is a good place with excellent microbrewery beer and cider. There's a relaxing, candlelit interior, heated terrace and heaps of choice at the taps. There's a huge downstairs space too, with comfy seating.

Nordic Gastropub PUB
(www.gastropub.net/nordic; Otavalankatu 3; ⊙3pm-2am Sun-Fri, noon-2am Sat) The range of perfectly poured microbrewed Finnish beers on tap, backed up by guest ales from around the Nordic lands, would tempt anybody in for a pint. There's a small selection of good-value, original Nordic-based dishes to back it up.

O'Connell's PUB
(www.oconnells.fi; Rautatienkatu 24; ⊙4pm-1am Sun-Mon, 4pm-2am Tue-Fri, 2pm-2am Sat) Popular with both Finns and expats, this rambling Irish pub is handy for the train station and has plenty of time-worn, comfortable seating and an air of bonhomie. Its best feature is the range of interesting beers on tap and carefully selected bottled imports. There's regular free live music.

Suvi BAR
(www.laivaravintolasuvi.fi; Laukontori; ⊙10am-2am Jun-Sep) Moored alongside Laukontori Quay, this is a typical Finnish boat bar offering no-nonsense deck-top drinking. Prepare a boarding party and lap up the afternoon sun.

Ruma CLUB, BAR
(www.ruma.fi; Murtokatu 1; ⊙6pm-4am Wed-Sat) A cool spot with offbeat decor, quirky lighting, friendly staff, and a mixture of Finnish and European pop and alternative rock. There's a cover of €3 to €6 on weekends. Opens 8pm in summer.

Entertainment

Klubi LIVE MUSIC
(www.klubi.net; Tullikamarinaukio 2; ⊙11am-10pm Mon-Tue, 11am-4am Wed-Sat) This cavernous place, near the train station, is Tampere's main indoor live-music venue; there are usually several bands playing every week, and big Finnish names regularly swing by for concerts.

Information

Visit Tampere (☎03-5656-6800; www.visittampere.fi; Hämeenkatu 14B; ⊙9am-5pm Mon-Fri Sep-May, 9am-6pm Mon-Fri, 10am-3pm Sat & Sun Jun-Aug; 📶) On the main street in the centre of town. Can book activities and events.

Getting There & Away

AIR

Finnair/Flybe Flies to Helsinki (though it's more convenient on the train) with connections to other Finnish cities.

Ryanair Daily services to several European destinations including London Stansted, Frankfurt, Milan and Girona.

SAS Flies direct to Stockholm.

BUS

Regular express buses run from Helsinki (€27, 2¾ hours) and Turku (€25.60, two to three hours) and most other major towns in Finland are served from here.

TRAIN

The train station is central. Express trains run hourly to/from Helsinki (€39, 1¾ hours) and there are direct trains to Turku (€33.30, 1¾ hours) and other cities.

Getting Around

The local bus service is extensive. A one-hour/24-hour ticket costs €2.60/6.50. Check route maps online at joukkoliikenne.tampere.fi.

Several car-hire companies operate at the airport and in town. **Bikes** can be hired from about €15 a day from several places, including **Holiday Inn Tampere** (03-245-5111; Yliopistonkatu 44; per 24hr €15). The **Citybike** (www.tamperecitybike.fi; mid-Jun–mid-Oct) scheme requires a €10 fee and €40 deposit – do this online. Get the key from the tourist office and you have access to a whole network.

TO/FROM THE AIRPORT

Tampere-Pirkkala airport is 15km southwest; arriving flights are met by a **bus** (0100-29400; www.paunu.fi; €4.70) to the centre (€4.70, 30 minutes). **Tokee** (0200-39000; www.airpro.fi) serves Ryanair flights, leaving from the railway station forecourt about 2½ hours before take-off (€6).

Hämeenlinna

03 / POP 67,800

Dominated by its namesake, majestic Häme Castle, Hämeenlinna (Swedish: Tavastehus) is Finland's oldest inland town, founded in 1649, though a trading post had existed here since the 9th century. The Swedes built the castle in the 13th century, and Hämeenlinna developed into an administrative, educational and garrison town around it. The town is quiet but picturesque, and its wealth of museums will keep you busy for a day or two. It makes a good stop between Helsinki and Tampere; you could head on to the latter by lakeboat.

Sights

★Hämeenlinna CASTLE

(Häme Castle; www.nba.fi; adult/child €8/4; 10am-4pm Mon-Fri, 11am-4pm Sat & Sun) Hämeenlinna means Häme Castle, so it's no surprise that this bulky twin-towered redbrick fortress is the town's pride and most significant attraction. Construction was begun in the 1260s by the Swedes, who wanted to establish a military redoubt against the power of Novgorod. It was originally built on an island, but, the lake receded and necessitated the building of new walls. It never saw serious military action and, after the Russian takeover of 1809, was converted into a jail.

Museo Militaria MUSEUM

(Tykistömuseo; www.museomilitaria.fi; adult/child €8/3; 11am-5pm Sep-May, 10am-6pm Jun-Aug) There are numerous museums devoted to Finnish involvement in WWII, but this takes the cake. It's huge. There are three floors packed with war memorabilia, including good information in English on the beginnings of the Winter War. Outside, and in a separate hall, is a collection of phallic heavy artillery big enough to start a war on several fronts.

Sibeliuksen syntymäkoti MUSEUM

(www.hameenlinna.fi; Hallituskatu 11; adult/child €5/2, incl Palanderin talo €8; 10am-4pm May-Aug, noon-4pm Tue-Sun Sep-Apr) Johan Julius Christian (Jean) Sibelius was born in Hämeenlinna in 1865 and was schooled here, but the town makes surprisingly little fuss about it. His childhood home is a small museum containing photographs, letters, his upright piano and some family furniture. It's a likeable place, although uninformative about his later life. Concert performances on summer Sundays are free with an entry ticket.

★Palanderin talo MUSEUM

(www.hameenlinna.fi; Linnankatu 16; adult/child €5/2, incl Sibeliuksen syntymäkoti €8; noon-4pm Tue-Sun May-Aug, Sat & Sun Sep-Apr) Finland loves its house-museums and this is among the best, offering a wonderful insight into well-off 19th-century Finnish life, thanks to excellent English-speaking guided tours. There's splendid imperial and art nouveau furniture as well as delicate little touches such as a double-sided mirror to spy on street fashion, and a set of authentic children's drawings from the period.

Sleeping & Eating

Aulanko Camping CAMPGROUND, COTTAGES €

(03-675-9772; www.aulankocamping.fi; Aulangonheikkiläntie 168; tent/van site incl 4 people €20/29, cottages €90-100; P wifi family) By the main entrance to Aulanko park, this offers good cottages and great grassy campsites on a spectacular lakeshore. There's a cafe, restaurant and sauna.

Hotelli Emilia HOTEL €€

(03-612-2106; www.hotelliemilia.fi; Raatihuoneenkatu 23; s/d €99/119; P air-con wifi) Located on the pedestrian street, this privately owned hotel is a good deal. Sizeable modern rooms, some of which can be connected for families, offer large windows, crisp white sheets and air-conditioning. There's a bar with terrace seating, a sauna, weekend nightclub and worthwhile buffet breakfast. Weekend prices (single/double €86/98) are also in place from June to August.

★ **Piparkakkutalo** FINNISH €€
(☎03-648-040; www.ravintolapiparkakkutalo.fi; Kirkkorinne 2; mains €16-28; ⏲11am-10pm Tue-Thu, 11am-11pm Fri, noon-11pm Sat) Pleasing for both eye and stomach, the 'gingerbread house' occupies a 1906 shingled house once home to artist Albert Edelfeldt; the interior still has a warm, domestic feel. Food includes Finnish classics as well as more adventurous fare, all served in generous portions. There's a cosy pub downstairs.

Information

Tourist Office (☎03-621-3373; www.hameenlinna.fi; Raatihuoneenkatu 11; ⏲9am-4pm Mon-Fri; 📶) In the Kastelli information centre.

Getting There & Away

Hämeenlinna is located on the Helsinki–Tampere motorway and rail line, so trains and express buses to both cities are frequent and fast. In summer you can cruise on a lake ferry to or from Tampere.

Rauma

☎02 / POP 39,870

The main attraction of this historic seaside settlement is its Old Town.

Sights

In the heart of modern Rauma, the Old Town remains a living centre, with cosy cafes, shops and a few artisans working in small studios; try to visit between Tuesday and Friday when everything's open and the town hums with life.

There are more than 600 18th- and 19th-century wooden buildings here, each with its own name – look for the small oval nameplate near the door. For a detailed history, pick up a free copy of *A Walking Tour in the Old Town* from the tourist office.

Sleeping & Eating

Poroholma CAMPGROUND €
(☎02-533-5522; www.poroholma.fi; Poroholmantie; campsites €10 plus per person €5, cottages €80-100; ⏲May-Aug; 👪) On beautiful Otanlahti bay, 2km northwest of Rauma, this five-star seaside holiday resort bursts at the seams with sun-browned families. Great facilities include a sauna, laundry, kitchen, on-site restaurant, and bike and canoe hire, even sailing ship cruises. Cottages are spick and span; higher-priced ones are just a few years old.

Hotelli Vanha Rauma HOTEL €€
(☎02-8376-2200; www.hotelvanharauma.fi; Vanhankirkonkatu 26; s/d €130/160; 📶) Once a warehouse in the old fish market, this is now the Old Town's only hotel. Its 20 rooms embrace modern Scandinavian design with lino flooring, leatherette chairs, flatscreen TV and views of the park or courtyard. Service is attentive, and the restaurant, SJ Nyyper, is well respected.

Café Sali CAFE, BISTRO €
(www.cafesali.fi; Kuninkaankatu 22; lunch mains €8.20-12.80, dinner mains €11-16.50; ⏲8am-10pm Jun-Aug, 9am-9pm Sep-May; 📶) Once you get over the shock of stepping from Vanha Rauma's 18th-century surroundings into a stark white space filled with giant photos of New York skyscrapers, Sali is a real buzz, with great lunch buffets (€9.50), a fine bistro menu in the adjoining lounge and a bustling terrace on the square.

★ **Wanhan Rauman Kellari** FINNISH €€
(☎02-866-6700; www.wrk.fi; Anundilankatu 8; mains €14.50-34; ⏲11am-10pm Mon, to 11pm Tue-Thu, to midnight Fri & Sat, noon-10pm Sun) A Rauma institution, this atmospheric former potato cellar and air-raid shelter has a sun-drenched rooftop summer terrace. Starters such as salmon salad or smoked reindeer and wild mushroom soup are followed by a huge choice of fresh fish, poultry and meat dishes (plus a solitary vegetarian option), and desserts such as seabuckthorn parfait or fried brie and cloudberry compote.

Information

Main Tourist Office (www.visitrauma.fi; Valtakatu 2; ⏲9am-6pm) Open year-round.
Summer Tourist Office (☎02-834-3512; www.visitrauma.fi; Kauppakatu 13; ⏲9am-6pm Jun-Aug) In Vanha Raatihuone (the Old Town Hall) on the kauppatori.

Getting There & Away

Rauma is connected by regular buses to Pori (45 minutes) and Turku (€22, 1½ hours), as well as destinations further afield.

Vaasa

☎06 / POP 66,405

The Gulf of Bothnia gets wasp-waisted around here and Sweden's a bare 45 nautical miles away, so it's no surprise that a cultural duality exists in Vaasa (Swedish: Vasa). A quarter of the population speaks Swedish and the city has a feel all of its own. You'll hear conversations between friends and colleagues in restaurants and bars flitting between Finnish and Swedish, often in the same sentence. Vaasa has a thriving art scene, with several galleries and plenty of public sculpture.

Sights

★Pohjanmaan Museo MUSEUM
(Ostrobothnian Museum; www.pohjanmaanmuseo.fi; Museokatu 3; adult/child €7/free, Fri free; noon-6pm Tue-Thu, noon-4pm Fri-Sun late May-late Aug, noon-5pm Tue, Thu & Sun, noon-8pm Wed late Aug-late May) Vaasa's dynamic, modern museum is divided into three sections. Downstairs, **Terranova** has a brilliant evocation of the region's natural history – complete with dioramas and storm-and-lightning effects – that includes information on the Kvarken Archipelago. On the ground floor, yesteryear Vaasa is brought to life in the **Pohjanmaan Museo**. Upstairs, the **Hedman collection** contains some 300 works of art, including a Tintoretto, a Botticelli Madonna, works from all the Finnish masters and a huge number of ceramics.

Wasalandia AMUSEMENT PARK
(020-796-1200; www.wasalandia.fi; Vaskiluoto; day pass €18, incl Tropiclandia €36; 11am-7pm late Jun-mid-Aug, 11am-5pm early Jun–mid-Jun, 11am-6pm mid-Jun–late Jun) Great for preteens, Wasalandia is the centrepiece of the island of Vaskiluoto, with lots of pirate-themed rides and a 'traffic park' for junior drivers. Across the road, the outdoor Tropiclandia has enough water slides, wave machines, Jacuzzis, saunas and spa treatments to keep both kids and adults happy. Packages can be arranged with the **spa hotel** here. The **Lilliputilla** (per person/family €5/15; 10.30am-5.30pm late Jun-early Aug) street train runs hourly from Vaasa's kauppatori to Vaskiluoto during summer.

Kuntsi GALLERY
(06-325-3920; http://kuntsi.vaasa.fi; Sisäsatama; adult/child €5/free; 11am-5pm Tue-Sun) The beautiful former customs house now hosts changing exhibitions of pop art, kinetic art, surrealism and postmodernism. At its core is the collection of Simo Kuntsi, who gathered almost a thousand modern Finnish works from the 1950s onwards.

> WORTH A TRIP
>
> ### KVARKEN ARCHIPELAGO
>
> Listed as a Unesco World Heritage Site in 2006, Kvarken stretches across to the Umeå region of Sweden and includes the sea and islands between the two countries. The land here is rising at an astonishing rate – around 8mm per year. During the last ice age, the weight of the ice covering Kvarken depressed the earth's crust by up to 1km. Since the ice melted, the pressure has been released and new islands are emerging – it's estimated that by the year 4500, a land bridge will join Sweden and Finland. Vaasa's Terranova is a great place to learn more; information is also available online at www.kvarkenworldheritage.fi.
>
> Kvarken's most accessible point is **Replot** (Finnish: Raippaluoto), a large island just off the Vaasa coast, linked by Finland's longest bridge.

Sleeping

Top Camping Vaasa CAMPGROUND €
(020-796-1255; www.topcamping.fi; Niemeläntie; tent sites €12 plus per person €8, 4-person cabins €70; mid-May–mid-Aug) This popular family getaway is 2km from town on Vaskiluoto. It hires bicycles (per two/six hours €3/6) and rowboats (per hour €4). Cabins require a minimum two-night stay. Ask about discount packages with nearby Wasalandia amusement park and **Tropiclandia** (020-796-1300; www.tropiclandia.fi; Sommarstigen 1, Vaskiluoto; spa & waterpark €23, incl Wasalandia €36, spa only €17; waterpark 10am-7pm Jun-early Aug, spa 8am-9pm Mon-Fri, 9am-9pm Sat, 10am-9pm Sun early Oct-late Aug;).

★Hotel Kantarellis BOUTIQUE HOTEL €€
(06-357-8100; www.hotelkantarellis.fi; Rosteninkatu 6; s/d €134/157;) Every room at this independent boutique gem has a private sauna, and most have Jacuzzis and air-con. The decor is dramatically dark, with spotlit wilderness-themed photos. Solid soundproofing means you won't hear your neighbours' giant flatscreen TV.

Hotel Astor HOTEL €€
(06-326-9111; www.astorvaasa.fi; Asemakatu 4; s €124, d €130-144;) Handy for the bus or train station, this great little hotel has a historic interior and personal feel, down to the fresh-baked cakes at breakfast. Rooms in the older wing feature polished floors and darkwood furnishings. Higher-priced doubles have their own sauna. Wi-fi can be patchy.

Eating

Sweet Vaasa CAFE €

(www.sweetvaasa.fi; Hovioikeudenpuistikko 11; mains €9-12; ⌚9am-6pm Mon-Fri, 10am-5pm Sat; 📶) Huge, healthy salads, such as a 'protein monster' (bell pepper, bacon, egg, chicken, tuna, salmon, seeds and nuts), and a daily special (anything from pesto chicken pasta to haloumi with chickpea salsa or smoked salmon cheesecake) are the mainstays of this buzzing post-industrial-style cafe; prices include gluten-free crispbread plus coffee or tea.

Strampen FINNISH €€

(☎041-451-4512; www.strampen.com; Rantakatu 6; lunch buffet €8.50-12, mains €18.50-29; ⌚11am-10pm Mon-Fri, noon-10pm Sat & Sun) Right on the water, this perennial favourite in a 19th-century pavilion serves top-end meals inside and affordable burgers et al on its terrace. In summer staff keep the outdoor bar pumping until late.

★**Gustav Wasa** MODERN FINNISH €€€

(☎050-466-3208; www.gustavwasa.com; Raastuvankatu 24; mains €18-36, 7-course tasting menu €69, with wine pairings €50; ⌚gastropub 5-10pm Mon-Fri, 3-10pm Sat, fine dining 6-10pm Mon-Fri, 4-10pm Sat) A former coal cellar is home to one of Finland's best restaurants, newly split into a casual gastropub with by-the-glass wines and on-tap Finnish beers, and an intimate candlelit fine-dining space serving sublime seven-course tasting menus. Cooking courses are available; you can also order food for its adjacent sauna (sauna €250 plus per person €6; sauna buffets €25 to €36).

Information

Tourist Office (☎06-325-1145; www.visitvaasa.fi; Raastuvankatu 30; ⌚9am-5pm daily Jul, 9am-5pm Mon-Fri Jun & Aug, 10am-4pm Mon-Fri Sep-May) Books accommodation and has bikes for hire (per day €10).

Getting There & Away

From the combined bus and train station, there are frequent buses up and down the coast, and trains connecting via Seinäjoki to Tampere (€40.80, 2½ hours) and Helsinki (€61.10, four to five hours) among other destinations.

Finnair/Flybe flies daily to Helsinki and Stockholm.

There's a ferry service from Vaasa to Umeå in Sweden with Wasaline.

Jakobstad

☎06 / POP 19,670

Stretching for several blocks north of the new town, Jakobstad's mainly residential Old Town, Skata, has around 300 of the best-preserved wooden houses in Finland.

Over half the population are Swedophone in Jakobstad (Finnish: Pietarsaari), one of the most distinctive and enchanting spots on this part of the Finnish west coast known as *parallelsverige* (parallel Sweden).

Sights

Most of the houses in Skata were originally occupied by sailors. While the 18th-century houses along Hamngatan are the oldest, the prettiest street is Norrmalmsgatan, with a stunning clock tower bridging the street.

The Gamla Hamn (Old Harbour) has a child-friendly swimming beach.

Sleeping & Eating

Jakobstad has a couple of lovely daytime cafes, but a dearth of decent evening options.

Hostel Lilja HOSTEL €

(☎06-781-6500; www.aftereight.fi; Storgatan 6; s/d/tr/ste €45/55/65/75; 📶) Eight restored rooms range over two storeys of a 19th-century barn at this friendly hostel. Most share bathrooms but the 'honeymoon suite' has a small en suite. Extras include laundry facilities, bike hire (per day €5) and a sauna. Breakfast is €6.50.

Westerlunds Inn GUESTHOUSE €

(☎06-723-0440; www.multi.fi/westerlund; Normalmsgatan 8; s/d/tr with shared bathroom €30/50/60) You'll forgive this charming inn's minuscule rooms (and shared bathrooms) given its peaceful location in Jakobstad's Skata (Old Town). The rooms still manage to cram in a tiny table and washbasin and there is, of course, a sauna. Breakfast is €6.

Hotel Epoque HOTEL €€

(☎06-788-7100; www.hotelepoque.fi; Jakobsgatan 10; s/d €116/136; ⌚reception 7am-10pm Mon-Fri, 8am-10pm Sat, 8am-4pm Sun; @📶) This restored customs house is the best place in town – service is great (although reception hours are limited), and with just 16 rooms, it feels quiet, private and exclusive.

After Eight CAFE €
(www.aftereight.fi; Storgatan 6; lunch €9.20; ⏲10am-7pm Mon-Fri) This smashing cafe and cultural centre is the best hang-out in town, with a relaxed atmosphere, well-spaced tables, chilled-out music and a grassy courtyard garden. Lunch (served from 10am to 1pm – don't be late!) offers simple but tasty dishes such as salmon soup, roast beef stew, Swedish meatballs and vegetable gratin. Homemade cakes are available throughout the day.

Information

Tourist Office (☎06-723-1796; www.jakobstad.fi; Salutorget 1; ⏲8am-6pm Mon-Fri, 9am-3pm Sat Jun-Aug, 8am-4pm Mon-Fri Sep-May) Next to the town square.

Getting There & Away

There are regular buses to Jakobstad from Vaasa (€22, 1¾ hours), Kokkola (€8.20, 45 minutes) and other west coast towns.

Bennäs (Finnish: Pännäinen), 11km away, is the closest railway station. A shuttle bus (€3.90, 15 minutes) meets arriving trains.

LAKELAND & KARELIA

Most of southern Finland could be dubbed 'lakeland', but this spectacular area takes it to extremes. It often seems there's more water than land here, and what water it is: sublime, sparkling and clean, reflecting sky and forests as cleanly as a mirror. It's a land that leaves an indelible impression on every visitor.

The greater Lakeland area encompasses Karelia, once the symbol of Finnish distinctiveness and the totem of the independence movement. Most of Karelia today lies over the other side of the Russian border; much of the gruelling attrition of the Winter and Continuation Wars against the Soviet Union took place in this area, and large swaths of territory were lost in ceasefire and reparation agreements.

Lappeenranta

☎05 / POP 72,680

The South Karelian capital of Lappeenranta was a frontier garrison town until the construction of the Saimaa Canal in 1856 made it an important trading centre. These days the canal is a major attraction for tourists, with boats cruising through Russia to the Baltic at Vyborg, Finland's second-largest city until it was lost to its large neighbour. Finland's largest lake, Saimaa, spreads out from Lappeenranta's harbour, and the town itself is vibrant, with plenty of historical links in its old fortress; it's a good place to sample Karelian food and culture.

Sights

Linnoitus FORTRESS, MUSEUM
(www.lappeenranta.fi/linnoitus; fortress free, adult/child combined museum ticket €9/free; ⏲10am-6pm Mon-Fri, 11am-5pm Sat & Sun Jun-late Aug, 11am-5pm Tue-Sun late Aug-May) Standing guard above the harbour, this hulking hilltop fortification was begun by the Swedes and finished by the Russians in the late 18th century. Today it contains galleries, craft workshops and fascinating museums, including the history-focused **South Karelian Museum** (Etelä-Karjalan Museo; adult/child €6.50/free), **Cavalry Museum** (Ratsuväkimuseo; adult/child €3/free; ⏲10am-6pm Mon-Fri, 11am-5pm Sat & Sun) and **South Karelia Art Museum** (Etelä-Karjalan Taidemuseo; adult/child €6.50/free). Its **Orthodox Church** (⏲10am-5pm Tue-Sun Jun–mid-Aug), Finland's oldest church, was completed in 1785 by Russian soldiers. Pick up the tourist office's free walking guide *The Fortress of Lappeenranta*.

Hiekkalinna SANDCASTLE
(http://hiekkalinna.lappeenranta.fi; ⏲10am-8pm early Jun-Aug) FREE Every summer around 30 sand artists from Finland and abroad gather to build the Hiekkalinna, a giant themed 'sandcastle' made from some three million kilograms of sand. Previous themes have included dinosaurs, a Wild West scene incorporating a gigantic steam train, and 'outer space' featuring ET and Darth Vader. Kids' entertainment here includes small carousel-style rides.

Tours

Saimaan Risteilyt CRUISE
(☎020-787-0620; www.saimaanristeilyt.fi; adult/child €16/2; ⏲departs 11am, 3pm & 6pm late May-Oct) Offers popular two-hour trips on Lake Saimaa and the Saimaa Canal aboard the M/S *El Faro*.

Saimaan Matkaverkko CRUISE
(☎05-541-0100; www.saimaatravel.fi; Kipparinkatu 1; ⏲9am-5pm Mon-Fri) Day cruises (Thursday and Saturday, June to August; from €59)

cross Lake Saimaa to Savonlinna aboard M/S *Brahe* (returning by bus). Also runs 'visa-free' trips along the canal to Vyborg and St Petersburg in Russia.

Sleeping

Contact the Lappeenranta tourist office for details of some of the many appealing farmhouse stays available in the area.

Huhtiniemi Tourist Resort HOSTEL, CAMPGROUND €
(☎05-451-5555; www.huhtiniemi.com; Kuusimäenkatu 18; tent sites €14 plus per person €5, 2-/4-person cottages €40/50, apt €80-98; ⏰mid-May–Sep; 📶) Situated 2km east of the city centre, this large lakeside campground has waterside sites, neat cottages and self-contained apartments that fill to the gills in summer – reservations are a must. Also here are two HI hostels, the simple **Huhtiniemi Hostel** (☎05-451-5555; www.huhtiniemi.com; dm €15; ⏰Jun-Aug) and hotel-style **Finnhostel Lappeenranta** (☎05-451-5555; www.huhtiniemi.com; s/d/tr €75/95/115). Bus 5 from the city stops here, as do most intercity buses.

★**Lappeenrannan Kylpylä** SPA HOTEL €€
(☎020-761-3761; www.kylpyla.info; Ainonkatu 17; s €80-110, d €120-160; ❄@📶🏊) Bronze- and gold-toned, minibar-equipped rooms – some opening to balconies overlooking the park and water – range over the revamped 1970s spa hotel housing reception and the upper floors of the lakefront art nouveau Wanha Kylpylä (Old Spa) building across the street. Facilities include a gym, a couple of pools and a waterfall that delivers a pounding shoulder massage.

Eating & Drinking

Stalls at the harbour, kauppatori and kauppahalli sell local Karelian specialities such as *vety* (bread roll or pie with ham, sliced boiled egg, mince and spices), the similar *atomi* (either smoked ham or egg), rice pies, or waffles with jam and whipped cream.

In town, Kauppakatu has a lively strip of bars.

Kahvila Majurska CAFE €
(www.majurska.com; Kristiinankatu 1; dishes €3-5; ⏰10am-5pm Mon-Sat, 11am-5pm Sun) If you can't border-hop to a genuine Russian teahouse, this is as close as you'll get in Finland. A former officer's club (check out the vintage furniture and august portrait of Mannerheim), it still serves tea from the samovar and does a range of homemade pastries.

Wanha Makasiini BISTRO €€
(☎010-666-8611; www.ravintolawanhamakasiini.fi; Satamatie 4; pizzas €13-15, mains €19-31.50; ⏰noon-10pm Mon, noon-11.30pm Tue-Sat, noon-6pm Sun; 🖉) High-quality dishes at this cosy spot range from fresh fish to horse steaks and seasonal delicacies such as chanterelle soup. Thin, crispy pizzas come with traditional toppings as well as local specialities like smoked *muikku* (vendace, or whitefish, a small lake fish) and pickled cucumber.

★**Wolkoff Restaurant & Wine Bar** FINNISH €€€
(☎05-415-0320; www.wolkoff.fi; Kauppakatu 26; lunch buffet €15, mains €21-30, 3-course menu €46; ⏰11am-11pm Mon-Fri, 4.30-11pm Sat) This grand old-world restaurant utilises organic produce and seasonal ingredients to create gourmet Finnish cuisine with adventurous flavour combinations such as reindeer tartare with Dijon mustard ice cream, and duck breast with plum, sweet potato and dark wheatbeer sauce. The laden lunch buffet is a veritable bargain.

Boat Bars BAR
In summer the best place for a drink is down at the harbour where boats welcome you to their busy beer terraces.

Information

Main Tourist Office (☎05-667-788; www.visitlappeenranta.fi; Valtakatu 37; ⏰10am-5pm Mon-Fri, 10am-2pm Sat) Has an accommodation booking service for €3.50.

Summer Tourist Office (☎040-352-2178; www.visitlappeenranta.fi; ⏰10am-8pm late Jun-early Aug, 10am-6pm early Aug-late Aug) Located at the sandcastle Hiekkalinna.

Getting There & Away

From Lappeenranta's airport, Ryanair serves Bergamo, Girona and Weeze. Take bus 4 to the airport (€3.30), a 20-minute walk from the centre.

The bus and train stations are together about 500m south of the centre along Ratakatu, though most buses stop in the centre too. Trains are significantly speedier than buses to Helsinki (€47.20, two hours) and Joensuu (€41.20, two hours). For Savonlinna, change trains at Parikkala. For Kuopio change at Mikkeli.

Savonlinna

015 / POP 27,420

Finland's prettiest town, Savonlinna shimmers on a sunny day as the water ripples around its centre. Set on two islands between Haapavesi and Pihlajavesi lakes, it's a classic Lakeland settlement with a major attraction: perched on a rocky islet, one of Europe's most visually dramatic castles lords it over the picturesque centre and hosts the world-famous opera festival in a spectacular setting.

Sights & Activities

From June to August, Savonlinna **passenger harbour** is buzzing with dozens of daily scenic cruises that last an hour to 90 minutes and cost around €12 to €20. Boats anchor alongside the kauppatori and you can soon see which is the next departure. There are also many boats available for charter.

★Olavinlinna CASTLE

(www.olavinlinna.fi; adult/child €8/4; 11am-6pm Jun–mid-Aug, 10am-4pm Mon-Fri, 11am-4pm Sat & Sun mid-Aug–mid-Dec & Jan-May) Standing immense and haughty, 15th-century Olavinlinna is one of the most spectacularly situated castles in northern Europe and, as well as being an imposing fortification, is also the stunning venue for the month-long Savonlinna Opera Festival. The castle's been heavily restored, but is still seriously impressive, not least in the way it's built directly on a rock in the middle of the lake. To visit the upper part of the interior, including the towers and chapel, you must join a guided tour (around 45 minutes).

Tours are multilingual depending on demand and depart on the hour. Guides are good at bringing the castle to life and furnish you with some interesting stories: the soldiers, for instance, were partly paid in beer – 5L a day and 7L on Sundays, which

Savonlinna

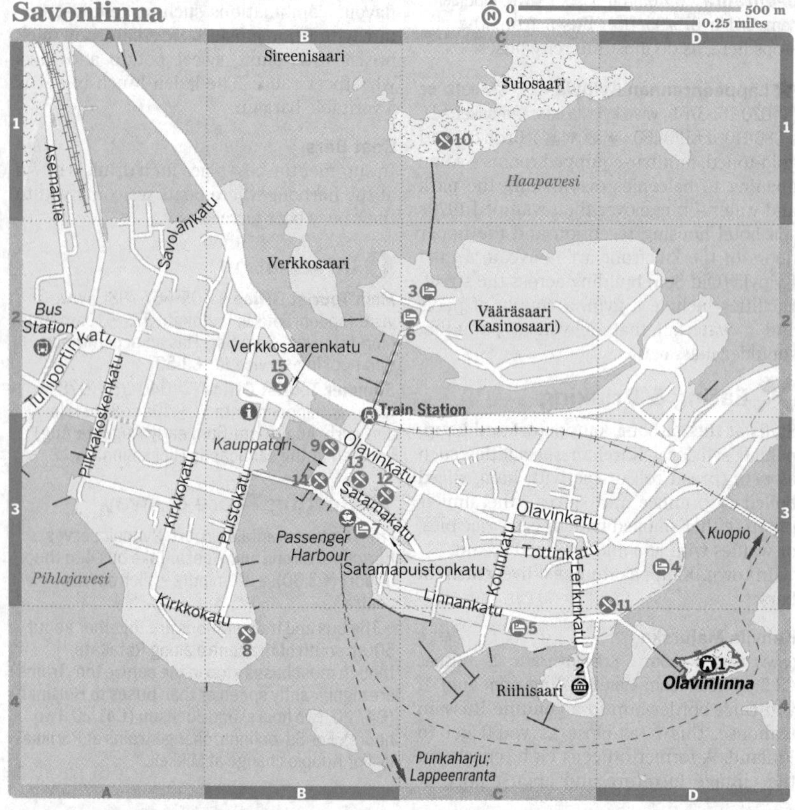

makes the castle's frequent changes of hands more understandable.

Savonlinna Maakuntamuseo MUSEUM
(www.savonlinna.fi/museo; Riihisaari; adult/child €5/3, incl Olavinlinna €9/4; 10am-5pm daily, closed Mon Sep-May) The town's provincial museum, in an old Russian warehouse near Olavinlinna Castle, tells of local history and the importance of water transport. There are old photographs, models and a changing art exhibition. Here also is **Nestori**, a national parks information centre, and a selection of **museum ships**, open from mid-May to mid-September during the same hours as the museum (included in ticket or €3 alone).

Festivals

★ Savonlinna Opera Festival OPERA
(015-476-750; www.operafestival.fi; Olavinkatu 27) Savonlinna Opera Festival is Finland's most famous festival, with an enviably dramatic setting: the covered courtyard of Olavinlinna Castle. It offers four weeks of top-class opera performances from early July to early August. The atmosphere in town during the festival is reason enough to come; it's buzzing, with restaurants serving post-show midnight feasts, and animated discussions and impromptu arias on all sides.

Savonlinna

Top Sights
1 Olavinlinna D4

Sights
2 Savonlinna Maakuntamuseo C4

Sleeping
3 Kesähotelli Vuorilinna C2
4 Lossiranta Lodge D3
5 Perhehotelli Hospitz C4
6 Spa Hotel Casino C2
7 SS Heinävesi B3

Eating
8 Huvila B4
9 Kalastajan Koju B3
10 Kalliolinna C1
11 Linnakrouvi D3
12 Majakka B3
13 Muikkubaari B3
14 Sirkan Torikahvio B3

Drinking & Nightlife
15 Olutravintola Sillansuu B2

Sleeping

Prices rise sharply during the opera festival, when several student residences are converted to summer hotels. Book July accommodation well in advance.

Kesähotelli Vuorilinna SUMMER HOTEL €
(015-73950; www.spahotelcasino.fi; Kylpylaitoksentie; dm/hostel/s/d €30/40/70/90; Jun-Aug; P) Set in several buildings used by students during term time, this is run by the Spahotel Casino and has an appealing location across a beautiful footbridge from the town centre. Rooms are clean and comfortable; the cheaper ones share bathroom and kitchen (no utensils) between two. Happily, dorm rates get you the same deal, and there's a HI discount.

SS Heinävesi BOAT €
(0500-653-774; www.savonlinnanlaivat.fi; d upper/lower deck €75/65; Jun-late Aug) After 5pm during high summer, this steamer offers cramped but cute two-bunk cabins. There's a good chance of getting a bed here, even during the opera festival, and it's moored right in the centre of things.

Vuohimäki CAMPGROUND €
(015-537-353; www.suncamping.fi; tent sites €15 plus per person €5.50, 4-person r €75-80, cabins €65-90; early Jun-late Aug; P @) Located 7km southwest of town, this campground has good facilities but fills quickly during July. You can hire canoes, bikes and rowing boats. Rooms and cabins are cheaper in June and August.

Perhehotelli Hospitz HOTEL €€
(015-515-661; www.hospitz.com; Linnankatu 20; s/d €88/98; Apr-Dec; P) This cosy Savonlinna classic was built in the 1930s and maintains that period's elegance. The rooms are stylish, although beds are narrow and bathrooms small; larger family rooms are available. Balconies cost a little extra. There's a pleasant terrace and orchard garden with access to a small beach. Opera atmosphere is great with a midnight buffet, but rates rise (single/double €130/155): book eons in advance.

Spa Hotel Casino HOTEL €€
(015-73950; www.spahotelcasino.fi; Vääräsaari (Kasinosaari); s/d €99/114, superior d €154; P @) Charmingly situated on an island across a footbridge from the kauppatori, this is old-fashioned in parts but

a good option. Nearly all rooms have a balcony; those that don't have their own sauna. Some have dreamy outlooks west over water. Try for a recently renovated room. Guests have access to the spa facilities; nonguests can use them for €10 in the afternoons.

★ **Lossiranta Lodge** BOUTIQUE GUESTHOUSE €€€
(☎044-511-2323; www.lossiranta.net; Aino Acktén Puistotie; d €160-200; P 📶) To get up close and personal with Olavinlinna Castle, this lakeside spot is the place to be: the impressive castle looms just opposite. Offering five snug little nests in an outbuilding, this is one of Finland's most charming hotels. All are very different but decorated with love and style; they come with a small kitchen (yes, that's it in the cupboard) and numerous personal touches.

Eating & Drinking

The lakeside **kauppatori** is the place for casual snacking. A traditional *lörtsy* (turnover) comes savoury with meat *(lihalörtsy)* or sweet with apple *(omenalörtsy)* or cloudberry *(lakkalörtsy)*. Savonlinna is also famous for fried *muikku* (vendace); try these in summer at **Kalastajan Koju** (www.kalastajankoju.com; Kauppatori; ⏲10.30am-9pm Mon-Thu, 10.30am-10pm Fri-Sat, 11am-6pm Sun Jun-Aug) on the kauppatori, or the **Muikkubaari** (www.sokoshotels.fi; Top fl, Sokos Hotel Seurahuone, Kauppatori 4-6; vendace €8-11; ⏲noon-10pm Mon-Thu, noon-midnight Fri-Sat, noon-8pm Sun May-Aug) on the top floor of the Seurahuone hotel. Restaurants open later during the Opera Festival.

Kalliolinna CAFE €
(http://kalliolinna.blogspot.com; Sulosaari; pancakes €3.50-5; ⏲10am-7pm late May–mid-Aug) Savonlinna's nicest cafe is this lovely spot, tucked away on a wooden island north of the town centre. It's a very pleasant stroll over bridges to get there; when you do, relax with a book and a cup of coffee or try the tasty choose-your-own-filling pancakes.

Sirkan Torikahvio CAFE €
(www.torikahvio.fi; Kauppatori; snacks €3-6; ⏲9am-7pm summer, 9am-3pm rest of year) Run by a stout grandmotherly figure, this is a worthwhile option on the square to try the local pastry speciality, *lörtsy,* available here with all sorts of fillings. Delicious!

★ **Huvila** FINNISH €€
(☎015-555-0555; www.panimoravintolahuvila.fi; Puistokatu 4; mains €20-28; ⏲4-11pm Mon-Fri, 2-11pm Sat Jun & Aug, noon-midnight Mon-Sat, noon-10pm Sun Jul; 📶) This noble wooden building was formerly a fever hospital then asylum, but writes happier stories now as an excellent microbrewery and restaurant across the harbour from the town centre. Food focuses on fresh local ingredients with some unusual meats sometimes featuring, all expertly prepared and served. Homebrewed beers are exquisite and the terrace is a wonderful place on a sunny afternoon, with occasional live music.

DON'T MISS

THE SEAL LAKES

Linnansaari (www.outdoors.fi) and **Kolovesi**, two primarily water-based national parks in the Savonlinna area, offer fabulous lakescapes dotted with islands; all best explored by hiring a canoe or rowing boat. Several outfitters offer these services, and free camping spots dot the lakes' shores. This is perhaps the best part of the Lakeland to really get up close and personal with the region's extraordinary natural beauty. It makes a good winter destination too, with laketop skating tracks, snowshoe walks and ice-fishing.

This is the habitat of the Saimaa ringed seal, an endangered freshwater species whose population levels have stabilised and are on the increase, although there remain only a precarious 300-odd of the noble greyish beasts. Late May is the best time to glimpse them.

A convenient place for information on these parks is the Nestori centre in the Savonlinna museum. **Saimaaholiday** (☎Oravi 015-647-290, Porosalmi 020-729-1760; www.saimaaholiday.net) can set you up with anything you need for Linnansaari, from maps and canoe/equipment hire to hostel and hotel accommodation at the two main embarkation points for park exploration, Oravi and Rantasalmi. For the Kolovesi park, **Kolovesi Retkeily** (☎040-558-9163; www.sealtrail.com) is the best and most experienced operator.

Majakka FINNISH €€
(☎015-206-2825; www.kattaasavon.fi; Satamakatu 11; mains €16-27; ⏰11am-11pm Mon-Thu, 11am-midnight Fri & Sat, noon-9pm or 10pm Sun; 📶👪) This restaurant has a deck-like terrace, fitting the nautical theme (the name means 'lighthouse'). Local meat and fish specialities are tasty, generously sized and fairly priced, and the select-your-own appetiser plate is a nice touch. It's child-friendly too.

Linnakrouvi FINNISH €€
(☎015-576-9124; www.linnakrouvi.fi; Linnankatu 7; mains €17-32; ⏰noon-10pm or later Mon-Sat, 3-10pm or later Sun late Jun–mid-Aug) Closest to Olavinlinna Castle, this is the best of the summertime food options that cater to the pre- and post-opera crowd. This offers tiered outdoor seating, an attractive interior and a range of fare, running from upmarket, tasty sandwiches and burgers to more elaborate fish and meat dishes with a gourmet flourish.

Olutravintola Sillansuu PUB
(Verkkosaarenkatu 1; ⏰2pm-2am Tue-Sat, 2pm-midnight Sun & Mon) Savonlinna's best pub is compact and cosy, offering an excellent variety of international bottled beers, a decent whisky selection and friendly service. There's a downstairs area with a pool table; during the opera festival amateur (and sometimes professional) arias are sung as the beer kegs empty.

Information

Savonlinna Travel (☎0600-30007; www.savonlinna.travel; Puistokatu 1; ⏰9am-4pm Mon-Fri Aug-Jun, 10am-6pm Mon-Sat, 10am-2pm Sun Jul) Tourist information including accommodation reservations, cottage booking, farmstays, opera festival tickets and tours. The Sokos Hotel Seurahuone can help with tourist information when this is closed.

Getting There & Away

AIR

Finnair/FlyBe fly daily between Helsinki and Savonlinna in summer (except late June and early August), weekdays in winter.

BOAT

M/S Puijo (☎015-250-250; www.mspuijo.fi; ⏰late Jun-early Aug) A standout lake trip, century-old M/S *Puijo* travels from Savonlinna to Kuopio on Monday, Wednesday and Friday at 9am (one way €90, 10½ hours), returning on Tuesday, Thursday and Saturday. The boat passes through scenic waterways, canals and locks, stopping en route at Oravi among others. You can book a return with overnight cabin accommodation for €175 or get a same-day bus back (€130 return).

M/S Brahe (☎05-541-0100; www.saimaatravel.fi) Heads to/from Lappeenranta (€69, 8½ hours) roughly twice weekly from early June to mid-August; the fare includes return bus transfer to Savonlinna. The *Brahe* also sails from Helsinki to Lappeenranta, so you could combine all these routes into a Helsinki–Kotka–Lappeenranta–Savonlinna–Kuopio extravaganza.

BUS

Savonlinna is not on major bus routes, but there are several express buses a day from Helsinki (€49.90, five to 5½ hours), and buses run regularly from Mikkeli (€24, 1½ hours). There are also direct services to Joensuu (€26.30, 2¾ hours) and Jyväskylä (€43.90, 3½ hours).

TRAIN

Trains from Helsinki (€65.70, 4¼ hours) and Joensuu (€34, 2¼ hours) both require a change in Parikkala. The station is right in the centre of things, near the kauppatori.

A COTTAGE BY A LAKE

The Lakeland is a particularly enticing place to search out a waterside cottage retreat or cosy rural farmstay for a true Finnish holiday. Around 100,000 rental cabins and cottages are dotted around the myriad lakes.

A good first point of investigation is the nationwide operators – Lomarengas (p203) has heaps of options and also links to farmstays and rural B&Bs. A local operator with a decent portfolio is **Saimaa Tours** (www.saimaatours.fi). Savonlinna's travel website, www.savonlinna.travel, and Mikkeli's, www.visitmikkeli.fi, both link to farmstay and cottage-rental providers.

Around Savonlinna

Punkaharju

Situated between Savonlinna and Parikkala, Punkaharju is a renowned sand ridge covered with pines; the surrounding forest and lakes are beautiful and it is a great area for cycling or walking.

Lusto (www.lusto.fi; adult/child €10/5; ⏰10am-5pm Tue-Sun Oct-Apr, 10am-5pm May & Sep, 10am-7pm Jun-Aug) museum is dedicated to forests and forestry and is a good visit, with plenty of English information. There's also tourist information here.

Trains between Savonlinna and Parikkala stop at Retretti, Lusto and Punkaharju train stations (35 minutes, five to six daily). You can also get here on less regular buses from Savonlinna.

Kerimäki

Unexpectedly, the world's largest wooden **church** (Kerimäki Church; www.kerimaenseurakunta.fi; admission free; ⏲10am-6pm Jun & early Aug, to 7pm Jul, to 4pm late Aug) FREE can be found here, about 23km east of Savonlinna. It was built in 1847 to seat a (very optimistic) congregation of 5000 people. Regular buses run here from Savonlinna.

Jyväskylä

☎014 / POP 134,800

Vivacious and young-at-heart, western Lakeland's main town has a wonderful waterside location and an optimistic feel. Jyväskylä (*yoo*-vah-skoo-lah), thanks to the work of Alvar Aalto, is of global architectural interest, and petrolheads know it as a legendary World Rally Championships venue. The big student population and lively arts scenes give the town plenty of energy and nightlife.

Sights & Activities

It's a nice walk or cycle around the lake of about 12km, which you can cut in half using the road bridge. There are numerous boating options – check visit.jyvaskyla.fi for more choices, or wander along the pleasant harbour area, where there's everything: boat-bars, jet-ski hire, houseboats (www.houseboat.fi) and floating saunas for rent.

Alvar Aalto Museo MUSEUM

(www.alvaraalto.fi; Alvar Aallonkatu 7; adult/child €6/free; ⏲11am-6pm Tue-Sun) Alvar Aalto, a giant of 20th-century architecture, was schooled in Jyväskylä, opened his first offices here and spent his summers in nearby Muuratsalo. The city has dozens of Aalto buildings, but stop first at one of his last creations, this museum in the university area. It chronicles his life and work, with detailed focus on his major buildings, as well as sections on his furniture design and glassware. It's very engaging; you get a real feel for the man and his philosophy.

Päijänne Risteilyt Hilden CRUISE

(☎014-263-447; www.paijanne-risteilythilden.fi; ⏲early Jun–mid-Aug) The main cruise operator runs several vessels, including the *Suomi*, one of the oldest steamers plying the Finnish lakes. Short cruises depart daily from the passenger harbour (some are lunch or dinner cruises) and cost €18 to €24, half-price for kids. Longer trips include trips northwards to the Keitele canal or south to Lahti.

Sleeping

Kesähotelli Harju SUMMER HOTEL €

(☎010-279-2004; www.hotelharju.fi; Sepänkatu 3; s/d/tr incl breakfast €60/70/87; ⏲early Jun-early Aug; P@☏) Five minutes uphill from the city centre, this summer hotel has modern, light, spacious student rooms each with a kitchenette (no utensils) and good bathrooms. It's good value.

★ **Hotel Yöpuu** BOUTIQUE HOTEL €€

(☎014-333-900; www.hotelliyopuu.fi; Yliopistonkatu 23; s/d/ste €108/135/195; P❄@☏) Among Finland's most enchanting boutique hotels, this exquisite spot has lavishly decorated rooms, individually designed in markedly different styles. Service is warm and welcoming with an assured personal touch – including a welcome drink – that makes for a delightful stay. Renovating and improving is always going on here so standards are kept high. Suites offer excellent value.

Hotelli Milton HOTEL €€

(☎014-337-7900; www.hotellimilton.com; Hannikaisenkatu 29; s/d €85/120; P@☏) Right in the thick of things, this family-run hotel has an old-fashioned dark foyer, but the modern rooms offer plenty of natural light, space and attractive wooden floors; most have a balcony. An evening sauna on weekdays is included and it's very handy for the bus and train stations. Weekend prices are great (s/d €65/85).

Eating & Drinking

Soppabaari SOUP BAR €

(www.soppabaari.fi; Asemakatu 11B; soup, pasta €8.80; ⏲11am-8pm Mon-Thu, 11am-10pm Fri & Sat) This friendly licensed soup bar makes a great stop at any time but especially in colder weather. It does three daily soups and pasta specials, pretty much guaranteed to be delicious. There are also salads and tapas-sized portions of Finnish treats like meatballs.

★Figaro FINNISH €€

(☎020-766-9810; www.figaro-restaurant.com; Asemakatu 4; mains €24-29; ⊙11am-3pm Mon, 11am-11pm Tue-Fri, noon-11pm Sat; 👪) With a warm drawing-room feel and cordial service, this backs up the atmosphere with excellent food served in generous portions. The fish is especially good, served with creamy sauces and inventive garnishes. Sizeable steaks are a given, and reindeer and bear make occasional appearances. There are good vegetarian mains too, and it's youngster-friendly.

★Sohwi PUB

(www.sohwi.fi; Vaasankatu 21; ⊙2pm-midnight Tue-Thu, 2pm-2am Fri, noon-2am Sat, 2-10pm Sun-Mon; 📶) A short walk from the city centre is this excellent bar with a spacious wooden terrace, a good menu of snacks and soak-it-all-up bar meals with decent veggie options, and plenty of lively student and academic discussion lubricated by a range of good bottled and draught beers. A great place.

Information

Tourist Office (☎014-266-0113; visit.jyvaskyla.fi; Asemakatu 6; ⊙9am-4pm Mon-Fri, also 10am-2pm Sat Jul) Information and ticket sales.

Getting There & Away

AIR

Finnair operates flights Sunday to Friday (except July) from Helsinki to Jyväskylä. The airport is 23km north of the centre; a few buses between Jyväskylä and other towns stop in here (€6 to €10: check www.matkahuolto.fi for times). A taxi is around €40.

BUS & TRAIN

The bus and train stations share the Matkakeskus building. Daily express buses connect Jyväskylä to southern Finnish towns, including hourly departures to Helsinki (€50.20, four to five hours). Some services require a change.

There are regular trains from Helsinki (€56.10, four hours) via Tampere, and some quicker direct trains.

Kuopio

☎017 / POP 106,450

Most things a reasonable person could desire from a summery lakeside town are in Kuopio, with pleasure cruises on the azure water, spruce forests to stroll in, wooden waterside pubs and local fish specialities to taste. And what better than a traditional smoke sauna to give necessary impetus to jump into the chilly waters?

Sights

Puijo HILL

Even small hills have cachet in flat Finland, and Kuopio was so proud of Puijo that it was crowned with a tower. Views from the top of **Puijon Torni** (Puijo Tower; www.puijo.com; adult/child €6/3; ⊙10am-9pm Mon-Sat, 10am-7pm Sun Jun-Aug, 11am-7pm Mon-Thu, 11am-9pm Fri-Sat, 11am-4pm Sun Sep-May) are very impressive; the vast perspectives of lakes and forests represent a sort of idealised Finnish vista. Atop is a revolving restaurant, cafe and open-air viewing deck. Surrounding it is one of the region's best-preserved spruce forests, with trails for walking, biking and cross-country skiing.

Also here is a ski jump and chairlift. In high summer there's a public bus to Puijo, but it's a nice walk through the trees, or a short drive or cab ride.

Kuopion Museo MUSEUM

(www.kuopionmuseo.fi; Kauppakatu 23; adult/child €7.50/free; ⊙10am-5pm Tue-Sat) In a castle-like art nouveau mansion, this museum has a wide scope. The top two floors are devoted to cultural history, but the real highlight is the natural history display, with a wide variety of beautifully presented Finnish wildlife, including a mammoth and an ostrich wearing snowboots. The ground floor has temporary exhibitions. Pick up English explanations at the ticket desk.

Kuopion Korttelimuseo MUSEUM

(Old Kuopio Museum; www.korttelimuseo.kuopio.fi; Kirkkokatu 22; adult/child €5.50/free; ⊙10am-5pm Tue-Sat mid-May–Aug, 10am-3pm Sep–mid-May) This block of old town houses forms one of Kuopio's delightful museums. Several homes – all with period furniture and decor – are very detailed and thorough and the level of information (in English) is excellent. **Apteekkimuseo** in building 11 contains old pharmacy paraphernalia, while in another building it's fascinating to compare photos of Kuopio from different decades. There's also a cafe serving a delicious *rahkapiirakka* (a local sweet pastry).

Activities

The **Rauhalahti** (www.rauhalahti.com; Katiskaniementie 8) estate is full of summer and winter activities for families.

★ Jätkänkämppä SAUNA

(☎030-60830; www.rauhalahti.fi; adult/child €12/6; ⊙4-10pm Tue, also Thu Jun-Aug & Nov-Dec, 4-11pm Jun-Aug) This giant *savusauna* (smoke sauna) is a memorable, sociable experience that draws locals and visitors. It seats 60 and is mixed: you're given towels to wear. Bring a swimsuit for lake dipping – devoted locals and brave tourists do so even when it's covered with ice. Repeat the process several times. Then buy a beer and relax, looking over the lake in Nordic peace.

The **restaurant** (adult/child buffet plus hot plate €21/10.50; ⊙4-8pm) in the adjacent loggers' cabin serves traditional Finnish dinners when the sauna's on, with accordion entertainment and a lumberjack show. Buses 7 and 9 head to Rauhalahti hotel, from where it's a 600m walk, or take a summertime cruise from the harbour.

Tours

Koski-Laiva Oy CRUISE

(☎0400-207-245; www.koskilaiva.com; adult/child €15/8; ⊙mid-May–late Aug) Offers 90-minute scenic cruises, lunch trips and trips to Rauhalahti, a nice way of reaching the smoke sauna there.

Roll Cruises CRUISE

(Kuopion Roll Risteilyt; ☎017-277-2466; www.roll.fi; adult/child €15/8; ⊙mid-May–late Aug) Runs regular 90-minute scenic cruises from Kuopio's harbour, as well as trips to a local berry wine farm.

Festivals & Events

Kuopion Tanssii ja Soi DANCE

(www.kuopiodancefestival.fi) In mid-June this is the most interesting of Kuopio's annual events. There are open-air classical and modern dance performances, comedy and theatre gigs, and the town is buzzing.

Sleeping

Matkailukeskus Rauhalahti CAMPGROUND €

(☎017-473-000; www.visitrauhalahti.fi; Rauhankatu 3; tent sites €15-16 plus per person €6, cabins €33-60, cottages €120; ⊙mid-May–late Aug; P) Near the Rauhalahti hotel complex, this place has a great location, plenty of facilities and is well set up for families. Bus 20 will get you here. The upmarket cottages are open year-round.

Hostelli Hermanni HOSTEL €

(☎040-910-9083; www.hostellihermanni.fi; Hermanninaukio 3D; dm/s/d €35/55/65; P@) Tucked away in a quiet area 1.5km south of the kauppatori (follow Haapaniemenkatu and bear left when you can: the hostel's in the Metsähallitus building), this is a decent hostel with comfy wooden bunks and beds, bright bedspreads, high ceilings and reasonable shared bathrooms and kitchen. Bus 3 from the town centre makes occasional appearances nearby. No breakfast.

Hotel Atlas HOTEL €€

(☎020-789-6101; www.hotelatlas.fi; Haapaniemenkatu 22; s/d €130/150; P@) An historic Kuopio hotel that reopened in 2012 after complete remodelling, the Atlas is now the town's most appealing option, not least for its prime location on the kauppatori. The commodious modern rooms are of good size, with a sofa, are well soundproofed and offer perspectives over the square, or, more unusually, the interior of a department store.

Hotelli Jahtihovi HOTEL €€

(☎017-264-4400; www.jahtihovi.fi; Snellmaninkatu 23; s/d €94/114; P@) Well located near the harbour on a quiet street, this cordial independent hotel makes a good address. Regular rooms are good-sized and pleasant (twins are a fair bit larger than doubles); the superiors (s/d €104/124), in a modern wing, add big windows, extra mod-cons and

SHE AIN'T HEAVY, SHE'S MY WIFE

What began as a heathenish medieval habit of pillaging neighbouring villages in search of nubile women has become one of Finland's oddest – and most publicised – events. Get to Sonkajärvi, in the northern Lakeland, for the **Wife-Carrying World Championships** (www.eukonkanto.fi) in early July.

It's a race over a 253.5m obstacle course, where competitors must carry their 'wives' through water traps and over hurdles to achieve the fastest time. The winner gets the wife's weight in beer and the prestigious title of World Wife-Carrying Champion. To enter, men need only €50 and a consenting female. There's also a 40-plus and team competition, all accompanied by a weekend of drinking, dancing and typical Finnish frivolity.

a stylish look. A session in the smart sauna is included, and parking's free. Prices drop €20 on weekends.

Spa Hotel Rauhalahti SPA HOTEL €€
(030-60830; www.rauhalahti.fi; Katiskaniementie 8; s/d €114/146;) Though it feels faded in parts, this spa hotel 6km south of town still makes a great place to stay, largely because of the huge scope for activities. The pool complex is good (available to nonguests for €12.50), and the modernised rooms are spacious and attractive. Excellent family packages are offered on its website. Take bus 7/9, or it's €25 in a cab.

Kuopion Asemagrilli GUESTHOUSE €€
(Hostal Asema; 017-580-0569; www.kuopionasemagrilli.com; Asemakatu 1; s/d €55/79;) Let's get one thing straight: sleeping as close as you can to transport terminals isn't lazy, it's practical. True. This friendly place, operating out of the grilli (fast-food outlet) in the train station, actually offers ensuite rooms in the building itself – very comfortable, exceedingly spacious and surprisingly peaceful. It's a good deal. Decent rooms for groups available.

Eating

Kaneli CAFE €
(www.kahvilakaneli.net; Kauppakatu 22; cakes €4-5; 11am-5pm Mon-Fri, 11am-4pm Sat, 11am-3pm Sun) This cracking cafe just off the kauppatori evokes a bygone age with much of its decor, but offers modern comfort in its shiny espresso machine, as well as many other flavoured coffees to accompany your toothsome, sticky *pulla*. It opens earlier in winter.

Lounas-Salonki FINNISH €
(www.lounassalonki.fi; Kasarmikatu 12; lunches €7.50-9.50; 9am-9pm Mon-Sat, noon-9pm Sun;) This charming wooden building west of the town centre is warm and friendly, with little rooms sporting elegant imperial furniture. It serves a salad buffet and daily hot lunch (11am to 3pm) featuring traditional Finnish fare. It's reliably delicious and offers excellent value, including dessert, soft drinks and coffee. There are also à la carte options including vegetarian choices. On Sundays the expanded lunch buffet costs €16.70.

Kauppahalli MARKET €
(8am-5pm Mon-Fri, 8am-3pm Sat;) At the southern end of the kauppatori is a classic Finnish indoor market hall, beautifully restored. Here stalls sell local speciality *kalakukko,* a large rye loaf stuffed with whitefish and then baked. It's delicious hot or cold. A whole one – a substantial thing – costs around €25, but you can buy halves.

★Kummisetä FINNISH €€
(www.kummiseta.com; Minna Canthinkatu 44; mains €17-30; kitchen 3-9.30pm Mon-Sat) The sober brown colours of the 'Godfather' give it a traditional feel replicated on the menu, with sauces featuring fennel, berries and morel mushrooms garnishing prime cuts of beef, tender-as-young-love lamb and succulent pike-perch. Food is hearty rather than gourmet; it and the service are both excellent. In summer, eating on the spacious two-level back terrace is an absolute pleasure.

Sampo FINNISH €€
(www.wanhamestari.fi; Kauppakatu 13; dishes €14-18; 11am-10pm Mon-Thu, 11am-midnight Fri & Sat, noon-10pm Sun) Have it stewed, fried, smoked or in a soup, but it's all about *muikku* here. This is one of Finland's most famous spots to try the small lakefish that drives Savo stomachs. The 70-year-old restaurant is cosy, and classically Finnish.

★Musta Lammas FINNISH €€€
(017-581-0458; www.mustalammas.net; Satamakatu 4; mains €28-33, degustation menu €59; 5-9pm Mon-Thu, 5-11pm Fri & Sat;) One of Finland's best restaurants, the Black Sheep has a golden fleece. Set in an enchantingly romantic brick-vaulted space, it offers a short menu of delicious gourmet mains using top-quality Finnish meat and fish, with complex sauces that complement but never overpower the natural flavours. Wines include a fabulous selection of generously priced special bottles (healthy credit card required). There's also a roof terrace.

Drinking & Nightlife

Kuopio's nightlife area is around Kauppakatu, east of the kauppatori. There are many options in this block, some with summer terraces.

Wanha Satama PUB
(www.wanhasatama.net; 11am-11pm Mon-Thu, 11am-4am Fri & Sat, noon-9pm Sun May-Aug) In a noble blue building by the harbour, this has one of Lakeland's best terraces, definitely the place to be on a sunny day to watch the boats come and go. There's decent Finnish fish and meat dishes, and regular live music. Hours reduce at the beginning and end of the season.

WORTH A TRIP

VALAMO MONASTERY

Finland's only Orthodox monastery, **Valamo** (☎017-570-111; www.valamo.fi; Valamontie 42, Uusi-Valamo) is one of Lakeland's most popular attractions. One of the great, ancient Russian monasteries, old Valamo was eventually re-established here, after the Revolution and the Winter War. Monks and novices, almost a thousand strong at old Valamo a century ago, now number in single figures, but the complex in general is thriving.

The first church was made by connecting two sheds; the rustic architecture contrasts curiously with the fine gilded icons. The new church, completed in 1977, has an onion dome and is redolent of incense. Visitors are free to roam and enter the churches. A guided tour is highly recommended for insights into the monastery and Orthodox beliefs.

The **monastery** (☎017-570-1810; www.valamo.fi; s/d without bathroom €45/66, hotel s/d from €70/110; P 🛜) makes an excellent place to stay, especially peaceful once evening descends. Guesthouses in picturesque wooden buildings provide comfortable, no-frills sleeping with shared bathroom; there are also two grades of hotel room offering a higher standard. Prices drop midweek and outside summer. The complex's eatery, **Trapesa** (www.valamo.fi; Valamon Luostari; buffet lunch €14, high tea €10; ⏲7am-6pm Mon-Thu, to 9pm Fri-Sat), has high-quality buffet lunches. There's no monastic frugality: try their own range of berry wines.

Valamo is clearly signposted 4km north of the main Varkaus–Joensuu road. A couple of daily buses run to Valamo from Joensuu and from Helsinki via Mikkeli and Varkaus.

The most pleasant way to arrive in summer is on the M/S *Puijo* (p171) from Kuopio. The cruise uses a combination of the regular Kuopio to Savonlinna boat and road transport (adult return €80).

Helmi PUB
(www.satamanhelmi.fi; Kauppakatu 2; ⏲11am-11pm Mon-Thu, 11am-2am Fri, noon-2am Sat, noon-8pm Sun) This historic 19th-century sailors' hang-out by the harbour has recently been remodelled and is a cosy, comfortable spot with a range of local characters. There's a decent pool table, tasty pizzas (€8 to €10) and a sociable enclosed terrace.

Ilona CLUB
(www.ilonacity.fi; Vuorikatu 19; ⏲10pm-4am) The city's best nightclub has an attractive London-themed bar with a smoking cabin done out like a red bus, and a separate karaoke bar where enthusiastic punters belt out Suomi hits. There's a fat list of English-language songs if you don't fancy trying out your Finnish vowels. There's a 22-year-old minimum entry on weekends.

☆ Entertainment

Henry's Pub LIVE MUSIC
(www.henryspub.net; Käsityökatu 17; ⏲9pm-4am; 🛜) An atmospheric underworld with bands playing several times a week, usually free, and usually at the heavier end of the rock/metal spectrum. Opens at 11pm Sunday and Monday.

Shopping

Pikku-Pietarin Torikuja CRAFTS
(www.pikkupietarintorikuja.fi; ⏲10am-5pm Mon-Fri, 10am-3pm Sat Jun-Aug) An atmospheric narrow lane of renovated red wooden houses converted into quirky shops stocking jewellery, clothing, handicrafts and other items. Halfway along is an excellent cafe (open from 8am) with cosy upstairs seating and a great little back deck for the summer sun.

ℹ Information

Kuopio Info (☎0800-182-050; www.visitkuopio.fi; Apaja Shopping Centre, Kauppakatu 45; ⏲8am-3pm Mon-Fri) Underneath the kauppatori. Information on regional attractions and accommodation. May open on Saturday in the future.

ℹ Getting There & Away

Finnair flies daily to Helsinki.

BOAT

See M/S *Puijo* (p171) for transport between Kuopio and Savonlinna.

BUS

Express services to/from Kuopio (change in Varkaus for Savonlinna):

Helsinki (€66.30, 6½ hours)
Jyväskylä (€25.60, 2¼ hours)

TRAIN

Daily trains:
Helsinki (€68, 4½ to five hours)
Kajaani (€30.70, 1¾ hours)
Oulu (€53.70, four hours)

Change at Pieksämäki or Kouvola for other destinations.

Joensuu

☎013 / POP 74,475

The capital of North Karelia is a bubbly young university town, with students making up almost a third of the population. Today Joensuu looks pretty modern – bombing raids during the Winter and Continuation Wars flattened many of its older buildings. It's also the gateway to the deep, quiet depths of the Karelian wilderness. The gentle Pielisjoki rapids divide the town into two parts: most of the town centre is west of the river, but the bus and train stations are to the east.

Sights

Carelicum MUSEUM
(Koskikatu 5; adult/child €5/3; 9am-5pm Mon-Fri, 10am-3pm Sat year-round plus 10am-3pm Sun Jul) Themed displays – on the region's prehistory, its war-torn past, the Karelian evacuation, the importance of the sauna etc – cover both sides of the present-day border at this excellent museum.

Pielisjoki Cruise CRUISE
(☎050-566-0815; www.satumaaristeilyt.fi; adult/child from €15/7) From June to mid-August, the M/S *Vinkeri II* and M/S *Satumaa* run two-hour scenic cruises on the Pielisjoki, departing from the passenger harbour south of Suvantosilta bridge. Sailing schedules are posted online; buy tickets on board.

Festivals

Ilosaari Rock Festival MUSIC
(www.ilosaarirock.fi; 2-day ticket €95) Held over a weekend in mid-July, this massive rock festival attracts Finnish and international acts. It has received awards for its environmental record.

Sleeping

Hotel GreenStar HOTEL €
(☎010-423-9390; www.greenstar.fi; Torikatu 16; r €59-69; reception 8am-8pm Mon-Fri, 9am-8pm Sat, 9am-1pm & 3-7pm Sun;) Eco initiatives at this contemporary hotel include water heating rather than air-con and small communal areas to reduce heating. Clean, comfortable rooms sleep up to three for the same price (a pull-out armchair converts into a single bed). Breakfast (€7) is optional. Try to arrive when reception is staffed as the lobby's automatic check-in kiosk can be temperamental.

Finnhostel Joensuu HOSTEL €
(☎013-267-5076; www.islo.fi; Kalevankatu 8; s €54, without bathroom €44, tw €64, 4-person apt €84, all incl breakfast; reception 3-8pm;) The great-value, sizeable rooms come with mini

WORTH A TRIP

MARVELS OF MECHANICAL MUSIC

It's worth visiting the timber-pulp town of Varkaus for a wonderful attraction, **Mekaanisen Musiikin Museo** (☎050-590-9297; www.mekaanisenmusiikinmuseo.fi; Pelimanninkatu 8; adult/child €14/7; 11am-6pm Tue-Sat, to 5pm Sun Mar–mid-Dec, to 6pm daily Jul).

'You must understand', says the personable owner, 'it's not a normal museum; more a madhouse'. A truly astonishing collection of mechanical musical instruments ranges from a ghostly keyboard-tinkling Steinway to a robotic violinist to a full-scale orchestra emanating from a large cabinet. This is just the beginning; political cabaret in several languages and an overwhelming sense of good humour and imagination make it a cross between a Victorian theatre and Willy Wonka's chocolate factory. It's an extraordinary place.

Entry is by guided tour that lasts around 75 minutes. Having a coffee outside under the steely gaze of a sizeable macaw seems like a return to normality. The museum is signposted 1km west of the main north–south highway.

kitchens and small balconies; some share bathroom and kitchen facilities with one other room. Prices include access to a private sauna session and a gym in the sports institute across the road that handles reception. HI discount.

Linnunlahti CAMPGROUND €
(☎010-666-5520; www.linnunlahti.fi; Linnunlahdentie 1; tent sites €7 plus per person €2, cottages €119-160;) This bargain almost-lakeside campground is mobbed during the rock festival, but otherwise has sites to spare. Cottages sleeping two to six people have free wi-fi.

Eating

The kauppatori is packed with grillis (a type of fast-food outlet) and stalls selling cheap snacks: try the *karjalanpiirakka*, a savoury rice pastry of local origin but eagerly munched all over Finland.

★**Teatteri** KARELIAN €€
(☎010-231-4250; www.teatteriravintola.fi; Rantakatu 20; lunch buffet €8.60-10.50, mains €16.50-26.50; 11am-10pm Mon & Tue, 11am-11pm Wed & Thu, 11am-midnight Fri, 11.30am-midnight Sat) Locally sourced ingredients prepared in innovative ways are served in the town hall's art deco surrounds and beautiful summer terrace. Dishes span braised, smoked pork neck with wild boar sausage and rhubarb compote to thyme-crusted chicken with blackcurrant sauce; lush desserts like liquorice jelly, vanilla-infused strawberries and liquorice meringue are the icing on the cake.

Astoria HUNGARIAN €€
(☎013-229-766; www.astoria.fi; Rantakatu 32; mains €18-30; 4-10pm Mon, 4-11pm Tue-Fri, noon-midnight Sat, noon-8pm Sun) In a former girls' school built in brick-Gothic style, this wood-panelled restaurant is a stylish affair with a Hungarian menu of paprika- and garlic-laced goulashes and hefty steaks complemented by Hungarian wines. Finish with a chilled *slivovitz* (plum brandy).

Ravintola Kielo KARELIAN €€€
(☎013-227-874; www.ravintolakielo.fi; Suvantokatu 12; mains €22-29, tasting menu €46; 4-10pm Mon-Fri, noon-10pm Sat) At the high end of Karelian cuisine, artfully presented miniature starters such as whitefish escabeche with ratatouille and sour cream set the stage for mains like ravioli and pan-fried pikeperch in fish broth, and horsebean risotto with overnight-braised pork. Wine pairings are available.

Information

Karelia Expert (☎0400-239-549; www.visitkarelia.fi; Koskikatu 5; 9am-5pm Mon-Fri year-round plus 10am-3pm Sat & Sun Jun-Aug) In the Carelicum, enthusiastic staff handle tourism information and bookings for the region.

Getting There & Away

Finnair (www.finnair.com) operates several flights a day between Helsinki and Joensuu.

Major bus services:

Helsinki (€60.10, 7½ hours, up to 14 daily)
Jyväskylä (€43.90, four hours, six daily)
Kuopio (€29.90, 2½ hours, up to two per hour)
Lappeenranta (€43.90, 4½ hours, two daily)

Train services:

Helsinki (€78.90, 4½ hours, seven daily)
Lieksa (€15.10, 1¼ hours, two daily)
Nurmes (€22.50, two hours, two daily)
Savonlinna (€31.80, two hours, five daily); change at Parikkala

Ilomantsi

☎013 / POP 5690

Pushing up against the border that separates Finland from Russia, Ilomantsi is Finland's most Karelian, Orthodox and eastern municipality, and the centre of a charming region where a wealth of wilderness hiking opens up before you.

The excellent tourist centre, **Karelia Expert** (☎0400-240-072; www.visitkarelia.fi; Kalevalantie 13; 9am-5pm Mon-Fri Jun-Aug, 8am-4pm Mon-Fri Sep-May) can help with just about everything, from cottage reservations to information on trekking routes and hire of camping equipment, snowshoes and cross-country ski gear.

Parppeinvaara (www.parppeinvaara.fi; Parppeintie; adult/child €7/5; 10am-4pm Jun-Aug, 10am-6pm Jul) is the oldest and most interesting of Finland's Karelian theme villages, where you can hear the *kantele* (Karelian stringed instrument) played and try traditional food at the excellent **Parppeinpirtti** (☎010-239-9950; www.parppeinpirtti.fi; lunch €22; 10am-6pm Jul, to 5pm Jun & Aug, to 3pm Mon-Fri, 11am-3pm Sat & Sun Sep).

Ilomantsi celebrates the traditional Orthodox festivals **Petru Praasniekka** on 28 and 29 June and **Ilja Praasniekka** on 19 and 20 July.

Contact Karelia Expert about cottages in the surrounding region.

Buses to/from Joensuu (€15.90, 1½ hours, nine daily Monday to Friday, fewer on weekends) stop in the centre of town.

Treks Around Karelia

Karelia's best trekking routes form the **Karjalan Kierros** (Karelian Circuit), a loop of really lovely marked trails with a total length of over 1000km between Ilomantsi and Lake Pielinen. For more information on these and other routes check out the www.outdoors.fi website or contact Karelia Expert in Ilomantsi or Lieksa (p180).

Karhunpolku

The **Bear's Trail** (not to be confused with the Bear's Ring near Kuusamo) is a 133km marked hiking trail of medium difficulty leading north from Patvinsuo National Park near Lieksa, through a string of stunning national parks and peaceful nature reserves along the Russian border. The trail ends at Teljo, about 50km south of Kuhmo. You will need to arrange transport from either end.

Susitaival

The 97km **Wolf Trail** is a marked trail running south from the marshlands of Patvinsuo National Park to the forests of Petkeljärvi National Park, 21km east of Ilomantsi. This links with the Bear's Trail. It's a three-day trek of medium difficulty (the marshland can be wet underfoot). It passes through some important Winter War battlegrounds near the Russian border.

Lake Pielinen Region

In a land full of lakes, Pielinen, Finland's sixth-largest, is pretty special. In summer it's the shimmering jewel of North Karelia and is surrounded by some of the most beautiful wilderness areas and action-packed countryside in the country.

Koli National Park

Finns, with reason, consider the stunning views from the heights of Koli, overlooking Lake Pielinen, as the best in the country – the same views inspired several Finnish artists from the National Romantic era. In summer, the national park offers scenic hiking routes; in winter, skiing, with two slalom centres and more than 60km of cross-country trails, including 24km of illuminated track.

The hill has road access with a short **funicular** (free) from the lower car park to the hilltop Sokos hotel. From here it's a brief walk to **Ukko-Koli**, the highest point with the best vistas. It really is an incredible panorama as you stand on weatherbeaten rocks with the vast island-studded lake stretched out far below you and pine forest as far as the eye can see.

By the hotel, **Luontokeskus Ukko** (☎020-564-5654; www.outdoors.fi; exhibition adult/child €5/2; ⏲9am-7pm mid-Jun–early Aug, shorter hours rest of year) is a modern visitor centre with exhibitions on history, nature and the park's geology, and information on hiking. There's a craft shop, free internet terminal and a cafe.

In Koli village, 3km below the Luontokeskus, **Karelia Expert** (☎045-138-7429; www.visitkarelia.fi; Ylä-Kolintie 4; ⏲10.30am-6pm Jun-Aug, 9am-5pm to 5pm Sep-May) books activities and has a comprehensive range of information and maps.

Vanhan Koulun Majatalo (☎050-343-7881; www.vanhankoulunmajatalo.fi; Niinilahdentie 47; s/d/tr/q from €36/52/72/88, 2-person apt €80-120; @ 📶 👪), on a gravel road 6km from Koli village (follow signs to Kolin Retkeilymaja), is a great place to base yourself for walking, skiing and exploring the area. A tranquil setting, with a grassy garden, smoke sauna and outdoor games, is complemented by large kitchen and common areas inside, and simple, comfortable private rooms with beds and bunks as well as studio apartments.

There's a summer car **ferry** (MF Pielinen; ☎0400-228-435; www.pielis-laivat.fi; one way adult/child/car/bicycle €18/10/12/5) between Koli and Lieksa (1½ hours). Apart from the boat, year-round *kimppakyyti* (shared) **shuttle taxis** (☎040-104-4687) run from Joensuu to Koli (one hour), picking up door-to-door, including the *majatalo*. It's best to book the service the day before; if your phone Finnish isn't great, get the tourist office or your hotel to call for you. There are also bus connections from Joensuu to Kolikylä (Koli village) via Ahmovaara.

KARELIAN COTTAGES

Karelia's gorgeous scenery, sparkling lakes and deep forests make it an appealing part of the country to rent a cabin or cottage and relax for a few days. As well as national operators, Karelia Expert has a great portfolio.

Lieksa & Ruunaa

013 / POP 12,570

The small lakeside town of Lieksa is primarily a base and service town for outdoor activities in the region. In winter, husky tours and snowmobile safaris along the Russian border are popular; in summer, hiking, fishing and white-water rafting are all the rage.

Sights & Activities

Pielisen Museo MUSEUM

(040-104-4151; www.lieksa.fi/museo; Pappilantie 2; adult/child €6/1.50; 10am-6pm mid-May–mid-Sep) Over 70 Karelian buildings and open-air exhibits at this outdoor museum are organised by century or trade (such as farming, milling, fire-fighting). A fascinating insight into the forestry industry includes a look at a logging camp and floating rafts and machinery used for harvest and transport.

In winter the only section open is the **indoor museum** (040-104-4151; www.lieksa.fi/museo; admission winter adult/child €3/1; 10am-3pm Tue-Fri mid-Sep–mid-May) featuring photographs and displays on Karelian history.

★ **Erä Eero** BEAR-WATCHING

(040-015-9452; www.eraeero.com; per person €175; 4pm-6am) Erä Eero runs awesome overnight trips to its observation cabin, where you may see bears, wolves and beavers between April and October, as well as birds of prey, wolverines and lynx.

Ruunaa Recreation Area ACTIVITY PARK

(www.outdoors.fi) Karelia Expert in Lieksa handles information and bookings for all manner of activities around Lieksa and at this park, 30km east. This is a superb, carefully managed wilderness area perfect for fishing, white-water rafting, wildlife spotting and easy hiking. The drawback is that public transport barely exists, but you should be able to hitch (or go with an organised tour) in summer.

Sleeping

There are numerous options in the countryside around Lieksa. In town, there's campsite, hostel and hotel accommodation.

Timitranlinna HOSTEL €

(044-333-4044; www.timitra.fi; Timitrantie 3; dm from €22, d €52; P) Once the national training centre for the Finnish border guard, this HI-affiliated hostel is peacefully situated about 800m south of the main street. Its 1st-floor rooms are standard fare, but kayaks are available for exploring the nearby river.

Ruunaa Hiking Centre CAMPGROUND €

(013-533-170; www.ruunaa.fi; tent sites €12 plus per person €3, cabins/cottages €35/100; P) Near the *pitkospuu* (boardwalk) to the Neitikoski rapids, this excellent hiking centre incorporates a large cafe, camping area, kitchen, sauna, luxurious four- to six-bed cottages and simple cabins. Mountain bikes, canoes and rowboats are available for hire.

Information

Karelia Expert (0400-175-323; www.visitkarelia.fi; Pielisentie 22; 9am-5pm Mon-Fri Jun & Aug, to 5pm Mon-Fri, to 2pm Sat Jul, 8am-4pm Mon-Fri Sep-May) Books tours and accommodation.

Getting There & Away

Buses head from Joensuu and Nurmes to Lieksa, as do trains. A car ferry (p179) runs across the lake to Koli in summer.

WORTH A TRIP

KESTIKIEVARI HERRANNIEMI

For a relaxing break, it's worth going out of the way and catching a train to Vuonislahti, 28km south of Lieksa, for **Kestikievari Herranniemi** (013-542-110; www.herranniemi.com; Vuonislahdentie 185; dm €16, s/d from €59/84, cabins €30-84, cottages €145;), a brilliant lakeside retreat. Attractive wooden buildings house a variety of excellent rooms and cottages, with some particularly appealing ones for families. The welcoming owners offer meals by arrangement and a variety of treatments, and there are all sorts of extras, with several saunas, rowing boats and a fantastic lakeside with its own pavilion and auditorium. It's a magically peaceful place that seems close to the soul of Finnishness. Various discounts are available in winter.

Nurmes

☎013 / POP 8360

On the northern shores of Lake Pielinen, Nurmes is another base for activities such as snowmobiling, ice fishing, dog-sledding and cross-country skiing tours in winter, and wildlife-watching, canoeing, hiking and farmhouse tours in summer. It's a pleasant town in its own right though, with an 'old town' area (Puu-Nurmes) of historical wooden buildings along Kirkkokatu. A highlight is Bomban Talo, the largest building of a re-created Karelian village 3km east of the centre featuring a summer market, craft shops and cafes.

Karelia Expert (☎050-336-0707; www.visitkarelia.fi; Kauppatori 3; ⏲9am-5pm Mon-Fri Jun-Aug, to 4pm Mon-Fri Sep-May) has local information and bookings. It's opposite the bus and train stations.

The best places to stay in Nurmes are side by side on the lake shore about 3.5km east of the centre. **Sokos Hotel Bomba** (☎020-123-4908; www.sokoshotels.fi; Tuulentie 10; s €105-119, d €111-131, Karelian cabins €160, spa for nonguests from €12.50; ⏲spa 10am-10pm May-Aug, to 9pm Sep-Apr;) has a great indoor pool and spa area overlooking the lake and slick modern rooms in a stylish new wing. There are also fully equipped apartment cottages available, and cheaper rooms in wooden buildings within the replica Karelian village. Prices can be up to 40% lower at quiet times. Just beyond, **Hyvärilä** (☎040-104-5960; www.hyvarila.com; Lomatie 12; campsites €10 plus per person €5, cabins €48-63, hostel dm €22, hotel s/d/f €81/98/118; ⏲camping Jun–mid-Sep; P) is a sprawling lakefront holiday resort with a manicured camping ground, hostel accommodation, cabins, upmarket cottages, a hotel, restaurant and even a golf course.

Buses run regularly to Joensuu, Kajaani and Lieksa. Trains go to Joensuu via Lieksa.

NORTH-CENTRAL FINLAND

Kuhmo

☎08 / POP 9270

Surrounded by wilderness, Kuhmo makes a natural base for hiking and wildlife-watching. Vast taiga forests run from here right across Siberia and harbour 'respect' animals such as wolves, bears and lynx. Kuhmo is also the unofficial capital of Vienan Karjala, the Karelian heartland now in Russia, explored by artists in the movement that was crucial to the development of Finnish national identity.

This likeable little town also has a great chamber music festival in July.

Sights & Activities

Hiking is the big drawcard in Kuhmo, but there are plenty of other ways to get active; Petola Luontokeskus has more walking info and can arrange fishing permits.

Juminkeko CULTURAL CENTRE

(www.juminkeko.fi; Kontionkatu 25; adult/child €4/2; ⏲noon-6pm Mon-Fri, daily in Jul) If you are interested in the *Kalevala* or Karelian culture, pay a visit to this excellent resource centre, a beautiful building made using traditional methods and modern styling. The fantastic staff can tell you anything you wish to know; there are also three to four detailed exhibitions here yearly.

Petola Luontokeskus NATURE CENTRE

(www.outdoors.fi; Lentiirantie 342; ⏲9am-4pm Mon-Fri May–mid-Jun & mid-Aug–Oct, 9am-5pm daily mid-Jun–mid-Aug) On the main road 3km from the town centre, this has an informative exhibition in various languages on Finland's quartet of large carnivores, known hereabouts as *karhu* (bear), *ilves* (lynx), *ahma* (wolverine) and *susi* (wolf), as well as wild reindeer, locally present in small numbers, and golden eagles. There's a summer cafe, national park information and a cute gift shop.

Wild Brown Bear WILDLIFE-WATCHING

(☎040-546-9008; www.wildbrownbear.fi; ⏲Mar-Sep) Runs bear-watching excursions (€120), with chances to view wolverines, wolves and other creatures. Accommodation available.

Taiga Spirit WILDLIFE-WATCHING

(☎040-746-8243; www.taigaspirit.com) Organises wildlife safaris and bear- and wolverine-viewing from hides.

Festivals & Events

★**Kuhmon Kamarimusiikki** MUSIC

(Kuhmo Chamber Music Festival; www.kuhmofestival.fi; tickets €17-24) This two-week festival in late July has a full program performed by a variety of Finnish and international musicians, many youthful. Most concerts, usually five or six short pieces bound by a tenuous theme, are held in the Kuhmo-Talo, a beautiful, comfortable hall that looks like a matchstick hobby model. Tickets are a steal at around €17 for most events.

Sleeping

Matkakoti Parkki GUESTHOUSE €
(08-655-0271; matkakoti.parkki@elisanet.fi; Vienantie 3; s/d €35/60; P) Run in a kindly manner, this quiet and handsome little family guesthouse offers excellent value near the centre of town. Rooms share bathrooms, which are spotless. There's a kitchen you can use, and tasty breakfast is included.

Hotelli Kalevala HOTEL €€
(08-655-4100; www.hotellikalevala.fi; Väinämöinen 9; s/d €98/132; P @) Four kilometres from central Kuhmo, this striking building of wood and concrete is the area's best place to stay. Pretty rooms in pastel colours mostly have tantalising lake views: the situation is gorgeous, and the hotel takes full advantage, with a relaxing Jacuzzi and sauna area with vistas and plenty of activity options in winter and summer.

Information

There's no tourist office. The town hall, sights and hotels give out info.

Getting There & Away

Several daily buses head to/from Kajaani (€20.40, 1¾ hours), and a couple to Nurmes, changing at Sotkamo. There's a bus Monday and Friday schoolday mornings to Suomussalmi. For other destinations, go via Kajaani.

Oulu

08 / POP 141,670

Prosperous Oulu (Swedish: Uleåborg) is one of Finland's most enjoyable cities to visit. In summer, angled sunshine bathes the kauppatori (market square) in light and all seems well with the world. Locals, who appreciate daylight when they get it, crowd the terraces, and stalls groan under the weight of Arctic berries.

The centre is spread across several islands, elegantly connected by pedestrian bridges and cycleways: Oulu's network of bike paths is one of Europe's best. Oulu is also a significant technology city; the university turns out top-notch IT graduates and the corporate parks on the city's outskirts employ people from all over the globe.

Sights & Activities

One of Oulu's best features is the extensive network of **bicycle paths** crossing bridges, waterways and islands all the way out to surrounding villages. Grab a cycle map from the tourist office.

A good 3km walk or ride is from the kauppatori, across the bridge to Pikisaari and across another bridge to Nallikari, where there's a lovely beach facing the Gulf of Bothnia.

Kauppatori SQUARE
Oulu has the liveliest market square of all Finnish towns, and its position at the waterfront makes it all the more appealing. The square is bordered by several old wooden storehouses now serving as restaurants, bars and craft shops. The squat *Toripolliisi* statue, a humorous representation of the local police, is a local landmark.

★**Tietomaa** MUSEUM
(www.tietomaa.fi; Nahkatehtaankatu 6; adult/child €15/11; 10am-5pm, 6pm or 8pm;) This huge, excellent science museum can occupy kids for the best part of a day with a giant IMAX screen, hands-on interactive exhibits on planets and the human body, and an observation tower. There's a yearly mega-exhibition that's the focal point.

Oulun Taidemuseo GALLERY
(www.ouka.fi/taidemuseo; Kasarmintie 7; adult/child €6/free; 10am-5pm Tue-Thu, Sat & Sun, noon-7pm Fri) Oulu's art museum is a bright spacious gallery with excellent temporary exhibitions of both international and Finnish contemporary art, and a cafe.

Festivals & Events

Air Guitar World Championships MUSIC
(www.airguitarworldchampionships.com) Part of the Oulu Music Video Festival in late August. Contestants from all over the world take the stage to show what they can do with their imaginary instruments.

Tervahiihto SKIING
(Oulu Tar Ski Race; www.tervahiihto.fi) Held in early March. This 70km skiing race (40km for women) has been running since 1889.

Sleeping

Forenom House HOTEL €
(020-198-3420; www.forenom.fi; Rautatienkatu 9; r €54-70; P) You can't beat this spot for convenience: it's bang opposite the train station.

Oulu

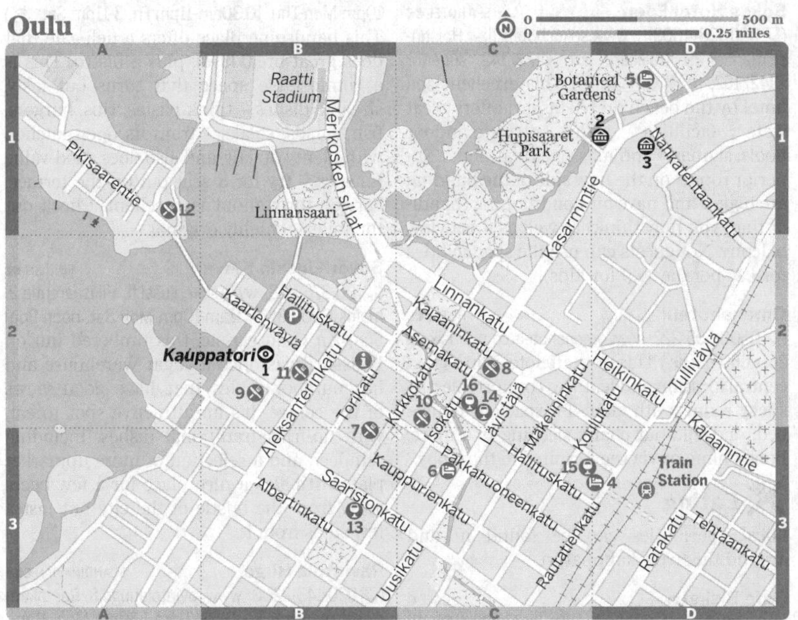

There's a range of rooms (sleeping up to five) with plenty of space, and as fridge and microwave. They could do with better curtains. Book online or via the lobby terminal. Rates can be excellent value. It also offers apartments elsewhere in Oulu. Reception is staffed Monday to Friday during working hours.

Nallikari Camping CAMPGROUND €
(☎044-703-1353; www.nallikari.fi; Hietasaari; campsite €13 plus per adult/child €4/2, cabins €40-45, cottages €105-145; P @ 🛜 👪) This excellent campground offers all sorts of options in a location close to the beach on Hietasaari, a 40-minute walk to the city centre via pedestrian bridges. Both summer and winter activities are on offer, plus a large variety of cabins and cottages, substantially cheaper outside of high season. It's very child-friendly. Take bus 15 from the city centre, or the summer tourist train.

★Hotel Lasaretti HOTEL €€
(☎020-757-4700; www.lasaretti.com; Kasarmintie 13; s/d €148/169, Sat & Sun €82/98; P ❄ @ 🛜 🏊) Bright, modern and optimistic, this inviting hotel sits in a group of renovated brick buildings, once a hospital. It's close to town but the parkside location by the bubbling-bright stream makes it feel rural. The artistically modern rooms are great: ask for one with a water view. Facilities and staff are excellent, and there's also a busy bar-restaurant with sun-kissed terrace spaces.

Oulu

Top Sights
1 Kauppatori ... B2

Sights
2 Oulun Taidemuseo ... D1
3 Tietomaa ... D1

Sleeping
4 Forenom House ... D3
5 Hotel Lasaretti ... D1
6 Omenahotelli ... C3

Eating
7 Café Bisketti ... B3
8 Hella ... C2
9 Oulun Kauppahalli ... B2
10 Puistola ... C2
11 Ravintola Hugo ... B2
12 Sokeri-Jussin Kievari ... A1

Drinking & Nightlife
13 45 Special ... B3
14 Never Grow Old ... C2
15 Snooker Time ... C3
16 St Michael ... C2

Sokos Hotel Eden SPA HOTEL €€
(☎020-123-4603; www.sokoshotels.fi; Holstinsalmentie 29, Nallikari; s/d €122/142, superior €142/162; P❄@📶🏊👪) This excellent spa hotel by the beach on Hietasaari offers great watery facilities – slides, intricate indoor pools, saunas – and massage treatments. Superior rooms on the new side of the building are bigger and have air-conditioning (handier than you may think) as well as a sea-view balcony. Nonguests can use the spa facilities for €15 per day (€9 for kids).

Omenahotelli HOTEL €€
(☎0600-555-222; www.omenahotels.com; Uusikatu 26; r €60-90; 📶) This no-staff hotel is in a good central location and features comfortable plasticky rooms with giant TV, spacious double bed, and fold-out chairs sleeping two more. Book online or via the terminal in the lobby.

Eating

Local specialities can be found in and around the lively kauppatori.

Café Bisketti CAFE €
(www.cafebisketti.fi; Kirkkokatu 8; lunches €6-10; ⏲7.30am-9.30pm Mon-Sat, 10am-8pm Sun; 📶) This top double-sided spot transforms itself throughout the day. Think twice before getting that pastry with your morning coffee; they're enormous and might not leave room for lunch, with cheap deals on soup, salad, coffee and a pastry, and hot dishes for not much extra. In the evenings, the terrace is a decent spot for a people-watching beer.

Oulun Kauppahalli MARKET €
(www.oulunliikekeskus.fi/kauppahalli; ⏲8am-5pm Mon-Thu, 8am-6pm Fri, 8am-3pm Sat; ✍) 🍃 On the square, the kauppahalli has freshly filleted salmon glistening in the market stalls and plenty of spots to snack on anything from cloudberries to sushi.

★**Hella** BISTRO €€
(☎08-371-180; www.hellaravintola.fi; Isokatu 13; mains €20-27; ⏲10.30am-10pm Mon-Thu, 10.30am-11pm Fri, 3-11pm Sat) This little corner spot is a two-person show offering excellent Italian-inspired fare. Attentive service is backed up by the food, which changes seasonally but features great salads, cannelloni stuffed with goat's cheese, and tender, well-treated meat dishes. Opens shorter hours in July.

Puistola BISTRO €€
(☎020-792-8210; www.ravintolapuistola.fi; Pakkahuoneenkatu 15; mains €16-26; ⏲bistro 10.45am-10pm Mon-Thu, 10.30am-11pm Fri, 3-11pm Sat; 📶) This handsome place offers a deli-cafe that does great breakfasts, plus a bistro. This is a comfortable space that turns out tasty, sizeable dishes – think pastas, ribs, burgers, fish, salads, steaks – from its open kitchen with plenty of flair, and also does good-value lunches – try for a seat out on the terrace. Service throughout is excellent. Check out the toilets – highly original.

Sokeri-Jussin Kievari FINNISH €€
(☎08-376-628; www.sokerijussi.fi; Pikisaarentie 2; mains €20-33; ⏲11am-10pm Mon-Sat, noon-9pm Sun) An Oulu classic, this timbered inn on Pikisaari was once a sugar warehouse and has outdoor tables that have good views of the centre. It's an attractive spot to eat, with no-frills traditional dishes, including reindeer, and a selection of more upmarket plates. It's also a nice place for a few beers away from the bustle of the city but just a few steps from it.

Ravintola Hugo SCANDINAVIAN €€€
(☎020-143-2200; www.ravintolahugo.fi; Rantakatu 4; set menus €38-70; ⏲11am-1.30pm Mon, 11am-1.30pm & 5-10pm Tue-Fri, 5-10pm Sat) Innovative gourmet dining generally using locally available products makes this a real Oulu highlight. There are some outstanding flavour combinations and a variety of degustation menu options with matched wines.

Drinking & Entertainment

There's plenty going on at night. The kauppatori is the spot to start in summer: bars set in traditional wooden warehouses have terraces that lick up every last drop of the evening sun.

★**St Michael** PUB
(www.stmichael.fi; Hallituskatu 13; ⏲2pm-2am; 📶) This convivial Irish pub has a brilliant selection of craft beer, including excellent guest ales, and a fine array of whisky. The large terrace makes it a top spot when the sun's shining.

Never Grow Old BAR
(www.ngo.fi; Hallituskatu 17; ⏲8pm-2am Sun-Tue, 6pm-2am Wed-Thu, 6pm-3am Fri & Sat) Enduringly popular, NGO hits its stride after 10pm, with dancing, DJs and revelry in the tightly packed interior. The goofy decor includes some seriously comfortable and extremely uncomfortable places to sit, and a log palisade bar that seems designed to get you to wear your drink. It opens earlier in summer.

Snooker Time BAR

(Asemakatu 28; ⊙4pm-1am Sun-Thu, 4pm-2am Fri & Sat) With a bohemian clientele and dive-bar feel, this characterful place is an Oulu favourite: locals describe it as the city's living room. Streetside seating, downstairs pool and snooker tables, and a graffiti-splashed smoking chamber are the highlights.

45 Special CLUB

(www.45special.com; Saaristonkatu 12; ⊙4pm-4am) This grungy three-level club pulls a good mix of people for its downstairs rock and chartier top floor. There's a €7.50 admission on selected nights and regular live gigs. It serves food until 3am.

Information

Wireless internet is available throughout the city centre on the PanOulu network.

Tourist Office (☎08-5584-1330; www.visitoulu.fi; Torikatu 10; ⊙9am-5pm Mon-Fri, plus 10am-4pm Sat Jun-Aug) Good range of information on Oulu and other Finnish destinations. Closes 4pm Fridays in winter.

Getting There & Away

AIR

There are daily direct flights from Helsinki with Finnair and Norwegian. SAS fly direct to Stockholm and Norwegian has a direct Alicante service. Bus 9 goes to the airport every 30 minutes (€4.70, 25 minutes).

BUS

Helsinki €98.30, 10 to 11½ hours
Kajaani €31.40, 2¾ hours
Rovaniemi €30 to €44, 3½ hours
Tornio €25.20, two to 2½ hours

TRAIN

Several direct trains run daily to Helsinki (€77 to €94, six to eight hours). There are also trains via Kajaani and trains north to Rovaniemi.

Kuusamo & Ruka

☎08 / POP 16,175

Kuusamo is a remote frontier town 200km northeast of Oulu and close to the Russian border, while Ruka is its buzzy ski resort 30km north. Both places make great activity bases: wonderful canoeing, hiking and wildlife-watching is available in the surrounding area.

Sights & Activities

There are many tour operators based in Kuusamo, Ruka and the surrounding area, offering a full range of winter and summer activities from husky-sledding to fishing to bear-watching. The Ruka webpage, www.ruka.fi, is a good place to look for active ideas. Apart from skiing (downhill and cross-country), there's also great hiking as well as fast, rugged rapids on the Kitkajoki and Oulankajoki.

★ **Kuusamon Suurpetokeskus** ZOO

(www.kuusamon-suurpetokeskus.fi; Keronrannantie 31; adult/child €10/5; ⊙10am-5pm Apr-Sep) There's a great backstory to this bear sanctuary 33km south of Kuusamo on the Kajaani road. Rescued as helpless orphans, the bears were nursed by their 'father' Sulo Karjalainen, who then refused to have them put down (they can't return to the wild) when government funding dried up. He casually takes them fishing and walking in the forest, but you'll meet them in their cages here; it's thrilling to see these impressive, intelligent animals up close and appreciate their different personalities. There are also lynx, foxes and reindeer.

Rukatunturi SNOW SPORTS

(www.ruka.fi; day/week €38/189) Busy Ruka fell boasts 34 ski slopes, dedicated snowboard areas, a vertical drop of 201m and a longest run of 1300m. The 200-day-plus season normally runs from November to May. Ruka also boasts cross-country trails totalling an impressive 500km, with 40km illuminated. Lift passes allow you to ski at Pyhä in Lapland too.

Sleeping & Eating

Ruka's very busy in winter; in summer, it's great value. There are numerous apartments in Ruka itself, and hundreds of cabins and cottages throughout the surrounding area. For cottages, contact Kuusamo tourist office, Lomarengas (p203) or **ProLoma** (☎020-792-9700; www.proloma.fi). For apartments and chalets in Ruka, contact **Ski-Inn** (☎08-860-0300; www.ski-inn.fi; apt €75-200) or **Ruka-ko** (☎020-734-4790; www.rukako.fi; Rukanriutta 7). There are links to more cabin and cottage providers on www.ruka.fi.

Kuusamo-opisto GUESTHOUSE €

(☎050-444-1157; www.kuusamo-opisto.fi; Kitkantie 35, Kuusamo; s/d €36/60, without bathroom €30/52; Ⓟ) Around the corner from

Kuusamo's bus station, this college offers great budget accommodation in comfortable spacious rooms with en suites (some share shower facilities) in a variety of buildings. There are kitchen and laundry facilities; the bad news is that you have to arrive during office hours (8am to 3.45pm Monday to Friday), though you may be able to arrange a key drop by calling ahead.

Royal Hotel Ruka HOTEL €€
(040-081-9840; www.royalruka.fi; Mestantie 1, Ruka; s/d €110/149, r Jul-Oct €100; Jul-Apr;) Down at the foot of the fell at the turn-off to Rukajärvi, this small and intimate hotel looks like a children's fort to be populated with toy soldiers. It's the closest to a boutique hotel in the Kuusamo area; service is excellent here, and the classy restaurant offers delicacies such as roast hare. From July to November it only opens for bookings.

Riipisen Riistaravintola GAME €€
(08-868-1219; www.ruka.fi; Kelo, Ruka; mains €16-45; 1-9pm Mon-Sat) At the Kelo ski-lift area, a five-minute walk from Ruka's main square, this friendly log cabin has an attractively rustic interior. It specialises in game dishes, and you'll find Rudolf, Bullwinkle and, yes, poor Yogi (€61) on the menu here in various guises, depending on availability and season. Arctic hare also features, while capercaillie in a creamy sauce will get bird lovers twitching too.

Information

Ruka has a free wi-fi network.

Karhuntassu (040-860-8365; www.ruka.fi; Torangintaival 2, Kuusamo; 9am-5pm Mon-Fri, 10am-2pm Sat, plus noon-4pm Sun Jun-Aug) This large visitor centre is at the highway junction, 2km from central Kuusamo. There's comprehensive tourist information, rental cottage booking and a cafe-shop. Hours vary through the year; there's also a wildlife photography exhibition and national park information desk here.

Ruka Info (08-860-0250; www.ruka.fi; Ruka; 9am-5pm early Jun & late Aug, 9.30am-7pm Sep & late Jun–mid-Aug, 10am-8pm daily Oct-May) In the Kumpare building in the main village. Tourist information and accommodation booking. In the same building is a self-service laundry, supermarket, gym and more.

Getting There & Away

Finnair hits Kuusamo airport, 6km northeast of town, from Helsinki. Buses meet flights (€7 to Kuusamo, €10 to Ruka). Call 0100-84200 for a taxi.

Buses run daily from Kajaani (€43.60, 3½ hours), Oulu (€40.80, three hours) and Rovaniemi (€34.50, three hours).

Buses run between Kuusamo and Ruka a few times daily (€6.80, 30 minutes). During the ski season there's a shuttle bus, stopping at major hotels.

Oulanka National Park

This is one of the most visited national parks in Finland, thanks mainly to the 82km **Karhunkierros** (Bear's Ring Trail), a spectacular three- or four-day trek through rugged hills, deep gorges and swinging suspension bridges, starting from either the Hautajärvi Visitor Centre or the Ristikallio parking area and ending at the resort village of Ruka, which is located 25km north of Kuusamo.

There are shelters and free overnight huts on the trail, which is very well marked. The best online resource is the excellent Metsähallitus website, www.outdoors.fi.

Juuma is another gateway to the region, with accommodation and accessibility to some of the main sights, such as the charming, idyllic **Myllykoski** and **Jyrävä** waterfalls. If you don't have the time or resources for the longer walk, you can do the 12km **Pieni Karhunkierros** (Little Bear's Ring) circuit from Juuma, where there's camping, cabin and lodge accommodation.

LAPLAND

Lapland casts a powerful spell and irresistibly haunts the imagination and memory. There is something lonely and intangible here that makes it magic.

The midnight sun, the Sámi peoples, the aurora borealis and wandering reindeer are all components of this, as is good old ho-ho-ho himself, who 'officially' resides here. Another part of the spell is in the awesome latitudes – at Nuorgam, the northernmost point, you have passed Iceland and nearly all of Canada and Alaska.

Lapland, which occupies 30% of Finland's land area but houses just 3% of its population, has vast and awesome wildernesses, ripe for exploring on foot, skis or sledge. The sense of space, pure air and big skies is what is memorable here, more than the towns.

Lapland's far north is known as Sápmi, home of the Sámi people, whose main communities are around Inari, Utsjoki and Hetta. Rovaniemi is the most popular gateway to the north.

Rovaniemi

016 / POP 60,890

A tourism boomtown, the 'official' terrestrial residence of Santa Claus is the capital of Finnish Lapland and a more-or-less obligatory northern stop. Its wonderful Arktikum museum is the perfect introduction to the mysteries of these latitudes, and Rovaniemi is a good place to organise activities from. It's also Lapland's transport hub.

Thoroughly destroyed by the retreating Wehrmacht in 1944, the town was rebuilt to a plan by Alvar Aalto, with the major streets in the shape of a reindeer's head and antlers (hint: the Keskuskenttä stadium is the eye). Its unattractive buildings are compensated for by its marvellous riverside location.

Sights & Activities

Rent bicycles from **Europcar** (040-306-2870; www.europcar.fi; Pohjanpuistikko 2; per 3/24hr €10/20).

★ **Arktikum** MUSEUM
(www.arktikum.fi; Pohjoisranta 4; adult/child/family €12/5/28; 9am-6pm Jun-Aug & Dec–mid-Jan, 10am-6pm Tue-Sun mid-Jan–May & Sep-Nov) With its beautifully designed glass tunnel stretching out to the Ounasjoki, this is one of Finland's best museums and well worth the admission fee if you are interested in the north. One side deals with Lapland, with information on Sámi culture and the history of Rovaniemi. The other side offers a wide-ranging display on the Arctic, with superb static and interactive displays focusing on flora and fauna, as well as on the peoples of Arctic Europe, Asia and North America.

Pilke Tiedekeskus MUSEUM
(www.sciencecentrepilke.fi; Ounasjoentie 6; adult/child €7/5; 9am-6pm Mon-Fri, 10am-6pm Sat & Sun Jun-Aug & mid-Dec–mid-Jan, closed Mon rest of year;) Downstairs in the Metsähallitus (Finnish Forest and Park Service) building next to the Arktikum, this is a highly entertaining exhibition on Finnish forestry. It has dozens of interactive displays that are great for kids of all ages, who can clamber up into a logging vehicle or play games about forest management. Multilingual touch-screens provide interesting background

THE AURORA

The northern lights, or aurora borealis, an utterly haunting and exhilarating sight, are often visible to observers above the Arctic Circle. They're particularly striking during the dark winter; in summer, the sun more or less renders them invisible.

The aurora appears as curtains of greenish-white light stretching east to west across the sky for thousands of kilometres. At its lower edge, the aurora typically shades to a crimson-red glow. Hues of blue and violet can also be seen. The lights seem to dance and swirl in the night sky.

These auroral storms, however eerie, are quite natural. They're created when charged particles (protons and electrons) from the sun bombard the earth. These are deflected towards the North and South Poles by the earth's magnetic field. There they hit the earth's outer atmosphere, 100km to 1000km above ground, causing highly charged electrons to collide with molecules of nitrogen and oxygen. The excess energy from these collisions creates the colourful lights.

To see the lights, you'd best have a dark, clear night with high auroral activity. October, November and March are often optimal for this. Then it's a question of waiting patiently outside, preferably between the hours of 9pm and 2am. There are several useful websites for predicting auroral activity:

Geophysical Institute (www.gi.alaska.edu/AuroraForecast) Change the view to Europe and away you go.

Service Aurora (www.aurora-service.eu) Daily and hourly forecasts and text-message notification service.

University of Oulu (http://cc.oulu.fi/~thu/Aurora/forecast.html) Finland-based page with links so you can make your own prediction.

Rovaniemi

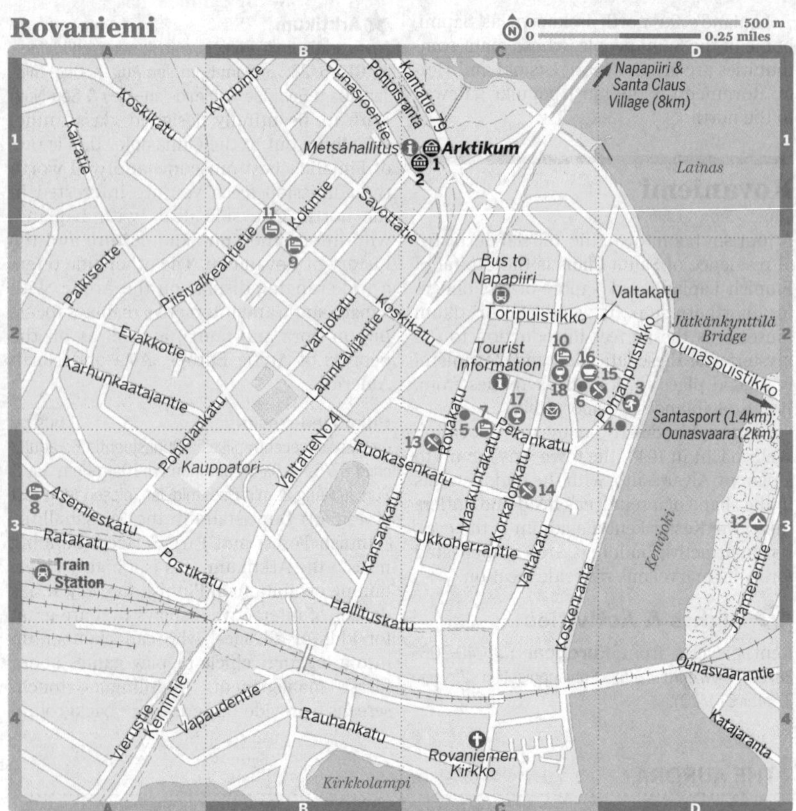

information. Sustainable forestry is the focus, though a bear-hunting simulation breaks the PC mould.

Ounasvaara SNOW SPORTS
(www.ounasvaara.fi; mountain-biking & toboggan run 11am-5pm late Jun–mid-Aug) This long fell across the river to the east of town is a place to get active. In winter there's a **ski centre**. There are ski jumps here, plus more than 100km of cross-country tracks. In summer there's a mountain-biking and toboggan run; walkers can take advantage of the cross-country skiing tracks. Bus 9 gets you here.

Tours

Rovaniemi is great for winter and summer activities, offering frequent departures with multilingual guides.

In summer, activities include guided walks, mountain biking (€55 to €70), river cruises (€30), visiting reindeer or huskies (€50 to €90), rafting, canoeing, moose-watching and wilderness camping.

Winter activities are snowmobiling (€100 to €170 for a two- to six-hour trip), snowshoe-walking (€55), reindeer-sledding (€100 to €130), husky-sledding (€75 to €250), cross-country skiing (€50 to €60), ice-fishing, aurora-watching, overnighting in a wilderness hut or a combination of any of these. All prices are based on two people sharing a snowmobile/sled; you'll pay up to 50% more if you want one all to yourself. You need a driving licence to operate a snowmobile.

Some recommended operators (most offices unstaffed in summer so call, or book via the tourist office) are listed here.

Lapland Safaris OUTDOORS
(016-331-1200; www.laplandsafaris.com; Koskikatu 1) Reliable and well-established outfit for most of the above activities.

Rovaniemi

Top Sights
1 Arktikum C1

Sights
2 Pilke Tiedekeskus C1

Activities, Courses & Tours
3 Europcar D2
4 Lapland Safaris D2
5 Lapland Welcome C2
6 Safartica C2

Sleeping
7 City Hotel C2
8 Guesthouse Borealis A3
9 Hostel Rudolf B2
10 Hotel Santa Claus C2
11 Hotelli Aakenus B1
12 Ounaskoski Camping D3

Eating
13 Cafe & Bar 21 .... C3
14 Mariza C3
Monte Rosa .... (see 7)
15 Nili D2

Drinking & Nightlife
16 Kauppayhtiö C2
17 Roy Club C2
18 ZoomIt C2

Lapland Welcome OUTDOORS
(016-439-148; www.laplandwelcome.fi; Rovakatu 26) Winter and summer excursions with good customer service.

Husky Point DOG-SLEDDING
(0400-790-096; www.huskypoint.fi; Kittiläntie 1638, Sinettä) From short rides to multiday treks. They also do summer dog-trips and reindeer visits.

Safartica OUTDOORS
(016-311-485; www.safartica.com; Koskikatu 9) One of the best for snowmobiling and river activities.

Festivals & Events

Christmas is a big time of the year and there are plenty of festive activities in December. In March, Rovaniemi hosts the **Napapiirinhiihto** (www.napapiirinhiihto.fi) with skiing and ski-jumping competitions as well as a reindeer race in the centre of town. **Jutajaiset** (www.jutajaiset.fi), in late June, is a celebration of Lapland folklore by various youth ensembles.

Sleeping

Most places offer good discounts in summer.

Guesthouse Borealis GUESTHOUSE €
(016-342-0130; www.guesthouseborealis.com; Asemieskatu 1; s/d/tr €53/66/89; P @) Cordial hospitality and proximity to trains make this family-run spot a winner. Rooms are simple, bright and clean; some have a balcony. The airy dining room is the venue for breakfast, featuring Finnish porridge. Guests have use of a kitchen (and sauna for a small charge), and there are two self-contained apartments. Prices are a little higher in winter; substantially so over Christmas.

Hostel Rudolf HOSTEL €
(016-321-321; www.rudolf.fi; Koskikatu 41; dm/s/d mid-Jan–Mar €52/64/92, Apr-Nov €42/49/63, Christmas period €58/73/108; P) Run by Hotel Santa Claus, where you inconveniently have to go to check-in, this staffless hostel is Rovaniemi's only one and can fill up fast. Rooms are private and good for the price, with spotless bathrooms, solid desks and bedside lamps; dorm rates get you the same deal. There's also a kitchen available but don't expect a hostel atmosphere. HI discount.

Ounaskoski Camping CAMPGROUND €
(016-345-304; www.ounaskoski-camping-rovaniemi.com; Jäämerentie 1; campsites €14 plus per adult/child €8/4; late May-late Sep; P) Just across the elegant bridge from the town centre, this campground is perfectly situated on the riverbank. There are no cabins, but plenty of grassy tent and van sites, with great views over the Ounaskoski.

★ **City Hotel** HOTEL €€
(016-330-0111; www.cityhotel.fi; Pekankatu 9; s/d/superior d €129/149/177; P @) There's something very pleasing about this welcoming central place. It retains an intimate feel, with excellent service and plenty of extras included free of charge. Rooms are commodious and compact; they look very stylish with large windows, arty silvery objects, good beds, and plush maroon and brown fabrics. Lux rooms offer a proper double bed, while smart suites have a sauna. Cheaper in summer.

Santasport HOTEL €€
(020-798-4200; www.santasport.fi; Hiihtomajantie 2; s €74-99, d €96-150; P @) A

SEEING SANTA

The southernmost line at which the sun doesn't set on at least one day a year, the Arctic Circle, is called **Napapiiri** in Finnish and crosses the Sodankylä road 8km north of Rovaniemi (although the Arctic Circle can actually shift several metres daily). There's an **Arctic Circle marker** here; around it is built the 'official' **Santa Claus Village** (www.santaclausvillage.info; ⏲10am-5pm mid-Jan–May & Sep-Nov, 9am-6pm Jun-Aug, 9am-7pm Dec–mid-Jan) FREE, a touristy complex of shops, winter activities and cottage accommodation.

Santa Claus Post Office (www.santaclaus.posti.fi) here receives over half a million letters yearly from children (and adults) all over the world. You can browse a selection of the letters, which range from rather mercenary requests for thousands of euros of electronic goods to heart-rending pleas for parents to recover from cancer. Santa answers as many as he can. Your postcard sent from here will bear an official Santa stamp, and you can arrange to have it delivered at Christmas. For €7.90, you can get Santa to send a Christmas card to you.

At the tourist information desk you can get your Arctic Circle certificate (€4.20) or stamp your passport (€0.50).

But the top attraction for most is, of course, **Santa** himself, who sees visitors year-round in a rather impressive **grotto** (www.santaclauslive.com) FREE, where a huge clock mechanism (it slows the earth's rotation so that Santa can visit the whole world's children on Christmas night) eerily surrounds those queuing for an audience. The portly saint is quite a linguist, and an old hand at chatting with kids and adults alike. A private chat (around 2 minutes) is absolutely free, but you can't photograph the moment, and official photos of your visit start at an outrageous €25.

Other things at the complex are Arctice/Snowman World with igloo accommodation, an ice bar and tyre tobogganing; Santamus; an atmospheric seasonal 'experience' restaurant; a husky park; reindeer rides; ice sculpture; and varying Christmassy exhibitions. There's also cottage accommodation and a cafe serving salmon smoked over a traditional fire.

Bus 8 heads here from the train station, passing through the centre (adult/child €6.60/3.80 return).

15-minute stroll from the town centre at the base of Ounasvaara, this sports complex offers great value. Functional modern rooms – including excellent family suites – offer heaps of space, fridge, microwave and drying cupboard. On-site is a full-size swimming pool, spa facilities, bowling, gym, indoor playpark, and bike and cross-country ski hire.

Hotelli Aakenus HOTEL €€
(☎016-342-2051; www.hotelliaakenus.net; Koskikatu 47; s/d €77/89; P @ wi-fi) Offering excellent summer value from mid-May to the end of August (s/d €65/69), this friendly, efficient little hotel is a short distance west of the town centre and a quick stroll from the Arktikum. The rooms are simple and spacious, with narrow beds. A sauna (switched on for several hours) and decent buffet breakfast are included. There are also some apartments out the back.

Santa Claus Holiday Village COTTAGES €€
(☎040-159-3811; www.schv.fi; Tähtikuja 2, Napapiiri; d €99-149; P wi-fi family) This cottage complex is right at Santa's Napapiiri home. It's run out of an enormous souvenir shop (there's a Santa in here too) but staff bend over backwards to be helpful and can arrange all sorts of activities. Cottages are at a decent distance from tour groups and offer modern, hotel-standard rooms with sauna and kitchenette.

Hotel Santa Claus HOTEL €€€
(☎016-321-321; www.hotelsantaclaus.fi; Korkalonkatu 29; s/d €168/203; P @ wi-fi) Thankfully this excellent hotel is devoid of sleighbells and 'ho-ho-ho' kitsch. It's right in the heart of town and very upbeat and busy, with helpful staff and a good bar and restaurant. Rooms have all the trimmings and are spacious, with a sofa and good-sized beds; a supplement gets you a slightly larger superior room. Unacceptably, wi-fi is charged. Prices can halve in summer.

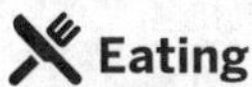

Eating

Cafe & Bar 21 CAFE €
(www.cafebar21.fi; Rovakatu 21; dishes €8-11; ⏲11am-9pm Mon-Tue, 11am-midnight Wed-Thu, 11am-2am Fri, noon-2am Sat, noon-9pm Sun; 📶) It's a surprise to find this artfully modern designer place here: a reindeer pelt collage on the grey concrete wall is the only concession to place. Modish black and white makes a stylish haunt for creative cocktails, espressos, hot chocolate and a very tasty selection of salads, tapas portions plus sweet and savoury waffles.

Mariza FINNISH €
(www.ruokahuonemariza.fi; Ruokasenkatu 2; lunch €7.50-9.50; ⏲10am-2pm Mon-Fri; 🌿) A couple of blocks from the town centre in untouristed territory, this simple lunch place is a real find, and offers a buffet of home-cooked Finnish food, including daily changing hot dishes, soup and salad. Authentic and excellent.

Monte Rosa FINNISH €€
(☎016-330-0400; www.monterosa.fi; Maakuntakatu 25; mains €25-35; ⏲11am-10.30pm Mon-Fri, 3-10.30pm Sat, 5-9.30pm Sun; 📶) Attached to the City Hotel, this goes for the romance vote with a low candlelit interior and chummy booth seating. Good-sized portions of Finnish and Lapland fare are very tasty; there's plenty of reindeer and local fish. Downstairs, the Bull Bar serves ribs and huge burgers out of the same kitchen.

Nili FINNISH €€
(☎0400-369-669; www.nili.fi; Valtakatu 20; mains €20-33; ⏲6-11pm Mon-Sat) There's much more English than Finnish heard at this popular central restaurant, with an attractive interior and a Lapland theme. The food's tasty rather than gourmet, but uses toothsome local ingredients, with things like reindeer, lake fish, wild mushrooms and berries creating appealing northern flavours. The overpriced wine list needs work.

Drinking & Entertainment

★Kauppayhtiö CAFE, BAR
(www.facebook.com/kauppayhtio; Valtakatu 24; ⏲11am-8pm Mon-Thu, 11am-4am Fri & Sat; 📶) Rovaniemi's most personable cafe, this is an oddball collection of retro curios with a coffee and gasoline theme and colourful plastic tables. All the knick-knacks are purportedly for sale here, but it's the espresso machine, charismatic outdoor lounge and stage area, salads, rolls, burgers, Wednesday-to-Sunday sushi, sundaes and bohemian Lapland crowd that keep the place ticking.

Roy Club BAR, CLUB
(www.royclub.fi; Maakuntakatu 24; ⏲10pm-4am) This friendly bar has a sedate, comfortable top half with cosy seating, cheap and long happy hours and regular karaoke. There's also a downstairs nightclub that gets cheerily boisterous with students and stays open late.

ZoomIt BAR
(www.hotelsantaclaus.fi; Koskikatu 14; ⏲2pm-midnight Mon-Thu, 2pm-2am Fri, noon-2am Sat, noon-11pm Sun; 📶) Large, light and modern, ZoomIt is a popular, buzzy central bar and cafe. Right in the heart of town, its terrace is the spot to be on a sunny afternoon and its spacious interior gives room to stretch out with a book if it's raining or snowing.

Information

There are lockers at both train and bus stations.

Metsähallitus (☎020-564-7820; www.outdoors.fi; Pilke, Ounasjoentie 6; ⏲8am-6pm Mon-Fri, 10am-6pm Sat & Sun) Information centre for the national parks, sells maps and fishing permits.

Tourist Information (☎016-346-270; www.visitrovaniemi.fi; Maakuntakatu 29; ⏲9am-6pm Mon-Fri, 9am-3pm Sat & Sun mid-Jun–mid-Aug & late Nov-early Jan, 9am-5pm Mon-Fri rest of year; 📶) On the square in the middle of town. Very helpful.

LAPLAND SEASONS

It's important to pick your time in Lapland carefully. In the far north there's no sun for 50 days of the year, and no night for 70-odd days. In June it's very muddy, and in July insects can be hard to deal with. If you're here to walk, August is great and in September the *ruska* (autumn leaves) can be seen. There's thick snow cover from mid-October to May; December draws charter flights looking for Santa, real reindeer and guaranteed snow, but the best time for skiing and husky/reindeer/snowmobile safaris is March and April, when you get a decent amount of daylight and less-extreme temperatures.

WORTH A TRIP

RANUA ZOO

Little Ranua is famous for its excellent **zoo** (Ranuan Eläinpuisto; www.ranuazoo.com; Ranua; adult/child €16/13; ⏲9am-7pm Jun-Aug, 10am-4pm Sep-May; 👪), focused almost entirely on Finnish animals, although there are also polar bears and musk oxen. A boardwalk runs past all the creatures, which include minks and stoats, impressive owls and eagles, wild reindeer, elk, a big bear paddock (they hibernate from November to March), lynx and wolverines. There's plenty more for kids, with horse rides, mini-karts, pettable domestic animals and assault courses. Ice-cream stops dot the route, and there's a cafe and lunch restaurant.

Ranua, 82km south of Rovaniemi on Rd 78, has hotel, cottage and camping accommodation; there are three to six daily buses from Rovaniemi (€17.30, 1¼ hours) as well as connections from Kajaani and Oulu.

Getting There & Away

AIR

Rovaniemi's airport is a major winter destination for charter flights and it's the 'official airport of Santa Claus': he must hangar his sleigh here. Finnair and Norwegian fly daily from Helsinki.

BUS

Frequent express buses go south to Kemi (€20 to €27, 1½ to 2½ hours), Oulu (€29 to €44, three to four hours), and there are night buses to Helsinki (€130.20, 12¾ hours). Daily connections serve just about everywhere else in Lapland. Some buses head on north into Norway.

TRAIN

The train between Helsinki and Rovaniemi (€84 to €102, 10 to 12 hours) is quicker and cheaper than the bus. There are three daily direct services (via Oulu), including overnighters (various berth options available) with car transport.

Getting Around

Rovaniemi airport is 10km northeast. **Minibuses** (☎016-362-222; www.airporttaxirovaniemi.fi) meet arriving flights, dropping off at hotels in the centre (€7, 15 minutes). They pick up along the same route about an hour before departures.

Major car-rental agencies have offices in the airport and in town.

Western Lapland

There's plenty going on in western Lapland, with Kemi's snow castle, several ski resorts (Levi, Ylläs, Olos), and a wonderful range of activities in Muonio, including memorable husky-sled treks. The long journey up Finland's left 'arm' culminates in Kilpisjärvi, tucked in between Sweden and Norway. These are Finland's 'highlands' and, though not especially high in altitude, they offer excellent walking and some outstanding views.

Kemi

☎016 / POP 22,285

Kemi is an industrial town and important deepwater harbour. Though in summer only the gem museum and wide waterfront have much appeal, it's home to two of Finland's blockbuster winter attractions.

Sights & Activities

★Lumilinna CASTLE

(SnowCastle; ☎016-258-878; www.visitkemi.fi; adult/child €15/7.50; ⏲10am-6pm late Jan-early Apr) Of all the marvels under the big sky, few things conjure the fairy-tale romance of a snow castle. First built in 1996 as a Unicef project, the castle is a Lapland winter highlight and favoured destination for weddings, honeymoons, or general marvelling at the weird light and sumptuously realised decoration of the interior. The design changes every year but always includes an ethereally beautiful chapel, a snow hotel, ice bar and restaurant (menus €43 to €50, must be prebooked).

Sampo CRUISE

(☎016-258-878; www.visitkemi.fi; 4hr cruise €270; ⏲cruises mid-Dec–mid-Apr, summer 10am-2pm Tue-Sat late Jun-late Aug) This retired icebreaker runs memorable, though overpriced, excursions. The four-hour cruise includes a meal and ice-swimming in special drysuits. For extra cost you can choose to approach and leave the ship on snowmobiles (reindeer visit included). The best experience is when the ice is thickest, usually March. Book well in advance. Note that kids under 12 aren't allowed to do the ice-swimming part.

Sleeping

Hotelli Palomestari HOTEL €€

(☎016-257-117; www.hotellipalomestari.com; Valtakatu 12; s/d €94/129; P📶) The 'fire chief' is a block south and one west of the train and bus stations on a pedestrian street, and offers friendly service and decent rooms with trademark Finnish furniture, including a desk and sofa. There's also a bar downstairs with outside seating. It's significantly better value on weekends and in summer.

★Lumihotelli SNOW HOTEL €€€
(☎016-258-878; www.visitkemi.fi; s/d/ste €190/320/350; ⊙late Jan-early Apr; P) The snow hotel's interior temperature is -5°C, but a woolly sheepskin and sturdy sleeping bag keep you warm(ish) atop the ice bed. There are also 'Olokolo' sleeping pods with a transparent ceiling for aurora-watching. In the morning you can thaw out in the sauna of a nearby hotel. It's cheaper midweek.

Information

Tourist Office (☎040-680-3120; www.visitkemi.fi; Valtakatu 26; ⊙8am-3.30pm Mon-Fri) In the town hall. Check out the views from the cafe upstairs in the same building.

Getting There & Away

Kemi-Tornio airport is 6km northwest. Finnair/FlyBe has regular Helsinki flights. Airport taxis cost €20.

Buses run to Tornio (€6.80, 35 minutes) more than hourly (fewer at weekends), Rovaniemi (€20 to €26, 1½ to two hours) and Oulu (€20 to €26, 1¾ hours), among other places.

There are trains from Helsinki (€79 to €85, nine hours), Oulu (€22.50, one hour) and Rovaniemi (€22.30, 1½ hours).

Tornio

☎016 / POP 22,525

Right on the impressive Tornionjoki, northern Europe's longest free-flowing river, Tornio is joined to its Swedish counterpart Haparanda by short bridges. Cross-border shopping has boomed here in recent years, with new malls popping up like mushrooms. Don't forget that Finland is an hour ahead of Sweden.

Sights

Aineen Taidemuseo GALLERY
(www.tornio.fi/aine; Torikatu 2; adult/child €4/free; ⊙11am-6pm Tue-Thu, 11am-3pm Fri-Sun) The attractive modern Tornio gallery comprises the private collection of Veli Aine, a local business tycoon. It displays Finnish art from the 19th and 20th centuries, and has decent temporary exhibitions and a good cafe.

Tornionlaakson Maakuntamuseo MUSEUM
(www.tornio.fi/museo; Keskikatu 22; adult/child €5/3; ⊙11am-6pm Tue-Thu, 11am-3pm Fri-Sun) The local historical museum has an interesting collection of old artefacts and costumes.

Activities

River-rafting is popular in summer on the Kukkolankoski, using inflatable rubber rafts or traditional wooden boats. There are also **kayaking** trips and winter excursions such as snowmobile, reindeer and husky **safaris**. The tourist office can make bookings for all trips and handles **fishing** permits; there are several excellent spots along the Tornionjoki.

Green Zone Golf Course GOLF
(☎016-431-711; www.torniogolf.fi; Näräntie; green fee €45; ⊙9am-8pm May-Oct, 8am-10pm late Jun-late Jul) This golf course straddles Finland and Sweden, allowing you to fire shots into a different country and time zone. There are various group discounts; there's also a driving range and pitch 'n' putt course (adult/child €10/5).

Sleeping & Eating

There's better accommodation choice across the border in Haparanda.

E-City GUESTHOUSE €€
(☎044-509-0358; www.ecity.fi; Saarenpäänkatu 39; s/d €75/90, with shared bathroom €60/75; P ☎) A friendly, clean guesthouse a 15-minute walk from central Tornio near the river. Some things could do with a tweak, but the comfortable, colourful rooms are fine. Shared bathrooms have decent showers, and breakfast includes traditional Finnish porridge.

Umpitunneli PUB FOOD €€
(www.umpitunneli.fi; Hallituskatu 15; mains €13-22; ⊙food Mon-Fri 3-10pm, Sat 1-10pm, Sun 1-8pm; ☎) The 'Dead-End Tunnel' may be a road to nowhere but it's a most enjoyable one, with a huge terrace, plenty of drunken locals adding entertainment value on weekends, and large plates of food, from creamy pastas to steaks and Tex-Mex. There are often live bands.

Information

Tourist Office (☎050-590-0562; www.haparandatornio.com; Krannigatan 5; ⊙9am-5pm Mon-Fri mid-Aug–May, 9am-7pm Mon-Fri, 10am-4pm Sat, 11am-5pm Sun Jun–mid-Aug; ☎) Tourist office for both towns in the shared Tornio-Haparanda bus station. These are the Finnish hours, though it's technically in Sweden.

Getting There & Away

Kemi-Tornio Airport is 18km east of town, with regular flights to/from Helsinki. Buses drop-off a kilometre away, or it's a €35 taxi from town.

From the shared Tornio-Haparanda bus station, there are a couple of direct services to Rovaniemi, but you usually must change (to bus or train) in Kemi (€6.80, 35 minutes, more than hourly, less at weekends). Swedish buses run to Luleå, from where buses and trains run to other Swedish destinations.

Levi (Sirkka)

016

Levi is one of Finland's two most popular ski resorts, but it's also a very popular destination for *ruska* (autumn) season hiking and a cheap base in summer.

Sights & Activities

Samiland MUSEUM

(www.samiland.fi; Tunturitie 205; adult/child €10/7; 10am-8pm) Attached to the Levi Panorama hotel at the top of the main ski lift, this museum is a Unesco project. The very worthwhile exhibition gives plenty of good multilingual information on the Sámi, including details about their traditional beliefs and reindeer herding, accompanied by excellent past and present photographs. Outdoors on the hillside is a collection of traditional kota huts and storage platforms.

Levitunturi SNOW SPORTS

(www.levi.fi) The ski resort has 43 downhill slopes, many lit, and 27 lifts. The vertical drop is 325m, and the longest run 2.5km. There are two half-pipes and a superpipe for snowboarders, a snow park, and several runs and free lifts for children. High-season lift tickets cost €41/195 per day/week. Equipment hire and lessons are available.

Sleeping

Virtually the whole town consists of holiday apartments and cottages. They typically sleep four to six, have a sauna, a fully equipped kitchen and many other mod-cons. In summer, they are a real bargain, costing €45 to €60 per night; in winter €1100 a week is average. **Levin Matkailu Keskusvaraamo** (0600-550-134; www.levi.fi; 9am-4.30pm Mon-Fri, 11am-4pm Sat & Sun Sep-May, 9am-7pm Mon-Fri, 11am-4pm Sat & Sun Jun-Aug), in the tourist office, is the place to book these.

★**Levi Panorama** HOTEL €€€

(016-336-3000; www.levipanorama.fi; Tunturitie 205; s/d winter €144/177, summer €80/89, superior summer €97/105, winter €160/193; Jun-Apr; P@) Halfway up the slopes, with a great ski-in-ski-out area downstairs, this stylish hotel has brilliant rooms with lots of space, modish furniture, big photos of Lapland wildlife and views over the pistes. Superiors add a balcony but most look the other way. The bar has a sensational outlook. You can nip up and down to town on the gondola. It's top value in summer.

Information

Tourist Office (0600-550-134; www.levi.fi; Myllyjoentie 2; 9am-4.30pm Mon-Fri, 11am-4pm Sat & Sun Sep-May, 9am-7pm Mon-Fri, 11am-4pm Sat & Sun Jun-Aug;) Behind the tepee-like building on the roundabout in the centre of the resort. The main accommodation booking agency is also here, and staff can book activities such as snowmobile safaris, dog-sled treks and reindeer rides.

Getting There & Away

Levi is on Rd 79, 170km north of Rovaniemi. All buses from Rovaniemi to Kittilä continue on to here, some continuing to Muonio.

Muonio

016

The last significant stop on Rd 21 before Kilpisjärvi and Norway, Muonio sits on the scenic Muonionjoki that forms the border between Finland and Sweden. It's a fine base for summer and winter activities, including low-key skiing at nearby Olos. Most of the town was razed during WWII, but the 1817 wooden church escaped that fate.

Activities

★**Harriniva** OUTDOORS

(0400-155-100; www.harriniva.fi; Harrinivantie 35) Three kilometres south of town, this excellent set-up has a vast program of summer and winter activities, ranging from short jaunts to multiday adventures. In summer these include canoe and boat trips and fishing on the salmon-packed Muonionjoki.

In winter wonderful dog-sledding safaris run from 1½ hours (€90) to two days (€580), or a week or more, perhaps adding reindeer-sledding and snowmobiling to the mix.

Harriniva has the **Arktinen Rekikoirakeskus** (Arctic sled-dog centre) with around 450 lovable dogs, all with names and personalities. A great guided tour of their town costs €7/4 per adult/child. There are two departures daily. You can also hire bikes, boats and rods here.

Hetta/Enontekiö & Pallas-Yllästunturi National Park

016 / POP 880

One of Lapland's signature long-distance walks is the excellent 55km trekking route between the northern village of Hetta (also known as Enontekiö) and **Hotelli Pallas** (016-323-355; www.laplandhotels.com; Pallastunturi; s/d winter €104/131, summer €78/92; Dec-late Sep; P). The marked trail crosses Pallas-Yllästunturi National Park, and can easily be completed in four days. There are free wilderness huts, but these pack out in summer so it's wise to carry a tent. See www.outdoors.fi for details of the route and huts.

Hetta has a large Sámi population and, though a bit spread-out, makes a good stop for a night or two. Here, **Skierri** (020-564-7950; www.outdoors.fi; Peuratie 15; 9am-5pm Mar-Apr & Jun-late Sep, 9am-4pm Mon-Fri late Sep-Feb & May;) is the combined local tourist office and national park visitor centre. At the trek's southern end, **Pallastunturi Luontokeskus** (020-564-7930; www.outdoors.fi; 9am-5pm Jun-Sep & mid-Feb–Apr, 9am-4pm Mon-Fri rest of year) by the Hotelli Pallas provides information and makes hut reservations.

Hetan Majatalo (016-554-0400; www.hetan-majatalo.fi; Riekontie 8; s/d hotel €68/94, guesthouse €42/68; P@) is in the centre of Hetta, but set back in its own garden away from the road. This welcoming pad offers two types of accommodation in facing buildings: clean and simple guesthouse rooms sharing bathrooms, and very handsome, spacious, wood-clad hotel rooms.

Buses head out to the main road to Rovaniemi (€56.90, five hours) and Kilpisjärvi (€31.10, 3¼ hours) via a swap-over at Palojoensuu. There are also buses to Hetta from Muonio.

Kilpisjärvi

016

The remote village of Kilpisjärvi, the northernmost settlement in the 'arm' of Finland, is in a memorable setting among lakes and snowy mountains on the doorstep of both Norway and Sweden. At 480m above sea level, this small border post, wedged between the lake of Kilpisjärvi and the magnificent surrounding fells, is also the highest village in Finland.

The Kilpisjärvi area offers fantastic long and short hikes. The ascent to slate-capped **Saana Fell** (1029m) takes two to three hours return. Also popular is the route through **Malla Nature Park** to the Kolmen Valtakunnan Raja, a concrete block in a lake that marks the **treble border** of Finland, Sweden and Norway. Alternatively, a summer **boat service** (0400-669-392; www.kilpisjarvi.org; single/return €20/25; Jul-late Sep) drops you a light 3km away.

Lining the main road are several camping grounds with cabins. Many places are open only during the trekking season, which is from June to September.

Two daily buses connect Rovaniemi and Kilpisjärvi (€72.90, six to eight hours) via Kittilä, Levi and Muonio, with connection to Hetta. In summer, one heads on to Tromsø, Norway.

Northeastern Lapland

North from Rovaniemi, Hwy 4 (E75) heads up to the vast, flat expanse of northern Lapland and Sápmi, home of the Sámi people and their domesticated reindeer herds wandering the forests and fells. Subtle landscape changes become more severe as you head north, and the feeling of entering one of Europe's last great wildernesses is palpable. The resort town of Saariselkä is the base for hiking or ski-trekking do-it-yourself itineraries in the wonderful UKK National Park, while the Sámi capital of Inari is the place to learn about their traditions and a base for visiting the Lemmenjoki National Park.

Sodankylä

016 / POP 5540

Likeable Sodankylä is the main service centre for one of Europe's least-populated areas, with a density of just 0.75 people per sq km. It makes a decent staging post on the way between Rovaniemi and the north.

The **tourist office** (040-746-9776; www.visitsodankyla.fi; Jäämerentie 3; 9am-5pm Mon-Fri 10am-4pm Sat & Sun) is at the intersection of the Kemijärvi and Rovaniemi roads. Next door, the **Vanha Kirkko** (☎0400-190-406; ⏰9am-6pm early Jun–mid-Aug, 9am-6pm Fri-Mon late Aug) FREE is the region's oldest church and dates back to 1689.

Sodankylä books out in mid-June for the **Midnight Sun Film Festival** (www.msff.fi), which has a comprehensive range of intriguing screenings in three venues.

Across the river from the town, **Camping Sodankylä Nilimella** (☎016-612-181; www.naturex-ventures.fi; tent sites €8 plus per adult/child €4/2, 2-/4-person cabins €38/54, apt €80-150; ⏰Jun-Aug; P 📶) has simple but spacious cabins, as well as cottage apartments with private kitchen and sauna.

Majatalo Kolme Veljestä (☎0400-539-075; www.majatalokolmeveljesta.fi; Ivalontie 1; s/d/tr €48/68/80; P @ 📶), 500m north of the centre, has small spotless rooms sharing a decent bathroom. Central **Hotelli Karhu** (Hotel Bear Inn; ☎040-122-8250; www.hotel-bearinn.com; Lapintie 7; r €105-115; P 📶) offers decent rooms with grey-wood floors and modern bathrooms. Some single rooms come with a cute mini-sauna.

There are regular buses from Rovaniemi, Ivalo and Kemijärvi. The bus terminal is on the main road.

Saariselkä

☎016

Between Sodankylä and Inari, this collection of enormous hotels and holiday cottages makes a great stop for the active. It's on the edge of one of Europe's great wilderness areas, much of which is covered by the Urho Kekkonen National Park. You could hike for weeks here; there's a good network of huts and a few marked trails. In winter, this is a ski resort and a very popular base for snowmobiling and husky trips. In the Siula centre there's tourist information and a **national parks office** (☎020-564-7200; www.outdoors.fi; Siula Centre; ⏰9am-5pm Mon-Fri, plus 10am-4pm Sat & Sun high season) that sells maps and reserves wilderness cabins. Hit the website www.saariselka.com for cottage accommodation; the cheapest place to stay is **Saariselän Panimo** (☎016-675-6500; www.saariselanpanimo.fi; Saariseläntie 10; s/d €53/63; P 📶), a cosy brewpub whose spacious, clean rooms are a real bargain. There are three to five daily buses from Rovaniemi (€47.20, 3½ to 4¼ hours), continuing to Ivalo (€7.40, 30 minutes).

Inari

☎016 / POP 550

The tiny village of Inari (Sámi: Anár), is Finland's most significant Sámi centre and is *the* place to begin to learn something of their culture. It boasts the wonderful Siida museum and Sajos, cultural centre and seat of the Finnish Sámi parliament, as well as excellent handicrafts shops. It's also a great base for locations like Lemmenjoki National Park and the Kevo Strict Nature Reserve.

The village sits on Lapland's largest lake, Inarijärvi, a spectacular body of water with more than 3000 islands in its 1153-sq-km area.

Sights & Activities

★Siida MUSEUM
(www.siida.fi; adult/child €10/5; ⏰9am-8pm Jun–mid-Sep, 10am-5pm Tue-Sun mid-Sep–May) One of Finland's finest museums, Siida, a comprehensive overview of the Sámi and their environment, should not be missed. The main exhibition hall consists of a fabulous nature exhibition around the edge, detailing northern Lapland's ecology by season, with wonderful photos and information panels. In the centre of the room is detailed information on the Sámi, from their former seminomadic existence to modern times.

Sajos CULTURAL CENTRE
(www.sajos.fi; Siljotie; ⏰9am-5pm Mon-Fri) FREE The spectacular wood-and-glass Sámi cultural centre stands proud in the middle of town. It holds the Sámi parliament as well as a library and music archive, restaurant, exhibitions and craft shop. In summer there are tours of the building, and Sámi handicraft workshops.

Visit Inari ACTIVITIES
(Lake & Snow; ☎040-179-6069; www.visitinari.fi; Inarintie 38) This outfit organises summer and winter excursions, including fishing, visits to reindeer farms, snowshoe walks, husky and snowmobile safaris, and aurora borealis hunting. It also operates cruises (adult/child €22/11) on Inarijärvi from June (as soon as the ice melts) to late September, with one or two daily departures from Siida car park. The destination is **Ukko Island** (Sámi: Äjjih), sacred to the Sámi.

RideNorth HORSES, HUSKIES
(Arctic Hysteria; ☎0400-814-424; www.ridenorth.fi; Kotiniemi, Inari; horse riding €55, husky-sledding from €100) This welcoming set-up offers sled excur-

sions with well-cared-for huskies, and year-round trips with beautiful, hardy Norwegian fjording horses. You can even go hiking in summer with the huskies pulling you along.

Tuula Airamo REINDEER
(☎043-200-1898; Tulvalahdentie 235, near Riutula; 1/2/3hr visit €28/39/60) Friendly Tuula offers a great experience here, 17km northwest of Inari off the Angeli road. The one-hour visit lets you meet and feed reindeer, the two-hour visit adds a Sámi handicrafts workshop, and the three-hour visit adds a visit to her typical Lapland home. Book in advance.

Festivals & Events

Skábmagovat FILM
(www.skabmagovat.fi) This indigenous-themed film festival in late January sees collaborations with groups from other nations. There's enough English content to make it worthwhile.

King's Cup REINDEER RACING
(www.paliskunnat.fi) Held over the last weekend of March or first weekend of April, this is the grand finale of Lapland's reindeer-racing season and a great spectacle as the beasts race around the frozen lake, jockeys sliding like water-skiers behind them.

Sleeping & Eating

Lomakylä Inari CAMPGROUND €
(☎016-671-108; www.saariselka.fi/lomakylainari; tent sites for 1/2/4 people €10/15/20, 2-/4-person cabins €67/79, without bathroom €40/50, cottages €85-170; P wi-fi) The closest cabin accommodation to town, this is 500m south of the town centre and a good option. There's a range of cabins and facilities that include a cafe. Lakeside cabins cost a little more but are worth it for the memorable sunsets. Camping and nonheated cabins are June to September only.

★ **Tradition Hotel Kultahovi** HOTEL €€
(☎016-511-7100; www.hotelkultahovi.fi; Saarikoskentie 2; s/d €78/102, annexe s/d €112/128; P @ wi-fi) This cosy place run by a Sámi family overlooks the Alakoski rapids and has spruce rooms, some with a great river view. The standard rooms have been recently renovated, while chambers in the annexe have appealing Nordic decor, drying cupboard, riverside balcony/terrace and (most) a sauna. The restaurant (open 11am to 10.30pm) serves delicious Lappish specialities (mains €20 to €31) with relaxing views.

Hotelli Inari HOTEL €€
(☎016-671-026; www.hotelliinari.fi; Inarintie 40; s/d €88/106, incl sauna €116/136; P wi-fi) In the heart of Inari, this has modernised, spacious rooms with good showers. Slightly cheaper 'small doubles' have two beds end-to-end. A modern annexe behind has top rooms, all modish greys and blacks with sauna and lovely lake views. The restaurant serves pizzas and reasonable local fish and reindeer dishes (mains €10 to €20). Watch the amazing sun at these latitudes out the windows.

Villa Lanca GUESTHOUSE €€
(☎040-748-0984; www.villalanca.com; s/d €63/85, incl kitchen €80/105; P wi-fi) On the main road through town, this is a very characterful lodging, with original rooms that are full of atmosphere and decorated with Asian fabrics, feather charms and real artistic flair. The cute attic rooms are spacious and cheaper but lack a bit of headroom. An excellent breakfast with delicious home-made bread is included. It's a great place to learn about Sámi culture and stories.

Information

Tourist Office (☎020-564-7740; www.inari.fi; Inarintie 46; ⌚9am-8pm Jun–mid-Sep, 10am-5pm Tue-Sun mid-Sep–May; wi-fi) Located in the Siida museum. There's also a nature information point here and internet access.

Getting There & Away

Buses run here from Ivalo (€8.20, 30 minutes), which has an airport. Two daily buses hit Inari from Rovaniemi (€60.10, five hours) and continue to Norway, one to Karasjok and on to Nordkapp in summer, another to Tana bru (four weekly in winter).

Lemmenjoki National Park

Lemmenjoki is Finland's largest national park, covering a remote wilderness area between Inari and Norway. It's prime hiking territory, with desolate wilderness rivers, rough landscapes and the mystique of gold, with solitary prospectors sloshing away with their pans in the middle of nowhere. Boat trips on the river allow more leisurely exploration of the park.

Lemmenjoki Nature Centre (www.outdoors.fi; ⌚9am-5pm mid-Jun–late Sep) is near the park entrance just before the village of Njurgulahti, about 50km southwest of Inari.

As well as hiking and gold panning, there's a boat cruise along the Lemmenjoki valley in summer, from Njurgulahti village to the Kultahamina wilderness hut at Gold Harbour. A 20km marked trail follows the course of the river, so you can take the boat one way, then hike back. There are departures at 10am and 5pm mid-June to mid-August; in early June and from mid-August to mid-September only the evening one goes (€20 one way, 1½ hours). There are several places offering camping and/or cabin accommodation, food and boat trips. Inside the park, a dozen wilderness huts provide free accommodation.

In school holidays (ie early June to early August) there's a taxi-bus service once daily Mondays to Fridays between Inari and Lemmenjoki (€10). During the school year, you may be able to squeeze onto the school taxi service, but it's far from guaranteed. Ask at the Inari tourist office.

UNDERSTAND FINLAND

History

Finnish history is the story of a people who for centuries were a wrestling mat between two heavyweights, Sweden and Russia, and the nation's eventful emergence from their grip to become one of the world's most progressive and prosperous nations.

Prehistory

Though evidence of pre–Ice Age habitation exists, it wasn't until around 9000 years ago that settlement was re-established after the big chill. Things are hazy, but the likeliest scenario seems to be that the Finns' ancestors moved in to the south and drove the nomadic ancestors of the Sámi north towards Lapland.

Sweden & Russia

The 12th and 13th centuries saw the Swedes begin to move in, Christianising the Finns in the south, and establishing settlements and fortifications. The Russians were never far away, though. There were constant skirmishes with the power of Novgorod, and in the early 18th century Peter the Great attacked and occupied much of Finland. By 1809 Sweden was in no state to resist, and Finland became a duchy of the Russian Empire. The capital was moved to Helsinki, but the communist revolution of October 1917 brought the downfall of the Russian tsar and enabled Finland to declare independence.

Winter & Continuation Wars

Stalin's aggressive territorial demands in 1939 led to the Winter War between Finland and the Soviet Union, conducted in horribly low temperatures. Finland resisted heroically, but was eventually forced to cede a tenth of its territory. When pressured for more, Finland accepted assistance from Germany. This 'Continuation War' against the Russians cost Finland almost 100,000 lives. Eventually Mannerheim negotiated an armistice with the Russians, ceding more land, and then waged a bitter war in Lapland to oust the Germans. Against the odds, Finland remained independent, but at a heavy price.

Recent Times

Finland managed to take a neutral stance during the Cold War, and once the USSR collapsed, it joined the EU in 1995, and adopted the euro in 2002.

In the new century, Finland has boomed on the back of the technology sector – which, despite the plunge of Nokia, continues to be strong – the traditionally important forestry industry, design and manufacturing, and, increasingly, tourism. Despite suffering economically along with most of the rest of the world in recent years, it's nevertheless a major success story of the new Europe with a strong economy, robust social values, and superlow crime and corruption.

The 2011 parliamentary elections in Finland sent a shock wave through Europe as the nationalistic, populist True Finns party came from nowhere to seize 19% of the vote. The success of what is now just called the Finns Party (Perussuomalaiset) reflected concerns about rising immigration and a feeling of frustration that Finnish taxpayers were being forced to pay for other countries' problems. It evoked a stereotype of the lonely Finn sitting at home and not caring much about the rest of the world. It remains to be seen if their influence is extended or diminished in the 2015 elections.

People

Finland is one of Europe's most sparsely populated countries, with 17 people per sq km, falling to fewer than one in parts of Lap-

THE SAUNA

Nothing is more traditionally or culturally Finnish than the sauna. For centuries it has been a place to bathe, meditate, warm up during cold winters and even give birth, and most Finns still use the sauna at least once a week. An invitation to bathe in a family's sauna is an honour.

There are three principal types of sauna around these days. The most common is the electric sauna stove, which produces a fairly dry harsh heat compared with the much-loved chimney sauna, which is driven by a log fire and is the staple of life at Finnish summer cottages. Even rarer is the true *savusauna* (smoke sauna), which is without a chimney.

Bathing is done in the nude (there are some exceptions in public saunas, which are almost always sex-segregated anyway) and Finns are quite strict about the nonsexual – even sacred – nature of the sauna.

Proper sauna etiquette dictates that you use a *kauha* (ladle) to throw water on the *kiuas* (sauna stove), which then gives off the *löyly* (sauna steam). At this point, at least in summer in the countryside, you might take the *vihta* (a bunch of fresh, leafy birch twigs) and lightly strike yourself. This improves circulation and has cleansing properties. When you are sufficiently warmed, you'll jump in the lake, river or pool, then return to the sauna to warm up and repeat the cycle several times. If you're indoors, a cold shower will do.

land. Both Finnish and Swedish are official languages, with some 5% of Finns having Swedish as their mother tongue, especially on the west coast and the Åland archipelago. Around 5% of all Finnish residents are immigrants, a low percentage but one that has increased substantially in recent years.

Finland's minorities include some 6000 Roma in the south and, in the north, the Sámi, from several distinct groups. Some 78% of Finns describe themselves as Lutherans, 1.5% are Orthodox and most of the remainder unaffiliated. Finns have one of the lowest rates of church attendance in the Christian world.

A capacity for silence and reflection are the traits that best sum up the Finnish character, though this seems odd when weighed against their global gold medal in coffee consumption, their production line of successful heavy bands and their propensity for a tipple. The image of a log cabin with a sauna by a lake tells much about Finnish culture: independence, endurance (*sisu* or 'guts') and a deep love of nature.

Arts

Architecture

Finland's modern architecture – sleek, functionalist and industrial – has been admired throughout the world ever since Alvar Aalto started making a name for himself during the 1930s. His works can be seen all over Finland today, from the angular Finlandia-talo in Helsinki to the public buildings and street plan of Rovaniemi. Jyväskylä is another obligatory stop for Aalto fans.

Earlier architecture in Finland can be seen in churches made from stone or wood – Kerimäki's oversized church is a highlight, as are the cathedrals at Turku and Tampere. Low-rise Helsinki boasts a patchwork of architectural styles, including the neoclassical buildings of Senate Square, the rich ornamentation of art nouveau (Jugendstil), the modern functionalism of Aalto's buildings and the postmodern Kiasma museum.

Design

Finland, like Scandinavia as a whole, is also famous for its design. Aalto again laid a foundation with innovative interior design, furniture and the famous Savoy vase. Finns have created and refined their own design style through craft traditions and using natural materials such as wood, glass and ceramics. Glassware and porcelain such as Iittala and Arabia are world famous, while Marimekko's upbeat, colourful fabric is a Finnish icon. A new wave of young designers is keeping things from stagnating. Stereotypes are cheerfully broken without losing sight of the roots: an innate practicality and the Finns' almost mystical closeness to nature.

Cinema

The best-known Finnish filmmaker is Aki Kaurismäki, famous for films such as *Le Havre* (2011), *Drifting Clouds* (1996), and the wonderful *Man Without a Past* (2002), an ultimately life-affirming story about a man who loses his memory. Aki Kaurismäki's brother, Mika, has made a reputation for insightful documentaries like *Sonic Mirror* (2008), partially looking at Finland's jazz scene.

Recent home-grown hits include *Musta jää* (*Black Ice*; 2007), a characteristically complex Finnish film of infidelity, and *The Home of Dark Butterflies* (2008), a stark look at a Finnish boys' home. For something completely different, check out *Dudesons Movie* (2006), featuring the painful madness of a group of Finnish TV nuts in the style of *Jackass, Miesten Vuoro* (*Steam of Life*; 2010), a fabulous doco-film featuring Finnish men sweating and talking about life in the confessional of the sauna, or the captivating *Kovasikajuttu* (The Punk Syndrome, 2012), a documentary tracking the progress of Pertti Kurikan Nimipäivät, a punk band whose members are mentally disabled.

Hollywood's most famous Finn is Renny Harlin, director of action movies such as *Die Hard II, Cliffhanger* and *Deep Blue Sea*.

Finland hosts some quality film festivals, notably the Midnight Sun Film Festival (p196) in Sodankylä and the Tampere Film Festival (p159).

Literature

The *Kalevala,* a collection of folk stories, songs and poems compiled in the 1830s by Elias Lönnrot, is Finland's national epic and a very entertaining read. As part of the same nationalistic renaissance, poet JL Runeberg wrote *Tales of the Ensign Ståhl*, capturing Finland at war with Russia, while Aleksis Kivi wrote *Seven Brothers* (1870), the nation's first novel, about brothers escaping conventional life in the forest, allegorising the birth of Finnish national consciousness.

This theme continued in the 1970s with *The Year of the Hare,* looking at a journalist's escape into the wilds by the prolific, popular and bizarre Arto Paasilinna. Other 20th-century novelists include Mika Waltari who gained international fame with *The Egyptian*, and FE Sillanpää who received the Nobel Prize for Literature in 1939. The national bestseller during the postwar period was *The Unknown Soldier* by Väinö Linna. The seemingly endless series of autobiographical novels by Kalle Päätalo and the witty short stories by Veikko Huovinen are also very popular in Finland. Finland's most internationally famous author is Tove Jansson, whose books about the fantastic Moomin family have long captured the imagination. Notable living writers (apart from Paasilinna) include the versatile Leena Krohn and Mikko Rimminen, who has attracted attention for both novels and poetry.

Music

Music is huge in Finland, and in summer numerous festivals all over the country revel in everything from mournful Finnish tango to soul-lifting symphony orchestras to crunchingly potent metal.

Revered composer Jean Sibelius (1865–1957) was at the forefront of the nationalist movement. His stirring tone-poem *Finlandia* has been raised to the status of a national hymn. Classical music is thriving in Finland, which is an assembly line of orchestral and operatic talent: see a performance if you can.

The Karelian region has its own folk-music traditions, typified by the stringed *kantele,* while the Sámi passed down their traditions and beliefs not through the written word but through the songlike chant called the *yoik*.

Finnish bands have made a big impact on the heavier, darker side of the music scale in recent years. The Rasmus, Nightwish, Apocalyptica, HIM and the 69 Eyes are huge worldwide. But there is lighter music, such as surf-rockers French Films, pop-rockers Sunrise Avenue, the Von Hertzen Brothers, indie band Disco Ensemble, emo-punks Poets of the Fall and melodic Husky Rescue.

Increasingly though, what young people in Finland are listening to is local hip-hop, or Suomirap. Artists such as Elastinen and Pyhimys have taken the airwaves by storm in recent years, and there's always some new underground project.

Dance

Finns' passion for dance is typified by the tango, which, although borrowed from Latin America, has been refined into a uniquely Finnish style. Older Finns are tango-mad and every town has a dance hall or dance restaurant. A similar form of Finnish dancing is the waltz-like *humppa*.

Visual Art

Finland's Golden Age in painting and sculpture was the 19th-century National Romantic era, when artists such as Akseli Gallen-Kallela, Albert Edelfelt, Pekka Halonen and the Von Wright brothers were inspired by the country's forests and pastoral landscape. Gallen-Kallela and Helene Schjerfbeck are probably Finland's most famous artists. Schjerfbeck is especially famous for her self-portraits, which seem to define the situation of Finnish women a century ago; Gallen-Kallela is known for *Kalevala*-inspired works – don't miss his frescos on display in the Kansallismuseo (National Museum) in Helsinki.

The best of Finnish art can be seen at Ateneum (National Gallery) in Helsinki, but there's an art gallery *(taidemuseo)* in just about every Finnish city.

Environment

People often describe Finland offhand as a country of 'forests and lakes', and the truth is that they are spot on. Some 10% of Suomi is taken up by bodies of water, and nearly 70% is forested with birch, spruce and pine. It's a fairly flat expanse of territory: though the fells of Lapland add a little height to the picture, they are small change compared to the muscular mountainscapes of Norway.

Measuring 338,000 sq km and weighing in as Europe's seventh-largest nation, Finland hits remarkable latitudes: even its southernmost point is comparable with Anchorage in Alaska, or the lower reaches of Greenland. Its watery vital statistics are also impressive, with 187,888 large lakes and many further wetlands and smaller bodies of water. Geographers estimate that its total coastline, including riverbanks and lakeshores, measures 315,000km, not far off the distance to the moon.

Finland has one of the world's highest tree coverages; much of this forest is managed, and timber-harvesting and the associated pulp-milling is an important industry.

Wildlife

Brown bears, lynx, wolverines and wolves are native to Finland, although sightings are rare unless you go on an organised excursion. You're more likely to see an elk, though hopefully not crashing through your windscreen; drive cautiously. In Lapland, the Sámi keep commercial herds of some 230,000 reindeer. Finland is a birdwatcher's paradise, with species like the capercaillie and golden eagle augmented by hundreds of migratory arrivals in spring and summer.

National Parks

Finland's excellent network of national parks and other protected areas is maintained by **Metsähallitus** (Finnish Forest & Park Service; www.outdoors.fi). In total, over 30,000 sq km, some 9% of the total area, is in some way protected land. The largest and most pristine national parks are in northern Finland, particularly Lapland, where vast swathes of wilderness invite trekking, cross-country skiing, fishing and canoeing.

Sustainable Finland

As a general model for environmentally sustainable nationhood, Finland does very well. Though it has a high per-capita carbon-emission rate, this is largely due to its abnormal heating requirements and is offset in many ways. As in much of northern Europe, cycling and recycling were big here decades ago, littering and waste-dumping don't exist, and sensible solutions for keeping the houses warm and minimising heat loss have long been a question of survival, not virtue. Finns in general have a deep respect for and understanding of nature and have always trodden lightly on it.

But the forest is also an important part of Finland's economy. Most of the forests are periodically logged, and privately owned plots are long-term investments for many Finns. Hunting is big here, and animals are kept at an 'optimum' population level by the keen shooting contingent.

Finland's own commitment to combating climate change is strong, having set a legally

WILDLIFE-WATCHING

The deep forests in eastern and north-eastern Finland offer excellent wildlife-spotting opportunities. While you're unlikely to spot bears, wolves, lynx or wolverines on a casual hike, there are plenty of reliable operators, especially in eastern Finland, that specialise in trips to watch these creatures in their domain. The excellent birdlife, both migratory and local, offers further opportunities. Ask at tourist offices for local services.

binding target in 2014 of 80% emissions reduction by 2050. A large nuclear power sector is backed by an increasing percentage of renewable energy.

Climate Change

Southern Finland has already noticed dramatically changed weather patterns, with much milder winters. The once-unthinkable prospect of a non-white Christmas in Helsinki is now a reality. Scientists in the Arctic are producing increasingly worrying data and it seems that northern nations like Finland may be some of the earliest to be seriously affected.

Food & Drink

Finland's eating scene has perked up dramatically in the last few years as a wave of gourmet restaurants in the major cities has added gastronomic innovation to the always-excellent fresh local produce.

Staples & Specialities

Finnish cuisine has been influenced by both Sweden and Russia and draws on what was traditionally available: fish, game, meat, milk and potatoes, with dark rye used to make bread and porridge and few spices employed.

Soups are a Finnish favourite, common in homes and restaurants. One light snack that you'll see everywhere is the rice-filled savoury pastry from Karelia, the *karjalanpiirakka*. Fish is a mainstay of the Finnish diet. Fresh or smoked salmon *(lohi)*, marinated herring *(silli)*, *siika* (lavaret, a lake whitefish), *kuha* (pike-perch or zander) and delicious Arctic char (*nieriä* or *rautu*) are common, and the tiny lake fish *muikku* (vendace) are another treat.

Two much-loved favourites that you'll see in many places are grilled liver, served with mashed potatoes and bacon, and meatballs. Reindeer has always been a staple food for the Sámi. Elk and bear make occasional appearances on menus.

Big towns all have a kauppahalli (market hall), the place to head for all sorts of Finnish specialities, breads, cheeses, deli produce, meat and a super variety of both fresh and smoked fish. It's also a top place for a cheap feed, with cafes and stalls selling sandwiches and snacks. The summer kauppatori (market square) also has food stalls, coffee stops and market produce, particularly vegetables and fruit.

Finns tend to eat their biggest meal of the day at lunchtime, so many cafes and restaurants put on a lounas special from Monday to Friday. This usually consists of soup plus salad or hot meal or both and includes a soft drink, coffee and sometimes dessert. Expect to pay around €8 to €14 for this deal.

Drinking

The Finns lead the world in coffee *(kahvi)* consumption, downing over 20 million cups per day – that's around four each for every man, woman and child.

Finns drink plenty of beer *(olut)* and among the big local brews are Karhu, Koff, Olvi and Lapin Kulta. The big brands are all lagers, but there's quite a number of microbreweries in Finland (look for the word panimo or panimo-ravintola), and these make excellent light and dark beers. Cider is also popular, as is *lonkero*, a ready-made mix of gin and fruity soft drink. A half-litre of beer in a bar costs around €5 to €7. Finns don't tend to drink in rounds; everybody pays their own.

Beer, wine and spirits are sold by the state network, Alko (www.alko.fi). There are stores in every town. The legal age for drinking is 18 for beer and wine, and 20 for spirits. Beer and cider with less than 4.8% alcohol can be bought at supermarkets, service stations and convenience stores. If you buy cans or bottles, you pay a small deposit (about €0.20). This can be reclaimed by returning them to the recycling section at a supermarket.

Wine is widely drunk, but very pricey in restaurants, where you might pay €45 for a bottle that would cost €10 in an Alko store.

Other uniquely Finnish drinks include *salmiakkikossu*, which combines dissolved liquorice sweets with the iconic Koskenkorva vodka (an acquired taste); *fisu*, which does the same but with Fisherman's Friend pastilles; and cloudberry or cranberry liqueurs.

Vegetarians & Vegans

Most medium-sized towns in Finland will have a vegetarian restaurant *(kasvisravintola)*, usually open weekday lunchtimes only. It's easy to self-cater at markets, or take the salad/vegetable option at lunch buffets (which is usually cheaper). Many restaurants also have a salad buffet. The website www.vegaaniliitto.fi has a useful listing of vegetarian and vegan restaurants; follow 'ruoka' and 'kasvisravintoloita' (the Finnish list is more up-to-date than the English one).

SURVIVAL GUIDE

Directory A–Z

ACCOMMODATION

Price Ranges

These price categories are based on the cost of a standard double room at its most expensive. In the budget category expect shared bathrooms; midrange will have private bathroom, good facilities and breakfast buffet included, while top end has business-class or five-star facilities. Double beds are rare; family or group rooms are common.

€ less than €70

€€ €70 to €160

€€€ more than €160

Camping

Most camping grounds are open only from June to August (ie summer) and popular spots are crowded during July and the Midsummer weekend. Campsites usually cost around €14 plus €5/2 per adult/child. Almost all camping grounds have cabins or cottages for rent, which are usually excellent value from €40 for a basic double cabin to €120 for a cottage with kitchen, bathroom and sauna.

The **Finnish Camping Association** (www.camping.fi) carries an extensive listing of campsites across the country.

Finland's *jokamiehenoikeus* (everyman's right) allows access to most land and means you can pitch a tent almost anywhere on public land or at designated free campsites in national parks.

Farmstays

A growing, and often ecologically sound, accommodation sector in Finland is that of farmstays. Many rural farms, particularly in the south, offer B&B accommodation, a unique opportunity to meet local people and experience their way of life. Plenty of activities are also usually on offer. **ECEAT** (www.eceat.fi) lists a number of organic, sustainable farms in Finland that offer accommodation. Local tourist offices keep lists of farmstay options in the surrounding area; the website www.visitfinland.com links to a few, and Lomarengas also has many listed on its website. In general, prices are good – from around €35 per person per night, country breakfast included. Evening meals are also usually available. Your hosts may not speak much English; if you have difficulties the local tourist office will be happy to help arrange the booking.

Hostels & Summer Hotels

For solo travellers, hostels generally offer the cheapest bed, and can be good value for twin rooms. Finnish hostels are invariably clean, comfortable and very well equipped, though most are in somewhat institutional buildings.

Some Finnish hostels are run by the Finnish Youth Hostel Association (SRM), and many more are affiliated. It's worth being a member of **HI** (www.hihostels.com), as members save 10% per night at affiliated places. You'll save money with a sleep sheet or your own linen, as hostels tend to charge €4 to €8 for this.

From June to August, many student residences are made over as summer hostels and hotels. These are often great value, as you usually get your own room, with kitchen (bring your own utensils though) and bathroom either to yourself or shared between two.

Hotels

Most hotels in Finland cater to business travellers and the majority belong to one of a few major chains, including the following:

Cumulus (www.cumulus.fi)

Finlandia (www.finlandiahotels.fi) An association of independent hotels.

Omenahotelli (www.omena.com) Offers good-value unstaffed hotels booked online.

Scandic (www.scandichotels.com)

Sokos (www.sokoshotels.fi)

Hotels in Finland are designed with the business traveller in mind and tend to charge robustly. But at weekends and during the July summer holidays, prices in three- and four-star hotels tend to drop by 40% or so.

Most hotel rooms have tiny Nordic bathrooms; if you want a bathtub, this can usually be arranged. Many hotels have 'allergy rooms', which have no carpet and minimal fabric.

Nearly all Finnish hotels have a plentiful buffet breakfast included in the rate and many include a sauna session.

Self-Catering Accommodation

One of Finland's joys is its plethora of cottages for rental, ranging from simple camping cabins to fully equipped bungalows with electric sauna and gleaming modern kitchen. These can be remarkably good value and are perfect for families. There are tens of thousands of cabins and cottages for rent in Finland, many in typical, romantic forest lakeside locations. Local booking agents are mentioned under individual destinations.

Local tourist offices and town websites also have lists.

Lomarengas (☎030-650-2502; www.lomarengas.fi) By far the biggest national agent for cottage rentals.

ACTIVITIES

Boating, Canoeing, Kayaking Every waterside town has a place (most frequently the camping ground) where you can rent a canoe, kayak or rowing boat by the hour or day. Rental cottages often have rowing boats that you can use free of charge to investigate the local lake and its islands. Canoe and kayak rentals range in price from €25 to €45 per day, and €90 to €200 per week, more if you need overland transportation to the start or end point of your trip.

Fishing Several permits are required of foreigners (between the ages of 18 and 64) who wish to go fishing in Finland, but they are very easy to arrange. The website www.mmm.fi has all the details. Ice fishing is popular and requires no licence.

Hiking Hiking is best from June to September, although in July mosquitoes and other biting insects can be a big problem in Lapland. Wilderness huts line the northern trails (both free and bookable ones, on a shared basis). According to the law, a principle of common access to nature applies, so you are generally allowed to hike in any forested or wilderness area. The website www.outdoors.fi provides comprehensive information on trekking routes and huts in national parks.

Saunas Many hotels, hostels and camping grounds have saunas that are free with a night's stay. Large towns have public saunas.

Skiing The ski season in Finland runs from late November to early May and slightly longer in the north, where it's possible to ski from October to May. You can rent all skiing or snowboarding equipment at major ski resorts for about €30/110 per day/week. A one-day lift pass costs around €35/170 per day/week. Cross-country skiing is popular: it's best during January and February in southern Finland, and from December to April in the north.

Snowmobiles (Skidoos) You'll need a valid drivers licence to use one.

CHILDREN

Finland is an excellent country to travel in with children, with many kid-friendly attractions and outdoor activities, whether you visit in winter or in summer.

All hotels will put extra beds in rooms, restaurants have family-friendly features and there are substantial transport discounts.

FOOD

The following price ranges refer to the price of an average main course:

€ less than €17

€€ €17 to €27

€€€ more than €27

GAY & LESBIAN TRAVELLERS

Finland's cities are open, tolerant places and Helsinki has a small but welcoming gay scene.

INTERNET ACCESS

Data Very cheap. If you've got an unlocked smartphone, you can pick up a local SIM card for a few euros and charge it with a month's worth of data at a decent speed for under €20. Ask at R-Kioski shops for the latest deals.

Public libraries Always have at least one free internet terminal.

Tourist offices Many have an internet terminal that you can use for free (usually 15 minutes).

Wireless internet access Very widespread; several cities have extensive networks, and nearly all hotels, as well as many restaurants, cafes and bars, offer free access to customers and guests.

MONEY

ATMs Using ATMs with a credit or debit card is by far the easiest way of getting cash in Finland. ATMs have a name, Otto, and can be found even in small villages.

Credit cards Widely accepted; Finns are dedicated users of plastic even to buy a beer or cup of coffee.

Currency Finland adopted the euro (€) in 2002. Euro notes come in five, 10, 20, 50, 100 and 500 denominations and coins in five, 10, 20, 50 cents and €1 and €2. Note that one- and two-cent coins are not used in Finland.

Moneychangers Travellers cheques and cash can be exchanged at banks; in the big cities, independent exchange facilities such as **Forex** (www.forex.fi) usually offer better rates.

Tipping Service is considered to be included in bills, so there's no need to tip at all unless you want to reward exceptional service.

OPENING HOURS

Many attractions in Finland, particularly outdoor ones, only open for a short summer season, typically mid-June to late August. Opening hours tend to shorten in winter in general.

Sample opening hours:

Alko (state alcohol store) 9am to 8pm Monday to Friday, to 6pm Saturday.

Banks 9am to 4.15pm Monday to Friday.

Businesses & Shops 9am to 6pm Monday to Friday, to 3pm Saturday.

Nightclubs 10pm-4am Wednesday to Saturday.

Pubs & Bars 11am to 1am (often later on Friday and Saturday).

Restaurants 11am to 10pm, lunch 11am to 3pm. Last orders generally an hour before closing.

PUBLIC HOLIDAYS

Finland grinds to a halt twice a year: around Christmas and New Year, and during the Midsummer weekend. National public holidays:

New Year's Day 1 January
Epiphany 6 January
Good Friday March/April
Easter Sunday & Monday March/April
May Day 1 May
Ascension Day May
Whitsunday Late May or early June
Midsummer's Eve & Day Weekend in June closest to 24 June
All Saints Day First Saturday in November
Independence Day 6 December
Christmas Eve 24 December
Christmas Day 25 December
Boxing Day 26 December

TELEPHONE

Public telephones Basically no longer exist in Finland, so if you don't have a mobile you're reduced to making expensive calls from your hotel room or talking over the internet.
Mobile phones The cheapest and most practical solution is to purchase a Finnish SIM card and pop it in your own phone. Make sure your phone isn't blocked from doing this by your home network. You can buy a prepaid SIM-card at any R-kioski shop. There are always several deals on offer, and you might be able to pick up a card for as little as €10, including some call credit. Top the credit up at the same outlets, online or at ATMs. Roaming charges within the EU are being phased out and should be abolishedby 2018.
Phonecards At the R-kioski you can also buy cut-rate phone cards that substantially lower the cost of making international calls.
Phone codes The country code for Finland is ☎358. To dial abroad it's ☎00.

TIME

Finland is on Eastern European Time (EET), an hour ahead of Sweden and Norway and two hours ahead of UTC/GMT (three hours from late March to late October).

TOILETS

Public toilets are widespread in Finland but expensive – often €1 a time. On doors, 'M' is for men and 'N' is for women.

TOURIST INFORMATION

The main website of the Finnish Tourist Board is www.visitfinland.com.

VISAS

For more information contact the nearest Finnish embassy or consulate, or check the website www.formin.finland.fi.

See the main Directory section (p484) for entry requirements.

Getting There & Away

AIR

Finland is easily reached by air, with direct flights to Helsinki from many European, American and Asian destinations. It's also served by budget carriers, especially Ryanair, from several European countries. Most other flights are with Finnair or Scandinavian Airlines (SAS).
Airports Most flights to Finland land at **Helsinki-Vantaa airport** (www.helsinki-vantaa.fi), 19km north of the capital. Winter charters hit **Rovaniemi** (www.finavia.fi), Lapland's main airport, and other smaller regional airports. Other international airports include Tampere (TMP), Turku (TKU) and Oulu (OUL). The website www.finavia.fi includes information for all Finnish airports.

LAND

There are several border crossings from northern Sweden and Norway to northern Finland, with no passport or customs formalities. There are nine main border crossings between Finland and Russia, including several in the southeast and two in Lapland. They are more serious frontiers; you must already have a Russian visa.

Sweden

The linked towns of Tornio (Finland) and Haparanda (Sweden), share a bus station from where you can get onward transport into their respective countries. A possible, if remote, crossing point is the Lapland villages of Kaaresuvanto (Finland) and Karesuando (Sweden), separated by a bridge and both served sporadically by domestic buses.

Norway

Three routes link Finnish Lapland with northern Norway, some running only in summer. These are operated by **Eskelisen Lapin Linjat** (www.eskelisen.fi), whose website has detailed maps and timetables, as does the Finnish bus website **Matkahuolto** (www.matkahuolto.fi).

All routes originate or pass through Rovaniemi; the two northeastern routes continue via Inari to Tana Bru/Vadsø or Karasjok. The Karasjok bus continues in summer to Nordkapp (North Cape). On the western route, a Rovaniemi–Kilpisjärvi bus continues to Tromsø in summer.

Russia

Bus

Daily express buses run to Vyborg and St Petersburg from Helsinki and Lappeenranta (one originates in Turku). These services appear on the website of **Matkahuolto** (www.matkahuolto.fi). Semi-official buses and minibuses can be cheaper options. **Goldline** (www.goldline.fi) runs three weekly buses from Rovaniemi via Ivalo to Murmansk.

Train

Three high-speed Allegro train services run daily from Helsinki to the Finland Station in St Petersburg (2nd/1st class around €86/140, 3½ hours). The evening train is usually cheaper. The Tolstoi sleeper runs from Helsinki via St Petersburg (Ladozhki station) to Moscow (2nd/1st class €128/188, 13½ hours). The fare includes a sleeper berth. There are a number of more upmarket sleeper options.

All trains go via Lahti, Kouvola, Vainikkala (26km south of Lappeenranta) and the Russian city of Vyborg. At Helsinki station tickets are sold at the international ticket counter.

You must have a valid Russian visa; immigration procedures are carried out on board.

There are significant discounts for families and small groups. See www.vr.fi.

SEA

For ferry company and route information, see p485.

Getting Around

Finland is well served by public transport.

AIR

Finnair/Flybe run a fairly comprehensive domestic service, mainly out of Helsinki. Standard prices are expensive, but check the website for offers. Budget carriers fly some routes.

Major airlines flying domestically:

Finnair (www.finnair.com) Extensive domestic network.

Flybe (☎0600-94477; www.flybe.com) Runs several domestic routes in partnership with Finnair.

BICYCLE

Bikes can be carried on most trains, buses and ferries.

Bike paths Finland is flat and as bicycle-friendly as any country you'll find, with many kilometres of bike paths. The Åland islands are particularly good cycling country.

Bike hire Daily/weekly hire around €20/80 is possible in most cities. Camping grounds, hotels and hostels often have cheap bikes available for local exploration.

BOAT

Lake and river passenger services were once important means of summer transport in Finland. These services are now largely kept on as cruises, and make a great, leisurely way to journey between towns. The site http://lautta.net is very handy for domestic lake-boat and ferry services.

Popular routes Tampere–Hämeenlinna, Savonlinna–Kuopio, Lahti–Jyväskylä.

Main coastal routes Turku–Naantali, Helsinki–Porvoo and the archipelago ferries to the Åland islands.

BUS

Discounts For student discounts (50% over long distances) you need to be studying full-time in Finland. If booking three or more adult tickets together, a 25% discount applies: great for groups.

Fares Buses may be *pikavuoro* (express) or *vakiovuoro* (regular). Fares are based on distance travelled. The one-way fare for a 100km trip is €18.70/22 for normal/express. Separate from the normal system – though their timetables appear on the Matkahuolto website, **OnniBus** (www.onnibus.com) runs a variety of budget inter-city routes in comfortable double-decker buses.

Ticket offices Long-distance bus ticketing is handled by **Matkahuolto** (www.matkahuolto.fi), whose excellent website has all timetables. Each town has a *linja-autoasema* (bus terminal), with local timetables displayed (*lähtevät* is departures, *saapuvat* arrivals). Ticket offices work normal business hours, but you can always buy the ticket from the driver.

CAR & MOTORCYCLE

Petrol is relatively expensive in Finland, though less so than Norway. Many petrol stations are unstaffed, with machines that take cards or cash. Change for cash is not given.

Hire

Costs Car rental is expensive, but with advance booking or with a group it can work out at a reasonable price. A small car is around €70/300 per day/week with 300km free per day. As ever, the cheapest deals are online.

Look out for weekend rates. These can cost little more than the rate for a single day, and you can pick up the car early afternoon on Friday, and return it late Sunday or early Monday.

Car-rental franchises with offices in many Finnish cities: **Budget** (www.budget.com), **Hertz** (www.hertz.com), **Europcar** (www.europcar.com) and **Avis** (www.avis.com). One of the cheapest is **Sixt** (www.sixt.com).

Road Conditions & Hazards

Wildlife Beware of elk and reindeer, which don't respect vehicles and can dash onto the road unexpectedly. This sounds comical, but elks especially constitute a deadly danger. Notify the police if there is an accident involving these animals. Reindeer are very common in Lapland; slow right down if you see one, as there will be more nearby.

Conditions Snow and ice on the roads, potentially from September to April, and as late as June in Lapland, make driving a serious undertaking. Snow chains are illegal: people use either snow tyres, which have studs, or special all-weather tyres. The website http://liikennetilanne.liikennevirasto.fi has road webcams around Finland, good for checking conditions. Select 'kelikamerat' on the map.

Road Rules

- Finns drive on the right.
- The speed limit is 50km/h in built-up areas, from 80km/h to 100km/h on highways, and 120km/h on motorways.
- Use headlights at all times.
- Seat belts are compulsory for all.
- Blood alcohol limit: 0.05%.

An important feature of Finland is that there are fewer give-way signs than most countries. Traffic entering an intersection from the right has right of way. While this doesn't apply to highways or main roads, in towns cars will often nip out from the right without looking: you must give way, so be careful at smaller intersections in towns.

TRAIN

State-owned **Valtion Rautatiet** (VR; www.vr.fi) runs Finnish trains: a fast, efficient service, with prices roughly equivalent to buses on the same route.

VR's website has comprehensive timetable information. Major stations have a VR office and ticket machines; tickets can also be purchased online, where you'll also find discounted advance fares. You can also board and pay the conductor, but if the station where you boarded had ticket-purchasing facilties, you'll be charged a small penalty fee (€2 to €5).

Classes

The main types of trains are the high-speed Pendolino (the fastest and most expensive class), fast Intercity (IC), Express and 2nd-class-only Regional trains (H on the timetable).

On longer routes there are two types of sleeping carriage. Traditional blue ones offer berths in one-/two-/three-bed cabins; newer sleeping cars offer single and double compartments in a double-decker carriage. There are cabins with bathroom, and one equipped for wheelchair use. Sleeper trains transport cars.

Costs

Fares vary slightly according to the type of train, with Pendolino the priciest. A one-way ticket for a 100km express train journey costs approximately €23 in 2nd ('eco') class. First-class ('extra') tickets cost around 35% more than a 2nd-class ticket. A return fare gives a 10% discount.

Children under 17 pay half; those under 6 travel free (but without a seat). A child travels free with every adult on long-distance trips, and there are also discounts for seniors, local students and any group of three or more adults travelling together.

Train Passes

International rail passes accepted in Finland include the Eurail Scandinavia Pass, Eurail Global Pass and InterRail Global Pass. For more information on these passes, see p489.

Finland Eurail Pass (www.eurail.com) Costs €137/182/245 for three/five/10 days' 2nd-class travel in a one-month period within Finland.

InterRail Finland Pass (www.interrail.eu) Offers travel only in Finland for three/four/six/eight days in a one-month period, costing €125/158/212/258 in 2nd class.It's about 33% cheaper for under-26s.

Tallinn

Includes ➡

Why Go?

Estonia doesn't have to struggle to find a point of difference; it's completely unique. Its closest ethnic and linguistic buddy is Finland, and although they both may love to get naked together in the sauna, 50 years of Soviet rule has created obvious differences.

If you're labouring under the misconception that 'former Soviet' means dull and grey, Estonia's capital city will delight in proving you wrong. Tallinn has charm by the bucketload, fusing the modern and medieval to come up with a vibrant vibe all of its own. It's an intoxicating mix of church spires, glass skyscrapers, baroque palaces, top-notch eateries, brooding battlements, run-down wooden houses and sunny squares – with a few Soviet throwbacks in the mix.

A visit from Helsinki is just too easy to pass up – ferries ply the 85km separating the two capitals so frequently that Finns almost think of Tallinn as a distant suburb.

Best Places to Eat

- ➡ Ö (p215)
- ➡ Tchaikovsky (p215)
- ➡ Leib (p215)
- ➡ Von Krahli Aed (p215)
- ➡ III Draakon (p214)

Best Places to Stay

- ➡ Hotel Telegraaf (p214)
- ➡ Yoga Residence (p214)
- ➡ Hotel Cru (p214)
- ➡ Euphoria (p214)
- ➡ Tallinn Backpackers (p214)

When to Go

Tallinn

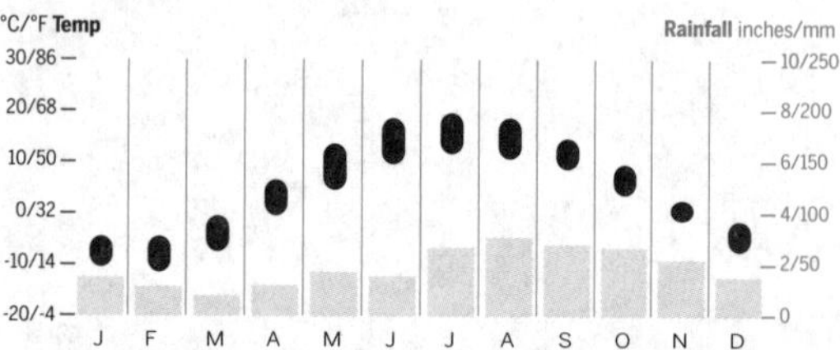

Apr–May See the city shake off winter's gloom, with forests thickening and gardens blooming.

Jun–Aug White nights, beach parties and loads of summer festivals.

Dec Christmas markets, mulled wine and long, cosy nights.

Sights

Old Town

Tallinn's medieval Old Town (Vanalinn) is without doubt the country's most fascinating locality. It's divided into Toompea (the upper town) and the lower town, which is still surrounded by much of its 2.5km defensive wall.

TOOMPEA

According to legend, Toompea is the burial mound of Kalev, the mythical first leader of the Estonians. When Tallinn was a German town (known as Reval), this large fortified hill was the preserve of the bishop and the feudal nobility, literally looking down on the traders and lesser beings below. A couple of wonderful lookouts offer sumptuous views across the Lower Town rooftops to the sea.

St Mary's Cathedral CHURCH

(Tallinna Neitsi Maarja Piiskoplik Toomkirik; www.eelk.ee/tallinna.toom/; Toom-Kooli 6; tower adult/child €5/3; ⏲9am-5pm daily May-Sep, 9am-3pm Tue-Sun Oct-Apr) Tallinn's cathedral (now Lutheran, originally Catholic) was founded by at least 1233, although the exterior dates mainly from the 15th century, with the tower added in 1779. This impressive, austere building was a burial ground for the rich and titled, and the whitewashed walls are decorated with the coats-of-arms of Estonia's noble families. Fit viewseekers can climb the tower.

Alexander Nevsky Cathedral CHURCH

(Lossi plats; ⏲9am-6pm) The positioning of this magnificent, onion-domed Russian Orthodox cathedral (completed in 1900), opposite the parliament buildings, was no accident: the church was one of many built in the last part of the 19th century as part of a general wave of Russification in the empire's Baltic provinces. Orthodox believers come here in droves, alongside tourists ogling the interior's striking icons and frescoes.

Kiek in de Kök CASTLE, MUSEUM

(☎644 6686; www.linnamuuseum.ee; Komandandi tee 2; adult/child €4.50/2.60; ⏲10.30am-6pm Tue-Sun) Built around 1475, this tall, stout fortress is one of Tallinn's most formidable cannon towers. Its name (amusing as it sounds in English) is Low German for 'Peep into the Kitchen'; from the upper floors medieval voyeurs could peer into the houses below. Today it houses a branch of the City Museum, focusing mainly on the development of the town's elaborate defences.

Museum of Occupations MUSEUM

(Okupatsioonide Muuseum; www.okupatsioon.ee; Toompea 8; adult/child €5/3; ⏲10am-6pm Tue-Sun) Displays illustrate the hardships and horrors of five decades of occupation, under both the Nazis (briefly) and the Soviets. The photos and artefacts are interesting but it's the videos (lengthy but enthralling) that leave the greatest impression – and the joy of a happy ending.

LOWER TOWN

Picking your way through the lower town's narrow, cobbled streets is like strolling into the 15th century – not least due to the tendency of local businesses to dress their staff up in medieval garb. The most interesting street is Pikk (Long St), which starts at the Great Coast Gate and includes Tallinn's historic guild buildings.

★**Raekoja Plats** SQUARE

(Town Hall Sq) Raekoja plats has been the heart of Tallinn life since markets began here in the 11th century. It's ringed by pastel-coloured buildings from the 15th to 17th centuries, and is dominated by the Gothic town hall. Throughout summer, outdoor cafes implore you to sit and people-watch; come Christmas, a huge pine tree stands in the middle of the square. Whether bathed in sunlight or sprinkled with snow, it's always a photogenic spot.

Tallinn Town Hall HISTORIC BUILDING

(Tallinna Raekoda; ☎645 7900; www.tallinn.ee/raekoda; Raekoja plats; adult/student €5/2; ⏲10am-4pm Mon-Sat Jul-Aug, by appointment Sep-Jun) Completed in 1404, this is the only surviving Gothic town hall in northern Europe. Inside, you can visit the Trade Hall (housing a visitor book dripping in royal signatures), the Council Chamber (featuring Estonia's oldest woodcarvings, dating from 1374), the vaulted Citizens' Hall, a yellow-and-black-tiled councillor's office and a small kitchen. The steeply sloped attic has displays on the building and its restoration.

NEED TO KNOW

Population 412,000

Country code ☎372, no area codes

Language Estonian

Currency Euro (€)

Tallinn

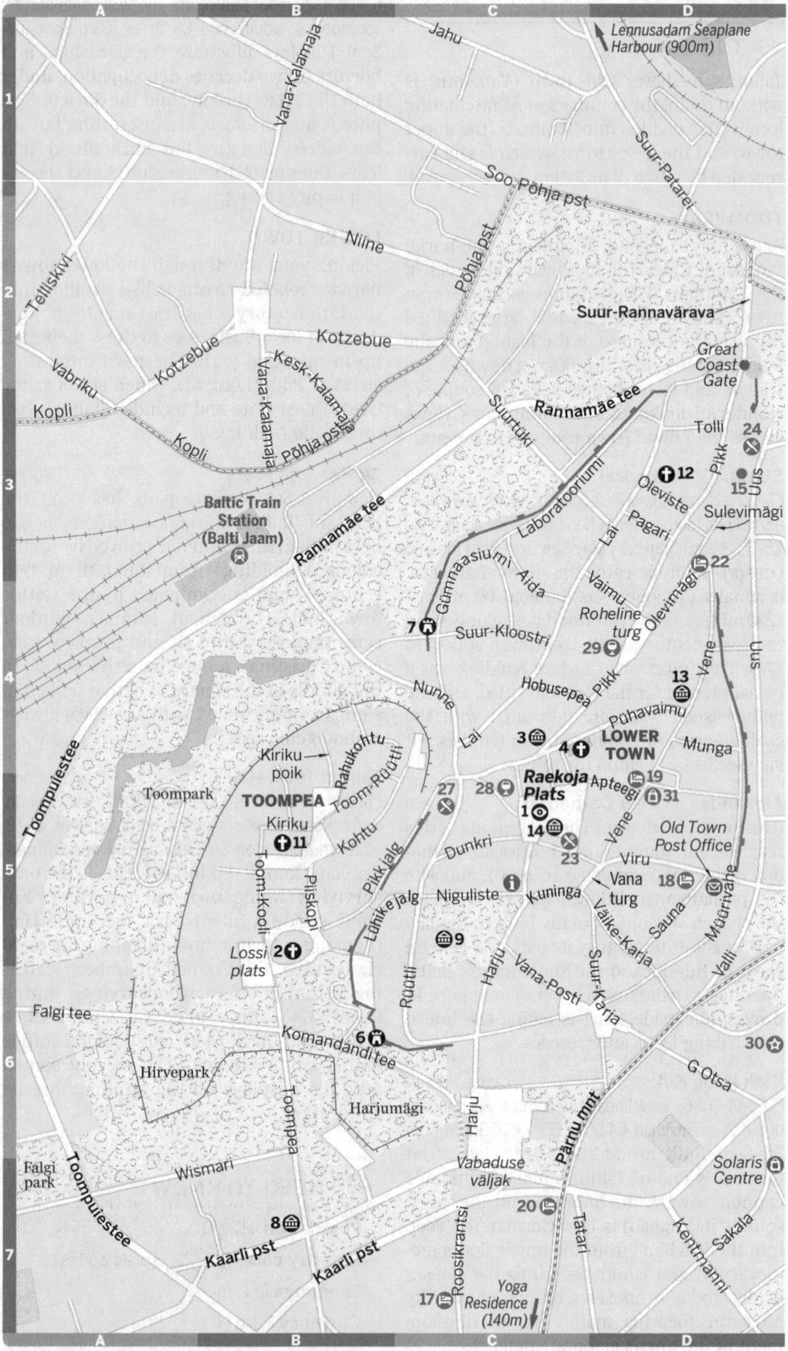

A B C D

1 2 3 4 5 6 7

Lennusadam Seaplane Harbour (900m)
Jahu
Vana-Kalamaja
Suur-Patarei
Soo
Põhja pst
Niine
Telliskivi
Kotzebue
Kesk-Kalamaja
Vabriku
Kopli
Põhja pst
Suur-Rannavärava
Great Coast Gate
Rannamäe tee
Suurtüki
Tolli
24
Pikk
12
Oleviste
15
Uus
Sulevimägi
Baltic Train Station (Balti Jaam)
Laboratooriumi
Pagari
Lai
22
Gümnaasiumi
Aida
Vaimu
Olevimägi
Roheline turg
7
Suur-Kloostri
29
Uus
13
Vene
Hobusepea
Pikk
Nunne
Pühavaimu
Lai
3
4
LOWER TOWN
Munga
Toompuiestee
Kiriku poik
Rahukohtu
Toom-Rüütli
Toompark
TOOMPEA
27
28
Raekoja Plats
Apteegi
19
31
1
14
Kiriku
11
Kohtu
Toom-Kooli
Piiskopi
Pikk jalg
Dunkri
23
Vene
Old Town Post Office
Viru
Vana turg
18
Niguliste
Kuninga
Lühike jalg
Väike-Karja
Sauna
Müürivahe
2
Lossi plats
9
Rüütli
Harju
Vana-Posti
Suur-Karja
Valli
Falgi tee
6
Komandandi tee
30
Hirvepark
Toompea
G Otsa
Harjumägi
Harju
Pärnu mnt
Falgi park
Toompuiestee
Wismari
Vabaduse väljak
Solaris Centre
20
Tatari
8
Sakala
Kaarli pst
Kaarli pst
Roosikrantsi
Kentmanni
17
Yoga Residence (140m)

A B C D

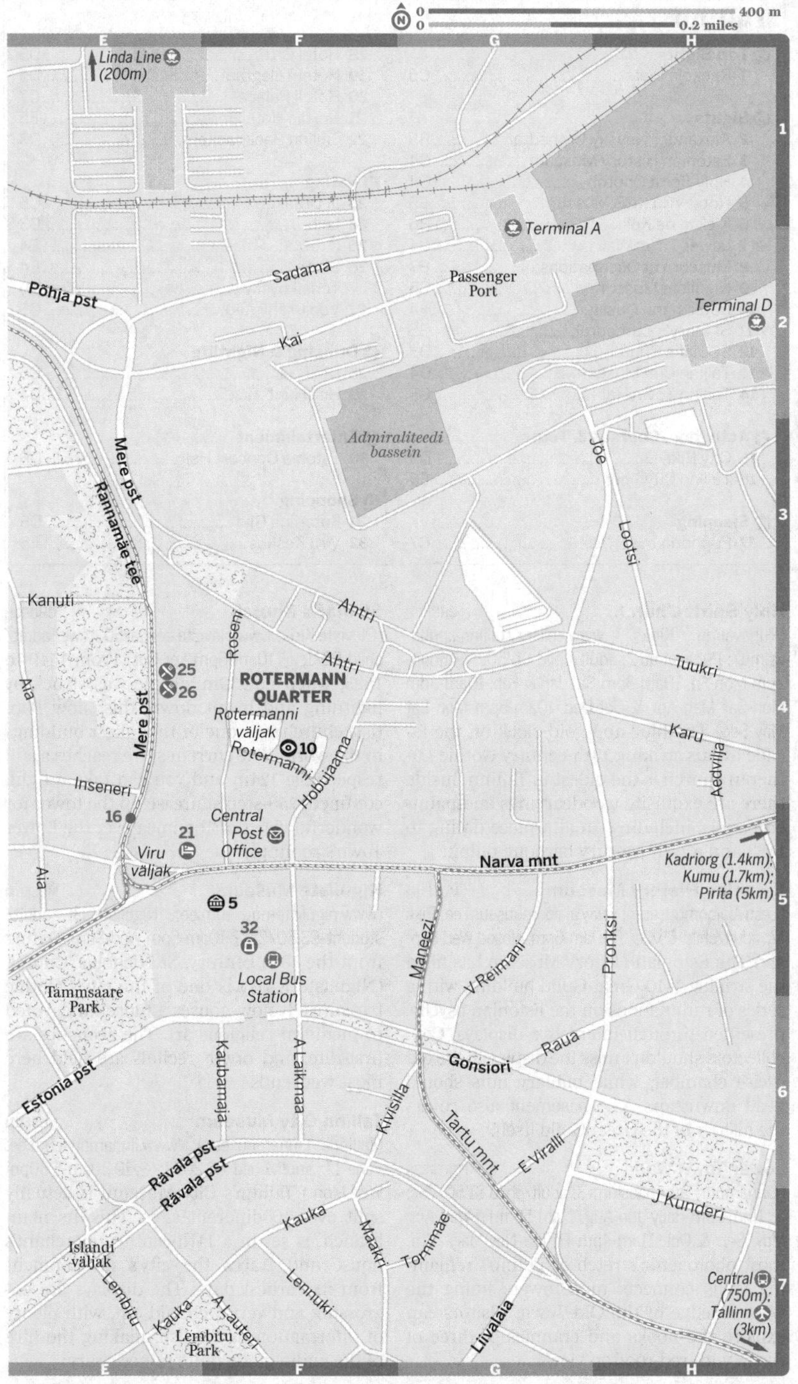

0 400 m
0 0.2 miles
Linda Line (200m)
Terminal A
Passenger Port
Terminal D
Sadama
Põhja pst
Kai
Admiraliteedi bassein
Mere pst
Rannamäe tee
Jõe
Lootsi
Kanuti
Roseni
Ahtri
Ahtri
Tuukri
25
26
ROTERMANN QUARTER
Rotermanni väljak
Aia
Karu
Aedvilja
10
Rotermanni
Hobujaama
Mere pst
Inseneri
16
Central Post Office
21
Viru väljak
Narva mnt
Kadriorg (1.4km); Kumu (1.7km); Pirita (5km)
Aia
5
32
Local Bus Station
Maneezi
V Reimani
Pronksi
Tammsaare Park
Raua
Gonsiori
Kaubamaja
A Laikmaa
Estonia pst
Kivisilla
Tartu mnt
E Viralli
Rävala pst
Rävala pst
J Kunderi
Kauka
Maakri
Tornimäe
Islandi väljak
Lennuki
Central (750m); Tallinn (3km)
Lembitu
Kauka
A Lauteri
Liivalaia
Lembitu Park
TALLINN

Tallinn

Top Sights
1 Raekoja Plats ... C5

Sights
2 Alexander Nevsky Cathedral ... B5
3 Estonian History Museum ... C4
4 Holy Spirit Church ... C4
5 Hotel Viru KGB Museum ... F5
6 Kiek in de Kök ... B6
7 Lower Town Wall ... C4
8 Museum of Occupations ... B7
9 Niguliste Museum ... C5
10 Rotermann Quarter ... F4
11 St Mary's Cathedral ... B5
12 St Olaf's Church ... D3
13 Tallinn City Museum ... D4
14 Tallinn Town Hall ... C5

Activities, Courses & Tours
15 City Bike ... D3
16 Tallinn City Tour ... E5

Sleeping
17 Euphoria ... C7
18 Hotel Cru ... D5
19 Hotel Telegraaf ... D5
20 Hotell Palace ... C7
21 Nordic Hotel Forum ... E5
22 Tallinn Backpackers ... D3

Eating
23 III Draakon ... C5
24 Leib ... D3
25 Ö ... E4
26 Sfäär ... E4
Tchaikovsky ... (see 19)
27 Von Krahli Aed ... C5

Drinking & Nightlife
28 DM Baar ... C5
29 Hell Hunt ... D4

Entertainment
30 Estonia Concert Hall ... D6

Shopping
31 Katariina Gild ... D5
32 Viru Keskus ... F5

Holy Spirit Church CHURCH
(Pühavaimu Kirik; www.eelk.ee/tallinna.puhavaimu/; Pühavaimu 2; adult/child €1/50c; noon-2pm Mon-Fri, 10am-3pm Sat Jan & Feb, 10am-3pm Mon-Sat Mar, Apr & Oct-Dec, 10am-5pm Mon-Sat May-Sep) The blue-and-gold clock on the facade of this striking 13th-century Gothic Lutheran church is the oldest in Tallinn. Inside there are exquisite woodcarvings and painted panels, including an altarpiece dating to 1483 and a 17th-century baroque pulpit.

Estonian History Museum MUSEUM
(Eesti Ajaloomuuseum; www.ajaloomuuseum.ee; Pikk 17; adult/child €5/3; 10am-6pm, closed Wed Sep-Apr) The Estonian History Museum has filled the striking 1410 Great Guild building with a series of ruminations on the Estonian psyche, presented through interactive displays. Coin collectors shouldn't miss the display in the old excise chamber, while military nuts should head downstairs. The basement also covers the history of the Great Guild itself.

Lower Town Wall FORTRESS
(Linnamüür; Gümnaasiumi 3; adult/child €1.50/75c; 11am-7pm daily Jun-Aug, 11am-5pm Fri-Wed Apr, May, Sep & Oct, 11am-4pm Fri-Tue Nov-Mar) The most photogenic stretch of Tallinn's remaining walls connects nine towers lining the western edge of the Old Town. Visitors can explore the nooks and crannies of three of them, with red-rooftop views.

St Olaf's Church CHURCH
(Oleviste Kirik; www.oleviste.ee; Lai 50; tower adult/child €2/1; 10am-6pm Apr-Oct) From 1549 to 1625, when its 159m steeple was struck by lightning and burnt down, this (now Baptist) church was one of the tallest buildings in the world. The current spire reaches a still respectable 124m and you can take a tight, confined, 258-step staircase up the tower for wonderful views of Toompea over the Lower Town's rooftops.

Niguliste Museum MUSEUM
(www.nigulistemuuseum.ee; Niguliste 3; adult/student €3.50/2; 10am-5pm Wed-Sun) Dating from the 13th century, St Nicholas' Church (Niguliste Kirik) is one of the city's Gothic treasures. It now houses a museum devoted to medieval religious art. The acoustics are first-rate, and organ recitals are held here most weekends.

Tallinn City Museum MUSEUM
(Tallinna Linnamuuseum; www.linnamuuseum.ee; Vene 17; adult/child €3.20/2; 10.30am-5.30pm Wed-Mon) Tallinn's City Museum is actually split over 10 different sites. This, its main branch, is set in a 14th-century merchant's house and traces the city's development from its earliest days. The displays are engrossing and very well laid out, with plenty of information in English, making the hire of the audio guide quite unnecessary.

City Centre

Hotel Viru KGB Museum MUSEUM
(☎680 9300; www.viru.ee; Viru väljak 4; tour €9; ⊙daily May-Oct, Tue-Sun Nov-Apr) When the Hotel Viru was built in 1972, it was not only Estonia's first skyscraper, it was the only place for tourists to stay in Tallinn – and we mean that literally. Having all the foreigners in one place made it much easier to keep tabs on them and the locals they had contact with, which is exactly what the KGB did from their 23rd-floor spy base. The hotel offers fascinating tours of the facility; bookings essential.

Rotermann Quarter NEIGHBOURHOOD
(Rotermanni Kvartal) With impressive contemporary architecture wedged between old brick warehouses, this development has transformed a former factory complex into the city's hippest new shopping and dining precinct.

Kadriorg

About 2km east of the Old Town (take tram 1 or 3), this beautiful park's ample acreage is Tallinn's favourite patch of green. Together with the baroque Kadriorg Palace, it was commissioned by the Russian tsar Peter the Great for his wife Catherine I soon after his conquest of Estonia (Kadriorg means Catherine's Valley in Estonian).

Kadriorg Art Museum PALACE, GALLERY
(Kardrioru Kunstimuuseum; www.kadriorumuuseum.ee; A Weizenbergi 37; adult/child €4.80/2.80; ⊙10am-5pm Tue & Thu-Sun, to 8pm Wed May-Sep, closed Mon & Tue Oct-Apr) Kadriorg Palace, built by Tsar Peter the Great between 1718 and 1736, now houses a branch of the Estonian Art Museum devoted to Dutch, German and Italian paintings from the 16th to the 18th centuries, and Russian works from the 18th to early 20th centuries (check out the decorative porcelain with communist imagery upstairs). The building is exactly as frilly and fabulous as a palace ought to be and there's a handsome French-style flower garden at the back.

Kumu GALLERY
(www.kumu.ee; A Weizenbergi 34; all exhibitions adult/student €5.50/3.20, permanent exhibitions €4.20/2.60; ⊙11am-6pm Tue & Thu-Sun, to 8pm Wed May-Sep, closed Mon & Tue Oct-Apr) This futuristic, Finnish-designed, seven-storey building (2006) is a spectacular structure of limestone, glass and copper, nicely integrated into the landscape. Kumu (the name is short for *kunstimuuseum* or art museum) contains the country's largest repository of Estonian art as well as constantly changing contemporary exhibits.

Other Neighbourhoods

★**Lennusadam Seaplane Harbour** MUSEUM
(www.lennusadam.eu; Vesilennuki 6, Kalamaja; adult/child €10/6; ⊙10am-7pm daily May-Sep, Tue-Sun Oct-Apr; P) When this triple-domed hangar was completed in 1917, its reinforced-concrete shell frame construction was unique in the world. Resembling a classic Bond-villain lair, the vast space was completely restored and opened to the public in 2012 as a fascinating maritime museum, filled with interactive displays. Highlights include exploring the cramped corridors of a 1930s naval submarine, and the icebreaker and minehunter ships moored outside.

Estonian Open-Air Museum MUSEUM
(Eesti Vabaõhumuuseum; www.evm.ee; Vabaõhumuuseumi tee 12, Rocca Al Mare; adult/child May-Sep €7/3.50, Oct-Apr €5/3; ⊙10am-8pm May-Sep, to 5pm Oct-Apr) If tourists won't go to the countryside, let's bring the countryside to them. That's the modus operandi of this excellent, sprawling complex, where historic buildings have been plucked and transplanted among the tall trees. In summer the time-warping effect is highlighted by staff in period costume performing traditional activities among the wooden farmhouses and windmills.

TV Tower VIEWPOINT
(Teletorn; www.teletorn.ee; Kloostrimetsa tee 58a; adult/child €8/5; ⊙10am-7pm) Opened in time for the 1980 Olympics, this futuristic 314m tower offers brilliant views from its 22nd floor (175m). Press a button and frosted glass disks set in the floor suddenly clear, giving a view straight down. Once you're done gawping, check out the interactive displays in the space-age pods. Daredevils can try the open-air 'edge walk' (€20) or rappel their way down (€49).

Tours

EstAdventures WALKING, BUS
(☎5308 3731; www.estadventures.ee; from €15; ⊙May-Sep) Offers offbeat themed walking tours of Tallinn (Soviet, Legends, Spys, Haunted, Beer etc). Full-day excursions further afield include Lahemaa National Park and Tartu.

Tallinn Traveller Tours WALKING, CYCLING
(☎5837 4800; www.traveller.ee) Entertaining, good-value tours – including a free, two-hour Old Town walking tour. There are also ghost tours (€15), pub crawls (€20), bike tours €16) and day trips to as far afield as Riga (€49).

City Bike CYCLING, WALKING
(☎511 1819; www.citybike.ee; Uus 33) Has a great range of Tallinn tours, by bike or on foot, as well as trips to Lahemaa National Park (€49). Two-hour cycling tours (€13 to €16) of Tallinn run year-round and include Kadriorg and Pirita.

Tallinn City Tour BUS
(☎627 9080; www.citytour.ee; 24hr pass adult/child €19/16) Runs red double-decker buses that give you quick, easy, hop-on, hop-off access to the city's top sights. A recorded audio tour accompanies the ride. Buses leave from Mere pst, just outside the Old Town.

Sleeping

The following price ranges are for a double room in high season:

€ less than €50

€€ €50 to €140

€€€ more than €140

Old Town

Tallinn Backpackers HOSTEL €
(☎644 0298; www.tallinnbackpackers.com; Olevimägi 11; dm €12-15; @ wi-fi) In an ideal Old Town location, this place has a global feel and a roll-call of traveller-happy features: free wi-fi and lockers, cheap dinners, a foosball table – one dorm even has its own sauna! There's also a regular roster of pub crawls and day trips to nearby attractions.

Hotel Cru HOTEL €€
(☎611 7600; www.cruhotel.eu; Viru 8; s/d from €100/135; wi-fi) Behind its pretty powder-blue facade, this boutique 14th-century offering has richly furnished rooms with plenty of original features (timber beams and stone walls) scattered along a rabbit warren of corridors. The cheapest are a little snug.

★ **Hotel Telegraaf** HOTEL €€€
(☎600 0600; www.telegraafhotel.com; Vene 9; s/d from €145/165; P ❄ wi-fi pool) This upmarket hotel, in a converted 19th-century former telegraph station, delivers style in spades. It boasts a spa, a pretty courtyard, an acclaimed restaurant, swanky decor and smart, efficient service.

City Centre

★ **Euphoria** HOSTEL €
(☎5837 3602; www.euphoria.ee; Roosikrantsi 4; dm/r from €12/40; P @ wi-fi) So laid-back it's almost horizontal, this hostel, just south of the Old Town, is an entertaining place to stay with a palpable sense of traveller community – especially if you like hookah pipes and impromptu late-night jam sessions (pack earplugs if you don't).

★ **Yoga Residence** APARTMENTS €€
(☎502 1477; http://yogaresidence.eu; Pärnu mnt 32; apt from €75; wi-fi) It's a strange name for what's basically a block of very modern, fresh and well-equipped apartments, a short stroll from the Old Town. You can expect friendly staff, a kitchenette and, joy of joys, a washing machine. There is a second block in an older building north of the Old Town.

Hotell Palace HOTEL €€
(☎680 6655; www.tallinnhotels.ee; Vabaduse väljak 3; s/d from €115/125; ❄ @ wi-fi pool) A recent renovation has swept through this architecturally interesting 1930s hotel, leaving comfortable, tastefully furnished rooms in its wake. It's directly across the road from Freedom Sq and the Old Town, and the complex includes an indoor pool, spa, sauna and small gym.

Nordic Hotel Forum HOTEL €€€
(☎622 2900; www.nordichotels.eu; Viru väljak 3; r from €135; P @ wi-fi pool) The Forum shows surprising personality for a large, business-style hotel – witness the artwork on the hotel's facade and the trees on the roof. Facilities include saunas and an indoor pool with an 8th-floor view.

Eating

These price ranges indicate the average cost of a main course:

€ less than €10

€€ €10 to €20

€€€ more than €20

Old Town

III Draakon CAFE €
(Raekoja plats; mains €1.50-3; ⏰9am-11pm) There's bucketloads of atmosphere at this Lilliputian tavern below the Town Hall, and

super-cheap elk soup, sausages and oven-hot pies. The historic setting is amped up – expect costumed wenches with a good line in tourist banter, and beer served in ceramic steins.

★Leib ESTONIAN €€
(☎611 9026; www.leibresto.ee; Uus 31; mains €15-17; ⏲noon-11pm) An inconspicuous gate opens onto a large lawn guarded by busts of Sean Connery and Robbie Burns. Welcome to the former home of Tallinn's Scottish club (really!), where 'simple, soulful food' is served along with homemade *leib* (bread). The slow-cooked meat and grilled-fish dishes are exceptional.

Von Krahli Aed MODERN EUROPEAN €€
(☎626 9088; www.vonkrahl.ee; Rataskaevu 8; mains €6-15; ⏲noon-midnight; 🌱) You'll find plenty of greenery on your plate at this rustic, plant-filled restaurant (*aed* means 'garden'). The menu embraces fresh flavours and wins fans by noting organic, gluten-, lactose- and egg-free options.

Tchaikovsky RUSSIAN €€€
(☎600 0610; www.telegraafhotel.com; Vene 9; mains €23-26; ⏲noon-3pm & 6-11pm Mon-Fri, 1-11pm Sat & Sun) Located in a glassed-in pavilion at the heart of the Hotel Telegraaf, Tchaikovsky offers a dazzling tableau of blinged-up chandeliers, gilt frames and greenery. Service is formal and faultless, as is the classic Franco-Russian menu, all accompanied by live chamber music.

City Centre

Sfäär MODERN EUROPEAN €€
(☎5699 2200; www.sfaar.ee; Mere pst 6e; mains €9-16; ⏲8am-10pm Mon-Wed, to midnight Thu & Fri, 10am-midnight Sat, 10am-10pm Sun) Chic Sfäär delivers an inventive menu highlighting the best Estonian produce in a warehouse-style setting that's like something out of a Nordic design catalogue. If you just fancy a tipple, the cocktail and wine list won't disappoint.

★Ö MODERN ESTONIAN €€€
(☎661 6150; www.restoran-o.ee; Mere pst 6e; 4-/6-/8-course menu €46/59/76; ⏲6-11pm Mon-Sat) Award-winning Ö (pronounced 'er') has carved a unique space in Tallinn's culinary world, delivering inventive degustation-style menus showcasing seasonal Estonian produce. The understated dining room nicely counterbalances the theatrical cuisine.

Drinking & Entertainment

DM Baar BAR
(www.depechemode.ee; Voorimehe 4; ⏲noon-4am) If you just can't get enough of Depeche Mode, this is the bar for you. The walls are covered with all manner of memorabilia, including pictures of the actual band partying here. And the soundtrack? Do you really need to ask?

Hell Hunt PUB
(www.hellhunt.ee; Pikk 39; ⏲noon-2am; 📶) Billing itself as 'the first Estonian pub', this trusty old trooper boasts an amiable air and a huge beer selection – local and imported. Don't let the menacing-sounding name put you off – it actually means 'gentle wolf'. In summer, it spills onto the little square across the road.

Estonia Concert Hall CLASSICAL MUSIC
(Eesti Kontserdisaal; ☎614 7760; www.concert.ee; Estonia pst 4) The city's biggest classical concerts are held in this double-barrelled venue. It's Tallinn's main theatre and houses the Estonian National Opera and National Ballet.

Shopping

Katariina Gild HANDICRAFTS
(Katariina käik; Vene 12) Lovely St Catherine's Passage (Katariina Käik) is home to several artisans' studios where you can happily browse ceramics, textiles, patchwork quilts, hats, jewellery, stained glass and beautiful leather-bound books.

Viru Keskus SHOPPING CENTRE
(www.virukeskus.com; Viru väljak; ⏲9am-9pm) Tallinn's showpiece shopping mall is home to fashion boutiques and a great bookstore (Rahva Raamat). At the rear it connects to the upmarket Kaubamaja department store.

Information

Tallinn Tourist Information Centre (☎645 7777; www.tourism.tallinn.ee; Kullassepa 4; ⏲9am-7pm Mon-Fri, to 5pm Sat & Sun May-Aug, 9am-6pm Mon-Fri, to 3pm Sat & Sun Sep-Apr) Brochures, maps, event schedules and other info.

Getting There & Away

AIR

Fourteen European airlines fly into Tallinn Airport, including the national carrier **Estonian Air** (www.estonian-air.ee).

LAND

➡ There are no direct bus connections from Tallinn to Scandinavian destinations, although there are services to Russia, Latvia and Lithuania.

➡ The only direct international train connections are to Moscow and St Petersburg.

SEA

Eckerö Line (www.eckeroline.fi; Passenger Terminal A, Varasadam; adult/child/car from €19/15/19) Twice-daily car ferry from Helsinki to Tallinn (2½ hours).

Linda Line (☎ 699 9333; www.lindaliini.ee; Linnahall Terminal) Small, passenger-only hydrofoils travel between Helsinki and Tallinn at least two times daily from late March to late December (from €25, 1½ hours). Weather dependent.

Tallink (☎ 640 9808; www.tallink.com; Terminal D, Lootsi 13) Four to seven car ferries daily between Helsinki and Tallinn (passenger/vehicle from €31/26). The huge *Baltic Princess* takes 3½ hours; newer high-speed ferries take two hours. They also have an overnight ferry between Stockholm and Tallinn, via the Åland islands (passenger/vehicle from €39/62, 18 hours).

Viking Line (☎ 666 3966; www.vikingline.com; Terminal A, Varasadam; passenger/vehicle from €29/26) Two daily car ferries between Helsinki and Tallinn (2½ hours).

Getting Around

TO/FROM THE AIRPORT

➡ **Tallinn Airport** (Tallinna Lennujaam; ☎ 605 8888; www.tallinn-airport.ee; Tartu mnt 101) is 4km from the centre.

➡ Bus 2 runs every 20 to 30 minutes (6am to around 11pm) from the A Laikmaa stop, opposite the Tallink Hotel, next to Viru Keskus. From the airport, bus 2 heads to the centre. Buy tickets from the driver (€1.60); journey time depends on traffic but rarely exceeds 20 minutes.

➡ A taxi between the airport and the city centre should cost less than €10.

TO/FROM THE FERRY TERMINALS

➡ Tallinn's main passenger terminal (Terminal A) is at the end of Sadama, 600m northeast of the Old Town.

➡ Bus 2 runs every 20 to 30 minutes between the bus stop by Terminal A and the city centre; if you're heading to the terminal, the bus stop is out the front of the Tallink Hotel on A Laikmaa.

➡ Trams 1 and 2, and bus 3 head from the city centre to the Linnahall stop, by the Statoil Petrol Station, five minutes' walk from Terminals A and the Linda Line terminal.

➡ Terminal D is at the end of Lootsi, better accessed from Ahtri; bus 2 services the terminal (the same bus route that services terminal A and the airport).

➡ A taxi between the city centre and any of the terminals will cost about €5.

PUBLIC TRANSPORT

Tallinn has an excellent network of buses, trams and trolleybuses that run from around 6am to 11pm. The major local bus station is on the basement level of Viru Keskus shopping centre, just east of the Old Town. Local public transport timetables are online at www.tallinn.ee.

Public transport is free for Tallinn residents. Visitors still need to pay, either with cash (€1.60 for a single journey) or by using the e-ticketing system. Buy a plastic smartcard (€2 deposit) and top up with credit, then validate the card at the start of each journey using the orange card-readers. Fares using the e-ticketing system cost €1.10/3/5 for an hour/day/three days.

TAXI

Taxis are plentiful, but each company sets its own fare. The base fare ranges from €2 to €5, followed by 50c to €1 per kilometre. To avoid suprises, try **Krooni Takso** (☎ 1212; www.kroonitakso.ee; base fare €2.50, per km 55c) and **Reval Takso** (☎ 1207; www.reval-takso.ee; base fare €2.30, per km 50c).

Iceland

Best Places to Eat

- ➡ Dill (p233)
- ➡ Þrír Frakkar (p232)
- ➡ Narfeyrarstofa (p241)
- ➡ Vogafjós (p254)
- ➡ Humarhöfnin (p260)
- ➡ Slippurinn (p267)

Best Places to Stay

- ➡ Hótel Egilsen (p241)
- ➡ Hótel Borg (p231)
- ➡ KEX Hostel (p229)
- ➡ Hótel Aldan (p256)
- ➡ Skjaldarvík (p248)
- ➡ Kaldbaks-Kot (p251)

Why Go?

Iceland is literally a country in the making, a vast volcanic laboratory where mighty forces shape the earth: geysers gush, mudpots gloop, sulphurous clouds puff from fissures and glaciers grind great pathways through the mountains. Experience the full weirdness of Icelandic nature by bathing in milky blue pools, kayaking under the midnight sun or crunching across a dazzling-white ice cap.

Iceland's creatures are larger than life too: minke, humpback and even blue whales are common visitors to the deeper fjords. Record-breaking numbers of birds nest in the sea cliffs: cutest are the puffins who flutter here in their millions.

Clean, green Reykjavík must contain the world's highest concentration of dreamers, authors, poets and musicians. Little wonder, as the magnificent scenery of this Atlantic island forged in fire and ice make it one of the world's most awe-inspiring sights.

When to Go

Reykjavík

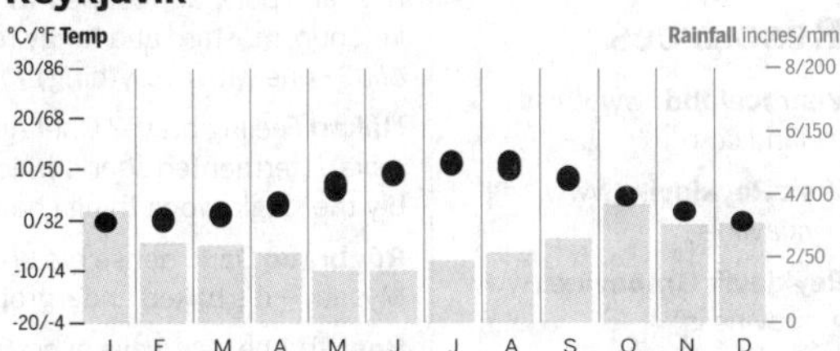

Jun–Aug Cons: high demand, high prices. Pros: best weather, loads of daylight, fun festivals.

May & Sep Shoulder season – smaller crowds, lower prices, cooler weather.

Oct–Apr Good for winter activities, including viewing the aurora borealis (northern lights).

AT A GLANCE

Capital Reykjavík

Area 103,000 sq km

Population 325,700

Country code ☎354

Language Icelandic

Currency króna (Ikr)

Exchange Rates

Australia	A$1	Ikr105
Canada	C$1	Ikr108
Euro Zone	€1	Ikr152
Japan	¥100	Ikr110
New Zealand	NZ$1	Ikr94
UK	UK£1	Ikr195
USA	US$1	Ikr120

Set Your Budget

Budget double room
Ikr12,000–Ikr15,000

Two-course evening meal
Ikr4000–Ikr5000

Museum entrance
free–Ikr1500

Beer (500mL)
Ikr800–Ikr1200

Reykjavík bus ticket
Ikr350

Resources

Visit Iceland (www.visiticeland.com)

Visit Reykjavík (www.visitreykjavik.is)

Reykjavík Grapevine (www.grapevine.is)

Icelandic Met Office (http://en.vedur.is)

Lonely Planet (www.lonelyplanet.com/iceland)

Connections

Iceland is well connected by regular flights from Keflavík airport to Scandinavian and other European capitals, as well as numerous North American cities.

The ferry from Denmark via the Faroe Islands to Seyðisfjörður (east Iceland, 660km from Reykjavík) is a superbly scenic way to arrive.

ITINERARIES

Three Days

Arrive in **Reykjavík** on Friday to join the notorious pub crawl. Sober up in Laugardalslaug geothermal pool, admire the views from Hallgrímskirkja, then absorb some Viking history at the National Museum. On Sunday, visit Gullfoss, Geysir and Þingvellir on a **Golden Circle** tour. Stop to soak in the **Blue Lagoon** on the way home.

One Week

Head for the countryside: chill out on serene **Snæfellsnes** in the west; view the volcanic **Vestmannaeyjar** in the south with their immense puffin colonies; or drive east to **Skaftafell** for wonderful hiking and glacier walking.

Essential Food & Drink

Protein power The superb local fish and lamb should be high on your culinary hit list. You may be enticed by the 'novelty value' of sampling whale or puffin, but please do consider your actions.

Skyr Rich and creamy yoghurtlike staple, sometimes sweetened with sugar and berries. You'll see it in local desserts, playing a starring role in cheesecake and crème brûlée (or even 'skyramisu') concoctions.

Pýlsur Icelandic hot dogs, made with a combination of lamb, beef and pork, and topped with raw and deep-fried onion, ketchup, mustard and tangy remoulade (ask for *'eina með öllu'* – one with everything).

Hákarl Feeling brave? Chef Anthony Bourdain described *hákarl* (fermented shark, which reeks of ammonia) as 'probably the single worst thing I have ever put in my mouth'.

Rúgbrauð Dark, dense rye bread. Look for *hverabrauð* in Mývatn – it's baked underground using geothermal heat.

Beer Try the new wave of craft beers from microbreweries such as Borg, Kaldi and Einstök.

REYKJAVÍK

POP 205,000

The world's most northerly capital combines colourful buildings, quirky people, eye-popping design, wild nightlife and a capricious soul to devastating effect.

In many ways Reykjavík is strikingly cosmopolitan for its size. After all, it's merely

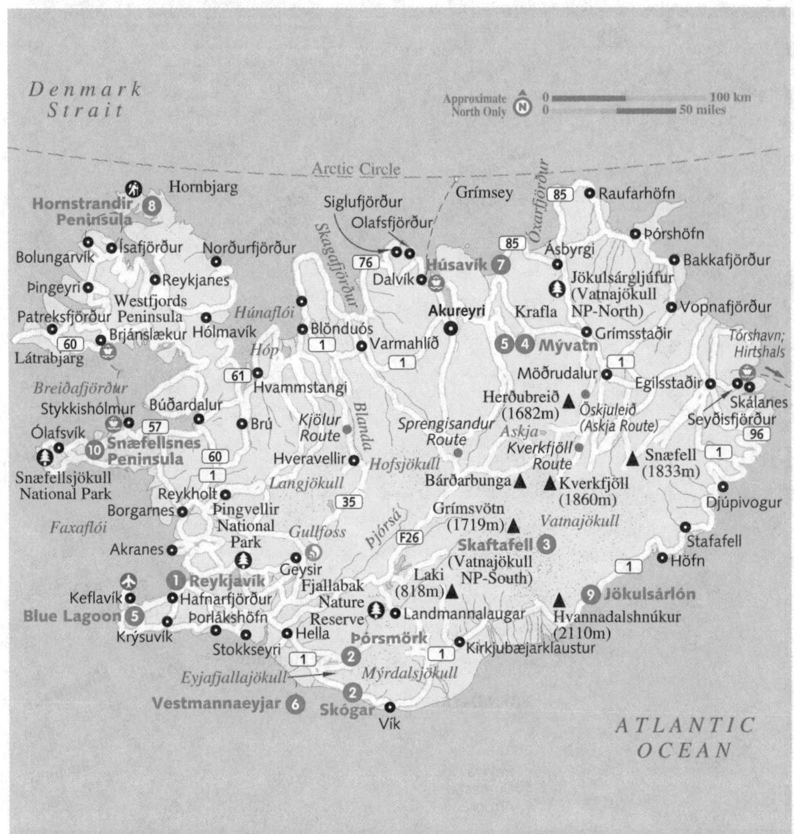

Iceland Highlights

1 Explore the boutiques, museums and galleries, restaurants and lively bars of **Reykjavík** (p219)

2 Hike from **Þórsmörk to Skógar** (p263) and see the lava formed in the 2010 Eyjafjallajökull eruptions

3 Don crampons for an easy but exhilarating glacier walk at glorious, view-blessed **Skaftafell** (p357)

4 Wander around the geological wonderland of otherworldly **Mývatn** (p251)

5 Soak in steaming lagoons at the world-famous **Blue Lagoon** (p238) or **Mývatn Nature Baths** (p252)

6 Set sail for **Vestmannaeyjar** (p264), with puffins galore and a small town tucked between lava flows

7 Admire the giants of the ocean on a whale-watching trip out of **Húsavík** (p250)

8 Rove around saw-toothed cliffs and lonely coves on an inspiring hike across remote **Hornstrandir** (p244)

9 Cruise among the ever-changing ice sculptures at the bewitching lagoon **Jökulsárlón** (p259)

10 Tour 'Iceland in miniature' – wild beaches, lava fields, a glacier-topped mountain – on the **Snæfellsnes Peninsula** (p240)

Reykjavík

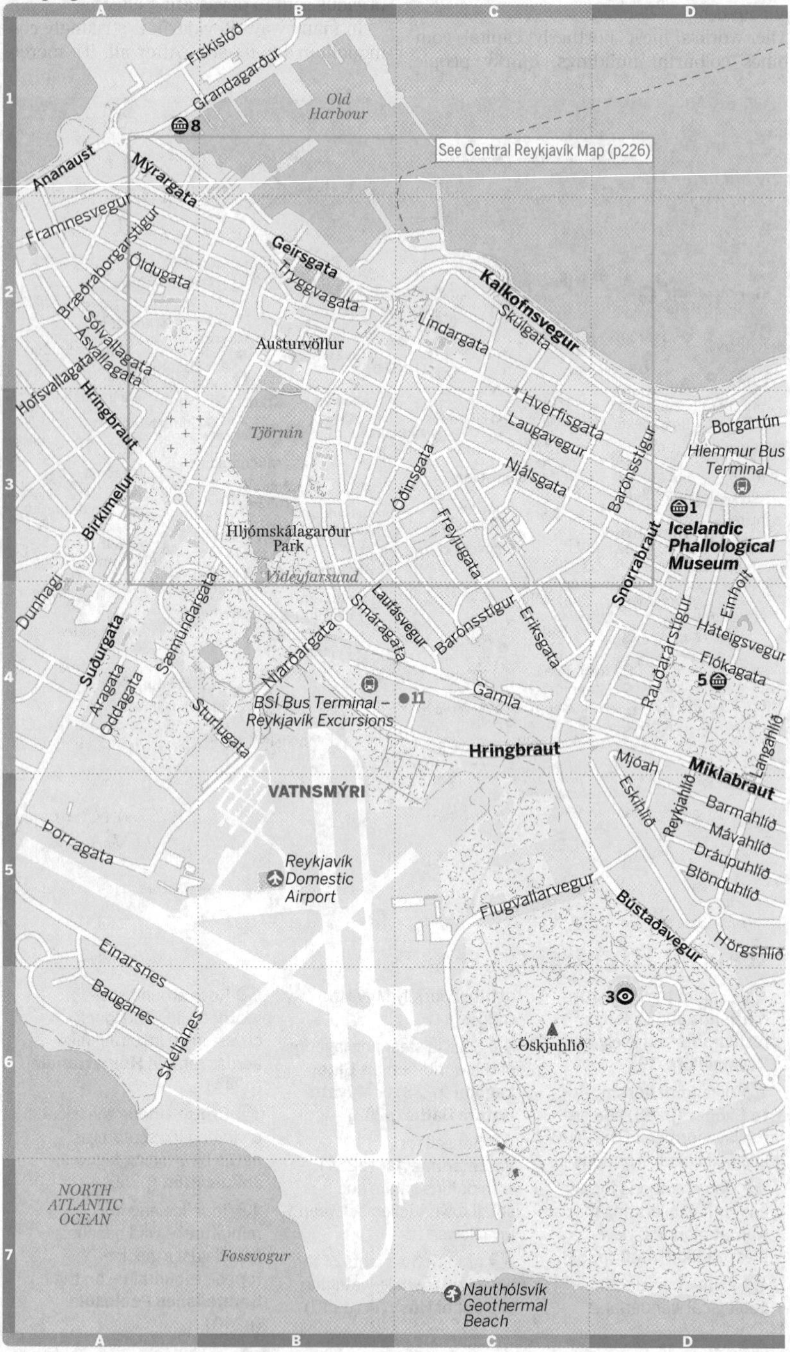

See Central Reykjavík Map (p226)

A B C D
1 2 3 4 5 6 7

Fiskislóð
Grandagarður
Old Harbour
8
Ananaust
Mýrargata
Framnesvegur
Bræðraborgarstígur
Öldugata
Geirsgata
Tryggvagata
Kalkofnsvegur
Skúlgata
Lindargata
Austurvöllur
Sólvallagata
Ásvallagata
Hofsvallagata
Hringbraut
Hverfisgata
Laugavegur
Borgartún
Hlemmur Bus Terminal
Tjörnin
Njálsgata
Barónsstígur
Óðinsgata
Freyjugata
Birkimelur
1 Icelandic Phallological Museum
Hljómskálagarður Park
Vídeyjarsund
Snorrabraut
Dunhagi
Suðurgata
Sæmundargata
Laufásvegur
Smáragata
Barónsstígur
Eiríksgata
Einholt
Rauðarárstígur
Háteigsvegur
Flókagata
5
Aragata
Oddagata
Njarðargata
Sturlugata
BSÍ Bus Terminal – Reykjavík Excursions
11
Gamla
Hringbraut
Mjóah
Eskihlíð
Reykjahlíð
Miklabraut
Langahlíð
Barmahlíð
Mávahlíð
Drápuhlíð
Blönduhlíð
VATNSMÝRI
Þorragata
Reykjavík Domestic Airport
Flugvallarvegur
Bústaðavegur
Hörgshlíð
Einarsnes
Bauganes
Skeljanes
3
Öskjuhlíð
NORTH ATLANTIC OCEAN
Fossvogur
Nauthólsvík Geothermal Beach

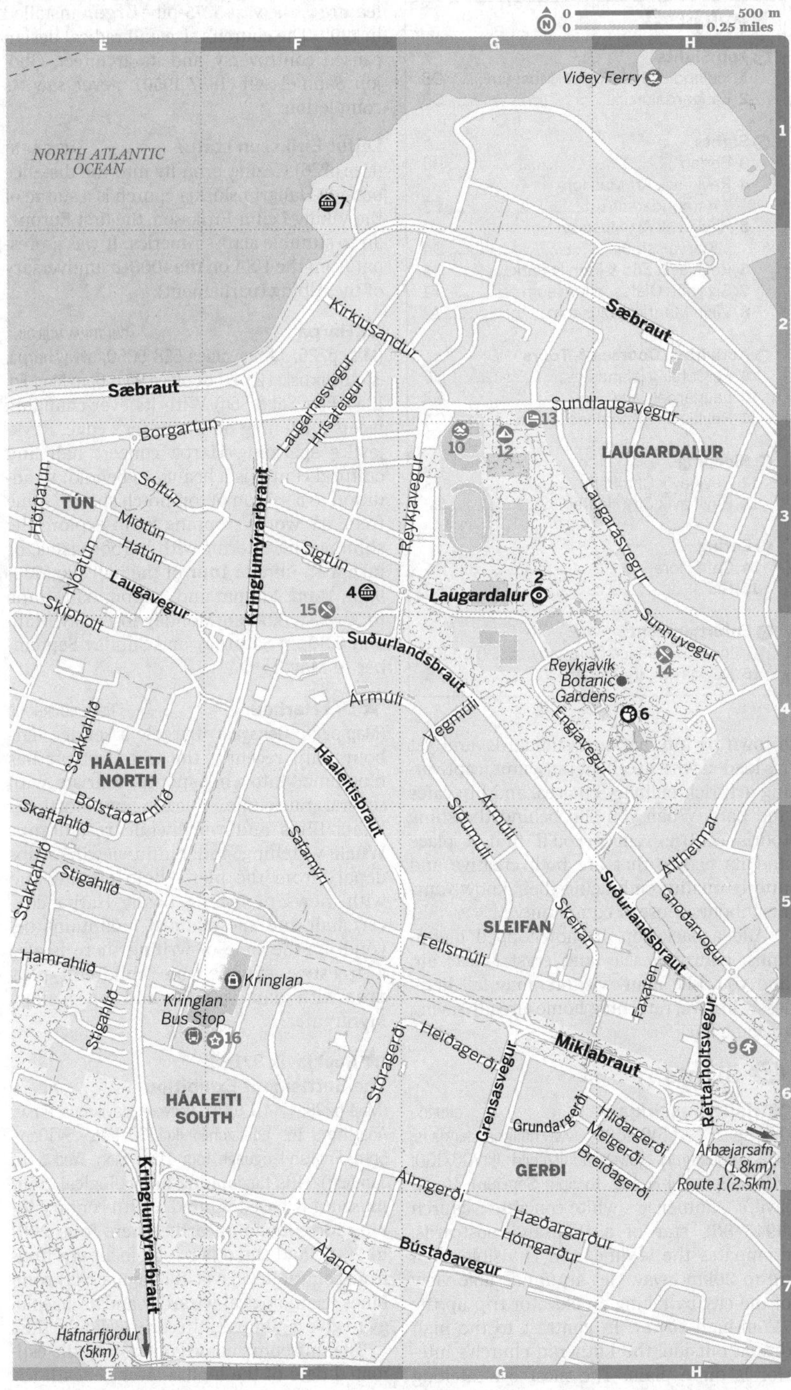

0 500 m
0 0.25 miles
E
F
G
H
1
2
3
4
5
6
7
Viðey Ferry
NORTH ATLANTIC OCEAN
7
Kirkjusandur
Sæbraut
Sæbraut
Laugarnesvegur
Hrísateigur
Sundlaugavegur
Borgartun
10
12
13
LAUGARDALUR
Höfðatún
TÚN
Sóltún
Miðtún
Hátún
Nóatún
Laugavegur
Skipholt
Kringlumýrarbraut
Reykjavegur
Sigtún
4
15
Laugardalur
2
Laugarásvegur
Sunnuvegur
14
Suðurlandsbraut
Reykjavík Botanic Gardens
6
Ármúli
Vegmúli
Engjavegur
Stakkahlíð
HÁALEITI NORTH
Bólstaðarhlíð
Skaftahlíð
Háaleitisbraut
Safamýri
Síðumúli
Ármúli
Álfheimar
Stakkahlíð
Stigahlíð
Suðurlandsbraut
Gnoðarvogur
Skeifan
SLEIFAN
Fellsmúli
Hamrahlíð
Kringlan
Kringlan Bus Stop
16
Stigahlíð
Faxafen
Réttarholtsvegur
Miklabraut
9
Heiðagerði
Stóragerði
Grensásvegur
HÁALEITI SOUTH
Grundargerði
Hliðargerði
Melgerði
Breiðagerði
GERÐI
Árbæjarsafn (1.8km); Route 1 (2.5km)
Álmgerði
Hæðargarður
Hólmgarður
Kringlumýrarbraut
Búståðavegur
Áland
Hafnarfjörður (5km)

Reykjavík

Top Sights
1 Icelandic Phallological Museum D3
2 Laugardalur G3

Sights
3 Perlan D6
4 Reykjavík Art Museum – Ásmundarsafn........F3
5 Reykjavík Art Museum – Kjarvalsstaðir D4
6 Reykjavík Zoo & Family Park........ H4
7 Sigurjón Ólafsson Museum........F1
8 Víkin Maritime Museum........ A1

Activities, Courses & Tours
9 Ferðafélag Íslands H6
10 Laugardalslaug........ G3
11 Reykjavík Excursions........ C4

Sleeping
12 Reykjavík Campsite........ G3
13 Reykjavík City Hostel........ G2

Eating
14 Café Flóra........ H4
15 Gló........F3

Entertainment
Icelandic Dance Company........ (see 16)
16 Reykjavík City Theatre F6

a town by international standards, and yet it's loaded with excellent museums, captivating art, rich culinary choices, and hip cafes and bars. When you slip behind the shiny tourist-centric veneer you'll find a place and its people that are both creative and utterly quaint, embracing their know-your-neighbours sense of community.

Add a backdrop of snow-topped mountains, churning seas and crystal-clear air, and you, like many visitors, may fall helplessly in love, returning home already saving to come back.

Sights

★Hallgrímskirkja CHURCH
(Map p226; ☎510 1000; www.hallgrimskirkja.is; Skólavörðustígur; tower adult/child Ikr700/100; ⏱9am-9pm Jul & Aug, to 5pm Sep-Jun) Reykjavík's immense white-concrete church (1945–86), star of a thousand postcards, dominates the skyline, and is visible from up to 20km away. Get an unmissable view of the city by taking an elevator trip up the 74.5m-high **tower**. In contrast to the high drama outside, the Lutheran church's interior is quite plain. The most eye-catching feature is the vast 5275-pipe **organ** installed in 1992. The church's size and radical design caused controversy, and its architect, Guðjón Samúelsson (1887–1950), never saw its completion.

Leifur Eiríksson statue MONUMENT
(Map p226) Gazing proudly into the distance outside Hallgrímskirkja church is a statue of the Viking Leifur Eiríksson, the first European to stumble across America. It was a present from the USA on the 1000th anniversary of the Alþing (parliament).

★Harpa CULTURAL BUILDING
(Map p226; ☎box office 528 5050; www.harpa.is; Austurbakki 2; ⏱box office 9am-6pm Mon-Fri, 10am-6pm Sat & Sun) With its ever-changing facets glistening on the water's edge, Reykjavík's sparkling Harpa concert hall and cultural centre is a beauty to behold. In addition to a season of top-notch shows (some free), it's worth stopping by to explore the shimmering interior with harbor vistas, or take a 45-minute **tour** of the hall (Ikr1500; 9am, 11am, 1.30pm and 3.30pm daily June to August, 3.30pm Monday to Friday, 11am and 3.30pm Saturday and Sunday September to May).

★Old Harbour NEIGHBOURHOOD
(Map p226; Geirsgata) Largely a service harbour until recently, the Old Harbour has blossomed into a hot spot for tourists, with several museums, volcano and northern lights films and worthwhile restaurants. Whale-watching and puffin-viewing trips depart from the pier. Photo ops abound with views of fishing boats, Harpa concert hall and snowcapped mountains beyond. At the time of writing there is also a freestyle summertime children's **play area** with giant spindles and ropes, along Mýrargata.

★Reykjavík 871±2: The Settlement Exhibition MUSEUM
(Map p226; ☎411 6370; www.reykjavikmuseum.is; Aðalstræti 16; adult/child Ikr1300/free; ⏱10am-5pm, English-language tour 11am Mon, Wed & Fri Jun-Aug) This fascinating archeological ruin/museum is based around a 10th-century **Viking longhouse** unearthed here from 2001 to 2002, and the other settlement-era finds from central Reykjavík. It imaginatively combines technological wizardry and archaeology to give a glimpse into early Icelandic life.

The museum's name comes from the estimated date of the tephra layer beneath the longhouse, but don't miss the fragment of **boundary wall**, at the back of the museum that is older still (and the oldest man-made structure in Reykjavík).

★Old Reykjavík NEIGHBOURHOOD
(Map p226) With a series of sights and interesting historic buildings, the area dubbed Old Reykjavík is the heart of the capital, and the focal point of many historic walking tours. The area is anchored by Tjörnin, the city-centre lake, and sitting between it and Austurvöllur park to the north are the Ráðhús (city hall) and Alþingi (parliament).

★Tjörnin LAKE
(Map p226) This placid lake at the centre of the city is sometimes locally called the Pond. It echoes with the honks and squawks of over 40 species of visiting birds, including swans, geese and Arctic terns; feeding the ducks is a popular pastime for the under fives. Pretty sculpture-dotted parks like Hljómskálagarður line the southern shores, and their paths are much used by cyclists and joggers. In winter hardy souls strap on ice skates and turn the lake into an **outdoor rink**.

★National Museum MUSEUM
(Þjóðminjasafn Íslands; Map p226; ☎530 2200; www.nationalmuseum.is; Suðurgata 41; adult/child Ikr1500/free, audioguide Ikr300; ⏰10am-5pm May–mid-Sep, 11am-5pm Tue-Sun mid-Sep–Apr; 🚌1, 3, 6, 12, 14) This superb museum displays artefacts from settlement to the modern age. Exhibits give an excellent overview of Iceland's history and culture, and the audioguide adds loads of detail. The strongest section describes the Settlement Era – including how the chieftains ruled and the introduction of Christianity – and features swords, drinking horns, silver hoards and a powerful little bronze figure of Thor. The priceless 13th-century **Valþjófsstaðir church door** is carved with the story of a knight, his faithful lion and a passel of dragons.

Perlan NOTABLE BUILDING
(Map p220; www.perlan.is; ⏰10am-10pm, cafe to 9pm; 🚌18) FREE The mirrored dome of Perlan covers huge geothermal-water tanks on Öskjuhlíð hill, about 2km from the city centre. The wrap-around viewing deck offers a tremendous 360-degree panorama of Reykjavík and the mountains. There's a cafe (often busy with tour groups), so in a

REYKJAVÍK IN...

One Day

Start with a walk around the **Old Reykjavík** quarter near **Tjörnin** then peruse the city's best museums, such as the impressive **National Museum**, **Reykjavík Art Museum** or **Reykjavík 871 +/-2**.

In the afternoon, wander up arty **Skólavörðustígur** to the immense **Hallgrímskirkja**. For a perfect view, take the elevator up the tower, then circle down to stroll **Laugavegur**, the main shopping drag.

Sit for people-watching and drinks at **Bravó** or **Tiú Droppar** then head to dinner. Many of the more lively restaurants – including **Vegamót** and **Kex** – turn into party hang-outs at night. On weekends, join Reykjavík's notorious pub crawl. Start at perennial favourite **Kaffibarinn** or beer-lovers' **Kaldi**, then tag along with locals to the latest drinking holes.

Two Days

After a late night out, enjoy brunch at **Bergsson Mathús**, **Grái Kötturinn** or **Laundromat Café**. Then head down to the **Old Harbour** for a wander, museums or a whale-watching tour.

For hot springs, gardens, beautiful Cafe Flóra and cool art, head to **Laugardalur** in the afternoon.

Book ahead if you'd like a swanky evening at one of Reykjavík's top Icelandic restaurants, such as **Dill** or **Þrír Frakkar**, then hit **Loftið**, one of the new breed of cocktail bars. Alternatively, catch a show at **Harpa** or a movie at **Bíó Paradís**.

'What about the **Blue Lagoon**?' we hear you ask. Well, here's the clever part – you can visit Iceland's number-one attraction on your way back to the airport tomorrow. Wallowing in its warm, sapphire-blue waters is a fantastic final memory to take home.

downpour you can admire the same views over coffee. The top of the dome contains the high-end Perlan dinner restaurant.

Two **artificial geysers** keep small children enthralled. Numerous **walking and cycling trails** criss-cross the hillside; one path leads down to Nauthólsvík beach.

Saga Museum MUSEUM
(Map p226; ☎511 1517; www.sagamuseum.is; Grandagarður 2; adult/child Ikr2000/800; ⏲9am-6pm) The endearingly bloodthirsty Saga Museum is where Icelandic history is brought to life by eerie silicon models and a multi-language soundtrack with thudding axes and hair-raising screams. Don't be surprised if you see some of the characters wandering around town, as moulds were taken from Reykjavík residents (the owner's daughters are the Irish princess and the little slave gnawing a fish!).

★**Icelandic Phallological Museum** MUSEUM
(Hið Íslenzka Reðasafn; Map p220; ☎561 6663; www.phallus.is; Laugavegur 116; adult/child Ikr1250/free; ⏲10am-6pm) Oh, the jokes are endless here, but though this unique museum houses a huge collection of penises, it's actually very well done. From pickled pickles to petrified wood, there are 283 different members on display, representing all Icelandic mammals and beyond. Featured items include contributions from sperm whales and a polar bear, miniscule mouse bits, silver castings of each member of the Icelandic handball team and a single human sample – from deceased mountaineer Páll Arason.

WORTH A TRIP

VIÐEY

On fine-weather days, the tiny uninhabited island of **Viðey** (www.videy.com) makes a wonderful day trip. Just 1km north of Reykjavík's Sundahöfn Harbour, it feels a world away. Surprising modern artworks, an abandoned village and great birdwatching add to its remote spell.

Viðey ferry (Map p220; ☎533 5055; www.videy.com; return adult/child Ikr1100/550; ⏲hourly 10.15am-5.15pm mid-May–Sep, reduced services Oct–mid-May) takes five minutes from Skarfabakki, 4.5km east of the centre. Two boats a day start from Elding at the Old Harbour and Harpa Concert Hall (check online).

Culture House ART MUSEUM
(Þjóðmenningarhúsið; Map p226; www.thjodminjasafn.is; Hverfisgata 15; adult/child Ikr1000/free; ⏲11am-5pm) At the time of writing this museum was being reimagined as a collaboration between the National Museum, National Gallery and four other organisations as a study of the artistic heritage of Iceland from settlement to today. It should have opened by the time you read this.

Víkin Maritime Museum MUSEUM
(Víkin Sjóminjasafnið; Map p220; ☎517 9400; www.sjominjasafn.is; Grandagarður 8; adult/child Ikr1200/free; ⏲10am-5pm Jun–mid-Sep, 11am-5pm Tue-Sun mid-Sep–May) Based appropriately in a former fish-freezing plant, this small museum celebrates the country's seafaring heritage, focusing on the trawlers that transformed Iceland's economy. Your ticket also allows you aboard coastguard ship *Óðinn* by guided tour (11am, 1pm, 2pm and 3pm, reduced hours during winter, closed January and February). The boat is a veteran of the 1970s Cod Wars, when British and Icelandic fishermen came to blows over fishing rights in the North Atlantic.

Einar Jónsson Museum ART MUSEUM
(Map p226; ☎561 3797; www.lej.is; Eriksgata; adult/child Ikr1000/free; ⏲1-5pm Tue-Sun Jun–mid-Sep, 1-5pm Sat & Sun mid-Sep–Nov & Feb-May) Einar Jónsson (1874–1954) is one of Iceland's foremost sculptors, famous for intense symbolist works. Chiselled representations of Hope, Earth and Death burst from basalt cliffs, weep over naked women and slay dragons. Jónsson designed the building, which was built between 1916 and 1923, when this empty hill was the outskirts of town. It also contains his austere penthouse flat and studio, with views over the city.

The sculpture garden behind the museum contains 26 bronzes, in the shadow of Hallgrímskirkja.

★**Reykjavík Art Museum** ART MUSEUM
(Listasafn Reykjavíkur; www.artmuseum.is; adult/child Ikr1300/free) The excellent Reykjavík Art Museum is split over three well-done sites: the large, modern downtown **Hafnarhús** (Map p226; ☎590 1200; Tryggvagata 17; ⏲10am-5pm Fri-Wed, to 8pm Thu) focusing on contemporary art; **Kjarvalsstaðir** (Map p220; ☎517 1290; Flókagata, Miklatún Park; ⏲10am-5pm), in a park just east of Snorrabraut, and displaying rotating exhibits of modern art; and **Ásmundarsafn** (Ásmundur Sveinsson Museum; Map

p220; ☎553 2155; Sigtún; ⏰10am-5pm May-Sep, 1-5pm Oct-Apr; 🚌2, 14, 15, 17, 19), a peaceful haven near Laugardalur for viewing sculptures by Ásmundur Sveinsson.

One ticket is good at all three sites, and if you buy after 3pm you get a 50% discount should you want a ticket the next day.

National Gallery of Iceland MUSEUM
(Listasafn Íslands; Map p226; www.listasafn.is; Fríkirkjuvegur 7; adult/child Ikr1000/free; ⏰10am-5pm Tue-Sun Jun-Aug, 11am-5pm Sep-May) This pretty stack of marble atriums and spacious galleries overlooking Tjörnin offers ever-changing exhibits drawn from the 10,000-piece collection. The museum can only exhibit a small sample at any time; shows range from 19th- and 20th-century paintings by Iceland's favourite sons and daughters (including Jóhannes Kjarval and Nína Sæmundsson) to sculptures by Sigurjón Ólafsson and others.

Árbæjarsafn MUSEUM
(www.reykjavikmuseum.is; Kistuhylur 4, Ártúnsholt; adult/child Ikr1300/free; ⏰10am-5pm Jun-Aug, by tour only 1pm Mon-Fri Sep-May; 👪; 🚌12, 19, 24) About20 quaint old buildings have been transported from their original sites to open-air Árbæjarsafn, 4km east of the city centre beyond Laugardalur. Alongside 19th-century homes are a turf-roofed church and various stables, smithies, barns and boathouses – all very picturesque. There are summer arts-and-crafts demonstrations and domestic animals, and it's a great place for kids to let off steam. Tickets also provide entry to Reykjavík 871 +/-2 (p222).

★**Laugardalur** NEIGHBOURHOOD, PARK
(Map p220; 🚌2, 14, 15, 17, 19) Laugardalur encompasses a verdant stretch of land 4km east of the centre. It was once the main source of Reykjavík's hot-water supply: it translates as 'Hot-Springs Valley', and in the park's centre you'll find relics from the old wash house. The park is a favourite with locals for its huge swimming complex, fed by the geothermal spring, alongside a spa, cafe (p231), skating rink, botanical gardens, sporting and concert arenas, and a kids' zoo/entertainment park.

Activities

Reykjavík is the main hub for activity tours to a range of destinations beyond the city limits.

SCRUB UP

Reykjavík's many outdoor swimming pools, heated by geothermal water, are the social hubs of the city: children play, teenagers flirt, business deals are made and everyone catches up with the latest gossip.

Geothermal pools are the nation's pride and joy. Volcanic heat keeps the temperature at a mellow 29°C, and most baths have *heitir pottar* (hot-pots): jacuzzi-like pools kept a toasty 37°C to 42°C. And as chemical cleaners like chlorine aren't used, it's vital that visitors wash thoroughly without a swimsuit before getting in. To do otherwise is to cause great offence.

For further information on all the capital's pools, see www.spacity.is.

You can rent bikes to zoom along lake or seaside trails, or pop into hot-pots all over town.

Laugardalslaug GEOTHERMAL POOL, HOT-POT
(Map p220; Sundlaugavegur 30a, Laugardalur; adult/child Ikr600/130, suit/towel rental Ikr800/550; ⏰6.30am-10pm Mon-Fri, 8am-10pm Sat & Sun; 👪) One of the largest pools in Iceland, with the best facilities: Olympic-sized indoor pool and outdoor pools, seven hot-pots, a saltwater tub, steam bath and a curling 86m water slide.

Tours

Walking, bike and bus tours are the main way to take in the city. Whale-watching, puffin-spotting and sea-angling trips allow a jaunt offshore.

As lovely as the capital's sights are, though, Reykjavík is also the main hub for tours to amazing landscapes and activities around Iceland. Those without wheels, time or the desire to travel the countryside independently can use Reykjavík as cosmopolitan base camp for all forms of tours from super-Jeeps and buses to horse riding, snowmobiling and heli-tours. If you have time, though, head out on your own.

Free Walking Tour Reykjavik WALKING TOUR
(Map p226; www.freewalkingtour.is; ⏰noon & 2pm Jun-Aug, reduced in winter) FREE One-hour, 1.5km walking tour of the centre, starting at the little clock tower on Lækjartorg Sq.

Central Reykjavík

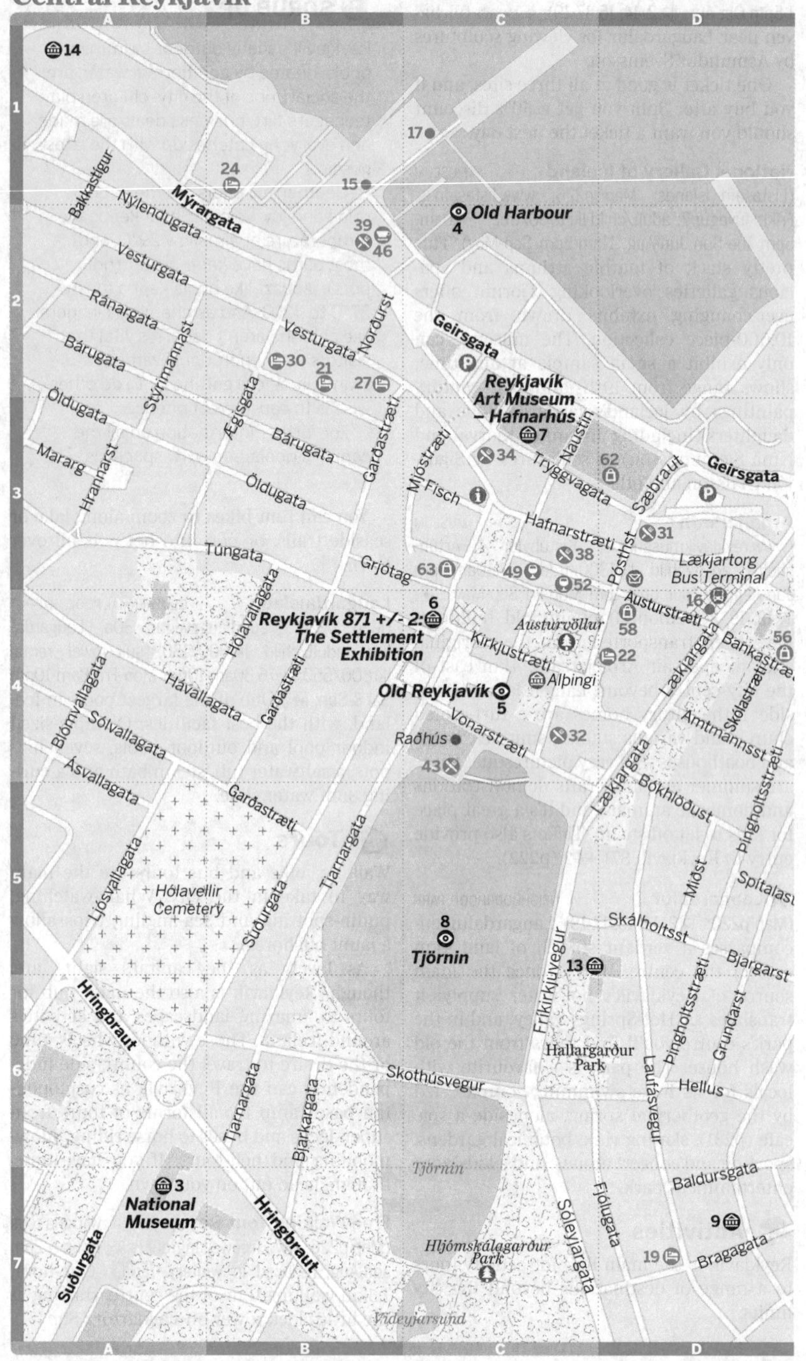

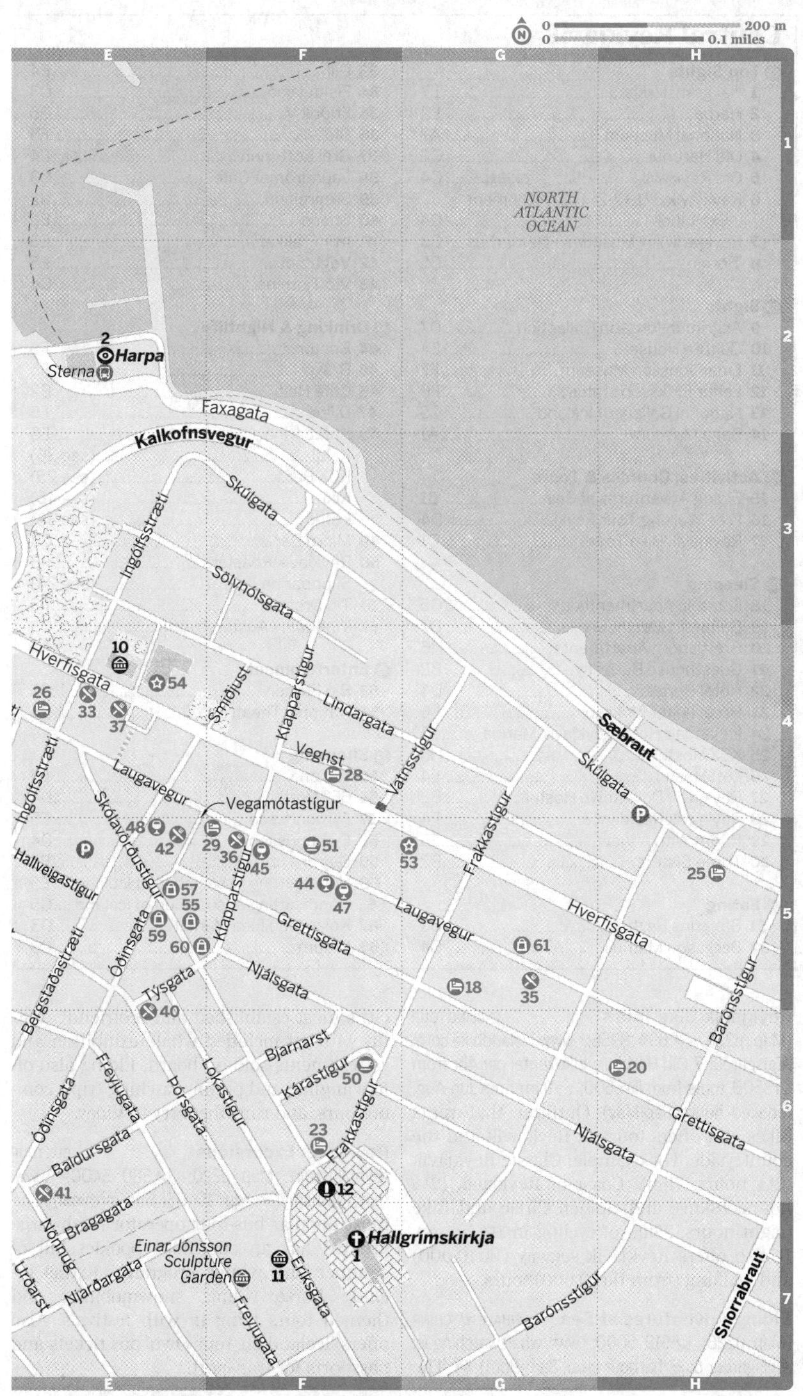
0 200 m
0 0.1 miles
NORTH ATLANTIC OCEAN
Harpa
Sterna
Faxagata
Kalkofnsvegur
Skúlagata
Ingólfsstræti
Sölvhólsgata
Hverfisgata
Smiðjust
Klapparstígur
Lindargata
Veghst
Vatnsstígur
Sæbraut
Skúlagata
Laugavegur
Vegamótastígur
Ingólfsstræti
Skólavörðustígur
Hallveigastígur
Frakkastígur
Laugavegur
Hverfisgata
Grettisgata
Óðinsgata
Bergstaðastræti
Klapparstígur
Týsgata
Njálsgata
Barónsstígur
Bjarnarst
Kárastígur
Freyjugata
Lokastígur
Þórsgata
Frakkastígur
Óðinsgata
Baldursgata
Grettisgata
Njálsgata
Bragagata
Nönnug
Hallgrímskirkja
Einar Jónsson Sculpture Garden
Eiríksgata
Urðarst
Njarðargata
Freyjugata
Barónsstígur
Snorrabraut

Central Reykjavík

Top Sights
1 Hallgrímskirkja F7
2 Harpa E2
3 National Museum A7
4 Old Harbour C2
5 Old Reykjavík C4
6 Reykjavík 871 +/-2: The Settlement Exhibition C4
7 Reykjavík Art Museum – Hafnarhús C3
8 Tjörnin C5

Sights
9 Ásgrímur Jónsson Collection D7
10 Culture House E4
11 Einar Jónsson Museum F7
12 Leifur Eiríksson statue F6
13 National Gallery of Iceland C5
14 Saga Museum A1

Activities, Courses & Tours
15 Elding Adventures at Sea B1
16 Free Walking Tour Reykjavik D4
17 Reykjavík Bike Tours C1

Sleeping
18 Forsæla Apartmenthouse G5
19 Galtafell Guesthouse D7
20 Grettisborg Apartments H6
21 Guesthouse Butterfly B2
22 Hótel Borg D4
23 Hótel Leifur Eiríksson F6
24 Icelandair Hotel Reykjavík Marina B1
25 KEX Hostel H5
26 Loft Hostel E4
27 Reykjavík Downtown Hostel B2
28 Reykjavík Residence F4
29 Room With A View F5
30 Three Sisters B2

Eating
31 Bæjarins Beztu D3
32 Bergsson Mathús C4
33 Dill E4
34 Fiskfélagið C3
35 Friðrik V G5
36 Gló F5
37 Grái Kötturinn E4
38 Laundromat Café C3
39 Sægreifinn B2
40 Snaps E6
41 Þrír Frakkar E6
42 Vegamót E5
43 Við Tjörnina C4

Drinking & Nightlife
44 Boston F5
45 Bravó F5
46 Café Haiti B2
47 Dillon F5
48 Kaffibarinn E5
Kaldi .... (see 36)
KEX Bar .... (see 25)
Kiki .... (see 45)
Loftið .... (see 38)
49 Micro Bar C3
50 Reykjavík Roasters F6
Slippbarinn .... (see 24)
51 Tiú Droppar F5
52 Vínbúðin - Austurstræti C3

Entertainment
53 Bíó Paradís G5
54 National Theatre E4

Shopping
55 12 Tónar E5
56 66° North D4
57 Eymundsson E5
58 Eymundsson D4
59 Geysir E5
60 Handknitting Association of Iceland E5
61 Handknitting Association of Iceland G5
62 Kolaportið Flea Market D3
63 Kraum C3

Reykjavík Bike Tours CYCLING TOUR
(Map p226; ☎694 8956; www.icelandbike.com; Ægisgarður 7, Old Harbour; bike rental per 4hr from Ikr3500, tours from Ikr5500; ⏱9am-5pm Jun-Aug, reduced hours Sep-May) Outfitter that rents bikes and offers tours of Reykjavík and the countryside. For example: Classic Reykjavík (2½ hours, 7km); Coast of Reykjavík (2½ hours, 18km); and Golden Circle and Bike (eight hours, 25km of cycling in 1½ hours). It also offers Reykjavík segway (Ikr10,000) and walking (from Ikr20,000) tours.

Elding Adventures at Sea WHALE WATCHING
(Map p226; ☎519 5000; www.whalewatching.is; Ægisgarður 5; ⏱harbour kiosk 8am-9pm) The city's most established and ecofriendly outfit, with an included whale exhibition and refreshments sold on board. Elding also offers angling and puffin-watching trips, combo tours, and runs the ferry to Viðey.

Reykjavík Excursions BUS TOUR
(Kynnisferðir; Map p220; ☎580 5400; www.re.is; Vatnsmýrarvegur 10, BSÍ Bus Terminal) The most popular bus-tour operator (with large groups) has an enormous booklet full of summer and winter programs. Extras include horse riding, snowmobiling and themed tours tying in with festivals. Also offers 'Iceland on Your Own' bus tickets and passports for transport.

Inside the Volcano ADVENTURE TOUR
(☎863 6640; www.insidethevolcano.com; admission Ikr37,000; ⊙mid-May–Sep) This one-of-a-kind experience takes adventure-seekers into a perfectly intact 4000-year-old magma chamber. Hike 50 minutes to the crater then a mining cart lowers groups of four 120m into the bottom of a vase-shaped chasm that once gurgled with hot lava. Lights are dim and time inside is limited. Participants must be over 12 years old.

Reykjavík Riding Center HORSE RIDING
(☎477 2222; www.reykjavikridingcenter.is; Brekknaás 9) Located near Reykjavík's main equestrian centre, this outift takes small groups (no more than 10) of all levels around the Rauðholar (Red Hills), and offers a midnight sun tour.

Festivals & Events

A great resource is at www.festivals.is.

Winter Lights Festival CULTURAL
(www.vetrarhatid.is) Mid-February, Reykjavík sparkles with this winter warmer encompassing Museum Night and Pool Night (late-opening museums and swimming pools), illuminated landmarks, light installations, concerts, and celebrations to mark International Children's Day.

Reykjavík Arts Festival PERFORMING ARTS
(www.listahatid.is) Culture vultures flock to Iceland's premier cultural festival, which showcases two weeks of local and international theatre performances, film, dance, music and visual art. In May/June.

Reykjavík Pride CULTURAL
(www.reykjavikpride.com) This festival brings Carnival-like colour to the capital on the second weekend of August. About 90,000 people (over one-quarter of the country's population) attended 2014's Pride march and celebrations.

Reykjavík Culture Night CULTURAL
(www.menningarnott.is) On Menningarnótt, held mid-August, Reykjavíkers turn out in force for a day and night of art, music, dance and fireworks. Many galleries, ateliers, shops, cafes and churches stay open until late. Your chance to get sporty and sophisticated on the same day: this event is held on the same date as the city's marathon.

Reykjavík Jazz Festival MUSIC
(www.reykjavikjazz.is) From mid-August, Reykjavík toe-taps its way through a week dedicated to jazz, man. Local and international musicians blow their own trumpets at events staged at Harpa.

Reykjavík International Film Festival FILM
(www.riff.is) This intimate 11-day event from late September features quirky programming that highlights independent film-making, both home-grown and international.

Iceland Airwaves MUSIC
(www.icelandairwaves.com) You'd be forgiven for thinking Iceland is just one giant music-producing machine. Since the first edition of Iceland Airwaves was held in 1999, this fab November festival has become one of the world's premier annual showcases for new music (Icelandic and otherwise).

Sleeping

Reykjavík has loads of accommodation choices, with hostels, midrange *gistiheimili* (guesthouses) and simple business-class hotels galore, but top-end boutique hotels and apartments seem to be opening daily.

From June through August accommodation books out entirely; reservations are essential. Everything is priced like any major European capital: high. Plan for hostels and camping if you're looking to save. Short-term apartment rentals are often the best value – airbnb.com has a huge and in-demand range.

Most guesthouses are in converted houses, so rooms often share bathrooms, kitchens and TV lounges. Some offer sleeping-bag accommodation.

Most places open year-round and many offer discounts or variable pricing online, and especially October to April. Summer prices are listed here. Prices and options (both in lodgings and in styles of room at each establishment) are growing fast. Check online to see each establishment's full range of room styles and up-to-date rates.

★**KEX Hostel** HOSTEL €
(Map p226; ☎561 6060; www.kexhostel.is; Skúlagata 28; 4-/16-bed dm Ikr6900/3900, d with/without bathroom Ikr28,500/19,700; @) An unofficial headquarters of backpackerdom and popular local gathering place, KEX is a megahostel with heaps of style (think retro Vaudeville meets rodeo) and sociability. Overall it's not as prim as the other hostels – and bathrooms are shared by many – but KEX is a perennial favourite for its friendly vibe and booming restaurant-bar with water views and interior courtyard.

Reykjavík Downtown Hostel HOSTEL €
(Map p226; ☎553 8120; www.hostel.is; Vesturgata 17; 4-/10-bed dm Ikr7900/5700, d with/without bathroom Ikr23,800/20,700; @) Squeaky clean and well run, this effortlessly charming hostel gets such good reviews that it regularly lures large groups and the nonbackpacker set. Enjoy friendly service, guest kitchen and excellent rooms. Discount Ikr700 for HI members.

Loft Hostel HOSTEL €
(Map p226; ☎553 8140; www.lofthostel.is; Bankastræti 7; dm/d from Ikr6650/23,800; @) Perched high above the action on bustling Bankastræti, this modern hostel attracts a decidedly younger crowd, including locals who come for its trendy bar and cafe terrace. This sociable spot comes with prim dorms, linen included, and en suite bathrooms in each. HI members discount dorm/double Ikr700/2800.

Reykjavík City Hostel HOSTEL €
(Map p220; ☎553 8110; www.hostel.is; Sundlaugavegur 34; dm/d from Ikr4150/17,900; P @) Reykjavík's original hostel is a large, ecofriendly complex with a fun backpacker vibe. Two kilometres east of the centre in Laugardalur, it abuts the campground and swimming pool, and is served by the Flybus and many tour operators. It boasts bike rental, three guest kitchens and a spacious deck. HI members discount Ikr700, kids four to 12 discount Ikr1500.

Reykjavík Campsite CAMPGROUND €
(Map p220; ☎568 6944; www.reykjavikcampsite.is; Sundlaugavegur 32; sites per adult/child Ikr1500/free; mid-May–mid-Sep; P @) Reykjavík's only campground (2km east of the centre in Laugardalur, next to the swimming pool and City Hostel) is popular in summer. There's space for 650 people in three fields, so you're likely to find a spot. Extensive, modern facilities include free showers, bike hire (five hours Ikr3500), kitchens and barbecue areas.

★ **Grettisborg Apartments** APARTMENT €€
(Map p226; ☎694 7020; www.grettisborg.is; Grettisgata 53b; apt from Ikr25,500;) Like sleeping in a magazine for Scandinavian home design, these thoroughly modern studios and apartments come in 50 shades of grey (no, not like that), sporting fine furnishings and sleek built-ins.

Room With A View APARTMENT €€
(Map p226; ☎552 7262; www.roomwithaview.is; Laugavegur 18; apt Ikr24,400-67,940;) This ridiculously central apartment hotel offers swanky studios and one- to four-bedroom apartments (that sleep 10!), decorated in luxe-Scandinavian style including kitchenettes, CD players, TVs and washing machines. They have those eponymous sea or city views, plus access to a sundeck and jacuzzi. Each apartment varies: check online for details. The only downside is Friday and Saturday nightlife noise.

Guesthouse Butterfly GUESTHOUSE €€
(Map p226; ☎894 1864; www.butterfly.is; Ránargata 8a; d with/without bathroom Ikr22,500/17,850; mid-May–Aug;) On a quiet, central residential street, Butterfly's flamboyant mural is hard to miss. Neat, simply furnished rooms, a guest kitchen, and friendly Icelandic-Norwegian owners make you feel right at home. The top floor has two self-contained apartments with kitchen and balcony (Ikr26,960).

Three Sisters APARTMENT €€
(Þrjár Systur; Map p226; ☎565 2181; www.threesisters.is; Ránargata 16; apt from Ikr24,500; mid-May–Aug; @) A twinkly-eyed former fisherman runs the Three Sisters, a corner townhouse in old Reykjavík, now divided into eight studio apartments. Comfy beds are flanked by old-fashioned chairs and state-of-the-art flat-screen TVs. Each room has a kitchen.

Hótel Leifur Eiríksson HOTEL €€
(Map p226; ☎562 0800; www.hotelleifur.is; Skólavörðustígur 45; d incl breakfast from Ikr26,000) This hotel glories in one of the best locations in Reykjavík: arty Skólavörðustígur just in front of Hallgrímskirkja, and more than half of the 47 rooms have excellent church views. Rooms are fairly small and basic, but you're paying for the hotel's coordinates rather than its interior design.

Galtafell Guesthouse GUESTHOUSE €€
(Map p226; ☎551 4344; www.galtafell.com; Laufásvegur 46; d/apt incl breakfast from Ikr18,500/29,300) In a quiet, lakeside neighbourhood within easy walking distance of the centre, the four one-bedroom apartments in this converted historic mansion contain fully equipped kitchens and cosy seating areas. Three doubles share a guest kitchen. The garden and entry spaces feel suitably lovely.

Forsæla Apartmenthouse GUESTHOUSE, APARTMENT €€
(Map p226; ☎551 6046; www.apartmenthouse.is; Grettisgata 33b; d without bathroom incl breakfast Ikr12,200, apt/house from Ikr36,000/78,000;) This lovely option in Reykjavík's centre stars a 100-year-old wood-and-tin house for four to eight people, which comes with all the old beams and tasteful mod cons you could want. Three apartments have small, cosy bedrooms and sitting rooms, kitchens and washing machines. Plus there's B&B lodging with shared bathrooms. Minimum three-night stay in apartments and the house.

★**Hótel Borg** LUXURY HOTEL €€€
(Map p226; ☎551 1440; www.hotelborg.is; Pósthússtræti 9-11; d from Ikr43,600; @) This historic hotel dates from 1930 and is now tricked out with supersmart beige, black and cream decor, parquet floors, leather headboards and flat-screen Bang & Olufsen TVs. The tower suite is two stories of opulence with panoramic views. At the time of writing, a huge renovation-expansion had shuttered gourmet Borg restaurant, which should be reopened when you read this under chef Völundur Völundarson; his bistro **Nora Magasin** is next door.

★**Reykjavík Residence** APARTMENT €€€
(Map p226; ☎561 1200; www.rrhotel.is; Hverfisgata 45; apt from Ikr29,300; @) Plush city-centre living feels just right in these two converted historic mansions. Linens are crisp, service attentive and the light a glowing gold. Accommodation comes in loads of configurations, from suites and studios with kitchenettes to two- and three-bedroom apartments. Recently established with all-modern fittings.

★**Icelandair Hotel Reykjavík Marina** BOUTIQUE HOTEL €€€
(Map p226; ☎560 8000; www.icelandairhotels.is; Mýrargata 2; d Ikr27,800-35,800; @) This large design hotel on the Old Harbour is adding a whole new wing. Captivating art, cool nautical-chic design elements, up-to-the-second mod cons and clever ways to conserve space make small rooms winners overall. Attic rooms on the harbour side have excellent sea views. The lively lobby sports a live satellite feed to sights all over Iceland, and the happening **Slippbarinn** (Map p226; ☎560 8080; www.slippbarinn.is; Mýrargata 2; 11.30am-midnight Sun-Thu, to 1am Fri & Sat).

Eating

From take-it-to-go hot dogs to gourmet platters on white-clothed tables, little Reykjavík has an astonishing assortment of eateries. Loads of seafood and Icelandic or 'new Nordic' restaurants serve tried-and-true variations on local fish and lamb, but the capital is also the main spot for finding international eats.

Reykjavík also has an amazing coffee culture and cafe scene. Cool, cosy cafes encourage lingering, and though they're tops for morning coffee and light lunches, as evening comes along, many undergo a Jekyll-and-Hyde transformation – coffee becomes beer, DJs materialise in dark corners, and suddenly you're in a kick-ass bar. Some restaurants morph into late-night bars too, with their kitchens closing around 10pm and the party rocking into the wee hours.

★**Gló** ORGANIC, VEGETARIAN €
(Map p226; ☎553 1111; www.glo.is; Laugavegur 20b; mains Ikr1700-2500; 11am-9pm;) Join the cool cats in this upstairs, airy restaurant serving fresh, large daily specials loaded with Asian-influenced herbs and spices. Though not exclusively vegetarian, it's a wonderland of raw and organic foods with your choice from a broad bar of elaborate salads, from root veggies to Greek. It also has branches in **Laugardalur** (Map p220; Engjateigur 19; 11am-9pm Mon-Fri, to 5pm Sat) and **Hafnarfjörður** (Strandgata 34; 11am-9pm Mon-Fri, to 5pm Sat & Sun).

★**Café Flóra** CAFE €
(Flóran; Map p220; ☎553 8872; www.floran.is; Botanic Gardens; cakes Ikr850, mains Ikr950-2500; 10am-10pm Jun-Aug;) Sun-dappled tables fill a greenhouse in the Botanic Gardens and spill onto a flower-lined terrace at this lovely cafe that specialises in wholesome local ingredients – some grown in the gardens themselves! Soups come with fantastic sourdough bread, and the snacks range from cheese platters with nuts and honey to pulled-pork sandwiches. Coffee and homemade cakes round it all out.

Bergsson Mathús CAFE €
(Map p226; ☎571 1822; www.bergsson.is; Templarasund 3; mains Ikr1300-2200; 7am-7pm Mon-Fri, to 5pm Sat & Sun;) This popular, no-nonsense cafe features homemade breads, fresh produce and filling lunch

ESSENTIAL TASTEBUD TOURING

Succulent specialities Icelandic lamb is some of the tastiest on the planet – sheep roam free in the mountains all summer, grazing on chemical-free grasses and herbs. Iceland also takes great pride in its fishing industry, and superfresh fish dishes grace most menus. Delicious yoghurtlike *skyr* is a unique treat, often sweetened with sugar and fruit. It's available in any supermarket, and you'll often see it in local desserts. Around Mývatn look out for a regional treat: *hverabrauð* (hot-spring bread) is a sweet, dark, sticky loaf, baked in the ground using geothermal heat. *Kleinur* (twisted doughnuts) are popular snacks with coffee.

Favourite drinks The traditional alcoholic brew *brennivín* is schnapps made from potatoes and caraway seeds. It's fondly known as 'black death'. A slew of local distilleries and breweries have sprung up in recent years, concocting whiskey, vodka and dozens of high-calibre craft beers. Coffee is a national institution (generally of the filtered kind).

Þorrablót The midwinter feast (named for the month of Þorri in the Old Norse calendar, mid-January to mid-February) features some traditional specialities that look more like horror-film props than food: brave souls might try *svið* (singed sheep's head), *súrsaðir hrútspungar* (pickled ram's testicles) and *hákarl* (fermented shark meat).

Tastebud challenges You can try cubes of *hákarl* at Kolaportið Flea Market in Reykjavík, but be warned that the smell alone makes many foreigners ill! Some restaurants serve *hval* (whale meat), some serve horse, and some serve *lundi* (puffin), which looks and tastes like calf liver. *Harðfiskur* is an everyday snack: these brittle pieces of wind-dried haddock are usually eaten with butter.

specials. Stop by on weekends when locals flip through magazines, gossip and devour scrumptious brunch plates.

Sægreifinn SEAFOOD €
(Seabaron; Map p226; ☎553 1500; www.saegreifinn.is; Geirsgata 8; mains Ikr1350-1900; ⏲11.30am-11pm) Sidle into this green harbourside shack for the most famous lobster soup (Ikr1300) in the capital, or to choose from a fridge full of fresh fish skewers to be grilled on the spot. Though the original sea baron sold the restaurant a few years ago, the place retains a homey, laid-back feel.

Grái Kötturinn CAFE €
(Map p226; ☎551 1544; Hverfisgata 16a; mains Ikr1000-2500; ⏲7.15am-3pm Mon-Fri, 8am-3pm Sat & Sun) Blink and you'll miss this tiny six-table cafe (a favourite of Björk's). It looks like a cross between an eccentric bookshop and an art gallery, and dishes up delicious breakfasts of toast, bagels, pancakes, or bacon and eggs served on thick, buttery slabs of freshly baked bread.

Tiú Droppar CAFE
(Ten Drops; Map p226; ☎551 9380; Laugavegur 27; ⏲9am-1am Mon-Thu, 10am-1am Sat & Sun) Tucked in a cosy teapot-lined basement, Tiú Droppar is one of those quintessential Reykjavík cafes that serves waffles, heaping brunches (Ikr640 to Ikr990) and sandwiches, then in the evenings morphs into a wine bar with occasional live music. It's said that the Sunday-night pianist can play anything by ear.

Bæjarins Beztu HOT DOGS €
(Map p226; www.bbp.is; Tryggvagata; hot dogs Ikr380; ⏲10am-2am Sun-Thu, to 4.30am Fri & Sat; 🚸) Icelanders swear the city's best hot dogs are at this truck near the harbour (patronised by Bill Clinton and late-night bar-hoppers). Use the vital sentence *Eina með öllu* ('One with everything') to get the quintessential favourite with sweet mustard, ketchup and crunchy onions.

★ **Þrír Frakkar** ICELANDIC, SEAFOOD €€
(Map p226; ☎552 3939; www.3frakkar.com; Baldursgata 14; mains Ikr3200-5300; ⏲11.30am-2.30pm & 6-11.30pm Mon-Fri, 6-11.30pm Sat & Sun) Owner-chef Úlfar Eysteinsson has built up a consistently excellent reputation at this snug little restaurant – apparently a favourite of Jamie Oliver's. Specialities range throughout the aquatic world from salt cod and halibut to *plokkfiskur* (fish stew) with black bread. Nonfish items run toward guillemot, horse, lamb and whale.

Snaps FRENCH €€
(Map p226; ☎511 6677; www2.snaps.is; Þórsgata 1; dinner mains Ikr3000-4000; ⊙11.30am-11pm Sun-Thu, to midnight Fri & Sat) Reserve ahead for this French bistro that's a megahit with locals. Snaps' secret is simple: serve scrumptious seafood and classic bistro mains (think steak or *moules frites*) at surprisingly decent prices. Lunch specials (11.30am to 2pm; Ikr1890) and scrummy brunches (11.30am to 4pm Saturday and Sunday; Ikr900 to Ikr3300) are a big draw too. Seats fill a lively glassed-in porch and have views of the open kitchen.

Við Tjörnina ICELANDIC €€
(Map p226; ☎551 8666; www.vidtjornina.is; Vonarstræti, Raðhús; mains Ikr3600-4600; ⊙noon-5pm & 6-10pm) Freshly relocated to the city hall, with wrap-around windows and lake views, this well-regarded restaurant has loyal followers due to its beautifully presented Icelandic seafood and other regional dishes like lamb fillet with barley. By day it's a relaxing cafe.

Laundromat Café INTERNATIONAL €€
(Map p226; www.thelaundromatcafe.com; Austurstæti 9; mains Ikr1000-2700; ⊙8am-midnight Mon-Wed & Sun, to 1am Thu & Fri, 10am-1am Sat; 👪) This popular Danish import attracts both locals and travellers who devour heaps of hearty mains in a cheery environment surrounded by tattered paperbacks. Go for the 'Dirty Brunch' (Ikr2690) on weekends, to sop up the previous night's booze. Oh, and yes, there are (busy) washers and dryers in the basement (per wash/15-minute dry Ikr500/100).

Vegamót INTERNATIONAL €€
(Map p226; ☎511 3040; www.vegamot.is; Vegamótastígur 4; mains Ikr2400-4000; ⊙11.30am-1am Mon-Thu, 11am-4am Fri & Sat, noon-1am Sun) A long-running bistro-bar-club, with a name that means 'crossroads', this is still a trendy place to eat, drink, see and be seen at night (it's favoured by families during the day). The 'global' menu ranges all over: from Mexican salad to Louisiana chicken. Weekend brunches (Ikr2000 to Ikr2500) are a hit too.

★**Dill** SCANDINAVIAN €€€
(Map p226; ☎552 1522; www.dillrestaurant.is; Hverfisgata 12; 3-course meals from Ikr8100; ⊙7-10pm Wed-Sat) Top 'New Nordic' cuisine is the major drawcard at this elegant yet simple bistro. The focus is very much on the food – locally sourced produce served as a parade of courses. The owners are friends with the famous Noma clan, and have drawn much inspiration from the celebrated Copenhagen restaurant. Popular with locals and visitors alike, so a reservation is a must.

Friðrik V ICELANDIC €€€
(Map p226; www.fridrikv.is; Laugavegur 60; lunch mains/3-course dinner Ikr1750/7500; ⊙11.30am-1.30pm Tue-Fri & 5.30-10pm Tue-Sat) One of the top spots to splash out on a gourmet Icelandic meal, Friðrik's eponymous master chef is known throughout the country for championing the 'slow food' movement. Each dish is a carefully prepared combination of locally sourced items presented in a forward-thinking manner.

Fiskfélagið INTERNATIONAL €€€
(Map p226; www.fishcompany.is; Vesturgata 2a; mains lunch Ikr1600-2800, dinner Ikr3800-5400; ⊙11.30am-2pm & 6-11.30pm) The 'Fish Company' takes Icelandic seafood recipes and spins them through a variety of far-flung inspirations from Fiji coconut to Spanish chorizo. Dine in an intimate-feeling stone-and-timber room with copper light fittings and quirky furnishings.

🍷 Drinking & Nightlife

Reykjavík is renowned for its weekend party scene that goes strong into the wee hours, and even spills over onto some of the weekdays (especially in summer). *Djammið* in the capital means 'going out on the town' (not to be confused with the infamous countryside *rúntur*, which involves Icelandic youth driving around their town in one big automotive party).

Beer is expensive. Most people visit a government-owned Vínbúð (the only shops licensed to sell alcohol), tipple at home, then hit the town from midnight to 5am. There's a central **Vínbúð** (Map p226; www.vinbudin.is; Austurstræti 10a; ⊙11am-6pm Mon-Thu & Sat, to 7pm Fri).

Most of the action is concentrated on Laugavegur and Austurstræti. Places usually stay open until 1am Sunday to Thursday and 4am or 5am on Friday and Saturday. You'll pay around Ikr800 to Ikr1200 per pint of beer, and cocktails hit the Ikr1800 to Ikr2600 mark. Some venues have cover charges (about Ikr1000) after midnight; many have early-in-the-evening happy hours that cut costs to between Ikr500 or Ikr700 per beer. Download the smartphone 'Reykjavík Appy Hour' app.

Things change fast – check *Reykjavík Grapevine* (www.grapevine.is) for the latest listings. You should dress up to fit in in Reykjavík, although there are some more relaxed pub-style joints. The legal drinking age is 20.

★ Kaffibarinn BAR

(Map p226; www.kaffibarinn.is; Bergstaðastræti 1; ⏲2pm-1am Sun-Thu, to 4.30am Fri & Sat) This old house with the London Underground symbol over the door contains one of Reykjavík's coolest bars; it even had a starring role in the cult movie *101 Reykjavík* (2000). At weekends you'll feel like you need a famous face or a battering ram to get in. At other times it's a place for artistic types to chill with their Macs.

★ KEX Bar BAR

(Map p226; www.kexhostel.is; Skúlagata 28; ⏲noon-11pm) Believe it or not, locals flock to this hostel bar-restaurant (mains Ikr1700 to Ikr2500) in an old cookie factory (*kex* means 'cookie') with broad windows facing the sea, an inner courtyard and loads of happy hipsters. The vibe is 1920s Vegas, with saloon doors, an old-school barber station, scuffed floors and happy chatter.

Micro Bar BAR

(Map p226; Austurstræti 6; ⏲2pm-midnight Jun-Sep, 4pm-midnight Oct-May) Boutique brews is the name of the game at this low-key spot near Austurvöllur. Bottles of beer represent a slew of brands and countries, but more importantly you'll discover 10 local draughts on tap from the island's top microbreweries: the best selection in Reykjavík. Its five-beer minisampler costs Ikr2500; happy hour (5pm to 7pm) offers Ikr600 beers.

Loftið COCKTAIL BAR

(Map p226; ☎551 9400; www.loftidbar.is; Austurstræti 9, 2nd fl; ⏲2pm-1am Sun-Thu, 4pm-4am Fri & Sat) Loftið is all about high-end cocktails and good living. Dress up to join the fray at this airy upstairs lounge with a zinc bar, retro tailor-shop-inspired decor, vintage tiles and a swanky crowd. The house booze here is the top-shelf liquor elsewhere, and it brings in jazzy bands on Thursday nights.

Kaldi BAR

(Map p226; www.kaldibar.is; Laugavegur 20b; ⏲noon-1am Sun-Thu, to 3am Fri & Sat) Effortlessly cool with mismatched seats and teal banquettes, plus a popular smoking courtyard, Kaldi is awesome for its full range of Kaldi microbrews, not available elsewhere. Happy hour (4pm to 7pm) gets you one for Ikr650. Anyone can play the in-house piano.

Bravó BAR

(Map p226; Laugavegur 22; ⏲6.30pm-1am Mon-Thu, to 4.30am Fri & Sat) Friendly, knowledgable bartenders, a laid-back corner-bar vibe with great people-watching, cool tunes on the sound system and happy-hour (5pm to 9pm) draught local beers for Ikr500 – what's not to love?

Reykjavík Roasters CAFE

(Map p226; www.reykjavikroasters.is; Kárastígur 1; ⏲8am-6pm Mon-Fri, 9am-7pm Sat & Sun) These folks take their coffee seriously. This tiny hipster joint is easily spotted on warm days with its smattering of wooden tables and potato sacks dropped throughout the paved square. Swig a perfect latte with a flaky croissant.

Café Haiti CAFE

(Map p226; ☎588 8484; www.cafehaiti.is; Geirsgata 7c; ⏲8am-10pm Mon-Thu, to 11pm Fri, 9am-11pm Sat, to 10pm Sun) If you're a coffee afficionado, this tiny cafe in the Old Harbour is the place for you. Owner Elda buys her beans from her home country Haiti, and roasts and grinds them on-site, producing what regulars swear are the best cups of coffee in the country.

Kiki GAY

(Map p226; www.kiki.is; Laugavegur 22; ⏲11pm-4.30am Fri & Sat) Ostensibly a queer bar, Kiki is also *the* place to get your dance on (with pop and electronica the mainstays), since much of Reyjavík's nightlife centres around the booze, not the groove.

Boston BAR

(Map p226; ☎577 3200; Laugavegur 28b; ⏲4pm-1am Sun-Thu, to 3am Fri & Sat) Boston is cool, arty and found up through a doorway on Laugavegur that leads to its laid-back lounge where DJs spin from time to time.

Dillon BAR, LIVE MUSIC

(Map p226; ☎578 2424; Laugavegur 30; ⏲2pm-1am Sun-Thu, to 3am Fri & Sat) Beer, beards and the odd flying bottle…atmospheric Dillon is a RRRRROCK pub with a great beer garden. Frequent concerts hit its tiny corner stage.

✩ Entertainment

The vibrant Reykjavík live-music scene is ever-changing. There are often performances at bars and cafes, and local theatres and Harpa concert hall (p222) bring in all of the performing arts.

To catch up with on Icelandic music and to see what's on, consult free English-language newspaper/website **Grapevine** (www.grapevine.is), **Visit Reykjavík** (www.visitreykjavik.is), **What's On in Reykjavík** (www.whatson.is/magazine), www.musik.is, or city music shops.

★Bíó Paradís CINEMA
(Map p226; www.bioparadis.is; Hverfisgata 54; adult Ikr1600) This totally cool cinema, decked out in movie posters and vintage officeware, screens specially curated Icelandic films with English subititles. It's a chance to see movies that you may not find elsewhere. Plus there's a happy hour from 5pm to 7.30pm.

National Theatre THEATRE
(Þjóðleikhúsið; Map p226; ☎551 1200; www.leikhusid.is; Hverfisgata 19; ⊙closed Jul) The National Theatre has three separate stages and puts on plays, musicals and operas, from modern Icelandic works to Shakespeare.

Reykjavík City Theatre THEATRE, DANCE
(Borgarleikhúsið; Map p220; ☎568 8000; www.borgarleikhus.is; Listabraut 3, Kringlan; ⊙closed Jul & Aug) Stages plays and musicals, and is home to the **Icelandic Dance Company** (Map p220; ☎588 0900; www.id.is).

Shopping

Reykjavík's vibrant design culture makes for great shopping: from sleek, fish-skin purses and knitted *lopapeysur* (the ubiquitous Icelandic woollen sweater) to unique music or lip-smacking Icelandic schnapps *brennivín*. Laugavegur is the most dense shopping street. You'll find interesting shops all over town, but fashion concentrates near the Frakkastígur and Vitastígur end of Laugavegur. Skólavörðustígur is strong for arts and jewellery. Bankastræti and Austurstræti have many touristy shops.

Don't forget – all visitors are eligible for a 15% tax refund on their shopping, under certain conditions.

★Kraum ARTS & CRAFTS
(Map p226; www.kraum.is; Aðalstræti 10; ⊙9am-6pm Mon-Fri, noon-5pm Sat & Sun) The brainchild of a band of local artists, Kraum literally means 'simmering', like the island's quaking earth and the inventive minds of its citizens. Expect a fascinating assortment of unique designer wares, like fish-skin apparel and driftwood furniture, on display in Reykjavík's oldest house.

66° North CLOTHING
(Map p226; ☎535 6680; www.66north.is; Bankastræti 5; ⊙9am-10pm) Iceland's premier outdoor-clothing company began by making all-weather wear for Arctic fishermen. This metamorphosed into costly, fashionable streetwear: jackets, fleeces, hats and gloves. Its kids' branch is a block away, and there are boutiques in Kringlan Shopping Centre.

Eymundsson BOOKS
(Map p226; www.eymundsson.is; Austurstræti 18; ⊙9am-10pm Mon-Fri, 10am-10pm Sat & Sun) This big central bookshop has a superb choice of English-language books, newspapers, magazines and maps, along with a great cafe. A second branch can be found on **Skólavörðustígur** (Map p226; Skólavörðustígur 11; ⊙9am-10pm Mon-Fri, 10am-10pm Sat & Sun).

★Kolaportið Flea Market MARKET
(Map p226; www.kolaportid.is; Tryggvagata 19; ⊙11am-5pm Sat & Sun) Held in a huge industrial building by the harbour, this weekend market is a Reykjavík institution. Don't expect much from the selection of secondhand clothes and old toys, just enjoy the experience. There's also a food section that sells traditional eats like *rúgbrauð* (geothermally baked rye bread), *brauðterta* ('sandwich cake', a layering of bread with mayonnaise-based fillings) and *hákarl* (fermented shark).

Geysir CLOTHING
(Map p226; ☎519 6000; www.geysir.com; Skólavörðustígur 16; ⊙10am-10pm) For traditional Icelandic clothing, Geysir boasts an elegant selection of sweaters, blankets, and men's and women's clothes, shoes and bags.

Handknitting Association of Iceland CLOTHING
(Handprjónasamband Íslands; Map p226; ☎552 1890; www.handknit.is; Skólavörðustígur 19; ⊙9am-9pm Mon-Fri, to 6pm Sat, 10am-6pm Sun) Traditional handmade hats, socks and sweaters are sold at this knitting collective, or you can buy yarn, needles and knitting patterns and do it yourself. The association's smaller **branch** (Map p226; ☎562 1890; Laugavegur 53b; ⊙9am-7pm Mon-Fri. 10am-5pm Sat) sells made-up items only.

12 Tónar MUSIC
(Map p226; www.12tonar.is; Skolavörðustígur 15; ⊙10am-8pm) A very cool place to hang out, 12 Tónar is responsible for launching some of Iceland's favourite bands. In the three-floor shop you can listen to CDs, drink coffee and

REYKJAVÍK CITY CARD

The **Reykjavík City Card** (24/48/72hr Ikr2900/3900/4900) offers free travel on the city's Straetó buses and on the ferry to Viðey, as well as free admission to Reykjavík's municipal swimming/thermal pools and to most of the main galleries and museums, discounts on some tours, shops and entertainment. The card is available at the tourist office, some travel agencies, 10-11 supermarkets, HI hostels and some hotels.

Kids enter free at many museums, but there is a reduced priced Children's City Card (24/48/72hr Ikr1000/2000/3000) for other services.

sometimes catch a live performance. There's a new branch in the Harpa concert hall too.

Information

EMERGENCY

For an ambulance, the fire brigade or the police, dial ☎112.

Landspítali University Hospital (☎543 1000; www.landspitali.is; Fossvogur) Casualty department open 24/7.

INTERNET ACCESS

Almost all accommodation options and many cafes have wi-fi. You can use terminals (Ikr250 per hour) at the main tourist-information office and libraries.

Aðalbókasafn (Reykjavík City Library; www.borgarbokasafn.is; Tryggvagata 15; ⏰10am-7pm Mon-Thu, 11am-7pm Fri, 1-5pm Sat & Sun) Excellent main library.

MONEY

Credit cards are accepted everywhere (except municipal buses); ATMs are ubiquitous. Currency-exchange fees at hotels or private bureaus can be obscenely high.

POST

Main Post Office (Map p226; www.postur.is; Pósthússtræti 5; ⏰9am-6pm Mon-Fri) Has poste restante.

TOURIST INFORMATION

Reykjavík has an excellent main tourist office, and loads of travel agencies that specialise in booking tours.

The excellent English-language newspaper the *Reykjavik Grapevine*, widely distributed (online at www.grapevine.is), has the low-down on what's new in town.

Main Tourist Office (Upplýsingamiðstöð Ferðamanna; Map p226; ☎590 1550; www.visitreykjavik.is; Aðalstræti 2; ⏰8.30am-7pm Jun–mid-Sep, 9am-6pm Mon-Fri, to 4pm Sat, to 2pm Sun mid-Sep–May) Friendly staff and mountains of free brochures, plus maps and Strætó city bus tickets for sale. Book accommodation, tours and activities. Also one site for getting your duty-free refund.

TRAVEL AGENCIES

Icelandic Travel Market (☎552 4979; www.icelandictravelmarket.is; Bankastræti 2; ⏰8am-9pm May-Aug, to 7pm Sep-Apr) Information, tour bookings and bike rental (Ikr3500 per five hours).

Getting There & Away

AIR

International flights operate through Keflavík International Airport (p278), 48km west of Reykjavík.

Reykjavík Domestic Airport (p278) is in the city and serves all domestic destinations, plus the Faroe Islands and Greenland. Internal flight operator **Air Iceland** (☎570 3030; www.airiceland.is) has an airport desk, but save money booking online.

BUS

You can travel from Reykjavík by day tour (many of which offer hotel pick-up), or use Strætó and several of the tour companies for transport, getting on and off their scheduled buses. They also offer various bus transport passes. The *Public Transport in Iceland* free map has a good overview of routes.

Bus service is reduced or cut in winter, and things are changing rapidly in Iceland. It pays to check websites for up-to-date information.

Bus operators from the capital:

Strætó (☎540 2700; www.straeto.is/english) Operates Reykjavík long-distance buses from Mjódd Bus Terminal, 8km southeast of the centre, which is served by local buses 3, 4, 11, 12, 17, 21, 24 and 28. Strætó also operates city buses and offers a smartphone app. For long distance buses *only* you can use cash, credit/debit card with PIN or (wads of) bus tickets.

Reykjavík Excursions (Map p220; ☎562 1011; www.bsi.is; Vatnsmýrarvegur 10) Reykjavík Excursions (and its Flybus) uses the BSÍ terminal (pronounced bee-ess-ee), south of the centre. There's a ticketing desk, tourist brochures, lockers, luggage storage (Ikr500 per bag per day), Budget car hire and a cafeteria with wi-fi. The terminal is served by Reykjavík buses 1, 3, 6, 14, 15 and 19. Reykjavík Excursions offers prebooked hotel pick-up to bring you to the terminal.

Sterna (Map p226; ☎551 1166; www.sterna.is) Sales and departures from the Harpa concert hall. Buses everywhere except the west and Westfjords.

Trex (☎587 6000; www.trex.is) Departs from the main tourist office or Harpa concert hall and Reykjavík Campsite. Buses to Þórsmörk and Landmannalaugar in the south.

Getting Around

TO/FROM THE AIRPORT

It's a 1km walk into town from the city airport terminal (domestic flights), or there's a taxi rank. Buses 15 and 19 run to Hlemmur bus station.

From Keflavík International Airport it's easy: the **Flybus** (☎580 5400; www.re.is) meets all international flights; it is not worth taking a taxi as they are expensive and take roughly the same amount of time as the bus. One-way bus ticket Ikr1950, or Ikr2500 for hotel pick-up/drop-off. Buy tickets from the booth just inside the airport doors. The journey to Reykjavík takes around 50 minutes.

BUS

Strætó operates regular, easy buses around Reykjavík and its suburbs.

Stations Hlemmur, at the eastern end of Laugavegur, and Lækjartorg Sq, in the centre of town

Stops Buses stop at designated bus stops, marked with a yellow letter 'S'.

Fare Adult Ikr350; buy tickets at the bus station or pay on board (exact change). One-/three-day pass available (Ikr900/2200).

Day buses At 20- or 30-minute intervals, running 7am to 11pm or midnight (from 10am Sunday).

Night buses Run until 2am Friday and Saturday.

Reykjavík City Card Acts as a Strætó bus pass.

Transfer ticket (*Skiptimiði*, valid 75 minutes) Available from driver if you need two buses to reach your destination.

BUSES FROM REYKJAVÍK

Below are sample routes and fares; check bus companies for current rates. Strætó usually offers the lowest fares. Private companies like Reykjavík Excursions (RE) and Sterna also ply some of these routes.

DESTINATION	COMPANY	PRICE (IKR)	DURATION	FREQUENCY	YEAR-ROUND
Akureyri	Strætó 57	7,700	6½hr	daily	yes
Blue Lagoon	Sterna/RE	2000	45min	daily	yes
Borgarnes	Strætó 57/58/59/82	1400	1¼hr	daily	yes
Geysir/Gullfoss	RE	5000	2½hr	daily	mid-Jun–mid-Sep
Höfn	Strætó 51	10,150	8½hr	daily	yes
Hólmavík	Strætó 59	5250	3½hr	daily	yes
Keflavík	REX	1500	40min	several daily	yes
Kirkjubæjarklaustur	Strætó 51	8100	5hr	daily	yes
Landmannalaugar	Trex/RE	8400/9000	5½hr	daily	mid-Jun–Aug
Mývatn	RE	20,500	12hr	three weekly	Jul-Aug
Selfoss	Strætó 51/52	1400	1hr	many daily	yes
Skaftafell	Sterna	7,200	6½hr	daily	yes
Skógar	Strætó 51/ Sterna	4200/3600	3¼hr	daily	Jun–mid-Sep
Stykkishólmur	Strætó 58	3150	3hr	two daily	yes
Landeyjarhöfn port for Vestmannaeyjar Islands	Strætó 52	3500	2¼hr	daily	yes
Vík í Mýrdal	Strætó 51	4900	4hr	two daily	yes
Þingvellir	RE	2500	45min	daily	mid-Jun-mid-Sep
Þórsmörk	Trex/RE	6800/7500	3½hr	two daily	Jun–mid-Sep

TAXI

Taxi prices are high; flag fall starts at around Ikr660. Tipping is not expected.

There are usually taxis outside the bus stations, airports, and bars (expect queues) on weekend nights. Alternatively, call **BSR** (☎561 0000; www.taxireykjavik.is) or **Hreyfill-Bæjarleiðir** (☎588 5522; www.hreyfill.is).

AROUND REYKJAVÍK

Blue Lagoon

As the Eiffel Tower is to Paris, as Disney World is to Florida, so the **Blue Lagoon** (Bláa Lónið; ☎420 8800; www.bluelagoon.com; Jun-Aug admission adult/14 & 15yr/under-14 from €40/20/free, visitor pass (no lagoon entry) €10; ⌚9am-9pm Jun & 11-31 Aug, to 11pm Jul-10 Aug, 10am-8pm Sep-May) is to Iceland…with all the positive and negative connotations that implies. Those who say it's too expensive, too commercial, too crowded aren't wrong, but ignore them anyway. The Blue Lagoon is a must-see, and you'll be missing something special if you don't go.

Set in a vast black lava field, the milky blue spa is fed by water (a perfect 38°C) from the futuristic Svartsengi geothermal plant, which provides an off-the-planet scene-setter for your swim. Add in rolling steam clouds and people coated in silica mud, and you're in another world.

Be careful on the slippery bridges and bring plenty of conditioner for your hair. There's a snack bar, top gourmet restaurant, rooftop viewpoint and gift shop on-site, plus masseurs, spa treatments (book these well in advance) and a VIP section.

The lagoon is 47km southwest of Reykjavík, and 23km southeast of Keflavík International Airport. Bus service runs year-round, as do tours (which sometimes offer better deals than a bus ticket plus lagoon admission). You must book in advance. See the 'Plan Your Visit' section of the website for detailed information.

Reykjavík Excursions (☎580 5400; www.re.is) runs buses to the lagoon from/to Reykjavík and from/to the airport. You can do a round trip from either Reykjavík or the airport, or stop off at the lagoon on your way between the two.

The Golden Circle

Gulp down three of Iceland's most famous natural wonders – Gullfoss, Geysir and Þingvellir – in one daylong circular tour. It's very easy to tour the Golden Circle on your own (by bike or car) – plus, it's fun to tack on additional elements that suit your interests.

DIYers can add the following elements to their tour:

Laugarvatn Located between Þingvellir and Geysir, this small lakeside town has two must-tries: Lindin, an excellent restaurant, and Fontana, a swanky geothermal spa.

Þjórsárdalur Largely untouristed, the quiet valley along the Þjórsá river is dotted with ancient Viking ruins and mysterious natural wonders such as Gjáin canyon. Ultimately it leads up into the highlands (a main route to Landmannalaugar, the starting point of the famous Laugavegurinn hike).

Reykholt and Flúðir On your way south from Gulfoss, you can go riverrafting on the Hvítá river from Reykholt or swing through the geothermal Flúðir area, to its new natural spa and to pick up fresh vegies for your evening meal.

Eyrarbakki and Stokkseyri These two seaside townships are strikingly different than others nearby. Feast on seafood and check out local galleries that informally set up shop each year.

Sights

Gullfoss WATERFALL

(www.gullfoss.is) FREE Iceland's most famous waterfall, Gullfoss (Golden Falls) is a spectacular double cascade dropping a dramatic 32m. As it descends, it kicks up magnificent walls of spray before thundering down a rocky ravine. On sunny days the mist creates shimmering rainbows, and in winter the falls glitter with ice. Although it's a popular sight, the remote location still makes you feel the ineffable forces of nature that have worked this landscape for millennia. Above, there's a small tourist-information centre, shop and cafe famous for its organic lamb soup.

Geysir GEYSER

All spouting hot springs are named after Geysir. Tourists clogged the Great Geysir in the 1950s with rocks and rubbish, thrown in an attempt to set it off. Since earthquakes in 2000, it has begun erupting again, though infrequently. Luckily, the world's most reliable geyser, Strokkur, is right next door. You rarely have to wait more than five minutes for the water to swirl up an impressive 15m to 30m plume before vanishing down what looks like an enormous plughole.

Þingvellir National Park HISTORIC SITE

(www.thingvellir.is) Þingvellir National Park is Iceland's most important historical site: the Vikings established the world's first democratic parliament, the Alþing, here in AD 930. It also has a superb natural setting, on the edge of an immense rift caused by the separating North American and Eurasian tectonic plates. Þingvellir was made a Unesco World Heritage Site in 2004. Above the park, on top of the rift, is an interesting **multimedia centre** exploring the area's nature and history.

Interesting features, concentrated in a small area of the park, include **Lögberg** (marked by a flagpole), the podium for the Alþing; the remains of **búðir** (booths) where Vikings attending Alþing camped; a **church** and **farm**, now the prime minister's summer house; **Drekkingarhylur**, where adulterous women were drowned; **Þingvallavatn**, Iceland's largest lake; and several fissures, including **Peningagjá** (wishing spring), **Flosagjá** (named after a slave who jumped his way to freedom) and **Nikulásargjá** (after a drunken sheriff discovered dead in the water).

Sleeping & Eating

There is a cafe at each of the sites.

Þingvellir Camping Grounds CAMPGROUND €

(☎482 2660; www.thingvellir.is; sites per adult/tent Ikr1300/100; ⏲Jun-Aug) The Park Service Centre oversees five camping grounds at Þingvellir. The best are those around Leirar (near the centre).

Hótel Geysir HOTEL, CAMPGROUND €€

(☎480 6800; www.geysircenter.is; Geysir; s/d from Ikr22,000/25,000, sites per person Ikr1500, buffet lunch Ikr3500, dinner mains Ikr2700-5700; ⏲Feb-Dec, campsite May-Sep; @) This alpine-style hotel across the street from Geysir is constantly busy because of its locale. There's a geothermal pool and two hot-pots, and during summer, the good restaurant can be completely overrun with tour buses at the buffet lunch. The hotel has a nearby campsite.

Hótel Gullfoss HOTEL €€

(☎486 8979; www.hotelgullfoss.is; d incl breakfast Ikr24,700) There's accommodation a few kilometres before the Gullfoss falls at Hótel Gullfoss, a modern bungalow hotel. Its clean en suite rooms overlook the moors (get one facing the valley) and there are two hot pots and a restaurant (mains Ikr2100 to Ikr5000) with sweeping views.

Information

On Rte 36, on the north side of the lake, **Þingvellir Information Centre** (Leirar Þjónustumiðstöð; ☎482 2660; www.thingvellir.is; ⏲9am-5pm May-Sep) has details about the national park, as well as a cafe.

Getting There & Away

From mid-June to mid-September the daily **Reykjavík Excursions** (☎580 5400; www.re.is) bus service 6/6A runs from Reykjavík's BSÍ bus terminal, stopping at various points around Þingvellir for 75 minutes, then continuing to Laugarvatn, Geysir, Gullfoss and back to Reykjavík.

WORTH A TRIP

GLJÚFRASTEINN LAXNESS MUSEUM

Nobel Prize–winning author Halldór Laxness (1902–1998) lived in Mosfellsbær all his life. His riverside home is now the **Gljúfrasteinn Laxness Museum** (☎586 8066; www.gljufrasteinn.is; Mosfellsbær; adult/child Ikr800/free; ⏲9am-5pm Jun-Aug, 10am-5pm Tue-Sun Sep-May, also closed Sat & Sun Jan-Feb & Nov) , easy to visit on the road from Reykjavík to Þingvellir (Rte 36). The author built this upper-class 1950s house and it remains intact with original furniture, writing room, and Laxness' fine-art collection (needlework, sweetly, by his wife Auður). An audio-tour leads you round. Look for his beloved Jaguar parked out front.

Reykjanesfólkvangur

For a taste of Iceland's raw countryside, visit this 300-sq-km wilderness reserve, a mere 40km from Reykjavík. Its three showpieces are **Kleifarvatn**, a deep mineral lake with submerged hot springs and black-sand beaches; the spitting, bubbling **Krýsuvík** geothermal zone at Seltún; and the southwest's largest bird cliffs, the epic **Krýsuvíkurberg**.

The whole area is crossed by **walking trails**. Get good maps at Keflavík, Grindavík or Hafnarfjörður tourist offices. You'll see parking turnouts at the head of the most popular walks: the loop around Kleifarvatn, and the tracks along the craggy Sveifluháls and Núpshliðarháls ridges.

THE WEST

Snæfellsnes

Sparkling fjords, dramatic volcanic peaks, sheer sea cliffs, sweeping golden beaches and crunchy lava flows make up the diverse and fascinating landscape of the 100km-long Snæfellsnes Peninsula. The area is crowned by the glistening ice cap Snæfellsjökull, immortalised in Jules Verne's *Journey to the Centre of the Earth*. Good roads and regular buses mean that it's an easy trip from Reykjavík, offering a cross-section of the best Iceland has to offer in a very compact region.

Stykkishólmur

POP 1090

The charming town of Stykkishólmur, the largest on the Snæfellsnes Peninsula, is built up around a natural harbour tipped by a basalt islet. It's a picturesque place with a laid-back attitude and a sprinkling of brightly coloured buildings from the late 19th century. With a comparatively good choice of accommodation and restaurants, and transport links, Stykkishólmur makes an excellent base for exploring the region.

Sights & Activities

★Breiðafjörður FJORD

Stykkishólmur's jagged peninsula pushes north into stunning Breiðafjörður, a broad waterway separating the Snæfellsnes from the looming cliffs of the distant Westfjords. According to local legend, there are only two things in the world that cannot be counted: the stars in the night sky and the craggy islets in the bay. You *can* count on epic vistas and a menagerie of wild birds (puffins, eagles, guillemots etc). Take **boat trips**, including whale watching and puffin viewing, from Stykkishólmur, Grundarfjörður and Ólafsvík.

Norska Húsið MUSEUM

(Norwegian House; ☎433 8114; www.norskahusid.is; Hafnargata 5; admission Ikr800; ⏰noon-5pm Jun-Aug) Stykkishólmur's quaint maritime charm comes from the cluster of wooden warehouses, shops and homes orbiting the town's harbour. Most date back about 150 years. One of the most interesting (and oldest) is the Norska Húsið, now the regional museum. Built by trader and amateur astronomer Árni Thorlacius in 1832, the house has been skilfully restored and displays a wonderfully eclectic selection of local antiquities. On the 2nd floor you visit Árni's home, an upper-class 19th-century residence, decked out in his original wares.

★Súgandisey ISLAND

The basalt island Súgandisey features a scenic **lighthouse** and grand views across Breiðafjörður. Reach it via the stone causeway from Stykkishólmur harbour.

Volcano Museum MUSEUM

(Eldfjallasafn; ☎433 8154; www.eldfjallasafn.is; Aðalgata 8; adult/child Ikr800/free; ⏰11am-5pm May-Sep) The Volcano Museum, housed in the town's old cinema, is the brainchild of vulcanologist Haraldur Sigurðsson, and features art depicting volcanoes, plus a small collection of interesting lava ('magma bombs'!) and artefacts from eruptions. A film screens upstairs. You can book a full-day geology tour (Ikr17,000) around the Snæfellsnes Peninsula with Haraldur.

Tours

Seatours BOAT TOUR

(Sæferðir; ☎433 2254; www.seatours.is; Smiðjustígur 3; ⏰8am-8pm mid-May–mid-Sep, 9am-5pm mid-Sep–mid-May) Various boat tours, including much-touted 'Viking Sushi', a 1½-hour/2¼-hour boat ride (Ikr5250/7090) taking in islands, bird colonies (puffins until August), and basalt formations. A net brings up shellfish to devour raw. Also offers dinner cruises, and runs the Baldur Ferry to Flatey. Partners with Reykjavík Excursions for Reykjavík pick-up. On-site shop and cafe.

Sleeping

Harbour Hostel HOSTEL €
(517 5353; www.harbourhostel.is; Hafnargata 4; dm/d without bathroom from Ikr3400/12,900;) Part of the Iceland Ocean Tours outfit, this new harbourside hostel offers some of the town's best cheap lodging, with dorm rooms, doubles and family rooms.

★ **Hótel Egilsen** BOUTIQUE HOTEL €€
(554 7700; www.egilsen.is; Aðalgata 2; s/d Ikr22,000/28,500; @) One of our favourite little inns in Iceland, this boutique hotel fills a lovingly restored timber house that creeks in the most charming way when winds howl off the fjord. The friendly owner has outfitted cosy (tiny!) rooms with traditional wool blankets, original artwork and organic Coco-Mat mattresses. Complimentary iPads and a homemade breakfast sweeten the deal.

Bænir og Brauð GUESTHOUSE €€
(820 5408; www.baenirogbraud.is; Laufásvegur 1; d Ikr15,900-17,900) A fine example of Stykkishólmur's quality guesthouse scene, this snug, immaculate house sits along the fjord, and some rooms have lovely views of the bay. Greta, the kindly owner, also owns Hótel Egilsen down the road.

Eating

★ **Narfeyrarstofa** ICELANDIC €€
(438 1119; www.narfeyrarstofa.is; Aðalgata 3; mains Ikr3600-5100; noon-10pm Apr–mid-Oct, 6-10pm Sat & Sun mid-Oct–Mar;) This charming restaurant run by an award-winning chef (known for his superlative desserts) is the Snæfellsnes' darling fine-dining destination. Book a table on the 2nd floor to dine under gentle eaves and the romantic lighting of antique lamps. Ask your waiter about the portraits on the wall – the building has an interesting history.

★ **Plássið** ICELANDIC, BISTRO €€
(436 1600; www.plassid.is; Frúarstígur 1; mains Ikr1400-4200; 11.30am-3pm & 6-10pm;) The newest creation of the owners of Narfeyrarstofa, this bistro-style old-town building is a perfect family-friendly spot, with elegant touches (wine glasses, mod furnishings) and friendly service. Using local ingredients, they serve up a full run of regional specials, and the catch of the day is usually delicious, paired with salad or barley risotto. Local beers too.

Information

Tourist Information Centre (433 8120; www.west.is; Borgarbraut 4; 9am-5pm Mon-Fri Jun-Aug) In the recreational complex wih the swimming pool. Friendly sports-centre staff offer tips when the information centre is closed.

Getting There & Away

You can get to Reykjavík (2½ hours) by changing in Borgarnes. **Strætó** (540 2700; www.bus.is) services: bus 58 to Borgarnes (1½ hours, two daily), bus 82 to Arnarstapi via Ólafsvík and Hellisandur (two daily).

The ferry **Baldur** (433 2254; www.seatours.is) operates between Stykkishólmur

WORTH A TRIP

SETTLEMENT CENTRE, BORGARNES

You could easily zip straight through the elongated settlement of **Borgarnes** without realising you were missing something special. The **Settlement Centre** (Landnámssetur Íslands; 437 1600; www.settlementcentre.is; Brákarbraut 13-15; 1 exhibition adult/child Ikr1900/1500, 2 exhibitions adult/child Ikr2500/1900; 10am-9pm Jun-Sep, 11am-5pm Oct-May) comprises two excellent multimedia exhibitions: one covers the settlement of Iceland, and the other recounts the most dramatic parts of *Egil's Saga*.

This is not your run-of-the-mill Icelandic folk museum: the Settlement Centre offers deep background into Iceland's history and flora and fauna, and a firm context in which to place your Icelandic visit. And *Egil's Saga* is one of the most nuanced and action-packed of the sagas.

The centre's restaurant, **Settlement Centre Restaurant** (437 1600; Brákarbraut 13; mains Ikr2400-5600; 10am-9pm), housed in one of the town's oldest building, is Borgarnes' best bet for food.

and Brjánslækur in the Westfjords (2½ hours), via Flatey (1½ hours). One-way fare per car/passenger is Ikr5250/5250. Advance booking strongly advised.

DEPART	EARLY JUN-LATE AUG	LATE AUG-EARLY JUN
Brjánslækur	12.15pm & 7pm	6pm Sun-Fri
Stykkishólmur	9am & 3.45pm	3pm Sun-Fri

Snæfellsjökull National Park & Around

The volcano Snæfell, at the tip of the peninsula, is the heart of **Snæfellsjökull National Park** (☎436 6860; www.snaefellsjokull.is).

Today, the park is criss-crossed with hiking trails, and during proper weather it is possible to visit the glacier with a tour/guide. Hellnar is home to the national-park visitor centre, and area tourist offices sell maps and give advice too. The park's online map is also excellent.

The dramatic glacial summit can be reached when conditions are right: the best option is to link up with a tour in Hellnar or Arnarstapi. They approach the peak from the south, on Rte F570; Rte F570's northern approach (near Ólafsvík) is frustratingly rutty (4WD needed) and frequently closed due to weather-inflicted damage.

HELLNAR

The spirit of the glacier, Bárður, once lived at tiny Hellnar, 6km outside the main park boundary on the south coast. He couldn't have chosen a more idyllic spot. The park's visitor centre, **Gestastofa** (Snæfellsjökull National Park Visitor Centre; ☎591 2000, 436 6888; www.snaefellsjokull.is; ⌚10am-5pm 20 May-10 Sep, reduced hours rest of year) FREE and a small cafe overlook a bay in a deep, narrow cleft between hills, echoing with the shrieks of seabirds.

Hótel Hellnar (☎435 6820; www.hellnar.is; s/d incl breakfast from Ikr22,800/26,200; ⌚May-Sep; P) , with its sun-filled, comfortable rooms, is the area's choice sleeping option (and thus often booked). Even if you're not overnighting, we highly recommend having dinner at the **restaurant** (dinner mains Ikr3450-4950; ⌚6-9.30pm May-Sep), which sources local organic produce for its Icelandic menu, plus offers heavenly *skyr* (a yoghurtlike dessert) cake for dessert. Reserve ahead.

THE WESTFJORDS

The Westfjords are where Iceland's dramatic landscapes come to a riveting climax – and where mass tourism disappears. Jagged bird cliffs and broad multihued dream beaches flank the south. Rutted dirt roads snake north along jaw-dropping coastal fjords and over immense central mountains revealing tiny fishing villages embracing traditional ways of life. In the far north, the Hornstrandir hiking reserve crowns the quiet region, and is home to cairn-marked walking paths revealing birdlife, Arctic foxes and ocean vistas.

Buses to, from and around the Westfjords are patchy and usually only possible in high season. The website www.westfjords.is is the best source for information (general info, and transport related).

Ísafjörður

POP 2527

Hub of Westfjords adventure tours, and by far the region's largest town, Ísafjörður (www.isafjordur.is) is a pleasant and prosperous place and an excellent base for travellers.

There's hiking in the hills around the town, skiing in winter and regular summer boats to ferry hikers across to the remote Hornstrandir Peninsula.

Sights

Westfjords Heritage Museum MUSEUM
(Byggðasafn Vestfjarða; ☎456 3293; www.nedsti.is; Neðstíkaupstaður; adult/child Ikr800/free; ⌚9am-6pm mid-May–mid-Sep) Part of a cluster of historic wooden buildings by the harbour, the Westfjords Heritage Museum is in the **Turnhús** (1784), which was originally a warehouse. It is crammed with fishing and nautical exhibits, tools from the whaling days, fascinating old photos depicting town life over the centuries, and accordions. To the right is the **Tjöruhús** (1781), now a pleasant seafood restaurant. The **Faktorhús** (1765), which housed the manager of the village shop, and the **Krambúd** (1757), originally a storehouse, are now private residences.

Tours

Borea KAYAKING TOUR, HIKING TOUR
(☎456 3322; www.borea.is; Aðalstræti 22b; ⌚8am-10pm) Borea is an adventure outfit-

ter offering fjord kayaking (from Ikr9900) and excellent hiking in Hornstrandir (from Ikr16,900). It also runs ferry services from Bolungarvík to Hornstrandir and operates Kviar, its private cabin in the reserve. Its base is at Bræðraborg cafe.

West Tours ADVENTURE TOUR
(Vesturferðir; ☎456 5111; www.vesturferdir.is; Aðalstræti 7; ⏰8am-6pm Mon-Fri, 8.30am-4.30pm Sat, 10am-3pm Sun Jun-Aug, 9am-5pm Sep-May) Popular, professional West Tours organises a mind-boggling array of trips throughout the Westfjords. There are tours of Vigur (Ikr8900), hiking in Hornstrandir (Ikr9600 to Ikr37,900) and kayaking trips (Ikr9900 to Ikr25,900). Biking, horse riding, boat and angling tours, birdwatching and cultural excursions are but a few of the other activities on offer.

Sleeping

Litla Guesthouse GUESTHOUSE €
(☎893 6993; www.guesthouselitla.is; Sundstræti 43; s/d without bathroom Ikr14,000/15,000) Wooden floors, crisp white linen, fluffy towels and TVs are available in the high-quality rooms of Litla, a cosy guesthouse with tasteful decor. Two rooms share each bathroom, and there's a guest kitchen.

★**Gamla Gistihúsið** GUESTHOUSE €€
(☎456 4146; www.gistihus.is; Mánagata 5; dm Ikr5100, s/d without bathroom incl breakfast Ikr16,000/20,000) Bright, cheerful and impeccably kept, this excellent guesthouse has simple but comfortable rooms with plenty of cosy touches. The bathrooms are shared, but each double room has telephone, washbasin and bathrobes. An annexe just down the road has a guest kitchen and more modern rooms.

Hótel Edda HOTEL, CAMPGROUND €€
(☎444 4960; www.hoteledda.is; Mantaskólinn; d with/without bathroom Ikr21,700/15,200; ⏰mid-Jun–mid-Aug) No-frills summer accommodation is available at the town's secondary school. Choose from basic sleeping-bag accommodation (Ikr5000) in the classrooms, or rooms with shared or private bathrooms.

Eating

Stock up in the supermarkets of Ísafjörður before heading to remote areas.

Bræðraborg CAFE €
(www.borea.is; Aðalstræti 22b; mains Ikr1190-1590; ⏰9am-7pm Mon-Sat, 10am-5pm Sun Jun-Aug, reduced hours Sep-May; 📶) Bræðraborg is a comfy travellers' cafe where people munch on healthy snacks and chat with other visitors. The cafe is the headquarters for Borea tours.

★**Húsið** INTERNATIONAL €€
(☎456 5555; Hrannargata 2; mains Ikr1290-2990; ⏰11am-10pm Sun-Thu, to 1am Fri & Sat) Sidle up to the varnished, rough-hewn wood tables inside this tin-clad house, or kick back on the sunny terrace for scrumptious, relaxed meals or local beer on tap. Groovy tunes play as hip staff sling soup, sandwiches, burgers, pizza and Icelandic staples like lamb. It's a fun hang-out regardless of what you're up to, and there are occasional DJs and live music.

Tjöruhúsið SEAFOOD €€
(☎456 4419; Neðstakaupstaður 1; mains Ikr2500-5000; ⏰noon-2pm & 6.30-10pm Jun-Sep, reduced hours Oct-May) The warm and rustic restaurant next to the heritage museum offers some of the best seafood around. Go for the *plokkfiskur* – flaked fish, potatoes and onions – or try the catch of the day, fresh off the boat from the harbour down the street.

Information

Westfjords Regional Information Centre (☎450 8060; www.isafjordur.is; Aðalstræti 7, Edinborgarhús; ⏰8am-6pm Mon-Fri, 8.30am-2pm Sat, 10am-2pm Sun Jun-Aug, reduced hours Sep-May) By the harbour in the Edinborgarhús (1907), helpful staff have loads of info on the Westfjords and Hornstrandir Reserve. Internet terminal with free 10-minute session; luggage storage Ikr200 per day.

Getting There & Away

AIR

Air Iceland (☎456 3000; www.airiceland.is) flies between Ísafjörður Airport (5km south on the fjord) and Reykjavík twice daily.

BUS

Ísafjörður is the major bus hub in the Westfjords. The long-distance bus stop is at the N1 petrol station on Hafnarstræti.

In 2014 buses were discontinued, but in 2015 buses to/from Holmavík are slated to run year-round, and summer only to/from Brjánslækur (Stykkishólmur ferry terminal) via Þingeyri and Dynjandi. Both Holmavík and Brjánslækur buses should have transfers to Reykjavík. Holmavík may have a transfer to Akureyri.

Hornstrandir Peninsula

Craggy mountains, precarious sea cliffs and plunging waterfalls ring the wonderful, barely inhabited Hornstrandir Peninsula at the northern end of the Westfjords. This is one of Europe's last true wilderness areas, covering some of the most extreme and inhospitable parts of the country. It's a fantastic destination for hiking, with challenging terrain and excellent opportunities for spotting Arctic foxes, seals, whales and teeming birdlife.

A handful of hardy farmers lived in Hornstrandir until the 1950s, but since 1975 the 580 sq km of tundra, fjord, glacier and alpine upland have been protected as **Hornstrandir Nature Reserve** (☎591 2000; www.ust.is/hornstrandir).

There are no services available in Hornstrandir and hikers must be fully prepared to tackle all eventualities. The passes are steep, heavy rains will make rivers impassable, fog can be dense and you'll need to carry all your gear, so hiking can be slower than you might expect. In addition, most trails are unmarked, primitive (and uneven), so it's essential to carry a good map, a compass and a GPS.

The best time to visit is in July. Outside the summer season (which runs from late June to mid-August; ferry boats run June to August) there are few people around and the weather is even more unpredictable. It is essential to plan ahead and get local advice. The two main operators running tours (boating, hiking, kayaking, skiing etc) into Hornstrandir are West Tours and Borea, based in Ísafjörður.

Where to hike? Locals and tourists agree: the **Royal Horn** (Hornsleið) is, hands down, your best option for getting a taste of all that the reserve has to offer. This four-to-five-day hike from Veiðileysufjörður to Hesteyri can also be easily modified if you run into bad weather. The Hornstrandir pages of www.westtours.is are a useful starting point for interested hikers.

Sleeping

Wild camping in Hornstrandir is free (carry out all rubbish). Camping on private grounds with facilities costs around Ikr1000. Expect to pay upwards of Ikr6500 for sleeping-bag space, which must be reserved well in advance, especially in Hesteyri.

Doctor's House in Hesteyri HOSTEL €
(☎845 5075, Hesteyri 899 7661; www.hesteyri.net; dm Ikr8000; ⏲mid-Jun–late Aug) By far the most developed lodging in Hornstrandir, Hesteyri has accommodation for 16 in the old doctor's house, with daytime coffee and pancakes available and a guest kitchen. Book well ahead.

Getting There & Away

Take a ferry boat from from Ísafjörður, Bolungarvík or Norðurfjörður (on the Strandir Coast) to Hornstrandir from June to August. One-way rides cost Ikr7200 to Ikr13,500, depending on your destination.

You need to book your return boat in advance; this serves as a safety measure, in case you don't turn up for it (in which case a search-and-rescue operation may be launched).

Látrabjarg

At the tip of the westernmost point of the Westfjords you'll find the renowned Látrabjarg bird cliffs. Extending for 12km along the coast and ranging from 40m to 400m, the dramatic cliffs are mobbed by nesting seabirds in early summer and it's a fascinating place even for the most reluctant of twitchers. Unbelievable numbers of puffins, razorbills, guillemots, cormorants, fulmars, gulls and kittiwakes nest here from June to mid-August.

Patreksfjörður tour operators offer guided birdwatching and hiking and can meet you on the Látrabjarg peninsula.

For accommodation, try the beautifully located **Breiðavík Guesthouse** (☎456 1575; www.breidavik.is; sites per person Ikr1900, d with/without bathroom incl breakfast Ikr27,000/18,500; ⏲mid-May–mid-Sep), 12km from the cliffs and located located behind an incredible cream-coloured beach of the same name. Prices are stiff for what they offer: basic rooms, sleeping-bag accommodation (Ikr10,000) and camping. But the setting is sublime. Alternatively, the largest village in this part of the Westfjords is Patreksfjörður.

Buses are slated to resume in 2015 between Patreksfjörður and Brjánslækur (where the *Baldur* ferry from Stykkishólmur docks), with connections to Látrabjarg.

THE NORTH

Siglufjörður

POP 1190

Sigló (as the locals call it) enjoys a dramatic setting at the top of the Tröllaskagi Peninsula, a road-trip-worthy destination of hair-raising road tunnels and ultrascenic panoramas.

In the past, herring fishing brought frenzied activity and untold riches to the town; today its appeal is its peaceful isolation and thrumming community spirit. New tunnels now link the town with Olafsfjörður and points further south, and these days Sigló is receiving warranted attention from travellers smitten by its hiking possibilities, its primary-coloured marina and its excellent diversions.

Sights

★Herring Era Museum MUSEUM
(Síldarminjasafnið; www.sild.is; Snorragata 10; adult/child Ikr1400/free; ⏲10am-6pm Jun-Aug, 1-5pm May & Sep, by appointment Oct-Apr) Lovingly created over 16 years, this award-winning museum does a stunning job of re-creating Siglufjörður's boom days between 1903 and 1968, when it was the herring-fishing capital of Iceland. Set in three buildings that were part of an old Norwegian herring station, the museum brings the work and lives of the town's inhabitants vividly to life. Start at the red building on the left, and move right.

Sleeping & Eating

★Siglunes Guesthouse GUESTHOUSE €
(☎467 1222; www.hotelsiglunes.is; Lækjargata 10; d with/without bathroom incl breakfast Ikr21,900/15,900) Personality shines through in this cool guesthouse, where vintage furniture is paired with contemporary art and ultramodern bathrooms in the hotel-standard wing. There's equally appealling guesthouse rooms, a big dining hall for breakfast (included in summer rates), and a cosy bar area celebrating happy hour from 5pm to 7pm.

★Herring Guesthouse GUESTHOUSE €€
(☎868 4200; www.theherringhouse.com; Hávegur 5; s/d without bathroom Ikr11,900/15,900, 4-person apt Ikr39,900) Þorir and Erla are charming, knowledgable hosts (he's a former town mayor) offering personalised service at their stylish, view-blessed guesthouse – now with two locations. There is a guest kitchen at the main house, and a lovely (optional) breakfast spread (Ikr1500). Families will appreciate the two-bedroom apartment.

★Hannes Boy ICELANDIC €€
(☎461 7730; www.raudka.is; mains Ikr3290-5990; ⏲noon-2pm & 6-10pm Jun-Aug, shorter hours Sep-May) Dressed in sunny yellow, this stylish, light-filled space is furnished with funky seats made from old herring barrels. The upmarket menu is fish focused (naturally), with lobster soup and catch of the day fresh from the boats outside. Reservations recommended.

Kaffi Rauðka ICELANDIC €€
(www.raudka.is; mains Ikr890-2990; ⏲11am-10pm Jun-Aug, shorter hours Sep-May) The counterpoint to neighbouring Hannes Boy, ruby red Rauðka has a more informal air, with an all-day menu of sandwiches, salads and hearty mains such as barbecue ribs, plus good-value weekday meal/soup of the day (Ikr1190/1590). At weekends, it often stages live music.

Getting There & Away

Strætó (☎540 2700; www.straeto.is) bus 78 conects Siglufjörður with Akureyri (Ikr2100, 70 minutes, three daily Monday to Friday, one daily Sunday).

Akureyri

POP 17,930

Akureyri nestles at the head of Iceland's longest (60km) fjord, at the base of snow-capped peaks. In summer flower boxes, trees and well-tended gardens belie the location, just a stone's throw from the Arctic Circle.

It's a wonder the city (which would be a 'town' in any other country) generates this much buzz - but this is Iceland's second city. Expect cool cafes, quality restaurants and something of a late-night bustle – a far cry from other towns in rural Iceland.

Sights & Activities

★Akureyrarkirkja CHURCH
(www.akirkja.is; Eyrarlandsvegur; ⏲generally 10am-4pm Mon-Fri) Dominating the town from high on a hill, Akureyri's landmark church was designed by Guðjón Samúelsson, the architect responsible for Reykjavík's Hallgrímskirkja. Although the basalt theme connects them, Akureyrarkirkja looks more like a stylised 1920s US skyscraper than its big-city brother.

Akureyri

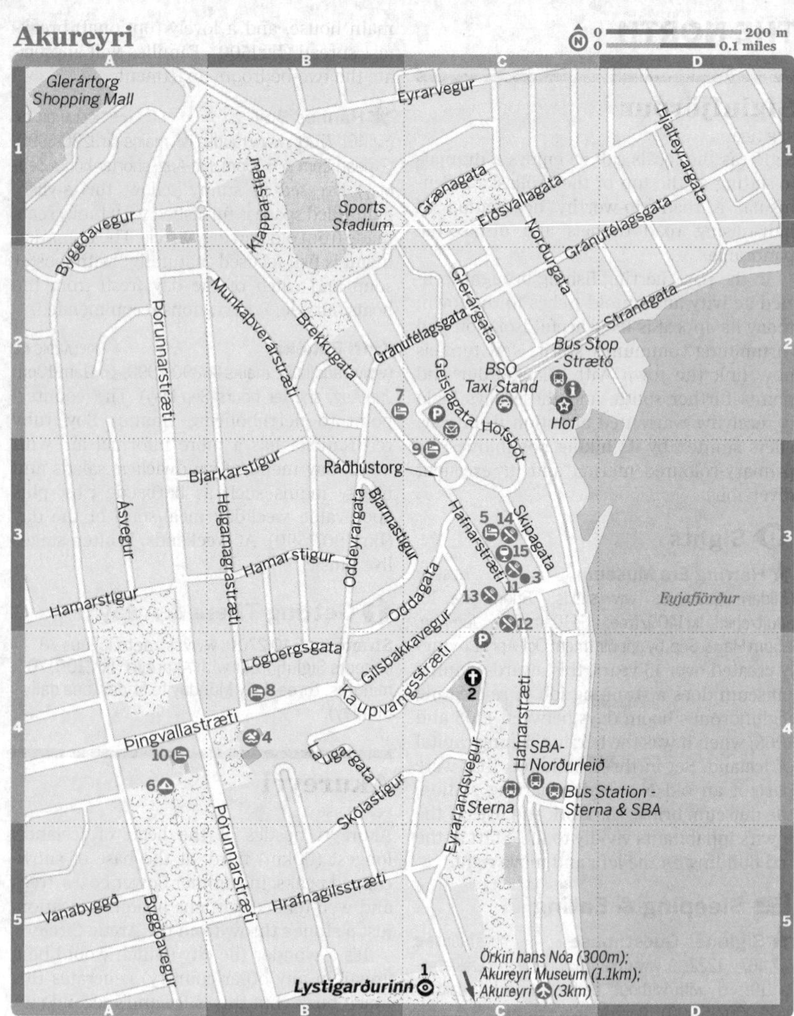

Akureyri Museum MUSEUM

(Minjasafnið á Akureyri; www.akmus.is; Aðalstræti 58; adult/child Ikr1000/free; 10am-5pm Jun–mid-Sep, 2-4pm Thu-Sun mid-Sep–May) This sweet, well-curated museum houses art and historical items relating to town life, including maps, photos and re-creations of early Icelandic homes. The **museum garden** became the first place in Iceland to cultivate trees when a nursery was established here in 1899.

★Lystigarðurinn GARDENS

(www.lystigardur.akureyri.is; Eyrarlandsholt; 8am-10pm Mon-Fri, 9am-10pm Sat & Sun Jun-Sep) FREE The most northerly botanical garden in the world makes a delightful picnic spot on sunny days. The wealth of plant life on display is truly astonishing considering the gardens' proximity to the Arctic Circle. You'll find examples of every species native to Iceland, as well as a host of high-latitude and high-altitude plants from around the world. There's also a beautifully situated cafe.

Akureyri

Top Sights
1 Lystigarðurinn C5

Sights
2 Akureyrarkirkja C4

Activities, Courses & Tours
3 Saga Travel C3
4 Sundlaug Akureyrar B4

Sleeping
5 Akureyri Backpackers C3
6 City Campsite A4
7 Gula Villan B2
8 Gula Villan II B4
9 Hrafninn C3
10 Icelandair Hotel Akureyri A4

Eating
11 Blaá Kannan C3
12 Hamborgarafabrikkan C3
13 Rub23 .... C3
14 Strikið C3

Drinking & Nightlife
Akureyri Backpackers .... (see 5)
15 Götubarinn C3

Entertainment
Græni Hatturinn .... (see 15)

Sundlaug Akureyrar SWIMMING POOL
(Þingvallastræti 21; adult/child Ik550/200; 6.45am-9pm Mon-Fri, 8am-7.30pm Sat & Sun;) The hub of local life: Akureyri's outdoor swimming pool is one of Iceland's finest. It has three heated pools, hot-pots, water-slides, saunas and steam rooms.

Tours

Horse-riding tours are available from a range of outlying farms. Most can arrange town pick-up if needed. The tourist-info centre has details and brochures for all tour operators.

★ **Saga Travel** ADVENTURE TOURS
(558 888; www.sagatravel.is; Kaupvangsstræti 4) Offers a rich and diverse year-round program of excursions and activities throughout the north: obvious destinations like Mývatn, Húsavík (for whale watching) and Askja in the highlands, but also innovative tours along themes such as food or art and design. Check out Saga's full program online, or drop by its office (open 7.30am to 10pm in summer).

Skjaldarvík HORSE RIDING
(552 5200; www.skjaldarvik.is; 90min ride Ikr7900) With a superb guesthouse and restaurant, Skjaldarvík, 6km north of town, offers 1½-hour tours along the fjord and into the surrounding hills, departing at 10am, 2pm and 5pm daily in summer. It also offers the good-value 'Ride & Bite': 5pm horse ride followed by access to the outdoor hot-pot and a two-course dinner (Ikr11,900).

Sleeping

Things fill fast in summer – book ahead. Bear in mind that there are plenty of options outside the town centre – Akureyri is surrounded by excellent rural farmstay properties (you'll need your own car for these). Consult the Icelandic Farm Holidays booklet or website (www.farmholidays.is). Another great source is **AirBnB** (www.airbnb.com), with strong coverage in Akureyri.

Akureyri Backpackers HOSTEL €
(571 9050; www.akureyribackpackers.com; Hafnarstræti 67; dm Ikr4500-5500, d without bathroom Ikr18,000; @) Supremely placed in the town's heart, this backpackers has a chilled travellers vibe and includes tour-booking service and popular bar. Rooms are spread over three floors: four- to eight-bed dorms, plus private rooms with made-up beds on the top floor. Minor gripe: all showers are in the basement, as is a sauna (toilets and sinks on all levels, however).

Linen hire (in dorms) costs Ikr990; breakfast is Ikr990.

Gula Villan GUESTHOUSE €
(896 8464; www.gulavillan.is; Brekkugata 8; s/d without bathroom Ikr10,500/14,700) Owner Sigriður has a background in travel and this cheerful yellow-and-white villa shines under her care. Bright, well-maintained rooms are in a good central location. In a second building, **Gula Villan II** (Þingvallastræti 14) is run by the same folks and offers extra space in summer. Both guesthouses have guest kitchens and breakfast served on request (quite steep at Ikr2000).

DON'T MISS

GOÐAFOSS

Goðafoss (Waterfall of the Gods) rips straight through the Bárðardalur lava field along Rte 1 about 50km east of Akureyri. Although smaller and less powerful than some of Iceland's other chutes, it's definitely one of the most beautiful. Take the path behind the falls for a less-crowded viewpoint.

City Campsite CAMPGROUND €
(Þórunnarstræti; sites per person Ikr1100, plus lodging tax per site Ikr100; ⏲ mid-Jun–mid-Sep) This central site has a washing machine, dining area and free showers, plus a car-free policy (except for loading and unloading). Note: no kitchen. Handily, it's close to the swimming pool and a supermarket.

★ **Skjaldarvík** GUESTHOUSE €€
(☎552 5200; www.skjaldarvik.is; s/d without bathroom incl breafast Ikr14,900/19,900; @ 👪) A slice of guesthouse nirvana, Skjaldarvík lies in a bucolic farm setting 6km north of town. It's owned by a young family and features quirky design details (plants sprouting from shoes, vintage typewriters as artwork on the walls). Plus: bumper breakfast buffet, horse-riding tours, hot-pot, book swap, and honesty bar in the comfy lounge.

★ **Icelandair Hotel Akureyri** HOTEL €€
(☎518 1000; www.icelandairhotels.com; Þingvallastræti 23; d incl breakfast from Ikr28,800; @) Icelandair added an Akureyri property to its portfolio in 2011, and did it in style. This high-class hotel showcases Icelandic designers and artists among its fresh, white-and-caramel-toned decor; rooms are compact but welldesigned. Added extras: outdoor terrace, lounge serving high tea of an afternoon and happy-hour cocktails in the early evening.

Hrafninn GUESTHOUSE €€
(☎462 2300; www.hrafninn.is; Brekkugata 4; s/d Ikr12,900/19,900) Priced below the competition yet delivering well above, Hrafninn (The Raven) feels like an elegant manor house without being pretentious or stuffy. All rooms have bathroom and TV; the 3rd-floor rooms have recently been renovated, and there's now a spacious 2nd-floor guest kitchen.

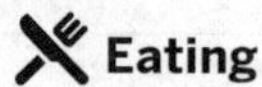

Eating

Blaá Kannan CAFE €
(Hafnarstræti 96; lunchtime buffet Ikr1490; ⏲ 9am-11.30pm Mon-Fri, from 10am Sat & Sun) Prime people-watching is on offer at this much-loved cafe (the 'Blue Teapot', in the dark-blue Cafe Paris building) on the main drag. The interior is timber lined and blinged up with chandeliers; the menu offers panini and bagels, and there's a cabinet full of sweet treats.

Hamborgarafabrikkan FAST FOOD €
(www.fabrikkan.is; cnr Hafnarstræti & Kaupvangsstræti; burger & fries Ikr1695-2395; ⏲ 11am-10pm Sun-Thu, to midnight Fri & Sat; 👪) Iceland is one of few countries without McDonald's, but who needs them? Part of a small chain, the Hamburger Factory gives you a choice of 16 square-patty bun-fillings (primarily beef, but also lamb and chicken options). Salads, spare ribs and classic desserts (banana split!) round out the menu.

Strikið INTERNATIONAL €€
(☎462 7100; www.strikid.is; Skipagata 14; light meals Ikr2400-3500, mains Ikr3800-5000; ⏲ from 11.30am Mon-Sat, from 6pm Sun) Huge windows with fjord views lend a magical glitz to this 5th-floor restaurant. The menu covers all options: go for burgers if you must, or order mains showcasing prime Icelandic produce (superfresh sushi, langoustine soup, beef tenderloin, slow-cooked duck breast). Strawberry *skyr* mousse makes for a sweet end.

Örkin hans Nóa SEAFOOD €€
(www.noa.is; Hafnarstræti 22; mains Ikr3000-5000; ⏲ noon-2pm & 4-10pm) Part gallery, part furniture store, part restaurant – 'Noah's Ark' is certainly unique, and offers a simple food concept done well. The menu features a selection of fresh fish options, which are pan-fried and served with vegetables, with the pan brought to the table. Classic, effective, tasty.

Rub23 INTERNATIONAL €€€
(☎462 2223; www.rub23.is; Kaupvangsstræti 6; lunch Ikr2190-2590, dinner mains Ikr4190-6290; ⏲ 11.30am-2pm Mon-Fri, from 5.30pm daily) This sleek restaurant revolves around a novel idea: you choose your protein (fish or meat), then pick one of the 11 'rubs' (marinades) to accompany it. Go with the chef's suggestions for cod with an Asian fusion rub, or lamb fillet with citrus-rosemary rub. There's also a separate sushi menu. Note that lunch is a more-standard (rub-less) affair.

Drinking & Entertainment

Compared to Reykjavík, Akureyri's nightlife is quite tame.

Akureyri Backpackers BAR

(www.akureyribackpackers.com; Hafnarstræti 67; ⏲7.30am-11pm Sun-Thu, to 1am Fri & Sat) Always a hub of convivial main-street activity, the fun, timber-clad bar at Akureyri Backpackers is beloved of both travellers and locals, for its occasional live music, good-value burgers (and weekend brunches), and wide beer selection - this is a fine spot to sample the local microbrews, Kaldi and Einstök.

Götubarinn BAR

(Hafnarstræti 95; ⏲5pm-1am Thu, to 4am Fri & Sat) The locals' favourite drinking spot, fun, central Götubarinn (the Street Bar) has a surprising amount of cosiness and charm for a place that closes at 4am. There's timber, mirrors, couches and even a downstairs piano for late-night singalongs.

Græni Hatturinn LIVE MUSIC

(Hafnarstræti 96) Tucked down a lane beside Blaá Kannan, this intimate venue is the best place in town to see live music - and one of the best in the country. If you get the chance, buy a ticket to anything going.

Information

Akureyri Hospital (☎463 0100; www.fsa.is; Eyrarlandsvegur) South of the botanical gardens.

Tourist Office (☎450 1050; www.visitakureyri.is; Hof, Strandgata 12; ⏲8am-6pm mid-May–Sep, 8am-4pm Mon-Fri, noon-5pm Sat, noon-3pm Sun Oct–mid-May) This friendly, efficient office is inside Hof. There are loads of brochures, maps, internet access and a great design store. Knowledgable staff can book tours and transport, and accommodation in the area (Ikr500).

Getting There & Away

AIR

Akureyri airport (www.akureyriairport.is) is 3km south of the city centre. **Air Iceland** (☎460 7000; www.airiceland.is) has flights up to eight times daily between Akureyri and Reykjavík (45 minutes), and daily in summer (three times a week in winter) from Akureyri to Grímsey (30 minutes).

BUS

Akureyri's **bus station** (Hafnarstræti 82) is the hub for bus travel in the north provided by SBA-Norðurleið and Sterna; Strætó operates from a stop in front of Hof.

SBA-Norðurleið (☎550 0700; www.sba.is; Hafnarstræti 82) services:

Bus 62 To Mývatn, Egilsstaðir and Höfn (one daily June to mid-September).

Bus 610a To Reykjavík via the Kjölur route (10½ hours, one daily mid-June to mid-September).

Bus 641 To Húsavík (1½ hours, two daily mid-June to August).

Sterna (☎551 1166; www.sterna.is; Hafnarstræti 77) services:

Bus 60a To Reykjavík via Rte 1 (5½ hours, one daily Monday to Friday mid-June to August).

Bus F35a To Reykjavík via the Kjölur route (13 hours, one daily mid-June to early September).

Strætó (☎540 2700; www.straeto.is) services generally run year-round:

Bus 56 To Mývatn (two daily) and Egilsstaðir (one daily); drops to four weekly services in winter.

Bus 57 To Reykjavík via Rte 1 (6½ hours, two daily).

Bus 78 To Siglufjörður (three daily Monday to Friday, one daily Sunday).

Bus 79 To Húsavík (1¼ hours, three daily).

Grímsey

Best known as Iceland's only true piece of the Arctic Circle, the remote island of Grímsey (population 77), 40km from the mainland, is a lonely little place where birds outnumber people by about 10,000 to one.

Grímsey's appeal probably lies less in the destination itself, and more about what it represents. Tourists flock here to snap up their 'I visited the Arctic Circle' certificate and pose for a photo with the 'you're standing on the Arctic Circle' monument. Afterwards, there's plenty of time to appreciate the windswept setting. Scenic coastal cliffs and dramatic basalt formations make a popular home for dozens of species of seabirds, including loads of puffins, plus the kamikaze Arctic tern.

Mid-May to August, the **Sæfari** (☎458 8970; www.saefari.is) ferry sails from Dalvík (44km north of Akureyri) to Grímsey at 9am Monday, Wednesday and Friday, leaving Grímsey at 4pm (giving you four hours on the island if you're not overnighting). The journey takes three hours and costs Ikr4830 one way.

From mid-June to mid-August, there are daily flights to/from Akureyri (three times weekly the rest of the year). The bumpy 25-minute journey takes in the full length of Eyjafjörður and is an experience in itself. Ticketing is handled by **Air Iceland** (☎570 3030; www.airiceland.is); one-way fares start around Ikr10,000. You can do a half-day air excursion with Air Iceland (Ikr28,200).

Húsavík

POP 2205

Most people visit the 'whale-watching capital of Iceland' to do just that; in season you're almost guaranteed to see these awe-inspiring ocean giants feeding in Skjálfandi Bay.

Sights

Húsavík Whale Museum MUSEUM

(Hvalasafnið; www.whalemuseum.is; Hafnarstétt; adult/child Ikr1400/500; 8.30am-6.30pm Jun-Aug, 9am-4pm Apr-May & Sep, 10am-3.30pm Mon-Fri Oct-Mar) This excellent museum tells you all you ever needed to know about the impressive creatures that come a-visiting Skjálfandi Bay. Housed in an old harbourside slaughterhouse, the museum interprets the ecology and habits of whales, conservation and the history of whaling in Iceland through beautifully curated displays, including several huge skeletons soaring high above (they're real!).

Culture House MUSEUM

(Safnahúsið; www.husmus.is; Stórigarður 17; adult/child Ikr800/free; 10am-6pm Jun-Aug, 10am-4pm Mon-Fri Sep-May) A folk, maritime and natural-history museum rolled into one complex, the Culture House is one of the north's most interesting regional museums. 'Man and Nature' nicely outlines a century of life in the region, from 1850 to 1950 (lots of local flavour), while the stuffed animals include a frightening-looking hooded seal, and a polar bear that was welcomed to Grímsey in 1969 with both barrels of a gun.

Tours

This is why you came to Húsavík. Although there are other Iceland locales where you can do whale-watching tours (Reykjavík and Eyjafjörður, north of Akureyri), this area has become Iceland's premier whale-watching destination, with up to 11 species coming here to feed in summer. The best time to see whales is between June and August.

Two large whale-watching companies operate from Húsavík harbour (plus a new, third player). Don't stress *too* much over picking an operator; prices are similar and services are comparable for the standard three-hour tour (guiding, warm overalls supplied, plus hot drinks and a pastry).

Where the differences are clear, however, is in the excursions that go beyond the standard. When puffins are around, all companies offer tours that incorporate whale watching with a sail by the puffin-festooned island of Lundey: North Sailing does this on board an atmospheric old schooner over four hours; Gentle Giants does it over 2½ hours in a high-speed RIB (rigid-inflatable boat).

Trips depart throughout the day (June to August) from around 8.30am to 8pm, and large signs at the ticket booths advertise the next departure time. Boats also run in April, May, September and October with less frequency (North Sailing even has a daily tour in November). You can't miss the offices on the waterfront.

North Sailing WHALE WATCHING

(464 7272; www.northsailing.is; Hafnarstétt 9; 3hr tour adult/child Ikr9280/4640) The original operator, with a fleet of lovingly restored traditional boats, including the oak schooners *Haukur* and *Hildur*. Its four-hour 'Whales, Puffins & Sails' tour is on board an old schooner; when conditions are right, there may be some sailing without the engine. Overnight sailing adventures to Grímsey are available in summer.

Gentle Giants WHALE WATCHING

(464 1500; www.gentlegiants.is; Hafnarstétt; 3hr tour adult/child Ikr9100/3900) Gentle Giants has a flotilla of old fishing vessels, plus recent additions of high-speed RIBs (rigid inflatable boats) and Zodiacs, offering a way to cover more ground in the bay. Gentle Giants also runs special trips to Flatey (Flat Island) for birdwatching, and fast (and pricey) RIB trips to Grímsey. There are also sea-angling expeditions.

Salka WHALE WATCHING

(464 3999; www.salkawhalewatching.is; Garðarsbraut 6; 3hr tour adult/child Ikr8640/4000) A new player on the scene, taking on the long-established companies with just one 42-passenger oak boat, cheaper prices (for now) and a tighter menu of offerings. It's base is its light-filled cafe on the main street.

Sleeping

Campground CAMPGROUND €

(sites per person Ikr1200; mid-May–mid-Sep) Next to the sports ground at the north end of town, this well-maintained spot has washing machines and limited cooking facilities, but not nearly enough to cope with summertime demand. Pay at the whale museum, or to the warden who visits nightly.

★**Kaldbaks-Kot** COTTAGES €€
(☎464 1504; www.cottages.is; 2-4 person cabins excl linen Ikr20,800-30,100, 2-night minimum stay; ⊙May-Sep; @) Located 3km south of Húsavík is this spectacular spread-out settlement of timber cottages that all feel like grandpa's log cabin in the woods (but with considerably more comfort). Choose your level of service: BYO linen or hire it, bring supplies or buy breakfast here (Ikr1550), served in the magnificent converted cowshed.

Minimum stay is two nights – perfect for enjoying the grounds, the hot-pots, the views, the serenity and the prolific birdlife. Options include larger houses sleeping up to 10.

Sigtún GUESTHOUSE €€
(☎864 0250; www.guesthousesigtun.is; Túngata 13; s/d without bathroom incl breakfast Ikr10,500/17,500; @) Free coffee machine, free laundry, a fancy kitchen and a help-yourself breakfast are draws at this small and cosy guesthouse.

Árból GUESTHOUSE €€
(☎464 2220; www.arbol.is; Ásgarðsvegur 2; s/d without bathroom incl breakfast Ikr10,600/18,100) This 1903 heritage house has a pretty stream and town park as neighbours. Spacious, spotless rooms are over three levels – those on the ground and top floor are loveliest (the pine-lined attic rooms are particularly sweet). Limited guest use of the kitchen is permitted of an evening.

Eating

Fish & Chips FAST FOOD €
(Hafnarstétt 19; fish & chips Ikr1500; ⊙11.30am-8pm Jun-Aug) Doing exactly what it says on the label, this small windowfront on the harbour doles out good-value fish (usually cod) and chips, with a few picnic tables out front and a simple seating area upstairs. To find it, walk down the stairs opposite the church, and turn left.

★**Naustið** SEAFOOD €€
(Naustagarði 4; mains Ikr1700-3500; ⊙noon-10pm) Quietly going about its business at the end of the harbour, sweetly rustic Naustið wins praise for its superfresh fish and a fun, simple concept: skewers of fish and vegetables, grilled to order. There's also fish soup (natch), salmon and langoustine, plus home-baked pie for dessert.

Gamli Baukur ICELANDIC €€
(www.gamlibaukur.is; Hafnarstétt 9; mains Ikr3100-4990; ⊙11.30am-11pm Sun-Wed, to 1am Thu, to 3am Fri & Sat Jun-Aug, shorter hours Sep-May) Among shiny nautical relics, this timber-framed restaurant-bar serves excellent food (juicy burgers, spaghetti with shellfish, organic lamb), plus the pun-tastic dessert *skyramisu*. Live music and a sweeping terrace make it one of the most happening places in northeast Iceland. Kitchen closes at 9pm.

Information

Tourist Information Centre (☎464 4300; www.visithusavik.is; Hafnarstétt; ⊙8.30am-6.30pm Jun-Aug, 9am-4pm Apr-May & Sep, 10am-3.30pm Mon-Fri Oct-Mar) At the Whale Museum, with plentiful maps and brochures.

Getting There & Away

AIR

Húsavík's airport is 12km south of town. **Eagle Air** (☎562 2640; www.eagleair.is) flies year-round between Reykjavík and Húsavík.

BUS

SBA-Norðurleið (☎550 0700; www.sba.is) services (depart from in front of Gamli Baukar restaurant, on the waterfront):

Bus 641/641a To Akureyri (two daily mid-June to August), and once daily east to Ásbyrgi and Dettifoss. From Dettifoss you can connect to bus 661a to Mývatn.

Bus 650a To Mývatn (two daily mid-June to August).

Strætó (☎540 2700; www.straeto.is) runs Bus 79 to Akureyri (Ikr2100, 1¼ hours, three daily) departing from N1 service station.

Mývatn

Mývatn (*mee*-vaht) is the calm, shallow lake at the heart of a volatile volcanic area. Nature's violent masterpieces are everywhere – crazy-coloured mudpots, huge craters and still-smouldering eruption debris. Once you've had your fill of geology gone wild, mellow out with cycle rides, bumper birdwatching and a bathe in the north's version of the Blue Lagoon.

Mývatn lake is encircled by a 36km sealed road (hire a bike and explore). The main settlement is **Reykjahlíð**, in the northeast corner, with an information centre and most sleeping and eating options. **Skútustaðir**, at the southern end, also has accommodation.

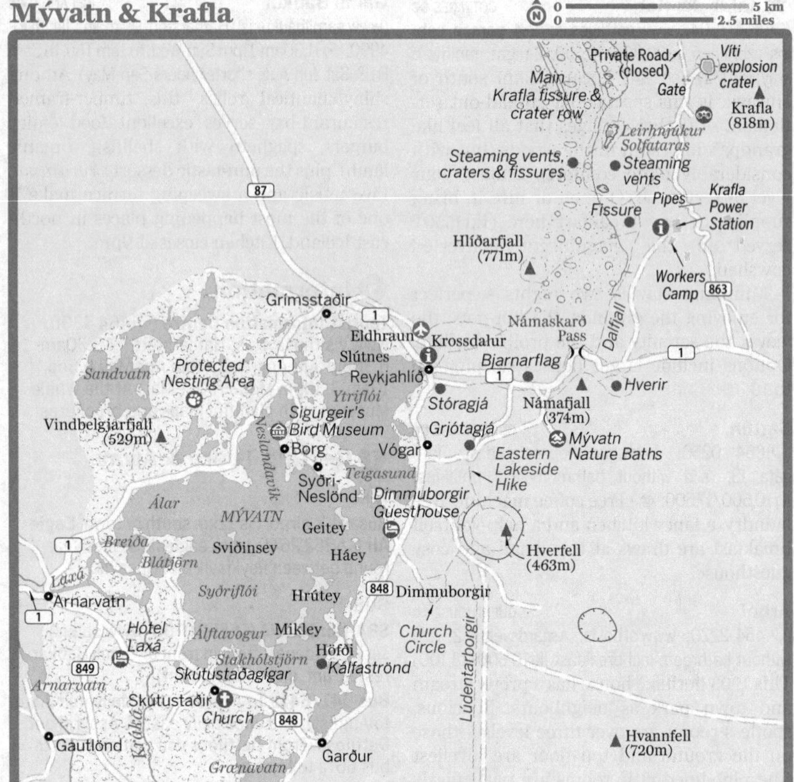

The down side to Mývatn (which means 'Midge Lake') are the dense midge clouds that appear during summer, intent on flying up your nose – you may want to buy a head net.

Sights & Activities

Most of the points of interest are linked by the lake's looping road, including the diverse lava formations in eastern Mývatn, the forested lava headland of Höfði, the cluster of pseudocraters near southern Mývatn, and the bird-friendly marsh plains around western Mývatn.

In northern Mývatn, the Ring Road (Rte 1) veers east, away from Reykjahlíð, and takes you over the Námaskarð pass to the Hverir geothermal area. Then, a turn-off to the north (Rte 863) leads to Krafla, 14km from Reykjahlíð.

With your own vehicle this whole area can be explored in a day, but on a bike allow at least two days. If you want to hike and explore more distant mountains and lava fields, allow three days or more.

★ Sigurgeir's Bird Museum MUSEUM

(Fuglasafn Sigurgeirs; ☎464 4477; www.fuglasafn.is; adult/child Ikr1000/500; ⊙10am-6pm Jun-Aug, reduced hours Sep-May) For some birdwatching background, swing by Sigurgeir's Bird Museum, housed in a beautiful lakeside building that fuses modern design with traditional turfhouse. Inside you'll find an impressive collection of taxidermic avians (more than 180 types), including every species of bird that calls Iceland home (except one – the grey phalarope). Designer lighting and detailed captions further enhance the experience.

★ Mývatn Nature Baths SPA

(Jarðböðin; www.jardbodin.is; adult/child Ikr3500/free; ⊙9am-midnight Jun-Aug, noon-10pm Sep-May) Northern Iceland's answer to the Blue Lagoon is 3km east of Reykjahlíð. Although it's smaller than its southern counterpart, it's also less hyped (probably a good thing), and it's a gorgeous place to soak in the powder-blue, mineral-rich waters and enjoy the panorama. After a relaxing soak, try one of the two natural steam baths and/or a meal at the on-site cafeteria.

Tours

Tourism reigns supreme at Reykjahlíð and for travellers without transport there are many sightseeing tours in the area (some originate in Akureyri). Tours fill up fast during summer, so try to book at least a day before. The information centre can help with bookings.

A number of operators run super-Jeep tours into the highlands, to Askja and surrounds, from mid-June (when the route opens) until as late into September as weather permits. From Akureyri it makes for a long day tour (up to 15 hours); 12-hour tours leave from Reykjahlíð. Both SBA-Norðurleið and Saga Travel offer Askja tours, including overnight options.

SBA-Norðurleið BUS TOUR
(☎550 0700; www.sba.is) For an abridged bus tour of Mývatn's top sights, consider linking up with the sightseeing tour operated by SBA-Norðurleið. It starts in Akureyri, but you can often hop aboard in Reykjahlíð (from Reykjahlíð in summer at 12.30pm: 3¾-hour tour, Ikr7700). There is also a winter trip.

Saga Travel ADVENTURE TOUR
(☎558 888; www.sagatravel.is) Akureyri-based Saga Travel operates an array of fabulous year-round tours in the Mývatn area (see the website for full selection). Join tours from Akureyri or Reykjahlíð.

Hike & Bike HIKING TOUR, CYCLING TOUR
(☎899 4845; www.hikeandbike.is; ⏲9am-5pm Jun-Aug) Hike & Bike has a booth by the Gamli Bærinn tavern in Reykjahlíð, offering tour bookings and mountain-bike rental (per day Ikr4000).

There's a summer program of cycling and hiking tours, including a four-hour guided walk to Hverfell and Dimmuborgir (Ikr7900); a three-hour pedal through the backcountry (Ikr8900); or a sightseeing cycle that ends with a soak at the Nature Baths (Ikr9900, including admission).

Sleeping

Mývatn's popularity means that room rates have soared, and demand is far greater than supply, so don't think twice about booking ahead. Most prices are overinflated, with €220 being the norm for a run-of-the-mill hotel double in summer's peak. Off-season rates are considerably cheaper (by up to 50%).

The website www.myvatn-hotels.com gives a rundown of most options. The following are in Reykjahlíð.

Hlíð CAMPGROUND, GUESTHOUSE €
(☎464 4103; www.myvatnaccommodation.is; Hraunbrún; sites per person Ikr1400, dm Ikr4700, d incl breakfast Ikr24,000, cottages Ikr35,000; @ⓘ) Sprawling, well-run Hlíð is 300m uphill from the church and offers a full spectrum: camping, sleeping-bag dorms and rooms with kitchen access, no-frills huts, self-contained cottages sleeping six, and en suite guesthouse rooms. There's also laundry, playground and bike hire.

EASTERN LAKESIDE HIKE

Although easily accessible by car, the sights along Mývatn's eastern lakeshore can also be tackled on a half-day hike.

A well-marked track runs from Reykjahlíð village to **Hverfell** (5km). This near-symmetrical crater appeared 2700 years ago in a cataclysmic eruption. Rising 463m from the ground and stretching 1040m across, it is a massive and awe-inspiring landmark; an easy track leads from the northwestern end to the summit and offers stunning views (of the crater itself and the surrounding landscape).

Then it's on to the giant jagged lava field at **Dimmuborgir** (another 3km) – the name means 'Dark Castles', and it's one of the most fascinating flows in the country. A series of nontaxing, colour-coded walking trails runs through the easily anthropomorphised landscape. The most popular path is the easy Church Circle (2.3km).

If you start in the late afternoon and time your hike correctly, you'll finish the day with a meal at Dimmuborgir while sunset shadows dance along the alien landscape. As an alternative, the walk from Hverfell's northwest corner to the Nature Baths is 2.3km – and the sunsets here are pretty special too.

DON'T MISS

GEOLOGICAL WONDERS

Travelling between Mývatn and Egilsstaðir, you'll quickly encounter the geological wonders of Hverir and Krafla, and no doubt be lured off the Ring Road to check out mighty Dettifoss.

➡ Vaporous vents cover the pinky-orange **Námafjall** ridge. At its foot, fumaroles and solfataras in the **Hverir** geothermal field scream steam and belch mud. The area rests on the mid-Atlantic rift (hence all the activity), and can be seen from quite a distance. It's just off the Ring Road 6km east of Reykjahlíð.

➡ A couple of kilometres past Hverir is the turn-off to **Krafla**, an active volcanic region (and geothermal power station) 7km north of the Ring Road. There's a walking track across the ominous-looking, sulphur-encrusted lava field known as **Leirhnjúkur**.

➡ The turn-off to mighty **Dettifoss** waterfall is 27km east of Reykjahlíð; it's then an easy 24km on sealed road to reach the falls. From the car park, a 2.5km loop walk takes you to the dramatic, canyon-edge viewpoint, where you can witness the power of nature in its full glory.

Eldá GUESTHOUSE €€
(☎464 4220; www.elda.is; Helluhraun 15; s/d without bathroom incl breakfast Ikr14,000/19,700; @) This friendly family-run operation owns three properties along Helluhraun and offers cosy, no-frills accommodation. There are guest kitchens and TV lounges, and buffet breakfast is included. All guests check in at this location.

Hótel Reynihlíð HOTEL €€€
(☎464 4170; www.myvatnhotel.is; s/d incl breakfast from Ikr25,400/32,300; @) The grand dame of Mývatn hotels is a smartly dressed 40-room hotel. The superior rooms aren't a noticeable upgrade; they only have slightly better views, plus a little more space. Also here is a restaurant, plus lounge-bar and sauna. We like the nine rooms at its cosier annexe, the pretty, lakeside **Hótel Reykjahlíð** (same prices).

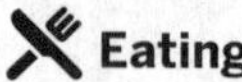

Eating

Look out for dark, sticky *hverabrauð* (rye bread), baked using geothermal heat.

★ **Vogafjós** ICELANDIC €€
(www.vogafjos.net; mains Ikr2550-4700; ⏲7.30am-11pm;) The 'Cowshed', 2.5km south of Reykjahlíð, is a memorable restaurant where you can enjoy views of the lush surrounds, or of the dairy shed of this working farm (cows are milked at 7.30am and 5.30pm). The menu is an ode to local produce: smoked lamb, house-made mozzarella, dill-cured Arctic char, geysir bread, home-baked cakes, homemade ice cream. It's all delicious.

Gamli Bærinn ICELANDIC €€
(www.myvatnhotel.is; mains Ikr1900-4900; ⏲10am-11pm) The cheerfully busy 'Old Farm' tavern beside Hótel Reynihlíð serves up pub-style meals, including lunchtime soups and burgers, and dinner-time fish and steak. In the evening it becomes a local hang-out; the opening hours are often extended during weekend revelry, but the kitchen closes at 10pm.

ℹ Information

Tourist Information Centre (☎464 4390; www.visitmyvatn.is; Hraunvegur 8; ⏲7.30am-6pm Jun-Aug, shorter hours Sep-May) The well-informed centre has good displays on the local geology, and can book accommodation, tours and transport. Pick up a copy of the hugely useful *Visit Mývatn* brochure and *Mývatn Lake* map.

ℹ Getting There & Around

All buses pick up/drop off passengers at the information centre in Reykjahlíð; many bus routes also stop in Skútustaðir.

SBA-Norðurleið (☎550 0700; www.sba.is) services include the following:

Bus 62/62a West to Akureyri, east to Egilsstaðir and Höfn (one daily June to mid-September).

Bus 650 To Húsavík (40 minutes, two daily mid-June to August).

Bus 661 To Krafla and Dettifoss (one daily mid-June to August). From Dettifoss you have the option of linking with bus 641a to Ásbyrgi, Húsavík or on to Akureyri.

Strætó (☎540 2700; www.straeto.is) runs Bus 56 west to Akureryi (1½ hours, two daily) or east to Egilsstaðir (two hours, one daily). Service drops to four weekly services in winter.

Reykjavík Excursions (☎580 5400; www.re.is) summer services run along the highland Sprengisandur route, to either Landmannalaugar or Reykjavík.

THE EAST

Wild reindeer roam the mountains of the east, and Iceland's version of the Loch Ness monster calls the area home. The empty highlands are a complete contrast to the sparkling, spectacular fjords, which are surrounded by tumbling waterfalls and dotted with tight-knit communities, such as those in picturesque Seyðisfjörður.

Egilsstaðir

POP 2330

Egilsstaðir isn't a ravishing beauty. It's the main regional transport hub, and a centre for local commerce, so its services are quite good. All amenities are clustered near the central crossroads.

The town's saving grace is its proximity to lovely **Lagarfljót**, Iceland's third-largest lake. Since saga times, tales have been told of a monster, the Lagarfljótsormurinn, who lives in its depths.

Sleeping & Eating

Book *well* ahead for Wednesday nights in summer, as the ferry to Europe sails from nearby Seyðisfjörður on Thursday mornings.

Campsite CAMPGROUND €
(Kaupvangur 17; sites per person Ikr1200; ⌚Jun-Sep; @) Camping pitches are in utilitarian rows, but it's central and facilities are reasonable: there's a laundry, and on-site cafe, but no camper kitchen. At reception you can rent bikes (Ikr3900 for 24 hours) or book tours through **Travel East** (☎471 3060; www.travel east.is; Kaupvangur 17), the agency based here.

Olga Guesthouse GUESTHOUSE €
(☎860 2999; www.gistihusolgu.com; Tjarnabraut 3; s/d without bathroom from Ikr12,400/14,700) In a good central location, dressed-in-red Olga offers five rooms that share three bathrooms and a kitchen; all rooms come with tea- and coffee-making facilities, TV and fridge. Two doors down is Olga's sister, yellow Birta Guesthouse, under the same friendly ownership and with similar high-quality facilities. Breakfast can be ordered for Ikr1550.

Egilsstaðir Guesthouse COUNTRY HOTEL €€€
(☎471 1114; www.lakehotel.is; s/d incl breakfast Ikr22,520/30,100; @) The town was named after this farm and splendid heritage guesthouse (now big enough to warrant the 'hotel' label) on the banks of Lagarfljót, 300m west of the crossroads. In its old wing, en suite rooms retain a sense of character. In contrast, a brand-new extension houses 30 modern, slightly anonymous hotel rooms. A great restaurant lives on-site.

Salt INTERNATIONAL €€
(www.saltbistro.is; Miðvangur 2; meals Ikr1290-3000; ⌚10am-11pm; 🌿👶) We totally get the appeal of this cool cafe-bistro, which offers one of the most interesting and varied menus in regional Iceland. Unfortunately, Salt can struggle with the large crowds it attracts. The food, however, is excellent: try the gourmet-topped flatbread pizza made with local barley, or opt for a burger, salad, crêpe or tandoori-baked Indian dish.

Information

Tourist Information Centre (☎471 2320; www.east.is; Miðvangur 2-4; ⌚8am-6pm Mon-Fri, 10am-4pm Sat & Sun Jun-Aug, 8am-4pm Mon-Fri Sep-May) Maps and brochures are plentiful here – you'll find everything you need to explore the Eastfjords and beyond.

Getting There & Away

AIR

Egilsstaðir's airport is 1km north of town. **Air Iceland** (Flugfélag Íslands; ☎570 3030; www.airiceland.is) flies daily year-round between Egilsstaðir and Reykjavík.

BUS

Egilsstaðir is a major crossroads on the Ring Road (note that there is no winter bus connection between Egilsstaðir and Höfn). Local buses run from Egilsstaðir to villages around the fjords.

SBA-Norðurleið (☎550 0720; www.sba.is) Bus 62/62a runs Akureyri–Mývatn–Egilsstaðir-Höfn (daily June to mid-September). Pick-up and drop-off at campground.

Strætó (☎540 2700; www.straeto.is) Bus 56 Akureyri–Mývatn–Egilsstaðir (daily June to mid-September, three to four weekly rest of year). Pick-up and drop-off opposite the N1, corner of Miðvangur.

Seyðisfjörður

POP 650

Things get lively when the Smyril Line's ferry *Norröna* sails up the 17km-long fjord and docks at pretty little Seyðisfjörður. The multicoloured wooden houses in the town, snow-capped mountains and cascading waterfalls make the perfect welcome for visitors to Iceland. It's also a friendly place with a community of artists, musicians and craftspeople.

Sights

Seyðisfjörður is stuffed with 19th-century timber buildings, brought in kit form from Norway; several of these have been transformed into cosy ateliers where local artisans work on various projects. Also worth a look is the gallery space above the Skaftfell cultural centre.

Bláa Kirkjan CHURCH
(www.blaakirkjan.is; Ránargata) The most prominent of Seyðisfjörður's timber buildings is the photogenic Blue Church. On Wednesday evenings from July to mid-August, it's the setting for a popular series of jazz, classical- and folk-music concerts (starting at 8.30pm; tickets Ikr2000); see the website for the program. If you're leaving on the Thursday ferry, this is a lovely way to spend your final night in Iceland.

Tours

Hlynur Oddsson KAYAKING
(☎865 3741; www.iceland-tour.com; ⊙Jun-Aug) For a sublime outdoor experience, contact Hlynur, a charming Robert Redford–esque character who spends his summers around town and offers tailor-made tours. With kids, you can opt for an easy half-hour paddling in the lagoon (Ikr1500); options on the fjord range from one to six hours, visiting a shipwreck or waterfalls (one/three hours Ikr4000/8000).

Sleeping

Hafaldan HI Hostel HOSTEL €
(☎611 4410; www.hafaldan.is; Suðurgata 8; dm Ikr4100, d with/without bathroom Ikr15,200/11,200; @ 👪) Seyðisfjörður's first-class budget digs are housed in two locations: the Harbour Hostel is at Ranárgata 9, a little out of town past the Blue Church; and the Hospital Hostel is the more-central summertime annexe at Suðurgata 8. The annexe houses the main reception for both from June to August.

Campsite CAMPGROUND €
(Ránargata; sites per person Ikr1150; ⊙May-Sep) There are two areas for camping – one sheltered, grassy site opposite the church for tents, and another nearby area for vans. The service building houses kitchen, showers and laundry facilities.

★ **Hótel Aldan** HOTEL €€
(☎472 1277; www.hotelaldan.com; reception at Norðurgata 2; s/d incl breakfast from Ikr17,900/23,900) This wonderful hotel is shared across three old wooden buildings: reception and bar-restaurant (where breakfast is served) are at the Norðurgata location. The Snæfell location (in the old post office at Austurvegur 3) is a creaky, characterful three-storey place with the cheapest rooms, fresh white paintwork and Indian bedspreads; a few new ground-floor suites have recently been added here, sleeping four. The Old Bank location (at Oddagata 6) houses a boutique guesthouse with antique furnishings and a refined air.

Eating

★ **Skaftfell Bistro** INTERNATIONAL €€
(http://skaftfell.is/en/bistro/; Austurvegur 42; meals Ikr1200-3100; ⊙from 11.30am daily; kitchen closes 10pm; 🖉 👪) This fabulous bistro-bar-cultural-centre is perfect for chilling, snacking and/or meeting locals. There's a short, daily-changing menu, plus popular pizza options (including 'reindeer bliss' and 'langoustine feast'). Be sure to check out the exhibitions in the gallery space upstairs.

Hótel Aldan ICELANDIC €€
(☎472 1277; www.hotelaldan.is; Norðurgata 2; lunch Ikr1550-2600, dinner mains Ikr3500-9400; ⊙7am-9pm mid-May–mid-Sep) Coffee and cakes are served all day in this country-chic spot, and lunches feature the likes of goat-cheese salad or catch of the day. In the evening, flickering candles prettify the tables, and the menu features traditional Icelandic ingredients (lamb, langoustine, reindeer, fish) with a contemporary touch. Reservations advised.

Information

Tourist Office (☎472 1551; ⊙8am-4pm Mon-Fri May-Sep) In the ferry terminal building, stocking local brochures, plus info on the entire country.

Getting There & Around

Contact kayaking guide Hlynur for rental of mountain bikes and route suggestions (half-day/one day/two days Ikr2500/3000/5000).

FAS (☎893 2669, 472 1515) runs a bus service between Egilsstaðir and Seyðisfjörður (Ikr1050, around 45 minutes). Extra services run to coincide with ferry arrivals and departures. An up-to-date schedule is at www.visitseydisfjordur.com. Details of the ferry service from mainland Europe are on p485.

THE SOUTH

Containing glittering glaciers, toppling waterfalls, the iceberg-filled Jökulsárlón lagoon and Iceland's favourite walking area, Skaftafell, it's no wonder that the south is the country's most visited region. Various places along the coast offer hiking, snowmobiling, dog sledding and glacier explorations; or head offshore to the charming, puffin-friendly Vestmannaeyjar (Westman Islands).

Vatnajökull

Mighty Vatnajökull is the world's largest ice cap outside the poles. At 8100 sq km, it's more than three times the size of Luxembourg, with an average thickness of 400m (and a maximum of almost 1km). Under this enormous blanket of ice are active volcanoes and mountain peaks. Yes, this is ground zero for those 'fire and ice' clichés.

Scores of outlet glaciers flow down from Vatnajökull's frosty bulk There are around 30 of them, with many visible (and accessible, to varying degrees) from the Ring Road in the southeast.

In 2008, **Vatnajökull National Park** (www.vjp.is) was founded, its boundaries encompassing the ice cap and the former Skaftafell and Jökulsárgljúfur national parks to form one giant megapark. With recent additions, the park now measures 13,900 sq km – nearly 14% of the entire country. There are major park visitor centres at Skaftafell in the south and Ásbyrgi in the north (east of Húsavík), as well as at Höfn and at Skriðuklaustur, near Egilsstaðir in Iceland's east.

WARNING

Dangerous crevasses criss-cross the ice cap and its outlet glaciers – hiking is not recommended without proper equipment and a knowledgable guide.

Around Vatnajökull

Skaftafell (Vatnajökull National Park – South)

Skaftafell, the jewel in the crown of Vatnajökull National Park, encompasses a breathtaking collection of peaks and glaciers. It's the country's favourite wilderness: 300,000 visitors per year come to marvel at thundering waterfalls, twisted birch woods, the tangled web of rivers threading across the sandar (sand deltas), and Vatnajökull with its lurching tongues of ice, dripping down mountainsides like icing on a cake.

Activities

Star of a hundred postcards, **Svartifoss** (Black Falls) is a stunning, moody-looking waterfall flanked by geometric black basalt columns. It's reached by an easy 1.8km trail leading up from the visitor centre via the campsite (about 1½ hours return).

DON'T MISS

SNOWMOBILING ON THE ICE CAP

One of the best ways to explore the whiteness of Vatnajökull is via an unforgettable snowmobile ride, and the easiest route is via the F985 4WD track (about 35km east of Jökulsárlón, 45km west of Höfn) to the broad glacial spur Skálafellsjökull. The 16km-long road is practically vertical in places, with iced-over sections in winter. Don't even think of attempting it in a 2WD car.

At 9.30am and 2pm daily from May to October, **Glacier Jeeps** (☎478 1000, 894 3133; www.glacierjeeps.is) collects people in a super-Jeep from the parking area at the start of the F985 (call ahead to reserve a space). At the top of the road, 840m above sea level, is Jöklasel, its base (where you can also get food, with epic views).

From here, the most popular tour option is the awesome one-hour **snowmobile ride** (Ikr21,000 including pick-up from the start of the F985). Prices are per person, with two people to a skidoo – there's Ikr8000 extra to pay if you want a skidoo to yourself. If the skidoo isn't your thing, you can also take a more-sedate **super-Jeep ride** onto the ice for the same price.

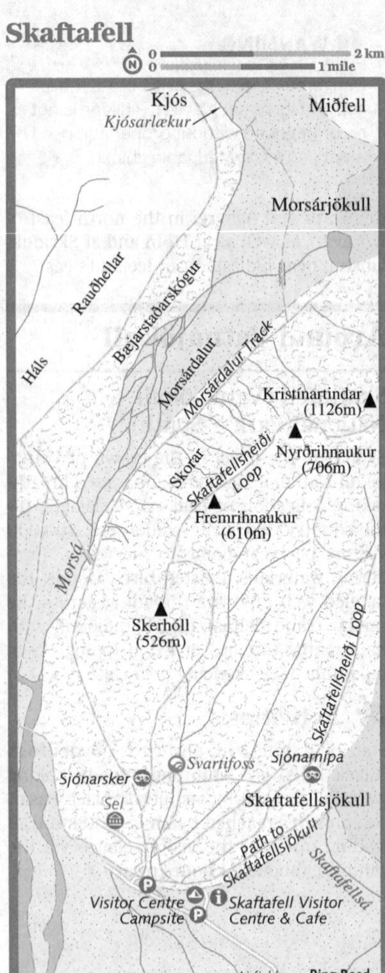

Another very popular trail is the easy one-hour return walk (3.7km) to **Skaftafellsjökull**. The marked trail begins at the visitor centre and leads to the glacier face, where you can witness the bumps and groans of the ice (although the glacier is pretty grey and gritty here).

On a fine day, the five- to six-hour (15.5km) loop walk around **Skaftafellsheiði** is a hiker's dream.

The highlight of a visit to Skaftafell is a **glacier hike**. It's utterly liberating to strap on crampons and crunch your way around a glacier. A number of authorised guides operate in the area. The largest companies, **Icelandic Mountain Guides** (☎587 9999; www.mountainguides.is; Stórhöfði 33) and **Glacier Guides** (☎Reykjavík office 571 2100, Skaftafell 659 7000; www.glacierguides.is), have info and booking huts in the car park at Skaftafell visitor centre. Both companies go further than just easy glacier hikes (two hours on the ice for around Ikr9000), offering more-challenging options and ice climbs, right up to summiting Iceland's highest peak. Both offer combos, such as a glacier hike plus ice lagoon boat trip or Ingólfshöfði visit.

Sleeping

Visitor Centre Campsite CAMPGROUND €
(☎470 8300; www.vjp.is; sites per person Ikr1400 plus per tent Ikr100; May-Sep;) Most visitors bring a tent to this large, gravelly, panorama-filled campsite (with laundry facilities, and hot showers for Ikr500). It gets very busy in summer (at capacity, it holds 400 pitches); reservations are only required for large groups (40-plus people). Wi-fi is available, as are storage lockers.

Hótel Skaftafell HOTEL €€
(☎478 1945; www.hotelskaftafell.is; Freysnes; s/d incl breakfast Ikr24,500/29,000; @) Formerly part of the Fosshotel chain, this is the closest hotel to Skaftafell. It's 5km east, at Freysnes, and one of very few hotels in the area, so it's in hot demand – prices reflect this. Its 63 rooms are functional rather than luxurious; staff are helpful. There's a decent restaurant (mains Ikr3500 to Ikr4100) plating up local produce.

Information

Visitor Centre (Skaftafellsstofa; ☎470 8300; www.vjp.is; 8am-9pm Jun-Aug, 9am-7pm May & Sep, 10am-5pm Mar-Apr & Oct, 11am-4pm Nov-Feb) The helpful year-round visitor centre has an information desk with free brochures and maps for sale, informative displays on the Öræfi area, a fascinating 10-minute film about the 1996 Grímsvötn *jökulhlaup* (flooding caused by volcanic eruption beneath an icecap), exhibitions, a summertime cafe and internet access. The staff here know their stuff.

Getting There & Away

Skaftafell is a stop on Reykjavík–Höfn bus routes and also a departure point for buses to wilderness areas such as Landmannalaugar and Lakagígar. There are frequent services to Jökulsárlón. Buses stop in front of the visitor centre.

Jökulsárlón

A ghostly procession of luminous-blue icebergs drifts through the astoundingly photogenic, 25-sq-km **Jökulsárlón glacier lagoon**, before floating out to sea. This surreal scene (right next to the Ring Road between Skaftafell and Höfn) is a natural film set: in fact, you might have seen it in *Batman Begins* (2005) and the James Bond film *Die Another Day* (2002). The ice breaks off from Breiðamerkurjökull glacier, an offshoot of Vatnajökull.

Take a memorable 40-minute trip in an **amphibious boat** (☎478 2222; www.icelagoon.is; adult/child Ikr4000/1000; ⏲9am-7pm Jun-Aug, 10am-5pm Apr-May & Sep-Oct), which trundles along the shore like a bus before driving into the water. On-board guides regale you with factoids about the lagoon, and you can taste 1000-year-old ice. There is no set schedule; trips run from the eastern car park (by the cafe) regularly – at least half-hourly in summer.

Countless day tours take in Jökulsárlón. Strætó and Sterna's Reykjavík–Skaftafell–Höfn buses pass here – on its eastbound run, the Sterna service stops long enough for you to take a boat ride. From mid-June to mid-September, Reykjavík Excursions bus 15 runs a loop between Skaftafell visitor centre and Jökulsárlón.

Höfn

POP 1700

Although it's no bigger than many European villages, the southeast's main town (pronounced 'herp', more or less) feels like a sprawling metropolis after driving through the emptiness on either side. Its setting is stunning; on a clear day, wander down to the waterside, find a quiet bench and just gaze at Vatnajökull and its brotherhood of glaciers.

Sights & Activities

Gamlabúð VISITOR CENTRE, MUSEUM

(www.vjp.is; ⏲8am-8pm Jun-Aug, 10am-6pm May & Sep, 10am-noon & 4-6pm Oct-Apr) The 1864 warehouse that once served as the regional folk museum has been moved from the outskirts of town to a prime position on the Höfn harbourfront. It's been refurbished to serve as the town's visitor centre, with good exhibits explaining the marvels of the region's flagship national park (including flora and fauna), plus documentaries being screened.

WORTH A TRIP

A CART RIDE TO INGÓLFSHÖFÐI

The dramatic, 76m-high Ingólfshöfði promontory is a nature reserve just east of Skaftafell. The only way to access this almost-island is by tour, operated by **Local Guide** (Öræfaferðir; ☎894 0894; www.localguide.is; tours adult/child Ikr6900/1000; ⏲tours 1.30pm Mon-Sat May-Aug, also 10.15am Mon-Sat Jun–mid-Aug). Tours begin with a fun ride across 6km of shallow tidal lagoon (in a tractor-drawn wagon), then a short but steep sandy climb, followed by a 1½-hour guided walk round the headland. The emphasis is on birdwatching, with mountain backdrops to marvel over. Confirm tour times via the website, where you can also book tickets (prebooking recommended).

Waterfront WALKING, BIRDWATCHING

There are a couple of short **waterside paths** where you can amble and gape at the views: one by Hótel Höfn, and another round the marshes and lagoons at the end of the promontory Ósland (about 1km beyond the harbour – head for the seamen's monument on the rise). The latter path is great for watching seabirds, though watch out for dive-bombing Arctic terns.

Sleeping

Höfn Camping & Cottages CAMPGROUND €

(☎478 1606; www.campsite.is; Hafnarbraut 52; sites per person Ikr1200, cabins Ikr17,000-22,000; ⏲May–mid-Oct; @) Lots of travellers stay at the campsite on the main road into town, where superhelpful owners and extensive local info are among the draws. There are 11 good-value cabins, sleeping up to six; some have private toilet, but all use the amenities block for showers. There's also a playground, laundry and a store selling camping gear.

HI Hostel HOSTEL €

(☎478 1736; www.hostel.is; Hvannabraut; dm/d without bathroom Ikr4500/11,200) Follow the signs from the N1 to find Höfn's sole budget option, hidden away in a residential area and with some primo views. It's a sprawling space (a former aged-care home) that's usually bustling with travellers in summer, with the requisite facilities including laundry and kitchen (but no lounge areas). There's Ikr700 discount for members; linen is Ikr1650.

★Guesthouse Dyngja GUESTHOUSE €€

(☎846 0161; www.dyngja.com; Hafnarbraut 1; d without bathroom incl breakfast from Ikr18,500; @) A lovely young couple have opened this petite five-room guesthouse in a prime harbourfront locale, and filled it with charm and good cheer: rich colours, record player and vinyl selection, self-service breakfast, outdoor deck and good local knowledge. There's a good new addition: a downstairs suite with private bathroom.

Eating

Humar (langoustine, or 'Icelandic lobster') is the speciality on Höfn menus. This is a town where it's well worth a splurge.

★Humarhöfnin ICELANDIC €€€

(☎478 1200; www.humarhofnin.is; Hafnarbraut 4; mains Ikr3900-7900; ⊙noon-10pm Jun-Aug, 6-10pm Apr-May & Sep) Humarhöfnin offers 'Gastronomy Langoustine' in a cute, cheerfully Frenchified space with superb attention to detail: herb pots on the windowsills, roses on every table. Mains centred on pincer-waving little critters cost upwards of Ikr6500, but there's also more budget-friendly dishes including a fine langoustine baguette (Ikr3900).

Pakkhús ICELANDIC €€€

(☎478 2280; www.pakkhus.is; harbourfront; mains Ikr3190-6000; ⊙noon-10pm May-Sep) Hats off to a menu that tells you the name of the boat that delivers its star produce. In a stylish harbourside warehouse, Pakkhús delivers a level of kitchen creativity you don't often find in rural Iceland. First-class local langoustine, lamb and duck tempt tastebuds, while clever desserts end the meal in style (who can resist a dish called '*skyr* volcano'?).

Getting There & Away

AIR

Höfn's airport is 6.5km northwest of town. **Eagle Air** (☎562 2640; www.eagleair.is) flies year-round between Reykjavík and Höfn.

BUS

Bus companies travelling through Höfn have different stops, so make sure you know what operator you're travelling with and confirm where they pick up from. Note: there is no winter bus link north to Egilsstaðir and beyond.

SBA-Norðurleið (☎550 0720; www.sba.is) Bus 62/62a to Egilsstaðir, Mývatn and Akureryi (one daily June to mid-September); stop at N1 petrol station.

Sterna (☎551 1166; www.sterna.is) Bus 12/12a to Reykjavík (10¾ hours, one daily June to mid-September); pick-up/drop-off at campground and hostel.

Strætó (☎540 2700; www.straeto.is) Bus 51 to Reykjavík (seven hours, one or two daily year-round); pick-up/drop-off out front of the swimming pool on Víkurbraut

Reykjavík Excursions (☎580 5400; www.re.is) Bus 19/19a to Skaftafell (one daily June to mid-September); from N1. Stops at Jökulsárlón for 2½ hours. From Skaftafell there are buses further west.

Landmannalaugar & Fjallabak Nature Reserve

The Fjallabak route (F208) is a spectacular alternative to the coast road between Hella and Kirkjubæjarklaustur. It passes through the scenic nature reserve to **Landmannalaugar**, an area of rainbow-coloured rhyolite peaks, rambling lava flows, blue lakes and hot springs, which can hold you captive for days. Much of the route is along (and in!) rivers and therefore unsuitable for 2WD vehicles.

The star attractions around Landmannalaugar are **Laugahraun**, a convoluted lava field; the soothing **hot springs** just 200m from the Landmannalaugar hut; multicoloured vents at **Brennisteinsalda**; the incredible red crater lake **Ljótipollur**; and the blue lake **Frostastaðavatn**, just over the rhyolite ridge north of Landmannalaugar.

The chaotic **hut and camping complex** (☎860 3335; N 63°59.600', W 19°03.660'; huts per person Ikr6500) is operated by Ferðafélag Íslands, like the huts on the Laugavegurinn hike, and its website (www.fi.is) is loaded with information. The base accommodates 75 people in closed (and close) quarters. There's a kitchen area, showers and several wardens on-site. Campers can pitch a tent in the designated areas (Ikr1500 per person); they have access to the toilet and shower facilities as well.

The complex opens for the season depending on when the roads are clear (any time from late May to sometime in June). It closes for sure by mid-October, but it can be earlier.

Getting There & Away

Landmannalaugar can be reached by rugged, semiamphibious buses that run from three different directions from about mid-June to mid-September (depending on road-opening dates). **Reykjavík Excursions** (☎ 580 5400; www.re.is) services:

Bus 10/10a Skaftafell–Landmannalaugar (four hours)

Bus 11/11a Reykjavík–Landmannalaugar (4¼ hours)

Bus 14/14a Mývatn–Landmannalaugar (10 hours, three weekly) via the Sprengisandur route (F26).

Laugavegurinn Trek

This 55km trek from Landmannalaugar to Þórsmörk, commonly known as Laugavegurinn, is where backpackers earn their stripes in Iceland. It means 'Hot Spring Road', and it's easy to understand why.

We highly recommend bringing along a map and GPS if you plan on tackling the walk without a guide. The track is almost always passable for hiking from early July through to mid-September. You shouldn't have problems if you're in reasonable condition, but don't take the walk lightly: it requires substantial river crossings, all-weather gear, sturdy boots and sufficient food and water.

Most people walk from north to south (because of the net altitude loss), taking three to four days. Some continue on to Skógar on the Fimmvörðuháls hike, which takes an extra day or two (about an additional 22km).

As the route is very well travelled, you'll find a constellation of carefully positioned huts along the way – all are owned and maintained by **Ferðafélag Íslands** (www.fi.is). These huts sleep dozens of people and must be booked *months* in advance.

You can also camp in the designated areas around the huts, although these spaces tend to be open to the elements. Campers do not need to reserve.

Ferðafélag Íslands breaks Laugavegurinn into four sections (see its website for a detailed description).

Part 1: Landmannalaugar to Hrafntinnusker (12km; three to five hours) A relatively easy start to your adventure, the walk to the first hut passes the boiling earth at Stórihver and sweeping fields of glittering obsidian.

Part 2: Hrafntinnusker to Álftavatn (12km; four to five hours) At Hrafntinnusker you can try a couple of short local hikes without your pack before setting off: there are views at Södull (20 minutes return) and Reykjafjöll (one hour return), and a hidden geothermal area behind the ice caves (three hours return); ask the warden for walking tips. Views aplenty are found on the walk to Álftavatn as well; hike across the northern spur of the Kaldaklofsfjöll ice cap for vistas from the summit. Walking into Álftavatn you'll see looming Tindfjallajökull, Mýrdalsjökull and the infamous Eyjafjallajökull before reaching the serenely beautiful lake at which you'll spend the night.

Part 3: Álftavatn to Emstrur (16km; six to seven hours) To reach Emstrur you'll need to ford at least one large stream – you can take your shoes off and get wet or wait at the edge of the river for a 4WD to give you a lift over. Not to be missed is the detour to Markarfljótsgljúfur – a gaping

WORTH A TRIP

SKÓGAR

Skógar nestles under the Eyjafjallajökull ice cap just off the Ring Road. This little tourist settlement is the start (or occasionally end) of the hike over the Fimmvörðuháls Pass to Þórsmörk, and is one of the activities centres in the southwest. At its western edge, you'll see a dizzyingly high waterfall, **Skógafoss**, shrouded in mist and rainbows, and on the eastern side you'll find the fantastic **Skógar Folk Museum** (Skógasafn; ☎ 487 8845; www.skogasafn.is; adult/child Ikr1750/free, outside stuctures only Ikr800; ⏲ museum 9am-6pm Jun-Aug, 10am-5pm May & Sep, 11am-4pm Oct-Apr), built by charming nonagenarian Þórður Tómasson. There are various restored buildings (church, turf-roofed farmhouse, cowsheds etc), and a hangarlike building at the back houses an interesting transport and communication museum, plus a cafe and souvenir shop.

Laugavegurinn Trek

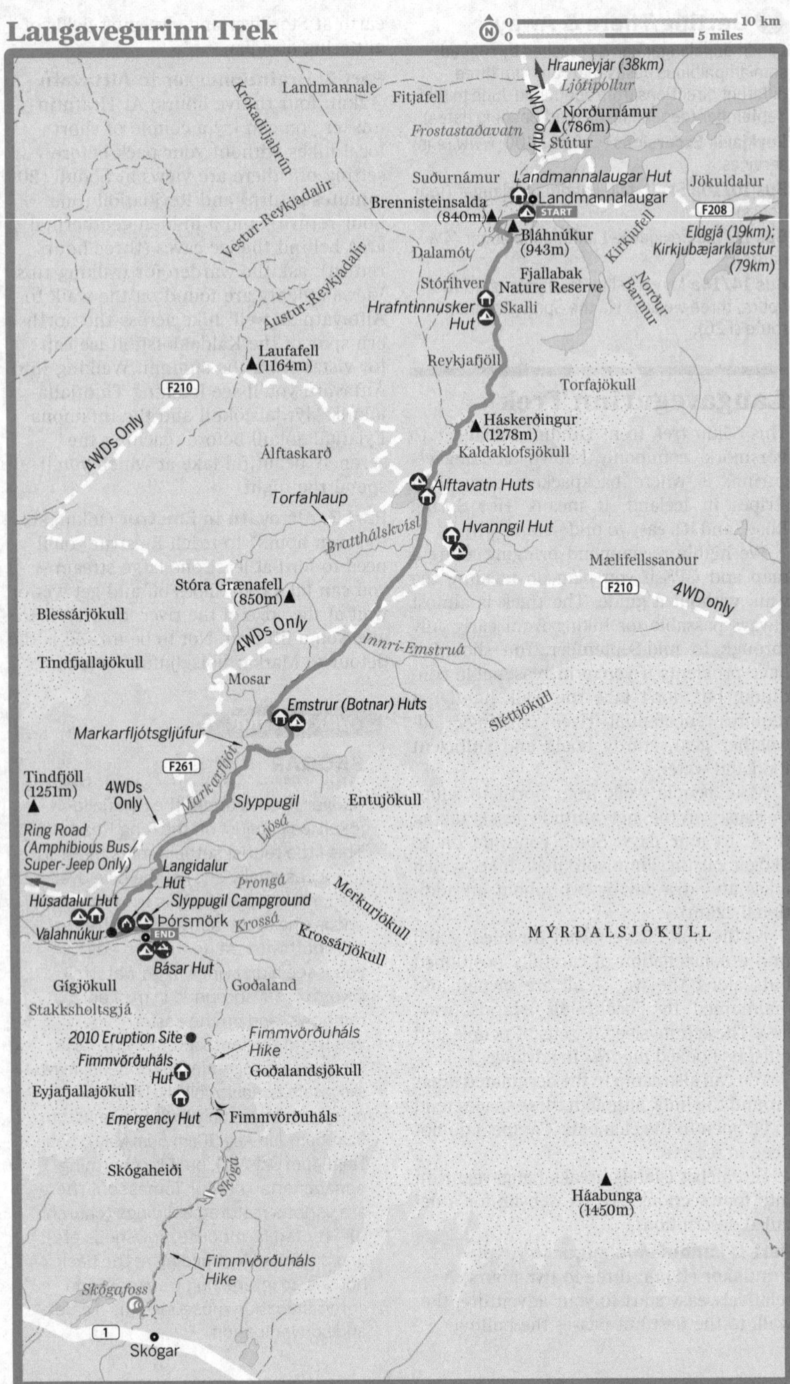

green canyon. It's well marked from Emstrur, and takes about an hour to reach (you come back the same way).

Part 4: Emstrur to Þórsmörk (15km; six to seven hours) Barrenness turns to the lush Arctic flowers of a brilliantly verdant kingdom. If you're not planning on staying in Þórsmörk, you need to arrive before the last bus leaves.

Þórsmörk

A hidden valley deep in the Icelandic wilderness, the 'Forest of Thor' is a verdant realm of forest and flower-filled lees that looks onto curling gorges, icy rivers and three looming glaciers that guard the hamlet from harsher weather. Be warned, though: Þórsmörk's lovely setting and proximity to Reykjavík (130km) make it a popular spot in summer.

Þórsmörk is the end of the Landmannalaugar–Þórsmörk four-day trek, although walkers can extend the journey with the spectacular 23km Þórsmörk–Skógar hike. It crosses **Fimmvörðuháls Pass**, where a new lava field was formed in the 2010 Eyjafjallajökull eruptions. Go prepared – the terrain is tough, the pass is high and bad weather can descend very quickly even in midsummer. The hut on this stretch, **Fimmvörðuhálskali** (☎893 4910; www.utivist.is; N 63°37.320', W 19°27.093'; per person Ikr4200), is run by Útivist. In bad weather it can be difficult to find; there's no campsite.

Sleeping

There are three lodging areas in the Þórsmörk area: Langidalur (sometimes referred to as Þórsmörk) with huts as well as at nearby Slyppugil; Básar (technically in Goðaland); and Húsadalur (also called Volcano Huts Thorsmork). All have huts and campsites, cooking facilities and running water. They get crammed during summer months, so it's crucial to book space in the huts in advance. We recommend bringing a sleeping bag and your own food. Note that wild camping is forbidden in the area, as it is a nature preserve.

Húsadalur HUT, CAMPGROUND €

(Volcano Huts Thorsmork; ☎552 8300; www.volcanohuts.com; sites per person Ikr1600, dm/s/d & tr/cottages without bathroom Ikr6500/15,000/19,000/25,000) Thriving Volcano Huts Thorsmork fills the Húsadalur area with dorm-style huts, private rooms, four- to five-person cottages (with basic kitchenettes), campground and a restaurant (breakfast/lunch/dinner costs Ikr2000/Ikr2500/Ikr4500). Lunch tends to be soup and fresh bread with coffee and cake, dinner a simple buffet. There's a guest kitchen, hot-pot and sauna, a masseuse/yoga instructor and lots of action. Linen costs Ikr3000.

Langidalur HUT, CAMPGROUND €

(Þórsmörk, Skagfjörðsskáli; ☎893 1191; www.fi.is; N 63°40.960', W 19°30.890'; sites per person Ikr1200, huts per person Ikr6500; ⊙mid-May–Sep) Langidalur – also referred to simply as Þórsmörk, or Skagfjörðsskáli – is the most rustic option of the four in Þórsmörk, but is well maintained. It sleeps 75, and there's well-tended camping space, a dining hut, large shower block and guest kitchens. Operated by Ferðafélag Íslands, which manages the Laugavegurinn huts.

Getting There & Away

Reykjavík Excursions (☎580 5400; www.re.is) bus 9/9a runs between Reykjavík and Þórsmörk (Ikr7500, 3¼ to four hours) once daily May to mid-October, stopping at Húsadalur, Stakksholtsgjá Canyon, Básar and Langidalur; there are two additional services in high summer (mid-June to August). Returning 9a buses have a slightly simplified route heading back towards Reykjavík.

Basically, forget about driving into Þórsmörk with your private vehicle. If you have your own 4WD with excellent clearance you can plough down Rtes 249 and F249 until the deep river ford, where you should leave your car. The bus that takes passengers is a special amphibious vehicle.

Vík

POP 295

The welcoming little community of Vík has become a booming hub for a very beautiful portion of the south coast. Iceland's southernmost town, it's also the rainiest, but that doesn't stop the madhouse atmosphere in summer when every room within 100km is booked solid. White waves wash up on black sands and the cliffs glow green from all that rain. Put simply, it's beautiful.

Sights

Reynisdrangur LANDMARK, BEACH

Vík's most iconic cluster of sea stacks is known as Reynisdrangur, which rise from the ocean like ebony towers at the western end of Vík's black-sand beach. They're traditionally believed to be trolls that got caught out in the sun. The nearby cliffs are good for puffin watching. A bracing walk up from Vík's western end takes you to the top of **Reynisfjall** ridge (340m), offering superb views.

★**Reynisfjara** LANDMARK, BEACH

On the west side of **Reynisfjall**, the high ridge above Vík, Rte 215 leads 5km down to the black-sand beach at Reynisfjara. The raw beach is backed by an incredible stack of **basalt columns** that look like a magical church organ, and there are outstanding views west to Dyrhólaey. The surrounding cliffs are pocked with caves formed from twisted basalt, and puffins bellyflop from here into the crashing sea during the summer.

★**Dyrhólaey** LANDMARK, WILDLIFE RESERVE

One of the south coast's most recognisable natural formations is the rocky plateau and huge stone sea arch at Dyrhólaey (deer-lay), which rises dramatically from the surrounding plain 10km west of Vík, at the end of Rte 218. The promontory is a nature reserve that's rich in bird life, including puffins. It's closed during nesting season (15 May to 25 June), but at other times you can visit its crashing black beaches and get awesome views from atop the archway.

Sleeping

Vík HI Hostel HOSTEL €

(Norður-Vík Hostel; ☎487 1106; www.hostel.is; Suðurvíkurvegur 5; dm/d without bathroom Ikr4100/11,200; @) Vík's small, homey, year-round hostel is in the beige house on the hill behind the village centre. Good facilities include guest kitchen and bike hire (per half/full day Ikr2000/Ikr3000). Staff also arrange 2½-hour glacier tours to Mýrdalsjökull. HI members discount Ikr700.

Vík Campsite CAMPGROUND €

(Tjaldsvæðið Vík; ☎487 1345; Austurvegur; sites per adult Ikr1300; ⊙Jun-Aug or early Sep) The campsite sits under a grassy ridge at the eastern end of town, just beyond the Hótel Edda. An octagonal building houses cooking facilities, washing machine, toilets and free showers. There are two little cottages (Ikr10,000) too.

★**Icelandair Hótel Vík** HOTEL €€

(☎487 1480, booking 444 4000; www.icelandairhotels.com; Klettsvegur 1-5; d from Ikr24,500) This sleek, black, window-fronted new hotel is improbably tucked just behind the Hótel Edda, on the eastern edge of town, near the campground. The hotels share a lobby (and have the same friendly owners), but that's where the resemblance ends. The Icelandair hotel has suitably swanky rooms, some with views to the rear cliffs or the sea. The light, natural decor is inspired by the local environment.

Eating

★**Suður-Vík** ICELANDIC, ASIAN €€

(☎487 1515; Suðurvíkurvegur 1; mains Ikr1750-4950; ⊙noon-10pm) The friendly ambience, from hardwood floors and interesting artwork to smiling staff, helps elevate this new restaurant beyond the competition. Food is Icelandic hearty, from heaping steak sandwiches with bacon and Béarnaise sauce, to Asian (think Thai satay with rice). In a warmly lit silver building atop town. Book ahead in summer.

Svarta Fjaran CAFE €€

(Black Beach; ☎859 7141; Reynisfjara; snacks Ikr990, dinner mains Ikr2400-5200; ⊙11am-9pm) Spectacularly set black volcanic cubes, meant to mimic the nearby black beach Reynisfjara with its famous basalt columns, house this new cafe that serves homemade cakes and snacks during the day and offers a full dinner menu at night. Plate-glass windows give views to the ocean and Dyrhólaey beyond.

Getting There & Away

Vík is a major stop for all Reykjavík–Höfn bus routes; buses stop at the N1 petrol station.

Strætó (☎540 2700; www.straeto.is) Runs bus 51 Reykjavík–Vík–Höfn (two daily).

Sterna (☎551 1166; www.sterna.is) Runs bus 12/12a Reykjavík–Vík–Höfn (one daily June to mid-September).

Vestmannaeyjar

POP 4260

Jagged and black, the Vestmannaeyjar (sometimes called the Westman Islands) form 15 eye-catching silhouettes off the southern shore. They were formed by sub-

Vestmannaeyjar

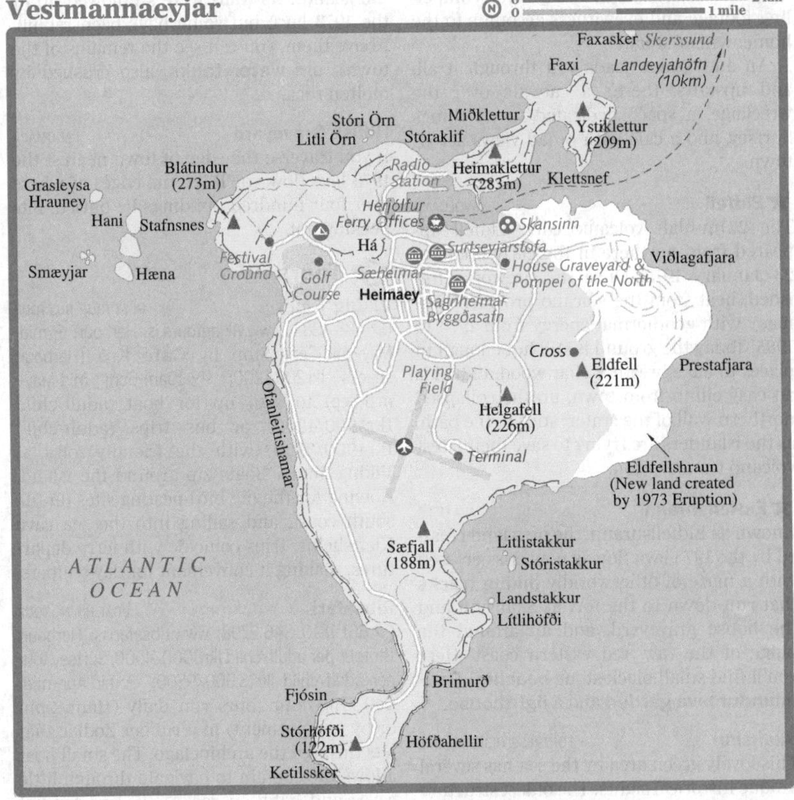

marine volcanoes around 11,000 years ago, except for Surtsey, the archipelago's newest addition, which rose from the waves in 1963. Surtsey was made a Unesco World Heritage Site in 2008, but its unique scientific status means that it is not possible to land there.

Heimaey is the only inhabited island. Its little town and sheltered harbour lie between dramatic *klettur* (escarpments) and two ominous volcanoes – blood-red Eldfell and conical Helgafell. In 1973 unforgettable pictures of Heimaey were broadcast across the globe when a huge eruption buried a third of the town under 30 million tonnes of lava. These days Heimaey is famous for its puffins (around 10 million birds come here to breed); Þjóðhátíð, Iceland's biggest outdoor festival, held in August; and its new volcano museum.

Sights & Activities

Heimaey's sights cluster in the main village, on the point around Skalinn and then in the fascinating fresh lava field and volcano, plus puffin-viewing cliffs.

★Eldheimar MUSEUM

(Pompeii of the North; ☎488 2000; www.eldheimar.is; Gerðisbraut 10; adult/10-18yr/child Ikr1900/1000/free; ⌚11am-6pm Jun–mid-Sep, reduced hours rest of year) Over 400 buildings lie buried under lava from the 1973 eruption, and on the edge of the flow 'Pompei of the North' is a new musuem revolving around one house excavated from 50m of pumice, along what was formerly Suðurvegur. The modern volcanic-stone building allows a glimpse into the home with its crumbling walls and intact but toppled knick-knacks, and is filled with multimedia exhibits on the eruption and its aftermath, from compelling footage and eyewitness accounts to the homeowners' story.

An audioguide leads you through it all, and upstairs, there's a catwalk over the wreckage, a space dedicated to all things Surtsey, and a cafe with broad views across town.

★ Eldfell VOLCANO

The 221m-high volcanic cone Eldfell appeared from nowhere in the early hours of 23 January 1973. Once the fireworks finished, heat from the volcano provided Heimaey with geothermal energy from 1976 to 1985. Today the ground is still hot enough in places to bake bread or char wood. Eldfell is an easy climb from town, up the collapsed northern wall of the crater; stick to the path, as the islanders are trying to save their latest volcano from erosion.

★ Eldfellshraun LAVA FIELD

Known as Eldfellshraun, the new land created by the 1973 lava flow is now criss-crossed with a maze of otherworldly **hiking tracks** that run down to the fort at Skansinn and the house graveyard, and all around the bulge of the raw, red eastern coast. Here you'll find small black-stone **beaches**, **Gaujulundur lava garden** and a **lighthouse**.

Skansinn FORTRESS, HISTORIC SITE

This lovely green area by the sea has several unique historical sights. The oldest structure on the island was Skansinn, a 15th-century fort built to defend the harbour (not too successfully – when Algerian pirates arrived in 1627, they simply landed on the other side of the island). Its walls were swallowed up by the 1973 lava, but some have been rebuilt. Above them, you can see the remains of the town's **old water tanks**, also crushed by molten rock.

House Graveyard LANDMARK

If you traverse the edge of town nearest the 1973 lava flow you'll see the edges of where over four hundred buildings lie buried, bits peeking out.

Tours

Viking Tours BOAT TOUR, BUS TOUR

(☎488 4884; www.vikingtours.is; Harbour; ⊗mid-May–mid-Sep) Stop by **Café Kró** (Harbour; snacks Ikr200-1200; ⊗10am-6pm mid-May–mid-Sep) to sign up for boat (adult/child Ikr5900/4900) or bus trips (adult/child Ikr4900/3900) with the friendly folks at Viking Tours. Boats zip around the island, slowing for the big bird-nesting sites on the south coast, and sailing into the sea cave Klettshellir. Trips coincide with ferry departures, making it convenient for day trippers.

Ribsafari BOAT, HIKING TOUR

(☎661 1810, 846 2798; www.ribsafari.is; Harbour; 1hr tour per adult/child Ikr8000/4500, Surtsey tour per adult/child Ikr16,500/9500; ⊗mid-Apr–mid-Oct) One-hour tours run daily (11am, 2pm or by appointment) in a rubber Zodiac that jets through the archipelago. The small boat allows the captain to navigate through little caves and between rocky outcrops for up-close views of bird colonies. Charter trips to Surtsey (note: you cannot get off the boat) require a minimum of 10 people.

PUFFINS – CLOWNS OF THE OCEAN

Iceland is famous for its puffins (*Fratercula arctica*, or *lundi* as they're called in Icelandic). It's hard not to get dewy-eyed over these sociable little 'clowns of the ocean', but really they're as tough as old boots, living out on the stormy winter seas.

It's easy to spot puffins: they're the clumsiest things in the air. Wings beat frantically 300 to 400 times per minute to keep them aloft, and the birds often crash-land. Underwater, it's a different story – their flight beneath the waves is so graceful that they were once thought to be a bird-fish hybrid.

Every spring, the puffins return to land to breed. From late May to August, the best places to see them include Látrabjarg, Grímsey and Heimaey, which has the world's biggest puffin colony. Pufflings start leaving their nests in August. On Heimaey, the young birds are often confused by the town's lights, so every year the town's children stay up late to collect them and point them seawards.

Sadly, a decline in sand eel numbers (the birds' main food source) has led to a corresponding drop in puffin numbers in Iceland's south. For twitchers, the good news is that puffins in Iceland's north seem unaffected (for now).

Festivals & Events

★Þjóðhátíð MUSIC

(National Festival; www.dalurinn.is; admission Ikr18,900) Three-day Þjóðhátíð is the country's biggest outdoor festival. Held at Herjólfsdalur festival ground over the last weekend in July or the first weekend in August, it involves music, dancing, fireworks, a big bonfire, litres of alcohol and, as the night progresses, lots of drunken sex (it's something of a teen rite of passage), with upwards of 17,000 people attending.

Sleeping

Sunnuhöll HI Hostel HOSTEL €

(481 2900; www.hotelvestmannaeyjar.is; Vestmannabraut 28; dm Ikr4500) We have a soft spot for homey Sunnuhöll hostel, with its handful of prim rooms. The recent surge in day trippers means that dorms are rarely full, and there's generally a quiet and laidback vibe. Reception is at Hótel Vestmannaeyjar. HI members discount Ikr700.

Campsite CAMPGROUND €

(Tjaldsvæði; sites per person Ikr1300; Jun-Aug) Cupped in the bowl of an extinct volcano, the Herjólfsdalur campsite has hot showers, a laundry room and cooking facilities. You can also pitch a tent inland and across the street next to the football field at Þórsheimili, which is less windy.

Hótel Vestmannaeyjar HOTEL €€

(481 2900; www.hotelvestmannaeyjar.is; Vestmannabraut 28; d/q incl breakfast Ikr24,700/30,500; @) Iceland's first cinema is now a pleasant hotel, with modern rooms (some with good town and harbour views), friendly staff and top restaurant Einsi Kaldi downstairs.

Eating

★Slippurinn ICELANDIC €€

(481 1515; www.slippurinn.com; Strandvegur 76; mains Ikr2000-3900; 5.30-11pm Sun-Thu, to 1am Fri & Sat) Lively Slippurinn fills the upper storey of a beautifully remodeled old machine workshop that once serviced the ships in the harbour and now has great views to it. The tool shelves are still in their original positions, with tables made from old boat scraps beneath them. The food is delicious Icelandic with a few bright flavours from the Med.

★Gott ORGANIC €€

(431 3060; Bárustigur 11; mains Ikr1290-2650;) Fresh fusion food is done with care, using organic, healthy ingredients in this jolly corner dining room. Think cod fillet with cauliflower purée or spelt-wrapped grilled chicken. Plus vegie options.

Information

Tourist Information Centre (www.vestmannaeyjar.is; Strandvegur; 9am-6pm Mon-Fri, 10am-5pm Sat, 1-5pm Sun Jun-Aug) The summer tourist office is staffed by local teens at a cafe-bookshop. Pick up pamphlets and trail maps.

Getting There & Away

AIR

There are two daily flights between Reykjavík's domestic airport and Vestmannæyjar on **Eagle Air** (562 4200; www.eagleair.is).

BOAT

Eimskip's ferry **Herjólfur** (481 2800; www.eimskip.is; adult/child/car/bicycle Ikr1260/630/2030/630) sails from Landeyjahöfn (about 12km off the Ring Road between Hvolsvöllur and Skógar) to Heimaey up to five times daily year-round. The journey takes about 30 minutes. You must always reserve ahead for cars, and passengers should book ahead in high season, especially at peak daytripper hours (the morning to Vestmannaeyjar and the afternoon back).

BUS

Strætó (540 2700; www.bus.is) bus 52 connects Reykjavík (Mjódd terminal) with Landeyjahöfn harbour (Ikr3500, 2¼ hours, three daily). Not all the ferry journeys have a bus connection, and there is nothing whatsoever to do or see at Landeyjahöfn, so check bus schedules carefully.

THE INTERIOR

Iceland's interior is so vast, barren and remote that the Apollo astronauts held training exercises here before the 1969 lunar landings. The highlands are true wilderness, with practically no services, accommodation or bridges, and no guarantees if things go wrong: careful preparations are essential.

Routes of Central Iceland

Historically, the interior routes were used as summer shortcuts between north and south, places of terror to be traversed as quickly as possible. Some *útilegumenn* (outlaws) fled into these harsh highlands: those who survived gained legendary status, like the superhuman Grettir; or Fjalla-Eyvindur, an Icelandic Robin Hood/Butch Cassidy figure.

Routes are only open to high-clearance 4WDs (river crossings are required, except on the Kjölur route); routes open anytime from mid-June to early July, and usually close again in September. Full details are at www.vegagerdin.is or by calling 1777. Note that summertime 4WD buses serve the Kjölur and Sprengisandur routes; tour operators offer super-Jeep vehicles and experienced drivers/guides. Petrol is not available in the highlands.

Many mountain huts are run by **Ferðafélag Íslands** (568 2533; www.fi.is); accommodation is in demand, so book in advance. Facilities tend to be spartan.

Kjölur Route

The Kjölur route (Rte 35) was once believed to be infested with bloodthirsty outlaws. Nowadays, it's a favourite with visitors: it's more hospitable than the Sprengisandur route, and it forms a neat shortcut between Reykjavík and Akureyri. It is still a mountain road, and while it's possible to drive a 2WD along the route, it is definitely not recommended. Car-hire companies expressly forbid the use of 2WD rentals on the route.

Kjölur's main attraction is **Hveravellir**, a geothermal area of fumaroles and multicoloured hot pools at the northern end of the pass. A **campground** (summer 452 4200, year-round 894 1293; www.hveravellir.is; sites/dm per person Ikr1200/4500; mid-Jun–mid-Sep) and two hiker huts are here. The **Kerlingarfjöll** mountain range (10km off Rte F35 on Rte F347) has superb hiking, and the **Kerlingarfjöll Highland Centre** (summer 664 7878, year-round 664 7000; www.kerlingarfjoll.is; sites per person Ikr1550, d with bathroom incl breakfast Ikr29,300; mid-Jun–mid-Sep) has huts, houses and camping, plus meals.

Daily from mid-June to early September, scheduled buses travel along the Kjölur route between Reykjavík and Akureyri (in both directions, with various stops). **SBA-Norðurleið** (550 0770, 550 0700; www.sba.is) bus 610/610a takes 10½ hours for the complete journey; **Sterna** (551 1166; www.sterna.is) bus F35/35a takes 13 hours.

Sprengisandur Route

The Sprengisandur route (F26) is long and desolate, but it does offer some wonderful

BÁRÐARBUNGA VOLCANO

In mid-August 2014, sensors began picking up increased seismic activity in and around Bárðarbunga, one of many volcanoes that lie underneath Vatnajökull ice cap (this immense volcano system is under the northwest part of the ice cap).

In late August a fissure eruption, complete with spectacular lava fountains, began in Holuhraun, a 200-year-old lava field about 5km away from the ice edge. Scientists are monitoring developments, preparing for various scenarios, including a more serious eruption underneath the ice. Any eruptions that occur under ice present danger of glacier melt (causing destructive meltwater floods), and a likelihood of ashcloud – potentially along the lines of the Eyjafjallajökull eruption of 2010, which grounded air traffic in Europe for six days (and tripped up newsreaders around the world thanks to its tricky pronunciation).

There is no way of knowing what developments may occur, or when. And can you visit? At the time of publication, the only option was to see the eruption from the air. The Holuhraun fissure eruption is occurring in a remote, uninhabited region (south of Askja), with the only immediate dangers as a result of the sulphuric gases being released and causing some nasty pollution countrywide (depending on wind strength and direction). But, the possibility of further eruptions and flooding mean that certain parts of the highlands are off limits to all. Roads are closed (these are remote, 4WD-access roads).

If and when the area is deemed safe for visitors, there will no doubt be tour operators ready to take tourists to it (and charge them handsomely!). The tour operators that visit Askja (usually from Mývatn) will be best placed to offer such tours, but be aware that this is a remote area, with tough access, so be prepared to cough up!

In the meantime, keep up to date on Bárðarbunga – and other volcanic activity – via various websites: the **Icelandic Meteorological Office** (www.vedur.is) and the **Icelandic National Broadcasting Service** (www.ruv.is) are good places to start.

views of Vatnajökull, Tungnafellsjökull and Hofsjökull ice caps, as well as Askja and Herðubreið. The northern section passes the photogenic waterfall **Aldeyjarfoss**, which topples over clustered basalt columns.

A good place to break your journey is **Nýidalur**, which has a campsite, two Ferðafélag Íslands **huts** (☎Jul-Aug 860 3334; www.fi.is; N 64°44.130', W 18°04.350'; site/dm Ikr1200/6500) and lots of hiking possibilities.

In July and August, **Reykjavík Excursions** (☎580 5400; www.re.is) operates two scheduled services along the Sprengisandur route. Bus 14/14a connects Landmannalaugar with Mývatn (10 hours, three weekly); bus 17/17a connects Reykjavík with Mývatn (11½ hours, three weekly).

Öskjuleið (Askja Route)

The Öskjuleið route runs across the highlands to Herðubreið, and to the desert's most popular marvel, the immense Askja caldera. The usual access road is Rte F88, which leaves the Ring Road 32km east of Mývatn (p251).

HERÐUBREIÐ

Iceland's most distinctive mountain, Herðubreið (1682m), has been described as a birthday cake and a lampshade, but the tourist industry calls it (more respectfully) the 'Queen of the Mountains'. The track around it makes a nice day hike from **Herðubreiðarlindir Nature Reserve**, a grassy oasis created by springs flowing from beneath the lava. There's a campsite and the 30-bed **Þorsteinsskáli hut** (☎822 5191; www.ffa.is; N 65°11.544', W 16°13.360'; sites/dm Ikr1200/6000), a comfy lodge with showers and kitchen.

ASKJA

Askja is an immense 50-sq-km caldera, created by a colossal explosion of tephra in 1875. Part of the volcano's collapsed magma chamber contains sapphire-blue **Öskjuvatn**, Iceland's second-deepest lake at 220m. Near its northeastern corner is **Víti**, a tepid pool in a tephra crater where the milky-blue water (around 25°C) is ideal for a soak.

The **Dreki huts** (Askja Camp; ☎822 5190; www.ffa.is; N 65°02.503', W 16°35.690'; site/dm per person Ikr1200/6500; ⏲mid-/late Jun-early Sep) at **Drekagil** (Dragon Ravine), 8km away, accommodate 60 people.

Loads of super-Jeep tours run to the Askja caldera, primarily from Mývatn.

UNDERSTAND ICELAND

History

Geologically young, staunchly independent and frequently rocked by natural (and more recently financial) disaster, Iceland has a turbulent and absorbing history of Norse settlement, literary genius, bitter feuding and foreign oppression.

Viking Beginnings

Irish monks were probably the first people to come to Iceland in around AD 700. Their solitude was rudely shattered by the Settlement Era (871–930), when a wave of Nordic people descended, driven from the Scandinavian mainland by political clashes. Many raided Ireland and the Scottish islands on the way, bringing Celtic slaves to the new country.

Ingólfur Arnarson, a Norwegian fugitive, became the first official Icelander (AD 871). He settled at Reykjavík (Smoky Bay), which he named after steam he saw rising from geothermal vents. According to 12th-century sources, Ingólfur built his farm on Aðalstræti. Recent archaeological excavations have unearthed a Viking longhouse on that very spot; the dwelling is now the focus of the Reykjavík 871+/-2 museum.

The settlers rejected monarchy and established the world's first democratic parliament at Þingvellir (Parliament Plains), outside Reykjavík. The country converted to Christianity in the year 1000.

Six-Hundred Years of Misery

Two hundred years of peace ended during the Sturlung Age (1230–62), when Iceland's chieftains descended into bloody territorial fighting. Under pressure from the Norwegian king and with few alternatives, Iceland ceded control of the country to Norway in 1262. In 1397 the Kalmar Union of Norway, Sweden and Denmark brought Iceland under Danish rule. For the next six centuries, the forgotten country endured a dark age of famine, disease and disastrous volcanic eruptions.

In the early 17th century, the Danish king imposed a trade monopoly that was exploited by foreign merchants. In an attempt to bypass the crippling embargo, weaving, tanning and wool-dyeing factories were built, which led to the foundation of the city of Reykjavík.

Iceland's next calamity was volcanic. In 1783 the vast crater row Lakagígar (Laki) erupted for 10 months, devastating southeastern Iceland and creating a lingering poisonous haze. Nearly 75% of Iceland's livestock and 20% of the human population perished in the resulting famine; an evacuation of the country was discussed.

Birth of a New Nation

In spite (or perhaps because) of such neglectful foreign rule and miserable living conditions, a sense of Icelandic nationalism slowly began to grow.

Perversely, while the rest of Europe endured the horrors of WWII, Iceland went from strength to strength: at the outbreak of war it was an independent state within the Kingdom of Denmark, asserting its neutrality; by war's end, it was a republic (triggered by the German occupation of Denmark). The Republic of Iceland was established on 17 June 1944, symbolically at Þingvellir.

British and then US troops were stationed at Keflavík (right up until 2006), bringing with them undreamt-of wealth. Subsistence farming gave way to prosperity and a frenzy of new building, funded mainly by American dollars. The Ring Road, Iceland's main highway that circles the whole country, was finally completed in 1974.

Boom...& Bust

A corresponding boom in the fishing industry saw Iceland extend its fishing limit in the 1970s to 200 miles (322km). This precipitated the worst of the 'cod wars', when the UK initially refused to recognise the new zone and continued fishing inside what were now deemed to be Icelandic waters. During the seven-month conflict, Icelandic ships cut the nets of British trawlers, shots were fired and ships on both sides were rammed.

Iceland's booming economy suffered when the world financial crisis dealt the country a sledgehammer blow in 2008, thanks to massive foreign debt and a severely overvalued currency. All three national banks went into receivership, and the country teetered on the brink of bankruptcy.

Help came in the form of International Monetary Fund (IMF) loans, and bailouts from Scandinavian neighbours. Protestors rioted in Reykjavík, suffering the effects of spiralling inflation and furious with a government they felt had betrayed them by not downsizing the bloated banking system.

The government fell, and in May 2009 a new left-wing government was elected, headed by Jóhanna Sigurðardóttir, Iceland's first female prime minister. Her first major act was to apply for EU membership, with the eventual aim of adopting the euro as the country's new currency in an effort to stabilise the economy. EU membership was then (and continues to be) a contentious issue.

The banking collapse was a terrible blow to Icelanders – its legacy included high household debt, high inflation, record unemployment and emigration for work.

But, incredibly, the economic situation has begun to right itself. Where other countries chose to bail out their financial institutions, the Icelandic government refused to use taxpayers' money to prop up the failing banks, and let the private banks' creditors take the hit.

Ash, Cash & the Road to Recovery

Icelanders went to the polls in April 2013 with the national economy on the path to recovery, but with the population smarting from the government's tough austerity measures (higher taxes, spending cuts). The results showed a clear backlash against the ruling Social Democrats; two centre-right parties formed a coalition government. In early 2014 the government halted all membership negotiations with the EU.

In volcano news, the ash cloud from the April 2010 eruption under Eyjafjallajökull glacier shut down European air traffic for six days, causing travel chaos across much of the continent. The Grimsvötn volcano, which erupted the following year, was a mere trifle by comparison: its ash cloud only managed three days of air-traffic disruption. In mid- to late 2014, all eyes were on the Bárðarbunga eruption (p268).

However, erupting volcanoes tickled people's interest and this, combined with the devalued króna, gave the nation's tourism industry an unforeseen jolt. Recently, Iceland has been registering record-breaking tourist numbers; the country hosted one million annual visitors in 2014 (doubling figures from 2010), and there are no signs of a slowdown in sight.

People

Centuries of isolation and hardship have instilled particular character traits in the small, homogenous Icelandic population. Their connection to their homeland, history and countrymen is deeply felt, even if the land reciprocates that love with some sharp edges (volcanic eruptions and earthquakes, for a start). The nation's 325,000 souls tend to respond to life's challenges with a compelling mix of courage, candour and creativity, edged with a dark, dry humour.

A visit to Iceland is as much about the people as it is about the landscapes. The warmth of Icelanders is disarming, as is their industriousness – they're working hard to recover from financial upheaval, and to transform Iceland into a destination that can host triple its population each year. And though they may initially come across as reserved, Icelanders are notably welcoming – the most welcoming of 140 countries, according to the World Economic Forum ranking in 2013.

Icelanders' names are constructed from a combination of their first name and their father's (or mother's) first name. Girls add the suffix *dóttir* (daughter) to the patronymic and boys add *son*. Therefore, Jón, the son of Einar, would be Jón Einarsson. Guðrun, the daughter of Halldór, would be Guðrun Halldórsdóttir. Icelanders always call each other by their first names – and yes, trivia buffs, the telephone directory is alphabetised by first name.

Further contributions to Iceland's whimsy factor: surveys suggest that more than half of Icelanders believe in (or at least entertain the possibility of) the existence of *huldufólk* (hidden people – elves, gnomes, dwarves etc).

Religious Beliefs

Iceland officially converted to Christianity around 1000, although followers of the old pagan gods were allowed to worship in private. The Danes imposed Lutheranism in the 1550 Reformation: today, as in mainland Scandinavia, most Icelanders (around 80%) belong to the Protestant Lutheran Church – but many are nonpractising.

Arts

Literature

Iceland produces the most writers and literary translations per capita of any country in the world.

Bloody, black, humorous and powerful, the late-12th- and 13th-century sagas are are some of Iceland's greatest cultural achievements. Written in Old Norse, these epics look back on the disputes, families, doomed romances and larger-than-life characters (from warrior and poet to outlaw) who lived during the Settlement Era. They continue to entertain Icelanders and provide them with a rich sense of heritage.

Iceland's most celebrated 20th-century author is Nobel Prize_winner Halldór Laxness (1902–98). His darkly comic work gives a superb insight into Icelandic life. His most famous book, *Independent People* (1934), concerning the bloody-minded farmer Bjartur and the birth of the Icelandic nation, is an unmissable read.

Modern Icelandic writers include Einar Kárason, who wrote the outstanding *Devil's Island* (1983; about Reykjavík life in the 1950s). Hallgrímur Helgason's *101 Reykjavík* is the book on which the cult film was based. Currently surfing the Nordic Noir tidal wave is Arnaldur Indriðason, whose Reykjavík-based crime fiction permanently tops the bestsellers list.

Music

Iceland punches above its weight in the pop-music world. Internationally famous Icelandic musicians include (of course) Björk, and her former band, The Sugarcubes. Sigur Rós have followed Björk to stardom; their biggest-selling album *Takk* (2005) garnered rave reviews around the world.

Indie-folk band Of Monsters and Men stormed the US charts in 2011 with their debut album *My Head is an Animal*. Most recently Ásgeir Trausti, who records simply as Ásgeir, had a breakout hit with *In the Silence* (2014), an English-language album, and he has been selling out concerts internationally.

Back home, Reykjavík has a flourishing music scene with a constantly changing

READY FOR ITS CLOSE-UP

Iceland has become a Hollywood darling for location shooting. Its alien beauty and the government's 20% production rebate for film-makers have encouraged Hollywood directors to make movies here. Try to spot the Icelandic scenery in blockbusters such as *Tomb Raider* (2001), *Die Another Day* (2002), *Batman Begins* (2005), *Flags of Our Fathers* (2006), *Stardust* (2007), *Journey to the Centre of the Earth* (2008), *Prometheus* (2012), *Oblivion* (2013), *Star Trek: Into Darkness* (2013), *The Secret Life of Walter Mitty* (2013), *Noah* (2104) and the HBO series *Game of Thrones*. The upcoming *Star Wars Episode VII* was shot here too.

line-up of new bands and sounds; see www.icelandmusic.is for an idea of the variety.

If your trip coincides with one of the country's many music festivals, go! The fabulous Iceland Airwaves music festival (held in Reykjavík in November) showcases Iceland's talent along with international acts, as does Secret Solstice (June) and ATP Festival (July).

Cinema

Iceland's film industry is young but distinctive, often containing quirky, dark subject matter and superb cinematography, using Iceland's powerful landscape as a backdrop.

Director Friðrik Þór Friðriksson is something of a legend in Icelandic cinema circles, although some of his films are better than others. *Children of Nature* (1992), *Cold Fever* (1994), *Angels of the Universe* (2000) and *The Sunshine Boy* (2009) are well worth watching.

If one Icelandic film put Reykjavík on the cinematic stage, it's *101 Reykjavík* (2000), directed by Baltasar Kormákur and based on the novel by Hallgrímur Helgason. This dark comedy explores sex, drugs and the life of a loafer in downtown Reykjavík. Kormákur's *Jar City* (2006) stars the ever-watchable Ingvar E Sigurðsson as Iceland's favourite detective, Inspector Erlendur, from the novels by Arnaldur Indriðason.

Environment

The Land

Contrary to popular opinion, Iceland isn't completely covered in ice, nor is it a treeless, lunar landscape of congealed lava flows and windswept tundra. Both of these habitats exist, but so too do steep-sided fjords, rolling emerald-green hills, glacier-carved valleys and bubbling mudpots.

A mere baby in geological terms, Iceland is the youngest country in Europe, formed by underwater volcanic eruptions along the joint of the North American and Eurasian plates 17 to 20 million years ago. At 103,000 sq km, it is roughly the size of Portugal, or the US state of Kentucky. Within its borders are some 30 active volcanoes. Its landscape is 3% lakes, 11% ice caps and glaciers, 23% vegetation and 63% wasteland. Its highest point, Hvannadalshnúkur, rises 2110m.

Iceland's active volcanic zone runs through the middle of the country, from southwest to northeast. Active-zone geological features include lava flows, tubes, geysers, hot springs and volcanoes, and rocks such as basalt, pumice and rhyolite. Geysir, Krýsuvík and Krafla are very accessible active areas.

There are few trees, although more are being planted to combat erosion. Most of the native flora consists of grasses, mosses, lichens and wildflowers.

Wildlife

Apart from birds, sheep and horses, you'll be lucky to have any casual sightings of land animals in Iceland. The only indigenous land mammal is the elusive Arctic fox. Reindeer were introduced from Norway in the 18th century and now roam the mountains in the east. Polar bears very occasionally drift across from Greenland on ice floes, but armed farmers make sure they don't last long.

In contrast, Iceland has a rich marine life. On whale-watching tours from Húsavík in northern Iceland (among other places), you'll have an excellent chance of seeing cetaceans, particularly dolphins, porpoises, minke whales and humpback whales. Sperm, fin, sei, pilot, killer and blue whales also swim in Icelandic waters. Seals can be seen in a handful of regions.

Birdlife is prolific, at least from May to August. On coastal cliffs and islands around the country you can see a mind-boggling array of seabirds, often in massive colonies. Most impressive for their sheer numbers are gannets, guillemots, gulls, razorbills, kittiwakes, fulmars and puffins.

National Parks & Nature Reserves

Iceland has three national parks and more than 100 nature reserves, natural monuments and country parks, with a protected area of 18,806 sq km (about 18% of the entire country).

Iceland's three national parks:

Snæfellsjökull In west Iceland. Protects the Snæfellsjökull glacier (made famous by Jules Verne), the surrounding lava fields and coast.

Þingvellir Part of the Golden Circle, southeast of the capital, and a Unesco World Heritage Site.

Vatnajökull Founded in 2008, joining the Vatnajökull ice cap and the former Skaftafell and Jökulsárgljúfur national parks to form one giant, 13,900-sq-km megapark.

Environmental Issues

Historically, sheep farming and timber extraction caused immense environmental damage. At the time of settlement (9th century) an estimated quarter of the country was covered by birch woodlands, whereas today forests only cover a little over 1%. Large-scale aerial seeding and intensive tree-planting programs are combating erosion.

WEIGHING UP THE WHALE DEBATE

After centuries of hunting, many whale species are now facing extinction. To give populations a chance to recover, the International Whaling Commission (IWC) called for a suspension of commercial whaling in 1986. Most countries complied; however, Iceland continued 'scientific' whaling, a loophole that allows whales to be hunted for DNA samples and then permits the meat to be sold to restaurants.

Following international pressure, there was a lull between 1989 and 2003, after which Icelandic whalers resumed 'scientific' whaling. In 2006, Iceland resumed commercial whaling, to the consternation of environmentalists worldwide. When asked 'why is Iceland whaling today?', the answer is not a simple one.

Iceland's authorities stress that the country's position has always been that whale stocks should be utilised in a sustainable manner like any other living marine resource. Its catch limits for common minke whales and fin whales follow the advice given by the Marine Research Institute of Iceland regarding sustainability – the advice for the 2014 and 2015 seasons is for an annual maximum catch of 229 minke whales and 154 fin whales. Those numbers stir passions – especially given that fin whales are classified as endangered on the Internaional Union for Conservation of Nature (IUCN) Red List.

The industry has attracted international condemnation: in September 2014 a formal diplomatic protest (known as a démarche) against whaling was delivered to the Icelandic government from 35 nations, including the US, Australia and members of the EU. But arguments against whaling hold little sway in Iceland, and past protests seem to have fallen on deaf ears.

It's interesting to note that a mid-2013 survey of Icelanders found close to 60% were in favour of the hunting of fin whales, 9% were against and 24% were neutral (even considering that 75% of Icelanders never buy whale meat, and much of the catch is exported to Japan). The fishing industry is of paramount importance to the country, and many believe that culling whales preserves fish stocks (although this is refuted by studies). Most of all, whaling has become intrinsically linked to national pride. Icelanders have a long tradition of not letting others dictate their actions, and in the face of worldwide criticism, asking Icelanders whether they support whaling is tantamount to asking whether they support Iceland.

Ironically, 35% to 40% of Icelandic whale meat consumption is by curious tourists. In 2012 the International Fund for Animal Welfare (IFAW) and IceWhale (Icelandic Whale Watching Association) launched a high-profile 'Meet Us Don't Eat Us' campaign to encourage visitors to go whale watching rather than whale tasting.

To ensure prosperity continues even if the tourism boom comes to a crashing halt, Iceland is shoring up its position as a green-energy superpower, looking at exporting its geothermal and hydroenergy know-how (and quite possibly its actual energy, transmitting via undersea cables) to foreign shores. It's also wooing more big-business energy-users to consider setting up shop (it already has large aluminium smelters here for the cheap, abundant power).

The most controversial project in Icelandic history was the Kárahnjúkar hydroelectric station in east Iceland. Completed in 2009, it created a network of dams and tunnels, a vast reservoir, a power station and kilometres of power lines to supply electricity to a fjordside smelter 80km away. In the process, it altered the courses of two glacial rivers and flooded a vast area of untouched wilderness. Environmentalists fear that other tracts of Iceland's wilderness may be threatened by industrial megaprojects.

An important debate is also taking place, questioning whether Iceland's fragile environment can withstand the pressure it is now under due to the rapid increase in visitor numbers. There is a nascent government proposal to introduce a one-off fee (perhaps an arrival tax payable at the airport, or a nature pass you purchase depending on the length of your stay), ensuring travellers contribute to the protection and maintenance of natural sites.

Food & Drink

If people know anything about Icelandic food, it's usually the punchline of a plucky population tucking into boundary-pushing dishes like fermented shark. It's a pity the spotlight doesn't shine as brightly on Iceland's delicious, fresh-from-the-farm ingredients, the seafood bounty hauled from the surrounding icy waters, the innovative dairy products (hello, *skyr*!) or the clever historic food-preserving techniques that are finding new favour with today's much-feted New Nordic chefs.

Where to Eat & Drink

Iceland's best restaurants are in Reykjavík, but some magnificent finds are mushrooming up beyond the capital. In rural Iceland you may not have a huge choice – the town's only eating place may be the restaurant in the local hotel, supplemented by the grill in the petrol station. And in peak summer, you may struggle to get a table without a reservation, and/or face long waits.

À la carte menus usually offer at least one fish dish, one vegie choice (invariably pasta) and a handful of meat mains (lamb stars, of course). Many restaurants also have a menu of cheaper meals such as hamburgers and pizzas. Soup will invariably appear as a lunchtime option (perhaps in the form of a soup-and-salad buffet), or as a dinner-time starter. Large petrol stations often have good, cheap, well-patronised grills and cafeterias attached.

Downtown Reykjavík has a great range of bohemian cafe-bars. The cafe scene is spreading too, with some cool new spots scattered around the country. Many of Reykjavík's cafes morph into wild drinking dens in the evenings (Fridays and Saturdays mostly).

Every town and village has at least one small supermarket. Bónus is the country's budget supermarket chain. Alcohol is available to people aged over 20 from licensed hotels, bars, restaurants and Vínbúð (state monopoly) stores.

SURVIVAL GUIDE

Directory A–Z

ACCOMMODATION

- Iceland has a full spectrum of accommodation options, from hikers huts to business-standard hotels via hostels, working farms, guesthouses, apartments and school-based summer rooms. Luxury and boutique hotels are predominantly found in Reykjavík and tourism hot spots in the southwest, with a select few in regional pockets.
- There's been a boom of new hotels and guesthouses, and many existing ones have expanded and upgraded to cater to the rapid increase in tourist numbers. Even still, demand often outstrips supply in tourist hot spots (eg the capital, the south, Mývatn). Summer prices are high, and getting higher with increased demand. We recommend that between June and August travellers book *all* accommodation in advance (note there is rarely any need to prebook campsites).

➡ For the prices charged, accommodation is often of a lower standard than you might expect from a developed European destination. Although rooms are generally spotless, they are usually small, with thin walls and limited facilities.

➡ Sleeping-bag accommodation is a peculiarly Icelandic concept, and a boon for those on a budget. Many hostels and guesthouses let you have a bed without bedding for a discount on their standard prices, if you use your own sleeping bag.

➡ We have given high-season prices throughout. Out of season, prices at some B&Bs, guesthouses and hotels drop by as much as 50%. Many places close in winter; check first.

Price Ranges

The following price categories are based on the high-season price of a double room with bathroom:

€ less than Ikr15,000 (€100)

€€ Ikr15,000–Ikr30,000 (€100–€200)

€€€ more than Ikr30,000 (€200)

Camping

➡ *Tjaldsvæði* (organised campsites) are found in almost every town, at some rural farmhouses and along major hiking trails. Wild camping is possible in some areas (although not on fenced land without permission, or in national parks and nature reserves), but is often discouraged.

➡ Make sure your tent is up to Icelandic weather: storm-force winds and deluges aren't uncommon throughout the year, even in summer.

➡ Camping with a tent or campervan/caravan usually costs Ikr1000 to Ikr1400 per person. Electricity is often an additional Ikr800. Many campsites charge for showers.

➡ A new 'lodging tax' of Ikr107 per site per night was introduced a few years ago; some places absorb this cost in the per-person rate, others make you pay it in addition to the per-person rate.

➡ Campfires are not allowed, so bring a stove. Butane cartridges and petroleum fuels are available in petrol stations and hardware shops.

➡ Most campsites open from around mid-May to mid-September. Large campsites that also offers huts or cottages may be open year-round.

➡ Consider purchasing the **Camping Card** (www.campingcard.is), which costs €105 and covers 28 nights of camping at 44 campsites throughout the country (but doesn't include the lodging tax, electricity or showers).

➡ A few car-rental places offer camping equipment for rent. Otherwise, rental places in Reykjavík include Iceland Camping Equipment and Reykjavík Backpackers.

Farmhouse Accommodation

➡ Many rural farmhouses offer campsites, sleeping-bag spaces, made-up guest rooms and cabins and cottages. Over time, some 'farmhouses' have evolved into large country hotels.

➡ Facilities vary: some farms provide meals or have a guest kitchen, some have outdoor hot-pots (hot tubs), and many provide horse riding or can organise activities such as fishing.

➡ Rates are similar to guesthouses in towns, with sleeping-bag accommodation around Ikr6000 and made-up beds from Ikr9000 to Ikr14,000 per person.

➡ Some 180 farm properties are members of **Icelandic Farm Holidays** (www.farmholidays.is), which publishes an annual listings guide called *Discover Rural Iceland*, available free from most tourist information centres.

Guesthouses

➡ The Icelandic term *gistiheimilið* (guesthouse) covers a wide variety of properties, from family homes renting out a few rooms to custom-built motels.

➡ Most are comfortable and homey, with guest kitchens, TV lounges and buffet-style breakfast (either included in the price or for around Ikr1500 to Ikr2000 extra). A surprisingly high number of them offer rooms only with shared bathroom.

➡ Some guesthouses offer sleeping-bag accommodation at a price significantly reduced from that of a made-up bed. Some places don't advertise a sleeping-bag option, so it pays to ask.

➡ As a general guide, sleeping-bag accommodation costs Ikr6000, double rooms Ikr14,000 to Ikr20,000, and self-contained units from Ikr15,000 per night.

Hostels

➡ Iceland has 32 well-maintained youth hostels administered by **Hostelling International Iceland** (www.hostel.is). In Reykjavík and Akureyri, there are also independent backpacker hostels. Bookings are recommended at all of them, especially from June to August.

➡ If you don't have a sleeping bag, you can hire linen (varies, but around Ikr1500 per stay). Breakfast (where available) costs Ikr1500 to Ikr2000.

➡ Join **Hostelling International** (www.hihostels.com) in your home country to benefit from HI member discounts of Ikr700 per person. Nonmembers pay around Ikr4100 for a dorm bed; single/double rooms cost Ikr6900/11,200 (more for private bathrooms). Children aged five to 12 get a discount of Ikr1500.

Hotels

- Every major town has at least one business-style hotel, usually featuring comfortable but innocuous rooms with private bathroom, phone, TV and sometimes minibar. Invariably the hotels also have decent restaurants.
- Summer prices for singles/doubles start at around Ikr16,000/22,000 and include a buffet breakfast. Rates for a double room at a nice but nonluxurious hotel in a popular tourist area in peak summer can easily top Ikr30,000.
- Prices drop substantially outside high season (June to August), and cheaper rates may be found via online booking engines.
- The largest local chains are **Icelandair Hotels** (www.icelandairhotels.is) and the expanding **Fosshótel** (www.fosshotel.is) and **Keahotels** (www.keahotels.is) chains. New hotels are cropping up: **Stracta Hótels** (www.stractahotels.is) is a new chain with plans to expand beyond its first base in Hella.

Summer Hotels

- Once the school holidays begin, many schools, colleges and conference centres become summer hotels offering simple accommodation. Most open from early June to late August (some are open longer), and 12 are part of a chain called **Hotel Edda** (www.hoteledda.is), overseen by the Icelandair Hotels chain.
- Rooms are plain but functional, usually with twin beds, a washbasin and shared bathrooms, although four of the 12 hotels offer 'Edda Plus' rooms, with private bathroom, TV and phone. Some Edda hotels have dormitory sleeping-bag spaces; most Edda hotels have a restaurant.
- Expect to pay around Ikr4000 for sleeping-bag accommodation, Ikr9,500/11,800 for a single/double with washbasin and Ikr17,500/21,900 for an 'Edda Plus' single/double.

Mountain Huts

- Private walking clubs and touring organisations maintain *skálar* (mountain huts; singular *skáli*) on many of the popular hiking tracks. The huts are open to anyone and offer sleeping-bag space in basic dormitories. Some also have cooking facilities, campsites and a summertime warden.
- The huts are open to anyone, but members get a discount. Book in advance, as places fill quickly.
- The main mountain-hut provider is **Ferðafélag Íslands** (www.fi.is), with 38 huts around Iceland.

ACTIVITIES

Glacier Walking

- Common-sense safety rules apply: don't get too close to glaciers or walk on them without the proper equipment and guiding.
- Several companies offer exhilarating guided walks, with crampons and ice axes, on the south-coast glaciers. A great place to organise your trip is Skaftafell, with companies guiding hikes on outlet glaciers of the mighty Vatnajökull ice cap.

Hiking & Mountaineering

- The opportunities for hiking in Iceland are endless, from leisurely hour-long strolls to multiday wilderness treks. However, the unpredictable weather is always a consideration, and rain, fog and mist can turn an uplifting hike into a miserable trudge. Always be prepared.
- In the highlands, straightforward hiking only becomes possible in July, August and early September. At other times, routes are impassable without complete winter gear; in late spring, melting snow turns many tracks into quagmires. Unbridged rivers can be difficult to cross at any time of year.
- Use caution when walking with children, especially in fissured areas such as Mývatn and Þingvellir, where narrow cracks in the earth can be hundreds of metres deep. Tough boots are needed for negotiating lava fields.
- For details on hiking and mountaineering, contact **Ferðafélag Íslands** (Iceland Touring Association; Map p220; ☎568 2533; www.fi.is; Mörkin 6, Reykjavík) or **Icelandic Mountain Guides** (☎587 9999; www.mountainguides.is; Stórhöfði 33).

Horse Riding

- The Icelandic horse is known for its *tölt*, a smooth, distinctive gait that makes riding easy, even for beginners.
- Many farms around the country offer short rides for neophytes – there are a handful of stables within a stone's throw of Reykjavík. Figure from around Ikr6000/9000 for a one-/two-hour ride.

Kayaking & Rafting

- Sea-kayaking opportunities abound in the Westfjords (organise these from Ísafjörður), while Seyðisfjörður in the east also has scenic paddling opportunities.
- White-water rafting bases are Varmahlíð in northern Iceland (tour pick-ups can be arranged from Akureyri; www.vikingrafting.com) and Reykholt, in the southwest (www.arcticrafting.com). Reykholt also has adrenalin-pumping jetboat rides.

Scuba Diving & Snorkelling

One of the most other-worldly activities in Iceland is strapping on a scuba mask (or snorkel) and dry suit and exploring the crystalline Silfra fissure in Lake Þingvellir on the Golden Circle, giving you the chance to dive between the North American and European continental plates. You must book ahead with a Reykjavík dive operator; **Dive.is** (☎578 6200; www.dive.is; 2 dives at Þingvellir Ikr34,990) runs daily tours year-round.

Skiing & Snowboarding

➡ Both Reykjavík and Akureyri have winter resorts for downhill skiing or snowboarding (one-day lift passes around Ikr3000):

Bláfjöll (www.skidasvaedi.is) Near Reykjavík.

Hlíðarfjall (www.hlidarfjall.is) Near Akureryri.

Swimming

➡ Thanks to Iceland's abundance of geothermal heat, swimming is a national institution, and nearly every town has at least one *sundlaug* (heated swimming pool – generally outdoors). Admission is usually around Ikr600 (half-price for children).

➡ A good online resource for pools and hot springs is **Swimming in Iceland** (www.swimminginiceland.com).

Whale Watching

➡ The most common sightings are of minke and humpback whales, but you can also spot fin, sei and blue whales, among others. Húsavík, Reykjavík and Akureyri all have tour operators.

➡ Prices hover around Ikr9000 for a two- or three-hour tour. Sailings do in fact run all year, with the best chances of success from June to August.

FOOD

In this chapter restaurant prices are based on the average cost of a main course, unless stated otherwise. The following price indicators apply:

€ less than Ikr2000 (approx €13)

€€ Ikr2000–Ikr5000 (€13–€32)

€€€ more than Ikr5000 (€32)

GAY & LESBIAN TRAVELLERS

➡ Icelanders have a very open, accepting attitude towards homosexuality, though the gay scene is quite low-key, even in Reykjavík.

➡ Check out www.gayice.is for news, events and LGBT travel tips.

INTERNET ACCESS

➡ Wi-fi is common in Iceland: you can get online in most sleeping and eating venues across the country. Often wi-fi is free for guests/customers, but occasionally there may be a small charge. In many places you'll need to ask staff for an access code. Most of the N1 service stations have free wi-fi.

MAPS

➡ Tourist-information centres have useful free maps of their town and region. They also stock the free tourist booklet *Around Iceland*, with information and town plans. Tourist-info centres, petrol stations and bookshops all sell road atlases and maps. Serious hikers can ask at info centres, which often sell excellent regional walking maps, or at national park visitor centres.

MONEY

Currency Iceland uses the króna (plural krónur; indicated by Ikr, ISK or simply kr). Coins come in denominations of 1, 5, 10, 50 and 100 krónur. Notes come in 500, 1000, 2000, 5000 and 10,000 krónur denominations.

Some accommodation providers and tour operators quote their prices in euro, but these must be paid in Icelandic krónur.

Value-added tax VAT is included in marked prices: spend over Ikr4000 in a shop offering 'Tax-Free Shopping' and you can claim back up to 15%. Shop staff will give you a tax-refund form; hand it in at the Reykjavík tourist office, the airport or the ferry terminal for a rebate.

ATMs Almost every town in Iceland has a bank with an ATM, where you can withdraw cash using MasterCard, Visa, Maestro or Cirrus cards.

Tipping Not required.

OPENING HOURS

➡ Many attractions and tourist-oriented businesses in Iceland are only open for a short summer season, typically June to August.

➡ As tourism increases at a rapid pace, some businesses are vague about their opening and closing dates (increasingly, seasonal restaurants or guesthouses may open sometime in May, or even April 'if there's enough tourists around'; conversely, they may stay open until the end of September or into October if demand warrants it). The best advice is to check websites, and ask around.

Opening hours in general tend to be far longer from June to August, and shorter from September to May. Standard opening hours:

Banks 9am–4pm Monday to Friday

Cafe-bars 10am–1am Sunday to Thursday, 10am to between 3am and 6am Friday and Saturday

Cafes 10am–6pm

Offices 9am–5pm Monday to Friday

Petrol stations 8am–10pm or 11pm

Post offices 9am–4pm or 4.30pm Monday to Friday (to 6pm in larger towns)

Restaurants 11.30am–2.30pm and 6–9pm or 10pm

Shops 10am–6pm Monday to Friday, 10am–4pm Saturday; some Sunday opening in Reykjavík malls and major shopping strips

Supermarkets 9am–8pm (later in Reykjavík)

Vinbuð (government-run alcohol stores) Variable; many outside Reykjavík only open for a couple of hours per day

PUBLIC HOLIDAYS

New Year's Day 1 January

Easter March or April (Maundy Thursday and Good Friday to Easter Monday; changes annually)

> **SAFE TRAVEL**
>
> A good place to learn about minimising your risks while travelling in Iceland is **Safetravel** (www.safetravel.is), an initiative of the Icelandic search-and-rescue association.
>
> In geothermal areas avoid thin crusts of lighter-coloured soil around steaming fissures and mudpots. Snowfields may overlie fissures, sharp lava chunks or slippery slopes of scoria (volcanic slag). Don't underestimate the weather: only attempt isolated hiking if you know what you're doing.

First Day of Summer First Thursday after 18 April
Labour Day 1 May
Ascension Day May or June (changes annually)
Whit Sunday and Whit Monday May or June (changes annually)
National Day 17 June
Commerce Day First Monday in August
Christmas 24 to 26 December
New Year's Eve 31 December

TELEPHONE

Public phones Elusive these days; there may be one outside the bus station, and at the local petrol station. Many payphones accept credit cards as well as coins.

Mobile phones The cheapest and most practical way to make calls at local rates is to purchase an Icelandic SIM card and pop it into your own mobile (cell) phone. You can buy a prepaid SIM card at bookshops, grocery stores and petrol stations throughout the country. Top-up credit is available from the same outlets. Starter packs including local SIM cards cost around Ikr2000 (including Ikr2000 in call credit).

Phone codes To make international calls while in Iceland, first dial the international access code ☎00, then the country code, the area/city code, and the telephone number. For dialling into Iceland from abroad, the country code is ☎354. Within Iceland there are no area codes: just follow the country code with the seven-digit number. Calling within Iceland, just dial the seven-digit number. Most Icelandic mobile-phone numbers begin with the digit ☎6, ☎7, or ☎8.

TIME

Iceland's time zone is the same as GMT/UTC (London), but there is no daylight-saving time.

TOURIST INFORMATION

Tourist-information centres are all over the country, and can be invaluable in helping you find accommodation, book tours or see the best an area has to offer.

The official tourism site for the country is **Visit Iceland** (www.visiticeland.com), which has comprehensive information. Visit its **Inspired by Iceland** (www.inspiredbyiceland.com) site to be, well, inspired.

VISAS

For more information contact the nearest Icelandic embassy or consulate, or check online at www.utl.is.

See the main Directory section (p484) for entry requirements.

ℹ Getting There & Away

AIR

Iceland's main airport is **Keflavík International Airport** (KEF; ☎425 6000; www.kefairport.is), 48km southwest of Reykjavík.

Internal flights and those to Greenland and the Faroes use the small **Reykjavík Airport** (Reykjavíkurflugvöllur; Map p220; www.reykjavikairport.is; Innanlandsflug) in central Reykjavík.

Airlines Flying to/from Iceland

A growing number of airlines fly to Iceland; some have services only from June to August.

- Air Berlin
- Air Greenland
- Air Iceland
- Atlantic Airways
- Austrian
- Delta
- easyJet
- flybe
- Germanwings
- Icelandair
- Lufthansa
- Norwegian
- SAS
- Transavia France
- WOW air

SEA

Smyril Line (www.smyrilline.com) operates a pricey but well-patronised weekly car ferry, the *Norröna*, from Hirsthals (Denmark) through Tórshavn (Faroe Islands) to Seyðisfjörður in east Iceland. For more information, see p485.

Getting Around

There is no train network in Iceland. The most common way for visitors to get around the island is to rent a car and drive.

There's a decent bus network operating from approximately mid-May to mid-September to get you between major destinations, but don't discount internal flights to help you maximise your time.

AIR

Iceland has an extensive network of domestic flights, which locals use almost like buses. In winter a flight can be the only way to get between destinations, but weather at this time of year can play havoc with schedules.

Note that almost all domestic flights depart from the small domestic airport in Reykjavík (ie *not* the major international airport at Keflavík).

Airlines

Air Iceland (Flugfélag Íslands; www.airiceland.is) Not to be confused with international carrier Icelandair. Destinations covered: Reykjavík, Akureyri, Grimsey, Ísafjörður, Vopnafjörður, Egilsstaðir and Þórshöfn. Offers some fly-in day tours. Online deals for one-way flights start at around Ikr9500.

Eagle Air (www.eagleair.is) Operates scheduled flights to five smaller airstrips from Reykjavík: Vestmannaeyjar, Húsavík, Höfn, Bíldudalur and Gjögur. One-way flights cost Ikr19,200 to Ikr28,300. There are also a number of day tours.

BICYCLE

- Cycling is a fantastic (and increasingly popular) way to see the country's landscapes, but you should be prepared for harsh conditions. Gale-force winds, driving rain, sandstorms, sleet and sudden flurries of snow are possible at any time of year. Bring the best waterproofing money can buy.
- Worth knowing: you can always put your bike on a bus if things become intolerable – space may be a problem so show up early or book ahead. It's free to take a bike on Strætó services; other companies (Sterna, SBA-Norðurleið) charge around Ikr3500.
- Puncture-repair kits and spares are hard to come by outside Reykjavík, so bring your own or stock up in the capital.
- A brilliant resource: the English pages of the website of the **Icelandic Mountain Bike Club** (http://fjallahjolaklubburinn.is). It links to the annually updated *Cycling Iceland* map – an invaluable source of info.
- Most airlines will carry your bike in the hold if you pack it correctly in a bike box. Reykjavík City Hostel (p230) offers facilities to assemble and disassemble bikes and will store bike boxes (it's adjacent to the Reykjavík Campsite).
- The Smyril Line ferry from Denmark transports bikes for €15 each way.
- Various places rent out mountain bikes, but in general these are intended for local use only, and often aren't up to long-haul travel. If you're planning a big trip, consider bringing your bike from home. Alternatively, Reykjavík Bike Tours (p228) has touring bikes for rent.

BOAT

The following Icelandic car ferries are in operation:

Dalvík–Hrísey/Grímsey (www.saefari.is)

Landeyjahöfn–Vestmannaeyjar (www.herjolfur.is)

Stykkishólmur–Brjánslækur (www.seatours.is)

From June to August, Bolungarvík and Ísafjörður have boat services to points in Hornstrandir (Westfjords).

BUS

- Iceland has an extensive network of long-distance bus routes with services provided by a number of companies.
- From roughly mid-May to mid-September there are regular scheduled buses to most places on the Ring Road, into the popular hiking areas of the southwest, and to larger towns in the Westfjords and Eastfjords and on the Reykjanes and Snæfellsnes Peninsulas. The rest of the year, services range from daily to nonexistent.
- In summer there are 4WD buses along a few F roads, including the highland Kjölur and Sprengisandur routes (inaccessible to 2WD cars).
- Worth knowing: many bus services can be used as day tours (the bus spends a few hours at the final destination before returning to the departure point, and may stop for a half-hour at various tourist destinations en route), or as regular transport, getting off at a certain point and travelling further a day or two later.
- Bus companies operate from different terminals. In small towns, buses usually stop at the main petrol station, but that's not a given – it pays to double-check.

Companies

Main bus companies:

Reykjavík Excursions (☎580 5400; www.re.is)

SBA-Norðurleið (☎550 0700; www.sba.is)

Sterna (☎551 1166; www.sterna.is)

Strætó (☎540 2700; www.straeto.is)

Bus Passes

Bus operators offer 'bus passports' every summer (valid from mid-June to the first week of September), with the aim of making public transport around the island as easy as possible. Note: at the time of writing, none of the passports cover the Westfjords, but services along the highland Sprengisandur and Kjölur routes can be included.

If you're considering touring Iceland by bus, do your homework before buying a bus pass. It's still significantly more convenient (and may be cheaper, if you are two or more) to hire your own vehicle.

Passes lock you into using the services of one company, and no Icelandic bus company offers the perfect network – each has significant geographic gaps in service, and most routes only run once per day. Strætó has the biggest bus network but is not a part of any pass. You may be better off buying separate tickets for each leg of your journey, using the bus service that offers you the best route at the time.

Visit www.re.is/iceland-on-your-own and www.sterna.is/en/bus-passport for list of passports and their coverage.

CAR & MOTORCYCLE

➡ Driving in Iceland gives you unparalleled freedom to discover the country and, thanks to good roads and light traffic, it's all fairly straightforward.

➡ The 1330km Ring Road (Rte 1) circles the country and, except for a couple of small stretches in east Iceland, is paved. Beyond the Ring Road, fingers of sealed road or gravel stretch out to most communities.

➡ In coastal areas driving can be spectacularly scenic, and incredibly slow as you weave up and down over unpaved mountain passes and in and out of long fjords. Even so, a 2WD vehicle will get you almost everywhere in summer (note: *not* into the highlands, or on F roads).

➡ In winter heavy snow can cause many roads to close; mountain roads generally only open in June and may start closing as early as September. For up-to-date information on road conditions, visit www.vegagerdin.is.

➡ Car hire in Iceland is very expensive, so taking your own vehicle to the country on the ferry from Denmark may not be as crazy as it sounds.

Fuel & Spare Parts

➡ In the highlands you should check fuel levels and the distance to the next station before setting off.

➡ At the time of writing, unleaded petrol and diesel cost about Ikr245 (€1.60) per litre.

➡ Most smaller petrol stations are unstaffed, and all pumps are automated – put your card in and follow the instructions (you'll need a card with a four-digit PIN). It's a good idea to check that your card will work by visiting a staffed station while it is open, in case you have any problems.

➡ Some Icelandic roads can be pretty lonely, so carry a jack, a spare tyre and jump leads just in case. In the case of a breakdown or accident, your first port of call should be your car-hire agency.

➡ The round-the-clock breakdown number for the Icelandic motoring association is ☎511 2112. Even if you're not a member, it can provide information and phone numbers for towing and breakdown services all around Iceland.

Hire

➡ Travelling by car is often the only way to get to parts of Iceland. Although hire rates are expensive, they compare favourably against bus or internal air travel within the country, especially if there are a few of you to split the costs.

➡ To rent a car you must be 20 years old (23 to 25 years for a 4WD) and hold a valid licence.

➡ The cheapest cars cost from around Ikr12,000 per day in high season (June to August). Figure on paying from around Ikr24,000 for the smallest 4WD. Rates include unlimited mileage and VAT, and usually CDW (collision damage waiver). Book well ahead in summer. From September to May you should be able to find considerably better daily rates and deals.

➡ Most companies are based in the Reykjavík and Keflavík areas, with city and airport offices. Larger companies have extra locations around the country (usually in Akureyri and Egilsstaðir).

➡ Ferry passengers entering Iceland via Seyðisfjörður will find car-hire agencies in nearby Egilsstaðir.

DRIVE SAFELY

Road Rules

➡ Drive on the right.

➡ Front and rear seat belts are compulsory.

➡ Dipped headlights must be on at all times.

➡ Blood-alcohol limit is 0.05%.

➡ Mobile-phone use is prohibited except with a hands-free kit.

➡ Children under six must use a car seat.

➡ Do not drive off-road (ie off marked roads and 4WD trails).

Speed Limits

➡ Built-up areas 50km/h.

➡ Unsealed roads 80km/h.

➡ Sealed roads 90km/h.

Car-Hire Companies

The following list is far from exhaustive.

Avis (www.avis.is)

Budget (www.budget.is)

Cheap Jeep (www.cheapjeep.is)

Europcar (www.europcar.is) The biggest hire company in Iceland.

Geysir (www.geysir.is) Lists its daily/weekly summer and winter prices for each of its vehicles on its website.

Go Iceland (www.goiceland.com) Also rents out camping equipment (tents, mattresses, stoves).

SADcars (www.sadcars.com) Older fleet, therefore (theoretically) cheaper prices.

Saga (www.sagacarrental.is)

Campervan Hire

Combining accommodation and transport costs into campervan rental is a popular option – and has extra appeal in summer, as it allows for some spontaneity (unlike every other form of accommodation, campsites don't need to be prebooked).

The large car-hire companies usually have campervans for rent, but there are some more offbeat choices, from backpacker-centric to family sized, or real 4WD set-ups.

Camper Iceland (www.campericeland.is)

Happy Campers (www.happycampers.is)

JS Camper Rental (www.js.is) Truck campers on 4WD pick-ups.

Kúkú Campers (www.kukucampers.is) Artwork-adorned campers, plus gear rental (tent, barbecue, guitar, surfboard etc).

Road Conditions & Hazards

Good main-road surfaces and light traffic make driving in Iceland relatively easy, but there are some specific hazards. Watch the 'Drive Safely on Icelandic Roads' video on www.drive.is.

Livestock Sheep graze in the countryside over the summer, and often wander onto roads.

Gravel roads Not all roads are sealed, and most accidents involving foreign drivers in Iceland are caused by the use of excessive speed on unsurfaced roads. If your car does begin to skid, take your foot off the accelerator and gently turn the car in the direction you want the front wheels to go. Do not brake.

F roads F-numbered roads are suitable for 4WD vehicles only. It's a good idea to carry emergency supplies and repair kit. Let someone know where you are going and when you expect to be back.

River crossings Few interior roads have bridges over rivers. Fords are marked on maps with a 'V', but you may need to check the depth and speed of the river by wading into it.

HITCHING & CARPOOLING

➡ Hitching is never entirely safe, and we don't recommend it. Travellers who hitch should understand that they are taking a small but potentially serious risk. Nevertheless, we met scores of tourists who were hitching their way around Iceland and most had positive reports.

➡ Check out www.samferda.is, a handy carpooling site that helps drivers and passengers to link up. Passengers often foot some of the petrol bill.

Norway

Includes ➡

Best Places to Eat

- ➡ Hos Thea (p295)
- ➡ Lysverket (p315)
- ➡ Emma's Under (p352)
- ➡ Gapahuken (p357)
- ➡ Huset (p363)

Best Places to Stay

- ➡ The Thief (p295)
- ➡ Stalheim Hotel (p325)
- ➡ Hotel Brosundet (p334)
- ➡ Svinøya Rorbuer (p345)
- ➡ Engholm Husky Design Lodge (p358)

Why Go?

Norway is a must-go-once-in-a-lifetime destination and the essence of its appeal is remarkably simple: this is one of the most beautiful countries on earth.

The drama of Norway's natural world is difficult to overstate. Impossibly steep-sided fjords cut deep gashes into the interior. But this is also a land of glaciers, grand and glorious, snaking down from Europe's largest ice fields, and of the primeval appeal of the Arctic.

The counterpoint to so much natural beauty is found in the country's vibrant cultural life. Norwegian cities are cosmopolitan and brimful of architecture that showcases the famous Scandinavian flair for design. At the same time, a busy calendar of festivals, many of international renown, are worth planning your trip around.

Yes, Norway is one of the most expensive countries on earth. But Norway will pay you back with never-to-be-forgotten experiences many times over.

When to Go

Oslo

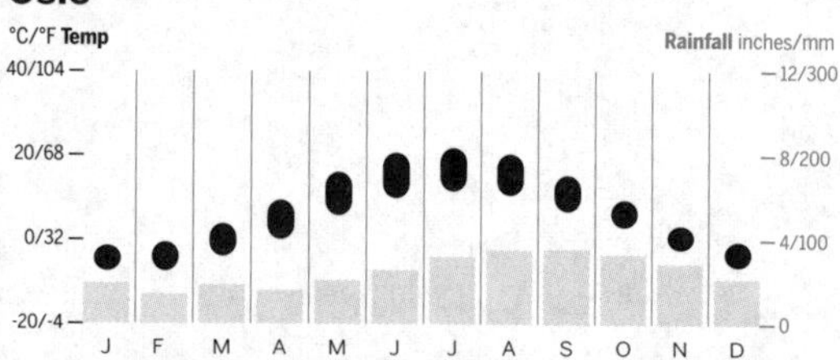

Mid-Jun–mid-Aug Summer fjords, endless days and accommodation prices fall.

Dec–Feb The aurora borealis (northern lights) and wonderful winter activities.

May–mid-Jun & mid-Aug–Sep Generally fine weather and without the crowds.

Connections

Trains and buses link Norway with Russia, Sweden and Finland. Frequent ferries head to Germany and Denmark from several Norwegian ports. Airports in Oslo and Bergen connect Norway to the world, with a handful of international flights to Stavanger, Trondheim and distant Tromsø, way up in the Arctic Circle.

ITINERARIES

One Week

Spend a day in Oslo, then take the Norway in a Nutshell tour to Bergen via Myrdal, Flåm and Nærøyfjorden. Spend two nights in Bergen before taking an unhurried jaunt around Hardangerfjord. Return to Sognefjord, stay at the Stalheim Hotel and visit glaciers around Fjærland. Return to Oslo.

Two Weeks

Instead of returning to Oslo, head back to Bergen and take the Hurtigruten along the coast, pausing for stays of a night or two in Ålesund and Trondheim, before continuing to the fishing villages of craggy Lofoten, where you should spend at least a couple of days exploring. Finally, take the Hurtigruten to Tromsø, the north's most vibrant city, before returning to Oslo.

Essential Food & Drink

- **Reindeer** Grilled or roasted, Scandinavia's iconic species is also its tastiest red meat; you'll find it on menus from Oslo to Svalbard.
- **Elk** Call it what you like (many prefer moose), but this tasty meat appears usually as steaks or burgers.
- **Salmon** World-renowned Norwegian salmon is so popular that you'll eat it for dinner (grilled) or breakfast (smoked).
- **Arctic char** The world's northernmost freshwater fish is a star of northern Norway's seafood-rich menus.
- **Arctic menu** A popular scheme (www.arktiskmeny.no) in northern Norway that encourages restaurants to use natural local ingredients.
- **Fish markets** Often the best (and cheapest) places to eat along the Norwegian coast, with the freshest seafood at fresh-off-the-boat prices.

AT A GLANCE

Capital Oslo

Area 385,186 sq km

Population 5.15 million

Country code ☎ 4

Language Norwegian

Currency kroner (Nkr)

Exchange Rates

Australia	A$1	Nkr5.49
Canada	C$1	Nkr5.45
Euro Zone	€1	Nkr8.15
Japan	¥100	Nkr5.88
New Zealand	NZ$1	Nkr5.09
UK	UK£1	Nkr10.04
USA	US$1	Nkr5.95

Set Your Budget

Budget hotel room up to Nkr750

Two-course evening meal Nkr400–Nkr500

Museum entrance free–Nkr120

Beer Nkr60–Nkr100

Oslo bus or tram ticket Nkr30–Nkr50

Resources

Fjord Norway (www.fjordnorway.com)

LonelyPlanet.com (www.lonelyplanet.com/norway)

Visit Norway (www.visitnorway.com)

Northern Norway (www.nordnorge.com)

Svalbard (www.svalbard.net)

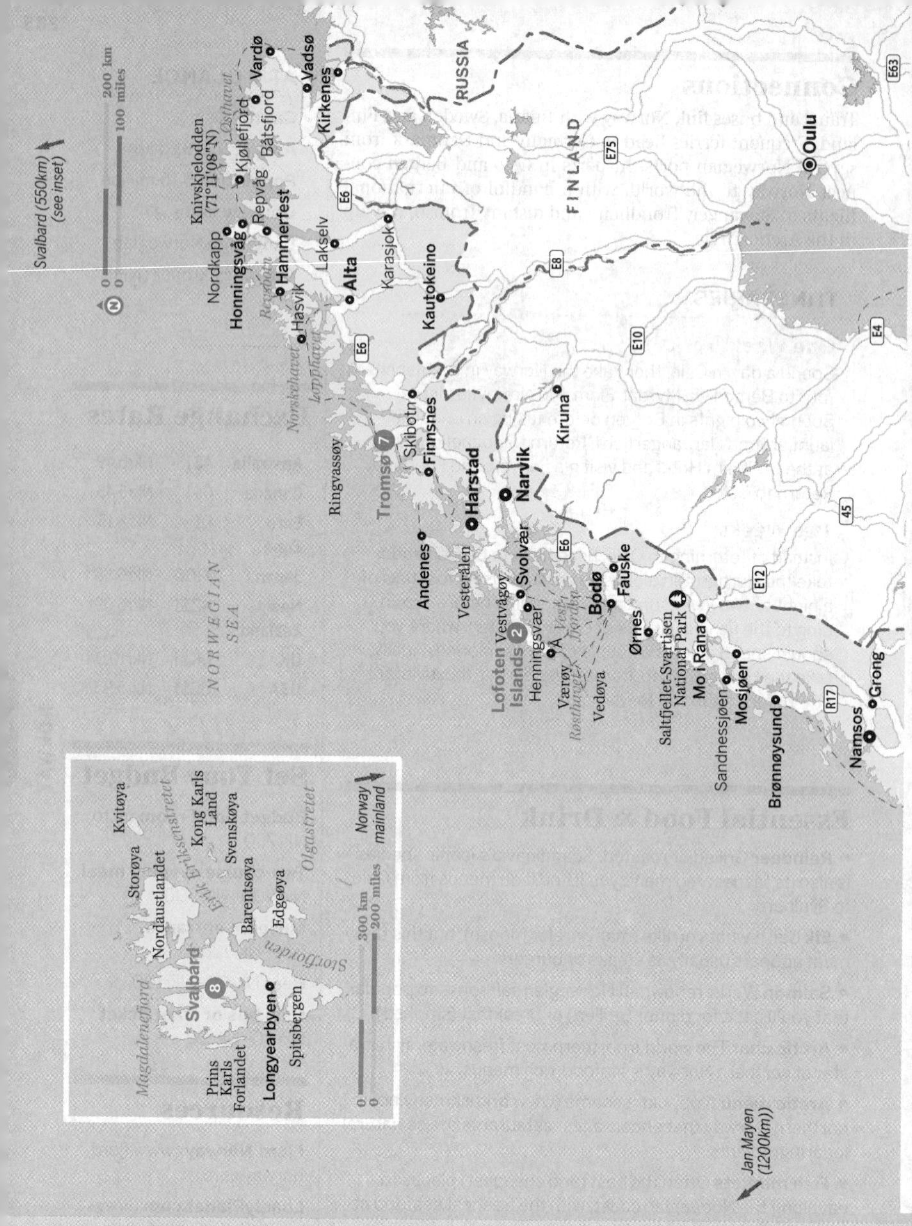

Norway Highlights

1 Take the ferry from **Flåm to Gudvangen** (p324) through some of Norway's most spectacular fjord scenery

2 Sleep in a fisherman's *robu* (shanty) on the craggy **Lofoten Islands** (p343)

3 Journey by train from **Oslo to Bergen** (p309), arguably Norway's most attractive coastal city

4 Ride Norway's jagged, beautiful coast aboard the **Hurtigruten coastal ferry** (p372)

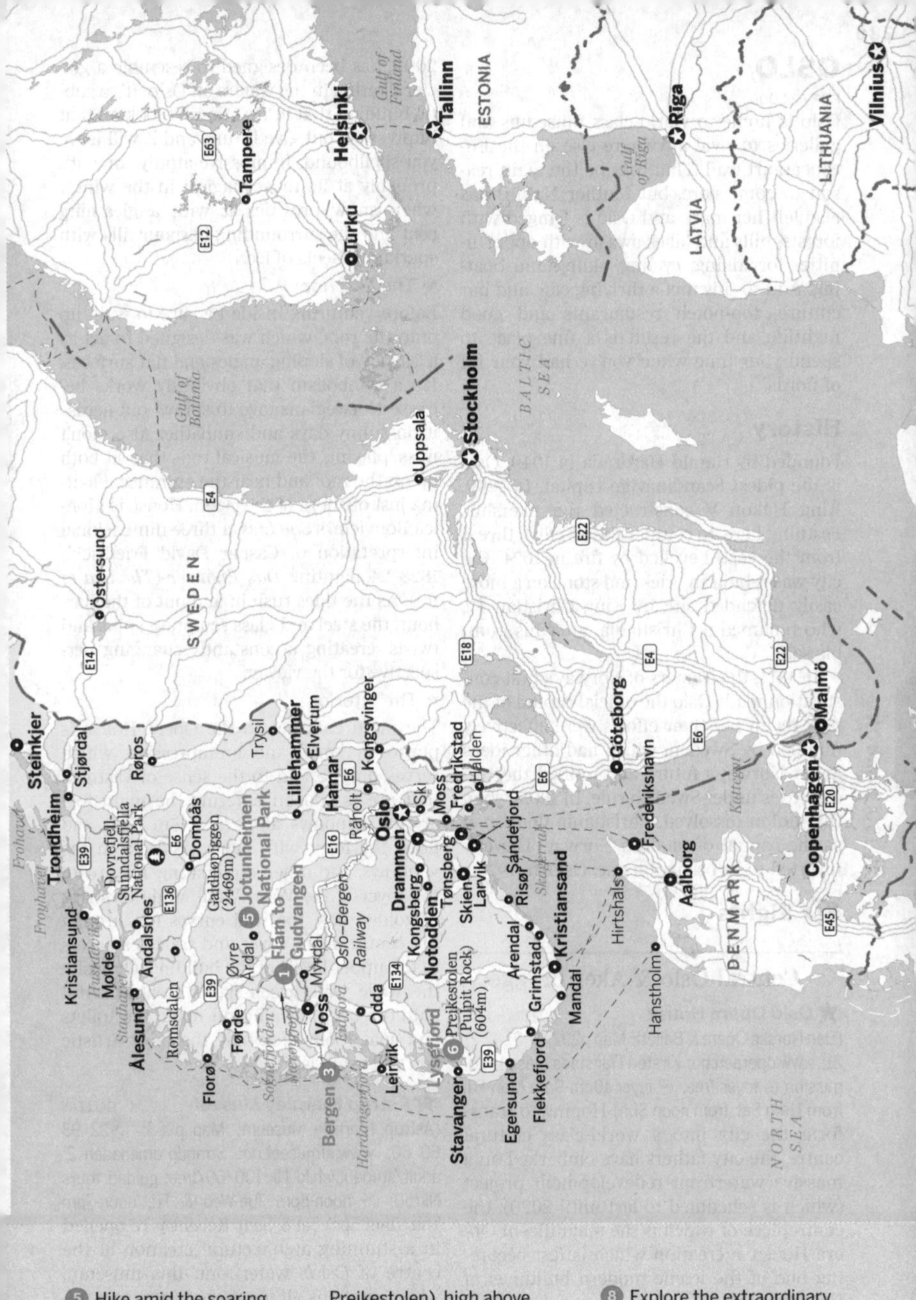

5 Hike amid the soaring peaks and countless glaciers of **Jotunheimen National Park** (p307)

6 Draw near to the edge at **Pulpit Rock** (p322; Preikestolen), high above glorious Lysefjord

7 **Dog-sled** (p350) out into the winter Arctic wilderness of Norway's far north

8 Explore the extraordinary landscapes of **Svalbard** (p360), Norway's otherworldly subpolar outpost

OSLO

POP 624,000

Oslo is home to world-class museums and galleries to rival anywhere else on the European art trail. That may be the main reason to come here, but Mother Nature has also left her mark and Oslo is fringed with forests, hills and lakes awash with opportunities for hiking, cycling, skiing and boating. Add to this mix a thriving cafe and bar culture, top-notch restaurants and good nightlife and the result is a fine place to spend your time when you've had your fill of fjords.

History

Founded by Harald Hardråda in 1049, Oslo is the oldest Scandinavian capital. In 1299, King Håkon V constructed the Akershus Festning here, to counter the Swedish threat from the east. Levelled by fire in 1624, the city was rebuilt in brick and stone on a more easily defended site by King Christian IV, who renamed it Christiania, after his humble self.

In 1814, the framers of Norway's first constitution made Oslo the official capital of the new realm but their efforts were effectively nullified by Sweden, which had other ideas about Norway's future and unified the two countries under Swedish rule. In 1905, when that union dissolved, Christiania flourished as the capital of modern Norway. The city reverted to its original name, Oslo, in 1925.

Sights

Central Oslo & Aker Brygge

★Oslo Opera House OPERA HOUSE

(Den Norske Opera & Ballett; Map p292; ☎21 42 21 21; www.operaen.no; Kirsten Flagstads plass 1; admission to foyer free; ⊙foyer 10am-9pm Mon-Fri, from 11am Sat, from noon Sun) Hoping to transform the city into a world-class cultural centre, the city fathers have embarked on a massive waterfront redevelopment project (which is scheduled to last until 2020), the centrepiece of which is the magnificent Opera House, a creation which is fast becoming one of the iconic modern buildings of Scandinavia.

➡ The Design

Designed by Oslo-based architectural firm Snøhetta and costing around €500 million to build, the Opera House, which opened in 2008, has been designed to resemble a glacier floating in the waters off Oslo. It's a subtle building that at first doesn't look all that impressive, but give it time and it will leave you spellbound. Impressive at any time, it's probably at its most magical in the winter when snow provides it with a gleaming coat and the surrounding harbour fills with sparkling sheets of ice.

➡ The Exterior

Before venturing inside be sure to walk up onto the roof, which was designed to act as a 'carpet' of sloping angles and flat surfaces. It's a symbolism that obviously works because Norwegians love to sprawl out across it on sunny days and sunbathe. Also, don't miss 'playing' the musical rods that sit both up on the roof and near the entrance. Floating just offshore of the Opera House is Monica Bonvicini's *She Lies,* a three-dimensional interpretation of Caspar David Friedrich's 1823–24 painting *Das Eismeer* (*The Sea of Ice*). As the tides rush in and out of the harbour, the steel and glass sculpture spins and twists, creating a constantly changing perspective for the viewer.

➡ The Interior

The main entrance to the Opera House is purposely small and unimpressive, which serves only to add to the sense of vastness that greets you on entering the main foyer (the windows alone are 15m high and flood the foyer with light). Aside from the windows, the other dominating feature of the foyer is the Wave Wall. Made of strips of golden oak, the wall curves up through the centre of the foyer and provides access to the upper levels of the building. Opposite the wave wall, green lights create playful patterns on the wall (and make the toilets and coat room they hide the most artistic you will ever visit!).

★Astrup Fearnley Museet GALLERY

(Astrup Fearnley Museum; Map p288; ☎22 93 60 60; www.afmuseet.no; Strandpromenaden 2; adult/student/child Nkr100/60/free, guided tours Nkr50; ⊙noon-5pm Tue-Wed & Fri, noon-7pm Thu, 11am-5pm Sat & Sun) Recently re-opened in a stunning architectural creation at the centre of Oslo's waterfront, this museum, which contains all manner of zany contemporary art, is Oslo's latest flagship project and the artistic highlight of the city.

Rather than containing a collection from a specific historical period, or from a certain artistic movement, the museum concentrates on individual pieces of work or artists who have pushed artistic boundaries. That said, the bulk of the original collection is focused on American artists from the 1980s, but today it has become far more wide-ranging in its outlook and the collection hosts pieces by Tom Sachs, Cindy Sherman and Cai Guo-Qiang. Its most famous piece is the gilded ceramic sculpture *Michael Jackson and Bubbles*, by Jeff Koons.

Nobels Fredssenter MUSEUM

(Nobel Peace Center; Map p292; ☎48 30 10 00; www.nobelpeacecenter.org; Rådhusplassen 1; adult/student/child Nkr90/60/free; ⏰10am-6pm daily mid-May–Sep, Tue-Sun rest of year) Norwegians take pride in their role as international peacemakers, and the Nobel Peace Prize is their gift to the men and women judged to have done the most to promote world peace over the course of the previous year. This state-of-the-art museum celebrates the lives and achievements of the winners with an array of digital displays intended to offer as much or as little information as the visitor desires.

Nasjonalgalleriet GALLERY

(National Gallery; Map p292; ☎21 98 20 00; www.nasjonalmuseet.no; Universitetsgata 13; adult/child Nkr50/free, Sun free; ⏰10am-6pm Tue, Wed & Fri, to 7pm Thu, 11am-5pm Sat & Sun) One of Oslo's major highlights, the National Gallery houses the nation's largest collection of Norwegian art, including works from the Romantic era, as well as more-modern works from 1800 to WWII. Some of Edvard Munch's best-known creations are on display here, including his most renowned work, *The Scream*. There's also an impressive collection of European art, with works by Gauguin, Picasso and El Greco, and impressionists such as Manet, Degas, Renoir, Matisse, Cézanne and Monet.

Museet for Samtidskunst GALLERY

(National Museum for Contemporary Art; Map p292; ☎21 98 20 00; www.nasjonalmuseet.no; Bankplassen 4; adult/child Nkr50/free, Sun free; ⏰11am-5pm Tue, Wed & Fri, to 7pm Thu, noon-5pm Sat & Sun) The National Museum of Contemporary Art features the National Gallery's collections of post-WWII Scandinavian and international art. Some works in the 3000-piece collection are definitely an acquired taste, but it does provide a timely reminder that Norwegian art didn't cease with Edvard Munch. There are frequent cutting-edge temporary exhibitions. The in-house cafe is also worthy of praise.

Rådhus ARCHITECTURE

(Map p292; Fridtjof Nansens plass; ⏰9am-6pm, guided tours 10am, noon & 2pm Mon-Sat, also 4pm Sun Jun-Aug, Wed only rest of year) FREE This twin-towered town hall, completed in 1950 to commemorate Oslo's 900th anniversary, houses the city's political administration. Something of an Oslo landmark, its red-brick functionalist exterior is unusual, if not particularly attractive. It's here that the Nobel Peace Prize is awarded on 10 December each year.

Akershus Festning FORTRESS

(Akershus Fortress; Map p292; ⏰6am-9pm) FREE Strategically located on the eastern side of the harbour, dominating the Oslo harbourfront, are the medieval castle and fortress, arguably Oslo's architectural highlights. The complex as a whole is known as Akershus Festning. Inside the expansive complex are a couple of museums and interesting buildings.

Akershus Slott CASTLE

(Akershus Castle; Map p292; ☎22 41 25 21; www.nasjonalefestningsverk.no; adult/child Nkr70/30, with Oslo pass free; ⏰10am-4pm Mon-Sat & noon-4pm Sun May-Aug, noon-5pm Sat & Sun Sep-Apr,

OSLO IN TWO DAYS

Start your day at the **Nasjonalgalleriet** for a representative dose of artwork by Edvard Munch. Afterwards try an al fresco, pier-side lunch of peel-and-eat shrimp on **Aker Brygge** from one of the local fishing boats, followed by a visit to the new **Astrup Fearnley Museet** (p286). Take a ferry from here to **Bygdøy** and spend your afternoon learning about the exploits of Norway's greatest explorers at the **Frammuseet** (p290) or **Vikingskipshuset** (p290).

On day two head to the breathtaking new **Oslo Opera House** (p286), after which take a look at all that's cool and modern at the **Museet for Samtidskunst**. In the afternoon, explore the medieval **Akershus Slott** (p287) and learn how to make the world a better place at the **Nobels Fredssenter**.

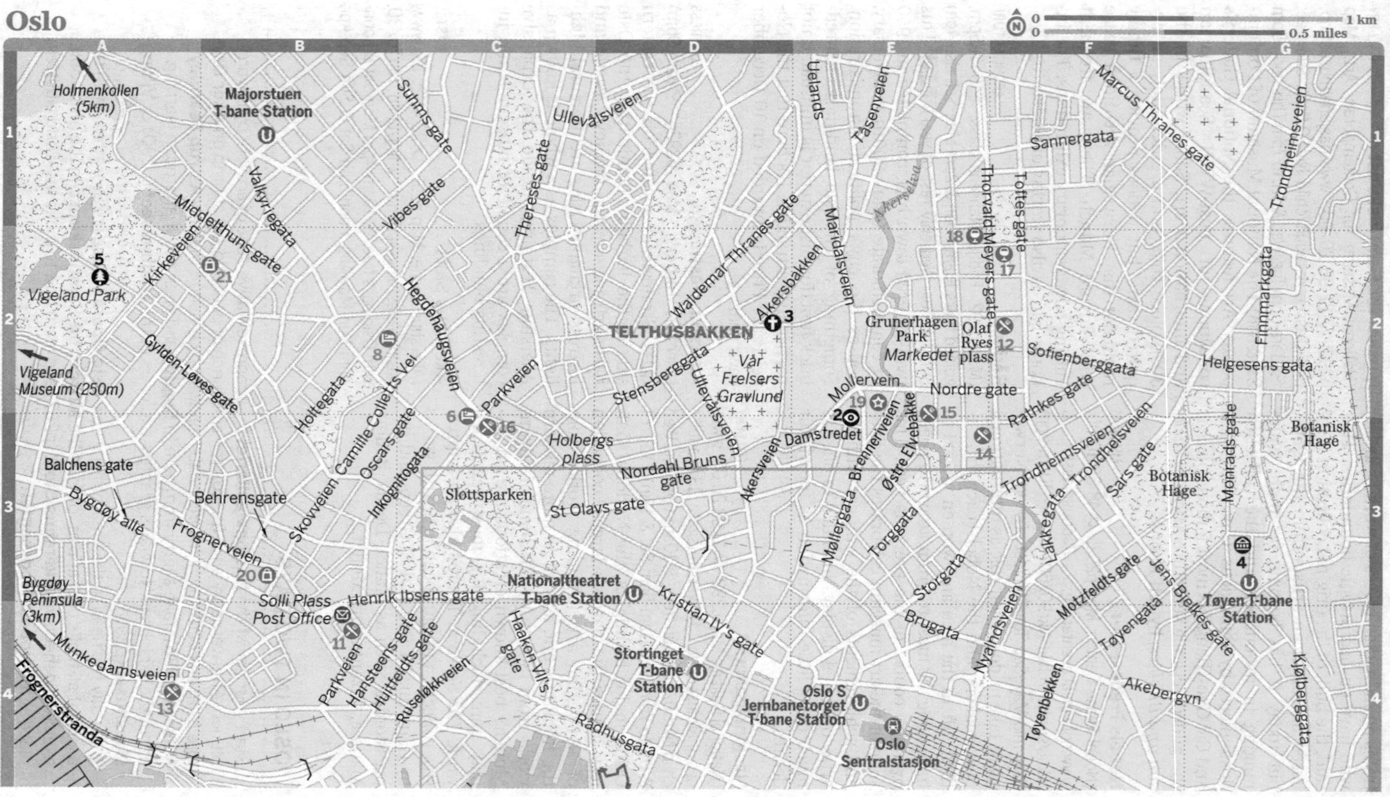
Oslo
0
1 km
0
0.5 miles
A
B
C
D
E
F
G
1
2
3
4
Holmenkollen (5km)
Majorstuen T-bane Station
Suhms gate
Ullevålsveien
Uelands
Tåsenveien
Marcus Thranes gate
Trondheimsveien
Sannergata
Akerselva
Valkyriegata
Middelthuns gate
Vibes gate
Thereses gate
Waldemar Thranes gate
Maridalsveien
Thorvald Meyers gate
Toftes gate
18
17
5
Vigeland Park
Kirkeveien
21
Akersbakken
3
Finnmarkgata
Hegdehaugsveien
TELTHUSBAKKEN
Grunerhagen Park
Markedet
Olaf Ryes plass
12
Sofienberggata
Helgesens gata
8
Vigeland Museum (250m)
Gylden-Løves gate
Holtegata
Camille Colletts Vei
Parkveien
Stensberggata
Vår Frelsers Gravlund
Ullevålsveien
Møllervein
19
Nordre gate
Rathkes gate
6
16
Oscars gate
2
15
Botanisk Hage
Holbergs plass
Akersveien
Damstredet
Brenneriveien
Østre Elvebakke
14
Balchens gate
Skovveien
Inkognitogata
Nordahl Bruns gate
Trondheimsveien
Trondheimsveien
Sars gate
Botanisk Hage
Monrads gate
Bygdøy allé
Behrensgate
Slottsparken
St Olavs gate
Møllergata
Torggata
Lakkegata
Frognerveien
4
20
Nationaltheatret T-bane Station
Storgata
Motzfeldts gate
Jens Bjelkes gate
Bygdøy Peninsula (3km)
Solli Plass
Post Office
Henrik Ibsens gate
Kristian IV's gate
Nyalndsveien
Tøyen T-bane Station
Haakon VII's gate
Brugata
Tøyengata
11
Munkedamsveien
Parkveien
Hansteens gate
Huitfeldts gate
Stortinget T-bane Station
Kjølberggata
13
Ruseløkkveien
Oslo S
Jernbanetorget T-bane Station
Tøyenbekken
Akebergvn
Frognerstranda
Rådhusgata
Oslo Sentralstasjon

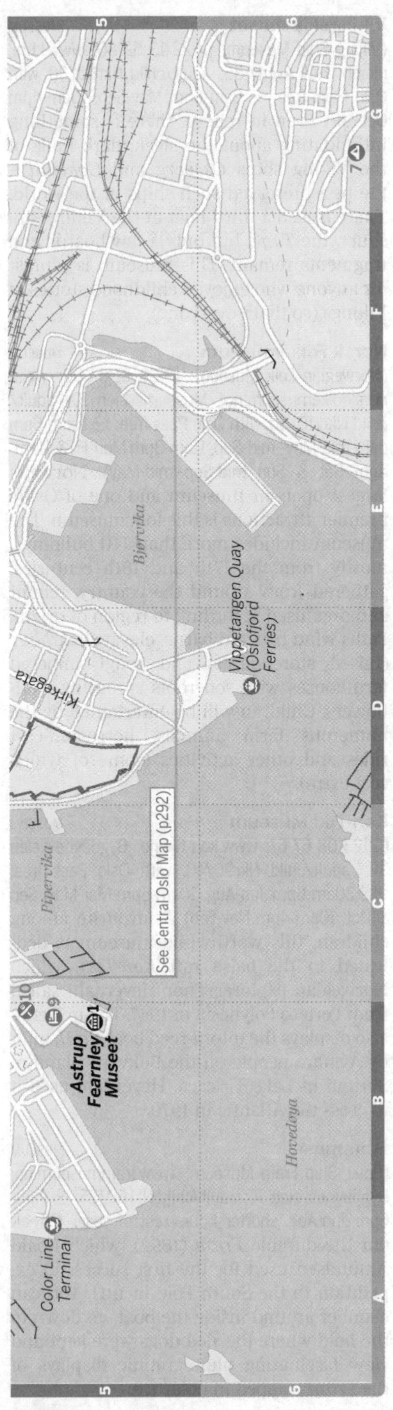

Oslo

Top Sights

1 Astrup Fearnley Museet B5

Sights

2 Damstredet E3
3 Gamle Aker Kirke D2
4 Munchmuseet G3
5 Vigeland Park A2

Sleeping

6 Cochs Pensjonat C3
7 Ekeberg Camping G6
8 Ellingsens Pensjonat B2
9 The Thief B5

Eating

10 Bølgen & Moi B5
11 Fauna B4
12 Fru Hagen F2
13 Hos Thea A4
14 Kolonihagen Grünerløkkha E3
15 Markveien Mat & Vinhus E2
16 Rust C3

Drinking & Nightlife

17 Bar Boca F2
18 Tea Lounge E2

Entertainment

19 Blå E2

Shopping

20 Hassan og Den Dama B3
21 Vestkanttorget Flea Market B2

guided tours 11am, 1pm, 3pm mid-Jun–mid-Aug, shorter hours May–mid-Jun & mid-Aug–Sep) In the 17th century, Christian IV renovated Akershus Castle into a Renaissance palace, although the front remains decidedly medieval. In its dungeons you'll find dark cubbyholes where outcast nobles were kept under lock and key, while the upper floors contained sharply contrasting lavish banquet halls and staterooms.

Damstredet OLD TOWN

(Map p288) The quirky 18th-century wooden homes of the Damstredet district and the nearby Telthusbakken are a nice change of pace from the modern architecture of the city centre. Once an impoverished shanty town, Damstredet has become a popular residential neighbourhood for artists. To get there, walk north on Akersgata and turn right on Damstredet gate. Telthusbakken is a little further up Akersgata, also on the right.

OSLO PASS

Oslo Pass (www.visitoslo.com/en/activities-and-attractions/oslo-pass; adult 1/2/3 days Nkr290/425/535, child & senior Nkr145/215/270), sold at the tourist office, is one popular way of cutting transport and ticket costs around the city. The majority of the city's museums are free with the pass, as is public transport within the city limits (barring late-night buses). Other perks include restaurant and tour discounts.

Ibsen Museet MUSEUM
(Ibsen Museum; Map p292; ☎40 02 36 30; www.ibsenmuseet.no; Henrik Isbens Gate 26; adult/child Nkr95/30; ⊗guided tours hourly 11am-6pm mid-May–mid-Sep, 11am-4pm Mon-Wed & Fri-Sun & 11am-6pm Thu rest of year) Housed in the last residence of Norwegian playwright Henrik Ibsen, the Ibsen Museum is a must-see for Ibsen fans. The study remains exactly as he left it, and other rooms have been restored to the style and colours popular in Ibsen's day. Visitors can even glance into the bedroom where he uttered his famously enigmatic last words 'Tvert imot!' ('To the contrary!'), before dying on 23 May 1906.

Bygdøy Peninsula

The Bygdøy Peninsula holds some of Oslo's top attractions.

Ferry No 91 (☎23 35 68 90; onboard adult/child Nkr50/25, from kiosks on departure jetty adult/child Nkr30/15, with the Oslo Pass free) makes the 15-minute run to Bygdøy every 20 minutes from 11.05am to 4.25pm from early April to early October, and every 30 minutes from 8.45am to 10.45am and 4.45pm to 8.45pm between mid-May and late August, with earlier final departures during the rest of the year.

The ferries leave from **Rådhusbrygge 3** (Map p292; opposite the Rådhus) and stop first at Dronningen ferry terminal, from where it's a 10-minute walk to the Norwegian Folk Museum and a 15-minute walk to the Viking Ship Museum. Beyond the ships it's a further 20 minutes' walk to Bygdøynes, where the Kon-Tiki, Polarship Fram and Norwegian Maritime Museums are clustered; the route is signposted and makes a pleasant walk. Alternatively, the ferry continues to Bygdøynes. You can also take bus 30 from Jernbanetorget T-bane station.

Vikingskipshuset MUSEUM
(Viking Ship Museum; ☎22 13 52 80; www.khm.uio.no; Huk Aveny 35; adult/child Nkr60/30, with Oslo Pass free; ⊗9am-6pm May-Sep, 10am-4pm Oct-Apr) Even in repose, there is something intimidating about the sleek, dark hulls of the Viking ships *Oseberg* and *Gokstad* – the best-preserved such ships in the world. There is also a third boat at the Vikingskipshuet, the *Tune,* but only a few boards and fragments remain. This museum is a must for anyone who enjoyed childhood stories of Vikings (so that's everyone).

Norsk Folkemuseum MUSEUM
(Norwegian Folk Museum; ☎22 12 37 00; www.norskfolkemuseum.no; Museumsveien 10; adult/child Nkr110/30, with Oslo Pass free; ⊗10am-6pm daily mid-May–mid-Sep, 11am-3pm Mon-Fri & 11am-4pm Sat & Sun mid-Sep–mid-May) Norway's largest open-air museum and one of Oslo's premier attractions is this folk museum. The museum includes more than 140 buildings, mostly from the 17th and 18th centuries, gathered from around the country, rebuilt and organised according to region of origin. Paths wind past old barns, elevated *stabbur* (raised storehouses) and rough-timbered farmhouses with sod roofs sprouting wildflowers. Children will be entertained by the numerous farm animals, horse-and-cart rides and other activities (some of which cost extra).

Kon-Tiki Museum MUSEUM
(☎23 08 67 67; www.kon-tiki.no; Bygdøynesveien 36; adult/child Nkr90/40, with Oslo Pass free; ⊗9.30am-6pm Jun-Aug, 10am-5pm Mar-May, Sep & Oct, 10am-4pm Nov-Feb) A favourite among children, this worthwhile museum is dedicated to the balsa raft *Kon-Tiki,* which Norwegian explorer Thor Heyerdahl sailed from Peru to Polynesia in 1947. The museum also displays the totora-reed boat *Ra II,* built by Aymara people on the Bolivian island of Suriqui in Lake Titicaca. Heyerdahl used it to cross the Atlantic in 1970.

Frammuseet MUSEUM
(Polar Ship Fram Museum; www.frammuseum.no; Bygdøynesveien 36; adult/child Nkr60/25; ⊗9am-6pm Jun-Aug, shorter hours rest of year) Check out the durable *Fram* (1892), which Roald Amundsen used for the first successful expedition to the South Pole in 1911. You can clamber around inside the boat, go down to the hold where the sled dogs were kept and view fascinating photographic displays of the *Fram* trapped in polar ice.

Greater Oslo

★Munchmuseet GALLERY
(Munch Museum; Map p288; ☎23 49 35 00; www.munchmuseet.no; Tøyengata 53; adult/child Nkr95/40, with Oslo Pass free; ⏰10am-5pm daily mid-Jun–Sep, 11am-5pm Wed-Mon rest of year) Fans of Edvard Munch (1863–1944) won't want to miss the Munch Museum, which is dedicated to his life's work and has most of the pieces not contained in the National Gallery. The museum provides a comprehensive look at the artist's work, from dark *(The Sick Child)* to light *(Spring Ploughing)*. With over 1100 paintings, 4500 watercolours and 18,000 prints and sketching books bequeathed to the city by Munch himself, this is a landmark collection.

Vigeland Park PARK
(Map p288) The centrepiece of Frognerparken is an extraordinary open-air showcase of work by Norway's best-loved sculptor, Gustav Vigeland. Statistically one of the top tourist attractions in Norway, Vigeland Park is brimming with 212 granite and bronze Vigeland works. His highly charged work ranges from entwined lovers and tranquil elderly couples to contempt-ridden beggars. His most renowned work, *Sinataggen* (*Little Hot-Head*), portrays a London child in a mood of particular ill humour.

Vigeland Museum GALLERY
(www.vigeland.museum.no; Nobelsgata 32; adult/child Nkr60/30, with Oslo Pass free; ⏰10am-5pm Tue-Sun May-Aug, 12-4pm Tue-Sun rest of year) For an in-depth look at Gustav Vigeland's work, visit the Vigeland Museum, opposite the southern entrance to Frognerparken. It was built by the city in the 1920s as a home and workshop for the sculptor in exchange for the donation of a significant proportion of his life's work. It contains his early collection of statuary and monuments to public figures, as well as plaster moulds, woodblock prints and sketches.

Gamle Aker Kirke CHURCH
(Map p288; Akersbakken 26; ⏰noon-2pm Mon-Sat) FREE This medieval stone church, located north of the centre on Akersbakken, dates from 1080 and is Oslo's oldest building. Take bus 37 from Jernbanetorget to Akersbakken, then walk up past the churchyard.

Activities

There are over 240 sq km of woodland, 40 islands and 343 lakes within the city limits.

Hiking

A network of 1200km of trails leads into Nordmarka from Frognerseteren (at the end of T-bane line 1), including a good trail down to Sognsvann lake, 6km northwest of the centre at the end of T-bane line 5. The Ekeberg woods to the southeast of the city centre is another nice place for a stroll; take bus 34 or 46 from Jernbanetorget to **Ekeberg Camping** (Map p288; ☎22 19 85 68; www.ekebergcamping.no; Ekebergveien 65; 4-person tent with/without car Nkr270/180; ⏰Jun-Aug; P).

Cycling

Mountain bikers will find plenty of trails on which to keep themselves occupied in the Oslo hinterland. Two especially nice rides within the city (which are also suitable to do on an Oslo city bike) are along the Akerselva up to Lake Maridal (Maridalsvannet; 11km), and in the woods around Bygdøy. For more serious cycling, take T-bane line 1 to Frognerseteren and head into the Nordmarka.

Skiing

Oslo's ski season runs roughly from December to March. There are over 2400km of prepared Nordic tracks (1000km in Nordmarka alone), many of them floodlit. Easy-access tracks begin at the end of T-bane lines 1 and 5. The **Skiservice Centre** (☎22 13 95 00; www.skiservice.no; Tryvannsveien 2; ⏰10am-8pm), at Voksenkollen station, one T-bane stop before Frognerseteren, hires out snowboards and Nordic skis. The downhill slopes at **Tryvann Vinterpark** (☎40 46 27 00; www.oslovinterpark.no; ⏰10am-10pm Mon-Fri, to 5pm Sat & Sun Dec–mid-Apr) are open in the ski season. Check out www.holmenkollen.com for more ski related info.

Tours

Norway in a Nutshell TOUR
(☎81 56 82 22; www.norwaynutshell.com) A range of tours in and around Oslo. See p315 for more on this company.

City Sightseeing BUS TOUR
(Map p292; www.citysightseeing.no; adult/child/family Nkr250/125/650; ⏰first departure 9.30am, last departure 5.25pm mid-May–mid-Sep) Oslo's version of the hop-on, hop-off phenomenon. There are departures every half-hour. Tickets are valid for 24 hours, and cover

Central Oslo

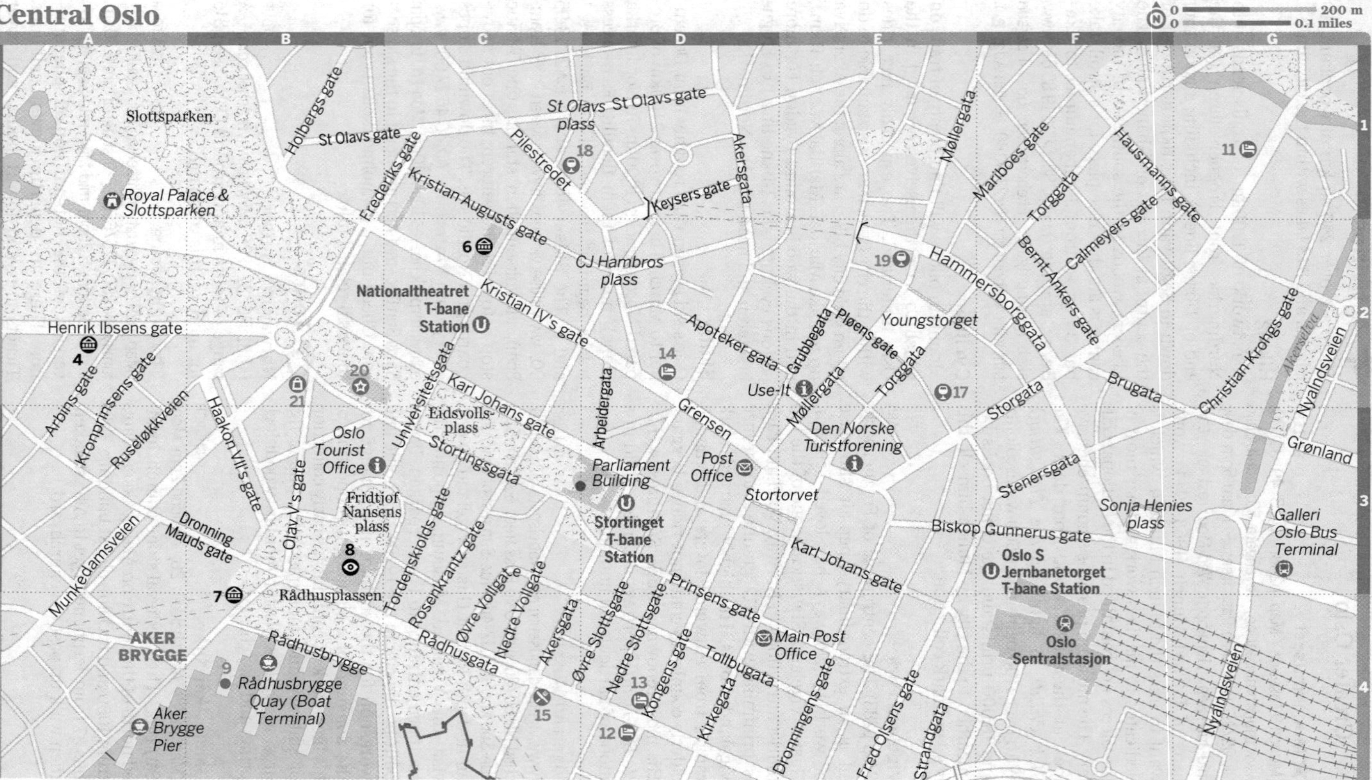

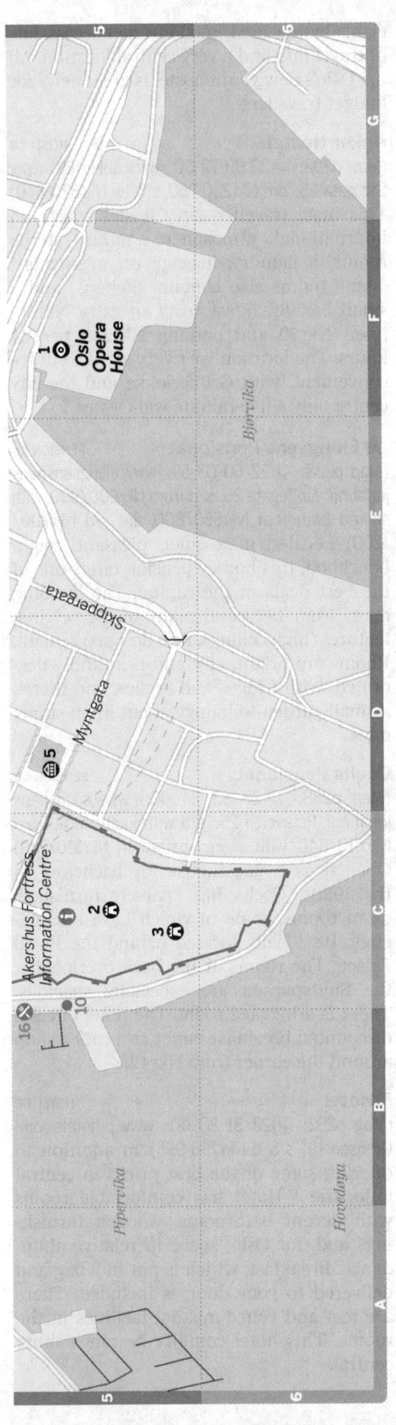

Central Oslo

Top Sights
1 Oslo Opera House.......F5

Sights
2 Akershus Festning.......C5
3 Akershus Slott.......C5
4 Ibsen Museet.......A2
5 Museet for Samtidskunst.......D5
6 Nasjonalgalleriet.......C2
7 Nobels Fredssenter.......B4
8 Rådhus.......B3

Activities, Courses & Tours
9 Båtservice Sightseeing.......B4
10 City Sightseeing.......C5
Oslo Promenade.......(see 8)

Sleeping
Anker Hostel.......(see 11)
11 Anker Hotel.......G1
12 Grims Grenka.......D4
13 Oslo Vandrerhjem Central.......D4
14 P-Hotel.......D2

Eating
15 Café Skansen.......C4
Oslo Opera House Restaurant.......(see 1)
16 Solsiden Seafood.......B5

Drinking & Nightlife
17 Fisk Og Vilt Club.......E2
18 Fuglen.......C1
19 Villa.......E2

Entertainment
20 Nationaltheatret.......B2
Oslo Opera House.......(see 1)

Shopping
21 Norway Designs.......B2

the overwhelming proportion of city sights, which you can explore at your own pace. The tourist office has a list of bus stops.

Oslo Promenade WALKING TOUR
(Map p292; ☎22 42 70 20; www.guideservice.no; adult/child Nkr150/free, with Oslo Pass free) Oslo Guide Service offers personalised city tours for groups of up to 25 people (Nkr2000 per group), which have to be booked in advance. There's also a 1½-hour evening city walk starting from in front of the Rådhus (town hall) at 5.30pm. The guides are knowledgeable and entertaining, making this a good option for getting an insider's view of Oslo.

Båtservice Sightseeing BOAT
(Map p292; ☎23 35 68 90; www.boatsightseeing.com; Pier 3, Rådhusbrygge; per person Nkr185-590; ⏲Apr-Sep) For a watery view of Oslo and the Oslofjord, Båtservice Sightseeing offers a whole array of tours aboard either a traditional wooden schooner or a more up-to-date motor boat. Some tours also combine with bus rides.

Festivals & Events

Oslo's most festive annual event is the **17 May Constitution Day** celebration, when city residents descend on the royal palace in the finery of their native districts.

Inferno Metal Festival MUSIC
(www.infernofestival.net) This festival in early April lets the dark lords of heavy metal loose on the good people of Oslo.

Norwegian Wood Festival MUSIC
(www.norwegianwood.n) Oslo plays host to dozens of music festivals but this is one of the bigger ones. The 2014 event saw Arcade Fire as one of many performers. Held in June

Oslo International Jazz Festival MUSIC
(www.oslojazz.no) Jazz and Oslo's long summer evenings go well together. This festival brings big names to the city in mid-August.

Oslo Opera Festival OPERA
(www.operafestival.no) Live opera fills the concert halls – and even the streets – of Oslo throughout October.

Sleeping

★**Oslo Vandrerhjem Central** HOSTEL €
(Map p292; ☎23 10 08 00; www.hihostels.no; Kongens gate 7; dm/tw/f Nkr395/835/1495) New and slickly run, this utterly immaculate hostel has plain and functional rooms, a big sociable lounge area, good internet access, lots of travel info and a very central location. All up, Oslo's new youth hostel is great news for budget travellers.

Anker Hostel HOSTEL €
(Map p292; ☎22 99 72 00; www.ankerhostel.no; Storgata 55; dm Nkr230-250, s & tw Nkr620-640) This huge traveller-savvy hostel boasts an international atmosphere, rather sterile rooms, a laundry, luggage room, kitchens (some rooms also contain kitchens) and a small bar. Breakfast costs an extra Nkr60, linen Nkr70 and parking Nkr230 per 24 hours. The location isn't very scenic, but it's convenient, with Grünerløkka and the city centre only a five-minute walk away.

★**Ellingsens Pensjonat** PENSION €€
(Map p288; ☎22 60 03 59; www.ellingsenspensjonat.no; Holtegata 25; s/d from Nkr600/990, with shared bathroom Nkr550/800, apt s/d Nkr700/1200) Located in a quiet, pleasant neighbourhood, this homey pension offers one of the best deals in the capital. The building dates from 1890 and many of the original features (high ceilings, rose designs) remain. Rooms are bright, airy and beautifully decorated, with fridges and kettles, and there's a small garden to lounge about in on sunny days.

Cochs Pensjonat PENSION €€
(Map p288; ☎23 33 24 00; www.cochspensjonat.no; Parkveien 25; s/d with kitchenette from Nkr610/840, with shared bathroom Nkr510/720) Opened as a guesthouse for bachelors in the 1920s, Cochs has sparsely furnished, clean rooms, some of which have kitchenettes. It's ideally located behind the Royal Palace. The rooms at the back overlooking the Slottsparken are especially spacious. There is a luggage room. The hotel offers a discounted breakfast buffet at a coffee shop around the corner from Nkr42.

P-Hotel HOTEL €€
(Map p292; ☎23 31 80 00; www.p-hotels.com; Grensen 19; s & d Nkr795-995) In addition to offering some of the best prices in central Oslo, the P-Hotel has comfortable rooms with decent bathrooms, wooden furnishings and, for Oslo, space in relative abundance. Breakfast, which is put in a bag and delivered to your door, is included. There are tea- and coffee-making facilities in the rooms. This hotel couldn't be much more central.

B&B IN THE CITY

One of the cheapest ways to stay in Oslo, and one that promises a much more personable stay than anything a hotel can offer, is to take a room in one of the city's handful of B&Bs. The tourist office can also point you towards some options (but only if you visit in person; see also **Use-It** (p297)

B&B Norway (www.bbnorway.com) is an online source of information that lists many of Norway's better-established B&Bs.

Anker Hotel HOTEL €€
(Map p292; ☎22 99 75 00; www.anker-hotel.no; Storgata 55; s/d from Nkr690/890) This busy place could be described as a 'budget business hotel'. The plain and simple rooms, which have everything you need in a hotel room and nothing more, are a perfect compromise between a hostel and an upper-crust hotel. A huge breakfast spread is included.

★ **The Thief** BOUTIQUE HOTEL €€€
(Map p288; ☎24 00 40 00; www.thethief.com; Landgangen 1; d from Nkr2890; ❄) Part of the new waterfront development, the Thief is a world-class hotel (albeit one with a strange name) overlooking the Astrup Fearnley Museum. The hotel's decoration is inspired by the next-door art: there's moving human images in the elevators, gold knitting clocks that don't tell the time, and swish rooms with piles of cushions.

Grims Grenka BOUTIQUE HOTEL €€€
(Map p292; ☎23 10 72 00; www.firsthotels.no; Kongens gate 5; s/d from Nkr1445/1645; P❄) Oslo's answer to the exclusive, cosmopolitan experience offered by boutique hotels in London and New York, Grims Grenka has minimalist, modern rooms, a hipster rooftop bar and an Asian-fusion restaurant, and is, without doubt, one of the most exciting hotels in Oslo.

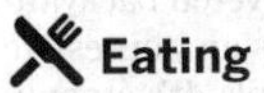

Eating

Central Oslo

Rust INTERNATIONAL €€
(Map p288; ☎23 62 65 05; www.rustoslo.com; Hegehaugsveien 22; tapas Nkr40-80, mains Nkr129-195; ⏲11am-1am Mon-Sat, noon-midnight Sun) On a small side street lined with cafes and restaurants, Rust is bright, colourful and 100% modern Oslo. It has plenty of outdoor seating and loads of blankets for when it gets cold. Good for a quiet cocktail, hearty salads or some creative tapas late into the night.

Café Skansen MEDITERRANEAN €€
(Map p292; ☎24 20 13 11; www.cafeskansen.no; Rådhusgata 32; mains Nkr110-230; ⏲11am-midnight Mon-Fri, noon-midnight Sat, noon-11pm Sun) One of the wave of sophisticated cafes and restaurants currently taking Oslo by storm. As in many such places, this one looks south to the Mediterranean for style and taste – and on sunny summer days its outdoor terrace does indeed feel very far from the popular images of a frozen Norway.

★ **Hos Thea** GOURMET €€€
(Map p288; ☎22 44 68 74; www.hosthea.no; Gabelsgata 11; menus from Nkr495, mains Nkr295-330; ⏲5-10pm Mon-Thu & Sun, to 10.30pm Fri & Sat) Kroner for Kroner, this place, with its creative dishes such as locally caught lobster ravioli with an apple and curry sauce or duck in rosehip sauce, is arguably the best place to eat in Oslo.

★ **Fauna** GOURMET €€€
(Map p288; ☎41 67 45 43; www.restaurantfauna.no; Solligata 2; menus from Nkr750; ⏲from 6pm Tue-Thu, from 5.45pm Fri & Sat) A stand-out choice in Oslo; the Fauna is all hip, modern elegance with its large, open kitchen, massive, well-stocked bar and a menu that turns stodgy old Norwegian food into culinary art that's good enough to have been blessed with a Michelin Star. Unlike some other Norwegian restaurants of this class it's quite a relaxed place to eat.

Aker Brygge

Solsiden Seafood SEAFOOD €€€
(Map p292; ☎22 33 36 30; www.solsiden.no; Søndre Akershus Kai 34; mains Nkr295-315; ⏲4.30-10pm Mon-Sat, to 9pm Sun) Solsiden means 'sunny side' in Norwegian, which explains why this place is so popular among sun-craving locals. Located inside a grey warehouse, and often overlooked by massive cruise ships, on the opposite side of Pipervika from Aker Brygge, Solsiden serves up some of the city's best seafood and has an ideal view over the fjord.

Bølgen & Moi SEAFOOD €€€
(Map p288; ☎22 44 10 20; www.bolgenogmoi.no; Tjuvholmen Allé 5; menu from Nkr565, mains Nkr189-356; ⏲noon-10pm Mon-Sat, 3-9pm Sun) Part of a small chain, Bølgen & Moi is cool, jazzy and serves decent seafood from a prime position overlooking the docks. It's as popular a place to just kick back on a summer evening with a drink as it is a place to eat.

Grünerløkka

Oslo's Greenwich Village, while always lively and frequented by a well-dressed, youthful crowd, is especially pleasant in summer, when life spills out onto the sidewalks from the numerous cafes, bars and restaurants around Olaf Ryes plass.

Kolonihagen Grünerløkkha NORWEGIAN €
(Map p288; ☎95 96 83 52; www.kolonihagen.no; Korsgata 25; mains Nkr110-140; ⏲11am-8pm Mon-Thu & Sun, to 10pm Fri & Sat) There's an old

farmhouse feel to this tucked-away little place with its incredibly friendly staff, exacting attention to detail and low prices (it's Oslo so this last statement is relative!). At lunchtime the food is mainly wholesome open sandwiches and such, while in the evening there's some fairly imaginative Norwegian dishes.

Fru Hagen CAFE €€
(Map p288; ☎45 49 19 04; www.fruhagen.no; Thorvald Meyers gate 40; mains Nkr159-189; ⏲11am-midnight Mon & Tue, 11am-1am Wed, 11am-2am Thu, 11am-3am Fri & Sat, midday-11pm Sun) The low-key and always full Fru Hagen (Mrs Garden) serves snacks, light meals and appealing mains such as local sausage with mushrooms and onion. Its location facing Olaf Ryes plass also makes it good for people-watching.

★Markveien Mat & Vinhus MODERN NORWEGIAN €€€
(Map p288; ☎22 37 22 97; Torvbakkgt 12; mains Nkr240-290, 3 courses Nkr495; ⏲4pm-1.30am Tue-Sun) With a hint of truffle oil or a dash of dill, the cooks at Markveien make Norwegian cooking unforgettable. The restaurant focuses on using local seafood and meat, as well as organic produce, to create its delectable dishes. You shouldn't miss the house specials of either lamb or crayfish.

Drinking & Nightlife

The tourist office's free monthly brochure *What's On in Oslo* lists current concerts, theatre and special events, but the best publication for night owls is the free *Streetwise*, published annually in English by Use-It.

Bars, Clubs & Live Music

The city's best neighbourhood bar scene is along Thorvald Meyers gate and the surrounding streets in Grünerløkka. The Youngstorget area has some of the most popular places close to the city centre and the new developments around Aker Brygge have brought more after-dark life to the waterfront, while the Grønland neighbourhood has a more alternative feel.

Note that many Oslo nightspots have an unwritten dress code that expects patrons to be relatively well turned out – at the very least, don't show up in grubby gear and hiking boots. For most bars and clubs that serve beer and wine, you must be over 18 years of age, but many places, especially those that serve spirits, impose a higher age limit. On weekends, most Oslo nightspots remain open until at least 3am.

★Fuglen COCKTAIL BAR
(Map p292; www.fuglen.com; Universitetsgaten 2; ⏲7.30am-10pm Mon & Tue, 7.30am-1am Wed & Thu, 7.30am-3am Fri, 11am-3am Sat, 11am-10pm Sun) By day this is a renowned coffee bar, but by night it transforms itself into what is hands down the hippest cocktail bar in town. And if you like the retro decorations and furnishings then why not take some home with you – all the furnishings are for sale!

Tea Lounge BAR
(Map p288; Thorvald Meyers gate 33b; ⏲11am-1am Mon-Wed, 11am-3am Thu-Sat, noon-1am Sun) During the bright and cheerful daylight hours, this split-personality bar is a teashop with a small range of brews and a chilled-out soundtrack, but in the dark of night it transforms itself into a hip bar, with a list of cocktails to suit.

Bar Boca BAR
(Map p288; Thorvald Meyers gate 30; ⏲noon-1am Sun-Tue, 11am-2pm Wed & Thu, 11am-3am Fri & Sat) Squeeze into what is quite possibly the smallest bar in Oslo and you'll find that you have slid back in time to the 1960s. It's retro cool and has a cocktail selection as great as its atmosphere.

Fisk Og Vilt Club CLUB
(Map p292; Pløens gate 1; ⏲8pm-3.30am Mon-Sat) DJs rock the crowd in the covered backyard of this bar-club, which boasts an impressive selection of beers and cocktails. It's a popular central spot, and on a Monday night it's really the only place worth considering.

Villa CLUB
(Map p292; www.thevilla.no; Møllergata 23; ⏲11pm-3am Fri & Sat) With arguably the best sound system in the city, this is a die-hard house- and electro-music club. In addition to Friday and Saturday, it's also open on some Thursdays.

☆ Entertainment

★Blå JAZZ
(Map p288; www.blaaoslo.no; Brenneriveien 9c; admission Nkr100-180) It would be a pity to leave Oslo without checking out Blå, which features on a global list of 100 great jazz clubs compiled by the savvy editors at the US jazz magazine *Down Beat*. As one editor put it, 'To get in this list means that it's quite the club'.

Theatre

Oslo Opera House OPERA
(Den Norske Opera & Ballett; Map p292; www.operaen.no; Kirsten Flagstads plass 1; tickets Nkr100-795;

foyer 10am-11pm Mon-Fri, 11am-11pm Sat, noon-10pm Sun) Apart from being one of Norway's most impressive examples of contemporary architecture, Oslo Opera House is also the venue for world-class opera and ballet performances.

Nationaltheatret THEATRE

(National Theatre; Map p292; www.nationaltheatret.no; Stortingsgata 15; tickets Nkr160-400) Norway's showcase theatre, with its lavish rococo hall, was constructed specifically as a venue for the works of Norwegian playwright Henrik Ibsen, whose works are still performed here.

Shopping

Oslo excels in upmarket shopping and there are many shops on Grensen and Karl Johans gate. For art, try the galleries on Frognerveien, for exclusive boutiques head to Hegdehaugsveien or Skovveien and for funky shoes or T-shirts go no further than Grünerløkka.

Vestkanttorget Flea Market MARKET

(Map p288; Amaldus Nilsens plass; 10am-4pm Sat) If you're happy with pot luck and sifting through heaps of junk, take a chance here. It's at the plaza that intersects Professor Dahls gate, a block east of Vigeland Park, and it's a more than pleasant way to pass a Saturday morning.

Hassan og Den Dama CLOTHES, JEWELLERY

(Map p288; www.hassanogdendama.no; Skovveien 4; 10am-6pm Mon-Fri, to 2pm Sat) One of many boutiques on Skovveien, this shop has clothing, shoes and jewellery produced by Scandinavian and international designers.

Norway Designs CLOTHES, JEWELLERY

(Map p292; www.norwaydesigns.no; Stortingsgata 28; 10am-6pm Mon-Wed & Fri, to 7pm Thu, to 4pm Sat) Features designer clothing and glassware, stationery and watches within a stone's throw of the National Theatre.

Information

EMERGENCY

Ambulance (113)

Fire (110)

Police (112)

MEDICAL SERVICES

Jernbanetorget Apotek (Fred Olsens gate; 24 hr) A 24-hour pharmacy opposite Oslo S.

Oslo Kommunale Legevakten (Oslo Emergency Clinic; 22 93 22 93; Storgata 40; 24hr) Casualty and emergency medical clinic.

TOURIST INFORMATION

Den Norske Turistforening Tourist Information Centre (DNT, Norwegian Mountain Touring Club; Map p292; www.turistforeningen.no; Storget 3; 10am-5pm Mon-Wed & Fri, to 6pm Thu, to 3pm Sat) Provides information, maps and brochures on hiking in Norway and sells memberships, which include discounted rates on the use of mountain huts along the main hiking routes. You can also book some specific huts and pick up keys. It also sells hiking gear.

Oslo Tourist Office (Map p292; 81 53 05 55; www.visitoslo.com; Fridtjof Nansens plass 5; 9am-6pm May-Sep, to 4pm Oct-Apr) The main tourist office is located just north of the Rådhus and can provide masses of information. Look out for its useful *Oslo Guide* or the monthly *What's On in Oslo* (both are available at all tourist offices in and around the city, as well as at many sights and hotels). Sells the Oslo Pass (p290).

Use-It (Map p292; 24 14 98 20; www.use-it.no; Møllergata 3; 10am-6pm Mon-Fri & noon-5pm Sat Jul & early Aug, 11am-5pm Mon-Fri & noon-5pm Sat rest of year) The exceptionally helpful and savvy Ungdomsinformasjonen (Youth Information Office, better known as Use-It) is aimed at, but not restricted to, backpackers under the age of 26. It makes (free) bookings for inexpensive or private accommodation and provides information on anything from current events to hitching possibilities.

Getting There & Away

AIR

Oslo Gardermoen International Airport (www.osl.no)

In addition to the main airport, Oslo Torp (123km south of the city) and Rygge Airport (60km southeast of Oslo) are secondary airports.

BUS

Galleri Oslo Bus Terminal (Map p292; 23 00 24 00; Schweigaards gate 8) Long-distance buses arrive and depart from the Galleri Oslo Bus Terminal; the train and bus stations are linked via a convenient overhead walkway for easy connections.

CAR & MOTORCYCLE

The main highways into the city are the E6 from the north and south, and the E18 from the southeast and west.

TRAIN

All trains arrive and depart from Oslo S in the city centre. It has reservation desks (6.30am to 11pm) and an **information desk** (81 50 08 88, press 9 for service in English), which provides details on routes and timetables throughout the country.

Major destinations include Stavanger via Kristiansand, Bergen via Voss, Røros via Hamar, and Trondheim via Hamar and Lillehammer.

Getting Around

Oslo has an efficient public-transport system with an extensive network of buses, trams, underground trains (T-bane) and ferries. In addition to single-trip tickets, day and transferable eight-trip tickets are also available. Children aged four to 16 and seniors over 67 years of age pay half price on all fares.

The Oslo Pass includes access to all public-transport options within the city, with the exception of late-night buses and trams.

Trafikanten (☎177; www.ruter.no; Jernbanetorget; ⊙7am-8pm Mon-Fri, 8am-6pm Sat & Sun) is located below Oslo S tower and provides free schedules and a public-transport map, *Sporveiskart Oslo*.

TO/FROM GARDERMOEN INTERNATIONAL AIRPORT

Flybussen (www.flybussen.no) Flybussen is the airport shuttle to Gardermoen International Airport, 50km north of Oslo. It departs from the bus terminal at Galleri Oslo three or four times hourly from 4.05am to 9.50pm. The trip costs Nkr120/220 one way/return (valid one month) and takes 40 minutes.

Flybussekspressen (www.flybussekspressen.no) Flybussekspressen connects Gardermoen with Majorstuen T-bane station (Nkr205) and other places, one to four times hourly.

Flytoget (www.flytoget.no) FlyToget rail services leave Asker station in the far southwest of the city for Gardermoen (Nkr190, 49 minutes) every 20 minutes between 4.18am and midnight, with departures also from the National Theatre and Oslo S.

NSB (www.nsb.no) Rail services between Oslo S and Gardermoen (Nkr90, 30 minutes)

TO/FROM TORP AIRPORT

Torp-Expressen (www.torpekspressen.no; one way/return adult Nkr220/380, child Nkr110/220) To get to/from Torp Airport in Sandefjord, 123km southwest of Oslo, take the Torp-Expressen bus between Galleri Oslo bus terminal and the airport (1½ hours). Departures from Oslo leave three hours before scheduled Ryanair departures, and leave from Torp after Ryanair flights arrive. Although the service operates primarily for Ryanair passengers (the bus will wait if the flight is delayed), passengers on other airlines may also use it.

TO/FROM RYGGE AIRPORT

Rygge-Expressen (www.ryggeekspressen.no; one way/return adult Nkr160/290, child Nkr80/160) Bus service.

BUS & TRAM

Most westbound buses, including those to Bygdøy and Vigeland Park, stop immediately south of the National Theatre.

Tickets for most trips cost Nkr30/15 adult/child if you buy them in advance (at 7-Eleven, Narvesen, Trafikanten) or Nkr50/25 if you buy them from the driver.

T-BANE

The six-line Tunnelbanen underground system, better known as the T-bane, is faster and extends further from the city centre than most city bus lines. All lines pass through the Nationaltheatret, Stortinget and Jernbanetorget (for Oslo S) stations. Ticket prices are the same as for the buses and trams.

SOUTHERN NORWAY

In the summer months, the curving south coast is a magnet for vacationing Norwegian families, who come to the area for its beaches, offshore islands and sailing opportunities. First-time foreign travellers generally visit the coast's sleepy wooden towns as a pit stop en route to more-exciting locales.

Arendal

POP 40,100

Arendal, one of the larger south-coast towns, has an undeniable buzz throughout summer, with the outdoor restaurants and bars around the harbour (known as Pollen) filling up with holidaymakers, and a full calendar of festivals.

Sights

Tyholmen NEIGHBOURHOOD

Rising up behind the Gjestehavn (Guest Harbour) is the harbourside Tyholmen district, home to beautiful 17th- to 19th-century timber buildings featuring neoclassical, rococo and baroque influences. Tyholmen was once separated from the mainland by a canal, which was filled in after the great sailing era. Look out for the **rådhus** (town hall), a striking wooden building dating from 1815.

Festivals & Events

Canal Street Jazz & Blues Festival MUSIC

(www.canalstreet.no) World-class jazz and blues, with surprise acts such as Patti Smith. July.

Sleeping & Eating

Clarion Tyholmen Hotel HISTORIC HOTEL €€€

(☎37 07 68 00; www.choice.no; Teaterplassen 2; s/d Nkr1520/1720; ❄) Undoubtedly Arendal's best hotel, the Clarion combines a prime waterfront position with attractive-enough rooms in a restored old building that seeks to emulate Tyholmen's old-world ambience. The corner suites offer magnificent sea views.

Thon Hotel Arendal HOTEL €€€
(☎37 05 21 50; www.thonhotels.no; Friergangen 1; s/d Nkr1345/1545; ❄) It might not have waterfront views, but this typical Thon is just 50m from the water's edge. Bland on the exterior, the rooms are modern, large and comfortable. There's a public pay carpark nearby.

Blom Restaurant SEAFOOD €€€
(☎37 00 14 14; www.blomrestaurant.no; Langbrygge 5; mains Nkr289-299; ⏰4-10pm Mon-Sat, 3-8pm Sun) The most upmarket of the Pollen harbour crowd, Blom provides a respite from the boozy vibe that sometimes wins at the other waterside bars. Dishes such as grilled scallops and smoked mackerel salad are tasty.

Information

Tourist Office (☎37 00 55 44; www.arendal.com; Sam Eydes plass; ⏰9am-5pm Mon-Fri & 11am-4pm Sat Jul–mid-Aug, 10am-3pm Mon-Fri mid-Aug–Jun) Note that outside the high season, hours can be erratic. Even if the office is shut, someone will be on hand to answer phone calls.

Getting There & Away

Nor-Way Bussekspress buses between Kristiansand (Nkr220, 1½ hours, up to nine daily) and Nessbuss services to Oslo (Nkr350, four hours) call in at the Arendal Rutebilstasjon, a block west of Pollen harbour. Local Timekspressen buses connect Arendal with Grimstad (Nkr76, 30 minutes, half-hourly).

Grimstad

POP 19,500

Grimstad, once a major shipbuilding centre, is at its most beautiful in the pedestrianised streets that lie inland from the waterfront; these streets are some of the loveliest on the Skagerrak coast. Grimstad was also the home of playwright Henrik Ibsen and has a good museum. It's officially the sunniest spot in Norway and has a large student population.

Sights

★**Ibsenhuset Museum** MUSEUM
(www.gbm.no; Henrik Ibsens gate 14; adult/child Nkr80/free; ⏰11am-4pm Mon-Sat, from noon Sun Jun–mid-Sep, closed mid-Sep–May) Norway's favourite playwright, Henrik Ibsen, washed up in Grimstad in January 1844. The house where he worked as a pharmacist's apprentice, and where he lived and first cultivated his interest in writing, has been converted into the Ibsenhuset Museum. It contains a re-created pharmacy and many of the writer's belongings, and is one of southern Norway's most interesting museums. The young staff here are wonderful, their tours full of fascinating detail and the odd spot of salacious gossip.

Sleeping & Eating

For camping, there are at least six nearby camping grounds that are listed on the tourist office website.

Rica Hotel Grimstad HISTORIC HOTEL €€
(☎37 25 25 25; www.rica.no; Kirkegata 3; s/d Nkr1145/1345; P ❄) At the town's heart, this historic hotel spans a number of converted and conjoined timber houses, with an atmospheric breakfast room and basement restaurant. Rooms here can be absolutely delightful, if a little staid, but make sure you're not allocated one of the dark, stuffy and very noisy internal rooms overlooking the lobby.

Café Ibsen B&B B&B €€
(☎90 91 29 31; www.cafeibsen.no; Løkkestredet 7; s/d Nkr600/900) This is a great central B&B option, run by the friendly owners of Café Ibsen. There are six simple, but character-filled rooms in a historic house, all with private bathrooms.

Café Ibsen CAFE €
(☎37 27 57 63; Henrik Ibsens gate 12; sandwiches Nkr89; ⏰10am-4pm Mon-Sat, from noon Sun) Come here for homemade pastries, slabs of cake, quiches and big sandwiches. It's in a lovely rambling space opposite the Ibsenhuset Museum.

★**Smag & Behag** CAFE, DELI €€
(www.smag-behag.no; Storgaten 14; mains Nkr115-165; ⏰10am-10pm Mon-Sat) We concur with this upmarket deli-cafe's name: 'taste and enjoy'. Come for lunch or a casual dinner and sample the region's best produce (which is also available from the deli counter) and a carefully selected wine list. A summer salad of beets and 40-degree cured salmon is a riot of colour, an open sandwich of pulled beef and coleslaw is a revelation.

Apotekergården SEAFOOD €€
(☎37 04 50 25; Skolegata 3; mains Nkr160-260, pizzas Nkr125; ⏰noon-midnight) The Apotekergården is a fun, busy restaurant with a cast of regulars who wouldn't eat anywhere else. It can be difficult to get a table out on the terrace in summer, especially as the night wears on. If so, head up the old wooden stairs for a beer and a game of shuffleboard.

Information

Tourist Office (www.visitgrimstad.com; Storgata 1a, Sorenskrivergården; ⏰9am-6pm Mon-Fri & 10am-4pm Sat mid-Jun–mid-Aug, 8.30am-4pm Mon-Fri Sep-May) Down on the waterfront inside the big white timber building. Staff run guided tours of the town every Wednesday and Friday in July at 1pm (adult/child Nkr100/free).

Getting There & Around

The Grimstad **Rutebilstasjon** is on Storgata at the harbour, though some buses only stop up at the highway, rather than coming into town. Nor-Way Bussekspress buses between Oslo (Nkr400, 4½ hours) and Kristiansand (Nkr220, one hour) call at Grimstad three to five times daily.

Kristiansand

POP 85,680

Kristiansand, Norway's fifth-largest city, calls itself 'Norway's No.1 Holiday Resort'. Sun-starved Norwegians do flock here in summer, but for everyone else it's a gateway to the charming seaside villages of Norway's southern coast.

Sights & Activities

★**Kristiansand Dyrepark** ZOO
(www.dyreparken.com; high season admission incl all activities adult/child from Nkr549/489; ⏰10am-7pm mid-Jun–mid-Aug, to 3pm mid-Aug–mid-Jun) Off the E18, 10km east of Kristiansand, Dyrepark is probably *the* favourite holiday destination for Norwegian kids. The former zoo is several parks rolled into one. There's a **fun fair** that includes rides such as the pirate-ship cruise, Captain Sabretooth's Treasure Trove and enchanted houses. **Cardamom Town** (Kardamomme By) is a fantasy village based on the children's stories of Thorbjørn Egner. There's a **water park** with heated pools and water slides. The biggest attraction, though, is still the **zoo** itself.

Posebyen NEIGHBOURHOOD
The Kristiansand Posebyen takes in most of the 14 blocks at the northern end of the town's characteristic *kvadraturen* (square grid pattern of streets). It's worth taking a slow stroll around this pretty quarter; its name was given by French soldiers who came to *reposer* here (it's French for 'relax').

Christiansholm Fortress FORTRESS
(Kristiansand Festning; ⏰grounds 9am-9pm mid-May–mid-Sep) FREE Strandpromenaden's hulking centrepiece is the distinctive Christiansholm Fortress. Built by royal decree between 1662 and 1672 to keep watch over the strategic Skagerrak Straits and protect the city from pirates and rambunctious Swedes, the construction featured walls up to 5m thick and an armoury buried within a concentric inner wall. It was connected to the mainland by a bridge over a moat (filled in during the 19th century) deep enough to accommodate tall ships.

One Ocean Dive Center DIVING
(☎38 09 95 55; www.oneocean.no; Dvergsnesveien 571; 1/2 dives with equipment from Nkr950/1300) A professional centre that runs dives to wrecks, including a downed plane and even a mine sweeper. It's 8km east of Kristiansand.

Sleeping

Kristiansand can be expensive for what you get, which may be nothing unless you book early for summer, especially during the July school-holiday period when prices soar.

★**Sjøgløtt Hotell** HOTEL €€
(☎38 70 15 66; www.sjoglott.no; Østre Strandgate 25; s/d Nkr895/975) This low-key 15-room hotel in a historic building is run by a lovely young couple. The rooms are, admittedly, small, but have big windows and are well designed, and include extras unusual at this price, such as Nespresso machines. Breakfast, afternoon tea-time waffles and evening pizza and wine are served in an atmospheric basement, or relax in the sun in the cute courtyard.

Scandic Kristiansand Bystranda HOTEL €€
(☎21 61 50 00; www.scandic-hotels.com; Østre Strandgate 76; s/d Nkr1290/1390; P @) This brand-new beachside place is big and brash, but very beautifully designed. It has a warm, textured and relaxed kind of style, and has all the facilities and extras you can expect in a hotel of this size. It's a wonderful spot for families with its beach, park and pool-side position.

Yess Hotel HOTEL €€
(☎38 70 15 70; www.yesshotel.no; Tordenskjolds gate 12; s/d Nkr748/848; P ❄) This good-value, 'back-to-basics' hotel chain steps in when B&Bs are in short supply. It does have a corporate sunniness that can be grating, but rooms are pleasant, with wall-to-wall photographs of trees, comfortable beds and pristine bathrooms.

Eating & Drinking

In summer, everyone ends up at the small, remodelled harbour around the **fish market**, where you'll find fresh seafood, beer and ice cream.

Snadderkiosken FAST FOOD €
(Østre Strandgate 78a; dishes Nkr89-115; ⏲8.30am-11.30pm Mon-Fri, 11.30am-1.30am Sat & Sun) We don't normally go out of our way to recommend fast-food kiosks, but Snadderkiosken is one of the best of its kind, plus it also feels apt for a seaside town. Just behind the beach, this lovely tiled, 1920s-style kiosk serves up hearty meatballs and mashed potatoes or grilled chicken with rice and salad to beachgoers and late-night wanderers.

★**Måltid** MODERN NORWEGIAN €€€
(☎47 83 30 00; www.maltid.no; Tollbodgata 2b; 1 to 9 courses Nkr395-920; ⏲5-9.45pm Tue-Sat, closed mid-Jun–mid-Aug) We advise booking well ahead to secure a table at this unassuming, elegant Kristiansand shopfront. It's been hailed Norway's 'fifth best restaurant' and offers top-notch Neo Nordic dining with extreme attention to detail and the best local produce.

★**Mean Bean** CAFE
(Kunstmuseet; Skippergata 24; ⏲8am-5pm Mon-Fri, 11am-5pm Sat, noon-4pm Sun) Owner Steinar Svenning roasts coffee for Mean Bean and its sibling, Cuba Life, under the Mean Bean name. This wonderful high-ceilinged space has, naturally, fabulous coffee, but the friendly staff here also serve up roast beef, salmon or roast-vegetable open sandwiches, fresh strawberry smoothies in summer, and more-ish sweets such as homemade Snickers slices.

Information

Tourist Office (☎38 12 13 14; www.visitkrs.no; Rådhusgata 6; ⏲8am-6.15pm Mon-Fri, 10am-6pm Sat & noon-6pm Sun Jul-Aug, 8am-3.30pm Mon-Fri Sep-Jun)

WORTH A TRIP

STAVE CHURCH & THE BLUES

Notodden, in the southern Norwegian interior, is an industrial town of little note, but the nearby **Heddal stave church** (www.heddalstavkirke.no; Heddal; adult/child Nkr70/free, entry to grounds free; ⏲9am-6pm Mon-Sat mid-Jun–mid-Aug, 10am-5pm May–mid-Jun & mid-Aug–Sep) rises out of a graveyard like a scaly wooden dragon. Of great interest are the 'rose' paintings, a runic inscription, the bishop's chair and the altarpiece. The church possibly dates from 1242, but parts of the chancel date from as early as 1147. It was heavily restored in the 1950s. Notodden's other claim to fame is the renowned and hugely popular **Notodden Blues Festival** (www.bluesfest.no), in early August.

Timekspressen buses run to Notodden from Kongsberg (35 minutes).

Getting There & Away

BUS

Departures from Kristiansand include Arendal (Nkr220, 1½ hours, up to nine daily), Oslo (Nkr400, 5½ hours, up to nine daily) and Stavanger (Nkr390, 4½ hours, two to four daily).

TRAIN

There are up to four trains daily to Oslo (Nkr299 to Nkr677, 4½ hours) and up to five to Stavanger (Nkr249 to Nkr474, 3¼ hours).

Rjukan

POP 5900

Sitting in the shadow of what is arguably Norway's most beautiful peak, Gausta (1881m), Rjukan is a picturesque introduction to the Norwegian high country as well as southern Norway's activities centre par excellence.

Sights

★**Industrial Workers Museum** MUSEUM
(Norsk Industriarbeidermuseet Vemork; www.visitvemork.com; adult/child Nkr80/50; ⏲10am-6pm mid-Jun–mid-Aug, to 4pm mid-Aug–Sep & May–mid-Jun, noon-3pm Oct-Apr) This museum, 7km west of Rjukan, is in the Vemork power station, which was the world's largest when completed in 1911. These days it honours the Socialist Workers' Party, which reached

the height of its Norwegian activities here in the 1950s. There's an interesting exhibition about the race in the 1930s and '40s to make an atom bomb, plus a fabulous miniature power station in the main hall.

Rjukanfossen WATERFALL

Believed to be the highest waterfall in the world in the 18th century (Angel Falls in Venezuela now has that claim), the 104m-high Rjukanfossen is still a spectacular sight, even if most of the water has been diverted to drive the Vemork power station. To get the best view, take the Rv37 heading west and park just before the tunnel 9.5km west of town; a 200m walk leads to a fine viewpoint.

★ Gaustabanen Cable Railway SCENIC RAILWAY

(www.gaustabanen.no; one way/return adult Nkr250/350, child Nkr125/175; ⏲10am-5pm late Jun–mid-Oct) Gaustabanen runs 860m deep into the core of Gausta before a different train climbs an incredible 1040m, alongside 3500 steps at a 40-degree angle, to 1800m, just below the Gaustahytte, not far from the summit. It was built by NATO in 1958 at a cost of US$1 million to ensure it could access its radio tower in any weather. Taking the railway is an incredible experience, although it's not for the claustrophobic. The base station is 10km southeast of Rjukan.

Activities

Bungee Jumping ADVENTURE SPORTS

(☎99 51 31 40; www.telemark-opplevelser.no; per session Nkr790; ⏲mid-May–Sep, exact times vary) Described as Norway's highest land-based bungee jump, this 84m plunge into the canyon from the bridge leading to the Industrial Workers Museum is Rjukan's biggest adrenaline rush. Book through the tourist office.

Ice-Climbing ADVENTURE SPORTS

If the idea of hauling yourself up a giant vertical icicle that looks suspiciously as if it's going to crack and send you tumbling to an early grave sounds like fun, then Rjukan is fast becoming known as *the* place for ice-climbing. There are more than 150 routes in the immediate area of the town.

Moose Safari WILDLIFE WATCHING

(☎35 06 26 30; www.visitrauland.com; adult/child Nkr350/250; ⏲book by 4pm for dusk depar-

HIKING & CYCLING FROM RJUKAN

To get an idea of what's possible, visit the tourist office (p303) to pick up the free *Rjukan – og Tinn*, which has a number of route suggestions.

Gausta

The most obvious goal for hikers is the summit of beautiful Gausta (1881m), from where you can see a remarkable one-sixth of Norway on a clear day. The popular, and easy, two- to three-hour, 4km hiking track leads from the trailhead of Stavsro (15km southeast of Rjukan) up to DNT's **Gaustahytta** (1830m). The summit is a further half-hour walk along the rocky ridge. A 13km road link (no public transport) runs from the far eastern end of Rjukan to Stavsro (altitude 1173m) at Heddersvann lake. **Taxis** (☎35 09 14 00) charge around Nkr450 one way.

Hardangervidda

The Hardangervidda Plateau, the biggest mountain plateau in Europe and home to Europe's largest herd of wild reindeer, rises up to the north of Rjukan and offers numerous fantastic hikes. From Gvepseborg, the summit of the **Krossobanen** (www.krossobanen.no; one way/return adult Nkr50/100, child Nkr20/40, bike Nkr50/100; ⏲9am-8pm mid-Jun–Aug, 10am-4pm Sun-Thu, to 8pm Fri & Sat rest of year) cable car, the most rewarding day hike is the five-hour round trip to the **Helberghytta DNT Hut**. The scenery takes in icy-cold lakes, snow-streaked hills, barren moorland and views back over towards Gausta.

Alternatively, follow the marked route that begins above Rjukan Fjellstue, around 10km west of Rjukan and just north of the Rv37. This historic track follows the **Sabotørruta** (Saboteurs' Route), the path taken by the members of the Norwegian Resistance during WWII. From late June until mid-August, the tourist office organises three-hour guided hikes along this route (Nkr220, noon Tuesday, Thursday and Sunday).

The best hiking map to use for this part of the plateau is Telemark Turistforening's *Hardangervidda Sør-Øst* (1:60,000), available from the tourist office (Nkr98).

ture, 28 Jun-23 Aug) You can get up close and personal to the largest member of the deer family in Europe on one of the moose safaris organised through the tourist office in the village of Rauland (on the Rt37 southwest of Rjukan), or head out in your own car with a downloadable map.

Sleeping & Eating

Rjukan's town centre has a few places to stay, but there are more choices up in the Gaustablikk area. For the busy winter season, contact **Gausta Booking** (☎45 48 51 51; www.gaustatoppenbooking.com), which can help track down a spare hut.

★Rjukan Hytteby & Kro CABINS €€
(☎35 09 01 22; www.rjukan-hytteby.no; Brogata 9; large cabins Nkr895-1400, small cabins with linen s/d Nkr950/1095) Easily the best choice in town, Rjukan Hytteby & Kro sits in a pretty spot on the river bank and has carefully decorated, very well-equipped huts that sweetly emulate the early-20th-century hydroelectric workers' cabins. The owner is exceptionally helpful. It's a pleasant 20-minute walk along the river bank to the town centre.

Gaustablikk Høyfjellshotell LODGE €€€
(☎35 09 14 22; www.gaustablikk.no; s/d from Nkr1075/1590; P) With a prime location overlooking the lake and mountain, this lodge is one of Norway's better mountain hotels. Rooms are modern and many have lovely views of Gausta, while the evening buffet dinner (Nkr385) is a lavish affair. Geared towards a winter skiing crowd (prices rise considerably in winter and advance reservations are necessary), it's also a great place in summer.

Kinokafeen INTERNATIONAL €€
(☎40 85 60 48; Storstulgate 1; mains Nkr120-179) Kinokafeen, at the cinema, has a pleasing art-deco style and its outdoor tables (summer only!) and fading interior make it the most memorable place to eat in the town centre.

Information

Tourist Office (☎35 08 05 50; www.visitrjukan.com; Torget 2) The tourist office in Rjukan is possibly the best in Telemark, with loads of information and knowledgeable staff.

Getting There & Away

Regular buses connect Rjukan to Oslo (Nkr390, 3½ hours) via Notodden (where you need to change buses) and Kongsberg (Nkr295, two hours).

CENTRAL NORWAY

The central region of Norway is strewn with stunning national parks, the most spectacular of which is Jotunheimen, a popular wilderness area and national park characterised by dramatic ravines and multiple glaciers. The immensely scenic Oslo–Bergen railway line slices east to west, crossing the stark and white snowscape of the Hardangervidda Plateau, a cross-country-skiing paradise. For a resort-town feel, try Lillehammer, close to several downhill slopes and host of the 1994 Winter Olympics.

Lillehammer

POP 27,050

Long a popular Norwegian ski resort, Lillehammer became known to the world after hosting the 1994 Winter Olympics, which still provide the town with some of its most interesting sights. Lying at the northern end of the lake Mjøsa and surrounded by farms, forests and small settlements, it's a laid-back place with year-round attractions, although in winter it becomes a ski town par excellence.

Sights & Activities

Maihaugen Folk Museum MUSEUM
(www.maihaugen.no; Maihaugveien 1; adult/child/family Jun-Aug Nkr150/75/375, Sep-May Nkr110/55/275; ⏲10am-5pm daily Jun-Aug, 11am-4pm Tue-Sun Sep-May) One of Norway's finest folk museums is the expansive, open-air Maihaugen Folk Museum. Rebuilt like a small village, the collection of around 180 buildings includes the transplanted Garmo stave church, traditional Gudbrandsdalen homes and shops, a postal museum and 27 buildings from the farm Bjørnstad. The three main sections encompass rural and town architecture, with a further section on 20th-century architecture.

Norwegian Olympic Museum MUSEUM
(www.ol.museum.no; Olympiaparken; adult/child Nkr110/55; ⏲10am-5pm daily Jun-Aug, 11am-4pm Tue-Sun Sep-May) The excellent Olympic museum is at the Håkons Hall ice-hockey venue. On the ground floor there is a well-presented display covering the ancient Olympic Games, as well as all of the Olympic Games of the modern era, with a focus on the exploits of Norwegian athletes and the Lillehammer games.

Upstairs, you can look down upon the ice-hockey arena, which is circled by corridors with displays and video presentations from the Lillehammer games.

★**Lygårdsbakkene Ski Jump** SKI JUMP
(⌚9am-7pm early Jul–mid-Aug, to 4pm late May–early Jul & mid-Aug–late Sep) The main ski jump (K120) drops 136m with a landing-slope angle of 37.5 degrees. The speed at takeoff is a brisk 86km/h, and the longest leap at the Olympics was 104m. During the Olympics, the site was surrounded by seating for 50,000 spectators and it was here that the opening ceremony was held; the tower for the **Olympic flame** stands near the foot of the jump. There's also a smaller jump (K90) alongside, where you'll often see athletes honing their skills.

Sleeping

★**Lillehammer Vandrerhjem** HOSTEL €
(☎61 26 00 24; www.stasjonen.no; 1st fl, railway station; dm/s/d/f from Nkr340/745/890/1200; P) If you've never stayed in a youth hostel, this one above the train station is the place to break the habit of a lifetime. The rooms are simple but come with a bathroom, bed linen and free wireless internet. There's a spick-and-span communal kitchen, but the downstairs cafe is pretty terrible (hot-dog soup anyone?!). Free parking.

Clarion Collection Hotel Hammer HOTEL €€
(☎61 26 73 73; www.clarionhotel.com; Stortorget 108b; s/d incl breakfast & dinner from Nkr1220/1320) In an architecturally pleasing mustard-yellow building, this hotel is considered the town's foremost address. The

CENTRAL NORWAY ACTIVITIES

It's possible to engage in a wide range of activities in central Norway. For more information, contact the following which have lists of operators and local accommodation, and can provide advice on hiking in nearby national parks:

Dombås Tourist Office & Dovrefjell National Park Centre (Dovrefjell Nasjonalparksenter; ☎61 24 14 44; www.rondane-dovrefjell.no; Sentralplassen; ⌚2-7pm Mon, 11am-2pm Tue, Fri & Sat)

Oppdal Booking (☎72 40 08 00; www.oppdal-booking.no; Olav Skasliens vei 10; ⌚9am-6pm mid-May–Oct)

Otta Tourist Office & Rondane National Park Centre (☎61 23 66 50; www.rondane-dovrefjell.no; Ola Dahls gate 1; ⌚8am-4pm Mon-Fri mid-Jun–mid-Aug)

For more possibilities, pick up the *Summer Adventures* brochure from any of the region's tourist offices.

Rafting

You can raft in Sjoa or Oppdal from the middle of May until early October. Prices start at Nkr775 for a 3½-hour family trip; there are also day trips and longer excursions available on request. In addition to rafting, most of the following operators also organise **riverboarding** (from Nkr990), low-level **rock climbing** (from Nkr490), **canyoning** (from Nkr820), **caving** (from Nkr690) and **hiking**.

Operators include the following:

Go Rafting (☎61 23 50 00; www.gorafting.no)

Heidal Rafting (☎61 23 60 37; www.heidalrafting.no)

Opplev Oppdal (☎72 40 41 80; www.opplevoppdal.no; Olav Skasliens vei 10; ⌚rafting early Jun–mid-Aug)

Sjoa Rafting (☎90 07 10 00; www.sjoarafting.com; Nedre Heidal)

Sjoa Rafting Senter NWR (☎47 66 06 80; www.sjoaraftingsenter.no; Varphaugen Gård)

Moose & Musk Ox Safaris

Your best chance of seeing one of Norway's last 80 musk oxen is to take a three- to five-hour morning **musk ox safari** (from Nkr325), either from Oppdal or Dombås. In both places, a three-hour evening **elk safari** (Nkr350) is also possible.

service is fast and efficient, and the inclusion of a dinner buffet in the price makes it very tempting for couples. For people travelling solo there are better-value options.

Mølla Hotell HOTEL €€
(☎61 05 70 80; www.mollahotell.no; Elvegata 12; s/d from Nkr990/1290; P) Although you wouldn't know it from the lurid yellow exterior, this hotel was built from the shell of an old mill. Fully refurbished with good-quality but slightly dated rooms, the hotel has mill memorabilia in the public areas, and flat-screen TVs and comfy beds in the rooms. The rooftop bar has fine views and the architecture is distinguished.

Eating

Café Opus SNACKS €
(Stortorget 63; baguettes from Nkr59; ⏲9am-6pm Mon-Fri, 9am-4pm Sat, 11am-4pm Sun) Hugely popular for its baguettes, rolls and cakes (and for its outdoor tables in summer), Café Opus gets the simple things right – tasty food, friendly service and smart-casual decor.

Nikkers INTERNATIONAL €€
(www.nikkers.no; Elvegata; mains Nkr150-200; ⏲11am-11pm) Right by Lillehammer's bubbling brook, this is a dark, warm and cosy pub where a moose has apparently walked through the wall (look outside for the full effect). It attracts masses of locals, and whether you have a craving for salad, coffee, a burger or even reindeer stew, this place delivers.

Blåmann INTERNATIONAL €€
(☎61 26 22 03; www.blaamann.com; Lilletorget 1; lunch mains & light meals Nkr109-189, dinner mains Nkr169-259; ⏲noon-11pm Mon-Sat, to 9pm Sun) This recommended spot has a clean-lined interior and a trendy menu that ranges from kangaroo fillet to Mexican dishes to reindeer. The decor is classy, yet the atmosphere is casual.

Information

Lillehammer Tourist Office (www.lillehammer.com; Lillehammer Skysstasjon; ⏲8am-6pm Mon-Fri & 10am-4pm Sat & Sun mid-Jun–mid-Aug, 8am-4pm Mon-Fri & 10am-2pm Sat rest of year) Inside the train station.

Getting There & Away

Bus Lavprisekspressen bus services run to/from Oslo (Nkr440, three hours, three to four daily) via Oslo's Gardermoen Airport (Nkr319, 2¼ hours). Nor-Way Bussekspress runs to Bergen (Nkr615, nine hours, two daily).

Train Trains run to/from Oslo (Nkr383, 2¼ hours, 11 to 17 daily) and Trondheim (from Nkr705, 4¼ to seven hours, four to six daily).

WORTH A TRIP

PEER GYNT VEGEN

Of all the beautiful mountain roads of central Norway, one stands out for its combination of scenery and storytelling: **Peer Gynt Vegen** (www.peergyntvegen.no; toll Nkr70; ⏲Jun-Sep). Running for 60km from Skei to Espedalen, it takes you along the trail followed by that ill-fated fictional character created by Henrik Ibsen and offers fine views of the Jotunheimen and Rondane massifs en route. Climbing up to 1053m above sea level at the Listulhøgda lookout point, it passes the Solbrå Seter farm, where Gudbrandsdal cheese was first made in 1863. An open-air arena next to Gålåvatn lake is the scene in early August for an opera concert of Edvard Grieg's *Peer Gynt*. To reach Skei, head north of Lillehammer along the E6 and at Tretten take the turn-off for the Rv254. At Svingvoll, Peer Gynt Vegen branches off to the northwest.

Røros

POP 5580

Røros, a charming Unesco World Heritage–listed site set in a small hollow of stunted forests and bleak fells, is one of Norway's most beautiful villages. The Norwegian writer Johan Falkberget described Røros as 'a place of whispering history' and this historic copper-mining town (once called Bergstad, or mountain city) has wonderfully preserved, colourful wooden houses that climb the hillside, as well as fascinating relics of the town's mining past. Røros has become something of a retreat for artists, who lend even more character to this enchanted place.

Sights

Røros' **historic district**, characterised by the striking log architecture of its 80 protected buildings, takes in the entire central area. The two main streets, **Bergmannsgata** and **Kjerkgata**, are lined with historical homes and buildings, all under preservation orders. The entire area is like an architectural museum of old Norway. For one of the loveliest turf-roofed homes you'll see, head up to the top of Kjerkgata to the house signposted as **Harald Sohlsbergs Plass 59**.

If Røros looks familiar, that's because several films have been made here, including Røros author Johan Falkberget's classic *An-Magrit*, starring Jane Fonda. Flanderborg gate starred in some of Astrid Lindgren's *Pippi Longstocking* classics and Røros even stood in for Siberia in *A Day in the Life of Ivan Denisovich*.

Røros Kirke CHURCH
(Kjerkgata; adult/child Nkr40/free; 10am-4pm Mon-Sat & 12.30-2.30pm Sun mid-Jun–mid-Aug, 11am-1pm Mon-Sat early Jun & mid-Aug–mid-Sep, 11am-1pm Sat rest of year) Røros' Lutheran church is one of Norway's most distinctive, and also one of the largest, with a seating capacity of 1640. The first church on the site was constructed in 1650, but it had fallen into disrepair by the mid-18th century and from 1780 a new baroque-style church (the one you see today) was built just behind the original at a cost of 23,000 *riksdaler* (at the time, miners earned about 50 *riksdaler* per year).

Smelthytta MUSEUM
(www.rorosmuseet.no; Malmplassen; adult/student/child Nkr80/70/free, incl guided tour in summer; 10am-6pm mid-Jun–mid-Aug, 11am-4pm Mon-Fri & 11am-3pm Sat & Sun early Jun & mid-Aug–mid-Sep, shorter hours rest of year, guided tours during summer in Norwegian 11am or 3.30pm, in English 12.30pm) Housed in old smelting works, which were central to Røros' *raison d'être* until 1953, this museum is a town highlight. The building was reconstructed in 1988 according to the original 17th-century plan. Inside you'll discover a large balance used for weighing ore, some well-illustrated early mining statistics, and brilliant working models of the mines and the water- and horse-powered smelting processes. Displays of copper smelting are held at 3pm Tuesday to Friday from early July to early August.

Activities

Dog-sledding, **canoeing**, **horse riding**, **sleigh rides** and **ice-fishing** are all possible. The tourist office has a full list of operators.

Husky Excursions

Alaskan Husky Tours DOG-SLEDDING
(62 49 87 66; www.huskytour.no; dog-sledding winter/summer adult from Nkr1400/1100, child Nkr700/550) Organises winter dog-sledding tours that last from a few hours to a few days. It also operates summer tours on wheel-sleds. Located some distance outside Røros; you can book through the tourist office.

Røros Husky DOG-SLEDDING
(91 51 52 28; www.roroshusky.no) Organises winter dog-sledding tours of varying lengths. It's located about 10km north of Røros, but bookings can be made via the tourist office.

Sámi Excursions

Røros Rein WINTER ACTIVITIES
(97 97 49 66; www.rorosrein.no; Hagaveien 17) Organises a winter program that includes sleigh rides, getting up close and personal with reindeer, and a traditional Sámi meal in a Sámi hut.

Tours

Guided Walking Tours WALKING
(adult/child Nkr80/free; tours 10.30am, 12.30pm, 2.30pm Mon-Sat, 11.30am & 1pm Sun mid-Jun–mid-Aug, 11am Mon-Sat early Jun & mid-Aug–mid-Sep) Run by the tourist office, these walking tours take you through the historic town centre. English tours are at 12.30pm Monday to Saturday and 1pm Sunday. They also run children's tours (Nkr60; in Norwegian only) at 12pm on Tuesdays and Thursdays throughout July and the first week of August.

Festivals & Events

Rørosmartnan MARKET
(Røros Market) The biggest winter event is Rørosmartnan, which began in 1644 as a rendezvous for hunters who ventured into town to sell their products to miners and buy supplies.

Fermund Race DOG-SLEDDING
(www.femundlopet.no) One of Europe's longest dog-sled races starts and ends in Røros in the first week of February.

Sleeping

Frøyas Hus B&B €€
(72 41 10 10; www.froyashus.no; Mørkstugata 4; s/d Nkr850/950) With only two rooms, this gorgeous place has an intimacy you won't find elsewhere. Rooms are small and have scarcely changed in over 300 years – it's rustic in the best sense of the word. Throw in friendly service, a lovely courtyard cafe and public areas strewn with local antiques and curiosities, and it's all perfectly integrated into the Røros experience.

Vertshuset Røros HISTORIC HOTEL €€
(☎72 41 93 50; www.vertshusetroros.no; Kjerkgata 34; s/d from Nkr1185/1540, 2-/4-bed apt Nkr1690/2140) In a historic 17th-century building on the main pedestrian thoroughfare, the Vertshuset Røros is a wonderful choice. The all-wood rooms are generously sized and have numerous period touches, such as wooden beds with columns – arguably the most comfortable beds in town.

★**Erzscheidergården** GUESTHOUSE €€€
(☎72 41 11 94; www.erzscheidergaarden.no; Spell Olaveien 6; s/d from Nkr1245/1590; P) This appealing, very cosy 24-room guesthouse is up the hill from the town centre and behind the church. The wood-panelled rooms are loaded with personality, the atmosphere is Norwegian-family-warmth and the breakfasts were described by one reader as 'the best homemade breakfast buffet in Norway'. We're inclined to agree.

Eating

Kaffestugu Cafeteria NORWEGIAN €€
(www.kaffestuggu.no; Bergmannsgata 18; mains Nkr88-225; ⌚9am-9pm daily mid-Jun–mid-Aug, 10am-6pm Mon-Fri & 10am-5pm Sat & Sun rest of year) This historic place offers a good range of coffee, pastries, snacks and light meals, as well as some more substantial main dishes such as reindeer steak. Its lunchtime specials are a little heavy on the potatoes, but the food in general is enduringly popular. The atmosphere wavers between old Norwegian tea room and informal cafeteria.

Peder Hiort Mathus INTERNATIONAL €€
(☎72 40 60 80; www.bergstadenshotel.no/peder_hiort_mathus; Bergmannsgata 1; barbeque buffet Nkr249, mains from Nkr120-170; ⌚2-10pm Mon-Thu, 2-11pm Fri, 11am-11pm Sat, noon-10pm Sun) With old photos of Røros and traditional decor, you might be forgiven for imagining this to be a bastion of traditional cooking, but this being modern Norway, it's mostly about pizza. Of more interest is its garden barbeque buffet served from 5pm Thursday to Sunday throughout the summer (weather depending). Its outdoor tables have views up this historic street.

★**Vertshuset Røros** NORWEGIAN €€€
(☎72 41 93 50; Kjerkgata 34; lunch mains Nkr 100-185, set menu from Nkr385; ⌚10am-9.30pm) Lunch dishes here include fairly standard soup, sandwiches and burgers, but from 4pm onwards the food is exquisite – the tenderest fillets of reindeer or elk, as well as Arctic char and desserts such as 'blue cheese and pear marinated in cinnamon, walnuts in honey and balsamico'. In short, it's one of the region's finest eating experiences. Book ahead.

Information

Tourist Office (☎72 41 00 00; www.roros.no; Peder Hiortsgata 2; ⌚9am-6pm Mon-Sat & 10am-4pm Sun mid-Jun–mid-Aug, 9am-3.30pm Mon-Fri & 10am-4pm Sat rest of year) The tourist office has loads of good info on things to see and do in and around the town but walkers wanting to explore the surrounding moorland peaks will find little of use in regards to route suggestions.

Getting There & Away

AIR

Røros has two **Widerøe** (www.wideroe.no) flights to/from Oslo daily except Saturday.

BUS

There are two daily buses from Røros to Trondheim (Nkr286, four hours).

TRAIN

Røros lies on the eastern railway line between Oslo (from Nkr249, five hours, six daily) and Trondheim (from Nkr249, 2½ hours).

Jotunheimen National Park

The Sognefjellet road (the highest mountain road in northern Europe) between Lom and Sogndal passes the northwestern perimeter of Jotunheimen National Park, Norway's most popular wilderness destination. Hiking trails lead to some of the park's 60 glaciers, up to the top of Norway's loftiest peaks, Galdhøpiggen (2469m) and Glittertind (2452m), and along ravines and valleys featuring deep lakes and plunging waterfalls. There are more than 275 summits above 2000m inside the park. There are **DNT huts** (Norwegian Mountain Touring Club; ☎22 82 28 22; www.turistforeningen.no; Storgata 7, Oslo) and private lodges along many of the routes.

Sights & Activities

Jotunheimen's hiking possibilities are practically endless and all are spectacular. The best maps are Statens Kartverk's *Jotunheimen Aust* and *Jotunheimen Vest* (1:50,000; Nkr99 each).

★ Sognefjellet Road SCENIC DRIVE
(www.turistveg.no) Town councillors of the world: you may have built a lot of roads in your time – many of them are probably very useful – but chances are none of them are as spectacular as this one. Snaking through Jotunheimen National Park (and providing access to most of the trailheads), the stunningly scenic Sognefjellet Rd (Rv55) connects Lustrafjorden with Lom, and is billed as 'the road over the roof of Norway'. With little doubt it's one of Norway's most beautiful drives.

Constructed in 1939 by unemployed youths, the road rises to a height of 1434m, making it the highest mountain road in northern Europe. It is one of Norway's 18 'National Tourist Routes'.

Access from the southwest is via multiple hairpin bends climbing up beyond the tree line to Turtagrø, with a stirring view of the Skagastølstindane mountains on your right. If you're coming from Lom, the ascent is more gradual, following beautiful Bøverdalen, the valley of the Bøvra River, with its lakes, glacial rivers, grass-roofed huts and patches of pine forest. The road summit on Sognefjell offers superb views.

The snow sometimes doesn't melt until early July, although the road is usually open from May to September. The road can get very narrow and snow is often piled metres high on either side. Ample camping and other accommodation options line the road.

Although this road is mainly traversed by motorised transport, the Sognefjellet Rd has legendary status among cyclists and frequently appears on lists of the world's most spectacular cycle routes. It's a serious undertaking that requires high levels of fitness and perfect brakes.

From mid-June to late August, a daily bus runs between Lom and Sogndal (Nkr250, 3½ hours) via Sognefjellet Rd.

Galdhøpiggen Summer Ski Centre SKI CENTRE
(☎61 21 17 50; www.gpss.no; ski & snowboard rental Nkr300, adult/child day lift pass Nkr370/300) This ski centre, at 1850m on the icy heights of Norway's highest mountain, is a stunning spot for summer skiing. From Galdesand on the Rv55, follow the Galdhøpiggen road (Nkr100 toll) to its end at 1841m. The main season runs from June to mid-November. Apart from the skiing opportunities, this road takes you to the highest point reachable by road in Norway.

Sleeping & Eating

Krossbu Turiststasjon MOUNTAIN LODGE €
(☎61 21 29 22; www.krossbu.no; dm from Nkr390, s Nkr490, d from Nkr900; P) Excellent value, cosy wood-lined rooms look out over a landscape of inspiring bleakness. Meals are available. Dozens of impressive walks start from here including a guided glacier walk (Nkr500 per person, minimum four people).

★ Elvesæter Hotell HOTEL €€
(☎61 21 99 00; www.ton.no; Bøverdalen; s/d from Nkr850/1150; P) Run by the sixth generation of the Elvesæter family, this gorgeous hotel has pretty rooms and lovely architecture. It's high on novelty value as it's adjacent to the Sagasøyla, a 32m-high carved wooden pillar tracing Norwegian history from unification in 872 to the 1814 constitution. Decent set three-course dinners are Nkr325. A great Jotunheimen base.

Røisheim Hotel HISTORIC HOTEL €€€
(☎61 21 20 31; www.roisheim.no; Bøverdalen; d from Nkr1500; P) This charming place combines architecturally stunning buildings that date back to 1858 with modern comforts, although there are no TVs. Some rooms have wonderful baths made out of old barrels. Apart from the charming accommodation, the appeal lies in the meals, which are prepared by Ingrid Hov Lunde, one of the country's best-loved chefs.

Turtagrø Hotel LODGE €€€
(☎57 68 08 00; www.turtagro.no; Fortun; camping Nkr125, dm from Nkr550, annexe tw Nkr770, s/d Nkr1850/2760, tower ste per person Nkr1595; P) This historic hiking and mountaineering centre is a friendly yet laid-back base for exploring Jotunheimen and Hurrungane, whatever your budget. The main building has wonderful views and supremely comfortable rooms. The hotel also conducts week-long climbing courses and guided day trips (hiking, climbing, skiing) and there's a great bar full of historic mountaineering photos.

Information

For park information, maps and glacier-walk arrangements contact **Lom tourist office** (☎61 21 29 90; www.visitjotunheimen.com; ⊙9am-4pm Mon-Sat & 9am-3pm Sun Jul–mid-Aug, 9am-4pm Mon-Sat mid-Aug–early Sep).

Getting There & Away

Three daily Nordfjordekspressen bus services run from Oslo to Lom (Nkr509, 6½ hours). There are local buses to/from Otta (Nkr129, 1½ hours, six daily). There's also a daily bus through the Jotunheimen National Park to Sogndal (Nkr250, 3½ hours, two daily) from late June to the end of August.

Oslo to Bergen

The Oslo–Bergen railway line, a seven-hour journey past forests and alpine villages, and across the starkly beautiful **Hardangervidda Plateau**, is Norway's most scenic long-haul train trip.

Midway between Oslo and Bergen is **Geilo**, a ski centre where you can practically walk off the train and onto a chairlift. There's also good summer **hiking** in the mountains around Geilo, where you'll find **Ro Hotell & Kro** (☎32 09 08 99; www.rohotell.no; Geilovegen 55; s/d Nkr730/950, with shared bathroom Nkr470/67/670) and **Geilo Tourist Office** (☎32 09 59 00; www.geilo.no; Vesleslåttveien 13; ⊙8.30am-6pm Mon-Fri, 9am-5pm Sat, 11am-5pm Sun).

From Geilo the train climbs 600m through a tundra-like landscape of high lakes and snow-capped mountains to the tiny village of **Finse**, near the **Hardangerjøkulen** icecap. Finse has year-round **skiing** and is in the middle of a network of summer **hiking trails**. One of Norway's most frequently trodden trails winds from the Finse train station down to the fjord town of **Aurland**, a four-day trek. There's breathtaking mountain scenery along the way as well as a series of DNT and private mountain huts a day's walk apart. There's also a bicycle route from Finse to Flåm (six hours, downhill) on the century-old **Rallarvegen** railway construction road.

Myrdal, further west along the railway line, is the connecting point for the spectacularly steep Flåm railway, which twists and turns its way down 20 splendid kilometres to **Flåm** on Aurlandsfjorden, an arm of Sognefjorden.

BERGEN & THE WESTERN FJORDS

This spectacular region has truly indescribable scenery. Hardangerfjord, Sognefjord, Lysefjord and Geirangerfjord are all variants on the same theme: steep crystalline rock walls dropping with sublime force straight into the sea, often decorated with waterfalls, and small farms harmoniously blending into the natural landscape. Summer hiking opportunities exist along the fjord walls and on the enormous Jostedalsbreen glacier. Bergen is an engaging and lively city with a 15th-century waterfront.

Bergen

POP 258,500

Surrounded by seven hills and seven fjords, Bergen is a beautiful, charming city. With the Unesco World Heritage–listed Bryggen and buzzing Vågen harbour as its centrepiece, Bergen climbs the hillsides with timber-clad houses, while cable cars offer stunning views from above. Throw in great museums and a dynamic cultural life and Bergen amply rewards as much time as you can give it.

With so much else going for it, it seems almost incidental that Bergen is also a terminus of the scenic Bergen–Oslo railway line and a convenient place to stay before excursions into fjord country. The *Hurtigruten* coastal ferry begins its journey to Kirkenes here.

History

During the 12th and 13th centuries, Bergen was Norway's capital and easily the country's most important city. By the 13th century, the city states of Germany allied themselves into trading leagues, most significantly the Hanseatic League, and the sheltered harbour of Bryggen drew the traders in droves. They established their first office here around 1360, transforming Bryggen into one of the league's four major headquarters abroad.

By the early 17th century Bergen was the trading hub of Scandinavia and Norway's most populous city, with 15,000 people. Bryggen continued as an important maritime trading centre until 1899, when the Hanseatic League's Bergen offices finally closed.

Sights

★Bryggen HISTORIC SITE

Bergen's oldest quarter runs along the eastern shore of Vågen Harbour (the name simply translates to 'wharf') in long, parallel and often leaning rows of gabled buildings with stacked-stone or wooden foundations and reconstructed rough-plank construction. It's enchanting, no doubt about it, but can be exhausting if you hit a cruise-ship and bus-tour crush.

KODE GALLERY

(☎55 56 80 00; kodebergen.no; adult/child Nkr100/free, Thu free for students) Bergen's art museums

Western Fjords & Central Norway

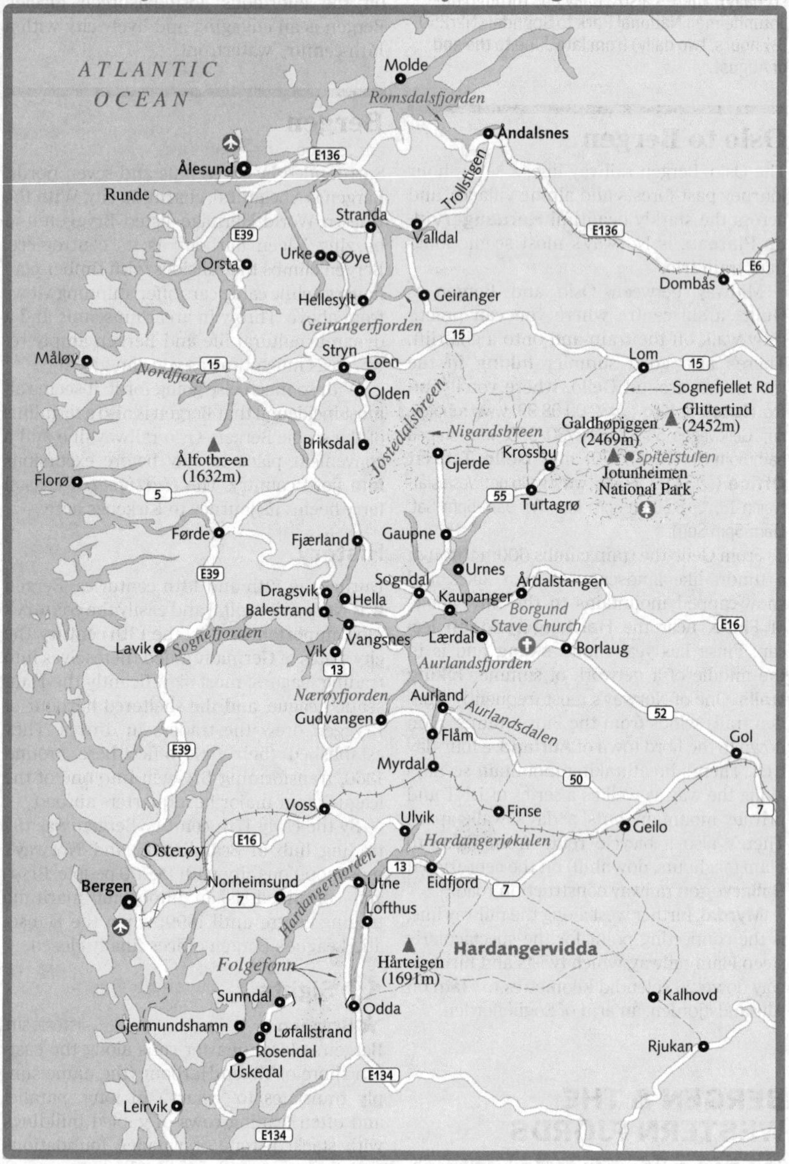

0 50 km
0 25 miles

are collected under the umbrella institution KODE and together form one of the largest art and design collections in Scandinavia. Four separate, and architecturally unique, buildings line up along the Lille Lungegård lake, each with its own specialist focus.

★ **Edvard Grieg Museum** MUSEUM
(Troldhaugen; www.griegmuseum.no; Troldhaugvegen 65, Paradis-Bergen; adult/child Nkr90/free; ⌚9am-6pm May-Sep, 10am-4pm Oct-Apr) The composer Edvard Grieg and his wife Nina Hagerup spent summers at this charming

Swiss-style wooden villa from 1885 until Grieg's death in 1907. Surrounded by fragrant, tumbling gardens and occupying a semi-rural setting on a peninsula by coastal Nordåsvatnet lake, south of Bergen, it's a truly lovely place to visit. Apart from the Griegs' original home, there is a modern exhibition centre, a 200-seat concert hall and, perhaps the most compelling feature of them all, a tiny, lake-side **Composer's Hut**.

Activities

Fløibanen Funicular CABLE CAR
(www.floibanen.no; Vetrlidsalmenning 21; adult/child return Nkr85/43; ⏲7.30am-11pm Mon-Fri, from 8am Sat & Sun) For an unbeatable view of the city, ride the 26-degree Fløibanen funicular to the top of Mt Fløyen (320m), with departures every 15 minutes. From the top, well-marked hiking tracks lead into the forest; the possibilities are mapped out on the free *Walking Map of Mount Fløyen,* which is available from the Bergen tourist office (p317).

Ulriken643 CABLE CAR
(www.ulriken643.no; adult/child return Nkr150/80, with bus Nkr250/140; ⏲9am-9pm daily May-Sep, 9am-5pm Tue-Sun Oct-Apr) Bergen's cable car ascends to the radio tower and cafe atop Mt Ulriken (642m), offering a fine panoramic view of the city and surrounding fjords and mountains. An antique shuttle bus to the cable-car lower station leaves every half-hour from the Torget fish market from 9am to 9pm mid-May to September. Otherwise, it's a 45-minute walk from the centre or a short bus ride (bus 2, 31, 50).

Tours

Guided Tours of Bryggen WALKING
(☎55 58 80 30; adult/child Nkr120/free; ⏲11am, in English noon Jun-Aug) Excellent walking tours through the timeless alleys of Bryggen are offered by the **Bryggens Museum** (www.bymuseet.no; Dreggsallmenning 3; adult/child Nkr70/free; ⏲10am-4pm mid-May–Aug, shorter hours rest of year). Tours last 90 minutes and leave from the museum. The commentary includes descriptions of life during Bergen's trading heyday. The ticket includes admission to Bryggens Museum, Schøtstuene and the Hanseatic Museum (plus re-entry later the same day).

Festivals & Events

For a full list of events, visit www.visitbergen.com.

Bergen International Festival CULTURAL
(www.fib.no) Held over 14 days in late May, this is the big cultural festival of the year, with dance, music, theatre and visual arts shows throughout the city.

Night Jazz Festival MUSIC
(www.nattjazz.no) May jazz festival that is popular with Bergen's large student population.

Bergenfest MUSIC
(www.bergenfest.no) International music festival in June.

Bergen Food Festival FOOD
(www.matfest.no) September showcase of local food producers (including whale meat).

Sleeping

Bergen has outstanding accommodation, but *always* book before arriving in town. The tourist office (p317) has an accommodation booking service both online and onsite.

Marken Gjestehus HOSTEL €
(☎55 31 44 04; www.marken-gjestehus.com; Kong Oscars gate 45; dm Nkr240, s/d Nkr705/810, with shared bathroom Nkr525/610) Midway between the harbour and the train station, this hostel-within-a-hotel has simple, modern rooms. White walls and wooden floors lend a sense of light and space, bright chairs and wall decals are cheery, and the communal areas are more stylish than you'd expect for the price.

Citybox HOSTEL €
(☎55 31 25 00; www.citybox.no; Nygårdsgaten 31; s/d/family Nkr650/950/1550, s/d with shared bathroom Nkr550/750) The Citybox mini-chain began in Bergen and is one of the

BERGEN CARD

The **Bergen Card** (www.visitbergen.com/bergencard; adult/child 24hr pass Nkr200/75, 48hr Nkr260/100) gives you free travel on local buses; free entrance to some museums, with discounted entry to the rest; free or discounted return trips on the Fløibanen funicular, depending on the time of year; free guided tours of Bergen; and discounts on city and boat sightseeing tours, concerts and cultural performances. It's available from the tourist office, some hotels, the bus terminal and online.

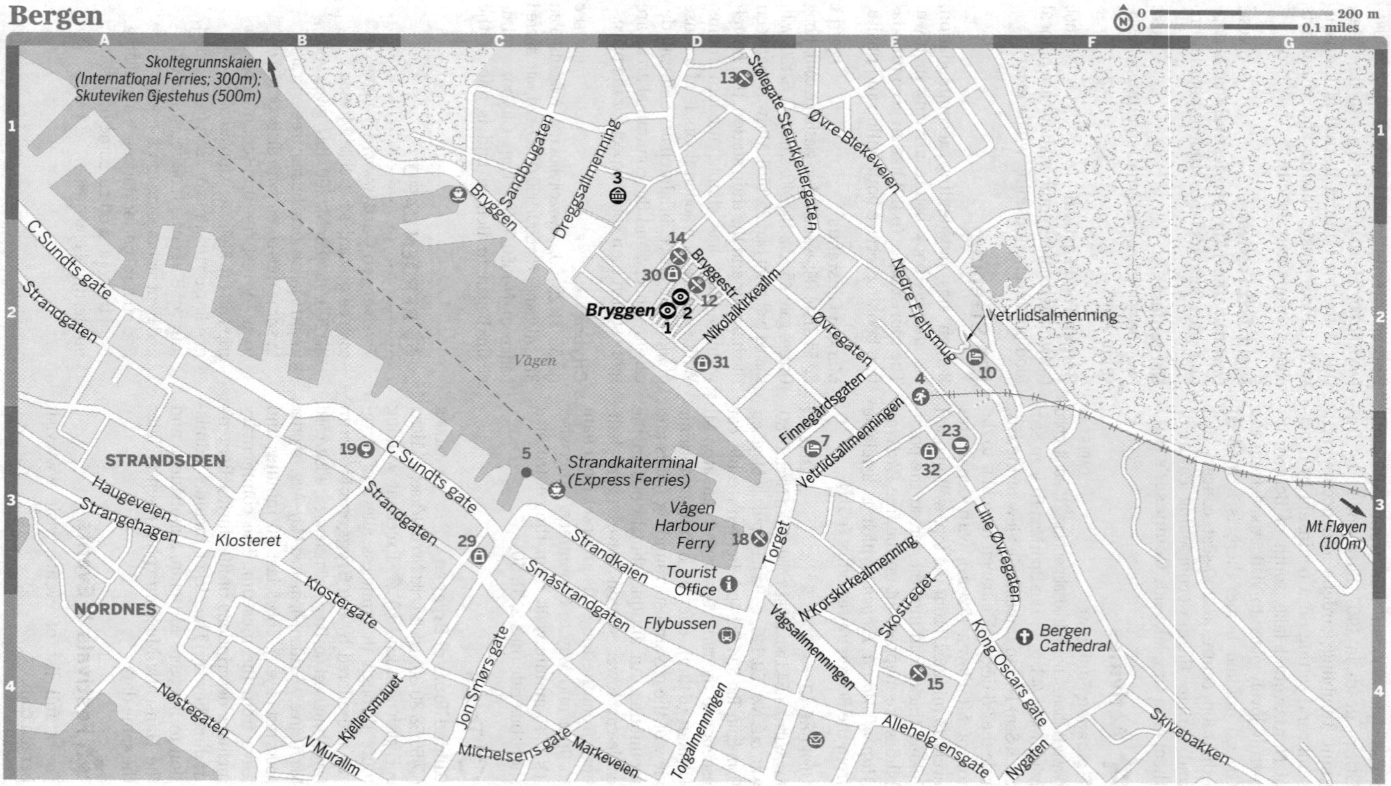

Bergen

0 200 m
0 0.1 miles

A B C D E F G
1 2 3 4

Skoltegrunnskaien (International Ferries; 300m); Skuteviken Gjestehus (500m)
13 Stølegate Steinkjellergaten
Øvre Blekeveien
Sandbrugaten
Dreggsallmenning
3
Bryggen
14
Bryggestr
30
12
Bryggen 2
1
Nikolaikirkeallm
C Sundts gate
Strandgaten
Vågen
31
Øvregaten
Nedre Fjellsmug
Vetrlidsalmenning
10
4
Finnegårdsgaten
7
Vetrlidsallmenningen
23
32
19
C Sundts gate
5
Strandkaiterminal (Express Ferries)
STRANDSIDEN
Haugeveien
Strangehagen
Klosteret
Strandgaten
29
Vågen Harbour Ferry
18
Torget
Strandkaien
Tourist Office
Småstrandgaten
N Korskirkealmenning
Skostredet
Lille Øvregaten
Mt Fløyen (100m)
NORDNES
Klostergate
Flybussen
Vågsallmenningen
Kong Oscars gate
Bergen Cathedral
15
Jon Smørs gate
Nøstegaten
Kjellersmauet
V Murallm
Michelsens gate
Markeveien
Torgalmenningen
Allehelg ensgate
Nygaten
Skivebakken

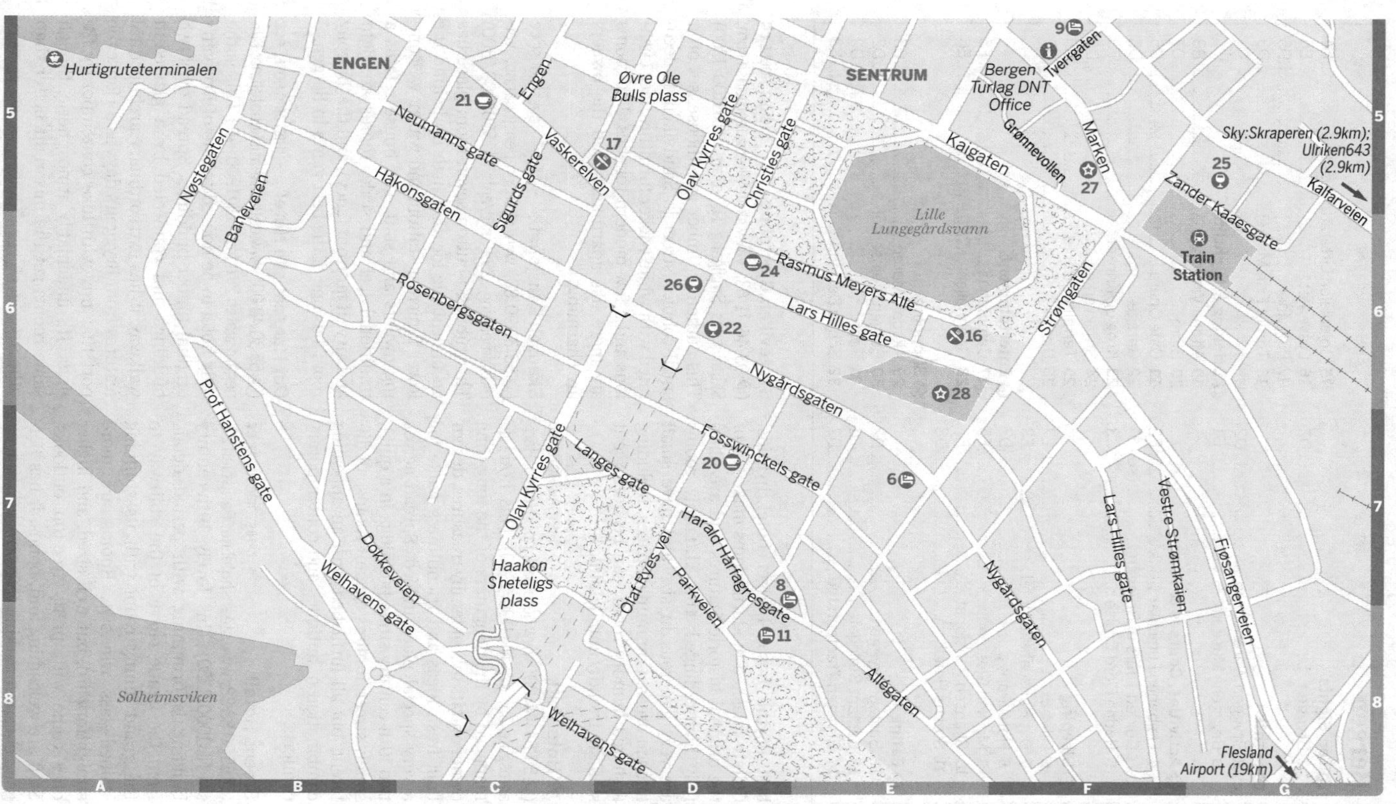

Hurtigruteterminalen
ENGEN
21
Engen
Øvre Ole Bulls plass
SENTRUM
Bergen Turlag DNT Office
Tverrgaten
9
Neumanns gate
Vaskerelven
17
Olav Kyrres gate
Christies gate
Kaigaten
Grønnevollen
Marken
27
Sky:Skraperen (2.9km); Ulriken643 (2.9km)
25
Kalfarveien
Zander Kaaesgate
Train Station
Nøstegaten
Baneveien
Håkonsgaten
Sigurds gate
Lille Lungegårdsvann
24
Rasmus Meyers Allé
26
Rosenbergsgaten
22
Lars Hilles gate
16
Strømgaten
Nygårdsgaten
28
Prof Hanstens gate
Olav Kyrres gate
Langes gate
20
Fosswinckels gate
6
Harald Hårfagresgate
Dokkeveien
Welhavens gate
Haakon Sheteligs plass
Olaf Ryes vei
Parkveien
8
11
Nygårdsgaten
Lars Hilles gate
Vestre Strømkaien
Fjøsangerveien
Allégaten
Solheimsviken
Welhavens gate
Flesland Airport (19km)
5
6
7
8
A
B
C
D
E
F
G

Bergen

Top Sights
1 Bryggen.......D2

Sights
2 Bryggen Warehouses.......D2
3 Bryggens Museum.......D1

Activities, Courses & Tours
4 Fløibanen Funicular.......E2
Guided Tours of Bryggen.......(see 3)
5 Rødne Fjord Cruise.......C3

Sleeping
6 Citybox.......E7
7 Det Hanseatiske Hotel.......E3
8 Hotel Park.......D7
9 Marken Gjestehus.......F5
10 Skansen Pensjonat.......E2
11 Steens Hotell.......D8

Eating
12 Bastant Bryggen.......D2
13 Bastant Stølegaten.......D1
14 Bryggen Tracteursted.......D2
15 Colonialen Litteraturhuset.......E4
16 Lysverket.......E6
17 Pingvinen.......D5
18 Torget Fish Market.......D3

Drinking & Nightlife
19 Altona Vinbar.......B3
20 Blom.......D7
21 Café Opera.......C5
22 Garage.......D6
23 Krog og Krinkel.......E3
24 Smakverket.......D6
25 Terminus Bar.......G5
26 Ujevnt.......D6

Entertainment
27 Café Sanaa.......F5
28 Grieghallen.......E6

Shopping
29 Aksdal i Muren.......C3
30 Bergen Steinsenter.......D2
31 Røst.......D2
32 Schau Design.......E3

best of the hostel-budget hotel hybrids. Colour-splashed modern rooms make use of the original historic features and are blissfully high-ceilinged; the XL/family rooms are very generous in size and have small kitchen areas. Communal spaces, including a shared laundry room, can be hectic, but staff are friendly and helpful.

★Hotel Park HISTORIC HOTEL €€
(☎55 54 44 00; www.hotelpark.no; Harald Hårfagresgate 35; s/d Nkr1190/1390) This hotel is managed by the daughters of the long-time owner and its mix of family treasures, design flair, fresh ideas and friendliness make for a very special place indeed. Spread across two 19th-century stone buildings in a quiet, stately street, it offers elegant rooms, all different, but all furnished with an appealing combination of antiques and contemporary comforts.

Steens Hotell HISTORIC HOTEL €€
(☎55 30 88 88; www.steenshotel.no; Parkveien 22; s/d Nkr1000/1350) This lovely 19th-century building is brimming with period detail, from the gentle curve of the stairway to the grand dining room with its stunning stained-glass windows. Rooms are more straightforward, but well sized, and higher ones come with pretty tree-top outlooks. Staff are welcoming and, bonus, it has Bergen's cheapest parking (Nkr50).

Skuteviken Gjestehus GUESTHOUSE €€
(☎93 46 71 63; www.skutevikenguesthouse.com; Skutevikens Smalgang 11; d/attic Nkr1100/1200) This authentic timber guesthouse, set on a small cobbled street in Sandviken, is decorated with white wicker furniture, lace cushions and a few modern touches. The rooms are more like apartments and the owners are charming.

Skansen Pensjonat GUESTHOUSE €€
(☎55 31 90 80; www.skansen-pensjonat.no; Vetrlidsalmenning 29; s/d/apt Nkr550/900/1100) This cute-as-a-button seven-room place has an unbeatable location high up behind the lower funicular station, and warm, welcoming owners and staff. The house retains a traditional feel and scale, rooms are light and airy (if far from fancy), and the 'balcony room' has one of the best views in Bergen.

Det Hanseatiske Hotel HISTORIC HOTEL €€€
(☎55 30 48 00; www.dethanseatiskehotell.no; Finnegårdsgaten 2; d from Nkr1900;) This is the only hotel to be housed in one of Bryggen's original timber buildings. Spread over two buildings and connected by a glassed-in walkway, it has extraordinary architectural features from Bryggen's days as a Hanseatic port that mix with luxe contemporary fittings. It's undeniably atmospheric, though some rooms get the mix right better than others.

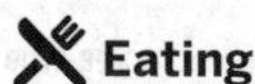

Eating

Torget Fish Market SEAFOOD €
(www.torgetibergen.no; Torget; ⏰7am-7pm daily Jun-Aug, to 4pm Mon-Sat Sep-May) For atmosphere, it's hard to beat the fish market. Right alongside the harbour and a stone's throw from Bryggen, you'll find everything from salmon to calamari, fish and chips, fish cakes, prawn baguettes, seafood salads, local caviar and, sometimes, reindeer and elk.

Pingvinen TRADITIONAL NORWEGIAN €
(www.pingvinen.no; Vaskerelven 14; daily special Nkr119, mains Nkr159-249; ⏰1pm-3am Sun-Fri, noon-3am Sat) Devoted to Norwegian home cooking, and with a delightfully informal ambience, Pingvinen is *everyone* in Bergen's old favourite. They come for meals their mothers and grandparents used to cook, and although the menu changes regularly, there'll be one or more of the following: fishcake sandwiches, reindeer, fish pie, whale, salmon, lamb shank and *raspeballer* (aka *komle*), west-coast potato dumplings.

Bastant Bryggen SOUP €
(☎40 07 22 47; Jacobsfjorden 4, Bryggestredet; soups Nkr99-129, sandwiches Nkr119, soup & half sandwich Nkr155; ⏰11am-5pm) Cuddle in or take away at this super-popular all-organic cafe in the heart of Bryggen's tiny alleyways. Daily soups always include a vegan, vegetarian and meat option, and sandwiches are hearty. There's homemade lemonade and strawberry frappes in summer, killer hot chocolates when it's cold and excellent coffee year-round. **Bastant Stølegaten** (Stølegaten 8a, Sandviken; ⏰11am-11pm) in Sandviken is roomier and open late.

Colonialen Litteraturhuset MODERN NORWEGIAN €€
(☎55 90 16 00; Østre skostredet 5-7; lunch Nkr145-175, dinner Nkr175-235; ⏰9-11am Mon-Fri, cafe 11am-9pm, brasserie 4-10pm Mon-Sat) This airy, open-plan space is subtly divided into two distinct venues by a bustling kitchen: one side for all-day breakfasting, snacking, lunching and drinking, the other an elegantly informal 'brassierie' where well-to-do Bergeners come for thoughtful dishes such as mackerel with apples, turnips, peas and horseradish. Staff know their wine, too.

★ **Lysverket** MODERN NORWEGIAN €€€
(☎55 60 31 00; lysverket.no; KODE 4, Rasmus Meyers allé 9; lunch 1/2/3 courses Nkr205/295/320, dinner 3/5/9 courses Nkr595/745/995, bar dishes Nkr75-195; ⏰noon-1am Tue-Thu, noon-3am Fri & Sat, 1-5pm Sun) Lysverket poetically translates as 'light plant', though it has a down-to-earth explanation: this building once housed a power company. The food is an intriguing combination of the everyday and the poetic, with chef Christopher Haatuft using seafood caught right on Bergen's doorstep and familiar seasonal vegetables in surprising combinations of colour, texture and flavour.

Sky:Skraperen MODERN NORWEGIAN €€€
(☎55 32 04 04; www.skyskraperen.no; Ulrikens topp; mains Nkr159-230, 4-course set menu with aperitif Nkr643; ⏰9am-9pm May-Sep, 10am-4pm Oct-Apr) You can drop in for a sausage

FJORD TOURS FROM BERGEN

Fjord Tours (☎81 56 82 22; www.fjordtours.com) has mastered the art of making the most of limited time with a series of tours into the fjords. Its popular year-round **Norway in a Nutshell** tour is a great way to see far more than you thought possible in a single day. The day ticket (adult/child Nkr1145/585) from Bergen combines a morning train to Voss, a bus to the Stalheim Hotel and then on to Gudvangen, from where a ferry takes you up the spectacular Nærøyfjord to Flåm, joining the stunning mountain railway to Myrdal, and then taking a train back to Bergen in time for a late dinner (or for Nkr1550/790 per adult/child you can continue on to Oslo to arrive at around 10pm).

From May to September, Fjord Tours also runs a range of train-bus-boat round trips from Bergen, including the 10-hour **Hardangerfjord in a Nutshell** (adult/child Nkr1180/490), which goes via Voss, Ulvik, Eidfjord and Norheimsund, and **Sognefjord in a Nutshell** (adult/child Nkr1340/670), which explores more of Sognefjord by boat. It also has four-day tours (adult/child Nkr5560/3460) that include Oslo, Sognefjorden, Geiranger and Ålesund.

Rødne Fjord Cruise (☎51 89 52 70; www.rodne.no; ⏰May-Aug) runs a seven-hour round-trip tour (adult/child Nkr725/325) to Rosendal that leaves Bergen at 9am, spends 3½ hours in Rosendal, which includes lunch and a guided tour of Baroniet Rosendal, and returns to Bergen at 4.15pm.

sandwich (Nkr39) or a fish soup (Nkr95) at this mountain-top restaurant any time during the day, though we suggest making an evening of it. The set dinner menu follows the seasons and showcases west-coast produce. Dishes pop with fresh, clean flavours and are prettily presented. Book at least one day ahead.

Bryggen Tracteursted MODERN NORWEGIAN €€€
(Bryggestredet 2, Bryggen; lunch mains Nkr185-215, dinner mains Nkr285-385; ⏲11am-10pm May-Sep) Housed in a 1708 building that ranges across the former stables, kitchen (note the stone floor, which meant that it was the only Bryggen building allowed to have a fire) and Bergen's only extant *schøtstuene* (dining hall), this restaurant serves traditional Norwegian dishes that change regularly; it's pubby and informal by day, traditionally upmarket by night.

Drinking & Nightlife

★Blom CAFE
(John Lunds plass 1; ⏲8.30am-5pm Mon-Fri, from 11am Sat & Sun) This cafe is known for its excellent coffee (this is where off-duty baristas come for a pour-over) and attracts a fashionable, young crowd. It's a simple, warm place, with sweet service, lots of room to pull out your laptop, big sandwiches and more-ish homemade muesli slices, brownies and fruit crumbles.

Altona Vinbar WINE BAR
(C Sundts gate 22; ⏲6pm-12.30am Mon-Thu, to 1.30am Fri & Sat) Set in a warren of vaulted underground rooms that date from the 16th century, Altona's huge, carefully selected wine list, soft lighting and murmured conversation make it Bergen's most romantic bar (particularly appealing when the weather's cold and wet). The bar menu tends towards tasty comfort food, such as Norwegian lamb burgers (Nkr175).

Krog og Krinkel CAFE
(Lille Øvregaten 14; ⏲11am-7pm Mon-Sat, noon-5pm Sun) Streetside tables line up along the cobbles in the warm weather, or you can venture down into the cosy, comfortable basement filled with painted vintage furniture, and, yes, books. The coffee is good and they make all their own *boller* and cakes onsite, including a *suksesskake* (almond meringue cake with custard topping; Nkr45) that will have you hooked at first bite.

Café Opera CAFE, CLUB
(Engen 18; ⏲11am-3am Mon-Sat, noon-12.15am Sun) By day, Café Opera has a literary-cafe feel, though on the weekends there's also a rota of DJs and a crowd that likes to pump up the jams. When the sun's out, its outside tables are some of the nicest in town to while a way a few hours.

Ujevnt WINE BAR
(www.ujevnt.no; Christiesgate 5-7; ⏲3pm-2.30am Mon-Sat, from 6pm Sun) You might find yourself in this moody little bar one afternoon, nursing a pint of the excellent Voss Bryggeri nut-brown ale on tap, but it's hard not to stay around for a cocktail once the music's turned up and the beautiful people arrive.

Garage LIVE MUSIC
(www.garage.no; Christies gate 14; ⏲3pm-3am Mon-Sat, from 5pm Sun) Garage has taken on an almost mythical quality for music lovers across Europe. It does have the odd jazz and acoustic act, but this is a rock and metal venue at heart, with well-known Norwegian and international acts drawn to the cavernous basement. Stop by for the Sunday jam sessions in summer.

Terminus Bar BAR
(Grand Terminus Hotel, Zander Kaaesgate 6; ⏲5pm-midnight) Consistantly voted one of the word's best whisky bars, this grand old bar in the Grand Hotel Terminus is the perfect place for a quiet dram. It promises over 500 different tastes, and the oldest whisky dates back to 1960. The 1928 room looks gorgeous both before and after you've sampled a few.

Entertainment

Grieghallen CLASSICAL MUSIC
(☎55 21 61 50; www.grieghallen.no; Edvard Griegs plass; ⏲Aug-Jun) Performances by the respected Bergen Philharmonic Orchestra.

Café Sanaa LIVE MUSIC
(www.sanaa.no; Marken 31; ⏲8pm-3am Fri & Sat) This little shopfront cafe just up from the lake spills over onto the cobblestones and draws a fun, alternative crowd with live music and, later, resident DJs that might be pumping out West African beats, tango, blues or jazz.

Shopping

The wooden alleyways of Bryggen have become a haven for artists and craftspeople, and there are stunning little shops and boutiques at every turn.

★Aksdal i Muren OUTDOOR WEAR
(www.aksdalimuren.no; Østre Muralmenning 23) This enticing shop in a historic landmark building has been ensuring the good people of Bergen are warm and dry since 1883. The city's best selection of rainwear includes cult Swedish labels such as Didriksons and big names like Helle Hansen and Barbour, but also local gems such as Blæst by Lillebøe. We can't think of a better Bergen souvenir than a stripey sou'wester.

Røst SOUVENIRS
(www.butikkenrost.no; Bryggen 15; ⏲10am-10.30pm Jul & Aug, to 6pm Sep-Jun) Short on souvenir-buying time and want something more up-market than a troll doll? This bright boutique in the centre of Bryggen has a large range of well-designed Norwegian and Scandinavian objects and homewares, as well as local fashion for women, children and babies.

Schau Design VINTAGE
(Lille Øvregaten 5; ⏲noon-5pm Tue-Fri, to 3.30pm Sat) Nice selection of reasonably priced Scandinavian mid-century objects and furniture, with lots of packable options such as lamps, vases and kitchenware.

Bergen Steinsenter GEMS
(www.bergen-steinsenter.no; Bredsgården, Bryggen; ⏲11am-4pm Tue-Fri, noon-3pm Sat Jun–mid-Sep, shorter hr rest of yr) Statisify your inner troll at this eccentric gem and crystal merchant, that stocks some stunning geological specimens from around Norway and further afield.

ℹ Information

Bergen Turlag DNT Office (☎55 33 58 10; www.bergen-turlag.no; Tverrgaten 4; ⏲10am-4pm Mon-Wed & Fri, to 6pm Thu, to 3pm Sat) Maps and information on hiking and hut accommodation throughout western Norway.

Tourist Office (☎55 55 20 00; www.visitbergen.com; Vågsallmenningen 1; ⏲8.30am-10pm daily Jun-Aug, 9am-8pm daily May & Sep, 9am-4pm Mon-Sat Oct-Apr) One of the best and busiest in the country, this tourist office distributes the free and worthwhile *Bergen Guide* booklet, as well as a huge stock of information on the entire region. They also sell rail tickets. If booking or making an enquiry, come early or be prepared to queue.

ℹ Getting There & Away

AIR

The airport is in Flesland, 19km southwest of central Bergen. Direct flights connect Bergen with major cities in Norway, plus a handful of international destinations.

BOAT

The Hurtigruten coastal ferry leaves from the **Hurtigruteterminalen**, southwest of the centre, at 8pm daily from mid-April to mid-September, and from 10.30pm the rest of the year.

Norled Bergen (☎51 86 87 00; www.norled.no; Kong Christian Frederiks plass 3) Norled offers at least one daily ferry from Bergen to Sogndal (Nkr645, five hours), with some services going on to Flåm (Nkr750, 5½ hours).

BUS

Express buses run throughout the western fjords region, as well as to Ålesund (Nkr686, 10 hours, one to two daily), Trondheim (Nkr848, 12½ hours, two daily) and Stavanger (Nkr550, 5½ hours, five daily).

TRAIN

The spectacular train journey between Bergen and Oslo (p309; Nkr349 to Nkr829, 6½ to eight hours, five daily) runs through the heart of Norway. Other destinations include Voss (Nkr189, one hour, hourly) and Myrdal (Nkr286, 2¼ hours, up to nine daily) for connections to the Flåmsbana railway.

ℹ Getting Around

TO/FROM THE AIRPORT

Flybussen (www.flybussen.no; one way/return adult Nkr90/160, child Nkr50/80) Runs up to four times hourly between the airport, the Radisson SAS Royal Hotel, the main bus terminal and opposite the tourist office on Vågsallmenningen.

CAR & MOTORCYCLE

Metered parking limited to 30 minutes or two hours applies all over central Bergen. The largest and cheapest (Nkr130 per 24 hours) indoor car park is the 24-hour Bygarasjen at the bus terminal; elsewhere you'll pay upwards of Nkr200. The tourist office has two brochures covering where to park in Bergen.

Voss

POP 14,000

Voss has two personalities. At one level, it's a lakeside town with fine views at every turn and the perfect place to break up a journey between Bergen and the fjords. At the same time, it has a world-renowned reputation as one of Norway's top adventure capitals, drawing both beginners and veterans of the thrill-seeking world for rafting, bungee jumping and just about anything you can do from a parasail; many of the activities take you out into the fjords.

Sights & Activities

Vangskyrkja & St Olav's Cross CHURCH

(Uttrågata; adult/child Nkr20/free; ⏲10am-4pm Mon-Sat & 2-4pm Sun Jun-Aug, shorter hours Sep-May) Voss' stone church occupies the site of an ancient pagan temple. A Gothic-style stone church was built here in the mid-13th century and although the original stone altar and unique wooden spire remain, the Lutheran Reformation of 1536 saw the removal of many original features. The 1923 stained-glass window commemorates the 900th anniversary of Christianity in Voss. The building escaped destruction during the intense German bombing of Voss in 1940.

Prestegardsmoen Recreational & Nature Reserve HIKING

The Prestegardsmoen Recreational and Nature Reserve extends south from Voss Camping in a series of hiking tracks through elm, birch and pine forests with hundreds of species of plants and birds.

Hangursbahnen CABLE CAR

(www.vossresort.no; adult/child Nkr100/60; ⏲10am-5pm Jun-Aug) This cable car whisks you to Mt Hangur (660m), high above Voss, for stunning panoramic views over the town and the surrounding mountains. There's a restaurant at the top as well as walking paths.

VOSS ACTIVITIES

For booking any of the following, contact individual operators or get in touch with the tourist office (p319).

Paragliding, Parasailing & Bungee Jumping

Nordic Ventures (☎56 51 00 17; www.nordicventures.com; ⏲Apr–mid-Oct) is one of the most professional operators of its kind in Norway, offering tandem paragliding flights (Nkr1500), parasailing (solo/dual flights Nkr575/950) and even 180m-high, 115km/h bungee jumps (Nkr1800) from a parasail! It claims to offer the highest bungee jump in Europe. As its motto says: 'Be brave. Even if you're not, pretend to be. No one can tell the difference'.

Kayak Fjord Expeditions

If you do one activity in Voss (or even anywhere in the fjords), make it this one. The guided kayak tours offered by Nordic Ventures are the perfect way to experience Hardangerfjord and stunning Nærøyfjord and beyond with neither hurry nor crowds. The tours come in a range of options.

One-day (nine-hour) tours cost Nkr995 (including lunch and transport to/from the fjord), while the two-day version costs Nkr2295 and allows you to camp on the shores of the fjord. But our favourite is the three-day kayaking and hiking expedition (Nkr3295), which explores the fjords in kayaks and then takes you high above them for unrivalled views.

Nordic Ventures also rents out kayaks (one/two/three days Nkr550/925/1295) if you'd rather branch out on your own.

White-Water Rafting

Voss Rafting Senter (☎56 51 05 25; www.vossrafting.no) specialises in white-water rafting (Nkr1150) with some gentler, more family-friendly options (from Nkr630). Not to be outdone in the motto stakes, the company's motto is: 'We guarantee to wet your pants'.

Skiing

The ski season in Voss usually lasts from early December until April. The winter action focuses on the cable-car route up Mt Hangur from Voss, where there's a winter ski school. On the plateau and up the Raundalen Valley at Mjølfjell, you'll also find excellent cross-country skiing.

Other Activities

Voss Rafting Senter organises **canyoning** (Nkr1150), **waterfall abseiling** (from Nkr990), **riverboarding** (Nkr1150), **fishing** (from Nkr630) and **hiking** (from Nkr530).

Voss tourist office can also provide details of **cycling routes** and **self-guided hikes**, and sells fishing permits.

Festivals

Vossajazz MUSIC
(www.vossajazz.no) An innovative jazz, folk and world-music festival held annually in late March/early April.

Extreme Sports Festival SPORT
(Veko; www.ekstremsportveko.com) A week-long festival at the end of June that combines all manner of extreme sports (skydiving, paragliding and base jumping) with local and international music acts.

Sleeping & Eating

Voss Camping CAMPGROUND €
(☎56 51 15 97; www.vosscamping.no; Prestegardsalléen 40; campsites Nkr170, cabins from Nkr600; ⊙Easter-Sep; P @) Lakeside and centrally located, Voss Camping offers basic facilities and a rather rowdy summer scene.

Fleischer's Hotel HISTORIC HOTEL €€
(☎56 52 05 00; www.fleischers.no; Evangervegen; s/d from Nkr1290/1790; P ≋) Fleischer's Hotel, which opened in its current form in 1889, has a quaint historic charm. Rooms tend towards old-fashioned rather than authentic, but some have lake views, there's a swimming pool (with children's pool) and a lavish dining hall. Celebrity guests include Edvard Grieg, in 1901.

★ **Tre Brør Café & Bar** CAFE €
(www.vosscafe.no; Vangsgata 28; sandwiches & light meals Nkr85-185; ⊙10am-3am Tue-Sat, to 11pm Sun & Mon) This casual cafe in one of Voss' few original buildings is a long-time favourite with both travellers and locals. The recent addition of a basement bar means the fun continues until late most nights. Upstairs, there's a selection of snacky staples – organic beef burgers, soups, wraps – and a changing daily special, often with an Asian twist.

Ringheim Kafé NORWEGIAN €€
(www.ringheimkafe.no; Vangsgata 32; mains Nkr160-220; ⊙lunch) One of numerous cafes lined up along the main Vangsgata thoroughfare, Ringheim has outdoor tables and a cafeteria-style interior. Far from fancy, it serves regional-style dishes, including elk burgers (Nkr165), baked trout (Nkr210) and *hjortekoru* (Nkr180), the local smoked sausage with potato and cabbage stew.

Information

Tourist Office (☎40 61 77 00; www.visitvoss.no; Vangsgata 20; ⊙8am-7pm Mon-Fri, 9am-7pm Sat & noon-7pm Sun Jun-Aug, 8.30am-4pm Mon-Fri Sep-May) Well-stocked tourist office that also offers a booking service for various activities.

Getting There & Away

BUS

Frequent bus services connect Voss with Bergen (Nkr163, two hours), Flåm (Nkr143, 1¼ hours) and Sogndal (Nkr299, three hours), via Gudvangen and Aurland.

TRAIN

The **NSB** (☎56 52 80 00) rail services to/from Bergen (Nkr189, one hour, hourly) and Oslo (Nkr349 to Nkr829, 5½ to six hours, five daily) connect at Myrdal (Nkr117, 50 minutes) with the scenic line down to Flåm.

Hardangerfjord

A notch less jagged and steep than Sognefjord, Hardangerfjord's slopes support farms and wildflowers, which picturesquely enhance the green hills as they plunge into the water. Norway's second-longest fjord network, it stretches inland from a cluster of rocky coastal islands to the frozen heights of the **Folgefonn** and **Hardangerjøkulen** icecaps. The area is known for its orchards (apples, cherries and plums) and bursts into bloom from mid-May to mid-June. Helpful regional information can be found at www.hardangerfjord.com.

At the innermost reaches of Hardangerfjorden you'll find the **Eidfjord** area, with sheer mountains, huge waterfalls, spiral road tunnels and the extraordinary **Kjeåsen Farm**, a deliciously inaccessible farm perched on a mountain ledge about 6km northeast of Eidfjord. Other Eidfjord highlights include Viking burial mounds and, on the road up to the Hardangervidda Plateau, the excellent **Hardangervidda Natursenter** (www.hardangerviddanatursenter.no; Øvre Eidfjord; adult/child/family Nkr120/60/280; ⊙9am-8pm mid-Jun–mid-Aug, 10am-6pm Apr–mid-Jun & mid-Aug–Oct) with wonderful exhibits on the plateau, and the 182m-high **Vøringfoss** waterfall. For information, contact **Eidfjord tourist office** (☎53 67 34 00; www.visiteidfjord.no; Simadalsvegen 3; ⊙9am-7pm Mon-Fri & 10am-6pm Sat & Sun mid-Jun–mid-Aug, 10am-5pm Mon-Fri mid-Aug–mid-Jun).

Tranquil **Ulvik** has extraordinary views from its fjord-side walking paths, while at picturesque **Utne** you'll find an interesting collection of old buildings at the **Hardanger**

Folk Museum (www.hardangerogvossmuseum.no; adult/child Nkr75/free; ⌚10am-5pm daily May-Aug, to 3pm Mon-Fri Sep-Apr), and the pretty Utne Hotel.

For glacier hikes on the Buer arm of the Folgefonn ice sheet, contact the excellent **Flat Earth** (☎47 60 68 47; www.flatearth.no; adult incl crampons & ice axes Nkr700) in Odda. The hike up to **Trolltunga**, a narrow finger of rock that hangs out over the void high above the lake Ringedalsvatnet, and one of Norway's most precipitous vantage points, is another highlight close to Odda. For more information, contact Odda's **tourist office** (☎53 65 40 05; www.visitodda.com; ⌚9am-7pm mid-Jun–mid-Aug, shorter hours May & Sep).

Sleeping & Eating

★Eidfjord Gjestegiveri GUESTHOUSE €
(☎53 66 53 46; www.ovre-eidfjord.com; Øvre Eidfjord; hut Nkr480, s/d with shared bathroom & incl breakfast Nkr690/980; ⌚May-Aug; P) This delightful guesthouse run by Dutch owners Eric and Inge has a homely feel with just five sweetly furnished double rooms and one single, upstairs in a beautifully maintained building dating from 1896. There's six cute camping huts that are self-catering and use facilities in the main house's basement.

Vik Pensjonat GUESTHOUSE €€
(☎53 66 51 62; www.vikpensjonat.com; Eidfjord; d/f with private bathroom Nkr1100/1580, cabins Nkr800/1150, s/d with shared bathroom Nkr500/880; P) This appealing place in the centre of Eidfjord, not far from the water's edge, is set in a lovely renovated old home. It offers a friendly welcome and cosy rooms. Rooms with balconies are sought after, but the modern six-person cabin on the riverbank is also outstanding.

The attached cafe is one of the better places to eat in town, with reasonable prices (mains Nkr165 to Nkr210) and everything from soups and sandwiches to main dishes such as mountain trout.

★Utne Hotel HISTORIC HOTEL €€€
(☎53 66 64 00; www.utnehotel.no; Utne; s/d annex Nkr1290/1690, historic main bldg Nkr1490/1890; P) The historic wooden Utne Hotel was built in 1722 after the Great Nordic War, giving it claim to the title of Norway's oldest hotel, and has an interesting lineage of female hoteliers. Rooms have a simple elegance that harks back to another time, although bathrooms are smart and modern.

Getting There & Away

While thorough exploration of Hardangerfjord is best accomplished with a car, those with little time and no wheels would do well to book the 11-hour round-trip **Hardanger in a Nutshell** tour run by **Fjord Tours** (☎81 56 82 22; www.fjordtours.com). Combining bus, boat and train, it runs from Bergen to Norheimsund, Eidfjord, Ulvik and Voss, then back to Bergen again. Tickets can be purchased at Bergen's tourist office or online.

Stavanger

POP 124,940

Stavanger is one of our favourite cities in Norway. Said by some to be the largest wooden city in Europe, its old quarter climbs up the slopes around a pretty harbour. Here and elsewhere, the city is home to almost two dozen museums. Stavanger is also one of Norway's liveliest urban centres – in summer, the city's waterfront invariably courses with people in the best tradition of port cities. Stavanger is also an excellent base from which to explore stunning Lysefjord.

Sights

★Gamle Stavanger NEIGHBOURHOOD
Gamle (Old) Stavanger, above the western shore of the harbour, is a delight. The Old Town's cobblestone walkways pass between rows of late-18th-century whitewashed wooden houses, all immaculately kept and adorned with cheerful, well-tended flowerboxes. It well rewards an hour or two of ambling.

★Norsk Oljemuseum MUSEUM
(Oil Museum; www.norskolje.museum.no; Kjeringholmen; adult/child/family Nkr100/50/250; ⌚10am-7pm daily Jun-Aug, 10am-4pm Mon-Sat & 10am-6pm Sun Sep-May) You could spend hours in this state-of-the-art, beautifully designed museum, one of Norway's best. Focusing on oil exploration in the North Sea from discovery in 1969 until the present, it's filled with high-tech interactive displays and authentic reconstructions.

Highlights include the world's largest drill bit, simulated rig working environments, documentary films on a North Sea dive crew's work day and a vast hall of amazing oil-platform models.

Stavanger Domkirke CHURCH
(Haakon VII's gate; Nkr30; ⌚11am-7pm daily Jun-Aug, 11am-4pm Mon-Sat Sep-May) This beautiful church is an impressive but understated medieval stone cathedral dating from approx-

imately 1125; it was extensively renovated following a fire in 1272 and contains traces of Gothic, baroque, Romanesque and Anglo Norman influences. Despite restoration in the 1860s and 1940, and the stripping of some features during the Reformation, the cathedral is, by some accounts, Norway's oldest medieval cathedral still in its original form.

Stavanger Museum MUSEUM
(☎51 84 27 00; www.museumstavanger.no; ⏰11am-4pm daily mid-May–Aug, Tue-Sun rest of year) The large 11-part museum, with its sites scattered around Stavanger, could easily fill a sightseeing day or more. Entrance to all is by one-day ticket (adult/child Nkr70/40), or there is a four-day MUSTpass (adult/family Nkr100/250). Museums include the **Norwegian Printing Museum**, the **Norwegian School Museum** and the **Medical Museum**.

Sleeping

This is an oil city and prices can soar on weekdays as businesspeople arrive, but they return to more reasonable levels on weekends – try to plan your visit accordingly. Do, however, be sure to avoid the end of August in even years (2016 is up next), when the Offshore Northern Seas Foundation (ONS) show entirely takes over town.

The tourist office website (www.regionstavanger.com) has a list of small B&Bs in and around Stavanger.

★Thompsons B&B B&B €
(☎51 52 13 29; www.thompsonsbedandbreakfast.com; Muségata 79; s/d with shared bathroom Nkr400/500; P) Housed in a 19th-century villa in a peaceful residential area, this four-bed B&B has a home-away-from-home vibe engendered by the warm and welcoming owner, Sissel Thompson. Rooms are cosy and comfortable, and traditional Norwegian breakfast, taken around the downstairs dining table, is generous.

Comfort Hotel Square HOTEL €
(☎51 56 80 00; www.nordicchoicehotels.no; Løkkeveien 41; d from Nkr749; ❄) In a wavy wooden building up behind Gamle Stavanger, this option from the Nordic Choice Comfort line does the hip boutique thing (think exposed concrete walls, creative lighting and wall-sized photos) with chain convenience, facilities and value. Weekend rates are particularly good value (under half that of weekdays) and the elevated location is a good one.

★Darby's Inn B&B €€
(☎47 62 52 48; www.darbysbb.com; Kong Oscars Gate 18; s/d from Nkr1180/1290; P ❄) The two front rooms at this understated, oppulent B&B might be Stavanger's nicest, even without a sea view. Traditional interiors in this historic house combine dark wood with antique furniture, paintings, Persian rugs and a baby grand in the lounge and dining room. The large guest rooms are simpler but still have luxury linen, plump cushions and suitably heavy curtains.

Stavanger B&B B&B €€
(☎51 56 25 00; www.stavangerbedandbreakfast.no; Vikedalsgata 1a; s/d Nkr790/890, with shared bathroom Nkr690/790; P) This low-key place offers simple, bright rooms with satellite TV, shower and a smile from the friendly owners. Packed lunches are available for a small fee and free coffee, tea and waffles are served nightly.

Skagen Brygge Hotel HOTEL €€€
(☎51 85 00 00; www.skagenbryggehotell.no; Skagenkaien 30; s/d from Nkr1890/1990; ❄) This large, waterfront Clarion Collection flagship is quietly luxurious and rooms at the front have the best views in town (unusually, this includes some single rooms). There's a gym and free afternoon waffles, and the waterfront lounge is delightful. Prices halve come the weekend.

Eating

★Renaa Matbaren INTERNATIONAL €€
(Breitorget 6, enter from Bakkegata; small dishes Nrk135-189, mains Nkr195-335; ⏰11am-1am Mon-Sat, 1-10pm Sun) Yes, that's a proper Tracey Emin on the far wall and an actual Anthony Gormley in the middle of the room. This perpetually bustling bistro is testament to just how cashed-up and cultured this North Sea port is. You'd be happy to be here just for the buzz, but the food is fabulous too.

NB Sørensen's Damskibsexpedition NORWEGIAN €€
(☎51 84 38 00; Skagen 26; mains Nkr125-329; ⏰11am-1.30am Mon-Sat, 1-10pm Sun) Our pick of the waterfront restaurant row, this large maritime-themed place serves everything from confit duck (Nkr310) to roast Atlantic makerel (Nkr290). It really hits its straps when it comes to hearty, meaty mains, which may not be elegant but use top-quality produce.

Renaa Xpress Sølvberget MODERN NORWEGIAN €€
(Stavanger Kulturhus; www.restaurantrenaa.no; Sølvberggata 2; lunch dishes Nkr69-98, pizza Nkr160-200; ⏲10am-midnight Mon-Sat) This newcomer has quickly won the heart of Stavangerites and is all things to everybody at all hours of the day. Grab a morning coffee as the *kanelbollene* (cinammon rolls) come out of the oven, line up for the daily soup deal (Nkr160) or huge salad (Nkr69 to Nkr98) at lunch, or come later for wood-fired wild-yeasted pizza.

Torget Fish Market FISH MARKET €€€
(Rosenkildetorget; mains Nkr269; ⏲market 9am-4.30pm Mon-Sat, restaurant 11am-9pm Mon-Wed, 11am-midnight Thu-Sat) With just a tiny wet market, this place is not a patch on the Bergen version. The prime waterfront restaurant, however, does a good changing menu of entrees such as tuna tataki (Nkr169) and has a super fresh catch of the day. It's also a favoured after-work watering hole.

Drinking

We can only scratch the surface of Stavanger's surfeit of places to drink, dance and stay out late; the waterfront bar strip is loud, brash and perpetually busy, especially in the warmer months, and definitely not hard to find.

★ **Bøker & Børst** CAFE, BAR
(Øvre Holmegate 32; ⏲10am-2am) There are many little cafes beckoning in the lanes climbing the hillside west of the oil museum, but our favourite is book-clad Bøker & Børst, with its bohemian decor, good coffee and Stavanger's most interesting crowd, day or night.

Renaa Xpress CAFE
(Breitorget 6, enter from Steinkargata) Not to be confused with Renaa Xpress Sølvberget, this little cafe sits at the back of the glass-roofed arcade, up the stairs from the other two Renaa outfits. It's a great spot to soak up the sun in the company of Stavanger's stylish mums and babes with great coffee and brownies.

B.brormann B.bar BAR
(Skansegata 7; ⏲6pm-2am Mon-Thu, from 4pm Fri & Sat) One of Stavanger's best-loved bars, this low-key shopfront place draws a discerning over-30s crowd and, later, local hospitality staff for post-shift beers and gun-mixed cocktails (Nkr120).

ℹ Information

Stavanger Turistforening DNT (off Muségata; ⏲10am-4pm Mon-Wed & Fri, to 6pm Thu, to 3pm Sat) Information on hiking and mountain huts.

Tourist Office (☎51 85 92 00; www.regionstavanger.com; Domkirkeplassen 3; ⏲9am-8pm daily Jun-Aug, 9am-4pm Mon-Fri & 9am-2pm Sat Sep-May) Local information and advice on Lysefjord and Preikestolen.

ℹ Getting There & Around

TO/FROM THE AIRPORT

Between early morning and mid-to-late evening, **Flybussen** (☎51 52 26 00; www.flybussen.no/stavanger) runs every half-hour between the bus terminal and the airport at Sola (one way/return Nkr110/160).

BOAT

International ferries and boat tours of Lysefjord from Stavanger are available. Other services include the **M/S Lysebotn** (☎91 65 28 00; www.kolumbus.no) car-and-passenger ferries from Stavanger to Lysebotn (adult/child/car Nkr173/87/356).

BUS

Nor-Way Bussekspress offers services to Oslo (Nkr820, 9½ hours, three daily) and to Bergen (Nkr440, 5½ hours, 13 daily).

TRAIN

Trains run to Oslo (Nkr929, eight hours, up to five daily) via Kristiansand (Nkr474, 3½ hours).

Lysefjord

All along the 42km-long Lysefjord (Light Fjord), the granite rock glows with an ethereal, ambient light, even on dull days, all offset by almost-luminous mist. This is many visitors' favourite fjord and there's no doubt that it has a captivating beauty. Whether you cruise from Stavanger, hike up to Preikestolen, or drive the switchback road down to Lysebotn, it's one of Norway's must-sees.

The area's most popular outing is the two-hour hike to the top of the incredible **Preikestolen** (Pulpit Rock), 25km east of Stavanger. You can inch up to the edge of its flat top and peer 604m straight down a sheer cliff into the blue water of the Lysefjord for some intense vertigo. The other option is the **Kjeragbolten** boulder (chockstone), lodged between two rock faces about 2m apart but with 1000m of empty space underneath.

Sognefjorden

Sognefjorden, Norway's longest (204km) and deepest (1308m) fjord, cuts a deep slash across the map of western Norway. In places, sheer walls rise more than 1000m above the water, while elsewhere a gentler shoreline supports farms, orchards and villages. The broad, main waterway is impressive but by cruising into its narrower arms, such as the deep and lovely Nærøyfjord (on the Unesco World Heritage list) to Gudvangen, you'll see idyllic views of abrupt cliff faces and cascading waterfalls.

ℹ Getting There & Away

Norled (www.norled.no) operates a daily express boat between Bergen and both Flåm (Nkr750, 5½ hours) and Sogndal (Nkr645, 4¾ hours), stopping along the way at 10 small towns including Vik (Nkr510, 3½ hours) and Balestrand (Nkr545, 3¾ hours). Several local ferries also link Sognefjord towns, and there's an extensive, if infrequent, bus network.

Flåm

POP 450

Scenically set at the head of Aurlandsfjorden, Flåm is a tiny village of orchards and a handful of buildings. It's a jumping-off spot for travellers taking the Gudvangen ferry, the Sognefjorden express boat or the Myrdal train. It all gets a little overrun with people when a cruise ship's in port; it sees an amazing 500,000 visitors every summer. To rediscover solitude, walking a few minutes from the centre is all it takes.

VISITING LYSEFJORD

For general information on the region, check out www.ryfylke.com or www.visit lysefjorden.no.

Pulpit Rock by Public Transport

From May to mid-September, five to seven ferries a day run from Stavanger's Fiskespiren Quay to Tau, where the ferries are met by a bus, which runs between the Tau pier and the Preikestolhytta Vandrerhjem. From there, the two-hour trail leads up to Preikestolen. The last bus from Preikestolhytta to Tau leaves at 7.55pm. **Tide Reiser** (www.tidereiser.no) offers all-inclusive round-trip tickets (adult/child Nkr250/125); there are timetables online or at the tourist office. You can buy tickets there, online or at Fiskespiren Quay.

Pulpit Rock by Car

If you've got your own vehicle, you can take the car ferry (adult/child/car Nkr42/21/125, 40 minutes, up to 24 departures daily) from Stavanger's Fiskespiren Quay to Tau. From the pier in Tau, a well-signed road (Rv13) leads 19km to Preikestolhytta Vandrerhjem (take the signed turn-off after 13km). It costs Nkr70/35 per car/motorcycle to park here.

An alternative route from Stavanger involves driving to Lauvik (via Sandnes along Rv13), from where a ferry crosses to Oanes (10 minutes, departures almost every half-hour).

Either way, the trip between Stavanger and the trailhead takes around 1½ hours.

Boat Tours to Lysefjord

Two companies offer three-hour boat cruises from Stavanger to the waters below Preikestolen on Lysefjord and back:

Rødne Fjord Cruise (☎51 89 52 70; www.rodne.no; Skagenkaien 35-37, Stavanger; adult/senior & student/child/family Nkr450/350/280/1150; ⏰ departures 10am & 2pm Sun-Fri & noon Sat Jul & Aug, noon daily May, Jun & Sep, noon Fri-Sun Oct-Apr)

Tide Reiser (☎51 86 87 88; www.tidereiser.no; adult/senior & student/child Nkr360/280/250; ⏰ departures noon daily late May-late Aug, noon Sat Sep-late May)

Round Trips to Kjeragbolten

From mid-May to late August Tide Reiser also runs 13½-hour bus–boat–hike return trips to Kjeragbolten (Nkr490), which can otherwise be difficult to reach. It includes a five-hour return hike.

Sights

Flåmsbana Railway SCENIC RAILWAY

(www.flaamsbana.no; adult/child one way Nkr300/150, return Nkr400/300) A 20km-long engineering wonder hauls itself up 864m of altitude gain through 20 tunnels. At a gradient of 1:18, it's the world's steepest railway that runs without cable or rack wheels. It takes a full 45 minutes to climb to Myrdal on the bleak, treeless Hardangervidda plateau, past thundering waterfalls (there's a photo stop at awesome Kjosfossen). The railway runs year-round, with up to 10 departures daily in summer.

Flåmsbana Museum MUSEUM

(9am-7pm May-Sep, shorter hours rest of year) FREE This little museum is right by the Flåmsbana Railway platform. It's not, however, just about railways: there are fascinating photos of construction gangs and life in and around Flåm before cars and buses made it this far up the fjords.

Activities

Riding the Rallarvegen CYCLING

(www.rallarvegen.com) Cyclists can descend the Rallarvegen, the service road originally used by the navvies who constructed the Flåmsbana railway, for 83km from Haugastøl (1000m) or an easier 56km from Finse. You can rent bicycles from the **Haugastøl Turistsenter** (32 08 75 64; Haugastølvegen, Haugastøl; 2-day bike hire weekday/weekend Nkr480/580, including return transport from Flåm) and the company also offers packages that include accommodation.

Njord KAYAKING

(91 31 66 28; www.njord.as) Njord operates from Flåm's handkerchief of a beach. It offers a two-hour sea-kayaking induction (Nkr350), three-hour gentle fjord paddle (Nkr550) and four-hour paddle and hike trips (Nkr710), plus multiday kayaking, hiking and camping trips.

Fjord Safari ADVENTURE

(www.fjordsafari.com) Bounce along in a Zodiac/RIB inflatable to see more of the fjord in less time. The team supplies full-length waterproof kit – you'll need it for this exhilarating scoot across the waters. Trips, with stops, last from 1½ hours (adult/child Nkr510/310) to three hours (adult/child Nkr610/380).

Sleeping & Eating

★**Flåm Camping & Hostel** HOSTEL, CAMPGROUND €

(57 63 21 21; www.flaam-camping.no; car/caravan site Nkr215/220, dm/s/tw/q Nkr300/500/865/1255, with shared bathroom Nkr230/390/650/950; Mar-Oct) Family-run and built on the site of the old family farm, there's a lot of love gone into every aspect of this operation. Rooms, from dorms to ensuite doubles, are spread across the lush site, each with a stylish simplicity of their own. Campsites are idyllically located too. In a gorgeous spot a few minutes' walk from the station.

Heimly Pensjonat GUESTHOUSE €€

(57 63 23 00; www.heimly.no; s/d Nkr795/1195) Overlooking the water on the fringe of the village and away from all the port hubbub, this 1930s home has basic rooms. The more expensive ones have magnificent views right down the fjord.

Fretheim Hotel HOTEL €€€

(57 63 63 00; www.fretheim-hotel.no; s/d Nkr1195/2190; P @) A haunt of fly-fishing English aristocracy in the 19th century, the vast, 122-room Fretheim, despite its size, manages to be intimate and welcoming. In the original 1870s building, 17 rooms have been restored to their historic selves, although with full

SOGNEFJORDEN BY BOAT

Nærøyfjord, its 17km length a Unesco World Heritage Site, lies west of Flåm. Beside the deep blue fjord (only 250m across at its narrowest point) are towering 1200m-high cliffs, isolated farms, and waterfalls plummeting from the heights.

The most scenic trip from Flåm is the passenger ferry up Nærøyfjord to Gudvangen (one way/return Nkr295/400). It leaves Flåm at 3.10pm year-round and up to five times daily between May and September. You can also hop aboard in Aurland. At Gudvangen, a connecting bus takes you on to Voss, where you can pick up the train for Bergen or Oslo. The tourist office sells all ferry tickets, plus the Flåm to Voss ferry-bus combination. From Flåm-Bergen, there's at least one daily express boat (Nkr695, 5½ hours) via Balestrand (Nkr265, 1½ hours).

modern comfort, while the American wings are straight-up contemporary luxe.

Information

Tourist Office (☎57 63 33 13; www.visitflam.com; ⏲8.30am-8pm Jun-Aug, to 4pm May & Sep) Within the train station.

Getting There & Away

Bus services run to Gudvangen (Nkr52, 20 minutess, four to eight daily), Aurland (Nkr36, 15 minutes, four to eight daily), Sogndal (Nkr184, 1¾ hours, two to six daily) and Bergen (Nkr330, three hours, two to six daily).

Aurland

Peaceful Aurland is Flåm's alter ego, so much less hectic than its neighbour a mere 10km south along the fjord. The views from here are more spectacular than than those from Flåm, and it's the starting point for some fine drives, hikes and boat trips.

Sleeping & Eating

Aurland Fjordhotell HOTEL €€
(☎57 63 35 05; www.aurland-fjordhotel.com; s/d from Nkr920/1240) At this 30-room, family-owned hotel, most rooms have fjord views and balcony. It's old-fashioned, but both comfortable and friendly.

Vangsgaarden HOTEL €€
(☎57 63 35 80; www.vangsgaarden.no; d/f Nkr1100/1350, 4-bed cabins Nkr1250 (linen per person Nkr65);) Four 18th-century buildings along with six cabins down at sea level and the **Duehuset (Dovecot) Cafe & Pub** (mains from Nkr129; ⏲3-11pm Jun-Aug) make up this friendly prime waterfront place. Some rooms are furnished in antique style, while others are simpler. It's atmospheric – the dining room, for example, could be your grandmother's parlour – and the gardens are pretty.

Information

Aurland Tourist Office (☎57 63 33 13; www.alr.no; ⏲9am-5pm Mon-Fri & 10am-5.30pm Sat & Sun Jun-Aug, shorter hours rest of year) The tourist office is beside the village church.

Getting There & Away

Buses run up to eight times daily between Aurland and Flåm (Nkr36, 15 minutes) and one to six times daily between Aurland and Lærdal (Nkr83, 30 minutes). Express buses to/from Bergen (Nkr300, three hours) call in up to six times daily.

SNØVEGEN

The 45km Snow Road, officially signed **Aurlandsvegen**, climbs from sea level, twisting precipitously to the desolate, boulder-strewn high plateau that separates Aurland and Lærdalsøyri (Lærdal). This heart-stopping drive – strictly for summertime as snow banks line the road and tarns are still deep-frozen even in late June – has been designated as a National Tourist Route, so get there before the coaches catch on. Even if you don't opt for the whole route, drive the first 8km from Aurland to the magnificent **Stegastein observation point**. Projecting out over the fjord way below, the biomorphic pine-clad structure is striking to look at, not to mention designed to push you just a little out of your comfort zone, rather like Norway itself.

Stalheim

POP 200

This gorgeous little spot high above the valley is an extraordinary place. Between 1647 and 1909, Stalheim was a stopping-off point for travellers on the Royal Mail route between Copenhagen, Christiania (Oslo) and Bergen. The mailmen and their weary steeds rested in Stalheim and changed to fresh horses after climbing up the valley and through the Stalheimskleiva gorge, flanked by the thundering Stalheim and Sivle waterfalls.

Sleeping

★ **Stalheim Hotel** HISTORIC HOTEL €€€
(☎56 52 01 22; www.stalheim.com; s/d/superior from Nkr1160/1750/2150; ⏲mid-May–mid-Sep; P @) Arguably Norway's most spectacularly sited hotel, this large '60s place has simple, spacious rooms, around half of which have glorious views (room 324, in particular, once featured in Conde Nast's 'best rooms with a view'). The stunning lounge, lobby and dining hall are filled with a truly exceptional collection of Norwegian mid-century design and historical paintings.

Despite the onslaught of tour groups during the day, the friendly staff and elegant owner maintain a sense of calm. The buffets at lunch (Nkr250) and dinner (Nkr450) are lavish, or there is an a la carte menu (mains Nkr245); meals work out cheaper on half-board rates.

HIKES FROM STALHEIM

Husmannsplassen Nåli This cotter's farm, along the ledge from Stalheim high above Nærøydalen, was occupied until 1930. The route there (two hours return) is not for the faint-hearted. The path beneath the cliff wall is extremely narrow in parts and there is nothing between you and the valley floor far below; don't even think of walking here after rain.

Brekkedalen This three-hour return hike leads up into the valley above Stalheim. Locals in the know claim it's the region's prettiest walk, and the views are certainly magnificent. It's a relatively easy way to leave the crowds behind and have this stunning high country all to yourself. The tourist office in Voss has route descriptions, or ask at Stalheim Hotel for directions.

Getting There & Away

To reach Stalheim from Voss (Nkr101, one hour, four to 11 daily), take any bus towards the towns of Gudvangen and Aurland, but you may have to hike 1.3km up from the main road unless you can persuade the bus driver to make the short detour.

Balestrand

POP 1340

Balestrand sits comfortably beside the fjord; at its rear is an impressive mountain backdrop. Genteel and low-key, it has been a tranquil, small-scale holiday resort ever since the 19th century and it's still one of our favourite bases for exploring Sognefjord.

Sights

Church of St Olav CHURCH

This charming wooden church (1897), in the style of a traditional stave church, was built at the instigation of English expat Margaret Green, who married a local hotel-owner. It's just up the hill; should you find it closed, the owner of Midtnes Hotel has the key.

Sognefjord Aquarium AQUARIUM

(adult/child Nkr70/35; 10am-7pm May-Sep) View the 15-minute audiovisual presentation then tour the 24 aquariums in which lurk saltwater creatures from Sognefjord, large, small and very small. The entry price includes an hour of canoe or rowing-boat hire.

Viking Age Barrows BURIAL MOUNDS

Less than 1km south along the fjord, excavation of this pair of barrows revealed remnants of a boat, two skeletons, jewellery and several weapons. One mound is topped by a statue of legendary **King Bele**, erected by Germany's Kaiser Wilhelm II. Obsessed with Nordic mythology, he regularly spent his holidays here prior to WWI (a similar monument, also funded by the Kaiser and honouring Fridtjof, the lover of King Bele's daughter, peers across the fjord from Vangsnes).

Activities

The tourist office's free pamphlet *Outdoor Activities in Balestrand* has plenty of suggestions for **hiking**, ranging from easy to demanding. If you need more detail, it also stocks *Balestrand Turkart* (Nkr70), a good walking map at 1:50,000 with trails marked up.

The tourist office hires out bicycles for Nkr70/170/270 per hour/half day/full day.

Sleeping & Eating

Sjøtun Camping CAMPGROUND €

(95 06 72 61; www.sjotun.com; campsite Nkr210, 4-/6-bed cabin with outdoor bathroom Nkr300/400; Jun–mid-Sep) At this green campsite, a 15-minute walk south along the fjord, you can pitch a tent on soft grass amid apple trees or rent a sweet cabin at a very reasonable price.

Balestrand Hotell HOTEL €€

(57 69 11 38; www.balestrand.com; s/d Nkr850/1340; mid-May–mid-Sep) This summertime-only, family-run hotel is a friendly, jolly, intimate place that eschews the tour groups that fill so many beds elsewhere in town. It's well worth paying more for inspirational views over the fjord.

Kvikne's Hotel HOTEL €€€

(57 69 42 00; www.kviknes.no; s/d from Nkr1110/1720; May-Sep; P @) The dreamy pale-yellow, timber exterior of Kvikne's Hotel belies the more-is-more late-19th-century Norwegiana aesthetic in its lounges and dining halls. Of its 190 rooms, all but 25 are in the newer building, erected in the 1960s. They're comfortable to a fault but a little dated for the price.

Balholm Bar og Bistro serves snacks and light meals and you can take your drinks into the salon where there's plenty to look at outside and in. The hotel is on a point just south of the ferry landing.

SOGNEFJORDEN STAVE CHURCHES

Borgund Stave Church (adult/child Nkr75/55; ⏲8am-8pm mid-Jun–mid-Aug, 10am-5pm May–mid-Jun & mid-Aug–Sep) Some 30km southeast of Lærdalsøyri along the E16, this 12th-century stave church was raised beside one of the major trade routes between eastern and western Norway. Dedicated to St Andrew, it's one of the best-known, most-photographed – and certainly the best-preserved – of Norway's stave churches. Beside it is the only freestanding medieval wooden bell tower still standing in Norway. Buy your ticket at the visitors centre, which has a worthwhile exhibition (included in the price of your admission) on this peculiarly Norwegian phenomenon. If you enjoy walking, build in time to undertake the two-hour circular hike on ancient paths and tracks that starts and ends at the church.

Hopperstad Stave Church (adult/child Nkr60/50; ⏲10am-5pm late May-late Sep) On the southern outskirts of the village of Vik is this splendid stave church, about 1km from the centre. Built in 1130 and Norway's second oldest, it escaped demolition by a whisker in the late 19th century. Inside, the original canopy paintings of the elaborately carved baldequin have preserved their freshness of colour. A combined ticket for the Hove stone church, 1km to the south, is Nkr80/70.

Urnes Stave Church (adult/child Nkr80/45; ⏲10.30am-5.45pm May-Sep) Norway's oldest preserved place of worship is a Unesco World Heritage Site. Directly across the fjord from Solvorn, it gazes out over Lustrafjord. The original church was built around 1070, while the majority of today's structure was constructed a century later. Highlights are elaborate wooden carvings – animals locked in struggle, stylised intertwined bodies and abstract motifs – on the north wall, all recycled from the original church, and the simple crucifixion carving, set above the chancel wall.

Ciderhuset NORWEGIAN €€
(☎98 47 77 65; www.ciderhuset.no; Sjøtunsvegen 32; mains Nkr140-250; ⏲4-10pm late Jun–mid-Aug) Within a fruit farm that produces organic juices, jams, bottled fruits, cider and cider brandy, this happy restaurant fuses Nordic and Mediterranean culinary traditions. They use local produce wherever possible; even the dinnerware is fired by a local potter. Dine on the first-floor terrace or inside the cosy glasshouse, where fresh herbs and cherry tomatoes climb the panes.

ℹ Information

Tourist Office (☎99 23 15 00; www.visitbalestrand.no; ⏲10am-5.30pm daily Jun-Aug, 10am-5pm Mon-Fri May & Sep) This tourist office, run by an extremely knowledgeable and helpful local, is opposite the ferry quay. It hires out bicycles for Nkr70/170/270 per hour/half day/full day.

ℹ Getting There & Away

BOAT

Express boats run to/from Bergen (Nkr545, 3¾ hours, twice daily) and Sogndal (Nkr240, 45 minutes, once daily). From June to August, a daily ferry (Nkr240/390 one way/return, 90 minute, twice daily) follows the narrow Fjærlandsfjorden to Fjærland, gateway to the glacial wonderlands of Jostedalsbreen.

BUS

Express buses link Balestrand and Sogndal (Nkr128, one hour, three daily).

Jostedalsbreen

With an area of 487 sq km, the many-tongued Jostedalsbreen dominates the highlands between Nordfjord and Sognefjord and is mainland Europe's largest icecap; in some places it is 400m thick. Protected as a national park, the icecap provides extraordinary opportunities for otherworldly glacier hiking.

Jostedalen & Nigardsbreen

The Jostedalen valley pokes due north from Gaupne, on the shores of Lustrafjord. This slim finger sits between two national parks and it's a spectacular drive as the road runs beside the milky turquoise river, tumbling beneath the eastern flank of the Nigardsbreen glacier. Of the Jostedalsbreen glacier tongues visible from below, Nigardsbreen is the most dramatic and easiest to approach.

Sights

Breheimsenteret Visitors Centre MUSEUM

(☎57 68 32 50; www.jostedal.com; adult/child Nkr60/free; ⏲9am-6pm mid-Jun–Aug, 10am-5pm May–mid-Jun & Sep) Jostedal's visitor centre has a small museum of geological displays, a shop and a cafe with spectacular views down the valley to the winding blue glacial tongue. The website collects together all the tour and activities operators.

Activities

Most of the following activities are only available from June to September, and some only operate in July and August.

Ice Troll GLACIER VISITS

(☎97 01 43 70; www.icetroll.com; 6hr excursions Nkr750, overnight Nkr1500) Andy – from New Zealand and with a decade of guiding experience on Nigardsbreen – and his team offer truly original glacier visits, where kayaks are used to get to isolated spots.

Most are suitable for first-timers as well as the more experienced, or there's a motorboat option for young families.

Jostedalen Breførarlag GLACIER VISITS

(☎57 68 31 11; www.bfl.no) Leads several guided glacier walks on Nigardsbreen. The easiest is the family walk to the glacier snout and briefly along its tongue (around one hour on the ice, adult/child Nkr260/130). Fees for the two-hour (Nkr460), three-hour (Nkr525) and five-hour (Nkr760) walks on the ice include the brief boat trip across Nigardsvatnet lake.

Riverpig RAFTING

(www.riverpig.no; ⏲Jun-Sep) Riverpig offers white-water rafting on the Jostedalen river (Nkr800) and, for the truly hardy, riverboarding (Nkr1300).

Sleeping

★**Jostedal Camping** CAMPGROUND €

(☎57 68 39 14; www.jostedalcamping.no; car/caravan sites Nkr180/190, cabins Nkr390-1300) Astrid, after many years travelling and working overseas, returned to her home village and with her partner runs this buccolic, well-kept campsite, right beside the Jostedal river. Facilities are impeccable, with a beautiful new terrace, communal kitchen, lounge and

WORTH A TRIP

GAMLE STRYNEFJELLSVEGEN: A DRIVING TOUR

This spectacular 130km route takes a comfortable four hours. Head eastwards from Stryn along the **Rv15** as it runs alongside the river that descends from Lake Strynevatnet, then follows the lake shore itself. It's an inspirational ride with mountain views as impressive as anywhere in the country.

After 20km, stop to visit the **Jostedalsbreen National Park Centre** (Jostedalsbreen Nasjonalparksenter; www.jostedalsbre.no; adult/child Nkr80/40; ⏲10am-4pm or 6pm May–mid-Sep) in the village of **Oppstryn**. At an interpretive panel and sign 17km beyond the National Park Centre, turn right to take the **Rv258**. The road, the Gamle Strynefjellsvegen, considered a masterpiece of civil engineering at the time, opened to traffic in 1894, and for more than 80 years it was the principal east-to-west route in this part of the country. Until well into the 1950s, a team of some 200 workers, armed only with spades, would keep it clear in winter.

The climb to the high plateau is spectacular. Savour, in particular, the viewing platform above Videfossen, where the water churns beneath you. Some 9km along the Gamle Strynefjellsvegen, you reach **Stryn Summer Ski Centre** (Stryn Sommerskisenter; www.stryn.no/sommerski); from late May until some time in July it offers Norway's most extensive summer skiing.

The steep ascent behind you, continue along a good-quality unsurfaced single-track road that runs above a necklace of milky turquoise tarns overlooked by bare, boulder-strewn rock. After crossing the watershed 10km beyond the ski centre, there begins a much more gentle descent to rejoin the Rv15. Turn left for a fast, smooth, two-lane run beside **Lake Breidalsvatn** before diving into the first of three long tunnels that will bring you back to the National Park Centre and onward, retracing your steps back to Stryn.

The Gamle Strynefjellsvegen is normally free of snow from June to October. Electronic signs along the Rv15 indicate if the 'Strynfjellet' (its official name) is indeed open.

dining space with floor-to-ceiling windows overlooking the river's rapid course.

Jostedal Hotel HOTEL €€

(☎57 68 31 19; www.jostedalhotel.no; s/d/f Nkr820/1070/1320; @) Just 2.5km south of the Breheimsenteret visitors centre, this friendly hotel has been run by the same family for three generations and is currently under Laila's care. Newly renovated rooms are very comfortable and light, and have very pretty views. There are also family rooms with self-catering facilities that can accommodate up to five guests.

Getting There & Around

If you're driving, leave the Rv55 Sognefjellet Rd at Gaupne and head north up Jostedal along the Rv604.

From mid-June to mid-September, **Jostedalsbrebussen** (No 160; Glacier Bus; www.jostedal.com/brebussen; adult/child Nkr136/68) runs from Sogndal (with connections from Flåm, Balestrand and Lærdal) via Solvorn to the foot of the Nigardsbreen glacier, leaving at 8.45am and setting out on the return journey at 4.50pm.

Fjærland

POP 310

The village of Fjærland, also called Mundal, at the head of scenic Fjærlandsfjorden, pulls in as many as 300,000 visitors each year. Most come to experience its pair of particularly accessible glacial tongues, Supphellebreen and Bøyabreen. Others come to be bookworms. This tiny place, known as the Book Town of Norway (www.bokbyen.no), is a bibliophile's dream, with a dozen shops selling a wide range of used books, mostly in Norwegian but with lots in English and other European languages.

The village virtually hibernates from October onwards, then leaps to life in early May, when the ferry runs again.

Sights

★**Norwegian Glacier Museum** MUSEUM

(Norsk Bremuseum; ☎57 69 32 88; www.bre.museum.no; adult/child Nkr120/60; 9am-7pm Jun-Aug, 10am-4pm Apr, May, Sep & Oct) For the story on flowing ice and how it has sculpted the Norwegian landscape, visit this well-executed museum, 3km inland from the Fjærland ferry jetty. You can learn how fjords are formed, see a 20-minute audiovisual presentation on Jostedalsbreen, touch 1000-year-old ice, wind your way through a tunnel that penetrates the mock ice and even see the tusk of a Siberian woolly mammoth who met an icy demise 30,000 years ago.

Supphellebreen GLACIER

You can drive to within 300m of the Supphellebreen glacier, then walk right up and touch the ice. Ice blocks from here were used as podiums at the 1994 Winter Olympics in Lillehammer.

Activities

The tourist office's free sheet, *Escape the Asphalt,* lists 12 marked walking routes, varying from 30 minutes to three hours. For greater detail, supplement this with *Turkart Fjærland* (Nkr70) at 1:50,000, which comes complete with route descriptions and trails indicated.

Fjærland Kayak & Glacier KAYAKING

(☎92 85 46 74; www.kayakandglacier.com; Sandaneset; 10am-4pm May-Aug, or by appointment) At the small fjord-side shack, you can hire a kayak, canoe, motor or rowing boat or join one of its daily guided kayaking trips, ranging from 2½ hours (Nkr420) to a full day (Nkr950).

Sleeping

Bøyum Camping CAMPGROUND €

(☎57 69 32 52; www.boyumcamping.no; campsites Nkr190, dm Nkr200, d with shared bathroom Nkr315-400, 4-/8-bed cabins Nkr890/1100; May-Sep) Beside the Glacier Museum and 3km from the Fjærland ferry landing, this place has something for all budgets and sleeping preferences, not to mention a great view of the Bøyabreen glacier at the head of the valley.

★**Hotel Mundal** HOTEL €€€

(☎57 69 31 01; www.hotelmundal.no; s/d Nkr850/1200, water view Nkr1200/2100; May-Sep; P @) Run by the same family ever since it was built in 1891, this beautiful hotel retains much of its period interior: original local furniture with the odd bit of Viennese Thonet, paintings, rugs, leather armchairs made by local craftsmen and a 'modern' remodel of a 1920s parlour. Rooms are traditional, but pretty and light.

Getting There & Away

A car ferry (Nkr275/360 one way/return, 1¼ hours) runs twice daily between Balestrand and Fjærland in July and August (in May, June and September there's a daily passenger-ferry run).

Buses bypass the village and stop on the Rv5 near the glacier museum. Three to six run daily to/from Sogndal (Nkr73, 30 minutes) and Stryn (Nkr200, two hours).

Geirangerfjord

Added to Unesco's World Heritage list in 2005, this king of Norwegian fjords boasts towering, twisting walls that curve inland for 20 narrow kilometres. Along the way abandoned farms cling to the cliffs and breathtakingly high waterfalls – with names such as the Seven Sisters, the Suitor and the Bridal Veil – drop straight into the sea from forests above.

The public ferry cruise between Geiranger and Hellesylt is extraordinarily beautiful.

Sights

Flydalsjuvet VIEWPOINT

Somewhere you've seen that classic photo, beloved of brochures, of the overhanging rock Flydalsjuvet, usually with a figure gazing down at a cruise ship in Geirangerfjord. The car park, signposted Flydalsjuvet, about 5km uphill from Geiranger on the Stryn road, offers a great view of the fjord and the green river valley, but doesn't provide the postcard view down to the last detail. For that, you'll have to drop about 150m down the hill, then descend a slippery and rather indistinct track to the edge. Your intrepid photo subject will have to scramble down gingerly and with the utmost care to the overhang about 50m further along; if it's a selfie, we advise care when walking backwards.

Dalsnibba VIEWPOINT

For the highest and perhaps most stunning of the many stunning views of the Geiranger valley and fjord, take the 5km toll road (Nkr85 per car) that climbs from the Rv63 to the **Dalsnibba lookout** (1500m). A bus (adult/child Nkr180/90 return) runs three times daily from Geiranger between mid-June and mid-August.

Norsk Fjordsenter MUSEUM

(www.verdsarvfjord.no; adult/child Nkr100/50; 10am-6pm) The Norwegian Fjord Centre has tools, artefacts and even whole buildings that have been uprooted and brought here, illustrating the essential themes – the mail packet, avalanches, the building of early roads and the rise of tourism – that have shaped the land and its people. It's located up the hill along the Rv63, just past the

Hotel Union (70 26 83 00; www.union-hotel.no; s/d Nkr 1600/2200; Feb–mid-Dec; P @).

Activities

All around Geiranger there are great signed **hiking** routes to abandoned farmsteads, waterfalls and vista points. The tourist office's aerial-photographed *Hiking Routes* map (Nkr10) gives ideas for 18 signed walks of between 1.5km and 5km.

Coastal Odyssey KAYAKING, HIKING

(91 11 80 62; www.coastalodyssey.com; sea kayaks per hr/half day/day Nkr150/450/800, kayaking-hiking trips Nkr800-1250) Based at Geiranger Camping (a short walk from the ferry terminal), this much-recommended company is run by Jonathan Bendiksen, a Canadian from the Northwest Territories who learnt to kayak almost before he could walk. He rents sea-kayaks and does daily hiking and canoeing trips to four of the finest destinations around the fjord.

Geiranger Adventure CYCLING

(47 37 97 71; www.geiranger-adventure.com; Gågata; per adult/child incl transport, bikes, helmet & other equipment Nkr450/225) This outfit will drive you up to Djupvasshytta (1038m), from where you can coast for 17 gentle, scenically splendid kilometres by bike down to the fjord; allow a couple of hours. It also rents bikes (Nkr50/200 per hour/day).

Geiranger Fjordservice BOAT

(70 26 30 07; www.geirangerfjord.no) This operation offers 1½-hour sightseeing boat tours (adult/child Nkr 110/45, sailing four times daily June to August). Its kiosk is within the Geiranger tourist office. From mid-June to August, it also operates a smaller, 15-seater boat (Nkr390/190) that scuds deeper and faster into the fjord.

Sleeping & Eating

Geirangerfjorden Feriesenter CAMPGROUND €

(95 10 75 27; www.geirangerfjorden.net; Grande; campsite Nkr260, cabins from Nkr850; late Apr–mid-Sep; @) An excellent camping option with well-maintained facilities and particularly pretty, well-decorated cabins. Good longer-stay rates are available.

★**Westerås Gard** CABIN €€

(93 26 44 97; www.geiranger.no/westeras; 2-bed cabin Nkr950, apt Nkr1150; May-Sep) This beautiful old working farm, 4km along the Rv63 towards Grotli, sits at the end of a

narrow road dizzingly high above the bustle. Stay in one of the two farmhouse apartments, or there are five pine-clad cabins. The barn, dating to 1603, is home to a restaurant, where Arnfinn and Iris serve dishes made with their own produce.

Olebuda & Cafe Olé RESTAURANT €
(☎70 26 32 30; www.olebuda.no; restaurant Nkr120-135; ⊙cafe 9am-7pm, restaurant from 6pm) In Geiranger's old general store, the pretty upstairs restaurant does a range of international-style dishes and good local standards like poached salmon roulade and house-smoked goat; all fish and meat are local. Downstairs is a casual cafe with great carrot cake (Nkr45), all-day snacks and good coffee.

Information

Tourist Office (☎70 26 30 99; www.geiranger.no; ⊙9am-6pm mid-May–mid-Sep) Located right beside the pier.

Getting There & Away

BOAT

The popular, hugely recommended run between Geiranger and Hellesylt (car with driver Nkr320, adult/child one way Nkr160/79, return Nkr215/115; one hour) is quite the most spectacular scheduled ferry route in Norway. It has four to eight sailings daily from May to September (every 90 minutes until 6.30pm, June to August).

Almost as scenic is the ferry that runs twice daily between Geiranger and Valldal (adult/child one way Nkr240/130, return Nkr370/190, 2¼ hours). A mini-cruise in itself, it runs from mid-June to mid-August.

BUS

From mid-June to mid-August two buses daily make the spectacular run over Trollstigen to Åndalsnes (Nkr265, three hours) via Valldal (Nkr85, 1½ hours). For Molde, change buses in Åndalsnes; for Ålesund, change at Linge.

Åndalsnes

POP 2240

Two of the three approaches to Åndalsnes are dramatic by any standards: by road through the Trollstigen pass or along Romsdalen as you ride (or follow the route of the spectacularly scenic Raumabanen). Badly bombed during WWII, the modern town, nestled beside Romsdalfjord, is nondescript, but the surrounding landscapes are magnificent.

Sights

Trollveggen CLIFF
From Dombås, the E136 and rail line drop in parallel northwest down to Romsdalen (you might have a sense of déjà vu if you've seen *Harry Potter and the Half-Blood Prince*, in which the valley features). Near Åndalsnes, dramatic Trollveggen (Troll Wall), first conquered in 1958 by a joint Norwegian and English team, rears skywards. The highest vertical mountain wall in Europe, its ragged and often cloud-shrouded summit, 1800m from the valley floor, is considered the ultimate challenge among mountaineers.

Raumabanen SCENIC RAILWAY
(tourist train adult/child return Nkr460/230; one child per adult travels free) Trains run daily year-round along this spectacular route, meeting the main line, after 114km, at Dombås. There's also a **tourist train** with on-board commentary that runs twice daily from June to August from Åndalsnes' lakeside station up to Bjorli, at 600m. Book at the station or tourist office.

Activities

Hiking

An excellent day hike, signed by red markers, begins in town and climbs to the summit of Nesaksla (715m), the prominent peak that rises above Åndalsnes. At the top, the

SVELE AHOY

Norway is well known for its devotion to the waffle, but the western fjords and coast have a sweet afternoon treat that's all its own. *Svele*, a fat folded pancake, can be found at cafes and hotels throughout the region, but traditionally it's the snack of choice for fjord crossings. Ferries have served *svele* in their cafeterias since the early 1970s and have their own closely guarded recipes. So what, apart from the experience of eating one in the presence of stunning fjord scenery, makes a *svele* unique? A particularly satisfying cake-like texture and flavour come from the addition of an unusual rising agent, salt of hartshorn, along with a measure of tart buttermilk. Plus it's in the toppings. Forget jam; *svele* come with either a sublimely simple smear of butter and sprinkle of sugar between the folds, or stuffed with a slice of *brunost*, the characteristic caramelised brown cheese of the region.

payoff for a steep ascent is a magnificent panorama.

Another fabulous (and strenuous) day hike is the Romsdalseggen, an all-day hike (at least seven hours) along the ridge of the same name. In summer, a bus (25 minutes) leaves from outside the Åndalsnes train station at 9.30am to the trailhead. The tourist office has detailed information on this hike.

Climbing

The best local climbs are the less extreme sections of the 1500m-high rock route on Trollveggen and the 1550m-high Romsdalshorn, but there are a wealth of others. Serious climbers should buy *Klatring i Romsdal* (Nkr300), which includes rock- and ice-climbing information in both Norwegian and English.

Skiing

Romsdalen is considered among the best skiing areas in the country, its ski up/ski down demands rewarding with with untouched power, continuous views to fjords and wild peaks.

Kirketaket (1439m) is one of the Romsdalen 'classics' and takes three to five hours to ascend but delivers over 1000 vertical metres of steep downhill slopes, from where you can kikør down to the fjord.

Festivals & Events

Norsk Fjellfestival OUTDOOR ACTIVITIES

(Norway Mountain Festival; www.norsk-fjellfestival.no) A week-long get-together for lovers of the great outdoors with plenty of folk events thrown in. Early July.

Rauma Rock ROCK MUSIC

(www.raumarock.com) Central Norway's largest outdoor rock gathering. Two days in early August.

Sleeping & Eating

Trollstigen Resort CAMPGROUND €

(☎71 22 68 99; www.trollstigenresort.com; car/caravan sites Nkr190/200, 4-/5-bed cabins from Nkr500/1150) Recognisable by the strapping wooden troll at its entrance, this well-kept campsite is 2km along the Rv63 highway from Åndalsnes in the direction of Geiranger. The welcome's warm and the location, overlooking the River Rauma and embraced by mountains, is scenic and peaceful. All but one of the cabins have bathrooms and the two-bedders are smartly renovated. Open year-round, it's popular with skiers in winter.

★ **Hotel Aak** HOTEL €€

(☎71 22 71 71; www.hotelaak.no; s/d Nkr995/1400; ⊙mid-Jun–Aug; P) One of the oldest tourist hotels in Norway is now in the hands of a charming young family. Kristine and Odd Erik Rønning – locals, dedicated travellers, super-experienced climbers, hikers and skiers – have imbued all with a light touch that beautifully encapsulates the region's rustic appeal but is super stylish and switched on to a new generation of traveller. The restaurant is open 4pm to 10pm.

Grand Hotel Bellevue HOTEL €€€

(☎71 22 75 00; www.grandhotel.no; Åndalgata 5; s/d Nkr1195/1550; P@) This large hotel, up on its own hill, is the town's true centre. After a recent, smart renovation its busy lobby is now rather glamorous. Most of its 86 rooms have fine views and lots of light. The **restaurant** (mains Nkr275-325; ⊙dinner Mon-Sat) is the town's most formal and is decorated with a fascinating collection of local paintings, though the food is less remarkable.

★ **Sødahl-Huset** CAFE €

(Romsdalsvegen 8; ⊙10am-3pm Mon-Thu, 10am-11pm Fri & Sat & 2-7pm Sun mid-Jun–mid-Aug, shorter hours rest of year) The blackboard declares 'local and home-made burgers, coffee, cake, ice cream – served by lovely ladies'. It's all true. Owners Mari, Rannveig and Sissel are indeed lovely and the food is proudly local, from the berry sorbets to the pour-over coffee to the *kraftkar* (local blue cheese) burger.

Kaikanten CAFE-RESTAURANT €€

(mains Nkr150-225; ⊙10am-9pm Mon-Thu, 10am-11pm Fri & Sat, noon-9pm Sun mid-May–Aug) Sit back and relax at the jetty's edge and enjoy a drink and one pretty panorama in this welcoming place. The menu takes in those old Norwegian favourites: *svele* (pancakes), pizza and burgers.

Information

Tourist Office (☎71 22 16 22; www.visitandalsnes.com; ⊙9am-8pm daily Jun-Aug, 9am-3pm Mon-Fri Sep-May) At Åndalsnes train station. They rent bikes (hour/day Nkr60/185).

Getting There & Away

BUS

Buses along the spectacular National Tourist Route to Geiranger (Nkr265, three hours), via Trollstigen, the Linge–Eidsdal ferry and the steep Ørnevegen (Eagle's Way), run twice daily between mid-June and mid-August.

WORTH A TRIP

TROLLSTIGEN

South of Åndalsnes, **Trollstigen** (Troll's Ladder; www.trollstigen.net; ⌚ Jun-Sep) is a thriller of a climb or descent. Recently declared a National Tourist Route, it was completed in 1936 after eight years of labour. To add an extra daredevil element to its 11 hairpin bends and a 1:12 gradient, much of it is effectively single lane. Several dramatic waterfalls, including the thundering 180m-high Stigfossen, slice down its flanks.

At the top, a visitors centre has been built from concrete, rusted steel and glass, to both withstand the extreme terrain and to mimic its many textures. Leading from here are dramatic viewing platforms that jut here and there over the abyss and offer panoramas of the snaking road and the lush valley below, as well as a perpetual waterfall soundtrack. Around you as you descend are the open reaches of Reinheimen National Park, established in 2006 and Norway's third largest, where wild reindeer still crop the mosses and soft grass.

The pass is usually cleared and open from late May to mid-October; early in the season it's an impressive trip through a popular cross-country ski field, between high walls of snow.

There are also services to Molde (Nkr145, 1½ hours, up to eight daily) and Ålesund (Nkr295, 2¼ hours, four times daily).

TRAIN

Trains to/from Dombås (Nkr230, 1½ hours) run twice daily in synchronisation with Oslo–Trondheim trains. Trains connect in Åndalsnes twice daily with the express bus service to Ålesund via Molde.

Ålesund

POP 23,000

The coastal town of Ålesund is, for many, just as beautiful as Bergen, if on a much smaller scale, and it is certainly far less touristy. Lucky for you, Ålesund burned to the ground in 1904. The amazing rebuilding created a town centre unlike anything else you'll see in Norway – a harmonious collection of pastel buildings almost entirely designed in the art nouveau tradition. All the loveliness is well staged on the end of a peninsula, surrounded by islands, water and hills.

Sights & Activities

★Jugendstil Senteret MUSEUM

(Art Nouveau Centre; ☎70 10 49 70; www.jugendstilsenteret.no; Apotekergata 16; adult/child Nkr75/40; ⌚10am-5pm daily Jun–Aug, 11am-4pm Tue-Sun Sep-May) The city's unique architectural heritage is documented in a former pharmacy, the first listed Jugendstil monument in Ålesund. Apart from the building's own exquisite and almost entirely extant interior, including a sinuous staircase and florid dining room, displays include textiles, ceramics, furniture, posters and other ephemera. Even if you're not a keen aesthete, a 'Time Machine' capsule is great fun, presenting 'From Ashes to Art Nouveau', a 14-minute multimedia story of the rebuilding of Ålesund after the great fire.

KUBE MUSEUM

(Møre and Romsdal County Museum of Art; Apotekergata 16; adult/child Nkr75/40; ⌚10am-5pm Jun-Aug, 11am-4pm Tue-Sun Sep-May) Ålesund's primary contemporary art space highlights Norwegian artists, as well as hosting the occasional design- and architecture-focused show. The old Bank of Norway building's upstairs gallery also has a wonderful view of the harbour.

Sunnmøre Museum MUSEUM

(www.sunnmore.museum.no; Borgundgavlen; adult/child Nkr80/30; ⌚10am-4pm Mon-Fri, noon-4pm Sun, closed Mon Nov-Apr) Ålesund's celebrated Sunnmøre Museum is 4km east of the centre. Here, at the site of the old Borgundkaupangen trading centre, active from the 11th to 16th centuries, over 50 traditional buildings have been relocated. Ship-lovers will savour the collection of around 40 historic boats, including replicas of Viking-era ships and a commercial trading vessel from around AD 1000. Take bus 613, 618 or 624.

Aksla VIEWPOINT

The 418 steps up Aksla hill lead to the splendid **Kniven viewpoint** over Ålesund and the surrounding mountains and islands. Follow Lihauggata from the pedestrian shopping street Kongensgata, pass the **Rollon statue**, and begin the 15-minute puff to the top of the hill. There's also a cheat's road to the crest; take Røysegata east from the centre, then follow the Fjellstua signposts up the hill.

Sleeping

Ålesund Vandrerhjem HOSTEL €
(☎70 11 58 30; www.hihostels.no; Parkgata 14; dm/s/d/apt incl breakfast Nkr285/690/890/1490; @) In a pretty residential area a few minutes' walk from the port, this attractive building has big, pristine rooms. There's a large self-catering kitchen. Most doubles come with bathroom and there are family-sized apartments with their own kitchen.

Scandic Hotel Ålesund HOTEL €€
(☎21 61 45 00; www.scandichotels.com; Molovegen 6; s/d Nkr1060/1255; @) The Scandic has many things going for it, postion being just one. Rooms all have hardwood flooring and the clean, bright Scandic look. While most have some harbour view, you can't beat the junior suites; they are not large but have stunning round 'lookout' windows that bring the sea seemingly within reach.

★ **Hotel Brosundet** HOTEL €€€
(☎70 11 45 00; www.brosundet.no; Apotekergata 5; s/d Nkr1330/1530, d with view Nkr1730; P@) Right on the waterfront and designed by superstar architects Snøhetta, this former warehouse is one of Norway's most charming hotels. Wonderful old beams and exposed brick walls are combined wtih contemporary comfort and style. Bedroom furnishings are of white oak, bathrooms are set behind smokey glass walls and beds are draped with brown velvet and sheepskins.

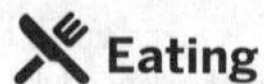

Eating

Invit CAFE €€
(☎70 15 66 44; www.invit.no; Apotekergata 9; salads Nkr135, Thu eve seafood buffet Nkr300-450; ⏲8.15am-4.30pm Mon-Fri, 6pm-midnight Thu, 10am-4.30pm Sat) Invit does central Ålesund's best coffee and is its most stylish lunch spot. Daily changing salads are super fresh and inventive, healthy soups are warming and the nutty, fragrant cakes are home made. If the streetside bar is full, spread out downstairs at one of the beautiful big wooden tables.

Lyspunktet CAFE, RESTAURANT €€
(www.lyspunktet.as; Kipervikgata 1; mains Nkr129-169; ⏲10am-10pm Tue-Fri, noon-5pm Sat & Sun) At this great-value place, join the youthful crowd on its deep sofa. There are free refills for coffee and soft drinks, and the west-coast pulled-pork and coleslaw sandwich is a local favourite, along with its fish soup. There's international cafe standards too, like chili con carne, as well as a 'slice of Sydney' focaccia.

XL Diner FISH RESTAURANT €€€
(☎70 12 42 53; Skaregata 1; mains Nkr289-340; ⏲5pm-midnight Mon-Sat) Nothing could be further from a trad greasy diner than this 1st-floor fish restaurant overlooking the harbour. Seductively lit *klippfisk* (salt-cod) line the entrance, so there's no doubt as to the house speciality. This quintessentially Norwegian dish is offered in a variety of *bacalao* (salt-cod stew) styles, such as Genovese (with pesto and potato) or Spanish (with 'red' sauce).

MOLDEJAZZ

Every July, Moldejazz pulls up to 100,000 fans and a host of jazz greats to the town of Molde. The lineup is primarily Scandinavian though every few years includes international top liners along the lines of Sonny Rollins, Bobby McFerrin and Herbie Hancock. The town parties all the way from Monday to Saturday. Of over 100 concerts, a good one-third are free, while big events are very reasonably priced at Nkr50 to Nkr600.

For this year's events, see www.moldejazz.no.

Information

Tourist Office (☎70 15 76 00; www.visitalesund-geiranger.com; Skaregata 1; ⏲8.30am-6pm daily Jun-Aug, 9am-4pm Mon-Fri Sep-May) Its booklet *Along the Streets of Ålesund* (Nkr30) details the town's architectural highlights in a walking tour.

Getting There & Away

AIR

Norwegian has direct summertime flights to Edinburgh and London (Gatwick). Internal destinations include Bergen (three times daily), Trondheim (twice daily) and Oslo (up to 10 times daily).

BOAT

The *Hurtigruten* docks at Skansekaia Terminal.

BUS

Local buses run to/from Åndalsnes (Nkr295, 2¼ hours, four times daily).

Express buses run to/from Bergen (Nkr686, 9¼ hours, one to three times daily), Hellesylt (Nkr190, 2¾ hours, up to five daily), Molde (Nkr155, 1½ hours, hourly), Oslo (Nkr915, 12½ hours, twice daily), Trondheim (Nkr1094, 7½ hours, one to three daily) via Molde (Nkr173, 2¼ hours), and Stryn (Nkr304, 3¾ hours, one to four daily).

NORTHERN NORWAY

A vast plateau reaches across much of the northern Norwegian interior, while small fishing villages cling to the incredibly steep and jagged Lofoten Islands, which erupt vertically out of the ocean. Medieval Trondheim, Norway's third-largest city, provides plenty of culture and charm, while Tromsø, the world's northernmost university town, parties year-round.

An alternative to land travel is the *Hurtigruten* coastal ferry, which pulls into every sizeable port, passing some of the best coastal scenery in Scandinavia. A good thing, too, since trains only run as far as Bodø.

Trondheim

POP 182,035

Trondheim, Norway's original capital, is Norway's third-largest city after Oslo and Bergen. With its wide streets and partly pedestrianised heart, it's an attractive city with a long history. Fuelled by a large student population, it buzzes with life. Cycles zip everywhere, it has some good cafes and restaurants, and it's rich in museums. You *could* absorb it in one busy day, but it merits more if you're to slip into its lifestyle.

Trondheim was founded at the estuary of the winding Nidelva in AD 997 by the Viking king Olav Tryggvason. After a fire razed most of the city in 1681, Trondheim was redesigned with wide streets and Renaissance flair by General Caspar de Cicignon. Today, the steeple of the medieval Nidaros Domkirke is still the highest point in the city centre.

Sights

From **Gamle Bybro** (Old Town Bridge) there's a superb view of the Bryggen, colourful 18th- and 19th-century riverfront warehouses. To the east, the one-time working-class neighbourhoods of **Møllenberg** and **Bakklandet** are all cobbles, car-free alleys, trim houses in pastel shades and gardens scarcely bigger than a towel that burst with flowers. Here, within old warehouses and renovated workers' housing, are some of the city's most colourful places to eat and drink.

★Nidaros Domkirke CATHEDRAL

(www.nidarosdomen.no; Kongsgårdsgata; adult/child/family Nkr70/30/170, tower Nkr30; ⌚9am-7pm Mon-Fri, to 2pm Sat, to 5pm Sun mid-Jun–mid-Aug, shorter hours rest of year) Nidaros Cathedral is Scandinavia's largest medieval building. Outside, the ornately embellished, altar-like west wall has top-to-bottom statues of biblical characters and Norwegian bishops and kings, sculpted in the early 20th century. Several are copies of medieval originals, housed nowadays in the museum. Within, the cathedral is subtly lit (just see how the vibrantly coloured, modern stained-glass glows, especially in the rose window at the west end), so let your eyes attune to the gloom.

There are ascents every half hour from its base in the south transept.

★Archbishop's Palace MUSEUM

(Kongsgårdsgata; adult/child/family Nkr70/30/170, crown jewels Nkr70/30/170; ⌚10am-5pm Mon-Fri, 10am-3pm Sat, noon-4pm Sun, shorter hours rest of year) The 12th-century archbishop's residence (Erkebispegården), commissioned around 1160 and Scandinavia's oldest secular building, is beside the cathedral. In its west wing, Norway's **crown jewels** shimmer. Its **museum** is in the same compound. After visiting the well-displayed statues, gargoyles and carvings from the cathedral, drop to the lower level, where a selection of the myriad artefacts revealed during the museum's construction in the late 1990s are on show. Also take a look at its 15-minute audiovisual program.

★Stiftsgården PALACE

(www.nkim.no/stiftsgarden; Munkegata 23; adult/child Nkr80/40; ⌚10am-5pm Mon-Sat & noon-5pm Sun Jun–late Aug, 10am-3pm Mon-Wed, Fri & Sat, noon-8pm Thu & noon-4pm Sun Sep–May) Scandinavia's largest wooden palace, the late-baroque Stiftsgården, was constructed as a private residence in the late 18th century, at the height of Trondheim's golden age. It is now the official royal residence in Trondheim. Admission is by tour only, every hour on the hour. The publicly accessible garden around the east side (enter via Dronningens gate) is one of Trondheim's loveliest corners.

Trondheim Kunstmuseum GALLERY

(☎73 53 81 80; trondheimkunstmuseum.no; Bispegata 7b; adult/child Nkr80/40; ⌚noon-4pm

COMBINATION TICKET

If you're planning to visit all three sights within the Nidaros Domkirke complex, it's worthwhile purchasing a combined ticket (adult/child/family Nkr140/60/340) that gives access to the cathedral, Archbishop's Palace museum and the crown jewels.

Tue-Sun) Trondheim's Art Museum, a stone's throw from the cathedral, houses a permanent collection of modern Norwegian and Danish art from 1800 onwards, including a hallway of Munch lithographs. It also runs temporary exhibitions.

★ Home of Rock MUSEUM

(www.rockheim.no; Brattørkaia 14; adult/child Nkr100/50; ⏲11am-7pm Tue-Fri, to 6pm Sat & Sun) This terrific museum is devoted to pop and rock music, mainly Norwegian, from the 1950s until yesterday. It's a dockside temple to R&B, where a huge projecting roof, featuring Norwegian record covers, extends above an equally vast converted warehouse. Within, there's plenty of action and interaction (mix your own hip-hop tape, for example). Home of Rock is on the quayside, very near Pirbadet and the fast-ferry landing stage.

★ Sverresborg Trøndelag Folkemuseum MUSEUM, ARCHITECTURE

(www.sverresborg.no; Sverresborg Allé 13; adult/child incl guided tour Nkr125/50; ⏲10am-5pm daily mid-May–Aug, 11am-3pm Mon-Fri & noon-4pm Sat & Sun rest of year) West of the centre, this folk museum is one of the best of its kind in Norway. The indoor exhibition, Livsbilder (Images of Life), displays artefacts in use over

Trondheim

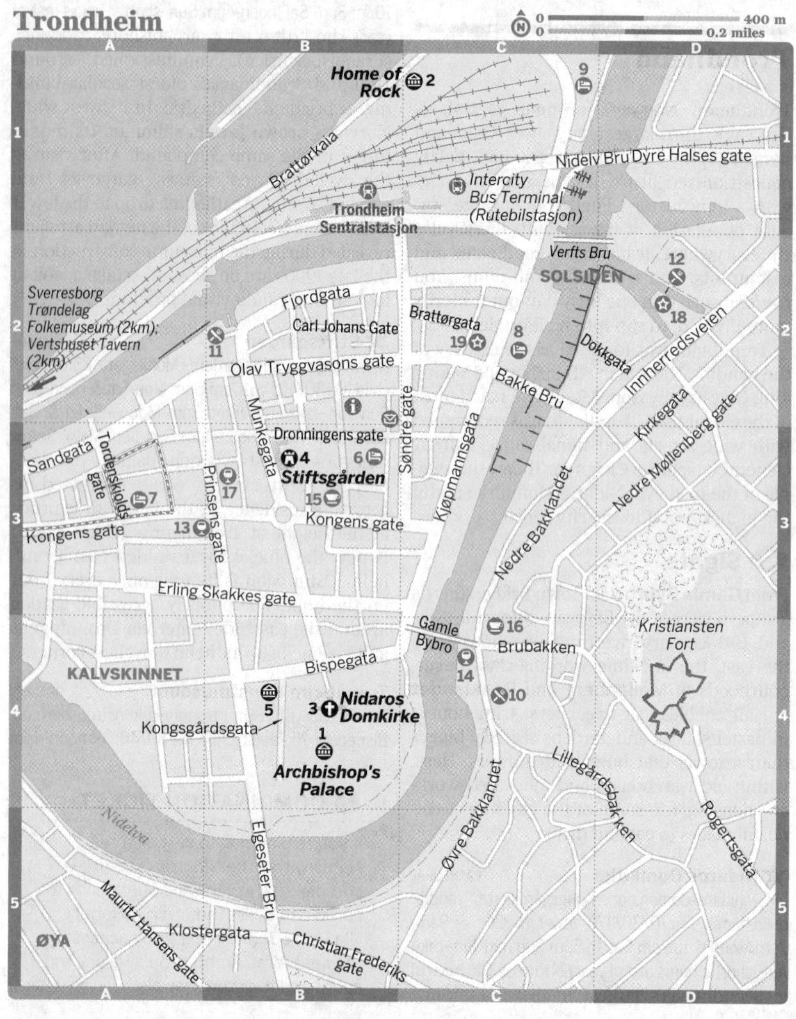

the last 150 years – from clothing to school supplies to bicycles – and has a short multimedia presentation. The rest of the museum, with over 60 period buildings, is open-air, adjoining the ruins of King Sverre's castle and giving fine hilltop views of the city.

Activities

West of town spreads the Bymarka, a gorgeous green woodland area laced with wilderness footpaths and ski trails. Take the Gråkallbanen tram, in itself a lovely scenic ride through the leafy suburbs, from the St Olavsgata stop to **Lian**. There you can enjoy excellent views over the city and a good swimming lake, **Lianvannet**.

The **Vassfjellet** mountains, south of town, offer both downhill and cross-country skiing. In season, a daily ski bus runs directly from Munkegata to the Vassfjellet Skisenter, only 8km beyond the city limits.

Trondheim Kajakk KAYAKING
(☎48 33 83 18; trondheimkajakk.no; 2hr tour incl rental Nkr300-400) A fine way to get an alternative perspective on Trondheim, these kayak tours paddle from where the Nidelven River meets the fjord and then right through the old town. Prices vary with the number of people.

Trondheim

Top Sights

1	Archbishop's Palace	B4
2	Home of Rock	C1
3	Nidaros Domkirke	B4
4	Stiftsgården	B3

Sights

5	Trondheim Kunstmuseum	B4

Sleeping

6	Britannia Hotel	B3
7	Pensjonat Jarlen	A3
8	Radisson Blu Royal Garden Hotel	C2
9	Rica Nidelven Hotel	C1

Eating

10	Baklandet Skydsstasjon	C4
11	Ravnkloa Fish Market	B2
12	Søstrene Karlsen	D2

Drinking & Nightlife

13	Bruk Bar	A3
14	Den Gode Nabo	C4
15	Dromedar Kaffebar	B3
16	Dromedar Kaffebar	C4
17	Trondheim Microbryggeri	B3

Entertainment

18	Dokkhuset	D2
19	Olavshallen	C2

Festivals & Events

Kosmorama FILM
(www.kosmorama.no) Trondheim's international film festival occupies an intensive week in late April, often spilling over into early May.

Nidaros Blues Festival MUSIC
(www.nidarosbluesfestival.com) A Who's Who of the international blues scene with local acts as well. Held in April.

Olavsfestdagene CULTURAL
(www.olavsfestdagene.no) In honour of St Olav and held during the week around his saint's day, 29 July. There's a medieval market and a rich program of classical music, folk, pop and jazz.

UKA CULTURAL
(www.uka.no) Trondheim's 25,000 university students stage this three-week celebration, Norway's largest cultural festival. Held every other year (in odd-numbered years) in October and November, it's a continuous party with concerts, plays and other festivities based at the round, red Studentersamfundet (Student Centre).

Sleeping

★ **Pensjonat Jarlen** GUESTHOUSE €
(☎73 51 32 18; www.jarlen.no; Kongens gate 40; s/d Nkr540/690) Price, convenience and value for money are a winning combination here. After a recent overhaul, the rooms at this central spot have a contemporary look and are outstanding value, although some bathrooms could do with a fresh look. Some rooms have polished floorboards, others carpet, and most have a hot plate and fridge thrown in.

Flakk Camping CAMPGROUND €
(☎72 84 39 00; www.flakk-camping.no; car/caravan site Nkr220/300, cabins Nkr490-650; ⊙May-Aug; P) Sitting right beside Trondheimfjord (there's minimal disturbance from the nearby ferry point), this welcoming campground is about 10km from the city centre. Take Rv715 from Trondheim.

Rica Nidelven Hotel HOTEL €€
(☎73 56 80 0073 56 80 00; www.rica.no; Havnegata 1-3; r Nkr945-1695; P @) A fabulous waterside location next to Solsiden and within a five-minute walk of the old part

of town, this stylish hotel has attractive rooms, all 343 of them, and many have river views. The hotel won the prize for Norway's best hotel breakfast, which is reason enough to stay here.

Britannia Hotel HOTEL €€
(☎73 80 08 00; www.britannia.no; Dronningens gate 5; s/d from Nkr506/806; P ❄ @ ☒) This mastodon of a hotel with nearly 250 rooms was constructed in 1897 and in 2013 became part of the Thon Hotel chain. It still exudes old-world grace from the mellow, wooden panelling of public areas to the magnificent oval Moorish-revival **Palmehaven restaurant** – just one of three places to eat – with its Corinthian pillars and central fountain. Rooms have a graceful, classical charm.

Radisson Blu Royal Garden Hotel HOTEL €€
(☎73 80 30 00; www.radissonblu.com; Kjøpmannsgata 73; s/d from Nkr795/995; P ❄ @ ☒) This first-class, contemporary riverside hotel (you can fish from your window in some rooms) is open and airy from the moment you step into the atrium, where the light streams in through the all-glass walls.

Eating

★Ravnkloa Fish Market SEAFOOD €
(☎73 52 55 21; www.ravnkloa.no; Munkegata; snacks from Nkr45, mains Nkr150-185; ⏲10am-5pm Mon-Fri, to 4pm Sat) Everything looks good at this fish market that doubles as a cafe with quayside tables out front. The fish cakes are fabulous and they also do shrimp sandwiches, mussels and a fine fish soup. In addition to seafood, they sell an impressive range of cheeses and other gourmet goods.

★Baklandet Skydsstasjon NORWEGIAN €€
(☎73 92 10 4473 92 10 44; www.skydsstation.no; Øvre Bakklandet 33; mains Nkr138-245; ⏲11am-1am Mon-Fri, from noon Sat & Sun) Within what began life as an 18th-century coaching inn are several cosy rooms with poky angles and listing floors. It's a hyperfriendly place where you can tuck into tasty dishes, such as its renowned fish soup ('the best in all Norway', a couple of diners assured us), or the lunchtime herring buffet (Nkr178) from Thursday to Saturday. Always leave room for a homemade cake.

Søstrene Karlsen NORWEGIAN, INTERNATIONAL €€
(☎73 60 00 25; www.sostrenekarlsen.no; Tmv-kaia 25; lunch mains Nkr135-239, dinner mains Nkr173-358; ⏲11am-midnight Mon-Thu, 11am-2am Fri & Sat, noon-11pm Sun) Despite the irresistible energy of the Solsiden waterfront area, most of the restaurants are of the chain variety – people tend to come here for the atmosphere rather than the quality of the food. Søstrene Karlsen is a cut above the rest and is wildly popular as a result. There's everything from sandwiches to more substantial mains of the usual fish and meat variety.

★Vertshuset Tavern NORWEGIAN €€€
(☎73 87 80 70; www.tavern.no; Sverresborg Allé 11; mains Nkr165-285; ⏲4-9pm Mon, 4-10pm Tue-Fri, 2-10pm Sat, 2-9pm Sun) Once in the heart of Trondheim, this historic (1739) tavern was lifted and transported, every last plank of it, to the Sverresborg Trøndelag Folkemuseum on the outskirts of town. Tuck into its rotating specials of traditional Norwegian fare or just graze on waffles with coffee in one of its 16 tiny rooms, each low-beamed, with sloping floors, candlesticks, cast-iron stoves and lacy tablecloths.

Drinking

As a student town, Trondheim offers lots of through-the-night life. The free paper *Natt & Dag* has listings, mostly in Norwegian. Solsiden (Sunnyside) is Trondheim's trendiest leisure zone. A whole wharf-side of bars and restaurants nestle beneath smart new apartment blocks, converted warehouses and long-idle cranes.

There's a cluster of nightclubs at the northern end of Nordre gate.

★Den Gode Nabo PUB
(www.dengodenabo.com; Øvre Bakklandet 66; ⏲4pm-1.30am Sun-Fri, from 1pm Sat) The Good Neighbour, dark and cavernous within, and nominated more than once as Norway's best pub, enjoys a prime riverside location. Indeed, part of it is on the water; reserve a table on the floating pontoon. There's a reproduction Wurlitzer jukebox; US visitors will find Sam Adams on tap while UK ale connoisseurs can savour Shepherd Neame's Bishop's Finger in the bottle.

★Trondheim Microbryggeri PUB
(Prinsens gate 39; ⏲5pm-midnight Mon, 3pm-2am Tue-Fri, noon-2am Sat) This splendid home-brew pub deserves a pilgrimage as reverential as anything accorded to St Olav from all committed *øl* (beer) quaffers. With up to eight of its own brews on tap and good light meals coming from the kitchen, it's a place to linger, nibble and tipple. It's down a short lane, just off Prinsens gate.

Bruk Bar BAR
(Prinsens gate 19; ⌚noon-1am Mon-Thu, noon-2am Fri & Sat, 1pm-midnight Sun) Inside, a stuffed elk head gazes benignly down, candles flicker and designer lamps shed light onto the 30-or-so-year-olds who patronise this welcoming joint. The music is eclectic, varying at the whim of bar staff, but guaranteed to be loud.

Dromedar Kaffebar CAFE
(Nedre Bakklandet 3; ⌚7am-6pm Mon-Fri, from 10am Sat & Sun) This longstanding local self-service coffee favourite serves what could be Trondheim's best coffee indeed, in all sizes, squeezes and strengths. Inside is cramped so, if the weather permits, relax on the exterior terrace bordering the cobbled street. There's a second **branch** (Nørdre gate 2), similar in style, also with a streetside terrace, that serves equally aromatic coffee, with further branches elsewhere around town.

✩ Entertainment

Dokkhuset CULTURAL CENTRE
(www.dokkhuset.no; Dokkparken 4; ⌚11am-1am Mon-Thu, 11am-3am Fri & Sat, 1pm-1am Sun) In an artistically converted former pumping station (look through the glass beneath your feet at the old engines), the Dock House is at once auditorium (where if it's the right night you'll hear experimental jazz or chamber music), restaurant and cafe-bar. Sip a drink on the jetty or survey the Trondheim scene from its roof terrace.

Olavshallen CONCERT HALL
(☎73 99 40 50; www.olavshallen.no; Kjøpmannsgata 44) Trondheim's main concert hall is within the Olavskvartalet cultural centre. The home base of the Trondheim Symphony Orchestra, it also features international rock and jazz concerts, mostly between September and May.

ℹ Information

Tourist Office (☎73 80 76 60; www.visittrondheim.no; Nordre gate 11; ⌚9am-6pm, closed Sun mid-Aug-mid-Jul) In the heart of the city with an accommodation booking service.

ℹ Getting There & Away

AIR

Værnes airport is 32km east of Trondheim. There are flights to all major Norwegian cities, as well as Copenhagen and Stockholm. Norwegian flies to/from London (Gatwick) and KLM covers Amsterdam.

> **GO TO HELL**
>
> It may be a cliché but who hasn't been tempted to pull over and snap a photo of themselves under the sign at Hell train station? If you give in to the temptation – and, hell, we have – you'll have the perfect riposte whenever someone tells you to go to hell. I've already been, you can reply, to Hell *and* back... Trondheim's Værnes airport is next door, but clearly naming Trondheim's main portal Hell International Airport was a road too far. For the record, the town's name means 'prosperity' in Norwegian.

BOAT

Trondheim is a major stop on the *Hurtigruten* coastal ferry route.

BUS

The **intercity bus terminal (Rutebilstasjon)** adjoins Trondheim Sentralstasjon (train station, also known as Trondheim S).

Nor-Way Bussekspress services run up to three times daily to/from Ålesund (Nkr587, seven hours, two to three daily) and once (overnight) to Bergen (Nkr848, 14½ hours).

TRAIN

There are two to four trains daily to/from Oslo (Nkr899, 6½ hours). Two head north to Bodø (Nkr1059, 9¾ hours).

ℹ Getting Around

TO/FROM THE AIRPORT

Flybussen (www.flybussen.no; one way/return Nkr130/220, 35 to 45 minutes) runs every 15 minutes from 4am to 9pm (less frequently at weekends), stopping at major landmarks such as the train station, Studentersamfundet and Britannia Hotel.

Trains run between Trondheim Sentralstasjon and the Værnes airport station (Nkr74, 30 to 40 minutes, half-hourly).

Bodø

POP 49,730

Travellers generally use Bodø as a gateway to the Lofoten Islands. Most get off their boat or train, poke around for a few hours and then get on the first ferry. Those that linger tend to do so to behold Saltstraumen, one of the world's most impressive maelstroms.

WORTH A TRIP

KYSTRIKSVEIEN COASTAL ROUTE

Longer, yes, more expensive, yes (gosh, those ferry tolls mount up). But if you've even a day or two to spare, divert from the Arctic Highway and enjoy the empty roads and solitary splendours of Kystriksveien, the coastal alternative that follows the coast for 650km. If the whole route seems daunting, it's quite possible to cut in or out from Steinkjer, Bodø or, midway, Mosjøen and Mo i Rana. It's one to drive; don't even attempt it by bus or you'll still be waiting when the first snows fall. Off the coast are around 14,000 islands, some little more than rocks with a few tufts of grass, others, such as Vega, supporting whole communities that for centuries have survived on coastal fishing and subsistence agriculture.

Sights

Norsk Luftfartsmuseum MUSEUM
(www.luftfart.museum.no; Olav V gata; adult/child Nkr110/55; 10am-6pm mid-Jun–mid-Aug, 10am-4pm Mon-Fri & 11am-5pm Sat rest of year) Norway's aviation museum is huge fun to ramble around if you have even a passing interest in flight and aviation history. Allow at least half a day to roam its 10,000 sq metres. Exhibits include a complete control tower, hands-on demonstrations and a simulator.

Nordlandmuseet MUSEUM
(www.nordlandsmuseet.no; Prinsens gate 116; adult/child Nkr50/10; 11am-6pm Mon-Fri, 11am-4pm Sat & Sun Jun-Aug, 9am-3pm Mon-Fri rest of year) Recounting the short history of Bodø, this little gem of a museum has a cheerily entertaining and informative 25-minute film with English subtitles on the town's development. Highlights include a mock-up of a fisherman's *rorbu* (hut), a section on Sámi culture complete with sod hut and ritual drum, regalia relating to the town's fishing heritage, and a small hoard of 9th-century Viking treasure that was discovered nearby in 1919.

Sleeping

City Hotell HOTEL €
(75 52 04 02; www.cityhotellbodo.no; Storgata 39; dm Nkr250, s/d Nkr650/750; @) This hotel has 19 smallish but well-priced standard rooms and plenty of flexibility. Three dorms sleeping three to six cater for backpackers. Beneath the eaves are a couple of very large family rooms and two rooms have a kitchenette.

★ **Skagen Hotel** HOTEL €€
(75 51 91 00; www.skagen-hotel.no; Nyholmsgata 11; s/d from Nkr850/1050; @) The Skagen occupies two buildings (one originally a butcher's, though you'd never guess it). Facing each other, they're connected by a passage that burrows beneath the street. Rooms are attractively decorated and a continent away from chain-hotel clones. There's a bar and free afternoon waffles and coffee, and excellent breakfasts. Staff can also give advice on a whole raft of vigorous outdoor activities.

★ **Thon Hotel Nordlys** HOTEL €€
(75 53 19 00; www.thonhotels.no; Moloveien 14; s/d from Nkr720/820) Bodø's most stylish hotel, with touches of subtle Scandinavian design throughout, overlooks the marina and runs a reasonable restaurant.

Eating & Drinking

Løvolds CAFE €€
(www.lovold.no; Tollbugata 9; mains Nkr155-175; 9am-6pm Mon-Fri, 9am-3pm Sat) This popular historic quayside cafeteria, Bodø's oldest eating choice, offers sandwiches, grills and hearty Norwegian fare with quality quayside views at no extra charge.

Farmors Stue CAFETERIA, NORWEGIAN €
(75 52 78 60; www.farmorsstue.no; Kongens gate 27; mains Nkr60-147; 10am-6pm Mon-Fri, 11am-4pm Sat) With all the warmth and charm of an old-fashioned tea room, this lovely little place serves up snacks and light meals, good coffee and a well-priced lunch buffet (Nkr148). Local produce dominates the simple but carefully chosen seasonal menu.

Bryggeri Kaia RESTAURANT-BAR €€
(75 52 58 08; www.bryggerikaia.no; Sjøgata 1; snacks from Nkr150, mains Nkr195-325; 11.30am-3.30am Mon-Sat, from noon Sun) Bryggeri Kaia is a firm favourite. You can dine well, snack, enjoy its weekday lunch buffet (Nkr175) or its Saturday herring buffet (Nkr175), or quaff one of its several beers. Enjoy your choice in its large pub-decor interior, on the streetside terrace or, best of all should you find a seat spare, on the veranda overlooking the harbour.

Information

Tourist Office (75 54 80 00; www.visitbodo.com; Sjøgata 15-17; 9am-8pm Mon-Fri &

10am-6pm Sat & Sun mid-Jun–Aug, 9am-3.30pm Mon-Fri rest of year) Publishes the excellent free *Bodø Guide* brochure and has two internet terminals (Nkr60 per hour) as well as free wifi.

 Getting There & Around

AIR

From Bodø's airport, southwest of the city centre, there are at least 10 daily flights to Oslo, Trondheim and Tromsø.

BOAT

Bodø is a stop on the *Hurtigruten* coastal ferry.

Car ferries sail five to six times daily in summer (less frequently during the rest of the year) between Bodø and Moskenes on Lofoten (car including driver/passenger Nkr646/180, three to 3½ hours). If you're taking a car in summer avoid a potential long wait in line by booking in advance (an additional Nkr100; online reservation at www.torghatten-nord.no).

There's also an express passenger ferry between Bodø and Svolvær (adult/child Nkr366/183, 3¾ hours) once daily.

BUS

Buses run to/from Narvik (Nkr280, 6½ hours) via Fauske (Nkr90, one hour) twice daily, with extra services to/from Fauske.

TRAIN

Bodø is the northern terminus of the Norwegian train network, with a service to Trondheim (Nkr1059, 10 hours, twice daily).

Around Bodø

At the 3km-long, 150m-wide Saltstraumen Strait, the tides cause one fjord to drain into another, creating the equivalent of a waterfall at sea. The result is the **Saltstraumen Maelstrom**, a churning, 20-knot watery chaos that shifts over 400 million cubic metres of water one way, then the other, every six hours. This maelstrom, claimed to be the world's largest, is actually a kinetic series of smaller whirlpools that form, surge, coalesce, then disperse. At its best – which is most of the time – it's an exhilarating spectacle. Should you be unlucky enough to hit an off day, it may recall little more than the water swirling around your bath plug.

Saltstraumen is 32km south of Bodø by road (and much nearer by boat). There are seven buses daily (two on Saturday and Sunday; one hour) between Bodø and Saltstraumen bridge.

Narvik

POP 18,705

Narvik, where the waterfront is obliterated by a monstrous trans-shipment facility, is pincered by islands to the west and mountains in every other direction, while spectacular fjords stretch north and south.

MIDNIGHT SUN & POLAR NIGHT

Because earth is tilted on its axis, polar regions are constantly facing the sun at their respective summer solstices and are tilted away from it in the winter. The Arctic Circle, at 66 degrees north latitude, is the northern limit of constant daylight on its longest day of the year.

The northern half of mainland Norway, as well as Svalbard and Jan Mayen Island, lie north of the Arctic Circle but, even in southern Norway, the summer sun is never far below the horizon. Between late May and mid-August, nowhere in the country experiences true darkness. Conversely, winters here are dark, dreary and long, with only a few hours of twilight to break the long polar nights.

TOWN/AREA	LATITUDE	MIDNIGHT SUN	POLAR NIGHT
Bodø	67° 18'	4 Jun to 8 Jul	15 Dec to 28 Dec
Svolvær	68° 15'	28 May to 14 Jul	5 Dec to 7 Jan
Narvik	68° 26'	27 May to 15 Jul	4 Dec to 8 Jan
Tromsø	69° 42'	20 May to 22 Jul	25 Nov to 17 Jan
Alta	70° 00'	16 May to 26 Jul	24 Nov to 18 Jan
Hammerfest	70° 40'	16 May to 27 Jul	21 Nov to 21 Jan
Nordkapp	71° 11'	13 May to 29 Jul	18 Nov to 24 Jan
Longyearbyen	78° 12'	20 Apr to 21 Aug	26 Oct to 16 Feb

Sights

Ofoten Museum MUSEUM
(Museum Nord; www.museumnord-narvik.no; Administrasjonsveien 3; adult/concession/child Nkr60/30/free; ⏲10am-4pm Mon-Fri & noon-3pm Sat & Sun Jul-early Aug, 10am-3pm Mon-Fri rest of year) The museum tells of Narvik's farming, fishing, railway-building and ore-shipment heritage. There's a rolling film about the Ofotbanen Railway and children will enjoy pressing the button that activates the model train. Linger too over the display case of Sámi costumes and artefacts and the collection of historic photos, contrasted with modern shots taken from the same angles. To reach the museum, take the minor road beside the restored building that served as Narvik's post office from 1888 to 1898.

Red Cross War Museum MUSEUM
(Krigsminnemuseum; ☎76 94 44 26; www.warmuseum.no; Kongens gate; adult/child Nkr75/25; ⏲10am-9pm Mon-Sat & noon-6pm Sun mid-Jun–mid-Aug, 10am-4pm Mon-Sat & noon-4pm Sun rest of year) This small but revealing museum illustrates the military campaigns fought hereabouts in the early years of WWII. The presentation may not be flash but it will still move you. Pick up a folder that explains each of the museum's sections.

WORTH A TRIP

RALLARVEIEN HIKE

This popular hike parallels the Ofotbanen Railway, following the Rallarveien, an old navvy (railway worker) trail. Few walkers attempt the entire way between Sweden's Abisko National Park and the sea, opting instead to begin at Riksgränsen, the small ski station just across the Swedish border, or Bjørnfell, the next station west. It's an undemanding descent as far as Katterat, from where you can take the evening train to Narvik.

For more exertion, drop down to Rombaksbotn at the head of the fjord and site of the main camp when the railway was being built (it's since returned to nature). From here, a boat (adult/child Nkr320/125) runs erratically to Narvik in summer. Check with the tourist office to avoid an unwelcome supplementary 10km trek at the end of the day.

Activities

★**Narvikfjellet** CABLE CAR
(www.narvikfjellet.no; Mårveien; adult one way/return Nkr100/150, under 7yr free; ⏲1-9pm Jun-Aug, shorter hours rest of year) Climbing 656m above town, this cable car offers breathtaking views over the surrounding peaks and fjords – even as far as Lofoten on a clear day. Several marked walking trails radiate from its top station or you can bounce down a signed mountain-bike route. From February to April, it will whisk you up high for trail, off-piste and cross-country skiing with outstanding views. It sometimes stays open later in the height of summer.

Sleeping

★**Norumgården Bed & Breakfast** B&B €€
(☎76 94 48 57; norumgaarden.narviknett.no; Framnesveien 127; s/d Nkr790/890; ⏲late Jan-Nov) This little treasure of a place (it has only four rooms so reservations are essential) offers excellent value. Used as a German officer's mess in WWII (the owner will proudly show you a 1940 bottle of Coca Cola, made under licence in Hamburg), nowadays it brims with antiques and character.

★**Spor 1 Gjestegård** HOSTEL, GUESTHOUSE €
(☎76 94 60 20; www.spor1.no; Brugata 2a; dm Nkr300, s/d with shared bathroom Nkr500/600) Britt Larsen and her partner, both Narvik born and bred and seasoned world travellers, run this delightful place right beside the railway track. It has the facilities of the best of hostels (especially the gleaming, well-equipped guest kitchen) and the comfort and taste of a guesthouse (bright, cheerful fabrics and decor, and soft duvets).

Rica Hotel Narvik HOTEL €€
(☎76 96 14 00; www.rica.no; Kongens gate 33; d Nkr845-1245) Towering over the downtown area, this striking glass edifice houses Narvik's most stylish hotel. Rooms are slick and contemporary and those on the upper floors have fabulous views. There's also a fine **restaurant** (mains from Nkr258; ⏲6-10.30pm Mon-Sat) and 16th-floor bar.

Eating

Fiskehallen CAFE €
(☎76 94 36 60; Kongens gate 42; mains Nkr80-150; ⏲9.30am-4.30pm Mon-Fri, 10am-2pm Sat) This tiny cafe, offshoot of the adjacent fish shop, offers tasty ready-to-eat dishes, such as

fish cakes, *bacalao* and whale stew, to eat in or take away.

Rallar'n BAR RESTAURANT €€€
(Kongens gate 64; daily specials NKr145, mains Nkr195-325; ⏲1pm-1am) The pub/restaurant of Quality Hotel Grand Royal is all atmospheric low ceilings, bare brick and dark woodwork. Divided into intimate compartments, it offers pizza, pasta and creative mains.

ℹ Information

Tourist Office (☎76 96 56 00; www.destinationnarvik.com; ⏲10am-7pm Mon-Fri & 10am-3pm Sat & Sun mid-Jun–mid-Aug, 9am-4.30pm Mon-Fri rest of year) At the train station, the tourist office holds Narvik og Omegns Turistforening cabin keys (Nkr100 deposit), has internet access (Nkr60 per hour) and rents bikes (Nkr250 per day).

ℹ Getting There & Away

AIR

Nearly all flights leave from Harstad/Narvik Evenes airport, 1¼ hours away by road. Narvik's tiny Framneslia airport, about 3km west of the centre, serves only Bodø, Tromsø and Andenes.

BUS

Express buses run northwards to Tromsø (Nkr240, 4¼ hours, three daily) and south to Bodø (Nkr280, 6½ hours, two daily) via Fauske (Nkr280, 5¼ hours). For Lofoten, two Lofotekspressen buses run daily between Narvik and Svolvær (from Nkr250, 4¼ hours) and continue to Å.

Between late June and early September, bus 91 runs twice a day up the E10 to Riksgränsen (45 minutes) in Sweden and on to Abisko and Kiruna (three hours).

TRAIN

Heading for Sweden, there are two daily services between Narvik and Riksgränsen (one hour), on the border, and Kiruna (three hours). Trains continue to Lulea (7¼ hours) via Boden, from where you can pick up connections to Stockholm.

Around Narvik

The spectacular mountain-hugging **Ofotbanen railway** (☎76 92 31 21) trundles beside fjord-side cliffs, birch forests and rocky plateaus as it climbs to the Swedish border. The railway, which opened in 1903, was constructed by migrant labourers at the end of the 19th century to connect Narvik with the iron-ore mines at Kiruna, in Sweden's far north. Currently it transports around 15 million tonnes of iron ore annually and is also a major magnet for visitors.

The train route from Narvik to Riksgränsen, the ski resort just inside Sweden (one way adult/child Nkr130/free, one hour), features some 50 tunnels and snowsheds. Towards the Narvik end of the rail line, you might make out the wreck of the German ship *Georg Thiele* at the edge of the fjord.

You can run the line as a day or half-day trip, leaving Narvik at 10.26am. The 11.39pm return train from Riksgränsen allows time for coffee and a quick browse or you can walk a trail in this stunning alpine country and catch the 4.02pm back to Narvik. For the best views, sit on the left side heading from Narvik.

Lofoten Islands

You'll never forget your first approach to the Lofoten Islands by ferry. The islands spread their tall, craggy physique against the sky like some spiky sea dragon and you wonder how humans eked a living in such inhospitable surroundings.

The main islands, Austvågøy, Vestvågøy, Flakstadøy and Moskenesøy, are separated from the mainland by Vestfjorden. On each are sheltered bays, sheep pastures and picturesque villages. The vistas and the special quality of the Arctic light have long attracted artists, represented in galleries throughout the islands.

The four main islands are all linked by bridges or tunnels, with buses running the entire length of the Lofoten road (E10) from Fiskebøl in the north to Å at road's end in the southwest.

Tourist information is available at www.lofoten.info.

Svolvær

POP 4460

The port town of Svolvær is as busy as it gets on Lofoten. The town once sprawled across a series of skerries, but the in-between spaces are being filled in to create a reclaimed peninsula. Although the setting is beautiful with a backdrop of high mountains, the hotch-potch of modern buildings clutter things somewhat.

Sights & Activities

★ Magic Ice ICE BAR

(☎76 07 40 11; www.magicice.no; Fiskergata 36; adult/child Nkr130/80; ⏱noon-10.30pm mid-Jun–late-Aug, 6-10pm rest of year) Housed, appropriately, in what was once a fish-freezing plant, this is the ultimate place to chill out, perhaps with something to warm the spirit, served in an ice glass. The 500-sq-metre space is filled with huge ice sculptures, illustrating Lofoten life. If you can't come back to northern Norway in winter, here's a great, if brief, approximation. Admission includes a drink in an ice glass.

★ Svolværgeita HIKING, CLIMBING

You'll see it on postcards all over Lofoten – some daring soul leaping between two fingers of rock high above Svolvær. To hike up to a point just behind the two pinnacles (355m), walk northeast along the E10 towards Narvik, pass the marina, and then turn left on Nyveien, then right on Blatind veg – the steep climb begins just behind the children's playground.

The climb takes around half an hour, or an hour if you continue up to the summit of Floya. To actually climb Svolværgeita and take the leap, you'll need to go with a climbing guide – ask the tourist office for recommendations or try **Northern Alpine Guides** (☎94 24 91 10; alpineguides.no; Havnegata 3).

Trollfjord CRUISE

(adult/child from Nkr695/300) From the port, several competing companies offer sailings into the constricted confines of nearby Trollfjord, spectacularly steep and narrowing to only 100m. Take the two-hour sea-eagle trip, the three-hour cruise or sign on for a four-hour trip that includes the chance to dangle a line and bring home supper. Buy your ticket at the **quayside** or at operators such as **Lofoten Explorer** (www.lofoten-explorer.no), **RiB Lofoten** (☎90 41 64 40; www.rib-lofoten.com) or **Trollfjord Cruise** (☎45 15 75 87; www.trollfjordcruise.com).

Kaiser Route CYCLING

For 83km of breathtaking cycling, head to Holandshamn and make your way back to Svolvær along the Kaiser Route. Lonely shoreline, jagged mountains and abandoned farms will be your constant companion. Unlike the west of Lofoten, this trip takes in parts of the island largely undiscovered by tourists. A long stretch runs parallel to Trollfjord. Ask at the tourist office for information about hiring bikes and getting to Holandshamn.

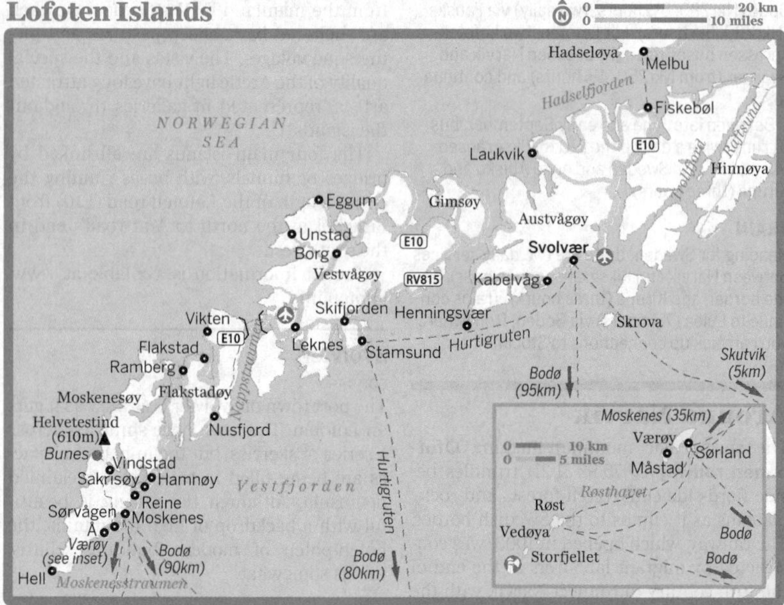

Sleeping & Eating

Svolvær Sjøhuscamp SEA HOUSE €
(☎76 07 03 36; www.svolver-sjohuscamp.no; Parkgata 12; d/q from Nkr540/880, d with kitchen Nkr590, all with shared bathroom) This friendly *sjøhus* (sea house) straddling the water is a convivial, excellent-value place to fetch up and meet fellow travellers. There's also a gem of a six-bed apartment with balcony and full facilities (Nkr1900).

★**Svinøya Rorbuer** CABIN €€
(☎76 06 99 30; www.svinoya.no; Gunnar Bergs vei 2; cabins & suites Nkr1150-3200) Across a bridge on the islet of Svinøya, site of Svolvær's first settlement, are several cabins, some historic, most contemporary, and all cosy and comfortable. Reception is a veritable museum, a restored and restocked *krambua* (general store), constructed in 1828, which was Svolvær's first shop. They've properties all over the area and they're some of the best *rorbuer* in Lofoten.

★**Thon Hotel Lofoten** HOTEL €€
(www.thonhotels.no; Torget; r from Nkr973; P) In a pleasing glass edifice overlooking the main square and harbour, Thon's Lofoten outpost has stylish modern rooms, most with fabulous views. Ask for a room on the upper floors (avoid the 2nd and 3rd floors) and facing the town for the best views - the binoculars in each room are a nice touch. Service is slick and the location couldn't be more central.

Lofoten Suite Hotel BOUTIQUE HOTEL €€€
(☎47 67 01 00; www.lofoten-suitehotel.no; Havnepromenaden; ste from Nkr1500) Right on the main harbour in Svolvær, in a lovely wood-and-glass structure, this suites-only hotel has attractive modern rooms with wooden floorboards, most of which have fine harbour views. Most have kitchenettes.

Bacalao BAR, CAFE €€
(☎76 07 94 00; www.bacalaobar.no; Havnepromenaden 2; mains Nkr145-175; ⏲10.30am-1am Mon-Thu, 10.30am-2.30am Fri & Sat, noon-1am Sun) With its upbeat interior, Bacalao offers leafy, innovative salads and sandwiches, and some equally creative pasta dishes; the *hot reke-pasta* (hot shrimp pasta) will set your taste buds tingling. Bacalao also expresses some of Lofoten's best coffee.

★**Børsen** RESTAURANT €€€
(☎76 06 99 30; www.svinoya.no; Gunnar Bergs vei 2; mains Nkr289-355; ⏲6-10pm) This Arctic Menu-restaurant brims with character. A former fish house, it was called the 'stock exchange' after the harbourfront bench outside, where older men of the town would ruminate endlessly over the state of the world. In its dining room, with its cracked and bowed flooring, stockfish is the house specialty – if you try it once, try it here – or try the Lofoten lamb.

Information

Tourist Office (☎76 06 98 07; www.lofoten.info; Torget; ⏲9am-10pm Mon-Fri, 9am-8pm Sat & 10am-8pm Sun mid-Jun–mid-Aug, shorter hours rest of year) Provides information on the entire archipelago.

Getting There & Away

AIR

From Svolvær's small airport there are up to six flights daily to Bodø.

BOAT

Svolvær is a stop on the *Hurtigruten* coastal ferry. Two other sea routes connect Svolvær to the mainland. For timetables and reservations, visit www.toghatten-nord.no:

To/from Skutvik (car/foot passenger Nkr325/95, 1¾ to 2¼ hours, up to 10 daily) The shortest, most popular crossing (from Skutvik you can connect by bus with Narvik).

To/from Bodø (Nkr366/183, 3½ hours) Daily express passenger boat calling by Skutvik (one hour).

BUS

Useful bus routes include the following:

Bus 8 To/from Sortland on Vesterålen (2¼ hours, three to five times daily), via Stokmarknes (1¾ hours).

Bus 9 To/from Leknes (1½ hours, four to six times daily), with connections to Å (3½ hours).

Lofotekspressen To/from Narvik (4¼ hours, twice daily).

Kabelvåg

Kabelvåg, 5km southwest of Svolvær, is an altogether more intimate and cosy place. At its heart is a small square and tiny harbour while its **Storvågen** district, 2km off the E10 to the south, has an enticing trio of museums and galleries.

Sights & Activities

Behind the old prison, a trail leads uphill to the **statue of King Øystein**, who in 1120 ordered the first *rorbu* (traditional seasonal house) to house fishermen who had been sleeping under their overturned rowing boats.

Lofoten Aquarium AQUARIUM
(Lofotakvariet; www.lofotakvariet.no; adult/child Nkr120/60; ⏲10am-6pm Jun-Aug, shorter hours Feb-May & Sep-Nov, closed Dec & Jan) Fish and sea animals of the cold Arctic waters inhabit this decent aquarium. Children will particularly enjoy the seal and sea otter feeding frenzies (noon, 3pm and 6pm) and there's a multimedia show five times daily.

Galleri Espolin GALLERY
(☎76 07 84 05; www.galleri-espolin.no; adult/child Nkr70/30; ⏲10am-6pm Jun–mid-Aug, shorter hours rest of year) This gallery features the haunting etchings and lithographs of one of Norway's great artists, Kaare Espolin-Johnson (1907–94). Espolin – his work all the more astounding as he was nearly blind for much of his life – loved Lofoten and often featured its fisherfolk and other Arctic themes.

Vågan Kirke CHURCH
(www.lofotkatedralen.no; Villaveien 9; admission Nkr40; ⏲10am-6pm Mon-Sat, from noon Sun late Jun–mid-Aug) Built in 1898 and Norway's second-largest wooden church, Vågan rises above the E10 just north of Kabelvåg. Built to minister to the influx of seasonal fisherfolk, its seating capacity of 1200 far surpasses Kabelvåg's current population.

Sleeping & Eating

Kabelvåg Hotell HOTEL €€
(☎76 07 88 00; Kong Øysteinsgate 4; summer s/d Nkr850/1250; ⏲Jun–mid-Aug & late Feb-Apr) On a small rise close to the centre of Kabelvåg, this imposing seasonal hotel has been tastefully rebuilt in its original art deco style. Rooms overlook either the port or mountains. It also functions as a centre for skiing and a host of other winter activities.

Nyvågar Rorbuhotell CABIN €€€
(☎76 06 97 00; www.classicnorway.no/hotell/nyvagar-rorbuhotell; Storvåganveien 22; 4-bed rorbu incl breakfast Nkr2300) At Storvågan, below the museum complex, this snazzy, modern seaside place owes nothing to history, but its strictly contemporary *rorbuer* are attractive and fully equipped. Guests can also rent bikes and motorboats.

Lorchstua Restaurant NORWEGIAN €€€
(☎76 06 97 00; mains Nkr195-389, 3-course menus Nkr525; ⏲6-10.30pm Jun–mid-Aug) The acclaimed Lorchstua restaurant, run by Nyvågar Rorbuhotell, serves primarily local specialities with a subtle twist, such as baked fillet of halibut in a cod brandade.

Henningsvær

A delightful 8km shore-side drive southwards from the E10 brings you to the still-active fishing village of Henningsvær, perched at the end of a thin promontory. Its nickname, 'the Venice of Lofoten', may be a tad overblown but it's certainly the lightest, brightest and trendiest place in the archipelago. It's also the region's largest and most active fishing port.

Sights & Activities

Ocean Sounds WHALE CENTRE
(☎91 84 20 12; www.ocean-sounds.com; Hjellskjæret; adult/child Nkr200/free; ⏲2-6pm Jul–mid-Aug, by request May-Jun & mid-Aug–Oct) Beside the Henningsvær Bryggehotel, this not-for-profit research centre is the initiative of one committed, hugely determined young biologist, Heike Vester. Enjoy a 45-minute multimedia presentation about cod, whales and other Arctic marine mammals, supplemented by an evocative 30-minute slide show featuring whales and other marine animals in the waters around Henningsvær.

North Norwegian Climbing School ROCK CLIMBING
(Nord Norsk Klatreskole; ☎90 57 42 08; www.nordnorskklatreskole.no; Misværveien 10; ⏲Mar-Oct) This outfit offers a wide range of technical climbing and skiing courses all around northern Norway. Climbing the peaks with an experienced guide costs around Nkr2200, including equipment, for one to four people.

Lofoten Adventure OUTDOORS
(☎90 58 14 75; www.lofoten-opplevelser.no; ⏲mid-Jun–mid-Aug) Based in Henningsvær, it offers a cluster of maritime tours and activities between mid-June and mid-August. Advance booking is essential. Tours include **sea-eagle safaris** (2.30pm, adult/child Nkr550/450, 1½ hours), **midnight safaris** (10pm, Nkr750, 2½ hours) and **snorkelling** sorties with equipment provided (11am, Nkr750, two hours).

Sleeping & Eating

Henningsvær Bryggehotel HOTEL €€€
(☎76 07 47 19; www.henningsvaer.no; Hjellskjæret; s/d from Nkr1150/1650) Overlooking the harbour, this attractive hotel is Henningsvær's finest choice. It's modern, with comfortable rooms furnished in contemporary design, yet constructed in a traditional style that blends harmoniously with its neighbours. **Bluefish**, its award-winning restaurant, is just as styl-

ish; it serves Arctic Menu dishes and succulent sorbets, using fresh berries in season.

★ Fiskekrogen RESTAURANT €€€
(☎76 07 46 52; www.fiskekrogen.no; Dreyersgate 29; mains Nkr195-295, lunch dishes Nkr145-275; ⏲1-4pm & 6-11pm Sun, 6-11pm Mon-Sat Jun-Aug, shorter hours rest of year) At the end of a slipway overlooking the harbour, this dockside restaurant, a favourite of the Norwegian royal family, is Henningsvær's other culinary claim to fame. Try, in particular, the outstanding fish soup (Nkr195), but there's everything else on the menu from fried cod tongues to smoked whale.

ℹ Information

Tourist Office (☎91 24 57 02; www.henningsvar.com; ⏲10am-6pm Mon-Fri, 11am-4pm Sat & Sun mid-Jun–mid-Nov) Henningsvær's tourist office is beside the main car park.

ℹ Getting There & Away

In summer, bus 510 shuttles between Svolvær (40 minutes), Kabelvåg (35 minutes) and Henningsvær 10 times on weekdays (three services Saturday and Sunday).

Nusfjord

A spectacular 6km diversion southwards from the E10 beneath towering bare crags brings you to the cutesy village of Nusfjord (www.nusfjord.no), sprawled around its tiny, tucked-away harbour. Many artists consider it to be the essence of Lofoten but be warned: so do tour operators. As a result, it costs Nkr50 just to walk around plus a further Nkr50 to see *The People & The Fish*, a 12-minute video about Nusfjord, past and present.

The country store recently celebrated its centenary and there's the old cod-liver oil factory, boat house, sawmill and a cluster of *rorbuer*, most of them modern and many available for rent (from Nkr1260 per night).

To snap the postcard-perfect shot of Nusfjord that you'll see everywhere around the island, you'll need to climb the rocky slope above the closed end of the little harbour. The path can be slippery after rain.

Parking is on a hill at the entrance to the village.

Reine

Reine is a characterless place but gosh, it looks splendid from various angles, beside its placid lagoon and backed by the sheer rock face of Reinebringen. You get a great view from the head of the road that drops to the village from the E10.

From June to mid-August, **Aqua Lofoten** (www.aqualofoten.no; adult/child from Nkr800/500) runs three-hour **boat trips** to the bird- and fish-rich Moskstraumen maelstrom.

Hamnøy Mat og Vinbu (☎76 09 21 45; Hamnøy; mains Nkr175-295; ⏲late May-early Sep) is a family-run place that serves stellar local specialities, including whale, *bacalao* and cod tongues. Grandmother takes care of the traditional dishes – just try her fish cakes – while her son is the main chef.

All buses from Leknes to Å stop in Reine.

Sakrisøy

Reine's rival for visual perfection, Sakrisøy is an incredibly charming and quiet village of ochre buildings set on some rocky outcroppings and surrounded by water, mountains and cod-drying racks. Here you can gawk at the scenery, grab a dockside fish cake, visit the **Museum of Dolls and Toys** (Dagmars Dukke og Leketøy Museum; ☎76 09 21 43; www.lofoten.ws; adult/child Nkr60/30; ⏲10am-6pm May & Sep, to 8pm Jun-Aug, by appointment rest of year), and sleep amid the postcard setting in a fine *robuer* at **Sakrisøy Rorbuer** (☎76 09 21 43; www.lofoten.ws; cabin Nkr1050-1950).

Sakrisøy is 1km west of Reine towards Hamnøy.

DON'T MISS

LOFOTR VIKINGMUSEUM

In 1981 at Borg, near the centre of Vestvågøy, a farmer's plough hit the ruins of the 83m-long dwelling of a powerful Viking chieftain, the largest building of its era ever discovered in Scandinavia. The resulting **Lofotr Vikingmuseum** (www.lofotr.no; adult/child incl guided tour mid-Jun–mid-Aug Nkr160/80, rest of year Nkr120/60; ⏲10am-7pm Jun–mid-Aug, shorter hours rest of year), 14km north of Leknes, offers a glimpse of life in Viking times. You can walk 1.5km of trails over open hilltops from the replica of the chieftain's longhouse (the main building, shaped like an upside-down boat) to the Viking-ship replica on the water.

Å

Å is a very special place at what feels like the end of the world on the western tip of Lofoten. A preserved fishing village perched on forbidding rocks connected by wooden footbridges, its shoreline is lined with red painted *rorbuer,* many of which jut into the sea. Racks of drying cod and picture-postcard scenes occur at almost every turn. Visitors enliven the tiny place in summer, while in winter it's stark, haunting and empty.

Sights & Activities

Lofoten Tørrfiskmuseum MUSEUM
(adult/child Nkr60/40; 11am-4pm or 5pm Jun-Aug) The Lofoten Stockfish Museum is housed in a former fish warehouse. You'll be bowled over by Steinar Larsen, its enthusiastic, polyglot owner, who meets and greets every visitor. This personal collection, a passionate hobby of his, illustrates well Lofoten's traditional mainstay: the catching and drying of cod for export, particularly to Italy. Displays, artefacts and a DVD take you through the process, from hauling the fish out of the sea through drying, grading and sorting to dispatch.

Norsk Fiskeværsmuseum MUSEUM
(Norwegian Fishing Village Museum; adult/child Nkr70/35; 10am-6pm daily mid-Jun–mid-Aug, to 3.30pm Mon-Fri rest of year) This museum takes in 14 of Å's 19th-century boathouses, storehouses, fishing cottages, farmhouses and commercial buildings. Highlights (pick up a pamphlet in English at reception) include Europe's oldest cod-liver oil factory, where you'll be treated to a taste and can pick up a bottle to stave off those winter sniffles; the smithy, who still makes cod-liver oil lamps; the still-functioning bakery, established in 1844; the old *rorbu* with period furnishings; and a couple of traditional Lofoten fishing boats.

Moskenesstraumen VIEWPOINT
Walk to the camping ground at the end of the village for a good hillside view of Værøy island, which lies on the other side of Moskenesstraumen, the swirling maelstrom that inspired the fictional tales of Jules Verne and Edgar Allen Poe.

Sleeping & Eating

Å-Hamna Rorbuer & Vandrerhjem HOSTEL €
(76 09 12 11; www.lofotenferie.com; Å; hostel dm/s/d/tr Nkr250/300/570/750, 4- to 8-bed rorbuer Nkr1000-1400) Sleep simple or sleep in more comfort; either way, this is an attractive choice. Newly affiliated to Hostelling International, this place has dorms above the Tørrfiskmuseum and in a quiet villa, set in its garden. For more space and privacy, choose one of the restored fishing huts, where prices drop significantly outside high summer.

Å Rorbuer CABIN €€
(76 09 11 21; www.a-rorbuer.com; d Nkr800-1100, apt Nkr1750-2000) *Rorbu* accommodation is dispersed throughout Å's historic buildings, the more expensive ones fully equipped and furnished with antiques. The newer sea house, above Brygga restaurant and with trim but plain rooms, has shared bathrooms, despite the hefty price.

Brygga Restaurant SEAFOOD €€€
(76 09 11 21; mains Nkr195-349, lunch specials from Nkr150; Jun-Sep) Hovering above the water, this is Å's one decent dining choice. The menu, as is right and proper in a village with such a strong fishing tradition, includes mainly things with fins.

Getting There & Away

BOAT

Car ferries sail five to six times daily in summer (less frequently during the rest of the year) between Moskenes and Bodø (car including driver/passenger Nkr597/167, 3½ hours).

BUS

Four to five buses connect Leknes and Å daily in summer, stopping in all major villages along the E10.

Vesterålen

Although the island landscapes of this region aren't as dramatic as those in Lofoten, they tend to be much wilder and the forested mountainous regions of the island of Hinnøya are a unique corner of Norway's largely treeless northern coast.

Sights & Activities

Hurtigrutemuseet MUSEUM
(www.hurtigrutemuseet.no; Markedsgata 1, Stokmarknes; adult/child Nkr90/35; 10am-6pm mid-Jun–mid-Aug, 2-4pm mid-Sep–mid-May) The Hurtigruten Museum portrays the history of the coastal-ferry line in text and image. Hitched to the quayside is the retired ship M/S *Finnmarken,* claimed to be the world's largest museum piece, which plied the coastal route between 1956 and 1993.

Nyksund Museum MUSEUM
(www.nyksund.as; 11am-5pm mid-Jun–mid-Aug) This small museum is in Nyksund, on Langøya, a former abandoned fishing village that's now re-emerging as an artists' colony. It contains a number of local artefacts and before-and-after photos that chart the village's transformation.

★ **Andøya Rocket Range** MUSEUM
(76 14 46 00; www.spaceshipaurora.no; exhibitions adult/child Nkr125/50, virtual missions Nkr350/175; 10am-6pm daily mid-Jun–mid-Aug, 9am-3pm Mon-Fri rest of year) Located 1km south of Andenes along the road to Bleik, this innovative space centre has a widescreen 16-minute movie and other exhibits about the aurora borealis (rockets sent up from here aid in the study of this phenomenon) and Norway's role in space research. To really get into the spirit, you can join a virtual mission (one hour to one hour 45 minutes) aboard the Spaceship Aurora and even send up a virtual rocket. Ring ahead to book.

Northern Lights Centre EXHIBITION
(Andenes; 10am-6pm late Jun-late Aug) FREE This impressive high-tech aurora borealis exhibition first featured at the 1994 Winter Olympics in Lillehammer.

★ **Hvalsenteret** MUSEUM
(Havnegate 1, Andenes; adult/child Nkr70/35; 8.30am-4pm late May–mid-Sep) The Whale Centre provides a perspective for whale-watchers, with displays on whale research, hunting and the life cycle of these gentle giants. Most people visit the centre in conjunction with a whale safari. There's also an onsite restaurant. It sometimes stays open as late as 8pm in July and August.

★ **Whale Safari** WHALE WATCHING
(76 11 56 00; www.whalesafari.no; Andenes; adult/child Nkr890/570) Far and away the island of Andøya's biggest outfit, Whale Safari runs popular whale-watching cruises between late May and mid-September. It also operates the Whale Centre. Tours begin with a guided visit to the centre, followed by a two- to four-hour boat trip. There's a good chance of spotting minke, pilot, humpback and orca (killer whale).

Sea Safari Andenes WHALE-WATCHING
(91 67 49 60; www.seasafariandenes.no; Andenes; adult/child Nkr995/800; late-May–mid-Sep) The smaller of Andenes' two whale-watching outfits, this place, with its base on the docks just off the road to the lighthouse, runs 1½- to three-hour whale-watching trips with up to two daily departures during the season. They also offer shorter seal- and bird-watching trips (1½ hours, adult/child Nkr450/400).

Sleeping & Eating

★ **Hotell Marena** BOUTIQUE HOTEL €€
(91 58 35 17, Andenes; www.hotellmarena.no; Storgata 15; s/d incl breakfast from Nkr800/1000) Hotell Marena is an exciting and particularly tasteful recent addition to Andenes' accommodation choices. Public areas feature nature photographs by local photographer Espen Tollefsen, as do each of the 12 bedrooms, individually designed with colours that match the tones of the blown-up images. There's free coffee around the clock, together with homemade cakes.

Holmvik Brygge GUESTHOUSE €€
(76 13 47 96; www.nyksund.com; Nyksund, Langøya s/d Nkr700/850) This cosy, hugely welcoming guesthouse and cafe in itself justifies the detour. You can either cater for yourself or eat at its Holmvik Stua, where the food's locally sourced and the fish smoked on the premises.

Information

Tourist Office (76 14 12 03; www.andoyturist.no; Andenes; Hamnegata 1; 10am-6pm mid-Jun–Aug, 10am-4pm early Jun & early Sep, by phone only rest of year) The tourist office covers the whole island and shares premises with the Hisnakul Natural History Centre. It produces a leaflet in English, *Andanes Vær* (Nkr35), which outlines a walking tour of the old quarter. There's internet access (Nkr60 per hour), free wi-fi and it rents bikes (Nkr150/200 per three hours/day).

Tourist Office (76 11 14 80; www.visitvesteralen.com; Kjøpmannsgata 2, Sortland; 9am-5.30pm Mon-Fri, 10am-3.45pm Sat, noon-3.45pm Sun mid-Jun–mid-Aug, 9am-2.30pm Mon-Fri rest of year) Covers the whole of the Vesterålen region.

Getting There & Away

Sortland is a stop on the *Hurtigruten* coastal ferry.

Bus services connect Sortland with Andenes, Narvik and Svolvær.

Tromsø

POP 67,300

Simply put, Tromsø parties. By far the largest town in northern Norway and administrative centre of Troms county, it's lively with cultural bashes, buskers, an animated street scene, a midnight-sun marathon, a respected university, the hallowed Mack Brewery – and more pubs per capita than any other Norwegian town. Its corona of snow-topped peaks provides arresting scenery, excellent hiking in summer and great skiing and dog-sledding in winter.

Although the city lies almost 400km north of the Arctic Circle, its climate is pleasantly moderated by the Gulf Stream. The long winter darkness is offset by round-the-clock activity during the perpetually bright days of summer.

Sights

Tromsø's city centre and airport are on the island of Tromsøya, which is linked by bridges to overspill suburbs on both the mainland and the much larger outer island Kvaløya. Storgata is the principal drag.

★Ishavskatedralen CHURCH

(Arctic Cathedral; www.ishavskatedralen.no; Hans Nilsensvei 41; adult/child Nkr40/free, organ recitals Nkr70-150; ⏲9am-7pm Mon-Fri & 1-7pm Sat & Sun Jun–mid-Aug, 3-6pm Apr, May & mid-Aug–Dec, 2-6pm Feb & Mar) The 11 arching triangles of the Arctic Cathedral (1965), as the Tromsdalen Church is more usually called, suggest glacial crevasses and auroral curtains. The magnificent glowing stained-glass window that occupies almost the whole of the east end depicts Christ descending to earth. Look back toward the west end and the contemporary organ, a work of steely art in itself, then up high to take in the lamps of Czech crystal, hanging in space like icicles. Take bus 20 or 24.

★Polaria MUSEUM, AQUARIUM

(www.polaria.no; Hjalmar Johansens gate 12; adult/child Nkr120/60; ⏲10am-7pm mid-May–Aug, 10am-5pm Sep–mid-May) Daringly designed Polaria is an entertaining multimedia introduction to northern Norway and Svalbard. After an excellent 14-minute film about the latter (screened every 30 minutes), plus another about the northern lights, an Arctic walk leads to displays on shrinking sea ice, a northern lights display, aquariums of cold-water fish and – the big draw – a trio of energetic bearded seals.

★Polar Museum MUSEUM

(Polarmuseet; www.polarmuseum.no; Søndre Tollbodgata 11; adult/child Nkr50/25; ⏲10am-7pm mid-Jun–mid-Aug, 11am-5pm rest of year) The 1st floor of this harbourside museum illustrates early polar research, especially the ventures of Nansen and Amundsen. Downstairs there's a well-mounted exhibition about the hunting and trapping of fuzzy Arctic creatures on Svalbard before coal became king there. Note the exploding harpoons outside; the whale didn't stand much of a chance.

Mack Brewery BREWERY

(Mack Ølbryggeri; ☎77 62 45 80; www.olhallen.no; Storgata 5) This venerable institution merits a pilgrimage. Established in 1877, it produces 18 kinds of beer, including the very quaffable Macks Pilsner, Isbjørn, Haakon and several dark beers. At 1pm year-round (plus 3pm June to August) tours (Nkr160, including a beer mug, pin and pint) leave from the brewery's own Ølhallen Pub, Monday to Thursday. It's wise to reserve in advance.

★Fjellheisen CABLE CAR

(☎77 63 87 37; www.fjellheisen.no; Solliveien 12; adult/child Nkr140/60; ⏲10am-1am late May–mid-Aug, shorter hours rest of year) For a fine view of the city and midnight sun, take the cable car to the top of Mt Storsteinen (421m). There's a restaurant at the top, from where a network of hiking routes radiates. Take bus 26 and buy a combined bus and cable-car ticket (adult/child Nkr145/65).

Activities

In and around Tromsø (operators will normally collect you from your hotel) there's a whole range of robust activities in the winter twilight. You can experience the aurora borealis, go cross-country skiing and snowshoeing (including snowshoe safaris), reindeer- and dog-sledding, and ice-fishing.

Tromsø Villmarkssenter SNOW SPORTS

(☎77 69 60 02; www.villmarkssenter.no) Tromsø Villmarkssenter offers dog-sled excursions ranging from a one-day spin to a four-day trek with overnight camping. The centre, 24km south of town on Kvaløya island, also offers a range of summer activities such as trekking, glacier hiking and sea-kayaking.

Active Tromsø ADVENTURE SPORTS

(☎48 13 71 33; activetromso.no) An excellent company offering the full range of summer and winter activities, with dog-sledding expeditions a particular speciality.

Tromsø Friluftsenter ADVENTURE SPORTS
(☎90 75 15 83; www.tromso-friluftsenter.no) Summer sightseeing, boat trips and a full range of winter activities (including trips to Sámi camps). One intriguing possibility is the five-hour humpback-whale safari from mid-November to mid-January.

Arctic Adventure Tours ADVENTURE SPORTS
(☎45 63 52 88; www.arcticadventuretours.no) A range of activities from dog-sledding and skiing in winter to fishing and hiking expeditions in summer.

Nordre Hestnes Gård HORSE RIDING
(☎90 98 26 40; www.nordre-hestnes-gaard.no) Midnight-sun horseback excursions, hikes and other summer (and also winter) activities.

Tromsø Outdoor EQUIPMENT RENTAL
(☎97 57 58 75; www.tromsooutdoor.no; Sjøgata 14; ⌚10am-5pm Mon-Fri & 10am-4pm Sat & Sun Jan, 9am-5pm daily Feb-Apr, 9am-4pm Mon-Fri & 10am-2pm Sat & Sun May-Aug, shorter hours Sep-Dec) This is for those who prefer a DIY approach to summer or winter activities, with equipment rental for everything from snowshoes and skis to bicycles.

Festivals & Events

Northern Lights Festival MUSIC
(www.nordlysfestivalen.no) Six days of music of all genres. Late January.

Sámi Week CULTURAL
Includes the national reindeer sledge championship, where skilled Sámi whoop and crack the whip along the main street. Early February.

Midnight Sun Marathon SPORT
(www.msm.no) The world's most northerly marathon. In addition to the full 42km, there's also a half-marathon and a children's race. Heald on a Saturday in June.

Insomnia Festival MUSIC
(www.insomniafestival.no) A long, loud weekend of electronic music in October.

Sleeping

Tromsø's peak tourist time is June, when the university's still in full throe, summer tourism has begun and reservations are essential. Check out the homestay section of the tourist office website (p352) for apartments and rooms in private homes.

Tromsø Camping CAMPGROUND €
(☎77 63 80 37; www.tromsocamping.no; Tromsdalen; car/caravan site Nkr240/280, cabins Nkr750-1690; ⌚Oct-Apr; P @) Tent campers enjoy leafy green campsites beside a slow-moving stream. However, bathroom and cooking facilities at this veritable village of cabins are stretched to the limit. Take bus 20 or 24.

★**Rica Ishavshotel** HOTEL €€
(☎77 66 64 00; www.rica.no/ishavshotel; Fredrik Langes gate 2; r Nkr1045-1695; @) Occupying a prime quayside position, this hotel is immediately recognisable by its tall spire resembling a ship's mast. It sometimes swallows as many as five tour groups per day so summer reservations are advisable. Almost half of its attractive rooms, including many singles, have superb views of the sound, and a recent expansion and overhaul of some rooms has added to the appeal.

Ami Hotel HOTEL €€
(☎77 62 10 00; www.amihotel.no; Skolegata 24; s/d Nkr740/910, with shared bathroom Nkr640/790; P @) Located beside a traffic-free road and park, this is a quiet, friendly, family-owned choice. There's a well-equipped kitchen for self-caterers and a couple of communal lounges, each with TV, internet access and free tea and coffee.

Clarion Hotel Aurora HOTEL €€
(☎77 78 11 00; www.nordicchoicehotels.no; Sjøgata 19/21; s/d from Nkr900/940; @) This stylish 121-room waterside hotel, poking towards the sea like the prow of a ship, is architecturally stunning with its odd angles, aluminium trim, pictures on bedroom ceilings, sauna – and a top-floor hot tub where you can savour the picturesque harbour and mountain views as you bubble and boil. Its restaurant too has great fjord views.

Eating

Driv CAFE, RESTAURANT €
(www.driv.no; Tollbodgata 3; mains Nkr115-185; ⌚kitchen 11am-6pm, bar 11.30am-1.30am) This student-run converted warehouse serves meaty burgers (try its renowned Driv burger) and great salads. It organises musical and cultural events and has a disco every Saturday. In winter you can steep yourself in good company within its open-air hot tub.

DON'T MISS

SENJA

Senja, Norway's second-largest island, rivals Lofoten for natural beauty yet attracts a fraction of its visitors.

A broad agricultural plain laps at Innersida, the island's eastern coast facing the mainland. By contrast, birchwoods, moorland and sweet-water lakes extend beneath the bare craggy uplands of the interior. Along the northwestern coast, Yttersida, knife-ridged peaks rise directly from the Arctic Ocean. Here, the Rv86 and Rv862, declared a National Tourist Route, link isolated, still-active fishing villages such as **Hamn** and **Mefjordvær**, and traffic is minimal. The at-times-flat, then mildly bucking road, almost always within sight of the shore, is a cyclist's dream. On the way, pause at the **Tungeneset viewing point**.

★ **Emma's Under** NORWEGIAN €€
(☎77 63 77 30; www.emmas.as; Kirkegata; mains Nkr155-295; ⏰11am-10pm Mon-Fri, from noon Sat) Intimate and sophisticated, this is one of Tromsø's most popular lunch spots, where mains include northern Norwegian staples such as reindeer fillet, lamb and stockfish. Upstairs is the more formal **Emma's Drømekjøkken** (mains Nkr295-365; ⏰6pm-midnight Mon-Sat), a highly regarded gourmet restaurant where advance booking is essential.

Aunegården NORWEGIAN €€
(☎77 65 12 34; www.aunegarden.no; Sjøgata 29; lunch mains Nkr112-196, dinner mains Nkr246-329; ⏰10.30am-11pm Mon-Sat) You could almost lose yourself in this wonderful cafe-cum-restaurant that's all intimate crannies and cubbyholes. In a 19th-century building that functioned as a butcher's shop until 1996, it's rich in character and serves excellent salads, sandwiches and mains. If you don't fancy a full meal, drop by just to enjoy a coffee and one of its melt-in-the-mouth cakes.

Fiskekompaniet SEAFOOD €€€
(☎77 68 76 00; www.fiskekompani.no; Killengrens gate; mains from Nkr325, 3-course meal Nkr565; ⏰4-11pm) This long-standing Tromsø fish and seafood favourite has a prime portside site. All starters and mains, subtly prepared and enhanced, are from the ocean and the atmosphere is classy and contemporary. Enjoy its delightful range of dinner desserts.

Drinking & Nightlife

Tromsø enjoys a thriving nightlife, with many arguing that it's the best scene in Norway. On Friday and Saturday, most nightspots stay open to 3.30am.

Ølhallen Pub PUB
(⏰9am-6pm Mon-Sat) At Mack Brewery's Ølhallen Pub you can sample its fine ales right where they're brewed. Perhaps the world's only, never mind most northerly, watering hole to be closed in the evening, it carries eight varieties on draught.

★ **Skibsbroen** COCKTAIL BAR
(⏰8pm-2am Mon-Thu, 6pm-3.30am Fri & Sat) For quite the most exceptional view of the harbour, fjord and mountains beyond, take the lift/elevator of the Rica Ishavshotel to the 4th floor. Skibsbroen (Ship's Bridge), its intimate crow's-nest bar, has friendly staff, great cocktails – and a superb panoramic view of all below.

Verdensteatret CAFE
(Storgata 93b; ⏰11am-2am Mon-Thu, 11am-3.30am Fri & Sat, 1pm-2am Sun) Norway's oldest film house will satisfy both cinephiles and those in search of great cafes. The bar is a hip place with free wi-fi and weekend DJs. At other times, the bartender spins from the huge collection of vinyl records, so expect anything from classical music to deepest underground. Ask staff to let you peek into the magnificent cinema, its walls painted roof-to-ceiling with early-20th-century murals.

Blå Rock Café BAR
(Strandgata 14/16; ⏰11.30am-2am) The loudest, most raving place in town has theme evenings, almost 50 brands of beer, occasional live bands and weekend DJs. The music is rock, naturally. Every Monday hour is a happy hour.

Information

Tourist Office (☎77 61 00 00; www.visittromso.no; Kirkegata 2; ⏰9am-7pm Mon-Fri, 10am-6pm Sat & Sun mid-May–Aug, shorter hours rest of year) Produces the comprehensive *Tromsø Guide*. Has two free internet points.

Getting There & Away

AIR

Destinations with direct SAS flights to/from **Tromsø Airport** (☎77 64 84 00; www.avinor.no), the main airport for the far north, include Oslo, Narvik/Harstad, Bodø, Trondheim, Alta,

Hammerfest, Kirkenes and Longyearbyen. **Norwegian** (www.norwegian.no) flies to and from London (Gatwick), Edinburgh, Dublin and Oslo.

BOAT

Express boats connect Tromsø and Harstad (2½ hours), via Finnsnes (1¼ hours), two to four times daily. Tromsø is also a major stop on the *Hurtigruten* coastal ferry route.

BUS

The main **bus terminal** (sometimes called Prostneset) is on Kaigata, beside the **Hurtigruten quay**. There are up to three daily express buses to/from Narvik (Nkr240, 4¼ hours) and one to/from Alta (Nkr560, 6½ hours); change in Alta for Nordkapp.

Getting Around

Tromsø's airport (p352) is about 5km from the town centre, on the western side of Tromsøya island. **Flybuss** (one way/return Nkr70/100) runs between the airport and Rica Ishavshotel (15 minutes), connecting with arriving and departing flights and stopping by other major hotels along the way.

FINNMARK

All along Norway's jagged northern coast, deeply cut by forbidding fjords, you'll find numerous isolated fishing villages, as well as some of the north's star attractions: Alta, with its Stone Age rock carvings; Kirkenes, a frontier-like town sharing a border with Russia; and Nordkapp, reportedly but not quite mainland Europe's northernmost point.

Those who head inland will find the vast and empty Finnmarksvidda Plateau, a stark expanse with only two major settlements: Karasjok and Kautokeino. They and Finnmarksvidda are part of the heartland of the Sámi people, where reindeer herding has occurred for centuries. Enjoy a dog-sled journey across empty tundra half lit under the bruise-blue winter sky.

One good source of information about the region is www.nordnorge.com.

Alta

POP 19,820

Although the fishing and slate-quarrying town of Alta lies at latitude N 70°, it enjoys a relatively mild climate. The Alta Museum, with its ancient petroglyphs, is a must-see, the Northern Lights Cathedral is stunning and the lush green Sautso-Alta Canyon is simply breathtaking.

Sights

The Altaelva hydroelectric project has had very little effect on the 400m-deep Sautso-Alta, northern Europe's grandest canyon.

Alta Museum MUSEUM

(www.alta.museum.no; Altaveien 19; adult/child May-Sep Nkr95/25, Oct-Apr Nkr65/15; 8am-5pm May–mid-Jun, 8am-8pm mid-Jun–Aug, 8am-3pm Mon-Fri & 11am-4pm Sat & Sun Sep-Apr) This superb museum is in Hjemmeluft, at the western end of town. It features exhibits and displays on Sámi culture, Finnmark military history, the Alta hydroelectric project and the aurora borealis (northern lights). The cliffs around it, a Unesco World Heritage Site, are incised with around 6000 late–Stone Age carvings, dating from 6000 to 2000 years ago, and it's these petroglyphs that will live longest in the memory.

Northern Lights Cathedral CHURCH

(Løkkeveien; 11am-3pm Mon-Fri, 10am-1pm Sat, services 11am Sun) Opened in 2013, the daringly designed Northern Lights Cathedral, next to the Rica Hotel Alta, promises to be one of the architectural icons of the north, with its swirling pyramid structure clad in rippling titanium sheets. The interior is similarly eye-catching, with an utterly modern 4.3m-high bronze *Christ* by Danish artist Peter Brandes – note how the figure gets lighter as your eyes move up the body.

Sleeping & Eating

★ **Rica Hotel Alta** HOTEL €€

(78 48 27 00; www.rica.no; Løkkeveien 61; s/d from Nkr850/1050; @) Alta's classiest hotel has attractive rooms (some have large photos of the northern lights) and excellent service. Try for one of the west-facing rooms with views over the cathedral. The **restaurant** (mains Nkr150-312; 6-11pm) is also also excellent and there's a bar (closed Sundays).

Thon Hotel Vica HOTEL €€

(78 48 22 22; www.thonhotels.no; Fogdebakken 6; s/d from Nkr820/1120; P@) Right from the stuffed brown bear that greets you at the door, the Vica beckons you in. In a timber-built former farmhouse, it was until recently a family-run concern, and still retains a more personal feel than many other hotels in this chain. There's a sauna (Nkr100), steaming outdoor hot tub (wonderful in winter when all around is snowcapped) and a good restaurant.

Sorrisniva Igloo Hotel HOTEL €€€
(☎78 43 33 78; www.sorrisniva.no; s/d Nkr2550/4500; ⏱early-Jan–mid-Apr; P) The 30 bedrooms – and beds too – are made entirely of ice, as are the chapel, bridal suite (no complaints of wedding-night frigidity so far) and stunning ice bar with its weird-and-wonderful sculptures lit by fibre-optics. Then again, you might just want to drop by and visit (adult/child Nkr200/50).

Alfa-Omega CAFE €€
(www.alfaomega-alta.no; Markedsgata 14-16; lunch mains from Nkr169, dinner mains Nkr216-329; ⏱8am-10pm Mon-Sat) As its name suggests, this place has two parts: Omega, its contemporary cafe, serves salads, sandwiches, pastas and cakes. Sink your teeth into its hugely popular Ole Mattis reindeer steak sandwich. Alfa, a pleasant, casual bar, comes into its own from 8pm. There's also a terrace, ideal for taking a little summer sunshine, overlooking Alta's bleak central square.

★ **Restaurant Haldde** NORWEGIAN €€€
(mains Nkr249-349; ⏱4-10pm Mon-Thu, 4-11pm Fri & Sat, 1-10pm Sun) This quality restaurant within Thon Hotel Vica relies almost entirely upon local ingredients in the preparation of choice dishes such as reindeer steak, grilled stockfish and its *Flavour of Finnmark* dessert of cloudberries and cowberry-blueberry sorbet.

Information

Tourist Office (www.alta-kommune.no; Markedsgata 3; ⏱10am-7pm Mon, Tue & Thu, 10am-4pm Wed & Fri, 11am-3pm Sat Jun-Aug, 10am-3.30pm Mon-Sat rest of year) In the library.

Getting There & Away

AIR

Alta's **airport** (☎78 44 95 55; www.avinor.no) is 4km northeast of Sentrum at Elvebakken. SAS has direct flights to/from Oslo, Tromsø, Hammerfest, Lakselv and Vadsø. Norwegian connects Alta with Oslo.

BUS

Buses leave from the terminal in Sentrum to Tromsø (Nkr560, 6½ hours, one daily), Hammerfest (Nkr315, 2¼ hours, two daily), Honningsvåg (Nkr475, four hours, one daily), Karasjok (Nkr475, 4¾ hours, two daily except Saturday) and Kautokeino (Nkr280, 2¼ hours, one daily except Saturday).

Hammerfest

POP 10,290

Welcome to Norway's, and perhaps even the world's, northernmost town – other Norwegian communities, while further north, are, Hammerfest vigorously argues, too small to qualify as towns!

If you're arriving on the *Hurtigruten* coastal ferry, you'll have only 1½ hours to pace around, pick up an Arctic souvenir and scoff some fresh shrimp at the harbour. For most visitors that will be ample. The town's most unusual experience is to be found at the Royal & Ancient Polar Bear Society.

Sights & Activities

★ **Royal & Ancient Polar Bear Society** MUSEUM
(www.isbjornklubben.no; ⏱8am-6pm daily Jun & Jul, 9am-4pm Mon-Fri & 10am-2pm Sat & Sun Aug-May) FREE Dedicated to preserving Hammerfest culture, the Royal & Ancient Polar Bear Society (founded in 1963) features exhibits on Arctic hunting and local history and shares premises with the tourist office. For Nkr180, you can become a life member, and get a certificate, ID card, sticker and pin. At times, the link to polar bears here can feel a little tenuous. But if you think of the place in terms of the Norwegian name (Isbjørklubben, simply Polar Bear Club), you're less likely to be disappointed.

★ **Hammerfest Kirke** CHURCH
(Kirkegata 33; ⏱7.15am-3pm Mon-Fri, 11am-3pm Sat, noon-1pm Sun mid-Jun–mid-Aug) The design of Hammerfest's contemporary church, consecrated in 1961, was inspired by the racks used for drying fish in the salty sea air all across northern Norway. Behind the altar, the glorious stained-glass window positively glows in the summer sun, while the wooden frieze along the organ gallery depicts highlights of the town's history. The chapel in the cemetery across the street is the only building in town to have survived WWII.

Gjenreisningsmuseet MUSEUM
(www.kystmuseene.no; Kirkegata 21; Feb-Nov adult/child Nkr50/free, Dec & Jan free; ⏱10am-4pm early Jun–late-Aug, 10am-2pm Mon-Fri & 11am-2pm Sat & Sun rest of year) Hammerfest's Reconstruction Museum is a great little museum with particularly thoughtful and sensitive panels and captions (each section has a synopsis in English). It recounts the forced evacuation and

decimation of the town during the Nazi retreat in 1944, the hardships that its citizens endured through the following winter, and Hammerfest's postwar reconstruction and regeneration.

Salen Hill VIEWPOINT

For panoramic views over the town, coast and mountains (there's a free pair of binoculars for you to sweep the bay), climb Salen Hill (86m), topped by the **Turistua restaurant** (☎94 15 46 25; mains Nkr160-225), a couple of Sámi turf huts and a lookout point. The 15-minute uphill walking trail begins at the small park behind the Rådhus.

Sleeping & Eating

Camping Storvannet CAMPGROUND €

(☎78 41 10 10; storvannet@yahoo.no; Storvannsveien; car/caravan site Nkr200/210, 2-/4-bed cabin Nkr450/500; ⏲Jun-Sep) Beside a lake and overlooked by a giant apartment complex, this pleasant site, Hammerfest's only decent camping option, is small so book your cabin in advance.

Rica Hotel Hammerfest HOTEL €€

(☎78 42 57 00; www.rica.no; Sørøygata 15; d Nkr890-1605; P @) Constructed in agreeable mellow brick, this hotel has an attractive if somewhat dated bar and lounge and well-furnished rooms – they're worth it if you get a harbour view, but overpriced if not. Its Arctic Menu restaurant, **Skansen Mat og Vinstue** (mains Nkr190-349; ⏲6-11pm), serves excellent local fare.

★**Redrum** CAFE €

(www.redrum.no; Storgata 23; snacks & mains Nkr69-190; ⏲11am-2pm Mon, 11am-6pm Tue-Thu, 11am-3am Fri, 11am-5pm & 9pm-3am Sat) A couple of blocks back from the waterfront, Redrum, with its attractive contemporary decor and flickering candles, saves its energy for weekend wildness, when there's regularly live music. To the rear, there's a deep, more relaxed wooden patio. Wherever you sit, the menu's divided into 'burgers' and 'non-burgers' – the latter includes fish and chips, Caesar salad and pulled pork.

Information

Tourist Office (www.hammerfest-turist.no; Hamnegata 3; ⏲8am-6pm daily Jun-Jul, 9am-4pm Mon-Fri & 10am-2pm Sat & Sun Aug-May) Has free internet access and rents electric bikes for Nkr130/325 per hour/day.

WHAT'S WITH THE POLAR BEARS?

A wild polar bear hasn't been seen in Hammerfest for thousands of years, and yet polar bears adorn the city's coat of arms, statues of polar bears guard various public buildings and there's even the Royal & Ancient Polar Bear Society. Cashing in without cause? Well, not quite. In the 19th and 20th centuries, Hammerfest was a major base for Arctic hunting expeditions to the Norwegian territory of Svalbard (or Spitsbergen as it was better known). Returning expeditions brought back numerous captive polar bears (particularly cubs) and from Hammerfest they were shipped to zoos around the world.

Getting There & Away

BOAT

The *Hurtigruten* coastal ferry stops in Hammerfest for 1½ hours in each direction. A *Hurtigruten* hop to Tromsø (11 hours) or Honningsvåg (five hours) makes a comfortable alternative to a long bus journey.

BUS

Buses run to/from Alta (Nkr315, 2¼ hours, two daily), Honningsvåg (Nkr425, 3½ hours, one to two daily) and Karasjok (Nkr410, 4¼ hours, twice daily except Saturday), with one service extending to Kirkenes (Nkr1050, 10¼ hours) via Tana Bru (Nkr740, eight hours) four times weekly.

Nordkapp

Yes, it's rip-off (more on that in a moment), but Nordkapp is a stunning, hauntingly beautiful place. Even after the novelty wears off, it's the view that thrills the most. In reasonable weather, you can gaze down at the wild surf 307m below, watch the mists roll in and simply enjoy the moment.

Nearer to the North Pole than to Oslo, Nordkapp sits at latitude 71° 10' 21"N, where the sun never drops below the horizon from mid-May to the end of July. Long before other Europeans took an interest, it was a sacrificial site for the Sámi, who believed it had special powers.

However, to reach the tip of the continent – by car, by bike, on a bus or walking in – you have to pay a toll (adult/child Nkr245/85). This allows unlimited entry

WORTH A TRIP

KNIVSKJELODDEN

Now here's a secret: Nordkapp isn't continental Europe's northernmost point. That award belongs to Knivskjelodden, an 18km round-trip hike away, less dramatic, inaccessible by vehicle – and to be treasured all the more for that. Lying about 3km west of Nordkapp, it sticks its finger a full 1457m further northwards. You can hike to the tip of this promontory from a marked car park 6km south of the Nordkapp toll booth. The 9km track, waymarked with giant cairns, isn't difficult despite some ups and downs, but it's best to wear hiking boots since it can be squelchy. When you get to the tall beehive-shaped obelisk at latitude 71° 11' 08"N, down at sea level, sign the guestbook. Allow five to six hours for the round trip.

over two days but it's small compensation for the majority who simply roll in, look around, take a snap or two and roll out.

There is a cheaper fee listed on the ticket-office window (adult/child Nkr160/80) which allows you to visit the site without entering the exhibits, but you may have to argue for it – the ticket officer on the day we visited had no idea of this cheaper fee's existence.

The closest town of any size is Honningsvåg, 35km from Nordkapp.

Sleeping

All of the following places are located in Honningsvåg.

Northcape Guesthouse HOSTEL €
(☎47 25 50 63; www.northcapeguesthouse.com; Elvebakken 5a; dm Nkr250, s/d/f with shared bathroom Nkr550/700/1400; ⊙May-Aug; P) A 15- to 20-minute walk from the Hurtigruten quay, this bright, modern hostel is an excellent budget choice. There's a cosy lounge, washing machine, well-equipped kitchen for self-caterers – and great views over the town below. It's often full so reserve well in advance.

Rica Hotel Honningsvåg HOTEL €€€
(☎78 47 72 20; www.rica.no; Nordkappgata 4; r from Nkr1290; P) The big plus of this hotel, reliable as all others in this Norway-wide chain, is its position, right beside the docks. **Grillen**, its à-la-carte restaurant, is worth a visit, whether you're staying at the hotel or elsewhere.

Information

Tourist Office (☎78 47 70 30; www.nordkapp.no; Fiskeriveien 4, Honningsvåg; ⊙10am-10pm Mon-Fri & noon-8pm Sat & Sun mid-Jun–mid-Aug, 11am-2pm Mon-Fri rest of year) Right on the waterfront and signposted all over town.

Getting There & Away

The *Hurtigruten* coastal ferry calls by Honningsvåg. Its 3½-hour northbound stop allows passengers a quick buzz up to Nordkapp.

An express bus connects Honningsvåg with Alta (Nkr475, four hours, one to two daily) and there's also a run to/from Hammerfest (Nkr425, 3½ hours, one to two daily).

Getting Around

Between mid-May and late August, a local bus (adult/child Nkr490/245, 45 minutes) runs daily at 11am and 9.30pm between Honningsvåg and Nordkapp. It sets off back from the cape at 1.15pm and 12.45am (so that you can take in the midnight sun at precisely midnight). From 1 June to 15 August, there's a supplementary run at 5pm, though this returns at 6.15pm, giving you barely half an hour at Nordkapp unless you want to hang around for the service that returns at 12.45am. Check precise departure times with the tourist office. Ticket prices include the Nkr245 per-passenger Nordkapp entry fee.

Kirkenes

POP 3680

This is it: you're as far east as Cairo, further east than most of Finland, a mere 15km from the border with Russia – and at the end of the line for the *Hurtigruten* coastal ferry. This tiny, nondescript place, anticlimactic for many, has a distinct frontier feel. You'll see street signs in Norwegian and Cyrillic script and hear Russian spoken by transborder visitors and fishermen.

The town reels with around 100,000 visitors every year, most stepping off the *Hurtigruten* to spend a couple of hours in the town before travelling onward. But you should linger a while here, not primarily for the town's sake but to take one of the many excursions and activities on offer.

Sights

On the last Thursday of most months, Russian merchants set up shop around the town centre, selling everything from craftwork to binoculars. Prices aren't as cheap as in Russia, but they're still a bargain for Norway.

Activities

Summer

The following activities are popular from late June to mid-August.

King-crab safari (adult/child Nkr1300/600)

Quad-bike safari (single/double Nkr1500/2500)

Half-day tours of the Pasvik Valley (adult/child Nkr900/450)

Visiting the Russian border and iron-ore mines (adult/child Nkr550/275)

Boat trips along the Pasvik river (adult/child Nkr1090/500, including meal)

Winter

Activities to try between December and mid-April include the following:

Snowmobile safaris (s/d Nkr1790/1990)

Ice fishing (from Nkr850)

Snowshoe walks (from Nkr850)

Dog-sledding (from Nkr1990)

King-crab safari (adult/child Nkr1300/600)

Tours

Arctic Adventure ADVENTURE TOURS
(☎78 99 68 74; www.arctic-adventure.no; Jarfjordbotn) Summer and winter activities such as snowmobiling, dog-sledding and king-crab safaris.

Barents Safari ADVENTURE TOURS
(☎90 19 05 94; www.barentssafari.no) Barents Safari runs a three-hour boat trip (at least twice daily from June to mid-September) along the Pasvik River to the Russian border at the historic village of Boris Gleb (Borisoglebsk in Russian). It also organises snowmobiling, king-crab safaris and summer quad biking.

Pasvikturist ADVENTURE TOURS
(www.pasvikturist.no; Dr Wessels gate 9) Offers a wealth of tours including a one-day trans-border visit to Russia's Pechenga valley and mining city of Nikel (around Nkr1500), and a guided weekend in Murmansk (around Nkr2400). For both you need to already have a Russian visa or be a Norwegian resident.

Radius ADVENTURE TOURS
(www.kirkenessnowhotel; Sandnesdalen 14) A full range of tours and safaris at the home of the Kirkenes Snow Hotel.

Sleeping & Eating

★**Sollia Gjestegård** HOTEL €€
(☎78 99 08 20; www.storskog.no; 1-/2-bed apt Nkr1090/1490, 2–4-bed cabin Nkr1050-1690, s/d Nkr650/800, breakfast Nkr95) The Sollia, 13km southeast of Kirkenes, was originally constructed as a tuberculosis sanatorium and you can see why. The air could scarcely be more pure or the atmosphere more relaxed at this wonderful getaway haven. The whole family can sweat it out in the sauna and outdoor tub, while children will enjoy communing with the resident huskies. Just below, beside the lake, its Gapahuken restaurant is just as enticing.

Thon Hotel Kirkenes HOTEL €€
(☎78 97 10 50; www.thonhotels.no/kirkenes; s/d from Nkr595/795) This newish waterside hotel is Thon-boxy from the exterior. Within, though, it's open, vast and exciting, offering great views of the sound and a cluster of laid-up Russian trawlers. The restaurant is just as architecturally stimulating, and you could easily dangle a line from the open-air terrace.

Rica Arctic Hotel HOTEL €€
(☎78 99 11 59; www.rica.no/arctic; Kongensgate 1-3; d from Nkr990; P@≋) The Rica Arctic, a pleasing modern block, boasts Norway's most easterly swimming pool, heated and open year-round. The other special attribute, its **Arctic Menu restaurant** (summer buffet Nkr350), is the best of the town's hotel dining options.

Kirkenes Snow Hotel HOTEL €€€
(☎78 97 05 40; www.kirkenessnowhotel.com; s/d half-board & sauna incl transfer from Kirkenes Nkr2500/5000; ⊙20 Dec–mid-Apr) Yes, the price is steep but you'll remember the occasion for life. And bear in mind that 25 tonnes of ice and 15,000 cu metres of snow are shifted each winter to build this ephemeral structure. For dinner, guests cook reindeer sausages over an open fire, then enjoy a warming main course of baked salmon.

★**Gapahuken** NORWEGIAN €€€
(☎78 99 08 20; mains Nkr220-550, buffet Nkr400; ⊙4-10pm Tue-Sat, 3-7pm Sun mid-Jun–Aug, on demand rest of year) From the broad picture windows of Gapahuken, Sollia Gjestegård hotel's restaurant, there's a grand panorama of the lake at its feet and the Russian frontier post beyond. Discriminating diners drive out from Kirkenes to enjoy gourmet Norwegian cuisine made with fresh local

ingredients such as reindeer, king crab, salmon and halibut. Sunday is buffet only.

Information

Kirkenes has no functioning tourist office – the website still works, but it's years out of date. Your best bet for information and brochures are the hotels or tour operators.

Getting There & Around

AIR

From **Kirkenes airport** (☎67 03 53 00; www.avinor.no), 13km southwest of town, there are direct flights to Oslo (SAS and Norwegian) and Tromsø (Widerøe). The airport is served by the Flybuss (Nkr85, 20 minutes), which connects the bus terminal and Rica Arctic Hotel with all arriving and departing flights.

BOAT

Kirkenes is the terminus of the *Hurtigruten* coastal ferry, which heads southwards again at 12.45pm daily. A bus (Nkr100) meets the boat and runs into town and on to the airport.

BUS

Buses run four times weekly to Karasjok (five hours), Hammerfest (10¼ hours) and many points in between.

Karasjok

POP 2875

Kautokeino may have more Sámi residents, but Karasjok (Kárásjohka in Sámi) is Sámi Norway's indisputable capital. It's home to the Sámi Parliament and library, NRK Sámi Radio, a wonderful Sámi museum and an impressive Sámi theme park.

Sights

Sápmi Park AMUSEMENT PARK, MUSEUM

(www.visitsapmi.no; Porsangerveien; adult/child Nkr130/65; ⏰9am-7pm mid-Jun–mid-Aug, 9am-4pm late Aug, 9am-4pm Mon-Fri & 11am-3pm Sat Sep–mid-Dec, 10am-2pm Mon-Fri Jan-May) Sámi culture is big business here, and this impressive theme park includes a wistful, high-tech multimedia introduction to the Sámi in the 'Magic Theatre', plus Sámi winter and summer camps and other dwellings to explore in the grounds. There's also, of course, a gift shop and cafe – and **Boble Glasshytte**, Finnmark's only glass-blowing workshop and gallery.

Sámi National Museum MUSEUM

(Sámiid Vuorká Dávvirat; ☎78 46 99 50; www.rdm.no; Museumsgata 17; adult/child Nkr75/free; ⏰9am-6pm daily Jun–mid-Aug, 9am-6pm Mon-Fri & 10am-4pm Sat & Sun late Aug, 9am-3pm Mon-Fri Sep–mid-Jun, 9am-3pm Tue-Fri mid-Aug–May) Exhibits at the Sámi National Museum, also called the Sámi Collection, include displays of colourful, traditional Sámi clothing, tools and artefacts, and works by contemporary Sámi artists. Outdoors, you can roam among a cluster of traditional Sámi constructions and follow a short trail, signed in English, that leads past and explains ancient Sámi reindeer-trapping pits and hunting techniques. In summer, a guided walk is included in the ticket price.

Sámi Parliament NOTABLE BUILDING

(Sámediggi; Kautokeinoveien 50; ⏰hourly tours 8.30am-2.30pm late Jun–mid-Aug, except 11.30am, 1pm Mon-Fri rest of yr) FREE The Sámi Parliament was established in 1989 and meets four times annually. In 2000 it moved into a glorious new building, encased in mellow Siberian wood, with a birch, pine and oak interior. The main assembly hall is shaped like a Sámi tent, and the **Sámi library**, lit with tiny lights like stars, houses over 35,000 volumes, plus other media. Tours last 30 minutes. There are similar Sámi parliaments in Finland and Sweden.

Activities

Engholm's Husky DOG-SLEDDING

(www.engholm.no; 1hr dog-sledding Nkr1000, 1-/4-/5-/8-day winter husky safari Nkr1700/7300/9800/16,800) Engholm's Husky, in the Engholm Husky Design Lodge, offers winter dog-sled tours. These are sometimes run by Sven Engholm, one of dog-sledding's most celebrated names. They can also arrange summer walking tours with a dog to carry at least some of your gear. Consult the website for the full range of activities.

Turgleder OUTDOORS

(☎91 16 73 03; www.turgleder.com) Run out of Engholm Husky Design Lodge by Sven Engholm's daughter Liv, this fine outfit offers a year-round range of activities, from four- to six-hour cross-country skiing excursions (per person Nkr950) to 24-hour 'Scout-for-a-day' experiences (Nkr1900).

Sleeping & Eating

★**Engholm Husky Design Lodge** CABINS €€

(☎91 58 66 25; www.engholm.no; full board from Nkr1400/2400, s/d hut only from Nkr700/1000; P) About 6km from Karasjok along the Rv92, Sven Engholm has built this wonderful haven in the forest with his own hands.

Each rustic cabin is individually furnished with great flair, with every item (from reindeer-horn toilet brushes to creative lampshades) hand-carved by Sven. All have kitchen facilities and two have bathrooms. You sink into sleep to the odd bark and yelp from the sled dogs.

Rica Hotel Karasjok HOTEL €€
(☎78 46 88 60; www.rica.no; Porsangerveien; d Nkr760-1560; P @) Adjacent to Sápmi Park, this is Karasjok's premier hotel lodging, with handsome rooms and Sámi motifs throughout, plus, outside in summertime, Gammen, an impressive Arctic Menu restaurant.

Biepmu Kafeà CAFE €€
(☎78 46 61 51; Finlandsveien; mains Nkr130-225; ⏲2-8pm) This simple cafeteria in the centre of town serves up hearty local dishes and snacks, with daily specials (starting at Nkr175) including reindeer on Sunday and a Wednesday fish buffet. There are also other dishes such as shredded reindeer meat. The heavy wooden benches resemble church pews and it's very much locals only in attendance.

★**Gammen** NORWEGIAN €€€
(☎78 46 88 60; mains Nkr225-385; ⏲11am-10pm mid-Jun–mid-Aug) It's very much reindeer or reindeer plus a couple of fish options at this summer-only rustic complex of four large interconnected Sámi huts run by the Rica Hotel. Although it may be busy with bus-tour groups, it's an atmospheric place to sample traditional Sámi dishes from reindeer stew to fillet of reindeer or simply to drop in for a coffee or beer.

Shopping

Knivsmed Strømeng HANDICRAFTS
(☎78 46 71 05; Badjenjárga; ⏲9am-4pm Mon-Fri) This shop calls on five generations of local experience to create original handmade Sámi knives for everything from outdoor to kitchen use. They're real works of art, but stay true to the Sámi need for durability, made with birch-and-brass handles and varying steel quality. Prices start at Nkr840 for a Sámi kid's knife and go up to Nkr1840 for the real deal.

To get here, turn southwest on Route 92 towards Ivalo at the lower of two main roundabouts along the E6 in the centre of town. It's on your left after crossing the bridge.

Information

Tourist Office (☎78 46 88 00; ⏲9am-7pm Jun–mid-Aug) The summer-only tourist office is in Sápmi Park, near the junction of the E6 and the Rv92. It will change money if you're stuck with euros after crossing the border from Finland.

WORTH A TRIP

KAUTOKEINO

While Karasjok has made concessions to Norwegian culture, Kautokeino, the traditional winter base of the reindeer Sámi (as opposed to their coastal kin), remains more emphatically Sámi. Some 85% of the townspeople have Sámi as their first language and you may see a few nontourist-industry locals in traditional dress.

The setting is pretty, and **Kautokeino Museum** (☎40 61 14 06; Boaronjárga 23; adult/child Nkr40/free; ⏲9am-6pm Mon-Sat & noon-6pm Sun mid-Jun–mid-Aug, 9am-3pm Tue-Fri rest of year) and **Kautokeino Kirke** (Suomalvodda; ⏲9am-8pm Jun–mid-Aug) both offer intriguing insights into Sámi life. And don't miss **Juhls' Sølvsmie** (Juhls' Silver Gallery; ☎78 48 43 30; www.juhls.no; Galaniitoluodda; ⏲9am-8pm mid-Jun–mid-Aug, to 6pm rest of year), a jewellery gallery and workshop that captures the essence of the Arctic.

The best place to stay in town is the **Thon Hotel Kautokeino** (☎78 48 70 00; www.thonhotels.no; Biedjovaggeluodda 2; s/d from Nkr1120/1320; P @), which also has a good restaurant. Budget travellers should try **Arctic Motell & Camping** (☎78 48 54 00; www.kauto.no; Suomaluodda 16; car/caravan sites Nkr200/250, cabins Nkr400-1800, motel r from Nkr900; ⏲Jun-Aug).

Kautokeino's **tourist office** (☎78 48 70 00; ⏲10am-6pm Mon-Fri, to 5pm Sun mid-Jun–mid-Aug) has had four different locations in our four recent visits. The Thon Hotel should know where it's migrated to.

Buses run between Kautokeino and Alta (Nkr280, 2¼ hours) daily except Saturday. From July to mid-August, the Finnish Lapin Linjat bus connects Kautokeino with Alta (1¾ hours) and Rovaniemi (eight hours), in Finland, once daily.

Getting There & Away

Twice-daily buses (except Saturday) connect Karasjok with Alta (Nkr475, 4¾ hours) and Hammerfest (Nkr410, 4¼ hours). There's a service to Kirkenes (Nkr529, five hours) four times weekly.

A daily Finnish Lapin Linjat bus runs to Rovaniemi (Nkr700, eight hours) via Ivalo (Nkr280, 3½ hours), in Finland.

SVALBARD

The world's most readily accessible piece of the polar north, and one of the most spectacular places imaginable, Svalbard is *the* destination for an unforgettable holiday. This wondrous archipelago is an assault on the senses: vast icebergs and floes choke the seas, and icefields and glaciers frost the lonely heights. It also hosts a surprising variety of flora and fauna, including seals, walrus, Arctic foxes and polar bears.

Plan your trip well in advance. When you arrive, you'll almost certainly want to participate in some kind of organised trek or tour, and many need to be booked early. If you don't travel outside Longyearbyen, you won't get Svalbard's appeal.

History

Although the first mention of Svalbard occurs in an Icelandic saga from 1194, the official discovery of Svalbard (then uninhabited) is credited to Dutch voyager Willem Barents in 1596. He named the islands Spitsbergen, or 'sharp mountains'. The Norwegian name, Svalbard, comes from the Old Norse for 'cold coast'; ancient Norse sagas referred to 'a land in the far north at the end of the ocean'. During the 17th century, Dutch, English, French, Norwegian and Danish whalers slaughtered the whale population. They were followed in the 18th century by Russians hunting walrus and seals. The 19th century saw the arrival of Norwegians, who hunted polar bears and Arctic foxes. In 1906, commercial coal mining began and is continued today by the Russians (at Barentsburg) and the Norwegians (at Longyearbyen and Sveagruva). The 1920 Svalbard Treaty granted Norway sovereignty over the islands.

Getting There & Away

Norwegian (www.norwegian.com) Norwegian flies three times a week between Oslo Gardermoen and Longyearbyen.

SAS (www.flysas.com) SAS flies to/from Oslo directly in summer (three flights weekly) or via Tromsø (three to five times weekly) year-round. There are as many as 11 different tariffs; book early to avoid paying the 11th least expensive.

SVALBARD TOUR COMPANIES

Companies that cover a range of activities include the followung:

Arctic Adventures (☎79 02 16 24; www.arctic-adventures.no) Small company offering the full range of activities.

Basecamp Spitsbergen (☎79 02 46 00; www.basecampspitsbergen.com) Basecamp Spitsbergen has a large portfolio of adventure trips and mainly offers winter activities, including a stay aboard the *Noorderlicht*, a Dutch sailing vessel that's set into the fjord ice as the long freeze begins each autumn. It also offers winter and summer stays at Isfjord Radio, the ultimate remote getaway on an upgraded, one-time radio station at the western tip of Spitsbergen.

Poli Arctici (☎79 02 17 05; www.poliartici.com) Poli Arctici is the trading name of Stefano Poli, originally from Milan, who has more than 15 years as a Svalbard wilderness guide.

Spitsbergen Outdoor Activities (☎91 77 65 95; www.spitsbergenoutdooractivities.com) Specialists in hiking, both on glacier and otherwise.

Spitsbergen Tours (☎79 02 10 68; www.terrapolaris.com) The owner of Spitsbergen Tours, Andreas Umbreit, is one of the longest-standing operators on the archipelago.

Spitsbergen Travel (p361)

Svalbard Wildlife Expeditions (p362)

Longyearbyen

POP 2100

Svalbard's only town of any size, Longyearbyen enjoys a superb backdrop including two glacier tongues, Longyearbreen and Lars Hjertabreen. The town itself is fringed by abandoned mining detritus and the waterfront is anything but beautiful, with shipping containers and industrial buildings. The further you head up the valley towards the glaciers, the more you'll appreciate being here. Even so, Longyearbyen is a place to base yourself for trips out into the wilderness rather than somewhere to linger for its own sake.

Sights

In addition to the main sights, keep an eye out for wild reindeer and even the Arctic fox in and around the town.

Svalbard Museum MUSEUM
(☎79 02 64 92; www.svalbardmuseum.no; adult/student/child Nkr75/50/15; ⏰10am-5pm Mar-Sep, from noon Oct-Feb) Museum is the wrong word for this impressive exhibition space. Themes include the life on the edge formerly led by whalers, trappers, seal and walrus hunters and, more recently, miners. It's an attractive mix of text, artefacts and birds and mammals, stuffed and staring. There's a cosy book-browsing area, too, where you can lounge on sealskin cushions and rugs.

Spitsbergen Airship Museum MUSEUM
(North Pole Expedition Museum; ☎91 38 34 67; www.spitsbergenairshipmuseum.com; adult/child Nkr75/40; ⏰9am-1pm) This fascinating private museum houses a stunning collection of artefacts, original newspapers and other documents relating to the history of polar exploration. With labels in English and intriguing archive footage, you could easily spend a couple of hours here reliving some of the Arctic's most stirring tales. Opening hours are in a state of flux. It's across the road from the back side of the museum and tourist office.

Activities

Summer Activities

There's a dizzying array of short trips and day tours that vary with the season. The tourist office's weekly activities list provides details of many more. All outings can be booked through individual operators (directly or via their websites) or online at the tourist office (p363).

BIRDWATCHING

More than 160 bird species have been reported in Svalbard, with the overwhelming number of these present during the summer months. Some tour operators run short boat trips to the 'bird cliffs' close to Longyearbyen, while birdwatchers should buy the booklet *Bird Life in Longyearbyen and Surrounding Area* (Nkr50), available from the tourist office.

BOAT TRIPS

Henningsen Transport & Guiding BOAT
(☎91 85 37 56, 79 02 13 11; www.htg.svalbard.no) Henningsen Transport & Guiding runs excellent trips to Barentsburg and Pyramiden (Nkr1550). En route, they tend to sail closer to shore than other companies, rather than sailing down the middle of the fjord. It also runs six-hour Friday-evening trips to Bore glacier for Nkr1190.

Polar Charter BOAT
(☎97 52 32 50; www.polarcharter.no) Polar Charter sends out the *MS Polargirl* to Barentsburg and the Esmark Glacier (Nkr1300, eight to 10 hours) four times a week, and to Pyramiden and Nordenskjöldbreen (Nkr1300, eight to 10 hours); prices include a lunch cooked on board. On Fridays, it also organises five-hour trips to the Borebreen glacier (Nkr900).

Spitsbergen Travel BOAT
(www.spitsbergentravel.com; 3/6hr Nkr640/990) One of the giants of the Svalbard travel scene, Spitsbergen Travel has a staggering array of tour options. It arranges up to 13 weekly boat cruises around Isfjord, which take in birdwatching, fossil-hunting and glacier views.

HIKING & FOSSIL-HUNTING

Summer hiking possibilities are endless and any Svalbard tour company worth its salt can organise half-, full- and multiday hikes. The easiest options are three-hour fossil-hunting hikes (from Nkr500), some of which take you up onto the moraine at the base of the Longyearbreen glacier.

Popular destinations for other hikes, many of which include glacier hikes, include **Platåberget** (three hours, Nkr450), up onto the **Longyearbreen glacier** itself (five hours, Nkr650), **Sarkofagen** (525m above sea level; six hours, Nkr620) and **Hiorthfjellet** (900m above sea level; 10 hours, Nkr1225).

Spitsbergen Outdoor Activities (p360) and Poli Arctici (p360) are among the better smaller operators.

KAYAKING

Svalbard Wildlife Expeditions ADVENTURE
(☎79 02 22 22; www.wildlife.no) Offering many of the usual and several unusual trips, including seven-hour kayaking expeditions to Hiorthamn (Nkr950), with an additional 10-hour hiking and kayaking challenge to Hiortfjellet (Nkr1225). Other options are the various excursions along Adventdalen.

Winter Activities

DOG-SLEDDING

Green Dog Svalbard DOG-SLEDDING
(☎79 02 61 68; www.greendog.no; 4hr Nkr1250) A range of dog-sledding adventures.

Svalbard Husky DOG-SLEDDING
(☎98 87 16 21, 98 40 40 89; www.svalbardhusky.no; 4hr Nkr1350) Year-round dog-sledding.

Svalbard Villmarkssenter DOG-SLEDDING
(☎79 02 17 00; www.svalbardvillmarkssenter.no; 3hr Nkr980; ⏲10am & 2pm) Experts in dog mushing, whether by sledge over the snow or on wheels during summer.

SNOWMOBILING

Most companies will offer snowmobile safaris. Spitsbergen Travel (p361) has a particularly wide range of excursions, while **Svalbard Snøscooterutleie** (☎79 02 46 61; www.scooterutleie.svalbard.no) offers snowmobile rental. Sample expeditions include the following (prices may vary between companies):

- Northern Lights Safari (three hours, Nkr1650)
- Coles Bay (four hours, Nkr1750)
- Elveneset (four hours, Nkr1750)
- East Coast Spitsbergen (10 hours, Nkr2350)
- Von Post Glacier (eight hours, Nkr2250)
- Pyramiden (11 hours, Nkr2350)
- Barentsburg (eight hours, Nkr2250)

Tours

Svalbard Maxi Taxi MINIBUS
(☎79 02 13 05; per person Nkr295; ⏲10am & 4pm Jun-Aug) This local taxi company offers two-hour minibus tours that take you further than you might think possible around Longyearbyen. From a number of the places it takes you there are stunning views when the weather's fine, and you can get much further than you would on foot, without needing a gun and guide.

Festivals & Events

Polar Jazz MUSIC
(www.polarjazz.no) A long winter weekend of jazz held in early February.

Sunfest CULTURAL
(www.solfest.no) Week-long celebrations beginning on 8 March to dispel the polar night.

Blues Festival MUSIC
(www.svalbardblues.co) Five-day jam session in October to warm you up before the onset of winter.

Sleeping

Spitsbergen Guesthouse GUESTHOUSE €
(☎79 02 63 00; www.spitsbergentravel.no; dm Nkr305-375, s Nkr510-900, d Nkr815-1210; ⏲mid-Mar–mid-Sep) This guesthouse is a subsidiary of Spitsbergen Travel (p361) and can accommodate up to 136 people. Spread over four buildings, one of which houses a large breakfast room (once the miners' mess hall), the rooms are simple, come with no frills and are terrific value for money.

★**Svalbard Hotell** HOTEL €€
(☎79 02 50 00; svalbardbooking.com/Accommodation/Svalbard-Hotell; s Nkr990-2190, d Nkr1190-2590) Svalbard's newest hotel offers stylish rooms with dark Scandinavian wood tones offset by stunning large photos above the beds and splashes of colour in the linens. There are flat-screen TVs, and you couldn't be more central for the main shops and restaurants of Longyearbyen

Spitsbergen Hotel HOTEL €€
(☎79 02 62 00; www.spitsbergentravel.no; s Nkr835-2580, d Nkr990-2900; ⏲Feb-Oct) This comfortable place (sink yourself low into the leather armchairs of its salon), run by the respected Rica Hotel chain, is where the mine bosses once lived. Rooms are comfortable with a vaguely old-world air.

★**Basecamp Spitsbergen** LODGE €€€
(☎79 02 46 00; www.basecampexplorer.com; s Nkr1100-2500, d Nkr1590-2890) Imagine a recreated sealing hut, built in part from recycled driftwood and local slate. Add artefacts and decorations culled from the local refuse dump and mining cast-offs. Graft on

21st-century plumbing and design flair and you've got this fabulous place, also known as Trapper's Lodge. The 16 cabin-like rooms are the definition of cosiness and comfort, and the breakfasts are splendid. It's a special place and easily the most atmospheric choice in Longyearbyen.

Eating

Fruene Kaffe og Vinbar CAFE €
(The Missus; ☎79 02 76 40; Lompensenteret; lunch mains from Nkr79; ⏰10am-6pm Mon-Fri, 10am-5pm Sat, 11am-5pm Sun) 'The Missus', run by three sprightly young women, is a welcoming and popular cafe, serving decent coffee, baguettes, pizza and snacks. There's free wi-fi, the walls are hung with stunning photography and the food's good – lunch specials usually include a soup or a salad. The soups are particularly outstanding.

★ **Huset** NORWEGIAN €€
(☎79 02 50 02; www.huset.com; cafe mains Nkr138-238, restaurant mains Nkr295-369, 4-/5-/6-course Arctic menu Nkr695/765/895; ⏰cafe 4-10pm Sun-Fri, 2-10pm Sat, restaurant 7-10pm) It's something of a walk up here but it's worth it. Dining in the cafe-bar is casual, with well-priced pasta, pizza and reindeer stew on the menu. Its signature dish is *hamburger med alt* (Nkr105) – a meaty burger with all the trimmings, so juicy, a researcher told us, that lonely scientists in their tents dream of it. The daily specials (Nkr109) are wonderful.

Kroa NORWEGIAN €€
(☎79 02 13 00; www.kroa-svalbard.no; lunch mains Nkr85-138, dinner mains Nkr206-245; ⏰11.30am-2am) This pub-restaurant was reconstructed from the elements of a building brought in from Russian Barentsburg (the giant white bust of Lenin peeking from behind the bar gives a clue), and it feels like a supremely comfortable and spacious trapper's cabin. Service is friendly and mains verge on the gargantuan.

Information

Tourist Office (☎79 02 55 50; www.svalbard.net; ⏰10am-5pm May-Sep, from noon Oct-Apr) Produces a helpful weekly activities list and has other information about the archipelago.

Getting Around

Longyearbyen Taxi (☎79 02 13 75) charges up to Nkr150 between the town and the airport. The airport bus (Nkr60) connects with flights.

Around Svalbard

Independent travel around Svalbard is heavily regulated in order to protect both the virgin landscape and travellers. Travel to the very few settlements is usually done as part of a tour package. One of these settlements is **Barentsburg** (population 400), a Soviet-era relic. This tiny Russian town still mines and exports coal and a statue of Lenin still stares over the bleak built landscape

POLAR BEARS UNDER THREAT

Polar bears are one of the most enduring symbols of the Arctic wilderness – loners, immensely strong and survivors in one of the world's most extreme environments. But for all the bears' raw power, some scientists predict that they could be extinct by the end of this century if the world continues to heat up.

Polar-bear numbers had been in decline since the late 19th century, when intensive hunting began. But ever since the 1973 treaty for the Conservation of Polar Bears and their Habitat, signed by all the countries whose lands impinge upon the Arctic, polar-bear numbers have been gradually increasing again and latest estimates suggest that there are between 20,000 and 25,000 left in the wild; Svalbard has a population of between 3000 and 3500.

But as is the case throughout the Arctic, Svalbard's glaciers are retreating and the ice sheet, the bears' natural habitat and prime hunting ground for seals, the mainstay of their diet (an adult bear needs to eat between 50 and 75 seals every year), is shrinking. Although polar bears are classified as marine mammals and are powerful swimmers, many risk drowning as they attempt to reach fresh ice floes that are ever more separated by open water. Less sea ice also means that some populations will become isolated and inbred, their genetic stock weakened. The birth rate may also fall since females need plenty of deep snow to dig the dens in which they will whelp. And hungry bears, on the prowl and desperate for food, could lead to increasing confrontations with humans.

and the impressive natural landscape that surrounds it. Almost-abandoned **Pyramiden** is a similar deal.

Tourist cruises might also bring you to **Ny Ålesund**, which, at latitude N79°, is a wild place full of scientists and downright hostile Arctic terns. Remnants of past glories include an **airship pylon**, used by Amundsen and Nobile on their successful crossing of the North Pole in 1926.

The lovely blue-green bay of **Magdalenefjord**, flanked by towering peaks and intimidating tidewater glaciers, is the most popular anchorage along Spitsbergen's western coast and is one of Svalbard's prettiest corners.

UNDERSTAND NORWAY

History

Norway's first settlers arrived around 11,000 years ago with the end of the ice age. As the glaciers melted, the earliest hunter-gatherers moved in from Siberia, pursuing migrating reindeer herds. You can see the prehistoric rock drawings of these hunters in the far north on Alta. Shortly afterwards, nomadic European hunters arrived in the south of the country.

The Vikings

Norway greatly affected Western civilisation during the Viking Age, a period usually dated from the plundering of England's Lindisfarne monastery by Nordic pirates (AD 793). Through the next century, the Vikings conducted raids throughout Europe and established settlements in the Shetland, Orkney and Hebridean islands, the Dublin area (Ireland) and in Normandy (named after the 'North men'). The Viking leader Harald Hårfagre (Fairhair) unified Norway after the decisive naval battle at Hafrsfjord near Stavanger in 872. King Olav Haraldsson, adopting the religion of the lands he had conquered, converted the Norwegians to Christianity and founded the Church of Norway in 1024. You can see Viking artefacts firsthand in Oslo's Vikingskipshuset (p290) and the Lofotr Vikingmuseum (p347) in Lofoten.

The Viking Age declined after 1066, with the defeat of the Norwegian king, Harald Hardråda, at the Battle of Stamford Bridge in England. Norwegian naval power was finished off for good when Alexander III, King of Scots, defeated a Viking naval force at the Battle of Largs (Scotland) in 1263.

Under Occupation

In the early 14th century, Oslo emerged as a centre of power. A period of growth followed until 1349 when the bubonic plague swept the country, wiping out two-thirds of the population. In 1380, Norway was absorbed into a union with Denmark that lasted more than 400 years.

Denmark ceded Norway to Sweden in 1814. In 1884 a parliamentary government was introduced in Norway and a growing nationalist movement eventually led to a constitutional referendum in 1905. As expected, virtually no one in Norway favoured continued union with Sweden. The Swedish king, Oskar II, was forced to recognise Norwegian sovereignty, abdicate and reinstate a Norwegian constitutional monarchy, with Håkon VII on the throne. His descendants rule Norway to this day, with decisions on succession remaining under the authority of the *storting* (parliament). Oslo was declared the national capital of the Kingdom of Norway.

Independent Norway

Norway stayed neutral during WWI. Despite restating its neutrality at the start of WWII, it was attacked by the Nazis on 9 April 1940, falling to the Germans after a two-month struggle. King Håkon set up a government in exile in England, and placed most of Norway's merchant fleet under the command of the Allies. Although Norway remained occupied until the end of the war, it had an active Resistance movement, which you can ponder in Bergen's Theta Museum and Narvik's Red Cross War Museum (p342).

The royal family returned to Norway in June 1945. King Håkon died in 1957 and was succeeded by his son, Olav V, a popular king who reigned until his death in January 1991. The current monarch is Harald V, Olav's son, who was crowned in June 1991.

In the late 1960s, oil was discovered in Norway's offshore waters, thereafter transforming Norway from one of Europe's poorest countries to arguably its richest. Although Norway joined the European Free Trade Association (EFTA) in 1960, it has been reluctant to forge closer bonds with other European nations, in part due to concerns about the effect on its fishing and small-scale farming industries. During 1994 a national referendum on joining the EU was held and rejected.

On 22 July 2011, a lone assailant killed 77 people in a bomb attack on government buildings in Oslo and a youth camp on the island of Utøya, close to Oslo. The killings, reportedly in protest at growing multiculturalism in the country, shocked and deeply traumatised the country. The perpetrator, a right-wing extremist, was later sentenced to 21 years for the attacks (the maximum possible sentence), with an option to renew the sentence thereafter.

People

Norway has one of Europe's lowest population densities. Most Norwegians are of Nordic origin (86.2% according to one recent study), and are thought to have descended from central and northern European tribes who migrated northwards around 8000 years ago. In addition, there are about 40,000 Sámi, the indigenous people of Norway's far north who now make up the country's second-largest ethnic minority (after the Polish community). Some Sámi still live a traditional nomadic life, herding reindeer in Finnmark.

Norway has become an increasingly multicultural society in recent years and was, at last count, home to around 635,000 immigrants (around 15% of the population) from 216 countries, (compared with just 1.5% of population in 1970).

Around 82% of Norwegians nominally belong to the Church of Norway, a Protestant Evangelical Lutheran denomination, although actual church attendance is low. A growing Muslim population (around 2.5% of the population) exists due to recent immigration.

Arts

In the late 19th century and into the early 20th century, three figures – playwright Henrik Ibsen, composer Edvard Grieg and painter Edvard Munch – towered over Norway's cultural life like no others. Their emergence came at a time when Norway was forging its path to independence and pushing the creative limits of a newly confident national identity.

Ibsen (1828–1906) became known as 'the father of modern drama', but to Norwegians he was the conscience of a nation. The enormously popular *Peer Gynt* (1867) was Ibsen's international breakthrough, while other well-known works include *The Doll's House* (1879), *Ghosts* (1881), *An Enemy of the People* (1882) and *Hedda Gabler* (1890).

Edvard Grieg (1843–1907) was greatly influenced by Norway's folk music and melodies and his first great, signature work, *Piano Concerto in A minor*, has come to represent Norway as no other work before or since. Thanks to his formidable repertoire, he became Norway's best-known composer. According to his biographer, it was impossible to listen to Grieg without sensing a light, fresh breeze from the blue waters, a glimpse of grand glaciers and a recollection of the mountains of Western Norway's fjords.

Edvard Munch (1863–1944), Norway's most renowned painter, was a tortured soul: his first great work, *The Sick Child*, was a portrait of his sister Sophie shortly before her death. In 1890 he produced the haunting *Night*, depicting a lonely figure in a dark window. The following year he finished *Melancholy* and began sketches of what would become his best-known work, *The Scream*, which graphically represents Munch's own inner torment.

Literature

In the 20th century, three Norwegian writers – Bjørnstjerne Bjørnson (1832–1910), the hugely controversial Knut Hamsun (1859–1952) and Sigrid Undset (1882–1949) – won the Nobel Prize in Literature.

One of the best-known modern Norwegian writers is Jan Kjærstad (b 1953), whose *The Seducer* (2003) combines the necessary recipes for a bestseller – a thriller with a love affair and a whiff of celebrity – with seriously good writing. Among other recent Norwegian winners of the prestigious Nordic Council Literature Prize is the prolific Per Petterson (b 1952), who won the prize in 2009. If you're lucky enough to get hold of a copy, Angar Mykle's *Lasso Round the Moon* (1954) might be the best book you've never read.

In the crime-fiction genre, it's Jo Nesbø (jonesbo.com/en) who is considered the king of Norwegian crime fiction. His stories are darker than many in the genre and are almost all set in Norway from World War II to the present.

Music

There's more to Norwegian music than a-ha and Kings of Convenience.

JAZZ

Norway has a thriving jazz scene, with world-class festivals throughout the year. Jazz saxophonist Jan Garbarek is one of the most enduring Norwegian jazz personalities. His work draws on classical, folk and world-music influences and he has recorded 30 albums. His daughter, Anja Garbarek, is seen as one of the most exciting and innovative performers on the Norwegian jazz scene, bringing pop and electronica into the mix.

Norway has some fine jazz festivals, including the following:

- Moldejazz (p334), Molde
- Oslo International Jazz Festival (p294)
- Canal Street Jazz & Blues Festival (p298), Arendal
- Night Jazz Festival (p311), Bergen
- Vossajazz (p319), Voss
- Polar Jazz (p362), Longyearbyen

ELECTRONICA

Norway is at once one of Europe's most prolific producers and most devoted fans of electronica. Röyksopp (www.royksopp.com) took the international electronica scene by storm with its debut album *Melody A.M.* in 2001 and it's never really left the dance-floor charts since.

METAL

Metal is another genre that Norway has taken to heart. Although traditional heavy metal is popular, Norway is particularly known for its black-metal scene. For a time in the early 1990s, black metal became famous for its anti-Christian, Satanist philosophy with a handful of members of black-metal bands burning down churches. Among the better-known Norwegian black-metal bands are Darkthrone, Mayhem, Emperor, Enslaved, Gorgoroth, Satyricon and Arcturus.

Environment

The Land

Norway's geographical facts tell quite a story. The Norwegian mainland stretches 2518km from Lindesnes in the south to Nordkapp in the Arctic North with a narrowest point of 6.3km wide. Norway also has the highest mountains in northern Europe and the fourth-largest landmass in Western Europe (behind France, Spain and Sweden).

Norway is also home to continental Europe's largest icecap (Jostedalsbreen), the world's second- and third-longest fjords (Sognefjorden and Hardangerfjord), the largest and highest plateau in Europe (Hardangervidda) and several of the 10 highest waterfalls in the world. Norway's glaciers cover some 2600 sq km (close to 1% of mainland Norwegian territory and 60% of the Svalbard archipelago).

Wildlife

Norway has wild and semidomesticated reindeer herds, thriving elk populations and a scattering of Arctic foxes, lynxes, musk oxen, bears and wolverines. Polar bears (population around 3000, or around one-eighth of the world's surviving population, and declining) and walrus are found in Svalbard. Several species of seal, dolphin and whale may be seen around most western and northern coasts. Birdlife is prolific in coastal areas.

National Parks

At last count, Norway had 44 national parks (including seven in Svalbard, where approximately 65% of the land falls within park boundaries). Thirteen new national parks have been created since 2003, with further new parks and extensions to existing parks planned. National parks cover 15% of the country. In many cases, the parks don't protect any specific features, nor do they necessarily coincide with the incidence of spectacular natural landscapes or ecosystem boundaries. Instead, they attempt to prevent development of remaining wilderness areas and many park boundaries simply follow contour lines around uninhabited areas.

Norwegian national parks are low profile and lack the traffic and overdeveloped facilities that have overwhelmed parks in other countries. Some parks, notably Jotunheimen and Rondane, are increasingly suffering from overuse, but in most places pollution and traffic are kept to a minimum.

Green Issues

Norway has led many contemporary environmental initiatives, such as the creation of the Svalbard Global Seed Vault (2008), where seeds are stored to protect biodiversity. In 2007 the government declared a goal of making Norway carbon-neutral and cutting net greenhouse gas emissions to zero by 2050, largely by purchasing offsets from developing countries. Around 98% of Norway's electricity supplies come from renewable (primarily hydro power) sources, with fossil fuels accounting for just 2%.

Loss of habitat has placed around 1000 species of plants and animals on the endangered or threatened species lists, and sport hunting and fishing are more popular here than in most of Europe. Hydroelectric schemes have devastated some mountain landscapes and waterfalls, and over-fishing perpetually haunts the economy.

Whaling in Norway is regulated by the International Whaling Commission. Norway resumed commercial whaling of minke whales in 1993, defying an international ban. The government, which supports the protection of threatened species, contends that minke whales, with an estimated population of 100,000, can sustain a limited harvest.

Food & Drink

Norwegian food *can* be excellent. Abundant seafood and local specialities such as reindeer are undoubtedly the highlights, and most medium-sized towns have fine restaurants in which to eat. The only problem (and it's a significant one) is that prices are prohibitive, meaning that a full meal in a restaurant may become something of a luxury item for all but those on expense accounts.

Striking a balance between eating well and staying solvent requires a clever strategy. For a start, most Norwegian hotels and some hostels offer generous buffet breakfasts, ensuring that you'll rarely start the day on an empty stomach. Many restaurants, especially in larger towns, serve cheaper lunch specials. These are often filling and well sized for those wanting more than a sandwich. Some hotels also lay on lavish dinner buffets in the evening – they're generally expensive, but excellent if it's your main meal of the day.

MUSK OX

The musk ox *(Ovibos moschatus)* is one of nature's great survivors; it has changed little in two million years. Although a member of the family Bovidae, the musk ox bears little resemblance to any other animal and its only known relative is the takin of northern Tibet.

Musk ox weigh between 225kg and 445kg, and have incredibly high shoulders and an enormous low-slung head with two broad, flat horns that cross the forehead, curving outwards and downwards before twisting upwards and forwards. Its thick and shaggy coat, with a matted fleece of soft hair underneath, covers the whole body. Only the bottom part of the legs protrude, giving the animal the appearance of a medieval horse dressed for a joust. During the rutting season, when the males gather their harems, they repeatedly charge each other, butting their heads together with a crash heard for miles around. This heated battle continues until one animal admits defeat and lumbers off. In winter, they stand perfectly still for hours to conserve energy, a position some scientists have described as 'standing hibernation'.

Traditionally, the musk ox's main predator has been the wolf; its primary defence is to form a circle with the males on the outside and females and calves inside, trusting in the force of its collective horns to rip open attackers. This defence has proven useless against human hunters, especially the Greenlandic Inuit, and numbers have been depleted.

The musk ox died out in Norway almost 2000 years ago, but in 1931, 10 animals were reintroduced to Dovrefjell-Sunndalsfjella from Greenland. Musk oxen all but vanished during WWII, but 23 were transplanted from Greenland between 1947 and 1953. The herd has now grown to around 300 animals and some have shifted eastwards into Femundsmarka National Park to form a new herd. Wild herds are also found in Greenland, Canada and Alaska.

Musk oxen aren't inherently aggressive towards humans, but an animal that feels threatened can charge at speeds of up to 60km/h and woe betide anything that gets in its way.

Staples & Specialities

Norwegian specialities include grilled or smoked *laks* (salmon), *gravat laks* (marinated salmon), *reker* (boiled shrimp), *torsk* (cod), *fiskesuppe* (fish soup), *hval* (whale) and other seafood. Roast reindeer *(reinsdyrstek)* is something every nonvegetarian visitor to Norway should try at least once; it's one of the tastier red meats.

Expect to see sweet brown goat's-milk cheese called *geitost*, and *sild* (pickled herring) with the breads and cereals in breakfast buffets. A fine Norwegian dessert is warm *moltebær syltetøy* (cloudberry jam) with ice cream. *Lutefisk* (dried cod made almost gelatinous by soaking in lye) is popular at Christmas but it's an acquired taste.

If Norway has a national drink, it's strong black coffee. Most of the beer you'll drink is pilsner. At the other end of the taste spectrum is Norway's bitter aquavit, which does the job at 40% proof.

Where to Eat & Drink

Common throughout Norway is the *konditori*, a bakery with tables where you can sit and enjoy pastries and relatively inexpensive sandwiches. Other moderately cheap eats are found at *gatekjøkken* (food wagons and street-side kiosks), which generally have hot dogs for about Nkr60 and hamburgers for Nkr100. Marginally more expensive, but with more nutritionally balanced food, are *kafeterias,* with simple, traditional meals from about Nkr120. Restaurants vary widely in price, with mains going for Nkr150 to Nkr385.

Vegetarians & Vegans

Being vegetarian in Norway is a challenge and vegan is almost impossible. In rural parts of the country, vegetarians will live out of a grocery store, though some cafes serve token dishes such as vegetables with pasta. Another easily found option is pizza, however Norwegian pizza is often bland and soggy. You'll find more options in bigger cities, although most menus are entirely based on fish and meat. About half of the kebab stands serve falafel.

Habits & Customs

Locals tend to eat breakfast at home, lunch between 11.30am and 2pm (often with their coworkers) and the evening meal between 6pm and 8pm (often later in larger cities).

SURVIVAL GUIDE

Directory A–Z

ACCOMMODATION

During summer, it's wise to book accommodation in advance.

The main tourist season runs from mid-June to mid-August. During the high season, accommodation prices are at their lowest and many hotels offer their best deals. During the rest of the year, prices are much higher, except on weekends.

Price Ranges

The following prices are for a high-season double room with private bathroom (usually including breakfast):

€ less than Nkr750

€€ Nkr750 to Nkr1400

€€€ more than Nkr1400

Bed & Breakfasts

Some places operate as B&Bs, where prices (usually with shared bathrooms) start from single/double Nkr450/600 and can go up to Nkr650/900.

Bed & Breakfast Norway (www.bbnorway.com) Bed & Breakfast Norway has extensive online listings for B&Bs throughout Norway; it also sells *The Norway Bed & Breakfast Book*, with listings throughout the country.

Camping

Norway has more than 1000 camping grounds. Tent space ordinarily costs from Nkr100 at basic camping grounds, up to Nkr225 for those with better facilities. Quoted prices usually include your car, motorcycle or caravan. A per-person charge is added in some places, electricity often costs a few kroner extra and most places charge Nkr10 for showers.

Most camping grounds also rent out cabins with cooking facilities, starting at around Nkr400 for a basic two- or four-bed bunkhouse. Bring a sleeping bag, as linen and blankets cost extra (from Nkr50 to Nkr100). There are also more-expensive deluxe cabins with shower and toilet facilities (Nkr750 to Nkr1500).

Norsk Camping (www.camping.no) A useful resource for general camping info, as well as the comprehensive *Camping* guide, available in book (they charge Nkr90 to send it out to you) or pdf format (free).

NAF Camp (www.nafcamp.no) An excellent online resource listing more than 250 campsites around Norway.

DNT & Other Mountain Huts

Den Norske Turistforening (DNT; Norwegian Mountain Touring Club; ☎22 82 28 22; www.turistforeningen.no) maintains a network of

460 mountain huts or cabins located a day's hike apart along the country's 20,000km of well-marked and maintained wilderness hiking routes. These range from unstaffed huts with two beds to large staffed lodges with more than 100 beds and renowned standards of service. DNT has lists of opening dates for each hut.

Guesthouses & Pensions

Many towns have *pensjonat* (pensions) and *gjestehus* (guesthouses). Some, especially the latter, are family-run and offer a more intimate option than a hostel or hotel. Prices for a room with a shared bathroom usually start at Nkr500/750 for singles/doubles but can cost significantly more; linen and/or breakfast will only be included at the higher-priced places.

Hostels

In Norway, reasonably priced *vandrerhjem* (hostels) offer a dorm bed for the night, plus use of communal facilities that usually include a self-catering kitchen (you're advised to take your own cooking-and-eating utensils), internet access and bathrooms. In most hostels, guests must bring their own sheet and pillowcase, although most hire sheets for a one-off fee (starting at Nkr50) regardless of the number of nights.

Most hostels have two- to six-bed rooms and beds cost from Nkr200 to Nkr400. Higher-priced hostels usually include a buffet breakfast, while other places may charge from Nkr50 to Nkr125 for breakfast.

A welcome recent addition to the budget end of the market are chains such as Citybox, Smarthotels and Basic Hotels. These hostel-hotel hybrids are slick and excellent value, but you'll only find them in larger cities.

Norske Vandrerhjem (☎23 12 45 10; www.hihostels.no) The Norwegian hostelling association, Norske Vandrerhjem is HI-affiliated and publishes the free *Hostels in Norway*, which contains a full listing of hostels and updated prices for the 77 hostels on its books; it's available from hostels and some tourist offices.

Hotels

Norway's hotels are generally modern and excellent, although those with any character are pretty thin on the ground. Comfortable nationwide chain hotels are the norm and the rooms can all start to look the same after a while, whether you're sleeping in Oslo or Kirkenes. The advantage of these chains or hotel networks, however, is that some offer hotel passes, which can entitle you to a free night if you use the chain enough times; some passes only operate in summer.

Best Western (www.bestwestern.no) The Best Western Rewards system operates at all Best Western hotels in Norway and beyond, in addition to occasional summer deals.

De Historiske (☎55 31 67 60; www.dehistoriske.no) Although it's less a chain than a collection of historic hotels and there are no membership options, it's always worth checking out the worthwhile De Historiske network, which links Norway's most historic old hotels and restaurants. The quality on offer is consistently high, every hotel is architecturally distinguished and many are family-run.

Fjord Pass (www.fjordpass.no; 2 adults & unlimited children under 15yr Nkr150) The Fjord Pass enables discounts at 120 hotels, guesthouses, cabins and apartments year-round; no free nights, but the discounts on nightly rates are considerable. Works best if you book in advance through its website, rather than simply turning up and hoping for a discount.

Nordic Choice Hotels (www.nordicchoicehotels.no) Covering Clarion, Quality and Comfort Hotels, with the Nordic Choice Club you can earn free nights if you stay in enough member hotels. In some Comfort Hotels, you get a light evening buffet included in the price. Watch out for their new upmarket, boutique brand, the Clarion Collection.

Scandic Hotels (Rica Hotels; www.scandichotels.no) Scandic recently bought the Rica brand. The process of rebranding will take some time, but expect the Rica name to disappear. The shape of the new rewards program is still being considered.

Thon Hotels (www.thonhotels.com) This program has free membership that qualifies you for discounts or free nights.

ACTIVITIES

Summer

Norway is a popular thrillseeker destination thanks to professional operators and spectacular settings. Extreme sports include **paragliding**, **parasailing**, **bungee jumping** and **skydiving**. Voss is the centre of most of the action.

Norway has some of Europe's best **hiking**, including around 20,000km of marked trails that range from easy strolls through the green zones around cities to long treks through national parks and wilderness areas. Many trails are maintained by **DNT** (Norwegian Mountain Touring Club; ☎40 00 18 68; www.turistforeningen.no) and marked with cairns or red Ts at 100m or 200m intervals.

The hiking season runs from late May to early October, with a much shorter season in the higher mountain areas and the far north. In the highlands, the snow often remains until June and returns in September, meaning many routes are only possible in July and August.

Norway's premier **kayaking** sites are clustered around the Western Fjords and there are numerous operators offering guided excursions. Kayaking is also possible in Svalbard.

The cascading, icy-black waters and white-hot rapids of central Norway are a **rafting** paradise from mid-June to mid-August. These range from Class II through to Class V.

Winter

Downhill and cross-country skiing is possible throughout the country in winter.

Dog-sledding is popular as it enables you to experience Arctic and sub-Arctic wilderness areas at a slow pace and free from engine noise. Expeditions can range from half-day to multiday trips with overnight stays in remote forest huts. Most operators will allow you to (depending on the number of travellers in your group) 'mush' your own sled (after a brief primer course) or sit atop the sled as someone else urges the dogs onwards.

Snowmobile operators usually allow you to ride as a passenger behind an experienced driver. For an additional charge you may be able to drive the snowmobile, but you will need a valid driving licence.

CHILDREN

Norway is a terrific destination in which to travel as a family. This is a country that is world famous for creating family-friendly living conditions, and most hotels, restaurants and many sights are accordingly child-friendly. It's worth remembering, however, that the old parental adage of not trying to be too ambitious in how far you travel is especially relevant in Norway – distances are vast and, due to the terrain, journey times can be significantly longer than for equivalent distances elsewhere.

FOOD

The price of an average main course:

€ less than Nkr125
€€ Nkr125 to Nkr200
€€€ more than Nkr200

GAY & LESBIAN TRAVELLERS

Norwegians are generally tolerant of alternative lifestyles and on 1 January 2009 Norway became the sixth country in the world to legalise same-sex marriage. That said, public displays of affection are not common practice, except perhaps in some areas of Oslo. Oslo is generally Norway's most gay-friendly city and has the liveliest gay scene.

INTERNET ACCESS

With wi-fi widely available, good cybercafes that last the distance are increasingly hard to find; ask at the local tourist office. Prices per hour range from Nkr25 to Nkr75; students sometimes receive a discount. Free internet access is available in most municipal libraries (biblioteket). As it's a popular service, you may have to reserve a time slot earlier in the day; in busier places, you may be restricted to a half-hour slot.

Wi-fi is widely available at most hotels, cafes and tourist offices, as well as some restaurants; it's generally (but not always) free and you may need to ask for a password.

MONEY

ATMs These machines accept most international cards and are available in most towns.

Currency The Norwegian kroner is most often written NOK in international money markets, Nkr in northern Europe and kr within Norway.

Changing money Not all banks will change money and in some places you may need to shop around to find one that does. Rates at post offices and tourist offices are generally poorer than at banks, but can be convenient for small amounts outside banking hours.

PUBLIC HOLIDAYS

Norway practically shuts down during the Christmas and Easter weeks.

New Year's Day (Nyttårsdag) 1 January
Maundy Thursday (Skjærtorsdag) March/April
Good Friday (Langfredag) March/April
Easter Monday (Annen Påskedag) March/April
Labour Day (Første Mai, Arbeidetsdag) 1 May
Constitution Day (Nasjonaldag) 17 May
Ascension Day (Kristi Himmelfartsdag) May/June, 40th day after Easter
Whit Monday (Annen Pinsedag) May/June, eighth Monday after Easter
Christmas Day (Første Juledag) 25 December
Boxing Day (Annen Juledag) 26 December

OPENING HOURS

Standard opening hours are for high season (mid-June to mid-September) and tend to decrease outside that time.

Banks 8.15am-3pm Mon-Wed & Fri, to 5pm Thu
Drinking 6pm-3am
Eating 8am-11am (breakfast), noon-3pm (lunch), 6-11pm (dinner)
Entertainment 6pm-3am
Offices 9am-5pm Mon-Fri, 10am-2pm Sat
Post offices 9am-5pm Mon-Fri, 10am-2pm Sat; large cities 8am-8pm Mon-Fri, 9am-6pm Sat
Shops 10am-5pm Mon-Wed & Fri, to 7pm Thu, to 2pm Sat

TELEPHONE

Mobile Phones

More than 90% of the country has GSM mobile access; wilderness areas and national-park hiking trails are exceptions.

Norwegian SIM cards can be purchased from any 7-Eleven store and some Narvesen kiosks;

prices start at Nkr200, including Nkr100 worth of calls. However, as the connection instructions are entirely in Norwegian, you're better off purchasing the card from any Telehuset outlet, where they'll help you connect on the spot.

NetCom (www.netcom.no) Norway's second-largest operator.

Mobile Norway (www.mobilenorway.no) Also known as Network Norway.

Telenor Mobil (www.telenor.com) The largest mobile-service provider.

Phone Codes

All Norwegian phone numbers have eight digits. Numbers starting with ☎800 usually indicate a toll-free number, while those beginning with ☎9 are mobile or cell-phone numbers.

International access code ☎00

Norway country code ☎47

Directory assistance ☎180 (calls cost Nkr9 per minute)

TIME

Time in Norway is one hour ahead of GMT/UTC, the same as Sweden, Denmark and most of Western Europe.

When telling time, in Norwegian the use of 'half' means 'half before' rather than 'half past'.

Norway observes daylight-saving time, with clocks set ahead one hour on the last Sunday in March and back an hour on the last Sunday in October.

TOURIST INFORMATION

It's impossible to speak highly enough of tourist offices in Norway. Most serve as one-stop clearing houses for general information and bookings for accommodation and activities. Nearly every city and town has its own tourist office and most tourist offices in reasonably sized towns or major tourist areas publish comprehensive booklets giving the complete, up-to-date lowdown on their town.

Offices in smaller towns may be open only during peak summer months, while in cities they're open year-round but with shorter hours in low season.

VISAS

Norway is one of 26 member countries of the Schengen Agreement, under which EU countries (all but Bulgaria, Cyprus, Ireland, Romania and the UK) plus Iceland, Norway and Switzerland have abolished checks at common borders. Citizens of the USA, Canada, Australia, Japan and New Zealand need a valid passport to visit Norway, but do not need a visa for stays of less than three months. Citizens of EU countries and other Scandinavian countries do not require visas.

ℹ Getting There & Away

Crossing most borders into Norway is usually hassle-free; travellers from non-Western countries or those crossing by land into Norway from Russia should expect more rigorous searches.

All travellers – other than citizens of Denmark, Iceland, Sweden and Finland – require a valid passport to enter Norway.

AIR

For a full list of Norwegian airports, visit www.avinor.no; the page for each airport has comprehensive information. The main international Norwegian airports are: Gardermoen (Oslo), Flesland (Bergen), Sola (Stavanger), Tromsø, Værnes (Trondheim), Vigra (Ålesund), Karmøy (Haugesund), Kjevik (Kristiansand) and Torp (Sandefjord).

Dozens of international airlines fly to/from Norwegian airports. Airlines that use Norway as their primary base include the following:

Norwegian (www.norwegian.com) Low-cost airline with an extensive and growing domestic and international network.

SAS (www.sas.no) The largest international network of Norway's carriers.

LAND

Finland

Eskelisen Lapin Linjat (☎016-342 2160; www.eskelisen-lapinlinjat.com) Most cross-border services between northern Norway and northern Finland are operated by this Finnish company.

FROM	DESTINATION	PRICE (€)	DURATION (HR)
Rovaniemi	Alta	82	10
Rovaniemi	Karasjok	66	7
Rovaniemi	Tromsø (Jun-Sep only)	93	8-10
Rovaniemi	Nordkapp	123	12

Russia

Russia has a short border with Norway and buses run twice daily between Kirkenes in Norway and Murmansk in Russia (one way/return Nkr400/Nkr675, five hours). Once in Murmansk, trains connect to St Petersburg and the rest of the Russian rail network.

To cross the border, you'll need a Russian visa, which must usually be applied for and issued in your country of residence.

Sweden

Bus

Swebus Express (☎0200 218 218; www.swebusexpress.se) has the largest (and cheapest) buses between Oslo and Swedish cities.

Among the numerous cross-border services along the long land frontier between Sweden and Norway, there are twice-daily services between Narvik and Riksgränsen (one hour), on the border, and Kiruna (three hours).

FROM	PRICE (SKR)	DURATION (HR)	FREQUENCY (DAILY)
Stockholm	from 329	8-13	five
Gothenburg (Göteborg)	from 189	3¾	5-10
Malmö	from 339	8	4-7

Train

Rail services between Sweden and Norway are operated by **Norwegian Railways** (NSB; ☎81 50 08 88; www.nsb.no) or **Swedish Railways** (SJ; ☎in Sweden 0771-75 75 99; www.sj.se). It's worth noting that some of the Stockholm–Oslo services require a change of train in the Swedish city of Karlstad.

ROUTE	PRICE	DURATION (HR)	FREQUENCY (DAILY)
Gothenburg (Göteborg)–Oslo	from Nkr204/ Skr221	4-6	up to 5
Stockholm–Oslo	from Skr341	6-7½	4
Stockholm–Narvik	from Skr916	20-22	19-16
Malmö–Oslo	from Skr530	7½-9	3-6

SEA

Ferry connections are possible between Norway and Denmark, Germany, Iceland, the Faroe Islands and Sweden.

Getting Around

Norway has an extremely efficient public transport system and its trains, buses and ferries are often timed to link with each other. *NSB Togruter*, available free at most train stations, details rail timetables and includes information on connecting buses. Boat and bus *ruteplan* (timetables) are available from regional tourist offices.

AIR

The major Norwegian domestic routes are competitive and you can travel for little more than the equivalent train fare if you're flexible about departure dates and book early.

Norwegian (www.norwegian.com) Low-cost airline with an extensive and growing domestic network that now includes Longyearbyen (Svalbard).

SAS (www.sas.no) Large domestic network on mainland Norway, plus flights to Longyearbyen (Svalbard).

Widerøe (www.wideroe.no) A subsidiary of SAS with smaller planes and a handful of flights to smaller regional airports.

BICYCLE

Given Norway's great distances, hilly terrain and narrow roads, only serious cyclists engage in extensive cycle touring, but those who do rave about the experience. Most of Norway's thousands of tunnels are closed to nonmotorised traffic; in many cases there are outdoor bike paths running parallel to the tunnels.

Rural buses, express ferries and nonexpress trains carry bikes for additional fees (around Nkr150), but express trains don't allow them. On international trains you'll need to pay excess baggage (around Nkr300). Nor-Way Bussekspress charges a child's fare to transport a bicycle.

Some tourist offices, hostels, camping grounds and *sykkelbutikken* (bicycle shops) rent bicycles (around Nkr60 for an hour, up to Nkr350 per day).

BOAT

An extensive network of ferries and express boats links Norway's offshore islands, coastal towns and fjord districts. The Norwegian Tourist Board has schedules and prices; try *Rutebok for Norge* (www.rutebok.no). Tourist offices have timetables for local ferries.

For more than a century, Norway's legendary **Hurtigruten Coastal Ferry** (☎81 00 30 30; www.hurtigruten.com) has served as a lifeline linking coastal towns and villages and it's now one of the most popular ways to explore Norway. Year in, year out, one of 11 *Hurtigruten* ferries heads north from Bergen every night of the year, pulling into 35 ports on to Kirkenes, where it then turns around and heads back south.

The northward journey takes six days; the return journey takes 11 days and covers a distance of 5200km. In agreeable weather (which is by no means guaranteed) the fjord and mountain scenery along the way is nothing short of spectacular. Most of the ships are modern, others are showing their age; the oldest ship dates from 1956, but all were substantially remodelled in the 1990s.

Onboard, meals are served in the dining room and you can buy snacks and light meals in the cafeteria.

BUS

Bus timetables (and some prices) can be found in the free *Rutehefte*, available from most bus stations and some tourist offices.

Advance reservations are rarely required; Nor-Way Bussekspress has a 'Seat Guarantee – No Reservation' policy.

Lavprisekspressen (www.lavprisekspressen.no) The cheapest buses are operated by Lavprisekspressen, which sells tickets over the internet. Its buses run along the coast between Oslo and Stavanger (via Kristiansand and most towns in between) and along two north–south corridors linking Oslo with Trondheim.

Nor-Way Bussekspress (www.nor-way.no) Nor-Way Bussekspress operates the largest network of express buses in Norway, with routes connecting most towns and cities.

CAR & MOTORCYCLE

Main highways, such as the E16 from Oslo to Bergen and the E6 from Oslo to Kirkenes, are open year-round. Cars in snow-covered areas should have studded tyres or carry chains.

Automobile Associations

Norges Automobil-Forbund (NAF; ☎92 60 85 05; www.naf.no) By reciprocal agreement, members affiliated with AIT (Alliance Internationale de Tourisme) national automobile associations are eligible for 24-hour breakdown recovery assistance from the Norges Automobil-Forbund. NAF patrols ply the main roads from mid-June to mid-August. Emergency phones can be found along motorways, in tunnels and at certain mountain passes.

Drivers Licence

Short-term visitors may hire a car with their home country's driving licence.

Fuel

Leaded and unleaded petrol and diesel are available at most petrol stations. Although prices fluctuate in keeping with international oil prices, prevailing prices at the time of research ranged from around Nkr13 per litre up to Nkr16. Diesel usually costs around Nkr1 per litre less. You can pay with major credit cards at most service stations.

In towns, petrol stations may be open until 10pm or midnight, but there are some 24-hour services. In rural areas, many stations close in the early evening and don't open at all on weekends. Some have unstaffed 24-hour automatic pumps operated with credit cards.

If driving a diesel vehicle: don't fill up at the pump labelled '*augiftsfri diesel*', which is strictly for boats, tractors etc.

Hire

Norwegian car hire is costly and geared mainly to the business traveller. Walk-in rates for a compact car (with 200km per day included) typically approach Nkr1200 per day (including VAT, but insurance starts at Nkr75 per day extra), although per-day rates drop the longer you rent. In summer, always ask about special offers.

Auto Europe (www.auto-europe.com) Online rental agency which acts as a clearing house for cheap rates from major companies.

Autos Abroad (www.autosabroad.com) UK-based clearing house for major companies.

Ideamerge (www.ideamerge.com) Information on the Renault company's car-leasing plan, motor-home rental and more.

Insurance

Third-party car insurance (unlimited cover for personal injury and Nkr1 million for property damage) is compulsory. If you're bringing a

ROAD TOLLS

Driving around Norway, you'll soon become accustomed to the ominous 'Bomstasjon – Toll Plaza' signs. Apart from on some smaller country roads, most of Norway's toll stations are automated. If you're driving a Norwegian rental car, they'll be fitted with an automatic sensor – after you return your car, the hire company adds up the accumulated tolls and charges your credit card.

If you're driving a foreign-registered car (including some rental cars from other countries), you're expected to register your credit card in advance online at www.autopass.no (and pay a deposit). The tolls are later deducted. The alternative is to stop at one of the pay stations (sometimes the first petrol station after the toll station) to pay there. If you don't pay, the authorities will, in theory, attempt to track you down once you return home (often six months later) and you may have to pay both the toll and a penalty fee of Nkr300.

MINIPRIS – A TRAVELLER'S BEST FRIEND

On every long-distance train route, for every departure, Norwegian State Railways sets aside a limited number of tickets known as *minipris*. Those who book the earliest can get just about any route for just Nkr249. Once those are exhausted, the next batch of *minipris* tickets goes for Nkr349 and so on. These tickets cannot be purchased at ticket counters and must instead be bought over the internet (www.nsb.no) or in ticket-vending machines at train stations. *Minipris* tickets must be purchased at least one day in advance; reservations are nonrefundable and cannot be changed once purchased.

vehicle from abroad, an insurance company Green Card outlines the coverage granted by your home policy. Make sure your vehicle is insured for ferry crossings.

Road Rules

- Blood-alcohol limit 0.02%
- Dipped headlights (including on motorcycles) required at all times
- Legal age to drive a car: 18 years
- Legal driving age to ride a motorcycle or scooter: 16 to 21 years (depending on the motorcycle's power); a licence is required
- Motorcycles may not be parked on the pavement (sidewalk)
- Red warning triangles are compulsory in all vehicles
- Drive on the right
- Speed limits: open road (80km/h); if passing a house or business (60km/h to 70km/h); in villages (50km/h to 60km/h); in residential areas (30km/h). A few roads have segments allowing 90km/h or 100km/h. The speed limit for caravans (and cars pulling trailers) is usually 10km/h less than for cars.

TRAIN

Norwegian State Railways (Norges Statsbaner, NSB; ☎ 81 50 08 88, press 9 for English; www.nsb.no) connects Oslo with Stavanger, Bergen, Åndalsnes, Trondheim, Fauske and Bodø; lines also connect Sweden with Oslo, Trondheim and Narvik.

Most long-distance day trains have 1st- and 2nd-class seats and a buffet car or refreshment trolley service.

Reservations sometimes cost an additional Nkr50 and are mandatory on some long-distance routes.

There's a 50% discount for seniors (67 years and older), for travellers with disabilities, and for children (aged four to 15 years); children under four travel free. The student discount is 25% to 40%.

STEVE ALLEN/GETTY IMAGES ©

Natural Wonders

Scandinavia's wide, wild expanses encompass forests, lakes, Arctic and volcanic landscapes, all governed by the seasons' spectacular swing. Life is abuzz in summer under the endless daylight, while winter's snowfall is a rapid scene change for the second act of this northern drama.

Above Blue Lagoon (p238), Iceland

JEPPE WIKSTROM/GETTY IMAGES ©

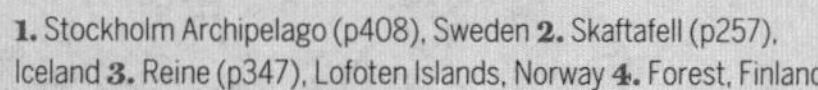

1. Stockholm Archipelago (p408), Sweden **2.** Skaftafell (p257), Iceland **3.** Reine (p347), Lofoten Islands, Norway **4.** Forest, Finland

DENNIS JANSSEN/GETTY IMAGES ©

PETER ADAMS/GETTY IMAGES ©

Great Outdoors

The scenery in Scandinavia is one of its great attractions. Wild, rugged coasts and mountains, hundreds of kilometres of forest broken only by lakes and the odd cottage, and unspoilt Baltic archipelagos make up a varied menu of uplifting visual treats.

Forests

Mainland Scandinavia has some of the world's top tree cover, and the forests stretch much further than the eye can see. Mainly composed of spruce, pine and birch, these forests are responsible for the crisp, clean, aromatic northern air.

Iceland

Thrown up in the middle of the Atlantic by violent geothermal activity, Iceland offers bleak and epic scenery that is at once both harsh and gloriously uplifting. The juxtaposition of frozen glaciers and boiling geysers make it a wild scenic ride.

Norway

Fjords are famous for a reason; coastal views here take the breath away. There are spectacular views the length of this long country. Near the top, the Lofoten Islands present picturesque fishing villages against the awesome backdrop of glacier-scoured mountains.

Lakes

Once the ice melts, Scandinavia is a watery land. A Finnish or Swedish lake under a midnight sun, pines reflected in the calm, chilly water and a stillness broken only by the landing of waterbirds: these are enduring images.

Archipelagos

Thousands of islands lie offshore and the Baltic is the place to grab a boat and find an islet to call your own. Out in the Atlantic, the Faroes offer stern cliffs housing vast seabird colonies.

MARKO NATRI/GETTY IMAGES ©

GORAN ASSNER/GETTY IMAGES ©

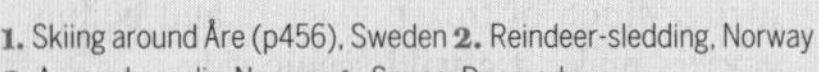

1. Skiing around Åre (p456), Sweden 2. Reindeer-sledding, Norway 3. Aurora borealis, Norway 4. Sauna, Denmark

PER-ANDRE HOFFMANN/GETTY IMAGES ©

ALTRENDO IMAGES/GETTY IMAGES ©

Winter Wonderland

Once the snows come, bears look for a place to sleep out the winter, but for the rest of us, there's no excuse. The ethereal beauty of the whitened land combines with numerous exciting activities to make this a great time to visit.

Skiing

There's not much you can teach Scandinavians about skiing; they invented it. There are numerous places to hit the powder, with excellent facilities for all levels. Cross-country is big, with lighted trails compensating for the long nights.

Winter Activities

Snowmobiles are a part of life up north, and it's lots of fun to whizz about on one. More sedate is ice fishing, but you'd better pack a warm drink. Ice climbing, nights in snow hotels, the aurora borealis (northern lights), snowshoe treks and kick sledding are other popular possibilities.

Sledding

The whoosh of the runners as a team of huskies or reindeer whisks you through the icy northern landscapes – it's tough to beat the feeling. Don't expect a pampered ride though – learn on the job or eat snow!

Landscapes

It's cold, but low winter light and the eerie blue colours the sky takes on make it spectacularly scenic. Trees glistening with ice crystals and snow carpeting the ground add to this magical landscape.

Saunas

If the cold has seeped into your bones, there's nothing like a log fire or, even better, a sauna, to warm the extremities again. Too hot? Get somebody to drill a hole in the lake and jump in. Good for the pores!

RICHARD CLARK/GETTY IMAGES ©

STEVE CASIMIRO/GETTY IMAGES ©

1. Snaefellsnes (p240), Iceland **2.** Trollfjord (p344), Norway
3. Log cabin, Sweden **4.** Midsummer celebrations, Sweden

MADELEINE SODER/GETTY IMAGES ©

2

WILLIAM GRAY/GETTY IMAGES ©

Summer Adventures

When the snows melt and the sun returns, it's like a blessing bestowed upon the land. Nature accelerates into top gear, and locals pack a year's worth of fun and festivals into the short but memorably vibrant summer season.

Nordic Peace

For many Scandinavians, summer is spent at a lakeside cottage or campsite where simple pleasures – swimming, fishing, chopping wood, picking berries – replace the stresses of urban life for a few blissful weeks.

Kayaking & Canoeing

It's a perfect time to get the paddles out and explore the rivers and lakes of the interior, or the coastal serrations and islands. Throughout the region, kayaking and canoeing are extremely popular and easy to organise.

Hiking

There's fabulous walking across the whole region, from the jaw-droppingly majestic Icelandic routes to the remote Finnish wilderness. Excellent facilities mean it's easy to plan short walks or multiday hiking adventures.

Midsummer

The summer solstice is celebrated throughout the region, whether with traditional midsummer poles and dancing, or beer, sausages and a lakeside barbecue and bonfire with friends.

Terraces

Once the first proper rays bathe the pavement, coat racks in bars and cafes disappear, and outdoor terraces sprout onto every square and street, packed with people determined to suck up every last drop of the precious summer sun.

4

Brown bear, Finland

Wildlife

Vast tracts of barely populated land away from the bustle of central Europe make Scandinavia an important refuge for numerous species, including several high-profile carnivores, myriad seabirds and lovable marine mammals.

Elk & Reindeer

If antlers are your thing, you won't be disappointed. The sizeable but ungainly elk (moose) is widespread in the mainland forests, often blundering onto roads or into towns. In Lapland, the domesticated reindeer is the herd animal of the indigenous Sámi.

Brown Bears

The ruler of the forest is deeply rooted in Finnish culture, and there's still a fairly healthy population of them in the east of the country, near the Russian border. Bear-watching trips offer a great opportunity to see these impressively large, shaggy beasts.

Polar Bears & Walrus

Svalbard is as close to the North Pole as most are going to get, and the wildlife is appropriately impressive. The mighty polar bear means you'll need a just-in-case weapon if you want to leave town, while the weighty walrus is also an impressive sight.

Whales & Seabirds

Iceland has important seabird colonies; they breed there in huge numbers. Off Iceland's and Norway's coastlines, several varieties of whale are in regular attendance, best seen on a dedicated boat trip.

Nordic Creatures

The region is stocked with a range of animals: lynx and wolves pace the forests, while golden eagles, ospreys, ptarmigans and capercaillie add feathered glory to the mix. Seals and dolphins are aplenty, and the lonely wolverine prowls the northern wastes in search of prey or carrion.

Sweden

Includes ➡

Best Places to Eat

- Kryp In (p399)
- Thörnströms Kök (p433)
- Bastard Restaurant (p421)
- Ájtte Museum Restaurant (p461)
- PM & Vänner (p442)

Best Places to Stay

- Treehotel (p457)
- Icehotel (p463)
- IQ Suites (p432)
- Rival Hotel (p399)
- Stora Hotellet Umeå (p458)

Why Go?

As progressive and civilised as it may be, Sweden is a wild place. Its scenery ranges from barren moonscapes and impenetrable forests in the far north to sunny beaches and lush farmland further south. Its short summers and long winters mean that people cling to every last speck of sunshine on a late August evening – crayfish parties on seaside decks can stretch into the wee hours. In winter locals rely on candlelight and *glögg* to warm their spirits. But lovers of the outdoors will thrive here in any season: winter sees skiing and dogsledding while the warmer months invite long hikes, swimming and sunbathing, canoeing, cycling, you name it – if it's fun and can be done outdoors, you'll find it here. For less rugged types, there's always restaurant and nightclub hopping and museum perusing in cosmopolitan Stockholm, lively Göteborg and beyond.

When to Go

Stockholm

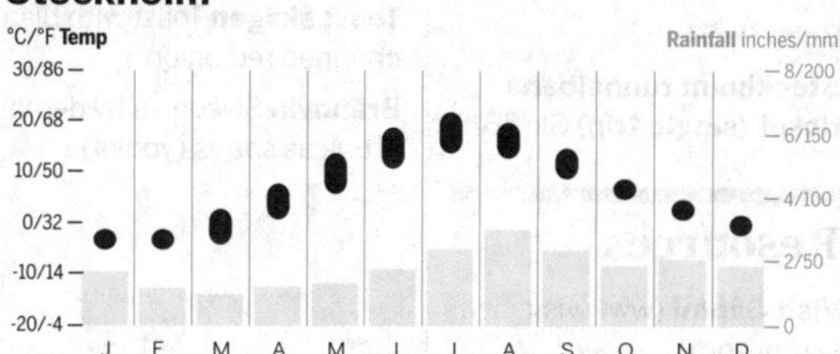

Jun–Aug Summers are short but intense, and the 'white nights' beyond the Arctic Circle magical.

Sep–Oct Nothing's open, but the countryside is stunning in autumn.

Mar–Apr Winter sports and the aurora borealis (northern lights) keep Norrland towns buzzing.

AT A GLANCE

Capital Stockholm

Area 449,964 sq km

Population 9.6 million

Country code ☎46

Languages Swedish, plus the officially protected minority languages Romani, Finnish, Yiddish, Meänkieli (Finnish dialects) and Sámi (10 languages)

Currency krona (Skr)

Exchange Rates

Australia	A$1	Skr6.32
Canada	C$1	Skr6.45
Euro Zone	€1	Skr9.12
Japan	¥100	Skr6.58
New Zealand	NZ$1	Skr5.63
UK	UK£1	Skr11.7
USA	US$1	Skr7.21

Set Your Budget

Budget hotel room from Skr820

Two-course evening meal Skr280

Museum entrance Skr70–120

Beer Skr54–65

Stockholm tunnelbana ticket (single trip) Skr36

Resources

Visit Sápmi (www.visitsapmi.com)

Visit Sweden (www.visitsweden.com)

White Guide (www.whiteguide.se)

Connections

Trains and buses link Sweden with Norway, Finland and Denmark. Flights connect Göteborg and Stockholm to Iceland. Stockholm Arlanda airport connects Sweden with the rest of the world, and domestic flights connect the capital with the country's northernmost and southernmost cities. Frequent ferries sail between Swedish ports and destinations in Denmark, Finland, Norway, Germany and parts of Eastern Europe.

ITINERARIES

One Week

Spend three days exploring Stockholm and Uppsala, and two days in and around Göteborg before continuing south to dynamic Malmö or flying to medieval Visby. In winter, get acclimatised in Stockholm before heading north to Kiruna and Abisko for dogsledding, the aurora borealis and stays at the Icehotel.

Two Weeks

In summer, include a trip northwards to the Lake Siljan region, then head further up towards Sundsvall to explore the dramatic cliffs of Höga Kusten and to Abisko for great hiking. Go in search of the lake monster in Östersund before detouring west to Åre for some extreme mountain biking and then head north to check out Sweden's most beautiful drive – the Wilderness Road.

Essential Food & Drink

Köttbullar och potatis Meatballs and mashed potatoes, served with *lingonsylt* (lingonberry jam).

Gravlax Cured salmon.

Sill & strömming Herring, eaten smoked, fried or pickled and often accompanied by capers, mustard and onion.

Toast skagen Toast with bleak roe, crème fraîche and chopped red onion.

Brännvin Sweden's trademark spirit, also called aquavit and drunk as *snaps* (vodka).

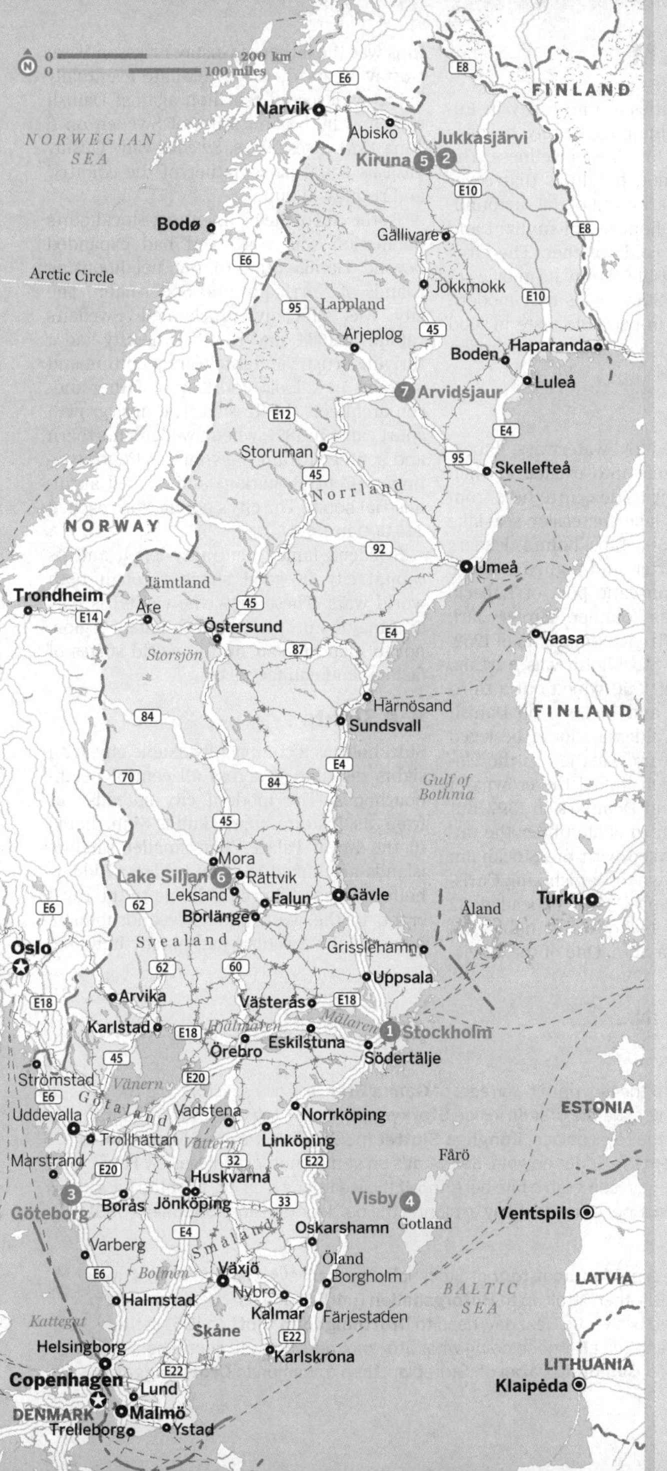

Sweden Highlights

1. Tour the urban waterways, exploring top-notch museums and wandering the labyrinthine Old Town of **Stockholm** (p386)
2. Hike through wild landscapes, spot herds of reindeer, absorb Sámi culture and sleep in the world-famous Icehotel in **Jukkasjärvi** (p463)
3. Dig into the art, fashion and originality that make Sweden's 'second city' of **Göteborg** (p426) first-rate
4. Join the feasting, archery and other medieval fun and frolics in historic **Visby** (p448)
5. Race a dog-sled under the northern lights near **Kiruna** (p463)
6. Celebrate Midsummer in the heartland villages surrounding lovely **Lake Siljan** (p415)
7. Take a car for a spin on a frozen lake near **Arvidsjaur** (p459)

STOCKHOLM

☎08 / POP 1.4 MILLION

Beautiful capital cities are no rarity in Europe, but Stockholm must surely be near the top of the list for sheer loveliness. The saffron-and-cinnamon buildings that cover its 14 islands rise starkly out of the surrounding ice-blue water, honeyed in sunlight and frostily elegant in cold weather. The city's charms are irresistible. From its movie-set Old Town (Gamla Stan) to its ever-modern fashion sense and impeccable taste in food and design, the city acts like an immersion school in aesthetics.

History

Its creation shaped by waterways, Stockholm originally came into existence when Vikings moved their trade centre here from northern Mälaren lake for easier sea–lake trade. Around 1250, Stockholm's leaders wrote a town charter and signed a trade treaty with the Hanseatic port of Lübeck. Stockholm's official founder, Birger Jarl, commissioned the Tre Kronor castle in 1252.

A century later, Stockholm was hurting. The Black Death of 1350 wiped out a third of the population, and in 1391 the Danish queen Margareta Valdemarsdotter besieged the city for four years. This led to the Union of Kalmar, which linked the crowns of Sweden, Norway and Denmark in 1397. But Sweden soon began to chafe under the union. Discontent peaked with the Stockholm Bloodbath of 1520, when Danish king Christian II tricked, trapped and beheaded 82 Swedish burghers, bishops and nobles on Stortorget in Gamla Stan. One of the 82 victims was the father of Gustav Eriksson Vasa; Gustav Vasa's quest to retaliate eventually led to widespread rebellion against Danish rule, and he became King of Sweden on 6 June 1523. These days, Swedes view Gustav Vasa as equal parts 'father of the country' and ruthless tyrant.

By the end of the 16th century, Stockholm's population was 9000 and had expanded beyond Gamla Stan to the neighbouring islands of Norrmalm and Södermalm. The city was officially proclaimed Sweden's capital in 1634, and by 1650 the city had a thriving artistic and intellectual culture and a grand new look, courtesy of father-and-son architects the Tessins. The next growth spurt came in 1871, when Sweden's northern and southern train lines met at Centralstationen (Central Station) and started an industrial boom. The city's population reached 245,000 in 1890.

Sweden's famed neutrality left it and its capital city in good shape through both world wars. These days, the capital is part of a major European biotechnology region, not to mention star on the world stages of fashion and culinary arts.

Sights

Stockholm is a compact, walkable city, with sights distributed across all central neighbourhoods. The modern city spreads out from its historic core, Gamla Stan, home to the Royal Palace. Two smaller satellite islands are linked to it by bridges: Riddarholmen, whose church is home to the royal crypt, to the west, and Helgeandsholmen, home of the Swedish parliament building,

STOCKHOLM IN...

Two Days

Beat the crowds to the labyrinthine streets of **Gamla Stan**, the city's historic old town. Watch St George wrestle the dragon inside **Storkyrkan** (p387), the old-town cathedral, and join a tour of the royal palace, **Kungliga Slottet** (p387). Then trek to **Södermalm** for dizzying views from the Söder heights. See what's on at the photography gallery **Fotografiska** (p395) – you can grab a bite here, too. If the weather's nice, party at the bars in Medborgarplatsen. Spend the next day exploring the outdoor museum **Skansen** (p391).

Four Days

On day three take a **guided boat tour** of Stockholm's waterways. Visit the impressive **Vasamuseet** (p391), then stroll up to **Hötorgshallen** (p400) for a big bowl of fish soup and speciality-food browsing. Next day, head to **Drottningholm Slott** (p406) in the morning, then spend the afternoon doing what Stockholmers do best: shopping. Start with pedestrianised **Biblioteksgatan** off Stureplan, then transition to **Drottninggatan** for souvenirs.

to the north. The tourist office is just across the street from Centralstationen, on the main island.

Many of Stockholm's best museums are on Djurgården, east of Gamla Stan, and the small island of Skeppsholmen. Södermalm, the city's funky, bohemian neighbourhood, lies south of Gamla Stan, just beyond the rather baffling traffic interchange called Slussen.

Gamla Stan

Once you get over the armies of tourists wielding ice-cream cones and shopping bags, you'll discover that the oldest part of Stockholm is also its most beautiful. The city emerged here in the 13th century and grew with Sweden's power until the 17th century, when the castle of Tre Kronor, symbol of that power, burned to the ground. While ambling along Västerlånggatan, look out for **Mårten Trotzigs Gränd** by No 81: this is Stockholm's narrowest lane, at less than 1m wide.

Kungliga Slottet PALACE

(Royal Palace; Map p392; 08-402 61 30; www.kungahuset.se; Slottsbacken; adult/child Skr150/75, valid for 7 days; 10am-5pm mid-May–mid-Sep, closed Mon rest of year; 43, 46, 55, 59 Slottsbacken, M Gamla Stan) Kungliga Slottet was built on the ruins of Tre Kronor castle, which burned down in 1697. The north wing survived and was incorporated into the new building. Designed by court architect Nicodemus Tessin the Younger, it took 57 years to complete. Free 45-minute tours in English start at 11am and 2pm mid-May to mid-September, and at 2pm and 3pm the rest of the year. The apartments are occasionally closed for royal business; closures are noted on the website.

Nobelmuseet MUSEUM

(Map p392; nobelmuseet.se; Stortorget; adult/child Skr100/70; 10am-8pm; M Gamla Stan) Nobelmuseet presents the history of the Nobel Prizes and their recipients, with a focus on the intellectual and cultural aspects of invention. It's a slick space with fascinating displays, including short films on the theme of creativity, interviews with laureates including Ernest Hemingway and Martin Luther King, and cafe chairs signed by the visiting prize recipients (flip them over to see!). The free guided tours are recommended (in English at 10.15am, 11.15am, 1pm, 3pm, 4pm and 6pm in summer).

Royal Armoury MUSEUM

(Livrustkammaren; Map p392; 08-402 30 30; www.livrustkammaren.se; Slottsbacken 3; adult/child Skr90/free; 10am-5pm; 43, 46, 55, 59 Slottsbacken, M Gamla Stan) Livrustkammaren is housed in the cellar vaults of the palace but has a separate admission fee. It's a family attic of sorts, crammed with engrossing memorabilia spanning more than 500 years of royal childhoods, coronations, weddings and murders. Meet Gustav II Adolf's stuffed battle steed, Streiff; see the costume Gustav III wore to the masquerade ball on the night he was shot, in 1792; or let the kids try on a suit of armour in the playroom.

Riddarholmskyrkan CHURCH

(Riddarholmen Church; Map p392; 08-402 61 30; www.kungahuset.se; Riddarholmen; adult/child Skr50/free; 10am-5pm mid-May–mid-Sep; 3, 53 Riddarhustorget, M Gamla Stan) The strikingly beautiful Riddarholmskyrkan, on the equally pretty and under-visited islet of Riddarholmen, was built by Franciscan monks in the late 13th century. It has been the royal necropolis since the burial of Magnus Ladulås in 1290, and is home to the armorial glory of the Seraphim knightly order. There's a guided tour in English at noon (included with admission) and occasional concerts. Holiday closures are frequent; check the website for updates. Admission fee is by credit card only.

Storkyrkan CHURCH

(Great Church; Map p392; www.stockholmsdomkyrkoforsamling.se; Trångsund 1; adult/child Skr40/free; 9am-4pm; M Gamla Stan) The one-time venue for royal weddings and coronations, Storkyrkan is both Stockholm's oldest building (consecrated in 1306) and its cathedral. Behind a baroque facade, the Gothic-baroque interior includes extravagant royal-box pews designed by Nicodemus Tessin the Younger, as well as German Berndt Notke's dramatic sculpture *St George and the Dragon*, commissioned by Sten Sture the Elder to commemorate his victory over the Danes in 1471. Keep an eye out for posters and handbills advertising music performances here.

Medeltidsmuseet MUSEUM

(Medieval Museum; Map p392; www.medeltidsmuseet.stockholm.se; Strömparterren; adult/child Skr100/free; noon-5pm Tue-Sun, to 7pm Wed; ; 62, 65, Gustav Adolfs torg) Tucked beneath the bridge that links Gamla Stan and Norrmalm, this child-friendly museum was established when construction workers preparing to build a car park here in the late 1970s

Stockholm

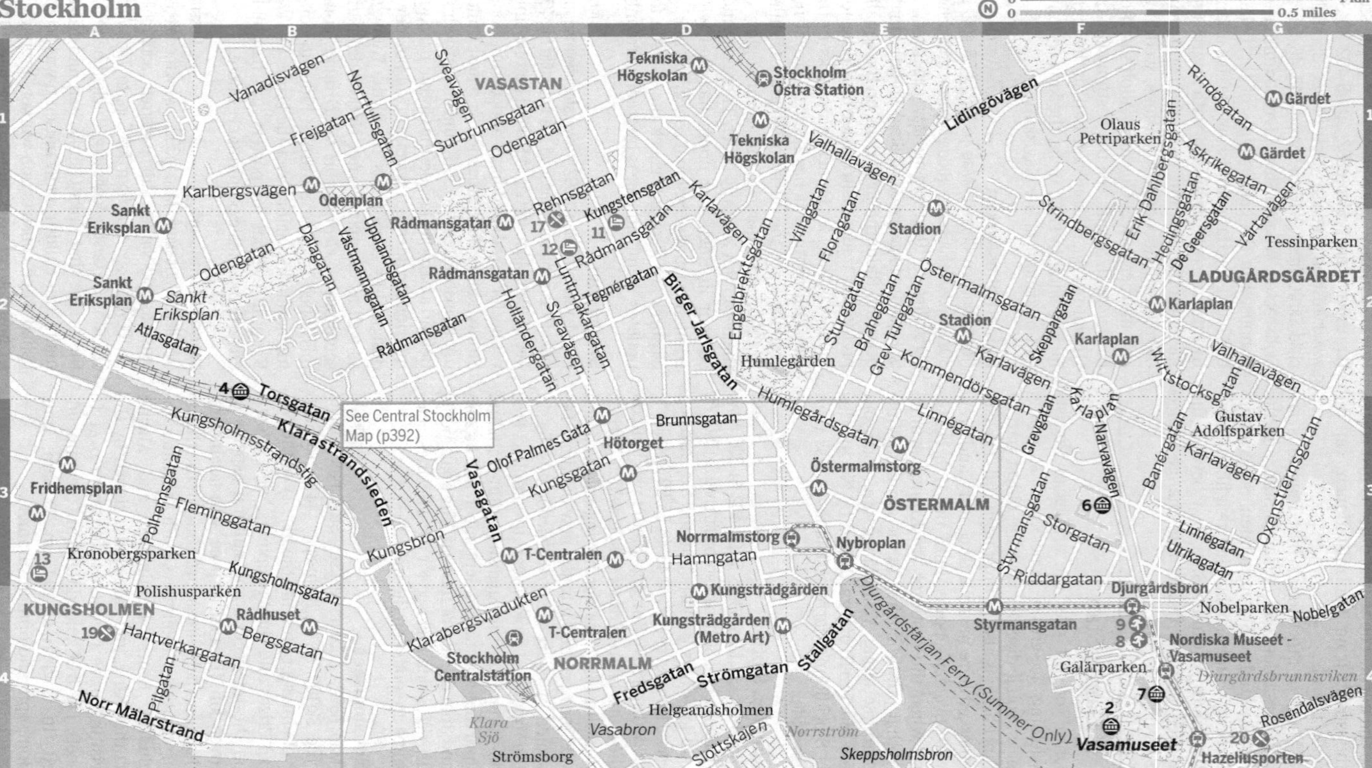
1 km
0.5 miles
VASASTAN
ÖSTERMALM
NORRMALM
KUNGSHOLMEN
LADUGÅRDSGÄRDET
See Central Stockholm Map (p392)
Djurgårdsfärjan Ferry (Summer Only)
Sankt Eriksplan
Odenplan
Rådmansgatan
Hötorget
T-Centralen
Stockholm Centralstation
Kungsträdgården (Metro Art)
Kungsträdgården
Normalmstorg
Nybroplan
Östermalmstorg
Stadion
Tekniska Högskolan
Stockholm Östra Station
Karlaplan
Gärdet
Styrmansgatan
Djurgårdsbron
Fridhemsplan
Rådhuset
Vasamuseet
Nordiska Museet - Vasamuseet
Galärparken
Nobelparken
Djurgårdsbrunnsviken
Hazeliusporten
Rosendalsvägen
Gustav Adolfsparken
Olaus Petriparken
Tessinparken
Humlegården
Kronobergsparken
Polishusparken
Helgeandsholmen
Strömsborg
Klara Sjö
Norrström
Skeppsholmsbron
Slottskajen
Vasabron
Sveavägen
Birger Jarlsgatan
Vasagatan
Klarastrandsleden
Torsgatan
Strömgatan
Fredsgatan
Stallgatan
Norr Mälarstrand
Lidingövägen
Valhallavägen
Karlavägen
Narvavägen
Kungsgatan
Kungsbron
Hamngatan
Linnégatan
Storgatan
Riddargatan
Hantverkargatan
Fleminggatan
Kungsholmsgatan
Bergsgatan
Odengatan
Dalagatan
Upplandsgatan
Västmannagatan
Norrtullsgatan
Surbrunnsgatan
Luntmakargatan
Holländergatan
Tegnérgatan
Kungstensgatan
Rehnsgatan
Engelbrektsgatan
Sturegatan
Floragatan
Villagatan
Grev Turegatan
Kommendörsgatan
Brahegatan
Skeppargatan
Strindbergsgatan
Erik Dahlbergsgatan
Oxenstiernsgatan
Banérgatan
Askrikegatan
Rindögatan
Värtavägen
Atlasgatan
Karlbergsvägen
Vanadisvägen
Frejgatan
Polhemsgatan
Pilgatan
Kungsholmsstrandstig
Klarabergsviadukten
Olof Palmes Gata
Brunnsgatan
Humlegårdsgatan
Östermalmsgatan
Ulrikagatan
Nobelgatan
Hedinsgatan
De Geersgatan
Wittstocksgatan
Grevgatan
Karlaplan

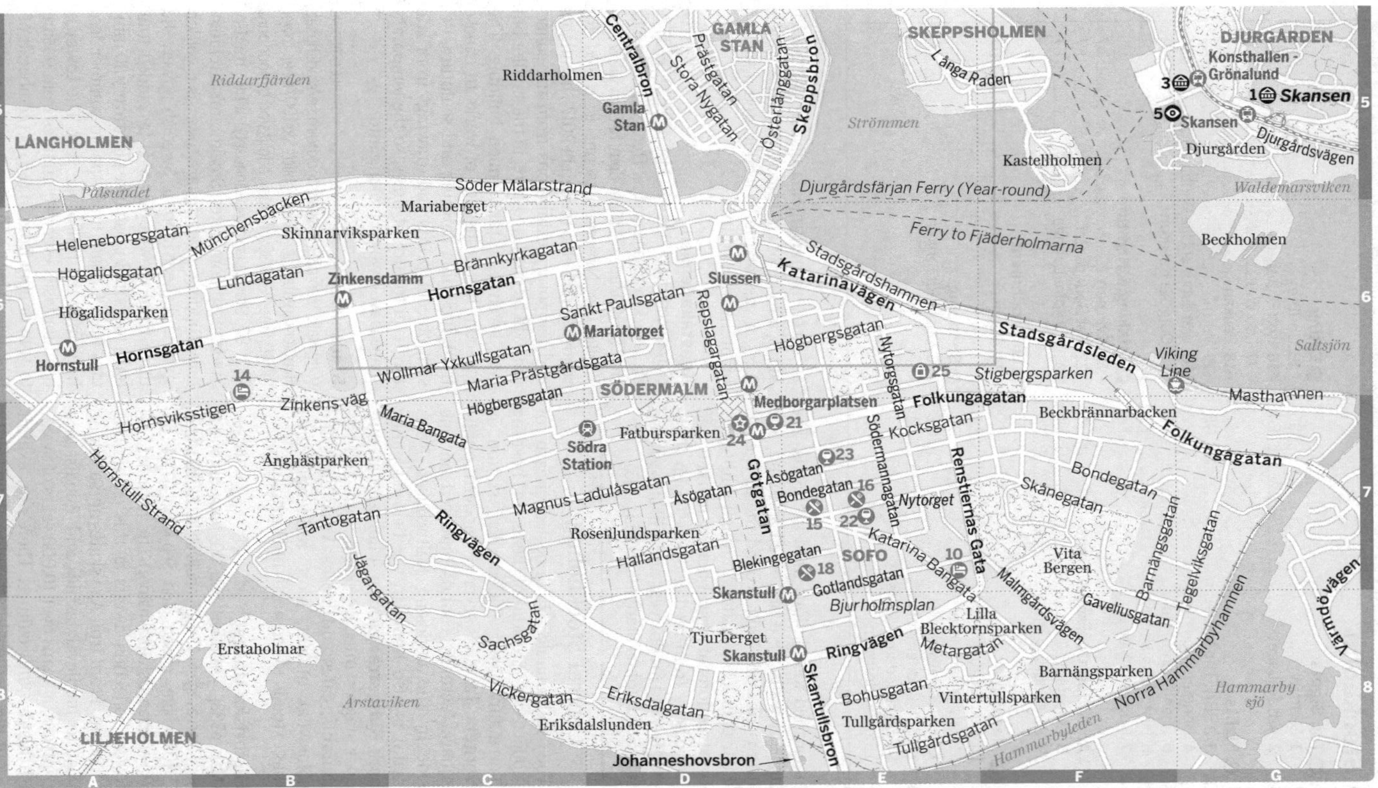

Riddarfjärden
Riddarholmen
Centralbron
Gamla Stan
GAMLA STAN
Prästgatan
Stora Nygatan
Österlånggatan
Skeppsbron
Strömmen
SKEPPSHOLMEN
Långa Raden
Kastellholmen
DJURGÅRDEN
Konsthallen - Grönalund
3
1 Skansen
5
Skansen
Djurgården
Djurgårdsvägen
Waldemarsviken
Beckholmen
LÅNGHOLMEN
Pålsundet
Söder Mälarstrand
Mariaberget
Djurgårdsfärjan Ferry (Year-round)
Ferry to Fjäderholmarna
Heleneborgsgatan
Münchensbacken
Skinnarviksparken
Högalidsgatan
Lundagatan
Brännkyrkagatan
Zinkensdamm
Hornsgatan
Slussen
Katarinavägen
Stadsgårdshamnen
Högalidsparken
Sankt Paulsgatan
Repslagargatan
Mariatorget
Högbergsgatan
Nytorgsgatan
Stadsgårdsleden
Viking Line
Saltsjön
Hornstull
Hornsgatan
Wollmar Yxkullsgatan
Maria Prästgårdsgata
25
Stigbergsparken
14
Högbergsgatan
SÖDERMALM
Medborgarplatsen
Folkungagatan
Masthamnen
Hornsviksstigen
Zinkens väg
Maria Bangata
21
Beckbrännarbacken
Södra Station
Fatbursparken
24
Södermannagatan
Kocksgatan
Folkungagatan
Ånghästparken
23
Renstiernas Gata
Hornstull Strand
Åsögatan
Götgatan
Bondegatan
16
Nytorget
Bondegatan
Skånegatan
Magnus Ladulåsgatan
Åsögatan
15
22
Tantogatan
Ringvägen
Rosenlundsparken
Hallandsgatan
Blekingegatan
18
SOFO
Katarina Bangata
10
Vita Bergen
Barnängsgatan
Tegelviksgatan
Jägargatan
Skanstull
Gotlandsgatan
Bjurholmsplan
Malmgårdsvägen
Gaveliusgatan
Värmdövägen
Lilla Blecktornsparken
Metargatan
Erstaholmar
Sachsgatan
Tjurberget
Skanstull
Ringvägen
Barnängsparken
Norra Hammarbyhamnen
Hammarby sjö
Årstaviken
Vickergatan
Eriksdalgatan
Skantullsbron
Bohusgatan
Vintertullsparken
Eriksdalslunden
Tullgårdsparken
Tullgårdsgatan
Hammarbyleden
LILJEHOLMEN
Johanneshovsbron

Stockholm

Top Sights
1 Skansen ... G5
2 Vasamuseet ... F4

Sights
3 ABBA: The Museum ... G5
4 Bonniers Konsthall ... B2
5 Gröna Lund Tivoli ... F5
6 Historiska Museet ... F3
7 Nordiska Museet ... F4

Activities, Courses & Tours
8 Sjöcaféet ... F4
9 Strandbryggan ... F4

Sleeping
10 Bed & Breakfast 4 Trappor ... E7
11 Birger Jarl Hotel ... D2
12 Hotel Hellsten ... C2
13 STF Fridhemsplan ... A3
14 Zinkensdamm Hotell & Vandrarhem ... B6

Eating
15 Chutney ... E7
16 Koh Phangan ... E7
17 Lao Wai ... C2
18 Pelikan ... E7
19 Vurma ... A4
20 Wärdshuset Ulla Winbladh ... G4
Östgöta Källaren ... (see 23)

Drinking & Nightlife
21 Kvarnen ... D7
22 Pet Sounds Bar ... E7
23 Vampire Lounge ... E7

Entertainment
24 Debaser ... D7

Shopping
25 Chokladfabriken ... E6

unearthed foundations from the 1530s. The ancient walls were preserved as found, and a museum was built around them. The circular plan leads visitors through faithful reconstructions of typical homes, markets and workshops from medieval Stockholm. Tickets are valid for one year and will also get you into Stockholms Stadsmuseum (p395).

Central Stockholm

The fashionable, high-heeled heart of modern-day Stockholm beats in bustling Norrmalm. Near T-Centralen station is **Sergels Torg**, a severely modern public square (actually round) bordered on one side by the imposing Kulturhuset. Norrmalm is also home to the beloved public park **Kungsträdgården** – home to an outdoor stage, winter ice-skating rink and restaurants, cafes and kiosks. Vasastan is the somewhat quieter, more residential area that extends to the north of Norrmalm.

Historiska Museet MUSEUM

(Map p388; 08-519 556 00; www.historiska.se; Narvavägen 13-17; adult/child Skr100/free; 10am-6pm, closed Mon Sep-May; 44, 56, M Karlaplan, Östermalmstorg) The national historical collection awaits at this enthralling museum. From Iron Age skates and a Viking boat to medieval textiles and Renaissance triptychs, it spans over 10,000 years of Swedish history and culture. There's an exhibit about the medieval Battle of Gotland (1361), an excellent multimedia display on the Vikings, a room of altarpieces from the Middle Ages, a vast textile collection and a section on prehistoric culture.

Konstakademien MUSEUM

(Royal Academy of Fine Arts; Map p392; 08-23 29 25; www.konstakademien.se; Fredsgatan 12; adult/child Skr100/free; 10am-6pm, to 8pm Tue & Thu) While the Nationalmuseum is closed for renovations (set to reopen in 2017), highlights and temporary exhibitions from the collection will be displayed here, in the smaller but very lovely Konstakademien building. The museum has thousands of works to choose from, including painting and sculpture, design objects, prints and drawings from late medieval to current times, so the temporary space is well worth looking into.

Stadshuset NOTABLE BUILDING

(City Hall; Map p392; www.stockholm.se/stadshuset; Hantverkargatan 1; adult/child Skr100/free, tower Skr40/free; 9.30am-4pm, admission by tour only; 3, 62 Stadshuset, M Rådhuset) The mighty Stadshuset dominates Stockholm's architecture. Topping off its square tower is a golden spire and the symbol of Swedish power: the three royal crowns. Entry is by guided tour only; tours in English take place every 30 minutes from 9.30am until 4pm in summer, less frequently the rest of the year. The **tower** is open for visits every 40 minutes from 9.15am to 4pm or 5pm from May to September; it offers stellar views and a great thigh workout.

Bonniers Konsthall GALLERY

(Map p388; 08-736 42 55; www.bonnierskonsthall.se; Torsgatan 19; adult/child Skr80/free; noon-8pm Wed, to 5pm Thu-Sun; St Eriksplan) This ambitious gallery keeps culture fiends busy with a fresh dose of international contemporary art, as well as a reading room, a fab cafe and a busy schedule of art seminars and artists-in-conversation sessions. The massive, transparent flatiron building was designed by Johan Celsing. There are discussions about the exhibitions in English at 1pm, 3pm, 5pm and 7pm Wednesdays, and 1pm and 4pm Thursday to Sunday. Sunday at 2pm there are free guided tours by the museum's curators.

Djurgården

A former royal hunting reserve, Djurgården is an urban oasis of parkland with some of Stockholm's best museums. To get here, take bus or tram 47, or the Djurgården ferry from Nybroplan or Slussen. Walking or cycling is the best way to explore the island; you can rent bikes near the bridge in summer.

★Vasamuseet MUSEUM

(Map p388; www.vasamuseet.se; Galärvarvsvägen 14; adult/child Skr130/free; 8.30am-6pm; ; 44, Djurgårdsfärjan, 7 Nordiska museet/Vasa) A good-humoured glorification of some dodgy calculations, Vasamuseet is the custom-built home of the massive warship *Vasa*. The ship, a whopping 69m long and 48.8m tall, was the pride of the Swedish crown when it set off on its maiden voyage on 10 August 1628. Within minutes, the top-heavy vessel tipped and sank to the bottom of Saltsjön, along with many of the people on board. Guided tours are in English every 30 minutes in summer.

★Skansen MUSEUM

(Map p388; www.skansen.se; Djurgårdsvägen; adult/child Skr160/60; 10am-10pm late Jun-Aug; ; 44, Djurgårdsfärjan, 7, Djurgården) The world's first open-air museum, Skansen was founded in 1891 by Artur Hazelius to give visitors an insight into how Swedes lived once upon a time. You could easily spend a day here and still not see it all (note that prices

MUSEUM ITINERARY: VASAMUSEET

As soon as you enter Vasamuseet, you can't help but marvel at the museum's centrepiece, subtly lit to great effect. The 17th-century **Vasa galleon**, built to be Sweden's greatest warship, instead became the subject of great controversy, sinking within minutes of sailing. Divided into six levels that allow you to admire the salvaged and restored *Vasa* from keel to stern, the museum itself resembles the insides of a giant ship, blending skilfully presented exhibits with a wood-panelled interior.

Duck into the **screening room** by the entrance for an excellent video introduction to the ship's conception on King Gustav Vasa's orders, its watery demise, its rescue in 1961 and the challenge of preserving the world's largest wooden museum exhibit.

Head down to Level 2, where a combination of paintings and models take you through the construction and sinking of **His Majesty's Ship**, including the fatal errors in the ship's construction that made her unseaworthy. The scale models at **Stockholm Shipyard** show how ships were built in 1620, and you can check out the *Vasa* during different stages of construction. Next, you come **Face to Face** with several of the ship's denizens through a mix of facial reconstruction and interactive displays. Fifteen skeletons from the ship have been dated by the radiocarbon method to determine age and health, their social status and possible occupation determined from their possessions and their location on the ship. Nearby, through a range of interactive displays, **Preserving the Vasa** explores various solutions to halting the ship's slow decomposition.

On the main Level 4, **The Salvaging** walks you through the delicate process of the ship's recovery from the bottom of the harbour in 1961 via its discovery in 1956 by amateur archaeologist Anders Franzén.

If it hadn't been for the *Vasa's* ignominious sinking, the ship's destiny would have been victory or destruction on the high seas; **Battle!** on Level 5 puts you in the middle of a nautical skirmish. A rich collection of period objects gives you an insight into day-to-day **Life on Board** in between battles.

Finally, on Level 6, **The Sailing Ship** showcases the original preserved sails from the *Vasa*, while **Imagery of Power** explains the symbolism of the *Vasa's* 700 ornaments and sculptures that added to the ship's fatal weight.

Central Stockholm

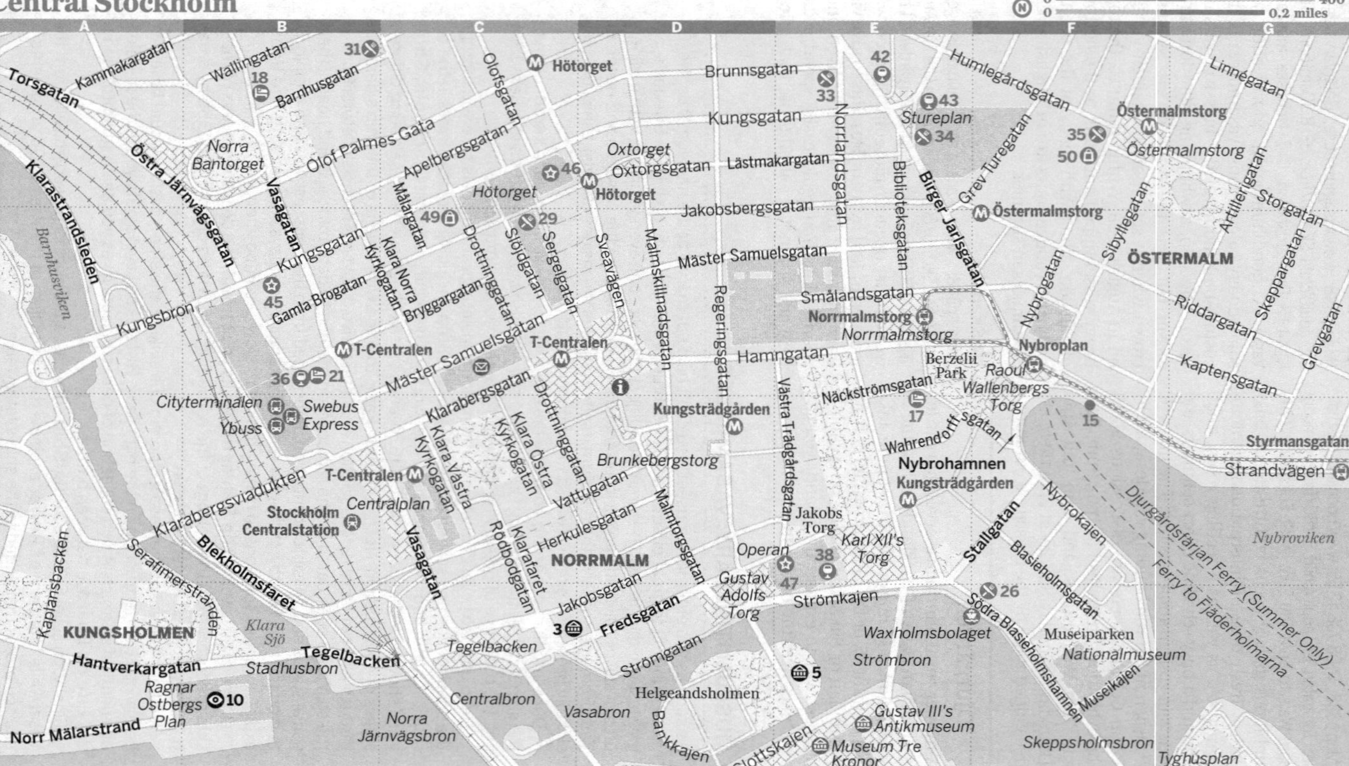

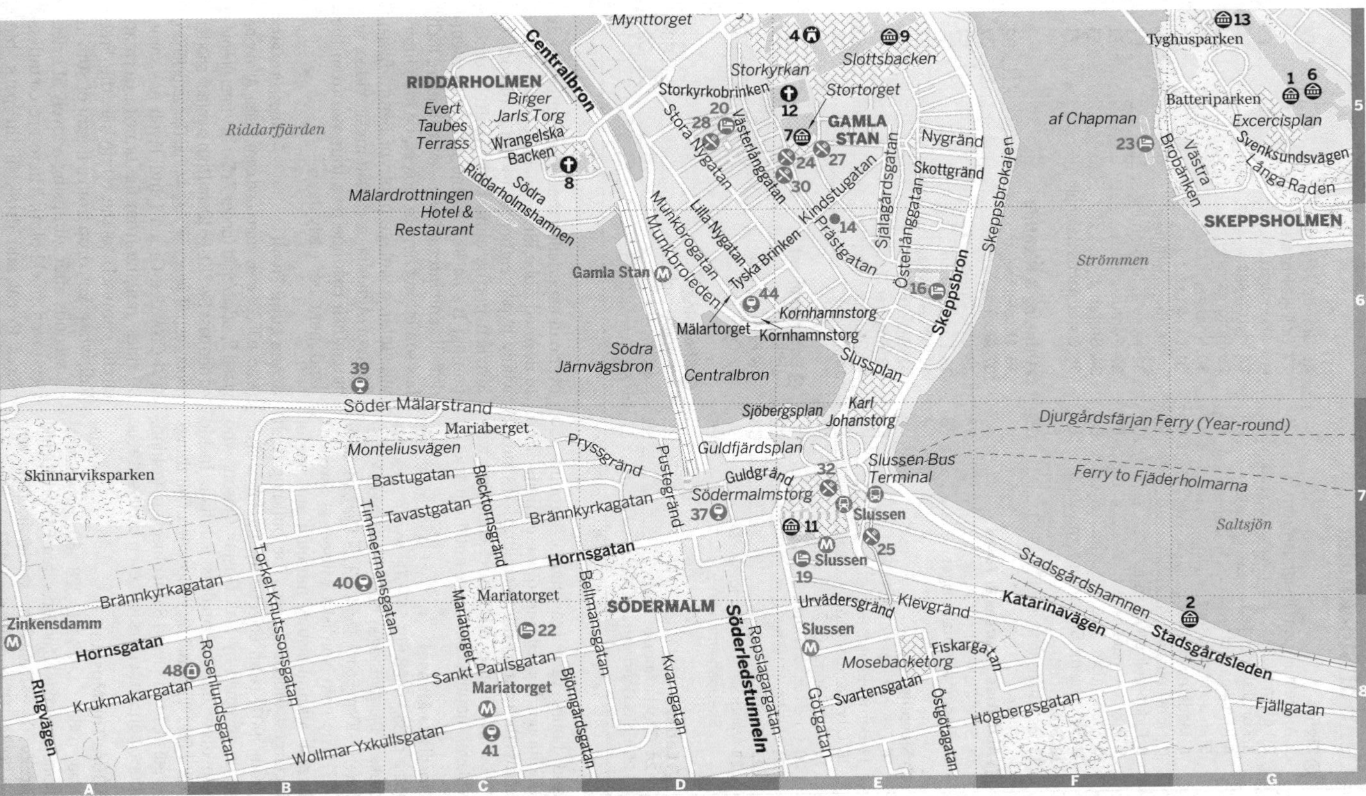
RIDDARHOLMEN
SKEPPSHOLMEN
GAMLA STAN
SÖDERMALM
Riddarfjärden
Strömmen
Saltsjön
Mynttorget
Centralbron
Birger Jarls Torg
Evert Taubes Terrass
Wrangelska Backen
Södra Riddarholmshamnen
Mälardrottningen Hotel & Restaurant
Storkyrkan
Slottsbacken
Storkyrkobrinken
Stortorget
Stora Nygatan
Västerlånggatan
Lilla Nygatan
Munkbrogatan
Munkbroleden
Tyska Brinken
Kindstugatan
Prästgatan
Själagårdsgatan
Österlånggatan
Nygränd
Skottgränd
Skeppsbrokajen
Skeppsbron
Gamla Stan
Kornhamnstorg
Mälartorget
Slussplan
Södra Järnvägsbron
Sjöbergsplan
Karl Johanstorg
Tyghusparken
Batteriparken
af Chapman
Excercisplan
Västra Brobänken
Svenksundsvägen
Långa Raden
Djurgårdsfärjan Ferry (Year-round)
Ferry to Fjäderholmarna
Söder Mälarstrand
Mariaberget
Monteliusvägen
Skinnarviksparken
Bastugatan
Tavastgatan
Pryssgränd
Guldfjärdsplan
Pustegränd
Guldgränd
Södermalmstorg
Slussen Bus Terminal
Slussen
Blecktornsgränd
Brännkyrkagatan
Hornsgatan
Timmermansgatan
Torkel Knutssonsgatan
Mariatorget
Bellmansgatan
Söderledstunneln
Repslagargatan
Urvädersgränd
Klevgränd
Katarinavägen
Stadsgårdshamnen
Stadsgårdsleden
Zinkensdamm
Rosenlundsgatan
Krukmakargatan
Ringvägen
Sankt Paulsgatan
Björngårdsgatan
Kvarngatan
Götgatan
Fiskargatan
Mosebacketorg
Svartensgatan
Östgötagatan
Högbergsgatan
Fjällgatan
Wollmar Yxkullsgatan

Central Stockholm

Sights
1 Arkitektur- och Designcentrum............G5
2 Fotografiska.............................G8
3 Konstakademien...........................C4
4 Kungliga Slottet.........................E5
5 Medeltidsmuseet..........................E4
6 Moderna Museet...........................G5
7 Nobelmuseet..............................E5
8 Riddarholmskyrkan........................C5
9 Royal Armoury............................E5
10 Stadshuset..............................B4
11 Stockholms Stadsmuseum..................E7
12 Storkyrkan..............................E5
13 Östasiatiska Museet.....................G5

Activities, Courses & Tours
14 Stockholm Ghost Walk....................E6
15 Strömma Kanalbolaget....................F3

Sleeping
16 2kronor Hostel Old Town.................E6
17 Berns Hotel.............................E3
18 City Backpackers........................B1
19 Hotel Anno 1647.........................E7
20 Lord Nelson Hotel.......................D5
21 Nordic 'C' Hotel........................B2
22 Rival Hotel.............................C8
23 Vandrarhem af Chapman & Skeppsholmen....F5

Eating
24 Chokladkoppen...........................E5
25 Eriks Gondolen..........................E7
26 Grands Verandan.........................F4
27 Grillska Husets Konditori...............E5
28 Hermitage...............................D5
29 Hötorgshallen...........................C2
30 Kryp In.................................E5
31 La Neta.................................B1
Mathias Dahlgren.....................(see 26)
32 Nystekt Strömming.......................E7
33 Pontus!.................................E1
34 Sturehof................................E1
35 Östermalms Saluhall.....................F1

Drinking & Nightlife
36 Absolut Icebar..........................B2
37 Akkurat.................................D7
38 Café Opera..............................E3
39 Lady Patricia...........................B6
40 Marie Laveau............................B7
41 Side Track..............................C8
42 Spy Bar.................................E1
43 Sturecompagniet.........................E1
44 Torget..................................D6

Entertainment
45 Fasching................................B2
46 Konserthuset............................C1
47 Operan..................................E3

Shopping
48 Papercut................................B8
49 PUB.....................................C2
50 Svensk Slöjd............................F1

and hours vary seasonally). Around 150 traditional houses and other exhibits from across the country dot the hilltop – it's meant to be 'Sweden in miniature', complete with villages, nature, commerce and industry.

Nordiska Museet MUSEUM
(Map p388; ☎08-519 547 70; www.nordiskamuseet.se; Djurgårdsvägen 6-16; adult/child Skr100/free; ⏲10am-5pm; 🚌44, 69, ⛴Djurgårdsfärjan, 🚊7) The epic Nordiska Museet is Sweden's largest cultural-history museum and one of its largest indoor spaces. The building itself (from 1907) is an eclectic, Renaissance-style castle designed by Isak Gustav Clason, who also drew up Östermalms Saluhall. Inside you'll find a sprawling collection of all things Swedish, from sacred Sámi objects to fashion, shoes, home interiors and even table settings.

ABBA: The Museum MUSEUM
(Map p388; ☎08-121 328 60; www.abbathemuseum.com; Djurgårdsvägen 68; adult/child Skr195/50; ⏲10am-8pm, shorter hours in winter; 🚌44, ⛴Djurgårdsfärjan, 🚊7) A sensory-overload experience that might appeal only to devoted Abba fans, this long-awaited and wildly hyped cathedral to the demigods of Swedish pop is almost aggressively entertaining. It's packed to the gills with memorabilia and interactivity – every square inch has something new to look at, be it a glittering guitar, a vintage photo of Benny, Björn, Frida or Agnetha, a classic music video, an outlandish costume or a tour van from the band members' early days.

Gröna Lund Tivoli AMUSEMENT PARK
(Map p388; www.gronalund.com; Lilla Allmänna gränd 9; adult/child (under 7) Skr110/free; unlimited ride pass Skr310; ⏲10am-11pm summer, shorter hours rest of year; 👪; 🚌44, ⛴Djurgårdsfärjan, 🚊7) Crowded Gröna Lund Tivoli has some 30 rides, ranging from the tame (a German circus carousel) to the terrifying (the Free Fall, where you drop from a height of 80m in six seconds after glimpsing a lovely, if brief, view over Stockholm). There are countless places to eat and drink in the park, but

whether you'll keep anything down is another matter entirely. The Åkband day pass gives unlimited rides, or individual rides range from Skr20 to Skr60.

Skeppsholmen

Moderna Museet MUSEUM

(Map p392; ☎08-52 02 35 01; www.modernamuseet.se; Exercisplan 4; adult/child Skr120/free, 6-8pm Fri free; ⊙10am-6pm Wed, Thu, Sat & Sun, to 8pm Tue & Fri, closed Mon; 🚌65; ⛴Djurgårdsfärjan) Moderna Museet is Stockholm's modern-art maverick, its permanent collection ranging from paintings and sculptures to photography, video art and installations. Highlights include work by Pablo Picasso, Salvador Dalí *(The Enigma of William Tell)*, Andy Warhol, Damien Hirst and Robert Rauschenberg (*Monograph*, affectionately known as 'the goat in a tyre'). There are important pieces by Francis Bacon, Marcel Duchamp and Matisse, as well as their Scandinavian contemporaries, and plenty of work by not yet household names.

Arkitektur- och Designcentrum MUSEUM

(Map p392; ☎08-587 270 00; www.arkdes.se; Exercisplan 4; adult/child Skr80/free, 4-6pm Fri free, combination ticket with Moderna Museet Skr180; ⊙10am-8pm Tue, to 6pm Wed-Sun; 🚌65, ⛴Djurgårdsfärjan) Adjoining Moderna Museet and housed in a converted navy drill hall, the architecture and design centre has a permanent exhibition spanning 1000 years of Swedish architecture and an archive of 2.5 million documents, photographs, plans, drawings and models. Temporary exhibitions also cover international names and work. The museum organises occasional themed architectural tours of Stockholm; check the website or ask at the information desk.

Östasiatiska Museet MUSEUM

(Museum of Far Eastern Antiquities; Map p392; www.ostasiatiska.se; Tyghusplan; adult/child Skr80/free; ⊙11am-8pm Tue, to 5pm Wed-Sun; 🚌65) This long, narrow building displays Asian decorative arts, including one of the world's finest collections of Chinese stoneware and porcelain from the Sing, Ming and Qing dynasties. The museum also houses the largest and oldest Asian library in Scandinavia, from which several notable specimens are displayed. The often refreshing temporary exhibitions cover a wide range of themes, with past shows including a look at Japanese *anime* characters and Chinese video art.

Södermalm

Once-working-class 'Söder' – the southern island – is Stockholm's coolest neighbourhood, jammed with up-and-coming boutiques and galleries, hip cafes and bars and a museum of city history. 'SoFo' (the area south of Folkungagatan) is the trendiest district.

Fotografiska GALLERY

(Map p392; www.fotografiska.eu; Stadsgårdshamnen 22; adult/child Skr120/90; ⊙9am-9pm Sun-Wed, to 11pm Thu-Sat; Ⓜ Slussen) A chic, upmarket photography museum, Fotografiska is a must for shutterbugs. Its temporary exhibitions are huge, interestingly chosen and well presented; examples have included a Robert Mapplethorpe retrospective and portraits by indie filmmaker Gus Van Sant. Recently the museum showed an enormous collection of black-and-white photos by Sebastião Salgado. There's also a strong permanent collection of photos from international and Swedish photographers. Follow signs from the Slussen tunnelbana stop to reach the museum.

Stockholms Stadsmuseum MUSEUM

(City Museum; Map p392; www.stadsmuseum.stockholm.se; Ryssgården, Slussen; adult/child Skr100/free; ⊙11am-5pm Tue-Sun, to 8pm Thu; 📶👪; Ⓜ Slussen) Evocative exhibits cover Stockholm's development from fortified port to modern metropolis via plague, fire and good old-fashioned scandal. The museum is housed in a late-17th-century palace designed by Nicodemus Tessin the Elder. Temporary exhibitions are fresh and eclectic, focused on the city's ever-changing shape and spirit. Admission gets you a card good for one year here and at Medeltidsmuseet (p387). Note that the museum is is closed for renovations until late 2016.

Ladugårdsgärdet

The vast parkland of Ladugårdsgärdet is part of the 27-sq-km **Ekoparken** (www.ekoparken.org), the world's first national park within a city. An impressive 14km long, its combo of forest and open fields stretches far into the capital's northern suburbs. Reached by bus 69 from Centralstationen or Sergels Torg, it boasts several fine museums and one of Stockholm's loftiest views.

Etnografiska Museet MUSEUM
(Museum of Ethnography; www.etnografiska.se; Djurgårdsbrunnsvägen 34; adult/child Skr80/free; ⏲11am-5pm Tue-Sun, to 8pm Wed; 👪; 🚌69 Museiparken) The Museum of Ethnography stages evocative displays on various aspects of non-European cultures, including dynamic temporary exhibitions and frequent live performances. Recent examples include a display about the cultural treasures of Afghanistan, Russian holiday traditions, and 'real-life' voodoo. If there's a dance or musical performance scheduled, don't miss it. The cafe is a treat, with great music, imported sweets and beverages, and authentic global dishes.

Magasin 3 GALLERY
(☎08-54 56 80 40; www.magasin3.com; Elevator 4, Magasin 3 Bldg, Frihamnen; adult/child Skr40/free; ⏲11am-7pm Thu, to 5pm Fri-Sun, closed Jun-Aug & Christmas holidays; 🚌1, 76, Ⓜ Ropsten) Though it's a bit out of the way and hours are limited, Magasin 3 is one of Stockholm's best contemporary art galleries and well worth seeking out. Located in a dockside warehouse northwest of Kaknästornet, its six to eight annual shows often feature specially commissioned, site-specific work from the likes of Pipilotti Rist or American provocateur Paul McCarthy.

Kaknästornet VIEWPOINT
(www.kaknastornet.se; Mörka Kroken 28-30; adult/child Skr55/20; ⏲9am-10pm Mon-Sat, to 7pm Sun; 🚌69 Kaknästornet) A handy landmark for navigating this part of town, the 155m-tall Kaknästornet is the automatic operations centre for radio and TV broadcasting in Sweden. Opened in 1967, it's among the tallest buildings in Scandinavia. There's a small visitor centre (mainly a gift shop) on the ground floor and an elevator up to the observation deck, restaurant and cafe near the top, from where there are stellar views of the city and archipelago.

LOFTY VIEWS IN STOCKHOLM

➡ There's a great panoramic view over Stockholm from the top of Katarinahissen lift, dating from the 1930s. Although the lift is currently closed, you can climb 38m up zigzagging wooden stairs to the balcony. At the top is one of the city's best restaurants, **Eriks Gondolen** (Map p392; ☎08-641 70 90; www.eriks.se; Stadsgården 6; mains Skr215-340; ⏲11.30am-11pm Mon, 11.30am-1am Tue-Fri, 4pm-1am Sat; Ⓜ Slussen).

➡ Take a ride up Fritt Fall at Gröna Lund Tivoli (p394) to cast your eye over the waterways…then scream as you plummet all the way down.

➡ Stadshuset (p390) – its tower offers stellar views and a great thigh workout.

Activities

Summer sees many head for the coast and the islands of the archipelago (with good swimming spots). Winter also sees some outdoor activity, including ice-skating on a rink set up in Kungsträdgården.

Stockholm City Bikes BICYCLE RENTAL
(www.citybikes.se; 3-day/season card Skr165/300) City Bikes has around 90 self-service bicycle-hire stands across the city. Bikes can be borrowed for three-hour stretches and returned at any City Bikes stand. You'll need to purchase a bike card online or from the tourist office, a Storstockholms Lokaltrafik (SL) centre, or most hotels (see the website for a list). Rechargeable season cards are valid April to October.

Strandbryggan YACHTING
(Map p388; ☎070-564 93 58, 08-660 37 14; www.strandbryggan.se; Strandvägskajen 27, Strandvägen; ⏲10am-dusk Apr-Sep; 🚋7) Across the water from **Sjöcaféet** (Map p388; ☎08-660 57 57; www.sjocafeet.se; Djurgårdsvägen 2; bicycles per hr/day Skr80/275, canoes Skr150/400, kayaks Skr125/400; ⏲9am-9pm Apr-Sep; 🚋7), floating restaurant-bar Strandbryggan offers yachts for charter for up to 12 passengers. Prices start at around Skr2000 per hour (minimum 2½ hours), and you can add catering from the restaurant.

Tours

You're spoiled for choice when it comes to tours of the capital. You can take to the water with **Strömma Kanalbolaget** (Map p392; ☎08-12 00 40 00; www.stromma.se; Strandvägen 8) for the excellent 'Under the Bridges of Stockholm' (Skr225, two hours) and trips to the archipelago, walk the streets in search of ghostly sightings and spooky tales with **Stockholm Ghost Walk** (Map p392; ☎07-614-666 00; www.stockholmghostwalk.com; Tyska Brinken 13; adult/child Skr200/100; ⏲6.45pm), follow in the footsteps of Blomqvist and Salander from *The Girl With the Dragon*

Tattoo with **Millennium Tour** (www.stadsmuseum.stockholm.se; per person Skr130; ⏲11.30am Sat) or soar above the city's spires and waterways in a hot-air balloon with **Far & Flyg** (☎08-645 77 00; www.farochflyg.se; per person Skr2345; ⏲flights late May–mid-Sep).

Festivals & Events

Smaka På Stockholm FOOD
(www.smakapastockholm.se) This five-day celebration of the Stockholm area's food scene is held in late May or early June. The program includes gourmet food stalls (including representatives from several archipelago restaurants) and entertainment on Kungsträdgården.

Stockholm Pride GAY & LESBIAN
(www.stockholmpride.org/en/) In late July or early August Stockholm goes pink with a week of parties and cultural events plus a pride parade.

Stockholm Jazz Festival JAZZ
(www.stockholmjazz.com) One of Europe's premier jazz festivals is held in October, headquartered at Fasching (p403).

Stockholm International Film Festival FILM
(www.stockholmfilmfestival.se) Held in November, this is a major celebration of local and international cinema whose guest speakers include top actors and directors.

Sleeping

Whether you choose youth hostels, B&Bs, boutique digs or big-name chains, you can expect high-quality (but generally expensive) accommodation in Stockholm. However, major hotel chains are invariably cheaper booked online and in advance, and most hotels offer discounted rates on weekends and in summer (mid-June to August), sometimes up to 50% off the listed price.

A number of services, including **Guestroom B&B** (☎070-206 71 69; www.gastrummet.com/eng/) and **Bed & Breakfast Agency** (☎070-739 05 15; www.bba.nu), can arrange apartment or B&B accommodation from around Skr400 per person per night, usually with a two-night minimum stay.

Stockholm's **Svenska Turistföreningen** (STF) hostels are affiliated with Hostelling International (HI), and a membership card yields a Skr50 discount. At **SVIF** (Sveriges vandrarhem i förening) hostels and independent hostels, no membership cards are required. Many have options for single, double or family rooms. Generally, you'll pay extra to use the hostel's linen and towels; bring your own to save Skr50 to Skr80 per night. Book in advance in summer.

Gamla Stan

2kronor Hostel Old Town HOSTEL €
(Map p392; ☎08-22 92 30; www.2kronor.se; Skeppsbron 40; dm/s/d Skr220/495/595; ⏲check-in 3-6pm; Ⓜ Gamla Stan, Slussen) This small, quiet, family-run hostel has a fantastic location and a friendly vibe. Rooms are on the basement level, slightly cavelike but pretty and well kept (and there are windows). Shared bathrooms are down the hall. Breakfast isn't available, but there's a guest kitchen and dining area by the reception upstairs. Dorms (six- and eight-bed rooms with bunks) are mixed.

Lord Nelson Hotel HOTEL €€€
(Map p392; ☎08-50 64 01 20; www.lordnelsonhotel.se; Västerlånggatan 22; s/d from Skr890/1890; Ⓜ Gamla Stan) Yo-ho-ho, me scurvy barnacles! It's a tight squeeze, but this pink-painted, glass-fronted building feels like a creaky old ship loaded with character. At just 5m wide, the 17th-century building is Sweden's narrowest hotel. Its nautical theme extends to brass and mahogany furnishings, antique sea-captain trappings and a model ship in each of the small rooms.

Central Stockholm

★ **STF Fridhemsplan** HOSTEL €
(Map p388; ☎08-653 88 00; www.fridhemsplan.se; St Eriksgatan 20; s/d Skr550/650, hotel s/d from Skr750/850; Ⓜ Fridhemsplan) This modern, inviting hostel near the Fridhemsplan tunnelbana stop on Kungsholmen has nice, modern, hotel-style rooms with shared bathrooms (the hotel-standard rooms are en suite). Some rooms have windows with city views. There's a cool lounge in the lobby to hang out in, and a vast and stylish breakfast room (with a better-than-average breakfast buffet, Skr70 for hostel guests).

★ **City Backpackers** HOSTEL €
(Map p392; ☎08-20 69 20; www.citybackpackers.org; Upplandsgatan 2a; dm Skr190-280, s/d/tr Skr500/650/870; Ⓜ T-Centralen) The closest hostel to Centralstationen has clean rooms, friendly staff, free bike hire and excellent facilities, including sauna, laundry and kitchen (with a free stash of pasta).

En suite private rooms are also available. Bonus for female guests: there are four- and eight-bed female-only dorms if you prefer, and you can borrow a hairdryer from reception.

★Hotel Hellsten HOTEL €€
(Map p388; ☎08-661 86 00; www.hellsten.se; Luntmakargatan 68; s/d from Skr1090/1490; ; MRådmansgatan) Hip Hellsten is owned by anthropologist Per Hellsten, whose touch is evident in the rooms and common areas, which are furnished and decorated with objects from his travels and life, including Congan tribal masks and his grandmother's chandelier. Rooms are supremely comfortable and individually styled, with themes ranging from rustic Swedish to Indian exotica; some even feature original tile stoves.

Birger Jarl Hotel HOTEL €€
(Map p388; ☎08-674 18 00; www.birgerjarl.se; Tulegatan 8; cabin r Skr690, s/d from Skr890, studios from Skr1890; ; 43 Tegnérgatan, MRådmansgatan) One of Stockholm's original design hotels, the Birger Jarl has recently had a full renovation and update of the lobby, plus about 30 new rooms and suites. Standard rooms are all done up in ultra-modern Swedish style, but each of the superior rooms is put together by a different Swedish designer, and they're well worth the price upgrade.

Nordic 'C' Hotel HOTEL €€
(Map p392; ☎08-50 56 30 00; www.nordicchotel.com; Vasaplan 4; s/d from Skr784/824; ; MT-Centralen) A fantastic deal if you time it right and book ahead, this sister hotel to the slightly more upmarket Nordic Light has smallish but sleek rooms, great service and a cool lobby lounge area with an impressive 9000L aquarium in the foyer. The cheapest rooms are windowless and very tiny but efficiently designed and totally comfortable.

Berns Hotel HOTEL €€€
(Map p392; ☎08-56 63 22 00; www.berns.se; Näckströmsgatan 8; s/d from Skr1490/1790; ; MKungsträdgården, 7 Kungsträdgården) The rooms at Berns come equipped with entertainment systems and styles ranging from 19th-century classical to contemporary sleek. Some are more impressive than others (the balcony rooms get our vote); room 431 was once a dressing room used by Marlene Dietrich and Ella Fitzgerald. The cheapest rooms don't include breakfast, but it can be added for Skr195.

Skeppsholmen

★Vandrarhem af Chapman & Skeppsholmen HOSTEL €
(Map p392; ☎08-463 22 66; www.stfchapman.com; Flaggmansvägen 8; dm/r from Skr260/590; ; 65 Skeppsholmen) The *af Chapman* is a storied vessel that has done plenty of travelling of its own. It's anchored in a superb location, swaying gently off Skeppsholmen. Bunks are in dorms below deck. Apart from showers and toilets, all facilities are on dry land in the Skeppsholmen hostel, including a good kitchen, a laid-back common room and a TV lounge.

Södermalm

Långholmen Hotell & Vandrarhem HOSTEL, HOTEL €
(☎08-720 85 00; www.langholmen.com; Långholmsmuren 20; hostel dm from Skr260, cell s/d Skr620/750, hotel r from Skr1075; ; 4, 40, 77, 94 Högalidsgatan, MHornstull) Guests at this hotel-hostel, in a former prison on Långholmen island, sleep on bunks in a cell, with either shared or private baths. (The friendly, efficient staff promise they will not lock you in.) The kitchen and laundry facilities are good, the restaurant serves meals all day, and Långholmen's popular summertime bathing spots are a towel flick away.

★Hotel Anno 1647 HOTEL €€
(Map p392; ☎08-442 16 80; www.anno1647.se; Mariagränd 3; budget s/d from Skr570/740, standard s/d from Skr890/990; ; MSlussen) Just off buzzing Götgatan, this historical hotel in two beautiful buildings has labyrinthine hallways, gorgeous wooden floors and spiral staircases, affable staff, and budget as well as standard rooms – both are recommended. The latter have antique rococo wallpaper, all modern amenities and the odd chandelier. The location and reduced high-season rates make this a fantastic deal.

Zinkensdamm Hotell & Vandrarhem HOTEL, HOSTEL €€
(Map p388; ☎08-616 81 00; www.zinkensdamm.com; Zinkens väg 20; dm Skr320, d without/with bathroom Skr700/950, hotel r from Skr1495; ; MZinkensdamm) In a cheery yellow building next to the adorable Tantolunden park, the Zinkensdamm STF is fun, attractive and well equipped – complete with a sleek guest kitchen and personal lockers in each room – and caters for families

with kids as well as pub-going backpackers. It can be crowded and noisy, but that's the trade-off for an upbeat vibe.

Bed & Breakfast 4 Trappor B&B €€
(Map p388; ☎08-642 31 04; www.4trappor.se; Gotlandsgatan 78; s/d Skr925/1250; P 📶; 🚌3, 53, 76, 96 Gotlandsgatan, M Medborgarplatsen) This great little apartment has a cosy, polished-floorboard bedroom (maximum two guests), a modern bathroom and a kitchen (with its own espresso machine). Note that there's no lift; you'll be climbing four flights of stairs. There's a two-night minimum stay, and the place is a huge hit, so book months ahead. Breakfast is served in the owners' apartment next door.

★ **Rival Hotel** HOTEL €€€
(Map p392; ☎08-54 57 89 00; www.rival.se; Mariatorget 3; s/d from Skr1895/2495; ; M Mariatorget) Owned by ABBA's Benny Andersson and overlooking leafy Mariatorget, this ravishing design hotel is a chic retro gem, complete with vintage 1940s movie theatre and art deco cocktail bar. The super-comfy rooms feature posters from great Swedish films and a teddy bear to make you feel at home. All rooms have good-size bathrooms and flat-screen TVs with Blu-ray players.

Ladugårdsgärdet

STF Vandrarhem Gärdet HOSTEL €
(☎08-463 22 99; www.svenskaturistforeningen.se; Sandhamnsgatan 59; s/d from Skr495/760; P; 🚌1 Östhammarsgatan, M Gärdet) Surrounded by forested trails and open fields in quiet Gärdet, this efficient hostel works more like a no-frills hotel. Rooms are tiny but well planned, and all have their own bathroom and TV. Towels, sheets and cleaning are included in the price; breakfast can be had for an extra Skr80, and there's a good guest kitchen.

Eating

Stockholm, with more than half a dozen Michelin-starred restaurants, has certainly earned its reputation as a foodie destination. For top-notch seafood with human scenery to match, head toward Östermalmstorg. Candlelit cafes dripping in history and charm line the crooked little streets of Gamla Stan. For solid everyman cuisine, head to Odenplan, and for inventive vegetarian fare try Södermalm's bohemian joints or Luntmakargatan and surrounding streets. Swedish food is not the only thing on offer; as in any cosmopolitan city worth its gourmet salt, you can easily find good Japanese, Thai, Italian and even Ethiopian gastronomic delights to tempt your tastebuds.

Gamla Stan

Grillska Husets Konditori BAKERY, CAFE €
(Map p392; ☎08-684 233 64; www.stadsmissionen.se/matochkonferens/grillska-huset/; Stortorget 3; sandwiches Skr25-75; ⏲9am-6pm Mon-Fri, 10am-6pm Sat & Sun; M Gamla Stan) The cafe and bakery run by Stockholms Stadsmission, the chain of secondhand charity shops, is a top-notch spot for a sweet treat or a sandwich, especially when warm weather allows for seating at the outdoor tables in Gamla Stan's main square. There's a bakery shop attached, selling goodies and rustic breads to take away.

Chokladkoppen CAFE €
(Map p392; www.chokladkoppen.se; Stortorget 18; cakes Skr40-80; ⏲9am-11pm summer, shorter hours rest of year; M Gamla Stan) Arguably Stockholm's best-loved cafe, hole-in-the-wall Chokladkoppen sits slap bang on the old town's enchanting main square. It's a gay-friendly spot, with cute waiters, a look-at-me summer terrace and yummy grub such as broccoli-and-blue-cheese pie and scrumptious cakes.

Hermitage VEGETARIAN €€
(Map p392; Stora Nygatan 11; lunch/dinner & weekends Skr110/120; ⏲11am-8pm Mon-Sat, noon-4pm Sun; ; M Gamla Stan) Herbivores love Hermitage for its simple, tasty, vegetarian buffet, easily one of the best restaurant bargains in Gamla Stan. Salad, homemade bread, tea and coffee are included in the price. Pro tip: don't miss the drawers of hot food hiding under the main buffet tabletop.

★ **Kryp In** SWEDISH €€€
(Map p392; ☎08-20 88 41; www.restaurangkryp-in.nu; Prästgatan 17; starters Skr135-195, mains Skr195-285; ⏲5-11pm Mon-Fri, 12.30-4pm & 5-11pm Sat & Sun; M Gamla Stan) Small but perfectly formed, this spot wows diners with creative takes on traditional Swedish dishes. Expect the likes of salmon carpaccio or smoked reindeer salad followed by a gorgeous, spirit-warming saffron aioli shellfish stew. The service is seamless and the atmosphere classy without being stuffy. The brief weekend lunch menu (Skr119 to Skr158) is a bargain. Book ahead.

Central Stockholm

Vurma CAFE €
(Map p388; www.vurma.se; Polhemsgatan 15-17; salads Skr108, sandwiches Skr60-80; 7am-7pm Mon-Fri, 8am-7pm Sat & Sun; ; M Rådhuset) Squeeze in among the locals at this friendly cafe-bakery, a reliably affordable place to get a healthy and substantial meal in an unfussy setting. The scrumptious sandwiches and salads are inspired, with ingredients including halloumi, falafel, cured salmon, avocado and greens over quinoa or pasta. The homemade bread that comes with your order is divine.

La Neta MEXICAN €
(Map p392; laneta.se; Barnhusgatan 2; 1/5 tacos Skr22/95; 11am-9pm Mon-Fri, noon-9pm Sat, noon-4pm Sun; M Hötorget) Competition for the title of 'Stockholm's Best Taqueria' is not fierce, but La Neta wins hands down. Fast-food pseudo-Mexican eateries are all over town, but this is the real deal, with home-made corn tortillas, nuanced flavours, and zero frills in the dining area (unless you count the bowls of delicious salsa). It's great value for money.

Hötorgshallen FOOD HALL €
(Map p392; Hötorget; 10am-6pm Mon-Thu, to 6.30pm Fri, to 6pm Sat, closed Sun; M Hötorget) Located below Filmstaden cinema, Hötorgshallen is Stockholm at its multicultural best, with stalls selling everything from fresh Nordic seafood to fluffy hummus and fragrant teas. Ready-to-eat options include Lebanese spinach parcels, kebabs and vegetarian burgers. For the ultimate feed, squeeze into galley-themed dining nook **Kajsas Fiskrestaurang** for a huge bowl of soulful *fisksoppa* (fish stew) with aioli (Skr95).

Lao Wai VEGETARIAN €€
(Map p388; 08-673 78 00; www.laowai.se; Luntmakargatan 74; dagens lunch Skr100, dinner mains Skr195-215; 11am-2pm Mon-Fri, 5.30-9pm Tue-Sat; ; M Rådmansgatan) Tiny, herbivorous Lao Wai does sinfully good things to tofu and vegetables, hence the faithful regulars. Everything here is vegan and gluten-free. A different lunch special is served each weekday; the dinner menu is more expansive, offering virtuous treats including Sichuan-style smoked tofu with shitake, chillies, garlic shoots, snow peas and black beans.

★ **Grands Verandan** SWEDISH €€€
(Grand Hôtel Stockholm; Map p392; 08-679 35 86; www.grandhotel.se; Södra Blasieholmshamnen 8; smörgåsbord Skr445, mains Skr185-275; noon-3pm & 6-10pm Mon-Fri, 1-4pm & 6-10pm Sat & Sun; M Kungsträdgården) Head here, inside the Grand Hôtel, for the famous smörgåsbord – especially during the Christmas holidays, when it becomes even more elaborate (reservations recommended). Arrive early for a window seat and tuck into both hot and cold Swedish staples, including gravad lax with almond potatoes, herring, meatballs and lingonberry jam. It's like a belt-busting crash course in classic Nordic flavours.

Mathias Dahlgren INTERNATIONAL €€€
(Map p392; 08-679 35 84; www.mathiasdahlgren.com; Södra Blasieholmenshamnen 6, Grand Hôtel Stockholm; Matbaren mains Skr145-295, Matsalen 5-/8-course menu Skr1500/1900; Matbaren noon-2pm Mon-Fri & 6pm-midnight Mon-Sat, Matsalen 7pm-midnight Tue-Sat, both closed mid-Jul–Aug; M Kungsträndsgården) Celebrity chef Mathias Dahlgren has settled in at the Grand Hôtel with a two-sided restaurant: there's the formal, elegant Matsalen ('the Dining Room'), which has been awarded two Michelin stars, and the bistro-style Matbaren ('the Food Bar'), boasting its own Michelin star. Both focus on seasonal ingredients, so menus change daily. Reservations are crucial.

Pontus! SWEDISH €€€
(Map p392; 08-54 52 73 00; Brunnsgatan 1; lunch Skr185, dinner mains Skr155-525; 11.30am-2pm & 6-10pm Mon-Fri, 6-10pm Sat, closed Sun; M Östermalmstorg) This Östermalm favourite has reconfigured its space, thankfully keeping the beloved library wallpaper and huge round booths in the main dining room. Indulge in set menus (Skr425 to Skr795) or a la carte mains featuring French-influenced treatments of seasonal ingredients – a chanterelle brioche with sorrel and onion, perhaps, or smoked *matjes* herring with new potatoes and egg-yolk confit.

Södermalm

Chutney VEGETARIAN €
(Map p388; 08-640 30 10; www.chutney.se; Katarina Bangata 19; dagens lunch Skr80; 11am-10pm Mon-Sat, noon-9pm Sun; ; M Medborgarplatsen) Sitting among a string of three inviting cafes along this block, Chutney is one of Stockholm's many well-established vegetarian restaurants, offering excellent value and great atmosphere. The daily lunch special is usually a deliciously spiced,

curry-esque heap of veggies over rice, and includes salad, bread, coffee and a second helping if you can manage it.

Nystekt Strömming SWEDISH €

(Map p392; Södermalmstorg; combo plates Skr35-75; 11am-8pm Mon-Fri, to 6pm Sat & Sun, closing times vary; M Slussen) For a quick snack of freshly fried herring, seek out this humble cart outside the tunnelbana station at Slussen. Large or small combo plates come with big slabs of the fish and a selection of sides and condiments, from mashed potato and red onion to salads and hardbread; more portable wraps and the delicious herring burger go for Skr55.

Pelikan SWEDISH €€

(Map p388; 08-556 090 90; www.pelikan.se; Blekingegatan 40; mains Skr172-285; 5pm-midnight or 1am; M Skanstull) Lofty ceilings, wood panelling and no-nonsense waiters in waistcoats set the scene for classic *husmanskost* at this century-old beer hall. The herring options are particularly good (try the 'SOS' plate, an assortment of pickled herring, Skr124 to Skr138) and there's usually a vegetarian special to boot. There's a hefty list of aquavit, too.

Koh Phangan THAI €€

(Map p388; 08-642 50 40; www.kohphangan.se; Skånegatan 57; starters Skr85-95, mains Skr155-285; 4pm-1am Mon-Fri, noon-1am Sat & Sun; M Medborgarplatsen) Best at night, this outrageously kitsch Thai restaurant has to be seen to be believed. Tuck into your *kao pat gai* (chicken fried rice) in a real *tuk-tuk* to the accompanying racket of crickets and tropical thunder, or kick back with beers in a bamboo hut. DJs occasionally hit the decks and it's best to book ahead.

Östermalm

Östermalms Saluhall MARKET €

(Map p392; www.ostermalmshallen.se/en/; Östermalmstorg; mains from Skr85; 9.30am-6pm Mon-Thu, to 7pm Fri, to 4pm Sat; M Östermalmstorg) Stockholm's historic gourmet food market feeds all the senses with fresh fish, seafood and meat, fruit, vegetables and hard-to-find cheeses, as well as cafes for a quick lunch or snack. The 1885 building, a Stockholm landmark, is showing its age and will be closed for renovations from 2015 to 2017, with a temporary market set up in the square.

Djurgården

★ Rosendals Trädgårdskafe CAFE €€

(08-545 812 70; www.rosendalstradgard.se; Rosendalsterrassen 12; mains Skr85-145; 11am-5pm Mon-Fri, to 6pm Sat & Sun May-Sep, closed Mon Feb-Apr & Oct-Dec; ; 44, 69, 76 Djurgårdsbron, 7) Set among the greenhouses of a pretty botanical garden, Rosendals is an idyllic spot for heavenly pastries and coffee or a meal and a glass of organic wine. Lunch includes a brief menu of eco-friendly soups, sandwiches (such as ground-lamb burger with chanterelles) and gorgeous salads. Much of the produce is biodynamic and grown on site.

Wärdshuset Ulla Winbladh SWEDISH €€€

(Map p388; 08-534 89 701; www.ullawinbladh.se; Rosendalsvägen 8; starters Skr125-265, mains Skr155-295; 11.30am-10pm Mon, 11.30am-11pm Tue-Fri, 12.30-11pm Sat, 12.30-10pm Sun; Djurgårdsfärjan, 7) Named after one of Carl Michael Bellman's lovers, this villa was built as a steam bakery for the Stockholm World's Fair (1897) and now serves fine food in intimate rooms and a blissful garden setting. Sup on skilfully prepared upscale versions of traditional Scandi favourites, mostly built around fish and potatoes – try the herring plate with homemade crispbread.

Drinking & Nightlife

From concrete-and-bare-bulb industrial spaces to raucous vintage beer halls and bricked-in underground vaults, there's a bar for every taste in this town. Good neighbourhood hang-outs *(kvarterskrog)* abound, but generally, the shiny-miniskirt crowd hangs out in Östermalm, while the hipsters and arty types slink around Södermalm – any of the bars along Skånegatan are a good bet.

Pet Sounds Bar BAR

(Map p388; www.petsoundsbar.se; Skånegatan 80; beer Skr72, cocktails Skr118; M Medborgarplatsen) A SoFo (south of Folkungagatan) favourite, this jamming bar pulls in music journos, indie culture vultures and the odd goth rocker. While the restaurant serves decent Italian-French grub, the real fun happens in the basement. Head down for a mixed bag of live bands, release parties and DJ sets. Hit happy hour (2pm to 6pm) for drink specials.

Akkurat BAR

(Map p392; 08-644 00 15; www.akkurat.se; Hornsgatan 18; beers Skr59-95, half/full order mussels Skr155/215; 11am-1am Mon-Fri, 3pm-1am

Sat, 6pm-1am Sun; Ⓜ Slussen) Valhalla for beer fiends, Akkurat boasts a huge selection of Belgian ales as well as a good range of Swedish-made microbrews, including Nynäshamn's Ångbryggeri. It's one of only two places in Sweden to be recognised by a Cask Marque for its real ale. Extras include a vast wall of whisky, and mussels on the menu.

Marie Laveau BAR

(Map p392; www.marielaveau.se; Hornsgatan 66; ⊙11am-3am; Ⓜ Mariatorget) In an old sausage factory, this kicking Söder playpen draws a boho-chic crowd. The designer-grunge bar (think chequered floor and tiled columns) serves killer cocktails, while the sweaty basement hosts club nights on the weekend. Its known for its monthly 'Bangers & Mash' Britpop night – check online for dates.

Kvarnen BAR

(Map p388; ☎08-643 03 80; www.kvarnen.com; Tjärhovsgatan 4; ⊙11am-1am Mon-Tue, 11am-3am Wed-Fri, 5pm-3am Sat, 5pm-1am Sun; Ⓜ Medborgarplatsen) An old-school Hammarby football fan hangout, Kvarnen is one of the best bars in Söder. The gorgeous beer hall dates from 1907 and seeps tradition; if you're not the clubbing type, get here early for a nice pint and a meal (mains Skr139 to Skr195). As the night progresses, the nightclub vibe takes over. Queues are fairly constant but justifiable.

Vampire Lounge BAR

(Map p388; www.vampirelounge.se; Östgötagatan 41; ⊙5pm-1am Mon-Fri, 7pm-1am Sat; Ⓜ Medborgarplatsen) The name says it all: this dark basement bar is bloodsucker-themed all the way through. There are perspex 'windows' in the floor showing buried caches of anti-vamp supplies such as holy water, crosses and garlic – just in case. Locals recommend the ice-cream cocktails. The lounge shares an entrance with **Östgöta Källaren** (Map p388; ☎08-643 22 40; Östgötagatan 41; mains Skr155-225; ⊙5pm-1am Mon-Fri, 3pm-1am Sat, 5pm-1am Sun; Ⓜ Medborgarplatsen) restaurant.

Absolut Icebar BAR

(Map p392; ☎08-50 56 35 20; www.icebarstockholm.se; Vasaplan 4, Nordic 'C' Hotel; prebooked online/drop in Skr185/195; ⊙11.15am-midnight Sun-Thu, to 1am Fri & Sat) It's touristy. Downright gimmicky! And you're utterly intrigued, admit it: a bar built entirely out of ice, where you drink from glasses carved of ice on tables made of ice. The admission price gets you warm booties, mittens, a parka and one drink. Refill drinks cost Skr95.

Café Opera CLUB

(Map p392; ☎08-676 58 07; www.cafeopera.se; Karl XII's Torg; admission from Skr160; ⊙10pm-3am Wed-Sun; Ⓜ Kungsträdsgården) Rock stars need a suitably excessive place to schmooze,

GAY & LESBIAN STOCKHOLM VENUES

Sweden's legendary open-mindedness makes homophobic attitudes rare, and party-goers of all persuasions are welcome in any Stockholm bar or club. For club listings and events, pick up a free copy of street-press magazine *QX*, found at many clubs, shops and cafes around town. Its website (www.qx.se) is more frequently updated and has listings in English. *QX* also produces a free, handy *Gay Stockholm Map*, available at the tourist office.

Good bars and clubs include the following:

Lady Patricia (Map p392; ☎08-743 05 70; www.patricia.st; Söder Mälarstrand, Kajplats 19; ⊙5pm-midnight Wed & Thu, to 5am Fri-Sun) Half-price seafood, nonstop *schlager* (campy, popular music, often synonymous with Eurovision Song Contest) music and decks packed with sexy Swedes and drag queens make this former royal yacht a gay Sunday night ritual (though you can now visit five nights a week). Head to the upper dance floor where lager-happy punters sing along to Swedish Eurovision entries with a bemusing lack of irony.

Side Track (Map p392; ☎08-641 16 88; www.sidetrack.nu; Wollmar Yxkullsgatan 7; ⊙6pm-1am Wed-Sat; Ⓜ Mariatorget) Claiming the title of Stockholm's oldest gay bar, this establishment in Södermalm is a particular hit with down-to-earth guys, with a low-key, pub-like ambience and decent bar food (fish and chips, curry, quesadillas).

Torget (Map p392; www.torgetbaren.com; Mälartorget 13; ⊙5pm-midnight, to 1am Sun; Ⓜ Gamla Stan) For camp and Campari, it's hard to beat this sparkling gay bar – think rotating chandeliers, mock-baroque touches and different themed evenings, from live burlesque to handbag-swinging *schlager*. The crowd is a good source of info on upcoming underground parties, so grab yourself a champers and chat away.

booze and groove, one with glittering chandeliers, ceiling frescoes and a jet-set vibe. This bar-club combo fits the bill, but it's also welcoming enough to make regular folk *feel* like rock stars. If you only have time to hit one primo club during your visit, this is a good choice.

Sturecompagniet CLUB
(Map p392; ☎08-54 50 76 00; www.sturecompagniet.se; Stureplan 4; admission Skr120; ⏰10pm-3am Thu-Sat; Ⓜ Östermalmstorg) Swedish soap stars, flowing champagne and look-at-me attitude set a decadent scene at this glitzy, mirrored and becurtained hallway. Dress to impress and flaunt your wares to commercial house. Big-name guest DJs come through frequently.

Spy Bar CLUB
(Map p392; Birger Jarlsgatan 20; admission from Skr160; ⏰10pm-5am Wed-Sat; Ⓜ Östermalmstorg) No longer the super-hip star of the scene it once was, the Spy Bar (aka 'the Puke' because *spy* means vomit in Swedish) is still a landmark and fun to check out if you're making the Östermalm rounds. It covers three levels in a turn-of-the-century flat (spot the tile stoves).

☆ Entertainment

For an up-to-date calendar see www.visitstockholm.com. Another good source if you can navigate a little Swedish is the Friday 'På Stan' section of Dagens Nyheter newspaper (www.dn.se). For most concerts and events, the tourist office can sell you tickets or tell you where to get them.

Live Music

Debaser LIVE MUSIC
(Map p388; ☎08-694 79 00; www.debaser.se; Medborgarplatsen 8; ⏰7pm-1am Sun-Thu, 8pm-3am Fri & Sat; Ⓜ Medborgarplatsen) This mini-empire of entertainment has its flagship rock venue (Debaser Medis) on Medborgarplatsen. Emerging or bigger-name acts play most nights, while the killer club nights span anything from rock-steady to punk and electronica. (There are also a couple of restaurants around town and a location in Malmö.)

Fasching JAZZ
(Map p392; ☎08-53 48 29 60; www.fasching.se; Kungsgatan 63; ⏰6pm-1am Mon-Thu, to 4am Fri & Sat, 5pm-1am Sun; Ⓜ T-Centralen) Music club Fasching is the pick of Stockholm's jazz clubs, with live music most nights. DJs take over with either Afrobeat, Latin, neo-soul or R&B on Friday night and retro-soul, disco and rare grooves on Saturday.

Concerts, Theatre & Dance

Konserthuset CLASSICAL MUSIC
(Map p392; ☎08-50 66 77 88; www.konserthuset.se; Hötorget; tickets Skr80-325; Ⓜ Hötorget) Head to this pretty blue building for classical concerts and other musical marvels, including the Royal Philharmonic Orchestra.

Operan OPERA
(Map p392; ☎08-791 44 00; www.operan.se; Gustav Adolfs Torg, Operahuset; tickets Skr100-750; Ⓜ Kungsträndsgården) The Royal Opera is the place to go for thunderous tenors, sparkling sopranos and classical ballet. It has some bargain tickets in seats with poor views, and occasional lunchtime concerts for less than Skr200 (including light lunch).

Shopping

A design and fashion hub, Stockholm offers shoppers everything from top-name boutiques to the tiniest secondhand shops. Good local buys include edgy street wear, designer home decor and clever gadgets, and edible treats such as cloudberry jam, pickled herring and bottles of *glögg*. Södermalm's SoFo district (the streets south of Folkungagatan) is your best bet for home-grown fashion and arty gifts, while Östermalm is the place for high-end names such as Marc Jacobs and Gucci.

Svensk Slöjd ARTS, HANDICRAFTS
(Map p392; Nybrogatan 23; ⏰10am-6pm Mon-Fri, 11am-6pm Sat; Ⓜ Östermalmstorg) If you like the traditional Swedish wooden horses but want one that looks a little unique (or maybe you'd prefer a traditional wooden chicken instead?), check out this shop. It's crammed with quirky hand-carved knick-knacks as well as luxurious woven textiles, handmade candles, ironwork, knitted clothing, and other high-quality gifts.

Papercut BOOKS
(Map p392; ☎08-13 35 74; www.papercutshop.se; Krukmakargatan 24; ⏰11am-6.30pm Mon-Fri, 11am-5pm Sat, noon-4pm Sun, closed Sun Jul; Ⓜ Zinkensdamm) This artfully curated shop sells books, magazines and DVDs with a high-end pop-culture focus. Pick up a new Field Notes journal and a decadent film journal or a gorgeous volume devoted to one of the many elements of style.

Chokladfabriken CHOCOLATE
(Map p388; www.chokladfabriken.com; Renstiernas Gata 12; ⏲10am-6.30pm Mon-Fri, 10am-5pm Sat; Ⓜ Medborgarplatsen, Slussen) For an edible souvenir, head to this chocolate shop, where seasonal Nordic ingredients are used to make heavenly treats. In addition to chocolate boxes and hot-cocoa mix in gift boxes, there's a cafe for an on-the-spot fix, occasional tastings, and a stash of speciality ingredients and utensils for home baking.

PUB DEPARTMENT STORE
(Map p392; Drottninggatan 72-6; ⏲10am-7pm Mon-Fri, 10am-6pm Sat, 11am-5pm Sun; Ⓜ T-Hötorget) Historic department store PUB is best known as the former workplace of Greta Garbo, and advertisements still work that angle pretty strongly. It's a major fashion and lifestyle hub, carrying fresh Nordic labels such as Stray Boys, House of Dagmar and Baum & Pferdgarten. Refuel at the slinky cafe-bar.

ℹ Information

EMERGENCY

24-Hour Medical Advice (☎08-32 01 00)

24-Hour Police Stations Kungsholmen (☎08-401 00 00; Kungsholmsgatan 37); Södermalm (☎08-401 03 00; Torkel Knutssonsgatan 20).

Emergency (☎112) Toll-free access to the fire service, police and ambulance.

INTERNET ACCESS

Most hostels and many hotels have a computer with internet access for guests, and nearly all also offer wi-fi access in rooms (sometimes for a fee). Wi-fi is also widely available in coffee shops and bars and in Centralstationen. Those without their own wi-fi enabled device have more-limited options, but the ubiquitous Sidewalk Express terminals are handy.

> **ℹ STOCKHOLM CARD**
>
> The **Stockholm Card** (visitstockholm.com; adult 24/48/72/120hr Skr450/625/750/950, accompanying child Skr215/255/285/315) is available from tourist offices, Storstockholms Lokaltrafik (SL) information centres, some museums, and some hotels and hostels, or online at www.visitstockholm.com. It gives you entry to 80 museums and attractions, travel on SL's public transport network, sightseeing by boat, some walking tours, and various other discounts.

MEDIA

Dagens Nyheter (www.dn.se) Daily paper with a great culture section and a weekend event listing ('På Stan'). The website (in Swedish) is a good place to look for bar and restaurant news.

Nöjesguiden (www.nojesguiden.se) Entertainment and pop-culture news and event listings.

MEDICAL SERVICES

Apoteket CW Scheele (www.apoteket.se; Klarabergsgatan 64; Ⓜ T-Centralen) A 24-hour pharmacy located close to T-Centralen.

CityAkuten (☎020-15 01 50; www.cityakuten.se; Apelbergsgatan 48; ⏲8am-6pm Mon-Thu, to 5pm Fri, 10am-3pm Sat) Emergency health and dental care.

Södersjukhuset (☎08-616 10 00; www.soderjukhuset.se; Ringvägen 52) The most central hospital.

MONEY

ATMs are plentiful, with a few at Centralstationen and airports; expect queues on Friday and Saturday nights.

The exchange company Forex has more than a dozen branches in the capital and charges Skr15 per travellers cheque.

Forex-Vasagatan (Vasagatan 16; ⏲5.30am-10pm Sun-Fri, to 6pm Sat) Near the tourist office and Centralstationen. There's also a branch in Terminal 2 at Arlanda airport.

POST

You can buy stamps and send letters at a number of city locations, including newsagencies and supermarkets – keep an eye out for the Swedish postal symbol (yellow on a blue background). There's a convenient outlet next to the Hemköp supermarket in the basement of central department store **Åhléns** (Map p392; Klarabergsgatan 50; Ⓜ T-Centralen).

TELEPHONES

Smartphones are ubiquitous in Stockholm; coin-operated public telephones are virtually nonexistent. The few remaining payphones are operated with phonecards purchased from Pressbyrån newsagents. Ask for a *telefon kort* for Skr50 or Skr120, which equate to roughly 50 minutes and 120 minutes of local talk time, respectively. (Be sure to specify that it's a payphone card). For mobile phones, check with your service provider to ensure your network is compatible with Sweden's. In many cases you can buy a local SIM card to use in your own phone. Barring that, buy a cheap mobile phone you can load with prepaid minutes and use as needed.

TOURIST INFORMATION

Stockholm Visitors Center (Map p392; ☎08-508 28 508; www.visitstockholm.com; Kulturhuset, Sergels Torg 3; ⏲9am-7pm Mon-Fri, to 6pm winter, 9am-4pm Sat, 10am-4pm Sun; Ⓜ T-Centralen) The main visitors centre occupies a space inside Kulturhuset on Sergels Torg.

Getting There & Away

AIR

Stockholm Arlanda (☎10-109 10 00; www.swedavia.se/arlanda) Stockholm's main airport, 45km north of the city centre, is reached from central Stockholm by bus and express train. Terminals two and five are for international flights; three and four are domestic; there is no terminal one.

Bromma Stockholm Airport (☎010-109 00 00; www.swedavia.se) Located 8km west of Stockholm, used for some domestic flights.

Stockholm Skavsta Airport (☎0155-28 04 00; www.skavsta.se) 100km south of Stockholm, near Nyköping, mostly used by low-cost carriers such as Ryanair.

BOAT

Both **Silja Line** (☎22 21 40; www.tallinksilja.com; Silja & Tallink Customer Service Office, Cityterminalen) and **Viking Line** (Map p388; ☎08-452 40 00; www.vikingline.fi) run ferries to Turku and Helsinki. **Tallink** (☎08-666 60 01; www.tallink.ee) ferries head to Tallinn (Estonia) and Riga (Latvia).

BUS

Most long-distance buses arrive at and depart from **Cityterminalen** (Map p392; www.cityterminalen.com; ⏲7am-6pm), which is connected to Centralstationen. The main counter sells tickets for several bus companies, including Flygbussarna (airport coaches).

Swebus Express (Map p392; www.swebus-express.com; Cityterminalen) destinations include the following:

Göteborg Skr389, 6½-7½ hours, six daily

Kalmar Skr369, 6½ hours, three daily

Mora Skr209, 4½ hours, one daily

Norrköping Skr169, 2¼ hours, 11 daily

Oslo Skr329, eight hours, three daily

Uppsala Skr59, 1¼ hours, nine daily

Västerås Skr99, 1½ hours, seven daily

Örebro Skr159, 2¾ hours, seven daily

Ybuss (Map p392; www.ybuss.se; Cityterminalen) runs services to the north of Sweden, including the following:

Gävle Skr235, 2¼ hours, six daily

Sundsvall Skr300, 5¼ hours, six daily

Umeå Skr445, nine to 9¾ hours, three daily

CAR & MOTORCYCLE

The E4 motorway passes through the west of the city, on its way from Helsingborg to Haparanda. The E20 motorway from Stockholm to Göteborg via Örebro follows the E4 as far as Södertälje. The E18 from Kapellskär to Oslo runs from east to west and passes north of central Stockholm.

LEFT LUGGAGE

There are three sizes of left-luggage boxes (per 24 hours Skr40 to Skr120) at Centralstationen. Similar facilities exist at the neighbouring bus station and at major ferry terminals.

TRAIN

Stockholm is the hub for national train services run by **Sveriges Järnväg** (SJ; ☎0771-75 75 75; www.sj.se). **Centralstationen** (Ⓜ T-Centralen) is the central train station.

Destinations include the following:

Copenhagen Skr831, 5¼ hours, six daily

Göteborg Skr388, 3¼ to 5¼ hours, twice hourly

Kiruna Skr649, 16¼ hours, one daily

Luleå Skr606, 13¼ hours, one daily

Malmö Skr535, 4½ to 5½ hours, twice hourly

Oslo Skr588, six hours, two daily

Åre via Östersund Skr649, 9½ hours, one daily

> **STOCKHOLM À LA CARTE**
>
> **Destination Stockholm** (☎08-663 00 80; www.destination-stockholm.com) offers discount hotel-and-sightseeing packages that can be booked online. Its Stockholm à la Carte package is available weekends year-round and throughout the summer.

Getting Around

TO/FROM THE AIRPORTS

Arlanda Express (www.arlandaexpress.com; one-way Skr260) The Arlanda Express train from Centralstationen takes 20 minutes to reach Stockholm Arlanda Airport; trains run every 10 to 15 minutes from about 5am to 12.30am. In peak summer season (mid-June to August), two adults can travel together for Skr280.

Airport Cab (☎08-25 25 25; www.airportcab.se) Runs from Stockholm to Arlanda for a flat fee of Skr365 to Skr390, and in the opposite direction for Skr475.

Flygbussarna (www.flygbussarna.se) The Flygbussarna service between Stockholm Arlanda, Bromma, Skavsta and Cityterminalen is the cheapest way to reach the airports. Buses for Arlanda leave every 10 to 15 minutes (one way/return Skr99/198, 40 minutes); for Bromma every 20 to 30 minutes, less frequently on weekends (Skr79/150, 20 minutes) and for Skavsta every 30 minutes (Skr149/259, one hour 20 minutes).

WORTH A TRIP

DROTTNINGHOLM

Home to the royal family for part of the year, the Renaissance-inspired **Drottningholm Slott** (08-402 62 80; www.kungahuset.se; adult/child Skr120/free, combined ticket incl Chinese Pavillion Skr180/free; 10am-4.30pm May-Aug, 11am-3.30pm rest of year, closed mid-Dec–Jan; P; M Brommaplan, then 301-323 Drottningholm, Stadshuskajen summer only) was designed by architectural great Nicodemus Tessin the Elder and begun in 1662, about the same time as Versailles. You can roam on your own, but it's worth taking a one-hour guided tour (Skr10; in English at 10am, noon, 2pm and 4pm June to August, noon and 2pm other months). Guides are entertaining and provide insight into the cultural milieu that influenced some of the decorations.

The unique **Drottningholms Slottsteater** (Court Theatre & Museum; www.dtm.se; entry by tour adult/child Skr100/free; tours hourly noon-3.30pm Fri-Sun Apr & Oct, 11am-4.30pm May-Aug, noon-3.30pm Sep) was completed in 1766 on the instructions of Queen Lovisa Ulrika. Remarkably untouched from the time of Gustav III's death (1792) until 1922, it's now the oldest theatre in the world still in its original state. The guided tour takes you into other rooms in the building, where highlights include hand-painted 18th-century wallpaper and an Italianate room (salon de déjeuner) with fake three-dimensional wall effects.

At the far end of the gardens is the 18th-century **Kina Slott** (Chinese Pavilion; adult/child Skr100/free, combined ticket incl royal palace Skr180/free; 11am-4.30pm), a lavishly decorated 'Chinese pavilion' – summer palace – that was built as a gift to Queen Lovisa Ulrika. Admission includes guided tours.

If you have time you could cycle out here, otherwise take the tunnelbana to Brommaplan and change to any bus numbered between 301 and 323. For a more scenic and leisurely approach, Strömma Kanalbolaget (p396) will take you to the palace by boat (about an hour one way, Skr145; round trip Skr195). Frequent services depart from Stadshusbron (Stockholm) daily between May and mid-September, with less frequent departures in September and October.

BICYCLE

Stockholm boasts a wide network of bicycle lanes, clearly marked with traffic signs. City Bikes (p396) has 90 self-service hire stands across the city.

Bicycles can be carried free on SL local trains as foldable 'hand luggage' only. They're not allowed in Centralstationen or on the tunnelbana.

BOAT

Djurgårdsfärjan city ferry services connect Gröna Lund Tivoli on Djurgården Nybroplan (summer only) and Slussen (year round) as frequently as every 10 minutes in summer and less frequently at other times. A single trip costs Skr36; it's free with an SL transport pass.

CAR & MOTORCYCLE

Driving in central Stockholm is not recommended. Skinny one-way streets, congested bridges and limited parking all present problems; note that Djurgårdsvägen is closed near Skansen at night, on summer weekends and some holidays. Don't attempt driving through the narrow streets of Gamla Stan.

Parking is a hassle, but there are *P-hus* (parking stations) throughout the city; they charge up to Skr100 per hour, though the fixed evening rate is usually lower.

PUBLIC TRANSPORT

Storstockholms Lokaltrafik (SL; 08-600 10 00; www.sl.se; Centralstationen, Sergels Torg; single trip Skr25-50, unlimited 24hr/72hr/7-day pass Skr115/230/300, students & seniors half-price) runs all tunnelbana (T or T-bana) metro trains, local trains and buses within the entire Stockholm county. There is an SL information office in the basement concourse at **Centralstationen** (6.30am-11.15pm Mon-Sat, from 7am Sun) and another near the **Sergels Torg entrance** (7am-6.30pm Mon-Fri, 10am-5pm Sat & Sun), which issues timetables and sells the Stockholm Card (p404) and SL Tourist Card (24/72 hours Skr115/230), both of which cover all travel on public transport and are the best choices for short-term stays.

SL also offers various other options for buses and tunnelbana travel, including individual tickets for one/two/three zones Skr36/54/72 and a pre-paid strip of 16 tickets (Skr200). International rail passes (eg Scanrail, Interrail) aren't valid on SL trains.

Bus

Ask any tourist office for the handy inner-city route map Innerstadsbussar. It's also available online (www.sl.se). Inner-city buses radiate from Sergels Torg, Odenplan, Fridhemsplan (on Kungsholmen) and Slussen. Bus 47 runs from Sergels Torg to Djurgården, and bus 69 runs from Centralstationen and Sergels Torg to the Ladugårdsgärdet museums and Kaknästornet. Useful buses for hostellers include bus 65, which goes from Centralstationen to Skeppsholmen, and bus 43 (Regeringsgatan to Södermalm).

Metro (Tunnelbana/T-Bana)

The most useful mode of transport in Stockholm is the tunnelbana, run by SL. Its lines converge on T-Centralen, connected by an underground walkway to Centralstationen. There are three main tunnelbana lines with branches.

Train

Local pendeltåg trains are useful for connections to Nynäshamn (for ferries to Gotland) and to Märsta (for buses to Sigtuna and the short hop to Stockholm Arlanda airport).

Tram

The historic No 7 tram connects Norrmalmstorg and Skansen, passing most attractions on Djurgården. The Stockholm Card, the SL Tourist Card and regular SL tickets are valid on board.

TAXI

Taxis are readily available but expensive, so check for a meter or arrange the fare first. The flag fall is Skr45, then about Skr10 to Skr13 per kilometre. Reputable firms include **Taxi Stockholm** (☎15 00 00; www.taxistockholm.se), **Taxi 020** (☎020-20 20 20; www.taxi020.se) and **Taxi Kurir** (☎0771-86 00 00; www.taxikurir.se).

AROUND STOCKHOLM

Most locals will tell you the one thing not to miss about Stockholm is leaving it – whether for a journey into the lovely rock-strewn archipelago or an excursion into the surrounding countryside. Within easy reach of the capital are idyllic islands, Viking gravesites, cute fishing villages and sturdy palaces.

Vaxholm

☎08 / POP 4857

Vaxholm is the capital of and gateway to the archipelago. It's a charming village, though its proximity to Stockholm (just 35km northeast, a quick bus ride) means it can be crowded in summer. Still, on a sunny spring day, its crooked streets and storybook houses are irresistible. It also has a thriving restaurant scene and a wildly popular Christmas market. If you plan an overnight stay, the tourist office keeps a list of private B&Bs.

Bus 670 from Stockholm's Tekniska Högskolan tunnelbana station runs regularly to the town. **Waxholmsbolaget** (Map p392; ☎08-679 58 30; www.waxholmsbolaget.se; Strömkajen; single trip Skr45-130, 5-day pass Skr440, 30-day pass regular/senior Skr770/470; ⏲8am-6pm; Ⓜ Kungsträdgården) boats sail frequently between Vaxholm and Strömkajen in Stockholm from 8am to 7.15pm (50 to 70 minutes, Skr75 one way). Strömma Kanalbolaget (p396) sails between Strandvägen and Vaxholm at noon and 3pm daily from April to December (three hours, Skr250 round trip).

WORTH A TRIP

BIRKA – PAST VIKING GLORY

On the island Björkö in Mälaren lake stand the remains of the Viking trading centre of **Birka** (www.stromma.se; return Skr360; ⏲May-Sep), founded around AD 760 and now a Unesco World Heritage Site. It is here that archaeologists have excavated the largest Viking cemetery in Scandinavia, consisting of more than 3000 graves, with most remains cremated, but some buried in coffins, which suggests the advent of Christianity. The harbour and fortress have also been excavated. Birka was abandoned in the late 10th century – either because it was eclipsed by the up-and-coming commercial settlement of Sigtuna or else because the water level in the lake had dropped, cutting the island off from the Baltic Sea. However, you can still see copies of the most magnificent objects from its heyday at the **Birka Museum** (☎08-560 514 45; ⏲11am-3pm Mon-Fri, 10am-4pm Sat & Sun), where a scale model of the village puts things into perspective.

Daily cruises to Birka run from early May to early September; the round trip on Strömma Kanalbolaget's (p396) *Victoria* from Stadshusbron, Stockholm, is a full day's outing. The cruise price includes a visit to the museum and a guided tour in English of the settlement's burial mounds and fortifications. Boats leave between 9am and 10am from early May to mid-September.

Stockholm Archipelago

South of the city, the land crumbles into myriad fragments. Depending on whom you ask, the archipelago has between 14,000 and 100,000 islands (the usual consensus is 24,000). Some are bare rocks sticking out of the water, others are covered in forest or dotted with the summer cottages of the well-do-to. The archipelago is the favourite time-off destination for Stockholm's locals, and everyone has their private spot to sunbathe and unwind.

Around Stockholm

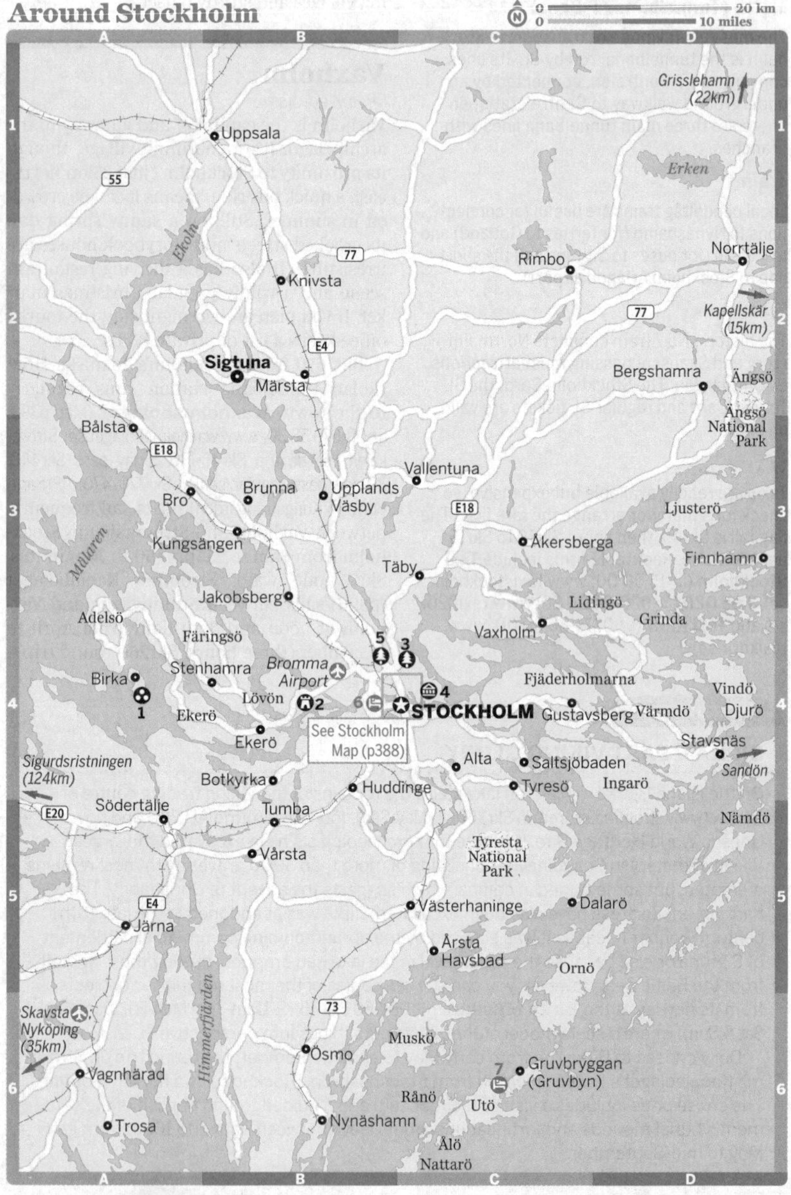

Waxholmsbolaget (p407), the main provider for island traffic, divides the archipelago into three sections: middle (Vaxholm, Ingmarsö, Stora Kalholmen, Finnhamn, Möja and Sandhamn), north (Ljusterö to Arholma), and south (Nämdö, Ornö and Utö). The Waxholmsbolaget office in Stockholm has maps and timetables for all routes and helpful staff to answer questions. There are endless possible itineraries for exploring the archipelago, including the four highlights listed here.

Sandhamn village on Sandön is popular with sailors and day trippers. One of the archipelago's best restaurants, **Seglarrestaurangen** (☎08-57 45 04 21; www.sandhamn.com; mains Skr225-295; ⏰year-round), inside the Seglarhotellet, serves high-end Swedish food, from exceptional seared Lofoten cod to coffee-roasted venison.

The 900m-long **Finnhamn**, northeast of Stockholm, combines lush woods and meadows with sheltered coves, rocky cliffs and visiting eagle owls. While it's a popular summertime spot, there are enough quiet corners to indulge your inner hermit. **STF Vandrarhem Utsikten** (☎08-54 24 62 12; www.finnhamn.se; dm/s/d Skr320/520/640; ⏰year-round; @📶) is a large wooden villa, with a killer view, tiny rooms and cheerful staff who go above and beyond. Advance booking is essential.

A cycling paradise in the southern archipelago, **Utö** has it all: sublime sandy beaches, lush fairy-tale forests, sleepy farms and abundant birdlife. **Utö Värdshus** (☎08-50 42 03 00; www.utovardshus.se; Gruvbryggan; hostel s/d Skr425/850, 2-person chalets incl breakfast per person from Skr995, hotel s/d Skr1750/2300) is the only hotel on the island, with a sterling gourmet restaurant and a very pretty STF hostel.

Fjäderholmarna, is the easiest of the 'feather islands' at the entrance to the archipelago to get to, with boats heading there every hour from Nybroplan (30 minutes). There are a couple of craft shops, restaurants and a great fish smokery selling smoked prawns here, though the main activity is sunbathing on the rocks. The last boats leave the islands at around midnight, making them a perfect spot to soak up the long daylight hours.

Around Stockholm

Sights

1	Birka	A4
2	Drottningholm Slott	B4
	Drottningholms Slottsteater & Teatermuseum	(see 2)
3	Ekoparken	C4
4	Etnografiska Museet	C4
5	Hagaparken	B4
	Kaknästornet	(see 4)
	Kina Slott	(see 2)
	Magasin 3	(see 4)

Activities, Courses & Tours

	Far & Flyg	(see 6)

Sleeping

6	Långholmen Hotell & Vandrarhem	B4
	STF Vandrarhem Gärdet	(see 4)
7	Utö Värdshus	C6

Eating

	Rosendals Trädgårdskafe	(see 4)

Sigtuna

☎08 / POP 8444

About 40km northwest of Stockholm, Sigtuna is one of the cutest, most historically relevant villages in the area. Founded around AD 980, it's the oldest surviving town in Sweden, and the main drag, Storagatan, is very likely Sweden's oldest main street.

Ten rune stones still stand in various places around Sigtuna, and 150 more dot the surrounding landscape. The mid-13th-century church **Mariakyrkan**, Sigtuna's most arresting sight, contains restored medieval paintings. The friendly **Sigtuna Museum** (☎08-5912 6670; www.sigtunamuseum.se; Storagatan 55; adult/child Skr20/free; ⏰noon-4pm Tue-Sun) displays finds from excavations of the area, including ample amounts of coins and jewellery.

Sigtuna is easily doable as a day trip from Stockholm. Out of the numerous cafes to choose from, don't miss the delightful **Tant Brun Kaffestuga** (☎08-59 25 09 34; Laurentii gränd; coffees & cakes from Skr35; ⏰10am-7pm), a 17th-century cafe with a worryingly saggy roof and pretty courtyard just off Storagatan.

To get here, take a local train (three hourly, 35 minutes) to Märsta, from where there are frequent buses to Sigtuna (570 or 575).

SVEALAND

This area, the birthplace of Sweden, offers evidence of the region's long history, including rune stones so plentiful you might stumble over them. Pre-Viking burial mounds in Gamla Uppsala light the imaginations of myth-builders and history buffs. There's also the trip into the bowels of the earth at the old mine in Falun, which accidentally provided the red paint for all those little cottages dotting the landscape. And in Mora, the definitive Swedish king's path towards the crown is still retraced today, by thousands of skiers each year in the Vasaloppet.

Uppsala

☎018 / POP 140,454

Drenched in history but never stifled by the past, Uppsala has the party vibe of a university town to balance out its large number of important buildings and general atmosphere of weighty cultural significance (the university is Scandinavia's oldest). It's a terrific combination, and one that makes the town both fun and functional, not to mention very rewarding for the interested traveller.

On the edge of the city is Gamla (Old) Uppsala, the original site of the town, which was once a flourishing 6th-century religious centre.

Sights

Gamla Uppsala ARCHAEOLOGICAL SITE

(www.arkeologigamlauppsala.se; 24hr; P; bus 2) FREE One of Sweden's largest and most important burial sites, Gamla Uppsala (4km north of Uppsala) contains 300 mounds from the 6th to 12th centuries. The earliest are also the three most impressive. Legend has it they contain the pre-Viking kings Aun, Egil and Adils, who appear in *Beowulf* and Icelandic historian Snorre Sturlason's *Ynglingsaga*. More recent evidence suggests the occupant of Östhögen (East Mound) was a woman, probably a female regent in her 20s or 30s.

Uppsala Slott CASTLE

(www.uppsalaslott.se; admission by guided tour only, adult/child Skr90/15; tours in English 1pm & 3pm Tue-Sun late Jun-Sep) Uppsala Slott was built by Gustav Vasa in the 1550s. It contains the state hall where kings were enthroned and Queen Kristina abdicated. It was also the scene of a brutal murder in 1567, when King Erik XIV and his guards killed Nils Sture and his two sons, Erik and Svante, after accusing them of high treason. The castle burned down in 1702 but was rebuilt and took on its present form in 1757.

Museum Gustavianum MUSEUM

(www.gustavianum.uu.se; Akademigatan 3; adult/child Skr50/40; 10am-4pm Tue-Sun Jun-Aug, from 11am rest of year) A wondercabinet of

WORTH A TRIP

SIGURDSRISTNINGEN

The vivid, 3m-long Viking Age rock carving **Sigurdsristningen** (http://www.eskilstuna.se/sv/Uppleva-och-gora/Sundbyholm/Sigurdsristningen; 24hr; bus 225) illustrates the story of Sigurd the Dragon Slayer, a hero whose adventures are described in *Beowulf* and the Icelandic sagas. The story inspired Wagner's *Ring Cycle*, and *The Hobbit* and *The Lord of the Rings* also borrow from it. Runes in the dragon's body, unrelated to the legend, explain that a woman named Sigrid raised a nearby bridge (the abutments can still be seen) in memory of her husband Holmger.

Carved into the bedrock around AD 1000, the carving shows Sigurd roasting the heart of the dragon Fafnir over a fire. Sigurd's stepfather Regin persuaded him to kill Fafnir for the dragon's golden treasure. Sigurd touches the heart to see if it's cooked, then sucks his finger, and voila – he tastes the dragon's blood and suddenly understands the language of birds. They warn him that Regin is plotting to kill him and keep the treasure, so Sigurd attacks first, chopping off his stepfather's head; the unfortunate fellow is shown in the left corner of the carving, among his scattered tools. Also depicted is Sigurd's horse Grani, a gift from Odin, tied to the tree where the birds perch.

A walking path along the river starts from the parking lot; ask at the tourist office about raft trips. The carving is situated near Sundbyholms Slott and Mälaren lake, 12km northeast of Eskilstuna.

wondercabinets, the Museum Gustavianum rewards appreciation of the weird and well organised. The shelves in the pleasantly musty building hold case after case of obsolete tools and preserved oddities: stuffed birds, astrolabes, alligator mummies, exotic stones and dried sea creatures. A highlight is the fascinating 17th-century **Augsburg Art Cabinet** and its thousand ingenious trinkets. Don't miss Olof Rudbeck's vertiginous **anatomical theatre**, where executed criminals were dissected. Admission includes a tour in English at 1pm Saturday and Sunday.

Linnémuseet MUSEUM
(www.linnaeus.se; Svartbäcksgatan 27; adult/under 16yr Skr60/free; ⌚11am-5pm Tue-Sun May-Sep) No matter how many times the brochures refer to the 'sexual system' of classification, the excitement to be had at Linnémuseet is primarily intellectual; still, botanists and vegetarians will enjoy a visit to the pioneering scientist's home and workshop, where he lived with his wife and five kids (1743–78). The adjoining **Linnéträdgården** (☎018-471 25 76; adult/child Skr60/free, admission with Linnémuseet ticket free; ⌚shop & exhibit 11am-5pm Tue-Sun May-Sep, park 11am-8pm Tue-Sun May-Sep) is a reconstructed version of Sweden's oldest botanical garden – Linné's playground – with more than 1300 species arranged according to the system he invented.

Domkyrka CHURCH
(Cathedral; www.uppsaladomkyrka.se; Domkyrkoplan; ⌚8am-6pm) FREE The Gothic Domkyrka dominates the city, just as some of those buried here, including St Erik, Gustav Vasa and the scientist Carl von Linné, dominated their country. Tours are available in English at 11am and 2pm Monday to Saturday, 4pm Sunday, in July and August.

Treasury MUSEUM
(Domkyrkan; ⌚10am-5pm Mon-Sat, 12.30-5pm Sun May-Sep) FREE Gustav's funerary sword, silver crown and shiny golden buttons are kept in the treasury in the Domkyrka's north tower, along with a great display of medieval textiles. Particularly fine are the clothes worn by the three noblemen who were murdered in the castle: they're the only example of 16th-century Swedish high fashion still in existence.

Carolina Rediviva LIBRARY
(www.ub.uu.se; Dag Hammarskjölds väg 1; ⌚exhibition hall 9am-8pm Mon-Fri, 10am-5pm Sat) FREE Rare-book and map fiends should go directly to Carolina Rediviva, the university library. In a small, dark gallery, glass cases hold precious maps and manuscripts, including illuminated Ethiopian texts and the first book ever printed in Sweden. The star is the surviving half of the *Codex Argentus* (AD 520), aka the Silver Bible, written in gold and silver ink on purple vellum; aside from being pretty, it's linguistically important as the most complete existing document written in the Gothic language.

UPPSALA KORTET

This handy little **discount card** (Skr149) gives 24 hours' free or discounted admission to many of the town's museums and attractions, plus free local bus travel and parking and free travel to Arlanda airport. There are also discounts at participating hotels, restaurants and shops. The card is valid from June to August, and can be bought from the tourist office. It covers one adult and up to two children.

Sleeping

STF Vandrarhem Sunnersta Herrgård HOSTEL €
(☎018-32 42 20; www.sunnerstaherrgard.se; Sunnerstavägen 24; dm Skr245, s/d incl breakfast from Skr650/770; ⌚Jan–mid-Dec; P@; 20) In a historic manor house about 6km south of the city centre, this hostel has a parklike setting at water's edge and a good restaurant on site. You can rent bikes (Skr50/200 per day/week) or borrow a boat, and there's free wi-fi. Hotel-standard rooms include breakfast; hostel guests can add it for Skr85.

Uppsala Vandrarhem & Hotell HOSTEL €
(☎018-24 20 08; www.uppsalavandrarhem.se; Kvarntorget 3; dm Skr190, s/d hostel Skr445/550, s/d hotel Skr750/895; P; 3 Kvarntorget) This hostel, attached to Hotell Kvarntorget, is away from the action but walkable from Uppsala Central Station. Spacious rooms, some with double beds, face an enclosed courtyard that works as a breakfast room; a newly designed dividing wall has greatly reduced the resulting noise. There's a guest kitchen and laundry. Bedding is included; towels (Skr30) and breakfast (Skr69) are extra.

Uppsala City Hostel HOSTEL €
(☎018-10 00 08; uppsalacityhostel.se/en/; Sankt Persgatan 16; dm/s/d from Skr220/400/500;

(reception 8am-11pm;) The no-nonsense Uppsala City Hostel is recommended for its sheer convenience – you really can't stay anywhere more central for these prices. Rooms, all named after famous Uppsala landmarks, are small but decent (although dorms suffer from traffic and level-crossing noise). There's wi-fi access in parts of the hostel. Breakfast costs Skr50, and a kitchen is available.

Best Western Hotel Svava HOTEL €€
(018-13 00 30; www.bestwestern.se; Bangårdsgatan 24; s/d Skr1350/1450;) Named after one of Odin's Valkyrie maidens, Hotel Svava, right opposite the train station, is a very comfortable top-end business-style hotel with summer and weekend discounts that make it a smashing deal.

Eating

Casual dining options can be found inside **Saluhallen** (Sankt Eriks Torg; 10am-6pm Mon-Thu, to 7pm Fri, to 4pm Sat, restaurants 11am-4pm Sun), an indoor market between the cathedral and the river. Find groceries at the central **Hemköp supermarket** (Stora Torget; 8am-10pm).

Ofvandahls CAFE €
(Sysslomansgatan 3-5; cakes Skr35, snacks Skr55-75; 8am-6pm Mon-Fri, 9am-5pm Sat, 11am-5pm Sun) Something of an Uppsala institution, this classy but sweet *konditori* (bakery-cafe) dates back to the 19th century and is a cut above your average coffee-and-bun shop. It's been endorsed by no less a personage than the king, and radiates old-world charm – somehow those faded red-striped awnings just get cuter every year.

Magnussons Krog SWEDISH €€
(www.magnussonskrog.se; Drottninggatan 1; dagens lunch Skr109, mains Skr175-225; 11am-late) Try any of the specials on the chalkboard at this sleek corner hangout. Late-night bar snacks (Skr109 to Skr129) help soak up delicious cocktails, which you can enjoy at outdoor tables on a busy riverside corner in fair weather. Great for people-watching.

Hambergs Fisk SEAFOOD €€
(www.hambergs.se; Fyristorg 8; mains Skr125-295; 11.30am-10pm Tue-Sat) Let the aromas of dill and seafood tempt you into this excellent fish restaurant, in a tiny storefront facing the river. Self-caterers should check out the adjoining fresh fish counter.

Amazing Thai THAI €€
(Bredgränd 14; buffet Skr159; lunch & dinner) This small, family-friendly spot inside a shopping centre is popular for its good-value buffet (both lunch and dinner) and welcoming atmosphere. The evening menu features a good selection of fragrant stir-fries, noodle dishes and curries.

Information

Tourist Office (018-727 48 00; www.destinationuppsala.se; Kungsgatan 59; 10am-6pm Mon-Fri, to 3pm Sat, plus 11am-3pm Sun Jul & Aug) Relocated to a prime spot directly in front of the train station, the tourist office has helpful advice, maps and brochures for the whole county.

Getting There & Away

Flygbuss (bus 801) runs to Arlanda airport (adult/child Skr125/75, 45 minutes, every 30 minutes) from Uppsala train station.

Swebus Express (0200-21 82 18; www.swebus.se) has services to Stockholm (Skr59, one hour, at least hourly), Västerås (via Stockholm, Skr139, 3½ hours, six daily), Örebro (via Stockholm, from Skr179, 4½ hours, four to seven daily) and Falun (change in Stockholm and Borlange, Skr259, nine hours, daily).

SJ (www.sj.se) trains run to/from Stockholm (Skr70 to Skr110, 35 to 55 minutes one way), Gävle (from Skr143, 50 minutes, at least seven daily), Östersund (Skr560, five hours, two daily) and Mora (Skr213, 3¼ hours, two daily).

Getting Around

Upplands Lokaltrafik (0771-14 14 14; www.ul.se) runs traffic within the city and county. City buses leave from Stora Torget and the surrounding streets. Tickets for unlimited travel for 90 minutes cost from Skr25.

Örebro

019 / POP 107,038

A substantial, culturally rich city, Örebro buzzes around its central feature: the huge and romantic castle surrounded by a moat filled with water lilies. The city originally sprang up as a product of the textile industry, but it's now decidedly a university town – students on bicycles fill the streets, and other relaxed folk gather on restaurant patios and in parks. It's an ideal spot to indulge in standard holiday activities, like nursing a beer in a terrace cafe or shopping unhurriedly along a cobbled street.

Sights

Slottet CASTLE
(☎019-21 21 21; www.orebroslott.se; tours adult/child Skr60/30; ⊙daily Jun-Aug, 1pm Sat & Sun rest of year, history exhibition 10am-5pm daily May-Aug) The magnificent Slottet is now the county governor's headquarters. It was originally built in the late 13th century, but most of what you see today is from 300 years later. The outside is far more dramatic than the interior. To explore you'll need to take a tour; those in English start at noon, 2pm and 4pm daily in summer, and at 1pm weekends otherwise. Book through the tourist office. The northwestern tower holds a small **history exhibition**.

Länsmuseum MUSEUM
(County Museum; www.orebrolansmuseum.se; Engelbrektsgatan 3; ⊙9am-6pm Tue & Thu, noon-9pm Wed, noon-4pm Fri-Sun) FREE The Länsmuseum has strong and topical temporary exhibits – for example, a collection of protest posters from the '60s, or a consideration of the era's clothing and home furnishings as cultural indicators. It's also home to a permanent collection of artwork grouped by theme, and historical displays about the region (mostly in Swedish). The grounds are often dotted with sculptures or outdoor art installations.

Stadsparken PARK
(⊙11am-5pm Tue-Sun; P 🚸) Stadsparken is an idyllic and kid-friendly park once voted Sweden's most beautiful. It stretches alongside Svartån (the Black River) and merges into the **Wadköping museum village** (admission Skr25; ⊙11am-4pm or 5pm Tue-Sun, tours 1pm & 3pm Aug; 🚸). The village, named after what author Hjalmar Bergman called his hometown in his novels, is a cobblestone maze of workshops, cafes, a bakery and period buildings – including Kungsstugan (the King's Lodgings; a medieval house with 16th-century ceiling paintings) and Cajsa Warg's house (home of an 18th-century celebrity chef).

St Nikolai Kyrka CHURCH
(⊙10am-5pm) The 13th-century St Nikolai Kyrka has some historical interest: it's where Jean Baptiste Bernadotte (Napoleon's marshal) was chosen to take the Swedish throne.

Just opposite, on Drottninggatan, is the **Rådhus** (town hall); if you're around at the right time, stop to hear the chimes (12.05pm and 6.05pm year-round, plus 9pm June to September), when sculptures representing the city's past, present and future come wheeling out of a high arched window.

Sleeping & Eating

Gustavsvik Camping CAMPGROUND, CABINS €€
(☎019-19 69 50; www.gustavsvik.se; Sommarrovägen; sites/cabins from Skr325/890; ⊙year-round; P 🏊 🚸; 🚌11) This camping facility is 2km south of the city centre, and it's attached to a family-oriented water park that can be a bit of a madhouse in summer. There are various swimming and soaking pools, minigolf, a cafe, a gym, a restaurant-pub and bike rental (Skr60 per day). Cabins have full kitchens, TV and wireless internet. Book ahead in summer.

Behrn Hotell HOTEL €€€
(☎019-12 00 95; www.behrnhotell.se; Stortorget 12; s/d Skr1375/1855; P ❄ @ 📶) Excellently situated on the main square, the Behrn Hotell goes the extra mile with individually decorated rooms – ranging from strictly business to farmhouse or edgy modern Scandinavian. Do it right and get a room with a balcony or a suite with old wooden beams, chandeliers and a Jacuzzi. There's also a spa, and a restaurant serving dinner Tuesday to Friday.

Hälls Konditori Stallbacken CAFE €
(www.hallsconditori.se; Engelbrektsgatan 12; pastries Skr20-45, lunch specials Skr79, brunch buffet Skr85; ⊙7.30am-6pm Mon-Fri, 10am-4pm Sat; 🚸) One of two locations of this bakery-cafe (the other's in Järntorget), Hälls is a classic old-style *konditori* and a favourite hangout for locals. Go for *fika* (coffee and cake) or more substantial salads, quiche and sandwiches. If the weather's nice, sit out back in the hidden courtyard area – part of Stallbacken, the tiny Old Town block.

Creperiet CAFE €
(Nikolaigatan; mains Skr59-85; ⊙11am-9pm Mon-Fri, 10am-5pm Sat & Sun; 🚸) This large underground space is extremely kid-friendly; a play area occupies about a third of the room. But it's no frumpy parental refuge; the long, low room is neatly designed, with subdued colours and well-chosen lighting. There are also tables outdoors on a terrace. The menu is mostly healthy salads and crepes filled with fresh veggies.

Information

Tourist Office (☎019-21 21 21; www.orebrotown.se; ⊙10am-5pm summer, noon-4pm Sat & Sun rest of year) The tourist office is inside the castle on the lower level.

Getting There & Away

Long-distance buses, which leave from opposite the train station, operate pretty much everywhere in southern Sweden. From here, **Swebus Express** (0771-218 218; www.swebus.se) has connections to Norrköping, Karlstad and Oslo (Norway), Mariestad and Göteborg, Västerås and Uppsala, and Eskilstuna and Stockholm.

Train connections are also good. Direct SJ trains run to/from Stockholm (Skr219, two hours) every hour with some via Västerås (Skr128, one hour), and frequently to and from Göteborg (Skr410, three hours). Other trains run to Gävle (Skr240 to Skr430, three to four hours, five daily) and Borlänge (Skr296, 2¼ hours, twice daily), where you can change for Falun and Mora.

Falun

023 / POP 37,291

An unlikely combination of industrial and adorable, Falun is home to the region's most important mine and, as a consequence, the source of the deep-red paint that renders Swedish country houses so uniformly cute. It's the main city of the Dalarna region, putting it within easy striking distance of some of Sweden's best attractions – including the home of painter Carl Larsson, a work of art in itself.

Sights & Activities

★ Falu Kopparbergsgruva MINE

(023-78 20 30; www.falugruva.se; tours adult/child Skr210/80, above-ground only Skr80/40; tours hourly 10am-5pm Jun-Aug, less frequent rest of year; P; 53, 708 Timmervägen) Falun's copper mine was the world's most important by the 17th century; called 'Sweden's treasure chest,' it drove the small country's international aspirations. Entrance to the mining complex is west of town at the top end of Gruvgatan. You can opt to take a one-hour underground tour of the mines or simply explore above-ground. For the mine tour, bring warm clothing and good shoes. In summer, tours in English happen hourly; from October to April you should book ahead.

Carl Larsson-gården HISTORIC BUILDING

(023-600 53; www.clg.se; Sundborn; tours adult/child/family Skr160/60/550; frequent tours in English 10am-5pm May-Sep, 11am Mon-Fri & 1pm Sat & Sun Jan-Apr; ; 64) Whatever you do, don't miss Carl Larsson-gården, home of artist Carl Larsson and his wife, Karin, in the picturesque village of Sundborn. After the couple's deaths, their early-20th-century home was preserved in its entirety by their children, but it's no gloomy memorial. Lilla Hyttnäs is a work of art, full of brightness, humour and love.

Tours (45 minutes) run hourly; call in advance for the times of English tours (alternatively, borrow an English handbook and follow a Swedish tour).

Dalarnas Museum MUSEUM

(www.dalarnasmuseum.se; Stigaregatan 2-4; 10am-5pm Tue-Fri, noon-5pm Sat-Mon, to 9pm Wed summer;) FREE Dalarnas Museum is a super introduction to Swedish folk art, music and costumes. It's kid-friendly, too, with the opposite of the usual 'Do not touch' signs (these say 'Be curious! Please touch!'). Selma Lagerlöf's study is preserved here, and there are ever-changing art and craft exhibitions, including a great regional collection of textiles. Don't miss the graphic-arts hall, with a display on the history of Swedish sketching and engraving techniques, or the gallery of traditional costumes from all parts of Dalarna.

Sleeping & Eating

Falu Fängelse Vandrarhem HOSTEL €

(023-79 55 75; www.falufangelse.se; Villavägen 17; dm/s/f Skr270/370/680; reception 8am-6pm; @) This hostel really feels like what it is – a former prison. Dorm beds are in cells, with heavy iron doors and thick walls, concrete floors and steel lockers for closets. The shower and toilet facilities are somewhat limited, so it's worth asking if a room with a bathroom is available.

Scandic Hotel Lugnet Falun HOTEL €€

(023-669 22 00; falun@scandic-hotels.com; Svärdsjögatan 51; s/d from Skr1100/1300; P@) This large, modern building stands out a mile with its ski-jump design. It has something of a college-dorm feel and heaps of facilities, including a restaurant, a bar and even a bowling hall in the basement. Steep summer and weekend discounts make it a smoking deal. The hotel is about 2km east of the centre off E16, close to Lugnet.

Kopparhattan Café & Restaurang CAFE €€

(Stigaregatan 2-4; lunch buffet Skr89, mains Skr142-210;) An excellent choice is this funky, arty cafe-restaurant below Dalarnas Museum. Choose from sandwiches, soup or a good vegetarian buffet for lunch; and light veggie, fish and meat evening mains. There's an outside terrace overlooking the river, and live music on Friday nights in summer.

Banken Bar & Brasserie SWEDISH €€€
(☎023-71 19 11; www.bankenfalun.se; Åsgatan 41; mains Skr185-225; ⏰11.30am-11pm Mon-Thu, 11.30am-midnight Fri, 1pm-midnight Sat) Based in a former bank, classy Banken has a splendid interior and matching service. The menu features decadent preparations of Swedish traditional meals, such as reindeer carpaccio with truffles, or saffron-scented roast salmon; there's also a simpler daily lunch special available weekdays.

Information

Tourist Office (☎023-830 50; www.visit-sodradalarna.se; Trotzgatan 10-12; ⏰10am-6pm Mon-Fri, to 4pm Sat) This tourist office has a nice gift shop and can book accommodation. Staff can help with questions about the whole region.

Getting There & Away

Falun isn't on the main train lines – change at Borlänge when coming from Stockholm or Mora. There are direct trains to and from Gävle (Skr188, 1¼ hours, every two hours) and regional buses (Skr120, two hours) equally often.

Swebus Express (☎0771-21 82 18; www.swebus.se) has buses on the Göteborg–Karlstad–Falun–Gävle route, and connections to buses on the Stockholm–Borlänge–Mora route.

Regional transport is run by **Dalatrafik** (☎0771-95 95 95; www.dalatrafik.se), which covers all corners of the county of Dalarna. Tickets cost Skr26 for trips within a zone and Skr15 extra for each new zone. Regional bus 70 goes hourly to Rättvik (Skr56, one hour) and Mora (Skr86, 1¾ hours).

Lake Siljan Region

Swedes tend to get all dewy-eyed at the mention of this picture-perfect, most intensely 'Swedish' region, complete with cute little red cottages with white window frames, rolling meadows and blue lakes. This gorgeous part of the country is an immensely popular summer destination (as testified by oodles of traffic around the lakes in peak season) and great for winter sports. **Dalarna** is well-known for its crafts, particularly those ubiquitous painted Dala horses you see everywhere, and its summer festivals; there's no better place to spend Midsummer, complete with the phallic pagan maypoles that Christianity couldn't get rid of.

Maps of **Siljansleden**, an excellent network of walking and cycling paths extending for more than 300km around Lake Siljan, are available from tourist offices for Skr20. Another way to enjoy the lake is by boat: in summer, **MS Gustaf Wasa** (☎070-542 10 25; www.wasanet.nu; tickets Skr125-150, with meal Skr300-400) runs a complex range of lunch, dinner and sightseeing cruises from the towns of Mora, Rättvik and Leksand. Ask at any tourist office or go online for a schedule.

Leksand

☎0247 / POP 15,292

Leksand's claim to fame is its Midsummer Festival, the most popular in Sweden, in which around 20,000 spectators fill the bowl-shaped green park on Midsummer Eve (a Friday between 19 and 25 June) to sing songs and watch costumed dancers circle the maypole. **Leksands Kyrka** (Kyrkallén; ⏰10am-6pm Jun–mid-Aug), with its distinctive onion dome, dates from the early 13th century, while the 19th-century **Munthe's Hildasholm** (☎0247-100 62; www.hildasholm.org; Klockaregatan 5; admission by guided tour only, adult/child Skr120/40, garden only Skr30; ⏰11am-5pm mid-Jun–mid-Aug, Sat & Sun mid-Aug–Sep) is a sumptuously decorated National Romantic–style mansion, set in beautiful gardens with stunning views over Lake Siljan. The **tourist office** (☎0248-79 72 00; info@siljan.se; Norsgatan 27E; ⏰9am-6pm Mon-Fri, 10am-4pm Sat & Sun) is on the main drag.

Tiny **Tällberg**, midway between Rättvik and Leksand, is cuteness personified, with its smattering of adorable gingerbread houses scattered like a handful of rubies along a hillside. It's predictably expensive if you want to stay the night, with eight upmarket hotels for a population of around 200.

Bus 58 between Rättvik and Leksand stops in the village regularly, and it's worth going just for the scenic landscape along the route. Tällberg is also on the train line that runs along Lika Siljan; the station is around 2km below the village.

Rättvik

☎0248 / POP 4686

Laidback Rättvik has sandy lakeside beaches in summer and ski slopes in winter. Don't miss the longest wooden pier in Sweden, the

625m **Långbryggan**. Views from surrounding hills are excellent.

By the lake northwest of the train station is the 13th-century **church**, rebuilt in 1793. Nearby, **Hembygdsgård Gammelgård** (0248-514 45; 11am-5pm mid-Jun–mid-Aug) FREE showcases a 1909 collection of buildings that were moved here during the 1920s from villages around Rättvik parish (the oldest is from the 1300s).

Inviting all sorts of bad puns about rocking out, **Dalhalla** (0455-61 97 00; www.dalhalla.se; tickets Skr600-900) is an old limestone quarry 7km north of Rättvik used as an open-air theatre and concert venue in summer; the acoustics are incredible and the setting is stunning.

The **tourist office** (0248-79 72 00; Riksvägen 40; 9am-6pm Mon-Fri, 10am-4pm Sat & Sun) is at the train station.

Sleeping & Eating

Siljansbadets Camping CAMPGROUND €
(0248-561 18; www.siljansbadet.com; sites Skr285, cabins from Skr610;) Near the train station, this shady, woodsy campground is on the lakeshore and boasts its own Blue Flag beach.

STF Vandrarhem Rättvik HOSTEL €
(0248-561 09; Centralgatan; s/d from Skr400/500; reception 8-10am & 5-6pm;) Toward the edge of town is this comfortable hostel with cosy rooms in three wooden buildings clustered around a grassy courtyard. It's a quiet place with good facilities, including a nice kitchen with a large dining/TV room in the main building, and picnic tables on the lawn for alfresco meals. Reception is at the Enåbadet campground office.

Frick's Konditori CAFE €
(www.frickskonditori.se; Stora Torget; sandwiches from Skr45) An old-fashioned bakery-cafe with a casual, neighbourhoody feel, Frick's offers sandwiches, quiches and salads but specialises in decadent cakes and pastries. It's opposite the train station and is a local gossip hang-out.

Jöns-Andersgården SWEDISH, ITALIAN €€€
(0248-130 15; www.jonsandersgarden.se; Bygatan 4; mains Skr165-255; 5-10pm late May-Aug; 74) If you can stir your stumps and make it up the hill, you'll find this rather sweet restaurant tucked at the top, attached to the hotel of the same name. Dishes such as lemony chicken with gremolata potatoes, shellfish cannelloni, or herb-and-parmesan roasted lamb over gnocchi bring a taste of Italy to this very Swedish establishment.

A HORSEY HISTORY

The Dalecarlian or Dala horse originated as a simple wooden toy for children but grew into an art form, and its characteristic sturdy form, traditionally painted bright red but with a harness in green, yellow, white and blue, came to symbolise Dalarna. Why a horse? Because horses were the most valuable possession of farm workers, and by the 19th century these wooden creations were used as a form of barter.

A good place to see how today's Dala horses are made, and pick up some of your own, is **Nils Olsson Hemslöjd** (0250-372 00; www.nohemslojd.se; 8am-4pm Mon-Fri, 10am-4pm Sat) at Nusnäs, 10km southeast of Mora (bus 108, three per day Monday to Friday).

Getting There & Away

Buses depart from outside the train station. Dalatrafik's bus 70 runs regularly between Falun, Rättvik and Mora. A couple of direct intercity trains per day from Stockholm (Skr396, 3½ hours) stop at Rättvik. Local trains run often between Rättvik and Mora (Skr56, 25 minutes).

Mora

0250 / POP 10,900

Legend has it that in 1520 Gustav Vasa arrived here in a last-ditch attempt to start a rebellion against the Danish regime. The people of Mora weren't interested, and Gustav was forced to put on his skis and flee for the border. After he left, the town reconsidered and two yeomen, Engelbrekt and Lars, volunteered to follow Gustav's tracks, finally overtaking him in Sälen and changing Swedish history.

Today the world's biggest cross-country ski race, **Vasaloppet**, which ends in Mora, commemorates this epic chase. Around 15,000 people take part on the first Sunday in March. In summer, you can walk the route on the 90km **Vasaloppsleden**.

Sights

Vasaloppsmuseet MUSEUM

(0250-392 00; www.vasaloppet.se; Vasagatan; adult/child Skr50/25; 8am-4.30pm Mon-Wed & Fri, to 3pm Thu, closed noon-1pm daily) Even if you have no interest in skiing, you may be pleasantly surprised by the excellent Vasaloppsmuseet, which really communicates the passion behind the world's largest cross-country skiing event. There's some fantastic crackly black-and-white film of the first race, a display about nine-times winner and hardy old boy Nils 'Mora-Nisse' Karlsson, and an exhibit of prizes. Outside the museum is the race finish line, a favourite place for holiday *snaps*.

Zornmuseet MUSEUM

(0250-59 23 10; www.zorn.se; Vasagatan 36; adult/child Skr60/free; 9am-5pm Mon-Sat, 11am-5pm Sun mid-May–mid-Sep, noon-4pm Sep–mid-May) Zornmuseet displays many of the best-loved portraits and characteristic nudes of Mora painter Anders Zorn (1860–1920), one of Sweden's most renowned artists. His naturalistic depictions of Swedish life and landscapes are shown here, as is the Zorn family silver collection.

Sleeping & Eating

Mora Parken CAMPGROUND, CABINS €

(0250-276 00; www.moraparken.se; sites Skr195, 2-/4-bed cabins from Skr495/645, hotel s/d Skr995/1245; @) This extra-fancy campground and hotel are in a great waterside spot, 400m northwest of the church. There's a beach, laundry, kitchen, minigolf, bicycle rentals and more. A hodgepodge of camping cabins are well equipped and full of rustic charm. The Vasaloppet track and Siljansleden trail pass through the grounds, and you can hire canoes to splash about on the pond.

Mora Hotell & Spa HOTEL €€

(0250-59 26 50; www.morahotell.se; Strandgatan 12; r from Skr1195; P) There's been a hotel here since 1830, although the current version is as modern as it gets, with all the facilities you'd expect from a big chain (it's a Best Western) – plus personality. Rooms combine clean lines, wooden floors and earthy tones with bright folk-art accents. Head to the spa for steam rooms, Jacuzzis, massage and body treatments.

WORTH A TRIP

WHERE THE WILD THINGS ARE

Fat-bottomed roly-poly bear cubs are the star attraction at **Grönklitt Björnpark** (0250-462 00; www.orsabjornpark.se; adult/child Skr240/160, family Skr680; 9am-6pm mid-Jun–Aug, hours vary rest of year; P; 103 or 104, then 118), the largest predator park in Europe, 16km from Orsa. Even if there are no cubs around during your visit, there's plenty to see: polar bears, Kodiak bears, leopards, Amur tigers, lynxes, wolves, red foxes and wolverines. The park and the various possible activities here continue to expand, and now include cycling tours, themed hikes and more.

Mora Kaffestuga CAFE €

(0250-100 82; Kyrkogatan 8; lunch specials Skr85; 9am-7pm Mon-Fri, to 5pm Sat, 10am-4pm Sun) For a quick lunch – such as basic salads, quiches and sandwiches – or a coffee-and-pastry break, this popular, stylish little coffee shop has a grassy garden out back.

Helmers Konditori CAFE €

(0250-100 11; helmers.se; Kyrkogatan 10; sandwiches from Skr47; 8am-7pm) This highly recommended bakery-cafe on the main pedestrian street draws a devoted local crowd with plenty of homemade bread, sandwiches and delicious pastries.

Information

Tourist Office (0250-59 20 20; mora@siljan.se; Köpmannagatan 3A; 9am-6pm Mon-Fri, 10am-4pm Sat & Sun) In a central location across from the library.

Getting There & Away

All Dalatrafik buses use the bus station at Moragatan 23. Bus 70 runs to Rättvik and Falun, while buses 103, 104, 105 and 245 serve Orsa.

Mora is an **SJ** (0771-75 75 75; www.sj.se) train terminus and the southern terminus of Inlandsbanan (Inland Railway), which runs north to Gällivare (mid-June to late September). The main train station is about 1km east of the town centre. The more central Mora Strand is a platform station in town, but not all trains stop there, so check the timetable. When travelling to Östersund, you can choose between Inlandsbanan (Skr494, 6¼ hours, one daily) or bus 45 (Skr269, 5¼ hours, two daily).

SKÅNE

Artists adore southern Sweden. Down here, the light is softer, the foliage brighter and the shoreline more dazzling and white. Sweden's southernmost county, Skåne (Scania) was Danish property until 1658 and still flaunts its differences. You can detect them in the strong dialect *(skånska)*, the half-timbered houses and Skåne's hybrid flag: a Swedish yellow cross on a red Danish background.

Malmö

040 / POP 280,415

Sweden's third-largest city has a progressive contemporary feel. Home to Scandinavia's tallest building, beautiful parks, edgy museums, head-turning architecture and some seriously good cuisine, the opening of the Öresund bridge in 2000 has also been undeniably positive, connecting the city to bigger, cooler Copenhagen and creating a dynamic new urban conglomeration.

Such a cosmopolitan outcome seems only natural for what is Sweden's most multicultural metropolis – 150 nationalities make up Malmö's headcount. Here, exotic Middle Eastern street-stalls, urbane Italian coffee culture and hipster skateboard parks counter the town's intrinsic Nordic reserve.

Sights & Activities

The cobbled streets and interesting buildings around **Lilla Torg** are restored parts of the late-medieval town. Many are now occupied by galleries, boutiques and restaurants.

OFF THE BEATEN TRACK

KRONETORPS WINDMILL

Located 7km north of Malmö on the way to Lund, the eye-catching **Kronetorps Mölla** (Dalbyvägen 63; 040-43 91 79) looms over the smattering of cottages that is Burlöv, as if challenging Don Quixote. This Dutch-style, fully functional windmill was built in 1841 by a wealthy landowner, and it's possible to peek inside at the giant cogs. Adjacent to the windmill is an indoor exhibition on life in bygone times. Guided tours are held on summer Sundays between 1pm and 4pm; the rest of the time visits are by appointment only.

★Malmö Museer MUSEUM

(www.malmo.se/museer; Malmöhusvägen; adult/child Skr40/free; audio guides Skr20; 10am-4pm Jun-Aug, shorter hours rest of year;) Various museums with diverse themes, including handicrafts, military materiel, art and transport, are located in and around Malmöhus Slott and make up the so-called Malmö Museer. There are gift shops and cafe-restaurants inside all the museums and plenty to keep the tots interested, including an **aquarium**. Renovated in 2014, don't miss the nocturnal hall here, wriggling with everything from bats to electric eels, plus local swimmers scuh as cod and pike.

★Malmöhus Slott CASTLE

FREE The addition of red-brick, Functionalist buildings in the 1930s might make it look slightly factory-like, but Malmöhus Slott has an intriguing history and houses some of the superb Malmö Museer.

After the Swedish takeover of Skåne in 1648, the Danes made a futile attempt to recapture the castle in 1677. When peace was restored, most of it became derelict and a devastating fire in 1870 left only the main building and two gun towers intact; these sections were revamped in 1930.

Moderna Museet Malmö MUSEUM

(www.modernamuseet.se; Gasverksgatan 22; admission Skr70; 11am-6pm Tue-Sun) Architects Tham & Videgård chose to make the most of the distinct 1901 Rooseum, once a power-generating turbine hall, by adding a contemporary annexe, complete with a bright, perforated orange-red facade. Venue aside, the museum's galleries are well worth visiting, with their permanent exhibition including works by such modern masters as Matisse, Dalí and Picasso.

Form/Design Center ARTS CENTRE

(www.formdesigncenter.com; Lilla Torg 9; 11am-5pm Tue-Sat, noon-4pm Sun) FREE Form/Design Center showcases cutting-edge design, architecture and art. The central cobbled courtyard is a remnant of the late-medieval town, while the historic half-timbered houses are now home to galleries and boutiques selling Scandi-cool art, fashion, crafts, toys and homewares. Pore over design magazines in the cafe and pick up one of the bicycle maps designed to guide you to design and architectural hot spots in the city.

Malmö

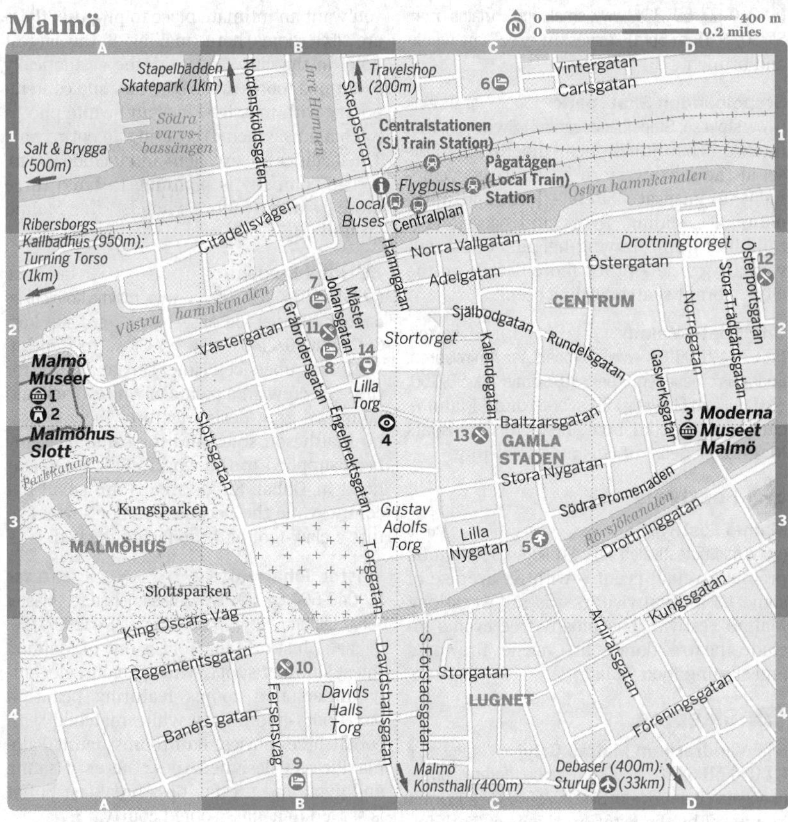

Malmö

Top Sights
1 Malmö Museer A2
2 Malmöhus Slott A2
3 Moderna Museet Malmö D3

Sights
4 Form/Design Center B2

Activities, Courses & Tours
5 City Boats Malmö C3

Sleeping
6 Comfort Hotel Malmö C1
7 Hotel Duxiana B2
8 Mäster Johan Hotel B2
9 STF Vandrarhem Malmö City B4

Eating
10 Atmosfär B4
11 Bastard Restaurant B2
12 Falafel No. 1 .... D2
13 Lilla Kafferosteriet C3

Drinking & Nightlife
14 Victors B2

Turning Torso NOTABLE BUILDING
In the distant northwest of the city, you may catch sight of the eye-boggling Turning Torso, an apartment block that twists through 90 degrees from bottom to top. Inaugurated at the end of August 2005, it's now Sweden's tallest building at 190m high.

Malmö Konsthall GALLERY
(www.konsthall.malmo.se; St Johannesgatan 7; 11am-5pm, to 9pm Wed;) **FREE** Malmö Konsthall, south of central Malmö, is one of Europe's largest contemporary-art spaces, with exhibitions spanning both Swedish and foreign talent. The museum cafe **Smak**

(040-50 50 35; www.smak.info; mains from Skr80; 11am-5pm) serves an excellent weekend brunch.

Stapelbädden Skatepark SKATE PARK
(www.stpln.se; Stapelbäddsgatan 1) Swing by this intense urban jungle near the Turning Torso, at the northwestern harbour redevelopment, to gasp at skaters – local and international – sliding, flying and occasionally tumbling from dizzying heights. Check out www.bryggeriet.org for more details on the city's vibrant skateboarding scene.

City Boats Malmö BOATING
(0704-71 00 67; www.cityboats.se; Amiralsbron, Södra Promenaden; per 30/60min Skr90/150; 11am-7pm May-Aug) To scoot round Malmö's canals in a pedal boat, head to City Boats Malmö, just east of Gustav Adolfs Torg.

Festivals

Malmö Festival MUSIC
(www.malmofestivalen.se; mid-Aug) Malmö's premier annual event – with an average of some 1.5 million visitors – is the week-long Malmö Festival. The mostly free events include theatre, dance, live music, fireworks and sizzling food stalls.

Sleeping

STF Vandrarhem Malmö City HOSTEL €
(040-611 62 20; www.svenskaturistforeningen.se; Rönngatan 1; dm/d from Skr230/560; @) Don't be put off by the exterior; this is a sparkling hostel right in the city centre with a bright and airy communal kitchen and an outdoor patio. Staff are enthusiastic and helpful.

Comfort Hotel Malmö HOTEL €
(040-33 04 40; www.choice.se; Carlsgatan 10C; s/d Skr690/800; P @) Not the right choice if you want an intimate place to propose: there are 293 rooms here, making it the largest hotel in the city. That said, the aesthetically revamped rooms are bright, airy and contemporary with massive black-and-white photos (with a music theme) covering an entire wall. The facilities are excellent and include a gym.

The company is planning to build three more similar-calibre hotels in Malmö around 2015–16.

★ **Hotel Duxiana** HOTEL €€
(040-607 70 00; www.malmo.hotelduxiana.com; Mäster Johansgatan 1; s/d/ste from Skr795/1090/2140; P @) Close to Centralstationen, ubersleek Hotel Duxiana is one for the style crew. In a palate of white, black and gunmetal grey, design features include Bruno Mattheson sofas and the same heavenly beds supplied to the world's first seven-star hotel in Dubai. Single rooms are small but comfy, while the decadent junior suites feature a claw-foot bathtub facing the bed.

Mäster Johan Hotel HOTEL €€€
(040-664 64 00; www.masterjohan.se; Mäster Johansgatan 13; r/ste from Skr1290/1790; P @) Just off Lilla Torg is one of Malmö's finest slumber spots, with spacious, elegantly understated rooms featuring beautiful oak floors and snowy white matched with cobalt blue fabrics. Bathrooms flaunt Paloma Picasso–designed tiles, there's a sauna and gym, and the faultless breakfast buffet is served in a glass-roofed courtyard.

Eating

Malmö isn't short on dining experiences, whether it's vegan dishes in a grungy leftwing hang-out or designer supping on contemporary Nordic flavours.

Lilla Kafferosteriet CAFE €
(040-48 20 00; www.lillakafferosteriet.se; Baltzarsgatan 24; sandwiches from Skr35; 8am-7pm Mon-Fri, 10am-5pm Sat, 11am-5pm Sun) Have a mosey around the warren of atmospheric rooms here before you bag your table, or head out to the pretty patio. This is a serious-about-coffee cafe with freshly ground (Fairtrade) beans, plus plenty of sweet and savoury goodies. You may just stay for a while; it's that kind of place.

Falafel No. 1 FELAFEL €
(040-84 41 22; www.falafel-n1.se; Österportsgatan 2; felafel from Skr35) Malmö residents are so fond of felafel that it even features in songs by local rapper Timbuktu. Falafel No.

GET YOUR KIT OFF!

Ribersborg is a fetching sandy beach backed by parkland, about 2km west of the town centre. Off the beach, at the end of a 200m-long pier, is an open-air naturist saltwater pool, **Ribersborgs Kallbadhus** (040-26 03 66; www.ribersborgskallbadhus.se; adult/child Skr55/free; 9am-8pm Mon, Tue & Thu, to 9pm Wed, to 6pm Fri-Sun May-Sep, shorter hours rest of year), with separate sections for men and women, and a wood-fired **sauna** dating from 1898. There is also a pleasant cafe.

1 (also known as the Orient House) is a long-standing favourite, or check out the website **Everything About Falafel** (www.alltomfalafel.se) for details on other venues.

★ Atmosfär SWEDISH €€
(☎040-12 50 77; www.atmosfar.com; Fersensväg 4; mains from Skr125; ⏰11.30am-11pm Mon-Fri, to 2am Sat) This classy neighbourhood restaurant changes its menu regularly depending on what's in season, but you can depend on flavourful, innovative combinations such as salads topped with young nasturtium leaves and veal with truffles, green peas and horseradish. The cocktails (Skr105) are similarly irresistible. Elderflower fizz, anyone?

Salt & Brygga SWEDISH €€
(☎040-611 59 40; www.saltobrygga.se; Sundspromenaden 7; lunch mains from Skr110, dinner mains from Skr145; ⏰11am-2pm & 5-11pm Mon-Fri, 12.30-4pm & 5-11pm Sat;) With an enviable view overlooking the Öresund bridge and the small harbour, this stylish slow-food restaurant presents updated Swedish cuisine with a clear conscience. Everything is organic (including the staff's uniforms), waste is turned into biogas, and the interior is allergy free. Flavours are clean and strictly seasonal.

★ Bastard Restaurant EUROPEAN €€€
(☎040-12 13 18; www.bastardrestaurant.se; Mäster Johansgatan 11; mains from Skr200; ⏰5pm-midnight Tue-Thu, to 2am Fri & Sat) This hipster restaurant is about as close as you'll get to a gastro-pub in Sweden. Meals here are both hearty and distinctive, ranging from gourmet meat platters to blackened grilled chicken for two or pizza with snails. The bar is a popular choice with well-heeled locals.

Drinking & Nightlife

Lilla Torg bars have a great atmosphere and outdoor terraces.

Victors COCKTAIL BAR
(www.victors.se; Lilla Torg 1; ⏰3-6.30pm Mon-Thu, noon-1am Fri & Sat) Glam cocktails on Lilla Torg with light late-night snacks available to accompany your tipple.

Debaser LIVE MUSIC
(www.debaser.se; Norra Parkgatan 2; ⏰7pm-3am Wed-Sun Apr-Sep; 🚌5, 32 Malmö Folkets park) After a temporary closure, Debaser opened again in mid-2014 with live gigs and club nights spanning anything from indie, pop and hip-hop to soul, electronica and rock. There's a buzzing outdoor bar-lounge overlooking Folkets Park.

MALMÖ CITY CARD

The **Malmö City Kort** (www.malmo-city.se) covers free bus transport, street parking, entry to several museums, and discounts at other attractions and on sightseeing tours. It costs Skr100 for one day and is now available as a smartphone app. Buy it at the tourist office.

Information

Tourist Office (☎040-34 12 00; www.malmotown.com; Skeppsbron 2; ⏰9am-7pm Mon-Fri, 10am-4pm Sat & Sun) Across from the Centralstationen.

Getting There & Away

TO/FROM THE AIRPORT

Flygbuss (www.flygbussarna.se) runs from Centralstationen to Sturup airport (adult/student Skr109/89, 40 minutes); check the website for the schedule. A taxi shouldn't cost more than Skr430.

Trains run directly from Malmö to Copenhagen's much larger main airport (Skr105, 35 minutes, every 20 minutes).

AIR

Sturup airport (☎010-10 945 00; www.swedavia.se) is situated 33km southeast of Malmö. **SAS** (☎0770-72 77 27; www.sas.se) has numerous daily flights to Stockholm Arlanda airport, as well as to Östersund. **Malmö Aviation** (www.malmoaviation.se) flies to Bromma Stockholm airport and Visby.

BUS

There are two bus terminals with daily departures to Swedish and European destinations. **Travelshop** (Malmö Buss & Resecenter; ☎33 05 70; www.travelshop.se; Carlsgatan 4A), north of the Centralstationen, services and sells tickets for several companies, including **Swebus Express** (☎0771-21 82 18; www.swebus.se), which runs two to four times daily direct to Stockholm (from Skr539, 8½ hours) and up to 10 times daily to Göteborg (from Skr139, three to four hours); five continue to Oslo (from Skr219, eight hours).

The second long-distance bus terminal, **Öresundsterminalen** (☎040-59 09 00; www.oresundsterminalen.se; Terminalgatan 10), is reached via bus 35 from Centralstationen towards Flansbjer (30 minutes). From here, **Svenska Buss** (☎0771-67 67 67; www.svenskabuss.se) runs to Stockholm (Skr420, 11 hours) via Karlskrona, six times weekly.

TRAIN

Pågatågen (local trains), operated by **Skånetrafiken** (www.skanetrafiken.se), run to Helsingborg (Skr103, one hour, half-hourly), Lund (Skr48, 15 minutes, every 20 minutes) and Ystad (Skr84, 50 minutes, half-hourly). Bicycles are not allowed during peak times, except mid-June to mid-August.

The Malmö to Copenhagen central station train leaves every 20 minutes (Skr105, 35 minutes).

Trains also serve Göteborg (from Skr235, 3¼ hours) and Stockholm (from Sk750, 4½ hours, hourly).

Getting Around

Skånetrafiken operates an extensive network of local buses, most leaving from in front of Centralstationen. A single journey costs Skr22, but tickets cannot be purchased on buses; purchase a reusable **Jojo** card at the Skånetrafiken customer service centres at Centralstationen or Triangeln and load it with an amount to cover your estimated local bus travel. Alternatively, purchase a 24- or 72-hour Timmarsbijett bus pass.

Lund

☎046 / POP 82,800

Centred around a striking cathedral (complete with a giant in the crypt and a magical clock), Lund is a soulful blend of leafy parks, medieval abodes and coffee-sipping bookworms. Like most university towns, however, it loses some of its buzz during the summer, when students head home for the holidays. Lund makes an easy day trip from Malmö.

Sights

★Domkyrkan CHURCH

(Kyrkogatan; ⏰8am-6pm Mon-Fri, 9.30am-5pm Sat, to 6pm Sun) FREE Lund's twin-towered Romanesque cathedral, Domkyrkan, is magnificent. Try to pop in at noon or 3pm (1pm and 3pm on Sunday and holidays) when the marvellous astronomical clock strikes up *In Dulci Jubilo* and the wooden figures at the top whirr into action. Within the crypt, you'll find Finn, the mythological giant who helped construct the cathedral, and a 16th-century well carved with comical scenes.

★Skissernas Museum ARTS CENTRE

(Sketch Museum; ☎046-222 72 83; www.skissernasmuseum.se; Finngatan 2; admission Skr50; ⏰noon-5pm Tue-Sun, to 9pm Wed) The exhibition rooms here with their visual feast of paintings and sculpture are designed for maximum impact and art immersion. Several sculptures and installations are huge, including the 6m-high *Women by the Sea* by Ivar Johnsson. Formerly a private collection, it includes works by some of the world's greats, including Joan Miró, Henri Matisse, Raoul Dufy, Sonia Delaunay and Fernand Léger. A sculpture park includes pieces by Henry Moore, and a Mexican gallery space has recently been completed.

★Kulturen MUSEUM

(www.kulturen.com; Tegnerplatsen; adult/child Skr90/free; ⏰10am-5pm May-Aug, noon-4pm Tue-Sat Sep-Apr; 👪) Kulturen, opened in 1892, is a huge open-air museum filling two whole blocks. Its 30-odd buildings include everything from the meanest birch-bark hovel to grand 17th-century houses. Permanent displays encompass Lund in the Middle Ages, vintage toys, ceramics, silver and glass (among many others); ask about guided tours in English. The popular outdoor cafe flanks several **rune stones**.

Historiska Museet MUSEUM

(History Museum; www.luhm.lu.se; Kraftstorg; admission Skr50; ⏰11am-4pm Tue-Fri, noon-4pm Sun) Behind the cathedral, the Historiska Museet has a large collection of pre–Viking Age finds, including a 7000-year-old skeleton. It's joined with **Domkyrkomuseet**, which explores the history of the church in the area; the rooms filled with countless statues of the crucified Christ are supremely creepy.

Sleeping

Lilla Hotellet i Lund HOTEL €€

(☎046-32 88 88; www.lillahotellet.com; Bankgatan 7; s/d Skr1350/1450; P 📶) Partly housed in an old shoe factory, this homely spot offers cosy rooms (think patchwork quilts and Laura Ashley–style wallpaper), as well as a sunny courtyard and guest lounge. Prices drop considerably on Friday and Saturday.

★Hotel Duxiana BOUTIQUE HOTEL €€€

(☎046-13 55 15; www.lundhotelduxiana.com; Sankt Petri Kyrkogatan 7; s/d 1695/1895; @📶) Top tip is that all rooms are priced the same, despite various levels of luxury, including a private sauna in one, a small kitchenette in another and still another which is split level with a sitting room. The decor is slickly contemporary and there is an oasis of a courtyard out the back, as well as a restaurant and bar.

Eating

★St Jakobs Stenugnsbageri BAKERY €
(☎046-13 70 60; www.stjakobs.se; Klostergatan 9; baked goods Skr15-50; ⏲8am-6pm Mon-Fri, to 4pm Sat, to 3pm Sun) Mouthwatering is the only way to describe the selection of stone-baked breads, knotted cardamom rolls, melt-in-your-mouth coconut-lemon towers and crisp sugar cookies overflowing from the countertops and baking trays at St Jakobs. During the summer you're likely to see an enormous bowl of strawberries at the centre of it all, served with fresh cream, of course.

Ved SWEDISH €€
(☎046-13 05 65; www.restaurangved.se; Mårtenstorget 3; mains from Skr120; ⏲10am-6pm Mon-Wed, 10am-7pm Thu & Fri, 9.30am-3pm Sat; 📶) Opened in 2014 and on the verge of expanding when we visited, this moodily lit bar and restaurant dishes up good-looking plates of Swedish-fusion dishes. Plates are midsized, so they're cheaper than you may expect, and the place hums with city-slick sophistication.

Information

Tourist Office (☎046-35 50 40; www.lund.se; Botulfsgatan 1A; ⏲10am-6pm Mon-Fri, to 2pm Sat) At the southern end of Stortorget.

Getting There & Away

Long-distance buses leave from outside the train station. Most buses to/from Malmö run via Lund.

It's 10 to 15 minutes from Lund to Malmö by train, with frequent local Pågatågen departures (Skr48). Some trains continue to Copenhagen (Skr135, one hour). Other direct services run from Malmö to Kristianstad and Karlskrona via Lund. All long-distance trains from Stockholm or Göteborg to Malmö stop in Lund.

Trelleborg

☎0410 / POP 28,290

Trelleborg is the main gateway between Sweden and Germany, with frequent ferry services (p486) but otherwise of little interest to the visitor; we suggest continuing on to Ystad or Malmö.

Simple and functional with shared bathrooms, **Night Stop** (☎0410-410 70; www.hotelnightstop.com; Östergatan 59; s/d/tr Skr300/400/500; 🅿📶) has the cheapest beds in town. Open 24 hours, it's about 500m from the ferry (turn right along Hamngatan after disembarking), diagonally opposite the museum.

Skånetrafiken bus 146 (Skr60, 45 minutes) runs roughly every half-hour between Malmö and Trelleborg's bus station, some 500m inland from the ferry terminals. Bus 165 has frequent weekday departures (and five on Saturdays) to Lund (Skr70, 1¼ hours).

Stena Line (www.stenaline.com) ferries connect Trelleborg to Sassnitz (twice daily each way, from Skr190) and Rostock (two or three daily, from Skr315). **TT-Line** (☎0450-280 181; www.ttline.com) ferries shuttle between Trelleborg and Travemünde (from Skr310) and Rostock (from Skr450) up to three to four times daily. Buy tickets inside the ferry building.

Ystad

☎0411 / POP 18,350

Half-timbered houses, rambling cobbled streets and the haunting sound of a nightwatchman's horn give this medieval market town an intoxicating lure. Fans of writer Henning Mankell know it as the setting for his best-selling Inspector Wallander crime thrillers, while fans of drums and uniforms head in for the spectacular three-day **Military Tattoo** (www.ystadtattoo.se) in mid-August.

Sights

Sankta Maria Kyrka CHURCH
(Stortorget; ⏲10am-6pm Jun-Aug, to 4pm Sep-May) FREE Among the church's highlights is a magnificent 17th-century baroque pulpit. This is also, famously, the place from where the nightwatchman sounds his horn. **Latinskolan**, next to Sankta Maria Kyrka, is a late-15th-century brick building and the oldest preserved school in Scandinavia.

Klostret i Ystad MUSEUM
(www.klostret.ystad.se; St Petri Kyrkoplan; adult/child Skr40/free; ⏲noon-5pm Tue-Fri, noon-4pm Sat & Sun) Klostret i Ystad, in the Middle Ages Franciscan monastery of Gråbrödraklostret, features local textiles and silverware. The monastery includes the 13th-century deconsecrated Sankt Petri Kyrkan (now used for art exhibitions), which has around 80 gravestones from the 14th to 18th centuries. Also included is the **Ystads Konstmuseum** (☎0411-57 72 85; www.konstmuseet.ystad.se; St Knuts Torg; ⏲10am-5pm Mon-Fri, noon-4pm Sat & Sun Jul–mid-Aug, noon-5pm Tue-Fri, noon-4pm Sat & Sun mid-Aug–Jun) FREE. In the same building as the tourist office, its superb collection of southern Swedish and Danish art includes work by the great Per Kirkeby.

OFF THE BEATEN TRACK

TO SAIL A STONE SHIP...

One of Skåne's most intriguing and remote attractions, **Ales Stenar** (admission free, tours adult/child Skr20/10; 24hr) has all the mystery of England's Stonehenge but without the commercialism and burnt-out druids. It's Sweden's largest stone ship setting, gorgeously located on a grassy knoll by the sea, 19km east of Ystad. According to legend, King Ale is buried there, but it may also have been a solar calendar. To get here, take bus 322 from Ystad (four times daily).

Sleeping & Eating

★Sekelgården Hotel HOTEL €€
(0411-739 00; www.sekelgarden.se; Långgatan 18; s/d Skr995/1395; P @) A family-run hotel in a half-timbered house (1793); staying here is a bit like staying with your (affluent) country cousins. Rooms are set around a garden and are all different, although typically decorated with a combination of William Morris–style wallpaper and pastel paintwork combined with colourful quilts, rugs and fabrics.

Host Morten CAFE €
(0411-134 03; Gåsegränd; mains from Skr75; 11am-5pm Mon-Fri, to 3pm Sat, 12.30-5pm Sun) Plunge into that Henning Mankell novel at this fabulous cafe – serving light meals such as filled baked potatoes, focaccias and piled-high salads – then pluck a book from one of the shelves and plan to stay awhile. In summer the 18th-century cobbled courtyard is a delight, especially when there's live music.

Store Thor INTERNATIONAL €€
(0411-185 10; www.storethor.se; Stortorget 1; mains from Skr105, tapas Skr39; 11.30am-4pm & 5pm-late Mon-Sat) Described as one of Ystad's best restaurants by Kurt Wallander in the movie *Täckmanteln*, Store Thor occupies the monastic arched cellar of the old town hall (1572). Nibble on such tapas as jalapeno peppers with cheese, tuck into succulent grilled meats or enjoy the cognac raw-spiced salmon with dill-stewed potatoes. The square-side terrace is a hit with summertime night owls.

Information

Tourist Office (0411-57 76 81; www.ystad.se; St Knuts Torg; 9am-7pm Mon-Fri, 10am-6pm Sat & Sun mid-Jun–mid-Aug;) Just opposite the train station with free internet access.

Getting There & Away

BOAT

Daily crossings (p486) between Ystad and Świnoujście are run by **Unity Line** (0411-55 69 00; www.unityline.se; adult one way Skr386) and **Polferries** (040-12 17 00; www.polferries.se; adult one way Skr353). Ystad's ferry terminal is within walking distance of the train station. **Faergen** (www.faergen.dk; adult one way Skr240) runs frequent ferries and catamarans between Ystad and Rønne, on the Danish island of Bornholm.

BUS

Buses depart from outside Ystad train station. Bus 190 runs from Ystad to Trelleborg (Skr72, one hour) hourly on weekdays, less frequently on weekends, while SkåneExpressen bus 5 runs to Lund (Skr96, 1¼ hours, hourly weekdays, less frequently on weekends).

TRAIN

Pågatågen trains run hourly or so to/from Malmö (Skr84, 50 minutes).

Helsingborg

042 / POP 97,122

At its heart, Helsingborg is a sparkly showcase of rejuvenated waterfront, metro-glam restaurants, lively cobbled streets and lofty castle ruins. With Denmark looking on from a mere 4km across the Öresund, its flouncy, turreted buildings feel like a brazen statement.

Sights & Activities

★Dunkers Kulturhus MUSEUM
(www.dunkerskulturhus.se; Kungsgatan 11; exhibitions adult/child Skr75/free; 10am-6pm Mon-Fri, to 8pm Thu, to 5pm Sat & Sun) Just north of the transport terminal, the crisp white Dunkers Kulturhus houses the main tourist office, an interesting town museum and temporary exhibitions (admission includes entry to both), plus a concert hall, an urbane cafe and a design-savvy gift shop. The building's creator, Danish architect Kim Utzon, is the son of Sydney Opera House architect Jørn Utzon.

From here, saunter along **Norra Hamnen** (North Harbour), where apartments, restaurants and bars meet yachts and preened locals in one rather successful harbour-redevelopment project.

Fredriksdals Friluftsmuseum MUSEUM
(www.fredriksdal.se; off Hävertgatan; May-Sep adult/child Skr70/free, Oct-Mar free; 10am-6pm May-Sep, shorter hours rest of year; P) One of Sweden's best open-air museums, based

around an 18th-century manor house (not open to the public), the houses and shops you see here once graced the streets of central Helsingborg; they were moved here, brick for brick, in the 1960s. Thankfully, this is no contrived theme park; the whole place is charming and there's plenty of scope for souvenir shopping at the art and craft workshops. There are also herb, rose and vegetable gardens and blissfully leafy grounds.

Kärnan RUIN
(adult/child Skr40/20; 10am-6pm Jun-Aug, closed Mon rest of year) Dramatic steps and archways lead up from Stortorget to the square tower Kärnan (34m), all that remains of the medieval castle. The castle became Swedish property during the 17th-century Danish-Swedish War, and was mostly demolished once the fighting stopped. The tower was restored from dereliction in 1894, and the view is regal indeed. There are plans to mount a permanent exhibition about the history of the castle.

Sleeping

★ Clarion Collection Hotel Helsing HOTEL €€
(042-37 18 00; www.choice.se; Stortorget 20; s/d Skr800/1050; P @) In an elegant, early-20th-century building at the foot of the stairs to the Kärnan tower, Hotel Helsing boasts distinct, boutique-style rooms with underfloor heating, a spa and a popular restaurant and nightclub. A buffet dinner is included in the room cost, a standard and great-value perk of the Clarion Collection chain.

Hotell Viking HOTEL €€
(042-14 44 20; www.hotellviking.se; Fågelsångsgatan 1; s/d from Skr940/1250; P @) Trendy and urbane, this hipster hotel sets the tone from the get-go with velvet cushions, modern bookshelves and brass candlesticks decorating the lobby. Rooms are similarly chic and stylish, although they do vary considerably: some are swing-a-cat size, while the most luxurious has a hot tub.

Eating

★ Holy Greens HEALTH FOOD €
(042-12 40 40; Nedre Långvinkelsgatan 7; mains from Skr69; 7.30am-6.30pm Mon-Fri, 11am-4pm Sat;) The key word here is fresh. Choose from set salad combos such as Asian Greens, Green Mexican, Salmon & Avocado and Nutty Chicken with various dressing choices. Then boost up the healthy-eating factor a notch by ordering a fresh fruit smoothie with ingredients including avocado, blackberries and mango (but not combined!).

Globe Trotter ASIAN €€
(042-37 18 00; Clarion Collection Hotel Helsing, Stortorget 20; tapas Skr39, mains from Skr100; 5-10pm Sun-Thu, to 1am Fri & Sat;) These beautifully presented gastro-Asian tapas and mains hit the spot and, combined with the mood music and superb Stortorget people-watching potential from the terrace, make it hard to get a table at weekends.

Olsons Skafferi ITALIAN €€€
(042-14 07 80; www.olsonsskafferi.se; Mariagatan 6; mains from Skr225; 11am-5.30pm & 7.30-11pm Mon-Sat) Olsons is a super little spot, with alfresco seating on the pedestrian square right in front of Mariakyrkan. It doubles as an Italian deli and cafe, with rustic good looks, spangly chandeliers and pasta that would make Bologna proud. Be sure to finish things off in proper Italian fashion with Vino Santo and *cantuccini* (almond biscotti). Lunch is more economical.

Information

Tourist Office (042-10 43 50; www.helsingborg.se; Kungsgatan 11; 10am-6pm Mon-Fri, to 8pm Thu, to 5pm Sat & Sun) Well stocked with a gift shop and conveniently located in the Dunkers Kulturhus museum.

Getting There & Away

BOAT

Knutpunkten is the terminal for the frequent **Scandlines** (042-18 61 00; www.scandlines.se) car ferry to Helsingør (car with passengers Skr420).

BUS

The bus terminal is at ground level in Knutpunkten. Regional Skånetrafiken buses dominate but long-distance services are offered by Swebus Express (p415).

Swebus runs north to Göteborg, continuing on to Oslo and south to Malmö. They also operate services northeast to Stockholm via Norrköping. Fares to Stockholm cost around Skr539 (7½ hours), to Göteborg Skr130 (three hours) and to Oslo Skr379 (seven hours).

TRAIN

Underground platforms in Knutpunkten serve trains, which depart frequently for Göteborg (from Skr285, 2½ to three hours), Lund (Skr84, 25 minutes) and Malmö (Skr103, 40 minutes), as well as Copenhagen and Oslo.

GÖTALAND

This region has a rich history and plenty to offer the visitor. For one, it's home to Sweden's second-largest city, Göteborg (also known as Gothenburg), with an amusement park for the kids and a huge range of grown-up entertainment. Norrköping, an urban-restoration achievement, has turned its workmanlike heart into a lovely showpiece. Linköping's medieval cathedral is one of Sweden's largest, and in Vadstena there's the abbey established by the country's most important saint, Birgitta. There's also the overwhelming natural beauty of the island-speckled Bohuslän coast.

Göteborg

031 / POP 549,839

Often caught in Stockholm's shadow, gregarious Göteborg (pronounced *yur*-te-borry, Gothenburg in English) socks a mighty good punch of its own. Some of the country's finest talent hails from its streets, including music icons José González and Soundtrack of Our Lives. Ornate architecture lines its tram-rattled streets and cafes hum with bonhomie. West of Kungsportsavenyn (dubbed the 'Champs Élysées' in brochures and 'tourist trap' by locals), the Haga and Linné districts buzz with creativity. Fashionistas design fair-trade threads while artists collaborate over mean espressos, and there's always some cutting-edge art and architecture to grab your attention.

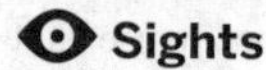

Sights

★Liseberg AMUSEMENT PARK

(www.liseberg.se; Södra Vägen; 1-/2-day pass Skr415/595; 11am-11pm Jun–mid-Aug; ; 2, 4, 5, 6, 8, 10 Korsvägen) The attractions of Liseberg, Scandinavia's largest amusement park, are many and varied. Adrenalin blasts include the venerable wooden roller coaster Balder, its 'explosive' colleague Kanonen, where you're blasted from 0km/h to 75km/h in under two seconds, AtmosFear, Europe's tallest (116m) free-fall tower, and the park's biggest new attraction: thrilling rollercoaster Helix that lets you experience weightlessness and loops the loop seven times. Softer options include carousels, fairy-tale castles, an outdoor dance floor, adventure playgrounds, and shows and concerts.

★Röda Sten GALLERY

(www.rodasten.com; Röda Sten 1; adult/under 21yr Skr40/free; noon-5pm Tue-Sun, to 7pm Wed; 3, 9 Vagnhallen Majorna) Occupying a defunct, graffitied power station beside the giant Älvsborgsbron, Röda Sten's four floors are home to such temporary exhibitions as edgy Swedish photography and cross-dressing rap videos by Danish-Filipino artist Lillibeth Cuenca Rasmussen that challenge sexuality stereotypes in Afghan society. The indie-style cafe hosts weekly live music and club nights, and offbeat one-offs such as punk bike races, boxing matches and stand-up comedy. To get there, walk towards the Klippan precinct, continue under Älvsborgsbron and look for the brown-brick building.

GÖTEBORG DISCOUNT CARDS

Göteborg City Card (www.goteborg.com/en/Do/Gothenburg-City-Card/; 24/48/72hr Skr355/495/655) The brilliant Göteborg City Card is particularly worthwhile if you're into intensive sightseeing: it gives you free access to most museums and Liseberg amusement park, discounted and free city tours, unlimited travel on public transport and free parking in the city with the most dedicated traffic wardens.

The card is available at tourist offices, hotels, Pressbyrån newsagencies and online at www.goteborg.com.

Göteborgspaketet (http://butik.goteborg.com/en/package; adult from Skr635) The Göteborgspaketet is an accommodation-and-entertainment package offered at various hotels, with prices starting at Skr635 per person per night in a double room. It includes the Göteborg Pass for the number of nights you stay; book online in advance.

Museum Discount Card (adult Skr40) If you're looking to visit more than one of the following: Stadsmuseum, Konstmuseet, Röhsska Museet, Sjöfartsmuseet and Naturhistoriska Museet, ask for the discount card that allows you to visit all five for a total of Skr40 – the price of a single museum admission – within the space of a year. (It's available at any of the five museums.)

Universeum MUSEUM
(www.universeum.se; Södra Vägen 50; adult/3-16yr Skr230/175; 10am-6pm; ; 2, 4, 5, 6, 8 Korsvägen) In what is arguably the best museum for kids in Sweden, you find yourself in the midst of a humid rainforest, complete with trickling water, tropical birds and butterflies flitting through the greenery and tiny marmosets. On a level above, roaring dinosaurs maul each other, while next door, denizens of the deep float through the shark tunnel and venomous beauties lie coiled in the serpent tanks. In the 'technology inspired by nature' section, stick your children to the Velcro wall.

Stadsmuseum MUSEUM
(City Museum; www.stadsmuseum.goteborg.se; Norra Hamngatan 12; adult/under 25yr Skr40/free; 10am-5pm Tue-Sun, to 8pm Wed; ; 1, 3, 4, 5, 6, 9 Brunnsparken) At Stadsmuseum, admire the remains of the *Äskekärrkeppet*, Sweden's only original Viking vessel, alongside silver treasure hoards, weaponry and jewellery from the same period in the atmospheric semigloom. Walk through the history of the city from its conception to the 18th century, spiced up with period wares, including an impressive booty of East Indian porcelain, and play 'Guess the Object!'. Temporary art and photography exhibitions are also worth a peek.

Konstmuseet GALLERY
(www.konstmuseum.goteborg.se; Götaplatsen; adult/under 25yr Skr40/free; 11am-6pm Tue & Thu, to 8pm Wed, to 5pm Fri-Sun; ; 4, 5, 7, 10 Berzeliigatan) Göteborg's premier art collection, Konstmuseet hosts works by the French Impressionists, Rubens, Van Gogh, Rembrandt and Picasso; Scandinavian masters such as Bruno Liljefors, Edvard Munch, Anders Zorn and Carl Larsson have pride of place in the **Fürstenburg Galleries**.

Other highlights include a superb sculpture hall, the **Hasselblad Center** with its annual *New Nordic Photography* exhibition, and temporary displays of next-gen Nordic art.

The unveiling of the bronze **Poseidon** fountain out front scandalised Göteborg's strait-laced citizens, who insisted on drastic penile-reduction surgery.

Maritiman MUSEUM
(www.maritiman.se; Packhuskajen; adult/5-15yr Skr100/50; 11am-6pm Jun-Aug; ; 5, 10 Lilla Bommen) Near the opera house, the world's largest floating ship museum is made up of 20 historical crafts, including fishing boats, a light vessel and a firefighter, all linked by walkways. Shin down into the 69m-long submarine *Nordkaparen* for a glimpse into underwater warfare. Inside the labyrinthine 121m-long destroyer *Småland*, in service from 1952 to 1979, hunched figures listen to crackling radio messages, and the bunks look just-slept-in – you half expect to meet uniformed sailors in the dim, twisting passages...

Sjöfartsmuseet MUSEUM
(www.sjofartsmuseum.goteborg.se; Karl Johansgatan 1-3; adult/under 25yr Skr40/free; 10am-5pm Tue-Sun, to 8pm Wed; ; 3, 9, 11 Stigbergstorget) Sjöfartsmuseet focuses on the city's maritime history through an entertaining collection of maps, model ships, recreated sailors' quarters, and period objects. Most compelling is the large darkened hall where you're surrounded by soaring figureheads – some regal, some pensive, some vicious. You may spot some scrimshaw and a tiny weaving loom in a bottle among the nautical booty.

The attached **aquarium** wriggles with goofy North Sea flatfish, lobsters and upside-down jellyfish, and you can find Nemo in the tropical fish tank.

Naturhistoriska Museet MUSEUM
(Natural History Museum; www.gnm.se; Museivägen 10; adult/under 25yr Skr40/free; 11am-5pm Tue-Sun; ; 1, 2, 6 Linnéplatsen) The Natural History Museum is home to an incredible range of taxidermied wildlife, from the horned and hoofed denizens of the savannah to all the big cats, the extinct Stellers sea cow, all manner of birds and pickled creatures of the deep. Its tour de force is the world's only stuffed blue whale. Visitors were allowed inside until an amorous couple was caught *in flagrante*, but Santa Claus still holds court here in the lead-up to Christmas.

Röhsska Museet MUSEUM
(www.designmuseum.se; Vasagatan 37; adult/under 25yr Skr40/free; noon-8pm Tue, to 5pm Wed-Fri, 11am-5pm Sat & Sun; 3, 4, 5, 7, 10 Valand) Sweden's only art and design museum captures the style of different eras from 1851 to the present day. Exhibitions cleverly contrast the classic and the cutting edge, whether it's Josef Frank and Bruno Mathsson furniture or 18th-century porcelain and Scandi-cool coat stands, allowing you to see how the the idea of utility and beauty changed with each successive historical period. Temporary

Göteborg

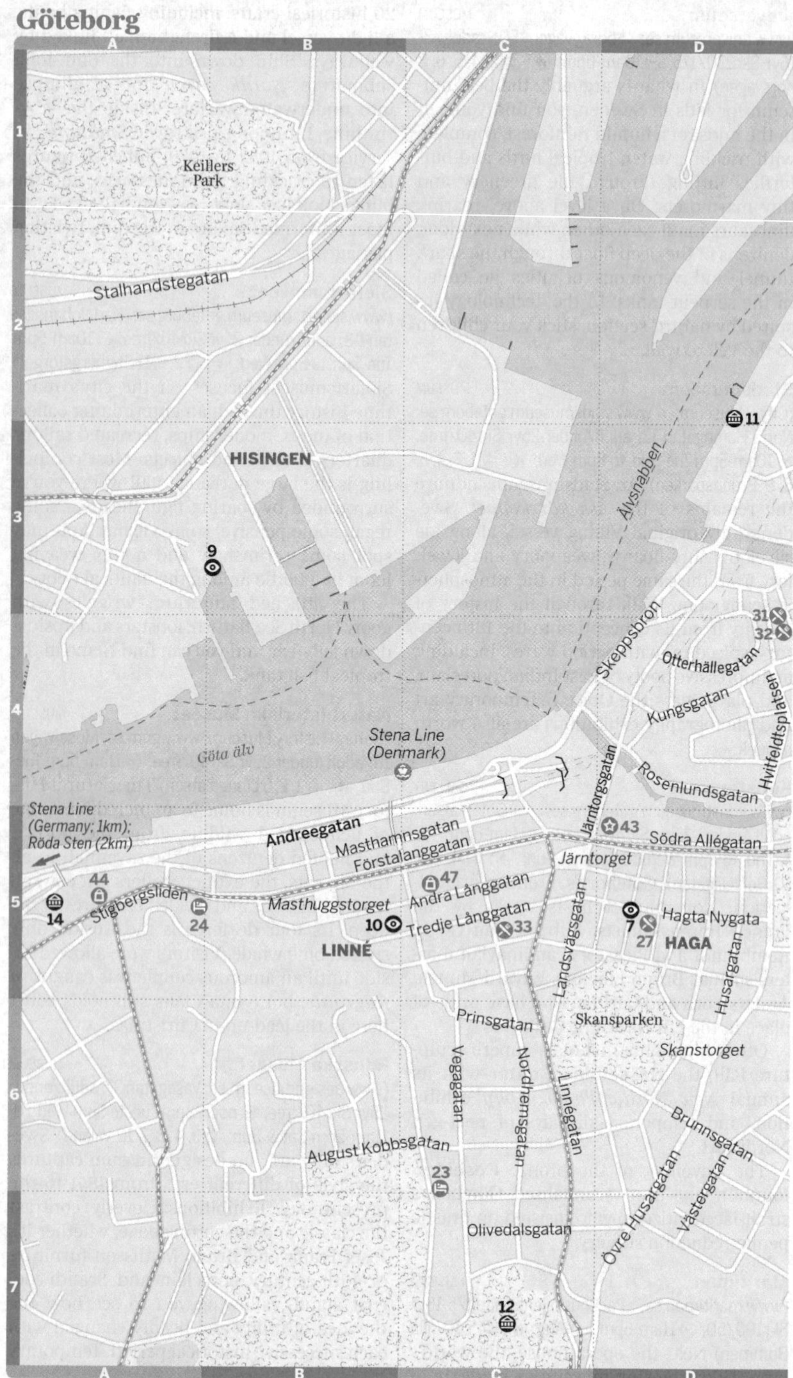

Keillers Park
Stalhandstegatan
HISINGEN
9
Älvsnabben
11
Göta älv
Stena Line (Denmark)
Skeppsbron
31
32
Otterhällegatan
Kungsgatan
Hvitfeldtsplatsen
Rosenlundsgatan
Järntorgsgatan
43
Södra Allégatan
Stena Line (Germany; 1km); Röda Sten (2km)
Andreegatan
Masthamnsgatan
Förstalanggatan
Järntorget
44
14
Stigbergsliden
24
47
Andra Långgatan
Masthuggstorget
10
Tredje Långgatan
33
7
27
Hagta Nygata
HAGA
LINNÉ
Landsvägsgatan
Husargatan
Prinsgatan
Skansparken
Skanstorget
Vegagatan
Nordhemsgatan
Linnégatan
Brunnsgatan
August Kobbsgatan
23
Övre Husargatan
Västergatan
Olivedalsgatan
12

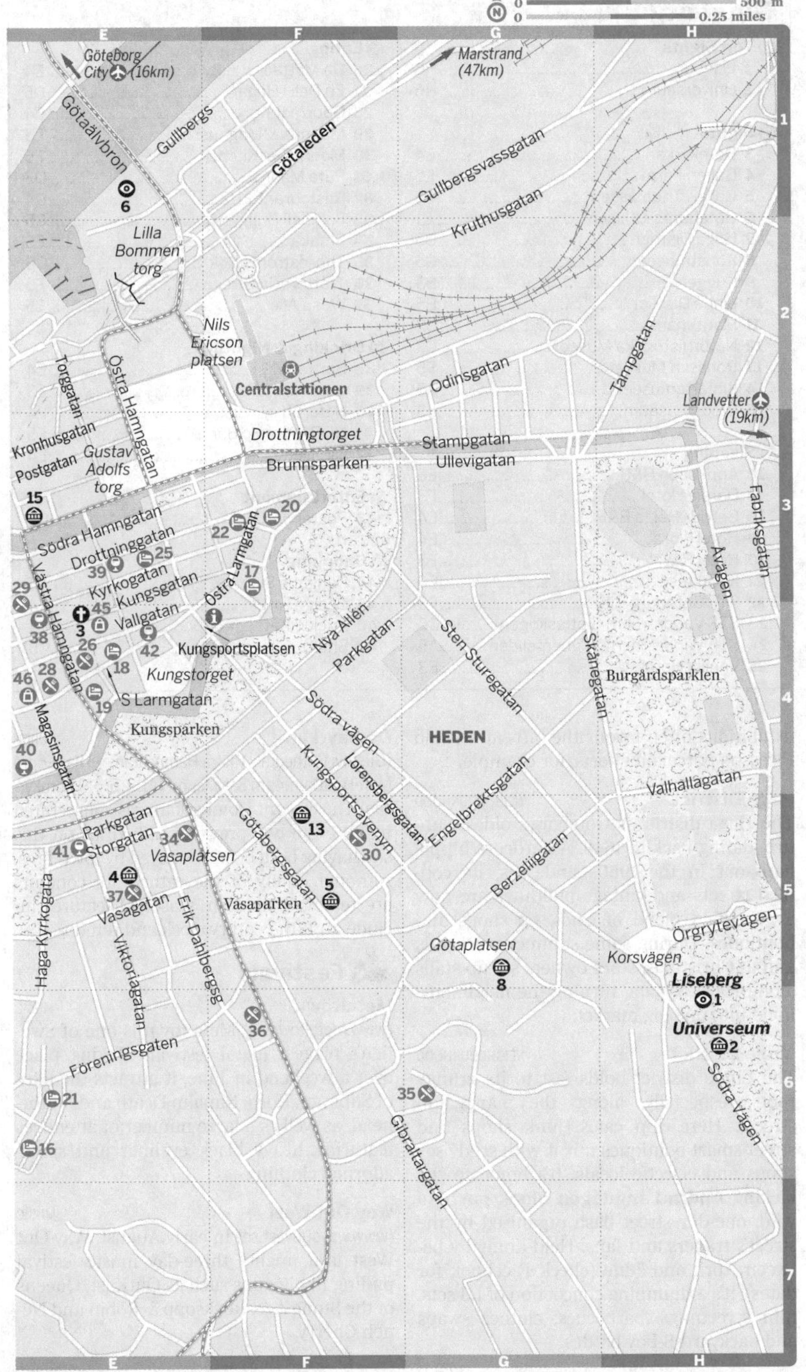
0
500 m
0
0.25 miles
Göteborg City (16km)
Marstrand (47km)
Götaälvbron
Gullbergs
Götaleden
Gullbergsvassgatan
Kruthusgatan
Lilla Bommen torg
Nils Ericson platsen
Centralstationen
Odinsgatan
Tampgatan
Landvetter (19km)
Torggatan
Östra Hamngatan
Kronhusgatan
Postgatan
Gustav Adolfs torg
Drottningtorget
Brunnsparken
Stampgatan
Ullevigatan
Fabriksgatan
Södra Hamngatan
Drottninggatan
Kyrkogatan
Kungsgatan
Vallgatan
Västra Hamngatan
Östra Larmgatan
Kungsportsplatsen
Kungstorget
S Larmgatan
Kungsparken
Magasinsgatan
Nya Allén
Parkgatan
Sten Sturegatan
Skånegatan
Åvägen
Burgårdsparklen
Södra vägen
HEDEN
Lorensbergsgatan
Kungsportsavenyn
Engelbrektsgatan
Valhallagatan
Parkgatan
Storgatan
Vasaplatsen
Götabergsgatan
Berzeliigatan
Vasagatan
Erik Dahlbergsg
Vasaparken
Götaplatsen
Örgrytevägen
Korsvägen
Haga Kyrkogata
Viktoriagatan
Liseberg
Universeum
Föreningsgaten
Södra Vägen
Gibraltargatan

Göteborg

Top Sights
1 Liseberg ... H6
2 Universeum ... H6

Sights
3 Domkyrkan ... E4
4 Galleri Ferm ... E5
5 Galleri Thomassen ... F5
6 Göteborgs-Utkiken ... E1
7 Haga District ... D5
8 Konstmuseet ... G5
9 Kuggen ... B3
10 Linné District ... B5
11 Maritiman ... D2
12 Naturhistoriska Museet ... C7
13 Röhsska Museet ... F5
14 Sjöfartsmuseet ... A5
15 Stadsmuseum ... E3

Sleeping
16 Aprikosen B&B ... E6
17 Dorsia Hotel ... F3
18 Gerdur Helga B&B ... E4
19 Hotel Flora ... E4
20 Hotel Royal ... F3
21 IQ Suites ... E6
22 STF Göteborg City ... F3
23 STF Vandrarhem Slottsskogen ... C6
24 STF Vandrarhem Stigbergsliden ... A5
25 Vanilla Hotel ... E3

Eating
26 Da Matteo ... E4
27 En Deli i Haga ... D5
28 Gourmet Korv ... E4
29 Magnus & Magnus ... E3
30 Moon Thai Kitchen ... F5
31 Puta Madre ... D3
32 Restaurant 2112 ... D4
33 Saluhall Briggen ... C5
34 Smaka ... E5
35 Thörnströms Kök ... G6
36 Trattoria la Strega ... F6
37 Wasa Allé ... E5

Drinking & Nightlife
38 Barn ... E4
39 Greta's ... E3
40 Nefertiti ... E4
41 NOBA Nordic Bar ... E5
42 Ölhallen 7:an ... E4

Entertainment
43 Pustervik ... D5

Shopping
44 Bengans Skivor & Café ... A5
45 DesignTorget ... E4
46 Prickig Katt ... E4
47 Shelta ... C5

exhibitions often favour the offbeat – Pablo Picasso's porcelain efforts, for example.

Haga District — NEIGHBOURHOOD

The Haga district is Göteborg's oldest suburb, dating back to 1648. A hardcore hippie hang-out in the 1960s and '70s, its cobbled streets and vintage buildings are now a gentrified blend of cafes, op shops and boutiques. During some summer weekends and at Christmas, store owners set up stalls along Haga Nygata, turning the neighbourhood into one big market.

Linné District — NEIGHBOURHOOD

The Linné district holds fast to its grungy roots, especially along the Långgatan streets. Here, hip cafes, junk shops and street-smart boutiques mix it with seedy sex shops and eclectic locals. It's home to the kicking **Andra Långdagen block party**, a wild, one-day street bash organised by the street's traders and fans. Held annually between April and June (check Facebook for dates), it's a thumping concoction of DJ sets, film screenings, barbecues, clothes swaps and backyard B-boy battles.

Domkyrkan — CHURCH

(Gustavi Cathedral; Västra Hamngatan; 8am-6pm Mon-Fri, 10am-4pm Sat & Sun; 1, 2, 5, 6, 9 Domkyrkan) The elegant Domkyrkan was consecrated in 1815, the two previous cathedrals on this site having both been destroyed by town fires. Although many of the cathedral's contents are relatively modern, seasoned features include an 18th-century clock and reredos.

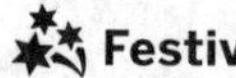

Festivals

Metaltown — MUSIC

(www.metaltown.se) Metaltown is one of Sweden's biggest metal festivals. Taking place over a weekend in June, it attracts the likes of Slipknot, Korn, Napalm Death and Motörhead, as well as a large number of attendees featuring heavy black eyeliner and spike-adorned clothing.

Way Out West — MUSIC

(www.wayoutwest.se) In early August, Way Out West is a mighty three-day music festival pulling in big guns such as OutKast, Queens of the Stone Age, Röyksopp & Robin and Neneh Cherry.

Sleeping

★STF Göteborg City HOSTEL €
(031-756 98 00; www.svenskaturistforeningen.se; Drottninggatan 63-65; s/d from Skr545/988; ; 1, 4, 6, 9, 11 Brunnsparken) Brand new and gleaming, this large super-central hostel is all industrial chic in the cafe/dining area and lounge and plush comfort on each of its individually themed floors. All rooms are private, with en suite bathroom, plush carpeting and comfortable bed-bunks, and – rarity of rarities! – your bed linen and towels are provided for you.

Gerdur Helga B&B B&B €
(031-13 55 29; www.inomvallgraven.com; Södra Larmgatan 18; d/q Skr800/1400; ; 1, 3, 5, 6, 9, 11 Grönsakstorget) This very central B&B consists of just two rooms – a quad and a twin – in a spacious apartment. Bed linen is included, and nothing is too much trouble for the friendly proprietress. Common spaces are shared with other guests and four adorable felines.

STF Vandrarhem Slottsskogen HOSTEL €
(031-42 65 20; www.sov.nu; Vegagatan 21; hostel dm/s/d from Skr195/395/540, hotel s/d Skr620/940; P@; 1, 2, 6 Olivedalsgatan) Like a good university dormitory, big, friendly Slottsskogen is a cracking place for meeting people. The facilities are top-notch, with comfortable beds, individual reading lights, lockable storage under the beds, a dressing table in the women's dorm and a good ratio of guests per bathroom. Proximity to the nightlife area is a bonus and the buffet breakfast (Skr70) is brilliant.

STF Vandrarhem Stigbergsliden HOSTEL €
(031-24 16 20; www.hostel-gothenburg.com; Stigbergsliden 10; dm/s/d/f from Skr185/475/675/875; reception 4-6pm; @; 3, 9, 11 Stigbergstorget) Rooms at Stigbergsliden have a certain monastic simplicity to them, in keeping with the hostel's history as a 19th-century seaman's institute. Staff are especially helpful, and besides the usual stuff (big kitchen, laundry, TV room) there is a pleasant sheltered garden. On the downside, the showers don't lock.

Vanilla Hotel BOUTIQUE HOTEL €€
(031-711 62 20; www.vaniljhotel.se; Kyrkogatan 38; s/d Skr1195/1345; P@; 1, 3, 5, 6, 9 Domkyrkan) This petite slumber spot has the cosy, welcoming feeling of a Swedish home. The compact rooms are pleasantly light and decorated in sparing Scandinavian style, with wooden floors and furniture, crisp sheets and immaculate bathrooms, but they get rather hot in summer. Ask for a garden-view room, as the street gets noisy from early morning. Weekend rates drop sharply.

DON'T MISS

CONTEMPORARY ART & ARCHITECTURE HIGH IN GÖTEBORG

Göteborg has imagination and creativity to spare, with new art galleries opening up and architectural flights of fancy made flesh. Here are four of our favourites:

Galleri Ferm (www.galleriferm.se; Karl Gustavsgatan 13; 11am-6pm Mon-Thu, to 5pm Fri, noon-3pm Sat & Sun; 1, 2, 3, 7, 10 Viktoriagatan) Constant surprises, mainly from Scandinavian artists such as Per Cederbank, Emil Olsson and Yrjö Edelmann, plus works by internationally renowned contemporary artists.

Galleri Thomassen (www.gallerithomassen.se; Götabergsgatan 32; noon-6pm Tue-Thu, to 4pm Fri-Sun; 1, 2, 3, 7, 10 Vasaplatsen) Showcases up-and-coming talent in its Lilla Galleriet and contemporary art from all over Scandinavia as well as Berlin.

Kuggen (Lindholmsplatsen) Across the river and next to the Science Park is the city's most exciting new building – the epitome of green engineering. Kuggen, or 'Cogwheel', resembles a bright red Colosseum, only with triangular windows that make maximum use of daylight and a host of eco-credentials that include adaptive ventilation and interactive heating and cooling systems. Take the Älvsn ferry from the Rosalund stop along Skeppsbron to Lindholmspiren.

Göteborgs-Utkiken (Lilla Bommen torg 1; adult/child Skr40/20; 11am-4pm; 6, 13 Nordstan) The red-and-white 'skyscraper' Göteborgs-Utkiken, nicknamed 'The Lipstick' for obvious reasons, has killer views of the harbour from the top.

Hotel Flora BOUTIQUE HOTEL €€
(☎031-13 86 16; www.hotelflora.se; Grönsakstorget 2; r from Skr840; @ 📶; 🚋1, 5, 6, 9, 10 Grönsakstorget) Fabulous Flora's slick, individually themed rooms flaunt black, white and a-dash-of-bright-colour interiors, designer chairs, flat-screen TVs and sparkling bathrooms, though lack of storage facilities may dismay those with extensive sartorial needs. The top-floor rooms have air-con, several rooms offer river views, and rooms overlooking the chic split-level courtyard are for night owls rather than early birds.

Hotel Royal HOTEL €€
(☎031-700 11 70; www.hotelroyal.nu; Drottninggatan 67; s/d from Skr1165/1495; @ 📶; 🚋1, 2, 5, 6, 9 Domkyrkan) Göteborg's oldest hotel (1852) has aged enviably. The grand entrance has been retained, complete with its flowery, art nouveau painted ceiling and sweeping staircase, and the elegant, individually styled rooms make necessary 21st-century concessions such as flat-screen TVs and renovated bathrooms. There's also homemade cake for guests, and an excellent breakfast. Check the website for special offers.

Aprikosen B&B B&B €€
(☎031-41 40 50; www.aprikosenbab.se; Muraregatan 5; s/d/f Skr695/895/1295; P 📶; 🚋2 Brunnsgatan) There's a pleasant contrast between the historic 1880s building this B&B is located in and the contemporary furnishings in the spacious rooms. The congenial hostess is happy to assist with the exploration of the city, there are tea/coffee-making facilities in each room, and the breakfast spread is excellent.

★ **IQ Suites** APARTMENTS €€€
(☎031-760 80 40; www.iqsuites.com; Besvärsgatan 3; s/d Skr1500/1800; P 📶; 🚋2 Brunnsgatan) Short of scanning your retinas upon entry, these luxurious, industrial-chic apartments are as high-tech as they come and are within walking distance of the city's main attractions, to boot. The fully equipped Miele kitchens are a boon for self-caterers, while the smaller of the two apartments comes with its own sauna and jacuzzi, for the ultimate in pampering.

★ **Dorsia Hotel** BOUTIQUE HOTEL €€€
(☎031-790 10 00; www.dorsia.se; Trädgårdsgatan 6; s/d/ste from Skr1900/2500/5800; ❄ @ 📶; 🚋3, 4, 5, 7, 10 Kungsportsplatsen) If Heaven had a bordello, it would resemble this lavish, flamboyant establishment that combines old-world decadence with cutting-edge design. Rooms delight with their heavy velvet curtains, a purple-and-crimson colour scheme and opulent beds; thick carpet in the corridors muffles your footsteps; and the fine art adorning the walls comes from the owner's own collection.

Eating

Cool cafes, cheap ethnic gems and foodie favourites abound around the Vasastan, Haga and Linné districts, often with lower prices than their Avenyn rivals. Göteborg also boasts plenty of great epicurean experiences in the form of Slow Food and Michelin-starred delights. For something quick, the Nordstan shopping complex has loads of fast-food outlets.

Gourmet Korv SAUSAGES €
(www.gourmetkorv.se; Södra Larmgatan; mains Skr25-85; ⏰10am-6pm Mon-Fri, to 4pm Sat, to 3pm Sun; 🚋1, 6, 9) A sausagefest to sate the hungriest of the carnivorously inclined. Choose from the likes of currywurst, bierwurst and the immensely satisfying, cheese-squirting käsekrainer and have it in a bun or with a full spread of salad and mash.

En Deli i Haga DELI €
(Haga Nygata 15; salad buffet from Skr75; ⏰8am-7pm Mon-Fri, 10am-5pm Sat & Sun; 🌿; 🚋1, 3, 5, 6, 9 Järntorget) En Deli dishes out great Mediterranean-style salads and meze, as well as good soup and sandwiches. An extra perk is the locally brewed beer and organic wine to accompany your meal.

Da Matteo CAFE €
(www.damatteo.se; Vallgatan 5; sandwiches & salads Skr50-95; ⏰8am-7pm Mon-Fri, 9am-5pm Sat, 10am-5pm Sun; 🚋1, 3, 5, 6, 9 Domkyrkan) The perfect downtown lunch pit stop and a magnet for coffee lovers, this cafe serves wickedly fine espresso, more-ish mini *sfogliatelle* (Neapolitan pastries), sandwiches, pizza and great salads. There's a sun-soaked courtyard and a second branch on Viktoriapassagen.

Saluhall Briggen MARKET €
(www.saluhallbriggen.se; Nordhemsgatan 28; sandwiches Skr60; ⏰9am-6pm Mon-Fri, to 3pm Sat; 🌿; 🚋1,6,7 10 Prinsgatan) This covered market will have you drooling over its bounty of fresh bread, cheeses, quiches, seafood and ethnic treats. It's particularly handy for the hostel district.

★ **Moon Thai Kitchen** THAI €€
(www.moonthai.se; Kristinelundsgatan 9; mains Skr129-298; ⏰11am-11pm Mon-Fri, noon-11pm Sat

& Sun; ; 4, 5, 7, 10) The owners have opted for a 'Thailand' theme and decided to run with it a few miles, hence the kaleidoscopic whirl of tuktuks, flowers and bamboo everything. Luckily, the dishes are authentic, the whimsical menu features such favourites as *som tum* (spicy papaya salad) and the fiery prawn red curry will make you weep with pleasure and gratitude.

Puta Madre MEXICAN €€
(031-711 88 38; www.putamadre.se; Magasinsgatan 3; mains Skr179-262; 6pm-midnight Mon-Thu, 5pm-2am Fri & Sat; 1, 3, 5, 6, 9 Domkyrkan) This tribute to a Mexican brothel madam serves fresh, imaginative takes on classic Mexican dishes, such as *chile en nogada* (stuffed chilli), fish tacos, shrimp and crab enchiladas and jicama salad. And haven't you always wanted to toast your friends with a 'Rusty Puta'?

Trattoria la Strega ITALIAN €€
(031-18 15 01; www.trattorialastrega.se; Aschebergsgatan 23B; mains Skr120-220; 5pm-late Tue-Fri, from 4pm Sat & Sun; ; 1, 2, 3, 7, 10 Vasaplatsen) A genuine rustic trattoria in the middle of Göteborg, La Strega has a limited but beautifully executed menu of regularly changing dishes, complemented by wines from different Italian regions. Feast on the likes of black-truffle risotto, buckwheat pasta with Savoy cabbage and entrecôte with chestnut ragu and leave room for the organic gelato.

Restaurant 2112 BURGERS €€
(031-787 58 12; Magasinsgatan; burgers Skr189-399; 4pm-1am, from 2pm Sat; ; 1, 3, 5, 6, 9 Domkyrkan) Appealing to refined rockers and metalheads, this upmarket joint serves only burgers and beer. But what burgers! These masterpieces range from the superlative Smoke on the Water with its signature Jack Daniels glaze to the fiery Hell Awaits Burger, featuring habanero dressing. The hungriest of diners will meet their match in the 666g monster Number of the Beast.

Smaka SWEDISH €€
(www.smaka.se; Vasaplatsen 3; mains Skr130-225; 5pm-late; 1, 2, 3, 7, 10 Vasaplatsen) For top-notch Swedish *husmanskost*, like the speciality meatballs with mashed potato and lingonberries, it's hard to do better than this smart yet down-to-earth restaurant-bar. Mod-Swedish options might include hake with suckling pig cheek or salmon tartar with pickled pear.

★**Thörnströms Kök** SCANDINAVIAN €€€
(031-16 20 66; www.thornstromskok.com; 3 Teknologgatan; mains Skr255-285, 4-/6-/9-course menu Skr625/825/1125; 6pm-1am Mon-Sat; 7, 10 Kapellplatsen) Specialising in modern Scandinavian cuisine, chef Håkan shows you how he earned that Michelin star through creative use of local, seasonal ingredients and flawless presentation. Feast on the likes of sweetbreads with hazelnut and cured perch with rhubarb; don't miss the remarkable milk-chocolate pudding with goat's-cheese ice cream. A la carte dishes are available if a multi-course menu overwhelms you.

Magnus & Magnus MODERN EUROPEAN €€€
(031-13 30 00; www.magnusmagnus.se; Magasinsgatan 8; 2-/3-course menus Skr455/555; from 6pm Mon-Sat; 1, 2, 5, 6, 9 Domkyrkan) Ever-fashionable Magnus & Magnus serves inspired and beautifully presented modern European dishes in an appropriately chic setting. It's an unpretentious place in spite of its popularity, with pleasantly down-to-earth waitstaff. The menu tantalises with its lists of dish ingredients (pork belly, king crab, melon, feta cheese) and the courtyard draws Göteborg's hipsters in summer.

Wasa Allé SWEDISH €€€
(031-13 13 70; www.wasaalle.se; Vasagatan 24; business lunch from Skr225, mains Skr195-225; 11.30am-2pm Mon-Fri & 6pm-late Tue-Sat; ; 1, 2, 3 Vasa Viktoriagatan) At Wasa Allé, the flagship restaurant of Mats Nordström, most ingredients come from within four hours of the restaurant, year-round. The result is 'modern, conscious Swedish food': choose between the lunchtime buffet (Skr145), seasonal business-lunch dishes, stomach-filling classics (pork with potato pancakes and lingonberries) at the attached Wasa Basement, and the surprise three- to seven-course *stolen* (chair) evening menu.

Drinking & Nightlife

Kungsportsavenyn brims with beer-downing tourists; try the following places for a little more character. The Linné district is home to several student hang-outs serving extremely cheap beer.

Barn BAR
(www.thebarn.se; Kyrkogatan 11; beer from Skr50; 5pm-late Mon-Sat, from 2pm Sun; 1, 3, 5, 6, 9 Domkyrkan) As the name suggests, this bar is all roughly hewn wood and copper taps, and the beer/wine/cocktail selection is

guaranteed to get you merry enough to, erm, raise the barn. The burgers make fantastic stomach-liners, too.

NOBA Nordic Bar BAR
(www.noba.nu; Viktoriagatan 1A; beers from Skr52; ⌚4pm-1am Mon-Thu, to 3am Fri & Sat, 5pm-1am Sun; 🚋1, 2, 3, 7, 10 Viktoriagatan) With ye olde maps of Scandinavia on the walls and a glassed-over beer patio with birch tree stumps for stools, this bar takes its Nordic beers very seriously. From Iceland's Freja to Denmark's K:rlek, you name it, they've got it. The free-flowing whiskies liven up the scene on weekends.

Ölhallen 7:an BEER HALL
(Kungstorget 7; ⌚4pm-late; 🚋3, 4, 5, 7, 10 Kungsportsplatsen) This well-worn Swedish beer hall hasn't changed much in over 100 years. It attracts an interesting mix of bikers and regular folk with its homey atmosphere and friendly service. There's no food, wine or pretension, just beer, and plenty of choices.

Greta's GAY
(☎031-13 69 49; Drottninggatan 35; ⌚9pm-3am Fri & Sat; 🚋1, 3, 4, 5, 6, 9 Brunnsparken) Decked out with Greta Garbo memorabilia, Greta's is Göteborg's only gay club, featuring flamboyant Tiki parties, DJs and other kitsch-a-licious fun on Friday and Saturday nights.

Nefertiti CLUB
(www.nefertiti.se; Hvitfeldtsplatsen 6; admission Skr120-220; 🚋1, 5, 6, 9, 11 Grönsakstorget) Named rather incongrously after an Egyptian goddess, this Göteborg institution is famous for its smooth live jazz and blues, as well as club nights spanning everything from techno and deep house to hip hop and funk. Saturday's BEAT is all about soul.

Pustervik LIVE MUSIC, THEATRE
(www.pusterviksbaren.se; Järntorgsgatan 12; 🚋1, 3, 5, 9, 11 Järntorget) Culture vultures and party people pack this hybrid venue, with its heaving downstairs bar and upstairs club and stage. Gigs range from independent theatre and live music (anything from emerging singer-songwriters to Neneh Cherry) to regular club nights spanning hip hop, soul and rock.

Shopping

DesignTorget HOMEWARES
(www.designtorget.se; Vallgatan 14; ⌚10am-7pm Mon-Fri, to 5pm Sat, noon-4pm Sun; 🚋1, 2, 5, 6, 9 Domkyrkan) Cool, affordable designer kitchenware, jewellery and more from both established and up-and-coming Scandi talent.

Prickig Katt CLOTHING
(www.prickigkatt.se; Magasinsgatan 17; ⌚11am-6pm Mon-Fri, to 4pm Sat; 🚋1, 5, 6, 9, 11 Grönsaktorget) The outrageous 'Spotted Cat' has retro-clad staff and idiosyncratic fashion from Dutch, Danish and home-grown labels, as well as kitschy wares and out-there handmade millinery and bling.

Bengans Skivor & Café MUSIC
(☎031-14 33 00; www.bengans.se; Stigbergstorget 1; ⌚to 4pm Sat, noon-4pm Sun; 🚋3, 9, 11 Stigbergstorget) Göteborg's mightiest music store is set in an old cinema, complete with retro signage and indie-cool cafe.

Shelta SHOES
(☎031-24 28 56; www.shelta.eu; Andra Långgatan 21; ⌚11am-6.30pm Mon-Sat; 🚋3, 9, 11 Masthuggstorget) Pimp your style with limited-edition and must-have sneakers and streetwear from big players and lesser-known labels.

Information

INTERNET ACCESS

Sidewalk Express (www.sidewalkexpress.se; per hr Skr25) Sidewalk Express computers are found at Centralstationen and the 7-Eleven shop on Vasaplatsen. To log on, buy vouchers from the coin-operated machines and enter the username and password issued.

MEDICAL SERVICES

Apotek Hjärtat (☎0771-45 04 50; Nils Eriksongatan; ⌚8am-10pm) Late-night pharmacy inside the Nordstan shopping complex.

Sahlgrenska Universitetssjukhuset (☎031-342 00 00; www.sahlgrenska.se; 🚋1) Major hospital about 5km northeast of central Göteborg, near the terminus at the end of tram line 1.

MONEY

Forex (www.forex.se) Foreign-exchange office with branches at Centralstationen, Kungsportsavenyn 22, Kungsportsplatsen, Landvetter Airport and Norstan shopping complex.

TOURIST INFORMATION

Cityguide Gothenburg (www.goteborg.com/en/Do/Artiklar/Mobileapp/) Info on the city's attractions, events and more, available as an Android and iPhone app. City map available offline.

Gay Information (RFSL) (☎031-13 83 00; www.rfsl.se/goteborg) Comprehensive information on the city's gay scene, events and more.

Tourist Office (☎031-368 42 00; www.goteborg.com; Kungsportsplatsen 2; ⌚9.30am-8pm) Central and busy; has a good selection of free brochures and maps.

Getting There & Away

AIR

Göteborg Landvetter Airport (www.swedavia.se/landvetter) Twenty-five kilometres east of the city, Sweden's second-biggest international airpor has up to 12 direct daily flights to/from Stockholm Arlanda and Stockholm Bromma airports (with SAS, Malmö Aviation and Norwegian), as well as weekday services to Umeå and several weekly services to Borlänge, Falun, Visby and Sundsvall. Take Flygbuss from central Götborg.

Göteborg City Airport (www.goteborgairport.se) Some 15km north of the city at Säve, this airport is used for budget Ryanair and Wizz Air flights to destinations including London Stansted, Edinburgh, Paris, Malaga and Budapest, as well as domestic flights to Visby with Gotlandsflyg.

BOAT

Stena Line (Denmark) (www.stenaline.se; 🚋3, 9, 11 Masthuggstorget) Nearest to central Göteborg, the Stena Line Denmark terminal near Masthuggstorget (tram 3, 9 or 11) has around six daily departures for Frederikshavn in peak season (one way/return from Skr499/998).

Stena Line (Germany) (www.stenaline.se; 🚋3, 9 Jaegardorffsplatsen) Services to Kiel in Germany (one way/return from Skr1699/2998) depart from near the Älvsborgsbron bridge. Departures are daily at 6.45pm and the journey takes 14 hours.

BUS

Västtrafik (☎0771-41 43 00; www.vasttrafik.se) and **Hallandstrafiken** (☎0771-33 10 30; www.hlt.se) provide regional transport links. The bus station, Nils Ericson Terminalen, is next to the train station. The Västtrafik information booth provides information and sells tickets for all city and regional public transport within the Göteborg, Bohuslän and Västergötland area.

Swebus Express (p415) has an office located at the bus terminal and operates frequent buses to most of the major towns. Services include the following:

Copenhagen Skr239, five hours, four daily

Halmstad Skr109, 1¾ hours, five daily

Helsingborg Skr139, 2¾ hours, five to eight daily

Malmö Skr159, 3½ to four hours, five to eight daily

Oslo Skr189, 3½ hours, five to ten daily

Stockholm Skr379, seven hours, four to five daily

CAR & MOTORCYCLE

The E6 motorway runs north–south from Oslo to Malmö just east of the city centre and there's also a complex junction where the E20 motorway diverges east for Stockholm.

International car-hire companies **Avis** (www.avisworld.com), **Europcar** (www.europcar.com) and **Hertz** (www.hertz-europe.com) have desks at Landvetter and Göteborg City airports.

WORTH A TRIP

MARSTRAND

Looking like a Tommy Hilfiger ad, this former spa town and island is a Swedish royal favourite, conveying the essence of the Bohuslän fishing villages that dot the coast from Göteborg to the Norwegian border. Boasting the country's most popular *gästhamn* (guest harbour) and pedestrian-only cobbled streets, it's the weekend destination for yachting types.

The 17th-century **Carlstens Fästning** (www.carlsten.se; adult/7-15yr Skr80/40; ⏲11am-6pm late Jun-late Jul, to 4pm rest of Jun & Aug) fortress reflects the town's martial and penal history. There are smashing archipelago views from the top of its round tower; you can also explore the secret tunnel and in the prison cells learn the story of Lasse Maja, a cross-dressing thief and local Robin Hood figure.

Marstrand's numerous eating options include century-old local institution **Bergs Konditori** (www.bergskonditori.com; Hamngatan 9; sandwiches from Skr69; ⏲7am-5pm May-Aug), a dockside bakery selling fresh bread, cakes, quiches and sandwiches, while **Johan's Krog** (☎0303-612 12; www.johanskrogmarstrand.se; Kungsgatan 12; mains Skr265-345; ⏲6.30pm-late) tantalises with the likes of king crab paired with pickled carrot and entrecote with roasted beef marrow and port reduction.

From Göteborg, take the **Marstrands Expressen** (www.vasttraffik.se) directly to Marstrand passenger-only ferry terminal (50 minutes) that crosses over to the island every 15 minutes (Skr25).

TRAIN

From Centralstationen – Sweden's oldest train station – SJ and regional trains run to Stockholm (Skr476, 3¼ to 4¾ hours, twice hourly), Copenhagen (Skr450, 3¾ hours, hourly), Malmö (Skr343, 3¼ hours, hourly) as well as numerous other destinations.

Getting Around

Flygbuss (www.flygbussarna.se) services connect Nils Ericson Terminalen to the two airports.

Västtrafik runs the city's public transport system of buses, trams and ferries. There are Västtrafik information booths selling tickets and giving out timetables inside Nils Ericson Terminalen and in front of the train station on Drottningtorget.

Holders of the Göteborg City Card travel free. Otherwise a city transport ticket costs from Skr25. A 24-hour Dagkort (day pass) for the whole city area costs Skr80, or Skr160 for 72 hours.

The easiest way to cover lengthy distances in Göteborg is by tram. Lines, numbered 1 to 13, converge near Brunnsparken (a block from the train station).

Västtrafik has regional passes for 24 hours (adult Skr235) that give unlimited travel on all *länstrafik* buses, trains and boats within Göteborg, Bohuslän and the Västergötland area.

Cykelkungen (☎031-18 43 00; www.cykelkungen.se; Chalmersgatan 19; 24hr/3 days/1 week Skr200/400/700) offers bike rental.

Strömstad

☎0526 / POP 6288

A sparky resort, fishing harbour and spa town, Strömstad is laced with ornate wooden buildings echoing those of nearby Norway. There are several fantastic Iron Age remains in the area, and some fine sandy beaches at Capri and Seläter. Boat trips run to the Koster Islands, popular for cycling and swimming. One of Sweden's largest, most magnificent **stone ship settings** (24hr) FREE lies 6km northeast of Strömstad; ask for details at the tourist office.

A 10-minute walk from central Strömstad, the stately **Emma's Bed and Breakfast** (☎0916-65 046; www.emmasbedandbreakfast.se; Kebal 2; s/d from Skr700/1400; P 📶), dating back to 1734, sits amidst quiet wooded grounds. The rooms are bright and airy and the friendly hostess whips up a full Scandinavian spread at breakfast time.

One of the best places to try the fresh local *räkor* (shrimp) and delicious seafood is **Rökeri is Strömstad** (dnn.rokerietistromstad.se; Torksholmen; lunch mains Skr130-180, dinner mains Skr209-359; noon-5pm Tue-Sat, 5pm-late Fri & Sat), a family-run smokehouse, fish shop and restaurant.

The **tourist office** (☎0526-623 30; www.stromstad.se; Ångbåtskajen 2; 9am-8pm Mon-Sat, 10am-7pm Sun Jun-Aug) is located between the two harbours on the main square.

Buses and trains both use the train station near the southern harbour. **Västtrafik** (www.vasttrafik.se) runs bus 871 to Göteborg (Skr170, 2¼ hours, three to four daily). Direct trains connect Strömstad to Göteborg (Skr180, 2¼ to three hours, one to two hourly).

Norrköping

☎011 / POP 87,247

The envy of industrial has-beens across Europe, Norrköping has managed to cleverly regenerate its defunct mills and canals into a posse of cultural and gastronomic hang-outs fringing waterfalls and locks. Retro trams rattle down streets that are lined with eclectic architecture, while some 30km to the northeast, the animal park at Kolmården swaps urban regeneration for majestic Siberian tigers.

Sights

★Industrilandskapet HISTORIC SITE

Industrilandskapet, Norrköping's star turn, is the impeccably preserved industrial area near the river. Pedestrian walkways and bridges lead past magnificent former factory buildings and around the ingenious system of locks and canals. The most thunderous waterfall is **Kungsfallet**, near the islet Laxholmen.

Within the area are several interesting museums, all with free admission.

Arbetets Museum MUSEUM

(www.arbetetsmuseum.se; Laxholmen; 11am-5pm, to 8pm Tue) FREE The innovative Arbetets Museum documents working life. There's one permanent display about Alva Carlsson, a typical worker in the former cotton mill, and temporary exhibitions focusing mainly on gender issues, human rights or multiculturalism. The seven-sided building, completed in 1917 and dubbed the 'flatiron', is a work of art in itself.

Konstmuseum MUSEUM
(www.norrkoping.se/konstmuseet; Kristinaplatsen; ⏲noon-4pm Tue-Sun, to 8pm Wed Jun-Aug) FREE Over near Vasaparken, Konstmuseum is Norrköping's impressive art museum. Its collection boasts important early-20th-century works, including modernist and cubist gems, as well as one of Sweden's largest collections of graphic art.

Louis de Geer Konserthus CULTURAL CENTRE
(☎011-15 50 30; www.louisdegeer.com; Dalsgatan 15) A modern addition to the riverside scenery is the extraordinary 1300-seat Louis de Geer Konserthus concert venue, located in a former paper mill. Still containing the original balconies, it's a superb setting for concerts.

Stadsmuseum MUSEUM
(City Museum; www.norrkoping.se/stadsmuseet; Holmbrogränd; ⏲11am-5pm Tue-Fri, to 8pm Thu, noon-5pm Sat & Sun) FREE Stadsmuseum delves into the town's industrial past, complete with still-functioning machinery, a great cafe and dynamic temporary exhibitions.

Sleeping

STF Vandrarhem Abborreberg HOSTEL €
(☎011-31 93 44; www.abborreberg.se; dm/s/d Skr250/300/500; ⏲Apr–mid-Oct; P 👪; 🚌116) Stunningly situated in a coastal pine wood 5km east of town, this sterling hostel offers accommodation in huts scattered through the surrounding park. The associated ice-cream parlour is a hit with gluttons. Take bus 116 to Lindö (Skr35).

★ **Strand Hotell** BOUTIQUE HOTEL €€
(☎011-16 99 00; www.hotellstrand.se; Drottninggatan 2; s/d from Skr995/1295, apt Skr2100; @ 📶) A real gem in the heart of town, the Strand takes up the 2nd floor of a gorgeous 1890 building overlooking the Motala river and Drottninggattan. It's operated as a hotel since the 1930s, and the furniture and fabrics make the most of the building's existing features, such as cut-glass chandeliers and big bay windows.

Hotell Hörnan HOTEL €€
(☎011-16 58 90; www.hotellhornan.com; cnr Hörngatan & Sankt Persgatan; r with/without bathroom Skr865/665; ❄ 📶) These spacious rooms were fully renovated in 2013 and are excellent value. Glossy parquet floors, comfortable chairs, colourful rugs and scarlet drapes contrasting with dazzling white linen equal a contemporary, comfortable look. Pick up the key to your room in the adjacent pub.

> WORTH A TRIP
>
> ### THE KINGDOM OF THE TIGER
>
> **Kolmården** (www.kolmarden.com; adult/child Skr399/299; ⏲10am-7pm mid-Jun–mid-Aug; P) is Scandinavia's largest zoo, with some 750 residents from all climates and continents. There is a safari park, marine world and tiger world, plus dolphin shows and a separate superb **Tropicarium** (☎011-39 52 50; www.tropicarium.se; adult/child Skr120/60; ⏲10am-8pm daily Jul–mid-Aug, 10am-6pm Mon-Fri, to 7pm Sat & Sun May-Jun, shorter hours rest of year) with its motley crew of spiders, sharks, alligators and snakes.
>
> You'll need a whole day to fully appreciate the zoo. Kolmården lies 35km north of Norrköping, on the north shore of Bråviken. Take bus 432 or 433 from Norrköping (Skr80, 40 minutes).

Eating

There are plenty of eateries in the shopping district along Drottninggatan, in the little square off Skogatan and in the student quarter around Kungsgatan.

Mimmis Visthus DELI €
(www.mimmisvisthus.se; Skolgatan 1B; lunch Skr89; ⏲10am-6pm Mon-Fri, to 4pm Sat, noon-4pm Sun; 🌶) 🌿 With its emphasis on ecologically sound, local produce, this adorable little cafe serves heaped plates of superfood salads, spicy vegetarian lasagne, quiches, cakes, chicken satay and smoothies.

Fiskmagasinet SEAFOOD €€
(☎011-13 45 60; www.fiskmagasinet.se; Skolgatan 1; lunch Skr90, mains Skr135-285; ⏲11.30am-2pm & 5-10pm Mon-Fri, noon-10pm Sat) Housed in a converted 19th-century *snus* (snuff) factory, urbane Fiskmagasinet combines an intimate bar with a casually chic dining room serving savvy seafood dishes such as grilled scampi with mashed potato, truffle and port wine reduction, as well as cheaper Swedish classics.

Lagerqvist EUROPEAN €€
(☎011-10 07 40; www.restauranglagerqvist.se; Gamla Torget 4; mains Skr125-285; ⏲5-11pm Tue-Sun)

Norrköping

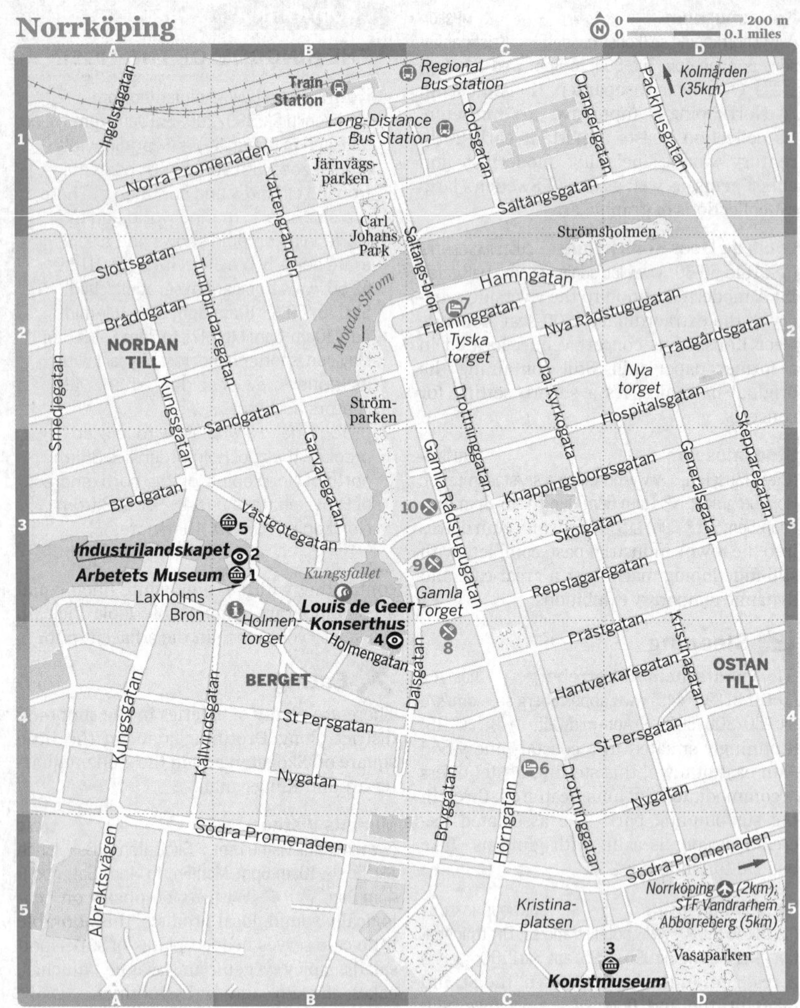

This perennially popular restaurant-pub has a great summer garden courtyard and snug vaulted cellar. Meat dishes are the speciality, with innovative sides including green beans with truffle butter. There are also platters for sharing.

Pappa Grappa Bar & Trattoria ITALIAN €€
(www.pappagrappa.se; Gamla Rådstugugatan 26-28; pizzas from Skr83, mains from Skr165; ⏲4-10pm Mon-Fri, noon-late Sat, to 9pm Sun, pizzeria also 4-11pm Sun) Gobble up a brilliant wood-fired pizza or slip into the vaulted restaurant for scrumptious antipasto.

Information

Tourist Office (☎011-15 50 00; www.norrkoping.se; Källvindsgatan 1; ⏲10am-6pm daily Jul–mid-Aug, shorter hours rest of year) The tourist office runs free one-hour walking tours of the industrial area in summer.

Getting There & Around

AIR

Sweden's third-largest airport, **Stockholm Skavsta** (www.skavsta.se), is 60km away. To get there take the train to Nyköping, then catch a local bus. **Norrköping airport** (☎011-15 37 22;

Norrköping

Top Sights

1 Arbetets Museum B3
2 Industrilandskapet B3
3 Konstmuseum D5
4 Louis de Geer Konserthus B4

Sights

5 Stadsmuseum B3

Sleeping

6 Hotell Hörnan C4
7 Strand Hotell C2

Eating

Fiskmagasinet .... (see 9)
8 Lagerqvist C4
9 Mimmis Visthus C3
10 Pappa Grappa Bar & Trattoria C3

www.norrkopingflygplats.se) has direct flights from Copenhagen, Helsinki and Munich.

BUS

The regional bus station is next to the train station, and long-distance buses leave from a terminal across the road. Swebus Express (p415) has frequent services to Stockholm (Skr149, 2¼ hours) and Jönköping (Skr219, 2½ hours), and several services daily to Göteborg (Skr299, five hours) and Kalmar (Skr269, four hours).

TRAIN

SJ trains depart for Stockholm (from Skr230, 1½ hours) and Malmö (from Skr370, 3¼ hours). Trains run roughly every hour north to Nyköping (from Skr93, one hour) and every 20 minutes south to Linköping (from Skr84, 25 minutes).

Linköping

013 / POP 104,232

Most famous for its mighty medieval cathedral, Linköping is Norrköping's more upmarket cousin and also the site of the 'bloodbath of Linköping'. Following the Battle of Stångebro (1598), many of King Sigismund's defeated Catholic army were executed here, leaving Duke Karl and his Protestant forces in full control of Sweden.

While quite the modern industrial city today (manufacturer Saab is the major employer), pockets of its past survive in its churches, castle, museums and the picture-perfect streets around Hunnebergsgatan and Storgatan.

Sights & Activities

★Gamla Linköping & Valla Fritidsområde HISTORIC SITE
(www.gamlalinkoping.info; P) FREE Located 2km west of the city, this is one of the biggest living-museum villages in Sweden. It's a gorgeous combo of cobbled streets, picket-fenced gardens and around 90 19th-century houses. Take bus 12 or 19 (Skr25).

Just 300m through the forest is Valla Fritidsområde, a recreation area with domestic animals, a children's playground, mini golf, small museums and vintage abodes.

Domkyrka CHURCH
(9am-6pm) FREE Made from blocks of handcarved limestone, the enormous Domkyrka was the country's largest and most expensive church in the Middle Ages. Its foundations were laid around 1250 and its 107m spire and vast interior still impress. Inside, the contemporary stained-glass windows may also catch your eye; they're the work of famous British stained-glass artist Brian Clarke. There are organ concerts on Thursday in summer.

Östergötlands Länsmuseum GALLERY
(www.ostergotlandsmuseum.se; Vasavägen; adult/child Skr70/free; 11am-4pm Tue-Sun) Has a decent European art collection (Cranach's painting of Eden, *Original Sin*, is wonderful, with a smiling Eve twiddling her toes), and Swedish art dating from the Middle Ages.

Kinda Canal CRUISE
While it's upstaged by the Göta Canal, Linköping boasts its own canal system, the 90km Kinda Canal. Opened in 1871, it has 15 locks, including Sweden's deepest. Cruises include evening sailings, musical outings and wine-tasting trips. For a simple day excursion, from late June to early August the **M/S Kind** (0141-23 33 70; www.kindakanal.se; adult/child Skr375/185; May-Sep) leaves Tullbron dock at 10am on Tuesday, Thursday and Saturday, and travels to Rimforsa (return by bus or train).

Sleeping & Eating

Most places to eat and drink are on the main square or nearby streets, especially along buzzing Ågatan.

City Hotel & STF Vandrarhem HOSTEL, HOTEL €
(013-35 90 00; www.lvh.se; Klostergatan 52A; hostel s/d Skr585/649, hotel s/d Skr690/1090;

🅿@📶👪; 🚌30, 52, 59, 72, 78) This slickly modern hostel has hotel-style accommodation too, mostly with kitchenettes. All rooms have TVs and private bathrooms – rooms for the hotels and hostels are similar, but the hotel price includes breakfast and linen.

Park Hotel HOTEL €€
(☎013-12 90 05; www.fawltytowers.se; Järnvägsgatan 6; s/d Skr1145/1345; 🅿@📶) Disturbingly billed as Sweden's 'Fawlty Towers', this smart family-run establishment resembles that madhouse in appearance only (yes, there's an elk head at reception). The public spaces sport chandeliers, oil paintings and clean, parquet-floored rooms, while the rooms are crisply modern.

★ **Café Berget** BAKERY €
(www.cafeberget.com; Klostergatan 38; cakes from Skr35; ⏲10am-6pm Mon-Fri, to 4pm Sat) Up a narrow set of stone stairs you'll find a sunny terrace, resplendent with flowers and ivy, which serves as the doorstep to this glorious little bolt-hole bakery. Café Berget serves up classic Swedish baked goodies – vanilla cream hearts and blueberry tartlets – as well as coffee, tea and sandwiches, in lovingly restored rooms in this 1905 building.

Yellow Fellow ASIAN €€
(☎913-12 22 26; Stora Torget 7; mains from Skr100; ⏲11am-11pm Mon-Thu, to 1.30am Fri & Sat, noon-9pm Sun) Overlooking the main square and making a change from the ubiquitous cafes, this Thai restaurant is great for a cold beer and a spicy curry. Check out the lavish frond-filled interior.

Stångs Magasin SWEDISH €€€
(www.stangsmagasin.se; Södra Stånggatan 1; lunch Skr115, mains Skr145-505; ⏲11.30am-2pm Mon-Fri, 6pm-midnight Tue-Fri, 5pm-midnight Sat Jul & Aug; 📶) In a 200-year-old warehouse down near the Kinda Canal docks, this elegant award-winner fuses classic Swedish cuisine with continental influences – think stuffed trout with beet aioli. There is an extensive wine list and a sommelier on hand to help you choose.

ℹ Information

Tourist Office (☎013-190 0070; www.visitlinkoping.se; Storgatan 15; ⏲10am-6pm Mon-Fri, to 4pm Sat, to 6pm Sun) Across from Sankt Lars Kyrka.

ℹ Getting There & Away

AIR

The **airport** (☎013-18 10 30; www.linkopingcityairport.se) is 2km east of town. There's no airport bus, but taxi company **Taxibil** (☎013-14 60 00) charges around Skr160 for the ride.

BUS

Regional and local buses, run by **ÖstgötaTrafiken** (☎0771-21 10 10; www.ostgotatrafiken.se), leave from the terminal next to the train station.

Up to five express buses per day go to Vadstena; otherwise change at Motala.

Long-distance buses depart from a terminal 500m northwest of the train station. Swebus Express (p415) runs to Göteborg (Skr289, four hours, seven daily), and north to Norrköping (Skr59, 45 minutes, nine daily).

TRAIN

Trains run to Stockholm (Skr285, 1¾ to 2½ hours, hourly), Malmö (Skr341, 2¾ hours, hourly) and Norrköping (Skr80, 25 minutes, every 20 minutes).

Vadstena

☎0143 / POP 5613

Sublimely situated aside Vättern lake, Vadstena is a legacy of both church and state power, and today St Birgitta's abbey and Gustav Vasa's castle compete with each other for admiration. The atmosphere in the old town, with its wonderful cobbled lanes, intriguing small shops and wooden buildings, makes it an especially satisfying place to end a day of touring along the Göta Canal.

👁 Sights & Activities

★ **Vadstena Slott** CASTLE
(www.vadstenadirect.se; Slottsvägen; tours adult/child Skr80/60; ⏲11am-4pm, to 6pm Jun-early Aug) Overlooking the lake, and considered one of the finest early Renaissance buildings in the Nordic region, Vadstena Slott was the family project of the early Vasa kings; their gloomy portraits are on view, along with a modest historical display. The furnished upper floors are the most interesting, and be sure to visit the chapel, with its incredible 17-second echo! There are guided tours (in English) mid-July to mid-September; call ahead for times.

Sancta Birgitta Klostermuseet MUSEUM
(www.sanctabirgitta.com; Lasarettsgatan; adult/child Sk60/30; ⏲10.30am-5pm Jul–mid-Aug, 11am-4pm Jun & rest of Aug) The Sancta Birg-

itta Klostermuseet is in Bjälboättens Palats (a royal residence that became a convent in 1384) and tells the story of St Birgitta's roller-coaster life and those of all her saint-and-sinner children. Artefacts include the coffin that carried her back from Rome.

Klosterkyrkan CHURCH

(Abbey Church; 9am-8pm Jul, to 7pm Jun & Aug) 'Of plain construction, humble and strong', Klosterkyrkan was built in response to one of St Birgitta's visions. After the church's consecration in 1430, Vadstena became *the* top pilgrimage site in Sweden. Step inside for medieval sculptures and carved floor slabs.

Sleeping & Eating

Pensionat Solgården B&B €

(0143-143 50; www.pensionatsolgarden.se; Strågatan 3; s/d from Skr540/790; May-Sep; P) Set in a classic 1905 wooden house, this family-run hotel boasts lovingly decorated rooms; some have private bathrooms and all have an art/artist connection. They're each *very* different – check the photos on the website to choose your favourite (number 25 is particularly grand).

Vadstena Klosterhotel HISTORIC HOTEL €€

(0143-315 30; www.klosterhotel.se; r from Skr1475; P@) History and luxury merge at this wonderfully atmospheric hotel in St Birgitta's old convent. The bathrooms are a wee bit dated, but the medieval-style rooms are great, with chandeliers and high wooden beds. Most boast lake views. The hotel also has simpler rooms with shared bathrooms and showers in a nearby cottage (singles/doubles Skr790/990).

★**Restaurant Munkklostret** EUROPEAN €€

(0143-130 00; lunch mains from Skr125, dinner mains from Skr169; noon-11pm daily Jun-Aug, from 6pm rest of year;) The Klosterhotel's ravishing restaurant is the best dining spot in town. Seasonal, succulent steak, lamb, game and fish dishes are flavoured with herbs from the monastery garden, and served in the monks' old dorms.

Rojas BISTRO €€

(0143-123 43; Storgatan 20; mains from Skr115; 10am-10pm Sun-Mon, to 11pm Wed-Sat) The interior here is cosily cluttered with a 1950s theme, kickback sofas and an eclectic display of art and antiques, while the terrace sprawls invitingly into the square. The menu has an interesting range of dishes, including excellent tacos.

Information

Tourist Office (0143-315 70; www.vadstena.se; 10am-6pm daily Jul, 10am-6pm Mon-Sat, to 4pm Sun Jun & early Aug, to 2pm Mon-Sat rest of year) Located in the Rödtornet (Sånggatan). A great place to get details about town walks, boat tours and festivals.

Getting There & Around

Only buses run to Vadstena – take bus 610 to Motala (for trains to Örebro) or bus 661 to Mjölby (for trains to Linköping and Stockholm). **Blåklints Buss** (0142-121 50; www.blaklintsbuss.se) runs one to three services daily from the Viking Line Terminal in Stockholm to Vadstena (Skr250).

SMÅLAND

The region of Småland is one of dense forests, glinting lakes and bare marshlands. Historically it served as a buffer zone between the Swedes and Danes; the eastern and southern coasts in particular witnessed territorial tussles. Today it's better known for the Glasriket (Kingdom of Crystal) in the central southeast.

Växjö

0470 / POP 60,887

A venerable old market town, Växjö (*vak-choo*, with the 'ch' sound pronounced as in the Scottish 'loch'), in Kronobergs *län*, is an important stop for Americans seeking their Swedish roots. In mid-August, **Karl Oscar Days** (www.karloskardagarna.se) commemorates the mass 19th-century emigration from the area, and the Swedish-American of the year is chosen. The town's glass museum, packed with gorgeous works of art and plenty of history, is another highlight.

Sights

★**Smålands Museum** MUSEUM

(www.kulturparkensmaland.se; Södra Järnvägsgatan 2; adult/child Skr70/free; 10am-5pm Tue-Fri, to 4pm Sat & Sun) Among the varied exhibits at Sweden's oldest provincial museum is a truly stunning exhibition about the country's 500-year-old glass industry, with objects spanning medieval goblets to cutting-edge contemporary sculptures. It even houses a Guinness World Records collection of Swedish cheese-dish covers – 71 in total. There's a great cafe and the ticket price covers the adjacent House of Emigrants.

WORTH A TRIP

ASTRID LINDGREN'S HOUSE

If you've grown up on stories of Pippi Longstocking, Karlsson-on-the-Roof, Kalle Blomkvist and other characters who'll stay with you all your life, you shouldn't miss the opportunity to visit the childhood home of Astrid Lindgren (1907–2002), Sweden's most prolific children's book author, whose books have been translated into dozens of languages.

In Vimmerby, halfway between Linköping and Växjö, **Astrid Lindgrens Näs** (tours 0492-76 94 00; www.astridlindgrensnas.se; Prästgården 24; adult/child Skr120/free, tours adult/child Skr95/50; 10am-6pm mid-Jun–end Aug, shorter hours rest of the year; P) presents both her restored childhood home – an adorable cottage surrounded by rosebushes and visited by guided tour in summer – and a superb permanent exhibition that takes you through this remarkable woman's life and achievements.

A girl with an idyllic childhood turned struggling single mother at 18, with energy to spare and a wild imagination, she took a stand against Hitler, was first published as an author in 1944, had a minor planet named after her and was found up a tree when she was well past the age of 70, saying that there's no rule that says that old women shouldn't climb trees. That's just the tip of the iceberg. To discover more, stop by.

House of Emigrants MUSEUM
(Utvandrarnas Hus; www.utvandrarnashus.se; Vilhelm Mobergs gata 4; adult/child Skr70/free; 10am-5pm Tue-Fri, to 4pm Sat & Sun) Boasts engrossing displays on the emigration of over one million Swedes to America (1850–1930) and includes a replica of Vilhelm Moberg's office and original manuscripts of his famous emigration novels.

Sleeping & Eating

B&B Södra Lycke B&B €€
(0706-76 65 06; www.sodralycke.se; Hagagatan 10; s/d Skr500/800; P) This charming B&B in an atmospheric mid-19th-century family house is in a residential area 10 minutes' walk southwest from the centre via Södra Järnvägsgatan (check online for a map). There are three rooms and an appealingly overgrown garden complete with vegetable plot, wildflowers, greenhouse and black hens.

★ **PM & Vänner** SWEDISH €€€
(0470-70 04 44; www.pmrestauranger.se; Storgatan 22; restaurant tasting menu Skr995, bistro mains Skr209-365; 11.30am-1.30pm Mon-Sat, plus 6-10pm Wed-Sat) A stylish bistro complete with black-and-white tiled floors and wicker chairs, PM & Vänner serves up new-school Swedish flavours with global twists. Local produce sparkles in dishes ranging from grilled cod with summer chanterelles to Småland veal. It also runs popular cocktail and lounge bar **Terrassen** (www.pmrestauranger.se; Västergatan 10; 6pm-midnight), which has live music Wednesday and Thursday.

Information

Tourist Office (0470-73 32 80; www.turism.vaxjo.se; Stortorget, Residencet; 9.30am-6pm Mon-Fri, 10am-2pm Sat Jun-Aug) On the main square.

Getting There & Away

Småland airport (0470-75 85 00; www.smalandairport.se) is 9km northwest of Växjö. SAS and **NextJet** (08-639 85 38; www.nextjet.se) have direct flights to Stockholm Arlanda airport, **Fly Smaland** (0900-20 71 720; www.flysmaland.com) to Stockholm's Bromma, and Ryanair to Düsseldorf Weeze. Bus 50 connects with Ryanair flights from Växjö's Centralstation; otherwise take a **taxi** (0470-135 00; www.vaxjotaxi.se).

Länstrafiken Kronoberg (0470-72 75 50; www.lanstrafikenkron.se) runs the regional bus network, with daily buses to Halmstad, Jönköping and Kosta. Long-distance buses depart beside the train station. Svenska Buss (p421) runs daily services to Eksjö (Skr250, 1½ hours), Linköping (Skr320, 3¼ hours) and Stockholm (Skr420, 6½ hours).

Växjö is served by SJ trains running to Kalmar (Skr146, 1¼ hours), Malmö (Skr195, two hours, hourly) and Karlskrona (Skr163, 1½ hours).

Glasriket

With its hypnotic glass-blowing workshops, **Glasriket** (www.glasriket.se), the 'Kingdom of Crystal', is the most visited area of Sweden outside Stockholm and Göteborg, featuring a dozen or so glass factories (look for *glasbruk* signs), most with long histories: Kosta, for example, was founded in 1742.

The glassworks have similar opening hours, usually 10am to 6pm Monday to Friday, 10am to 4pm Saturday and noon to 4pm Sunday. Expert glass designers produce some extraordinary avant-garde pieces, often with a good dollop of Swedish wit involved. Factory outlets have substantial discounts on seconds (around 30% to 40% off), and larger places can arrange shipping to your home country.

Pick up the **Glasriket Pass** (Skr95) if you want to try glass-blowing and buy some pieces, but if you're just browsing, skip it.

Kosta

Kosta is where it all began in 1742. Today, the **Kosta Boda** (☎0478-345 00; www.kostaboda.se; Stora vägen 96; ⏲shops 10am-6pm Mon-Fri, to 5pm Sat & Sun, glass-blowing demonstrations 9am-3.30pm Mon-Fri, 10am-4pm Sat & Sun, exhibition gallery 10am-5pm Mon-Fri, to 4pm Sat & Sun; P) complex pulls in coachloads of visitors, who raid the vast discount outlets. The exhibition gallery contains some inspired creations, there are plenty of glass-blowing demos in the old factory quarters and **Kosta Boda Art Hotel** (☎0487-348 30; www.kostabodaarthotel.com; Stora vägen 75; s/d Skr1100/2590; P 📶) combines seriously inspired design with seriously good smörgåsbord lunches (Skr245) at the attached Linnéa Art Restaurant.

Orrefors

Established in 1888, **Orrefors** (www.orrefors.se; Stora vägen 96; ⏲10am-6pm Mon-Fri, noon-4pm Sat & Sun; P) features arguably the most famous of Sweden's glassworks. Demonstrations abound and you're likely to spend hours admiring the unconventional creations in the sleek museum-gallery.

The friendly Orrefors Bed & Breakfast is located in an aesthetically renovated 19th-century cottage with simple yet comfortable rooms and shared facilities. The friendly owners run short summer courses in glass-blowing (three hours, Skr350) at the nearby **Riksglasskolan** (National School of Glass; ☎0481-302 64; www.riksglasskolan.se).

Nybro

Quiet Nybro has two excellent glassworks worth visiting and was once an important centre for hand-blown light bulbs! Of the two glassworks, 130-year-old (don't laugh) **Pukeberg** (www.pukeberg.se; Pukebergarnas väg; ⏲10am-5pm Mon-Fri, to 2pm Sat, noon-4pm Sun; P), just southeast of the centre, is perhaps more interesting for its quaint setting. **Nybro** (www.nybro-glasbruk.se; Herkulesgatan; ⏲10am-5pm Mon-Fri, to 3pm Sat, 11am-2pm Sun; P) is smaller and laced with quirky items (think Elvis Presley glass platters).

The local STF hostel near Pukeberg, **Nybro Lågprishotell & Vandrarhem** (☎0481-109 32; www.nybrovandrarhem.se; Vasagatan 22; dm/s/d Skr300/400/500, hotel s/d Skr550/850; P 📶), is comfortable, with a kitchen on each floor as well as a sauna. More expensive rooms have cable TV, nonbunk beds and private showers and toilets, with breakfast included.

Nybro's **tourist office** (☎0481-450 85; www.nybro.se; Stadshusplan; ⏲9am-5pm Mon-Fri, noon-4pm Sun) is at the train station.

Getting There & Around

Apart from the main routes, bus services around the area are practically nonexistent. The easiest way to explore is with your own transport (beware of elk). Bicycle tours on the unsurfaced country roads are excellent; there are plenty of hostels, and you can camp almost anywhere except near the military area on the Kosta–Orrefors road.

Kalmar Länstrafik (☎010-21 21000; www.klt.se) bus 139 runs from mid-June to mid-August only and calls at a few of the glass factories. The service operates four times daily on weekdays and once on Saturday, and runs from Nybro to Orrefors and Måleräs. Kosta is served by **Länstrafiken Kronoberg** (☎0470-72 75 50; www.lanstrafikenkron.se) bus 218 from Växjö (two or three daily).

Buses and trains run from Emmaboda to Nybro and Kalmar (roughly hourly).

Oskarshamn

TRANSPORT HUB

Oskarshamn is useful mostly for its regular boat connections with Gotland.

Vandrarhemmet Oscar (☎0491-158 00; www.forumoskarshamn.com; Södra Långgatan 15-17; hostel dm/s/d Skr180/305/410, hotel s/d Skr790/1060; P @ 📶), a shiny hotel-hostel hybrid, is a convenient budget option. Rooms have TV, fans and bathrooms – only the kitchen for self-caterers gives it away as a hostel.

Boats to Visby depart from the Gotland Ferry Terminal, daily in winter and twice daily in summer. The **MS Solund** (www.olandsfarjan.se) ferry to Öland departs in summer from the ferry terminal off Skeppsbron.

Long-distance bus services stop at the very central bus station. Regional bus services run up to six times daily from Oskarshamn to Kalmar (Skr64, 1½ hours).

Swebus Express (p415) has two to four daily buses between Stockholm and Kalmar calling in at Oskarshamn.

Kalmar

0480 / POP 36,392

Not only is Kalmar dashing, it claims one of Sweden's most spectacular castles, with an interior even more perfect than its turreted outside. Other local assets include Sweden's largest gold hoard, from the 17th-century ship *Kronan*, and the cobbled streets of Gamla Stan (Old Town) to the west of Slottshotellet.

The Kalmar Union of 1397, when the crowns of Sweden, Denmark and Norway became one, was agreed to at the castle.

Sights & Activities

Kalmar Slott CASTLE

(www.kalmarslott.kalmar.se; adult/child Skr120/100; 10am-6pm daily Jul–mid-Aug, shorter hours rest of year;) Fairy-tale turrets, a drawbridge, a foul dungeon and secret passages…yes, Kalmar Slott has everything that a proper castle should. This powerful Renaissance building was once the most important in Sweden, and it's fortified accordingly. It also boasts one of the best-preserved interiors from the period.

For more information, join one of the **guided tours** (in English at 11.30am, 1.30pm & 2.30pm Jun–mid-Aug, 11.30am only mid-Aug–early Oct), included in the admission price. There are also children's activities here in summer.

Kalmar Länsmuseum MUSEUM

(County Museum; www.kalmarlansmuseum.se; Skeppsbrogatan; adult/child Skr80/free; 10am-4pm Mon-Fri, to 8pm Wed, 11am-4pm Sat & Sun) The highlight of this fine museum, in an old steam mill by the harbour, are finds from the 17th-century flagship *Kronan*. The ship exploded and sank just before a battle in 1676, with the loss of almost 800 men. It was rediscovered in 1980, and over 30,000 wonderfully preserved items have been excavated so far, including a spectacular gold hoard, clothing and musical instruments.

Kalmar Konstmuseum MUSEUM

(www.kalmarkonstmuseum.se; Stadsparken; adult/child Skr50/free; noon-5pm Tue-Sun, to 7pm Wed) The striking Kalmar Konstmuseum, in the park near the Kalmar Slott, dishes out brilliant temporary exhibitions featuring local and global art-scene 'It' kids.

Domkyrkan CHURCH

(Cathedral; www.kalmardomkyrka.se; Stortorget; 8am-3.30pm Mon-Fri, to 6.30pm Wed, 9am-4pm Sat & Sun) Home to a spectacular pulpit, the baroque Domkyrkan was designed by Tessin, King Karl X Gustav's favourite architect.

Sleeping

★Clarion Collection Hotel Packhuset HOTEL €€

(0480-570 00; www.choicehotels.se; Skeppsbrogatan 26; s/d Skr1320/1420 ; P) The seafaring theme here extends from the 1950s-era trunks and suitcases that are incorporated into the decor as well as the nautical barometers and gauges, grainy 'ship-ahoy' photos and wood-panelled rooms (request a sea view). A lavish dinner buffet is included in the accommodation price, along with homemade cakes at teatime.

Slottshotellet HOTEL €€

(0480-882 60; www.slottshotellet.se; Slottsvägen 7; r/ste from Skr1395/1795, annexe s/d Skr795/995; P @) This wonderfully romantic, cosy hotel is housed in four buildings in a gorgeous green setting near the castle. Most rooms have antique furniture with textured wallpaper, crystal chandeliers and oriental rugs. New budget accommodation opened in an annexe across the road in 2013 sporting a white, minimalist look.

Eating

Restaurang Källaren Kronan SWEDISH €€

(0480-41 14 00; www.kallarenkronan.com; Ölandsgatan 7; mains Skr135-275; noon-2pm & 6-10pm Tue-Sun) Six cellars have been transformed into a high-calibre experience, with meals served under a cosy vaulted ceiling. There's even a 1660s menu, with mains such as salmon poached in wine with crayfish and root vegetables. Otherwise, the menu is replete with Swedish classics including meatballs and gravlax.

Gröna Stugan EUROPEAN €€€

(www.gronastuganikalmar.se; Larmgatan 1; mains Skr210-285; 5-11pm Mon-Sat, to 9pm Sun) Located in an unassuming sage-green building complete with round windows reminiscent of a ship, this gem of a restaurant serves up dishes that are gorgeous on the plate and even better to eat. Leave space for the blueberry pancakes with raspberry panna cotta.

Information

Tourist Office (☎0480-41 77 00; www.kalmar.com; Ölandskajen 9; ⏲9am-9pm Mon-Fri, 10am-5pm Sat & Sun Jun-Aug, shorter hours rest of year) Handy for information on the region.

Getting There & Away

AIR

The **airport** (☎480-45 90 00; www.kalmarairport.se) is 6km west of town. SAS (p476) flies several times daily to Stockholm Arlanda airport, while **Kalmarflyg** (www.kalmarflyg.se) flies to Stockholm's Bromma airport. The Flygbuss airport bus (Skr50) provides connections to central Kalmar.

BUS

Roughly three **Swebus Express** (☎0771-21 82 18; www.swebus.se) services daily run north to Norrköping (Skr289, four hours); and one to three services daily run south to Karlskrona (Skr69, 1¼ hours) and Malmö (Skr229, 4½ hours), among other destinations.

Svenska Buss (☎0771-67 67 67; www.svenskabuss.se) has similar routes and prices.

TRAIN

SJ trains run every hour or two between Kalmar and Alvesta (from Skr167, 1¼ hours), where you can connect with the main Stockholm–Malmö line and with trains to Göteborg. Trains run to Linköping up to nine times daily (Skr333, 3¼ hours), also with connections to Stockholm.

Öland

☎0485 / POP 24,640

Like a deranged vision out of *Don Quixote*, the skinny island of Öland is covered in old wooden windmills. Symbols of power and wealth in the mid-18th century, there are still 400 or so left.

At 137km long and 16km wide, the island is Sweden's smallest province. Formerly a regal hunting ground, Öland is doable as a long day trip from Kalmar, but is best explored at leisure. Having a car will allow you to reach such isolated spots as Trollskogen on the island's northernmost tip – a dense pine forest full of delightful walking trails – and the remains of the Iron Age fortresses is the southern half of the island. A slower, equally scenic way of exploring is by bicycle; check **Cykla På Öland** (www.cyklapaoland.se) for cycling routes and other handy info.

Färjestaden & Around

South of Färjestaden, half of the island has made it onto Unesco's World Heritage list. Its treeless, limestone landscape is hauntingly beautiful and littered with the relics of human settlement and conflict. Besides linear villages, Iron Age fortresses and tombs, this area is also a natural haven for plants and wildlife.

The bridge from Kalmar lands you on the island just north of Färjestaden, where there's a well-stocked **tourist office** (☎0485-890 00; www.olandsturist.se; ⏲9am-7pm Mon-Fri, to 6pm Sat, to 5pm Sun Jul–mid-Aug) at the Träffpunkt Öland centre. Staff can book island accommodation (for a fee). There are few hotels, but more than 25 camping grounds and at least a dozen hostels (book ahead). Camping between midsummer and mid-August can cost up to Skr320 per site.

Silverlinjen (www.silverlinjen.se) runs one or two direct buses from Öland to Stockholm (Skr320, six hours), calling at Kalmar – reservations essential.

Borgholm & Around

Öland's 'capital' and busiest town, Borgholm exudes a vaguely tacky air with its discount shops and summer crowds. Just outside town, **Borgholms Slott** (www.borgholmsslott.se; adult/child Skr70/40; ⏲10am-6pm Jun-Aug), Northern Europe's largest ruined castle, is a most dramatic sight. These four grey walls and towers were burnt and abandoned early in the 18th century, but now there's a terrific museum inside on the castle's history, and summer concerts in the courtyard. Three kilometres south of Borgholm and boasting exceptional gardens is the more compact **Solliden Palace** (Sollidens Slott; www.sollidens-slott.se; adult/child Skr75/45; ⏲11am-6pm mid-May–mid-Sep), still used by the Swedish royal family. Nine kilometres south, in Halltorp, is **VIDA Museum & Konsthall** (☎0485-774 40; www.vidamuseum.com; adult/child Skr50/free; ⏲10am-6pm daily Jul-early Aug, shorter hours rest of year; P), a strikingly modern museum and art gallery, its finest halls devoted to two of Sweden's top glass designers.

Sleeping & Eating

The tourist offices in Borgholm and Färjestaden can help you find inexpensive private rooms in the area.

Villa Sol B&B €
(☎0485-56 25 52; www.villasol.nu; Slottsgatan 30; s/d without bathroom from Skr450/800; 📶) The sunny yellow exterior sets the tone for this delightful accommodation located on a quiet residential street near Borgholm's centre. Rooms in the main house share two bathrooms, a fully equipped cottage-style kitchen and a homey living room, complete with board games and books. The marginally more expensive garden rooms are in separate chalets overlooking the flower-filled garden.

★ **Hotell Borgholm** HOTEL €€€
(☎0485-770 60; www.hotellborgholm.com; Trädgårdsgatan 15-19; s/d Skr1335/1535; ❄@📶) Cool grey hues, bold feature walls, pine wood floors and smart functionalist furniture make for stylish slumber at this urbane hotel. Rooms are spacious, with those on the top floor (Skr1885) especially chic. Owner Karin Fransson is one of Sweden's top chefs, so a table at the restaurant here is best booked ahead (tasting menu Skr1075).

Nya Conditoriet BAKERY €
(Storgatan 28; ⏲8am-5pm Mon-Fri, to 3pm Sat) This busy old-fashioned bakery-cafe in Borgholm serves yummy sandwiches and pastries.

Robinson Crusoe EUROPEAN €€
(www.robinsoncrusoe.se; Hamnvägen; lunch buffet Skr130, mains from Skr150; ⏲noon-10pm Apr-Sep) Slouch back on the plush purple terrace sofas for a cocktail or an (excellent) coffee, or make a date for the daily buffet. The setting is sublime, overlooking the bobbing boats in Borgholm harbour.

Karlskrona

☎0455 / POP 35,212

If you like your Swedes in uniform, you'll appreciate Karlskrona. Marine cadets pepper the streets of what has always been an A-league naval base. In 1998 the entire town was added to the Unesco World Heritage list for its impressive collection of 17th- and 18th-century naval architecture. Karlskrona's archipelago of almost 1000 islands makes for a great boat excursion in summer. Much of the town is still a military base, so for many sights you'll need to book a tour at the tourist office.

Sights & Activities

★ **Fortifications** HISTORIC BUILDING
(👪) Karlskrona's star is the extraordinary offshore Kungsholms Fort (guided tours adult/under 17yr Skr210/50; ⏲10am-2pm Jun-Aug), built in 1680 to defend the town. Two-hour guided **boat tours** (adult/child Skr220/free; ⏲10am mid-Jun–Aug) depart from Fisktorget, the tourist office or the Marinmuseum. Tickets must be prebooked through the tourist office. Another option is the boat operated by **Affärsverken** (www.affarsverken.se; adult/child Skr90/50; ⏲Jul & Aug), which runs from Fisktorget and circles the fort in June, July and August (adult/child Skr90/50); inform the tourist office of your visit in advance if you choose this second option.

Marinmuseum MUSEUM
(www.marinmuseum.se; Stumholmen; adult/child Skr100/free; ⏲10am-6pm Jun-Aug, shorter hours rest of year; P) The striking Marinmuseum is the national naval museum. Dive in for reconstructions of a battle deck in wartime, a hall full of fantastic figureheads, piles of model boats, and even some of the real thing – such as a minesweeper, the HMS *Västervik* and Sweden's royal sloop. There is also a pleasant **restaurant** (mains from Skr100).

Amiralitetskyrkan CHURCH
(Vallgatan 11; ⏲11am-4pm Mon-Fri, 9.30am-2pm Sat) FREE Sweden's oldest wooden church is the stocky Amiralitetskyrkan, with a gorgeous pastel interior. Outside, the wooden statue **Old Rosenbom** raises his hat to charitable visitors.

Sleeping & Eating

STF Vandrarhem Trossö Karlskrona HOSTEL €
(☎0455-100 20; www.karlskronavandrarhem.se; Drottninggatan 39; dm/s/d from Skr160/280/370; 📶👪) Modern, clean and friendly, this hostel has a laundry, a TV room, a backyard for kids to play in and handy parking across the street.

First Hotel Ja HOTEL €€
(☎0455-555 60; www.firsthotels.se; Borgmästaregatan 13; s/d Skr790/990; P@📶) Karlskrona's top slumber spot boasts fashionable rooms with stripey wallpaper and decorative fabrics. Hotel perks include a sauna, a bar-restaurant and a full-blown breakfast buffet

served in a pleasant atrium. There are also several more decorative 'Ladies Rooms', exclusively for women.

Glassiärens Glassbar ICE CREAM €
(Stortorget 4; cones from Skr25; ⏲9am-6pm May-Sep) The queues at this legendary ice-cream parlour are matched by the mammoth serves, piled high in a heavenly waffle cone. Go for three flavours if you can. Memories are made of this...

Nivå INTERNATIONAL €€
(☎0455-103 71; www.niva.nu; Norra Kungsgatan 3; mains from Skr190; ⏲5-11pm Mon-Thu, 4pm-1am Fri, noon-1am Sat) Just off Stortorget, this steakhouse has a variety of light, well-priced dishes (nachos, burgers, salads), as well as heartier meals from the grill and some veggie options such as a tasty haloumi burger. It's also a popular evening bar; the doors stay open until at least 1am.

ℹ Information

Tourist Office (☎0455-30 34 90; www.visitkarlskrona.se; Stortorget 2; ⏲9am-7pm Jun-Aug, shorter hours rest of year) Internet access and super-helpful staff.

ℹ Getting There & Away

AIR

Ronneby airport (☎010-109 54 00; www.swedavia.com) is 33km west of Karlskrona; the Flygbuss leaves from Stortorget (adult/child Skr90/45). There are several SAS and Blekinge-flyg flights to Stockholm Arlanda and Bromma, respectively.

BOAT

Ferries to Gdynia (Poland) on **Stena Line** (www.stenaline.com) depart from Verkö, 10km east of Karlskrona.

BUS

The bus and train stations are just north of central Karlskrona. **BlekingeTrafiken** (☎0455-569 00; www.blekingetrafiken.se) operates regional buses. **Svenska Buss** (www.svenskabuss.se) runs daily from Malmö to Stockholm, calling at Kristianstad (Skr420, 2¼ hours) and Karlskrona (Skr420, 3½ hours).

TRAIN

Direct trains run at least 13 times daily to Karlshamn (Skr85, one hour) and Kristianstad (Skr158, two hours), at least 10 times to Lund (Skr222, two hours and 40 minutes) and Malmö (Skr221, three hours).

GOTLAND

Gorgeous Gotland has much to brag about: a Unesco-lauded capital, truffle-sprinkled woods, A-list dining hot spots, talented artisans and more hours of sunshine than anywhere else in Sweden. It's also one of the country's richest historical regions, with around 100 medieval churches and countless prehistoric sites.

The island lies nearly halfway between Sweden and Latvia, in the middle of the Baltic Sea. Just off its northeast tip lies the island of Fårö, most famous as the home of Sweden's directing great, the late Ingmar Bergman. The island national park of Gotska Sandön lies 38km further north, while the petite islets of Stora Karlsö and Lilla Karlsö sit just off the western coast.

Information on the island abounds; both www.gotland.net and www.guteinfo.com are good places to start.

ℹ Getting There & Away

AIR

The cheaper local airline is **Gotlands Flyg** (☎22 22 22; www.gotlandsflyg.se), with regular flights between Visby and Stockholm Bromma (one to eight times daily) and daily flights (June to September) between Visby and Malmö. Prices start at Skr346 one way to Stockholm and to Malmö; book early for discounts. Another budget airline, **NextJet** (☎0771-90 00 90; www.nextjet.se) operates between two to three daily flights from Stockholm Arlanda to Visby (June to September). Prices start at Skr445 one way. Popular summer-only routes include Göteborg, Hamburg, Oslo and Helsingfors (Helsinki).

The island's **airport** (☎26 31 00) is 4km northeast of Visby. Catch a taxi into/from town (around Skr180); there is an airport bus during summer.

BOAT

Year-round car ferries between Visby and both Nynäshamn and Oskarshamn are operated by **Destination Gotland** (☎0771-22 33 00; www.destinationgotland.se). There are departures from Nynäshamn one to six times daily (about three hours). From Oskarshamn, there are one or two daily departures in either direction (three to four hours). **Gotlandsbåten** (www.gotlands-baten.se) run one to two daily ferries (June to August) from Västervik to Visby (from Skr250, about three hours).

Regular one-way adult tickets for the ferry start at Skr260, but from mid-June to mid-August there is a far more complicated fare system; some overnight, evening and early-morning sailings in the middle of the week have cheaper fares.

Transporting a bicycle costs Skr50; a car usually starts at Skr345, although, again, in the peak summer season a tiered price system operates and advance reservations are recommended.

Getting Around

There are several bike-rental places in Visby, including at **Gotlands Cykeluthyrning** (0498-21 41 33; www.gotlandscykeluthyrning.com; Skeppsbron 2), and cycling is a wonderful way to get around the quiet roads.

Kollektiv Trafiken (0498-21 41 12; www.gotland.se) runs buses via most villages to all corners of the island. The most useful routes, which have connections up to seven times daily, operate between Visby and Burgsvik in the far south, Visby and Fårösund in the north (also with bus connections on Fårö), and Visby and Klintehamn. A one-way ticket will not cost you more than Skr75 (although if you take a bike on board it will cost an additional Skr40).

Visby

0498 / POP 22,593

The port town of Visby is medieval eye candy and enough to warrant a trip to Gotland all by itself. Inside its thick city walls await twisting cobbled streets, fairy-tale wooden cottages, evocative ruins and steep hills with impromptu Baltic views. The city wall, with its 40-plus towers and the spectacular church ruins within, attest to the town's former Hanseatic glories.

Sights

★Gotlands Museum MUSEUM

(www.gotlandsmuseum.se; Strandgatan 14; adult/child Skr100/80; 10am-6pm) Gotlands Museum is one of the mightiest regional museums in Sweden. While highlights include amazing 8th-century pre-Viking picture stones, human skeletons from chambered tombs and medieval wooden sculptures, the star turn is the legendary Spillings horde. At 70kg it's the world's largest booty of preserved silver treasure. Included in the ticket price is entry to the nearby **Konstmuseum** (0498-29 27 75; Sankt Hansgatan 21; adult/under 20yr/senior Skr50/free/40; noon-4pm Tue-Sun, closed for Midsummer), which has a small permanent collection mainly focusing on Gotland-inspired 19th- and 20th-century art, plus temporary exhibitions showcasing contemporary local artists.

Medieval Churches CHURCH

Founded by Franciscans in 1233, **St Karins Kyrka** (Stora Torget) is one of the most stunning of Visby's medieval churches, with a beautiful Gothic interior. Other ruins include the magnificent **St Nicolai Kyrka**, built in 1230 by Dominican monks. The **Helge And Kyrka** ruin is the only stone-built octagonal church in Sweden. It was built in 1200, possibly by the Bishop of Riga; the roof collapsed after a fire in 1611.

Sleeping

Book accommodation well in advance if possible. Gotland's hotel prices increase on summer weekends and in the peak tourist months.

Fängelse Vandrarhem HOSTEL €

(0498-20 60 50; www.visbyfangelse.se; Skeppsbron 1; dm/s/d from Skr300/400/500; wi-fi) This hostel offers beds year-round in the small converted cells of an old prison. It's in a handy location, between the ferry dock and the harbour restaurants, and there's an inviting terrace bar in summer. Reception is open from 9am to 2pm, so call ahead if you are arriving outside these times.

Wisby Jernvägshotellet HOSTEL €

(0498-20 33 00; www.gtsab.se; Adelsgatan 9; 2-/4-bed r from Skr495/595; wi-fi) Run by the same folks as Hotel Villa Borgen next door, this is an excellent budget choice. The spotless rooms are more spacious than some

Visby

Top Sights
1 Gotlands Museum ... B4
2 St Karins Kyrka ... C4

Sights
3 Helge And Kyrka ... D3
4 Konstmuseum ... C4
5 St Nicolai Kyrka ... D2

Sleeping
6 Clarion Hotel Wisby ... B4
7 Fängelse Vandrarhem ... A5
8 Hotel St Clemens ... C3
9 Hotel Villa Borgen ... B5
10 Wisby Jernvägshotellet ... B5

Eating
11 Bakfickan ... C3
12 Donners Brunn ... B4
13 Surfers ... C4
14 Vinäger ... B4
15 Visby Crêperie & Logi ... C4

swing-a-cat hostels in these parts, and the kitchen–dining room is airy and bright, with an outside terrace.

Hotel Villa Borgen BOUTIQUE HOTEL €€
(☎0498-20 33 00; www.gtsab.se; Adelsgatan 11; s/d/apt Skr1050/1195/2000; @ 📶) This place has attractive rooms with lashings of white linen, pale grey walls and scarlet cushions. Accommodation is set around a pretty, quiet courtyard, and the intimate breakfast room with French doors and stained glass contributes to that boutique feeling. There is also a self-contained apartment that sleeps six.

Visby

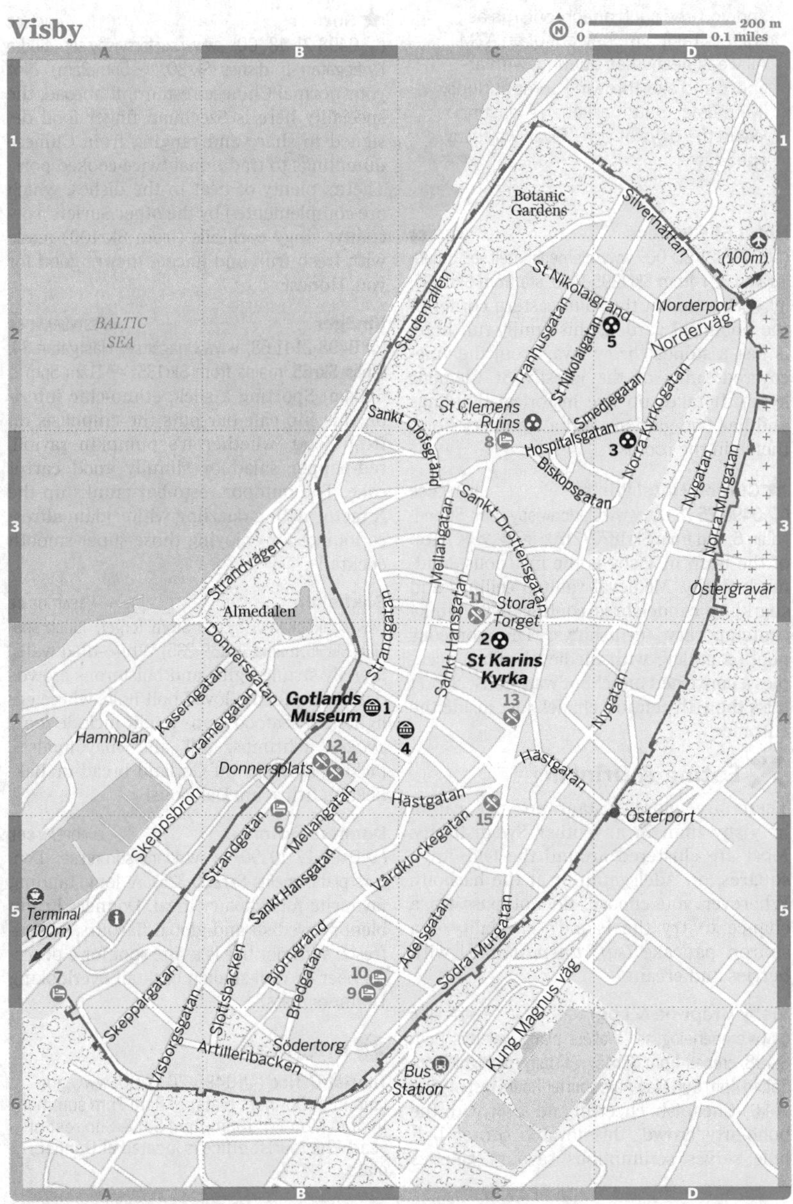

MEDIEVAL WEEK

Undoubtedly the most exciting time to be in Visby is during **Medeltidsveckan** (Medieval Week; www.medeltidsveckan.com) in early August, when everyone walks around dressed in medieval garb and you see such anachronisms as knights taking money out of an ATM. All week, festivities abound, with archery and axe-throwing competitions, live music, craft market and feasting like in the days of yore. Book way, way ahead.

Hotel St Clemens HOTEL €€
(☎0498-21 90 00; www.clemenshotell.se; Smedjegatan 3; r from Skr1295-1450, ste from Skr2195; P 📶) Located at the southeastern corner of the botanical garden, this family-run hotel is just a stone's throw away from the vine-covered ruins of the ghostly St Clemens kyrka. It takes up five historical buildings and has two gardens and a summery floral theme in the rooms.

★**Clarion Hotel Wisby** HOTEL €€€
(☎0498-25 75 00; www.clarionwisby.com; Strandgatan 6; s/d from Skr1870/2170; P @ 📶 🏊) Top of the heap in Visby is the luxurious, landmark Wisby. Medieval vaulted ceilings and sparkling candelabras contrast with funky contemporary furnishings. The gorgeous pool (complete with medieval pillar) occupies a converted merchant warehouse. Don't miss the 11th-century chapel, just inside the entrance.

Eating & Drinking

There are more restaurants per capita in Visby than in any other Swedish city. Most are clustered around the Old Town squares, on Adelsgatan or at the harbour. Wherever you choose, do not pass up a chance to try the island's speciality – a saffron pancake *(saffranspankaka)* with berries and cream.

Visby Crêperie & Logi CREPERIE €
(www.creperielogi.se; Wallérs plats; galettes from Skr98, crepes from Skr45; ⏲11am-midnight Mon-Sat, to 4pm Sun May-Aug, shorter hours rest of year; 🌿 👪) Cheapish, cheerful and a hit with the boho-arty crowd, this lovable corner bolt hole serves scrumptious savoury galettes and sweet crêpes, ranging from a moreish lamb, chèvre, honey, rocket and almond combo to a wicked chocolate composition further enhanced with white-chocolate chunks and ice cream. The recommended tipple is cider, with 10 varieties to choose from.

★**Surfers** ASIAN €€
(☎0498-21 18 00; www.surfersvisby.se; Södra Kyrkogatan 1; dishes Skr80; ⏲5pm-2am) Not your normal Chinese restaurant abroad, the speciality here is Szechuan finger food designed to share and ranging from Chinese dumplings to traditional twice-cooked pork. There's plenty of heat in the dishes, which are complemented by the other Surfers' speciality: zingy cocktails (from Skr100) made with fresh fruit and juice – they're good for you. Honest.

Vinäger RESTAURANT €€
(☎0498-21 11 68; www.vinager.se; Hästgatan 34; tapas Skr65, mains from Skr135; ⏲11am-5pm & 6-10pm) Sporting a slick, ethno-chic interior, this hip cafe-bar puts the emphasis on fresh food, whether it's pumpkin ravioli, red-pepper salad or sinfully good carrot cake. The outdoor resto-bar cranks up the X factor with a dazzling white, glam alfresco lounge for enjoying those super-smooth cocktails.

Bakfickan SEAFOOD €€
(www.bakfickan-visby.nu; Stora Torget; lunch specials Skr95, mains Skr139-235) White-tiled walls, merrily strung lights and boisterous crowds define this foodie-loved bolt hole, where enlightened seafood gems might include *toast skagen* (shrimps, dill and mayonnaise), pickled herrings on Gotland bread or Bakfickan's fish soup. Delicious!

Donners Brunn EUROPEAN €€€
(☎0498-27 10 90; www.donnersbrunn.se; Donners plats; mains Skr260-325) A longstanding favourite for a luxury meal, Donners Brunn blends Swedish and global flavours. The alfresco summer bar is a fine spot for a peaceful beer or well-shaken cocktail overlooking Donners plats.

Information

Tourist Office (☎0498-20 17 00; www.gotland.info; Donners plats; ⏲8am-7pm summer, to 4pm Mon-Fri, 10am-4pm Sat & Sun rest of year) The tourist office is located at Donners plats.

NORRLAND

In Norrland, the northern half of Sweden, the population is sparse – reindeer outnumber cars, and much of the landscape consists of deep-green forest. It's a paradise for nature lovers who enjoy hiking, skiing and other outdoor activities; in winter in particular, the landscape is transformed by snowmobiles, dog-sleds and the eerie aurora borealis. The north is home to the Sámi people, and it's possible to take part in traditional Sámi pastimes, such as reindeer herding.

Gävle

☎026 / POP 71,033

Founded in 1446, Gävle is a lively university town that's been a prosperous industrial centre since the late 19th century, when it exported local timber and iron. A vibrant culinary scene and a host of oddball attractions in and around town appeal to a motley crew of beachgoers, would-be arsonists, whisky connoisseurs and trainspotters.

Inside Gävle's former engine shed, **Sveriges Järnvägsmuseet** (Swedish Railway Museum; www.jarnvagsmuseum.se; Rälsgatan 1; adult/under 19yr Skr100/60; 10am-5pm Jun-Aug; P) traces the history of the railway in Sweden through seriously hands-on displays. Besides numerous old locomotives and carriages that you can clamber inside, there are collections of miniature train models, an X2000 simulator, toy railways, and a small railway for kids to ride.

A fire in 1869 wiped out most of the colourful old wooden buildings that formed the town's core. Today the little cluster that survived the fire is preserved in the rickety jumble that is **Gamla Gefle**, just south of the city centre. You can sample locally-distilled whiskies at the Mackmyra Svensk Whisky & Whiskyby, or else investigate an odd slice of China, Dragon Gate, 24km south of the city.

Sleeping & Eating

Gefle Vandrarhem HOSTEL €
(☎026-62 17 45; www.geflevandrarhem.se; Södra Rådmansgatan 1; dm/s/d Skr240/410/580; mid-Jan–early Dec) Set in one of Gamla Gefle's old-style wooden buildings around a flowering courtyard, this quiet hostel with a good guest kitchen is popular with travellers of all ages. The staff are lovely, with the exception of one crotchety member. Breakfast buffet costs Skr70.

Elite Grand Hotel Gävle HOTEL €€
(☎026-400 73 00; www.elite.se; Kyrkogatan 28; s/d from Skr729/999; P) This beautifully restored art deco hotel has a lot going for it, not least its super-central location and bright, contemporary decor. Light sleepers should opt for a room overlooking the river.

★**Matildas** FUSION €€
(www.matildas.nu; Timmermansgatan 23; 5pm-late Tue-Sat) The menu at this small, stylish bistro is short, sweet and seasonal, with a real depth of flavour to the dishes, wonderful attention to presentation and a relaxed ambience. Feast on lobster tacos, oysters paired with champagne, crispy pork belly and homemade black pudding with lingonberry. The home-brewed beer, served by the delightful owners, goes down very smoothly.

Church Street Saloon TEX-MEX €€
(☎026-12 62 11; Kyrkogatan 11; mains Skr190-513; 5pm-midnight Mon-Fri, noon-1am Sat;) Locals stampede this Wild West–themed saloon, encrusted with cowboy kitsch, looking to rustle up some Tex-Mex. The steaks (including the 'ridiculous size' 900g ribeye), enchiladas, ribs, buffalo wings and Macho Nachos arrive on plates the size of serving platters, so come ravenous. On weekends after 10pm the bar wenches hitch up their skirts and dance the can-can on the bar.

Getting There & Away

Long-distance bus services leave from behind the train station. For Ybuss departures, take a 'Busstaxi' from the train station to Gävlebro.

Ybuss (www.ybuss.se) runs daily to Sundsvall (Skr240, 2¾ to 3¼ hours, three to six daily) and Umeå (Skr390, 6½ to 7½ hours, three daily).

SGS Bussen (www.sgsbussen.nu) serves Stockholm (Skr150, two hours, five to seven daily).

GETTING GÄVLE'S GOAT

Gävle's most famous resident is a 13-metre tall straw **Gävle Goat** – a giant version of the traditional Yule Goat. It's been making an appearance at Slottstorget in early December since 1966 and every year extreme attempts are made to burn it down; one year an arsonist dressed as Santa shot flaming arrows at it. Bets are made locally and internationally as to whether the goat will go down before Christmas or New Year's Eve.

There are numerous daily services to Stockholm (Skr247, 1½ to 2¼ hours) via Uppsala (Skr97, 45 minutes to 1¼ hours), Sundsvall (Skr112, 2¼ hours, roughly hourly), one or two trains to Kiruna (Skr763, 14¼ hours, two daily) via Luleå (Skr691, 11¼ hours, daily), and three to Östersund (Skr232, 3½ hours).

Sundsvall

060 / POP 50,714

When Sundsvall burned to the ground in 1888, a decision was made to adopt the dragon as the town's symbol in a bid to fight fire with fire. Just in case, though, the old wooden houses were rebuilt in stone and separated by wide avenues, making the other towns along the Bothnian coast look like country bumpkins by comparison. You'll find brightly painted dragons all over the city centre, each annually decorated by a local artist.

Climb the Norra Berget for all-encompassing views of the city, or make for the **Kulturmagasinet** (www.sunsvall.se/kulturmagasinet; Sjögatan; 10am-7pm Mon-Thu, to 6pm Fri, 11am-4pm Sat & Sun) FREE, a beautifully restored old warehouse that's home to the **Sundsvall Museum**, with engaging exhibits of the history of the city and the area's natural history and geology. There's a permanent art display upstairs featuring 20th-century Swedish artists, while superb temporary exhibitions have recently included some rather risqué photography featuring aged but oddly beautiful burlesque dancers.

Sleeping

STF Sundsvall City HOSTEL €

(060-12 60 90; www.sundsvallcityhostel.se; Sjögatan 11; hostel s/d/tr/q Skr400/500/720/920, hotel s/d Skr500/595; P) Friendly but rather anonymous hostel in a super-central location. All the rooms are sparsely furnished but bright and have en suites; guests have use of the sauna and fully equipped kitchen; and reception is open all day – a miracle in the budget lodging category. 'Hotel' rooms are essentially hostel rooms but with bed linen and breakfast included.

Elite Hotel Knaust HOTEL €€

(060-608 00 00; www.elite.se; Storgatan 13; s/d from Skr990/1290; P) In a striking 19th-century building on Sundsvall's main pedestrian drag, this opulent hotel is full of old-world charm. Besides the grand, lobby-dominating (and much photographed) marble staircase, the rooms are decorated in classic Scandinavian style and have high ceilings. The breakfast buffet is excellent. Our only quibble is that wi-fi is not complimentary.

Eating & Drinking

Tant Anci & Fröcken Sara CAFE €

(Bankgatan 15; mains Skr85-115; 10am-10pm Mon-Thu, to 8pm Fri, 11am-5pm Sat;) Humongous bowls of soup or salad are the speciality at this frilly organic cafe, where you can also get hearty sandwiches, giant bowls of pasta and pastries.

★ **Udda Tapas Bar** TAPAS €

(073-098 66 07; http://uddatapasbar.wordpress.com; Esplanaden 17; tapas Skr40-75; 5-11pm Mon-Thu, to 2am Fri & Sat) Head for the roof terrace of this congenial bar on summer evenings to savour the likes of clams with lemongrass, smoked reindeer with Dijon mustard, lamb tacos and yellow beets with honey and feta, along with a glass of wine or a local brew. DJs kick it up a notch on weekends.

Oscar Matsal & Bar BAR

(www.oscarmatsal.se; Bankgatan 11; 5-11pm Mon-Thu, to 3am Fri & Sat) The hottest watering hole in town with retro decor triples as a sophisticated bistro and a nightclub where you can knock back Tom Collinses while checking out the latest live band.

Getting There & Away

Midlanda Airport (070-522 03 12; www.sdlairport.se) is 22km north of Sundsvall; buses run from the bus station three to eight times daily (Skr90) to connect with weekday SAS and City Airline flights to Göteborg, Luleå and Stockholm.

Buses depart from the Sundsvall bus station, near Kulturmagasinet. Ybuss (p477) runs to Gävle (Skr240, 2¾ to 3¾ hours, up to six daily) and Stockholm (Skr300, 4½ to six hours, up to six daily). Länstrafiken Västerbotten buses 10 and 100 run to Umeå (Skr310, 5¼ hours; up to five daily) via other coastal towns.

Trains run west to Östersund (Skr266, 2½ hours, up to eight daily) and south to Gävle (Skr265, 2¼ hours, hourly) and Stockholm (Skr373, 3½ to five hours, up to eight daily). The station is just east of the town centre on Landsvagsalen, which is a continuation of Köpmangatan.

Höga Kusten

☎0613

Cross the 1867m Höga Kustenbron – Norrland's answer to the Golden Gate Bridge – and you find yourself amidst some of the most dramatic scenery on the Swedish coastline. The secret to the rugged beauty of the Höga Kusten (High Coast) is elevation; nowhere else on the coast do you find such a mountainous landscape, with sheer rocky cliffs plunging straight down to the sea, as well as lakes, fjords and dozens of tranquil islands, covered in dense pine forest. The region, recognised as geographically unique, was recently listed as a Unesco World Heritage area.

It's a real delight to drive the scenic, winding roads between the minute fishing villages and even more rewarding to stay on the tiny islands of Högbonden, Ulvön and Trysunda, or to walk the 129km Höga Kustenleden, a hiking trail that spans the coast.

The Islands

HÖGBONDEN

A tiny island in the southern part of Höga Kusten, only 15 minutes by boat from Bönhamn or Barsta villages. It's famous for its 100-year-old lighthouse atop the forested island's rocky plateau. The main attractions here are sunset-watching or diving off the jetty; you have to make it a day trip, though, since the island's only lodgings have closed down.

ULVÖN

The largest island in the Höga Kusten archipelago, famous for its regatta (14 to 18 July) and for the production of *surströmming* – utterly noxious (or delightful, depending on your perspective) fermented herring, traditionally eaten in August. It's possible to do a day trip to Ulvöhamn, the island's one-street village with a tiny 17th-century chapel decorated with colourful murals inside. **Cafe Måsen** (mains Skr75-145; ⏲10am-6pm Jun-Aug) is the best place to try said *surströmming* and if you wish to linger overnight, **Ulvö Skarrgårdshotel** (☎0660-22 40 09; www.ulvohotell.se; Hamngatan 1; d Skr2190) is the most sumptuous of the island's limited lodgings with an excellent restaurant of its own.

TRYSUNDA

A small island with cute fishermen's houses clustered around a little U-shaped bay. There are also some great secluded spots for bathing, reachable by the walking paths through the woods. You can walk around the whole of Trysunda in an hour or two.

ℹ Information

Naturum (☎0613-700 200; www.naturumhogekusten.se; ⏲9am-7pm late Jun–mid-Aug) Naturum, off the E4, north of the village of Docksta, has exhibitions on the formation of the Höga Kusten and stocks brochures on the area. Adrenalin junkies can tackle the four via ferrata routes of varying difficulty (www.viaferrata.se; from Skr350 per person) along the flanks of Skuleberget mountain (285m) behind the visitor centre between May and October.

Tourist Office (☎0613-504 80; www.hogakusten.com; ⏲10am-6pm Jun-Aug) Inside Hotell

DON'T MISS

THE HIGH COAST TRAIL

Starting at the northern end of the Höga Kustenbron and finishing at the summit of the hill overlooking Örnsköldsvik, the 129km-long High Coast Trail spans the entire length of the Höga Kusten. The trail is divided into 13 sections, each between 15km and 24km in length, with accommodation at the end of each section consisting mostly of rustic cabins.

Parts of the trail involve an easy ramble, whereas other sections will challenge you with steep, uneven ground. Take food and plenty of drinking water with you.

The trail takes in some of the most beautiful coastal scenery in Sweden – from cliffs and sandy coves to lush countryside, dense evergreen forest, and the Slåtterdalskrevan, a 200m-deep canyon. The forest is home to lynx, roe deer and mink, as well as all four of Sweden's game birds: the black grouse, willow grouse, capercallie and hazel hen.

The trail is well-signposted but it's best to pick up a detailed booklet and map beforehand. Buses running along the E4 stop at either end of the trail, as well as at several villages along that way that are close to different sections of the trail.

Höga Kusten, just north of Höga Kustenbron suspension bridge. Has a detailed map of the scenic byways, boat timetables and guidebooks on the Höga Kusten trail.

Getting There & Around

This area is difficult to explore without your own set of wheels, though you can reach most boat departure points by public transport.

BUS

Frequent Länstrafiken Västerbotten buses 10 and 100 (at least six daily) stop at Ullånger, Docksta and Bjästa. From Örnsköldsvik, bus 421 runs to Köpmanholmen (Skr 59, 40 minutes, up to nine daily). The villages of Bönhamn and Barsta are not reachable by public transport.

BOAT

The **M/S Ronja** (www.hkship.se; one way/return Skr100/150) ferries to Högbonden run from Barsta only mid-May to mid-June and mid-August to October (noon Friday to Sunday), and from both Barsta and Bönhamn in peak summer (mid-June to mid-August) four times daily.

M/S Kusttrafik (☎0613-105 50; www.hkship.se) ferry to Ulvön leaves from Docksta daily at 9.30am, returning at 3pm between June and August.

Between mid-June and mid-August, **MF Ulvön & MF Minerva** (☎070-651 92 65; www.ornskolvikshamn.se; return adult/6-19yr Skr150/90) ferries leave Köpmanholmen for Ulvöham, three of them stopping at Trysun.

Östersund

☎063 / POP 44,327

This pleasant town by Storsjön lake, in whose chilly waters is said to lurk Sweden's answer to the Loch Ness monster, is an excellent gateway town for further explorations of Norrland.

STORSJÖODJURET – THE LAKE MONSTER

Just imagine...you're sitting by Lake Storsjön at dusk when you notice a dark shadow rise out of the water. Could it be the head of **Storsjöodjuret** (www.storsjoodjuret.com) – the lake monster that dwells somewhere in the 91m depths? There are new sightings every summer, and the lake monster has had such a grip on the public imagination that in 1894, an (unsuccessful) hunt for it was organised by King Oscar II.

Sights

★Jamtli MUSEUM

(www.jamtli.com; adult/under 18yr Skr250/free; ⏰11am-5pm; 👪) Jamtli, 1km north of the centre, consists of two parts. One is an open-air museum comprising of painstakingly reconstructed wooden buildings, complete with enthusiastic guides wearing 19th-century period costume.

The stars of the indoor museum are the **Överhogdal Tapestries**, the oldest of their kind in Europe – Christian Viking relics from AD 1100 that feature animals, people, ships and dwellings. Another fascinating display is devoted to Storsjöodjuret, including taped interviews with those who've seen the monster, monster-catching gear and a pickled monster embryo.

Frösön ISLAND

Large and peaceful Frösön island sits just across the bridge from central Östersund, reachable by road and by footbridge from Badhusparken. The island takes its name from Frö, the pagan god of fertility, worshipped by the Vikings originally residing here.

Just across the footbridge, outside Landstingshuset and near the Konsum supermarket, is Sweden's northernmost **rune stone**, which commemorates the 1050 arrival of Austmaður or 'East Man', the first Christian missionary on Frösön.

Exercishallen Norr GALLERY

(Infanterigatan 30; ⏰noon-4pm Thu-Sun) FREE A worthwhile contemporary art museum, Exercishallen Norr lives across the E14 motorway from Jamtli. It's a cavernous room with an ambitious curatorial scope and always something curious on show, from installations, paintings and sculpture to photography and soundscapes.

Sleeping & Eating

Hotel Jämteborg HOTEL €€

(☎063-51 01 01; www.jamteborg.se; Storgatan 54; hostel d/tr Skr590/840, B&B s/d/tr Skr590/690/890, hotel s/d from Skr1065/1250; 🅿📶) Just imagine: you're travelling with friends but you're all on different budgets. Hotel Jämteborg comes to the rescue, with its catch-all combo of hostel beds, B&B rooms and hotel rooms in several buildings next to each other. The cheerful hotel rooms come in cream-and-crimson, defying Sweden's 'earth tones only' rule.

WORTH A TRIP

VILDMARKSVÄGEN: THE WILDERNESS ROAD

Branching off Route 45 at Strömsund (located between Ostersund and Arvidsjaur) is one of the most spectacular drives in Sweden. Route 342, known as the **Wilderness Road** (www.wildernessroad.eu), stretches for around 500km, first running northwest towards the mountains before skirting the Norwegian border and then joining the E45 3km north of Vilhelmina. The first section runs through dense evergreen forest, punctuated by numerous lakes – perfect for skinny dipping, since you're unlikely to encounter anyone else. The surrounding forest is also home to elk, lynx, wolverine, fox and Sweden's highest population of bears, so if you're lucky (or unlucky!) you may well spot one.

Just left of Bågede, a rocky track leads towards the impressive 43m-high Hällsingsåfallet, a waterfall that tumbles into an 800m-long canyon.

Beyond Stora Blåsjon lake, Route 345 climbs up onto the enormous, desolate Stekkenjokk plateau dotted with stone cairns before descending to the tiny village of Klimpfjäll (this stretch of road is closed October to early June); 13km east, a turnoff leads to the late-18th-century Sámi church village at Fatmomakke where you find traditional Sámi *kota* and log cabins.

About 20km further east, you reach the fishing paradise of Saxnäs, a great base for all sorts of outdoor adventures. You'll soon reach the Vildmarksvägen/E45 junction. If you get here early enough, you can grab a meal at the excellent **Martin Bergmans Fisk smokery** (0940-250 90; E45 & Vildmarksvägen; mains Skr110-159; 9am-5.30pm Mon-Fri, 10am-5pm Sat) before driving the final 3km south to Vilhelmina for a well-earned rest.

Allow a full day for driving the Vildmarksvägen and fill up on petrol, as the only petrol station is in Gäddede, halfway along.

Hotel Emma HOTEL €€
(063-51 78 40; www.hotelemma.com; Prästgatan 31; s/d Skr950/1095; P) The individually styled rooms at super-central Emma nestle in crooked hallways on two floors, with homey touches including squishy armchairs and imposing ceramic stoves; some rooms have French doors facing the courtyard. The breakfast spread is a delight. Reception hours are limited, so call ahead if arriving late or early.

Törners Konditori CAFE €
(www.tornerskonditori.se; Storgatan 24; sandwiches Skr60-70; 7.30am-7pm Mon-Fri, 9am-5pm Sat, 11am-5pm Sun;) This large, cafeteria-style cafe seems perpetually filled with locals, who come for the cakes (Skr 35), chunky sandwiches – from open-faced prawn to toasted pulled-pork baguettes – as well as salads and daily lunch specials ranging from goulash to chicken curry.

★**Innefickan Restaurang & Bar** FUSION €€€
(063-12 90 99; www.innefickan.se; Postgränd 11; mains Skr210-295; 5pm-late Tue-Sat) With a cosy cellar ambience – all exposed brick and contemporary-art pieces – Innefickan packs a great deal of creativity into its succinct 13-item menu. We're floored by the carpaccio with wasabi and coriander, the veal with chanterelles and pumpkin puree is expertly seared, and rhubarb is transformed into something far greater than the raw material in their capable hands.

Information

Tourist Office (063-14 40 01; www.visitostersund.se; Rådhusgatan 44; 9am-5pm Mon-Fri, 10am-3pm Sat & Sun) The tourist office is opposite the town hall, and has free internet access.

Getting There & Away

AIR

Åre Östersund Airport (063-19 30 00; www.swedavia.se/ostersund) The Åre Östersund Airport is on Frösön, 11km west of the town centre. The airport bus leaves regularly from the Östersund bus terminal to meet Stockholm flights (adult/child Skr80/30). Destinations include Stockholm, Göteborg, Luleå, Umeå and Malmö.

BUS

Daily bus 45 runs north at 7.15am from Östersund to Gällivare (Skr507, 11¼ hours) via Arvidsjaur (Skr440, seven hours) and Jokkmokk (Skr507, 9½ hours), and south to Mora (Skr345, 5¼ hours, two daily).

TRAIN

In summer, the daily 7.05am **Inlandsbanan** (Inland Railway; www.inlandsbanan.se; late Jun–mid-Aug, reduced service to late Sep) train heads north to Gällivare (Skr1194, 14½ hours) via Arvidsjaur (Skr728, nine hours) and Jokkmokk (Skr993, 12½ hours). Inlandsbanan also runs south to Mora (Skr494, six hours, one daily at 7.45am). SJ departures include two trains daily to Stockholm (Skr670, five hours) via Uppsala and up to six daily trains heading west to Åre (Skr181, 1¼ hours).

Åre

0647 / POP 10,156

Beautifully situated in a mountain valley by the shores of Lake Åresjön, Åre is Sweden's most popular **ski resort** (www.skistar.com/are; one-day ski pass Skr425) and a party town during the November to mid-May season. In winter, you can also engage in heliskiing, kiteboarding, snowfering (windsurfing on snow) and other alternatives to resort-style skiing and snowboarding.

In July, Åre hosts the **Åre Bike Festival** (www.arebikefestival.com) and the hardcore **Åre Extreme Challenge** (www.areextremechallenge.se), with mountain boarding, hillcarting, hiking, rafting and paragliding also on the menu.

Sights & Activities

Kabinbanan CABLE CAR, VIEWPOINT
(adult/child Skr150/110; 10am-4pm daily late Jun-late Sep) Taking you almost to the top of Mt Åreskutan, the only gondola in Scandinavia is worth taking for the awesome views alone. The seven-minute ride departs from behind Åre's main square and whisks you up to a viewing platform (1274m) complete with Åre's most expensive cafe.

★ **Åre Bike Park** MOUNTAIN BIKING
(www.arebikepark.com) In summer the slopes of Mt Åreskutan become an enormous playground dedicated to downhill biking. More than 30 trails span 40km of track, ranging from beginner to extreme (the trails are graded using the same system as ski slopes). The Kabinbanan cable car, the Bergbanan funicular, and the VM6:an and Hummelliften chairlifts are fitted with bike racks.

Sleeping & Eating

Accommodation fills up quickly in winter; not all hotels stay open in summer.

STF Åre Torg HOSTEL €
(0647-515 90; www.svenskaturistforeningen.se/aretorg; Kabinbanevägen 22b; dm/s/d Skr295/540/690;) This large, renovated hostel sits right on the main square. All rooms are identical windowless cubes with four glossy dark-wood bunks, ventilated from the inside. All open onto an enormous common space, with an indoor 'patio' with picnic tables in front of each room and a cafe serving light bites during the day. Spotless guest kitchen and bathrooms.

★ **Copperhill Mountain Lodge** LODGE €€€
(0647-143 00; Åre Björnen; r from Skr2400;) Beautifully constructed of wood and stone with copper accents, this lodge looks down on Åre from its lofty mountain perch. Its stylish, contemporary rooms are grouped according to precious metals; the Gold Suites come equipped with Playstation 3 for après-ski gaming. Its spa offers facials, massages and mineral baths and the three-course seasonal dinner menu (Skr395) is a worthy splurge.

Åre Bageri BAKERY, SWEDISH €€
(www.arebageri.se; Årevägen 55; mains Skr165-235; 7am-4pm & 5-10pm;) This sprawling organic cafe and stone-oven bakery does an enormous all-you-can-eat breakfast spread for Skr89 (7am to 10.30am), great coffee, pastries and huge sandwiches. In the evenings, the upstairs restaurant serves the best of Norrland's seasonal cuisine.

Broken AMERICAN €€
(www.broken-are.com; Torggränd 4; mains Skr115-196; noon-11pm) Just off the main square, this American-style diner is where all the hungry bikers and skiers converge to replenish burned calories by hoovering down Philly cheese steak, fajitas the size of your head, rib platters and jumbo hamburgers, washed down with frozen margaritas.

Information

Tourist Office (0647-163 21; www.visitare.se; St Olafsväg 35; 10am-6pm Mon-Fri, to 3pm Sat & Sun) Inside the public library in the train-station building. Plenty of info on the area, including maps of hiking trails and brochures on outdoor activities.

Getting There & Away

Åre has east-bound trains for Östersund (Skr181, 1¼ hours, six daily) and Stockholm (Skr845, 10¼ hours, daily at 8.12pm). To get to Trondheim, Norway (Skr220, 2½ hours, two daily) change at Storlien.

Umeå

☎090 / POP 79,594

With the vibrant feel of a college town (it has around 30,000 students), Umeå is a welcome outpost of urbanity in the barren north. Since having the title of Culture Capital of Europe bestowed on it in 2014, its museums and other venues have been showcasing northern and Sámi culture; it also plays host to an annual metalfest, **House of Metal** (www.houseofmetal.se), in early February – the darkest time of year, of course.

The town's main attraction is Gammlia, an entertaining cluster of museums. The **tourist office** (☎090-16 16 16; www.visitumea.se; Renmarkstorget 15; ⊙9am-7pm Mon-Fri, 10am-4pm Sat, noon-4pm Sun) has plenty of info on attractions in and around town.

Sights

★Västerbottens Museum MUSEUM

(www.vbm.se; Gammliavägen; ⊙10am-5pm, to 9pm Wed) FREE The star of the Gammlia museum complex, the engrossing Västerbottens Museum traces the history of the province from prehistoric times to Umeå today. Exhibitions include an enormous skis-through-the ages collection starring the world's oldest ski (5400 years old), and an exploration of Sámi rock art and shaman symbols. Of the temporary exhibitions, a photographic portrayal of a single family through several decades, shot by Latvian photographer Inta Ruka, was particularly moving. Take bus 2 or 7.

Bildmuséet GALLERY

(www.bildmuseet.umu.se; Östra Strandgatan 30B; ⊙11am-8pm Tue, to 6pm Wed-Sun) In its new home next to the Umeå Academy of Fine Arts, this state-of-the-art modern-art museum showcases the likes of *Right is Wrong* – four decades of contemporary art in China, and *A Cry from the Expanses* by Carola Granh, a haunting sound installation that's all about the Sámi presence on the northern Swedish landscape. Take bus 1, 5, 6, or 8.

Umedalens Skulpturpark SCULPTURE

(www.umedalenskulptur.se; Umedalen; ⊙24hr) Perhaps appropriately located in the vast grounds of Umeå's former psychiatric hospital, this contemporary sculpture park features the efforts of Anthony Gormley and Sean Henry, among others. Works range from the eerie *New Perspective* sound installation by Lin Peng and humorous *Eye Benches* by Louise Bourgeois to the baffling *Untitled* by Carina Gunnars that consists of eight half-buried bathtubs. Take bus 1 or 61 to the Löftets gränd stop.

Sleeping & Eating

STF Vandrarhem Umeå HOSTEL €

(☎090-77 16 50; www.umeavandrarhem.com; Västra Esplanaden 10; dm/s/d from Skr170/300/500; @☜) This busy, efficient hostel has rooms of varying quality: try to nab a space in one of the newer rooms with beds, as opposed to the rather basic dorms with bunks. It's in a great location: a residential neighbourhood at the edge of

WORTH A TRIP

TREEHOTEL

A spaceship suspended high above ground. A mirror cube reflecting sunlight and surrounding spruce branches...The six individually styled tree-rooms that make up Sweden's most mind-boggling, award-winning lodgings sit just off Rte 97 in the midst of pristine forest, with saunas and hot tubs to relax stiff muscles after a day of hiking, kayaking or dogsledding.

The **Treehotel** (☎070-572 77 52, 0928-104 03; www.treehotel.se; Rte 97; r Skr4700-7200;) came into being in 2010, inspired by the film *The Tree Lover* by Jonas Selberg Augustsen, and its unique rooms were designed by some of Sweden's leading architects, such as Tham & Videgård and Bertil Harström, with an emphasis on minimal environmental impact and ecologically friendly construction. The toilets are a wonder in themselves. We have only one question: why is the Blue Cone red?

Guided tours of this architectural wonder are available on weekends at 1pm (Skr150) and at other times by prior arrangement. Even if you don't stay in the Treehotel itself, you can lodge at the retro **Britta's Pensionat** (doubles Skr750) by the road and treat yourself to a delicious weekday lunch buffet (11am to 3pm) at the cheerful cafe inside (open early July until the end of August); three-course dinners are available on request.

the town centre, and the facilities (kitchen, laundry) are very handy for self-caterers. Reception hours are limited.

★ **Stora Hotellet Umeå** BOUTIQUE HOTEL €€
(090-77 88 70; www.storahotelletumea.se; Storgatan 46; s/d/ste from Skr1000/1150/6000; P) We love the muted colours and the plush, old-style furnishings that give you the impression that you're adrift aboard a luxurious ship. Of the six categories of rooms, even the modest 'Superstition' presents you with luxurious queen-size bunks that real sailors could only dream of, while 'Passion' offers grander surroundings, velvet couches and his 'n' hers showers.

Rost Mat & Kaffe CAFE €
(www.rostmatochkaffe.se; Skolgatan 62; mains Skr83-98; 11am-8pm Mon-Fri, noon-5pm Sat & Sun;) Fresh, imaginative salads, dish-of-the-day lunches with a Mediterranean lean, some of the best coffee in town and scrumptous cakes await at this popular vegetarian cafe.

Rex Bar och Grill INTERNATIONAL €€€
(090-70 60 50; www.rexbar.com; Rädhustorget; mains Skr175-315; 11am-2pm & 5-11pm Mon-Thu, 11am-2am Fri & Sat) This popular bistro has northern Swedish cuisine meeting international brasserie in a convincing explosion of flavour. Choose the northern menu (bleak roe, smoked Arctic char and reindeer steak) or opt for Iberico pork cheek or grilled courgette with morels. Alternatively, stop by for the American-style pancake-and-bacon weekend brunch. Dinner reservations on weekends recommended.

Getting There & Away

Umeå Airport (www.swedavia.se/umea) is 5km south of the city centre. SAS and Norwegian fly daily to Stockholm's Arlanda and Bromma, Malmö Aviation to Göteborg and Stockholm and Direktflyg to Östersund. Airport buses connect it to the city centre (Skr40, 20 minutes).

RG Line (www.directferries.co.uk/rg_line.htm) ferries between Umeå and Vaasa (Finland) run once or twice daily (Skr349 one way, four hours, Sunday to Friday) from Holmsund, 20km south of Umeå.

Bus services from Ybuss run south to Gävle (Skr435, 6½ to 7½ hours, two daily) and Stockholm (Skr430, 9½ hours, two daily), stopping at all the coastal towns. Buses 20 and 100 head up the coast to Luleå (Skr310, four to five hours).

Train departures include five daily trains to Stockholm, including two overnighters (Skr804, nine hours), while the north-bound trains to Luleå (Skr295, five to 5½ hours, two daily) stop in Boden, from where there are connections to Kiruna (Skr647, 7½ to 8½ hours, two daily).

GETTING TO FINLAND

If you're moving on to Finland you'll need to pass through the Swedish town of Haparanda (accessed from Luleå), which shares a joint bus terminal with Tornio (p193) in Finland. This is the main border crossing between the two countries.

Luleå

0920 / POP 46,607

Pretty Luleå is a laidback university town with an appealing island archipelago off its coast, a sparkling bay with a marina and more than its fair share of good restaurants for a town of its size. The capital of Norrboten, Luleå moved to its present location from Gammelstad in 1649 because of the falling sea level (8mm per year), a result of postglacial uplift of the land.

Sights

Gammelstad VILLAGE
(0920-45 70 10; www.lulea.se/gammelstad) FREE This Unesco World Heritage–listed smattering of little red Swedish cottages with the white trim and lace curtains was the medieval centre of northern Sweden. The 1492-built stone Nederluleå church, with a reredos worthy of a cathedral and a wonderfully opulent pulpit, 424 wooden houses (where the pioneers stayed overnight on their weekend pilgrimages) and six church stables remain, some of them open to the public. Guided tours (Skr70) leave from the Gammelstad tourist office at 10am, 11am, 1pm and 3pm (mid-June to mid-August).

Norrbottens Museum MUSEUM
(www.norrbottensmuseum.nu; Storgatan 2; 10am-4pm Mon-Fri, noon-4pm Sat & Sun;) FREE Worth a visit for the collection of photos, tools, and dioramas depicting traditional reindeer-herding Sámi life and the 19th-century playrooms for kiddies.

Teknikens Hus SCIENCE MUSEUM
(www.teknikenshus.se; University Campus; adult/under 4yr Skr70/free; 10am-4pm mid-Jun–Aug; ; 4, 5) Hands-on displays let you fly a rocket, sit in a helicopter, attend a simulated mine explosion and learn about the northern lights.

Sleeping & Eating

Citysleep HOSTEL €
(☎0920-420 002; www.citysleep.se; Skeppsbrogatan 18; dm Skr450) The only budget digs in central Luleå don't come more anonymous than this: book online to get the door code, since there's no reception, then let yourself into a featureless room with two-tiered beds. There are no windows but reasonably good in-room ventilation and a large guest kitchen.

Elite Luleå HOTEL €€
(☎0920-27 40 00; www.lulea.elite.se; Storgatan 15; s/d from Skr790/990; P ✱ ☈) One of Luleå's most sumptuous hotels, the grand Elite is more than a hundred years old, with classically decorated and beautifully refurbished rooms. All bathrooms are decked out in Italian marble and the plusher suites come with whirlpool tubs as well. Bargains are to be had on weekends and the breakfast buffet is extensive.

★ **Hemmagastronomi** FUSION €€
(www.hemmagastronomi.se; Norra Strandgatan 1; tapas from Skr75; ⌚8am-11pm Mon-Fri, to 1am Sat) Is it a bakery? Is it a deli? Is it a bar? Is it a bistro? Hemmagastronomi wears many hats and we love them all. Come for a leisurely breakfast, grab a light bite at lunchtime, or romance your sweetie in the evening under dimmed lights over softshell-crab tapas and seafood platters, complemented by the wide-spanning wine list.

Baan Thai THAI €€
(Kungsgatan 22; mains Skr130-250; ✎) All dark wood and gold Buddha images, this authentic Thai restaurant on the main drag is perpetually filled with locals. Dishes such as the *chu chi pla* (deep-fried fish curry) are particularly good, but ask the staff to spice it up if you want the true Thai fire.

Information

Tourist Office (☎0920-45 70 00; www.visitlulea.se; Skeppsbrogatan 17; ⌚10am-7pm Mon-Fri, to 4pm Sat & Sun) The tourist office is inside Kulturens Hus.

Getting There & Around

AIR

The **airport** (☎010-109 48 00; www.swedavia.se/lulea) is 10km southwest of the town centre. SAS and Norwegian fly daily to Stockholm, while Direktflyg serves Kiruna, Sundsvall, Umeå and Östersund. Bus 4 connects it to the city centre.

DON'T MISS

LULEÅ ARCHIPELAGO

This extensive archipelago consists of some 1700 islands, most of them uninhabited and therefore perfect for skinny dipping, berrypicking, camping wild...we can go on! The larger islands are accessible by boat from Luleå in summer (ask the tourist office for updated boat schedules). Here's our Top 5 island-in-a-nutshell guide:

Sandön The largest island, with an attractive beach in Klubbviken bay.

Junkön Famous for its 16th-century windmill.

Rödkallen Numerous seabird species and an 1872 lighthouse.

Kluntarna Holiday cottages, pine forest, seabird colonies and fishing villages.

Brändöskär Bleakly beautiful, wind-lashed dot in the outermost archipelago.

BUS

Buses 20 and 100 run south to Umeå (Skr310, four to five hours, seven daily), stopping at all the coastal towns, and north to Haparanda (Skr178, 2¼ to 2½ hours, nine daily) and Finland. Bus 44 connects Luleå with Gällivare (Skr311, 3½ to 4½ hours) and Jokkmokk (Skr237, three hours) up to five times daily.

TRAIN

There are two overnight trains to Stockholm (Skr829, 14 to 15 hours) via Gävle (same price, 11¾ to 12½ hours) and Uppsala (same price, 14 hours), while two daily trains connect Luleå with Narvik, Norway (Skr477, 7¼ to 8¼ hours) via Kiruna (Skr292, 3¾ to 4¼ hours, four daily) and Abisko (Skr457, 5½ to 6½ hours).

Arvidsjaur

☎0960 / POP 4635

If you've ever dreamed of taking a fast car for a spin on a frozen lake, or flying through the snowy wilderness on a snowmobile or dog-sled, here's your chance. The small settlement of Arvidsjaur was established as a Sámi marketplace, but it's most famous now as a centre for winter activities.

The first church was built in Arvidsjaur in 1607, in hopes of introducing the Sámi to Christianity. Church attendance laws imposed a certain amount of pew time upon the nomadic Sámi, so to give them a place to rest

WORTH A TRIP

THE SILVER & THE SÁMI

Tiny Arjeplog, 85km northwest of Arvidsjaur, is well worth a detour for two big reasons: Sámi silver and Sámi culture. The tour de force of the wonderful **Silver Museum** (www.silvermuseet.se; Torget; adult/child Skr80/free; 10am-noon & 1-6pm Mon-Fri, 10am-2pm Sat) is the vast collection of Sámi silver objects – the most extensive of its kind – including belt buckles, ornate spoons and goblets and collars decorated with the Gothic letter 'M' (a reference to Holy Mary) that would traditionally have been passed down from mother to daughter. Linger in the basement and delve into Sámi medical lore by focusing on native plant exhibits and their traditional uses.

If you want to learn more about reindeer herding and Sámi livelihood, watch reindeer being lassoed, stay in a Sámi *kåta* (traditional Forest Sámi dwelling) and have your dinner cooked over a campfire, take the road running immediately south of Arjeplog or else the E45 west of Arvidsjaur for 50km and turn north at the village of Slagnäs; the **Båtsuoj Sami Camp** (0960-65 10 26; www.batsuoj.se; short tour/long tour/overnight stay Skr290/600/1100) is signposted near the village of Gasa.

their weary heads after travelling from afar, they built small cottages, or *gåhties*. Some 80 of these are preserved now in **Lappstaden** (Lappstadsgatan; tours Skr50; tours 6pm mid-Jun–mid-Aug) FREE – the biggest Sámi church town in Sweden – and are still in use.

In winter, **Nymånen** (070-625 40 32; www.nymanen.com) organise dogsledding trips in the area, while **Super Safari** (0960-104 57; www.supersafari.info; Idrottsgatan 9A; 2hr tours Skr950) takes visitors out on guided snowmobile tours. Lapland Lodge can arrange both, plus lessons in driving on ice (Skr5900).

Sleeping & Eating

★ Lapland Lodge B&B, HOTEL €€
(0960-137 20; www.laplandlodge.se; Östra Kyrkogatan 18; B&B s/d/f Skr690/850/950, hotel s/d Skr1490/1890; P) Next to the church, this friendly B&B offers a range of room configurations (some en suite) in a pretty yellow house. Contemporary comforts sit amid antique style accented with old wooden skis, antlers and snowshoes. The new hotel wing is all en suite. An outdoor hot tub and sauna are available, and snowmobile, ice-driving and husky-sledding tours run in winter.

Hotell Laponia HOTEL €€
(0960-555 00; www.hotell-laponia.se; Storgatan 45; s/d/ste Skr1190/1290/1990; P) All heavy dark wood inside, Arvidsjaur's only hotel gets booked out by drivers in winter who come to test the Mercedes, BMWs and Porsches on ice. This is also one of the nicer places to eat in town – the bistro-pub serves a very good weekday buffet (Skr85) – and there's a spa.

Laponiakåtan BARBECUE €€
(www.hotell-laponia.se; Storgatan; mains Skr145-325; 4-10pm Mon-Fri, noon-10pm Sat & Sun mid-Jun–Sep) Belonging to Hotell Laponia, this enormous Sámi hut on the lakeside delivers on its promise of 'BBQ with a view'. A single concession to vegetarianism aside (gnocchi), this place attracts discerning carnivores with its burgers, troll-sized portions of hickory ribs and tender reindeer steaks. Outside the summer season, the culinary action moves back inside the hotel.

Getting There & Away

Arvidsjaur airport (0960-173 80; www.ajr.nu), 11km from town, has daily links to Stockholm Arlanda with **NextJet** (www.nextjet.se).

From the bus station on Västlundavägen bus routes include bus 45 south to Östersund (Skr440, 7¼ hours, daily) and north to Gällivare (Skr311, 3¾ hours, daily) via Jokkmokk (Skr215, 2¼ hours), as well as daily bus 104 to Arjeplog (Skr130, one hour).

Arvidsjaur is connected by daily Inlandsbanan (p478) trains in summer/autumn to Östersund (Skr728, 8¼ hours), Gällivare (Skr420, 5¾ hours) and Jokkmokk (Skr265, 3½ hours).

Jokkmokk

0971 / POP 2786

The capital of Sámi culture and the biggest handicraft centre in Lappland, Jokkmokk not only has the definitive Sámi museum, but it's also the only town in Sweden with a further education college that teaches reindeer husbandry, craft-making and ecology using the Sámi language. Jokkmokk is the jumping-off point for visiting the four nearby national parks which are part of the **Laponia World Heritage Site** (www.laponia.nu) and for all manner of outdoor adventures year-round.

Sights

★Ájtte Museum MUSEUM
(www.ajtte.com; Kyrkogatan 3; adult/child Skr80/40; ⊙9am-6pm) This illuminating museum is Sweden's most thorough introduction to Sámi culture. Follow the 'spokes' radiating from the central chamber, each dealing with a different theme – from traditional costume, silverware, creatures from Sámi folk tales and 400-year-old painted shamans' drums, to replicas of sacrificial sites and a diagram explaining the uses and significance of various reindeer entrails. The beautifully showcased collection of traditional silver jewellery features heavy collars, now making a comeback among Sámi women after a long absence.

Sameslöjdstiftelsen Sami Duodji GALLERY
(www.sameslojdstiftelsen.se; Porjusvägen 4; ⊙10am-5pm Mon-Fri) This centrally located Sámi gallery and crafts centre is your one-stop shop for diverse, authentic Sámi handicrafts of the highest quality: from leatherwork, clothing in Sámi colours and silver jewellery to bone-inlaid wood carvings and Sámi knives in reindeer-antler sheaths. Most items are available for purchase.

Sleeping & Eating

Book your accommodation months in advance for the Jokkmokk Winter Festival.

STF Vandrarhem Åsgård HOSTEL €
(☎0971-55 977; www.svenskaturistforeningen.se; Åsgatan 20; dm/s/d from Skr250/300/600; @📶👪) This family-run STF hostel has a lovely setting among green lawns and trees, right near the tourist office. It's a creaky, cheerful old wooden house with numerous bunk beds, compact private rooms, guest kitchen, TV lounge and basement sauna (Skr30 per person). Walls are on the thin side, so you may feel as if you're in bed with your neighbours.

Hotel Jokkmokk HOTEL €€
(☎0971-777 00; www.hoteljokkmokk.se; Solgatan 45; s/d Skr935/1130; P📶) Overlooking picturesque Lake Talvatis, Jokkmokk's nicest hotel has thoroughly modern, if unmemorable rooms, a superb tiled sauna in the basement and another by the lake (for that refreshing hole-in-the-ice dip in winter). The large restaurant, shaped like a Sámi *kåta* (hut), appropriately serves the likes of elk fillet and smoked reindeer with juniper-berry sauce.

★Ájtte Museum Restaurant SWEDISH €€
(www.restaurangattje.se; Kyrkogatan 3; mains Skr95-140; ⊙noon-4pm) This Sámi restaurant makes it possible to enhance what you've learned about the local wildlife by sampling some of it – from *suovas* (smoked and salted reindeer meat) to reindeer steak and grouse with local berries. The weekday lunchtime buffet (Skr90) serves home-style Swedish dishes.

Joik evenings and Sámi storytelling events take place here occasionally.

Thai Muang Isaan THAI €€
(Porjusvägen 4; mains Skr120-140; ⊙11am-8pm Mon-Fri, noon-8pm Sat; 🌶) This central, authentic Thai place fills the spice gap in the local dining scene with noodle, rice and stir-fry dishes, but it's the curries that really hit the spot.

JOKKMOKK WINTER MARKET

Winter travellers shouldn't miss the annual Sámi **Jokkmokk Winter Market** (www.jokkmokksmarknad.com), held the first Thursday through Saturday in February. The oldest and biggest of its kind, it attracts some 30,000 people annually; it's the biggest sales opportunity of the year for the Sámi traders to make contacts and see old friends, while visitors can splurge on the widest array of Sámi *duodji* (handicrafts) in the country and watch the merry chaos of reindeer races on the frozen Talvatissjön lake behind Hotel Jokkmokk.

The event has been going strong since 1605, when King Karl XI decreed that markets should be set up in Lappland to increase taxes, spread Christianity and exert greater control over the nomadic Sámi. The Winter Market is preceded by the opening of the smaller Historical Market and several days of folk music, plays, parades, local cinematography, photography exhibitions, food-tasting sessions and talks on different aspects of Sámi life – all of which segues into the Winter Market itself. It's the most exciting (and coldest!) time to be in Jokkmokk, with temperatures as low as -40°C, so wrap up warm!

Information

Tourist Office (0971-222 50; www.turism.jokkmokk.se; Stortorget 4; 10am-6pm Tue-Sat, noon-3pm Sun) Stocks numerous brochures on activities and tours in the area.

Getting There & Away

From the bus station on Klockarvägen, daily bus 45 connects Jokkmokk with Östersund (Skr507, 9¾ hours) via Arvidsjaur (Skr215, 2¼ hours), while bus 44 runs northeast to Luleå (Skr237, 2¾ hours, one or two daily) via Gällivare (Skr142, 1½ hours, five daily).

In summer and early autumn, daily Inlandsbanan (p478) trains head south to Östersund (Skr993, 12 hours) via Arvidsjaur (Skr129, 3¾ hours) at 9.17am, and north to Gällivare (Skr154, 2¼ hours) at 7.34pm.

Gällivare

0970 / POP 8449

Gällivare – the last stop on the Inlandsbanan – and its northern twin, Malmberget, are surrounded by forest and dwarfed by the bald Dundret hill. After Kiruna, Malmberget ('Ore Mountain') is the second-largest iron-ore mine in Sweden, and – you've guessed it! – Gällivare's main attraction is a trip into the bowels of the earth. The Gällivare tourist office runs daily mine tours in summer: one to the **LKAB iron-ore mine** (admission Skr340; tours 9.30am daily) and the other to the **Aitik open-pit copper mine** (admission Skr340), both being less touristy than Kiruna's equivalent.

Even if you don't descend into the subterranean gloom, a visit to Malmberget casts a melancholy spell, many of its houses abandoned in anticipation of their imminent destruction. You can also take a **midnight sun tour** (return Skr200) up **Dundret** (821m), a nature reserve and excellent vantage point for watching the midnight sun. The tourist office organises special taxi transfers (11pm early June to mid-July, 10pm mid-July to early August) from the train station and the price includes ice cream and waffles at the cafe at the top.

Sleeping & Eating

Stay In HOSTEL €
(070-216 69 65; Lasaretsgatan 3; s/d Skr350/650; wi-fi) This rambling complex, across the road from the train/bus station, may look a bit institutional, but it's clean, functional, super-central and a godsend to self-caterers: guests share several fully equipped kitchens and TV lounges with more long-term local hospital-staff residents. Reserve in advance to get an access code.

Grand Hotel Lapland HOTEL €€
(0970-77 22 90; www.ghl.se; Lasarettsgatan 1; s/d from Skr850/1077; P wi-fi) This modern, business-set-oriented hotel opposite the train station was a building site when we visited but should be fully revamped by the time you do, with a new gym, pool and steakhouse to complement its airy, comfortable rooms. The ground-level **Vassara Pub** serves local specialities such as reindeer, Arctic char and cloudberry tiramisu.

Nittaya Thai THAI €€
(www.nittayathaicatering.se; Storgatan 21B; mains Skr110-120; 10am-2pm Mon, to 9pm Tue-Fri, 1-9pm Sat & Sun; veg) Authentic Thai cuisine in attractive surroundings. The changing weekday lunch buffet (Skr85) is a crowd-pleaser, but we prefer the curries and stir-fried dishes.

Information

Tourist Office (0970-166 60; www.gellivarelapland.se; Central Plan 4; 7am-10pm daily late Jun-Aug, 9am-5pm Mon-Fri rest of year) Inside the train station. Can organise mine and midnight-sun tours. Baggage storage available.

Visit Sápmi (070-688 15 77, 070-346 56 06; www.visitsapmi.com; Östra Kyrkallén 2) Started in 2010, Visit Sápmi is an initiative owned by the **Swedish Sámi Association** with an emphasis on sustainable ecotourism. It aims to be the first port of call for visitors with an interest in any aspect of Sámi life, be it staying with reindeer herders, attending a *yoik* (Sámi song) session or purchasing *duodji* from the best craftspeople.

Getting There & Away

Regional buses depart from the train station. Daily bus 45 runs to Östersund (Skr483, 11 hours) via Jokkmokk (Skr142, 1½ hours, three daily) and Arvidsjaur (Skr311, 3¾ hours, daily), while buses 44 and 10 serve Luleå (Skr311, 3½ to 4¾ hours, two daily) via Kiruna (Skr178, 1¾ to two hours).

The **Inlandsbanan** train runs south to Östersund (Skr507, 11¼ hours, one daily at 9.15am) via Jokkmokk (Skr154, two hours) and Arvidsjaur (Skr420, six hours). Other departures include Narvik (Skr360, 4¾ to 5¼ hours, two daily) via Kiruna (Skr133, one to 1¼ hours, five daily), and Luleå (Skr247, 2½ to three hours, five daily).

Kiruna

☎0980 / POP 18,148

Thousands of visitors flock to Kiruna every year and, at first glance, it's difficult to say why: it's a sprawl of a mining town that's due to be moved from 2016 onwards to stop it from collapsing into the enormous pit mine. However, Kiruna is also an important centre for Sámi culture and the gateway to nearby Jukkasjärvi's Icehotel – northern Sweden's biggest attraction – and the Kungsleden in Abisko. It's also a fantastic base for all manner of outdoor adventures: dogsledding, snowmobiling and northern lights tours in winter and biking, hiking and canoeing in summer.

Whether you consider it a marvel of modern engineering or a monumental eyesore, a descent 540m into the depths of the **LKAB iron-ore mine** (adult/student Skr295/195) – the world's largest iron ore mine – is an eye-opener. Some of the stats you'll hear on the tour are mind-blowing and you'll find yourself dwarfed by the immense machinery. Tours leave daily from the tourist office mid-June to mid-August; book English tours via the tourist office.

Activities

★Nutti Sami Siida CULTURAL TOUR, ADVENTURE TOUR
(☎0980-213 29; www.nutti.se) One of Nature's Best (an endorsement given to tour operators who have certain eco-credentials), this specialist in sustainable Sámi ecotourism arranges visits to the Ráidu Sámi camp to meet reindeer herders (Skr1880), reindeer-sledding excursions (from Skr2750), northern-lights tours (Skr2700) and four-day, multi-activity Lappland tours that take in dogsledding and more (Skr9450).

Kiruna Guidetur SNOW SPORTS, OUTDOORS
(☎0980-811 10; www.kirunaguidetur.com; Vänortsgatan 8) These popular all-rounders organise anything from overnighting in a self-made igloo, snowmobile safaris and cross-country skiing outings in winter to overnight mountain-bike tours, rafting and quad-biking in summer.

ICEHOTEL

Every winter, from December onwards, the **Icehotel** (☎0980-668 00; www.icehotel.com; Marnadsvägen 63; s/d/ste from Skr2300/3200/5300, cabins from Skr1900; P) seems to grow organically from ice blocks taken from Torne river, while international artists flock from all over to carve the ice sculptures that make its frozen rooms masterpieces. Besides the experience of sleeping in the world's largest igloo, there's much to tempt active travellers, with warm accommodation available year-round.

From a humble start in 1989 as a small igloo, originally built by Yngve Bergqvist to house an art gallery, the Icehotel has grown into a building comprising an entrance hall and a main walkway lined with ice sculptures and lit with electric lights, with smaller corridors branching off towards the 67 suites. The beds are made of compact snow and covered with reindeer skins, and you are provided with sleeping bags used by the Swedish army for Arctic survival training, guaranteed to keep you warm despite the –5°C temperature inside the rooms (and in winter that's nothing – outside the hotel it can be as low as –30°C).

There are heated bathrooms near the reception, and you leave most of your possessions in lockers so that they don't freeze. Stuff your clothes into the bottom of your sleeping bag, otherwise they'll soon resemble a washboard. Come morning, guests are revived with a hot drink and a spell in the sauna. Guests spend just one night in the Icehotel itself (it's not a comfortable night's sleep for most), so the hotel provides 30 satellite Aurora Houses – bungalows decorated in contemporary Scandinavian style, with skylights for viewing the northern lights.

This custom-built 'igloo' also has an **Ice Church**, popular for weddings (giving new meaning to the expression 'cold feet')! Outside the winter season the hotel offers 'From River to River' tours (Skr150) that initiate visitors into the process of building this unique hotel, year after year.

Winter adventures on offer include snowmobile safaris, skiing, ice fishing, dogsledding (you can even arrange a dogsled pickup from the airport!), Sámi culture tours and northern-lights safaris, while summer activities comprise hiking, rafting, paddleboarding, canoeing, fishing and Ranger all-terrain-buggy tours.

Sleeping & Eating

STF Vandrarhem & Hotell City HOSTEL, HOTEL €€
(☎0980-666 55; www.kirunahostel.com; Bergmästaregatan 7; dm/s/d from Skr250/450/500, hotel s/d/tr Skr750/850/1100;) This catch-all hotel-and-hostel combo has a gleaming red-and-white colour scheme in its modern hotel rooms and cosy dorms. Sauna and breakfast cost extra for hostel guests, but there are handy guest kitchens.

★**Hotel Arctic Eden** BOUTIQUE HOTEL €€
(☎0980-611 86; www.hotelarcticeden.se; Föraregatan 18; s/d Skr900/1200;) At Kiruna's most luxurious lodgings, the rooms are a chic blend of Sámi decor and modern technology, there's a plush spa and indoor pool, and the friendly staff can book all manner of outdoor adventures. A fine breakfast spread is served in the morning and the on-site Arctic Thai & Grill is flooded with spice-seeking customers on a daily basis.

Thai Kitchen THAI €
(Vänortsgatan 8; mains Skr80-130; 11.30am-9pm;) Don't let the plastic tablecloths fool you – this informal joint cooks up excellent Thai dishes, though if you want authentic spice levels, ask them to kick it up a notch. We particularly love one of the specialities: the sour and spicy glass noodles.

Landströms Kök & Bar SWEDISH €€
(☎0980-133 55; www.landstroms.net; Föreningsgatan 11; mains Skr165-280; 6-11pm Mon-Thu, to 1am Fri & Sat) Take a stylish, monochrome interior, throw in some reindeer steak, haloumi burgers, racks of lamb and crayfish sandwiches, add a concise, well-chosen wine menu and beers that span the world, and you've got a winning recipe for a perpetually buzzy bistro.

Information

Tourist Office (☎0980-188 80; www.kirunalapland.se; Lars Janssonsgatan 17; 8.30am-9pm Mon-Fri, to 6pm Sat & Sun) Inside the Folkets Hus visitor centre; has internet access and can book various tours.

Getting There & Away

AIR

The **airport** (☎010-109 46 00; www.swedavia.com/kiruna), 7km east of town, has flights with SAS and Norwegian to Stockholm (two to three daily), as well as several weekly flights to Luleå and Gällivare. The airport bus (Skr100 one way) is timed to meet Stockholm flights and runs between the tourist office and airport during peak season.

BUS

Bus 91 runs daily to Narvik, Norway (Skr280, 2¾ hours) via Abisko (Skr175, 1¼ hours). Other departures include bus 501 to Jukkasjärvi (Skr40, 30 minutes, two to six daily), and buses 10 and 52 to Gällivare (Skr178, 1¾ hours, two or three daily).

TRAIN

There is a daily overnight train to Stockholm (Skr960, 17½ hours) via Uppsala (Skr960, 16¾ hours) at 3.46pm. Other destinations include Narvik, Norway (Skr227, 3½ to 3¾ hours, two daily) via Abisko (Skr119, 1½ to two hours), Luleå (Skr281, 4¼ hours, five daily) and Gällivare (Skr133, 1¼ hours, five daily).

Abisko

☎0980

The one-elk town of Abisko is the main gateway to the Kungsleden – a 500km-long hiking trail that starts in the 75-sq-km **Abisko National Park**, by the southern shore of Torneträsk lake. This is the driest part of Sweden, giving the area a completely distinct landscape – it's wide open and arid, and consequently has a relatively long (for northern Sweden) hiking season.

Abisko's location far beyond the Arctic Circle and its relative remoteness make it an ideal location for observing the northern lights and the midnight sun. From December through March, and also between mid-June and mid-July a chairlift takes you up the local mountain Nuolja to the viewpoint **Aurora Sky Station** (www.auroraskystation.se; northern lights Skr595, midnight sun adult/child return Skr220/110; 8pm-midnight Dec-Mar, 9.30am-4pm & 10pm-1am Tue, Thu & Sat mid-Jun–mid-Jul). From October to March, **Lights Over Lapland** (☎0760-754 300; www.lightsoverlapland.com; 3hr photography tours Skr1195, 4-day expeditions Skr18,500) organise photo safaris for amateur photographers who come to chase the aurora borealis.

The STF Abisko Turiststation provides information on local hikes and runs a variety of tours, from hiking excursions and Sámi camp tours to dogsledding in winter. **Naturum** (☎0980-788 60; www.lansstyrelsen.se; 9am-6pm Tue-Sat early Jul-Sep & Feb-Apr), next to STF Turiststation, has detailed maps, booklets and extensive information on the Kungsleden.

Activities

Hikes HIKING

Hiking is the big draw in the Abisko National Park, aided by the microclimate that makes this one of the driest places in Sweden. Trails are varied in both distance and terrain, and while most people come here to tackle part (or all) of the 450km-long Kungsleden, there are plenty of shorter rambles.

Before you set off, arm yourself with *Fjällkartan BD6* or *Calazo Kungsleden*; both maps are available at the STF lodge and Naturum.

Sleeping & Eating

Abisko Fjällturer HOSTEL €

(☎980-401 03; www.abisko.net; dm/d from Skr225/600; P) This backpackers' delight is spread over two buildings, with comfortable doubles and dorms with wide bunks, sharing guest kitchens and a wonderful wooden sauna. Brothers Tomas and Andreas keep a large team of sled dogs; dogsledding packages (from Skr1200) and northern-lights tours (from Skr600) are not to be missed in winter. Cross the railway tracks 150m east of Abisko Östra station.

STF Abisko Turiststation & Abisko Mountain Lodge HOSTEL €€

(☎0980-402 00; www.abisko.nu; hostel dm/tw Skr295/885, hotel d Skr1540; P) This 300-bed place overlooking Torneträsk lake is a massive hiker destination. The dorms, cabins and private rooms are overpriced for what they are, but there's huge demand for the excellent facilities: guest kitchens, a basement sauna, a supply shop and an excellent restaurant to treat yourself to a sumptuous post-hike three-course dinner (Skr395). Guided day treks, caving and tours are available.

Getting There & Away

Abisko has two train stops: Östra station puts you in the centre of the tiny village, while Abisko Turiststation is across the highway from the STF lodge – where most visitors are heading.

Bus 91 runs east to Kiruna (Skr175, 1¼ hours, two daily) and west to Narvik, Norway (Skr185, 1½ hours, one daily).

Trains run to Kiruna (Skr119, 1¼ hours, two daily) and to Narvik (Skr116, 1¾ hours, two daily).

Kungsleden

Kungsleden (The King's Trail) is Sweden's most important hiking and skiing route that runs for around 500km from Abisko to Hemavan through Sámi herding lands consisting of spectacular mountainous wilderness that includes Sweden's highest mountain, Kebnekaise (2106m), fringed with forests, speckled with lakes and ribboned with rivers. The route is split into five mostly easy or moderate sections, with **STF mountain huts** (dm Skr370, sites Skr85; ⊙mid-Feb–early May & late Jun–mid-Sep), each manned by a custodian, spaced out every 10km to 20km. Eleven of the 16 huts sell provisions, and full kitchen facilities (including wood-burning stoves) are provided. You'll need your own sleeping bag. There's no electricity. The section between Kvikkjokk and Ammarnäs is not covered by STF, so you can stay in private accommodation in villages or camp wild. Insect repellent is essential.

Abisko to Kebnekaise (Five to Seven Days; 105km)

From Abisko it's 86km to Kebnekaise Fjällstation and 105km to Nikkaluokta if you're leaving the trail at Kebnekaise. This section of Kungsleden runs through the dense vegetation of Abisko National Park, mostly following the valley, with wooden boardwalks

WHICH MAP?

There are two series of detailed maps (1:100,000) that cover every section of the Kungsleden: Fjällkartan and **Calazo** (www.calazo.se). Fjällkartan maps cover a slightly wider area around the Kungsledenand and are one-sided, whereas Calazo are double-sided and water-resistant.

Maps for specific trail sections:

Abisko–Nikkaluokta Fjällkartan BD6 Calazo Kungsleden

Nikkaluokta–Saltoluokta Fjällkartan BD8/Calazo Kebnekaisefjällen

Saltoluokta–Kvikkjokk Fjällkartan BD10/Calazo Sarek & Padjelanta

Kvikkjokk–Ammarnäs Fjällkartan BD14 (north), BD16 (south)/ Calazo Kvikkjokk-Ammarnäs

Ammarnäs–Hemavan Fjällkartan AC2/ Calazo Ammarnäs-Hemavan

over the boggy sections and bridges over streams. The highest point along the trail is the Tjäkta Pass (1150m), with great views over the Tjäktavagge Valley. There are five STF huts along the trail: Abiskojaure, Alesjaure, Tjäktja, Sälka and Singi. The STF has mountain lodges at Abisko (p465) and **Kebnekaise** (☎0980-550 00; www.svenskaturistforeningen.se/kebnekaise; dm/d/q Skr420/1550/2100; ⊙mid-Feb–early May & mid-Jun–mid-Sep).

Kebnekaise to Saltoluokta (Three to Four Days, 52km)

South of Singi, 14km from Kebnekaise, this quieter section of the trail runs through peaceful valleys and beech forest. Row yourself 1km across lake Teusajaure and then cross the bare plateau before descending to Vakkotavare through beech forest.

A bus runs from Vakkotavare to the quay at Kebnats, where there's an STF ferry across the Langas lake to Saltoluokta Fjällstation. STF has a mountain lodge at **Saltoluokta** (☎0973-410 10; www.svenskaturistforeninggen.se/saltoluokta; dm/d/q Skr325/1295/1580; ⊙Mar, Apr & mid-Jun–mid-Sep), and four huts en route at Singi, Kaitumjaure, Teusajaure and Vakkotavare.

Saltoluokta to Kvikkjokk (Four Days, 73km)

From Saltoluokta, it's a long and relatively steep climb to Sitojaure (six hours), where you cross a lake using the boat service run by the hut's caretaker, followed by a boggy stretch with wooden walkways. At Aktse, on the shores of Laitaure Lake, you are rewarded with expansive views of the bare mountainous terrain, before you cross the lake using the rowboats provided and pass through pine forest to reach Kvikkjokk.

STF has a lodge at **Kvikkjokk** (☎0971-210 22; www.svenskaturistforeningen.se/kvikkjokk; dm/s/d Skr295/610/815; ⊙mid-Feb–May & mid-Jun–Oct), and huts at Sitojaure, Aktse and Pårte.

Kvikkjokk to Ammarnäs (Eight to Ten Days, 157km)

This is the wildest and most difficult section of the park, recommended for experienced hikers only. Bring your own tent, as accommodation is very spread out.

Take the boat across Saggat lake from Kvikkjokk before walking to Tsiellejåkk, from where it's 55km to the next hut at Vuonatjviken. Then cross Riebnesjaure lake and another one from Hornavan to the village of Jäkkvikk, from where the trail runs through Pieljekaise National Park. From Jakkvikk it's only 8km until the next hut, followed by another stop at the village of Adolfström. Cross Iraft lake before making for the cabins at Sjnjultje. Here the trail forks: either take the direct 34km route to Ammarnäs, or take a 24km detour to Rävfallet with an additional 20km to Ammarnäs.

You'll find private accommodation at Tsielejåkk, Vuonatjviken, Jäkkvikk, Pieljekaise, Adolfström, Sjnjultje, Rävfallet and **Ammarnäs** (☎0952-600 03; www.ammarnasgarden.se; Tjulträskvägen 1; hostel s/d Skr250/440, hotel s/d Skr595/795; P ♨).

Ammarnäs to Hemavan (Four Days, 78km)

This trail is the easiest of the five sections, mostly consisting of a gentle ramble through beech forest and wetlands, and over low hills. There's a long steep climb (8km) through beech forest between Ammarnäs and Aigert, but at the top you are rewarded with an impressive waterfall.

To reach Syter, cross the wetlands using the network of bridges, stopping at the hut by Tärnasjö Lake for a spell in the sauna. The hike up to Syter peak (1768m) from Syter hut is greatly recommended and the view on the way down to Hemavan, taking in Norway's Okstindarnas glaciers, is particularly spectacular.

The STF has a hostel at **Hemavan** (☎0954-300 02; www.svenskaturistforeningen.se/hemavan; s/d from Skr330/430; P @ ♨), and five huts en route at Aigert, Serve, Tärnaskö, Syter and Viterskalet.

ℹ Getting There & Away

If you're aiming for a more remote part of the trail, you may have to contend with limited (and practically nonexistent outside peak season) bus services.

Frequent trains stop at Abisko en route from Kiruna to Narvik, Norway. Inlandsbanan stops at Jokkmokk in summer.

The bus routes to other starting points along the Kungsleden:

Kiruna to Nikkaluokta On bus 92 (Skr110; 1¼ hours, two daily)

Gällivare to Ritsem Via Kebnats and Vakkotavare on bus 93 (Skr198, 3¼ hours, one daily)

Jokkmokk to Kvikkjokk On bus 47 (Skr178, 2¾ hours, daily)

Arjeplog to Jäkkvik On bus 104 (Skr105, 1¼ hours, one daily on weekdays)

Sorsele to Ammarnäs On bus 341 (Skr115, 1¼ to 1¾ hours, one to three daily)

Umeå via Tärnaby to Hemavan On bus 31 (Skr261, six hours, one to three daily)

Kallax Flyg (☎0980-810 00; www.kallaxflyg.se; adult/2-11yr Skr850/500) helicopters transport hikers twice daily between Nikkaluokta and Kebnekaise between late June and late August (9am & 5pm) and daily until late September (9am), while **Fiskflyg** (☎072-512 77 70; www.fiskflyg.se) has flights from Kvikkjokk and between Ritsem and Staloluokta. If you wish to be dropped off in a wilderness location of your choice, that can also be arranged.

UNDERSTAND SWEDEN

History

Sweden's history can be seen as a play in three acts.

Act I Fur-clad hunter-gatherers – the predecessors of the Sámi – are followed by the Vikings' raiding and plundering, only to be subdued by the Christians.

Act II The action is split between the court and the battlefield. Royal dynasties follow one another in rapid succession: there's fratricide by poisoned pea soup; an androgynous girl-king; a king is assassinated at a masked ball and another during battle. Sweden's territory expands and then rapidly contracts.

Act III Sweden is largely untouched by the turmoil of the world wars and focuses on improving the lives of her own citizens before turning her sights to the rest of the world. Sweden welcomes scores of refugees and the homogenous-looking cast quickly becomes a diverse one.

From First Settlement to Christianity

Around 9000 BC, hunter-gatherers followed the retreating ice into Sweden.

By 600 AD, the Svea people of the Mälaren valley (just west of Stockholm) had gained supremacy, and their kingdom, Svea Rike, gave the country of Sweden its name: Sverige.

The Viking Age was under way by the 9th century, and initial hit-and-run raids along the European coast were followed by major military expeditions, settlement and trade.

Stubbornly pagan for many centuries, Sweden turned to Christianity in the 10th century and by 1160, King Erik Jedvarsson (Sweden's patron saint, St Erik) had virtually wiped out paganism.

Intrigue & Empire-building

In 1319 Sweden and Norway were united as one kingdom, but after the Black Death in 1350 created a shortage of candidates for the throne, Denmark intervened and, together with Norway, joined Sweden in the Union of Kalmar in 1397, resulting in Danish monarchs on the Swedish throne.

A century of Swedish nationalist grumblings erupted in rebellion under the young nobleman Gustav Vasa. Crowned Gustav I in 1523, he introduced the Reformation and a powerful, centralised nation state. The resulting period of expansion gave Sweden control over much of Finland and the Baltic countries. Gustav Vasa's sons did not get on – to the point of Johan dispatching King Erik to the afterlife via some poisoned pea soup.

The last of the Vasa dynasty – Kristina – was a tomboy and a willful, controversial character who eventually abdicated the throne in 1654 and fled to Rome, dressed as a man.

King Karl XII's adventures in the early 18th century cost Sweden its Baltic territories. The next 50 years saw greater parliamentary power, but Gustav III led a coup that brought most of the power back to the crown.

NOBEL ACHIEVEMENTS

In his will, Alfred Nobel (1833–96), the inventor of dynamite, used his vast fortune to establish the Nobel Institute and the international prizes in 1901. This idea was reportedly sparked by an erroneous report in a French newspaper, a premature obituary in which the writer condemned Nobel for his explosive invention ('the merchant of death is dead,' it declared). Prizes are awarded annually for physics, chemistry, medicine and literature, as well as the Peace Prize. An awards ceremony is held in Stockholm on 10 December, while the Peace Prize is awarded in Oslo in the presence of the King of Norway.

An aristocratic revolt in 1809 fixed that (and lost Finland to Russia). The constitution produced in that year divided legislative powers between king and *riksdag* (parliament).

During a gap in royal succession, Swedish agents chose Napoleon's marshal Jean-Baptiste Bernadotte (renamed Karl Johan) as regent. He became king of Norway and Sweden in 1818, and the Bernadotte dynasty still holds the Swedish monarchy.

World Wars & Beyond

In spite of rapid industrialisation, around one million Swedes fled poverty for a brighter future in America in the late 19th and early 20th centuries.

Sweden declared herself neutral in 1912, and remained so throughout the bloodshed of WWI. Swedish neutrality during WWII was ambiguous: letting German troops march through to occupy Norway and selling iron ore to both warring sides tarnished Sweden's image, leading to a crisis of conscience at home and international criticism.

At the same time, Sweden was a haven for refugees from Finland, Norway, Denmark and the Baltic states; downed allied aircrew who escaped the Gestapo; and many thousands of Jews who escaped persecution and death.

Throughout the 1950s and 1960s the Social Democrats continued with the creation of *folkhemmet* (the welfare state), with the introduction of unemployment benefits, childcare and paid holidays. The standard of living for ordinary Swedes rose rapidly.

MURDER MOST MYSTERIOUS

In 1986, Social Democrat Prime Minister Olof Palme (1927–86) was shot dead by a mystery man as he walked home from the cinema with his wife on a frigid February night. What followed resembles an absurd play, complete with a cast of incompetent police, a hysterical wife, a number of improbable suspects including members of the Kurdish separatist movement (PKK), a violent alcoholic and a right-wing ladies' man, and various assorted lunatics. Decades later, conspiracy theories abound and the murderer has still not been brought to justice, though it is widely thought that the South African secret service may have been responsible, given Palme's strong anti-apartheid stance.

Recent Years

World recession of the early 1990s forced a massive devaluation of the Swedish krona, and with both their economy and national confidence shaken, Swedes voted narrowly in favour of joining the European Union (EU) in 1995.

Since then, Sweden's economy has improved considerably, with falling unemployment and inflation. A 2003 referendum on whether Sweden should adopt the euro resulted in a 'no' vote.

The global economic crisis again affected Sweden towards the end of 2008. As ever, economic tensions fed social anxieties. An annual survey about ethnic diversity, conducted by Uppsala University researchers, indicated twice as many Swedes had an 'extremely negative' attitude towards racial diversity in 2008 than in 2005.

Sweden has been embroiled in the extradition scandal involving Wikileaks founder Julian Assange. Wanted in Sweden on sexual assault charges, Assange has opted to take refuge in the Ecuador embassy in London, as the Swedish courts cannot guarantee that he would then not be turned over to the Americans afterwards.

People

With 9.6 million people spread over the third-largest area in Western Europe, Sweden has one of the lowest population densities on the continent. Most Swedes live in the large cities of Stockholm, Göteborg, Malmö and Uppsala. Conversely, the interior of Norrland is sparsely populated.

The majority of Sweden's population is considered to be of Nordic stock, and about 30,000 Finnish speakers form a substantial minority in the northeast, near Torneälven (the Torne river). More than 180,000 citizens of other Nordic countries live in Sweden.

Around 20% of Sweden's population are either foreign born or have at least one non-Swedish parent. The 10 largest immigrant groups are from Finland, former Yugoslavia, Iraq, Poland, Iran, Germany, Denmark, Norway, Turkey and Somalia, and there are around 45,000 Roma.

Swedish music stars José González and Salem Al Fakir and film director Josef Fares are testament to Sweden's increasingly multicultural make-up. Some 200 languages are now spoken in Sweden.

THE SÁMI IN SWEDEN

Europe's only indigenous people, the ancestors of the Sámi migrated to the north of present-day Scandinavia, following the path of the retreating ice, and lived by hunting reindeer in the area spanning from Norway's Atlantic coast to the Kola Peninsula in Russia, collectively known as Sápmi. By the 17th century, the depletion of reindeer herds had transformed the hunting economy into a nomadic herding economy. Until the 1700s, the Sámi lived in *siida* – village units or communities, migrating for their livelihoods, but only within their own defined areas. Those areas were recognised and respected by the Swedish government until colonisation of Lappland began in earnest and the Sámi found their traditional rights and livelihoods threatened both by the settlers and by the establishment of borders between Sweden, Norway, Finland and Russia.

Sweden's Sámi population numbers around 15,000 to 20,000, and there are 10 Sámi languages spoken across Sápmi, which belong to the Finno-Ugrian language group and are not related to any Scandinavian language. Sámi education is now available in government-run Sámi schools or regular municipal schools. Of the 6000 or so Sámi who still speak their mother tongue, 5000 speak the North Sámi dialect.

Sámi beliefs and mythology have traditionally revolved around nature, with the *noaidi* (shamans) bridging the gap between the physical and the spiritual worlds. From 1685, the Sámi were forcibly converted to Christianity and Sweden's policies regarding the Sámi were tinted with social Darwinism, deeming them to be an inferior race fit only for reindeer herding, up until after WWII, when the Sámi began to actively participate in the struggle for their rights, forming numerous associations and pressure groups.

The Sámi in Sweden are represented by the Sámediggi (Sámi parliament), which oversees community matters and acts in an advisory capacity to the Swedish government, though it does not have the power to make decisions regarding land use. The Swedish state is yet to ratify the International Labour Organisation's Convention 169, which would recognise the Sámi as an aboriginal people with property rights, as opposed to just an ethnic minority.

From the 1970s onwards, there has been a revival of traditional Sámi handicraft, such as leatherwork, textiles, knife-making, woodwork and silverwork. Since then, high-quality Sámi handwork that uses traditional designs and materials has borne the Sámi Duodji trademark and can be found all over Lappland.

The booklet *The Saami – People of the Sun & Wind*, published by Ájtte, the Swedish Mountain and Saami Museum in Jokkmokk, is a fantastic introduction to the Sámi and is available at tourist shops around the area. Visit Sápmi (p462) is an excellent resource for all things Sámi. Also, look for the 'Naturenș Bäst' logo, which indicates that an excursion or organisation has been approved by **Svenska Ekoturismföreningen** (www.ekoturism.org), the country's first ecotourism regulating body.

Sweden first opened its borders to mass immigration during WWII. At the time it was a closed society, and new arrivals were initially expected to assimilate and 'become Swedish'. In 1975 parliament adopted a new set of policies that emphasised the freedom to preserve and celebrate traditional native cultures.

Not everyone in Sweden is keen on this idea, with random hate crimes – including the burning down of a Malmö mosque in 2004 – blemishing the country's reputation for tolerance. As hip-hop artist Timbuktu (himself the Swedish-born son of a mixed-race American couple) told the *Washington Post,* 'Sweden still has a very clear picture of what a Swede is. That no longer exists – the blond, blue-eyed physical traits. That's changing. But it still exists in the minds of some people.'

Gender equality has made great inroads in Swedish society, with plenty of childcare leave allocated to both parents, and legislation in place to prevent sexual discrimination.

Arts

Painting & Sculpture

Sweden's 19th-century artistic highlights include the warm art nouveau oil paintings of Carl Larsson (1853–1919), the nudes and portraits of Anders Zorn (1860–1920), August Strindberg's violently moody seascapes, and the nature paintings of Bruno Liljefors (1860–1939). Carl Milles (1875–1955) is Sweden's greatest sculptor, once employed as Rodin's assistant.

Literature

Well-known Swedish writers include the poet Carl Michael Bellman (1740–95), playwright August Strindberg (1849–1912), Nobel Prize winner Selma Lagerlöf (1858–1940) and prolific children's writer Astrid Lindgren (1907–2002) – the 18th most translated author in the world. Vilhelm Moberg (1898–1973) won international acclaim with *Utvandrarna* (The Emigrants; 1949) and *Nybyggarna* (The Settlers; 1956). More recently, Stieg Larsson's Millennium trilogy *(The Girl with the Dragon Tattoo)* has become a worldwide phenomenon and has inspired at least two feature-film adaptations.

Design

Sweden is a living gallery of inspired design, from Jonas Bohlin 'Tutu lamps' to Tom Hedquist milk cartons. While simplicity still defines the Nordic aesthetic, new designers are challenging Scandi functionalism with bold, witty work. A claw-legged 'Bird Table' by Broberg Ridderstråle and a table made entirely of ping-pong balls by Don't Feed the Swedes are two examples of playful creations from design collectives such as Folkform, DessertDesign and Defyra.

Aesthetic prowess also fuels Sweden's thriving fashion scene. Since the late 1990s and continuing today, local designers have aroused global admiration: Madonna dons Patrik Söderstam trousers, and Acne Jeans sell like hot cakes at LA's hip Fred Segal. In fact, these days Sweden is exporting more fashion than pop.

Frozen art – the ice sculptures at the Icehotel (p463) – has become a focus for collaboration between Swedish artists and designers and those from around the world.

And if you haven't come across IKEA furniture, then you've probably been living on a desert island for the last few decades.

Cinema

Swedish cinema is inextricably linked with the name of Ingmar Bergman. His deeply contemplative films *(The Seventh Seal; Through a Glass Darkly; Persona)* explore alienation, the absence of god, the meaning of life, the certainty of death and other light-hearted themes. Recently, Trollhättan and Ystad have become film-making centres, thanks to younger directors such as Lukas Moodysson, whose *Lilja 4-Ever, Show Me Love* and *Tillsammans* have all been hits. Director Tomas Alfredson's atmospheric teen-vampire film *Let the Right One In* also became a cult hit and inspired an American remake and Stieg Larsson's trilogy, starting with *The Girl With a Dragon Tattoo,* has been immortalised on the big screen as well.

Pop Music

Any survey of Swedish music must at least mention ABBA, the iconic, dubiously outfitted winners of the 1974 Eurovision Song Contest (with 'Waterloo'). More current Swedish successes are pop icon Robyn, indie melody-makers Peter Björn & John, and the exquisitely mellow José González, whose cover of the Knife's track 'Heartbeats' catapulted the Göteborg native to international stardom. Other Swedish exports include Roxette, The Hives, Mando Diao, The Cardigans, Kent, Lisa Ekdahl, The Hellacopters, Nicolai Dunger and Ace of Base, while Swedish songwriters and producers have been sought after by the likes of JLo and Madonna.

Environment

Sweden occupies the eastern side of the Scandinavian peninsula, sharing borders with Norway, Finland and Denmark (the latter a mere 4km to the southwest of Sweden and joined to it by a spectacular bridge and tunnel).

Sweden's surface area (450,000 sq km) is stretched long and thin. Around one-sixth of the country lies within the Arctic Circle, yet Sweden is surprisingly warm thanks to the Gulf Stream: minimum northern temperatures are around –20°C (compared with –45°C in Alaska).

The country has a 7000km-long coastline, with myriad islands – the Stockholm archipelago alone has up to 24,000. The largest and most notable islands are Gotland and Öland on the southeast coast, and the best sandy beaches are down the west coast, south of Göteborg.

Forests take up nearly 60% of Sweden's landscape and the land is dotted with around 100,000 lakes. Vänern is the largest lake in Western Europe, at 5585 sq km. Kebnekaise (2111m), part of the glaciated Kjölen Mountains along the Norwegian border, is the highest mountain in Sweden. The southern part of the country is mostly farmland.

Wildlife

Thanks to Sweden's geographical diversity, it has a great variety of European animals, birds and plants. The big carnivores – bear, wolf, wolverine, lynx and golden eagle – are all protected species. The elk (moose in North America), a gentle, knobby-kneed creature that grows up to 2m tall, is the symbol of Sweden. Elk are a serious traffic hazard, particularly at night: they can dart out in front of your car at up to 50km/h. Around 260,000 domesticated reindeer, also no fun to run into on a highway, roam the northern areas under the watchful eyes of Sámi herders. The musk ox is another large herbivore. Forests, lakes and rivers support beaver, otter, mink, badger and pine marten and hundreds of bird species (including numerous sea birds) populate the country.

National Parks

Sweden had the distinction of being the first country in Europe to establish a national park (1909). There are now 29, along with around 2600 smaller nature reserves; together they cover about 9% of the country. The organisation **Naturvårdsverket** (www.swedishepa.se) oversees and produces pamphlets about the parks in Swedish and English, along with the excellent book *Nationalparkerna i Sverige* (National Parks in Sweden).

Four of Sweden's large rivers (Kalixälven, Piteälven, Vindelälven and Torneälven) have been declared National Heritage Rivers in order to protect them from hydroelectric development.

ARCTIC PHENOMENA

The north of Sweden offers two unparalleled shows of nature. The mesmerising **aurora borealis** (p187; northern lights) consists of ghostly wisps, streaks and haloes of faint green, yellow and even crimson light, caused by the interaction of charged particles in the atmosphere and best seen between October and March.

Beyond the Arctic Circle, the **midnight sun** can be seen between mid-June and early July and the endless hours of daylight give lakes and rivers a wonderful pearly sheen.

Environmental Issues

Ecological consciousness in Sweden is very high and reflected in concern for native animals, clean water and renewable resources. Swedes are fervent believers in sorting and recycling household waste – you'll be expected to do the same in hotels, hostels and camping grounds. Most plastic bottles and cans can be recycled in supermarkets with around Skr1 returned per item.

Two organisations that set standards for labelling products as ecologically sound are the food-focused **KRAV** (www.krav.se), a member of the International Federation of Organic Agriculture Movements, and **Swan** (www.svanen.se), which has a wider scope and certifies entire hotels and hostels.

Linked to the environmental concerns is the challenge of protecting the cultural heritage of the Sámi people. The harnessing of rivers can have massive (negative) impact on what has historically been Sámi territory, whether by flooding reindeer feeding grounds or by diverting water and drying up river valleys. In general, the mining, forestry and space industries have wreaked havoc on Sámi homelands.

Food & Drink

Epicureans around the world are smitten with Sweden's new-generation chefs and their inventive creations. Current luminaries include Bocuse d'Or recipient Mathias Dahlgren, TV chef Niklas Ekstedt and New York–based Marcus Samuelsson.

Staples & Specialities

While new-school Swedish cuisine thrives on experimentation, it retains firm roots in Sweden's culinary heritage. Even the most avant-garde chefs admire simple, old-school *husmanskost* (everyman cuisine) such as *toast skagen* (toast with bleak roe, crème fraiche and chopped red onion) and *köttbullar och potatis* (meatballs and potatoes, usually served with lingonberry jam, or *lingonsylt*). Seafood staples include caviar, gravlax (cured salmon) and the ubiquitous *sill* (herring), eaten smoked, fried or pickled and often accompanied by capers, mustard and onion. The most contentious traditional food is the pungent *surströmming* (fermented Baltic herring), traditionally eaten in August and September in a slice of *tunnbröd* (thin, unleavened bread) with boiled potato and onions and ample amounts of *snaps*. In the north of Sweden, the bounty of the wilderness enhances the menu, from reindeer and elk steak and Arctic char (fish) to mushrooms and berries (including cloudberry-based desserts).

Where to Eat & Drink

Most hotels and some hostels provide breakfast buffets laden with cereals and yogurt plus bread, fruit, cold cuts, cheese and the like. Sweden is the inventor of the smörgåsbord – a vast buffet of Swedish specialities and served as brunch in many establishments. Many cafes and restaurants offer a daily lunch special called *dagens rätt* or *dagens lunch* (main course, salad, bread, cold drink and coffee) at a fixed price between 11.30am and 2pm, which makes it considerably cheaper to eat out in the middle of day than in the evenings.

To counter the mid-afternoon slump, Swedes enjoy *fika,* an almost mandatory coffee break. *Konditori* are old-fashioned bakery-cafes where you can get a pastry or a *smörgås* (sandwich), but there are also many stylish, modern cafes where you can enjoy people-watching over pricier Italian coffees, gourmet salads, bagels and muffins.

Pure vegetarian restaurants (especially buffets) are increasingly common, and there will usually be at least one vegetarian main-course option on the menu at ordinary restaurants.

Drinking

Lättöl (light beer, less than 2.25% alcohol) and *folköl* (folk beer, 2.25% to 3.5% alcohol) can be bought in supermarkets everywhere. *Mellanöl* (medium-strength beer, 3.6% to 4.5% alcohol), *starköl* (strong beer, over 4.5% alcohol) and wines and spirits can be bought only at outlets of the state-owned alcohol store – Systembolaget – which is open until about 6pm on weekdays and slightly shorter hours on Saturday.

Sweden's trademark spirit, *brännvin,* also called aquavit and drunk as *snaps,* is a fiery and strongly flavoured drink that's usually distilled from potatoes and spiced with herbs.

The legal drinking age in Sweden is 18 years, although you have to be 20 years old to buy alcohol at a Systembolaget.

SURVIVAL GUIDE

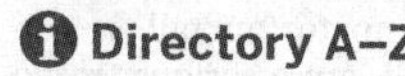

ACCOMMODATION

In much of Sweden prices go *down* in high season (July and August) by up to 50%. Most hotels in Sweden also offer steep discounts (up to 50%) on Friday and Saturday nights and from mid-May through August. Many hotels also have discounts for rooms booked online ahead of time. The following price categories are for a standard double room with private bathroom in high season (June to August):

€ less than Skr800

€€ Skr800 to Skr1600

€€€ more than Skr1600

Cabins & Chalets

Daily rates for *stugor* (cabins and chalets, often found at camping grounds or in the countryside) offer good value for small groups and families, and range in both quality and price (Skr350 to Skr950). Some are simple, with bunk beds and little else (you share the bathroom and kitchen facilities with campers); others are fully equipped with their own kitchen, bathroom and living room. Local and regional tourist offices have listings of cabins and cottages that may be rented by the week; these are often in idyllic forest, lakeside or coastal locations. See the **Stuga** (www.stuga.nu) website for more.

Camping

Sweden has hundreds of camping grounds; a free English-language guide with maps is available from tourist offices. Some are open year-round, but the best time for camping is from May to September. Prices vary with facilities, from Skr150 for a basic site to around Skr250 for the highest standards. Most camping grounds have kitchens and laundry facilities, and many have the works – swimming pool, bike and canoe rental, restaurant, store and laundry facilities.

You must have a Camping Key Europe card (Skr150) to stay at most Swedish camping grounds. Buy one online at the **Sveriges Camping & Stugföretagares Riksorganisation** (www.camping.se) website; otherwise pick up a temporary card at your first campsite.

Visit www.camping.se for lots of useful information.

Hostels

Sweden has well over 450 hostels *(vandrarhem)*, usually with excellent facilities. Outside major cities, hostels aren't backpacker hang-outs but are used as holiday accommodation by Swedish families, couples or retired people. Another quirk is the scarcity of dormitories; hostels are more likely to have singles and doubles of almost hotel quality, often with en suite bathrooms. About half of hostels are open year-round; many others open from May to September, some only from mid-June to mid-August.

Be warned, Swedish hostels keep very short reception opening times: generally from 5pm to 7pm, and 8am to 10am. The secret is to prebook by telephone – reservations are recommended in any case, as good hostels fill up fast. If you're stuck arriving when the front desk is closed, you'll usually see a number posted where you can phone for instructions.

Breakfast is usually available (Skr65 to Skr95). Most hostels, mountain huts and lodges are affiliated with **Svenska Turistföreningen** (STF; ☎08-463 21 00; www.svenskaturistforeningen.se), part of Hostelling International (HI); non-members pay Skr50 extra per night. Others are affiliated with **Sveriges Vandrarhem i Förening** (SVIF; ☎031-828 800; www.svif.se), but there are also unaffiliated hostels with high standards of accommodation.

Hotels

Most hotels in Sweden tend to belong to big hotel chains. Hotel prices include a breakfast buffet unless stated otherwise. Visit the website www.hotelsinsweden.net; budget travellers should check out **Ibis** (www.ibishotel.com), with simple and cheap rooms with private facilities. Midrange Scandic is known for being environmentally friendly, while the top-end Countryside chain has the most characterful rooms, in castles, mansions, monasteries and spas.

BED SHEETS & BROOMS

The vast majority of Swedish youth hostels do not include bedding in the price, so you either have to pay an extra Skr55 to Skr70 to rent sheets on a nightly basis, or – if you don't wish to drift into insolvency – bring your own. Sleeping bags are usually allowed if you have a sheet and pillowcase. Giving the room a sweep with the cleaning materials provided helps to avoid the nightly cleaning fees.

ACTIVITIES

Sweden is a **canoeing** and **kayaking** paradise (canoes are more common). The national canoeing body is **Kanotförbundet** (Kayak & Canoe Federation; www.kanot.com). It provides general advice and lists approved canoe centres that hire out canoes.

There are thousands of kilometres of hiking trails in Sweden, particularly in the north. The best hiking time is between late June and mid-September, when trails are mostly snow-free.

Large ski resorts cater to downhill **skiing** and **snowboarding**. **SkiStar** (www.skistar.com) manages the largest resorts and has good information on its website.

Winter activities in the north include dogsledding, snowmobiling, and cross-country skiing.

CHILDREN

Sweden is a very easy, friendly place to travel with children. Museums almost always have dedicated playrooms with hands-on learning tools. Restaurants offer high-chairs and kids' menus. There are safety features for children in hire/rental cars. Hostels generally have family rooms and camping grounds are often equipped with swimming pools and playgrounds.

DISCOUNT CARDS

Göteborg, Malmö, Stockholm and Uppsala offer tourist cards that offer discounts on major attractions, transport and more (see individual city sections for details).

The **International Student Identity Card** (ISIC; www.isic.org; fee $25) offers discounts on admission to museums, sights, public transport and more. **Hostelling International** (HI) cards get you discounts on accommodation.

Seniors get discounts on entry to museums, sights, cinema and theatre tickets, air tickets and other transport. No special card required. Show your passport as proof of age (the minimum qualifying age is 60 or 65).

FOOD

The following price ranges refer to a standard main course:

€ less than Skr100

€€ Skr100 to Skr200

€€€ more than Skr200

GAY & LESBIAN TRAVELLERS

Sweden recognises civil unions or 'registered partnerships' that grant general marriage rights to gay and lesbian couples.

Riksförbundet för Sexuellt Likaberättigande (RFSL; ☎08-501 62 900; www.rfsl.se; Sveavägen 57-59) The national organisation for gay and lesbian rights is Riksförbundet för Sexuellt Likaberättigande, with an attached bookshop, restaurant and nightclub.

QX (www.qx.se) Free monthly magazine in Stockholm, Göteborg, Malmö and Copenhagen.

INTERNET ACCESS

Sweden is a wired country. Most hotels have wireless LAN connections. Hostels and tourist offices frequently have at least one internet-enabled computer available for use, often free of charge.

Nearly all public libraries offer free internet access, but often the time slots are booked in advance by locals.

Internet cafes are rarely found outside big cities and typically charge around Skr1 per online minute, or Skr50 per hour. Wireless internet is almost universal (and free) at coffee shops, bars, cafes and hotels, although there's a fee for access at train stations, bus stations and airports.

Bring a universal AC adaptor and plug adaptor for your laptop.

MONEY

Sweden uses the krona (plural: kronor), denoted Skr (or SEK in Sweden) and divided into 100 öre. Coins are one, five and 10 kronor, and notes are 20, 50, 100, 500 and 1000 kronor. Swedes round to the nearest krona when paying cash, as there are no öre coins any more.

ATMs

ATMs are easy to find in all major towns and cities. They accept major credit cards as well as Plus and Cirrus.

Credit Cards

Visa and MasterCard are widely accepted; American Express, Discover and Diners Club less so.

Moneychangers

Forex (☎0771-22 22 21; www.forex.se) is the biggest foreign money exchange company in Sweden; it has branches in major airports, ferry terminals and city centres.

Tipping

Hotels Optional; Skr10 per day for housekeeping appreciated.

Restaurants 10% is customary at dinner to reward good service.

Taxis Optional; round up the bill to the nearest 10Skr.

OPENING HOURS

Opening hours can vary significantly between high and low seasons. Any hours provided here are for the high season, from June to August.

Banks 9.30am to 3pm Monday to Friday; some city branches open 9am to 5pm or 6pm.

Bars & pubs 11am or noon to 1am or 2am.

Department stores 10am to 7pm Monday to Saturday (sometimes later), noon to 4pm Sunday.

Government offices 9am to 5pm Monday to Friday.

Post offices 9am to 5pm Monday to Friday.

Restaurants Lunch from 11.30am to 2pm, dinner 5.30pm to 10pm; often closed on Sunday and/or Monday.

Shops 9am to 6pm Monday to Friday, 9am to 1pm Saturday.

Supermarkets 8am or 9am to 7pm or 10pm.

Systembolaget 10am to 6pm Monday to Friday, 10am to 2pm (often to 5pm) Saturday, sometimes with extended hours on Thursday and Friday evenings.

PHOTOGRAPHY

Photographing military establishments is forbidden. Ask permission before taking photos of the Sámi.

PUBLIC HOLIDAYS

Many businesses close early the day before and all day after official public holidays, including the following:

Nyårsdag (New Year's Day) 1 January

Trettondedag Jul (Epiphany) 6 January

Långfredag, Påsk, Annandag Påsk (Good Friday, Easter Sunday & Monday) March/April

Första Maj (Labour Day) 1 May

Kristi Himmelsfärds dag (Ascension Day) May/June

Pingst, Annandag Pingst (Whit Sunday & Monday) Late May or early June

Midsommardag (Midsummer's Day) First Saturday after 21 June

Alla Helgons dag (All Saints' Day) Saturday, late October or early November

Juldag (Christmas Day) 25 December

Annandag Jul (Boxing Day) 26 December

TELEPHONE

Directory Assistance (☎118 118) Within Sweden.

Directory Assistance (☎118 119) International.

Mobile phones Using a mobile phone from another EU country is relatively inexpensive due to standardised rates. For longer stays in Sweden, consider buying a Swedish SIM card (around Skr100) from one of the three main providers: **Telia**, **Tele2** or **Telenor**.

Phone codes Swedish phone numbers have area codes followed by varying numbers of digits. To call Sweden from abroad, dial the country code (☎46) followed by the area code and telephone number (omitting the first zero in the area code). For international calls dial ☎00 followed by the country code and the local area code. Toll-free codes include ☎020 and ☎0200 (but not from public phones or abroad). Mobile phone numbers usually begin with ☎010, ☎070, ☎073, ☎076 and ☎0730.

Phonecards All public pay phones take coins and prepaid phonecards are available at Pressbyrån newsagents.

TIME

Sweden is one hour ahead of GMT/UTC and observes daylight-saving time (with changes in March and October). Timetables and business hours generally use the 24-hour clock.

TOILETS

Public toilets in parks, shopping malls, libraries and bus or train stations are rarely free in Sweden. Except at the larger train stations (where an attendant is on duty), pay toilets are coin operated and usually cost Skr5 to Skr10 (so keep coins handy).

TOURIST INFORMATION

Most Swedish towns have a centrally located tourist office *(turistbyrå)*, with plenty of brochures on attractions, accommodation and transport. Most are open long hours in summer and short hours (until 4pm on weekdays or not at all) during winter.

TRAVELLERS WITH DISABILITIES

Sweden is one of the easiest countries to travel around in a wheelchair. People with disabilities will find transport services with adapted facilities, ranging from trains to taxis, but contact the operator in advance for the best service. Public toilets and some hotel rooms have facilities for people with disabilities; **Hotels in Sweden** (www.hotelsinsweden.net) indicates whether hotels have adapted rooms.

De Handikappades Riksförbund (☎08-685 80 00; www.dhr.se) Provides information on disability-friendly venues in Stockholm.

VISAS

Non-EU passport holders from the USA, Canada, Australia and New Zealand do not need a visa for stays of less than three months. Citizens of EU countries and other Scandinavian countries with a valid passport or national identification card do not require visas. Other nationalities should check with **Migrationsverket** (☎0771-235 235; www.migrationsverket.se) to see whether they require a visa before arriving in Sweden.

ℹ Getting There & Away

AIR

The main airport is Stockholm Arlanda (p405), which links Sweden with major European and North American cities. Göteborg Landvetter (p435) is Sweden's second-biggest international airport. Stockholm Skavsta (p405) (100km south of Stockholm, near Nyköping) and Göteborg City (p435) both act as airports for the budget airline Ryanair. Stockholm's Västerås airport also serves Ryanair.

Reliable Scandinavian Airlines System (SAS) is the regional carrier. Most of the usual airlines fly into Sweden, including the following:

Air France (www.airfrance.com)

British Airways (www.britishairways.com)

Lufthansa (www.lufthansa.com)

Norwegian Air (www.norwegian.com)

Ryanair (www.ryanair.com)

SAS (www.flysas.com)

LAND

Direct access to Sweden by land is possible from Norway, Finland and Denmark (via the Öresund toll bridge). Border-crossing formalities are nonexistent.

Train and bus journeys between Sweden and the continent go directly to ferries. Include ferry fares (or Öresund tolls) in your budget if you're driving from continental Europe.

Eurolines Scandinavia (www.eurolines.se) Has an office in Malmö. Full schedules and fares are listed on the company's website.

Nettbuss Express (☎0771-15 15 15; www.nettbuss.se) Long-distance buses within Sweden and to Oslo (Norway) and Copenhagen.

Sveriges Järnväg (SJ; ☎0771-75 75 99; www.sj.se) Train lines with services to Copenhagen.

Swebus Express (☎0200-21 82 18; www.swebusexpress.se) Long-distance buses within Sweden and to Oslo and Copenhagen.

Continental Europe

Regular Eurolines services run between Göteborg and London via Copenhagen and Brussels and Göteborg and Berlin (Sk1500, 15 hours, five weekly) via Copenhagen.

Denmark

Bus

Eurolines runs buses between Göteborg and Copenhagen (Skr299, 4½ hours, daily). Swebus Express and Nettbuss Express both run regular buses on the same routes. All companies offer student, youth (under 26) and senior discounts.

Train

Öresund trains operated by **Skånetrafiken** (www.skanetrafiken.se) run every 20 minutes from 6am to midnight (and once an hour thereafter) between Copenhagen and Malmö (one way Skr105, 35 minutes) via the bridge. The trains usually stop at Copenhagen airport.

From Copenhagen, change in Malmö for Stockholm trains. Frequent services operate directly between Copenhagen and Göteborg (Skr416, four hours) and between Copenhagen, Kristianstad and Karlskrona.

Car & Motorcycle

You can drive from Copenhagen to Malmö across the Öresund bridge on the E20 motorway. Tolls are paid at Lernacken, on the Swedish side, in either Danish or Swedish currency (single crossing per car Skr435), or by credit or debit card.

Finland

Bus

Express coaches on **Tapanis Buss** (www.tapanis.se) run from Stockholm to the joint Tornio/Haparanda bus terminal twice weekly (Skr695, 15 hours). **Länstrafiken i Norrbotten** (☎ 0771-10 01 10; www.ltnbd.se) operates buses as far as Karesuando, across the bridge to Kaaresuvanto (Finland).

There are also regular services from Haparanda to Övertorneå; you can walk across the border at Övertorneå and pick up a Finnish bus to Muonio, with onward connections to Kaaresuvanto and Tromsø (Norway).

Car & Motorcycle

The main routes between Sweden and Finland are the E4 from Umeå to Kemi and Rd45 from Gällivare to Kaaresuvanto.

Norway

Bus

Nettbuss Express runs from Stockholm to Oslo (Sk632, 7½ hours, five daily), and from Göteborg to Oslo (Skr209, four hours, at least three daily).

In the north, buses run once daily from Umeå to Mo i Rana (eight hours) and from Skellefteå to Bodø (nine hours, daily except Saturday); for details, contact **Länstrafiken i Västerbotten** (☎ 077-10 01 10; www.tabussen.nu)and **Länstrafiken i Norrbotten** (☎ 0771-10 01 10; www.ltnbd.se) .

Train

Trains run daily from Stockholm to Oslo (Skr588, six to seven hours, two daily) and at night to Narvik (Skr916, 21 hours, daily). There are also trains from Helsingborg via Göteborg to Oslo (Skr837, seven hours, two daily).

Car & Motorcycle

The main roads between Sweden and Norway are the E6 from Göteborg to Oslo, the E18 from Stockholm to Oslo, the E14 from Sundsvall to Trondheim, the E12 from Umeå to Moi i Rana and the E10 from Kiruna to Bjerkvik.

SEA

Ferry connections between Sweden and its neighbours are frequent and straightforward. See p485 for full details.

Getting Around

AIR

Domestic airlines in Sweden tend to use Stockholm Arlanda (p405) as a hub, but there are 30-odd regional airports. Flying domestic is expensive on full-price tickets, but substantial discounts are available on internet bookings, student and youth fares, off-peak travel, return tickets booked at least seven days in advance and low-price tickets for accompanying family members and seniors.

Sweden's internal flight operators and their destinations include the following:

Malmö Aviation (☎ 040-660 28 20; www.malmoaviation.se) Göteborg, Stockholm and Umeå.

SAS (☎ 0770-72 77 27; www.flysas.com) Arvidsjaur, Borlänge, Gällivare, Göteborg, Halmstad, Ängelholm-Helsingborg, Hemavan, Hultsfred, Jönköping, Kalmar, Karlstad, Kiruna, Kramfors, Kristianstad, Linköping, Luleå, Lycksele, Norrköping, Malmö, Mora, Örebro, Örnsköldsvik, Oskarshamn, Skellefteå, Stockholm, Storuman, Sundsvall, Sveg, Torsby, Trollhättan, Umeå, Vilhelmina, Visby and Västerås.

BOAT

Canal Boat

The canals provide cross-country routes linking the main lakes. The longest cruises, on the Göta Canal from Söderköping (south of Stockholm) to Göteborg, run from mid-May to mid-September, take at least four days and include the lakes between.

Rederiaktiebolaget Göta Kanal (☎ 031-80 63 15; www.gotacanal.se) operates three ships over the whole distance at fares from Skr12,295 to Skr17,125 per person for a four-day cruise, including full board and guided excursions.

Ferry

An extensive boat network and the five-day Båtluffarkortet boat passes (Skr420) open up the attractive Stockholm archipelago. Gotland is served by regular ferries from Nynäshamn and Oskarshamn, and the quaint fishing villages off the west coast can normally be reached by boat with a regional transport pass – enquire at the Göteborg tourist offices.

BUS

Swebus Express (p475) has the largest network of express buses, but they serve only the southern half of the country (as far north as Mora in Dalarna).

Svenska Buss (p421) and Nettbuss Express (p475) also connect many southern towns and cities with Stockholm; prices are often slightly cheaper than Swebus Express, but services are less frequent.

North of Gävle, regular connections with Stockholm are provided by several smaller operators, including **Ybuss** (☎060-17 19 60; www.ybuss.se), which has services to Sundsvall, Östersund and Umeå.

Länstrafiken i Norrbotten (☎0771-10 01 10; www.ltnbd.se) serves many destinations in the north of the country, as does its sister company, **Länstrafiken i Västerbotten** (☎077-10 01 10; www.tabussen.nu). Services are well integrated with the regional train system, with one ticket valid on any local or regional bus or train. Rules vary but transfers are usually free if used within one to four hours.

You don't have to reserve a seat on Swebus Express services. Generally, tickets are cheaper if they're for travel between Monday and Thursday, or if they're purchased online or more than 24 hours before departure. If you're a student or senior, ask about fare discounts.

Bus Passes

Good-value daily or weekly passes are usually available from local and regional transport offices, and many regions have 30-day passes for longer stays, or a special card for peak-season summer travel.

CAR & MOTORCYCLE

Sweden has good-standard roads, and the excellent E-class motorways rarely have traffic jams.

Automobile Associations

The Swedish national motoring association is **Motormännens Riksförbund** (☎020-21 11 11; www.motormannen.se).

Bring Your Own Vehicle

If bringing your own car, you'll need your vehicle registration documents, unlimited third-party liability insurance and a valid driving licence. A right-hand drive vehicle brought from the UK or Ireland should have deflectors fitted to the headlights to avoid blinding oncoming traffic. You must carry a reflective warning breakdown triangle.

> **LOCAL TRANSPORT**
>
> In Sweden, public transport is heavily subsidised and well organised. It's divided into 24 regional networks *(länstrafik)*, with local transport always linked to regional transport. Town and city bus fares are typically around Skr20, but it works out cheaper to get a day card or travel pass.

Driving Licence

An international driving permit isn't necessary; your domestic licence will do.

Hire

To hire a car you have to be at least 20 (sometimes 25) years of age, with a recognised licence and a credit card.

International rental chains Avis, Hertz and Europcar have desks at Stockholm Arlanda and Göteborg Landvetter airports and offices in most major cities. The lowest car-hire rates are generally from larger petrol stations (such as Statoil and OK-Q8).

Avis (☎0770-82 00 82; www.avisworld.com)
Europcar (☎020-78 11 80; www.europcar.com)
Hertz (☎0771-211 212; www.hertz-europe.com)
Mabi Hyrbilar (☎08-612 60 90; www.mabirent.se) National company with competitive rates.
OK-Q8 (☎020-85 08 50; www.okq8.se) Click on *hyrbilar* in the website menu to see car-hire pages.
Statoil (☎08-429 63 00; www.statoil.se/biluthyrning) Click on *uthyrningsstationer* to see branches with car hire, and on *priser* for prices.

Road Hazards

In the northern part of Sweden, reindeer and elk (moose, to Americans) are serious road hazards, particularly around dawn and dusk. Look out for black plastic bags tied to roadside trees or poles – this is a sign from local Sámi that they have reindeer herds grazing in the area. Report all incidents to police – failure to do so is an offence. In Göteborg and Norrköping, be aware of trams, which have priority; overtake on the right.

TRAIN

Sweden has an extensive and reliable railway network, and trains are almost always faster than buses. Many destinations in the northern half of the country, however, cannot be reached by train alone, and Inlandsbanan, the historic train line through Norrland, runs only during

ROAD RULES

- You drive on and give way to the right.
- Dipped headlights must be on at all times when driving.
- Seatbelt use is obligatory and children under the age of seven should be in the appropriate harness or car seat.
- The maximum blood-alcohol limit is a stringent 0.02%; a single drink will put you over.
- The speed limit on motorways (signposted in green and called E1, E4, etc) is 110km/h; highways 90km/h; narrow rural roads 70km/h and built-up areas 50km/h. Police using hand-held radar speed detectors impose on-the-spot fines (Srk1200).

summer/early autumn. Sveriges Järnväg (p475) runs services to Copenhagen. The other main train operators in the country include: the following

Inlandsbanan (☎0771-53 53 53; www.inlandsbanan.se) One of the great rail journeys in Scandinavia is this slow and scenic 1300km route from Kristinehamn to Gällivare. Several southern sections have to be travelled by bus, but the all-train route starts at Mora. It takes seven hours from Mora to Östersund (Skr494) and 15 hours from Östersund to Gällivare (Skr1149). A pass allows two weeks' unlimited travel for Skr1795.

Tågkompaniet (☎0771-44 41 11; www.tagkompaniet.se) Operates excellent overnight trains from Göteborg and Stockholm north to Boden, Kiruna, Luleå and Narvik, and the lines north of Härnösand.

Costs

Ticket prices vary tremendously, depending on the type of train, class, time of day and how far in advance you buy the ticket. Super-fast X2000 trains are pricier than other trains. Full-price 2nd-class tickets for longer journeys cost about twice as much as equivalent bus trips, but there are various discounts available, especially for booking in advance or at the last minute. Students, pensioners and people aged under 26 get a steep discount.

All Sveriges Järnväg (SJ) ticket prices drop from late June to mid-August. Most SJ trains don't allow bicycles to be taken onto trains (they have to be sent as freight), but those in southern Sweden do; check when you book your ticket.

Train Passes

The Sweden Rail Pass and international passes, such as Inter-Rail and Eurail, are accepted on SJ services and most regional trains.

The **Eurail Scandinavia Pass** (www.eurail.com) entitles you to unlimited rail travel in Denmark, Finland, Norway and Sweden; it is valid in 2nd class only and is available for three, four, five, six, eight or 10 days of travel within a one-month period (prices start at youth/adult US$276/368). The X2000 trains require all rail-pass holders to pay a supplement of Skr62. The pass also provides free travel on Scandlines' Helsingør–Helsingborg route, and 20% to 50% discounts on various ship routes, including the following:

Frederikshavn–Göteborg Stena Line
Grenå–Varberg Stena Line
Helsinki–Åland–Stockholm Silja Line
Stockholm–Tallinn Silja Line
Stockholm–Riga Silja Line
Turku–Åland–Stockholm/Kappelskär Silja Line

Survival Guide

Directory A–Z

Accommodation

Accommodation listings have been divided into budget, midrange and top-end categories.

Cheap hotels are virtually unknown in far-northern Europe, but hostels, guesthouses, private rooms, farm accommodation and B&Bs can be good value. Self-catering cottages and flats are an excellent option if travelling in a family or group. The following options are useful for bookings:

Train stations Often have a hotel-booking desk.

Tourist offices Have extensive accommodation lists. Usually for a small fee, the more helpful offices will go out of their way to find you somewhere to stay.

Internet A powerful resource both for scope and discounted rooms.

B&Bs, Guesthouses & Hotels

- B&Bs, where you get a room and breakfast in a private home, can often be real bargains. Pensions and guesthouses are similar but usually slightly more upmarket.
- Most Scandinavian hotels are geared to business travellers and have prices to match. But excellent hotel discounts are often available at certain times (eg at weekends and in summer in Finland, Norway and Sweden) and for longer stays. Breakfast in hotels is usually included in the price of the room.
- If you think a hotel is too expensive, ask if it has a cheaper room. In non-chain places it can be easy to negotiate a discount in quiet periods.

Camping

- Camping is immensely popular throughout the region. The **Camping Key Europe** (www.campingkey.com) card offers good benefits and discounts.
- Campsites tend to charge per site, with a small extra charge per person. Tent sites are often cheaper than van sites.
- National tourist offices have booklets or brochures listing camping grounds all over their country.
- In most larger towns and cities, camping grounds are some distance from the centre. If you've got no transport, the money you save by camping can quickly be outweighed by the money spent commuting in and out of town.
- Nearly all mainland Scandinavian camping grounds rent simple cabins – a great budget option if you're not carrying a tent. Many also have more upmarket cottages with bedrooms, bathrooms and proper kitchens, perfect for families who want to self-cater.
- Camping other than in designated camping grounds is not always straightforward but in many countries there's a right of common access that applies. Tourist offices usually stock official publications in English explaining your rights and responsibilities.

Hostels

Hostels generally offer the cheapest roof over your head. In Scandinavia hostels are geared for budget travellers of all ages, including families, and most have dorms and private rooms.

Most hostels are part of national Youth Hostel Associations (YHA), known collectively throughout the world as **Hostelling International** (HI; www.hihostels.com).

You'll have to be a YHA or HI member to use some affiliated hostels (indicated by a blue triangle symbol) but most are open to anyone. Members get substantial discounts; it's worth joining, which you can do at any hostel, via your local hostelling organisation or online. There's a particularly huge network of HI hostels in Denmark and Sweden.

Comfort levels and facilities vary markedly. Some hostels charge extra if you don't want to sweep your room out when you leave.

Breakfast Many hostels (exceptions include most hostels in Iceland) serve breakfast, and almost all have communal kitchens where you can prepare meals.

Bookings Some hostels accept reservations by phone; they'll often book the next hostel you're headed to for a small fee. The HI website has a booking form you can use to reserve a bed in advance – but not all hostels are on the network. Popular hostels in capital cities can be heavily booked in summer and limits may be placed on how many nights you can stay.

Linen You must use a sleeping sheet and pillowcase or linen in hostels in most Scandinavian countries; sleeping bags are not permitted. It's worth carrying your own sleeping sheet or linen, as hiring these at hostels is comparatively expensive.

Travellers with disabilities Specially adapted rooms for visitors with disabilities are common, but check with the hostel first.

Self-Catering

- There's a huge network (especially in Norway, Sweden, Denmark and Finland) of rental cottages that make excellent, peaceful places to stay and offer a chance to experience a traditional aspect of Scandinavian life.
- Many Scandinavians traditionally spend their summers in such places. Renting a cottage for a few days is highly recommended as part of a visit to the region.

University Accommodation

Some universities and colleges rent out students' rooms (sometimes called 'summer hotels') to tourists from June to mid-August, usually single or twin rooms with a kitchenette (but often no utensils). Enquire directly at the college or university, student information services or local tourist offices.

HOSPITALITY WEBSITES

Organisations such as **Couchsurfing** (www.couchsurfing.org) or **Hospitality Club** (www.hospitalityclub.org) put people in contact for informal free accommodation offers – a bit like blind-date couch surfing. Even if you're not comfortable crashing in a stranger's house, these sites are a great way to meet and socialise with locals. **Airbnb** (www.airbnb.com) is a community that has a whole range of options, from private rooms in people's flats to top-value holiday rentals and almost anything else you can think of.

Children

Most of Scandinavia is very child friendly, with domestic tourism largely dictated by children's needs. Iceland is something of an exception: children are liked and have lots of freedom, but they're treated as mini-adults, and there aren't many attractions tailored particularly for children.

Accommodation Bigger camping grounds and spa hotels are particularly kid-conscious, with heaps of facilities and activities designed with children in mind. Cots (cribs) are standard in many hotels but numbers may be limited.

Activities In Denmark, Finland, Norway and Sweden you'll find excellent theme parks, water parks and holiday activities. Many museums have a dedicated children's section with toys, games and dressing-up clothes.

Food Choice of baby food, infant formula, soy and cow's milk, disposable nappies (diapers) etc is wide in Scandinavian supermarkets.

Restaurants High chairs are standard in many restaurants but numbers may be limited. Restaurants will often have children's menu options, and there are lots of chain eateries aimed specifically at families.

Transport Car-rental firms hire out children's safety seats at a nominal cost, but advance bookings are essential.

Want more? Pick up a copy of Lonely Planet's *Travel with Children*.

Customs Regulations

From non-EU to EU countries For EU countries (ie Denmark, Sweden, Finland and Estonia), travellers arriving from outside the EU can bring duty-free goods up to the value of €430 without declaration. You can also bring in up to 16L of beer, 4L of wine, 2L of liquors not exceeding 22% vol or 1L of spirits, 200 cigarettes or 250g of tobacco.

Within the EU If you're coming from another EU country, there is no restriction on the value of purchases for your own use.

Åland islands Arriving on or from the Åland islands (although technically part of the EU), carries the same import restrictions as arriving from a non-EU country.

Other Nordic countries Norway, Iceland and the Faroe Islands have lower limits.

Discount Cards

Seniors Cards Discounts for retirees, pensioners and those over 60 (sometimes slightly younger for women; over 65 in Sweden) at museums and other sights, public swimming pools, spas and transport companies. Make sure you carry proof of age around with you.

Student Cards If you are studying in Scandinavia, a local student card will get you mega-discounts on transport and more.

Camping Key Europe (www.campingkey.com) Discounts at many camping grounds and attractions, with built-in third-party insurance. In Denmark and some Swedish camping grounds, it's obligatory to have this or a similar card. Covers up to a whole family with children under 18. Order through regional camping websites, or buy from campsites throughout the region (this is sometimes cheaper). It costs around €16 depending on where you get it.

Camping Card International (www.campingcardinternational.com) Widely accepted in the region, this camping card can be obtained from your local camping association or club.

European Youth Card (www.eyca.org) If you're under 30, you can pick up this card in almost any European country (some specify a maximum age of 26 though). It offers significant discounts on a wide range of things through the region. It's available for a small charge to anyone, not just European residents, through student unions, hostelling organisations or youth-oriented travel agencies.

Hostelling International (HI; www.hihostels.com) The HI membership card gives significant discounts on accommodation, as well as some transport and attractions.

International Student Identity Card (ISIC; www.isic.org) Discounts on many forms of transport, reduced or free admission to museums and sights, and numerous other offers – a worthwhile way of cutting costs. Check the website for a list of discounts by country. Because of the proliferation of fakes, carry your home student ID as back up. Some places won't give student discounts without it.

The same organisation also issues an International Youth Travel Card for under-26ers, and the International Teacher Identity Card.

Electricity

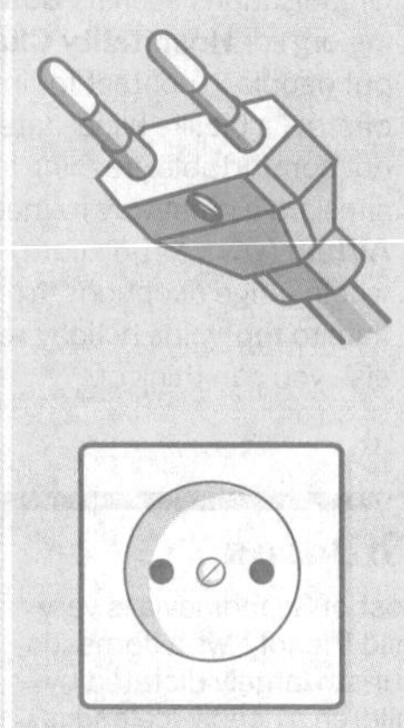

230V/50Hz

Gay & Lesbian Travellers

- Denmark, Finland, Iceland, Norway and Sweden are very tolerant nations, although public displays of affection are less common in rural areas, particularly Lapland.
- See individual country chapters for more information.

Health

Travel in Scandinavia presents very few health problems. The standard of health care is extremely high and English is widely spoken by doctors and medical-clinic staff. Tap water is safe to drink, the level of hygiene is high and there are no endemic diseases.

Extreme climate risks Be aware of hypothermia and frostbite. Biting insects, such as mosquitoes, are more of an annoyance than a real health risk.

Health insurance (EEA) Citizens of the European Economic Area (EEA) are covered for emergency medical treatment in other EEA countries (including Denmark, Finland, Iceland, Norway and Sweden) on presentation of a European Health Insurance Card (EHIC), though they may be liable to pay a daily or per-appointment fee as a local would. Enquire about EHICs at your health centre, travel agency or (in some countries) post office well in advance of travel.

Health insurance (Non-EEA) Citizens from countries outside the EEA should find out if there is a reciprocal arrangement for free medical care between their country and the country visited. If not, travel health insurance is recommended.

Vaccinations Not specifically required for visitors to Scandinavia.

Insurance

A travel-insurance policy to cover theft, personal liability, loss and medical problems is recommended. Travel insurance also usually covers cancellation or delays in travel arrangements, for example, if you fall seriously ill two days before departure.

- Buy insurance as early as possible. If you buy it the week before you are due to fly, you may find that you're not covered for delays to your flight caused by strikes or other industrial actions that may have been in force before you took out the insurance.
- Online comparison sites are the best places to unearth good deals on travel insurance.
- Get a policy that covers you for the worst-possible health scenario if you aren't already covered by a reciprocal health-care agreement. Make sure your policy also covers you for any activities you plan to do, like skiing – check the small print. Find out in advance if your insurance plan will make payments directly to providers or reimburse you later for overseas health expenditure.

➡ If you plan to travel more than once in a 12-month period, you may find it cheaper to take out an annual policy rather than two single-trip policies.

➡ Paying for your airline ticket with a credit card often provides limited travel accident insurance. Certain bank accounts also offer their holders automatic travel insurance.

➡ Worldwide travel insurance is available at www.lonelyplanet.com/bookings. You can buy, extend and claim online anytime – even if you're already on the road.

Internet Access

➡ Wireless (wi-fi) hotspots are rife. Numerous cafes, bars, hostels and hotels offer the service for free. A growing number of towns and cities in the region have free public wi-fi across the centre.

➡ Data is cheap. Buy a local SIM card, pop it in an unlocked phone, laptop or USB modem, and away you go. Deals may mean you pay as little as €15 to €20 for a month's unlimited access.

➡ Internet cafes are increasingly uncommon, but libraries provide free or very cheap internet service.

Money

ATMs Widespread, even in small places. This is the best way to access cash in Scandinavia. Find out what your home bank will charge you per withdrawal before you go as you may be better off taking out larger sums.

Cash cards Much like debit or credit cards but are loaded with a set amount of money. They also have the advantage of lower withdrawal fees than your bank might otherwise charge you.

Changing money All Scandinavian currencies are fully convertible.

SCANDINAVIAN CURRENCIES

COUNTRY	CURRENCY
Denmark	Danish krone (Dkr; DKK)
Estonia (Tallinn)	euro (€; EUR)
Finland	euro (€; EUR)
Iceland	Icelandic króna (Ikr; ISK)
Norway	Norwegian krone (Nkr; NOK)
Sweden	Swedish krona (Skr; SEK)

Charge cards Includes cards like American Express and Diners Club. Less widely accepted than credit cards because they charge merchants high commissions.

Debit and credit cards Scandinavians love using plastic, even for small transactions, and you'll find that debit and credit cards are the way to go here.

Foreign currencies Easily exchanged, with rates usually slightly better at exchange offices rather than banks. Avoid exchanging in airports if possible; you'll get better rates downtown. Always ask about the rate and commission before handing over your cash.

Tax A value-added tax (VAT) applies to most goods and services throughout Scandinavia. International visitors from outside the EEA can claim back the VAT above a set minimum amount on purchases that are being taken out of the country. The procedure for making the claim is usually pretty straightforward.

Tipping Not required in Scandinavia. But if you round up the bill or leave a little something in recognition of good service, it won't be refused.

Travellers cheques Rapidly disappearing but still accepted in big hotels and exchange offices.

Telephone

To call abroad dial ☎00 (the IAC, or international access code from Scandinavia), the country code (CC) for the country you are calling, the local area code (usually dropping the leading zero if there is one) and then the number.

Emergencies The emergency number is the same throughout Scandinavia: ☎112.

Internet Calling via the internet is a practical and cheap solution for making international calls, whether from a laptop, tablet or smartphone.

Mobile phones Bring a mobile that's not tied to a specific network (unlocked) and buy local SIM cards.

Phone boxes Almost nonexistent in most of Scandinavia.

Phonecards Easily bought for cheaper international calls.

TELEPHONE CODES

COUNTRY	CC	IAC
Denmark	☎45	☎00
Finland	☎358	☎00
Iceland	☎354	☎00
Norway	☎47	☎00
Sweden	☎46	☎00
Estonia (Tallinn)	☎372	☎00

Use the country code (CC) to call into that country. Use the international access code (IAC) to call abroad from that country.

TIME ZONES

CITY	TIME IN WINTER	TIME IN SUMMER
New York	11am (UTC -5)	noon (UTC -4)
Reykjavík	4pm (UTC)	4pm (UTC; no summer time)
London	4pm (UTC)	5pm (UTC +1)
Oslo, Copenhagen, Stockholm	5pm (UTC +1)	6pm (UTC +2)
Helsinki, Tallinn	6pm (UTC +2)	7pm (UTC +3)

Reverse-charge (collect) calls Usually possible, and communicating with the local operator in English should not be much of a problem.

Roaming Roaming charges within the EU are set to be abolished in late 2015.

Time

Scandinavia sprawls across several time zones. The 24-hour clock is widely used. Note that Europe and the US move clocks forward and back at slightly different times.

Tourist Information

Facilities Generally excellent, with piles of regional and national brochures, helpful free maps and friendly employees. Staff are often multilingual, speaking English and perhaps other major European languages.

Locations Offices at train stations or centrally located (often in the town hall or central square) in most towns.

Opening hours Longer office hours over summer, reduced hours over winter; smaller offices may open only during peak summer months.

Services Will book hotel and transport reservations and tours; a small charge may apply.

Websites Most towns have a tourist information portal, with good information about sights, accommodation options and more.

Travellers with Disabilities

➡ Scandinavia leads the world as the best-equipped region for the traveller with disabilities. By law, most institutions must provide ramps, lifts and special toilets for people with disabilities; all new hotels and restaurants must install disabled facilities. Most trains and city buses are also accessible by wheelchair.

➡ Some national parks offer accessible nature trails, and cities have ongoing projects in place designed to maximise disabled access in all aspects of urban life.

➡ Iceland is a little further behind the rest of the region – check access issues before you travel. Scandinavian tourist-office websites generally contain good information on disabled access.

➡ Before leaving home, get in touch with your national support organisation – preferably the 'travel officer' if there is one. They often have complete libraries devoted to travel and can put you in touch with agencies that specialise in tours for the disabled. One such agency in the UK is **Can Be Done** (☎+44 (0)20-8907 2400; www.canbedone.co.uk).

Visas

➡ Denmark, Estonia, Finland, Iceland, Norway and Sweden are all part of the Schengen area. A valid passport or EU identity card is required to enter the region.

➡ Most Western nationals don't need a tourist visa for stays of less than three months. South Africans, Indians and Chinese, however, are among those who need a Schengen visa.

➡ A Schengen visa can be obtained by applying to an embassy or consulate of any country in the Schengen area.

Women Travellers

➡ Scandinavia is one of the safest places to travel in all of Europe and women travellers should experience little trouble.

➡ In smaller towns, and especially in northern Sweden and Finland, bars can be fairly unreconstructed places, and women may get a bit of nonthreatening but very boring hassle from drunk locals.

Transport

GETTING THERE & AWAY

Scandinavia is easily accessed from the rest of Europe and beyond. There are direct flights from numerous destinations into Sweden, Norway, Denmark and Finland, and less choice to Iceland.

Denmark, Sweden and Norway can be accessed by train from Western Europe, while Baltic and North Sea ferries are another good option for accessing these Nordic countries.

Flights, tours and rail tickets can be booked online at lonelyplanet.com/bookings.

Air

As well as the many national carriers that fly directly into Scandinavia's airports, there are several budget options. These routes change frequently and are best investigated online.

The following are major hubs in Scandinavia:

Stockholm Arlanda Airport (www.swedavia.com/arlanda) Sweden.

Helsinki Vantaa Airport (www.helsinki-vantaa.fi) Finland.

Copenhagen Kastrup Airport (www.cph.dk) Denmark.

Reykjavík Keflavík Airport (www.kefairport.is) Iceland.

Oslo Gardermoen Airport (www.osl.no) Norway.

Land

Bus

Without a rail pass, the cheapest overland transport from Europe to Scandinavia is the bus, though a cheap flight deal will often beat it on price. **Eurolines** (www.eurolines.com), a conglomeration of coach companies, is the biggest and best-established express-bus network, and connects Scandinavia with the rest of Europe. Advance ticket purchases are usually necessary and sometimes cheaper.

Car & Motorcycle

Driving to Scandinavia means driving into Denmark from Germany (and on to Sweden via the bridge-tunnel), going through Russia or taking a car ferry.

Train

➡ Apart from trains into Finland from Russia, the rail route into Scandinavia goes from Germany into Denmark, then on to Sweden and then Norway via the Copenhagen–Malmö bridge-tunnel connection. Hamburg and Cologne are the main gateways in Germany for this route.

➡ See the exceptional **Man in Seat 61** (www.seat61.com) website for details of all train routes.

➡ Contact **Deutsche Bahn** (www.bahn.com) for details of frequent special offers and for reservations and tickets.

➡ For more information on international rail travel (including Eurostar services), check out www.voyages-sncf.com.

Sea

Services are year-round between major cities: book ahead in summer, at weekends and if travelling with a vehicle. Many boats are amazingly cheap if you travel deck class (without a cabin). Many ferry lines offer 50% discounts for holders of Eurail, Scanrail and InterRail passes. Some offer discounts for seniors, and for ISIC and youth-card holders; inquire when purchasing your ticket. There are usually discounts for families and small groups travelling together. Ferry companies have detailed timetables and fares on their websites. Fares vary according to season.

Baltic Countries

There are numerous sailings between Tallinn, Estonia and Helsinki, Finland, operated by Eckerö Line, Linda Line (fast boats), Tallink/Silja Line and Viking Line. Tallink/Silja also sails from Tallinn to Stockholm via Mariehamn and DFDS Seaways runs from Paldiski (Estonia) to Kappelskär (Sweden). Navirail crosses from Paldiski to Hanko (Finland).

Stena Line runs from Nynäshamn, Sweden to Ventspils, Latvia. Tallink/Silja does a Stockholm to Riga run.

DFDS operates between Karlshamn (Sweden) and Klaipėda (Lithuania).

Germany

Denmark Bornholmer Færgen runs between the island of Bornholm and Sassnitz, in eastern Germany. Scandlines runs from Rødby, on the island of Lolland, to Puttgarten, and between Gedser, on the island of Falster, and Rostock. There's also a service from Havneby, at the southern tip of the Danish island of Rømø, to List on the German island of Sylt; this is run by Syltfaehre.

Finland Finnlines runs from Helsinki to Travemünde and Helsinki to Rostock.

Norway Color Line runs daily from Oslo to Kiel.

Sweden Stena Line runs Trelleborg to Rostock, Trelleborg to Sassnitz and Göteborg to Kiel. TT-Line runs Trelleborg to Travemünde and Trelleborg to Rostock. Finnlines runs Malmö to Travemünde.

Poland

Sweden Polferries runs Ystad to Świnoujście, as does Unity Line, while TT-Line runs Trelleborg to Świnoujście. Polferries also links Nynäshamn with Gdańsk. Stena Lines runs between Karlskrona and Gdynia.

GETTING AROUND

Getting around the populated areas of Scandinavia is generally a breeze, with efficient public transport systems and snappy connections. Remote regions usually have trustworthy but infrequent services.

Air

➡ Flights are safe and reliable. Can be expensive, but often cheaper than land-based alternatives for longer journeys, and can save days of travelling time.

FERRY COMPANIES

The following is a list of the main ferry companies operating to and around Scandinavia, with their websites and major routes. See websites for contact telephone numbers, times, durations and sample fares.

BornholmerFærgen (www.faergen.com) Denmark (Bornholm)–Sweden, Denmark (Bornholm)–Germany.

Color Line (www.colorline.com) Norway–Denmark, Norway–Germany, Norway–Sweden.

DFDS Seaways (www.dfdsseaways.com) Denmark–Norway, Sweden–Lithuania, Sweden–Estonia.

Eckerö Line (www.eckeroline.fi) Finland (Åland)–Sweden, Finland–Estonia.

Finnlines (www.finnlines.com) Germany–Sweden, Sweden–Finland, Germany–Finland.

Fjord Line (www.fjordline.com) Denmark–Norway.

Linda Line (www.lindaline.fi) Finland–Estonia.

Navirail (www.navirail.com) Finland–Estonia.

Polferries (www.polferries.com) Sweden–Poland, Denmark–Poland.

Regina Line (www.reginaline.dk) Denmark–UK.

Scandlines (www.scandlines.com) Sweden–Denmark, Denmark–Germany.

Smyril Line (www.smyrilline.com) Denmark–Faroe Islands–Iceland.

St Peter Line (www.stpeterline.com) Sweden–Russia, Finland–Russia, Estonia–Russia.

Stena Line (www.stenaline.com) Denmark–Norway, Denmark–Sweden, Sweden–Germany, Sweden–Poland, Sweden–Latvia.

Syltfaehre (www.sylt-ferry.com) Denmark–Germany (Sylt).

Tallink/Silja Line (www.tallinksilja.com) Finland–Sweden, Finland–Estonia, Sweden–Estonia, Sweden–Latvia.

TT-Line (www.ttline.com) Sweden–Germany, Sweden–Poland.

Unity Line (www.unityline.pl) Sweden–Poland.

Viking Line (www.vikingline.com) Sweden–Finland, Finland–Estonia.

Wasaline (www.wasaline.com) Finland–Sweden.

- There are reduced rates for internet bookings on internal airline routes. The main budget operators in the region are Ryanair and Norwegian, one of Europe's fastest-growing airlines.
- Good bus and train networks between airports and city centres.
- Visitors flying **SAS** (www.flysas.com) or code-shared flights on a return ticket to Scandinavia from Asia or the USA can buy Visit Scandinavia/Europe Airpass coupons. The passes allow one-way travel on direct flights between any two Scandinavian cities serviced by SAS and some other operators. They can be purchased after arriving in Scandinavia if you have a return SAS international ticket.

Bicycle

Scandinavia is exceptionally bike friendly, with loads of cycle paths, courteous motorists, easy public transport options and lots of flattish, picturesque terrain.

The **Cyclists' Touring Club** (www.ctc.org.uk) offers cycling conditions, routes, itineraries, maps and specialised insurance.

Bike shops Widespread in towns and cities.

Hire Often from train station bike-rental counters, tourist offices and campsites; in some cases it's possible to return hire bikes to another outlet so you don't have to double back. Several cities have bike-sharing schemes accessible for a small fee.

No-nos Cycling across the Øresund bridge between Denmark and Sweden is prohibited.

On public transport Bikes can be transported as luggage, either free or for a small fee, on slower trains and local buses in Scandinavia.

Theft Not uncommon in big cities; take a decent lock and use it when you leave your bike unattended.

Boat

Ferry

You can't really get around Scandinavia without using ferries extensively. The shortest routes from Denmark (Jutland) to Norway and from southern Sweden to Finland are ferry routes. Denmark is now well connected to mainland Europe and Sweden by bridges.

Ferry tickets are cheap on competitive routes, although transporting cars can be costly. Bicycles are usually carried free. On some routes, train-pass holders are entitled to free or discounted travel.

Weekend ferries, especially on Friday night, are significantly more expensive. Teenagers are banned from travelling on some Friday-night ferries due to problems with drunkenness.

Denmark–Faroe Islands–Iceland Smyril Line run the popular *Nörrona* ferry from Hirtshals, Denmark to Seyðisfjörður, Iceland via Tórshavn on the Faroe Islands.

Denmark–Norway There are several connections. From Hirtshals, Fjord Line sails to Bergen, Kristiansand, Langesund and Stavanger. Color Line goes to Kristiansand and Larvik. From Frederikshavn, Stena Line goes to Oslo. From Copenhagen, DFDS Seaways also goes to Oslo.

Denmark–Sweden Stena Line runs the connections Grenå to Varberg and Frederikshavn to Göteborg. The short Helsingør to Helsingborg crossing is covered by Scandlines, while BornholmerFærgen goes from Rønne on Bornholm to Ystad.

Norway–Sweden Color Line connects Strömstad, Sweden, with Sandefjord, Norway.

Sweden–Finland Connections from Stockholm to Helsinki or Turku via Mariehamn are operated by Tallink/Silja and Viking Line. Eckerö Line runs from Grisslehamn to Eckerö on Åland, Finnlines runs Kapellskär to Naantali, while further north, Wasaline connects Umeå with Vaasa.

Steamer

- Scandinavia's main lakes and rivers are served by boats during summer, including some historic steamers. Treat these as relaxing, scenic cruises; if you view them merely as a way to get from A to B, they can seem quite expensive.
- Sweden has numerous routes. Most leave from Stockholm and sail east to the Stockholm archipelago and west to historic Lake Mälaren. You can also cruise the Göta Canal, the longest water route in Sweden.
- Legendary *Hurtigruten* ferry provides a link between Norway's coastal fishing villages.
- In Finland, steamships ply the eastern lakes, connecting the towns on their shores.

Bus

Buses provide a viable alternative to the rail network in Scandinavian countries, and are the only option in Iceland and parts of northern Sweden, Finland and Norway.

Cost Compared to trains, they're usually cheaper and slightly slower. Connections with train services (where they exist) are good.

Advance reservation Rarely necessary. But you do need to prepurchase your ticket before you board many city buses, and then validate your ticket on board.

International routes There are regular bus services between Denmark and Sweden, and Sweden and Norway. Services between Finland and Norway run in Lapland, and you can change between Swedish and Finnish buses at the shared bus station of the border towns of Tornio/Haparanda.

Car & Motorcycle

Travelling with a vehicle is the best way to get to remote places and gives you independence and flexibility.

Scandinavia is excellent for motorcycle touring, with good-quality winding roads, stunning scenery and an active motorcycling scene – just make sure your wet-weather gear is up to scratch. The best time for touring is May to September. On ferries, motorcyclists rarely have to book ahead as they can generally be squeezed in.

Bringing Your Own Vehicle

Documentation Proof of ownership of a private vehicle should always be carried (this is the Vehicle Registration Document for British-registered cars). You'll also need an insurance document valid in the countries you are planning to visit. Contact your local automobile association for further information.

Border crossings Vehicles crossing an international border should display a sticker showing their country of registration. The exception is cars with Euro-plates.

Safety It's compulsory to carry a warning triangle in most places, to be used in the event of breakdown, and several countries require a reflective jacket. You must also use headlamp beam reflectors/converters on right-hand-drive cars.

Driving Licence

An EU driving licence is acceptable for driving throughout Scandinavia, as are North American and Australian licences, for example. If you have any other type of licence, you should check to see if you need to obtain an International Driving Permit (IDP) from your motoring organisation before you leave home.

If you're thinking of going snowmobiling, you'll need to bring your driving licence.

Fuel

Fuel is heavily taxed and very expensive in Scandinavia. Most types of petrol, including unleaded 95 and 98 octane, are widely available; leaded petrol is no longer sold. Diesel is significantly cheaper than petrol in most countries. Usually pumps with green markings deliver unleaded fuel, and black pumps supply diesel.

Hire

Cost Renting a car is more expensive in Scandinavia than in other European countries. Be sure you understand what's included in the price (unlimited or paid kilometres, injury insurance, tax, collision damage waiver etc) and what your liabilities are. Norway is the most expensive so it may pay to rent a car in neighbouring Sweden and take it across.

Insurance Decide whether to take the collision damage waiver. You may be covered for this and injury insurance if you have a travel-insurance policy: check.

Companies The big international firms – Hertz, Avis, Budget and Europcar – are all present. Sixt often has the most competitive prices. Using local firms can mean a better deal. Big firms give you the option of returning the car to a different outlet when you've finished with it, but this is normally heavily charged.

Booking Prebooking always works out cheaper. Online brokers often offer substantially cheaper rates than the company websites themselves.

Fly/drive combination SAS and Icelandair often offer cheaper car rentals to their international passengers. Check their websites for deals.

Border crossings Ask in advance if you can drive a rented car across borders. In Scandinavia it's usually no problem.

Age The minimum rental age is usually 21, sometimes even 23, and you'll need a credit card for the deposit.

Motorcycle and moped rental Not particularly common in Scandinavian countries, but possible in major cities.

Insurance

Third-party motor insurance A minimum requirement in most of Europe. Most UK car-insurance policies automatically provide third-party cover for EU and some other countries. Ask your insurer for a Green Card – an internationally recognised proof of insurance (there may be a charge) – and check that it lists all the countries you intend to visit.

Breakdown assistance Check whether your insurance policy offers breakdown assistance overseas. If it doesn't, a European breakdown-assistance policy, such as those provided by the AA or the RAC, is a good investment. Your motoring organisation may also offer reciprocal coverage with affiliated motoring organisations.

Road Conditions & Hazards

Conditions and types of roads vary widely across Scandinavia, but it's possible to make some generalisations.

Iceland Specific challenges include unsealed gravel roads, long, claustrophobic single-lane tunnels, frequent mist and the wild, lonely, 4WD-only F-roads. See the video at www.drive.is for more info.

Main roads Primary routes, with the exception of some roads in Iceland, are universally in good condition. There are comparatively few motorways.

Minor roads Road surfaces on minor routes are not so reliable, although normally adequate.

Norway Has some particularly hair-raising roads; serpentine examples climb from sea level to 1000m in what seems no distance at all on a map. These roller coasters will use plenty of petrol and strain the car's engine and brakes, not to mention your nerves! Driving a campervan on this kind of route is not recommended.

Tolls In Norway, there are tolls for some tunnels, bridges, roads and entry into larger towns, and for practically all ferries crossing fjords. Roads, tunnels, bridges and car ferries in Finland and Sweden are usually free, although there's a hefty toll of €49 per car on the **Øresund bridge** (www.oresundsbron.com) between Denmark and Sweden.

Winter Snow tyres are compulsory in winter, except in Denmark. Chains are allowed in most countries but almost never used.

Livestock on roads Suicidal animals, including sheep, elk, horses and reindeer, are a potential hazard. If you are involved in an animal incident, by law you must report it to the police.

Road Rules

- Drive on the right-hand side of the road in all Scandinavian countries.
- Seatbelts are compulsory for driver and all passengers.
- Headlights must be switched on at all times.
- In the absence of give-way or stop signs, priority is given to traffic approaching from the right.
- It's compulsory for motorcyclists and their passengers to wear helmets.
- Take care with speed limits, which vary from country to country.
- Many driving infringements are subject to on-the-spot fines in Scandinavian countries. In Norway they are stratospheric. Drink-driving regulations are strict.

Hitching & Car-Ride Services

- It's neither popular nor particularly rewarding to hitch in most of the region. In fact, it's some of the slowest in the world. Your plans need to be flexible.
- Hitching is better in Denmark and Sweden than Norway and Finland.
- It's sometimes possible to arrange a lift privately: scan student notice boards in colleges.

After hitching, the cheapest way to get around is as a paying passenger in a private car. Various car-sharing websites are good places to start. Try www.blablacar.com, www.ridefinder.eu, www.mitfahrzentrale.de or www.joinants.com. There are numerous others.

Train

Trains in Scandinavia are comfortable, frequent and punctual. As with most things in the region, prices are relatively expensive, although train passes can make travel affordable. There are no trains in Iceland, far-north Finland or Norway.

Costs Full-price tickets can be expensive; book ahead for discounts. Rail passes are worth buying if you plan to do a reasonable amount of travelling. Seniors and travellers under 26 years of age are eligible for discounted tickets in some countries, which can cut fares by between 15% and 40%.

Reservations It's a good idea (sometimes obligatory) to make reservations at peak times and on certain train lines, especially long-distance trains. In some countries it can be a lot cheaper to book in advance and online.

Express trains There are various names for fast trains throughout Scandinavia. Supplements usually apply on fast trains.

Overnight Trains

These trains usually offer couchettes or sleepers. Reservations are advisable, particularly as sleeping options are generally allocated on a first-come, first-served basis.

Couchettes Basic bunk beds numbering four (1st class) or six (2nd class) per compartment are comfortable enough, if lacking a little privacy. In Scandinavia, a bunk costs around €25 to €50 for most trains, irrespective of the length of the journey.

Sleepers The most comfortable option, offering beds for one or two passengers in 1st class and two or three passengers in 2nd class.

Food Most long-distance trains have a dining car or snack trolley – bring your own nibbles to keep costs down.

Car Some long-distance trains have car-carrying facilities.

Train Passes

There are a variety of passes available for rail travel within Scandinavia, or in various European countries including Scandinavia. There are cheaper passes for students, people under 26 and seniors. Supplements (eg for high-speed services) and reservation costs are not covered by passes, and terms and conditions change – check carefully before buying. Pass-holders must always carry their passport on the train for identification purposes.

EURAIL PASSES

Eurail (www.eurail.com) offers different passes available to residents of non-European countries; purchase before arriving in Europe.

Eurail Scandinavia Pass Gives a number of days of travel in a two-month period, and is valid for travel in Denmark, Sweden, Norway and Finland. It costs €261 for four days, up to €403 for 10 days. A similar but cheaper pass includes Sweden and one of Norway, Denmark or Finland. There are also single-country passes.

Eurail Global Pass Offers travel in 23 European countries – either 10 or 15 days in a two-month period or unlimited travel from 15 days up to three months. It's much better value for under-26s, as those older have to buy a 1st-class pass.

Discounts Most passes offer discounts of around 25% for under-26-year-olds, or 15% for two people travelling together. On most Eurail passes, children aged between four and 11 get a 50% discount on the adult fare. Eurail passes give a 30% to 50% discount on several ferry lines in the region; check the website.

INTERRAIL PASSES

If you've lived in Europe for more than six months, you're eligible for an **InterRail** (www.interrail.eu) pass. InterRail offers two passes valid for train travel in Scandinavia.

InterRail One Country Pass Offers travel in one country of

Train & Ferry Routes

your choice for three/four/six/eight days in a one-month period, costing €125/158/212/255 in 2nd class for Denmark or Finland, and €190/216/281/326 for Sweden or Norway.

Global Pass Offers travel in 30 European countries and costs from €281 for five days' travel in any 10, to €668 for a month's unlimited train travel.

Discounts On both the InterRail-passes, there's a 33% discount for under-26s. InterRail passes give a 30% to 50% discount on several ferry lines in the region; check the website for details.

Language

This chapter offers basic vocabulary to help you get around Scandinavia. If you read our coloured pronunciation guides as if they were English, you'll be understood. Note that the stressed syllables are indicated with italics.

Some phrases in this chapter have both polite and informal forms (indicated by the abbreviations 'pol' and 'inf' respectively). The abbreviations 'm' and 'f' indicate masculine and feminine gender respectively.

DANISH

Danish has official status in Denmark and the Faroe Islands.

All vowels in Danish can be long or short. Note that aw is pronounced as in 'saw', eu as the 'u' in 'nurse', ew as 'ee' with rounded lips, oh as the 'o' in 'note', ow as in 'how', and dh as the 'th' in 'that'.

Basics

Hello.	*Goddag.*	go·*da*
Goodbye.	*Farvel.*	faar·*vel*
Excuse me.	*Undskyld mig.*	*awn*·skewl mai
Sorry.	*Undskyld.*	*awn*·skewl
Please.	*Vær så venlig.*	ver saw *ven*·lee
Thank you.	*Tak.*	taak
You're welcome.	*Selv tak.*	sel taak
Yes.	*Ja.*	ya
No.	*Nej.*	nai

How are you?
Hvordan går det? — vor·*dan* gawr dey

Good, thanks.
Godt, tak. — got taak

What's your name?
Hvad hedder De/du? (pol/inf) — va *hey*·dha dee/doo

My name is ...
Mit navn er ... — mit nown ir ...

Do you speak English?
Taler De/du engelsk? (pol/inf) — *ta*·la dee/doo *eng*·elsk

I don't understand.
Jeg forstår ikke. — yai for·*stawr i*·ke

Accommodation

campsite	*campingplads*	*kaam*·ping·plas
guesthouse	*gæstehus*	*ges*·te·hoos
hotel	*hotel*	hoh·*tel*
youth hostel	*ungdoms-herberg*	*awng*·doms·heyr·beyrg

Do you have a ... room?	*Har I et ... værelse?*	haar ee it ... *verl*·se
single	*enkelt*	*eng*·kelt
double	*dobbelt*	*do*·belt

How much is it per ...?	*Hvor meget koster det per ...?*	vor *maa*·yet *kos*·ta dey peyr ...
night	*nat*	nat
person	*person*	per·*sohn*

WANT MORE?

For in-depth language information and handy phrases, check out Lonely Planet's *Western Europe Phrasebook*. You'll find it at **shop.lonelyplanet.com**.

Signs – Danish

Indgang	Entrance
Udgang	Exit
Åben	Open
Lukket	Closed
Forbudt	Prohibited
Toilet	Toilets

Eating & Drinking

Can you recommend a ...?	*Kan De/du anbefale en ...?* (pol/inf)	kan dee/doo *an*·bey·fa·le in ...
bar	*bar*	baar
cafe	*café*	ka·*fey*
restaurant	*restaurant*	res·toh·*rang*

What would you recommend?
Hvad kan De/du anbefale? (pol/inf) — va kan dee/doo *an*·bey·fa·le

Do you have vegetarian food?
Har I vegetarmad? — haar ee vey·ge·*taar*·madh

I'll have ...
..., tak. — ... taak

Cheers!
Skål! — skawl

I'd like the ..., please.	*Jeg vil gerne have ..., tak.*	yai vil *gir*·ne ha ... taak
bill	*regningen*	*rai*·ning·en
menu	*menuen*	me·*new*·en

breakfast	*morgenmad*	*morn*·madh
lunch	*frokost*	*froh*·kost
dinner	*middag*	*mi*·da
beer	*øl*	eul
coffee	*kaffe*	*ka*·fe
tea	*te*	tey
water	*vand*	van
wine	*vin*	veen

Emergencies

Help!	*Hjælp!*	yelp
Go away!	*Gå væk!*	gaw vek

Call ...!	*Ring efter ...!*	ring *ef*·ta ...
a doctor	*en læge*	in *le*·ye
the police	*politiet*	poh·lee·*tee*·et

I'm lost.
Jeg er faret vild. — yai ir *faa*·ret veel

I'm ill.
Jeg er syg. — yai ir sew

I have to use the telephone.
Jeg skal bruge en telefon. — yai skal *broo*·e en tey·ley·*fohn*

Where's the toilet?
Hvor er toilettet? — vor ir toy·*le*·tet

Shopping & Services

I'm looking for ...
Jeg leder efter ... — yai *li*·dha *ef*·ta ...

How much is it?
Hvor meget koster det? — vor *maa*·yet *kos*·ta dey

That's too expensive.
Det er for dyrt. — dey ir for dewrt

Where's ...?	*Hvor er der ...?*	vor ir deyr ...
an ATM	*en hæve-automat*	in *he*·ve·ow·toh·mat
a foreign exchange	*et veksel-kontor*	it *veks*·le·kon·tohr

market	*marked*	*maar*·kedh
post office	*postkontor*	*post*·kon·tohr
tourist office	*turist-kontoret*	too·*reest*·kon·toh·ret

Transport & Directions

Where's ...?
Hvor er ...? — vor ir ...

What's the address?
Hvad er adressen? — va ir a·*draa*·sen

Numbers – Danish

1	*en*	in
2	*to*	toh
3	*tre*	trey
4	*fire*	feer
5	*fem*	fem
6	*seks*	seks
7	*syv*	sew
8	*otte*	*aw*·te
9	*ni*	nee
10	*ti*	tee

Can you show me (on the map)?
Kan De/du vise mig det (på kortet)? (pol/inf) — kan dee/doo *vee*·se mai dey (paw *kor*·tet)

Where can I buy a ticket?
Hvor kan jeg købe en billet? — vor ka yai *keu*·be in bi·*let*

What time's the ... bus?	*Hvad tid er den ... bus?*	va teedh ir den ... boos
first	*første*	*feurs*·te
last	*sidste*	*sees*·te

One ... ticket (to Odense), please.	*En ... billet (til Odense), tak.*	in ... bee·*let* (til *oh*·dhen·se) taak
one-way	*enkelt*	*eng*·kelt
return	*retur*	rey·*toor*

boat	*båden*	*w*·dhen
bus	*bussen*	*boo*·sen
plane	*flyet*	*flew*·et
train	*toget*	*taw*·et

ESTONIAN

Double vowels in written Estonian indicate they are pronounced as long sounds.

Note that air is pronounced as in 'hair', aw as in 'law', ea as in 'ear', eu as in 'nurse', ew as ee with rounded lips, oh as the 'o' in 'note', ow as in 'how', uh as the 'a' in 'ago', kh as in the Scottish *loch*, and zh as the 's' in 'pleasure'.

Basics

Hello.	*Tere.*	*te*·re
Goodbye.	*Nägemist.*	*nair*·ge·mist
Excuse me.	*Vabandage.* (pol) *Vabanda.* (inf)	*va*·ban·da·ge *va*·ban·da
Sorry.	*Vabandust.*	*va*·ban·dust
Please.	*Palun.*	*pa*·lun
Thank you.	*Tänan.*	*tair*·nan
You're welcome.	*Palun.*	*pa*·lun
Yes.	*Jaa.*	yaa
No.	*Ei.*	ay

How are you?
Kuidas läheb? — *ku*·i·das *lair*·hep

Fine. And you?
Hästi. Ja teil? — *hairs*·ti ya tayl

What's your name?
Mis on teie nimi? — mis on *tay*·e *ni*·mi

My name is ...
Minu nimi on ... — *mi*·nu *ni*·mi on ...

Signs – Estonian

Sissepääs	Entrance
Väljapääs	Exit
Avatud/Lahti	Open
Suletud/Kinni	Closed
WC	Toilets

Do you speak English?
Kas te räägite inglise keelt? — kas te *rair*·git·te *ing*·kli·se keylt

I don't understand.
Ma ei saa aru. — ma ay saa *a*·ru

Eating & Drinking

What would you recommend?
Mida te soovitate? — *mi*·da te *saw*·vit·tat·te

Do you have vegetarian food?
Kas teil on taimetoitu? — kas tayl on *tai*·met·toyt·tu

I'll have a ...
Ma tahaksin ... — ma *ta*·hak·sin ...

Cheers!
Terviseks! — *tair*·vi·seks

I'd like the ..., please.	*Ma sooviksin ..., palun.*	ma *saw*·vik·sin ... *pa*·lun
bill	*arvet*	*ar*·vet
menu	*menüüd*	*me*·newt

breakfast	*hommikusöök*	*hom*·mi·ku·seuk
dinner	*õhtusöök*	*uhkh*·tu·seuk
lunch	*lõuna*	*luh*·u·na
beer	*õlu*	*uh*·lu
coffee	*kohv*	kokv
tea	*tee*	tey
water	*vesi*	*ve*·si
wine	*vein*	vayn

Emergencies

Help!	*Appi!*	*ap*·pi
Go away!	*Minge ära!*	*ming*·ke *air*·ra

Call ...!	*Kutsuge ...!*	*ku*·tsu·ge ...
a doctor	*arst*	arst
the police	*politsei*	po·li·*tsay*

I'm lost.
Ma olen ära eksinud. — ma *o*·len *air*·ra *ek*·si·nud

Where are the toilets?
Kus on WC? — kus on *ve*·se

Numbers – Estonian

1	*üks*	ewks
2	*kaks*	kaks
3	*kolm*	kolm
4	*neli*	*ne*·li
5	*viis*	vees
6	*kuus*	koos
7	*seitse*	*say*·tse
8	*kaheksa*	*ka*·hek·sa
9	*üheksa*	*ew*·hek·sa
10	*kümme*	*kewm*·me

Shopping & Services

I'm looking for ...
Ma otsin ... ma *o*·tsin

How much is it?
Kui palju see maksab? *ku*·i *pal*·yu sey *mak*·sab

That's too expensive.
See on liiga kallis. sey on *lee*·ga *kal*·lis

bank	*pank*	pank
market	*turg*	turg
post office	*postkontor*	*post*·kont·tor

Transport & Directions

Where's the ...?
Kus on ...? kus on ...

Can you show me (on the map)?
Kas te näitaksite mulle (kaardil)? kas te *nair*·i·tak·sit·te *mul*·le (*kaar*·dil)

Where can I buy a ticket?
Kust saab osta pileti? kust saab *os*·ta *pi*·let·ti

What time's the ... bus?	*Mis kell väljub ... buss?*	mis kel *vairl*·yub ... bus
first	*esimene*	*e*·si·me·ne
last	*viimane*	*vee*·ma·ne

One ... ticket (to Pärnu), please.	*Üks ... pilet (Pärnusse), palun.*	ewks ... *pi*·let (*pair*·nus·se) *pa*·lun
one-way	*ühe otsa*	*ew*·he *o*·tsa
return	*edasi-tagasi*	*e*·da·si·*ta*·ga·si

boat	*laev*	laiv
bus	*buss*	bus
plane	*lennuk*	*len*·nuk
train	*rong*	rongk

FINNISH

Double consonants are held longer than their single equivalents. Note that eu is pronounced as the 'u' in 'nurse', ew as 'ee' with rounded lips, oh as the 'o' in 'note', ow as in 'how', and uh as the 'u' in 'run'.

Basics

Hello.	*Hei.*	hay
Goodbye.	*Näkemiin.*	*na*·ke·meen
Excuse me.	*Anteeksi.*	*uhn*·tayk·si
Sorry.	*Anteeksi.*	*uhn*·tayk·si
Please.	*Ole hyvä.*	*o*·le *hew*·va
Thank you.	*Kiitos.*	*kee*·tos
You're welcome.	*Ole hyvä.*	*o*·le *hew*·va
Yes.	*Kyllä.*	*kewl*·la
No.	*Ei.*	ay

How are you?
Mitä kuuluu? *mi*·ta *koo*·loo

Fine. And you?
Hyvää. Entä itsellesi? *hew*·va *en*·ta *it*·sel·le·si

What's your name?
Mikä sinun nimesi on? *mi*·ka *si*·nun *ni*·me·si on

My name is ...
Minun nimeni on ... *mi*·nun *ni*·me·ni on ...

Do you speak English?
Puhutko englantia? *pu*·hut·ko *en*·gluhn·ti·uh

I don't understand.
En ymmärrä. en *ewm*·mar·ra

Eating & Drinking

What would you recommend?
Mitä voit suositella? *mi*·ta voyt *su*·o·si·tel·luh

Do you have vegetarian food?
Onko teillä kasvisruokia? *on*·ko *teyl*·la *kuhs*·vis·ru·o·ki·uh

I'll have a ...
Tilaan ... *ti*·laan ...

Cheers!
Kippis! *kip*·pis

Signs – Finnish

Sisään	Entrance
Ulos	Exit
Avoinna	Open
Suljettu	Closed
Kielletty	Prohibited
Opastus	Information

I'd like the ..., please.	*Saisinko ...*	*sai*·sin·ko ...
bill	*laskun*	*luhs*·kun
menu	*ruoka-listan*	*ru*·o·kuh·*lis*·tuhn

breakfast	*aamiaisen*	*aa*·mi·ai·sen
lunch	*lounaan*	*loh*·naan
dinner	*illallisen*	*il*·luhl·li·sen

bottle of (beer)	*pullon (olutta)*	*pul*·lon (*o*·lut·tuh)
(cup of) coffee/tea	*(kupin) kahvia/teetä*	(*ku*·pin) *kuh*·vi·uh/*tay*·ta
glass of (wine)	*lasillisen (viiniä)*	*luh*·sil·li·sen (*vee*·ni·a)
water	*vettä*	*vet*·ta

Emergencies

Help!	*Apua!*	*uh*·pu·uh
Go away!	*Mene pois!*	*me*·ne poys

Call ...!	*Soittakaa paikalle ...!*	*soyt*·tuh·kaa *pai*·kuhl·le ...
a doctor	*lääkäri*	*la*·ka·ri
the police	*poliisi*	*po*·lee·si

I'm lost.
Olen eksynyt. o·len *ek*·sew·newt

Where are the toilets?
Missä on vessa? *mis*·sa on *ves*·suh

Shopping & Services

I'm looking for ...
Etsin ... *et*·sin ...

How much is it?
Mitä se maksaa? *mi*·ta se *muhk*·saa

That's too expensive.
Se on liian kallis. se on *lee*·uhn *kuhl*·lis

Where's the ...?	*Missä on ...?*	*mis*·sa on ...
bank	*pankki*	*puhnk*·ki
market	*kauppatori*	*kowp*·pa·*to*·ri
post office	*posti-toimisto*	*pos*·ti·*toy*·mis·to

Transport & Directions

Where's ...?
Missä on ...? *mis*·sa on ...

Numbers – Finnish

1	*yksi*	*ewk*·si
2	*kaksi*	*kuhk*·si
3	*kolme*	*kol*·me
4	*neljä*	*nel*·ya
5	*viisi*	*vee*·si
6	*kuusi*	*koo*·si
7	*seitsemän*	*sayt*·se·man
8	*kahdeksan*	*kuhk*·dek·suhn
9	*yhdeksän*	*ewh*·dek·san
10	*kymmenen*	*kewm*·me·nen

Can you show me (on the map)?
Voitko näyttää sen minulle (kartalta)? *voyt*·ko *na*·ewt·ta sen *mi*·nul·le (*kar*·tuhl·tuh)

Where can I buy a ticket?
Mistä voin ostaa lipun? *mis*·ta voyn *os*·taa *li*·pun

What time's the ... bus?	*Mihin aikaan lähtee ... bussi?*	*mi*·hin *ai*·kaan *lah*·tay ... *bus*·si
first	*ensimmäinen*	*en*·sim·mai·nen
last	*viimeinen*	*vee*·may·nen

One ... ticket, please.	*Saisinko yhden ... lipun.*	*sai*·sin·ko *ewh*·den ... *li*·pun
one-way	*yksisuun-taisen*	*ewk*·si·*soon*·tai·sen
return	*meno-paluu*	*me*·no·*pa*·loo

Where does this ... go?	*Minne tämä ... menee?*	*min*·ne *ta*·ma ... *me*·nay
boat	*laiva*	*lai*·vuh
bus	*bussi*	*bus*·si
plane	*lentokone*	*len*·to·*ko*·ne
train	*juna*	*yu*·nuh

ICELANDIC

Double consonants are given a long pronunciation. Note that eu is pronounced as the 'u' in 'nurse', oh as the 'o' in 'note', ow as in 'how', öy as the '-er y-' in 'her year' (without the 'r'), dh as the 'th' in 'that', and kh as the throaty 'ch' in the Scottish *loch*.

Basics

Hello.	*Halló.*	*ha*·loh
Goodbye.	*Bless.*	bles
Please.	*Takk.*	tak
Thank you.	*Takk fyrir.*	tak *fi*·rir

Signs – Icelandic

Inngangur	Entrance
Útgangur	Exit
Opið	Open
Lokað	Closed
Bannað	Prohibited
Snyrting	Toilets

You're welcome.	*Það var ekkert.*	thadh var e·kert
Excuse me.	*Afsakið.*	*af*·sa·kidh
Sorry.	*Fyrirgefðu.*	*fi*·rir·gev·dhu
Yes.	*Já.*	yow
No.	*Nei.*	nay

How are you?
Hvað segir þú gott? kvadh *se*·yir thoo got

Fine. And you?
Allt fínt. En þú? alt feent en thoo

What's your name?
Hvað heitir þú? kvadh *hay*·tir thoo

My name is ...
Ég heiti ... yekh *hay*·ti ...

Do you speak English?
Talar þú ensku? *ta*·lar thoo *ens*·ku

I don't understand.
Ég skil ekki. yekh skil *e*·ki

Eating & Drinking

What would you recommend?
Hverju mælir þú með? *kver*·yu *mai*·lir thoo medh

Do you have vegetarian food?
Hafið þið grænmetisrétti? *ha*·vidh thidh *grain*·me·tis·rye·ti

I'll have a ...
Ég ætla að fá ... yekh *ait*·la adh fow ...

Cheers!
Skál! skowl

I'd like the ..., please.	*Get ég fengið ... takk.*	get yekh *fen*·gidh ... tak
bill	*reikninginn*	*rayk*·nin·gin
menu	*matseðillinn*	*mat*·se·dhit·lin

breakfast	*morgunmat*	*mor*·gun·mat
lunch	*hádegismat*	*how*·de·yis·mat
dinner	*kvöldmat*	*kveuld*·mat

bottle of (beer)	*(bjór)flösku*	*(byohr)*·*fleus*·ku
(cup of) coffee/tea	*kaffi/te (bolla)*	*ka*·fi/te (*bot*·la)
glass of (wine)	*(vín)glas*	*(veen)*·glas
water	*vatn*	vat

Emergencies

Help!	*Hjálp!*	hyowlp
Go away!	*Farðu!*	*far*·dhu

Call ...!	*Hringdu á ...!*	*hring*·du ow ...
a doctor	*lækni*	*laik*·ni
the police	*lögregluna*	*leu*·rekh·lu·na

I'm lost.
Ég er villtur/villt. (m/f) yekh er *vil*·tur/vilt

Where are the toilets?
Hvar er snyrtingin? kvar er *snir*·tin·gin

Shopping & Services

I'm looking for ...
Ég leita að ... yekh *lay*·ta adh ...

How much is it?
Hvað kostar þetta? kvadh *kos*·tar *the*·ta

That's too expensive.
Þetta er of dýrt. *the*·ta er of deert

Where's the ...?	*Hvar er ...?*	kvar er ...
bank	*bankinn*	*bown*·kin
market	*markaðurinn*	*mar*·ka·dhu·rin
post office	*pósthúsið*	*pohst*·hoo·sidh

Transport & Directions

Where's ...?
Hvar er ...? kvar er ...

Can you show me (on the map)?
Geturðu sýnt mér (á kortinu)? *ge*·tur·dhu seent myer (ow *kor*·ti·nu)

Numbers – Icelandic

1	*einn*	aydn
2	*tveir*	tvayr
3	*þrír*	threer
4	*fjórir*	*fyoh*·rir
5	*fimm*	fim
6	*sex*	seks
7	*sjö*	syeu
8	*átta*	*ow*·ta
9	*níu*	*nee*·u
10	*tíu*	*tee*·u

Where can I buy a ticket?
Hvar kaupi ég miða? kvar köy·pi yekh *mi*·dha

What time's the ... bus?	*Hvenær fer ... strætisvagninn?*	*kve*·nair fer ... *strai*·tis·vag·nin
first	*fyrsti*	*firs*·ti
last	*síðasti*	see·dhas·ti

One ... ticket (to Reykjavík), please.	*Einn miða ... (til, Reykjavíkur) takk.*	aitn *mi*·dha ... (til *rayk*·ya·vee·kur) tak
one-way	*aðra leiðina*	*adh*·ra *lay*·dhi·na
return	*fram og til baka*	fram okh til *ba*·ka

Is this the ... to (Akureyri)?	*Er þetta ... til (Akureyrar)?*	er *the*·ta ... til (*a*·ku·ray·rar)
boat	*ferjan*	*fer*·yan
bus	*rútan*	*roo*·tan
plane	*flugvélin*	*flukh*·vye·lin

NORWEGIAN

There are two official written forms of Norwegian, *Bokmål* and *Nynorsk*. They are actually quite similar and understood by all speakers. It's estimated that around 85% of Norwegian speakers use *Bokmål* and about 15% use *Nynorsk*. In this section we've used *Bokmål* only.

Each vowel can be either long or short. Generally, they're long when followed by one consonant and short when followed by two or more consonants. Note that aw is pronounced as in 'law', eu as the 'u' in 'nurse', ew as 'ee' with pursed lips, and ow as in 'how'.

Basics

Hello.	*God dag.*	go·*daag*
Goodbye.	*Ha det.*	*haa*·de
Please.	*Vær så snill.*	veyr saw snil
Thank you.	*Takk.*	tak
You're welcome.	*Ingen årsak.*	*ing*·en *awr*·saak
Excuse me.	*Unnskyld.*	*ewn*·shewl
Sorry.	*Beklager.*	bey·*klaa*·geyr
Yes.	*Ja.*	yaa
No.	*Nei.*	ney

How are you?
Hvordan har du det? *vor*·dan haar doo de

Fine, thanks. And you?
Bra, takk. Og du? braa tak aw doo

What's your name?
Hva heter du? vaa *hey*·ter doo

My name is ...
Jeg heter ... yai *hay*·ter ...

Do you speak English?
Snakker du engelsk? *sna*·ker doo *eyng*·elsk

I don't understand.
Jeg forstår ikke. yai fawr·*stawr i*·key

Accommodation

campsite	*campingplass*	*keym*·ping·plas
guesthouse	*gjestgiveri*	*yest*·gi·ve·ree
hotel	*hotell*	hoo·*tel*
youth hostel	*ungdoms-herberge*	*ong*·dawms·heyr·beyrg

Do you have a single/double room?
Finnes det et enkeltrom/dobbeltrom? *fi*·nes de et *eyn*·kelt·rom/*daw*·belt·rom

How much is it per night/person?
Hvor mye koster det pr dag/person? vor *mew*·e *kaws*·ter de peyr daag/*peyr*·son

Eating & Drinking

Can you recommend a ...?	*Kan du anbefale en ...?*	kan doo *an*·be·fa·le en ...
bar	*bar*	baar
cafe	*kafé*	ka·*fe*
restaurant	*restaurant*	res·tu·*rang*

I'd like the menu.
Kan jeg få menyen, takk. kan yai faw me·*new*·en tak

What would you recommend?
Hva vil du anbefale? va vil doo *an*·be·fa·*le*

Do you have vegetarian food?
Har du vegetariansk mat her? har doo ve·ge·ta·ree·*ansk* maat heyr

I'll have ...
Jeg vil ha ... yai vil haa ...

Signs – Norwegian

Inngang	Entrance
Utgang	Exit
Åpen	Open
Stengt	Closed
Forbudt	Prohibited
Toaletter	Toilets

Numbers – Norwegian

1	*en*	en
2	*to*	taw
3	*tre*	trey
4	*fire*	*fee*·re
5	*fem*	fem
6	*seks*	seks
7	*sju*	shoo
8	*åtte*	*aw*·te
9	*ni*	nee
10	*ti*	tee

Cheers!
Skål! — skawl

I'd like the bill.
Kan jeg få regningen, takk. — kan yai faw *rai*·ning·en tak

breakfast	*frokost*	*fro*·kost
lunch	*lunsj*	loonsh
dinner	*middag*	*mi*·da
beer	*øl*	eul
coffee	*kaffe*	*kaa*·fe
tea	*te*	te
water	*vann*	van
wine	*vin*	veen

Emergencies

Help!	*Hjelp!*	yelp
Go away!	*Forsvinn!*	fawr·*svin*

Call a doctor/the police!
Ring en lege/politiet! — ring en *le*·ge/po·lee·*tee*·ay

I'm lost.
Jeg har gått meg vill. — yai har gawt mai vil

I'm ill.
Jeg er syk. — yai er sewk

I have to use the telephone.
Jeg må låne telefonen. — yai maw *law*·ne te·le·*fo*·nen

Where are the toilets?
Hvor er toalettene? — vor eyr to·aa·*le*·te·ne

Shopping & Services

I'm looking for ...
Jeg leter etter ... — yai *ley*·ter e·*ter* ...

How much is it?
Hvor mye koster det? — vor *mew*·e kaws·ter de

That's too expensive.
Det er for dyrt. — de eyr fawr dewrt

Where's ...?	*Er det ...?*	eyr de ...
an ATM	*en minibank*	en *mi*·nee·bank
a foreign exchange	*valuta veksling*	va·*lu*·ta·vek·sling
market	*marked*	*mar*·ked
post office	*postkontor*	*pawst*·kawn·tawr
tourist office	*turist-informasjon*	tu·*reest*·in·fawr·ma·*shawn*

Transport & Directions

Where is ...?
Hvor er ...? — vor ayr ...

What is the address?
Hva er adressen? — va ayr aa·*dre*·seyn

Can you show me (on the map)?
Kan du vise meg (på kartet)? — kan du vee·se ma (paw *kar*·te)

Where can I buy a ticket?
Hvor kan jeg kjøpe billett? — vor kan yai *sheu*·pe bee·*let*

One one-way/return ticket (to Bergen), please.
Jeg vil gjerne ha enveisbillett/ returbillett (til Bergen), takk. — yai vil *yer*·ne haa en·veys·bee·*let*/ re·*toor*·bi·*let* (til *ber*·gen) tak

What time's the ... bus?	*Når går ... buss?*	nawr gawr ... bus
first	*første*	*feur*·ste
last	*siste*	*si*·ste

boat	*båt*	bawt
bus	*buss*	bus
plane	*fly*	flew
train	*tåg*	tawg

SWEDISH

Swedish is the national language of Sweden and it also has official status in neighbouring Finland.

Vowel sounds can be short or long – generally the stressed vowels are long, except when followed by double consonants. Note that aw is pronounced as in 'saw', air as in 'hair', eu as the 'u' in 'nurse', ew as 'ee' with rounded lips, oh as the 'o' in 'note', and fh is a breathy sound pronounced with rounded lips, like saying 'f' and 'w' at the same time.

Basics

Hello.	*Hej.*	hey
Goodbye.	*Hej då.*	*hey* daw

Please.	*Tack.*	tak
Thank you.	*Tack.*	tak
You're welcome.	*Varsågod.*	var·sha·*gohd*
Excuse me.	*Ursäkta mig.*	oor·*shek*·ta mey
Sorry.	*Förlåt.*	feur·*lawt*
Yes.	*Ja.*	yaa
No.	*Nej.*	ney

How are you?
Hur mår du? hoor mawr doo

Fine, thanks. And you?
Bra, tack. Och dig? braa tak o dey

What's your name?
Vad heter du? vaad *hey*·ter doo

My name is ...
Jag heter ... yaa *hey*·ter ...

Do you speak English?
Talar du engelska? taa·lar doo *eng*·el·ska

I don't understand.
Jag förstår inte. yaa feur·*shtawr in*·te

Accommodation

campsite	*campingplats*	*kam*·ping·*plats*
guesthouse	*gästhus*	*yest*·hoos
hotel	*hotell*	hoh·*tel*
youth hostel	*vandrarhem*	*van*·drar·hem

Do you have a single/double room?
Har ni ett enkelrum/ dubbelrum? har nee et *en*·kel·rum/ *du*·bel·rum

How much is it per night/person?
Hur mycket kostar det per natt/person? hoor *mew*·ket *kos*·tar de peyr nat/*peyr*·shohn

Eating & Drinking

Can you recommend	*Kan du rekommendera*	kan doo re·ko·men·*dey*·ra
a bar?	*en bar?*	eyn bar
a cafe?	*ett kafé?*	et ka·*fey*
a restaurant?	*en restaurang?*	en res·taw·*rang*

I'd like the menu.
Jag skulle vilja ha menyn. yaa *sku*·le *vil*·ya *haa* me·*newn*

What would you recommend?
Vad skulle ni rekommendera? vaad *sku*·le nee re·ko·men·*dey*·ra

Do you have vegetarian food?
Har ni vegetarisk mat? har nee ve·ge·*taa*·risk maat

Signs – Swedish

Ingång	Entrance
Utgång	Exit
Öppet	Open
Stängt	Closed
Förbjudet	Prohibited
Toaletter	Toilets

I'll have ...
Jag vill ha ... yaa vil haa ...

Cheers!
Skål! skawl

I'd like the bill.
Jag skulle vilja ha räkningen. yaa *sku*·le *vil*·ya *haa reyk*·ning·en

breakfast	*frukost*	*froo*·kost
lunch	*lunch*	lunsh
dinner	*middag*	*mi*·daa
beer	*öl*	eul
coffee	*kaffe*	*ka*·fe
tea	*te*	*tey*
water	*vatten*	*va*·ten
wine	*vin*	veen

Emergencies

Help!	*Hjälp!*	yelp
Go away!	*Försvinn!*	feur·*shvin*

Call a doctor!
Ring efter en doktor! ring *ef*·ter en *dok*·tor

Call the police!
Ring efter polisen! ring *ef*·ter poh·*lee*·sen

I'm lost.
Jag har gått vilse. yaa har got *vil*·se

I'm ill.
Jag är sjuk. yaa air fhook

I have to use the telephone.
Jag måste använda telefonen. yaa *maws*·te *an*·ven·da te·le·*foh*·nen

Where are the toilets?
Var är toaletten? var air toh·aa·*le*·ten

Shopping & Services

I'm looking for ...
Jag letar efter ... yaa *ley*·tar *ef*·ter ...

How much is it?
Hur mycket kostar det? hoor *mew*·ke *kos*·tar de

Numbers – Swedish

1	*ett*	et
2	*två*	tvaw
3	*tre*	trey
4	*fyra*	*few*·ra
5	*fem*	fem
6	*sex*	seks
7	*sju*	fhoo
8	*åtta*	*o*·ta
9	*nio*	*nee*·oh
10	*tio*	*tee*·oh

That's too expensive.
Det är för dyrt. de air feur *dewrt*

Where's ...?	*Var finns det ...?*	var fins de ...
an ATM	*en bankomat*	eyn ban·koh·*maat*
a foreign exchange	*ett växlings-kontor*	et *veyk*·slings·kon·tohr

market	*torghandel*	*tory*·han·del
post office	*posten*	*pos*·ten
tourist office	*turistbyrå*	too·*rist*·bew·raw

Transport & Directions

Where's ...?
Var finns det ...? var finns de ...

What's the address?
Vilken adress är det? *vil*·ken a·*dres* air de

Can you show me (on the map)?
Kan du visa mig (på kartan)? kan doo *vee*·sa mey (paw *kar*·tan)

Where can I buy a ticket?
Var kan jag köpa en biljett? var kan yaa *sheu*·pa eyn bil·*yet*

A one-way/return ticket (to Stockholm), please.
Jag skulle vilja ha en enkelbiljett/returbiljett (till Stockholm). yaa *sku*·le *vil*·ya haa eyn *en*·kel·bil·*yet*/*re*·*toor*·bil·*yet* (til *stok*·holm)

What time's the ... bus?	*När går ... bussen?*	nair gawr ... *bu*·sen
first	*första*	*feursh*·ta
last	*sista*	*sis*·ta

boat	*båt*	bawt
bus	*buss*	bus
plane	*flygplan*	*flewg*·plaan
train	*tåg*	tawg

Behind the Scenes

SEND US YOUR FEEDBACK

We love to hear from travellers – your comments keep us on our toes and help make our books better. Our well-travelled team reads every word on what you loved or loathed about this book. Although we cannot reply individually to your submissions, we always guarantee that your feedback goes straight to the appropriate authors, in time for the next edition. Each person who sends us information is thanked in the next edition – the most useful submissions are rewarded with a selection of digital PDF chapters.

Visit **lonelyplanet.com/contact** to submit your updates and suggestions or to ask for help. Our award-winning website also features inspirational travel stories, news and discussions.

Note: We may edit, reproduce and incorporate your comments in Lonely Planet products such as guidebooks, websites and digital products, so let us know if you don't want your comments reproduced or your name acknowledged. For a copy of our privacy policy visit lonelyplanet.com/privacy.

OUR READERS

Many thanks to the travellers who used the last edition and wrote to us with helpful hints, useful advice and interesting anecdotes:

Arkadiusz Rubajczyk, Mikala Kuchera, Ralf van Veen, Rejane Strieder, Stephanie Schuterman, Stephanie Kasdas

AUTHOR THANKS

Andy Symington

I owe a large *kiitos* to many across Finland, including the Campbell and Schulman families, Eira Torvinen, Satu Natunen, Alexis Kouros, Heikki Paltto, Ari-Matti Piippo, Tuomo Polo and Laura Klefbohm. Thanks too to Finland co-author Catherine Le Nevez, editor Gemma Graham and the great team of Scandinavia authors that have been an absolute pleasure to work with. Thanks to my parents for constant support and to the friends who keep things ticking over at home during my frequent absences.

Carolyn Bain

I could list half the Icelandic phonebook given the amount of friendly, generous and wise locals who helped me out on this trip – they made it a joy to research. A sincere *takk fyrir* to everyone I met along the way, and a special shout-out to my very talented co-author on the Iceland guidebook, Alexis Averbuck.

Cristian Bonetto

Tusind tak to Martin Kalhoj, Christian Struckmann Irgens, Mette Cecilie Perle Smedegaard, Grete Seidler, Mia Hjorth Lunde, Jens Lunde, Henrik Lorentsen, Gitte Kærsgaard, Henrik Sieverts Ørvad, Brian Jakobsen and René Ørum for their insights and generosity. Last but not least, many thanks to the ever-diligent Andy Symington and Carolyn Bain.

Peter Dragicevich

It's a special treat to be able to meet up with friends on the road, and on this trip it was wonderful to enjoy the company of Kaspars Zalitis and Ivica Erdelja. Thanks guys!

Anthony Ham

Special thanks to Gemma Graham; to my fine co-authors Stuart and Donna; to Miles Roddis; to Ron and Elaine for first igniting my love of Norway. As always, so many Norwegians I met were unfailingly helpful ambassadors for their country – I am deeply grateful to all of them. And it gets harder with each journey to be away from my family – to Marina, Carlota and Valentina, heartfelt thanks for enduring my absences. Os quiero.

Anna Kaminski

Many thanks to Team Scandinavia, not least to Gemma for entrusting me with this chapter. I'm grateful to everyone who helped me along the way, including Britta at STF Kebnekaise, Joran and the Kallaxflyg team in Nikkaluokta, Ali in Luleå, Amelie, Erik and the other medieval doom metal rockers in Gävle, Nandito in Gothenburg, Doris in Vilhelmina and Sven in Kiruna.

ACKNOWLEDGEMENTS

Climate map data adapted from Peel MC, Finlayson BL & McMahon TA (2007) 'Updated World Map of the Köppen-Geiger Climate Classification', Hydrology and Earth System Sciences, 11, 163344.

Cover photograph: Swedish forest, Claus Christensen/Getty.

THIS BOOK

This 12th edition of Lonely Planet's *Scandinavia* guidebook was researched and written by Andy Symington, Carolyn Bain, Cristian Bonetto, Peter Dragicevich, Anthony Ham and Anna Kaminski. This guidebook was produced by the following:

Destination Editor Gemma Graham

Product Editors Elin Berglund, Kate James

Senior Cartographer Valentina Kremenchutskaya

Book Designer Mazzy Prinsep

Assisting Editors Katie Connolly, Carly Hall, Charlotte Orr, Christopher Pitts, Jeanette Wall

Assisting Cartographers Mark Griffiths, Alison Lyall

Cover Researcher Naomi Parker

Thanks to Ryan Evans, Samantha Forge, Claire Naylor, Karyn Noble, Diana Saengkham, Lauren Wellicome, Tony Wheeler

Index

Map Pages **000**
Photo Pages 000

Map Pages **000**
Photo Pages **000**

Map Pages **000**
Photo Pages 000

Map Pages **000**
Photo Pages **000**

Map Legend

Sights
- Beach
- Bird Sanctuary
- Buddhist
- Castle/Palace
- Christian
- Confucian
- Hindu
- Islamic
- Jain
- Jewish
- Monument
- Museum/Gallery/Historic Building
- Ruin
- Shinto
- Sikh
- Taoist
- Winery/Vineyard
- Zoo/Wildlife Sanctuary
- Other Sight

Activities, Courses & Tours
- Bodysurfing
- Diving
- Canoeing/Kayaking
- Course/Tour
- Sento Hot Baths/Onsen
- Skiing
- Snorkelling
- Surfing
- Swimming/Pool
- Walking
- Windsurfing
- Other Activity

Sleeping
- Sleeping
- Camping

Eating
- Eating

Drinking & Nightlife
- Drinking & Nightlife
- Cafe

Entertainment
- Entertainment

Shopping
- Shopping

Information
- Bank
- Embassy/Consulate
- Hospital/Medical
- Internet
- Police
- Post Office
- Telephone
- Toilet
- Tourist Information
- Other Information

Geographic
- Beach
- Hut/Shelter
- Lighthouse
- Lookout
- Mountain/Volcano
- Oasis
- Park
- Pass
- Picnic Area
- Waterfall

Population
- Capital (National)
- Capital (State/Province)
- City/Large Town
- Town/Village

Transport
- Airport
- Border crossing
- Bus
- Cable car/Funicular
- Cycling
- Ferry
- Metro station
- Monorail
- Parking
- Petrol station
- S-Bahn/S-train/Subway station
- Taxi
- T-bane/Tunnelbana station
- Train station/Railway
- Tram
- Tube station
- U-Bahn/Underground station
- Other Transport

Note: Not all symbols displayed above appear on the maps in this book

Routes
- Tollway
- Freeway
- Primary
- Secondary
- Tertiary
- Lane
- Unsealed road
- Road under construction
- Plaza/Mall
- Steps
- Tunnel
- Pedestrian overpass
- Walking Tour
- Walking Tour detour
- Path/Walking Trail

Boundaries
- International
- State/Province
- Disputed
- Regional/Suburb
- Marine Park
- Cliff
- Wall

Hydrography
- River, Creek
- Intermittent River
- Canal
- Water
- Dry/Salt/Intermittent Lake
- Reef

Areas
- Airport/Runway
- Beach/Desert
- Cemetery (Christian)
- Cemetery (Other)
- Glacier
- Mudflat
- Park/Forest
- Sight (Building)
- Sportsground
- Swamp/Mangrove

Anthony Ham

Norway Anthony fell in love with Norway the first time he laid eyes on her and there aren't many places in Norway he hasn't been, from Lindesnes in the south to the remote fjords of Svalbard in the far north. His true passion is the Arctic north whether dog-sledding and spending time with the Sámi around Karasjok or drawing near to glaciers and scouring the horizon for polar bears in the glorious wilderness of Svalbard. When he's not travelling for Lonely Planet to the Arctic (or, his other great love, Africa), he lives in Melbourne and Madrid and writes and photographs for magazines and newspapers around the world. See more at www.anthonyham.com.

Read more about Anthony at:
lonelyplanet.com/members/anthony_ham

Anna Kaminski

Sweden Anna got her first taste of Sweden as a youngster in the Soviet Union through the books of Astrid Lindgren and Selma Lagerlöf and has had a great affinity for it ever since. During this research trip, she roamed both of Sweden's coastlines by boat, drove close to 3000 miles, descended into three mines and flew over the Arctic tundra in a helicopter. This is the third time she researched Sweden for Lonely Planet and this seemingly sedate country never fails to surprise her.

OUR STORY

A beat-up old car, a few dollars in the pocket and a sense of adventure. In 1972 that's all Tony and Maureen Wheeler needed for the trip of a lifetime – across Europe and Asia overland to Australia. It took several months, and at the end – broke but inspired – they sat at their kitchen table writing and stapling together their first travel guide, *Across Asia on the Cheap*. Within a week they'd sold 1500 copies. Lonely Planet was born.

Today, Lonely Planet has offices in Franklin, London, Melbourne, Oakland, Beijing and Delhi, with more than 600 staff and writers. We share Tony's belief that 'a great guidebook should do three things: inform, educate and amuse'.

OUR WRITERS

Andy Symington

Coordinating author; Finland Andy hails from Australia, lives in Spain, learned to ski as a child in Norway, was entranced by wintertime Finland as a backpacking teenager and has been a regular visitor to the Nordic lands ever since. He has travelled extremely widely throughout the region, and is a regular contributor on Finland and Scandinavia for Lonely Planet guides and other publications. His highlights have included close encounters with bears, rowing-boat odysseys on enormous lakes and a near-terminal swim in a seriously cold Arctic Ocean. In a never-ending bid for honorary citizenship of the north, he has a huge stockpile of Nordic CDs ranging from contemporary Sámi yoiks to epic eighties Viking metal.

Read more about Andy at:
lonelyplanet.com/members/andy_symington

Carolyn Bain

Iceland Melbourne-born Carolyn has had an ongoing love affair with the Nordic region, ignited as a teenager living in Denmark and regularly rekindled over 14 years of writing guidebooks to glorious northern destinations such as Iceland, Denmark, Sweden and Nordic-wannabe Estonia (see more at carolynbain.com.au). Carolyn has worked on six editions of this book (dating back to 2003); for this edition she got to feed her addiction to skyr, fjords, secret hot-pots and glacier trails, puffins, lopapeysur and the music of Ásgeir.

Cristian Bonetto

Denmark Cristian is proudly addicted to Henningsen lamps, Herning sweaters, and *kanelsnegle*. He has contributed to many Scandinavian titles for Lonely Planet, and his musings on Danish food, design and culture have featured in numerous media outlets, including San Francisco magazine *7x7* and UAE radio station Dubai Eye 103.8. When he's not Tweeting on his Danish bike, you'll find him hunting down the next big thing in Italy, New York City, Singapore and his native Australia. He tweets @CristianBonetto.

Peter Dragicevich

Tallinn After a dozen years working for newspapers and magazines in both his native New Zealand and Australia, Peter ditched the desk and hit the road. After contributing to literally dozens of Lonely Planet titles (including the *Estonia, Latvia & Lithuania* guidebook) he wholeheartedly rates Tallinn as one of his favourite cities in the world.

OVER PAGE MORE WRITERS

Published by Lonely Planet Publications Pty Ltd
ABN 36 005 607 983
12th edition – June 2015
ISBN 978 1 74321 569 2

10 9 8 7 6 5 4 3 2 1
Printed in China